# CHRONOLOGY OF WORLD HISTORY

# CHRONOLOGY OF WORLD HISTORY

*A Calendar of Principal Events*
*from 3000 BC to AD 1976*

SECOND EDITION

## G.S.P. Freeman-Grenville

ROWMAN AND LITTLEFIELD
TOTOWA, NEW JERSEY

This edition published in the United States 1978
by Rowman and Littlefield, Totowa, New Jersey

First published 1975
Second Edition 1978

© Rex Collings 1978

ISBN 0-8476-6040-0

Printed in Great Britain

FOR TERESA

O teach us to number our days: that we may apply our hearts unto wisdom.

Psalm 90(89), 12

History is the record of human society, or world civilization; of the changes that take place in the nature of that society . . . of revolutions and uprisings by one set of people against another with the resulting kingdoms and states, with their various ranks; of the different activities and occupations of men, whether for gaining their livelihood or in the various sciences and crafts; and, in general, of all the transformations that society undergoes by its very nature.

Ibn Khaldun, Muqaddamah

For now we see in a glass darkly . . .

I Corinthians 13, 12.

# PREFACE

TO THE FIRST EDITION

The aim of this chronology is to provide a book of reference to human history. It offers a skeletal outline of the principal events and dates from c.3000 BC to 31 December AD 1973; it gives a comparative panorama of events contemporary to each other in different parts of the world.

Man, as Aristotle observed, is a political animal; history, as E. A. Freeman remarked, is yesterday's politics. If we study the history of man, no part of the world can be ignored: omission of what we know can only produce distortion. If we regard politics in its broadest sense in relation to all human activity, a division between history and prehistory emerges: by definition the only survivals of prehistoric societies are non-perishable artefacts. The men who made them are no more than shadows. In its true sense history begins only when, some sooner, some later, the records of human societies and of individuals begin to reveal it in different parts of the world. There is a distinct point in the human story when the first societies begin to be apparent. The historical period, the past some 5000 years, is of course but a fragment of the human story, which extends back in time for some millions of years. It is all that can be set out in a calendrical fashion in terms of men and events. A beginning at c. 3000 BC is thus not arbitrary in the way Steinberg took 58 BC as a starting-point for European history, ignoring, to say the least, its roots in ancient Greece, but much more besides.[1] On the contrary, the date of c.3000 BC is imposed by the nature of historical materials.

Our perspectives cannot remain those of our fathers. As Lord Acton foresaw,[2] in recent years the study of archives has greatly enlarged our knowledge; no one could foresee the advances in historical archaeology and in the opening of new provinces of history that the past seventy years have seen. A kind reviewer of my *Chronology of African History* remarked that history, as it emerges, 'seems to resemble an old-fashioned sugar sprinkler, from which events are shaken, slowly and with difficulty at first, but in ever-increasing quantity at an ever-increasing pace.'[3] There is still much to discover, especially in Africa. We can only set out the dates available to us, and these are often hard to seek before modern times. We know in great detail of the wars and raids and wanderings of the Mongols, but next to nothing of the Bantu migrations which populated very much of Africa somewhat before and during much of the same time. We must understand the limitations of our material. Quite often such dates as we have are disputable: *c.* (*circa*), about, has been used liberally, and its absence should not always be taken to imply that a date cannot be a matter for dispute. Similarly, a mark of interrogation has been used in cases of dubiety. Many dates rely in the last resort upon the arbitrary, albeit considered, judgements of archaeologists and historians: many have been painstakingly calculated and disputed by numerous scholars. If a reasonable date now seems available, say, for the *Periplus of the Erythraean Sea*[4] (a key to our earlier knowledge of the countries bordering the Indian Ocean), it remains that different dates and sequences of dates have been proposed by more than fifty scholars. The date at present judged the most accurate could be confirmed or set aside if fresh material were discovered tomorrow. Nor is our assessment of an event or series of events always correct. To one Portuguese chronicler the discovery of the Indies was 'the most important event in the history of the world since the Incarnation and Death of him who created it.' He was in no position to foresee the future of the Americas. The dating and assessment of events must always be a matter of controversy, and this makes the selection of datable events more difficult in modern times, when our records become overwhelmingly prolific. We can only be sure that our successors will see things differently.

This chronology is not a mere list of dates. Nor is it a history of all mankind. It is necessarily selective. It is a skeleton because chronology is the backbone of history, and because without a system of chronology history is unintelligible. The panoramic form adopted invites the reader to study the course of events in different parts of the world at the same time, and, if remote in space, to see them as contemporary. It is an attempt to reproduce on paper something of the pictorial effect of the *camera-obscura*. This is the primary reason for separating the chronological information into columns.

It is of course possible to set out a chronology simply as a calendar, allowing a page or more for each year, without any divisions of geography, or, for that matter, of subject. Until very recent times events, say, in China impinged little upon Europe, and still less on the Americas. A purely calendrical method is unsatisfactory because it juxtaposes events and men geographically remote from each other. The idea of a division into subjects or periods, or into civilizations, is at first sight attractive, but can only produce confusion, because these quite invariably overlap.

This chronology is therefore presented in a panoramic tabular form with reference to specified geographical areas. There are six columns on each pair of opposite pages, making six in each opening. As will be seen, the first five vary from time to time as the quantity and impetus of events accelerate or decelerate in different areas. The titles of these areas are printed at the head of each column in each opening. The sixth column of each opening bears the same title throughout, Religion and Culture. At first it seemed more appropriate to include such matters in one or the other of the first five columns. Experiment showed this to be confusing, because in these spheres so many events and discoveries, and so many religious events, transcend a geographical frame-work. The geographical divisions are of wholly arbitrary convenience: many events are significant in relation to more than one column: on such occasions either the place of the event or its greatest impact have determined the placing. From 3000 BC Western Europe occupies the first column; the second is devoted to Central and Eastern Europe; the third to Egypt and Africa; the fourth to the Near East; and the fifth to the Far East. At the turn of the Christian Era, but not because of it, more becomes known of Western, Northern and Central Europe, and this gives a new title to the first column: the second becomes Spain, Italy and Eastern Europe. These titles are retained until 1099, but after 700 more becomes known of Africa, and the third column is retitled Africa and Egypt. After 1100 the pressure of events increases in the West: the first column is retitled Western and Northern Europe, the second Central, Southern and Eastern Europe. Between 3000 BC and AD 1399 there is no change in the titles of other columns. The Spanish and Portuguese discovery of the Americas makes a new grouping necessary in the fifteenth century: while other columns retain their titles, the fourth column now combines the Near and Far East; the fifth column is entitled the Americas throughout the rest of the work. From 1600-99 other adjustments are necessary. The quantity of events in the extreme West of Europe compels us to devote the first column to Western Europe exclusively; the second column is entitled Northern, Central and Southern Europe. By now Egypt was a mere Turkish province, while other parts of Africa steadily become more known to us: henceforward the third column is entitled Africa, and the fourth column abbreviated to the East. After 1700 the first column is retitled Western and Northern Europe, and the second Central and Southern Europe. The fourth column now becomes the East and Australasia because of the discovery of the latter. Thenceforward the divisions and titles remain constant. If they lay some stress upon Europe, it is because the quantity of European events is great, and has so often affected the rest of the world in one way or another.

There is no bibliography. If one were included, it would occupy 400 pages or more. Similarly, justificatory footnotes have been omitted, because frequently they would occupy more space than the text. Nor does this preface attempt to discuss the problems of chronological theory, because any proper discussion would cover some hundreds of pages. Abbreviations have been used frequently. Other than the most common ones, they have been listed following this preface.

A chronology without an index is like a dog without a nose. Mr A. T. Howat has prepared the present index. It refers directly to years, not to page numbers: the reader need not scan an entire page for the reference he seeks; he has only to verify the year from the index and scan the appropriate column for the reference required. The index gives the briefest possible reference to personal and place names, to countries and the more important subjects. For persons terminal dates of birth and death, or of reigns, or in many cases simply the *floruit*, the period during which an individual's actions are known or pertinent, alone are shown. It would be burdensome to note every year in which the more important personages are named, for it would simply be a repetition of the text. Countries are given the names current at particular times: we speak of Britain in Roman times and before, and then of England until the Act of Union with Scotland in 1707, when the island became Great Britain. The same rule applies to African countries, some of which have changed their names several times during this century. Such names are cross-referenced. For these, and for select subjects of importance, general entries are listed first, and, where appropriate, by sub-headings. Where a consecutive series of dates is given, say, between 1925 and 1930, this has been abbreviated to 1925–1930. This seems the quickest method to guide the reader to the date sought, each year being printed in bold in the body of the work so as to meet the eye instantly. The first and last years mentioned in each opening are also shown in bold at the top of each page. Throughout the index strict alphabetical order has been maintained, the first complete name in any series determining the order. In languages which possess surnames, the order is that of surnames. Otherwise the order is determined by the name by which a man is customarily known, or by the first of a succession of names, as customary in the Arab world and much of Africa and the East. In some cases a double reference is given: for example, Mustafa Kemal Atatürk is more familiar as Mustafa Kemal, albeit he adopted the surname Atatürk.

In a work of this kind orthography presents serious problems. Innumerable languages are involved, and plainly a preface cannot give an account of all the conventions. The Oxford *Atlas* has been used as the standard for geographical names. For personal names some arbitrary decisions have been necessary, but generally the usage of the best English authors has been followed. The English conventions have been preferred, and thus, for example, the numerous Johns who have reigned in different places have all been called John. We should not easily recognize Pope John XXIII as Johannes XXIII or Giovanni XXIII. The same applies to many other personal names. In Arab names diacritical marks, *'ain, hamzah*, and indications of vowel length have been discarded. They are confusing to the ordinary reader, and can be supplied at once by any Arabist. The assimilation of *al-* has been ignored: al-Shaikh, not ash-Shaikh, has been written. Diacritical marks have been deleted from all other languages transliterated from non-Roman scripts. But so many Arab names occur in many African languages, notably Hausa and Swahili, and likewise in Persian and in the Indic languages—to name only some examples—that in some cases the deviations followed by the best authors have been allowed to stand. Accents, however, have been retained in the relevant languages. Even so, there are certain English conventions which it would be pedantic not to follow. We write Lyons, not Lyon; Rome, not Roma. Thus Aden is preferred to the correct Adn, Mecca to the classical al-Makkah, Medina to al-Madinah, and so on. French orthography has been retained for the names of many northern African cities and towns, because such usage is conventional, even in English. For many readers a failure to follow conventional usage would obscure the meaning.

So many scholars have taught, assisted or advised me during many years of historical study that a list of acknowledgements would be too long to set out here. I am unwilling to select some rather than others for fear of seeming invidious. They all have my warmest gratitude. My neighbour, D. H. T. Lancaster, and my son, the Master of Kinloss, have kindly helped me sort more than 33,000 slips. I owe a debt of great gratitude to Mr A. T. Howat for making the index, and to his wife Olga Howat for her patience and precision in typing the entire work. Both have kindly corrected me on many points of literal accuracy as well as the orthography of some Polish, Portuguese and Spanish names. They have been invaluable friends and allies. I am ever grateful to my wife, whose ingenuity and critical sense have helped me overcome many problems.

SHERIFF HUTTON, YORK
*Anniversary of the battle of Lepanto,*
*7 October 1974.*

G.S.P.F.-G.

1.  S. H. Steinberg, *Historical Tables, 58 B.C.-A.D. 1972*, 9th edn., 1973, first appeared in 1939, concentrating chiefly upon Europe, with less attention to Africa, the Americas, Asia or Australasia.
2.  Lord Acton, *Lectures on Modern History* (1906), Fontana Library, 1960, 'Inaugural Lecture on the Study of History', pp. 22-3, esp. p. 23, 'We are still at the beginning of the documentary age . . .'
3.  Anon., *Times Literary Supplement*, 3 May 1974, p. 482. Mr Thomas Hodgkin has since kindly told me that he wrote the review.
4.  Cf. D. W. MacDowall and N. G. Wilson, 'The references to the Kusanas in the Periplus, and further Numismatic Evidence for its Date', *Numismatic Chronicle*, 1970.

## PREFACE TO THE SECOND EDITION

This edition is updated to the end of 1976. Some minor amendments have been made, and some 2,000 new entries provided. Many are in the column headed Religion & Culture, some generated by new discoveries. New perspectives are ever opening. Outstanding are the hitherto unknown literate civilization of Ebla in Syria and finds of Roman and Egyptian pottery on the Somali coast.

    I am grateful for many kindly comments and criticisms.

SHERIFF HUTTON, YORK                                          G.S.P.F.-G.

29 April 1978

# ABBREVIATIONS

| | |
|---|---|
| ± | a radio-carbon dating |
| *ABAKO* | *Association des Bakongo* (Congo, L) |
| Abp | Archbishop |
| AD | after the birth of Christ |
| *ad int.* | *ad interim* (used for acting appointments) |
| *AEF* | *Afrique Equatoriale Française* |
| *ALN* | *Armée de Libération Nationale,* (Algeria) |
| *AML* | *Amis du Manifeste et de la Liberté,* (Algeria) |
| ANC | African National Congress, (SA) |
| *AOF* | *Afrique Occidentale Française* |
| *ante* | before |
| b. | *bin* or *ibn* (Arabic, son of) |
| b. | born |
| BC | before the birth of Christ |
| Bp | Bishop |
| BSA Co. | British South Africa Co., Ltd |
| C | Central |
| C. | Cape |
| c.(cc.) | century, centuries |
| c. | *circa* (about) |
| CDW(A) | Colonial Development and Welfare (Act) |
| C.E. | Church of England |
| CENTO | Central Treaty Organization |
| *CFA* | *Côte Française d'Afrique* |
| *CFLN* | *Comité Français de la Libération Nationale* |
| CFS | Congo Free State |
| *CGT* | *Confédération Générale de Travail* |
| C.-in-C. | Commander-in-Chief |

| | |
|---|---|
| CMS | Church Missionary Society |
| *CNF* | *Comité National Français* |
| *CNRA* | *Conseil National de la Révolution Algérienne* |
| Co. | Company |
| Con. | Conservative Party, Britain |
| Congo (B) | Congo (Brazzaville) |
| Congo (K) | Congo (Kinshasa), later Zaïre |
| Congo (L) | Congo (Léopoldville), later Congo (K) |
| CP | Communist Party |
| CPP | Convention People's Party, (Ghana) |
| *CRF* | *Comité pour le Renaissance de France,* (Algeria) |
| *CRUA* | *Comité Révolutionnaire pour l'Unité et l'Action,* (Algeria) |
| CSSp | Congregation of the Holy Ghost, or Holy Ghost Fathers |
| d. | died |
| DEI | Dutch East Indies |
| Dem. | Democratic Party, USA |
| Dept., | Department |
| DP | Destour Party, (Tunisia) |
| Dr. | Doctor |
| DRC | Dutch Reformed Church |
| E | East |
| EA | East Africa |
| ECD | European Defence Community |
| EEC | European Economic Community |
| EFTA | European Free Trade Association |
| EIC | East India Co., or East Indies Co. |
| *ENA* | *Etoile Nord Africaine,* (Algeria) |
| EOKA | Greek Cypriot Nationalist Movement for union with Greece. |

| | |
|---|---|
| FAO | Food and Agriculture Organization, UN |
| FCA | Federation of Central Africa |
| *FFL* | *Force Française Libre* |
| *fl.* | *floruit,* period at which an individual is believed to have been alive |
| *FLN* | *Front de Libération Nationale* |
| Fr. | Father |
| *frs.* | *francs* |
| *FRELIMO* | Liberation Front of Mozambique |
| GATT | General Agreement on Tariffs and Trade |
| GMBA | General Council of Burmese Associations |
| HMS | His (Her) Majesty's Ship |
| IBEA | Imperial British East Africa Co. |
| IMP | Independence of Malaya Party |
| INC | Indian National Congress |
| IRA | Irish Republican Army |
| Is. | Island, Islands |
| IWA | International Workers of Africa, (SA) |
| KADU | Kenya African Democratic Union |
| KANU | Kenya African National Union |
| KAU | Kenya African Union |
| L. | Lake |
| Lab. | Labour Party, Britain |
| LAFTA | Latin American Free Trade Association |
| Leg. Co. | Legislative Council |
| Lib. | Liberal Party, Britain |
| LSSP | Lanka Sama Samaja Party, (Ceylon) |
| Ltd | Limited |
| m. | married |
| m. | million(s) |
| MCA | Malayan Chinese Association |
| MCP | Malayan Communist Party |

| | |
|---|---|
| MDU | Malay Democratic Union |
| *MEP* | *Mahajana Eksath Peramuna,* Ceylon |
| Mgr | Monsignor |
| MIC | Malayan Indian Congress |
| MNP | Malayan Nationalist Party |
| *MNR* | *Movimento Nacional Revolucionista,* (Bolivia) |
| MPAJA | Malayan People's anti-Japanese Army |
| *MPLA* | Popular Movement for the Liberation of Angola |
| Mt(s). | Mount, Mountains |
| N | North |
| NAC | Nyasaland African Congress |
| NATO | North Atlantic Treaty Organization |
| NE | North East |
| NEP | New Economic Policy, (USSR) |
| NS | New Style |
| NSW | New South Wales |
| NZ | New Zealand |
| *OAS* | *Organisation Armée Secrète,* (Algeria) |
| OAU | Organization for African Unity |
| OBU | One Big Union, (Canada) |
| *OCAM* | *Organisation Commune Africaine et Malgache* |
| OEEC | Organization for European Economic Co-operation |
| OFS | Orange Free State |
| OP | Order of Preachers, (Dominicans) |
| OPEC | Organization of Petroleum Exporting Countries |
| ORS | Orange River Sovereignty |
| OS | Old Style |
| *OS* | *Organisation Spéciale,* (Algeria) |
| OSB | Order of St Benedict |
| *PCA* | *Parti Communiste Algérien* |
| pop. | population |
| *PPA* | *Parti Populaire Algérien* |

| | |
|---|---|
| *post* | after |
| ps. | pseudonym |
| R. | Royal |
| RAF | Royal Air Force |
| R(s) | River, Rivers |
| Rep. | Republican Party, USA |
| Rev. | Reverend |
| RN | Royal Navy |
| *RPF* | *Rassemblement du Peuple Français* |
| Rt. | Right |
| S | South |
| SA | South Africa |
| SANU | Sudan African National Union |
| SCAP | Supreme Commander for Allied Powers |
| SEAC | South East Asia Command |
| SEATO | South East Asia Treaty Organization |
| SJ | Society of Jesus, (Jesuits) |
| SPG | Society for the Propagation of the Gospel |
| St | Saint |
| succ. | successor, succeeded |
| SWA | South West Africa |
| TAA | Tanganyika African Association |
| TANU | Tanganyika (later Tanzania) African National Association |
| UAR | United Arab Republic, (Egypt) |
| UDA | Ulster Defence Association |
| UK | United Kingdom of Great Britain and Northern Ireland |
| UMCA | Universities' Mission to Central Africa |
| UN(O) | United Nations (Organization) |
| UNP | United Nationalist Party,(Ceylon) |
| UNRRA | United Nations Relief and Rehabilitation Administration |
| *UPA* | *Union Populaire Algérienne* |

| | |
|---|---|
| US(A) | United States (of America) |
| USAAF | United States Army Air Force |
| USN | United States Navy |
| USPG | United Society for the Propagation of the Gospel |
| USSR | Union of Soviet Socialist Republics |
| UTP | United Tanganyika Party |
| *via* | by way of |
| W | West |
| W. | Wadi |
| WCC | World Council of Churches |
| WF | White Fathers |
| WI | West Indies |
| YMBA | Young Men's Buddhist Association |
| ZANU | Zimbabwe African National Union, (Rhodesia) |
| ZAPU | Zimbabwe African People's Union, (Rhodesia) |

| WESTERN EUROPE | CENTRAL & EASTERN EUROPE | EGYPT & AFRICA |
|---|---|---|
| c. 3rd millenium Neolithic tools gradually replaced by copper in Italy. | 3rd millenium Ancient Minoan period in Crete. | c. post 3100 ff. First Dynasty (Thinite) in Egypt. |
| | 2nd millenium Celts, or (in Asia Minor) Galati, emerge as a people in upper Danube basin. | c. 3000—2000 Period of pyramid building in Egypt. |
| | | c. post 2850—c. 2700 Second Dynasty in Egypt. |
| | | c. 2700 Earliest pyramid, Step Pyramid at Sakkara, and complex of adjacent buildings, erected by Pharaoh Djoser: architect, Imhotep. c. post 2700—2620 Third Dynasty in Egypt: capital at Memphis. |
| | | c. post 2620 Pharaoh Snofru's expedition against Nubia: 7,000 captives and 200,000 cattle said to have been brought back. Further expedition against Libya. Trade with Byblos: forty vessels return with Lebanon cedar-wood. c. 2620—c. 2480 Fourth Dynasty in Egypt. |
| | | c. post 2580 Pyramids of Giza built: Great Pyramid of Cheops 481 ft. high: spires of Cologne Cathedral the only higher stone buildings erected by man. c. post 2574 Pyramid of Chephren built; Sphinx (image of god Atum) carved. |

**THE NEAR EAST & INDIA**　　　　**THE FAR EAST**　　　　**RELIGION & CULTURE**

**ante 3000** The loom used in Mesopotamia and Egypt. Farming communities in existence in the Indus valley.

**c. 3000** Semites beginning to people Mesopotamia. Lead known as a metal. Weights and measures standardized in Mesopotamia and Egypt. First pictograms in Indus valley. Nineveh culture in N Iraq. Proto-literate period in S Iraq. Cotton cultivation begins in Indus valley.
**post 3000** Seed drills attached to ploughs in Mesopotamia.
**c. 3000–2750** Early Bronze Age II in Palestine.
**c. 3000–c. 1500** Indus Valley Civilization or Harappan Culture in India.

**c. 2800–2500** Jemdet-Nasr culture.
**c. 2750–2550** First Dynasty of Uruk.
**2750** Traditional date of foundation of Tyre.
**c. 2750–2650** First Dynasty of Kish.
**c. 2750–2500** Early Bronze Age III in Palestine.
**c. 2750–c. 2400** Dynasty of Lagash.
**c. 2725** Royal cemetery of Ur.

**c. 2675** Gilgamesh, ruler of Uruk.
**c. 2650–2500** Second Dynasty of Kish. First Dynasty of Ur.

**post 2585** Commercial relations develop between Syria and Egypt.

**c. 3000** Proto-Malays of Tibetan-Mongoloid affinities spread from Yunnan into Malaysia.

**2879–258** Legendary Vietnamese Kingdom of Van Lang, or Van Tang, under Hong Bang Dynasty.

**c. ante 3000** Reed boats made in Mesopotamia and Egypt. The first ploughs made in Mesopotamia and Egypt. Discovery of bronze alloy of tin and copper, made in (? )Syria or Anatolia.
**c. 3000** Science of survey already known in Egypt. Moulded copper axe-heads and knives made in Palestine. Coast of Peru occupied by sedentary fishermen and agriculturalists, ignorant of the art of pottery.

| WESTERN EUROPE | CENTRAL & EASTERN EUROPE | EGYPT & AFRICA |
|---|---|---|
| c. 2500 First invaders cross from mainland Europe into Britain: Salisbury Plain, first notable population centre. Neolithic civilization in Scotland. Small colonies from E Mediterranean, using bronze and dwelling in fortified cities, settle in S Spain and Portugal. | c. 2500 Camb pottery in C Russia. Laudanum extracted from cultivated poppies in Cyprus. | c. 2500 The phalanx used in Egypt. Wheeled scaling ladders used in Egypt. Building of wooden boats developed in Egypt. Sea-going vessels built in Egypt: rowing now in usage. Stone bowl industry in Egypt: drills used for hollowing stone. Papyrus reed manufactured for writing material in Egypt: pictograms and, later, hieroglyphic used: ink made. |
| | | c. post 2480 City of On (now Heliopolis, Cairo) and Pyramids of Abusir built. c. 2480–c. 2340 Fifth Dynasty in Egypt: capital at Memphis. |
| | c. 2300–2150 Old Minoan Period II. | c. 2340–c. 2137 Sixth Dynasty in Egypt. |
| | 2150–1950 Old Minoan Period III. | ante c. 2134 Seventh, Eighth, Ninth and Tenth Dynasties in Egypt either spurious or representing lines of pretenders. c. 2134–1991 Eleventh Dynasty in Egypt: capital at Thebes. c. 2134–1575 Middle Kingdom in Egypt. |
| | c. 2000 Knossos, Crete, developed as a trading centre. Ionians reach Greece. Pottery from Ukraine reaching China and the Balkans. | ante 2000 Beads and faience begin to be manufactured in Egypt. c. ante 2000 Bronze-smelting introduced into Egypt. c. 2000 The *shaduf*, water-lifting device, already used in Egypt and Mesopotania. Horizontal loom used in Egypt. |

## THE NEAR EAST & INDIA

## THE FAR EAST

## RELIGION & CULTURE

**c. 2500** Early Bronze Age IV in Palestine. Gudea, Ruler of Lagash. The phalanx used in Mesopotamia. Chariots used in Mesopotamia. Beer-making introduced into Egypt and Mesopotamia. Third Dynasty of Kish. Amorites immigrate from Arabia into the Fertile Crescent.

**c. 2500–2400** Second Dynasty of Uruk.
**c. 2500–2350** Second Dynasty of Ur.
**2500–2300** First civilization at Troy.

**c. 2450–2300** Fourth Dynasty of Kish.
**c. 2400–2371** Third Dynasty of Uruk.
**c. 2371–2230** Dynasty of Akkad.
**c. 2371–2316** Sargon I, Akkadian ruler: extends dominions from Mesopotamia into Syria: object possibly to control sources of tin for bronze-making.

**c. 2300 (or c.2350)–2250** Dynasty of Ebla (now Tell Mardikh), near Aleppo.

**c. 2260–2230** Fourth Dynasty of Uruk
**c. 2250–2120** Dynasty of Gutium.

**2120–2114** Fifth Dynasty of Uruk.
**c. 2113–2006** Third Dynasty of Ur.
**c. 2060–1950** Sumerian law code of Ur-nammu of Ur promulgated.
**c.2050–1761** Eshnunna Dynasty.
**c. 2050– 609** Assyrian Dynasty.
**c. 2025–1763** Dynasty of Larsa.
**c. 2017–1794** Isin Dynasty.

**ante 2000** Glass first made in Mesopotamia.
**c. 2000** Indo-Europeans entering Iran. Hittites entering Anatolia. Middle Bronze Age I in Palestine. Sledge·transport used in Mesopotamia.

**c. 2300** Domestication of the horse by Indo-Europeans in the steppes of Asia.

**c. 2200–1700** Hieroglyphic writing appears in Far East.

**ante 2000** Agricultural settlements in China.

**c. 2500** Fine metal-work made in Mesopotamia. Cone mosaic made in Mesopotamia. Wagons in existence amongst steppe nomads. Oil pressed from plants and other flora in Egypt: flowers and herbs cultivated for scent.

**c. 2000** First known pharmacopeia compiled at Ur.

| WESTERN EUROPE | CENTRAL & EASTERN EUROPE | EGYPT & AFRICA |
|---|---|---|
| | c. 2000 High-sterned wooden ships made in Crete. | c. 2000 The battering-ram, covered with reeds or hides, used in Egypt. Egyptian stone weights found in Sinai. The balance known in Egypt. Grape cultivation for wine and wine presses introduced in Egypt and Mesopotamia. |
| c. post 2000 Palafitte (pile-dwellings) appear in Italy: evidence of new culture entering from the north. | **First half of the 2nd millenium** Middle Minoan period in Crete. Cretan hegemony develops in the Mediterranean. Crete develops commercial relations with Syria. | post 2000 Furnace bellows worked by foot introduced into Egypt from Mesopotamia. |
| | | c. 1991–c.?1786 Twelfth Dynasty in Egypt: capital at Diospolis. |
| c. 1900 'Beaker' folk people invade Britain: tin first used: bronze made: Avebury and Stonehenge circles built. | c. 1900–1700 First Palace of Hagia Triada built. | |
| | | c. 1786–1700 Thirteenth and Fourteenth Dynasties in Egypt. |
| | c. 1700–1400 Apogee of the Cretan civilization: commercial relations with Cyprus, Egypt and Syria. | c. 1700–c. 1575 Fifteenth to Seventeenth Dynasties in Egypt: Hyksos Period. |
| c. 1600 or 1500 Terremare settlements begin in Italy. | | c. 1600 The horse first known in Egypt. |
| | | c. 1575–c. 1550 Amosis, Pharaoh. c. 1575–c.?1308 Eighteenth Dynasty in Egypt. Period of the New Kingdom. c. 1550–c. 1528 Amenophis I, Pharaoh. c. 1528–c. 1510 Tuthmòsis I, Pharaoh. |

THE NEAR EAST & INDIA     THE FAR EAST     RELIGION & CULTURE

c. **2000** Indus Valley over-run by northern Aryans.

**post 2000** The bellows invented: enables advances in furnace temperature.
c. **between 2000 and 1500** Abraham migrates from Haran to southern Palestine with a clan possessing 318 fighting men.

c. **1900—1750** Assyrian trading colonies in Asia Minor. Middle Bronze Age IIA in Palestine
c. **1894—1595** First Dynasty of Babylon.
c. **1870** Sumerian law code of Lipit-Ishtar promulgated.
c. **1850—1767** Mari Dynasty.
**18th or 17th c.** Babylonian mathematicians already understand cube and square roots.
c. **1792—1750** Hammurabi, ruler of Babylon, lawgiver: literature flourishes: Babylonian epics of the Creation and the Flood written.

c. **1780** Zimri-Lim, King of Mari, warns his wife Shibtu of contagious disease.
c. **1763** Larsa overthrown.
**ante c. 1761** Akkadian law code of Eshnunna promulgated.
c. **1750—c. 1625** Middle Bronze Age IIB in Palestine.
c. **1750—1600** Sealand Dynasties.
c. **1750—1500** Old Hittite Kingdom in Anatolia.
c. **1746—1162** Kassite Dynasty in Babylonia.
c. **1700** Harappa culture in decline.

**?c. 1690** Law code of Hammurabi promulgated.
c. **1625—c. 1525** Middle Bronze Age IIC in Palestine.

**1595—1168** Kassite Dynasty in Babylonia.

c. **2000** Huang Ti (Yellow Emperor) ruling in Yellow River area. Period of transition from Neolithic to Bronze Age. Stock-breeding and farming already established. Dams and irrigation canals in use. Art of writing and of silk-weaving known.
**post 2000** Hsia Dynasty in China founded by Yu.

c. **1700** Ukrainian pottery reaching China.

| WESTERN EUROPE | CENTRAL & EASTERN EUROPE | EGYPT & AFRICA |
|---|---|---|
| | | c. 1510–c. 1490 Tuthmosis II, Pharaoh. |
| | c. 1500 Bronze age in E Siberia and the Danube. | c. 1500 Egyptian chariots more elaborately made: more sophisticated types of wooden ships constructed. Egyptian vessels with double rudder constructed. Queen Hatshepsut sends expedition to Punt. |
| | c. 1500–1100 Recent Minoan period in Crete: time of artistic decadence: brachycephalic replace dolichocephalic people. | c. 1500–c. 1250 The Hebrews in Egypt. |
| | | c. 1490–1468 Hashepsowe, Pharaoh. |
| | | c. 1490–c. 1436 Tuthmosis III, Pharaoh. |
| | c. 1482 Cretan fleet carries wood from Lebanon to Egypt. | |
| c. 1450 Wessex invaded from European mainland: more refined techniques of metal-work introduced. | | |
| | | c. 1436–c. 1413 Amenophis II, Pharaoh. |
| | | c. 1413–c. 1405 Tuthmosis IV, Pharaoh. |
| | c. 1400 Second Palace of Hagia Triada built. | c. 1405–c. 1367 Amenophis III, Pharaoh. |
| | c. 1400 Achaean invasion of Crete. | |
| | c. 1400 or 1250–8th c. Gandja-Qarabagh culture. | |
| | c. 1400–1100 Period of the apogee of Mycenaean civilization. | |
| | c.?1400–1100 Chtetkovo Treasure. | |
| | c. 1400–1100 Ramparts of the Acropolis, Athens, built. | |
| | | c. 1367–c. 1350 Amenophis IV and Akhenaten, Pharaohs. |
| | | c. 1350–c. 1347 Smenkhare, Pharao[h] |
| | | c. 1347–c. 1339 Tutankhaten, name later changed to Tutankhamun, Pharaoh: buried in an elaborate tom[b] discovered in 1922. |
| | | c. 1339–c. 1335 Ay, Pharaoh. |
| | | c. 1335–c.?1308 Haremhab, Pharao[h] intermediate ruler between Eighteenth and Nineteenth Dynastie[s] |
| | | c. 1309–1291 Sethos I, Pharaoh. Tablet of Abydos depicts Sethos I making offerings to seventy-six of his ancestors, all of whom are name[d] in hieroglyphics. |
| | | c. 1308 Ramesses I, Pharaoh. |

| THE NEAR EAST & INDIA | THE FAR EAST | RELIGION & CULTURE |
|---|---|---|

**c. 1525** Egyptian campaign in Syria.
**c. 1525–c. 1200** Later Bronze Age in Palestine.

**?1523–?1027** Shang Dynasty in China. Agriculture principal occupation. Wheeled vehicles and horses common. Many specialized tools made in bronze. Cowries used as currency. Pictographs beginning to be standardized.

**c. 1500** Iron weapons become common in the Near East.
post c. **1500** Lead used as an ingredient in casting bronze and glass. *Cire-perdu* process evolved.
**c. 15th–13th c.** The camel first domesticated in Arabia.
**c. 1500–1190** Hittite Empire.

**c. 1500** Bronze Age in W Siberia. Bronze becomes used in China.

**c.1500** Hymns of the Rig-Veda begin to be composed.

**c. 1475** Egypt conquers part of Syria.

**14th c.** Tushratta, King of Mitanni, sends Babylonian physicians to Egypt.

**c. 1400** Siberian axes and lances imitated in China.

**c. 1375–1335** Arnuwandas II Suppilaliumas, Hittite ruler.

**1365–1330** Ashur-uballit I, ruler of Assyria.

**1334–1306** Mursilis II, Hittite ruler.

| WESTERN EUROPE | CENTRAL EASTERN EUROPE | EGYPT & AFRICA |
|---|---|---|
| | | c. 1308—c.?1194 Nineteenth Dynasty in Egypt. |
| | c. ?1300 Staromishastovskaya Treasure of gold and silver.<br>c. 1300—1200 Pekrovsk tomb bronze culture.<br>c. ?1300—1100 The Borodino Treasure.<br>1300—800 Seima culture near Nijni Novgorod. | c. 1300 Spokes of chariot axle wheels increased from four to six in Egypt. |
| | | c.1300—600 Saharan bronze age: sources from Mauritania and Senegal. Dessication of the Sahara progressing: horse-drawn carts depicted in drawings show trade routes Morocco to Senegal and R. Niger; and Tripoli to R. Niger.<br>c. 1290—c. 1224 Ramesses II, Pharaoh. Hall of the temple of Karnak built. |
| | c. 1250 Dorians appear in Greece. | post c. 1250 Exodus of the Israelites from Egypt. |
| | | c. 1224—c. 1214 Merenptah (or Meneptah), Pharaoh.<br>c. 1214—1208 Sethos II, Pharaoh.<br>c. 1208 Amenmesse, Pharaoh.<br>c. 1208—c. 1202 Siptah, Pharaoh.<br>c. 1202—c.?1194 Queen Twosre, Pharaoh, followed by a short interregnum. |
| | c. 1200 Talych culture. Bronze age in C Siberia. Iron age begins in the Aegaean. Cimmerians reach Russian steppe N of the Black Sea.<br>c. ?1200 Piatigorsk treasure. Abramovka bronzes.<br><br>c. ?1200—1000 Bronze age of Koban.<br>c. 1200—700 Scythian culture appears first at Khralinsk. | |
| | | c. 1184—c. ?1182 Setnakhte, Pharaoh<br>c. 1184—c. 1087 Twentieth Dynasty in Egypt.<br><br>c. ?1182—c. 1151 Ramesses III, Pharaoh. |

| THE NEAR EAST & INDIA | THE FAR EAST | RELIGION & CULTURE |
|---|---|---|

c. 1306—1282 Mutawallis, Hittite
ruler.
13th c. Inscription in Phoenician on
tomb of Ahiram at Byblos.

c. 1300 Chariots with more than four
spokes found in China and S Russia.

1285 Battle of Qadesh between
Egypt and Hittites.
1275—1250 Hattusilis II, Hittite
ruler.
1274—1245 Shalmaneser I, ruler of
Assyria.
1269 Treaty between Egypt and
Hittites.
c. 1250—c. 1200 Israelite conquest
of Palestine.
1244—1208 Tukulti-Ninurti I, ruler
of Assyria.
c. 1225 Babylonia ruled by Assyria
for seven years.

1275—1250 Physicians from Babylon
sent to Hittite King Hattusilis III.

1259 Isthmian Games said to have
been inaugurated.

c. 1200 Representatives of
Israelitic tribes assemble at Shechem
to celebrate conquest of the
Promised Land. Hide shaped copper
ingots traded from S Turkey.
c. 1200—1020 Period of the Judges
in Palestine.
c. 1200—c. 1000 Beginning of the
Iron Age in Palestine. Philistines
settling in Palestine.
c. 1200 or after Siege of Troy.
c. 1190 Phrygians invade Asia Minor.

12th c. Tchin-la (later Cambodia)
mentioned in Chinese Chronicles.

c. 1200 Minaean script already
developed in S Arabia.

c. 1200—1000 Art of Pottery
becomes known in Peru.

1183 Traditional date of fall of Troy.

1171 Elamite invasion of Babylonia.
c. 1168—1162 Kassite Dynasty in
Babylonia overthrown by Elamites.

| WESTERN EUROPE | CENTRAL & EASTERN EUROPE | EGYPT & AFRICA |
|---|---|---|
| | | c. 1151–1145 Ramesses IV, Pharaoh. |
| | c. 1150–950 Cimmerian culture develops N of the Black Sea. | |
| | | c. 1145–c. 1141 Ramesses V, Pharaoh. |
| | | c. 1141–c. 1134 Ramesses VI, Pharaoh. |
| | | c. 1134 Ramesses VII, Pharaoh. Ramesses VIII, Pharaoh. |
| | | c. 1134–c. 1117 Ramesses IX, Pharaoh. |
| | | c. 1117–c. 1114 Ramesses X, Pharaoh. |
| | | c. 1114–c. 1087 Ramesses XI, Pharaoh. |
| 1100 Traditional date of founding of Agadir (modern Cadiz) by Phoenicians. | c. ?1100 Bronze foundry at Nicolaiev. c. 1100–900 Dorian invasion of Crete. | c. 1100 Phoenicians found Lixus and Utique (Utica). |
| | | c. 1087–c. 945 Twenty-first Dynasty in Egypt. |
| c. ?1052 Cumae founded. | | |

| THE NEAR EAST & INDIA | THE FAR EAST | RELIGION & CULTURE |
|---|---|---|

**c. ? 1162–1152** Marduk-kabit-aheshu, ruler of Babylon.
**c. 1162–1046** Fourth Dynasty of Babylon.
**c. ? 1151–1143** Itti-marduk-balatu, ruler of Babylon.

**c. 1150–c. 1100** Deborah and Gideon, Judges in Israel.

**c. 1125** Aramaeans established in Syria.
**1124–1103** Nebuchadrezzar I, ruler of Babylon.

**1115–1077** Tiglathpileser I, ruler of Assyria.

**1100** Tadmor (Palmyra) already in existence as a city.
**c. 1100** Syria conquered by Tiglathpileser I of Assyria. Israelites conquer Canaan.
**c.1100–c. 500** 'Painted-Grey Ware' sites of agricultural communities in the western Ganges valley: horses and cattle bred: copper used.
**11th c.** The camel introduced into Syria.

**c. 1077–911** Aramaeans invade Mesopotamia.
**1074–1057** Ashur-bel-Kala, ruler of Assyria.

**post 1050** Battle of Aphek: Israel defeated by the Philistines: the Ark of the Covenant taken, but later restored. Fall of Shiloh.
**fl. post 1050–post 1020** Samuel the Prophet.
**1049–1031** Ashurnasipal I, ruler of Assyria.
**c. 1046–1015** Fifth Dynasty of Babylon.
**1030–1019** Shalmaneser II, ruler of Assyria.

**?1017–256** Chou Dynasty in China.

**c. 1020–c. 1000** Saul, King of Israel.
**c. post 1020** Saul defeats the Ammonites, the Philistines and the Amalekites: simple capital at Gibeah.
**c. 1010–970** Ashur-rabi II, ruler of Assyria.

**c. 1010–c. 970** Hebrew Alphabet developed from earlier Semitic script.

| WESTERN EUROPE | CENTRAL & EASTERN EUROPE | EGYPT & AFRICA |
|---|---|---|

**c. end of 2nd millenium** 'Dorian Invasion from Greece into Italy.
**c. ante 1000** Iron Age begins in Italy: known as Villanova culture: probable evidence of immigration from N.: Bologna founded.

**c. 1000** Alban Hills cease to be volcanically active: 'Latin' villages begin to be built. Sickles with shaped handles evolved in Switzerland.
**c. 1000–500** Celtic immigration into central Germany.

**c. 1000** Crude anchors evolved in the Mediterranean.
**c. ? 1000** Date of the earliest Homeric traditions.
**c. 1000–900** Iron-working occurs in Lelvar culture, Georgia.
**c. 1000–800** Phoenician alphabet adopted by the Greeks.

**c. 1000** Dessication of the Sahara progressing: drawings of horse-drawn carts show routes from Morocco and Tripoli to Rs Senegal and Niger. Pre-Carthaginian settlement at Salammbo, near Carthage.

**?10th–9th c.** Aristocracy giving way to monarchy in Ionia, and subsequently throughout Greece.

**c. 945–924** Shoshenk I, Pharaoh. unifies upper and lower Egypt.

| THE NEAR EAST & INDIA | THE FAR EAST | RELIGION & CULTURE |
|---|---|---|

**c. ante 1000** Glazing of bricks and tiles begun.
**ante 1000** David, living as an outlaw, harries the Amalekites and other S Palestinian tribes. Deeper plough share evolved.

**c. ante 1000** White nomads encounter Mongol hunters and gatherers in the western steppes: mounted nomadism develops.
**ante 1000** White ware with feldspar glazes made for a short while in China .
**c. 1000** Composite bow evolved in China: development from western techniques.

**c. ante 1000** Earliest *Rig-Veda* collection of 1528 verses begins to be memorized and collected.

**c. 1000—600** Heavier chariots evolved in Assyria.

**c. 1000—700** *Ramayana* and *Mahabharata* historical epics composed in India; the *Mahabharata* the longest epic in existence: both of partial historical reliability.
**c. 10th c.** J documents in the OT first written down.

**c. post 1000** Coronation of David at Hebron (-c. 961): campaign against Philistines: Jerusalem seized from the Jebusites: the Ark of the Covenant solemnly transferred to Jerusalem: campaigns against Ammonites and Aramaeans, and as far as Syria, capturing important copper mines: empire extends from Wadi al-Arish to Gulf of Aqaba, and includes all central and southern Syria.
**c. 969—936** Hiram I, King of Tyre, provides Solomon with hardwood in exchange for wheat and olive oil.
**966-935** Tiglathpileser ll, ruler of Assyria.
**c. ante 961** Absalom rebels against David, abortively: Sheba also rebels and is assassinated.
**c. 961—c. 922** Solomon, King of Israel.
**c. 961** Solomon consolidates his throne by executions; foreign policy consolidated by diplomatic marriages; army strengthened by increase in chariots and building of fortified cities.
**c. post 961** Solomon develops Red Sea trade from Ezion-geber and caravan trade with Saba (Sheba), principal power in S Arabia.
**c. 958** Building of Solomon's Temple begun by a Tyrian architect.
**c. 951** Solomon's Temple completed and dedicated: construction follows Phoenician models.
**c. 948** 'House of the Forest of Lebanon' (armoury), judgement hall and palace for his wife, Pharaoh's daughter, completed by Solomon. Period of intense literary activity: Court History of David written.

**c. post 1000** Urban societies beginning in China.

**post 951** Israelitic music and psalmody developed: composition of proverbs, some, ascribed to Solomon, popular.

| WESTERN EUROPE | CENTRAL & EASTERN EUROPE | EGYPT & AFRICA |
|---|---|---|
| | | c. 945—c. 730 Twenty-second Dynasty in Egypt. |
| | | c. 924—c. 888 Osorkon I, Pharaoh. |
| | | c. 920 Kushite Dynasty begins to rule at Nepata. |
| | | c. 918±70—207±50 Nok figurine culture in Nigeria. |
| c. 900 ff. Celts invade Britain. | ?9th or 8th c. Slavery first recorded in Greece. | c. 900 Beginning of Phoenician colonial maritime expansion. |
| c. post 900—6th c. Celts entering Spain. | 900—750 Last phase of Cimmerian culture. | |
| | c. 900—700 Formation of Ionian confederacy. Hallstatt iron age culture. | |
| | | c. 888—c. 881 Takelot I, Pharaoh. |
| | | c. 881—c. 852 Osorkon II, Pharaoh. |

## THE NEAR EAST & INDIA    THE FAR EAST    RELIGION & CULTURE

**934–912** Ashur-dan II, ruler of
Assyria.

**c. 922** Schism between the Kingdoms
of Israel and Judah.
**c. 922–722/1** Kingdom of Israel.
**c. 922–587** Kingdom of Judah.
**c. 922-915** Rehoboam, King of
Judah: speedily loses ten northern
tribes and Syrian possessions by
tactlessness and arrogance.
**c. 922–901** Jeroboam I, King of
Israel.

**c. 918** Judah invaded by Egypt:
150 places claimed as taken:
Rehoboam forced to pay massive
tribute: Egyptians lay waste
Kingdom of Israel.
**c. 915–913** Abijah, King of Judah:
frontier fighting with Israel,
continued into next reign.
**c. 913–873** Asa, King of Judah:
further fighting with Egypt ended
by Asa's success at battle of
Mareshah.
**911–891** Adad-Nirari II, ruler of
Assyria.
**c. 901–900** Nadab, King of Israel.
**c. 900** Nadab assassinated by Baasha,
one of his officers.
**c. 900** Military pontoon bridges
evolved in Assyria. Aramaeans
expelled from Assyria.
**c. 900–877** Baasha, King of Israel.
**c. post 900** Baasha seizes Judaean
territory to within five miles of
Jerusalem: forced to withdraw by
alliance between Judah and
Benhadad I of Damascus.
**post 900** Kingdom of Urartu
founded: struggles with Syria ensue.
**890–884** Tukulti-Ninurta II, ruler
of Assyria.

**883–859** Ashurnasirpal II, ruler of
Assyria.

**877** Ashurnasirpal II occupies
Carchemish: reaches Mediterranean.
**c. 877–876** Elah, King of Israel:
very shortly assassinated.
**c. 876** Zimri, King of Israel: ruled
one week, then committed suicide:
period of confusion follows.
**c. 876–869** Omri, King of Israel:
takes some time to consolidate
power.
**873–849** Jehosaphat, King of Judah:
responsible for legal reforms.
**c. ante 869** New capital at Samaria
built as Israel's capital: an 'ivory
house' (palace) built: many other
cities fortified.

**9th c.** 'J' document in the Hexateuch
written. Maize already cultivated
in Peru.

| WESTERN EUROPE | CENTRAL & EASTERN EUROPE | EGYPT & AFRICA |
|---|---|---|
| | | c. 858 Takelot II becomes co-ruler with Osorkon II. |
| c. 850–800 Etruscans arrive in Central Italy. | | c. 852–827 Takelot II, Pharaoh: a weakling: independent principalities in much of Egypt. |
| | | c. 827–c. 788 Shoshenk III, Pharaoh |
| | | c.?817–c. 730 Twenty-third Dynasty in Egypt of usurpers: period of anarchy. |

| THE NEAR EAST & INDIA | THE FAR EAST | RELIGION & CULTURE |
|---|---|---|

**869–850** Ahab, King of Israel: m. Jezebel, daughter of Ittobaal, King of Tyre: alliance important economically and diplomatically. Ahab allies also with Benhadad of Damascus, following Aramaean raids into Israelite territory, acknowledging him as overlord.

**fl. c. 869–849** Elijah, prophet in Israel.

**858–824** Shalmaneser III, ruler of Assyria: conquers Syria from the Euphrates to the Mediterranean: coalition of Kings of Cilicia, Damascus, Ammon, Hamath and Israel formed against him: Ahab contributes 2,000 chariots and 2,000 infantry.
**c. 854** First mention in literature of camels owned by Arabs.
**853** Shalmaneser III again raids Syria: checked at Karkar on the Orontes by the coalition under Ahab of Israel.

**850** Ahab d. fighting the Aramaeans.
**c. 850–849** Ahaziah, King of Israel: d. of a fall after a few month's reign.

**fl. c. 850** Homer, poet.
**c. 850 (or c. 750–650)** *Iliad* and *Odyssey* composed.

**c. 849–842** Jehoram, King of Israel: Moab, under King Mesha, revolts successfully.
**c. 849–842** Jehoram, King of Judah: puts to death all his brothers to eliminate rivals.

**c. 849–c. post 842** Elisha, prophet in Israel.

**c. post 849** Edom becomes independent of Judah: Judah thus loses port of Ezion-Geber, and ? Araba copper mines.
**842** Jehu kills Jehoram of Judah and Ahaziah of Israel: succ. as King of Israel (–815): Jezebel thrown out of a window in Jezreel: worshippers of Baal butchered.
**c. 842–837** Athaliah, Queen of Judah: Baal Melqart worshipped in Jerusalem as well as Yahweh.
**841** Shalmaneser III again attacks Syria and reaches coast: tribute taken from Tyre, Sidon and Israel.
**837** Shalmaneser III again raids Western Syria.
**c. 837–800** Joash (or Jehoash), King of Judah, aged seven, made king after murder of Athaliah.
**836** The Medes first mentioned in an inscription listing Assyria's enemies.

**823–811** Shamshi-Adad V, ruler of Assyria.

| WESTERN EUROPE | CENTRAL & EASTERN EUROPE | EGYPT & AFRICA |
|---|---|---|
| | | **814** Traditional date of foundation of Carthage, seat of western Phoenician trading empire. |
| **c.?800** Probable date of founding of Cadiz by Phoenicians: art of writing and knowledge of mining and smelting introduced.<br>**c. 800** Etruscans settle in twelve cities between Rs Tiber and Arno. Carthaginian trading colony founded at Nora, Sardinia. , Intercourse between Aegaean seafarers and Tuscany.<br>Urn cemeteries in Scotland. | **c. 800** Spartans conquer and settle Lacedaemonia.<br><br><br>**800** Ship building evolved in Greece. | **c. ante 800** Greek colony set up on Plataea Is., Marmarica. |
| **8th–7th c.** Bronze industry in Italy reaches lighest development.<br>**8th–6th c.** Greek settlements in Sicily and in S Italy: Italy becomes an important market for Greek exports: vine and olive cultivation introduced. | **8th–7th c.** Cimmerians occupying much of present Russia.<br>**8th c.** Athenian citizens divided into four classes: landed proprietors; knights; peasants with two oxen; wage-earners. Greek cities begin to form states.<br>**c. mid 8th c.** Thraco-Phrygeans occupying Balkans and Asia Minor. | **c. 788—c. 782** Pemay, Pharaoh. |
| | | **c. 782–745** Shoshenk IV, Pharaoh.<br><br>**c. 780** Kashta, a Sudanese, intervenes in Thebes. |
| **c. 753** Traditional date of foundation of Rome. | | **c. ante 751** Alara, ruler of Kush: succ. by brother Kashta: obtains control of Upper Egypt.<br>**c. 751–730** Piankhy, King of Napata-Meroe. |

| THE NEAR EAST & INDIA | THE FAR EAST | RELIGION & CULTURE |
|---|---|---|

**c. ante 815** Trans-Jordan lost by
Israel to Damascus.
**c. 815—801** Jehoahaz, King of
Israel.

**810—783** Adad-Nirari III, ruler of
Assyria.
**801—786** Jehoash, King of Israel:
regains much lost territory.

**c. 800** Siege towers evolved in
Assyria. Aryan culture and the use
of iron spreading in India.
Tripoli, Lebanon, founded.

**c. 800—783** Amaziah, King of
Judah: regains Edom; but taken
prisoner by Jehoash of Israel, who
retires after sacking Jerusalem.

**8th and 7th c.** Detailed catalogues of
stars written in Babylon.
**8th c.** Temple and palace architecture
begins to be developed in Greece:
sculpture follows.

**8th c.** Population of Judah probably
exceeds 250,000. Kingdom of
Lydia founded by Mermnades
Dynasty: commercial intercourse
grows up with Greek cities.

**c. 786—746** Jeroboam II, King of
Israel: much territory regained.
**c. 783** Amaziah of Judah
assassinated. Uzziah (Azariah), King
of Judah, at age of sixteen: walls of
Jerusalem restored: Edom recovered:
Ezion-Geber regained: forts erected
in Negeb and in Philistine territory:
period of prosperity ensues.
**782—772** Shalmaneser IV, ruler of
Assyria.

**fl. c. 786—746** Amos, prophet in
Israel.

Olympiad Era begins.
**c. 776** First Olympic Games.

**771—754** Ashur-dan III, ruler of
Assyria.

**c. 770** Chou capital, Hao, invaded by
Jung nomads. Capital moved to
Loyang.

**753—746** Ashur-nirari V, ruler of
Assyria.

| WESTERN EUROPE | CENTRAL & EASTERN EUROPE | EGYPT & AFRICA |
|---|---|---|
| c. 750 Large numbers of Celts reach Britain: plough introduced. Chalcidian Greek colony founded in Campania, W Italy.<br>c. post 750 Chalcidian Greek colonies founded in the strait of Messina and at Naxos and Catania, E Sicily. | c. 750–700 Cimmerians lose the Russian steppes to the Scythians from Turkestan and W Siberia. Cimmerians enter Hungary, Thrace, Colchis and Asia Minor.<br><br>747–657 Bacchiads govern Corinth. | c. 750 Gebel Barkal the capital of an independent Ethiopian kingdom. |
| | c. ?736 Corinth colonizes Corcyra. | |
| c. 733 Syracuse founded by Corinthians: other Greek colonies follow in Sicily and on the Italian mainland. | | |
| | | c. 730 Piankhy conquers Egypt.<br>c. 730–715 Twenty-fourth Dynasty. Pharaoh Tefnakht a vassal of Piankhy. |

## THE NEAR EAST & INDIA      THE FAR EAST      RELIGION & CULTURE

**c. mid 8th c.** Scythians living N of Caspian Sea.
**c. 750–742** Jotham, co-regent of Judah.
**fl. c. 750–115** Sabaean kingdom in S Arabia.

**747** Nabu-nasir, King of Babylon, corrects lunar calendar by intercalation.
**c. 746–745** Zechariah, King of Israel.
**746–734** Ninth Dynasty of Babylon.
**c. 745** Shallum, King of Israel.
**c. 745–738** Menahem, King of Israel.
**c. 745–725** Tiglathpileser III, King of Assyria.
**745–20** Assyrians conquer Neo-Hittite Kingdoms in N Syria.
**743 ff.** Tiglathpileser campaigns frequently in Syria.
**c. 742–735** Jotham, King of Judah.

**c. 740** Kingdom of the Medes founded by Deioces (Daiakku).
**c. 738–737** Pekahiah, King of Israel.
**c. 737** Pekahiah of Israel assassinated.
**c. 737–732** Pekah, King of Israel: kingdom in a state of collapse.

**735–733** Isaiah urges Ahaz of Judah not to co-operate with the Aramean-Israelite coalition against Assyria.
**c. 735–715** Ahaz, King of Judah: Judah a vassal of Assyria.

**c. 732–724** Hoshea, King of Israel.
**732–626** Tenth Dynasty of Babylon.

**728** Tayma and people of the Sabai send tribute to Tiglathpileser III.
**725–722** Shalmaneser V, ruler of Assyria.
**724** Shalmaneser V attacks Hoshea, King of Israel, and takes him prisoner. Samaria besieged by Shalmaneser (to 722 or 721).
**722 or 721** later summer or autumn, Samaria falls: 27,290 citizens deported to upper Mesopotamia and Media.

**c. 750** Hesiod, poet.
**fl. c. post 750** Hosea, prophet in Israel.

**fl. c. 742–688** Isaiah, prophet in Judah. Micah, prophet, in Judah.

**c. 722–c. 481** Spring and Autumn eras of the Chou Dynasty in China, with authority divided amongst virtually independent warring states. Iron replaces bronze in common use.

| WESTERN EUROPE | CENTRAL & EASTERN EUROPE | EGYPT & AFRICA |
|---|---|---|
| | | c. 716—695 Kushite ruler Shabaka conquers all Egypt. c. 716—656 Twenty-fifth (Kushite) Dynasty. |
| c. 708 Tarentum founded by Greeks. | 710 ff. Rulers of Greek towns in Cyprus pay homage to Sargon II of Assyria. | |
| c. 700 Tyrians first arrive on Tuscan coast. | c. 700 Sparta begins to expand. c. 700—550 Centre of Scythian culture SE Russia. | |
| | 7th c. Argos, in the Peloponnese, annexes port of Nauplia: system of weights and measures initiated by King Phaedon. Athens annexes state of Eleusis: Eleusis, under Athenian direction, becomes a religious centre for all Greece. c. 7th c. Amphictyonic Leagues begin to emerge in different parts of Greece: Delphi becomes an important centre. | 7th c. The camel introduced into Egypt. |
| | | 695—690 Shabataka, Pharaoh. |
| | | 689—664 Taharka, co-Pharaoh with Shabataka. |

721—705 Sargon II, ruler of Assyria.
c. 721—675 Cyaxeres I, ruler of the
Medes.
c. 720 Cimmerians reach Phrygia.

715 Sargon II subjugates Arabs of
Tamud (Thamud) and Ibadid.
c. 715—687/6 Hezekiah, King of
Judah: cautious policy to maintain
independence.
c. 714 Ashdod rebels against
Assyria.
c. 714—712 Isaiah warns Hezekiah
of Judah not to ally with Egypt
against Assyria.
710—705 Sargon II, vice-regent of
Babylon.

708 Empire of the Medes founded
by Deioces.
705 General rebellion of Assyrian
provinces and vassals, supported by
Egypt. Isaiah warns Hezekiah of
Judah against Egypt.
c. 704—681 Sennacherib, King of
Assyria.
c. 704 Hezekiah of Judah refuses
tribute to Sennacherib of Assyria.
c. ante 701 Hezekiah of Judah allies
with Egypt against Assyria:
fortification of Jerusalem improved
by tunneled water supply.
c. 700 Phoenicians invent the bireme.
Greeks increase length of ships.
c. ?700 Writing becomes known by
Aryans of India.
c. 700—675 Achaemenes, founder of
the Achaemenean Dynasty of Persia.
c. 700—c. 300 Minaean (Ma'an)
Kingdom in S Arabia: capital Qarnaw.

c. post 700 Gyges, King of Lydia,
allied with Greek towns.

694 Sennacherib campaigns in
Chaldaea.
c. ?690—689 Hezekiah regains
independence for Judah.
689 Babylon sacked by Sennacherib.

688 Sennacherib reduces Adumu,
'fortress of Arabia.'

post 721 J and E documents in the
OT combined.

c. 700—c. AD 100 Chavin
civilization in Peru.
c. 700 Demotic script evolved from
hieratic script in Egypt. True
potter's wheel developed.

7th c. Earliest known Greek
inscriptions: knowledge of writing
thought to be confined to a minority.
Shrine of Delphi begun.

post 700 Kapila, Indian philosopher.
7th—6th c. Mystery religions begin to
spread in Greece. Artemis of Delos and
Artemis of Delos and Winged Victory
of Delos sculpted. Apollos of Naxos,
Thera and Melos carved. Earliest
monuments abd paintings at the
Acropolis, Athens.

| WESTERN EUROPE | CENTRAL EASTERN EUROPE | EGYPT & AFRICA |
|---|---|---|

CENTRAL
EASTERN EUROPE

EGYPT & AFRICA

**686–5** List of archons of Athens begins.
**c. 680** Parians found Thasos.

**680–669** Egypt made a colony by Esarhaddon of Assyria.

**677** Chalcedon founded by Megarians.

**c. 675** Cyzicus founded by Milesians.

**c. ?670** Beginning of iron-working at Meroe.

**c. 667** Pharaoh Taharka regains Memphis: loses it shortly to Ashurbanipal of Assyria.
**c. 665** Psammetichus becomes master of the Delta. Treaty with Gyges of Lydia to provide mercenaries.
**c. 664–656** Tanuatamun, an Ethiopian, Pharaoh at Memphis.
**664–610** Psammetichus I, ruler of Egypt.
**c. 664–525** Twenty-sixth Dynasty.
**c. 663** Tanuatamun driven from Memphis by Ashurbanipal: retires to Napata. Greek colony founded at Naucratis.

**664** Naval battle between Corinth and Corcyra.

**c. 660** Byzantium founded by Megarians.

**c. 657** Bacchiads expelled from Corinth: Cypselos becomes tyrant.

**c. 654** Tanwetamani renounces claims in Egypt: retires to Napata.

| THE NEAR EAST & INDIA | THE FAR EAST | RELIGION & CULTURE |
|---|---|---|

**c. 688** Sennacherib takes many Judaean cities. Hezekiah of Judah defends Jerusalem, supported by Isaiah. Sennacherib's army, crippled by plague, retires.
**c. 687/6** Hezekiah of Judah d.
**c. 687/6—642** Manasseh, King of Judah: peace made between Judah and Assyria: policy of loyalty to Assyria.

**680** Sennacherib of Assyria murdered: succ. Esarhaddon (—669).
**c. 678** Cimmerians enter Assyrian Empire. Party of Scythians contact Assyria under their king Ichpakai: attack unsuccessful.

**676** Rebellion of Arabs against Esarhaddon.
**675—653** Phraortes, King of the Medes.
**674/3** Esarhaddon's attack on Egypt checked at the frontier.
**671** Esarhaddon again attacks Egypt: Memphis seized.

**668** Esarhaddon d. on expedition against Egypt: succ. Ashurbanipal (—627).

**c. 685** Lowest level of Kawa temple built: opened 679.

**660** Jimmu Tenno, reputed first Emperor of Japan and founder of present dynasty: alleged by Japanese tradition to have founded capital S of present Kyoto: first twelve emperors alleged to live average of 100 years each.

**653—585** Cyaxares II, King of the Medes: shortly overcome by the Scythians: tribute paid for twenty-eight years.
**652** Shash-shum-ukin, brother of Ashurbanipal, rebels, supported by many elements in the Assyrian Empire.

| WESTERN EUROPE | CENTRAL & EASTERN EUROPE | EGYPT & AFRICA |
|---|---|---|
| c. 650 Etruscans invade Latium and Campania: Capua founded. | c. 650 Chalcidians settle on Thracian coast; Megarians settle on both sides of the Bosphorus; Miletus founds 100 towns and marts during the following 150 years: the Mediterranean becomes virtually a Greek lake. Messena revolts against Sparta: King Aristomenes put down by Spartans. | c. 650 Tanwetamani d.: his dynasty endures at Napata and Meroe for 1,000 years. Beginning of iron-working in Egypt. |
| | c. 646 Olbia founded. | |
| | | c. 640 Syrian and Jewish colonists settle at Elephantine: Ionian traders settling; Greek mercenaries recruited. |
| | 632/1 Megacles, Archon of Athens. War against Megara. | |
| 630 King of Tartessos, (Spain), visited by a Samian Greek: rich cargo of silver obtained. | | c. 630 Greek colony at Cyrene founded. |
| | 627—585 Periander, tyrant of Corinth. | |

| THE NEAR EAST & INDIA | THE FAR EAST | RELIGION & CULTURE |
|---|---|---|

**THE NEAR EAST & INDIA**

c. 650 Cimmerians reach Cappadocia and Cilicia. Cimmerians from the N coast of the Black Sea invade Lydia: Gyges killed in battle: Sardis taken: Magnesia and Temple of Artemis near Ephesus destroyed. Dam constructed at Marib.
650–648 Ashurbanipal besieges Shamash-shum-ukin in Babylon.
648 Sumer and Akkad pacified: Kandalanu, Viceroy of Babylon. Babylon regained by Ashurbanipal: Shamash-shum-ukin commits suicide.

c. 642–640 Amon, King of Judah.
c. 642 Jeremiah the prophet b.
c. ?642 or 600 Saisunaga Dynasty of Magadha, India, founded: first ruler Sisunaga (or Sisunaka): capital at Girivraja or old Rajagriha, Gaya District.
c. 640 Amon assassinated.

c. 640–610 Josiah, King of Judah: ascends throne aged eight.
640–600 Cyrus I, King of Persia.
639 Assyrian conquest of Elam completed: Susa devastated.
c. 638 Scythians from Assyria sent to destroy Cimmerians in Pontus.

c. 629/8 Judah gains independence from Assyria: Samaria, Megiddo, and possibly Gilead, added to Judah.
628 Madyes with Scythian army allies with Assyria against the Medes: Media submits: Cyaxares forms new army: Scythian chiefs murdered: remainder flee to the Caucasus.

627 Nabu-apal-usur (Nabopolassar) Aramaean governor of the Sealand, revolts against Assyria.
627–612 Ashurbanipal of Assyria d.: succ. Ashur-etil-ilani.
626 Nabopolassar seizes Babylon: proclaimed King: Eleventh Dynasty (−539) known as Chaldaean or Neo-Babylonian: Babylonian Chronicles record events almost daily.
626–615 Continuous war between Assyrians and Babylonians.
c. 625 Cyaxares II murders Scythian leaders at a banquet.
623–612 Sin-shar-ishkun, King of Assyria jointly with his brother.

**RELIGION & CULTURE**

c. 650 Archilochos of Paros, poet.
c. 650–627 Habbakkuk, prophet.
c. 650–560 Sappho, poetess.

640–548 Thales of Miletus, philospher.

c. 628–551 Zoroaster: Zendavesta: origin of Mazdaism in Persia.

    CENTRAL &
EASTERN EUROPE    EGYPT & AFRICA

c. ?616 Establishment of the Tarquin
Dynasty at Rome.

c. 621 Dracon, law-giver, at Athens.

c. 612 Athens takes Salamis from
Megara.

c. 610–595 Necho II, Pharaoh.
c. 610 Necho attempts to build Red
Sea-Nile canal: alleged to have sent
Phoenicians to circumnavigate Africa.

c. 607 Athens occupies Sigea.

THE NEAR EAST & INDIA          THE FAR EAST          RELIGION & CULTURE

c. 622 Josiah of Judah initiates
widespread legal and religious
reforms. Bethel and Samaritan
shrines destroyed.

c. post 622 Zephaniah, prophet, in
Judah. Jeremiah (−587) begins to
prophesy.

616 Nabopolassar takes Nippur, and
all Sumer and Akkad, Harran and
Kirkuk: Assur besieged without
success. Egyptians ally with Sin-
shar-ishkun.
615 Medes invade Assyria and take
Arrapha.
614 Medes take Assur: treaty made
between Cyaxares and Nabopolassar:
his son, Nebuchadrezzar m.
Cyaxares' daughter.
613 Nabopolassar campaigns on the
Euphrates.
612 Nabopolassar takes Nineveh
after two months' siege: assisted by
Medes under Cyaxares: Assur,
Nineveh and (?)Nimrud, destroyed.
Sin-shar-ishkun killed: shadow
Assyrian monarchy continued under
Ashur-uballit (−610) at Harran.
612/611 Egyptian aid sent to Sin-
shar-ishkun.

610 Babylonians and Medes attack
Harran: abandoned by Ashur-uballit
and Egyptian allies. Babylonians in
full possession of Assyria. End of
the Assyrian Empire.
c. 610 Pharaoh Necho II attempts to
save Assyria by attacking the
Babylonians: Josiah of Judah killed
in battle at Megiddo. Change of
title in the Sabaean Kingdom.
c. 610−115 Second period of the
Sabaean Kingdom: capital at Marib,
famous for its dam.
c. 609 Jehoahaz, King of Judah:
reigned three months: then deposed
and deported to Egypt by Pharaoh
Necho.
609 Ashur-uballit disappears.
c. 609−598 Jehoiakim, King of
Judah, as an Egyptian vassal: poll tax
paid to Egypt: Jeremiah the prophet
openly contemptuous of Egypt.
607−605 Nebuchadrezzar (Nabu-
kudurri-usur), Crown Prince of
Chaldaea, campaigns against
Egyptians in Syria.

fl. 606 Alcaeus, lyric poet.

605 May−June, Nebuchadrezzar
defeats Egyptians at Karkemish:
Egyptian army massacred:
Nebuchadrezzar reaches Pelusium:
returns to Babylon on news of his
father's death: 23 Sept.,
Nebuchadrezzar crowned in Babylon
(−562)

c. 605−520 Lao-Tse, founder of
Taoism.

| WESTERN EUROPE | CENTRAL & EASTERN EUROPE | EGYPT & AFRICA |
|---|---|---|

**ante 600** Etruscans adopt alphabet from the Greeks.
**c. 600** Rome the 'City of the Four Regions'. Marseilles founded by Ionians: other Ionian colonies founded as far as E Spain.

**c. 600** Thrasybulus, tyrant of Miletus; Pythagoras, tyrant of Ephesus. Epidamnus founded. Currency commonly minted by Greek cities.

**c. 600** Carthage the leading city of the W Mediterranean.

**c. 6th or 5th c.** Etruscan kings replaced by annually elected magistrates.

**6th c.** Practice of mortgaging land in Greece first known: probably practised earlier. Serfs first recorded in Greece. Sparta expands territories: Spartan League formed with adjacent cities. Dyarchy in Sparta: two kings with aristocratic deliberative assembly. Avars, horde of Turkish origin, pushed into Russia, and then into Hungary.

**6th c.** Habashat (Abyssinians) emerging in present Ethiopia as evidenced by inscriptions.

**c. 597** Necho II constructs fleet.

**c. 595–589** Psammetichus II, Pharao At war with Napata-Meroe.

**c. 594/3** Solon, Archon of Athens, elected by Areopagus: economic reformer: jury system introduced. laws engraved on stone tablets in the Agora.

**c. 594–588** Greek inscriptions on monuments at Abu Simbel: commemorate Greek aid in Psammetichus II's expedition against Ethiopia.

**c. 593–568** Aspelta, King of Napata Meroe: builds temple of the Sun at Meroe.

| THE NEAR EAST & INDIA | THE FAR EAST | RELIGION & CULTURE |
|---|---|---|

**604** Nebuchadrezzar, with an army, takes tribute from Damascus, Tyre, Sidon and Jerusalem: Ascalon destroyed.
**601** Nebuchadrezzar fights indecisive battle with Egyptian army.

**c. 600** Psammetichus II leads expedition against Chaldaeans in Syria. The trireme first built in the Levant and Egypt. Medes take Armenia and Cappadocia. Many kingdoms and republics established in N India: monarchies chiefly in Ganges plain: republics in hill country.
**post 600** Nabataean nomads occupy present Jordan.

**c. 600** Seismographs made in China. Greeks evolve long-boat. More sophisticated type of potter's wheel evolved in Greece: slip ware first produced.

**c. post 600** Gold coin or bars first used in China.

**c. 600—559** Cambyses I, King of Persia: m. the daughter of Astyages, his original overlord.

**6th c.** Indians already trading in Malaysia.
**6th—4th c.** Mythical period of Sinhalese history.

**6th c.** Buddhism spreads as far as Japan. First map of the world, inscribed on clay, made at Nineveh. Classical Sanskrit begins to break down into derived languages.
**?6th c.** Beginning of oracle of Delphi in Thessaly.

**599** Nebuchadrezzar sends detachments against the Arabs of Qedar.
**598 Dec.,** Jehoiakim of Judah d.: possibly assassinated.
**c. 597** Jehoiachin, King of Judah: 16 March surrenders Jerusalem to Babylon after three months' reign: Judah in captivity: some 3,000 Jews taken to Babylon.
**c. 597—587** Zedekiah, King of Judah: title nominal only.
**post 597** Population of Judah reduced to c. 125,000.

**c. 595/4** Revolt of Jews in Babylon quickly put down.
**c. 595—570** Pharaoh Apries takes Gaza: attacks Tyre and Sidon.
**594/3** Ambassadors of Ammon, Edom, Moab, Sidon and Tyre meet in Jerusalem with Zedekiah to discuss plans for revolt against Babylon: meeting a failure: Zedekiah of Judah assures Babylon of his loyalty.

**593** The prophet Ezekiel begins to prophesy amongst Jewish exiles in Babylon (—c. 573).

| WESTERN EUROPE | CENTRAL & EASTERN EUROPE | EGYPT & AFRICA |
|---|---|---|
| | | c. 591 Psammetichus II sacks Napata: Meroe becomes Kushite capital. |
| | | c. 589–568 Apries (Hophra) Pharaoh: sends expedition to raise Babylonian siege of Jerusalem. |
| | | c. 588 Libyans ally with Greeks of Cyrene. |
| | | c. 587 Prophet Jeremiah and other Jews take refuge in Egypt. |
| | c. 585–582 Psammetichus, last tyrant of Corinth. | |
| | | c. 570 Libyan chief Adicran applies to Egypt for aid against Greeks: Egyptians badly defeated. |
| | | c. 570–526 Amaris, Pharaoh, following civil war: allies with Greeks of Cyrene: takes parts of Cyprus. |
| c. 565 Alalia, a colony of Phocaea, founded in Corsica. | c. 565 Pisistratus defeats the Megarians: takes Nisaia. | |
| | 561–556/5 Pisistratus, tyrant of Athens: body-guard installed on the Acropolis. | |

| THE NEAR EAST & INDIA | THE FAR EAST | RELIGION & CULTURE |
|---|---|---|

590 Delphic Games first celebrated.

588 Jerusalem blockaded by the Babylonians.

587 June; Jerusalem, having revolted under Zedekiah, taken by Nebuchadrezzar after eighteen months' siege: Jerusalem sacked: Solomon's Temple destroyed: many thousand Jews deported.
587–538 The Babylonian Captivity of the Jews.

585 Cyaxares of Media and Alyattes of Lydia meet at 'Battle of the Eclipse': Nebuchadrezzar acts as mediator: R. Halys fixed as boundary: Nebuchadrezzar occupies Cilicia.
c. 585 Kingdom of Urartu overthrown.
584–550 Astyages, King of the Medes.
582 Further deportation of Jews to Babylon: many more killed or d. of starvation.

c. 582 Pythagoras, mathematician and philosopher, b.
582 Isthmiad Era begins.
570–530 Statues of the Branchides at Miletus.

c. 563–483 Life of Gautama, the Buddha. Original Shwedagon pagoda stated by tradition to have been built in Burma.

562 Nebuchadrezzar d.: succ. his son, Awel-Marduk (Evil-Merodach).

560 Awel-Marduk supplanted as King of Babylon by Nergal-shar-usur (–556).
560–546 Croesus, King of Lydia: first ruler to mint coinage.
559–530 Cyrus II (the Great), King of Persia: capital at Pasargadae.
556–539 Nabonidus (Nabu-na-id), ruler of Babylon: principal residence at Tayma.
554 Nabonidus in Arabia: al-Jauf besieged: Belshazzar (Bel-shar-usur) regent at Babylon.

| WESTERN EUROPE | CENTRAL & EASTERN EUROPE | EGYPT & AFRICA |
|---|---|---|
| c. 550 Etruscans cross Apennines: Bologna founded: Adriatic coast seized and N to Mantua and the lakes.<br>post 550 Silver or bronze coinage becomes common among Greek towns of Sicily and Italy. | c. 550 Cylon attempts to become tyrant of Athens by force. Pittacus, philosopher, tyrant of Mitylene.<br><br>c. 550–527 Pisistratus again tyrant of Athens: Mediterranean commerce actively encouraged: agricultural loan bank instituted: travelling magistrates sent round countryside.<br>c. 550–500 Peloponnesian League formed.<br>c. 550–450 Scythian culture spreads in Ukraine.<br><br>c. 540 Thessalian cavalry defeated by *hoplites* (heavy infantry) of Thebes in invasion of central Greece near Thespies. | c. 550 Euthymenes voyages to Senegal: describes Carthaginian settlements in Mediterranean and Moroccan coast. |
| | | c. 539 Greeks defeat Carthage. |
| c. 535 Carthaginians and Etruscans in possession of Corsica: Carthage predominant. | | |
| | | c. 533 Carthage imposes tribute on on neighbouring tribes. |
| | c. 530 Polycrates, tyrant of Samos: great builder and maritime leader. | |
| | c. 527 Pisistratus d.: succ. jointly by his sons, Hipparchus and Hippias.<br>c. post 527 Hipparchus assassinated: Hippias rules alone (−510). | |

| THE NEAR EAST & INDIA | THE FAR EAST | RELIGION & CULTURE |
|---|---|---|

**c. 551—479** Confucius, correctly Kung (Master) Fu Tsu, principal amongst many other scholars in China. His *Analects* (or Select Sayings) crystallize Chinese philosophy and outlook.

**550** Cyrus takes Media from his father-in-law, Astyages: Media and Persia united: Assyria, Mesopotamia, Armenia and Cappadocia tributary.
**547** Cyrus II takes Lydia from Croesus at battle of Pteryum: Ionia follows: all Asia Minor now under Cyrus: Parthis, Aria, E Iran, Sogdia, Bactria and Afghanistan subsequently taken.
**546** Croesus of Lydia advances beyond R. Halys: defeated and taken prisoner by Cyrus of Persia: Sardis seized and made a satrapy: satrap of Lydia takes Cyprus.

**c. 540** The 'second Isaiah' prophesying amongst the Jews in exile.
**c. 540—475** Heraclitus of Ephesus, philosopher.
**c. 540—468** Mahavira, founder of Jainism.
**c. 540—530** Treasure of Siphnos.
**540—500** Cores of the Acropolis, Athens, sculpted.

**539** Cyrus attacks Babylonia: Oct., Akkad at Opis: Belshazzar killed: Nabonidus massacres Akkadians: Cyrus seizes Sippar: Nabonidus flees: Cyrus takes Babylon without a battle: Oct.-Nov., Cyrus enters Babylon: policy of complete magnanimity towards the vanquished: restoration of Jewish community and cult ordered: Temple to be rebuilt: Shesh-bazzar, governor of Jerusalem.
**538** Cambyses, son of Cyrus, made viceroy of Babylonia.
**c. 538** Population of Judah only *c.* 20,000 even after return of first exiles.
**post 538** Zerubbabel, governor of Judah: cult resumed in Jerusalem.

**536—515** Pediments of the Temple of Apollo at Delphi constructed.

**post 534** Tragedy emerges as a dramatic *genre*.

**c. ante 530** Cyrus invades NW India: receives tribute from Kamboja, Gandhara and trans-Indus tribes: Gandhara made a satrapy, with capital at Takshashila (or Taxila).
**c. 529** Cyrus II campaigns against the Massagetes: Scythians settled E of Khiva.
**529** Cyrus II killed: succ. Cambyses (−522).

**c. 530** Treasure of Cnidus at Delphi.

| WESTERN EUROPE | CENTRAL & EASTERN EUROPE | EGYPT & AFRICA |
|---|---|---|
| | | 526–525 Psammetichus III, Pharaoh. |
| | | 525 Egypt conquered by Cambyses: becomes part of Persian Empire. |
| | | c. 525 The camel introduced into Egypt from Persia. |
| | | 525–404 Twenty-seventh (Persian) Dynasty: Cambyses, Pharaoh: expedition to Siwa and Batn-al-Hagar. |
| | | 522 Libyan Greeks revolt successfully against Persia. Persian satrap Aryandis installed in Egypt: declares himself independent: rebellion put down by Darius I. |
| | c. 519 Alliance between Athens and Sparta. | 517 Canal built from R. Nile to Red Sea. |
| | | c. 517 Darius I visits Egypt: laws codified. |
| | c. 514–512 Darius campaigns against the Scythians in Thrace and Bessarabia: Greek towns of Hellespont submitted: northern shores of Black Sea explored: Thrace conquered: following Scythian withdrawal, Darius retires. | |
| | 510 Sparta attacks Athens: Hippias capitulates and flees to Sigea. Tyranny discredited: new Athenian constitution with *demes* as basis: *Boule* (council) of 500 members: Clisthenes author of reforms. | post c. 510 Egyptian voyages to Punt (? Hadhramaut). Greek colonies in N. Africa expanding trade. Carthage allies with Libyans against Greeks of Leptis. |
| c. 509 Revolution in Rome: Tarquin Dynasty ended: Rome becomes a republic: combats Etruscan chief, Porsenna: Latin League of eight cities, exluding Rome, formed. | | |
| c. ?509 Treaty between Rome and Carthage: Roman suzerainty on adjacent coast implied. | | |
| | c. 506 Sparta and her allies decisively defeated by Athens at battle of Eleusis. | |
| ante 500 Etruscan exports reaching the Rhineland. | | c. 500 Barca founded. Carthage destroys attempted Spartan colony in Libya. |

| THE NEAR EAST & INDIA | THE FAR EAST | RELIGION & CULTURE |
|---|---|---|

**c. 526** First codes of law issued in China.

**525–456** Aeschylus, tragedian.

**522** Cambyses commits suicide: succ. Darius I (−486), first Persian ruler to issue coinage.
**522** Oct. Dec., Nebuchadrezzar III, a son of Nabonidus, rebels and holds Babylon: defeated by Darius.
**c. 522–494** Bimbisara (or Srenika) fifth ruler of the Saisunaga Kingdom: capital at New Rajagriha (Rajgir).
**521** Aug., Babylonians again rebel under an Armenian pretender as Nebuchadrezzar IV: 27 Nov., executed.
**520** Persian imperial administration reformed and re-organized.
**520–460** Persepolis built as capital of Persia.

**520** Haggai and Zechariah, prophets in Judah: effort to rebuild Temple and revival of Judaism demanded.
**post 520** 'P' document of the Hexateuch written.

**518–442** Pindar, poet.
**517** A Chief Physician appointed in Egypt. Sais Library rebuilt.
The Olympeion, Athens, begun.
Canal built from R. Nile to Red Sea.

**c. post 516** Skylax of Karyanda sent by Darius I to explore sea route between the Indus and the Persian gulf: Darius's annexation of the Indus valley follows.

**515** Rebuilding of the Temple at Jerusalem completed, with solemn ceremony of rededication (March).

**fl. 510** Hecataeus of Miletus, *The Survey of the Earth*, lost work describing geography, especially of ancient Egypt.

**c. 500** Site of Pnyx, Athens, organized as a place of assembly.
Carthaginian tombs near Tipasa constructed.

| WESTERN EUROPE | CENTRAL & EASTERN EUROPE | EGYPT & AFRICA |
|---|---|---|
| c. 500 Further Celts arrive in Britain: iron introduced, and iron bar currency. Approximately 500 *gentes*, or patricians, in Rome: commons represented by *Comitia Curiata*, subject to Senate. Royal power put in commission under *praetors* (headmen) and later, consuls.<br>c. 500–c. post 300 'Conflict of the Orders' in Rome.<br>c. post 500 End of epoch of Greek colonization. Written records first come into use in Italy.<br>early 5th c. War between Rome and the Volsci. | c. 500 Greeks adopt the bireme. Aristagoras, tyrant of Miletus: proposes conquest of Aegaean Is. to Artaphernes, satrap of Lydia: Naxos unsuccessfully besieged for four months: expedition fails (499). Celts migrate into Britain, France and Spain.<br>c. 500–300 or 200 Pre-Turkish Altaic culture in Siberia.<br><br>5th c. Earliest known written treaties between Greek states: oral treaties doubtless earlier: beginning of diplomacy in Europe: elementary principles of the law of nations begin to emerge. Kings of Macedon adopt Attic Greek as the official language. | c. ?post 500 Proto-Karanga reaching Rhodesia: other Bantu groups spread in E. Africa.<br>5th c. Carthaginian traders open up trade in Cornish tin, and in gold and ivory from W Africa. |
| | c. 499 Hippocratus tyrant of Gela: most of eastern Sicily under his authority. | |
| 496 Battle between Romans and Latins at L. Regillus. | | |
| 493 Treaty between Rome and the Latins. | 492 Second Persian expedition across the Hellespont: Mardonius attacked by Thracians: half of fleet lost in a gale: garrisons established in Thrace and Macedonia. | |

| THE NEAR EAST & INDIA | THE FAR EAST | RELIGION & CULTURE |
|---|---|---|
| c. 500 Nabataeans established NE of Sinai. Punches and chisels evolved for sculpture work.<br>c. 500—c. AD 100 Megalithic culture in S India. | c. 500 Mons entering Burma from the E. | fl. c. 500 Euphronius, master potter.<br>c. 500 Obadiah, prophet, in Judah. Writing a normal accomplishment in India.<br>c. 500—432 Pheidias, sculptor.<br>c. 500—425 Polygnotus, painter.<br>c. 500—c. AD 500 *Puranas* or early historical legends collected in India. |
| | c. 500—300 Minoussinsk and Tagarskoie bronze culture in E Siberia. Viets moving into SE China and towards Indo-Chinese peninsula. | |
| 5th c. Persians settle Greek exiles in Bactria (Bukhara). | 5th c. Tibeto-Burmese peoples, led by Pyus, entering Burma from N. Glass first imported into China from the Near East. | 5th c. The *Book of Songs, The Book of History, The Spring and Autumn Annals*, the *Book of Rites*, and the *Book of Music* composed: sometimes ascribed to Confucius. China producing both cast iron and wrought iron: fusion of both producing steel. Athens, following Ionic alphabet, spreads it throughout Greece. Prodicus of Ceos, grammarian. Empedocles, chemist and biologist. Anaxagoras, physicist.<br>5th c.—AD 914 Lists, some legendary, of Kings of Tibet.<br>5th c. Corinna, Greek poetess. |
| 498 General revolt of Greeks of Asia Minor against Persians led by Aristagoras: Sparta, Athens and Eretria send military and naval support: Sardis taken: Hellespont and Caria again independent: Cyprus rises successfully.<br>497 Persian armies retake Sardis and check Ionian infantry: Hellespont and Aeolis recovered: fleet built by Phoenicians for Persians.<br>496 Aristagoras leaves Miletus for Thrace: Persian fleet victorious off Miletus: Ionian fleet defeated: Miletus sacked and pillaged. | | |
| 494 Remainder of population of Miletus deported to Babylonia. Ajatashatru murders his father Bimbisara, King of Magadha: becomes ruler to 467; builds Pataligrama, later Mauryan metropolis of Pataliputra: Magadha Kingdom expanded: becomes the most powerful Kingdom on Ganges plain: successful wars against Vaisali and Kosali. | | c. 495—406 Sophocles, poet and playwright. |

| WESTERN EUROPE | CENTRAL & EASTERN EUROPE | EGYPT & AFRICA |
|---|---|---|
| | **490** Persian fleet attacks central Greece: Naxos seized: Eretria taken by assault: Persians land troops on mainland near Marathon: Athens, Sparta and Plataea ally: 10,000 Greeks assemble under Miltiades and gain decisive victory. | c. **490** Zeno of Elis, philosopher, b. **489** Treasure of the Athenians at Delphi. |
| | **490 ff.** Athenian army re-organized: fleet built up by Themistocles, Archon of Athens: Piraeus harbour reconstructed. | |
| | **489** Abortive Athenian expedition against Paros: Miltiades d. of a wound. | |
| | **487** Relatives of Hippias and other traitors ostracized by Athens. | |
| c. **486** Further treaty between Rome and the Latins. | | **486** Egypt revolts against Persia. |
| **485** Gelon succ. Hippocrates as tyrant of Gela: seizes Syracuse and makes it his capital: power increased by cavalry and by dynastic marriages with Theron tyrant of Agrigentum. | **485** Discovery of rich silver mine in Laurion region greatly enriches Athens: Themistocles persuades Assembly to build a large fleet. | |
| | | c. **484–483** Treaty between Carthage and Persia. |
| | **481** Sacred League of Greek City states formed at Corinth: isthmus of Corinth fortified. | |
| c. **480** Hamilcar of Carthage invades Sicily with an army and a fleet: Himaera besieged: relieved by cavalry under Gelon: Syracuse thus becomes principal Hellenic centre in W Mediterranean. Romans attempt to drive Etruscans from Latin territory near Fidenae: badly defeated. | **480** July, Greek fleet of more than 300 vessels assembled: allied Greek armies under Leonidas await Persians at defile of Thermopylae. 29 Sept., battles of Thermopylae and Salamis. Persians cross Hellespont with (*sic*) 1,700,000 men: supported by fleet carrying victuals. Athenian fleet already 200 triremes, making it the largest in the Hellenic world. | **480–470** Sculptures of the Temple of Aphaea carved. |
| | **479** Persian fleet burnt by Greeks while drawn up on the beach near Cape Mycales. Battle of Plataea. Athens fortified, including the Piraeus. | c. **479** Carthaginian constitution revised. c. **post 479** Carthage expands agriculture in hinterland: further trading centres in Morocco. |
| | **477** League of Delos established under Athenian leadership: federated city states pay into common fund to preserve freedom of shipping and trade in the Aegaean. | |
| | **474** Fleet of Syracuse, under Hieron, succ. of Gelon, decisively defeats Etruscan fleet off Cyme. | c. **474** Theseum built. |
| | **472** Themistocles ostracized for alleged contact with Persians. Pausanias put to death. | |
| | | c. **470** Hanno the Carthaginian's alleged voyage to Cameroun. |

| THE NEAR EAST & INDIA | THE FAR EAST | RELIGION & CULTURE |
|---|---|---|

**486–465** Indians provide mercenaries for Persian wars against the Greeks.

**485–465** Xerxes I, King of Persia.

**c. 485** Aeschylus: *The Suppliants*, first of his plays.

**fl. c. 484–429** Herodotus of Halicarnassus, known as 'the father of history',

**482** Babylonians rebel: put down by Megabyzus.

**481–256** Warring states era in China: use of iron more widespread. Many schools of philosophy, known as 'The Hundred Schools of Thought', arise. Constant struggles between warring feudal lords.

**480–410** Protagoras of Abdera, philosopher: adumbrates theory of relativity.

**480–406** Euripides, poet and playwright.

**c. inter 479 and 381** School of Mo Ti teaches austere anti-Confucian philosophy.

**c. 478** The *Auriga* of Delphi.

**472** Aeschylus: *The Persians.*

**c. 470–430** Myron, sculptor.

| WESTERN EUROPE | CENTRAL & EASTERN EUROPE | EGYPT & AFRICA |
|---|---|---|
| | **468** Fleet of League of Delos under Cimon, son of Miltiades, destroys Persian fleet of 200 vessels off Pamphylia. | |
| | **466** Thrasybulus, last of Gelon's brothers, expelled from Syracuse by a popular rising. | **c. 465–454** Inaros, a Libyan, rebels against Persians in Egypt, Egyptians helped by Athenian allies. |
| | **462** Abortive Athenian expedition in Messania: Argos and Thessaly ally with Athens: Cimon ostracized: Sparta allies with Aegina, Corinth and Thebes against Athens. **461** Ephialtes murdered in Athens. | **460** Egypt rebels against satrap Achaemenes. |
| **c. 460** Sabine chief Appius Herdonius raids Capitol in Rome. Sabine and Aequian wars. **460** Cincinnatus, consul. | | |
| | **455–454** Athenian fleet cruises off Sparta and N of Peloponnese. **454** Athens makes five year truce with Sparta. | **454** Division of the Athenian fleet joins in revolt of Egypt against Persia: sails up Nile to Memphis: destroyed by Persians: second Athenian naval division from Cyprus destroyed by Persians in Nile estuary. Persian general Megabyzus regains Egypt. |
| **c. 450** (or before) Roman army re-organized: *Comitia Centuriata* set up to organize conscription. *Code of the Twelve Tables* collected in Rome. **c. post 450** Oscans seize Capua and adjacent Etruscan cities. **449** Roman *plebs* elect *tribunes* to reject the Twelve Tables: two *aediles* represent merchants: *plebs* at first ignored by patricians. | **450** Athenian fleet of 200 triremes wins two engagements with the Phoenicians off Cyprus. **c. 450** Total Greek population estimated at 4 m.: population of Athens *c.* 100,000. **449–448** Treaty between Athens and Persia: Persians abandon all claims in W Asia Minor: Athens recognizes Persian claims in Cilicia, Cyprus and Egypt. **448–429** Pericles, effective ruler of Athens. **447** Boeotia rises against Athens: defeats army sent by Pericles: Euboea and Megara expel Athenian garrisons. Pericles invites delegates of Greek city states to discuss freedom of navigation and the keeping of peace: Spartan ill-will precludes pan-Hellenic union: other states ally with Athens. | **c. 450** Herodotus' description of Egypt and N. Africa. Brisk gold trade between Libya and W. Africa. Himilcon of Carthage sends expedition to Ireland. |

## THE NEAR EAST & INDIA

## THE FAR EAST

## RELIGION & CULTURE

468–457 Temple of Zeus at Olympia constructed.
c. 468–399 Socrates, philosopher.

c. 467–443 Darsaka, son of Ajatasatru, Saisunaga ruler.

467 Aeschylus: *Seven against Thebes.*

465–424 Artaxerxes I, King of Persia.

c. 464–402 Thucydides, historian.

c. 460 Herodotus visits Babylon: states that 'it surpasses in splendour any city in the world.'
fl. 460–400 Murashu family of Nippur, bankers: interest rates from 40% to 70%.

c. 460 Competitions for comedy introduced in Athens.
c. 460–367 Hippocrates, physician: keeps first known medical school at Cos.
c. 460–361 Democritus, philosopher.
458 Temple of Delphi destroyed by fire. Aeschylus: *Orestia.*
458–380 Lysias, orator.
c. 456 First tragedies of Euripides appear.
c. 455–369 Theaitetes, mathematician.

c. 452–412 Polyclitus of Argos. sculptor.
c. 450 Malachi, prophet in Judah.
c. post 450 The Acropolis of Athens built.
post 450 Gorgias of Sicily, philosopher: Leucippus and Democritus of Abdera, philosophers.

c. 450–c. AD100 Kingdom of Hadhramaut: capital Shabwah (Sabota). Phoenicians begin to mint coinage.

fl. 449–423 Cratinos, poet.

c. 448 Pheidias' statue of Zeus at Olympia.
c. 448–400 Agathon, tragedian.
c. 447–432 The Parthenon built.

| WESTERN EUROPE | CENTRAL & EASTERN EUROPE | EGYPT & AFRICA |
|---|---|---|
| **446** Agrigentum taken by Syracuse. | **446** Athenian treaty with Sparta expires: Peloponnesian army invades Attica, camping at Eleusis: new peace treaty between Athens and Sparta for thirty years: Athens abandons claims in Megara and Peloponnese: Sparta abandons claim to Aegina and Euboea: treaty ratified by popular assembly. Chalcis brings criminal cases for judgement in Athens. | |
| | **444/3** Thourioi founded: peopled by colonists from many parts of Greece. | |
| | **442** Five divisions established for sharing expense of maintaining Athenian league, its fleet, garrisons and commissariat.<br>**440** Samos and Byzantium quarrel with Athens: Samos capitulates after a nine month siege: garrisoned by Athens: Byzantium submits. | |
| | **437** Amphipolis founded, and other Greek cities on the Black Sea. | |
| **433 ff** Military tribunes, at first three, later six, instituted at Rome. | **435/4** Epidamnus, a colony of Corcyra, seeks aid from Corcyra against Illyrians: following refusal, aid sought from Corinth: Corinth sends colonists to Epidamnus with garrison and fleet of 75 vessels: Corcyra defeats Corinthians, and applies to Athens for aid.<br>**433** Indecisive sea battle between Corinth and Corcyra: Athenian fleet prevents Corcyran defeat.<br>**432** Athens attacks Potidaea: Corinth sends forces to occupy and assist Potidaea.<br>**431–421** The Peloponnesian War: Sparta sides with Corinth against Athens: Peloponnesian League formed: Attica invaded by 25,000 armed men. | |
| **c. 430** Volsci decisively defeated by Romans.<br>**post c. 430** A *dictator* agreed in Rome in times of military emergency. | **430** Second Peloponnesian attack on Attica: (?) bubonic plague breaks out in Piraeus: Pericles dismissed from power.<br>**430/29** Potidaea taken by Athens; Athens defeated in Chalcis: Pericles restored to power, and then d. | |

**THE NEAR EAST & INDIA**     **THE FAR EAST**     **RELIGION & CULTURE**

**445–433** Nehemiah, prophet, reforms politics and administration in Judah: fortifications of Jerusalem rebuilt.  Population of Judah now *c.* 50,000.

**c. 443–410** Udasin or Udaya, son of Darsaka, Saisunaga ruler: city of Kusumapura built.

**post 437** Many Jewish names recorded in business documents found at Nippur, showing evidence of Jewish settlement.

**c. ?431–c. post 428** Nehemiah again Governor of Judah.

**c. post 445** Herodotus: *The Histories* (in various recensions to *c.* 429).
**c. 445–c. 385** Aristophanes, comic poet.
 **445** Odeon, Athens, built by Pericles.
**c. 444–365** Antisthenes, philosopher.

**c. 442** Sophocles: *Antigonē.*

**438** Propylaea built on the Acropolis. Euripides: *Alcestis.*
**c. 437–432** Propylaea built on the Acropolis.

**436–338** Isocrates, rhetorician.
**c. 435** Erechtheion built on the Acropolis.

**433** Meton reforms the Greek calendar.

**c. 430–356** Xenophon, historian.

| WESTERN EUROPE | CENTRAL & EASTERN EUROPE | EGYPT & AFRICA |
|---|---|---|
| | **429** Sitalces, King of Odryses in Thrace, invades Macedonia at instigation of Athens.<br>**429—427** Plataea besieged by Peloponnesians.<br>**429** Two Athenian naval victories off Naupactus: abortive Spartan attack on Piraeus. | |
| **428** Oscans reach Bay of Naples: Cumae taken: Lucania occupied: Bruttians driven into heel and toe of Italy: Greeks confined to coast. | **428** Lesbos revolts against Athens: fleet sent by Athens to blockade Mytilene: another off the Laconian coast: and another off the isthmus of Corinth.<br>**428, 427, 425** Further attacks upon Attica each spring. | |
| **c. 427** *Comitia Centuriata* makes itself arbiter of peace and war. | **427** Mytilene capitulates: Plataean garrison surrenders: all killed: town razed. Gorgias leads embassy to Athens seeking protection for Sicilian towns against Syracuse: small naval force sent.<br>**426** Following initial defeat, Demosthenes takes Acarnania and Ambracia. | |
| **c. 425** Romans defeat Veii near Fidenae. | **425** Decisive naval blockade of Sphacteria: Athenians take island, and 300 Spartans prisoner.<br>**424** Abortive Athenian naval attacks on Cythera and Sicily: expedition against Megara fails. Thucydides *strategos* of Athens.<br>**422** Athenian army defeated under the walls of Amphipolis. | |
| **421** *Quaestors* raised from two to four: two for civil duties in Rome: two for army. | **421** Peace made between Athens and Sparta.<br><br>**420** Alcibiades becomes *strategos* of Athens: alliance made with Argos.<br>**419** Athens and Sparta make defensive and offensive alliance for fifty years. Argos invades Epidaurus: Sparta and Athens send help.<br>**418** Battle of Mantinea: Spartans defeat Argos: unsatisfactory treaty follows. | |
| **415** Athenian expedition to Sicily: 134 triremes and more than 20,000 men: ineffective attack on Syracuse.<br>**414** Syracuse besieged: Sparta intervenes against Athens: Syracusans take most of Athenian fleet and defeat army. | | **c. 415** Carthage enlarges fleet for w: on Sicily. |
| | **413/412** New fleet constructed at Athens.<br><br>**412** Sparta allies with satraps of Lydia and Phrygia against Athens.<br>**411** Alcibiades makes agreement with Tissaphernes, satrap of Lydia. Assembly abolished in Athens: replaced by Council of 400: oligarchy in power: Peloponnesian fleet defeated off Hellespont. | |

| THE NEAR EAST & INDIA | THE FAR EAST | RELIGION & CULTURE |
|---|---|---|
| | | 429—411 Eupolis, comic poet. |
| | | 428 Euripides: *Hippolytus.*<br>c. ?post 428 Ezra, priest, scribe and prophet in Judah: systematic reform of religious abuses.<br>c. 428—347 Plato, philosopher. |
| | | 427 Aristophanes' first comedy. |
| 424—404 Darius II, King of Persia. | | |
| | | 420—407 The Erechtheion completed. |
| 413 Shishunaga appointed King of Magadha (−393): becomes founder of a dynasty. | | 413—323 Diogenes the Cynic, philosopher. |
| | | 411 Antiphon of Rhamnontum advocate d.: author of *Tetralogics.* |

| WESTERN EUROPE | CENTRAL & EASTERN EUROPE | EGYPT & AFRICA |
|---|---|---|
| | **410** Peloponnesian fleet destroyed by Alcibiades near Cyzicus. Syracuse breaks off relations with Sparta. Council of 500 restored in Athens. | **410** Riots against the Jews in Elephantine led by priests of Khnum. Jewish Temple destroyed. |
| **409** Carthage takes Segesta, Selinontum and Himaera in N Sicily: 10,000 men killed in Selinontum: Himaera razed. | **409–408** Athens suffers further reverses. | **c. 409** Carthage invades Sicily: 100 years war. |
| | **407** Alcibiades elected *strategos* of Athens: given dictatorial powers: Thasos, Abdera and Ionia recovered. | |
| **406** Carthaginians besiege Agrigentum: opposed by army of 30,000 led by Syracuse: Dionysius becomes tyrant of Syracuse. | **406** Sparta makes fresh treaty with Cyrus, now satrap of Lydia. Alcibiades not re-elected *strategos:* succ. Conon: Peloponnesian fleet defeated. Agis, King of Sparta offers peace on principle of *status quo:* Athens declines. | |
| **405** Dionysius of Syracuse resists rising of aristocrats. Carthage again campaigns against Greeks in Sicily: army destroyed by plague while besieging Syracuse: armistice made: Carthage retains its conquest: Dionysius and other Sicilian towns retain independence. | **405** Sparta re-organizes former Athenian Empire: Spartan garrison in Athens: autocratic government introduced. Athenian fleet decisively defeated in Bay of Aigos-Potamos: Sparta dictates peace: Athens remains independent: keeps Attica and Salamis: required to join Peloponnesian League: fleet reduced to twelve vessels. | **405** Treaty between Carthage and Syracuse. |
| **405–396** Romans besiege Veii. | | |
| **404** Military rebellion in Syracuse put down. | **404–403** Thrasybulus rebels: seizes frontier of Attica and Boeotia with fortress of Phylae: occupies Piraeus: government of Athens flees to Eleusis: Sparta blockades Piraeus: Peloponnesian army attacks Attica under Pausanias: truce agreed and general amnesty: democracy re-established in Athens. | **c. 404** Chabrias, an Athenian, put in command of Egyptian army by Nectanebo (−373). |
| | | **404–369** Harsiyotef, King of Meroe conducts expeditions against Beja and Rehreh. |
| | | **404–399** Twenty-eighth Dynasty: struggle against Persians continues. |
| | **401** Athens recovers Eleusis: leaders of oligarchy put to death. 10,000 mercenaries recruited by Cyrus in Ionia. | |
| | **401–397** Tissaphernes attempts to re-conquer Ionia: Greek cities resist. | |
| **400** Dionysius of Syracuse takes further towns in E Sicily. | **c. 400** Archelaus of Macedon makes abortive expedition against Thessaly. | |
| **c. 400** Celtic bodies cross Alps into Italy. | **post 400** Celtic tribes begin to move from central Europe: Balkans invaded. | |
| **post 400** *Comitia Curiata* declines: authority of *Comitia Centuriata* increases, both as a legislative body and court of appeal. | **c. post 400–300** Federal monarchy in Epirus: Kings subject to Thessaly, and then to Macedon. | |

| THE NEAR EAST & INDIA | THE FAR EAST | RELIGION & CULTURE |
|---|---|---|

**post 410** Nandivardhana, and then Mahandandiu, Saisunaga rulers: no dates or events known.

409 Sophocles: *Philoctetes.*

408 Euripides: *Orestes.*
c. 408—355 Eudoxus, mathematician and astronomer.

404—358 Artaxerxes II Mnemon, King of Persia.

401 Following battle of Cynaxa, heroic retreat of the 10,000, led by Xenophon.

403 Critias, orator, d. at Athens.
fl. 403—387 Lysias, orator.
End of 5th c. Bimetallic coinages begin to be struck in the Near East.

c. 400 population of India believed to be c. 181 m.
400—50 Kingdom of Qataban in S Arabia: capital Tamna (Kuhlan).

c. 400—100 Chinese give up eating beef and mutton, principally eating pork and dog meat.

c. 400 Bouleuterion, or Senate House, built at Athens.

| WESTERN EUROPE | CENTRAL & EASTERN EUROPE | EGYPT & AFRICA |
|---|---|---|
| | **4th c.** Sarmatian culture in Orenburg region, near the Ural Mts. Population of Macedonia *c.* ½ m.: state gradually influenced by Hellenic culture. Scythian state in the Taurian Chersonese friendly to Athens: stretches from the Caucasus to R. Don. Sparta, last Greek town to abandon iron coinage. | |
| | **399** Archelaus of Macedon d.: period of palace revolutions, with nine successive kings follows (−359). Socrates condemned to death. | **399** Nepherites I of Mendes expels Persians from Egypt. |
| | | **399—380** Twenty-ninth Dynasty in Egypt. |
| | **397** Sparta sends army against Tissaphernes under its king, Agesilaus. Carthage attacks Panormos (Palermo) with fleet of 250 vessels: Syracuse loses 100 ships in battle off Catania: evacuates W Sicily: Syracuse besieged. | |
| **396** Romans take Veii by assault. | **396** Peloponnesian towns send fleet to aid Syracuse: Carthaginian army suffers casualties from malaria and plague: Dionysius attacks Carthaginian fleet in Syracuse harbour: Himilcon withdraws army and forty vessels only to Carthage. | **396—393** Egyptian treaty of alliance with Sparta. |
| | **396—395** Delegation from Rhodes visits Athens, Argos, Thebes and Corinth with bribes of Persian gold. | |
| | **395** Conon, former *strategos* of Athens, made admiral by Euagoras, King of Salamis, Cyprus: fleet of 50 triremes: expels Spartans from Rhodes. Thebes attacks Spartan allies: Spartan army defeated at Haliartos: Lysander killed: Pausanias makes peace with Boeotians: Theban embassy visits Athens and gains support for coalition against Sparta, including Argos and Corinth. | |
| | **394** Agesilaus defeats allies in the plain of Corinth: is wounded: obliged to evacuate Boeotia: Spartan fleet defeated by Conon off Cnidus. Conon delivers all the Greek towns of Asia and the Cyclades, except the Hellespont, from their Spartan garrisons: returns to Athens: fortifications restored: Athens recovers Andros and Lemnos. | |

## THE NEAR EAST & INDIA

c. 4th c. Shishunaga Dynasty of Magadha usurped by Mahapadma Namda, founder of Nanda Dynasty: large army and systematic administration and taxation inaugurated.

396—395 Brilliant campaigns by Agesilaus in Phrygia, Lydia and Paphlagonia, but without permanent result.

## THE FAR EAST

4th c. First known issues of silver coins by Arakan Kingdom in Burma: gold coins also issued, but none survive. The cross-bow developed in China.

## RELIGION & CULTURE

4th c. First iron working in China, of cast iron. Xenophon: *Cyropaedia*: reflections on the education of a good king. Academy of the Gate of Chi set up as a centre for scholars, together with many other academies. Criminal law codified by Li K'uei. Peruvian culture disturbed by unknown invaders. First Jewish silver coinage known issued. Aramaic beginning to replace Hebrew amongst the Jews. Beginning of Maya civilization in Mexico.
4th to 1st c. Maya astronomy at its peak: accurate calendar calculated.
?4th or 6th c. Lao Tzu, mystical philosopher.
c. early 4th c. Samaritan Temple built on Mount Gerizim.
4th c.—AD 2nd c. Devotion to God under name Vasudeva practised in India.

397 Thucydides: *Histories*.

c. 396 Tyrian cults being replaced by Greek cults at Carthage.
396 First *Dialogues* of Plato.

394 Latest known hieroglyphic inscription found at Philae.

| WESTERN EUROPE | CENTRAL & EASTERN EUROPE | EGYPT & AFRICA |
|---|---|---|
| **393** Carthage sends new expedition against Sicily: fleet defeated: peace made with Syracuse: Carthage retains possessions in NW Sicily only. | | **393** Egyptian treaty with Salamis, Cyprus. |
| **391** Gauls under Brennus enter Etruria near Clusium: town appeals to Rome: Senate warns them not to proceed. **c. 390** Romans defeat Etruscan attempt to recover Veii. **390** Celtic army defeats Romans on banks of R. Allia, near Rome: Gauls pillage and burn Rome: Capitol besieged for seven months: capitulates: Gauls bought off with a ransom in gold. Dionysius of Syracuse campaigns against Greeks of Italy. **389** Successful Roman campaign against the Aequi. **c. 389–c. 380** Successful Roman campaigns against the Volsci. | **c. 391** Thibron of Sparta defeated by Strouthas, satrap of Ionia.<br><br>**390** Sparta makes peace with Persia. Athens re-arms, constructing a new fleet: Iphicrates of Athens defeats Spartans near Corinth.<br><br>**389** Spartan naval squadron, established at Aegina, obstructs shipping in the Gulf of Saronica: coasts of Attica terrorized: penetrates Piraeus. **388** Iphicrates defeats Spartans in the Chersonese. | |
| **388** Dionysius again campaigns in Italy: wins battle of Eleporus: country under control as far as the Abruzzi: Rhegion surrenders: Syracuse now controls Strait of Messina: colonies founded on Illyrian coast as far as the mouth of R. Po: naval demonstration off Etruscan coast: naval station established in Corsica. | | |
| | **387** Spartan fleet of eighty vessels controls the Hellespont. **387–386** Tiribazes, satrap of Lydia, calls conference of Athenians and their allies: treaty agreed: Athens retains irs fortifications and fleet: each city to have right of 'autonomy' (self–determination). **386** Spartan garrisons occupy Arcadia and Phlius: support sent to Amyntas, King of Macedonia, against Chalcis: Olynthus taken. **post 386** Spartan population declines sharply. | **c. 386–383** Egypt attacked by Persia Egyptians carry war into Palestine. |
| | **384** Illyrians gain control of part of Macedon. **382** Sparta occupies Cadmean citadel, Thebes. | |
| **380** Dionysius of Syracuse attacks Carthaginian colonies in NW Sicily: five year campaign begins. **?c. 380** Euagoras, King of Salamis, suffers siege by land and sea from Carthaginians: honourable peace made. | | **380** Egypt and Persia make peace. |
| | | **380–343** Thirtieth Dynasty: earliest parts of Philae temple built. |

392 Gorgias appeals for the unity of
all Greeks at the Olympic Games.
392—388 Last comedies of
Aristophanes.

c. 390 Xenophon: *Anabasis.*

c. 389 Plato's first visit to Syracuse.
389—314 Aeschines, orator.

388 The orator Lysias begs for Greek
unity at the Olympic Games.
c. 388—567 'Nabonassar' (Nabu-nasir)
calendar standardized in Babylon.

387 The *Academy* founded by Plato.

11. c. 385—40 Scopas, sculptor.
c. 384—322 Demosthenes, orator.
384—322 Aristotle, philosopher.

380 Isocrates, rhetorician: *Panegyrics:*
calls for Greek unity.

c. 380—375 Temple of Asclepius
built in Epidaurus.

| WESTERN EUROPE | CENTRAL & EASTERN EUROPE | EGYPT & AFRICA |
|---|---|---|
| | 379 Seven men banished from Thebes enter the city secretly: members of the government murdered: Spartan garrison expelled: Spartan army makes abortive demonstration: Sphodrias garrisons Thespia. | 379 Libyan mercenaries rebel against Carthage. Some small independent Kingdoms existing in Morocco. |
| | 378 Athens organizes league against Sparta: new financial laws in Athens. Sphodrias attacks Piraeus: Athens makes alliance with Thebes: Agesilaus fails in attack on Thebes. | 378 Persian invasion defeated at Memphis. |
| | | 378–360 Nectanebo I, Pharaoh. |
| | 377 Agesilaus again attacks Thebes without success. | |
| | 376 Agesilaus of Sparta falls sick: replaced as King by Cleombrotus: abortive expedition against Boeotia. | |
| 375 Dionysius of Syracuse defeats Carthaginians at Cabala: Carthaginians re-arm: peace made, allowing Carthaginians to remain in NW Sicily. | 375 Athenian fleets in the Aegaean and Ionian seas: further city states join Athenian league. Peace treaty between Athenian league and Sparta. | |
| | 374 Ignoring treaty, Sparta attacks Athenians at Corcyra and Zacynthos: army defeated at Corcyra: fleet retires. | |
| | 373 Chabrias recalled from Egypt by Athens. | 373 Abortive Persian attacks on Pelusium and Memphis. |
| | 372 Jason, son of Lycophron, master of all Thessaly: allied with Thebes. | |
| | 371 July, 10,000 Peloponnesians beaten by 7,000 Boeotians under Epaminondas of Thebes at Leuctres: only 1,000 Peloponnesians, including 400 Spartans under King Cleombrotus, remain alive: end of Peloponnesian League. Pan-Hellenic congress at Sparta: peace made between Peloponnedian League and Athenian confederation: Epaminondas of Thebes and Boeotian League refused recognition. | |
| | 370 Epaminondas leads abortive expedition into Spartan territory. Jason assassinated: succ. his nephew, Alexander of Phaeres: nobility rise against him and against Alexander of Macedon, having taken Larissa: aid sought from Thebes: Epaminondas campaigns in Thessaly. | |
| | 369 Epaminondas campaigns against Corinth in spite of Athenian and Spartan armies: defeated before Corinth: compelled to retire by reinforcements from Syracuse. | |
| | 368 Following death of Amyntas, King of Macedon, and assassination of his eldest son, Alexander, Eurydice the Queen Mother applies to Athens to support her second son, Perdiccas: Thebes forces alliance on Macedon: the third son, Philip, kept as a hostage in Thebes. Sparta campaigns in the Peloponnese: Arcadians defeated. | |

**THE NEAR EAST & INDIA**     **THE FAR EAST**     **RELIGION & CULTURE**

post 378 Many temples and other
buildings constructed in Egypt.

375 Kidinnu (Cidenas), astronomer,
at Babylon: calculates motion of the
sun accurately.

372—359 Rising of Persian satraps
in Asia Minor, supported by Sparta.

373 Temple of Apollo at Delphi burnt:
rebuilt by national subscription.
c. 372—289 Meng Tsu (Mencius),
philosopher.

c. 370—330 Praxiteles, sculptor.
c. 370—286 Theophrastus, philosopher.

| WESTERN EUROPE | CENTRAL & EASTERN EUROPE | EGYPT & AFRICA |
|---|---|---|

**368** Sparta campaigns in the Peloponnese: Arcadians defeated.
**367** Theban campaign restores federal regime to Thessaly.

**367** Dionysius of Syracuse campaigns abortively against Carthaginians in Sicily: then d. Roman tribunes enact law to prevent enclosure of common land by sheepfarmers. Consulate made open to plebeians in Rome.
**367–366** Reconstruction of the magistracy in Rome.
**366** *Praetors* instituted as consular deputies. Sextius, first plebeian to become a consul. Henceforward curule *aediles* elected in alternate years from the Senate and the *plebs*.

**366** Epaminondas seizes Achaia: pro-Theban democracies given power: aristocrats replace them with oligarchies on his departure: Sparta invokes Persia: Persians propose conditions favourable to Thebes, including disarmament of Athenian fleet: Athenian ambassadors at Susa refuse conditions: abortive conference held at Thebes: Theban garrison installed at Oropos, cutting off the grain of Euboea from Athens.
**365** Timoleon of Corinth overthrows his brother for attempting to set up a tyranny. Timotheos seizes Samos for Athens. Sestos ceded to Athens for aiding revolt of Ariobarzanes in Asia Minor: Athenians under Timotheos campaign in Chalcis with little effect (–361). Sparta seizes territory in N Laconia: Elis allies with Sparta: invades Arcadia and are repulsed: Arcadians take the sanctuary of Olympus.
**365–359** Perdiccas, King of Macedon.
**364** Thebes completes new fleet: Epaminondas seizes Byzantium. Indecisive battle at Cynocephaloi between Thessalian league and Alexander of Phaeres. Olympic Games celebrated under Arcadian presidency: raid by Elis repulsed.
**363** Orchomenum revolts against Thebes: following a siege, all males executed: women and children sold. Alexander of Phaeres submits to Thessalian league.
**362** Battle of Mantinea: Thebes defeated by Athenians: Epaminondas d. of wounds.

**360** Gauls invade Alban Hills: Romans retire behind newly constructed stone fortifications.
**c. 360** Tibur, Praeneste and Hernici campaign against Romans: following their defeat, Rome imposes treaty reforming Latin league under Roman control.
**359** Tarquinii attack Rome.

**360** First coinage minted in Egypt: taxation paid in kind.

**360–341** Nectanebo II, Pharaoh.

**359** Amyntas, King of Macedon, abdicates in favour of his uncle, Philip.
**359–336** Philip II, King of Macedon: conqueror of all Greece.

367 Plato's second visit to Syracuse.

c. ?362—322 Mahapadma, followed
by some of his eight sons, successor
of Saisungaya Dynasty.

360 Egypt attacks  Phoenicia with
Spartan aid.

361 Plato's third visit to Syracuse.
360—327 Callisthenes, philosopher.

| WESTERN EUROPE | CENTRAL & EASTERN EUROPE | EGYPT & AFRICA |
|---|---|---|

**358** Senate recognizes *Concilium Plebis* by agreeing to a law forbidding canvassing at elections.

**357** Dion of Syracuse attacks his nephew Dionysius the Younger, ruler of Syracuse, with 3,000 mercenaries and Carthaginian aid. Council of the *Plebs* fixes maximum borrowing rate at 10%.

**356** Etruscan League makes war on Rome: defeated by Rome with Latin allies. C. Marcus Rutilus, first plebeian to be elected *dictator*.

**357** Philip of Macedon takes Amphipolis and Pydna, commanding district of Olympus: Athens declares war: desultory hostilities follow.

**356** Alexander the Great b. Dion seizes Syracuse: Dionysius flees to Leucres. Philomelos of Phocis seizes Delphi: wealth of the temple enables Phocis to hire mercenaries: allies with Athens, Corinth and Sparta: killed in battle by Thebans. Athens sends two fleets against Mausoleus, son of Hecatomnos, ruler of Caria, for seizure of Chios, Cos and Rhodes: Timotheos checked off Chios: tried, fined and disgraced.

**355** Athenian expedition against Persians in Asia Minor retires in face of superior forces: Chios, Cos and Rhodes become independent: subsequently garrisoned by Caria.

**354** Dion assassinated: Dionysius returns to Syracuse. Alliance between Samnites and Romans, possibly against the Gauls.

**353** Caere joins Roman allies.

**354** Demosthenes speaks in Athens against a war with Persia. Philip of Macedon invades Thessaly: defeated twice by Phocis.

**353** Philip again invades Thessaly: wins decisive action near Leucres: all Thessaly falls to Macedon: attacks Phocis: checked by Athenians at Thermopylae.

**353–352** Athens builds fleet of 350 triremes.

**351** Roman allies overrun cities of Falerii and Tarquinii: made to accept forty years' truce.

**c. 350** Celts take Felsina, later Bologna: area becomes known later as Cisalpine Gaul: Celts spread out and raid in N Italy (–*c.* 150).

**350–270** Series of Roman coastguard colonies established from Etruria to Campania.

**351** Philip makes Kings of Epirus and Illyria vassals: forces alliance with Kersobleptos, King of Odryses.

**351** Persian invasion of Egypt defeated with the aid of Athenian and Spartan mercenaries.

**c. 350–250** Scythian culture at the height in Ukraine.

**349** Gauls again invade Alban Hills: Latin allies of Rome called out: Gauls retire without battle. Latins restive: threaten Rome to withold aid against Gaul.

**349** Philip invades Chalcis: Athens sends reinforcements: revolt in Euboea organized by Philip neutralizes Athenians.

**348** Towns of Chalcis incorporated into Macedonia.

**348** Trade treaty between Carthage and Rome.

**347** *Plebs* lower borrowing rate to 5%.

**346** Demosthenes, Philocrates and Aeschines sent by Athens as ambassadors to Philip of Macedon: *status quo* accepted: Philip seizes fortresses in Thrace and Kingdom of Kersobleptos: Phocis capitulates: inhabitants deported.

## THE NEAR EAST & INDIA   THE FAR EAST   RELIGION & CULTURE

**358—337** Artaxerxes III, King of
Persia.

**356** Temple of Artemis (Diana) at
Ephesus burnt.

**354** Isocrates: *Areopagitica.*
Demosthenes' first speech.

**351** Demosthenes: first *Philippic.*

**c. 350 or 400** Active Sogdian
merchants travelling between India,
Persia and China.

**c. 350—258** Zeno of Citium,
originator of Stoicism.
**fl. c. 350—320** Apelles, painter.

**347—270** Epicurus, philosopher.

**346** Isocrates: *Philip.*

| WESTERN EUROPE | CENTRAL & EASTERN EUROPE | EGYPT & AFRICA |
|---|---|---|

**345** Alliance between Philip of Macedon and Persia. Syracuse requests aid from Corinth: party antipathetic to Dionysius take refuge at Leontinoi: Corinth sends relief squadron under Timoleon: siege of Syracuse by Hiketas raised.

**c. 343** Tarentum requests Spartan aid against local enemies. Second Roman treaty with Carthage.
**343** Capua invites Roman alliance: Romans assist Capuans in driving Samnites out of Campania.
**343–341** First Samnite War.

**343** Philip of Macedon sends embassy to Athens to renegotiate treaty of 346: met with intransigence led by Demosthenes: preparations for war demanded. War between Carthage and Timoleon of Corinth.

**343** Persia successfully invades Egypt: Thirty-first (Persian) Dynasty (-332).

**342** Roman troops mutiny. *Plebs* forbid usury.

**342** Athenian detachment prevents Philip of Macedon from seizing Ambracia: Corinth and Corcyra ally with Athens. Philip takes Kingdom of Kersobleptos and makes it a Macedonian province.
**341–340** Athenian campaign against Philip of Macedon: Euboea recovered: Athenian fleet compels Philip to halt siege of Byzantium: Demosthenes made inspector-general of Athenian navy: Athens recognized as leader of almost all Greece.

**341** Henceforward one consul generally elected from the *plebs*. Treaty between Rome and Samnites renewed. Carthaginian fleet defeated off the Crimisos, W Sicily, by Timoleon of Corinth.
**post 341** Timoleon restores democracy in Syracuse: retires there as ordinary citizen: fresh revolt put down.
**340** Latins demand parity of rights with Rome: Rome refuses: Latins now ally with Campanians and Volsci: Romans and Samnites coalesce: 'Great Latin War' begins: Campanians neutralized by offer of terms.
**339** Plebiscites made binding on whole Roman community, subject to senatorial assent. Q. Publilius Philo, dictator, abolishes senatorial veto.
**339–338** Romans defeat Latins: Antium taken from Volsci: their prows (*rostra*) used as speakers' platforms in the *forum*.
**338** Archidamus, King of Sparta, killed in battle near Tarentum. Roman military control now established throughout central Italy: policy of isolation and annexation followed.

**339** Philip of Macedon seizes strong point at Elatea, commanding Boeotian plain: Thebes and Athens ally: Athenians assemble army of 40,000 allies.

**338** Philip seizes Amphissa, destroying allied force: enters Boeotia: force under his son Alexander (the Great) defeats Thebans and Athenians at Cheronea: battle becomes a rout: Thebes surrenders: Athens prepares naval blockade: Philip dictates terms to Athens, including end of Athenian confederation: holds conference in autumn of all Greek states: all to retain liberty and autonomy: all to be united in single league with headquarters at Corinth: all to join in defensive and offensive alliance with Macedon.
**337** Philip of Macedon sends army of 10,000 beyond the Hellespont.

345 Aeschines: *Against Timarchus.*

344 Demosthenes: second *Philippic.*

342–292 Menander, comic dramatist.

341 Demosthenes: third and fourth *Philippics.*

c. 340 The umbrella first recorded in Greece.

c. 338 Shang Yang (or Shang Tzu) legalist philosopher, d.: ideas the foundation of Chin state organization.

| WESTERN EUROPE | CENTRAL & EASTERN EUROPE | EGYPT & AFRICA |
|---|---|---|
| | **336** Philip of Macedon assassinated: succ. Alexander the Great (−323): accepted by Corinthian League with little difficulty.<br>**335** Alexander campaigns as far as the Danube and against revolt in Illyria: Thebes revolts: put down by Alexander with a massacre: town razed: population sold. | |
| **334** Rome allies with Tarentum: Samnites offended. Romans secure Capua.<br>**334–333** All of S Italy submits to Alexander, King of Epirus. | **334** Antipater made regent of Macedon: Alexander crosses the Hellespont to Troas with *c.* 40,000 men from all Greece: Persians defeated at battle of Granica: many cities surrender without a struggle. | |
| | | **332** Alexander the Great takes Egypt: recognized as Pharaoh: Ptolemy, commander of the army. |
| **331** Alexander of Epirus loses control of S Italy: defeated and killed by Lucanians. Senones, section of the Gauls, make peace with Rome.<br>**c. 330–320** Disputes in Syracuse between democrats and aristocrats. | **331** Agis, King of Sparta, attempts to seize Crete behind Alexander's back: defeated and killed at Megalopolis. | **c. 331** Alexandria founded: many Greeks, Jews and Macedonians settle.<br>**331** Oracle of Siwa confirms Alexander's divine origin. |
| **328** Romans expel Volsci from Liris valley: colony established at Fregellae.<br>**327–304** Second Samnite War.<br>**327** First appointment of a *proconsul.* Peace between Samnites and Tarentum: Neapolis (Naples) garrisoned: Rome seizes Naples from Samnites.<br>**326** *Lex Poetelia* mitigates bond-servitude. | | **328–308** Nastasan, last King of Kush to be buried at Napata.<br>**327** Trade treaty between Carthage and Rome. |
| **325** Romans traverse central Apennines to the Adriatic: Marsi and Paeligni made allies: Vestini conquered. | | |

| THE NEAR EAST & INDIA | THE FAR EAST | RELIGION & CULTURE |
|---|---|---|

**335–330** Darius III, last
Achaemenian King of Persia.

**334** Aristotle founds the *Lyceum.*

**333** Memnon put in charge of
Persian fleet: Chios taken: Memnon
d. before Mitylene: Mitylene,
Tenedos, Miletus and Halicarnassus
taken. Alexander forces the
Cilician Gates: Darius defeated at
Issus: Persian army flees: Alexander
takes Levant coast piece-meal,
cutting off Persian fleet: Egypt
surrenders without fighting.

**333** Viet Kingdom in lower
Yangtze Valley destroyed by the
Chinese.

**331–330** 1 Oct., Alexander routs
Darius utterly at battle of Arbela:
enters Babylonia and Susa without
further fighting: Persepolis burnt:
Darius assassinated by satrap Bessus:
Bessus proclaims himself as
Artaxerxes: Alexander enters Bactria
(Afghanistan) in pursuit.
**329** Alexander crosses Hindu Kush:
enters Balkh: seizes Bessus: passes
Samarkand: raids up to R. Jaxartes:
Sogdiana and Bactria pacified.

**330** Lycurgus: *Against Leocrates.*
Aeschines: *Against Ctesiphon.*
Demosthenes: *On the Crown.*
**c. 330–283** Euclid, mathematician,
at Alexandria.

**327** Alexander enters India *via*
Kabul. June–Dec., Alexander
campaigns in Bajaur and Suwat(Swat).

**326** June to July, battle of Hydaspes:
Alexander defeats Poros: all
elephants captured or killed.
Alexander enters the Punjab:
welcomed by Rajah of Taxila:
operation against Poros: all Punjab
pacified. Poros made Viceroy of
Alexander's conquests in India. Oct.,
Alexander's fleet sails, protecting
retreat of army.
**325** Jan., Malavas (Malloi) defeated
by Alexander. Oct., Alexander
marches through Gedrosia; Nearchus
starts voyage to Persian Gulf.

**326** Lycurgus, orator, d.

| WESTERN EUROPE | CENTRAL & EASTERN EUROPE | EGYPT & AFRICA |
|---|---|---|

CENTRAL & EASTERN EUROPE

EGYPT & AFRICA

**324** Harpalus, treasurer of Alexander, flees from Babylon with 5,000 gold talents to start a rising in Greece: disappears mysteriously.
**323** Demosthenes recalled to Athens: coalition formed to free Greece from Macedonian Empire.
**323–322** Winter, Athenians under Leosthenes occupy Thermopylae.

**323** Embassy from Carthage to Alexander the Great.
**323–30** Ptolemaic Dynasty in Egypt.

**322** Spring, Athenian fleet defeated near Amorgos: indecisive land battle at Crannon: Athens requests peace: harsh terms imposed: Demosthenes commits suicide.
**321** Perdiccas d.: succ. Antipater as regent of Macedon.

**321** Roman army of 20,000 trapped in the Caudine Forks by Samnites: Fregellae and other outposts surrendered to Samnites: peace made for five years.

**c. 320** Agathocles raises small army in Syracuse to oppose aristocrats.

**320** Ptolemy I Soter formally recognized as ruler of Egypt (−285). Libya included as a province.

**319–318** Carthage arbitrates in Syracuse: Agathocles given military power on condition of respecting the laws: takes control after riot: aristocrats flee, seeking help from Sparta: naval battle between Sparta and Tarentum follows: Spartans defeated.

**319** Philip Arrhidaeus grants to Greek towns all the privileges enjoyed under Philip and Alexander.
Antipater d.: coalition formed against succ. Polyperchon.

**318–317** Athens submits to Cassander: new constitution agreed: Demetrius of Phalerus, philosopher, given position of tyrant.

**316** Cassander, ruler of all Greece, Macedon included.
**315** Antigonus takes over parts of Greece from Cassander.

**315** Rome repudiates treaty with Samnites: Roman army reaches 35,000 to 40,000: attempt to take Samnites in rear *via* Apulia foiled: Romans defeated at Lautulae.
**314** Rome drives Samnites from Terracina: Capua surrenders: Luceria captured.
**313** Agathocles in control of all Sicily, except Messina and Agrigentum.
**312** *Comitia Centuriata* reformed: number of centuries fixed at 193. Construction of *Via Appia* from Rome to Terracina and Capua begun.

**314** Cyrene revolts unsuccessfully against Egypt.

**313** Athenian population c.21,000.

**312** Seleucus Nicator takes Babylon: assumes title of King of Syria: attempts to recover Alexander's Indian conquests: defeated: compelled to cede Indian provinces and modern Afghanistan; beginning of Seleucid Dynasty.

## THE NEAR EAST & INDIA

**post c. 325** Petra most-important entrepôt between Mediterranean and Saba.
**324** Feb., Alexander's army in Karmania. May, Alexander arrives at Susa, Persia.

**323** June, Alexander the Great d. council of regency set up pending pregnancy of his queen, Roxane: posthumous son, Alexander, b.: brother, Philip Arrhidaeus, an imbecile, nominal regent: quarrels amongst Alexander's generals (*diadochi*) ensue, leading to break-up of empire.
**c. 322** Nanda Dynasty of Magadha usurped by Chandragupta Maurya, founder of Maurya Dynasty.
**322–AD 7th c.** Maurya Dynasty in India.
**321** Poros awarded charge of the Indus valley; Ambhi of the Punjab. Province of Triparadeisos divided between Alexander's generals: Antigonus sent against Eumenes.
**c. 321–305** Chandragupta expands Maurya territories.
**320** Antigonus head of Alexander's former armies in Asia. Seleucus I Nicator prominent.
**c. 320** Indian population estimated at 181 m.
**319** Ptolemy, commanding general in Egypt, seizes Syria.

**318** Antigonus campaigns against Eumenes in Asia.

**317** Eumenes deserted by his troops: executed by Antigonus.

**315** Antigonus takes Syria from Ptolemy. Antigonus ruler from the Indus to N Greece.

**314–313** General war in Asia and Greece: Antigonus prepares to invade Europe.

## THE FAR EAST

**316** Au Lac allegedly liquidated by Chinese.

## RELIGION & CULTURE

**324** Alexander deified by the Greek states.

**c. 323–245** Manetho, first Egyptian historian: *History of Egypt.*

**322** Aristotle d.: Theophrastus becomes head of the *Lyceum.*
**fl.c. 322–298** Kautalya, author of *Arthashastra*, treatise on government and economics.
**321** First comedy of Menander.

**c. 320–c. 295** Tson Yeu, influential politico-scientific philosopher.

**c. 318** Academy of the Gate of Chi (Chi-Hsia) founded.
**316–241** Archesilaus, philosopher.

**314** Zeno teaching at Athens.

| WESTERN EUROPE | CENTRAL & EASTERN EUROPE | EGYPT & AFRICA |
|---|---|---|

**post 312** Election to the Senate made open to the *plebs*.

**311** Carthaginian expedition under Hamilcar disembarks in Sicily: Agathocles defeated by army of 45,000 at Ecnomos: Syracuse alone left to Agathocles. Samnites persuade Etruscans to attack Rome: joined by Marsi, Paeligni and Hernici. Roman flotilla instituted to patrol coast.
**311–304** Romans fight Etruscans to a standstill: Samnites sue for peace.
**310** Romans outflank Etruscans and defeat them in Tuscany: Etruscan League accepts armistice.

**310** Agathocles of Syracuse seizes Tunis and besieges Carthage: Carthaginians withdraw some troops from Sicily without serious effect: Agathocles gathers rich booty from Carthaginian hinterland.
**309** Agathocles receives reinforcements of 10,000 men from Ophellas, tyrant of Cyrene: Ophellas assassinated: troops used to gain control of Carthaginian Libya: Agathocles returns to Syracuse: his son, Archagathos, put in command.

**309–308** Ptolemy attempts to gain power over Greece, and to reconstruct the Corinthian League.

**c. 308** Bomilcar's conspiracy in Carthage.
**307** Agathocles defeated in Africa: compelled to raise siege of Carthage.
**c. 307** Libyans replace war chariots by cavalry.
**306** Peace between Carthage and Agathocies.

**307** Agathocles returns to Syracuse: W Sicily restored to Agathocles: all E Sicily under Syracuse except Agrigentum.

**306** Agathocles takes title of King.

**307** Antigonus sends Demetrius with fleet of 200 vessels to Athens: garrison expelled: Athenians greet him with joy: Pan-Hellenic League proposed: walls of Athens repaired.
**306** Fleet of 163 vessels leaves Athens to attack Egypt: Demetrius attacks and defeats Egyptian fleet at Salamis, Cyprus.

**c. 306** Trade treaty between Carthage and Rome, defining spheres of influence.

**post 305** Agathocles conducts a series of campaigns against the Italiots.

**305** Abortive expedition against Egypt led by Antigonus and his son Demetrius Poliorcetes. Ptolemy I proclaimed Pharaoh.

**304** Demetrius unsuccessfully besieges Rhodes; peace made leaving Rhodes independent.
**303** Demetrius regains the Peloponnese.

**302** Pyrrhus, son of Aiacidas, King of Epirus, expelled after a revolution. Corinthian League revived.

| THE NEAR EAST & INDIA | THE FAR EAST | RELIGION & CULTURE |
|---|---|---|

**312** Ptolemy and Seleucus take Syria from Antigonus: Seleucus sets up in Babylon. Ghassanids maintain independence against Antigonus I.
**311** Demetrius, son of Antigonus, regains Syria. Treaty between Antigonus and other generals follows. Antigonus recognized as ruler of near East.
**post 311** Seleucus campaigns in India: treaty with Chandragupta ceding to him the Punjab and Indus regions.

**310** Roxane, widow of Alexander the Great, and their son Alexander assassinated: principal former generals of Alexander the Great style themselves kings.

**c. 310—267** Theocritus, poet.
**310** Aristarchus of Samos, astronomer, b.

**307—306** Theophrastus exiled.

**306** Epicurus opens school at Athens.
**c. 306** The Winged Victory of Samothrace sculpted.

**305** Seleucus proclaims himself King (−281).
**305—63** Seleucid Dynasty. Seleucus's abortive invasion of India. Chandragupta campaigns against him.

**c. 305—250** Callimachus, poet and grammarian.

**303** Chandragupta adds Seleucid provinces of India to Maurya empire.
**c. 302** Seleucus I sends Megasthenes as ambassador to India: author of treatise on geography, institutions and produce of India.
**302** Lysimachus campaigns in Asia with Thessalian army: instals himself in new Syrian capital of Antigoneia after taking most of Asia Minor.
**301** Lysimachus receives large reinforcements from Seleucus: Antigonus killed at battle of Ipsos, Phrygia: Demetrius flees with remnant of army. Peace now made: Macedon and Greece awarded to Cassander: Lysimachus, Thrace and

**302** Temple of Salus at Rome decorated with paintings.
**c. 302** Zeno opens Stoic school in Athens.

| WESTERN EUROPE | CENTRAL & EASTERN EUROPE | EGYPT & AFRICA |
|---|---|---|

**c. 300** First Italian mints: exchange by weight still persisting in rural areas. Tiles begin to be used for roofs.
**300 ff** Pontiffs and augurs raised in number from four to nine each: five each to be co-opted from the *plebs.*
**post 300** Veneti of Brittany become middlemen for Cornish tin, transporting it into Gaul.
**3rd c.** Road system begins to develop in Italy: Greek communications almost exclusively by sea. Greek coinage and local imitations current in Gaul.

**3rd c.** Outriggers appear on Greek ships.

**ante 300** Beja raiding Kawa and other settlements on the Nile. Trade treaty between Carthage and Egypt.
**c. 300** Rock paintings in C Sahara. ·Elaborate cemetery with 45,000 graves at Garama.

**3rd—2nd c.** Iron Age begins in Scotland. Celts begin to populate Scotland: 'Gallic Forts' built.
**3rd—1st c.** Sarmatian jewellery spreads in S Russia.

**299** Roman colony established at Narnia.
**298** Lucania invites Roman aid against Samnites: relief force sent under L. Scipio Barbatus.
**298—290** Third Samnite War.

**298** Agathocles expels the Spartan garrison from Corcyra.

**298** Pyrrhus sent as a hostage to Alexandria: given troops and a subsidy to re-establish himself in Epirus.

**296** Statue of wolf with Romulus and Remus set up near the Roman forum. Samnites break through Romans into Campania: main army joins with Etrurians and Gauls.
**295** L. Scipio Barbatus defeated by Gauls and Samnites at Camerinum: Roman army of 40,000 defeats Gauls and Samnites at Sentinum.
**294** Etruscans make peace with Rome.
**293** L. Papirius Cursor attacks Samnites.

**293** Boeotia revolts against Demetrius.

**291** Lysimachus taken prisoner in campaign against the Getae: Demetrius seizes opportunity to invade Thrace: Lysimachus set free: Demetrius retreats in haste. Boeotia again revolts against Demetrius: Thebes surrenders after a long siege.

**290** M. Curius Dentatus attacks Samnites, who sue for peace: given generous terms.

| THE NEAR EAST & INDIA | THE FAR EAST | RELIGION & CULTURE |
|---|---|---|

Asia Minor up to the Taurus: Seleucus, all the Syrian provinces: Ptolemy, Coele-Syria with Egypt.

**ante 300** Caste system already in existence in India.
**300** 22 May, Antioch on the Orontes founded.
**c. 300** Lower Deccan sites in contact with Megalithic culture of S India.

**300** Chinese merchants believed to have reached Peru: ? oriental techniques imported.
**c. 300** Deutero-Malays from Yunnan entering Malaysia: armed with iron weapons superior to stone weapons of Proto-Malays. Feudalism breaking up in China. King Wu-ling of Chao takes part of Shangsi from the Huns. Asoka's mission of Buddhist monks convert Mon kingdom of Thaton Burma, to Buddhism.
**post 300** City of Anuradhapura founded in Ceylon. Japanese traders believed to be visiting and trading in Ecuador.
**3rd c.** Trousers, in imitation of the Huns, adopted by Chinese cavalry. Hiong-nou, or Huns, first mentioned in Chinese annals as living N of Yellow River: ruler a king, with a military organization. The name Nam Viet first used for the present Vietnam.
**c. 300–200** Iron age begins in E. Siberia.

**300** *Jatakas,* early Buddhist scriptures, composed.
**c. 300** Euclid: *elements of Geometry.* The lathe invented in Egypt. Royal burials begun at Meroe.

**3rd c.** Jain scriptures collated and written down from oral tradition. Asclepiades of Samos, post. Cult of Osiris-Apis spreads throughout Greek world. Livius Andronicus, epic poet.

**298** Deimachos succ. Megasthenes as ambassador in India.

**c. 298–c. 238** Hsun Tzu, philosopher.

**297** Chandragupta d.: succ. Bindusara (−272): campaigns in Deccan as far as Mysore expand Maurya empire, which stretches from the Indian Ocean to the Bay of Bengal: S India voluntarily subject to him, Kalinga (Orissa) alone independent.
**296–294** Demetrius Poliorcetes loses his Asian possessions to Seleucus and Ptolemy.

**290** *Mouseion* founded by Ptolemy I at Alexandria: 400,000 scrolls collected.

| WESTERN EUROPE | CENTRAL EASTERN EUROPE | EGYPT & AFRICA |
|---|---|---|
| **289** Agathocles d.: Syracusan kingdom falls to pieces: city-states taken over by different tyrants. Messana put under former Campanian mercenaries, known as Mamertines. | **289** Having constructed a fleet of 500 vessels, Demetrius campaigns in Epirus: Pyrrhus attacks Macedonia. <br><br> **288** Pyrrhus allies with Lysimachus: joint invasion of Macedonia: Demetrius deserted by his troops: flees to Athens gathering more troops: Demetrius forced to cede Macedon to Pyrrhus of Epirus. | |
| | **ante 285** Secret treaty between Pyrrhus and Antigonus: Lysimachus takes Macedonia from Pyrrhus. <br> **285** Sparta re-fortified. | **285–247** Ptolemy II Philadelphus. |
| **284** Gauls invade Etruria: besiege Arretium. Curius Dentatus defeats Gauls and lays their territory waste. <br> **283** Incursion of the Boii into Etruria: reach within fifty miles of Rome: defeated near L. Vadimo by P. Cornelius Dolabella. <br> **282** Renewed incursion of Boii: made to sue for peace. Rome sends relieving force at request of Thurii, besieged by Lucanians: Roman force expelled by Tarentum. <br> **281** Tarentum hires Pyrrhus, King of Epirus, with 25,000 mercenaries, against Rome. | | |
| **280** Pyrrhus of Epirus, with 20,000 men disembarks in Italy: defeats Roman army near Heraclea: gains all S Italy: Pyrrhus abortively raids Latium. <br> **280–274** The Pyrrhic War. | | **280** Pharos (lighthouse) built by Sostratus of Cnidus at Alexandria. Nile–Red Sea canal completed. Trade develops between Egypt and India. <br> **280 ± 120** Nok culture site at Tarunga: abundant evidence of iron working. |
| **279** Pyrrhus leads army of 40,000–50,000 men into Apulia: battle of Asculum won by Pyrrhus's elephants: casualties about equal: offers Rome peace with evacuation of all S. Italy: rejected in the Senate by Appius Claudius: Carthage offers Rome aid. | **post 279** Bands of Celts reach Thrace, the Axios valley and Illyria, towards Macedonia: horde reaches Thessaly under Brennus: Galatians ravage Macedonia. | **279** Treaty between Carthage and Rome against Pyrrhus. |

## THE NEAR EAST & INDIA     THE FAR EAST     RELIGION & CULTURE

**c. 288** Theophrastus, author of
*Historia Plantarum* d.: first to refer to
Sabaean Kingdom.

**287** Demetrius Poliorcetes flees to
Asia.
**287—285** Demetrius carries on
guerrilla warfare in territory of
Lysimachus and Seleucus:
eventually taken prisoner by
Seleucus.

**287—212** Archimedes, mathematician,
at Alexandria.

**285** Herophilos and Erasistros,
physicians, d.

**283 or 282** Demetrius Poliorchetes
d.

**283** Ptolemy I accorded a cult
as Soter.

**281** Pitched battle between Seleucus
and Lysimachus at Courupaion,
Phrygia: Lysimachus killed: Seleucus
controls almost all Greece: makes
his son Antiochus I Soter regent of
his Asiatic domains: retires to
Macedon: assassinated on arrival by
Ptolemy Keraunos, thereby
acquiring territory of Lysimachus.
**281—261** Antiochus I Soter,
Seleucid.

**c. 280** Chrysippus, philosopher.

| WESTERN EUROPE | CENTRAL & EASTERN EUROPE | EGYPT & AFRICA |
|---|---|---|
| **278** Carthaginians besiege Syracuse: many city-states seek Roman protection.<br>**278–275** Pyrrhus campaigns in Sicily. Roman campaigns against Oscans. | | |
| | **277** Celts decisively defeated by Antigonus.<br>**276** Antigonus Gonatas established as founder of new dynasty in Macedonia.<br>**275** Pyrrhus returns to Epirus. | |
| **275** Oscans, pressed by Rome, request Pyrrhus to return: Pyrrhus defeated by Romans: flees to Epirus. | | |
| | **274** Antigonus reinforces Macedonian army with local Galatians: Pyrrhus returns and takes much of Macedonia. | **274** War between Egypt and Syria. Magas, half-brother of Ptolemy II, Governor of Cyrene, revolts: reaches within two days' march of Alexandria: recalled by revolt in Cyrenaica. |
| **273** Treaty between Rome and Ptolemy II of Egypt. Rome annexes Caere.<br>**272** Pyrrhus withdraws remainder of his troops from Tarentum: town made over to the Romans: Romans subjugate Bruttians, Lucanians and Samnians. | **272** Following victories of Pyrrhus, Antigonus left with a few coastal towns only. Pyrrhus d. in Epirus: Antigonus recovers Macedonia and mainland Greece. Alexander becomes King of Epirus. | |
| | | **c. 269** Port of Ptolemais Epitheras (Ptolemais of the Hunts) developed on Eritrean coast. |
| **267** *Quaestores Italici* or *classici* inaugurated to supervise naval defence. | | |
| | **265** Antigonus besieges Athens. | |
| **264** Messana besieged by Hiero, King of Syracuse: Carthaginian fleet induced to stop siege: Messana seeks alliance with Rome to evict Carthaginians from town: Romans send relief force: Carthaginians retire: Carthaginians then return with Hiero of Syracuse and besiege Messana: Appius Claudius persuades both to withdraw by diplomacy.<br>**264–241** First Punic War.<br>**264–201** Consulate in Rome rarely attained outside the Senate.<br>**264–133** Principal period of Roman foreign expansion.<br>**263** Romans besiege Syracuse: Hieron detached from Carthaginian alliance: Carthaginians cut off.<br>**262** Romans besiege Agrigentum to forestall Carthaginian attack: city taken by storm. | **264** Antigonus defeats Spartan army near Corinth.<br><br>**262** Spartan army defeated by Aristodemus, tyrant of Megalopolis and ally of Antigonus.<br>**262–261** Athens surrenders to Antigonus: Greece re-organized, with Macedonian garrisons. | |

**275** Antiochus defeats the
Galatians in Phrygia.

**c. 275** Callimachus: *Hymn to Zeus.*
Manetho, *History of Egypt.*

**275−200** Eratosthenes of Cyrene,
mathematician and philosopher.

**273** Asoka succ. Bindusara (−232):
apogee of the Mauryan Empire: his
acts recorded on inscribed pillars.
**c. 272** Egyptian possession of Coele-
Syria recognized by Antiochus.

**c. 273** Callimachus: *Hymn to Delos.*

**272** Livius Andronicus brought to
Rome as a slave: translates the
*Odyssey* and Greek plays into Latin.

**270** Epicurus d.
**c. 270−200** Cn. Naerius, author of
epic poem on First Punic War.
**269−232** Indian agriculturalists move
to Ceylon, bringing Buddhism: Asoka's
son Mahinda principal missionary.

**269** Coronation, or consecration,
of Asoka (−232).

**c. 265** Hydraulic organ invented by
Ctesibius: also inventor of force-pump.
**c. 264** Zeno d.: succ. Cleanthes.

| WESTERN EUROPE | CENTRAL & EASTERN EUROPE | EGYPT & AFRICA |
|---|---|---|
| **261** Indecisive Roman campaign in Sicily. Romans begin to construct fleet. | | |
| **260** Roman fleet defeats Carthaginians off Mylae.<br>**259** Abortive Roman campaigns against Corsica and Sardinia: Roman army takes central Sicily. | | |
| | | **256** Roman army under Regulus campaigns near Carthage. Carthaginian fleet defeated off Cap Ecnomos. |
| **254** Romans take Panormos, Sicily. | | |
| | **253** Macedonian fleet in the Aegaean defeats Egyptian fleet off Cos.<br>**251** Aratos overthrows tyrant of Sicyon. | **253** Romans raid Tripolitanian coast. |
| **250** Abortive Carthaginian attempt to recapture Panormos. | **Second half of 3rd c.** Sarmatians drive Scythians out of Ukraine into Crimea. | **c. 250** Inscriptions in ancient Libya found in Fezzan and C. Sahara. |
| **249** Roman fleet defeated off Drepanum: second division destroyed by a gale.<br>**248–242** Armistice between Rome and Carthage.<br>**247** Hamilcar Barca made Carthaginian commander in Sicily: raids Roman territory. | | **247** Ptolemy II Philadelphus d.: succ. Ptolemy III Euergetes (–221) trade missions sent to Ethiopia: port of Adulis (Massawa) founded.<br>**247–183** Hannibal, Carthaginian leader. |
| | **c. 245** Naval battle off Andros between Antigonus and Egyptian fleet.<br>**243** Aratos seizes Acro-Corinth. | |
| **242** New Roman fleet invests Drepana and Lilybaeum.<br>**241** Rome obtains control of all Sicily. Carthage accepts peace: all claims to Sicily abandoned: substantial indemnity paid.<br>**240** Roman office of *praetor peregrinus* instituted to deal with cases involving foreigners. | | **240** Carthaginian army mutinies. |

| THE NEAR EAST & INDIA | THE FAR EAST | RELIGION & CULTURE |
|---|---|---|

**261** Antiochus I defeated by Pergamum at Sardis: d. in battle: succ. Antiochus II. Bactria becomes independent. Asoka conquers Kalinga, on the Bay of Bengal.
**261—246** Antiochus II, Seleucid.

**259** Antiochus II allies with Macedonia: retakes cities on Ionian coast from Egypt.

**258—207** Van Lang allegedly conquered by King of Thuc: second Vietnamese Kingdom of Au Lac.

**post 258** Callimachus: *Hymn to Artemis.*

**c. 256** First Rock Edict of Asoka.

**c. 256—206** Ch'in Dynasty rules China, gradually absorbing other states. Success due partly to introduction of cavalry.

**c. 254—184** T. Maccius Plautus, comic poet and dramatist.

**250** Buddhists meet in council at Pataliputra to re-organize Buddhism.
**c. 250** Hebrew scriptures translated into Greek (Septuagint) in Alexandria.

**c. 250** Diodotos, satrap of Bactria, makes his province an independent kingdom (−230). Arsaces (−248) leads nomadic band out of Turkestan into NE Iran, founding Parthian Dynasty (−AD 226).

**c. 250** Ch'in state develops high degree of centralized bureaucratic administration.
**250—210** Tissa, ruler of Anaradhapura: recognized as king by Asoka: takes new name 'Devanampiya' (dear to the gods).

**c. 249** Asoka abolishes royal hunt: makes pilgrimage to Buddhist holy places.
**248—211** Tiridates I, King of Parthia.

**249** *Ludi Tarentini* held in Rome to propitiate Dis and Proserpine.

**c. 248** Callimachus: *Hymn to Apollo.*

**c. 247** Lu Pu-Wei, a commoner, Regent of Ch'in state: shortly replaced as Emperor by his son Shih Huang-Ti (Cheng), who replaces his father's peaceable policy with one of rapid military expansion (230—222).

**246** Antiochus II d.: succ. Seleucus II (−226). Ptolemy III invades Syria to avenge murder of his sister: reaches Antioch: then recalled to Egypt.

**240** Treaty between Seleucus II and Ptolemy III: Seleucus gains N Syria: Ptolemy retains Ephesus and Seleucia near Antioch. Quarrel between Seleucus II and Antiochus Hierax, his brother.

| WESTERN EUROPE | CENTRAL & EASTERN EUROPE | EGYPT & AFRICA |
|---|---|---|
| | **239** Antigonus d.: succ. Demetrius. | |
| **238** Romans occupy Carthaginian stations in Sardinia: Carthage protests: Rome declares war: Carthage cedes Corsica to Rome without fighting. | | **238** Hamilcar given command in Carthage: peace restored.<br>**237** Hamilcar Barca defeats Libyan and other mercenaries. |
| **236** Boii restive: Roman army sent to Ariminum: quiet restored. | | |
| | **235** Cleomenes, King of Sparta.<br>**234** Epirus becomes a republic. | |
| **230** Senate sends embassy to Hamilcar to ascertain his intentions in Spain: protection promised to Saguntum. | **230** Roman embassy sent to Illyria: legate assassinated by Queen Teuta: Teuta takes Corcyra and Epidamnus: Aetolian and Achaean fleets beaten at Paxos.<br>**229** Demetrius d.: regency follows. | |
| **228—221** Hasdrubal in command of Carthaginian Spain. | **228** War between Sparta and the Achaeans. Epidamnus and Corcyra taken by Roman fleet: Teuta sues for peace: Roman protection instituted over cities of W Greece. Roman embassies visit Athens and Corinth. | |
| **227** Sicily, and Sardinia and Corsica, constituted Roman provinces.<br>**post 227** Number of praetorships increased: consulate reserved to ex-praetors: censorship and dictatorship reserved to ex-consuls.<br>**226** Second embassy from Senate to Hasdrubal: Carthaginians agree not to cross R. Ebro. Carthago Nova (Cartagena) becomes the centre of Carthaginian power in Spain.<br>**225** Celtic tribes in N Italy, together with mercenaries, mobilize 70,000 men against Rome: cut down at battle of Telamon by army of 130,000.<br>**224** Romans take Cispadane Gaul. | **c. 227** Cleomenes introduces reforms in Sparta: defeats the Achaeans.<br><br><br><br><br><br><br><br>**224** Treaty between Antigonus Doson and the Achaeans: Argolis and Arcadia taken from Cleomenes. | **227** Antiochus Hierax surrenders to Ptolemy: then escapes: killed fighting in Thrace.<br><br><br><br><br><br>**225—200** Arkamani, King of Meroe: maintains friendly relations with Alexandria. |
| **223** C. Flaminius crosses R. Po: destroys its bridges: defeats Insubres. | | |
| **222** M. Claudius Marcellus kills chief of the Insubres in single combat.<br>**221—218** Hannibal in command of Carthaginian Spain: extends Carthaginian domain to Salamanca region.<br>**220** Circus built in the Campus Martius, Rome. | **222** Battle of Sellasia: Antigonus Doson takes Sparta.<br>**221** Philip V succ. Antigonus Doson.<br><br><br>**220 or 219** Cleomenes d. | **221** Ptolemy III d.: succ. Ptolemy IV Philopator (−200): further trading stations developed in Red Sea. |

| THE NEAR EAST & INDIA | THE FAR EAST | RELIGION & CULTURE |
|---|---|---|
| | | **239** Ennius b. |
| | | **237** Ptolemy III Euergetes issues Decree of Canopus rectifying 365 day Egyptian calendar by the addition of an additional day in each fourth (Leap) year: decree not observed in practice. |
| | | **c. 235** First tragedy written in Latin by Naevius. |
| | | **c. 233** Han Fei Tzu, legalist philosopher, d. |
| **232** Asoka d.: empire divided between his grandsons: Dasaratha receives Magadha: Samprati receives Ujjain. | | **232–147** M. Porcius Cato, historian and writer on agriculture. |
| **230–227** Diodotos II, ruler of Bactria. | | |
| **229–228** Antiochus Hierax defeats various bands of Galati. | | |
| **c. 228–167** Bactrian Greek, or Yavana, Dynasty. | | |
| **227–189** Euthydemus, ruler and real founder of Kingdom of Bactria. (−167). | | |
| **226** Seleucus II d.: succ. Seleucus III Soter (−223). | | **226** Temple of Virtue and Honour built at Rome. |
| **223** Antiochus III the Great succ. Seleucus III Soter (−187). | | |
| **223–220** Achaios proclaims himself King in Asia Minor. | | |
| **222–221** Molon revolts against Antiochus III in Syria. | | **c. 222–180** Apollonius Rhodius, grammarian and poet. |
| **221** Molon defeated and killed. | **c. 221** Ch'in Dynasty overcomes the last of the feudal states: Shih Huang-Ti Emperor of all China: attempts to exterminate Confucianism. | |
| | | **ante 220** *Ludi Romani* (Roman Games) celebrated annually in Rome. |

| WESTERN EUROPE | CENTRAL & EASTERN EUROPE | EGYPT & AFRICA |
|---|---|---|
| **220** Romans receive submission of almost all Gallic tribes: Placentia and Cremona founded: *Via Flaminia* extended to Ariminum.<br>**c. 220** *Via Aurelia* built.<br>**219** Hannibal seizes Saguntum. | **219—217** Philip V at war with Aetolians.<br>**218** Demetrius of Pharos takes to piracy on coast of W Greece: halted by Roman fleet. | |
| **218** March, Rome declares war on Carthage. Hannibal crosses Alps: takes Po valley: P. Cornelius Scipio falls back on Apennines: defeated by Hannibal at Trebia. Rome equips fleet of 160 vessels, superior to Carthage's 130.<br>**218—201** Second Punic War. | | |
| **217** P. Cornelius Scipio and Cnaeus Scipio destroy Carthaginian fleet in R. Ebro. Hannibal defeats Romans near Lake Trasimene: campaigns fruitlessly in Campania and Apulia. | **217** Peace of Naupactus. Philip Alexander invades Illyria. | **217** Risings in Egypt. |
| **216** Many minor Roman successes in Spain under Cnaeus Scipio. Battle of Cannae: Hannibal, with 40,000 men, annihilates Roman army of 50,000: most of S Italy deserts Rome. | **216** Philip Alexander makes alliance with Carthage. | |
| **215** Scipio brothers defeat Hasdrubal near Dertosa. Hiero of Syracuse d.: succ. Hieronymus shortly murdered. Sardinia rebels: quickly put down by Roman expedition.<br>**215—211** Roman campaigns continue in Spain.<br>**214** Roman fleet prevents Philip V of Macedon from re-inforcing Hannibal. | **215—214** Philip Alexander leads expeditions into the Peloponnese: coalition formed against him. | **215** Pact of mutual assistance between Hannibal and Philip V of Macedon. |
| **213** Romans sack Leontinoi: Syracuse besieged: Carthage establishes base at Agrigentum. | **213** Aratos d. | |
| **212** Marcellus takes suburbs of Syracuse: many Carthaginians d. of malaria. Romans take Syracuse. Hannibal takes Tarentum. | **212** Rome makes treaties with Aetolian League and with Attalus I of Pergamum. | |
| **211** Capua regained by Rome. Hasdrubal reinforced in Spain: Roman army destroyed. Syracuse taken. | | |
| **210** P. Scipio the Younger sent to Spain. Following Carthaginian mutiny, Rome recovers Agrigentum. | **210** Roman fleet takes Aegina and parts of the Peloponnese. | |
| **209** Rome recovers Tarentum. Carthago Nova (Cartagena) taken by Scipio. | | |
| **208** Indecisive battle between Hasdrubal and P. Scipio at Baecula: Hasdrubal retires into France. | **208** Philopoemen of Megalopolis elected *strategos* of the Achaeans: army of 15,000 to 20,000 raised: Sparta taken: peace rapidly made. | |

| THE NEAR EAST & INDIA | THE FAR EAST | RELIGION & CULTURE |
|---|---|---|
| **220–187** Antiochus III, Seleucid. | | |
| **219** Antiochus III regains mastery of of Asia Minor. | | |
| **217** Ptolemy IV defeats Antiochus III at Raphia, S of Gaza: peace rapidly made. | | **217** Cult of Venus of Mount Eryx inaugurated in Rome. Cults of Baal (Saturn) and Tanith (Caelestis) introduced in Rome. Ceremonies of the *Saturnalia* at Rome enriched. |
| **216** Attalus I receives grant ofMysia from Antiochus III: Achaios kept in check by Attalus and Prusias, King of Bithynia. | | **216** Order of Sibylline oracle to bury alive a Greek and a Gallic couple obeyed. |
| **215–213** Siege of Sardis: ended by death of Achaios. | **c. 215** Great Wall of China built to keep out Hsiung-Nu or Huns. Hun state coming into being outside the wall: employing Chinese clerks and administrators. Hsiung-Nu states endure until *c.* AD 500. | **ante 215** Plautus: *Menechmes.* <br> **215** *Lex Oppia de Luxu Feminarum,* sumptuary law, enacted against luxury in Rome. |
| | | **213** All Confucianist books burnt except a single copy of each in the Chinese State Library. <br> **212** *Ludi Apollinares* instituted in Rome. Archimedes d. |
| **211** Antiochus III compels Armenia to recognize his authority. <br> **211–191** Artabanus I, King of Parthia. <br> **210–205** Antiochus III compels Kings of Parthia and Bactria to recognize his suzerainty; and other kings as far as the Punjab. | **c. 210–209** Huns under leader Teuman attack Yu-Che W of Yellow River. | **c. 210** Hypostyle hall built at Delos. |
| **208** Antiochus the Great recognizes Bactrian independence. Euthydemus King of Bactria, occupies Sogdiana, Ferghana and Chinese Turkestan. Prusias of Bithynia invades Pergamum. | | |

| WESTERN EUROPE | EASTERN EUROPE | EGYPT & AFRICA |
|---|---|---|

**207** Hasdrubal brings large army from Spain to N Italy: defeated by Romans on R. Metaurus.
**206** P. Scipio defeats Hasdrubal at Ilipa: Carthaginian army in Spain destroyed: Gades surrenders to Rome: P. Scipio master of all Spain.

**207** Roman fleet and military detachments recalled from Greece.

**205** Treaty between Rome and Macedon. P. Scipio returns to Rome: takes charge of army in Sicily.

**205** Peace of Phoenice between Romans and Philip Alexander.

**204** Scipio lands Roman army near Utica: gains Masinissa as an ally: Carthaginian army enlarged with Numidians under Syphax: Scipio destroys enemy in night attack: enemy raise fresh army: destroyed by Scipio in valley of Bagradas.
**203** Syphax expelled from Cirta: territory given to Masinissa: Carthage sues for peace: Rome demands cession of Spain, reduction of navy and indemnity.

**202** Philip V Alexander invades Thrace: Abydos sacked.

**202** Hannibal returns to Carthage with 15,000 men: armistice broken off: Hannibal utterly defeated at battle of Zama.

**201** Embassy from Attalus I of Pergamum to Rome. Peace made between Rome and Carthage on terms already stipulated.
**201–200** Ambassadors of Egypt, Pergamum and Rhodes meet in Rome.

**201** Macedonian fleet takes Samos.

**200** Cisalpine Gaul in revolt. Roman embassy sent to Macedon to demand indemnity for Attalus I.
**200–134** The Roman consulate chiefly filled from about twenty-five families.
**c. 200** Belgae, mixture of Celts and Germans, occupy area N of Rs Seine and Marne.

**200–181** Ptolemy V Epiphanes.

**c. 200** Population of Alexandria **c.** ½ m. Nigerian Nok culture at its zenith. Nubai living in Dongola region.

| THE NEAR EAST & INDIA | THE FAR EAST | RELIGION & CULTURE |
|---|---|---|
| | **207** Nam Viet over-run by armies from SW China: divided into provinces. | **207** *Ludi Tarentini* again held in Rome to propitiate Dis and Proserpine. |
| **206** Antiochus crosses Hindu Kush: defeats minor Indian King Subhagasena, ruler of Kabul valley: returns with large booty. | **206– AD 220** Han Dynasty.<br>**206– AD 9** Former Han Dynasty in China: Liu Chi (Liu Pang or Kao Tsu) Emperor: development of the 'gentry state', which continued until the 1948 revolution. | |
| | | **205** Cult of Cybele from Phrygia inaugurated in Rome on the Vatican Hill.<br>**204** *Ludi Megalenses* instituted in Rome.<br>**204–122** Polybius, historian. |
| **203** Antiochus III begins to seize territory of the Ptolemies in Syria. | | |
| | | **ante 202** *Ludi Ceriales* instituted in Rome. |
| **201** Antiochus III attacks Coele-Syria: abortive Roman expedition to Illyria. | | |
| **201–200** Antiochus III takes S Syria and Palestine. | **c. 201** Huns invade Shansi province of China. | |
| | **ante 2nd c.** Pyu Kingdom founded in N Burma. Mons establish kingdom in Lower Burma: Suvarnabhumi, capital. | **ante 200** Livius Andronicus d.<br>**ante c. 200** Antiquarian study of the past already in existence in China. |
| **200** Antiochus III routs Egyptians at Panion: Coele-Syria taken. | | **200** Plautus: *Stichus.* |
| | | **Between 200 and AD 200** The 'Laws', or Code, of Manu. |
| **c. 200** Arsacids established S of the Caspian: origin of Parthian Dynasty. The fluked anchor evolved in Syria.<br>**c. 200–175** Demetrius, fourth King of Bactria, 'King of India'.<br>**c. 200–AD 300** Mercantile community steadily develops in India: extensive network of internal roads and routes connecting with China and with Parthia: Indian Ocean routes dominated by Arabs: W India linked by sea with China: guilds, coinage, banking developed: extensive trade in textiles, minerals and luxury goods, especially with Rome. | **c. 200** War between Han and Hsiung-Nu states: Han barely victorious in N Shansi. | **c. 200** Fabius Pictor and Cincius Alimentus, historians: Naevius and Ennius, poets.<br>**fl. 200–160** Crates of Mallos, grammarian.<br>**c. 200–AD 300** Astronomy and mathematics developed in India: includes medical encyclopaedias and pharmacopoeias: literary works, law, poetry and drama develop. |

| WESTERN EUROPE | CENTRAL & EASTERN EUROPE | EGYPT & AFRICA |
|---|---|---|
| **post 200** Roman coinage and local imitations current in Gaul. | **2nd c.** Basternes, of German origin, occupy lower Dnieper valley. | **post 200** Masinissa extends his dominions at Carthaginian expense agriculture greatly developed. |
| **199** Right of appeal to Rome extended to citizens outside Rome. Rome intervenes half-heartedly in Second Macedonian War. | **199** Roman Consul Sulpicius defeats Philip V of Macedon.<br><br>**198** T. Quinctius Flamininus, with Roman army, takes Thessaly: much of Greece submits voluntarily. | |
| **197** Romans pacify Cisalpine Gaul. Spain organized as two Roman provinces.<br><br>**197–179** Almost continuous war against the Romans in Spain. | **197** T. Quinctius Flamininus defeats Achaeans at Cynocephaloi: Philip V Alexander cedes all possessions outside Macedonia.<br><br>**196–195** Antiochus III obtains foothold on N Gallipoli peninsula.<br>**196–192** Prolonged negotiations between Rome and Greek States. T. Quinctius Flamininus and ten commissioners established to regulate Greek affairs. | **196** Rosetta Stone, in hieroglyphic and demotic Egyptian scripts, and Greek, engraved in honour of Ptole V Epiphanes. |
| **195** Roman citizens exempted from scourging.<br>**195–192** Romans defeat Boii: migration ensues, eventually founding Bohemia.<br>**194–192** Puteoli and other Roman settlements made in S Italy. | **194** T. Quinctius Flamininus withdraws Roman troops from Greece.<br><br>**192** Antiochus III enters Greece with army of 10,000: takes Chalcis and raids Thessaly.<br>**191** Roman army of 20,000 joins Macedonian army against Antiochus III: Antiochus routed at Thermopylae: Roman fleet patrols Aegaean with support of Rhodes.<br><br>**190** Roman army of 13,000 under P. Scipio, with his brother Scipio Africanus, disembarks in Epirus: Greek allies increase army to 30,000. | **195–184** Hannibal, suffete of Carthage.<br><br>**191** Carthage pays off forty instalments of indemnity to Rome Carthaginian finances reformed by Hannibal.<br>**191–148** Masinissa gradually encroaching on Carthaginian territory. |

| THE NEAR EAST & INDIA | THE FAR EAST | RELIGION & CULTURE |
|---|---|---|

**2nd c.** Tamil navy built: Ceylon attacked and partly seized in N: Tamils shortly expelled.
**2nd—1st c.** Technique of glass-blowing improved.

**2nd c.** Dutugemunu, legendary ruler of Ceylon. Manufacture of paper invented in China.

**2nd c.** Agatharcides of Cnidus, geographer and historian. Great Stupa consecrated by King of Ceylon: ceremony attended by monks from Kelasa monastery, Burma.
Classical texts of pre-Ch'in times re-written in a standardized orthography. Parchment first made in Pergamum. Lantern bellows developed in China.
**2nd—1st c.** The water-clock, the water-organ and the fire-engine invented.

**198** Conference of Nicaea: Philip V Alexander meets T. Quinctius Flamininus with delegates from Achaia, Aetolia, Pergamum and Rhodes: negotiations abortive. Battle of Panium (Baniyas): Antiochus III seizes Palestine from the Ptolemies: Jews given special privileges.
**197** Antiochus III takes S Asia Minor: Ephesus made his second capital.

**198** Sex. Aelius Paetus, consul: author of first Roman work on jurisprudence.

**c. 197—159** Great Altar built at Pergamum.

**196** Eumenes III of Pergamum asks for protection of Rome against Antiochus III.

**196** Kao Tsu sends embassy to Canton, and incorporates nascent Cantonese state within Han 'federation'.

**196** Isthmian Games: T. Quinctius Flamininus proclaims liberty for all Greek towns and states.

**195** Hannibal takes refuge with Antiochus III at Ephesus.

**195** Kao Tsu d.: succ. his widow, Lu: attempt to revive feudal system fails.

**c. 195—159** Terence (P. Terentius Afer), comic poet, b.

**194** Antiochus III sends abortive embassy to Rome.
**193** Rome offers to negotiate with Antiochus III at Ephesus.

**c. 193** Siao Ho, elaborator of Li K'uei's legal code, d.

**191—190** Antiochus III enlarges his fleet: principal fleet of Rhodes destroyed off Samos: second Rhodian fleet destroys Phoenician navy under Hannibal off Myonnesus: Rome gains control of the sea.
**191—176** Priapatius, King of Parthia.
**190** Roman army sent *via* Macedonia into Asia Minor under L. Scipio: c. 30,000 Romans face 72,000 men under Antiochus III: battle of Magnesia: Roman army stampedes Antiochus III's elephants into a rout: Antiochus evacuates Asia Minor.
**190—180** Pantaleon and Agathocles, Kings of Taxila.

**191** Roman Calendar revised to include intercalated days. Plautus: *Pseudolus*.
**c.191** Water clocks introduced into Rome from Greece.

| WESTERN EUROPE | CENTRAL & EASTERN EUROPE | EGYPT & AFRICA |
|---|---|---|
| 189 Bononia founded. | 189 The Aetolians become Roman vassals. | |
| 186–180 Roman campaigns in Liguria. | | |
| 184 Cato holds office as *Censor*. Roman citizens exempted from summary execution while on military service. Basilica Porcia, law court and market, built by Cato: Roman drainage system repaired. 183 Parma founded. | | ?184 Hannibal exiled from Carthage |
| 181 Romans suppress revolt in Corsica. 180 *Lex Villia* forbids election of Romans to the same magistracy in successive years. | | 181–145 Ptolemy VI Philometor. |
| 179 First stone bridge built in Rome. Three quarters of the Roman Senate comprised of plebeians. Tib. Sempronius Gracchus makes peace in Spain (−154). | 179 Philip V d.: succ. Perseus. | |
| post c. 177 *Latifundia* increases in Italy: improvements made in cultivation. 177–176 Romans suppress revolt in Sardinia: many Sardinians carried off into slavery. | 177 Rebellion in Lycia. | |
| | | 173 Roman treaty with Egypt renewed. |
| 172 Plebeians enabled to hold both consulates. 171 Roman Senate institutes court to hear complaints from Spanish provinces. | 172–168 War between Rome and Perseus. | |

| THE NEAR EAST & INDIA | THE FAR EAST | RELIGION & CULTURE |
|---|---|---|

**189** Romans under Cn. Manlius Vulso raid Galatia.
**189—169** Demetrius, King of Bactria.

**188** Asia Minor shared between Eumenes and Rhodes: Romans withdraw from E Mediterranean: Antiochus III pays Rome indemnity of 15,000 talents.
**187** Antiochus III d.: succ. Seleucus IV Philopator (—175).
**c. 187—184** Demetrius of Bactria takes Seleucid provinces of Aria, Arachosia and Seistan: reaches Sind and Gujarat.
**186** Prusias I of Bithynia attacks Eumenes of Pergamum: complies with Roman order to cease.
**c. 185** Bridhadratha, last Maurya King, d.: succ. Shunga Dynasty (—73).

**186** Cult of Bacchus banned in Rome.

**183** Hannibal commits suicide in Bithynia. Minor war in Pontus.

**c. 181** Jewish Temple erected at Leontopolis.

**c. 180—160 (or 160—140)** Menander (Milinda), first ruler of the Indo-Greek Dynasty: holds Punjab, but fails to gain Ganges valley: capital at Kabul.

**180** City of Cumae requested by Rome to replace Oscan with Latin: Campanian, Apulian and Umbrian dialects beginning to disappear.
**c. 180** Cursive script replaces hieroglyphic at Meroe.

**179—157** Wen Ti, Han Emperor: period of peace and prosperity and Confucianist revival.

**179—104** Tung-Chung Tsu, Confucianist philosopher, re-states Confucianism in a legal form.

**175** Seleucus IV d.: succ. Antiochus IV Epiphanes (—164): policy of Hellenization of the Jews.
**c. 175** Eucratides usurps throne of Bactria: new dynasty, with forty undated rulers, founded.

**c. 174—160** Yueh—Chi migrate from China to borders of India.

**171—137** Mithradates I, King of Parthia.

| WESTERN EUROPE | EASTERN EUROPE | EGYPT & AFRICA |
|---|---|---|
| **170** Lucretius Gallus impeached and fined in Rome for ill-treatment of Roman allies in Greece. | | **170–168** Antiochus IV attacks Ptolemy VI of Egypt: Alexandria besieged. |
| | **168** Romans defeat Perseus of Macedon near Pydna: made to surrender unconditionally: Macedonian monarchy suppressed: four republics set up as vassals of Rome. Rome destroys Rhodes. Delos made a free port. | **168** Rome compels Antiochus IV to raise siege of Alexandria by threatening war. |
| **167** Land tax no longer imposed in Italy. | | |
| | | **162** Masinissa takes Syrta region. |
| **155** Romans take Lower Dalmatia. **154–139** Viriatus, a shepherd, principal anti-Roman guerrilla leader in Spain. **154–133** Further Spanish wars. | | **154** Libya bequeathed to Rome by Ptolemy VI. Carthage mobilizes against Masinissa. **c. 153** Cato in Africa. |
| **151** Córdoba (Córdova) founded as a Roman colony. **150** Death penalty for Roman citizens disused in Rome. **c 150** *Lex Aelia* and *Lex Fufia* curb right of popular assembly in Rome: power very rarely invoked. | | **150** Carthage at war with Masinissa: Masinissa takes further Carthaginian territory. Cato demands the destruction of Carthage: Roman embassy sent to Carthage protesting at breaches of treaty of 201: Carthage re-arms. |

| THE NEAR EAST & INDIA | THE FAR EAST | RELIGION & CULTURE |
|---|---|---|

**169** The Temple at Jerusalem plundered by Antiochus IV.
**168** Galatian rebellion: Roman Senate declares Galatia autonomous.

**169** Ennius d.

**167** Rome asserts authority over Eumenes of Pergamum. Jerusalem sacked by Antiochus IV: Seleucid garrison installed. Eucratides conquers Bactria: Demetrius killed: eastern provinces recovered for Antiochus IV Epiphanes.

**167** Dec., cult of Zeus installed in the Temple at Jerusalem: Jewish law and circumcision forbidden: many copies of the Scriptures destroyed. Polybius, historian, in Rome.

**c. 166—5** *Book of Daniel* composed.
**166—160** Terence: *Comedies.*

**165** Eucratides invades India. Maccabaean revolt against Antiochus IV begins: led by Judas Maccabaeus (the Hammer).
**164** Antiochus IV d.: succ. Antiochus V Eupator ( 162): Rome named tutor for his heir: Lysias regent. Seleucid general Lysias defeated at Beth-zur by Judas Maccabaeus: Jerusalem regained: Feast of *Hanukkah* (dedication) inaugurated in commemoration.
**162—150** Demetrius I Soter, Seleucid ruler.
**161** Rome makes treaty with Judas Maccabaeus.
**160—143** Mithradates I conquers Iranian plateau: reaches R. Tigris: camp made at Ctesiphon.

**160—140** Further sporadic fighting between Han and Hsiung-nu.

**161—144** Jonathan the Maccabee, High Priest at Jerusalem.
**c. 160** Library built at Pergamum.

**159** Eumenes of Pergamum d.: succ. Attalus II (−139). Eucratides d.

**153** Roman official year advanced from 15 March to 1 January: origin of present New Year's Day.

**152** Rome encourages Alexander Balas to supplant Seleucid Demetrius.

**150—145** Alexander Balas succ. Demetrius I.
**150—129** Jews autonomous in Judaea.
**150—128** Val-Arsaces, King of Armenia: throws off Seleucid suzerainty.

**c. 150** Educated Romans proficient in both Latin and Greek.
Cato: *On Agriculture.*
**post 150** Metroon built at Athens.

| WESTERN EUROPE | EASTERN EUROPE | EGYPT & AFRICA |
|---|---|---|
| **149** Sulpicius Galba acquitted in Rome for massacre and plunder in Spain. Senatorial court set up to hear charges of extortion by provincial governors. Roman criminal courts reformed.<br>**c. 148–132** Numantia, on R. Douro, defies Romans in Spain. | **148** Rome annexes Macedonia. | **149–146** Third Punic War. Rome besieges Carthage. Polybius voyages along W coast of Africa.<br>**149** Masinissa d.: succ. Micipsa (–118). |
| **146** *Lex Provinciae* embodies Roman provincial code of law: enables governors to legislate locally. | **146** Critolaus, dictator of Corinth, challenges Roman authority in Greece: put down by Caecilius Metellus. Achaean League dissolved: Governor of Macedonia authorized to preserve peace amongst autonomous Greek city states. Andriscos, pretender to the Macedonian throne, put down by Romans: general unrest in Greece put down with severe measures: Macedonia made a Roman province. | **147** P. Cornelius Scipio Aemilianus appointed Roman commander against Carthage.<br>**146** Scipio takes Carthage: 50,000 inhabitants sold into slavery: city razed: hinterland constituted Roman Province of Africa: capital at Utica. |
| **144** First high level aqueduct constructed in Rome. | | **145–116** Ptolemy VII Euergetes II. Jewish scholars invited to settle in Alexandria. |
| | **139** Viriatus assassinated. | |
| **135** Slave revolt in Sicily. | | **135** Scipio Aemilianus sent from Rome to investigate the state of Egypt. |
| **134** Scipio Aemilianus besieges Numantia with 60,000 men: 4,000 defenders hold out for sixteen months.<br>**133** Tiberius Gracchus's land act. P. Cornelius Scipio Aemilianus decisively defeats Spanish insurgents: end of pacification of Spain.<br>**133–132** Roman campaign against rebellious slaves in Sicily. | | |

| THE NEAR EAST & INDIA | THE FAR EAST | RELIGION & CULTURE |
| --- | --- | --- |

148 Mucius Scaevola: *Annales Maximi.*

146–138 Demetrius II, Seleucid.

144 Apollodorus of Athens:
*Chronology of History.*
144–135 Simon the Maccabee, High
Priest at Jerusalem.

143–80 Sang Hung-Yang, Chinese
economist, advocating state
monopoly of trade.
141–86 Wu, or Wu Ti, Han Emperor.
Commerce with Middle East highly
developed.

141 Parthians penetrate as far as
Babylon.
c. 140–130 Bactria taken by
nomadic peoples of Scythian origin:
Greek King Heliocles driven out.
139 Demetrius II defeated and
taken prisoner by the Parthians.
138–129 Antiochus VII Sidetes,
Seleucid.

139 Jews and astrologers banished
from Rome.

138–125 Chang Ch'ien travels widely
in central Asia, producing reports on
trade and politics to the Imperial
Court.

137–128 Phraates II, King of
Parthia.

135 Ssu-ma Chi, author of Shih Chi,
first known systematic Chinese
historian, b.
c. 135 Poseidonius of Apamaea b.
c. 135–106 *The Book of Enoch.*
John Hyrcanus, High Priest at
Jerusalem.

33 Attalus III d.: end of the
Dynasty of Pergamum: his will
makes Rome his heir: Aristonicus,
pretender to Pergamum, rebels.

133–119 Continuous war between
Han and Hsiung-nu.

| WESTERN EUROPE | CENTRAL & EASTERN EUROPE | EGYPT & AFRICA |
|---|---|---|

**132** Special tribunal constituted at Rome by Consul Papilius with power to award death sentence. Tiberius Gracchus clubbed to death. Numantia falls to Scipio.
**131** Secret ballot introduced at Rome at legislative assemblies.

**129** Land Commission suspended in Rome.

**129** Rome takes remainder of Illyria and Dalmatia.

**125** M. Fulvius Flaccus fails to extend Roman franchise to Italy.
**125—121** Romans conquer Narbonese Gaul, from Riviera to Auvergne, Nîmes and Toulouse.
**123** Romans take Balearic Is.
**123—122** Caius Gracchus, tribune: Tiberius Gracchus's land law and the land commission revived: Popilian tribunal abolished: Popilius impeached: jury system reformed: financial regulations enacted for Province of Asia.
**122** Caius Gracchus's franchise act defeated. Land law revised by Livius Drusus. Senate declares state of emergency: Caius Gracchus and over 3,000 others killed by general levy of Roman citizens.
**c. 120** Land acts of Tiberius and Caius Gracchus revised. Fabius Maximus erects first triumphal arch in Rome.

**122** Caius Gracchus initiates Roman colony of Iunonia near Carthage: visits Africa.

**119** Eudoxus voyages from Red Sea to India.

**118** Micipsa, King of Numidia d., leaving territory divided between three sons: succ. Jugurtha (−104) rids himself of his brothers.

**116** Adherbal, brother of Jugurtha, appeals successfully to Roman Senate.
**116—108/7** Ptolemy VIII Soter II (first reign).

## THE NEAR EAST & INDIA        THE FAR EAST        RELIGION & CULTURE

c. 132–131 Olympeion, Athens, completed.

131 Roman force defeated by Aristonicus.
130 Romans destroy Aristonicus: Pergamum made Roman province of Asia.

c. 130 Agatharcides of Cnidus describes the Red Sea.

129 Huns raid country-side near modern Peking.
128 Chinese embassy visits Yue-tche, inhabitants of Sogdiana: capital probably Samarqand. Overland caravan from India to China attested in Burma.

c. 129 Hipparchus of Nicaea describes the equinoxes.

128–124 Artabanus II, King of Parthia.

127 Hymeros rebels in Babylon.

c. 127–111 Emperor Wu Ti founds military colonies to keep out the Huns.
c. 126 Scythians cross R. Oxus.

c. 125 *Annales maximi* or calendar first published annually at Rome.

125–95 Antiochus VIII, Seleucid.

124–96 Asclepiades, physician.

123–88 Mithradates II, King of Parthia: kingdom extended into India.

120–63 Mithradates VI, King of Pontus: creator of an empire on the Black Sea.

120 Temple of Apollo at Delphi built.

119 Han cavalry action compels Hsiung-Nu to withdraw northwards and to end war.

116–27 M. Terentius Varro, writer.

c. 115–c. AD 300 Himyarite Kingdom of 'Saba and dhu-Raydan': capital Zafar, near Sanaa: gold, silver and copper currency issued imitating Greek coinage: wealth derived from camel transport and from incense trade between Indian Ocean and Fertile Crescent.

| WESTERN EUROPE | CENTRAL & EASTERN EUROPE | EGYPT & AFRICA |
|---|---|---|
| | **114** Scordisci (from modern Yugoslavia) defeat Romans under C. Porcius Cato: raids reach Delphi. | |
| **113** Cimbri and Teutones, Germanic or Celtic tribesmen, encounter Roman force: Cn. Papirius Carbo's army beaten off: movement temporarily halted. | | |
| | **112** M. Livius Drusus drives Scordisci back to the Danube. | **112** Jugurtha makes war on Adherba besieges him at Cirta (present Constantine): Cirta taken: Italian residents massacred. |
| **111** Consolidating land act passed in Rome. | | **111** Jugurtha allowed safe-conduct to plead his case in Rome.<br>**111–106** The Jugurthine War.<br>**110** Roman army of 40,000 fails to defeat Jugurtha: Jugurtha again allowed safe-conduct to Rome: on return, forces Roman army to capitulate.<br>**109** Q. Caecilius Metellus takes command of Roman army in Africa: Cirta taken. |
| **109** Cimbri and Teutones invade E France: met by Roman army near Narbonne: offer to serve Rome as mercenaries: declined by Senate: Roman army under M. Iunius Silanus defeated.<br>**108 ff** C. Marius re-organizes Roman army: proletarian recruitment organized on a voluntary basis: new equipment issued. | | **108** Metellus forces Jugurtha to offe submission: Jugurtha allies with Gaetuli and Bocchus, King of Mauretania: C. Marius takes command as consul.<br>**108/7–88** Ptolemy IX Alexander I. |
| **107** Roman army ambushed in Gascony by Tigurini and defeated. | | **107** C. Marius destroys Capsa: Jugurtha's treasury captured near R. Muluccha: Roman army drives o Jugurtha near Cirta without defeating him. |
| **106** Tigurini retreat from Gascony. | | **106** Bocchus, King of Mauretania, changes sides: L. Cornelius Sulla persuades him to kidnap Jugurtha: Jugurtha sent to Rome.<br>**105** Bocchus rewarded with much Numidia. Jugurtha captured: executed in Rome (104).<br>**105–c. 88** Gauda, King of Numidia |
| **104** Cimbri and Teutones apply to Rome to settle in Gaul: refused: defeat Romans near Aransio (now Orange). Cimbri enter Spain.<br>**104–100** C. Marius elected consul five times in succession. | | |
| **102** Cimbri rejoin Teutones in Gaul: three-pronged invasion of Roman frontier: Roman army under C. Marius defeats them near Aquae Sextiae (now Aix-en-Provence).<br>**103–101** Slave revolt in Spain.<br>**101** Cimbri again defeated by C. Marius near Vercellae: Tigurini defeated by Cornelius Sulla in eastern Alps. | | |

| THE NEAR EAST & INDIA | THE FAR EAST | RELIGION & CULTURE |
|---|---|---|
| | | **114** A Vestal Virgin killed by lightning at Rome: a number of virgins executed for unchasteness: Sibylline oracle orders the burial alive of a Greek and a Gallic couple. |
| | **111** Vietnam conquered by China. | **c. 111** Eudoxus of Cyzicus fails to reach India via the Cape. |
| **108** W Korea conquered by the Han. | | |
| | | **106—105** Aristobulus, High Priest at Jerusalem.<br>**106—43** M. Tullius Cicero, lawyer, orator and philosopher. |
| **104** Mithradates VI of Pontus occupies Galatia and Cappadocia. | **104** Hsiung-nu defeat Han in battle, but without follow-up.<br>**104 and 102** Han military expeditions under General Li Kuang-Li reach Ferghana: states of Tarim basin and some of W Turkestan subject to Han. Foreign consumer goods enter China: plants, including grapes, peaches and pomegranates, brought in. | |
| **103** Alexander Jannaeus, King of Judaea.<br>**102** Roman naval detachment stationed off Pamphylia and Cilicia to put down piracy. | | **102—44** C. Julius Caesar, soldier, statesman and historian. |

| WESTERN EUROPE | CENTRAL & EASTERN EUROPE | EGYPT & AFRICA |
|---|---|---|
| **late 2nd c.** Arverni of C. Gaul unite Gallic tribes from the Atlantic and the Pyrenees to the Rhine: colleges of Druid priests a bond of unity: government of Gaul principally warring nobles.<br>**100** Riots in Rome put down by C. Marius.<br>**c. 100** Germanic peoples move into Celtic territory between the Main and the Danube. Capua extends trade in bronze articles to N Europe. | | |
| **1st c.** Roads built in Gaul. First cities begin to develop. | **1st c.** Water mills already in use in N Greece for grinding corn. | **1st c.** Arabian colonists from Yemen and Hadhramaut settle in Ethiopia: Kingdom of Axum founded. |
| | | **97** Cyrenaica independent of Egypt. |
| | | **96** Cyrenaica bequeathed to Rome by Ptolemy Apion: no governor sent for twenty years: Greek cities govern themselves. |
| **91—83** The Italian Wars. | | |
| **90** Italian confederacy formed to extort Roman citizenship by force: rebellion based on Corfinium: rebels initially successful against Roman force of 150,000: Rome grants franchise to Italian loyalists.<br>**89** Asculum surrenders: confederacy defeated in central Italy. Romans fight successful campaign in S Italy.<br>**88** Most of Italy pacified: Italians enjoy Roman citizenship: reforms made by P. Sulpicius Rufus. Cornelius Sulla, consul: seizes Rome in a *coup d'état*. | | **ante c. 88—c. 68** Hiemsal, King of Numidia.<br>**88—80** Ptolemy VIII restored. |

| THE NEAR EAST & INDIA | THE FAR EAST | RELIGION & CULTURE |
|---|---|---|
| | | **End of 2nd c.** Samaritan Scriptures (Pentateuch) codified. |
| **c. 100** Mithradates II invades Armenia. Laws of Manu crystallize Indian concepts of kingship. Antialkidas, King of Taxila. Paper first made in China.<br>**1st c. BC—AD 2nd c.** Satavahana or Andhra Dynasty in NW Deccan. | **c. 100—AD 1904** Admission to Chinese civil service based on an examination system. State and Court Secretariat developed.<br><br>**1st c. or ante** Halingyi city founded in central Burma.<br>**1st c.** Turks reach Altai Mts, Mongolia. Prome, capital of Pyu (Sri Ksetra) Kingdom in Burma: eighteen kingdoms in Burma and Malaya said to be subject to it.<br>**1st c.±** Peikthanomyo (Vishnu City) founded in central Burma.<br>**1st c.** Economic decline in China.<br>**c. 1st c.** Salt trade, based on salt wells, developed in Szechwan. | **c. 100** L. Aelius Stilo and Varro, grammarians. Cult of Isis and Sarapis brought to Italy. Ball bearings used in Danish cart wheels.<br><br>**1st c.** Latest date for the entry of Buddhism into China at the hands of merchants from India or C Asia. Pomponius Mela, geographer. Cornelius Nepos, historian. P. Valerius Cato, grammarian and poet. Paper money first used in Szechwan: leads eventually to banking system. Caesar notes that the ships of the Gauls were superior to those of the Romans: chain anchors used: vessels more sturdily built. Roman ships adopt jib-sails in addition to mainsail. Tall horses of western breed introduced from Sogdiana into China.<br>**c. 99—55** Lucretius Carus, poet and philosopher.<br>**97** Human sacrifices forbidden by the Senate. |
| **95** Nicomedes II of Bithynia complains of Mithradates VI to Rome: Senate orders evacuation of Cappadocia. Tigranes, King of Armenia. | | **95** Persecution of the Pharisees by the Sadducees.<br>**c. 95** Q. Mucius Scaevola: treatise on civil law.<br><br>**c. 94** First school of Latin rhetoric opened at Rome opened by Plotius Gallus. |
| **93** Tigranes over-runs Cappadocia.<br>**92** Tigranes, King of Armenia, prevented by C. Sulla from taking Cappadocia. Mithradates II sends embassy to Sulla proposing an alliance between Parthia and Rome.<br>**91 or 90** Mithradates VI and Tigranes seize Cappadocia: Roman army ejects them without a battle.<br>**90** Pharisees rebel against Alexander Jannaeus. | **91** Hsiung-nu again defeat Han in battle, but with no follow-up. | **fl. c. 90—50** Pasiteles, sculptor, at Rome. |
| **88** Mithradates seizes Cappadocia and all Roman Asia Minor: 80,000 Italian residents said to have been massacred. | | |

| WESTERN EUROPE | CENTRAL & EASTERN EUROPE | EGYPT & AFRICA |
|---|---|---|
| **87** Cornelius Cinna and C. Marius march on Rome: short siege followed by reign of terror: Cinna and Marius declare themselves consuls: Marius d. **ante 86** Roman Senate sets up court to hear cases of misappropriation and embezzlement of public funds by officials.<br>**86–84** Cornelius Cinna virtual dictator of Rome: L. Cornelius Sulla outlawed. | **87** Mithradates VI seizes C and S Greece.<br><br>**86** C. Sulla recovers Athens: defeats Mithradates at Chaeronea and Orchomenus. | **c. 86** Julius Maternus allies with Garamantes against 'Ethiopians': visits Agisymba (? Air). |
| **83** Sulla lands at Brindisi: reaches Campania.<br><br>**82** Sulla takes Rome and finally N Italy: provinces submit: his opponents murdered: L. Valerius Flaccus nominated *interrex:* Sulla made dictator: Italians admitted to the Senate: constitution reformed. | | **82** Tingis (Tangier) occupied by Sertorius.<br>**c. 81** Wheat, olives and the vine introduced into Roman Africa, 'the granary of Rome'.<br>**80–51** Ptolemy XI Auletes. |
| **80–71** Sertorius' rebellion in Spain.<br><br>**79** Plague, followed by fire, in Rome. Sulla resigns dictatorship and retires.<br>**78** Attempted *coup d'état* by M. Aemilius Lepidus. | | |
| | | **74** Roman garrison established at Cyrene. |
| **73** Spartacus's Slave War in Italy. | | |
| | **72** Pirates defeat Roman fleet off Crete. | |
| **70** Pompey and Crassus elected consuls. Cicero (M. Tullius Cicero) prosecutes C. Verres, former governor of Sicily: the *Verrine Orations.*<br>**69** Pirates active off Brindisi and Ostia. | **69** Pirates sack Delos. | |

| THE NEAR EAST & INDIA | THE FAR EAST | RELIGION & CULTURE |
|---|---|---|

**c. 87—62** al-Harith (Aretas III) Ghassanid king: first Ghassanid to strike coins.

**86—34** Sallust (C. Sallustius Crispus), historian.

**85** C. Flavius Fimbria invades Asia Minor: Mithradates driven from Pergamum: peace made at Dardanus: Romans recover territory in Asia Minor: Mithradates surrenders fleet and pays indemnity.

**?84—54** Gaius Valerius Catullus, poet. **post 83** Temple of Jupiter Capitolinus at Rome rebuilt. Public Record Office erected.

**83—82** Second Mithradatic war: ended on previous terms.

**81** Cicero's first speech: *Pro Quinctio.*

**c. 80—30** Shaka Dynasty at Gandhara, India.

**78** P. Servilius attacks Lycian pirates. Tigranes again over-runs Cappadocia: takes part of Mesopotamia from Parthia with Syria and Cilicia.

**77—37** Ching Fang, Chinese musicologist.

**76** P. Servilius destroys Pamphylian pirates.
**75** P. Servilius puts down bandits in Cilicia.
**74** Mithradates VI invades Roman territory in Asia: Bithynia over-run: Chalcedon destroyed: L. Licinius Lucullus cuts Mithradates' communications.
**74—70** Third Mithradatic War.
**73—28** Kanva or Kanyavama Dynasty in India.
**73** Roman fleet defeats Mithradates' fleet off Lemnos: Lucullus raids Galatia.
**72** Lucullus defeats army of Pontus at Cabira: Mithradates escapes to Armenia.

**70—19** Vergil (P. Vergilius Maro), poet.

**69** L. Licinius Lucullus invades Armenia: defeats Tigranes at Tigranocerta.
**69—37** Phraates III, King of Parthia.

**69** Cicero: *Pro Fonteio.*

| WESTERN EUROPE | CENTRAL & EASTERN EUROPE | EGYPT & AFRICA |
|---|---|---|
| **68** Pirates cut out Roman fleet at Ostia: Roman corn supply intercepted. | | **c. 68** Juba I, King of Numidia: capital at Zama. |
| **68—67** Q. Metellus seizes Crete to put down piracy: made a Roman province. | | |
| **67** Pompey (Cn. Pompeius Magnus) given command of fleet of 270 sail and 100,000 infantry: end of piracy in the Mediterranean. | | |
| **c. 65—60** German settlers move into present Alsace under Ariovistus. Helvetii enter Switzerland. | | |
| **64** Cicero and C. Antonius elected consuls. | | |
| **63** Cataline's conspiracy to seize Rome prevented. | | |
| **62** Pompey returns to Rome: disbands his army. | | |
| **61** Caesar in Spain. | | |
| **59** Caesar, Pompey and Crassus form First Triumvirate. Caesar consul: brings in land act by force: obtains *Lex Vatinia,* making him governor of Gaul and Illyria for five years. | | **59** Caesar enforces recognition of Ptolemy Auletes as ruler of Egypt. |
| **58** Cicero banished from Rome. Caesar defeats Helvetii: Gauls unite under Ariovistus: Caesar expels him from Gaul and routs Suebi: territory of Aedui and Sequani (near Besançon) annexed. | | |
| **58—51** Conquest of Gaul by the Romans. | | |
| **57** Belgae unite against Caesar: Roman army reduces N France: Nervii defeated: W France submits to P. Crassus. Pompey commissioned to relieve grain shortage in Rome. | | |
| **56** Veneti and Atlantic coastal tribes unite against Caesar in Gaul: Veneti defeated: Caesar occupies N France from Brittany to Flanders. | | **56** Gabinius, Roman Proconsul in Syria, intervenes in Egypt. |
| **55** Pompey and Crassus, consuls: Caesar's proconsulate extended for five years: Crassus appointed proconsul of Syria; Pompey of Spain. German tribes in Gaul pushed back beyond the Rhine: most of Gaul under Roman domination: Julius Caesar's first campaign in Britain. | | |
| **54** Gaul and the Belgae revolt against the Romans: Ambiorix, chief of the Eburons, massacres a Roman legion: Caesar defeats the Nervii: Labienus defeats the Trevi. Caesar again invades Britain for two to three months. | | |

| THE NEAR EAST & INDIA | THE FAR EAST | RELIGION & CULTURE |
|---|---|---|

**68** Lucullus pursues Tigranes and Mithradates: Roman army mutinies in winter.

**67** Part of Lucullus' army drafted to assist Pompey: Lucullus retreats from Nisibis to Pontus. Pompey takes over Lucullus' army.

**66** Phraates III makes alliance with Pompey. Mithradates loses support of Tigranes: Armenia invaded by Parthia: Pompey defeats Mithradates at Nicopolis: Mithradates escapes: Tigranes submits to Pompey.

**65–63** Mithradates raises a fresh army.

**64** Pompey restores order in Syria.

**63** Pompey besieges Jerusalem: taken after three months' siege: general settlement made in the Near East. Seleucid Dynasty ended.

**66** Cicero: *Pro lege Manilia.*

**65–8** Horace (Quintus Horatius Flaccus), poet.

**63** Caesar (Caius Iulius Caesar) made Pontifex Maximus (high priest) at Rome. Cicero: *Catalinares: Pro Murena.* c. **63–AD 25** Strabo, geographer.

c. **60** Pythagorean philosophy revived at Alexandria by P. Nigidius Figulus. c. **59** Diodorus Siculus, geographer. **59–AD 17** Livy (Titus Livius), historian.

**57–55** Judaea revolts against Rome.

**58** Rival rulers amongst Hsiung-nu: period of great weakness: Shensi and Shansi provinces lost. Hsien-pi and Wu-huan revert to nomadism: S Hsiung-nu becomes part of Han dominions.

c. **57–51** Julius Caesar: *de Bello Gallico.*

**post 56–c. 37** Orodes II, King of Parthia: Ctesiphon made the capital of Parthia.

**56** Cicero: *Pro Sestio: Pro Caelio.*

**55** Cicero: *De Oratore.* **55–AD 41** M. Annaeus Seneca, rhetorician.

**54** Crassus succ. Gabinius as proconsul of Syria.

**54** Cicero: *De Somno Scipionis.* c. **54–19** Albius Tibullus, elegiac poet.

| WESTERN EUROPE | CENTRAL &<br>EASTERN EUROPE | EGYPT & AFRICA |
|---|---|---|

**53** Caesar puts down minor rebellions in Gaul.

**52** Rioting in Rome: Pompey appointed virtual dictator to restore order: Pompey's (nominal) command in Spain extended by five years. Rising of Gauls under Vercingetorix: Caesar takes Avaricum (Bourges): beaten by Vercingetorix and compelled to retire: Caesar again attacks, besieging Vercingetorix in Alesia: famine compels Vercingetorix to surrender.

**51** Caesar conducts mopping up actions in Gaul. End of resistance in Gaul: under Roman rule to AD 406.

**51—30** Cleopatra, last independent Egyptian ruler.

**49** 7 Jan., Senate decrees state of emergency: Pompey given virtual sole powers: Caesar crosses R. Rubicon and invades Italy: takes all Italy: Pompey flees to Thessalonica. Caesar nominated dictator: shortly abdicates. Caesar withdraws from Gaul: all Gaul now subject to Rome. Caesar's dictatorship prolonged by Rome: Mark Anthony (M. Anthonius) acts as viceroy: quells rebellion: Oct-Dec. Caesar in Rome: Dec., embarks for Africa.

**49** Juba I supports Pompey: Caesarion Curion defeated.

**48** Caesar crosses to Greece: attempts siege of Pompey at Petra: Caesar retreats to Thessaly: Pompey with 35,000 to 40,000, attacks Caesar, with 22,000, near Pharsalus: Pompey's army routed: many of Pompey's forces change sides: Caesar visits Egypt.

**48** Pompey flees to Egypt and d. Alexandria rises against Caesar.

**48—47** Caesar in Egypt: rebellion put down. Library of Alexandria burnt.

**47** Caesar receives Mithradates of Pergamum as an ally: defeats Egyptians: Ptolemy XII killed: succ. Ptolemy XIII with Cleopatra. Caesar returns to Rome. Sallust Governor of Africa.

**47—46** Caesar's campaign in N Africa

**46** Caesar campaigns against Pompeia army reinforced by Juba of Numidia: defeats Q. Metellus Scipio at Thapsus M. Cato commits suicide: Caesar returns to Rome.

**46—45** Caesarion campaigns against Pompey's son in Spain: enemy army destroyed at Munda. Caesar re-elected dictator in Rome for ten years.

**45** Caesar recognized master of the Roman world: magnanimity shown to opponents: re-organization of government begun: Pontine marshes to be drained: other public works put in hand: provincial taxation reduced. C. Octavius, grand-nephew of Caesar, adopted as his heir.

| THE NEAR EAST & INDIA | THE FAR EAST | RELIGION & CULTURE |
|---|---|---|

**53** Crassus invades Parthia: defeated at Carrhae: Crassus killed: 40,000 Romans perish.
**52** Civil war between Mithradates II and Orodes of Parthia.

**52** Cicero: *Pro Milone: De Legibus.*

**51–50** Parthians invade Syria.

**c. 50** Kalinga regains independence from Magadha under King Kharavela.
**c. 50–AD 100** Roman trade with S India flourishing.
**c. 50–c. AD 225** Satavahana Dynasty in NW Deccan.

**51** Hsiung-nu state finally submits to Han rule.

**51** Cicero: *De Republica.*

**50** Canal locks in existence in China.
**c. 50** The Tower of the Four Winds built at Athens. Basilica Aemilia restored. Publishing and book trade flourishing in Rome.
**c. 50–c. 16** S. Aurelius Propertius, poet.
**post 50** Art of glass-blowing discovered in Sidon.

**47** Caesar leaves Egypt for Palestine: Jewish tribute reduced: five day campaign against Pharnaces of Pontus: battle of Zela: Caesar exhibits placard *VENI, VIDI, VICI* (I came, I saw, I conquered).

**47** Varro: *Antiquities.* Caesar(? ): *De Bello Civili.*

**46** Cicero: *Orator: Brutus.* The Julian Calendar instituted.

**45** Cicero: *Hortensius: De finibus: Tusculanes.*

| WESTERN EUROPE | CENTRAL &<br>EASTERN EUROPE | EGYPT & AFRICA |
|---|---|---|

**44** 14 Feb., Caesar elected dictator for life: 15 March, Caesar assassinated in the Senate: government passes to Mark Anthony and M. Aemilianus Lepidus: 17 March, conspirators granted an amnesty: dictatorship abolished. C. Octavius takes the name C. Iulius Caesar Octavianus (Octavian). 2 Sept., Cicero delivers his *First Philippic* in the Senate. Oct., Anthony trumps up a charge against Octavian. 20 Dec., Cicero: *Third Philippic*.
**43** 1 Jan., Cicero: *Fifth Philippic:* proposes Octavian as propraetor. Anthony defeated at Mutina: declared a public enemy by the Senate: commanders in Cisalpine Gaul desert to him. July, Octavian marches on Rome: enters unopposed: amnesty for conspirators revoked: Anthony offered peace at meeting at Bononia: Octavian, Anthony and Lepidus proclaimed *triumvirs* for three years: end of Roman republic. Cicero d. Anthony and Octavian defeat Brutus and Cassius at Philippi: both commit suicide. Lepidus elbowed out of the triumvirate. Roman colony founded at Lugdunum (Lyons).
**43—30** More than forty colonies established by Rome.

**44—43** M. Brutus forms an army in the Balkans.

**42/41** Anthony spends winter in Egypt.
**42 and 38** Bogud, King in W Mauretania, takes part in expeditions in Spain.

**41** L. Anthonius (brother of Mark Anthony) seizes Rome. Octavian takes Gaul.
**40** Mark Anthony returns to Italy: besieged by Octavian's army at Brindisi: peace made: Octavian's authority over Gaul, Spain and Illyria recognized: Lepidus sent to Africa: Anthony m. Octavia, Octavian's sister. S. Pompeius cuts off grain supplies to Rome.

**39** Minor Roman campaign in Gaul. Abortive attempt by Anthony to make peace with S. Pompeius.
**38** Octavian's fleet defeated by S. Pompeius: new fleet built: triumvirate extended for five years.

**38** Bocchus II seizes Bogud's kingdom Tingis (Tangier) made a Roman city.

**37** Mark Anthony m. Cleopatra.

**36** Octavian's fleet defeats S. Pompeius at Naulochus: S. Pompeius flees to Phrygia: executed.

**36** Anthony becomes dependent on Cleopatra's finance: 'Donations of Alexandria': Media and Parthia declared Egyptian possessions, with Cyprus, Cyrene and S Syria: N Syria and Cilicia awared to Caesarion.

| THE NEAR EAST & INDIA | THE FAR EAST | RELIGION & CULTURE |
|---|---|---|
| | | 44–43 Cicero: *Philippics: De Officiis.* |
| 43 Cassius takes command of Asia Minor and eastern provinces. Mark Anthony tours eastern provinces, receiving tribute. | | 43–AD 17 Ovid (P. Ovidius Naso), poet. |
| 42 Fortress of Massada begun by Herod.<br>42–41 Mark Anthony makes abortive attempt to take Palmyra (Tadmor). | | 42 Caesar venerated as a god. |
| 41 Mark Anthony meets Cleopatra in Cilicia. | | 41 Horace: first *Epodes.* |
| 40 Herod made King of Judaea by the Romans. Parthians over-run Syria and Asia Minor.<br>39–38 Parthians driven out of Syria and Asia Minor by forces sent by Mark Anthony. | | c. 40 Dionysius of Halicarnassus describes flourishing state of Italian agriculture.<br>39 Vergil: *Eclogues.* |
| 37 Jerusalem recaptured: Herod installed (king from 40).<br>37–2 Phraates IV of Parthia.<br>36 Mark Anthony invades Parthia with little effect. | | 36 Varro: *De re rustica.* |

| WESTERN EUROPE | CENTRAL & EASTERN EUROPE | EGYPT & AFRICA |
|---|---|---|
| **35–34** Valerius Messala campaigns against the Salassi: approaches to St Bernard Pass cleared. | **35–33** Octavian campaigns in the Balkans. | **34** Mark Anthony divides the east between Cleopatra and her children. **33** Rome annexes Mauretania. Bocchus ll d. **33–25** Mauretania governed by Roman prefects. **32** Octavian sends declaration of war to Cleopatra. |
| **32** Octavian takes control of Rome: consuls and 300 senators expelled. Anthony divorces Octavia. | **32** Anthony moves into Greece with thirty legions and 500 sail. | |
| **31** Octavian elected consul: triumvirate allowed to lapse: war declared on Cleopatra. | **31** Agrippa sails with fleet of 600 against Anthony: Octavian encamps near Actium: 31 Sept., battle of Actium: Anthony escapes to Egypt: Anthony's troops and fleet desert. | **31–30** Octavian enters Egypt with army at Pelusium: Ptolemaic fleet burnt by Nabataeans: Anthony and Cleopatra commit suicide: Octavian makes Egypt a Roman province: royal treasure taken to Rome. |
| **30** M. Valerius Messala conducts minor Roman campaign in Gaul. **30–AD 14** More than forty Roman colonies established by Octavian. | | |
| **29** Romans repel an attack by the Suebi. Octavian returns to Rome: Senate purged: reduced from 1000 to 800. **28** Disused temples in Rome systematically repaired. Italian census 4 m. **27** Octavian offers to resign: 16 Jan., Senate refuses: title of Augustus conferred: provinces divided into senatorial and imperial provinces: Augustus given *imperium proconsulare,* virtual full powers. *Consilium Principis,* similar to Privy Council, instituted in Rome. **27–24** Augustus visits Gaul and Spain. **27–AD 14** Augustus (Octavianus) Roman Emperor. **26** Fire brigade instituted in Rome. **26–19** Augustus' campaigns in Spain. **25** Salassi rounded up and sold as slaves by Terentius Varro Murena: road built across Little St Bernard Pass. | **27** Augustus re-organizes Spain into three provinces: Baetica in the NE; Lusitania, chiefly modern Portugal; and Hispania Citerior, renamed Tarraconensis. | **27** Augustus re-organizes Roman Africa.

**26** L. Cornelius Gallus, governor, recalled from Egypt for setting up statues of himself. **c. 25–24** Aelius Gallus, Roman prefect of Egypt, visits 1st Cataract in company with Strabo, geographer. **c. 25–AD 23** Juba II, King of Mauritania. |

| THE NEAR EAST & INDIA | THE FAR EAST | RELIGION & CULTURE |
|---|---|---|

**35** Horace: first *Satires.*

**34** Mark Anthony takes Armenia.

**34–33** Cicero's *Letters* published.

**33** Artaxias seizes Armenia: all Romans in the country massacred. Tiridates, a nobleman, revolts against Parthia: Phraates flees: Tiridates proclaimed king (−30). Mark Anthony makes abortive campaign against Phraates.

**32–7** Ch'eng Ti, Emperor: virtual ruler, his mother, widow of Emperor Yuan Ti, with her nephew Wang Mang.

**30** Phraates restored.

**30** Horace: second *Satires.* Octavian imposes Julian calendar on Egypt.
**c. 30** Phaedras, writer of fables, b.
**fl. c. 30** Dionysius of Halicarnassus, historian.
**29** Horace: *Epodes.* Vergil: *Georgics.*
**29–19** Vergil: *The Aeneid.*

**27** Worship of Mithras alleged to have been brought to Rome by Pompey: spreads gradually, especially in the Roman army.

**c. 26** Tibullus: *Elegies.*

**25** Galatia annexed by Rome. Military colony set up at Antioch in Pisidia.
**25** Indian embassy visits Rome with tigers, pheasants, snakes and a Buddhist monk.
**25–24** C. Aelius Gallus, prefect of Egypt, sent to invade the Kingdom of Saba: treaty of friendship with Saba, guaranteeing freedom of navigation in the Bab al-Mandab.
**24** Ghassanids collaborate nominally in Gallus's expedition.

**25–12** Agrippa's baths built in Rome.
**post 25** Juba II explores Atlas Mts with his physician Euphorbius.

| WESTERN EUROPE | CENTRAL & EASTERN EUROPE | EGYPT & AFRICA |
|---|---|---|
| **23** Augustus ill: resigns consulate: given *tribunicia potestas: proconsulare imperium* renewed: provinces redistributed. Riots in Rome. | | **23** Petronius defeats Queen of Meroe: Napata sacked. |
| **c. 20** Agrippa settles Ubii near present Cologne.<br>**20** Highways board set up in Rome. | | **22** Roman frontier of Egypt advanced beyond 1st Cataract: Nubia army defeated: frontier shortly drawn back.<br>**c. 20–AD 15** Natakamani, King of Meroe: trades with India *via* Axum.<br>**c. 20** Volubilis, Babba Campestris and Banasa built. |
| **19** Augustus revises marriage laws in Rome. Riots in Rome. | | **19** L. Cornelius Balbus, Proconsul of Africa, ordered to prevent Garamantes raiding oasis of Jerma: his expedition claimed to have reached R. Niger. |
| **18** Senate reduced to 600. | | |
| **16** Sugambri attack Roman army on the Rhine: a standard captured. Celtic tribes raid Styria, Austria and W Hungary (Pannonia) and Istria.<br>**15** Lyons made the principal imperial mint. Tiberius and Drusus, Augustus's stepsons, campaign against the Raeti: Roman boundary extended to the upper Danube.<br>**15–13** Augustus again visits Gaul.<br>**14** Liguri cleared from the present Riviera: province of the Maritime Alps established.<br>**13** Italian census 5 m.<br>**12–10** Roman army under Drusus campaigns in Germany as far as the Elbe: fleet in R. Rhine and Zuyder Zee.<br>**12–9** Tiberius campaigns in Pannonia.<br>**9** Drusus d. near R. Elbe. Roman marriage laws again revised: bachelors and widowers required to marry: adultery to be punished with death or banishment.<br>**8–7** Drusus replaced by Tiberius: insubordinate German populations moved to Gaul. | | |
| **5** L. Domitius Ahenobarbus campaigns beyond the Elbe. | | |
| **2** Augustus given title of *Pater Patriae* (father of the fatherland). *Lex Fufia Caninia* forbids indiscriminate manumission of slaves. | **2** Callaecia and Asturia transferred to Spanish province of Tarraconensis (Tarragona). | |

| THE NEAR EAST & INDIA | THE FAR EAST | RELIGION & CULTURE |
|---|---|---|
| **23** Phraates restores the seven Roman standards captured at Carrhae: peace between Rome and Parthia.  Tigranes made King of Armenia.<br>**c. 23–AD 200** Roman settlement of Podouke (Arikamedu), near Pondichery.<br>**22–19** Augustus visits the eastern provinces. | | **23** Horace: *Odes I–III.*<br><br>**22** Caesarea built by Herod. |
| **20** Indian embassy sent to Rome. Artaxias assassinated: Tiberius, stepson of Augustus, sent to crown Tigranes King of Armenia (−6BC). | | **c. 20** Rebuilding of the Temple at Jerusalem begun by Herod. Lion Temple at Naga restored.<br>**20** Horace: *Epistles I.*<br><br>**19** *Aqua Virgo* aqueduct and *Thermae,* public baths, built in Rome.<br><br>**17** *Ludi Saeculares* celebrated in Rome in honour of Apollo and Diana. Horace: *Carmen saeculare.*<br>**16** *Maison Carrée,* Roman temple, built at Nîmes. |
| | **c. 14–AD 49** Campaigns under General Ma Yuan add Yunnan, Annam and Tongking to Chinese territory. | **c. 13** Horace: *Odes IV.* |
| **Between 12 and 4** Homonadeis bandits put down in Cilicia.<br>**9** Palmyra already an important entrepôt between Rome and Parthia.<br>**9–AD 40** Harithath IV (Aretas IV): Ghassanid Kingdom extends to Damascus. | | **8** Maecenas d.  Horace d.<br><br>**7** Agrippa's map of the world. |
| | **6–1** Ai Ti, Han Emperor, but under control of Wang Mang and his family. | |
| **4** Herod the Great d.: kingdom divided among his three sons.  Herod Archelaus awarded Jerusalem.<br>**2** Phraates IV murdered: succ. Phraataces. | | **?4** Birth of Jesus Christ.<br>**4–AD 65** L. Annaeus Seneca, Stoic philosopher. |

| WESTERN EUROPE | CENTRAL & EASTERN EUROPE | EGYPT & AFRICA |
|---|---|---|

**c. 1** Belgae set up petty kingdoms in SE Britain: heavy plough and coinage introduced.

| WESTERN, NORTHERN & CENTRAL EUROPE | SPAIN, ITALY & EASTERN EUROPE | AFRICA & EGYPT |
|---|---|---|

**1st c. AD** Roman water supply conveyed by nine aqueducts.

**1st c. AD** The camel introduced into the Sahara. About 1 m. Jews in Egypt: Alexandria the real centre of world Jewry.
**1st—6th** centuries Stamped Ware Stone Age communities penetrate S of R Zambezi: mining of gold, copper and tin begin.

**1** Beginning of the Christian Era as fixed by Dionysius the Little in the 5th c.
**c. 1** Roman imperial population estimated between 70 m. and 100 m.

**c. 1** Gaetuli raiding Numidia.

**AD 4—5** Tiberius again campaigns in Germany.

**6** Tiberius campaigns against the Marcomanni. Rebellion in Pannonia and Dalmatia while Tiberius was campaigning in Bohemia: Roman residents massacred.
**c. 6** Roman Province of Moesia established on lower Danube: Roman boundary now coterminous with the Danube.

**7** Tiberius receives reinforcements: army nearly 100,000: Pannonians quelled.

**4** *Lex Aelia Sentia* strengthens law against indiscriminate manumission of slaves.
**6** Estate duty introduced in Rome. Tiberius acknowledged as Augustus's successor.

**c. 6** Hippalus, an Alexandrine, discovers the periodicity of the monsoons in the Indian Ocean: trade increases between Alexandria and the East.

## THE NEAR EAST & INDIA

## THE FAR EAST

## RELIGION & CULTURE

**ante 1** The horse introduced into Syria and Arabia.
**1** Peace treaty between Rome and Parthia. Caius Caesar enthrones Ariobarzanes as King of Armenia.
**c. 1** Roman fleet destroys Aden because of infringement of treaty of 24 BC.

**1** Two infants succeed on Han throne: Wang Lang real ruler.

**end of 1st c.** State of Langkasuka, earliest of Malay states, in existence: Bhagadatta, King.

**ante 1** *Cire-perdu* method of casting practised in Peru.

## THE NEAR EAST

## THE FAR EAST

## RELIGION & CULTURE

**1st c. AD** Jews said to have settled in Cochin. Chola emerge as chieftains in Tamil-nad.
**1st—4th c.** Early Chola dynasty in S India.

**ante 1st c. AD** Perak and Johore already centres of Indian bead trade.
**1st c.—627** Funan Empire of the Mekong Delta: originally consists of towns between Chandoc and Phnom Penh: capital, Vyadhapura.
**1st—6th c.** Port of Go Oc Eo, opposite Kelantan, flourishing.

**1st c. AD** Manilius, astronomer and poet. Hero of Alexandria, scientist. Wang Ch'ung, *Lun Heng, Critique of Opinions,* rationalist philosopher. Books in codex form beginning to replace scrolls. Reaping machine evolved in Gaul. Water wheels in use in Italy for grinding corn. The saddle first becomes known in Europe.
**? 1st c.** Chinese script first imitated in Japan, *via* Korea.

**c. 1** The saddle first used in China.

**c. 1** Ovid: *Ars Amatoria.*

**2** Rome and Parthia agreed on Armenia.

**6** Herod Archelaus, son of Herod the Great, deposed by Augustus: Judaea and Samaria made a Roman Province: Galilee under Herod Antipas. Herod Archelaus banished to Gaul.
**6—9** Varus's expedition against Parthia.

**7** Rising of the Zealots in Judaea against the Romans.

| WESTERN, NORTHERN & CENTRAL EUROPE | SPAIN, ITALY & EASTERN EUROPE | AFRICA & EGYPT |
|---|---|---|

**9** German revolt led by Arminius: Roman army of 20,000 annihilated. Tiberius and Drusus (later called Germanicus) make retaliatory raids. Gothic kingdom established on lower Vistula. Marbodus, King of the Marcomanni, conquers Bohemia. **10** Roman army on the Rhine reorganized.

**9** Germanicus defeats Bato of Dalmatia: Pannonia made a separate province: Illyria renamed Dalmatia. *Lex Papia Poppaea* on marriage.

**13** Tiberius made co-regent with Augustus.
**14** 19 Aug., Augustus d.at Nola: succ. Tiberius (Tiberius Caesar Augustus) (−37). Drusus and Germanicus put down mutiny in Pannonia and Dalmatia.
**14** Augustus d.: succ. Tiberius (Tiberius Caesar Augustus) (−37). Drusus and Germanicus put down mutiny in Pannonia and Dalmatia.
**c. 14** Roman army numbers 250,000 to 300,000 men.
**c. 14** Roman army numbers 250,000 to 300,000 men. Romans fortify Vindomina, later Vienna.

**14—16** Germanicus campaigns in Germany.

**17— 24** Roman campaigns against Tacfarinas, Numidian chief.

**19** Jews and devotees of Isis expelled from Rome: 4000 Jews sent to Sardinia. *Lex Junia Norbana* on manumission.

**c. 20—96** Earliest datable iron-working in Zambia.

**21** Florus and Sacrovir rebel in Gaul.

**23** L. Aelius Seianus concentrates all praetorian troops in a single camp outside Rome: gains ascendancy over Tiberius. Drusus assassinated.

**23** Juba II of Mauritania d.

**24** Tacfarinas killed: Numidia pacified by P. Cornelius Dolabella.

**25** Revolt suppressed in Thrace.

**c. 25** Greek and Latin, official languages in Egypt.

**26** Tiberius retires to Capri: Seianus in virtual full power in Rome.

**28** Frisians make themselves independent.

**29** Agrippina and Nero banished. Germanicus' family poisoned by Seianus.

| THE NEAR EAST | THE FAR EAST | RELIGION & CULTURE |
|---|---|---|
| | c. 8 or 9—23 Hsin dynasty under Wang Mang usurps China. Wang Mang known as the 'first socialist on the throne of China' because of his egalitarian policies. Sends embassy to (? ) Acheh, Sumatra. | 8 Ovid exiled to the Black Sea. |
| 9 Varus taken prisoner by the Parthians. | | |
| | 12 Wang Mang abrogates his reformist legislation. | |
| 17 Severe earthquakes in Asia Minor: taxation remitted in twelve cities. Kingdom of Cappadocia and the Commagene made a Roman Province. Palmyra already remitting customs dues to Rome. | | 17 Livy, historian, d. |
| 18 Artaxias, King of Armenia (−35): crowned at Artaxata by Tiberius' nephew, Germanicus. Peace between Rome and Parthia renewed. | 18 Rising of peasants in China: rebels called 'Red Eyebrows' appalling fighting and murder: rebels joined by many soldiers sent against them. | |
| c. 20 Regular voyages, by as many as 120 vessels, between the Red Sea and India. | | |
| ?c. 20—48 Gondophernes (or Gondophares), ruler of Arachosia and Taxila. | | |
| | 22 Wang Mang's head cut off by a soldier whilst seated on the throne. | |
| | | 23—79 Pliny the Elder (C. Plinius Secundus), geographer. |
| | 25—220 Later Han dynasty in China: new capital at Loyang. | 25 Strabo, geographer, d. |
| c. 25—50 Kadphises I becomes King of the Kushans (or Yue-che) in Bactria: conquers Kabul. | | |
| | | 26—37 Pontius Pilate, Procurator of Judaea. |
| | | ?27 or 30 St John Baptist beheaded. |

| WESTERN, NORTHERN & CENTRAL EUROPE | SPAIN, ITALY & EASTERN EUROPE | AFRICA & EGYPT |
|---|---|---|
| | **30** Drusus (II) banished. | |
| | **31** Seianus disgraced and executed. | |
| | **37** Tiberius d.: succ. Caligula (Caius Caesar) (−41): reckless and poor administrator. | |
| | **38** Taxation organized in Spain. Date of beginning of 'Spanish era'. | **38** Jews mobbed by Greeks in Alexandria. |
| | **39** Conspiracy against Caligula. | |
| **40** Caligula visits Gaul as far as Boulogne. Cunobelin (Cymbeline), King of the Trinovantes: capital Camulodunum (Colchester): expels son from kingdom: son goes to Rome, offering submission of the Trinovantes. | | |
| **41** Cunobelin d. | **41** Caligula murdered by Praetorian Guard: succ. Claudius (−54): proclaimed by Praetorian Guard: wife Messalina a vicious voluptuary. | **41** Juba, King of Mauretania, put to death, Jews revolt in Alexandria. |
| | **c. 41−54** Imperial chancery developed in Rome. | **41−2** Revolt in Mauretania suppress by C. Suetonius Paulinus: Mauretani divided into two provinces: Mauretania Caesariensis (Cherchell) and Mauretania Tingitana (Tangier). |
| | | **c. 41−54** Diogenes voyages along eastern African coast as far as Rhapta (? R. Rufiji). |
| **43** 50,000 men under Aulus Plautius land in Kent: Emperor Claudius takes command: Caratacus, son of Cunobelin (Cymbeline) defeated: Camulodunum (Colchester) captured: Claudius returns to Rome: Roman army quickly takes E Anglia and S England. | | |
| | **46** Thrace made a Roman province. | |
| **47−52** P. Ostorius Scapula takes area between Rs Severn and Trent. | | |
| | **48** Conspiracy against Claudius fails. Messalina executed. | |

| THE NEAR EAST | THE FAR EAST | RELIGION & CULTURE |
|---|---|---|
| | | **30 or 33** Crucifixion and Resurrection of Jesus Christ.<br>**30—117** Dio Chrysostom, rhetorician.<br>**c. 40** See of Alexandria said to have been founded by St. Mark. Red Sea porphyry quarries exploited for export of stone to Rome. |
| **34** Arsaces installed by Artabanus of Parthia as King of Armenia.<br>**35** Mithradates installed by Tiberius as King of Armenia: shortly d.: Arsaces murdered: Pharasmanes, King of Iberia, takes Armenia: Romans appoint Tiridates.<br>**36** Artabanus III of Parthia campaigns ineffectually in Syria. Tiridates of Armenia takes Ctesiphon: crowned King of Parthia: Artabanus III shortly regains throne.<br>**37** Peace treaty between Rome and Parthia: Armenia ceded to Rome. | | **c. 36** Conversion of St Paul. |
| **40** Caligula orders his statue to be put up in Jerusalem: general rebellion in Palestine: Herod Agrippa apointed King of Judaea. Artabanus of Parthia d.<br>**40—6** Vardanes and Gotarzes, sons of Artabanus, struggle for Parthian throne.<br>**40—70** Malchus II, Ghassanid ruler: Arabic ordinary language: Aramaic script, used for learning and trade, eventually emerges as Nabataean script. | **40—2** Rebellion in Vietnam against China. Ruled by Trung sisters for two years. | **39—65** Lucan (Marcus Annaeus Lucanus), poet.<br>**c. 40** Quintilian (M. Fabius Quintilianus), rhetorician, b. Philo, Jewish Platonist, d. at Alexandria.<br>**c. 40—c. 104** Martial (Marcus Valerius Martialis), poet and epigrammatist. |
| | | **41** Seneca exiled to Corsica.<br>**fl. 41—54** Quintius Curtius, orator. |
| **43** Lycia and Pamphylia made a Roman province. | | **c. 42—67** St Peter, first Pope.<br>**c. 43** Helen, Queen of Adiabene, Mesopotamia, visits Jerusalem: converted to Judaism with her children. |
| **44** Herod Agrippa d. | | **c. 44** Herod Agrippa persecutes Christians in Jerusalem.<br>**c. 44—57** St. Paul's missionary journeys. |
| **45** Gotarzes, sole ruler of Parthia. | **45** Severe droughts and plagues of locusts in Hsiung territory. | **c. 45—130** D. Iunius Iuvenalis (Juvenal), satirist.<br>**c. 46—post 120** Plutarch, biographer and philosopher.<br>**c. 47** Council of Jerusalem relieves Gentile Christians of obedience to the Jewish Law.<br>**c. 47** Pomponius Mela, geographer: *De situ orbis .* |
| **48** Kadphises I seizes Taxila: succeeds Gondophernes: operations against Parthia. | | |

| WESTERN, NORTHERN & CENTRAL EUROPE | SPAIN, ITALY & EASTERN EUROPE | AFRICA & EGYPT |
|---|---|---|
| | **49** Jews banished from Rome. Claudius m. Agrippina. **50** Claudius adopts Nero as his son and successor. | **c. 50** Brisk trade between Alexandria and India. |
| **c. 50** Red-glazed pottery (*terra sigillata)* begins to be produced in the Cévennes. Sarmatians invade Hungary. | | |
| | **54** Claudius assassinated: succ. Nero, a dilettante aged sixteen (–68). **55** Britannicus murdered. | |
| | **58** Agrippina, mother of Nero, murdered. | |
| **59** Suetonius Paulinus campaigns in N Wales. **c. 60** The Roxolani appear on the lower Danube. | | |
| **61** Rebellion in E Anglia led by Iceni: Boudicca (Boadicaea) vigorously attacks Romans: Camulodunum, Londinium and Verulamium burnt: Romans then rout Boudicca. Romans take N Wales and Anglesey. **c. 62** 100,000 Dacians settled S of the Danube. Roman garrison sent to the Crimea. | | **61–3** Roman reconnaissance expedition in the Sudan halted by the Sudd marshes. |
| | **62** Nero's adviser Burrus d.; Seneca retires: Nero becomes profligate. | |
| | **63** Earthquake at Pompeii. | |
| | **64** Fire at Rome burns much of the city: Nero popularly accused: wrath of populace turned against Christians: first persecution. | |
| | **65** Further fire and plague in Rome. Conspiracy to assassinate Nero. **65–66** Tiridates crowned King of Armenia in Rome. | |
| | | **66** Alexandrian Jews rebel: Prefec of Egypt, Tiberius Alexander, pu them down with severity. |
| | **67–8** Nero tours Greece: exhibitions of charioteering and singing given: public business neglected: reign of terror conducted by Nero's agents. | |

| THE NEAR EAST | THE FAR EAST | RELIGION & CULTURE |
|---|---|---|
| | | 49 Seneca made tutor to Nero. |
| | | **ante 50** Cult of Attis introduced in Rome.<br>**c. 50** Christianity first preached in France by St Lazare. Edessa claimed to have been converted to Christianity. |
| **1** Vologeses of Parthia invades Armenia against Corbulo and Quadratus.<br>**2—61** Claudius Felix, governor of Judaea: corrupt and repressive. | | 52 St Thomas the Apostle's second visit to India: churches established on coast and near Madras.<br>54 Jews ordered to leave Rome following tumults about 'Chrestus'.<br>55 Seneca: *De Clementia.*<br>**c. 55—c. 120** P. Cornelius Tacitus, historian. |
| **8—60** Roman campaign in Armenia: Tigranes installed as king. | 58—75 Ming Ti, Han Emperor. | **fl. c. 55—138** Epictetus, philosopher.<br>58 St Paul: *Epistle to the Romans.* |
| **4** Vologeses raids Mesopotamia. | **c. 60—70** Northern Hsiung-nu atempt to gain control of Turkestan, but without disturbance to Chinese trade. | 59 *Iuvenalia* festival inaugurated at Rome.<br>60 *Neronia* festival instituted at Rome: Nero takes part as a singer.<br>**60—125** Apollodorus of Damascus, architect.<br>**c. 61—96** P. Papinius Statius, poet.<br>**61—c. 113** Pliny the Younger (C. Plinius Caecilius Secundus), letter writer. |
| Rome at war with Parthia: Roman army defeated.<br>**—3** Tiridates re-takes Armenia.<br>Rome and Parthia make agreement on Armenia. | | **c. 63** St Paul: *Epistle to the Colossians.*<br>63 St Paul: *Epistle to the Philippians,* from Rome. |
| **ante 64** Kadphises II seizes NW India.<br>Romans abortively invade Armenia. Eastern Pontus incorporated into Roman province Galatia. | | 65 Seneca d. First Buddhist missionaries arrive in China: White Horse monastery established at Loyang.<br>**c. 65** St Mark's *Gospel.* |
| Gentiles of Caesarea massacre Jews: rising in Jerusalem led by Zealot party: Roman garrison murdered: Romans besiege and then abandon Jerusalem: rebellion spreads throughout Judaea, Galilee and Transjordan (—68). Tiridates of Parthia formally invested by Nero. Emperor Titus, assisted by 1000 horse and 5000 foot sent by Malchus of Ghassan, attacks Jerusalem. Flavius Vespasianus (Vespasian) appointed to command in Palestine: Galilee recovered. | | 66 Petronius, satirist and writer of romances, d. Plutarch studying in Athens.<br><br>67 Crucifixion of St Peter and martyrdom of St Paul at Rome.<br>**67—c. 79** St Linus, Pope. |

| WESTERN, NORTHERN & CENTRAL EUROPE | SPAIN, ITALY & EASTERN EUROPE | AFRICA & EGYPT |
|---|---|---|

**68** Vindex rebels in Gaul.

**68** Nero deposed, commits suicide: succ. Servius Sulpicius Galba (Galba), a Gaul.

**68–9** Winter, party of horsemen from Russia raid Moesia: defeated by Romans.

**69** 1 Jan., Roman legions in Germany refuse to renew oath of allegiance to Galba: M. Piso Licinianus made co-emperor by Galba: 15 Jan., Otho proclaimed emperor: Galba lynched: Rhine army invades Italy under Vitellius: Otho defeated at Cremona: commits suicide: Vitellius proclaimed. Vitellius defeated by troops supporting Vespasian at Cremona: Vitellius lynched: Vespasian accepted by the Senate (−79). Autumn, Dacian raid checked. Insurrection of Batavians on the Rhine organized by Iulius Civilis.

**68** Rebellion in N. Africa.
**69** War between Oea and Leptis
**70** Garamantes pillage Tripolitania: Septimius Flaccus's expedition pursues them to the Fezzan, and perhaps Bilma.

**70** Temple of Jupiter Capitolinus burnt in Rome. Rising of the Treviri in NE Gaul: Gauls attempt to start their own empire: Assembly of Rheims: put down by Q. Petilius Civilis.
**70–100** Frequent trade intercourse between Roman Empire and China *via* Balkh and Merv.

**71** Q. Petilius Cerialis appointed Governor of Britain: Vale of York taken from Brigantes: Eboracum (York) founded: connected line of forts built to Deva (Chester).
**c. 72–74** Roman fort built at Manchester.

**71** Roman army re-organized by Vespasian.

**73** Vespasian revives the censorship.
**73–4** Rights of Latin citizens conferred in Spain.

**74** Raids of Suebi into Raetia checked by Pinarius Clemens.
**c. 74–7** Sextus Iulius Frontinus conducts campaigns in Wales.
**75** Roman occupation includes York, Chester, Wroxeter, Caerleon and Exeter.

**75** Helvidius Priscus condemned.

**c. 75** Septimius Flaccus crosses th⟨e⟩ Sudan.

**77–85** Agricola (Caius Iulius Agricola), Governor of Britain: remainder of Wales occupied: northern boundary extended to Clyde and Forth: policy of Romanization of British tribesmen: road system laid down.

| THE NEAR EAST | THE FAR EAST | RELIGION & CULTURE |
|---|---|---|
| 68 Vespasian recovers trans-Jordanian territory: Judaea encircled. | | 68 St Thomas the Apostle martyred at Mylapore, near Madras. |
| 69 1 July, eastern armies proclaim Vespasian emperor. | | |
| 0 Titus, after six months' siege, akes Jerusalem: survivors reduced o slavery: Sanhedrin abolished: ewish Temple burnt down: ebuilding forbidden: Jews forbidden ɔ proselytize and subjected to pecial poll tax: 'Patriarch' of the ews appointed *vice* the High Priest. 0—106 Rabbi II, last independent hassanid ruler. | | fl. 70 Nagardjuna, Mahayan Buddhist theologian. L. Valerius Flaccus, poet. post 70 Judaism spreads in Arabia. |
| 2 Vespasian deposes Kings of ommagene and Lesser Armenia: iddle Euphrates made the Roman ontier. | | 72 Vespasian founds chairs of rhetoric in Rome. St. Mark martyred in Alexandria. |
| 3 Massada, Jewish stronghold, falls. | 73 Chinese campaign against Turkestan led by Tou Ku: all Turkestan annexed to Han China. | |
| Parthian empire over-run by ani. | | 74—5 Last known dated cuneiform text: a calendar. c. 75 Flavius Josephus: *The Jewish Wars.* 75—82 The *Colosseum* built. c. 75—150 C. Suetonius Tranquillus, historian. |
| Vologeses of Parthia d.: succ. corus (—105). 77 or 78 Kadphises I d.: succ. ma Kadphises II: territory expanded. | 76—88 Chang Ti, Han Emperor: policy of isolation in foreign relations. | |
| 8 Beginning of Saka era. | 78 Han Emperor neglecting Turkestan: no supplies or money sent. Saka era introduced into Burma from India: Buddhist Era abandoned. Indonesia already known to the Romans. | |

| WESTERN, NORTHERN & CENTRAL EUROPE | SPAIN, ITALY & EASTERN EUROPE | AFRICA & EGYPT |
|---|---|---|
| **79–80** Agricola campaigns in the Cheviots and Tweed-dale. | **79–81** Titus, Roman Emperor.<br>**79** Military conspiracy to dethrone Titus led by A. Caecina. Vesuvius erupts: Herculaneum, Pompeii and Stabiae destroyed. Plague breaks out in Rome. | **79** Emperor Titus visits Egypt. |
| **81** Agricola builds chain of signalling forts between the Clyde and the Forth: makes reconnaissance of Ireland: invasion of Ireland forbidden by Domitian.<br>**82–3** Agricola campaigns in Scotland: army reinforced by fleet: combined Caledonian chiefs defeated.<br>**83** Emperor Domitian leads expedition against the Chatti.<br>**84** Agricola recalled from Britain: three legions left, at Caerleon-on-Usk, Deva and Eboracum: economic development in Britain greatly encouraged. | **81–96** Domitian, Roman Emperor.<br><br><br><br><br><br><br><br>**85** Domitian becomes permanent censor. | **c. 81–96** Growing of wheat, olives and vines increased in N. Africa, making it the granary of Rome. |
| **86** Dacians under Decebalus overwhelm Romans in Moesia: Romans counter-attack. | | |
| **88** Abortive military conspiracy on the Rhine led by L. Antonius Saturninus. Fortification of the *limes* begun.<br>**88 or 89** Dacians severely defeated by Tettius Iulianus.<br>**89** Domitian makes preventive war against Suebi, Quadi and Marcomanni: Decebalus made a Roman vassal: Danubian frontier fortified. Emperor Domitian leads further expedition against the Chatti. | | |
| **92–3** Domitian campaigns again on the Danube. | **92** Roman law restricts viticulture in favour of corn.<br>**93** Agricola d. | |
| | **96** Domitian assassinated: Nerva elected Emperor by the Senate (−98). | |

| THE NEAR EAST | THE FAR EAST | RELIGION & CULTURE |
|---|---|---|
| | c. 78 First Indian colonists reach Java. | c. 78 Pliny the Elder: *Natural History*. |
| | | 79 Fire at Rome destroys many libraries. Pliny the Elder d. Valerius Flaccus: *Aeronautica*. c. 79–c. 91 St Anacletus or Cletus, Pope. |
| c. 80 Kshaharata Sakas occupy W Deccan. | c. post 80 Chinese political situation deteriorating: inter-provincial rivalry between groups of court eunuchs and scholars. | 80 Martial: *Epigrams*. c. 80 St Luke's *Gospel*. |
| | 84 King of Yue-tche's aid sought by Chinese general Pan Tchao. | |
| | | c. 85 St Matthew's *Gospel*. 85 Last Buddhist Council at Peshawar. Schism between Hinayana and Mahayana Buddhists. |
| 7 Kadphises II asks the hand of a hinese princess in marriage: fused: war follows: Kadphises made pay tribute. | | |
| | | 88 *Ludi Saeculares* celebrated in Rome. |
| | 89 Chinese campaign against Turkestan: country a Chinese possession until 102. 89–105 Ho Ti, Han Emperor: his mother at first regent. | 89 Astrologers persecuted in Rome. |
| | | c. 90–168 Claudius Ptolemy, geographer. c. 92–c. 101 St Clement, Pope. |
| | c. 94 Vikrama dynasty of Sri Ksetra (Prome) collapses: Varman dynasty follows. | 94–5 Further persecution of astrologers. |
| | | c. 95 St John's *Gospel*. c. 95–c. 170 Arrian, historian. 96 St Clement of Rome: *Epistle to the Corinthians*. c. 96 Persecution of Christians by Domitian. |

**AD 97—114**

**WESTERN, NORTHERN
& CENTRAL EUROPE**

**SPAIN, ITALY
& EASTERN EUROPE**

**AFRICA & EGYPT**

98 Nerva d.: M. Ulpianus Traianus
(Trajan) succ. in fulfilment of Nerva's
designation (—117).

98—117 Trajan alienates Berber land
to Rome and allies.

2nd c. Berbers and Mandingos begin
to populate ancient Ghana.

2nd—3rd cc. Roman and Egyptian
pottery reaching Somalia.

c. 100 Earlier inhabitants of Ireland
rebel against Celts: put down by
Tuathal: united kingdom of
Connacht and Meath formed.

post 100 Germans settling and taking
to agriculture, especially in Bohemia.
101—2 Trajan's first campaign in
Dacia: King Decebalus left in control:
Roman garrisons in certain fortresses.
105—6 Decebalus destroys or besieges
Roman garrisons in Dacia: invades
Moesia: Trajan counter-attacks with
120,000 men: Decebalus commits
suicide: Dacia surrenders, paying
tribute of £27 m.: Roman colonies
established.

107 Law on the personal possessions
of senators. Dacia formally annexed.
109 Quintilius Maximus sent to put
the finances of cities in Achaea in
order.

| THE NEAR EAST | THE FAR EAST | RELIGION & CULTURE |
|---|---|---|
| **97** Chinese envoy Kan-Ying visits governor of Syria at (?) Antioch: favourable report on Roman empire written by Kan-Ying. | **97** Roman embassy to China travels overland from India *via* Burma. | |
| | | **98** Tacitus: *Agricola* and *Germania.* |
| | **2nd c.** Valagam Ba, King of Ceylon: kingdom recovered from the Tamils. Chinese records mention an Indianized kingdom in Vietnam. | **2nd c.** Many Chinese peasants become Buddhists. Masterly stone sculptures at Amaravati and in the Deccan. Jain sect divides into Svetambara (white-robed) and Digambara (sky-clad) sects. Pausanias, geographer. Appian, historian, at Alexandria. Religion of Mithras becomes widespread throughout the Roman empire. |
| | | **2nd or 3rd c.** Diogenes Laertius, biographer. |
| **c. 100** Pacorus makes his son, Exedares, King of Armenia. Herodian principality in Trans-Jordan incorporated into Syria. | | **c. 100** Paper invented in China. Juvenal: *Satires.* |
| | | **c. 100–165** Justin Martyr, Christian Platonist. |
| | | **c. 100–170** M. Cornelius Fronto, grammarian and letter-writer: tutor of Marcus Aurelius. |
| | | **post 100** Library of Pantainos, Athens, built. |
| | | **c. 101–9** St Evaristus, Pope. |
| **105** Nabataean Arabia taken over by Trajan: made the 'Province of Arabia': Damascus attached to Province of Syria. | | |
| **106–129** Osroes, King of Parthia. | | **106** Trajan's column erected at Rome. |
| | | **c. 106** *Periplus of the Erythraean Sea* written as an official report at Alexandria on the trade of the Red Sea, East Africa, S Arabia and India. |
| **107** Trajan sends embassy to India. | | |
| | | **c. 109–19** St Alexander I, Pope. |
| **c. 110** Kadphises II d.: succ. by a nameless king. | | **c. 110** Ignatius, Bishop of Antioch, martyred at Rome: writes *Epistles* to various churches during his captivity: the first writer known to use the expression 'Catholic Church'. |
| **c. post 110** Kanishka succ. the nameless king as ruler of Gandhara: capital at Peshawar: ardent supporter of Buddhism. | | |
| | | **111–13** Pliny the Younger, Legate in Bithynia, takes action against the Christians: so-called persecution of Trajan. |
| **112** Khusru I seizes Parthia. | | |
| **113** Parthamasiris made King of Armenia. | | **113** Pliny the Younger d. |
| **114** Parthamasiris deposed by Emperor Trajan: Armenia made a Roman Province. | | |

| WESTERN, NORTHERN & CENTRAL EUROPE | SPAIN, ITALY & EASTERN EUROPE | AFRICA & EGYPT |
|---|---|---|
| | **115** Jewish revolt in Cyprus. | **115** Jewish revolt in Leptis Magna and Cyrene: some flee to Fezzan and Hoggar. Public disturbances amongst Jews in Alexandria. |
| | | **116** Unrest amongst Jews in Egypt: Jews in Libya and Cyprus follow suit: rebellion quashed by Q. Marcius Turbo: end of Jewish resistance to Roman government in all areas. |
| **117** Ninth Legion defeated by the Brigantes. | **117–138** Hadrian, Roman Emperor. | |
| | **118** Conspiracy of Cornelius Palma, Lusius Quietus and others: sentenced to death by the Senate. | |
| c. **119** Rising against Romans in Britain: IXth Legion completely destroyed. | | |
| | **121–6** Emperor Hadrian visits frontiers on the Rhine and the Danube; Britain; Mauretania and Africa; Asia Minor and Greece. | |
| **122–7** Hadrian's wall built by A. Platorius Nepos, governor of Britain, from the Solway Firth to the Tyne. | | |
| | | **123** Hadrian campaigns in Mauretania: Roman occupation limited to borders of Atlas Mts. |
| | **128–34** Hadrian's second imperial progress. | |
| | | **130** Emperor Hadrian visits Egypt: new capital for Upper Egypt built at Antinopolis. |

| THE NEAR EAST | THE FAR EAST | RELIGION & CULTURE |
|---|---|---|
| **115** Trajan visits Babylon: sacrifices to the spirit of Alexander the Great. Jewish revolt in Palestine. | | **115** Dio Chrysostom d. |
| **115–116** Emperor Trajan sails down R. Tigris to the Persian Gulf: Mesopotamia now in Roman hands. **116** Trajan makes Parthamaspates ruler of Ctesiphon and Babylonia: middle Euphrates made into Province of Mesopotamia. Unrest amongst Jews in Palestine, following withdrawal of Roman legions: quashed by Lusius Quietus. **117** Seleucia and Judaea revolt. Hadrian evacuates Trajan's eastern conquests. | | **c. 116** Tacitus: *Annals.* <br><br> **ante 117** Earlier part of the *Epistle to Diognetus* written. |
| | | **c. 119–25** St Sixtus I, Pope. |
| | **120** Roman embassy to China passes along overland route from India *via* Burma, and then by sea to Loyang. | **120** Tacitus d. Plutarch d. Suetonius: *Lives of the Twelve Caesars.* **c. 120** Marcion, gnostic, b., teaching in Rome, 139–42. **121–80** Marcus Aurelius, philosopher. |
| **122** Emperor Hadrian meets Osroes of Parthia on Euphrates: cordial relations established. | | |
| | | **c. 125–36** St Telesphorus, Pope. **c. 125–90** Lucian, satirist. |
| **c. 126** Gautamiputra Satakarni, ruler of Satavahana kingdom: expels Sakas. | **c. 126** Yue-tche take Transoxiana. | |
| **129–34** Hadrian visits eastern provinces. **130** Emperor Hadrian visits Khusru I: boundary agreement made. Palmyra visited by Emperor Hadrian. **c. 130** Vasishthiputra Satakarni, ruling the Satavahana kingdom. | | **129** The *Olympeion* dedicated at Athens. **ante 130** Carpocrates, philosopher and gnostic, teaching at Alexandria. **c. 130** Basilides, gnostic, d. after teaching in Alexandria. **?c. 130** *Epistle of Barnabas* composed. **130–200** Galen, physician. **post 130** Aristides, Christian philosopher: *Apologia.* |
| **131** Hadrian founds Roman colony of Aelia Capitolina at Jerusalem: shrine of Jupiter Capitolinus built on the site of the Jewish Temple: Jewish rising follows under Bar-Cochba (–134). **132–4** Jewish rebellion under Bar-Cochba put down by C. Iulius Severus: fifty fortresses, 455 villages and 585,000 men, destroyed and killed: surviving Jews allowed to visit Jerusalem once only a year. | **131** Roman embassy to China uses portage route *via* Tenasserim, Burma, then by sea. <br><br> **?c. 132** Possible embassy from Indonesia to China. | **132–5** Final diaspora of Jews from Palestine. |

|  |  |  |
|---|---|---|
|  | **136** Servianus executed for conspiracy against Hadrian. **138–161** Antoninus Pius, Roman Emperor. |  |
| **c. 142–3** Following rising of the Brigantes in N Scotland, Antoninus' wall built by Q. Lollius Urbicus between the Firths of Clyde and Forth. |  |  |
|  |  | **144–152** Continuous Gaetulian raids on the Romans in Mauretania. |
|  | **146** Marcus Aurelius made associate ruler of the Empire. |  |
| **c. 150** Goths reach Black Sea. | **c. 150** Roman Empire *c.* 17 m. square miles. | **c. 150–350** General decline in Egypt as a result of excessive corn tax. |
| **post 150** German tribes crossing the Danube. |  |  |
| **155–162** Frequent repairs needed to Roman walls in Britain because of local attacks. |  |  |
|  | **161–180** Marcus Aurelius, Roman Emperor. | **c. 161** Peasants revolt near Alexandria. |

| THE NEAR EAST | THE FAR EAST | RELIGION & CULTURE |
|---|---|---|

**133** Alans raid Parthia.

**c. 133–203** Irenaeus, Bp of Lyons, theologian.
**c. 136–40** St Hyginus, Pope.

**140** Wei population *c.* 29 m.; Wu population *c.* 11.7 m.; Shu Han *c.* 7½ m.; Hsiung Nu, *c.* 3 m.

**?c. 140** Hermas: *The Shepherd.*
**c. 140–155** St Pius I, Pope.
**140–161** Valentinus, gnostic, teaching in Alexandria.

**c. 144** Marcionite heresy begins.

**148–91** Vologeses III, King of Parthia.

**150** Gaius: *Institutiones.*
Stone Buddha found at Palembang: alleged as evidence of visits by Indian trading vessels.
**c. 150** Ptolemy: *Geographia,* first recension.

**c. 150** State of Palembang in existence. Tong-king, with capital Hanoi, already the terminus of a sea-route from the Red Sea.

**c. 150–235** Dio Cassius, historian.

**post 150** Constant struggles for power between provincial generals. 'Yellow Turban' popular movement begins amongst peasantry, led by Chang Ling: religious aspect influenced both by Iranian Mazda'ism and by ideas of Lao Tzu.

**c. 153** St Justin: *Apologia.*
**154** Discussion of the date of Easter by St Polycarp of Smyrna and Pope Anicetus.

**155** Vologeses III of Parthia invades Armenia: withdraws at request of Emperor Hadrian.

**c. ante 155** Catechetical School founded at Alexandria by Pantaenus.
**c. 155** St Polycarp, Bp of Smyrna, martyred.
**c. 155–66** St Anicetus, Pope.
**c. 155–220** St Clement of Alexandria. bp and theologian, makes Alexandria the centre of advanced Christian theological study.
**c. 160** Appian: *History of Rome.*
First Buddhist missionaries reach China.
**c. 160–240** Tertullian, apologist and theologian, at Carthage.

**161** Vologeses of Parthia instals a puppet king in Armenia: defeats Roman governors of Cappadocia and Syria.

**post 161** Gaius: *Institutiones.*
**c. 162** St Felicitas and her seven sons martyred in Rome.
**c. 163** St Justin, apologist, martyred at Rome with six others.

**?c. 162** Huvishka succ. Kanishka as Kushan ruler (−*c.* 182).
**163** L. Verus, co-Emperor with Marcus Aurelius, attacks Parthia: takes Armenia and Mesopotamia: Armenian capital Artaxata captured.

| WESTERN, NORTHERN & CENTRAL EUROPE | SPAIN, ITALY & EASTERN EUROPE | AFRICA & EGYPT |
|---|---|---|
| | | **160** Siwa visited by Pausanias. Odeon of Herodes Atticus, Athens, built. |
| **165** Costobocae from Dacia or Sarmatia raid as far as the Aegaean: German tribes over-run middle Danube. | | |
| **167** Marcomanni, Quadi and Vandals cross Roman frontier on middle Danube: Pannonia and Noricum crossed: raiding as far as N Italy: Aquileia besieged. <br> **168–80** Marcus Aurelius campaigns on Danube frontier. | **167** Great Plague throughout Roman Empire. <br><br> **169** Lucius Verus d. | **170–6** Berber raids on Mauretania and Spain. |
| **172** Marcus Aurelius compels the Marcomanni to make peace. | | |
| | **175–6** Marcus Aurelius visits Roman provinces in the Mediterranean. | |
| **177–80** Fresh campaigns against the Marcomanni and Quadi. | **177–80** Berber invasions in Spain. | |
| **180** Marcus Aurelius makes peace with the Marcomanni and Quadi. Marcus Aurelius d. in Vienna: succ. Commodus (−193). | | **180±100** Iron working at Mabveni, Rhodesia. <br><br> **182** Rights of tenant farmers clarified in Roman Africa. |
| **c. 183** Ulpius Marcellus, governor of Britain, repels attack on Antoninus' wall. | **183** Abortive attempt to assassinate Commodus by his sister Lucilla and her stepson Pompeianus. | |
| **c. 185** Antonine Wall abandoned. | **185** Commodus executes Perennis for alleged treason. Cleander given command of Praetorian guards. | |
| **c. 186** P. Helvius Pertinax suppresses mutiny of Roman soldiers in Britain. | | **186** Regular service of grain ships from N Africa to Rome instituted. |

| THE NEAR EAST | THE FAR EAST | RELIGION & CULTURE |
|---|---|---|

**164** Battle of Dura-Europus: Romans take Seleucia and Ctesiphon: both destroyed: Media raided. Sohaemus, a Roman senator, made King of Armenia: Osrhoene made a Roman dependency: colony of veterans set up.

**166** Roman trade delegation to China uses portage route *via* Tenasserim, Burma, and then by sea to Tong-king: visits Chinese Emperor at Loyang.

**166** Persecution of Christians by Marcus Aurelius throughout the Roman Empire. c. 166—74 or 5 St Soter, Pope.

**c. 170—200** Gautamiputra Yajna Sri, Satavahana ruler.

**c. 170** Apuleius d.

**171—83** Theophilus, Bp of Antioch: first writer on the Trinity.

**174** Marcus Aurelius: *The Thoughts* begun.
**c. 174 or 5—89** St Eleutherius, Pope.
**175—250** Ammonius Saccas, founder of Neo-Platonist school at Alexandria.
**c. post 175** Montanist heresy begins in Phrygia.

**175** Avidius Cassius, governor of the eastern provinces, proclaims himself Emperor: rebellion suppressed by Marcus Aurelius.
**c. 175** Demetrius, son of Euthydemos, or Menander, King of the Punjab: invades India, making extensive conquests.

**176** Marcus Aurelius founds four chairs of philosophy at Rome.
**177** Vettius Epagathus, and many other Christians, martyred at Lyons.
**177—202** St Pothinus and St Irenaeus, Bishops of Lyons: Christianity spreads in the interior of France.
**c. 179** Bardesanes, a Syrian of Edessa: *Dialogue on Fate.*
**180** Christians martyred at Madaura and Scilli, Africa. St Irenaeus: *Adversus Haereses.*

**c. 182** Vasudeva succ. Huvishka as Kushan ruler (—c. 220).

**184** Abortive armed rising of 'Yellow Turbans'.

**185—254** Origen of Alexandria, theologian.

186–200

WESTERN, NORTHERN
& CENTRAL EUROPE

SPAIN, ITALY
& EASTERN EUROPE

AFRICA & EGYPT

186±150 Channelled ware people near Sesheke, Rhodesia: possible earliest arrival of Bantu speakers.

189 Cleander executed.

192 31 Dec., Emperor Commodus throttled in his bath: succ. P. Helvius Pertinax: finances and military discipline restored.
193 28 March, Emperor Pertinax murdered by the Praetorian Guard: empire put up to auction: Guard appoint Didius Iulianus Emperor: three rival emperors elected by the troops: Decimus Clodius Albinus in Britain: L. Septimius Severus (−211) in Pannonia: C. Pescennius Niger in Syria: Septimius Severus captures Rome. 1 July, Iulianus executed. Albinus given title 'Caesar'.
193–4 Septimius Severus defeats Pescennius Niger.

193 Albinus, general in Britain, declares himself Emperor: takes legions from Britain to contest claim: Caledonians or Picts over-run Scottish Lowlands reaching Hadrian's Wall: rebellion put down by Septimius Severus.

197 Septimius Severus defeats Albinus near Lugdunum: Septimius Severus now undisputed sole emperor: Lugdunum sacked.

c. 197 Leptis Magna made a Roman city.

late 2nd c. Caledonians and Maeatae over-run Britain as far as York and Chester: governor Virius Lupus bribes them to retire behind Hadrian's Wall.

199 Alexandria made a municipality

c. 200 Goths of Scandinavian origin reach present Russia: divide into Ostrogoths, occupying Lower Don valley to Lower Dnieper: and Visigoths, who eventually reach Spain and Italy *via* Germany , and N Africa. Romans construct mound from R. Aluta to the Danube. Viticulture introduced into the Moselle valley. Central and southern kingdoms formed in Ireland: rule by 'High Kings' (−1022).
post 200 Belgic tribesmen invading England and Scotland.

?c. 3rd–4th c. Elaborate steles, throne and palace built at Axum.

# THE NEAR EAST

# THE FAR EAST

# RELIGION & CULTURE

187—226 Vietnamese territories in Red R Valley virtually independent of China: Che Sie, governor.

190—220 Hsien Ti, last Emperor of the Han dynasty: several times captured by warring generals.
c. 192 Champa emerges as an independent state NE of Funan in present Vietnam.

189 Demetrius, Bp of Alexandria.
c. 189—98 or 9 St Victor I, Pope.
c. 190 Tertullian converted to Christianity.

195 Septimius Severus establishes Roman garrison at Nisibis.
197 Septimius Severus expels Parthians from Osrhoene and Adiabene.

197 Lam Ap state founded in Vietnam.

ante 197 Minucius Felix: *Octavius*.
197 Tertullian: *Ad Nationes: Apology*.

198 Septimius Severus destroys Ctesiphon: Mesopotamia annexed.

ante 3rd c. State of Tun-hsun made a dependency of Funan: divided between five vassal kings: a centre of trade between Tong-king and India, Parthia, and the West: probably at Klang, Port Swettenham.
early 3rd c. Pan Pan, ruler of Funan, hands over government to general Fan Che Man, 'Great King of Funan'.
3rd c. State of Funan already in possession of a navy. Tea-drinking spreads in China from Tibet: Szechwan and SE China main centres of tea-production. Paper money becomes current in China.

c. 198 or 9—217 St Zephyrinus, Pope.
198—217 Sabellius, gnostic, teaching in Rome.
late 2nd c. Monarchian heresy agitates the Church of Rome.

3rd c. Tanukh tribe from central Arabia settle at al-Hirah, three miles S of al-Kufah: origin of Lakhmid kingdom: officially Christian.

3rd c. Many Chinese encyclopaedias compiled: that of Lu Pu-wei the first; *Shan Hai Ching*, Book of the Mountains and Seas, the best known. Hindu works of art first found in Indonesia. Commodianus of Gaza, first Christian poet.

c. 200 Three principal parties in China: Ts'ao Ts'ao in N, controlling the emperor; Szechwan controlled by Liu Pei; SE by brother of Sun Ts'e. Use of gold for coin or in bars disappears in China.

200 Tertullian: *De Spectaculis*.
200—55 Beirut (Berytus) famous for its law school.
c. 200 Runic script first appears.
?c. 200 Text of the *Mahabharata* complete in its present form.
c. 200—215 St Clement, Bp of Alexandria.
c.200 *Mishnah* completed.

post 200 Local vernaculars begin to emerge from Latin.

| WESTERN, NORTHERN & CENTRAL EUROPE | SPAIN, ITALY & EASTERN EUROPE | AFRICA & EGYPT |
|---|---|---|
| | **203** Hippodrome constructed in Byzantium. | **c. 203** Roman fort built at Premis, Nubia: furthest known Roman penetration. |
| **205** Alfenius Senecio beats off attacks on Hadrian's Wall. | **205** Plautianus' conspiracy. | |
| **208–11** Septimius Severus visits Britain. **208** Septimius Severus rebuilds Hadrian's Wall. **209** Septimius Severus attempts to crush Caledonians and Maeatae. **211** Septimius Severus d. at York: Caracalla and Geta, his sons, withdraw behind Hadrian's Wall. | **211–17** Caracalla, Roman Emperor. | |
| | **212** *Constitutio Antoniana*: Roman coinage devalued: Caracalla extends Roman citizenship to all freemen within the Roman empire. Emperor Caracalla murders his brother, Geta. Papinian d. | **c. 212** Rebellion in Alexandria. |
| **213–4** Caracalla campaigns on the Danube against the Alemanni and the Goths: wall completed along the Rhine and upper Danube. | | |
| | **217–8** Macrinus, Roman Emperor. | |
| | **218–22** Elagabalus, Roman Emperor. | |
| **c. 220** Goths begin entering Balkans and Asia Minor. | | |
| | **222** Elagabalus murdered: succ. Severus Alexander, aged under fourteen (–235): his mother, Iulia Mamaea, regent and *de facto* ruler to 235. | **c. 222** Hoard of coins found at Debra Damo. Ethiopia, includes imports from India. |
| | | **225–300** Arkamani (Ergamanes), King of Meroe: friendly relations with Egypt. |

## THE NEAR EAST

## THE FAR EAST

## RELIGION & CULTURE

**202—c. 211** Edict of Emperor Septimius Severus forbids conversions to Judaism and Christianity: persecution of Christians especially fierce in Egypt and Africa.
**c. 203** Origen becomes head of the Catechetical School in Alexandria.
**203** St Perpetua martyred at Carthage.
**c. 205—70** Plotinus, neo-Platonist philosopher and mystic, at Alexandria.
**c. 206** Baths of Caracalla begun.
**c. 207** Tertullian adheres to Montanism.

**c. 215** Oriental trade with Roman Empire in decline.

**215** St Clement of Alexandria d.

**216** Vologeses V, King of Armenia, deposed by Caracalla: Armenia made a Roman province. Caracalla raids Media.
**217** Caracalla murdered by his staff: M. Opellius Macrinus (Emperor as Macrinus) leader of the conspiracy, succ.: Roman army driven out of Mesopotamia by Artabanus of Parthia: Kingdom of Armenia restored: Tiridates king.
**218** An impostor, M. Antonius Aurelius, Elagabalus, aged fourteen, made emperor by the army in Syria: quickly gains all eastern provinces.
**?c. 220** Vasudeva, Kushan ruler d.: empire gradually dissolved.

**217** Hippolytus, antipope.
**217—22** St Calixtus, Pope.

**220** Last Han Emperor abdicates.
**220—65** Period of the three kingdoms in China. Wei dynasty in N China, founded by Ts'ao P'ei, son of Ts'ao Ts'ao: takes name of Wen Ti (—226).
**220—80** Wu dynasty in SE China.
**221—63** Shu Han dynasty in SW China: claimed to be the representatives of the former Han dynasty.

**222** Tertullian d.
**222—30** St Urban I, Pope.

**c. 225** End of Satavahana dynasty: Chutus continue to rule near Vanavasi.

**c. 225** Origen: *Hexapla*.

226–244

**WESTERN, NORTHERN**
**& CENTRAL EUROPE**

**SPAIN, ITALY**
**& EASTERN EUROPE**

**AFRICA & EGYPT**

**228** Ulpianus, prefect of the guard, murdered by his men.

**234** Preparations made by Alexander for an expedition against the Alemanni: tribesmen bought off. Alexander and Iulia Mamaea assassinated by C. Iulius Maximinus: latter succ. in spite of disapproval by the Senate (−258).

**235** Revolt of Roman cc El Djem: Gordian, Rom of Africa, proclaimed em down by Carpillinus.

**236–7** Maximinus campaigns on the Rhine and Danube.

**238** March, Gordian I (M. Antonius Gordianus) and his son Gordian (Gordianus II) appointed co-emperors by the Senate: Apr., both killed in a war against the Governor of Numidia. Apr., M. Clodius Pupienus and D. Caelius Balbinus named co-emperors by the Senate: June, Maximinus murdered by his army while invading Italy: Pupienus and Balbinus murdered: Gordianus III, aged fifteen, appointed (−244), with C. Furius Timesitheus as regent.

**244–9** Philip, Roman Emperor.

| THE NEAR EAST | THE FAR EAST | RELIGION & CULTURE |
|---|---|---|
| **226** Ardashir (Artaxerxes), King of Persia, defeats Artabanus V of Parthia: end of Parthian dynasty: Sassanid dynasty (–641): Ardashir I proclaims himself Emperor of Persia (–241). | **226** Roman traders reach Canton. | **226–234** Chu-Ko Liang, premier of Shu Han. |
| | **227–233** Ming Ti, Wei Emperor; almost powerless in the hands of the Ssu-ma family. | |
| **230–51** Origen teaching in Palestine. | | **230** Origen exiled from Alexandria.<br>**230–5** St Pontian, Pope. |
| **231** Ardashir I besieges Romans at Nisibis.<br>**232** Alexander Severus invades Persia: peace made with Ardashir. Armenia annexed by Ardashir. | | **c. 232–304** Porphyry, philosopher, opponent of Christianity, at Alexandria. |
| | **234** Chu-Ko Liang d.: Shu Han state in decline. | |
| | | **235** Maximinus persecutes the Christians.<br>**235–6** St Anterus, Pope. |
| | | **236–50** St Fabian, Pope. |
| **237–8** Persia takes Nisibis and Carrhae. | **237** Wei annihilate Yen state in present-day Manchuria. | |
| | **c. 240** Fan Chan, ruler of Funan, sends embassy to Kushan ruler in India. | |
| **241** Armenia and Hatra rebel against Persia.<br>**241–271** Shapur I, Emperor of Persia. | | |
| | | **fl. 242–276** Manes, dualistic gnostic, originator of Manichaeism. |
| **243** Timesitheus repels invasion of Antioch by Shapur, son of Ardashir: Gordianus III murdered and supplanted by M. Iulius Philippus (Philip), an Arab. Peace made with Shapur.<br>**244** Peace between Persia and Rome. | **243** Fan Chan of Funan sends embassy to China. | **244** Beryllus, Bp of Bostra, Arabia, condemned by a Council for refusing to acknowledge Christ as God: subsequently recanted.<br>**244–70** Plotinus teaching in Rome. |

245—261

WESTERN, NORTHERN
& CENTRAL EUROPE

SPAIN, ITALY
& EASTERN EUROPE

AFRICA & EGYPT

**248** Successful Roman campaign on the Danube.

**248** Numerian d. mysteriously. Millenary of Rome celebrated.
**249** C. Traianus Decius kills Philip, and makes himself Emperor (−251).

c. **250** Aphilas, King of Axum: first Ethiopian monarch to issue coinage.
c. **250—350** Beja raid upper Egypt.

**251** Goths invade Macedonia and Thrace. Decius killed in an engagement with the Goths: C. Trebonianus Gallus proclaimed Emperor (−253).

c. **251—3** Embassy from Meroe to Rome.

**253** Civil war in Italy: Gallus defeated and killed at Interamna (Terni) by M. Aemilius Aemilianus: Aemilianus killed by his own men: P. Licinius Valerianus (Valerian) proclaimed Emperor (−260).

**253** Berber revolt in Numidia and Mauretania.

**255** Roman army under Atilius Regulus defeated by Carthaginians in Bagradas valley, near Carthage. Romans win further sea battle off Cape Hermaeum: fleet founders on way home.

**256** Goths and Alemanni seize Danube frontier: Franks coalesce and break through lower Rhine.
**256—7** Gallienus defeats the Alemanni.
**257** Visigoths and Ostrogoths divide.

**258** Ingenuus usurps Pannonia. Posthumus proclaimed Emperor of the Gauls.
c. **258** Saxons from Jutland and Frisia conducting piratical raids. Franks settle in Gaul and NE Spain.

**258** Goths raid the Balkans as far as Byzantium: Bithynia seized: piratical raids made in the Aegaean.
**258 or 9** Gallienus defeats the Alemanni at Milan.

**260** Alemanni, in two columns, overrun the Rhone valley and Auvergne; and traverse Brenner Pass, reaching Ravenna: halted by Gallienus assisted by other generals.
**260—8** Posthumus engaged in frequent actions to expel Franks from Gaul and Spain.

**260** Gallienus made Emperor (−268): makes Odaenathus King of Palmyra: Gallienus threatened by many mushroom pretenders.

**261** Aureolus puts down the sons of Macrianus, who had proclaimed themselves emperors. Gallienus excludes senators from military command.

| THE NEAR EAST | THE FAR EAST | RELIGION & CULTURE |
|---|---|---|
| | c. 245 Fan Chan of Funan murdered: succ. Fan Hsun: Chinese embassy visits Funan.<br>247—9 Sirisangabo, King of Ceylon.<br>248 Abortive Vietnamese rebellion against China led by Trieu Au. | 246 Cyprian becomes a Christian.<br>247—84 Dionysius, theologian, head of the Catechetical School of Alexandria, and Bp of Alexandria.<br>248 Origen: *Contra Celsum.*<br><br>249—58 St Cyprian, Bp of Carthage.<br><br>250 Christians persecuted by Emperor Decius. St Fabian, Pope, martyred.<br>c. 250 St Paul of Thebes (—c. 299) becomes the first hermit.<br>c. 250 (—356) St Anthony the Hermit, father of monks, b. in the Fayoum.<br>post 250 Ceramic and glass industries in decay in the western Roman provinces.<br>251—68 Novatian, antipope: theological writer, and holder of subordinationist views.<br><br>253—4 St Lucius, Pope. |
| | | 254—7 St Stephen I, Pope.<br>c. 255 Plotinus, *Enneads.*<br><br>c. 256 Arius b. in Libya.<br>256 Controversy between St Cyprian and Pope Stephen on the baptism of heretics. |
| 256 Shapur takes Antioch: Syria over-run. | | |
| | | 257 Assemblies of Christians forbidden by Emperor Valerian: bishops threatened with death.<br><br>257—8 St Sixtus II, Pope.<br>258 Further edict of Valerian against Christianity. 6 Aug., Pope Sixtus martyred. 14 Sept. St Cyprian of Carthage beheaded. |
| 258 Valerian recovers Antioch: defeated by Shapur near Edessa and taken prisoner. Goths invade Asia Minor. | | |
| 259 Valerian d. in captivity.<br>260 Shapur invades Syria and Asia Minor: Palmyrene army under P. Septimius Odaenathus raids Mesopotamia. Shapur compelled to retreat. Odaenathus drives Sassanid Shapur I out of Syria: pursued as far as Ctesiphon.<br>261—317 Tiridates III, King of Armenia: country converted to Christianity: becomes an ally of Rome. | | 259—68 St Dionysius, Pope.<br>260 Persecution of Christians suspended by Emperor Gallienus: Christianity recognized as a lawful religion, and the Church as a corporation. |

262–280

**WESTERN, NORTHERN
& CENTRAL EUROPE**

**SPAIN, ITALY
& EASTERN EUROPE**

**AFRICA & EGYPT**

**262** Berbers revolt near Sétif.

**267** Goths besiege Thessalonica;
Heruli temporarily seize Athens:
driven out by Dexippus.
**268** Claudius defeats the Goths at
Lake Garda.

**268** Conspiracy of M. Acilius
Aurelius. Gallienus assassinated by
his staff: succ. Claudius II (–270)
(M. Aurelius Claudius, or Claudius
Gothicus). Posthumus lynched by
his men: followed by three usurpers.
**268–70** Claudius reconquers Spain.

**269** Claudius II Gothicus destroys
Gothic forces at Nish. The Bagaudae
first appear in Gaul.
**269–70** Remaining Goths settled in
colonies on the Danube.

**271** Claudius Gothicus d. of plague:
succ. L. Domitius Aurelianus
(Aurelian)(–275). Aurelian restores
Danube frontier: Dacia evacuated:
Alemanni invade Italy: annihilated
by Aurelian.

**271** Roman currency reformed.

**274** Firmus leads uprising in
Alexandria: put down by Probus:
Probus leads expedition against the
Blemmyes.

**273** Aurelian regains complete
control of Gaul.

**275–300** Cormac, son of Art, High
King of Ireland: capital at Tara:
triennial assemblies of the nation
instituted.

**275** Aurelian murdered by his officers.
M. Cornelius Tacitus appointed
Emperor by the Senate (–276).

**276** Florian, Roman Emperor.
**276–82** Probus, Roman Emperor.

**278–9** Probus campaigns on the
lower Danube and in Asia Minor.
**280** Bonosus proclaims himself
Emperor at Cologne: suppressed by
Probus.

| THE NEAR EAST | THE FAR EAST | RELIGION & CULTURE |
|---|---|---|

**262** Chief of Palmyra appointed by Romans *dux orientis* (Chief of the East): given honorary title of *Imperator* by Emperor Gallienus.
**263** The Goths take Ephesus.
**264** Odaenathus recovers Mesopotamia for the Romans, except Ctesiphon.

**263** Wei state subjugates Shu Han.

**264—340** Eusebius of Caesarea, first church historian.
**264—73** Paul, Bp of Samosata, theatrical preacher: condemned as a heretic by three synods.

**265—89** Wu Ti, formerly Ssu-ma, first W Chin Emperor.
**265—317** Western Chin dynasty replaces Wei in China: unstable period of union of all China.

**266 or 7** Zenobia, his widow, succ. Odaenathus.

**269—74** St Felix I, Pope.

**270** Zenobia expands territory of Palmyra to Ancyra (Ankara) and Alexandria: supported by generals Zabbay and Zabda.
**271** Zenobia invades Asia Minor: driven back by Probus. Shapur I d.: succ. Hormuzd I (−272).

**c. 270—80** Fan Hsun of Funan allies with Champa: aids Champa in attack on Chinese in Annam.

**270** St Anthony becomes a hermit.
**c. 270—80** Porphyry: *Contra Christianos.*

**272** Emperor Aurelian defeats Zabda near Hims: enters Palmyra: Zenobia flees: later captured and taken to Rome: Roman garrison stationed in Palmyra.
**272—5** Bahram I, Emperor of Persia.
**273** Palmyra laid waste by Aurelian.

**273 or 4** Mani, author of Manichaean gnosticism, executed.
**c. 274** The *Bible* translated into Coptic.
**275—83** St Eutychian, Pope.

**275—83** Bahram II, Emperor of Persia: succ. Bahram III, for four months: succ. Narses (−302).

**276** Emperor Tacitus defeats Goths and Alans in Asia Minor: Tacitus murdered: his half-brother proclaimed Emperor and then killed: M. Aurelius Probus (Probus) made Emperor.

**276—303** Mahasena, last Mahavamsa King of Ceylon.

**280** Peace made between Champa, China and Funan: Funan embassy to China.

**280** Iamblichus b.

| WESTERN, NORTHERN & CENTRAL EUROPE | SPAIN, ITALY & EASTERN EUROPE | AFRICA & EGYPT |
|---|---|---|

282 Probus lynched in Pannonia: succ. M. Aurelius Carus (Carus) (—284).

284—305 Diocletian, Roman Emperor.
c. post 285 San Marino founded.

284 Diocletian reforms administration of Roman Africa. Nobatae introduced into lower Nubia as a defence against raiding Blemmyes.

285 Diocletian defeats Carus's son, Carinus, pretender, near R. Margus (Morava): beginning of period of stability. Maximian (Marcus Aurelius Valerius Maximianus) made Caesar.
285—6 Rising of Bagaudae, peasants in N Gaul, put down by Maximian.
286 M. Aurelius Carausius, commander of the Channel fleet, proclaims himself Augustus in Britain.

286 Diocletian makes Maximian his assistant Augustus.

289—95 Berber revolts in Kabylia and Hodna.

290 Maximian and Carausius make a formal peace. Line of forts built from Norfolk to Isle of Wight to resist Saxon raiders: Count of the Saxon Shore appointed to control them.

292 ff. Roman currency reformed by Diocletian.

292—3 Roman general Achilles proclaims himself emperor in Alexandria: besieged and defeated by Diocletian: Egyptian administration reformed: frontier drawn at Aswan.

293 Carausius d.: his murderer Allectus put down by Constantine Chlorus.

293 Flavius Valerius Constantine (known as Constantius Chlorus) and Galerius Valerius Maximianus (Maximian) appointed: Domitian retains eastern provinces as Augustus: Maximian given Italy and Africa as Augustus: Galerius the Danube provinces: western regions to Constantine Chlorus, both as Caesars.

294 Galerius defeats the Iazyges.
295 Galerius defeats Marcomanni.
296 The Picts first appear in history.

296 Egyptian frontier withdrawn to Elephantine: Kharqa oasis fortified: first camel corps enlisted.

| THE NEAR EAST | THE FAR EAST | RELIGION & CULTURE |
|---|---|---|
| | **280** Wu state absorbed by Chin. General disarmament ordered to restore economic and political situation, but order ineffective.<br>**281** Mu-jung tribes, of Mongolian linguistic affinity, occupy Peking area. | |
| **283** Carus campaigns against Bahram II, Emperor of Persia, following his occupation of Armenia and Mesopotamia: Carus takes Ctesiphon: then killed by lightning: succ. his son, Numerian (−284).<br>**284** Peace made between Diocletian and Persia: Armenia and Mesopotamia ceded to Rome. | | **283—96** St Gaius, Pope.<br>**284** Coptic Era of the Martyrs begins. |
| | | **c. 285** Pappus of Alexandria, engineer and mathematician. Monastic life beginning in Egypt: spreads rapidly. |
| **286** Diocletian makes Tiridates King of Armenia. | | |
| | **287** Liu Yuan, principal leader of Hsiung-nu or Hun tribes.<br>**289** Mu-jung recognize Chinese overlordship.<br>**290—306** Hui Ti, W Chin Emperor. | |
| **c. 290** Gupta Kingdom established in Bengal. | **290** Empress Chia secures assassination of her predecessor Yang and her whole family: Chia family in the ascendant. | **c. 290** Lactantius teaching at Nicomedia. |
| | | **c. 293—346** St Pachomius, organizer of monasteries. |
| **296** Narses attacks eastern Roman provinces: deposes Tiridates of Armenia: defeated by Galerius: Tigris basin added to Roman Mesopotamia. | | **296** St Menas d.: cult city and monastery subsequently grows up round his tomb near Alexandria.<br>**296—304** St Marcellinus, Pope. |

| WESTERN, NORTHERN & CENTRAL EUROPE | SPAIN, ITALY & EASTERN EUROPE | AFRICA & EGYPT |
|---|---|---|
| | **297** System of counting periods of time by indictions introduced by Diocletian. **post 297** Provincial governments reformed by Diocletian. | |
| **298** Constantius Chlorus defeats the Germans at Langres and at Vindonissa. | | |
| **late 3rd c.** Saxons raiding E coast of Britain. | | **300±100–900±100** Ziwa culture at Inyanga. |
| **4th c.** Huns begin to terrorise area between the Caspian Sea and Carpathian Mts. | | **4th c.–c. 750** Berber Maga dynasty rules Mandingo as Kings of Ghana. |
| **c. 300** Forts built on Welsh and Cumberland coasts. London and York fortified. Roman army reorganized. The Franks reach Zeeland. Gepids arrive in Transylvania. | | **c. 300** Kalomo, Zambia, first inhabited by mound-dwellers. Iron artefacts appear at Saharan sites. King of Axum in control of Himyar, Saba, Raydan and Salhen. **?c. 300–400** Beginning of Saharan camel-borne trade in gold and salt. |
| | **305** Diocletian formally abdicates: Maximian also abdicates: Constantius Chlorus (306) and Galerius (−311) become Augusti. | **305** Domitius Alexander, Roman general commanding Egypt, proclaimed emperor: Emperor Maxentius begins long struggle to suppress revolt. |

| THE NEAR EAST | THE FAR EAST | RELIGION & CULTURE |
|---|---|---|
| **297** Roman army under Galerius attacks Persia: five provinces taken. | | **c. 297** Diocletian's edict against the Manichaeans. |
| | **299** Chia family murder heir to the throne and another prince. | **298** *Ludi saeculares* celebrated for the last time. **298 or 9** St Athanasius, later Patriarch of Alexandria, b. |
| **4th c.** Banu Kindah tribe first mentioned in hsitory. | | **c. ante 300** Nabataean script develops into Northern Arabian script, ancestral to *Naskhi* script. **early 4th c.** First monasteries founded on Mount Athos. St Ephraim Syrus, theologian. Buddhism already present in Kedah. |
| | | **4th c.–16th c.** Period of Maya civilization in Mexico. |
| **c. 300** Hadhramaut made subject to Kingdom of Saba: Yemen mountains and coastal plain shortly added. | **300** Empress Chia assassinated by Prince Lun. **c. 300** Su Chun comes to prominence in S China as a bandit leader. Merchants in China required by law to wear a white turban, with name and place of business, and one white, and one black, shoe. **c. 300–600** Rice becomes main staple food of S Chinese. | **c. 300** Diocletian's palace at Spalato built. Moulded pottery in Peru. **c. 300–11** Peter, Bp of Alexandria. **c. 300–800** Mochica civilization in Peru. |
| **302–9** Hormuzd II, Emperor of Persia. | **post 300** State of Kedah, Malaya, in existence: already a major port. **301** Prince Lun declares himself Emperor: assassinated by Prince of Chi. **302** Prince of Chi murdered by Prince of Chang-sha. **302–6** Prince of Ho-chien seizes power, but is murdered. **303** Prince of Chang-sha killed by Prince of Tung-hai. Prince of Chengtu attempts to seize power. | **302** Christians banned in the Roman army. **c. 302–51** St Gregory the Illuminator Bp of Armenia at Etchmiadzin: evangelization of Armenia begun. **303** 23 Feb., Diocletian publishes general edict ordering destruction of churches and Christian writings; and reducing all Christians to slave status. March, second edict of Diocletian against the Christians. 21 Dec., Diocletian publishes a general amnesty (third edict) to celebrate the twentieth anniversary of his accession: Christian clergy not to be set free until they recant. **c. 303–5** Arnobius: *Adversus Nationes.* |
| | **304–439** Period of confusion of the 'Sixteen Kingdoms' in N China. **305** Prince of Chengtu conquers capital (removed in 306). | **304** April, Diocletian's fourth edict imposes the death penalty on Christians. **305** Donatist movement begins. **c. 305–6** St Anthony begins to organize monastic life. **305–11** Christians in the east persistently persecuted by Emperor Galerius: virtually no persecution in the west. **?c. 305** Proconsul of Africa ordered to burn Manichaeans. |

**306** Constantius Chlorus d. at York: succ.; his son, Constantine the Great (—337): Maxentius becomes Caesar in Italy and Africa. Maximian reassumes office.
**306 ff.** Constantine campaigns again against the Franks and the Alemanni.
**306—12** Maxentius (Marcus Aurelius Valerius Maxentius), Roman Emperor.

**307** Alliance between Maxentius and Constantine. Conference of Carnuntum. Licinius becomes an Augustus (—324).

**308** Constantine takes Gaul. Maxentius takes up arms against Constantine and Maximian.

**310** Constantine executes Maximian.

**311** Galerius d.: Licinius and Maximinus Daia take over his possessions.

**311** Maximin Daia persecutes Christians in Egypt: St Anthony visits Alexandria from the desert.

**312** 28 Oct., Constantine defeats Maxentius at battle of the Milvian Bridge: Maxentius d.: adopts *labarum* as personal standard: proclaims himself champion of Christ: Galerius d.: Constantine sole master of the west: contest for succession between Maximinus Daia and Licinius.

**313** Maximinus Daia attacks Licinius. Battle of Adrianople. Maximinus Daia and Diocletian d.

**314** Constantine defeats Licinius in Pannonia: Licinius cedes all Balkans except Thrace.

**315** Constantine adopts the style of 'the Great'.

**315** Crucifixion and the breaking of legs forbidden in the Roman Empire.

| THE NEAR EAST | THE FAR EAST | RELIGION & CULTURE |
|---|---|---|
| | | **306** Beginning of the Meletian schism. Council of Elvira, Spain: first enjoinment of clerical celibacy. Peter of Alexandria: *Letter on Penitence.* Cologne bridge begun. |
| | **307** Hun Han dynasty established by Liu Yuan at Ping-Cheng in S China: later called Earlier Chao dynasty. | |
| | | **308** 'Year of Terror' for Christians in the east. **308—9** St Marcellus I, Pope. |
| **309—79** Shapur II, the Great: b. posthumously. | **309** Hun Han attack Chinese capital, Loyang. | **309 or 310** St Eusebius, Pope. **309—92** Ausonius, poet. |
| | **310** Liu Yuan d.: succ. Liu Tsung (—318). Loyang taken with Emperor Huai Ti. | **310** Emperor Galerius issues proclamation granting tolerance to Christians, allowing churches to be rebuilt. **310—403** St. Epiphanius, theologian. **311** Caccilian, Bp of Carthage. |
| | | **311—4** St Miltiades, Pope. **311—81** Ulfilas, missionary to the Goths. **312** St Lucian of Antioch martyred. |
| | | **312—26** Alexander, Bp and then Patriarch of Alexandria. |
| **313** Maximinus attacks Licinius: captures Byzantium: Licinius drives Maximinus back to Tarsus: Maximinus d. suddenly: Licinius in full control of east. | **313** Emperor Huai Ti executed by the Huns. **313—6** Min Ti, Chinese Emperor at Changan. | **313** Constantine and Licinius issue rescript at Milan confirming Galerius' edict tolerating Christians: privileges granted to clergy. Three French and fifteen Italian bishops appointed under Pope Miltiades to inquire into the Donatists. |
| | **314—5** Further parts of NE China brought under control by Shih Lo. | **314** Council of Arles: attended by three English bishops. Constantine declines to celebrate the *ludi saeculares* at Rome because of their pagan associations. **314—35** St Sylvester I, Pope. **314—93** Libanius, sophist: tutor of Emperor Julian. **315** Lands of the clergy in the Roman Empire exempted from taxation. Arch of Constantine built in Rome. |
| | | **315—86** St Cyril of Jerusalem, theologian. |
| | **317—420** Eastern Chin dynasty, controlling S China only: Yuan Ti, first Emperor. Population of lower R. Yangtze and creation of manors begun. **316** Huns take Changan: Western Chin dynasty ended. | **316** The Donatists condemned by Constantine. c. **316—400** St Martin, Bp of Tours. |

| WESTERN, NORTHERN & CENTRAL EUROPE | SPAIN, ITALY & EASTERN EUROPE | AFRICA & EGYPT |
|---|---|---|
| | | **c. 320–55** Aezanas, King of Axum: ruler also of Saba, Himyar and Beja. Many Syrian merchants visiting Axum. |
| **323** Constantine defeats Licinius at Adrianople: Licinius surrenders: Roman Empire united under Constantine. **324** Battles of Adrianople and Chrysopolis. Licinius d. Constantine sole emperor. | **324** Nov., Constantine the Great begins the building of Constantinople. | |
| | **326** Crispus and Fausta executed. | |
| | **330** 11 May, Constantinople solemnly inaugurated as capital of the Roman Empire: court moved from Rome. | **330±90** Earliest traces of occupation at Engaruka, Tanzania. **330±150** Earliest traces of occupation at Zimbabwe. |

| THE NEAR EAST | THE FAR EAST | RELIGION & CULTURE |
|---|---|---|

**318** Constantine recognizes the jurisdiction of ecclesiastical courts.
**c. 318** Arius, a Libyan priest, preaches his own doctrine of the Incarnation at Alexandria.
**318–20** Edicts forbidding consultation of auspices and magic.
**319** Liu Tsung d.: succ. Liu Yao (−329).
**319** Licinius renews persecution of Christians in Egypt.
**320** Lactantius: *De mortibus persecutorum*. First dated Maya inscription.

**320** 26 Feb., beginning of Gupta era.
**c. 320–35** Chandra Gupta I: extends dominion over Oudh and as far as Prayaga (Allahabad).
**320–c. 647** Imperial Gupta dynasty in India based on Magadha and parts of E Uttar Pradesh.

**321** Arius excommunicated by Alexander, Bp of Alexandria: disturbances in Egypt follow: Hosius, Bp of Córdoba, sent by Constantine to mediate. Manumission in churches declared valid. Constantine grants the Donatists liberty to act in accordance with their consciences.
**323** Arius condemned and expelled from Alexandria. First monastery founded at Tabennisi, near Thebes, by St Pachomius.
**324** Constantine writes to Alexandria concerning Arianism.

**325** June, First General Council of the Church held at Nicaea: Eusebius of Caesarea and St Athanasius (later Bp of Alexandria), leading figures: Arianism condemned: first creed promulgated.

**326–42** Cheng, Eastern Chin Emperor, initially with his mother as regent; General Yu Liang actual ruler.

**327** Empress Helena 'rediscovers' Holy Places at Jerusalem: Holy Sepulchre and Bethlehem basilicas built. St Catherine's Monastery, Sinai, founded.

**328** Imru al-Qays I, first certain Lakhmid monarch, d.
**328** Su Chun kidnaps Eastern Chin Emperor, but defeated by Yu Liang. Emperor d: succ. his brother (−330).
**329** Shih Lo, follower of Liu Yuan, in control of NE China, after slaughter of more than 100,000 Chinese, including forty-eight princes: all of Liu Yao's empire annexed.
**329–52** Later Chao dynasty in NE China (Hun).
**328** Dated stele of Uaxactun, Mexico.
**328–73** St Athanasius Bp of Alexandria.
**328–73** St Athanasius Patriarch of Alexandria.
**329–89** St Gregory of Nazianzus, theologian.
Georgia converted. St Makarios settles in Scetis. Donatist Council at Carthage.
**330** Iamblichus, philosopher, d.
**c. 330** Frumentius (Abba Salama) begins evangelization of Kingdom of Axum.
**c. 330–79** St Basil the Great, Bp of Caesarea in Cappadocia, monk and theologian.
**c. 330–400** Ammianus Marcellinus, historian.

331—352

WESTERN, NORTHERN
& CENTRAL EUROPE

SPAIN, ITALY
& EASTERN EUROPE

AFRICA & EGYPT

332 Constantine defeats the Goths.

334 Edict forbidding splitting up of
slave families by sale issued.
335 Constantine divides the empire
between his sons and nephews.

336 Kingdom of Axum correspondin[g]
with Constantinople: its subjects
treated as equal with Romans.

337 Baptism and death of Constantine
the Great: his sons Constantine II,
Constans and Constantius II divide
the Empire, having massacred his
nephews.

340 Constantine II attacks Constans:
killed at Aquileia.

341—2 Constans campaigns against
the Franks.

343 Constans campaigns against the
Picts and Scots.

c. 341—6 Frumentius (Abuna
Salama) first Abuna of Ethiopia.

345 Circumcellions begin to rebel i[n]
N Africa.
347 Troops sent against Donatists.

c. 350 Britain supplying Roman
garrisons on the Rhine with wheat.
Huns invade Europe.

350 Constans killed by Maxentius:
Constantine, sole emperor (−361).
Vetranio and Nepotianus, usurpers.

350 Meroe destroyed by Aezanas o[f]
Axum: campaigns against the Nob[a]

351 Gallus made Caesar. Battle of
Mursa.

| THE NEAR EAST | THE FAR EAST | RELIGION & CULTURE |
|---|---|---|
| | | **331** Constantine forbids heretical gatherings and also divorce.<br>**c. 331—96** St Gregory of Nyssa, theologian. |
| | **333** Shih Lo d.: succ. 334 by Shih Hu (—349): capital transferred to Weh. | **333—451** Schnoudi of Atripe, founder of monasteries.<br>**333** Frumentius converts Axumite court. |
| **c. 335—85** Samudra Gupta: emperor over N India, and with Deccan and S India Kings as vassals. | | **335** St Athanasius accused of murder before the Synod of Tyre: rebutted by his production of the man alleged to be murdered alive. Buddhism officially tolerated in China.<br>**336** St Athanasius banished to Trèves for alleged high treason. Arius d. St Mark, Pope. |
| **337—50** Shapur II's first war with Rome. | | **337** 23 Nov., St Athanasius, released from exile, returns to Alexandria: visited in Alexandria by St Anthony the Hermit.<br>**337—52** St Julius I, Pope. |
| **338** Nisibis besieged by Persia. | **338—76** Tai state, first Toba (Turkish) dynasty in N Shansi. | |
| **c. 340—78** Kingdom of Himyar under rule of Axum. | | **339** Christians persecuted in Persia: Mar Shimun, five bishops and 100 priests executed at Susa.<br>**340** St Athanasius exiled a second time for alleged fraud: on appeal to Rome, cleared by a synod of fifty bishops. First monastery for women founded. Christians persecuted in Persia.<br>**c. 340—97** St Ambrose, theologian and Bishop of Milan.<br>**340—400** Theon of Alexandria, mathematician.<br>**c. 340—420** St Jerome, translator of the Vulgate. |
| **341** Treaty between Persia and Armenia: Arsaces made King. | | **341** Ulfilas, an Arian, begins to evangelize the Goths. Pagan sacrifices forbidden in the Roman Empire. Council of Antioch.<br>**343** Councils of Sardica (Sofia) and Philippopolis.<br>**344** Athanasius again returns to Alexandria.<br>**344 or 7—407** St John Chrysostom. |
| | **345—61** Mu Ti, Eastern Chin Emperor: ascends throne aged two. | **c. 345—410** Symmachus (Quintus Aurelius Symmachus), writer and protagonist of paganism. |
| **346** Shapur again besieges Nisibis. | **347** Huan Wen, gentleman adventurer, reconquers Szechwan for Eastern Chin dynasty: initiates campaigns against northern states. | |
| **348** Shapur invades Mesopotamia: indecisive battle at Singara.<br>**350—7** Shapur campaigns against the Huns. | **c. 350** Funan in an unsettled condition: Chandana, an Indian usurper, ruler. | **348—c. 405** Aurelius Clemens Prudentius, Spanish Latin poet.<br>**c. 350** Ulfilas translates the Bible into Gothic: Arian Christianity begins to spread amongst the Ostrogoths and Visigoths.<br>**c. 350—400** Ki Kai-chih, Chinese artist.<br>**351** First Creed of Sirmium. |
| **352** Treaty between Armenia and Rome. | **351—94** Earlier Chin (Tibetan) dynasty in N China.<br>**352—70** Earlier Yen (proto-Mongol) dynasty in NE China. | **352—66** St Liberius, Pope. |

**353** Maxentius defeated and killed.
**354** Gallus murdered. Treaty
between Constantius and the
Alemanni.
**355** Julian made Caesar. Alemanni,
Franks and Saxons invade Gaul. The
Huns reach Russia. Attempted
usurpations of Africanus and
Silvanus.

**356** Julian takes Cologne.

**357** Battle of Argentoratum.

**360** Julian acclaimed as emperor in
Paris.
**361–3** Julian (the Apostate), Roman
Emperor.

**363–4** Jovian, Roman Emperor.

**363** Leptis Magna appeals to Rome
for aid against raids of the
Austuriani.

**364** Alemanni invade Gaul.

**364–75** Valentinian I, Emperor, with
brother, Valens, as co-ruler.
**364** Brother Emperors Valentinian
and Valens divide the empire into
East and West.
**365** Attempted usurpation of
Procopius.

**364–75** Nomads invading
Tripolitanian ports. Firmus rebels in
Kabylia: Caesarea and Icosium taken

**366** Procopius defeated and killed
by Valens. Alemanni defeated.
**367** Roman legions withdrawn from
Britain to combat barbarians: Saxons
and Picts break through Hadrian's
Wall. Burgundians fight the
Alemanni.

| THE NEAR EAST | THE FAR EAST | RELIGION & CULTURE |
|---|---|---|

**THE NEAR EAST**

356 Embassy from Constantius to
S Arabia: led by Theophilus Indus,
an  Arian: church built at Aden and
two others in Himyar.

359—61 War between Rome and
Persia.
360 Embassy from King of Ceylon
to Samudragupta.
361 Constantius d. fighting against
Persia in Cilicia. Julian sole Emperor.

363 Julian leads expedition against
Persia: killed in battle: succ., Jovian
—364), makes peace: the five
provinces restored to Persia.

**THE FAR EAST**

354 Southern Chinese Empire
defeated by Chia dynasty.

357—85 Fu Chien, of the Earlier Chin
dynasty: state and army re-organized
on a Tibetan basis, ignoring family
and tribal ties.

**RELIGION & CULTURE**

353—431 St Paulinus of Nola.
354—430 St Augustine, Bp.

355 Council of Milan: St Athanasius
and other orthodox bishops removed
from their sees: intruder, George of
Cappadocia, installed in Alexandria.
355—8 St Felix II, Pope *ad int.* during
exile of St Liberius by the Arians
(d. 365).
356 Constantius closes pagan temples:
sacrifices forbidden. St Athanasius
flees to the desert.
357 St Athanasius: *Life of St Anthony*:
beginning of monastic life in the west
follows. Constantius orders the
removal of the Altar of Victory from
the Roman Senate. Second Creed, or
'Blasphemy of Sirmium'.
358 Third Creed of Sirmium.
359 Fourth, or Dated, Creed of
Sirmium. Council of Rimini.
c. 360—420 Pelagius, British theologian
and author of Pelagianism.
361 Julian reopens pagan temples and
permits sacrifices: openly declares
himself pagan. St Athanasius returns.
362 Emperor Julian orders the
expulsion of St Athanasius from
Alexandria: replaced by one George, a
pork-contractor, later murdered by the
mob. Following Emperor Julian's
apostasy from Christianity, a number
of Christians martyred in different
localities. Julian forbids Christians
from teaching: Christians forbidden to
attend pagan schools. St. Athanasius
returns from the Desert to Alexandria:
Council held.
Julian: *Misopogon* ('The Beard-hater').
c. 362 Apollinarius the Elder and the
Younger: translates the Psalms into
Pindaric odes: the Pentateuch into
hexameters; and the Gospels into
Platonic dialogues.
c. 363—425 Sulpicius Severus, writer.
364—75 Cathedral of Trêves (Trier)
begun as a basilica.

365 St Athanasius expelled from
Alexandria for the fifth time, but
shortly restored.
366—7 Ursicinus, antipope.
366—84 St Damasus I, Pope.

| WESTERN, NORTHERN & CENTRAL EUROPE | SPAIN, ITALY & EASTERN EUROPE | AFRICA & EGYPT |
|---|---|---|

**367** Roman Province of Britain invaded by Picts, Scots, Angles, Franks and Attacotti.
**367–9** Valens campaigns against the Goths.
**368–9** Theodosius in Britan.
**c. 370** The Huns reach R. Don: Ostrogoths defeated.

**367–75** Valentinian I and Gratian, Roman Emperors.

**373–5** Theodosius campaigns in N Africa: Firmus put down.

**374** Alliance between Valentinian and the Alemanni. Theodosius the Younger campaigns on the Danube.
**375** Valentinian defeats the Quadi.

**375–9** Gratian and Valentinian II, Roman Emperors.

**376** The Ostrogoths cross the Danube: battle of Marcianopolis. The Huns reach Dacia. Theodosius executed.
**377** The Goths invade Thrace. Gratian defeats the Alemanni.

**378** Goths defeat and kill Valens at Adrianople: Pannonia invaded.
**379** Theodosius and Gratian halt the Goths in Epirus and Dalmatia: expelled from Thrace and Moesia: allowed to settle in Pannonia.
**380** Niall of the Three Hostages, High King of Ireland.

**379–95** Theodosius I (the Great), Roman Emperor.
**379–457** Theodosian Dynasty of Byzantium.

**382** Visigoths allowed to settle in Moesia.

**383** Maximus kills Gratian: recognized as emperor by Theodosius.

| THE NEAR EAST | THE FAR EAST | RELIGION & CULTURE |
|---|---|---|
| | 370 Earlier Yen Kingdom annexed by Fu Chien. | c. 370 Beginning of Priscillian heresy.<br>370–447 Ho Cheng-tien, Chinese musicologist. |
| 371 Indecisive hostilities between Rome and Persia. | 371 Huan Wen deposes Eastern Chin Emperor, replacing him first with a dotard, and then with a child: then d. himself. | 371–400 St Martin, Bp of Tours, Roman army officer, and founder of monasticism in Gaul. |
| | 373–96 Hsiao Wu Ti, Eastern Chin Emperor: ascends throne as a child. | 372 Abbey of Marmoutiers founded by St Martin.<br>373 St Athanasius d.<br>373–97 St Ambrose, Bp of Milan.<br>c. 373–414 Synesius, Bp and scholar.<br>c. 375 Church of the Ascension on the Mount of Olives built. |
| 376 Peace treaty between Rome and Persia. | 376 Earlier Liang and Turkish Toba kingdoms annihilated by Fu Chien. | |
| | | 377 or 8 Synod of Rome condemns Apollinarianism. |
| c. 378 Himyarite kings regain independence from Axum (–c. 525).<br>379–83 Ardashir III, Emperor of Persia. | | 379 Synod of Antioch condemns Apollinarianism. |
| c. 380–415 Chandra Gupta II. | | 380 Council of bishops at Saragossa: Priscillianism condemned. Feb. 28, Theodosius publishes Edict ordering the acceptance of Christianity by all nations: Arians condemned.<br>c. 380 St Jerome translates Eusebius' *Ecclesiastical History* into Latin.<br>c. 380–456 Eutyches, heretic.<br>381 Second Ecumenical Council of Constantinople: Macedonianism condemned: Nicene Creed re-affirmed. Arians, Photinians and Eunomians forbidden to build churches. The Altar of Victory finally removed from the Roman Senate.<br>381–97 St John Chrysostom, Bp of Antioch, preacher and theologian. |
| 383–8 Shapur III, Emperor of Persia. | 383 Fu Chien, with army of 1 m., campaigns against S China: defeated in skirmishes: army flees in panic. Chin dominions thereafter disintegrate. | 382 Manichaeans ordered to be sought out by *inquisitores*.<br>382 and 383 Further assemblies of the Council of Constantinople.<br>c. 382 St Jerome revises the Latin translation of the *Psalms*.<br>383 July, heretical worship and ordinations forbidden throughout the Roman Empire. |

**386** Theodosius prevents the Goths from crossing the Danube.

**c. 386** Gildon appointed Count of Africa.

**387** Maximus takes Italy from Valentinian II.

**388** Maximus takes Rome: defeated and killed by Theodosius.

**390** Rising in Thessalonica.

**392** Stilicho destroys army of Alans, Bastarnes, Goths and Huns on the Danube.

**393—423** Honorius, Western Roman Emperor. Stilicho, *de facto* ruler of the west.

**393** Gildon declines to aid Theodosius.

**395—410** Alaric, the Bold, King of Visigoths.
**395** The Visigoths, led by Alaric, enter Moesia, Thrace and Macedonia and then Greece: Athens alone not pillaged.

**395—408** Arcadius, Eastern Roman Emperor.

**396** Gildon again revolts: grain convoys to Rome stopped.

**397** Stilicho fails to recover the Peloponnese from Alaric.

**398** Gildon's rebellion suppressed.

| THE NEAR EAST | THE FAR EAST | RELIGION & CULTURE |
|---|---|---|
| **384** Armenia partitioned between Rome and Persia. | **384–94** W Yen dynasty. **384–409** Later Yen dynasty, founded by a Tibetan in central Hopei. **384–417** Later Chin dynasty (Tibetan) chiefly in Shensi. **385–431** W Chin dynasty in the Ordos region. **385–550** Toba (Turkish) dynasty in N of Shansi. **386–403** Later Liang dynasty, founded by Lu Kuang, in Turkestan: includes many heterogeneous elements with Chinese, Hsien-pi, Huns and Tibetans. **386–535** Northern Wei and four minor dynasties in N China (−581). | **384** Buddhism reaches Korea. **384–99** Siricius, Pope. **c. post 384** Pope Siricius the first to enjoin celibacy on all the clergy. **385–412** Theophilus, Patriarch of Alexandria. **386** St Jerome settles at Bethlehem: translation of the Bible into Latin (the Vulgate) begun. Council of Trêves. Priscillian executed. **386–7** St Augustine: *Philosophical Dialogues*. **386** Basilica of St Ambrose, Milan, founded. **c. 390–459** St Simon Stylites. |
| **387** Rising in Antioch. **388–99** Bahram IV, Emperor of Persia. **388–401** Chandra Gupta II campaigns against the Shakas: annexes W India. | | **c. 389** Daughter Library at Alexandria burnt by order of Theodosius. **390** Dispute between St Ambrose and Theodosius. **c. 390** Apollinarius, Bp of Laodicaea in Syria, d.: theologian: denied existence of human soul in Christ. St. Makarios d. **391** Serapaeum destroyed in Alexandria. **392** Altar of Victory restored in the Roman Senate: all pagan worship forbidden by Theodosius. St Jerome: *De viris illustribus*. **393** Last Olympic Games. Synod of Hippo. **394** Olympic Games forbidden. |
| **395** Hun invasion reaches Antioch. | | **395** Sulpicius Severus: *Life of St Martin*. **395–430** St Augustine, Bp of Hippo, near Carthage: the first cathedral monastery initiated. |
| | **396–409** Later Yen dynasty disintegrates: five rulers in thirteen years. **396** Eastern Chin Emperor Hsiao Wu Ti d.: succ. by his five year old son: quarrels between rival cliques ensue. **397–439** Northern Liang dynasty founded by Huns: quickly absorbs later Liang Kingdom. | **397** St Ninian begins missionary work amongst the Picts. **397–8** St Augustine: *Confessions*. **398–404** St John Chrysostom, Patriarch of Constantinople. **late 4th c.** The 'Four Congregations' founded in Scetis. |
| **399** Gainas, a Goth, defeats imperial troops in Asia Minor: Eutropius exiled. **399–414** Fa-hien (or Fa-hsien) travelling in India. **399–420** Yazdagird I, the Wicked, Emperor of Persia. | | **399–401** Anastasius I, Pope. |

400–413

WESTERN, NORTHERN
& CENTRAL EUROPE

SPAIN, ITALY
& EASTERN EUROPE

AFRICA & EGYPT

**400** Gainas assassinated by the Huns: end of Gothic problem in the Roman Empire. The Huns reach R. Elbe.

**c. 400** Kingdom of Ulster founded.

**c. 400** Kalambo Falls, Zambia, first settled.

**401–3** Alaric leads the Visigoths into Italy: repelled by Stilicho.
**402** Ravenna made the imperial capital.

**406** Rebellion in Britain under pretender Constantine: reaches Rome.
**406 ff** Suevi, Vandals and Alans invade France.

**406** Ostrogoth invasion checked by Stilicho at Fiesole.

**407** Alaric again in Italy.
**407–11** Constantine III, usurper, Western Roman Emperor.
**408** Alaric takes tribute from Rome.
**408–14** Anthemius, regent of the Empire.
**408–10** Second Visigoth invasion of Italy: Alaric attacks Rome.
**408–50** Theodosius II, the Younger: succ. aged six: Yazdagird of Persia appointed guardian in Arcadius's will.

**408** The Saxons attack Britain. Stilicho d.

**409–19** N Gaul conquered by the Franks; E Gaul taken by the Bagaudae (Burgundians): Spain taken by the Suevi and Vandals.

**409** Alaric proclaims Attalus emperor.

**410** Emperor Honorius sends message to Britons that they must henceforward protect themselves. Attalus deposed. 24 Aug., Alaric takes Rome and then d.: succ. Athaulf.

**c. 413** Burgundians settle in the Rhone valley.

**413** Theodosian wall built at Constantinople.

## THE NEAR EAST

## THE FAR EAST

## RELIGION & CULTURE

**5th c.** Small Indianized kingdoms begin to emerge in Java and Borneo. Khmers emerge as a nation under Srutavarman. Dravidian rulers established in N Ceylon. Sirigiya palace and rock fortress built in Ceylon.

**400** Liu Yu, army commander in Eastern Chin dominions, suppresses popular rebellion in the S led by secret society similar to Yellow Turbans.
**c. 400** Gunavarman, son of Kundungga, King of E Borneo. Indonesian kingdom in E Borneo: ruler, Mulavarman. Hiung-nu cavalry force Chinese to abandon chariots in favour of cavalry.
**400–550** Second Kaundinya dynasty in Funan: Kaundinya, first ruler.

**fl. 400–18** Numan I al-Awar, Lakhmid ruler: famous in poetry and legend: builder of castle for Bahram Gor, son of Sassanid Yazdagird I.

**5th c.** Stirrups in common use in China. Water mill with controlled dam and sluice gates evolved. Decimal system and numerals already in use in India. *Samantapasadika,* account of early history of Ceylon.
**c. 5th c.** Chinese script officially adopted in Japan.
**5th to 6th c.** Best period of the Ajanta cave paintings. Daphni monastery founded.
**400** Java converted to Buddhism. Macrobius: *Saturnales.* Council of bishops at Toledo: Nicene creed endorsed.
**c. 400** Final recension of C. Ptolemy's *Geography* shows Byzantine knowledge of Africa and India. Marcian of Heraclea the first to record Arabs as Saracens. Codex Syriacus, Syriac text of the Gospels, written. Palestinian *Talmud* completed.
**post 400** Ravenna Cathedral built.
**401–17** Innocent I, Pope.

**403** St John Chrysostom exiled and then restored.
**404** St Jerome's translation of the Old Testament into Latin completed. St John Chrysostom again exiled.

**404** Liu Yu seizes Eastern Chin capital and restores Emperor.
**404–15** Liu Yu undertakes various campaigns against N Chinese rulers.

**407–31** Hun Kingdom of Hsia in the Ordos region.

**409** Christians permitted to worship openly in the Persian empire.

**410** Council of Seleucia organizes church in Persia. First recorded Bp of al-Hirah.
**c. 410** St Honoratus founds Abbey of Lérins.
**411** Donatist schism ended by Council of Carthage.
**412–26** St Augustine: *The City of God.*
**412–444** St Cyril, Patriarch of Alexandria.

| WESTERN, NORTHERN & CENTRAL EUROPE | SPAIN, ITALY & EASTERN EUROPE | AFRICA & EGYPT |
|---|---|---|
| | **414** Visigoths take Barcelona.<br>**414—6** Pulcheria, regent. | |
| | | **415** Hypatia murdered in Alexandria. |
| | **418** Visigothic campaigns against the Alans in Spain. | |
| **c. 419** Visigoths settle south of the Loire, with capital at Toulouse.<br>**420** The Franks invade northern France. | | **c. 420** Axum trading with India. |
| | **421** Constantine III, Western Roman co-Emperor. | |
| | **423—5** John, usurper, Western Roman Emperor.<br>**425—55** Valentian III, Western Roman Emperor.<br>**425** The vandals take Seville and Carthagena. | |
| **427—48** Clodion, King of Merovingian Franks.<br>**428** Aetius drives the Franks back beyond the Rhine. Genseric becomes King of the Vandals. | | **427** Boniface, Count of Africa, revolts. |
| | **429—39** Theodosian Code of law compiled. | **429—77** Genseric, Vandal King of Africa.<br>**429** Vandals under Genseric seize Roman Africa (—533).<br>**430—1** Vandals besiege Hippo. |
| **435** Riparian Franks reach Trèves.<br>**435—7** Bagaudae rebel in Gaul. | | **435** Vandals occupy Mauretania and Numidia: their conquest recognized by Valentinian III.<br>**436** Kharqa oasis raided by (? ) Tuaregs. |
| | **439** Genseric attacks Sicily: takes Lilybaeum. | **439** 19 Oct., Genseric takes Carthage builds fleet. |
| **441** Franks re-appear on the Rhine.<br>**441—2** Angles and Saxons occupy S and E England. | **441—9** War between Attila and Theodosius II. | |

| THE NEAR EAST | THE FAR EAST | RELIGION & CULTURE |
|---|---|---|
| | | **414** Fa Hsien, Buddhist monk, voyages from Ceylon to China *via* Borneo: records that few Indonesians are willing to become Buddhists. |
| **415–55** Kumara Gupta succ. Chandra Gupta II. | **c. 415** Purnavarman, King of W Java, mentioned in an inscription. | **415** Council of Diospolis rules Pelagianism orthodox. |
| | | **416** Council of Carthage rules Pelagianism heretical. |
| | | **417–8** St Zosimus, Pope. |
| **418–62** al-Mundhir I, Lakhmid ruler. | | **418** Pelagius excommunicated by the Pope. Council of Carthage defines doctrine of grace: Donatist schism virtually ended. |
| | | **418–9** Eulalius, antipope. |
| | | **418–22** St Boniface I, Pope. |
| | **419** Eastern Chin Emperor killed by Liu Yu: puppet installed. | |
| **420–40** Bahram V Gur, Emperor of Persia. | **420** Liu Yu removes puppet Eastern Chin Emperor and becomes first Emperor of the Liu-Sung dynasty (–478). | |
| **420–1** Bahram V campaigns against Rome. | **c. 420** Gunavarman, a prince from Kashmir, comes to Java or Sumatra. | |
| | **420–589** Period of Southern Dynasties in China. | |
| **422** Hundred Year peace made between Rome and Persia: kept until 442. | | **422–32** Celestine I, Pope. |
| **c. 425** White Huns, or Ephthalites, cross the Oxus: defeated by Bahram V. | | **425** University of Constantinople greatly expanded. |
| | | **426–7** St Augustine: *Retractationes.* |
| | | **428** Theodora of Mopsuestia, commentator on the Scriptures, d. |
| | | **428–31** Nestorius, Patriarch of Constantinople, alleged author of 'Nestorianism'. |
| | | **430–80** Sidonius Apollinaris. writer. |
| | | **431** Council of Ephesus: 'Nestorianism' condemned: Nestorius deposed and exiled: Pelagianism condemned. |
| | | **432** St Patrick begins the conversion of Ireland: bishopric of Armagh established. |
| | | **432–40** Sixtus III, Pope. |
| | | **438–85** Proclus teaching in Athens. |
| **440–57** Yazdagird II, Emperor of Persia. | **c. 440** After steady expansion, Toba empire dominates all N China. | **440–61** St Leo, Pope: doctrine of the supreme authority of the Roman Pontiff proclaimed by words and action. |
| | | **c. 440** Deir Anba Schenouda, Sohag, built. |

| WESTERN, NORTHERN & CENTRAL EUROPE | SPAIN, ITALY & EASTERN EUROPE | AFRICA & EGYPT |
|---|---|---|
| | | **442** Treaty between Genseric and the Empire. |
| **c. 446** Attila unites all the Huns under his rule.<br>**448** Mérovée recognized as chief of all the Franks.<br>**448–752** Merovingian dynasty in France.<br>**c. 449** Angles, Saxons and Jutes begin conquest of Britain. | | |
| **c. 450** Hengist and Horsa invited to Britain by Voltigern as mercenaries. Hengist ruler of Kent (−488). | **450–71** Aspar, a general of Alan descent, principal political influence in the Empire.<br>**450–7** Marcian, Eastern Roman Emperor (with Augusta Pulcheria to 453). | **c. 450** Philae raided by Beja and Nobatae. |
| **451** Aetius, with aid from Goths in Aquitania, beats off invasion of Attila the Hun into central France. The Huns under Attila reach Gaul: beaten at Châlons-sur-Marne by mixed force of Gauls and Romans. | | |
| | **452** Huns invade Italy. Rome re-occupied.<br>**453–66** Theodoric, King of the Visigoths<br>**454** Attila d. suddenly: chaos follows in Italy. Aetius murdered. | **453** Roman expedition against Beja and Nobatae: thirty year peace made. Rebellion in Alexandria. |
| **c. 455** The Alemanni take Alsace and parts of Germany. Battle of Aylesford: Hengist and Horsa defeat Voltigern: Horsa killed. | **455** Maximus, usurper, Western Roman Emperor. Rome plundered and devastated by Vandal Gaiseric.<br>**455–6** Avitus, Western Roman Emperor.<br>**456** Suevi defeated in Spain. | **455** Genseric takes Zingitana. Genseric prepares expedition against Rome. |
| **457–9** War between Majorian and Theodoric II.<br>**457–81** Childeric, King of the Franks. | **457–61** Majorian, Western Roman Emperor.<br>**457–74** Leo I, Eastern Roman Emperor.<br>**457–518** Leonine Dynasty. | |
| | | **460** Majorian's expedition to recover Africa fails. |
| **ante 461** War between Leo I and the Ostrogoths.<br>**461** Majorian killed: succ. Severus (−465).<br>**463** Burgundians occupy the Rhone valley.<br>**466** Euric kills Theodoric II: succ. him (−484).<br>**468** Euric defeats the Suevi. | **467–72** Anthemius, Western Roman Emperor. | **468** Byzantine fleet burnt by Vandals off Cape Bon. Treaty between Vandals and Visigoths. |

| THE NEAR EAST | THE FAR EAST | RELIGION & CULTURE |
|---|---|---|

**443–51** Yazdagird II campaigns on eastern Roman frontiers.

**444–51** Dioscorus, Patriarch of Alexandria.

**448** Eutyches condemned.

**449** The *Tome* of Pope Leo: judgement pronounced on the doctrine of the two natures of Christ. 'Robber Council' of Ephesus (Latrocinium): disorders caused by monks: Monophysitism accepted.

**c. 450** Dam of Marib collapses: shortly restored.

**c. 450** Liu-Sung dynasty expands in the S and in Annam. Toba campaign down the Yangtze R.: Liu Sung heavily defeated: tribute paid to Toba.

**c. 450–500** Hsieh-ho, Chinese artist.
**post 450** Mausoleum of Galla Placidia, Ravenna, built.

**451** Ecumenical Council of Chalcedon: Monophysitism condemned: the *Tome* of St. Leo upheld: Robber Council of Ephesus condemned: Coptic Church separates: twenty-eighth Canon accords supremacy to the See of Rome, placing Constantinople next, and before Alexandria and Antioch: repudiated by St Leo. Proterios imposed by government as Patriarch of Alexandria.
**c. 451** Nestorius d.
**454** Proterios assassinated by mob: henceforward two patriarchs, Coptic and Melkite.
**457–77** Timothy, Coptic Patriarch.

**455–70** Skanda Gupta: state weakened by Hun invasions.

**457–9** Hormuzd III, Emperor of Persia.

**459–83** Firuz, Emperor of Persia: frequent campaigns against the White Huns.
**c. 460** Gupta forces rally against the Huns.

**post 460** Numerous risings of princes against Liu-Sung dynasty: court occupied with drinking, licentiousness and frequent murders.

**c. 461** Gnyan-tsan, King of Tibet: first Buddhist objects reputed to have reached Tibet.

**463** Sinhalese clan wrests control of Ceylon from the Tamils.

**c. 460** Toba state, including Chinese, converted to Buddhism: a Buddhist monk, Tan-yao, made head of the 'state church', and given large endowments for temples and slaves.
**461** St Patrick d.
**461–8** Hilary, Pope.
**463** Monastery of Studion, Constantinople, founded.
**468–post 552** Magnus Aurelius Cassiodorus, author.

**468–83** St Simplicius, Pope.

469—482

WESTERN, NORTHERN
& CENTRAL EUROPE

SPAIN, ITALY
& EASTERN EUROPE

AFRICA & EGYPT

**469—76** Euric conquers Gaul.
**470** Fergus Mac Erc, prince of
Dalriada in N Antrim, founds
Kingdom of Dalriada in Scotland.
Ostrogoths take Dacia.
**470—90** Franks and Goths divide
central France and Provence between
them.
**471—3** War between Leo I and the
Ostrogoths.

**471** Aspar and members of his family
murdered in Constantinople by
imperial order.

**472** Olybrius, usurper, Western
Roman Emperor: besieges Rome
and d.
**473** Glycerius, usurper, Western
Roman Emperor.
**473—5** Julius Nepos, Western Roman
Emperor.
**474** Leo II, Eastern Roman Emperor.
**474—91** Zeno, an Isaurian, Emperor:
Isaurians preponderant influence at
court: Augusta Ariadne, Empress.
**474—6** War between Zeno and
Basiliscos.
**475** Julius Nepos replaced by his son
Romulus Augustulus (—476).
Visigothic sovereignty over Spain
recognized by Rome.
**476** Odovacar dethrones western
Emperor Romulus Augustulus: made
a Roman patrician by Theodosius II,
and given charge of Italy (—493).

**476** Masties, a Berber chief, proclaim
himself Roman Emperor. Vandal
kingdom formally recognized by
Emperor Zeno.
**477** Genseric, Vandal king, d.: succ.
Huneric (—484).

**?c. 477** Kingdom of Sussex founded.
**477—83** Renewed hostilities with
the Ostrogoths.

**480** Emperor Zeno invites settlement
of the Bulgars on the Danube and in
the Balkans in order to repel the
Goths.

**481** Odavacar conquers Dalmatia.
**481—511** Clovis, King of the Franks:
Gaul divided amongst six peoples:
Franks in Belgium; Alemanni
between the Vosges and the Rhine;
Burgundians in Rhone and Saône
valleys; Visigoths between the Loire
and the Pyrenees; Armoricans in
Brittany, Anjou and Maine; Romans
surviving in Marne and Oise valleys.
**482** Odovacar takes Noricum.

## THE NEAR EAST                THE FAR EAST                RELIGION & CULTURE

**470** Latest known demotic inscription: Coptic script, adapted from Greek script with seven additional characters, the norm in Egypt.
**470–543** St Caesarius of Arles.
**470** St Euphrosyne (a woman) d., having lived for forty years in a monastery for men.

**471–99** Toba Emperor Wen Ti: foreign languages banned: ministry for religious affairs created: Toba (Tibetan) state made entirely Chinese in culture.

**c. 475–909** At least ten cities built in Mexico.
**c. 475–545** Clotilde, wife of Clovis I.
**477** Peter, Coptic Patriarch. Catholics and Manichaeans persecuted in N Africa.

**477** Hsiao Tao-cheng has Liu-Sung Emperor murdered: a puppet installed, with himself as regent. Land equalization system first proposed in Toba Empire by Li An-shih.
**478–514** Jayavarman, ruler of Funan.
**479** Hsiao Tao-cheng has puppet emperor and all the imperial family murdered: proclaims himself first Emperor of the Southern Chi dynasty (–501): renewed fighting with the Toba.

**480** Hujr Akil al-Murar, first al-Kindah ruler in central Arabia.
**c. 480–5** Pura Gupta.
**c. 480–90** Gupta empire partly breaks up.
**481–3** Armenia rebels against Persia.

**c. 480–547** St Benedict, founder of Benedictine Order.

**482** Zeno issues the *Henoticon* in attempt to reconcile orthodox and Monophysites: rejected both in Rome and Alexandria.

| WESTERN, NORTHERN & CENTRAL EUROPE | SPAIN, ITALY & EASTERN EUROPE | AFRICA & EGYPT |
|---|---|---|

**484** Alaric II succ. Euric.

**484–96** Gunthamund, Vandal king.

**486** Clovis defeats Syagrius, King of the Romans, at Soissons: capital established at Paris: definitive end of Roman occupation.

**487** Theodoric revolts against Zeno: Italy conquered by Theodoric.
**488** Zeno grants Italy to Theodoric, making him King of Italy. Romans evacuate Noricum.
**489** Theodoric defeats Odovacar.

**c. 490** The Lombards reach Lower Austria.

**490–3** Theodoric besieges Odovacar in Ravenna.

**491** Anderida, near Pevensey, stormed by Saxons.

**491–518** Anastasius I (with Augusta Ariadne to 515).

**493** Clovis m. Clotilde.
**493–8** Slavs and Bulgars invade the Balkans.
**495** Cerdic, founder of the Kingdom of Wessex, arrives.

**493** Odovacar assassinated by Theodoric.
**493–8** Revolt of Isaurians in the imperial army put down by Anastasius.
**493–526** Theodoric, King of Italy: capital, Ravenna.

**?c. 495** Kingdom of Wessex founded.
**496** Clovis defeats the Alemanni near Strasbourg.

**496–523** Thrasamund, Vandal king: Berbers become independent in many towns: Cabaon, with Tripolitanian camel cavalry, defeats Thrasamund.

**498** Anastasius reforms currency.

**6th c.,** Avars reach lower Danube, pushing Slavs towards R. Dnieper. Slavs practising slash and burn agriculture.

**500** Clovis's first campaign against the Burgundians. Bavarians settle in Noricum. The Danes settle in Jutland.
**c. 500** First Scottish kingdoms established. Battle of Mount Badon: Bretons defeat invaders. The Huns ᴐplace the Ostrogoths in the Balkans.

**c. post 500** 'Silent trade' between Red Sea coast and African interior.

| THE NEAR EAST | THE FAR EAST | RELIGION & CULTURE |
|---|---|---|
| **484** Firoz, Emperor of Persia, killed by the Huns: succ. Vologeses (Balas) (−487). | **484** Jayavarman of Funan sends embassy to China with presents.<br><br>**485** Land equalization system put into operation in China (−c. 750), granting land on life tenure basis.<br>**post 485** Social classes in Toba empire fixed by law. | **483–92** St Felix (II) III, Pope.<br>**484** Pope Felix III excommunicates Patriarch Acacius of Constantinople on account of the *Henoticon:* first schism between East and West (−519).<br><br>**486** Monastery of St Sabas, near Jerusalem, begun. |
| **487–98** Kavadh (commonly Kobad), Emperor of Persia, first reign. | | **489** Christian school of Edessa destroyed: Nestorians move to Persia, setting up school at Nisibis: others reach India. |
| **c. 490** Maitrakas, possibly of Iranian origin, established dynasty at Valabhi (−770). | | **491** Council of Yagharshapat (now Echmiadzin): Armenian Church rejects Council of Chalcedon.<br>**491–518** Blachernae Palace, Constantinople, erected.<br>**492–6** St Gelasius, Pope.<br>**c. 494–565** Belisarius, general. |
| | **493/4** Toba capital moved to Loyang: Confucianism the official religion of the capital and the state.<br><br>**494** Southern Chi Emperor murdered: further fighting with the Toba and internal conflicts. | **496** Clovis baptized in Reims.<br>**496–8** Anastasius II, Pope. |
| **498–501** Kobad imprisoned: Jamasp usurps the Persian throne. | | **498–505** Lawrence, antipope.<br>**498–514** St Symmachus, Pope.<br>**fl. 499** Aryabhata, Indian astronomer, first to separate his discipline from mathematics.<br>**c. late 5th c.−post 558** Procopius, historian. |
| **6th c.** Apogee of Lakhmid dynasty of al-Hirah. Gurjara and kindred peoples enter India: various small kingdoms set up. | **mid 6th c.** 100,000 Koreans and Manchurian Chinese domiciled in Japan.<br>**6–7th c.** Turkish power N of Gobi desert in Orkhon basin: rule by Khans, with decimal military organization. | **6th c.** Chichén−Itza founded by the Itzás, and then abandoned.<br>Doncho, Korean artist. Monastery of Debra Libanos, Eritrea, founded.<br>**5th–6th c.** Arian Baptistery, Ravenna, built.<br>**c. 500** Pseudo-Dionysius, theologian. |
| **c. 500–10** Toramana, Hun King in N India. | | **c. 500** Faymiyun (Phemion), a Syrian, said to have introduced Monophysitism into Najran. |

500–519

WESTERN, NORTHERN
& CENTRAL EUROPE

SPAIN, ITALY
& EASTERN EUROPE

AFRICA & EGYPT

**501** Burgundians united by
Gondeband.

**c. 505** Theodoric defeats Byzantine
army. The Lombards replace the
Huns in Transylvania.
**507** Franks under Clovis defeat
Visigoths at Vouillé: Visigothic
Kingdom of Toulouse annexed. The
Salic Law promulgated. Byzantine
embassy to Clovis.
**508–10** Theodoric expels the
Franks from Provence.
**c. 509** Riparian Franks recognize
Clovis.

**511** Clovis d.: kingdom divided
among his four sons.

**512** *Trisagion* riots in Constantinople.
Anastasius builds the 'Long Wall'
from the Sea of Marmora to the
Black Sea.
**513–5** Vitalian rebels in Thrace.

**513** Theodoric defeats the Franks
and Burgundians.

**c. 514–43** Caleb (Ela Atsbeha),
King of Axum.

**516–23** Sigismond, Burgundian
ruler.

**518–27** Justin I, Eastern Roman
Emperor.
**518–610** Justinian Dynasty.

**519** Kingdom of Wessex founded by
Cerdic.

| THE NEAR EAST | THE FAR EAST | RELIGION & CULTURE |
|---|---|---|
| | | c. 500 Aztecs fully established in C and S Mexico. Maya cities inhabited in Yucatan peninsula. Chavin already reaching S American coast.<br>c. 500—post 562 Procopius, historian.<br>post 500 Kalidasa: *The Ring of Shakuntala*. The 'Nine Saints' translate the Scriptures into Geez, together with Syriac religious works. St Apollinare Nuovo, Ravenna, built. Debra Damo Monastery, Ethiopia, founded. Qalaat Monastery, Syria, founded. |
| 501—31 Kobad restored. | 502 Hsiao Yen, a member of the Southern Chi imperial family, makes himself Emperor: name of dynasty changed to Liang. Emperor takes name of Wu Ti (−549): famous for his love of literature and of Buddhism.<br>502—15 Almost continuous fighting between Toba and Liang dynasty.<br>502—57 Liang dynasty in S China. | |
| 503—5 Persia at war with Rome.<br>503—13 Successful Persian campaigns against the White Huns. | 503 Chinese Emperor recognizes Jayavarman, ruler of Funan, as 'Emperor of the Pacified South'. | 503—43 St Cesarius, Bp of Arles.<br>503 25 Dec., Clovis baptized. |
| 505—54 al-Mundhir III, Lakhmid ruler. | | ante 504—70 Gildas, writer.<br>505 Varahamihira, astronomer, b. |
| | 507 Toba badly defeated by Liang forces. | |
| c. 510—34 Mihirakula, son of Toramana, Hun king in N India: driven into Kashgir: impetus of Hun invasion lost: India now divided into many small kingdoms. | | 510 Practice of *sati* (suttee) first recorded. |
| | | 512—19 Severus, Monophysite Patriarch of Antioch. |
| | | 513 Council of Tyre: Severus of Antioch procures condemnation of the Council of Chalcedon.<br>514—23 St Hormisdas, Pope. |
| | 514 Jayavarman of Funan d.: succ., his son, Gunavarman: murdered by his brother Rudravarman, last independent King of Funan. | |
| | | 515 Chinese chronicle of *Leang Shu*. |
| 517 Caleb of Axum takes Yemen (−c. 570). | | |
| | | 518 Justin takes orthodox attitude, persecuting Monophysites. |
| | | 519 Severus of Antioch deposed. Schism between East and West terminated. |

| WESTERN, NORTHERN & CENTRAL EUROPE | SPAIN, ITALY & EASTERN EUROPE | AFRICA & EGYPT |
|---|---|---|
| | **520** Vitalian assassinated at command of Justin I. | |
| **523** Burgundians wiped out by the Franks and Theodoric. | **523** Riots in Constantinople put down. c. **523** Justinian m. Theodora. | |
| | | **523–30** Hilderic, Vandal king: Berber in control except on the coast. |
| **524** Godomar, brother of Sigismond, expels the Franks. | | c. **524** Cosmas Indicopleustes sails from near Suez to Ceylon *via* Adulis: visits Axum: trade route from Adulis to the interior. |
| **526–61** Clothair I, King of Orléans. | **526–34** Amalasuntha, ruler of Italy. | |
| | **527–65** Justinian I, Eastern Roman Emperor, (with Augusta Theodora to 548). **529** Justinian's *Code* promulgated. Tribonian, Quaestor of the Palace. | |
| | | **530** Hilderic deposed: succ. Gelimer (–534). Justinian sends mission to Ceylon *via* Adulis. **530±120–840±100** Gokomere culture in Mashonaland. |
| **531** Belisarius defeated at Callinicum. The Franks occupy Thuringia. | **531** Childebert defeats the Visigoths in Spain. | **531** Justinian requests Axum for an alliance against Persia. |
| **532–4** The Franks recover Burgundy. | **532** The *Nika* revolt in Constantinople: 30,000 to 40,000 killed by troops under Belisarius in the Hippodrome. Justinian concludes 'endless' peace with Persia. **533** Franks take Pamplona from the Visigoths: Saragossa unsuccessfully besieged. The *Digest* and the *Institutes* published. **533–48** Byzantium at war with the Vandals. | **533** Belisarius recovers all N Africa from the Vandals for Byzantium. |
| **534** The Slavs cross the Danube. **534–47** Theodebert, King of Austrasia. **534–61** Clothair I, King of Burgundy. | **534–65** Justinian's *Novellae*: additional imperial laws. | **534** Justinian re-organizes Roman Africa: Solomon, prefect: rebellion in Mauretania and Numidia. Military revolt in Africa led by Stotzas: put down by Belisarius. |
| | **535** Justinian reforms Byzantine administration and taxation. Belisarius occupies Sicily and Dalmatia. Amalasontha murdered by Theodahad. **535–40** Belisarius re-conquers Italy from the Goths. | |

| THE NEAR EAST | THE FAR EAST | RELIGION & CULTURE |
|---|---|---|

<table>
<tr><td>

**ante 523** Dhu-Nuwas, last Himyarite king, a Jew: many Jews resident in Yemen to 1948.
**523 Oct.,** Christians massacred by Jews in Najran: appeal made to Emperor Justin I: 70,000 men sent by Axum defeat Dhu-Nuwas.
**524—31** Byzantium at war with Persia.

**525** Axumites under Abraha again defeat Dhu-Nuwas: end of the Himyaritic kingdom: Axumites control Yemen until 575: Abraha, first viceroy: Cathedral of Sanaa built.

**529** Lakhmid al-Mundhir III defeated by Ghassanid al-Harith II: Emperor Justinian appoints al-Harith lord over all the Arabs of Syria.
**c. 529—69** al-Harith II b. Jabalah, ruler of Ghassan.
**530** Belisarius defeats the Persians at Dara.

**531—79** Chosroes I (Khusru Anusharvan), Emperor of Persia.

**532** Peace between Byzantium and Persia.

</td><td>

**post 530** Many risings in the Toba state.

**534—50** State of Yeh set up by eastern Chinese, with a puppet emperor.

</td><td>

**522—88** Agathias, historian.
**523** Mazdakites massacred in Persia.
**c. 523** Boethius: *de Consolatione Philosophiae.*
**523—6** St John I, Pope.

**525** Boethius murdered. Pope John I visits Constantinople.
**c. 525—622** Heroic age of Arabic literature.
**c. 525—615** Antarah (or Antar) b. Shaddad al-Absi, Arab poet and warrior.

**526—30** St Felix (III or) IV, Pope.
**526—46** Church of San Vitale built in Ravenna.
**527** Philosophical schools suppressed by Justinian.
**527—36** Little Sta Sophia built.
**529** Council of Orange condemns Pelagianism. Justinian recalls exiled Monophysites. Monastery of Monte Cassino founded by St Benedict.
**530** Dioscorus, antipope, Defensive walls of St Catherine's Monastery, Sinai, built.
**530—2** Boniface II, Pope.

**531** Mazdak put to death with 100,000 followers.
**c. 531** Muhalil d.: reputed first composer of Arabic *qasidah* (odes).
**532—7** St Sophia, Constantinople, built by Anthemius of Tralles.

**533—5** John II, Pope.

**c. 534** The *Rule* drawn up by St Benedict.
**534—9** St Apollinare in Classe built in Ravenna.

**535** Anthimus, Patriarch of Constantinople, a Monophysite.
**535—6** St Agapetus I, Pope.

</td></tr>
</table>

| WESTERN, NORTHERN & CENTRAL EUROPE | SPAIN, ITALY & EASTERN EUROPE | AFRICA & EGYPT |
|---|---|---|
| | **535–54** Byzantium at war with the Ostrogoths. | |
| **536–7** The Franks take Provence. | **536** Belisarius in Italy: Naples taken. Vitiges becomes King of the Goths. Belisarius takes Rome. | |
| **?c. 537** Arthur, King of the Britons, killed in battle at Camlan. | **537–8** The Goths besiege Rome. | |
| **538** The Huns invade Scythia and Mysia. | **538** Siege of Rome raised. | |
| | **539** Vitiges retakes Rome. The Franks invade Italy. | **539** Solomon campaigns successfully in Aurès: killed at Tebessa. |
| | **540** Ravenna, Ostrogothic capital, taken by Belisarius: ruler, Vitiges, taken prisoner to Constantinople. | **c. 540** Three kingdoms in Nubia: Nobatia, Alodia and Mukurra. |
| | **541** Theodora disgraces John of Cappadocia. **541–2** Clotaire and Childebert in Spain. **541–52** Totilas, King of the Goths in Italy. **542** Serious outbreak of plague in Egypt spreads to Syria, and thence to Constantinople and southern Europe. Belisarius disgraced. | |
| | **543** Totilas takes Naples. | **543** King of Nobatae converted to Monophysite Christianity: shortly moves capital to Faras. |
| **544–65** Diarmait, first Christian High King of Ireland. | **544** Totilas besieges Rome. | **544** Berber revolt in N Africa. |
| | **545** Pope Vigilius taken prisoner by the Goths. **546** Totilas takes Rome. | **546** Berbers take, and then lose, Carthage. **546–8** John Troglita campaigns against Berber rebels. |
| **547** The Slavs devastate Illyricum. **?c. 547** Kingdom of Bernicia (–670) founded by Ida (–559). **547–55** Theodebald, King of Austrasia. | **547** Belisarius recaptures Rome. | |
| | **548** Theodora d. of cancer. | |
| **549** Agala, King of the Visigoths. | | |
| **550** Avars form an empire. | **550** Byzantine naval force retakes numerous cities in southern Spain from the Visigoths. Totilas retakes Rome. | **c. 550** Yemeni Arabs settle in Ethiopia: Habashat chief tribe: country called Habashat (Abyssinia |
| | **551** Byzantine army under Narses lands in Italy. | |

| THE NEAR EAST | THE FAR EAST | RELIGION & CULTURE |
|---|---|---|
| | | **536** Anthimus deposed by the Pope.<br>**536–7** St Silverius, Pope.<br>**536–46** Church of the Holy Apostles built in Constantinople.<br>**537** Sancta Sophia dedicated. Monophysites persecuted.<br>**537–55** Vigilius, Pope.<br>**?c. 538–93** St Gregory of Tours, historian. |
| **539–62** War between Byzantium and Persia. | **539** Embassy from Funan to China. | |
| **540** Chosroes takes Antioch.<br><br>**540–5** Chosroes of Persia campaigns in Syria. | **c. 540** Bharvavarman, ruler of Chela, seizes throne of Funan. | **540** Bishoprics already in existence in Herat and Samarqand.<br>**c. 540** St Finnian makes Clonard a centre of learning.<br>**c. 540–80** Christian missions active in Nubia.<br>**540** Imru al-Qais d.: known as *amir* (prince) of Arab poets. |
| | **542** Ly Ben leads Vietnamese rebellion against China. | |
| **Between 542 and 570** Marib dam collapses: Banu Ghassan migrate to Hauran: Banu Lakhm migrate to Hirah area: many other tribes move N from Yemen.<br>**543** Marib dam again restored. | | **543** The 'Three Chapters': Theodore of Mopsuestia, Theodoret of Cyrus, and Ibas of Edessa anathematized by Justinian.<br>**c. 543–56** Church of St Germain-des-Prés founded in Paris. |
| **c. 544** War between Ghassan and al-Hirah: Lakhmid al-Mundhir III captures a son of al-Harith II of Ghassan. | | **c. 545–615** St Columban, missionary. |
| **546** Justinian purchases peace with Persia with an annuity: Byzantium retains Lazica. | **546** Tu-chueh, or Gok Turks, send embassy to N Chou, making an alliance. | |
| | **547** Hou Ching, powerful in the N as a military leader, tries to negotiate a formal alliance with the Liang: Northern Chi attempt a similar alliance.<br>**548** Hou Ching attacks Liang territory. | **c. 547** Cosmas Indicopleustes: *Christian Topography,* written in Alexandria. Gildas, British monk: *De excidio Britanniae.* San Vitale, Ravenna, consecrated.<br>**548–54** Pope Vigilius in Constantinople: condemns the 'Three Chapters'.<br>**549** Sant' Apollinare in Classe, Ravenna, consecrated. |
| **c. 550** Pulakesin I, Chalukya ruler.<br>**post 550–c. 850** Conflict in S India between Chalukya dynasty of Badami, Pallava dynasty of Kanchipuram, and Pandya dynasty of Madurai.<br>**551** Beirut entirely destroyed by an earthquake: 250,000 killed in the Levant. | **549** Hou Ching takes Liang capital and murders Wu Ti: instals puppet emperor for eighteen months, and then ascends throne.<br>**550** Puppet emperor at Yeh deposed: Kao Yang set up in his place as founding Emperor of the Northern Chi dynasty (–577). | **c. 550** Chess introduced into Persia from India. Jordanes, historian. Kingdom of Mukurra (Dongola) converted to Christianity. |

| WESTERN, NORTHERN & CENTRAL EUROPE | SPAIN, ITALY & EASTERN EUROPE | AFRICA & EGYPT |
|---|---|---|
| c. 552–60 Cynric, King of Wessex. | 552 Narses defeats the Goths. Totilas d. after defeat at Busta Gallorum, Umbria. Naples retaken. 552–5 Narses recovers Italy from the Goths. 553 Factional fights in the Hippodrome at Constantinople. | 553–4 Justinian reforms Egyptian administration. |
| | 554 Byzantine force sent by Justinian aids Athanagild to gain Visigothic throne: Byzantines retain Baetica and part of Carthaginensis. Italy, Dalmatia and Sicily reunited with the Empire. The Pragmatic Sanction: land taken by the Ostrogoths restored. King Athanagild of the Visigoths makes Toledo his capital. 555 Final capitulation of the Goths in Italy. | |
| 558 Following the deaths of his brothers, Clotaire, King of all Gaul (–561). 560–88 Aelle, King of Deira. 560–92 Ceawlin, King of Wessex. 560–616 Ethelbert, King of Kent. 561 Clotaire d.: kingdom again divided between his four sons. 561–752 Constant struggles for power between the descendants of Clotaire. 562 Avars attack Thuringia. | 558–9 Kotrigurs (Huns) invade Thrace, Macedonia and Greece: Constantinople besieged. 563 al-Harith II of Ghassan pays state visit to Constantinople. | |
| 565 ·Brude MacMaelcon, King of Picts, established near Inverness. 567 Charibert d.: kingdom divided among his sons. Gepid kingdom destroyed by the Avars and Lombards. c. 568 The Avars attack the Franks. 569–75 Lombards invade Gaul. 570–95 Childebert, King of the Franks. | 565–78 Justin II, Eastern Roman Emperor (with Augusta Sophia). 568–72 Lombards conquer N Italy: shortly reach S Italy. 568–86 Leovigild, Visigothic King of Spain: first Spanish ruler to issue coinage: Byzantine court usages followed. 569 Leovigild takes León and Zamora from the Suevi. 569–71 Byzantium at war with the Avars. | 565 Thomas, Prefect of Africa. Berber risings. fl. c. 570 Sef b. Dhi Yazan, reputed founder of Maghumi (Sefawa) dynasty of Bornu. |

| THE NEAR EAST | THE FAR EAST | RELIGION & CULTURE |
|---|---|---|
| | **552** Hou Ching driven out by Chinese princes and killed. | |
| | | **553** Fifth Ecumenical Council in Constantinople: Vigilius makes excuses for non-attendance: exiled with other bishops. |
| **554** al-Harith II defeats and slays Lakhmid al-Mundhir II at Qinnasrin: known as 'Day of Halimah'.<br>**554–69** Amr, known as Ibn al-Hind, Lakhmid ruler: liberal patron of poetry: convent founded at al-Hirah. | | |
| | **555** Juan-juan annihilated.<br>**555–87** Later Liang dynasty: capital Hankow: dependent on N Chou dynasty, with the result that most of S China was dependent upon it.<br><br>**557–80** Northern Chou dynasty founded by Yu-wen family, possibly of Turkish origin: Toba empire thus split between N Chi and N Chou.<br>**557–89** Ch'en dynasty in S China. | **555** Academy of medicine and philosophy founded at Jundi-Shapur by Chosroes of Persia.<br>**c. 555** Buddhist cave-temples created at Lung-men, near Loyang.<br>**556–60** Pelagius I, Pope. |
| | | **558** St Apollinare Nuovo dedicated in Ravenna. |
| | | **560 or 561–74** John III, Pope.<br>**c. 560–636** Isidore of Seville, encyclopaedist. |
| **561 or 562** Fifty year peace made between Byzantium and Persia. | | |
| | **563** Indecisive fighting between N Chou and N Chi. | **563** Monophysite Bp Jacob Baradaeus appointed prelate over Syrian Arabs: origin of Syrian Jacobite Church. Hasan b. Thabit, poet, b. at Medina.<br>**c. 563** St Columba settles in Iona: evangelization of Picts begun. |
| | | **565** Christianity reaches the Fezzan.<br>**569** Kingdom of Alodia converted to Christianity. |
| | **568** Embassy sent from Langkasuka to China. | |
| **570 or 571** Battle of the Elephant: Axumite army destroyed by smallpox: Persians occupy Yemen. | | **570 or 571** Prophet Muhammad b. |

571—589

WESTERN, NORTHERN
& CENTRAL EUROPE

SPAIN, ITALY
& EASTERN EUROPE

AFRICA & EGYPT

**572** Leovigild takes Córdoba from the Byzantines.

**573** War between Childeric and Sigebert. Suevi and nobility rebel against Leovigild. Rhydderch Hael defeats Votadini at Arthuret, near Glasgow.

**575** Sigebert murdered: Childebert II, King of Austrasia. (—596).

**578** The Bretons take Vannes.

**578—82** Tiberius II, Eastern Roman Emperor.

**579** Bretons invade region of Nantes and Rennes.
**579—82** Byzantines renew war against the Avars: Sirmium lost.
**580** The Slavs establish themselves in Thrace and Macedonia.

**580—5** Hermenigild, Governor of Baetica, revolts against his father, Leovigild: grounds afforded by Hermenigild's Catholic wife against Arian rule in Toledo.

**581—3** Leovigild defeats the Suevi and the Byzantines.

**582—602** Maurice, Eastern Roman Emperor, (with Augusta Constantina).

**582—602** Roman Africa re-organized as two provinces: Tripolitania transferred to Egypt.

**?c. 584** Kingdom of Mercia founded.
**?c. 584—93** Creoda, King of Mercia.

**584** Hermenigild surrenders to his father. Exarchates of Ravenna and Carthage founded. Exarch of Ravenna campaigns against the Lombards. Frank allies enter Italy.
**585** Hermenigild put to death: venerated as a martyr for the Catholic faith.

**585** Leovigild finally destroys the Suevi.
**586** Leovigild d.: succ. Reccared (--601).
**586—93** Ethelric, King of Bernicia and Deira.
**587** Gascons take Aquitaine. Slavs again invade Balkans.

**587** Gennadius, Exarch of Carthage.

| THE NEAR EAST | THE FAR EAST | RELIGION & CULTURE |
|---|---|---|

**571** N Chi gains some territory from N Chou; but loses some territory to S China.

**572** Justin II refuses to continue annuity to Persia: war ensues (−591).

**572** Persian Armenia rebels.

**572** Justin II persecutes Monophysites.

**c. 573** St Mungo, first Bp of Glasgow, installed.

**574** Daras taken by Persia. A year's truce secured by Byzantium by payment to Persia of 45,000 gold pieces.
**575** Chosroes defeated at Melitene: Maurice invades Persia. Saif ibn dhi-Yazan receives 800 reinforcements from Persia: Axumites finally evicted from Yemen: made a Persian satrapy.
**576** Byzantines defeated by Persians.

**574–8 or 9** Benedict I, Pope.

**c. 575** John Malalas: *Chronica*.

**576–7** N Chi defeated by N Chou.
**576–9** N Chou controls all N China.

**578** Byzantine and Persian armies devastate each other's territories. Persians seize Lakhmid kingdom.
**579** Byzantine raids across the Tigris.
**579–90** Hormuzd IV, Emperor of Persia.
**580** al-Mundhir of Ghassan sacks Lakhmid capital of al-Hirah: later taken a prisoner to Constantinople for alleged treachery.
**c. 580–602** al-Numan III, last Lakhmid ruler, only Christian king.
**581** Persians defeated at Constantia.

**578 or 9–90** Pelagius II, Pope.
**578–604** Damian Melkite Patriarch of Alexandra, a Monophysite.

**580** Council of Toledo concerning Arianism.

**581** Yang Chien declares himself Emperor of China: beginning of Sui dynasty.

**587** Reccared converted from Arianism to Catholicism: followed by majority of Visigoths. 12 Apr., First church on site of Toledo Cathedral dedicated.

**588** Byzantine army opposing Persia mutinies. Persians defeat Turkish invaders.
**589** Persians defeated invading Lazica.

**c. post 589** Numerous canals constructed by order of Emperor Wen Ti, to facilitate transport of grain: lighters of 500 and 800 tons capacity. Confucian examination for civil servants reformed.
**589–618** Sui dynasty controls all China: Wen Ti, first Sui Emperor: policy of financial austerity: fighting with the Turks and Koreans.

**589** Reccared summons third Council of Toledo: both Catholic and Arian bishops invited: Arian bishops accept Catholic faith.
**589–694** Eleven general councils of the Church held in Toledo: Abp of Toledo obtains prerogative of crowning the king.

590–608

**WESTERN, NORTHERN**
**& CENTRAL EUROPE**

**SPAIN, ITALY**
**& EASTERN EUROPE**

**AFRICA & EGYPT**

**591** Childebert II makes peace with Agilulf.
**591–7** Ceol, King of Wessex.
**591–602** War between the Slavs and the Avars.
**592–3** Mutiny of Roman troops in Europe.
**593** Agilulf takes Pérouse.
**c. 593–618** Ethelfrith, King of Bernicia and Deira.
**c. 593–606** Pybba, King of Mercia.
**595** Duke installed in Bavaria by Childeric.
**596** Avars attack Thuringia.
**596–617** Nectan MacDerili, King of Picts: first Pictish King to be converted to Christianity.
**597–611** Coelwulf, King of Wessex.
**597–616** King of Kent the chief in England.

**593** Rome besieged: defended by Gregory the Great.

**598–9** Priscus defeats the Avars.

**598–601** Truce between Lombards and Byzantines.

**c. 7th c.** Camels reach S Sahara. Dia Aliamen, ruler of Kukia. Frequent trade relations develop between N and W Africa.
**c. 7th or 8th c.** Zawila founded as a caravan station.

**7th c.** Bulgars, under Khan Asparuh, cross the Danube and settle in Moesia. Original nucleus of Slavs established along R. Dnieper.
**7th–8th c.** Witanagemots emerge in Kent, Mercia, Northumberland and Wessex: kings elected.

**c. 600** Bavarians occupy the Austrian Alps. Norwegians occupy the Shetland and Orkney Is.
**?c. 600** Votadini attack Catterick.
**post 600** Serbs and Croats settle in Illyricum.
**601** Reccared d.

**c. 600–900** Yoruba ancestors said to have left the Near East.
**c. 600–1000** Tuareg men adopt the veil.

**602** Revolt in Constantinople against Emperor Maurice. Padua taken by the Lombards.
**602–10** Phocas, Eastern Roman Emperor.
**603** Cremona and Mantua taken by the Lombards.

**603** Aidan, Scottish King, possesses a fleet: defeated by Angles at (?) Dawston.

**605** Conspiracy against Phocas put down with savagery.

**c. 606–26** Cearl, King of Mercia.

**607** New conspiracy against Phocas.

**608–9** Berbers sack Alexandria.

| THE NEAR EAST | THE FAR EAST | RELIGION & CULTURE |
|---|---|---|
| **590** Bahram Chubin revolts in Persia.<br>**590–628** Chosroes II (Khusru Parviz), Emperor of Persia.<br><br>**591** Bahram Chubin defeated and killed. | | **590** Irish monks in Gaul. St Columban sets up at Luxeuil. Lausanne made a bishopric.<br>**590–604** St Gregory (the Great), Pope.<br>**590–615** St Columban teaching in Lombardy and Burgundy. |
| | | **c. 596** Muhammad m. Khadijah. |
| | | **597** St Columba d. Benedictine monks from Rome begin mission in Kent under St Augustine of Canterbury. Conversion of King Ethelbert of Kent. Breach between Rome and Constantinople. |
| **7th c.** Many Persians, following Arab conquest, flee to India. | **598** Bharvavarman of Chenla and Funan d.: succ. his brother, Sitrasena.<br>**7th c.** Mons of the lower Menam found kingdom of Dvaravati: capital at Lavapura (Lopburi). Mon federation instituted. Cloves of the 'Spice Islands' first mentioned in a Greek report. | **7th c.** Khazars of the lower Don and Volga partly converted to Judaism. |
| **c. 600** Pulakesin I, Chalukya ruler of Vatapi.<br>**c. 600–25** Mahendra-varman, founder of Pallava dynasty: establishes Tamil culture. | | **c. 600** Amr b. Kulthum d.: celebrated Arab poet.<br><br>**c. 600–50** Han Kan, Chinese artist. |
| **602–11** Iyas b. Qabisa of the Tayyi, ruler of former Lakhmid kingdom as vassal of Persia, at al-Hirah. | | **602** Canterbury made an archbishopric: bishops consecrated for London and Rochester. |
| **603** Persians renew war against Byzantium. | | |
| **604** Byzantine army defeated at Edessa. | **604** 'Constitution of Seventeen Articles' (ethical precepts) promulgated by Japanese Prince Shotoku. | **604** St Paul's Cathedral, London, founded; 26 May, St Augustine of Canterbury d.<br>**604–6** Sabinian, Pope.<br>**c. 605** Hatim al-Tai d.: Beduin celebrated for his hospitality. |
| **605** Persians take Daras.<br>**605–9** Persia occupies eastern imperial provinces.<br>**c. 606–47** Harsha, reviver for a while of part of the Gupta empire.<br>**607** Persians take Harran, Edessa, and Aleppo: Cappadocia, Phrygia, Galatia and Bithynia ravaged.<br>**c. 608–42** Pulakesin II, Chalukya ruler of Vatapi. | | **607** Boniface III, Pope.<br><br>**608** The Kaaba rebuilt at Mecca.<br>**608–15** Boniface IV, Pope. |

| WESTERN, NORTHERN & CENTRAL EUROPE | SPAIN, ITALY & EASTERN EUROPE | AFRICA & EGYPT |
|---|---|---|

**609 or 610—21** Sisebut, King of the Visigoths.

**610—41** Heraclius, Eastern Roman Emperor.
**610—711** Heraclian Dynasty of Byzantium.

**611—43** Cynegils, King of Wessex.

**613—29** Clotaire II, sole King of the Franks.

**616** Assembly of Bonneuil.
**616—40** Eadbald, King of Kent.
**617** Slavs invade the Balkans.
**617—32** Edwin King of Bernicia and Deira.
**617—85** Northumbria leading monarchy in England.

**616** Constantinople besieged by Avars, Bulgarians, Persians and Slavs.
**617—19** Slavs ravage the Aegaean Is.

**616—17** Chosroes II besieges Alexandria.

**618 or 619** The Persians occupy Egypt: Alexandria taken (—629).

**619** Slavs and Avars besiege Thessalonica. Peace made between Byzantium and the Avars. Eleutherius, Exarch of Ravenna, attempts to usurp the empire.

**?c. 620** Normans invade Ireland.

**c. 620** Copper wire in use at Dambwa, Zambia.

**622** Pippin I, Mayor of the Palace in Austrasia.

**621** Svinthila, King of the Visigoths.

**623** Dagobert I, King of Austrasia.
**623—8** Samo, first Slav state, formed by Frankish merchant Samo.

| THE NEAR EAST | THE FAR EAST | RELIGION & CULTURE |
|---|---|---|

**09** The Persians reach Chalcedon.

c. **610** St Columban begins to convert the Alemanni. Muhammad begins to preach at Mecca.

**11** Persia attacks Syria: Antioch occupied.
. **611** Persian campaign against Hirah.
**11–33** Lakhmid domains ruled by Sassanid governors.
**12** Harsha's subjugation of upper India completed: solemnly enthroned: capital at Kanauj.

**612** All Jews in Spain ordered to be baptized.
c. **612** Monasteries of St Gall and Bobbio founded.

**14** Chosroes II takes Damascus: Jerusalem besieged and taken: the Holy Cross taken to Ctesiphon: 0,000 Christians killed.

**614** Two Seng-Chi (Zanj) slave women brought to the Chinese court by Javanese envoys.
**615** Sui badly defeated by the Turks.

**614** Council of Paris: clerics removed from lay jurisdiction.

**615** Meccan Muslims under Uthman b. Affan seek refuge in Axum.
**615–8** Deusdedit, Pope.
**616** Sisebut persecutes Jews.

**17** Chosroes II besieges and takes Chalcedon.

**617** Li Shih-min besieges the Sui capital, Changan, with an army supported by Turkish allies.

**618** Changan falls: Sui dynasty collapses: many independent governments formed. Li Yuan, father of Li Shih-Min, enthroned as the first Tang Emperor.
**618–906** Tang dynasty in China.

c. **618–26** Islam preached in Canton.

**619** Umar b. al-Khattab, future Caliph, converted to Islam.
**619–25** Boniface V, Pope.

**20** Harsha campaigns against Palakeshin II of the Deccan: defeated.
**2** Heraclius liberates Asia Minor from the Persians.

**621** Prince Shotoku d.

**622** Muhammad invited to settle at Yathrib (Medina): 16 July, traditional date of Muhammad's migration from Mecca: official year of beginning of Hijra Era (Muslim Calendar): 24 Sept., Muhammad arrives at Medina: theocratic state evolves.

**3** Heraclius campaigns in Armenia and Media.
**4** Ramadhan, Battle of Badr: 300 Muslims under Muhammad defeat more than 1000 Meccans.
Byzantines defeat three Persian armies.

**623** End of internal fighting: all China united under the Tang dynasty: equalization of land reformed to prevent formation of large estates.
c. **624** Turkish allies of the Tang attempt to take the capital, but withdraw for no apparent reason.
**624** General reform of Tang administration: technical departments set up, comparing favourably with eighteenth century Europe.

| WESTERN, NORTHERN & CENTRAL EUROPE | SPAIN, ITALY & EASTERN EUROPE | AFRICA & EGYPT |
|---|---|---|

**625** Edwin of Northumbria m. Ethelburga, Princess of Kent.

**c. 626–55** Penda, King of Mercia.

**627** Assembly of Clichy.

**626** Avars and Slavs abortively besiege Constantinople.

**628–39** Dagobert I, King of Franks: victorious over Saxons and Bretons: era of prosperity: capital at Soissons.

**629** Svinthila expels the Byzantines from Spain.

**629** Egypt recovered by Heraclius. Muslim exiles return to Mecca from Axum.

**c. 630** Kings of Gobir claim to have left Yemen for the Sudan.
**630–40** Arab pirates active in Red Sea.

**631** Cyrus (al-Muqauqis) acting Monothelite Patriarch of Alexandria also Ethnarch of Egypt.

**632** Edwin of Bernicia killed by English and Welsh coalition at battle of Hatfield Chase: succ. Oswald of Northumbria (–642): monks of Canterbury flee to Kent.
**632–3** Osric, King of Deira.
**633** Svinthila deposed: Sisenand elected: Visigothic monarchy made elective.

**c. 634–40** Slav rebellion in the Balkans. Thessalonica blockaded. St Oswald defeats the Britons.

**634** Arabs occupy Massawa.

## THE NEAR EAST

**625** Meccans under Abu Sufian defeat Muslims: Prophet Muhammad wounded. Byzantines defeat Persians in Cilicia.
**625—60** Narasimha-varman, Pallava ruler: ally of King of Ceylon.
**626** The Persians again reach Chalcedon.
**627** Meccans with Beduin and Ethiopian mercenaries besiege Medina: besiegers withdraw after a month: Muhammad campaigns against Jews for siding with Meccans: 600 Jews killed: other Jews in Medina expelled. Heraclius takes Tiflis: Persians defeated near Nineveh: Ctesiphon taken.
**628** Heraclius campaigns in Persia. Chosroes II d.: succ. Kavadh (Kobad) II Sheroe (—629): peace made between Persia and Byzantium. Peace made between Medina and Mecca: Muhammad leads pilgrimage of 1400 Muslims to Mecca.
**629** Shar-Baraz usurps Persia: murdered after two months: anarchy in Persia (—634). Jews expelled from Khaibar oasis by Muhammad. Sept., Byzantine army defeats a column sent by the Prophet at Mutah. Syria reconquered by Emperor Heraclius.

**630** Jan., Muhammad conquers Mecca: 365 idols expelled from the *haram* (sanctuary) of Mecca. Peace made between Byzantium and Persia.
**630—1** Muhammad stations garrison at Tabuk, in Ghassanid territory: treaties concluded with Christian and Jewish oases: Beduins and pilgrims from Hadhramaut, Oman and Yemen come to Medina to accept Islam and to do homage to Muhammad.
**631/2** Muhammad makes final pilgrimage to Mecca.

**632** 8 June, Muhammad d.: buried in the courtyard of his house, later the mosque of Medina.
**632—4** Abu Bakr, Caliph.
**632—61** Period in Islam of the four orthodox Caliphs.
**633** al-Hirah submits to army of Khalid b. al-Walid. Sergius, Patrician of Palestine, defeated at Wadi al-Arabah by Yazid b. Abi Sufian.

**634** 4 Feb., troops of Yazid retire: defeat remnant of Sergius's army at Dathin. Easter Day, Khalid b. al-Walid defeats Ghassanids at Marj Rahit; 30 July, battle of Ajnadain:

## THE FAR EAST

**c. 625** Militia system set up by the Tang, with average of 600,000 serving one month in five near the capital.

**626** Further Turkish attack on Chinese capital.
**627** Disturbances amongst the eastern Turks. Isanavarman, ruler of Chenla, finally incorporates all Funan into his state. Following a struggle with his brothers Li Shih-Min instals himself as Tang Emperor, with throne name Tai Tsung (—649).

**629—30** Chinese campaigns against eastern Turks: Turkish armies destroyed: the Khan taken prisoner: Chinese Emperor proclaimed as the 'Heavenly Khan'.
**c. 629—50** Srong-tsan Gampo, King of Tibet: Nepal occupied: Buddhism introduced into Tibet.
**c. 630** Gnam-ri Srong Btsan, King of Tibet d.: knowledge of arithmetic and medicine reaches Tibet from China: salt mining begun.

## RELIGION & CULTURE

**625** St Paulinus' mission at York.
**625—38** Honorius I, Pope.

**626** Abbey of St. Dénis, Paris, founded.

**627** Edwin, King of Bernicia, baptized by St Paulinus in York: many Northumbrians converted.

**628** Badhan, Persian satrap of Yemen, accepts Islam.

**629** Hiuen Tsang (or Yuan Chwang), Buddhist traveller in India (—645): leaves extensive description of Harsha's empire. Alleged date of foundation of first mosque in Canton.

**630** Heraclius restores the Holy Cross to Jerusalem. The Benedictine Rule popularized in Gaul.
**630—1** All Arabia submits to Islam.

**c. 632** Conversion of E Anglia begun.

**633** Mission to Northumbria led by St Aidan from Lindisfarne, or Holy Island. Fourth Council of Toledo: bishops made the second estate, with right to vote for elections to the crown: Reccared obtains right to appoint and dismiss bishops.
**634** Ecclesiastical provinces of Canterbury and York created.

| WESTERN, NORTHERN & CENTRAL EUROPE | SPAIN, ITALY & EASTERN EUROPE | AFRICA & EGYPT |
|---|---|---|

**635—56** Clovis II, King of Neustria and Burgundy.

**639—752** Period of 'les rois fainéants' in France: real power in the hands of mayors of the palace.

**639** 12 Dec., Amr ibn al-As, with Arab army of 4,000, enters Egypt at al-Arish.

**640—64** Eorcenberht, King of Kent.

**640** Arab fleet sent by Caliph Uma defeated by Ethiopia. Fortress of Babylon (Old Cairo) besieged by Amr: Cyrus (al-Muqauqis) surrenders himself to Amr. Jan., al-Farama (Pelusium) taken by Am July, Byzantine army routed by A at Ain Shams.

**641** Constantine III and Heracleonas, Eastern Roman Emperor.
**641—68** Constans II, Eastern Roman Emperor.

**641** 6 Apr., Babylon taken: 13 Ma Nikiu surrenders: 8 Nov., Alexandr surrenders to Amr: Byzantines allowed to embark: freedom of worship guaranteed: Abdallah b. Saad campaigns in Nubia: tribute paid.
**641—2** Mosque of Amr built at al-Fustat outside Fortress of Babylon al-Fustat made the capital of Egyp (—969): ancient canal linking R. Nile with Red Sea cleared.

**642** St Oswald defeated and killed by Penda of Mercia.

**642** Chindaswinth becomes King of the Visigoths (—653): Visigothic nobility massacred.

**642** Sept., Byzantine evacuation o Alexandria completed.

## THE NEAR EAST

## THE FAR EAST

## RELIGION & CULTURE

Khalid takes all Palestine; Busra falls to Khalid with little fighting. Basrah and al-Kufa founded. 26 Nov., Muslim army almost annihilated at Battle of the Bridge, over R. Euphrates, by Persian army.
**634—42** Yazdagird III, Emperor of Persia.
**634—44** Umar b. al-Khattab, Caliph.
**635** 23 Jan., al-Fihl taken by the Muslims. 25 Feb., Muslims rout Byzantines at Marj al-Suffar. March-Sept., Muslims besiege Damascus: Sept., following treachery, Muslims take Damascus from Byzantines.
**c. 635—6** Christians of Yemen deported by Caliph Umar to Iraq.
**635—6** Jews expelled from Khaibar; Christians expelled from al-Najran.
**636** 20 Aug., Muslims defeat Byzantines decisively in Yarmuk valley: Syria lost to the Byzantines.
**637** Jalula taken by Muslims. Muslims under Saad b. al-Waqqas take Ctesiphon: booty of nine billion dirhams taken. 31 May or 1 June, Saad b. Abi Waqqas defeats Rustam, administrator of Persia at al-Qadisiyah: Rustam killed: Sassanid army flees in disorder: all Iraq falls into Muslim hands.
**638** Jerusalem taken by the Muslims.

**635** Ishavavarman I, King of Cambodia d.: succ. Jayavarman I (*—post* 681).

**635** Stele erected at Sian Fu, relating history of Nestorian missions in China. Tripoli, Lebanon, already a walled city.

**636** St Isidore, Bp of Seville for nearly forty years d.: scholar, author of *Etymologiae*.

**ante 638** Burmese emerge as a separate entity. Sassanid ruler Yazdagird sends embassy to China requesting military aid against the Arabs.
**c. 639** Lhasa founded by Srong Tsan Gam-po, King of Tibet: Buddhism and art of writing introduced. Western Turks take Kao-chang (Khocho): affords pretext for Chinese counter-attack.
**639—48** Chinese conquests of Turkestan and Korea.
**640** Embassy to China from Ho-ling, either in C Java or Borneo. All Turkestan now under Chinese dominance.
**640—50** Tribal risings amongst the Turks: the Uighur Turks rise to dominance among them.

**638** Caliph Umar visits Jerusalem: avoids praying in the Church of the Holy Sepulchre so as not to make it a mosque. Heraclius issues the *Ecthesis* approving Monothelitism. Torcello Cathedral founded.

**640** Khuzistan occupied by the Muslims. Abortive Muslim attempt to take Armenia. Oct., Caesarea, after seven years of raids and sieges, surrenders to the Muslims.

**640** Severinus, Pope.
**640—2** John IV, Pope.
**c. 640—708** Jacob of Edessa, Bp and writer.

**641** Mosul taken: Muslims defeat main Persian army at Nihawand.

**641** Srong-tsan Gampo m. a Chinese and a Nepalese princess.

**642** Pulakesin II, Chalukya ruler, defeated and killed by Narasimha-varman, Pallava King of Kanchi.

| WESTERN, NORTHERN & CENTRAL EUROPE | SPAIN, ITALY & EASTERN EUROPE | AFRICA & EGYPT |
|---|---|---|
| **642–51** Oswine, King of Deira.<br>**642–70** Oswy, King of Bernicia. | | **642–3** Amr b. al-As attacks Libyan Pentapolis: Barqa occupied: Berber tribes submit voluntarily. Succ. Abdallah b. al-As takes Tripoli and Carthage: Fezzan raided. |
| **643** Donald Breac, Scottish king, killed by Britons at Strathcarron. Grimaud, son of Pepin, mayor of the palace in Austrasia.<br>**643–5** Cenwalh, King of Wessex, first reign. | | |
| **645–8** Penda, King of Mercia, also King of Wessex. | | **645** Amr b. al-As replaced by his brother Abdallah as Governor of Egypt. Alexandria revolts against Abdallah b. al-As.<br>**646** Alexandria recaptured by Abdallah. Gregory, governor of Africa, proclaims himself Roman emperor.<br>**647** Abdallah b. Saad defeats Byzantines under Gregory at Sbeitla Gregory killed.<br>**647–710** Arabs slowly conquer Berbers. |
| **648–72** Cenwalh, King of Wessex, restored. | | |
| | **649** Muawiyah, with Egyptian fleet, seizes Cyprus from the Byzantines. | |
| **c. 650** The Khazars settle on the Don steppes. | **650–2** Olympius, Exarch of Ravenna, usurps throne. | **c. 650** Villages on Batoka plateau, Zambia, import glass beads. |
| **651–55** Ethelwald, King of Deira. | | **651** Arab expedition against Nubia. |
| | **652** First Arab attack on Sicily: Syracuse pillaged. | **652** Abdallah b. al-As makes treaty between Egypt and Christian Kingdom of Nubia. Byzantine fleet repulsed off Alexandria. |
| **653** Aripert I becomes King of the Lombards. Recceswinth becomes King of the Visigoths.<br>**653–7** Talorcan, King of the Picts.<br>**654** Penda of Mercia takes East Anglia.<br><br>**c. 655–6** Peada, King of Mercia.<br>**655–70** Oswy, King of Bernicia, also King of Deira.<br>**656–70** Clotaire III, King of Neustria and Burgundy.<br>**656** Grimaud usurps the throne of Austrasia for his son, Childeric II (–675)<br>**656–9** Oswy, King of Bernicia, also King of Mercia. | **654** Rhodes pillaged by the Arabs. *Liber judiciorum*: Visigothic law code promulgated in Spain by Reccared.<br>**655** Joint Syro-Egyptian fleet under Muawiyah and Abdallah b. al-As defeat Byzantine fleet of 500 vessels off Lycian coast: known as 'Battle of the Masts'. | **656** Rebellion in Egypt: 500 malcontents deported to Medina. |

## THE NEAR EAST

**642–80** Vikamaditya, Chalukya ruler of Vatapi.

**643** Mukran, Baluchistan, taken by the Muslims. Harsha campaigns against Ganjam. Embassy from Tang Emperor to court of Harsha.

**644** 3 Nov., Caliph Umar assassinated.
**644–5** Arabs conquer Armenia.
**644–56** Uthman, Caliph.

**647** Embassy from Tang Emperor to Harsha finds him dead: throne seized by Arjuna: Chinese ambassador raises army in Nepal and Assam: Arjuna defeated and exiled to China.

**649/50** Istakhr (Persepolis) taken by the Muslims.

**650** Arwad taken by Egyptian fleet.

**651** Yazdagird of Persia flees: assassinated by a miller.
**652** Armenia finally taken by the Muslims. Rising in Persia. Arab force from Basrah invades Seistan: Kabul, Nishapur, Herat, and Merv, taken.

**656** 17 June, Caliph Uthman murdered. 24 June, Ali proclaimed Caliph at Medina (−661). 9 Dec., Caliph Ali defeats army of opposition led by Talhah and al-Zubayr outside Basrah.

## THE FAR EAST

**644–5** Embassy to China from Malayu, on Jambi R., Sumatra.
**645** Nakatomino-Kamatari (Fujiwara Kamatari) defeats Soga clan, and initiates administrative reforms in Japan in imitation of Tang China.

**647–8** Chinese army, with Tolos Turkish allies, establishes itself firmly in Turkestan.

**648** Chinese pilgrim Hsuan-tsang describes Sri Ksetra and Cambodian kingdom of Dvaravati.

**post 650** Tibetans expanding and gaining power.
**650–683** Kao Tsung, Tang Emperor: Chinese empire at its zenith: caravans from western and central Asia stream in with goods.

**655** Empress Wu, formerly a slave concubine, enthroned.

**656** Collapse of Sri Ksetra following change of Irawaddy delta: name probably still used for Pyu Kingdom.

## RELIGION & CULTURE

**642–9** Theodore I, Pope.

**643** Harsha holds Buddhist assemblies at Kanauj and Prayaga.

**644** Windmills first mentioned in Persia.

**c. 645** Adoptionist heresy spreads in the east.

**648** Constans II issues the *Typus* or 'Type of Faith'.

**649–55** Martin I, Pope.
**649** Pope Martin I condemns the *Typus* at the Lateran Synod.
**fl. c. 650** Paul of Aegina, physician and writer.

**651** Committee set up by Uthman to collate and revise the Koran.

**653** Penda of Mercia baptized by a monk from Lindisfarne. Pope Martin I exiled by Constans II.

**654** Abbey of Jumieges founded.
**654–7** Eugenius I, Pope.
**655** *Qasr* built against nomads at Deir al-Baramus: Church of al-Adra, Deir al-Suriani, begun: sanctuary of Benjamin, Deir Makarios, consecrated.

| WESTERN, NORTHERN & CENTRAL EUROPE | SPAIN, ITALY & EASTERN EUROPE | AFRICA & EGYPT |
|---|---|---|
| **657–80** Ebroin, Mayor of the Palace in Neustria.<br>**658** Mercia rebels against Oswy.<br>**658–792** Mercia the principal kingdom in Britain.<br>**659 75** Wulfhere, King of Mercia. | | **658–64** Amr b. al As, governor of Egypt: policy of conciliation: Trajan's canal re-opened: new capital built at al-Fustat. |
| **660** The Bulgars occupy Dobruja. | | **660–800** Governors of Ifriqiya (Africa) appointed by Caliphate. |
| | **663–8** Constans II makes Syracuse the temporary capital. | |
| **664–73** Egbert I, King of Kent. | | **665** Muawiya b. Hodaij leads expedition against Berbers.<br>**666** Uqba b. Nafi raids Fezzan. |
| | **668** Constans II murdered in a bath. Romuald of Beneventum takes Tarentum and Brindisi.<br>**668 or 669** Sicily pillaged by Egyptian Egyptian fleet.<br>**668–85** Constantine IV Pogonatos, Eastern Roman Emperor.<br>**669** Yazid (then heir apparent) and Fadhalah b. Ubaid al-Ansari briefly besiege Byzantium. | |
| **670–85** Ecgfrith, King of Northumberland: domain includes Bernicia and Deira.<br>**670–91** Thierry III, King of Neustria and Burgundy. | | **671** Qayrawan founded by Arabs under Uqbah b. Nafi: centre for operations against Berbers. |
| **672–4** Seaxburg, Queen of Wessex.<br>**672–93** Brude, son of Bile, ruler of all Picts.<br>**673** Childeric II, sole King.<br>**673–85** Hlothere, King of Kent. | **672** Arabs occupy Rhodes.<br><br>**673** Arab fleet appears off Constantinople. | |
| **674–6** Escwine, King of Wessex.<br><br>**675** Childeric II murdered: succ. Dagobert II (–679).<br>**c. 675** Aquitaine independent.<br>**675–704** Ethelred, King of Mercia.<br>**676–85** Centwine, King of Wessex. | **674** Arabs occupy Crete.<br>**674–80** 'Seven Years War' between the Byzantines and the Arabs. | |
| **678–81** Constantine IV makes peace with the Lombards.<br><br>**679** Constantine IV defeated by the Bulgars in Dobruja: Bulgars occupy Moesia and Dobruja as an independent kingdom. | **677** Abortive Arab siege of Constantinople raised: Arabs defeated.<br>**678** Truce between Muawiya and Byzantium. | **678** The Old Testament translated into Geez. |

| THE NEAR EAST | THE FAR EAST | RELIGION & CULTURE |
|---|---|---|
| **657** 26 July, abortive battle of Siffin between Caliph Ali and Muawiyah: submitted to arbitration.<br>**658 or 659** Muawiyah makes truce with Emperor Constans II in return for annual payment.<br>**659** Jan., arbitrators depose Caliph Ali: Ali defeats Kharijites on Nahrawan canal. | | **657—72** Vitalian, Pope.<br>**658** Muslim policy tolerant towards Copts in Egypt. |
| **661** 24 Jan., Caliph Ali murdered by a Kharijite at al-Kufah: succ. Muawiyah (—680), founder of Umayyad dynasty (—750): capital at Damascus. al-Hasan, son of Caliph Ali, proclaimed Caliph in Iraq: subsequently abdicates in favour of Muawiyah.<br>**663—71** Khurasan conquered by Arabs.<br>**c. 664—7** First Arab raids on India | **661** Chinese war against Korea.<br><br>**663** Tibet subdues Tukuhun Mongols: attack on China repelled: palace burnt at Lhasa. | **663 or 664** Synod of Whitby resolves differences between Celtic and English Christianity: Roman obedience confirmed. Irish monks expelled from Northumbria. |
| **c. 669** al-Hasan b. Caliph Ali d.: possibly poisoned. | | **669—90** Theodore of Tarsus, Abp of Canterbury. |
| | **670** Tibetans occupy Kashgaria.<br>**670—3** Embassy from Palembang to China: later known as Sri Vijaya.<br>**671—81** I-Ching, Chinese Buddhist pilgrim, makes first voyage to Malaysia and India.<br>**c. 671—92** I-tsing describes Kingdom of Sri Ksetra (Sumatra or Java): finds theology and philosophy flourishing: collects many MSS. | **670—5** Great Mosque of Qayrawan built.<br><br><br><br>**672—6** Adeodatus, Pope. |
| | | **673** Council of Hertford.<br>**c. 673—735** The Venerable Bede, first English historian. |
| **674** Bukhara raided by Muslim army. A son of Pulakesin II captures Kanchi. | **675** Peruz, last Sassanid ruler, takes refuge at Tang court. | **676—8** Donus, Pope. |
| | **678** Regional armies created in China. Tibetans inflict heavy defeat on China. | **678** St Wilfrid of York evangelizes the Frisians.<br>**678—81** Agatho, Pope. |

| WESTERN, NORTHERN & CENTRAL EUROPE | SPAIN, ITALY & EASTERN EUROPE | AFRICA & EGYPT |
|---|---|---|
| c. 680–6 Pepin I, mayor of the palace in Neustra: defeated by Ebroin of Neustria. | | |
| | | 681 Uqba b. Nafi, governor of Ifriqiyah, campaigns in Algeria: Kosaila, hero of Berber resistance. |
| c. 683 Ebroin murdered. | | 683 Kosaila kills Uqba b. Nafi in battle at Biskra: Kosaila holds Ifriqiyah with Qayrawan as capital. |
| 684–6 Eadric, King of Kent. | | |
| 685 Brude, son of Bile, defeats Ecgfrith, King of Northumbria, at Nechtansmere.<br>685–8 Caedwalla, King of Wessex.<br>685–704 Alfrith, King of Northumbria.<br>686–94 Interregnum and anarchy in Kent.<br>686–714 Pepin II, mayor of the palace in Neustria. | 685–95 Justinian II Rhinotmetos, Eastern Roman Emperor. | |
| 688–726 Ine, King of Wessex. | 688–9 Justinian II campaigns against the Bulgars. | |
| 691–5 Clovis III, King of Neustria and Burgundy. | 690 Justinian II defeats the Slavs in Macedonia. | c. 690 Beja penetrating Eritrea. Traditional date of foundation of Kingdoms of Gao and Bamba.<br>c. 691 Sulaiman and Said said to have settled in East Africa from Om |
| 694–725 Wihtred, King of Kent. | | 693–700 Hasan b. al-Numan al-Ghassani, Governor of Ifriqiyah, en Byzantine and Berber resistance in N Africa. |

| THE NEAR EAST | THE FAR EAST | RELIGION & CULTURE |
|---|---|---|
| **680—3** Yazid I b. Muawiyah Caliph.<br>**680** al-Husain, brother of al-Hasan b. Caliph Ali refuses to acknowledge Yazid, son and succ. of Caliph Muawiyah: defeated 10 Oct. 680 at Karbala and killed: origin of Shi'ite sects. | **680** Empress Wu removes Tang heir-apparent in favour of her son. | **680—1** Sixth Ecumenical Council held in Constantinople: Monothelitism condemned.<br>**681** Council of Toledo: canons against the Jews. |
| | **post 681** Cambodia ruled by a queen, Jayadevi. | **681—3** Leo II, Pope. |
| **683** Rebellion in Medina put down by force: Mecca subsequently sacked.<br>**683—4** Muawiyah II b. Yazid Caliph: ruled for three months only. | **683—6** Sri Vijaya, with capital at Palembang, conquers kingdoms of Bangka, Malayu and Taruma.<br>**683—1270** Sri Vijaya a great power in the E Indies.<br>**683** Empress Wu becomes regent of China for her infant son. | |
| **684—5** Marwan I b. al-Hakam Caliph. | **684** Manavamura, with help of S Indian Pallava ruler, makes himself ruler of Ceylon: dynasty lasts 200 years. | **684—5** Benedict II, Pope. |
| **685—705** Abd al-Malik b. Marwan Caliph. | **685—9** I-Ching resident in Palembang (Foche). | **685—6** John V, Pope.<br>**c. 685** Beginning of Kharijism. |
| | | **686—7** Conon, Pope. |
| | | **687—92** Pascal, antipope.<br>**687** Sept.-Oct., Theodore, antipope.<br>**687—91** The Dome of the Rock (Qubbat al-Sakhrah) erected in Jerusalem by Caliph Abd al-Malik.<br>**687—701** Sergius I, Pope. |
| **689** Oman conquered for the Caliphate by al-Hajjaj b. Yusuf.<br>**689—90** Caliph Abd al-Malik pays tribute to the 'tyrant of the Romans'. | | |
| | **690** Empress Wu declares herself Empress regnant, and first ruler of the Chou dynasty (—701): capital moved to Loyang. | |
| | | **691** Council of Constantinople, known as the Trullan or the *Quinisextum*: not accepted by Pope Sergius. |
| **692** Emperor Justinian II defeated by Arabs near Sebastopolis, Cilicia. Hijaz in revolt: 25 March, al-Hajjaj besieges Mecca for six and a half months: al-Hajjaj made governor of Arabia: Hijaz, Yemen and Yamamah pacified. | | |
| **694** Dec., al-Hajjaj puts down dissidents in Iraq: 100,000 said to have been killed. | | |

| WESTERN, NORTHERN & CENTRAL EUROPE | SPAIN, ITALY & EASTERN EUROPE | AFRICA & EGYPT |
|---|---|---|
| **695** Pepin II pushes the Frisians back beyond the Rhine.<br>**695–711** Childebert III, King of Neustria and Burgundy. | **695–8** Leontius, Eastern Roman Emperor. | **695** Hasan b. al-Numan takes Carthage: then defeated by Kahina, woman Berber patriot leader.<br>**c. 696** Alleged settlement of thirty-five eastern African towns by Syrians: possibly a commercial relationship. |
| | **698–705** Tiberius III, Eastern Roman Emperor. | **698** al-Hasan b. al-Numan ejects Byzantine fleet from Tunis.<br>**699** Jiddah attacked by Ethiopian pirates. |
| **8th c.** Varangian Norsemen penetrating present Russia, reaching as far as R. Volga, and thence to Constantinople and Baghdad for trade. | | **c. 8th c.** Sosso kingdom of Kaniaga founded. |
| **c. 700** Gottfried, Duke of the Alemanni, proclaims himself independent. Minting gold coinage and use of Latin ceases in Gaul. | | **?c. 700–1500** Madagascar gradually populated from Indonesia.<br>Ethiopians attack Jiddah and raid in Red Sea. |
| | | **702** Kahina finally defeated and d. |
| **704–5** Eardwulf I, King of Northumbria.<br>**704–9** Cenred, King of Mercia.<br>**705–16** Osred I, King of Northumbria. | **705–11** Justinian Rhinotmetos, Eastern Roman Emperor. | **c. 705** Musa b. Nusayr, governor of Africa: vigorous campaigns reach Atlantic and Sijilmasa: numerous conversions to Islam. |
| | | **706** Arabic made the official language of Egypt.<br>**707** Tangier taken by the Arabs. |
| **709–12** Pepin campaigns against the Alemanni.<br>**709–16** Ceolred, King of Mercia.<br>**c. 710** Nechtan, King of Picts. | **710** Tariq b. Ziyad leads reconnaissance party of 500 from N Africa to S Spain. Wittiza, Visigothic King of Spain d.; succ. Achila: promptly deposed: Roderic elected.<br>**711** Toledo succeeds in maintaining independence from Arabs for over 200 years. | **710** Count Julian, Visigothic governor of Ceuta, sides with Achila in succession dispute: comes to terms with Musa, Arab leader, in order to overthrow Roderic: Arab invasion of Spain follows. |

| THE NEAR EAST | THE FAR EAST | RELIGION & CULTURE |
|---|---|---|
| **695** First gold dinars and silver dirhams struck in Damascus. Postal service (*barid*) inaugurated in the Caliphate.<br>**696** Silver coinage struck in al-Kufah. | **695** Embassy from Sri Vijaya to China: policy of friendship maintained by later embassies. | **695—734** St Willibrord, or Boniface, sent from Winchester to convert the Frisians.<br><br>**c. 696—767** Abu Hanifa, theologian and jurisconsult.<br>**697** The Roman Calendar accepted in Ireland. |
| **698 or 699** Azraqi movement put down.<br>**699—700** Abd al-Rahman b. Muhammad b. al-Ashath leads Arab expedition against Zunbil, Turkish King of Kabul.<br>**8th c.** Arabs begin to settle on the W coast of India: Islam practised, but little proselytization. Arabs occupy Sind: abortive conflict with Chalukya. Pala dynasty in control of Bengal and Bihar: ruler, Gopala, elected: founder of Pala dynasty. | **699** Chinese break up Tibetan dominions.<br><br>**early 8th c.** Nara built as capital of Japan: many palaces and Buddhist temples constructed.<br>**8th c.** Khazar Turks pressed out of C Asia towards Russia. Nucleus of Tais established in Yunnan: slow beginning of Tai penetration. State of Nan-Chao founded in Yunnan peninsula. Mon kingdom of Haripunjaya (Lamphun) set up. Standing army, subsequently hereditary, organized in Japan against the Ainu.<br>**8th c. ff** Retired Chinese state officials granted pensions at 50% of final salary.<br>**post 700** Chinese annals record embassies from Indonesia. | **c. 699—754** St John of Damascus, theologian.<br><br>**8th c.** Japanese myths of origin first recorded in writing: *Kojiki* and *Nihon* chronicles.<br>**8th or 9th c.** Book-binding begins amongst Muslims in Egypt: derived from Copts.<br>**8th or 9th c.—13th c.** Toltec-Teotihuacán civilization in Mexico. |
| **703** Nepal and Tirhut become independent of Tibet.<br>**704** Qutaybah appointed Muslim governor of Khurasan. | | **c. 700** Lindisfarne *Gospels* copied and illustrated.<br>**700—30** *Beowulf,* epic.<br>**c. 700—50** Wu Tao-Tzu, Chinese artist.<br>**c. 700—54** St John of Damascus.<br>**701—5** John VI, Pope.<br>**701—62** Li Tai-po, poet. |
| | **705—12** Empress Wei, Empress regnant of China. | **705** Cathedral of Damascus reconstructed as the Great Mosque. Diocese of Sherborne established.<br>**705—7** John VII, Pope. |
| **705** Qutaybah takes Tukharistan, with capital Balkh.<br>**705—15** al-Walid I b. Abd al-Malik Caliph.<br>**706—9** Qutaybah takes Sogdiana (Sughd), with capital Bukhara.<br>**707** Arabs take Tyana, Cappadocia. | **c. post 706** Cambodia divided into two parts: general anarchy. | **c. 705** al-Aqsa Mosque, Jerusalem, begun. |
| | **708** First copper coinage struck in Japan. | **708** Sisinnius, Pope.<br>**708—15** Constantine, Pope.<br>**709** Last bilingual Greco-Arabic papyrus. Abbey of Mont St Michel founded. |
| **710** Arab army under Muhammad b. al-Qasim takes Mukran and Baluchistan.<br>**710—12** Qutaybah takes Samarqand and Khwarizm (Khiva).<br>**711—12** Muhammad b. al-Qasim takes Sind, including Daybul and Hyderabad. | | **711** Pope Constantine I visits Constantinople: last papal visit before Paul VI. |

| WESTERN, NORTHERN & CENTRAL EUROPE | SPAIN, ITALY & EASTERN EUROPE | AFRICA & EGYPT |
|---|---|---|

**SPAIN, ITALY & EASTERN EUROPE**

**711** Tariq b. Ziyad, as lieutenant of Musa b. Nusayr, leads Arab-Berber force of 7,000 into Spain *via* Gibraltar (Jabal al-Tariq): 19 July, Roderic, King of Spain, defeated at Barbate R.: southern Spain rapidly over-run: Gothic royalty sent as prisoners to Damascus.
**711–13** Philippikus Bardanes, Eastern Roman Emperor.
**711–17** Period of anarchy in Byzantium.
**712 June, Musa, Governor of Ifriqiya, follows Tariq to Spain with 10,000** Arabs: takes towns and strongholds avoided by Tariq.
**712** June–**713** June, Seville besieged by Musa.
**712** June–**713** 1 June, Merida besieged.
**713 Musa imprisons Tariq for alleged disobedience: northern Spain taken: Abd al-Aziz b. Musa left in charge.**

**713–16** Anastasius II, Eastern Roman Emperor.
**713–44** Liutprand, King of the Lombards.

**WESTERN, NORTHERN & CENTRAL EUROPE**

**711–15** Dagobert III, King of Neustria and Burgundy.

**714–41** Charles Martel, mayor of the palace.
**715–20** Chilperic II, King of Neustria, appointed by the Neustrians.

**AFRICA & EGYPT**

**715** Christian officials replaced by Muslims in Egypt.

**716–18** Cenred, King of Northumbria.
**716–19** Charles Martel subjects Neustria.
**716–57** Ethelbald, King of Mercia.
**717–20** Clotaire IV, King of Neustria and Burgundy, appointed by Charles Martel.
**720–37** Thierry IV, King of Neustria and Burgundy.

**716** Aug.–**717** Sept., Arabs besiege Constantinople.
**716–17** Theodosius III, Eastern Roman Emperor.

**717** Theodosius III deposed by Leo III, the Isaurian.
**717–18** Rhodes occupied by the Arabs. Muslim army and fleet besiege Constantinople: repulsed by Leo III with severe losses.
**717 or 718** al-Hurr b. Abd al-Rahman al-Thaqafi, first Arab ruler of Spain to cross the Pyrenees: raids until 720.
**717–820** The Isaurian dynasty in Byzantium.
**718** Battle of Covadonga: Pelayo of Asturia checks Muslim advance: regarded by Spanish historians as beginning of the *reconquista*.

**718–29** Osric, King of Northumbria.

**719–38** Charles Martel campaigns against the Saxons.
**720** Charles Martel defeats the Aquitanians.

**720** The ex-emperor Anastasius II executed. al-Samh b. Malik al-Khawlani, Governor of Spain: seizes Septimania and Narbonne.

| THE NEAR EAST | THE FAR EAST | RELIGION & CULTURE |
|---|---|---|

712 Toledo Cathedral turned into a mosque.
712–70 Tu Fu, poet.

712 Arabs conquer Sind with little difficulty: further expansion prevented by Pratiharas and Rashtrakutas. Hajjaj b. Yusuf d.

713 Muhammad b. al-Qasim takes Multan and S Punjab.
713–15 Qutaybah takes Farghanah and other Jaxartes provinces.

713–55 Hsuang Tsung, Emperor of China: 'second blossoming' of Tang culture: capital returned to Chang-an.

714 Kutayba d.

715–17 Sulaiman b. Abd al-Malik, Caliph.
715 Feb., Musa enters Damascus with 400 Visigothic princes, prisoners, slaves and booty from Spain: Musa despoiled of all his property and disgraced by Caliph Sulaiman: ends life as a beggar.

715–31 Gregory II, Pope.
c. 715–95 Malik b. Anas, founder of Malikite school of jurisprudence.

716 St Boniface (Willibrord) sent to evangelize the Frisians, Nilometer built at Cairo.

717 Syro-Egyptian fleet wrecked by storm off the Syrian coast.
717–20 Umar II b. Abd al-Aziz, Caliph.

717 Tibetan alliance with Arabs against China.

c. 717 A mosque built at Constantinople by Maslamah.
717 Benedictine monastery already in existence at Montserrat.

718–19 Caliph Umar II forbids sale of *Kharaj* (Christian or Jewish tax-paying lands) to Muslims.

719 St Boniface sent to evangelize Thuringia and Hesse.
720 Utrecht Cathedral founded.
720–59 St Gall Abbey Church begun.
c. 720–50 fl. Wu Tao-tsu, painter.
720–99 Paul the Deacon, author of *Historia Langobardorum*.

720 King of Kashmir invested by China.
720–4 Yazid II b. Abd al-Malik, Caliph.

| WESTERN, NORTHERN & CENTRAL EUROPE | SPAIN, ITALY & EASTERN EUROPE | AFRICA & EGYPT |
|---|---|---|
| **721** al-Samh checked at Toulouse by Eudes, Duke of Aquitaine: al-Samh d. | **721** Abd al-Rahman b. Abdallah al-Ghafiqi, Governor of Spain. | |
| | | **722** Caliph Yazid orders destruction of Christian images and pagan statues. |
| **725—48** Eadberht, King of Kent. | | **725** Copts revolt in Egypt. |
| **726—40** Ethelheard, King of Wessex. | | |
| | **727** Rebellion in Greece and the Cyclades against iconoclasm. | |
| **728** Charles Martel subjects Bavaria. **729—37** Ceolwulf, King of Northumbria. **730** Charles Martel finally subjects the Alemanni. | | **c. 730** Alleged Arab settlement in Pemba. |
| **732** Abd al-Rahman b. Abdallah al-Ghafiqi defeats Eudes of Aquitaine: storms Bordeaux: meets Charles Martel between Tours and Poitiers: Oct., Abd al-Rahman defeated and killed: Arabs withdraw to Narbonne. **733—4** Charles Martel conquers the Frisians. **734** Arabs temporarily seize Avignon. **734—9** Rebellion in Burgundy. | **732—55** Twenty-three Arab governors succeed each other in Spain: period of anarchy. | **732—3** Fleet re-organized at Tunis. **734—42** Berber rebellion against the Arabs. **c. 734—50** Habib b. Abi Ubaida's expedition to the Sudan: fails to locate source of gold. |
| **735** Charles Martel attempts to conquer Aquitaine. | | |
| **737** Arabs defeated by Charles Martel near Narbonne. **737—42** Interregnum in Neustria and Burgundy. **737—58** Eadberht, King of Northumbria. | | **737** Crusade of Ethiopians and Nubians to free the Coptic Patriarch. |
| | **739** Liutprand, King of the Lombards, besieges Rome: Charles Martel declines to assist the Pope. | **739—40** Maisara leads Berber revolt: captures Tangier: proclaims himself Caliph: beginning of Kharijite movement in N Africa. |

| THE NEAR EAST | THE FAR EAST | RELIGION & CULTURE |
|---|---|---|
| | | 721—59 Wang Wei, landscape painter and poet. |
| | 722 Vietnam in revolt against China. | 722 St Boniface consecrated Bp. |
| | | 723 St Boniface at the court of Charles Martel. |
| 724 Su-Lu, Khakan of the Turgesh, defeats Arabs under Muslim b. Said al-Kilabi near Ferghana: known as battle of the 'Day of Thirst'. | | 724 Pirminus evangelizes the Alemanni: Reichenau monastery founded. John, Bp of Seville, translates Bible into Arabic for Arabicized Christians and Moors. |
| 724—43 Hisham b. Abd al-Malik, Caliph. | | Between 724 and 743 al-Jad b. Dirham put to death for teaching that the Koran was created; Ghaylan al-Dimashqi executed for teaching the doctrine of free will. |
| 725 Pratihara dynasty established by Nagabhata I in Ujjain. | | 725 The Venerable Bede: *De temporum ratione*. c. 725 Mutazilite heresy appears in Islam. |
| 726 Arab offensive in Asia Minor. The *Ecloga* published, codifying civil, and some criminal, law. | | 726 Leo III issues first iconoclast edicts. 726—80 First period of Iconoclasm. |
| | | 727 Iconoclasm condemned by Rome. post 727 *Gesta Regum Francorum* composed. |
| 730 or 731 Junayd b. Abd al-Rahman defeats Khakan of the Turgesh. | 730 Peace made between China and Tibet. | 730 Germanus, Patriarch of Constantinople, deposed by Leo III. General edict of iconoclasm. |
| 731 Yasovarman, King of Kanauj, sends embassy to China. | | 731—41 Gregory III, Pope. 731 Pope Gregory III condemns iconoclasm. |
| 731 or 732 Junayd b. Abd al-Rahman relieves Turkish siege of Samarqand. | | |
| | c. 732—c.?822 Sanjaya dynasty ruling in Java as vassals of the Sailendra dynasty. | c. 732 The Venerable Bede: *Ecclesiastical History of the English Nation.* 732 al-Zaytuna Mosque, Tunis, built. |
| 733 King of Kashmir again invested by China. | | |
| 734 Junayd b. Abd al-Rahman d.: Harith b. Suraj revolts and occupies Balkh: defeated in attack on Merv. | | |
| | | 735 The Venerable Bede d. York made an Archbishopric: Egbert, first abp (—766). Mayence Cathedral founded. 735—804 Alcuin, theologian and educationist. |
| 736 The Tibetans conquer Kashmir. Dhillika (first city of Delhi) founded by the Tomaras. Arabs recover Balkh: Su-Lu assassinated. | 736—52 Li Lin-fu, a distant relative of the emperor, virtual dictator of China. | |
| | | 737 Buddhist church organized in Japan. 738 St Boniface sent to organize the church in Germany. |
| 738—40 Nasr b. Sayyar appointed by Caliph Hisham Governor of Transoxiana: has to reconquer most of the territory gained by al-Qutaybah. | | |
| 739 Leo III defeats the Arabs at Akroinion. | | |

| WESTERN, NORTHERN & CENTRAL EUROPE | SPAIN, ITALY & EASTERN EUROPE | AFRICA & EGYPT |
|---|---|---|
| **740** —56 Cuthred, King of Wessex. | | **c. 740** Zaidites said to have settled on the E African coast. |
| **741** Charles Martel d.<br>**741**—52 Pépin le Bref and Carloman, mayors of the palace: successful campaign against the Franks in E and N: Bavarians, Germans and Saxons forced to submit.<br>**742**—52 Childeric III, nominal King of the Franks. | **741** Artavasdes revolts at Constantinople.<br>**741**—75 Constantine V Kopronymos, Eastern Roman Emperor.<br><br>**742** Constantine V regains Constantinople from Artavasdes. Artavasdes d. Liutprand of Lombardy at war with Beneventum and Spoleto. Office of Doge instituted at Venice. | **741** Caliph Hisham sends army of 27,000 to quell Berber revolt: about one-third cross over and settle in Spain.<br><br>**742** Kharijites defeated at El Qarn and El Asnam. Sijilmasa founded by the Midrarids: centre of Tuareg trade in gold and salt. |
| **743** Arabs pillage Lyons. | | |
| | **744**—9 Ratchis, King of the Lombards. | **744** Kharijites take Qayrawan and Tripoli: two armies from Egypt defeated. |
| | | **745** Nubians invade Egypt: Cairo temporarily occupied. |
| | **746**—7 Serious outbreak of plague in Italy and SE Europe. | |
| **747** Carloman abdicates: Pépin le Bref sole mayor of the palace.<br><br>**748**—62 Ethelberht, King of Kent. | | **c. 747**—54 Qanbalu alleged to have been seized by Muslims: Zanj inhabitants enslaved. |
| **750** Angles occupy Kyle. | **749** The Lombards again besiege Rome.<br>**749**—56 Astulf, King of the Lombards.<br>**750** Saragossa becomes virtually independent of Córdoba. | **c.745**—75 Nile to Red Sea canal abandoned.<br>**?c. 750** First building at Zimbabwe.<br>**750** Jan., Caliph Marwan II flees to Egypt following defeat by Abbasids: Abbasids seize Egypt. |
| | **751** The Lombards occupy Ravenna. | |
| **752** Childeric dep. by Pépin le Bref with papal dispensation: Pépin le Bref proclaimed king at Soissons: crowned at Mayence: Carolingian dynasty in France (−987). Ethelbald of Mercia defeated by Cuthbert of Wessex at Burford.<br>**752**—9 Pépin conquers Septimania.<br>**752**—61 Angus MacFergus, King of Scots. | **752** Astulf attacks Rome. | |
| **754** Pépin again crowned at Reims by Pope Stephen II. | **754** Pépin le Bref campaigns against Lombards in defence of the Pope. First treaty of Pavia. | |

| THE NEAR EAST | THE FAR EAST | RELIGION & CULTURE |
|---|---|---|

**740** Yasovarman of Kanauj defeated and killed by Lalitaditya, King of Kashmir.

**741—52** Zacharias, Pope.

**742** Carloman requests St Boniface to reform the Frankish clergy.

**743—4** al-Walid II b. Yazid II, Caliph.
**744** Shi'ite rebellion in Persia. Yazid III b. al-Walid I, Caliph. Ibrahim b. al-Walid I, Caliph.
**744—50** Marwan II b. Muhammad, Caliph.

**743—89** Khri Srong Ide Tsan, King of Tibet, social reformer.

**743** Austrasian synod at Estinnes.

**744** Neustrian synod at Soissons. Abbey of Fulda founded by St Boniface.
Earthquake destroys Hisham Palace at Jericho.
**c. 744** The Koran translated into Berber.

**746** Constantine V invades Syria.
**746—53** Kirtivarman II, Chalukya ruler of Vatapi.
**747** Constantine V recovers Cyprus. Abbasid rising in Khorasan led by Abn Muslim.
**c. 750** Several embassies exchanged between Baghdad and China. Paper introduced into Samarqand from China.

**747—96** Liu Tsung-yuan, essayist.

**748—c. 828** Abu al-Atahiyah, potter and tragic poet.

**749—50** The Chinese expel the Tibetans from the Pamir Mrs.

**c. 750** Gopala elected King of Bengal: founder of the 'Pala' dynasty. Several embassies exchanged between Baghdad and China. Paper introduced into Samarqand from China.
**750—4** Abu al-Abbas al-Saffah, first Abbasid Caliph.
**750—1258** Abbasid Caliphate of Baghdad.
**751** Constantine V takes Theodosiopolis and Melitene. Arabs occupy Tashkent. Chinese army campaigns in Ferghana: defeated by Ziyad at Samarqand.

**post 750** Military governorates in Chinese Empire become hereditary: central government greatly weakened.
**750—? 832** Sailendra dynasty ruling in C Java.

**fl. 750** Cynewulf, Northumbrian poet.
**c. 750—850** Buddhist shrine erected at Barabudur, C Java.

**751** Chinese defeated by Arabs and Turks at Athlash.

**fl. 752** Bhanu, ruler of Sailendra dynasty of C Java.

**752** 23-25 March, St Stephen II, Pope.
**752—7** Stephen III, Pope.

**753—60** Dantidurga, first Rashtrakuta ruler.
**754—75** al-Mansur, Abbasid Caliph.
**754** Abdallah, uncle of Caliph al-Mansur, disputes the succession: defeated at Nisibis. Abu Muslim, Governor of Khorasan, murdered.

**753—4** Iconoclastic Council of Hieria.

**754** St Boniface martyred.

| WESTERN, NORTHERN & CENTRAL EUROPE | SPAIN, ITALY & EASTERN EUROPE | AFRICA & EGYPT |
|---|---|---|
| | **755** Byzantium at war with Bulgaria. | **755** Abd al-Rahman b. Muawiyah takes refuge in Ceuta: gathers Umayyad followers in defiance of Abbasid Caliphate. |
| **756** Angles, with allied Picts, defeat Britons at Dumbarton. <br> **756–7** Sigeberht, King of Wessex. | **756** Astulf again attacks Rome: Pépin le Bref again defends the Pope: second treaty of Pavia. 14 May, Abd al-Rahman I defeats Yusuf, Governor of Spain on R. Guadalquivir: captures Córdoba. <br> **756–64** Abd al-Rahman I steadily conquers all Spain. <br> **756–74** Didier, King of the Lombards. <br> **756–75** Constantine V leads six expeditions against the Bulgars. <br> **756–88** Abd al-Rahman I, Amir of Córdoba. <br> **756–961** Umayyad Amirs of Córdoba. | |
| **757** Beornred, King of Mercia. <br> **757–86** Cynewulf, King of Wessex. <br> **757–96** Offa the Great, King of Mercia: first to call himself 'King of all England': originator of silver penny coinage. <br> **758** Oswulf, King of Northumbria. | | **757** Tafilalet founded. <br> **757–923** Dynasty of Imams of Nefusa. |
| **759** Arabs withdraw from Narbonne. <br> **759–65** Ethelwald Moll, King of Northumbria. <br> **760–8** Pépin subjects Aquitaine. | | **760** Ismail b. Jafar d.: recognized by Ismaili Khoja sect as seventh Imam, and ancestor of Agha Khan. <br> **761** Ibn al-Ashatti, governor of Egypt, retakes Qayrawan from the Kharijites. <br> **761–908** Dynasty of Rustamid Imams of Tahert. |
| **762–98** Kent, subject to Mercia, divided between several kings. | | |
| **765–74** Alhred, King of Northumbria. | **765** Seven year peace between Byzantium and the Bulgars. | |
| | | **c. 766** Alleged expedition by Caliph to eastern African coastal towns: possibly a trade mission. <br> **767** Cyrenaica annexed to Egypt. <br> **767–72** Copts again in revolt. |

| THE NEAR EAST | THE FAR EAST | RELIGION & CULTURE |
|---|---|---|

**755** Sunbad (Sinbadh), a Magian rebel in Khurasan, put down.

**756** An Lu-shan rebels and proclaims himself Emperor of China: capital at Chang-an: then abdicates.
**756—62** Su Tsung, Chinese Emperor: flees to Shensi.

**757** Dantidurga overthrows the last Chalukya ruler.

**757** An Lu-shan defeated by Uighur Turks near Loyang: Tang government restored.

**757** Ibn al-Muqaffa, author of apothegms, executed.
**757—67** St Paul I, Pope.

**758** Rawandiyah, Persian sect identifying the Caliph with God, put down.
**c. 758—91** Sibawahi, philologist.
**759—812** Theodore of Studium, theologian and epigrammatist.

**760—75** Krishna I, Rastrakuta ruler.

**c. 760—80** Panangkaran, Sanjaya ruler.

**761** Caliph al-Mansur appoints al-Ala b. Mughith as Governor of Spain: body returned to Baghdad decapitated.

**762** Foundation stone of Baghdad laid by Caliph al-Mansur: constructed in four years by c. 100,000 architects, craftsmen and labourers. 6 Dec., Muhammad al-Nafs al-Zakiyah, Shi'a rebel, executed at Medina.
**763** 4 Feb., Ibrahim, Shi'a rebel, executed at al-Kufah.

**762** Tengri, Khan of the Uighur Turks, attempts to make himself Chinese emperor.

**764** Beginning of persecution by the iconoclasts: St Stephen the Younger martyred.
**765** Jafar al-Sadiq, sixth Imam, d.: Shias henceforward divided.
**c. 765** Jundi-Shapur, Khuzistan, Persia, famous for its hospital and medical knowledge.
**766—82** Alcuin and Ethelbert make York a centre of learning.

**765** Khalid b. Barmak (first Barmecide) puts down rebellion in Tabiristan: appointed governor. Frank embassy received in Baghdad.

**767—8** Rebellion of Ustadhsis suppressed.

**767** Vietnam invaded by 'Javanese': driven out by Chinese governor.

**767** Abu Hanifah al-Numan b. Thabit d.: founder of Hanifite school of jurisprudence. Muhammad b. Ishaq of Medina d.: first biographer of the Prophet Muhammad.
**767—8** Constantine, antipope.
**767—820** Muhammad b. Idris al-Shafii, founder of Shafiite school of jurisprudence.

| WESTERN, NORTHERN & CENTRAL EUROPE | SPAIN, ITALY & EASTERN EUROPE | AFRICA & EGYPT |
|---|---|---|
| **768** Pépin le Bref d.: kingdom partitioned between his sons Charles (later Charlemagne) and Carloman. | | |
| | **769** Battle of Veregava: Bulgars defeat Byzantium. | |
| | | **c. 770** Berber dynasty of Ghana driven out by Soninke of Wagudu: Soninke dynasty in Ghana (−1240). |
| **771** Following death of Carloman, Charlemagne seizes his possessions. | | **771** Kharijite Berbers invest Qayrawan: retaken by Caliphal army of 90,000. |
| | | **771—976** Dynasty of Midrarid rulers of Sijilmasa. |
| **772—6** Charlemagne at war with the Saxons. | **772** Didier attacks Rome. | |
| | **773** Charlemagne campaigns in Italy: Pavia besieged. | |
| **774** Kent and Wessex taken by Offa. Offa mints gold *dinar* in imitation of Islamic coinage. | **774** Lombards attack Carolingian domains: Charles crosses Alps and seizes Pavia: is proclaimed King of the Lombards at Monza, near Milan. | |
| **774—9** Ethelred I, King of Northumbria, first reign. | **775—80** Leo IV, Eastern Roman Emperor (with the Augusta Irene). | |
| **777** Charlemagne invited by confederacy of Arab chiefs of N Spain to invade as an ally of the Abbasids. | | |
| **777—85** Following Saxon invasion, Charles defeats them, beheading 4,500 prisoners. | | |
| **778** Widukind rebels in Saxony. | **778** Charlemagne campaigns in Spain as ally of Caliph of Baghdad against Abd al-Rahman I: sacks Pamplona: advances on Saragossa: city shuts its gates: withdraws ignominiously, harassed by guerrillas: his nephew Roland ambushed at Roncevaux. | |
| **ante 779** Charlemagne reforms coinage. | | |
| **779—80** Charlemagne campaigns in Saxony. | | |
| **779—88** Elfwald I, King of Northumbria. | **780—97** Constantine VI, Eastern Roman Emperor (with the Augusta Irene). | |
| **781** Tassilo, Duke of Bavaria, acknowledges Charlemagne as suzerain. | **781** Revolt of Slavs put down in the Balkans. | |

| THE NEAR EAST | THE FAR EAST | RELIGION & CULTURE |
|---|---|---|
| | | 767—822 Dengyo-Daishi, founder of the Japanese Tendai sect.<br>c. 768 Willibald: *Life of St Boniface.*<br>768 31 July-6 Aug., Philip, antipope.<br>768—72 Stephen IV, Pope.<br>768—825 Han Yu, essayist.<br>769 Lateran Council condemns Iconoclasm.<br>c. 770 Wood block printing first known in China. |
| 770 Arab fleet sent from Basrah to the Indus delta against pirates molesting Juddah. | | |
| | | 771 Muhammad b. Ibrahim al-Fazari (d. between 796—806) translates into Arabic *Siddhanta,* Indian treatise on astronomy.<br>c. 771 Indian numeral system introduced into the Arab world, whence present system of Arabic numerals.<br>772--4 Great Mosque of Qayrawan largely rebuilt.<br>772—95 Adrian I, Pope.<br>772—846 Po Chui, poet. |
| | 774 'Javanese' raids on Malay peninsula. | 774—835 Kobo-Daishi, founder of the Japanese Shingon sect. |
| 775—85 al-Mahdi, Caliph. | 775 Sri Vijaya in control of Ligor, N Malaya: Kedah its northern capital: Buddhist temple built.<br>c. 775—82 Vishnu or Dharmatunga, ruler of the Sailendra dynasty. | c. 775—82 Vishnu or Dharmatunga builds temple of Chandi Borobudur as mausoleum of the Sailendra dynasty. |
| | | fl. 776 Jabir b. Hayyan, pharmacist and alchemist: the first to be entitled a Sufi.<br>777 The Khan of the Bulgars baptized at Constantinople. Assembly of Paderborn: evangelization of Saxony organized.<br>c. 777 Ibrahim al-Fazari d.: first Muslim to construct an astrolabe. Ibrahim b. Adham of Balkh, quietist, d.<br>777—857 Yuhanna b. Masawayh, medical writer and translator: dissector of apes: opthalmologist.<br>778 Temple of Kalasan built by Vishnu, of the Sailendra. |
| 78 Leo IV invades Syria. | | |
| | | 779—831 Yuan Chen, poet. |
| | 780 System of land equalization abolished by the Tang.<br>c. 780—800 Panungulan, Sanjaya ruler: kingdom extended to C Java.<br><br>781 Attempt to end inheritance of military governorates provokes a rising in China. | 780 Veneration of images restored by Empress Irene. Alleged Manichaeans crucified in Aleppo.<br>780—c. 850 Muhammad b. Musa al-Khwarizmi, mathematician and algebraist.<br>781 Stele erected at Sian Fu, China, to commemorate sixty-seven Nestorian missionaries. |

| WESTERN, NORTHERN & CENTRAL EUROPE | SPAIN, ITALY & EASTERN EUROPE | AFRICA & EGYPT |
|---|---|---|
| **782–5** Charlemagne conquers and annexes Saxony. | **782** Harun b. al-Mahdi encamps at Scutari: tribute hastily paid by Empress Irene. | |
| | **783** Peace between Byzantium and the Arabs. Slav revolt in Macedonia, Greece and the Peloponnese quelled. | |
| **c. 784** Offa's Dyke built, to keep the Welsh out of Mercia. | | **c. 784–1846** Saifawa dynasty of Kanem, and, later, of Bornu: Dugu, first ruler. |
| **785–850** Norwegians occupy Shetland, Orkney and Caithness. | **785** Gerona taken by Charlemagne. Subjects of the Papal States required to swear fealty to him. | |
| **786** Papal mission sent to visit Offa, King of Mercia. <br> **786–802** Beorhtric, King of Wessex. | **786** Renewal of war between Byzantines and the Arabs: Byzantines defeated. | **786** Idris b. Abdallah settles at Ouli[ |
| **787** Egbert crowned King of Mercia during his father's life time: first English religious coronation. Charles at war with Bavaria, which is annexed. <br> **788–90** Osred II, King of Northumbria. <br> **788–96** Charles at war with Avars. <br> **789–821** Constantine MacAngus, King of Picts. <br> **790–6** Ethelred I, King of Northumbria, restored. | **788** Byzantium defeated by the Bulgars. <br> **788–96** Hisham I, Amir of Córdoba. <br><br> **790** Byzantine army mutinies: Empress Irene abdicates. <br> **791–5** Renewed war between Byzantium and the Arabs. <br> **791–842** Alfonso II, King of Asturias: capital at Oviedo. | **788–974** Idrisid dynasty of Fez: first Shi'ite dynasty: founded by Idris b. Abdallah. <br><br> **790–823** Abu Mansur al-Yasa, rule[ of Sijilmasa. <br> **c. 790** Kaya Maghan Sisse, King of Ghana, extends boundaries. |
| **793** Famine in Mercia. East Anglia taken by Offa. Lindisfarne Abbey destroyed by the Danes. <br> **793–805** Saxons again attack Carolingian dominions: defeated: many Saxons deported and settled in different parts of France. <br> **794** Jarrow Monastery destroyed by the Danes. | **793** Hisham I retakes Gerona: invades Septimania. | **793–4** Idris b. Abdallah poisoned [ Caliph Harun al-Rashid's instigatio[ succ. two days later by posthumou[ Idris II (–828). <br><br> **794** Rebellion against taxation in Egypt. |
| **795** Iona Abbey destroyed by the Danes. Norwegians attack Ireland. <br> **796** Charlemagne makes commercial treaty with Offa of Mercia. The Avars become vassals of the Franks. Ecgfrith, King of Mercia. Osbald, King of Northumbria. <br> **796–808** Eardwulf II, King of Northumbria, first reign. <br> **796–821** Coenwulf, King of Mercia. | **795** The Franks attack the Arabs in Spain. <br> **796** Constantine VI defeats the Bulgars. <br> **796–822** al-Hakam I, Amir of Córdoba. | |

| THE NEAR EAST | THE FAR EAST | RELIGION & CULTURE |
|---|---|---|
| **782** Arab expedition reaches Chrysopolis. | **782** Strike of merchants in Chang-an following a forced loan. Maritime Chenla taken by Indra of the Sailendras. **?c. 782–?812** Indra (Sangramadhanamajaya), Sailendra ruler. **783** Tang attempt to make tea trade a state monopoly. Military governors again rise against central government in China. | **ante 782** Adoptionist heresy appears in Spain. **782** Alcuin of York summoned by Charlemagne to organize education in the Empire. Buddhist temple built at Kelurak, Java. |
| **783–814** Govinda III, Rashtrakuta ruler. | | |
| | | **784** Lichfield made an archbishopric. |
| **785** Idris b. Abdallah, great-grandson of al-Hasan, rebels in Medina: then flees to Morocco: Alids massacred in Medina. **785–6** al-Hadi, Abbasid Caliph. **786–809** Harun al-Rashid, Caliph. Harun al-Rashid appoints Yahya b. Khalid b. Barmak *wazir* with unrestricted power (–805). | | **785** Pope Adrian I condemns Adoptionism. Thawafil (Theophilus) b. Tuma of al-Ruba d.: translator of part of the *Iliad* into Arabic. al-Mufaddah al-Dabbi d.: collector of Arab poetry. **786** Attempt to hold a Council to restore the veneration of images prevented by riot of troops in Constantinople. **fl. 786–833** al-Hajjaj b. Yusuf b. Matar, translator of Euclid and Cl. Ptolemy. **787** Seventh Council of Nicaea: veneration of images restored. |
| | | **788** Great Mosque of Córdoba founded. See of Bremen founded. **c. 788–820 fl.** Sankhara Acharya, Brahmin theologian. **789** Charlemagne orders all monasteries to open schools. |
| **791–5** Constantine VI at war with the Arabs. | | |
| **792** Byzantine troops mutiny in Armenia. **793** Yahya b. Abdallah rebels in Daylam. | | |
| | **794** Heian-kyo, later known as Miyako or Kyoto, made imperial capital of Japan. **794–1185** Heian period of Japanese history: Fujiwara clan the real rulers. | **794** Council of Frankfurt condemns Adoptionism. Paper mill established in Baghdad. **795–816** Leo III, Pope. **Between 796 and 806** Abu Yahya b. al-Batriq d.: translator into Arabic of Galen and Hippocrates. **c. 796–843** Abu Tammam, philologist. **796–804** Cathedral of Aix-la-Chapelle begun. |

| WESTERN, NORTHERN & CENTRAL EUROPE | SPAIN, ITALY & EASTERN EUROPE | AFRICA & EGYPT |
|---|---|---|

**797** Assembly of Aix-la-Chapelle: *Capitulare Saxonicum.*

**797** Alfonso II of Asturias seeks alliance with Charlemagne: prevented by his own nobles. Rising in Toledo against Arab domination. The Franks reach Huesca. The Augusta Irene overthrows Constantine VI: sole Empress (−802).

**798–805** Cuthred of Mercia, also King of Kent.

**798** Peace between Byzantium and the Caliphate: Byzantium to pay an annuity. Lisbon recovered from the Arabs.

**799** Synod of Aix-la-Chapelle.

**9th c.** Bielozorsk, Rostov on Kliazma and other Slav towns already in existence: Slavonic coinage first minted: trade in agricultural products in exchange for Byzantine luxuries and Scandinavian arms. Danes conquer Estonia.

**800** The Celts masters of Ireland. First Norman raids on France. Charlemagne proclaimed Western Roman Emperor: 25 Dec., crowned in Rome by Pope Leo III.

**c. 800–30** The Varangians make themselves the principal traders of western Russia.

**c. 800** Bornu said to be invaded by Beri-Beri from Yemen. Soninke mov into Kaniaga. Agriculturalists in C Africa in touch with east coast: evidenced by burials at Kisale. Tiloutane creates Berber empire in W Sahara.

**800–11** Ibrahim I b. Aghlab, govern of Ifriqiya, makes himself independe Aghlabid dynasty established in Tun (−909): capital Qayrawan.

**c. 9th c.** Audaghost founded by Lemtuna Tuareg. Commercial settlement at Irodo, Madagascar in existence.

**801** Louis the Pious, son of Charlemagne, takes Barcelona and all Catalonia. Charlemagne receives embassy from Harun al-Rashid.

**802** Military rising in Qayrawan.

**802–29** Further rebellion in Egypt.

**802** Charlemagne codifies German tribal laws.
**c. 802–3** *Lex Frisionum* published.
**802–25** Danish Vikings begin to settle and dominate Ireland.
**802–39** Egbert, King of Wessex, with title 'King of the English'.
**803** Peace of Salz between Charlemagne and the Saxons. Breach of relations between Charlemagne and Nicephorus I.

**802** Empress Irene dethroned and exiled: succ. Nicephorus I (−811).

**805–6** Charlemagne takes Bohemia.
**805–23** Baldred, King of Kent, probably subject to Mercia.

**804** Frankish fleet off Dalmatia.
**805** Unsuccessful conspiracy against al-Hakam I. Venice recognizes suzerainty of Charlemagne. Cyprus pillaged by a Muslim fleet.
**806** The Arabs attack Corsica.

**807** Amrus b. Yusuf appointed Governor of Toledo: city quietened by slaughter of 100 notables. Beginning of war between Krum, Khan of the Bulgars, and Byzantium. Krum pillages Macedonia.

**807** Ibrahim I builds al-Abbasiah: entertains embassy from Charlema

**808** Elfwald II, King of Northumbria.
**808–10** Eardwulf II, King of Northumbria, restored.

| THE NEAR EAST | THE FAR EAST | RELIGION & CULTURE |
|---|---|---|

**797** Harun al-Rashid campaigns as far as Ephesus and Ankara.
**797–806** Diplomatic intercourse between the Caliphate and Charlemagne.

**c. 798** Abu Yusuf d. at Baghdad: first to be appointed *qadi al-qudah,* chief justice of the Caliphate.

**end of 8th c.** Dharmapala succ. Gopala: dominant power in E India.

**9th c.** Chandel dynasty of Jijhoti or Bundelkand emerges. Devapala, son of Dharmapala, 'Pala' ruler: Assam and Kalinga annexed. Shahiya Turks establish dynasty in Kabul valley and Gandhara.

**03** Jafar the Barmecide murdered: ahya and his son Fadhl imprisoned.

**06** Arab expedition against yzantines: Heraclea and Tyana ken.

---

**late 8th c.** Tai kingdom of Nan-Chon takes control of Burmese trade routes between India and China.
**9th c.** Turks reach Kashgar region. Arab traders already visiting Kedah, Malay, for tin. Ceylon invaded by Pandyans from S India: plundered, and forced to a humiliating peace.

**c. 800** Nan-Chao raids in present Burma: fall of Pyu Kingdom.

**801** Embassy from Pyu Kingdom to China.

**802–1432** Cambodia an independent kingdom.
**802** Kingdom of Chenla absorbed into Cambodia. Jayavarman II (–850) proclaims himself King of Cambodia and independent of Java: capital near Angkor. Indravarman I of Champa d.: succ. Harivarman I.
**803** Harivarman I campaigns in China.

---

**c. 797–806** The *Rule* of Theodore of Studium.

**ante 800** al-Fazari, astronomer, refers to Ghana as the land of gold.

**9th c.** Copper mines first operated in Katanga. *The Book of Deer.*
**9th–11th c.** Danakil and Somali Islamized. Yezidi relegion, propitiating the Devil, founded in Iraq.

**800** Patriarch of Jerusalem sends Charlemagne the keys of the Church of the Holy Sepulchre.
**c. 800** Nennius, a Welshman: *History of the Britons. Bimaristan,* first hospital, built in Baghdad. Imported Chinese porcelain reaching Baghdad. Hinduism replaces Buddhism in Kashmir. George Syncellus, chronicler, d. St Irene, Constantinople, built.
**800–1300** Inscriptions give disconnected history of the Chola Kingdom.
**801** Jurjus b. Bakhtishu d.: chief physician of hospital in Baghdad.

**804** 19 May, Alcuin of York d.
**805** Tendai sect instituted in Japan. Archbishopric of Lichfield ended: Canterbury again the primatial see.

**807** Harun al-Rashid recognizes Frank rights in the Holy Places.

**808** Beginning of the quarrel between the western and eastern churches on the *Filioque* clause.

| WESTERN, NORTHERN & CENTRAL EUROPE | SPAIN, ITALY & EASTERN EUROPE | AFRICA & EGYPT |
|---|---|---|
| | **809** Krum takes Sardica.<br>**809–10** Pépin conquers Venetia.<br>Arabs pillage Corsica and Sardinia. | **809** Fez built by Idris II. |
| **810** The Danes pillage Frisia.<br>**810–40** Eanred, King of Northumbria. | | |
| | **811** Emperor Nicephorus I killed in battle at Virbitza against the Bulgars under Krum: succ. Stauracius, deposed and d. shortly: succ. Michael I (−813).<br>**812** Bulgars invade Thrace. | |
| **812** Charlemagne's title as Emperor recognized by Byzantium. Aquitaine revolts.<br>**813** Louis the Pious puts down Aquitaine. | **813** The Arabs pillage Nice and Corsica. Louis the Pious occupies Navarre. Krum defeats Michael I at Versinikia: besieges Constantinople: defeated by Byzantines at Mesembria. Michael I deposed: succ. Leo V the Armenian (−820). | |
| **814** Harald II of Denmark becomes a vassal of Charlemagne. Charlemagne d.: his sons Pépin donated Italy; Charles Germany; and Louis Aquitaine: Pépin d.: heir Bernard; Charles d.: heir Louis I the Pious (Holy Roman Emperor −840). | **814** Uprising in Córdoba against al-Hakam I: put down ruthlessly: 8,000 families expelled to Morocco; 15,000 sent to Alexandria. Krum d.: Omurtag, Khan of the Bulgars (−831).<br><br>**815 or 816** Peace treaty between Byzantium and the Bulgars. | **814 (or 817–8)** Spanish refugees settle in Fez, Alexandria, and Crete.<br>**815** Coptic weavers at Tanais complain at being taxed five times the correct amount. |
| | | **816** 15,000 refugees from Spain take Alexandria: Egypt then seized: order restored by Abdallah b. Tahir.<br>**816–36** Nubia refuses tribute to Egypt.<br>**817–38** Ziyadat-Allah I, Aghlabid.<br>**818–25** Fez grows rapidly. |
| | **817** Agreement between Franks and Byzantium on Danubian frontier.<br>**817–8** Revolt led by Bernard, King of Italy.<br>**818** Rising in Córdoba against Arab domination. | |
| **819** Harald II takes Jutland. | | |
| **ante 820** Noirmoutier and Ré pillaged by Normans.<br>**820** Normans settle in the Hebrides: Seine estuary raided.<br><br>**821** Coenwulf, King of Mercia, d.: end of Mercian supremacy: succ. Ceolwulf I (−823).<br>**821–33** Angus II, King of Picts. | **820** Leo V, the Armenian, murdered.<br>**820–9** Michael II, the Amorian, Eastern Roman Emperor.<br>**820–67** Amorian, or Phrygian, dynasty of Byzantium.<br>**821** Thomas the Slav rebels. | |

| THE NEAR EAST | THE FAR EAST | RELIGION & CULTURE |
|---|---|---|
| **809** Rebellion in Samarqand put down by Harun al-Rashid: d. at Meshed.<br>**809–13** al-Amin, Caliph. | **809** Harivarman I again campaigns in China. | **809–73** Hunayn b. Ishaq: translator of scientific treatises into Arabic: head of a school of translators: Aristotle, Dioscorides, Galen, Hippocrates, and the Old Testament translated: personal physician to Caliph al-Mutawakkil.<br>**c. 810** The rosary, subsequently Christianized, first mentioned in Arabic literature: a borrowing ultimately of Hindu origin. Abu Nuwas, poet and raconteur, d.<br>**810–70** Muhammad b. Ismail al-Bukhari, collected 600,000 traditions (*hadith*) of the Prophet: selected 7275 as genuine. |
| **c. 810** King of Kanauj deposed by Dharmapala, King of Bengal: Dharmapala master of most of N India. | | |
| | **?812–32** Samaratunga, Sailendra ruler. | **c. 811** Hamburg grows rapidly.<br>**813** Dar al-Hikmah (House of Wisdom) instituted at Baghdad by Caliph al-Mamun. |
| **813** Alids seize Mecca and Medina.<br>**813–6** Rebellions in the Caliphate.<br>**813–33** al-Mamun, Caliph. | | **813** Leo V the Armenian revives Iconoclasm.<br>**813–43** Second Period of Iconoclasm. |
| **815–77** Amoghavarsha, Rastrakuta ruler: capital at Manyakheta, Hyderabad: Chalukya made feudatories: patron of Jainism. | | **815** Council of St. Sophia: Theodore of Studium exiled: Iconoclastic council of 754 re-affirmed. al-Fadhl b. Nawbakht d.: translator of astronomical works. Maaruf al-Karkhi, mystic, d. |
| | **816** Nagabhata II captures Kanauj. | **816–7** Stephen V, Pope. Council of Aix-la-Chapelle. |
| **817** Ali Riza, head of the house of Ali, proclaimed heir-apparent of the Caliphate. | | **817** *Pactum Hludovicianum* defines papal territory. Scetis monasteries sacked. |
| **818** Ali Riza d. | | **817–24** Paschal I, Pope.<br>**c. 817** Further rebuilding of Great Mosque of Qayrawan begun. |
| **819** Following quarrel between Caliph al-Mamun and his brother al-Amin, much of Baghdad in ruins.<br>**819–22** Tahir b. al-Husayn of Khurasan appointed governor of all lands of the Caliphate E of Baghdad: founder of Tahirid dynasty (–872): capital at Merv, later Nishapur. | **ante 819** Warak, Sanjaya ruler.<br>**819 or 29–38** Garung, Sanjaya ruler. | **819** Hisham al-Kalbi of al-Kufah d.: historian of pre-Islamic Arabia. |
| | | **820–91** Photius, philologist. |
| | **821** Treaty of peace between Tibet and China. | **ante 821** Einhard: *Life of Charlemagne*. |

| WESTERN, NORTHERN & CENTRAL EUROPE | SPAIN, ITALY & EASTERN EUROPE | AFRICA & EGYPT |
|---|---|---|
| | 822 Thomas the Slav besieges Constantinople. 822–52 Abd al-Rahman II, Amir of Córdoba. | |
| 823 Norwegians raid Ireland. Bangor monastery destroyed. 823–5 Beornwulf, King of Mercia. | 823 Thomas the Slav defeated by Omurtag: taken prisoner and executed by Michael II. 824 *Constitutio Romana:* imperial control of Rome affirmed. 825 The Arabs take Crete. | |
| 825 Egbert, King of Wessex, conquers Kent: battle of Ellundun: defeats Beornwulf of Mercia. 825–7 Ludeca, King of Mercia. 825–39 Ethelwulf, King of Wessex, also King of Kent. | | c. 825±150 Dimple-based pottery used at Nsongezi, Uganda. |
| 827 Harald II expelled from Denmark. 827–9 Wiglaf, King of Mercia, first reign. | 826 Euphemius rebels in Sicily. 827 Bernard of Septimania defeats the Arabs near Barcelona. Euphemius brings Arab allies into Sicily: Euphemius killed by Byzantines: Arabs occupy greater part of the island. | 827 Spanish refugees expelled by Caliph al-Mamun from Alexandria: take refuge in Crete. |
| 828 Egbert, King of Wessex, becomes first King of England (–839). | | 828 Idris II d.: kingdom divided amongst his ten sons. |
| 829–30 Egbert, King of Wessex, annexes Mercia: Eanred of Northumbria does homage. | 829–42 Theophilus, Eastern Roman Emperor. | 829 Fresh revolts in Cairo suppressed |
| 830 State of Grand Moravia, including Bohemia, Moravia, and parts of Poland, Silesia and Pannonia, founded. Viking invasion compels monks to abandon Iona. 830–9 Wiglaf, King of Mercia, restored. | c. 830 Hungarians reach the Sea of Azov. 830–1 The Arabs take Palermo. | |
| 831–45 Turgesius, a Viking, makes himself High King of Ireland. 832–60 Kenneth MacAlpin, King of Kintyre. | 831 Omurtag, Khan of the Bulgars, d.; succ. Malamir (–852). Aghlabids capture Palermo from Byzantines. | 831 Egyptian treaty with Beja halts raiding: Beja required to pay tribute 831–2 Last armed Coptic rising in Egypt. 832–4 Kaider, first Turkish governor of Egypt. |
| 833 June, Emperor Louis I deposed by his sons. | | |
| 834 Louis I restored. | | 834 Beja raid Egypt. |

| THE NEAR EAST | THE FAR EAST | RELIGION & CULTURE |
|---|---|---|

**822** Tahir al-Husayn d.: succ., his son, Talha.

**824—7** Eugenius II, Pope.

**825** Thaton Kingdom of the Mons founds capital at Pegu.

**c. 825** First mechanical crank and first rotary grindstone recorded in Holland.

**826** Evangelization of Denmark begun.
**827** Valentine, Pope. Caliph al-Mamun proclaims Mutazilite dogma of the creation of the Koran, as opposed to the orthodox doctrine that it was uncreated. Mosque of Amr, Cairo, enlarged and repaired.
**827/8** C. Ptolemy's *Almagest* translated into Arabic.
**827—44** Gregory IV, Pope.
**828** Assembly of Aix-la-Chapelle: clergy oppose Louis the Pious. Relics of St Mark brought to Venice.
**829** *Annales Regni Francorum* completed.
**fl. c. 829—56** Leo of Salonika, encyclopaedist.
**ante 830** Astrolabes commonly made in Damascus and Baghdad.
**ante 830 or 831** Astronomical observatory built in Baghdad.
**830** Bait al-Hikmah (House of Wisdom) established in Baghdad by Caliph al-Mamun: combined academy, library and bureau of translation, chiefly Greek into Arabic; translators chiefly Christians and Jews.
**c. 830** Jibril b. Bakhtishu d.: court physician to Harun al-Rashid and his successors. Relics of St James the Apostle at Santiago de Compostela.

**831** The Arabs take Tarsus.

**831** Hamburg made a bishopric.
**831 or 832** Iconoclastic Council of Blachernae.
**post 831** Conversion to Islam accelerates in Egypt.

**832** Uighur Turks disintegrate. Sanjaya rulers cease to be subordinate to the Sailendras: Patapan of Sanjaya effective ruler of Java.
**post 832** Sailendra dynasty in control of Sri Vijaya.

**833** Caliph al-Mamun issues edict that no one may be appointed *qadi* who does not believe the Koran to have been created. *Mihnah,* inquisition, appointed to try and punish those denying this dogma.
**833—42** al-Mutasim, Caliph: first Caliph to employ a Turkish bodyguard.
**834** Rebellion of Jatt, or Zott, put down on lower Tigris.

**c. 833** Ibn Hisham, editor of Ibn Ishaq's life of the Prophet Muhammad, d. in Egypt.

**834** Rayhani, calligrapher, d.

| WESTERN, NORTHERN & CENTRAL EUROPE | SPAIN, ITALY & EASTERN EUROPE | AFRICA & EGYPT |
|---|---|---|
| **835** Temporary Danish settlement on Is. of Sheppey.<br>**836** London sacked by the Danes. | | **836** New treaty between Egypt and Nubia. |
| | **837** Aghlabids intervene in struggle in Naples. | |
| **838** Coronation of Charles the Bald. Normans raid up the Loire valley and pillage Orléans. Pépin, King of Aquitaine, d. | **838** The Arabs sack Marseilles. Arab settlements founded in S Italy. First Varangian embassy to Constantinople.<br>**c. 838** The Bulgars take the Vardar and Morava valleys. | |
| **839** Kenneth MacAlpin becomes King of Scots.<br>**839–c. 840** Athelstan, King of Wessex, also King of Kent.<br>**839–52** Beorhtwulf, King of Mercia.<br>**839–55** Ethelwulf, King of England.<br>**840–4** Ethelred II, King of Northumbria, first reign.<br>**840–55** Lothair I, Holy Roman Emperor: struggles with Louis the German and Charles the Bald.<br>**841** 25 June, battle of Fontenoy-en-Puisaye: Lothair I defeated by his brothers.<br>**841–8** Norman raids on N France.<br>**842** Oath of Strasbourg: sons of Louis the Pious ally. Varangian band fights Khazars in S Russia: attacks Byzantine colony on Euxine Sea. | **840** The Arabs take Bari. Diplomatic relations opened between Córdoba and Byzantium.<br><br><br><br>**842** The Arabs take Messina and Taranto. The Arabs pillage Arles.<br>**842–67** Michael III, Byzantine emperor, known as the Drunkard.<br>**842–56** Theodora, regent of Byzantium. | **c. 840** Tiboutiane, Tuareg chief, conquers W Sahara and twenty African chiefs. |
| **843** Kenneth MacAlpin becomes King of Picts: former dynasties of Dalriada and Caledonia now fused. Treaty of Verdun partitions the Empire: Charles the Bald takes France (−877): Louis the German retains Germany (−876): Lothair retains Lotharingia and Italy (−855). | **843** Aghlabids take Messina. Abortive Byzantine expedition against Crete. | |
| **844** Raedwulf, King of Northumbria.<br>**844–8** Ethelred II, King of Northumbria, restored.<br>**845** Malachy, King of Meath, murders Turgesius: makes himself High King of Ireland. The Normans raid up the Seine and pillage the outskirts of Paris.<br>**846–70** Rastie, or Ratislaus, Prince of Grand Moravia. | **845** Varangians first spoken of by Byzantines as *Rhos* (Russians). Arab raids on S Italy.<br>**845–6** Malamir of Bulgaria invades Macedonia: Philippopoli taken.<br>**846** Arabs land at Ostia: fail to take Rome: St Peter's and St Paul-without-the-Walls pillaged.<br>**c. 846** Empress Theodora forces Malamir to make peace.<br>**847** Louis II re-takes Beneventum. | **845** al-Nazzam, Mutazilite, d.<br><br><br>**846** Normans take Arzila. |
| **848** Malachy crushes Viking army at Sciath Nechtain.<br>**c. 848** Alfred, later the Great, King of England, b.<br>**848–66** Osberht, King of Northumbria. | **848** Fleet of Córdoba amounts to 300 vessels: sent to quell risings in the Balearic Is. | |

| THE NEAR EAST | THE FAR EAST | RELIGION & CULTURE |
|---|---|---|
| | | **835** First reference to a printed book in China. St Castor, Coblenz, founded. |
| **...36** Samarra built as new capital of ...e Caliphate (−892). | | **836—901** Thabit b. Qurrah, a Sabaean, translator and head of school of translation of Greek mathematics and philosophy. |
| **...37** Theophilus takes Samosata and ...elitene. Pigeon post first instituted ... the Caliphate. | | |
| **...38** al-Mutasim leads large expedition ...gainst the Byzantines: Amorium ...aken: withdrawn following news of ...conspiracy in Baghdad. | **c. 838—51** Pikatan, Sanjaya ruler: m. Queen Pramodavardhani, daughter of Samaratunga, Sailendra ruler. | **838—923** Abu Jafar Muhammad b. Jarir al-Tabari, distinguished historian. |
| **...40** Byzantine counter-offensive in ...sia Minor. **...40—90** Bhoja (Mihira Pratihara), ...ing of Kanauj. | | **840—50** Deir Anba Bishoi built. **c. 840** Bryas palace built in Constantinople. Mar Petrus, last known Bp of Sanaa and Yemen. |
| **...2—847** al-Wathiq, Caliph. | **842** Tibetan Empire falls to pieces: King Langdarma murdered: Buddhist clergy become all-powerful. | **842** Great Mosque of Samarra built. |
| | | **843** Methodius elected Patriarch of Constantinople. Council of Constantinople rejects Iconoclasm: 11 March, images solemnly restored in St Sophia: day still kept as the Feast of Orthodoxy. Alien religions, including Manichaeism, Mazdaism, Nestorianism and Islam, proscribed in China. 4,600 Buddhist temples, and 40,000 shrines and monasteries, secularized. 260,500 monks ordered to return to lay state. Only Taoism and Confucianism permitted. **844** Jan., John, antipope. **844—7** Sergius II, Pope. |
| | | **ante 845** John Scotus Erigena at the court of Charles the Bald. |
| | **846** Buddhist Confucians again tolerated. | |
| **...7—61** al-Mutawakkil, Caliph. | | **847—55** Leo IV, Pope: fortifies Rome against the Arabs. |

| WESTERN, NORTHERN & CENTRAL EUROPE | SPAIN, ITALY & EASTERN EUROPE | AFRICA & EGYPT |
|---|---|---|
| | **849** Arab fleet destroyed by Italians off Ostia. The Arabs retake Beneventum. | |
| **850** Norman settlements made in Seine and Loire estuaries. Normans granted a fief in Frisia. | **c. 850** The Republic of St Mark at Venice becomes a separate state. | **c. 850** Nubian embassy to Baghdad to protest against stoppage of food supplies by Cairo. Saifawa dynasty take Bornu.<br>**850** Ali b. Sahl Rabban al-Tabari: *Firdaws al-Hikmah* (Paradise of Wisdom), compendium of medicine<br>**c. 851–900** Betsine, son of Tiboutiane, Zenata ruler. |
| **851** Danes take Canterbury: London sacked: defeated by Ethelwulf at Oakley. Charles the Bald recognizes Breton independence.<br>**852** Dublin founded by the Vikings.<br>**852–74** Burgred, King of Mercia. | **852–86** Muhammad I, Amir of Córdoba.<br>**852–89** Boris (or Bogoris), Khan of Bulgaria. | |
| **853–7** Normans raid the Loire valley. | **854** Boris attacks Montenegro. | **853** Byzantine raid on Chata and Damietta.<br>**854** Conflict between Nubia and Egypt prevents Ethiopia from obtaining a new Abuna: Ethiopia gains Massawa. Beja refuse tribut Egyptian punitive expedition open gold mines.<br>**855** Ahmad b. Hanbal, founder of Hanbalite school of jurisprudence, |
| **855–60** Ethelbald, King of England, in rebellion against Ethelwulf.<br>**855–75** Louis II, Holy Roman Emperor and King of Italy.<br>**856–8** Ethelwulf, King of Wessex, again also King of Kent.<br>**856–61** Norman raids in present Normandy and as far as Paris. | **856** Michael III assumes power. The Arabs pillage Naples. | **856–8** Revolts in Alexandria and the Fayoum. |
| **858–60** Ethelberht, King of Wessex, also King of Kent. | **858** Theodora exiled. | |
| | **859** The Arabs take Castro Giovanni. The Normans pillage Navarre.<br>**860** 18 June, Russian attack on Constantinople with fleet of 200. | **859** Byzantine raid on al-Farama (Pelusium). Michael III campaign on the Euphrates with success. |
| **c. 860** Norse Vikings reach Iceland *via* the Faroe Is.<br>**860–3** Donald I, brother of Kenneth MacAlpin, King of Scots.<br>**860–6** Ethelbert, King of England. | | |

c. 849 Pagan city, Burma, built.

849 Alids and Mutazilites persecuted by the Caliph. Walahfrid Strabo d.: author of *Glossa ordinaria*. Yahya, jurist, d.: introduced Malikite rite into Spain.

850 Balaputra, last surviving male of the Sailendra dynasty, succeeds to throne of Sri Vijaya.
850–77 Jayavarman III, King of Cambodia.
c. 850–900 Unstable conditions in Upper Burma: overland route between India and China blocked.

850 Perfectus, a priest of Córdoba, reviles Muhammad and curses Islam: executed: acclaimed a saint by Bp of Córdoba and populace: eleven others follow suit. Debra Nguadguad founded.
c. 850 Pseudo-Isidorian Decretals forged. al-Khwarizmi d.: author of astronomical tables. The term *Sufi* used for Muslim religious ascetics. *Journey of the Merchant Sulaiman* describes E Indies. Kose-no-Kanaoka, Japanese artist.
c. 850–900 Borobodur temples built in Java.
fl. c. 850 Abu Yusuf Yaqub b. Ishaq al-Kindi, philosopher, alchemist, astrologer, musical theorist and optician.

c. 851–82 Kayuwani, Sanjaya ruler.

851 John Scotus Erigena: *De Praedestinatione*.
852 Church of St Rémi, Reims, begun.
853 Fraumünster monastery founded at Zurich.

fl. 854 Vikrantavarman III, Champa ruler.

855 Sept., Anastasius, antipope.
855–8 Benedict III, Pope.

856 Boris receives Greek missionaries.

857 Yuhanna b. Masawayh d.: translator into Arabic of medical and other works.
ante 858 Photius: *Myriobiblion*.
858 Ignatius, Patriarch of Constantinople, deposed: Photius installed (–867).
858–67 Nicholas I, Pope.
859 Eulogius, Bp of Córdoba, martyred.

9–90 Ashot I, Bagratid (or gratuni) King of Armenia: allies th Byzantium.

860 Popular rising caused by famine in Chekiang province.
860–90 Town of Angkor-Thom built by Khmer ruler Jayavarman III.

860 Cyril and Methodius, Greeks from Salonica, create a Slavonic alphabet in order to translate the Gospels and the Liturgy: evangelization of Russia begun in the Crimea. Dhu al-Nun al-Misri, Sufi theosophist, d. at Gizah.
860–940 Ibn Abd al-Rabbih, author, of Córdoba.

| WESTERN, NORTHERN & CENTRAL EUROPE | SPAIN, ITALY & EASTERN EUROPE | AFRICA & EGYPT |
|---|---|---|

**861** Normans attack Winchester.

**862** First Hungarian raids in Germany. Three Varangian chiefs ruling north-eastern Slavs: Rurik at Novgorod, Sinéous on the White Lake, and Trouvor at Izborsk.

**862–6** Bardas, uncle of Michael III, Caesar.

**863–4** Charles the Bald subjects Aquitaine.
**863–5** Norman raids on Auvergne and Poitou.
**863–77** Constantine I, King of Scots.
**863–933** Harold Fair Hair, King of Norway.

**863** Umar, Arab governor of Melitene sacks Amisus (Samsun): army subsequently annihilated at Poson: Umar killed.

**866–8** Further revolts in Alexandri and the Fayoum.

**864–1169** Grand Princes of Kiev, rulers of Russia: capital at Kiev.

**865** Danish 'Great Army' lands in England.

**865** Charles the Bald detaches Catalonia from northern territory: re-named Marca Hispanica.

**866** Nov., Danes take York. Norwegians attack Dumbarton. Frequent Norman raids on France.
**866–7** Elle, King of Northumbria.
**866–71** Ethelred I, King of England.
**c. 866–72** Harald Harfager unites Norway.
**867** The Normans take York. Treaty of Metz between Louis II and Charles the Bald.
**867–72** Egbert I, King of Northumbria.

**866** Bardas assassinated.
**866–7** Louis II expels the Arabs from S Italy.
**866–910** Alfonso III of Asturias: takes new territory as far as Coimbra.

**867** Michael III assassinated: succ. Basil I (–886).
**867–1059** Macedonian Dynasty.

**868** Normans take Nottingham.

**868** Ragusa taken by Byzantium.

**868–84** Ahmad b. Tulun, governor of Egypt, makes Egypt independen of the Caliphate: remission of taxation refused: Egypt enters era of prosperity.
**868–905** Tulunid dynasty in Egyp

**869** Danish 'Great Army' ravages East Anglia: Edmund, King of East Anglia, martyred at Thetford.
**870** Danes make a base at Reading: defeated by Wessex army under Alfred the Great at Ashdown: Danes occupy East Anglia. Norwegian republic of Iceland founded. Dumbarton sacked by the Danes. 9 Aug., treaty of Mersen: Lotharingia partitioned between France and Germany.
**870–94** Swietopolk, or Swatopluk, Prince of Grand Moravia.
**871–99** Alfred, the Great, King of England.

**869** Arabs take Malta.
**869–71** Louis II allies with Byzantium: Bari taken from the Arabs.

**c. 870** Ahmad b. Tulun refuses tribute to Baghdad: Egypt begins to emerge as an independent state. Ibn al-Sufi rebels: beaten at Akhm

**871** Basil I at war with the Caliphate.

**861–2** al-Muntasir, Caliph. Dec., Caliph al-Mutawakkil murdered at Samarra by Turkish guard: beginning of period of Turkish domination over the Caliphate.
**862–6** al-Musta'in, Caliph.

**861** Nilometer (device for measuring the Nile flood) restored on Roda Is., near Fustat by Abu al-Abbas Ahmad al-Farghani: includes first so-called 'Gothic' arch.
**862** The New Testament translated into German by Otfried of Wissemburg. Sts Cyril and Methodius evangelizing Moravia. Karaouine university mosque built at Fez. Lothair divorced.
**c. 862–9** John Scotus Erigena: *De divisione naturae.*
**863** Pope Nicholas I orders inquiry into Lothair's divorce. Tuan Cheng-Shih, *Yu-yang-tsu.*

**864** Lothair submits to Pope Nicholas I. Boris of Bulgaria converted to Christianity, with name of Michael. Sts Cyril and Methodius working in Bulgaria.
**865–925** Abu Bakr Muhammad b. Zakariya al Razi (Rhazes), physician and prolific writer: inventor of the seton.
**866** Boris (Michael) of Bulgaria requests Latin missionaries from Rome.

**866–9** al-Mutazz, Caliph.

**867–908** Saffarid dynasty in Sijistan and Persia.

**867** Council of Constantinople condemns and anathematizes the Pope for adding *Filioque* to the Creed.
**867–70** Schism of Photius between Rome and Constantinople: Photius suspended and replaced as Patriarch by Ignatius.
**867–72** Adrian II, Pope.
**868/9** Abu Uthman Amr b. Bahr al-Jahiz, zoologist and man of letters: founder of a Mutazilite sect.

**868–883** Revolt of the Zanj negroes Lower Iraq.

**869–70** al-Muhtadi, Caliph.

**870–92** al-Mutamid, Caliph.

**869** St Cyril d. Latin missionaries leave Bulgaria. Council of Constantinople restores Photius. Unity between Rome and Constantinople restored.
**870** First bishop sent to Russia by Constantinople: evangelization of Russia steadily progresses. St Methodius imprisoned.
**870–85** St Methodius, Abp of Pannonia.

**871** Ibn Abd al-Hakam, historian of Arab conquest of Egypt, d.

872–885

WESTERN, NORTHERN
& CENTRAL EUROPE

SPAIN, ITALY
& EASTERN EUROPE

AFRICA & EGYPT

**872** al-Umari revolts in Egypt.

**873–6** Ricsige, King of Northumbria.

**874** Ceolwulf, King of Mercia: Mercia conquered by the Danes.
**c. 874** Norse migration to Iceland.

**874** Independent County of Barcelona founded by Wilfred the Shaggy.

**874–902** Ibrahim II, Aghlabid: completes Great Mosque of Qayraw begun by Ziyadat-Allah I.

**875** Danish fleet attacks Poole Harbour: scattered by a storm.
**c. 875** Reykjavik, Iceland founded, subject to Norway.
**875–77** Charles II, the Bald, Holy Roman Emperor.
**876** Rollo or Robert I, son of Rognvald the Mighty, Earl of Möre. a Norwegian noble, commences ravaging northern France: founder of dynasty of Dukes of Normandy.
**876 fl.** Egbert II, King of Northumbria.
**877** 14 June, Edict of Quierzy: Charles the Bald makes fiefs hereditary.
**877–8** Aedh, King of Scots: said to have been killed by his subjects.
**877–9** Louis II le Bègue, King of France.
**877–87** Charles III, the Fat, succ. Charles II.
**878** Danes under Guthrum attack Wessex near Gloucester: King Alfred with small band takes refuge on Is. of Athelney: Danes encamp at Chippenham: defeated by Alfred at Ethandun (Edington): treaty made at Wedmore: Guthrum submits to baptism: Danes retain East Anglia, Essex and parts of Mercia.
**878–89** Giric, King of Scots: Scottish church re-organized.
**879–82** Louis III, King in N France.
**879–84** Carloman, King in S France. Normans pillaging N France.
**880** The Hungarians reach the Carpathians. The Normans annihilate the Saxons at Hamburg. Treaty of Ribemont: Lorraine ceded to Louis II by Charles III.
**881** Feb., Charles III crowned as Emperor (–887). 3 Aug., Louis III defeats Normans at Saucourt-en-Vimeu.
**882** Louis III d.: Carloman sole ruler of France (–884).

**875** Louis II d.: Bari reverts to Byzantium.

**876** Byzantium garrisons Bari.

**877** Byzantine authority demonstrated in Dalmatia.

**878** Aghlabids take Syracuse after nine months' siege.

**880** Taranto taken from the Arabs. Naval battle at Lipari: S Italy accepts Byzantine protection.

**882** Burgos founded as capital of Castile.

**883** Ibn Tulun d.: succ. Khumara

**884–95** Khumarawayh b. Tulun, ruler of Egypt: reprobated by Muslims for his extravagance and luxury.

**885** Normans besiege Paris.

**885–6** Byzantines reoccupy S Italy at the Pope's request.

| THE NEAR EAST | THE FAR EAST | RELIGION & CULTURE |
|---|---|---|
| 872 Tahirid dynasty overthrown by Yaqub b. Laith, founder of Saffarid dynasty.<br>873 Byzantium recovers Zapetra and Samosata. | | c. 872 First hospital built in Cairo by Ibn Tulun.<br>872–82 John VIII, Pope.<br>873 St Methodius freed at the instance of Pope John VIII. Abdallah b. Maimun al-Kaddah, an oculist, founds esoteric Ismaili sect. Münsterkirche, Essen, founded. |
| 874 Samanid dynasty of Samarqand Ferghana, Shash and Herat emerges (–909). | 874 Rising led by peasant, Wang-Hsien-chih, and salt merchant Huang Chao: eastern China quickly seized. | 874 Muhammed b. Nusayr d.: founder of Nusayri sect in Syria. |
| | 875 New dynasty established in Champa at Indaputra: ruler takes name of Indravarman (II). | 875 Great Mosque of Shiraz built. Muslim b. al-Hajjaj, traditionalist, d.<br>c. 875 Bayazid al-Bistami d.: introduced doctrine of self-annihilation into Sufism. |
| | | 876–9 Mosque of Ibn Tulun and other important buildings erected in Cairo. |
| 877 Ahmad ibn Tulun occupies Syria: naval base developed at Acre. | 877 Jayavarman III d.: succ. Indravarman (–889). | fl. 877–918 Abu Abdallah Muhammad b. Jabir al-Battani, astronomer. |
| 878 Byzantine campaigns in Cappadocia and Cilicia. Nepal revolts from Tibet, setting up kingdom which is still independent.<br>878–903 Amr b. Laith, ruler of Khorasan. | 878 Peasant rebels in eastern China defeated by Turk Sha-to: Wang beheaded. | 878 Guthorm, King of Denmark, baptized. |
| | 879 Canton burnt by Huang Chao: in addition to Chinese, 120,000 foreign merchants killed.<br>880 Chang-an captured by Huang Chao: proclaims himself Emperor: dynasty termed Chi. | 880 Nunnery founded at Montserrat. |
| | 881 Battle for Chang-an: Huang Chao holds out. | |
| | 883 Huang Chao compelled to flee from Chang-an.<br>884 Huang Chao killed by the Sha-to Turks. | 882 Pope John VIII murdered by Roman nobility.<br>882–4 Marinus I, Pope: first Bp to be so elected.<br>883–931 Ibn Masarrah, esoteric philosopher, at Córdoba.<br>884–5 Adrian III, Pope. |
| 885 Kingdom of Armenia restored: Ashot I, King. | 885 Tang emperor returns to Chang-an. | 885–91 Stephen V, Pope. |

| WESTERN, NORTHERN & CENTRAL EUROPE | SPAIN, ITALY & EASTERN EUROPE | AFRICA & EGYPT |
|---|---|---|
| **886** King Alfred occupies London: new treaty with Danes: Danelaw defined.<br>**886—7** Normans besiege Paris for eleven months.<br>**887** Charles the Fat dep.: Eudes elected King of France (−898): Arnulf, King of Germany.<br>**887—94** Guido, Holy Roman Emperor.<br>**888** Eudes defeats the Normans at Montfaucon. Charles the Fat d.<br>**888—98** Odo, Count of Paris.<br>**889—900** Donald II, King of Scots. | **886—8** al-Mundhir, Amir of Córdoba.<br>**886—912** Leo VI, Eastern Roman Emperor.<br><br><br><br>**888—912** Abdallah, Amir of Córdoba.<br>**888—924** Berengar, King of Italy.<br>**889** Guy of Spoleto elected King of Italy by the bishops. Boris of Bulgaria retires to a monastery: succ. Vladimir (−893). | **c. 887** Traditional date of foundatio of Mogadishu. The Seven Brothers o al-Hasa said to have settled in easter: Africa.<br><br>**c. 890** Songhai Kings of Kukia exter dominions to Gao. |
| | **891—4** Guy of Spoleto, Emperor. | |
| **892** Flanders and Aquitaine revolt against Eudes.<br><br>**893** Charles the Simple at war with Eudes. Abortive Danish invasion of Kent.<br>**893—8** Charles the Simple at war with<br>**894—6** Lambert, Holy Roman Emperor. | **893** Vladimir of Bulgaria dethroned by Boris: succ. Simeon (−927).<br><br>**894** War between Byzantium and the Bulgars: alliance between Byzantium and Hungary. | **893** Dai Abu Abdallah preaching: beginning of Fatimid movement. |
| **895** The Hungarians establish themselves in the Danube valley. Kingdom of Lorraine created for Zwentibold, bastard son of Arnulf. The Hungarians invade Bulgaria.<br>**896** Occupation of Normandy by the Normans recognized by France.<br>**896—9** Arnulf, Holy Roman Emperor.<br>**897** Peace between Charles the Simple and Eudes. | **896** The Bulgars pay tribute to Byzantium.<br><br>**897** Lambert of Spoleto crowned Emperor by the Pope (−898). | **895—6** Jaysh, ruler of Egypt.<br><br>**896—904** Harun, ruler of Egypt.<br><br>**c. 897/8—1285** Makhzumi dynasty eastern Shoa. |
| **898—929** Charles the Simple, sole king of France.<br>**899—911** Louis III the Child, King of Germany.<br>**899—925** Edward the Elder, King of England.<br>**10th c.—1598** Princes of Rostov and Souzda reign at Moscow. | **10th c.** Counts of Castile fight to make themselves independent of León. Communal constitution organized in San Marino. | |

| THE NEAR EAST | THE FAR EAST | RELIGION & CULTURE |
|---|---|---|
| | | **886** Photius forced to relinquish Patriarchate of Constantinople by Leo VI: Stephen, brother of Leo VI, appointed. **886—940** Ibn Muqlah, calligrapher, d. **c. 887** Alfred the Great: *Enchiridion.* |
| | **889** Indravarman d.: succ. Yasovarman (−*c.* 900). | **889** Latest known Maya stele. Friday Mosque of Nishapur built. Muhammad b. Muslim al-Dinawari d.: historian. |
| **890—910** Mahendrapala, King of Kanauj. | **890** Open war between rival generals in China. | **c. 890** Hamdan Qarmat founds Batinite Qarmatian sect near al-Kufah. *Cantilène de Ste Eulalie,* first known French poem. **c. 890—977** Ibn al-Qutiya, grammarian. **891** Photius d. Over 100 booksellers reported in Baghdad. **891—2** Ibn Wadih al-Yaqubi, geographer: *Kitab al-Buldan.* **891—6** Formosus, Pope. **892** al-Biladhuri, geographer, d. |
| **892—902** al-Mutadid, Caliph. **892** Baghdad again the capital under Caliph al-Mutadid. | | |
| | | **893** Asser, Bp of Sherborne: *Life of King Alfred the Great.* **893—974** Yahya b. Adi, Jacobite Bp and translator, principally of Aristotle. **894** King Alfred: translation of Pope Gregory the Great, *Cura Pastoralis,* and other works into Anglo-Saxon: education encouraged. **c. 894** *Anglo-Saxon Chronicle* begun. |
| | **895** Separate dynasties set up by governors of Szechwan and Chekiang. | |
| | | **896** 11—26 Apr., Boniface VI, antipope. |
| | | **897** May—Oct., Stephen VII, Pope. Aug.—Nov., Romanus, Pope. Theodore II, Pope. Anthony Caulias, Patriarch of Constantinople, restores unity in the eastern Church between the supporters of Photius and Ignatius. **897—961** Muhammad b. Yusuf al-Kindi, historian. **897—967** Abu al-Faraj al-Isfahani, compiler of *Kitab al-Aghani* (Book of Songs). **898—900** John IX, Pope. |
| **899** Qarmatian independent state founded with capital al-Ahsa, Persian Gulf. | | |
| **10th c.** Jews settle on Malabar coast. Inscription at Uttaramerur, a Brahman village, records method of election of *sabha* (village council). | | **10th c.** Metal working first known in Mexico. Theodosius the Deacon, panegyrist. Deir al-Banat, church hall, built in Cairo. |

**WESTERN, NORTHERN & CENTRAL EUROPE**  |  **SPAIN, ITALY & EASTERN EUROPE**  |  **AFRICA & EGYPT**

**900** The Hungarians invade Bavaria. Zwentibold defeated by Louis the Child: Gebhardt of Franconia made Duke of Lorraine. Donald II of Scots killed by the Danes: succ. Constantine II (−942). Kingdom of Denmark founded by Gorm (−935).
**c. 900** All the Icelandic coast occupied: republican government by the Althing (assembly of the people).
**901—11** Lewis III, the Blind, of Provence, Holy Roman Emperor.

**906** The Hungarians destroy Moravia.

**910** 5 Aug., Edward the Elder defeats Danes at Tettenhall.

**911** Treaty of St Clair-sur-Epte: Charles the Simple grants Rollo or Robert I the Duchy of Normandy (−927), and, contingent on his baptism, his daughter Giselle in marriage, with object of ending Norman raids.
**911—15** Conrad I, Holy Roman Emperor.
**911—8** Ethelfleda, sister of Edward the Elder, harasses Danes from Mercia. Conrad of Franconia, King of Germany.

**900** Louis of Provence elected king by Italian feoffees.

**901** The Byzantines take Reggio.

**ante 902** Ibrahim II, Aghlabid, campaigns in Calabria.
**902** Aghlabids seize Taormina, last Byzantine possession in Sicily: Malta and Sardinia seized later.
**902—4** Berengar of Friuli usurps the Empire.

**904** Cretan pirate Leo of Tripoli attacks Constantinople: Salonica taken: raiders retire to Syria. Peace between Byzantium and the Bulgars.
**905** Navarre becomes a kingdom.

**906** Byzantine admiral Himerius defeats Arab fleet in the Aegaean.
**907** Russian Prince Oleg attacks Constantinople: preliminary peace made.

**909** Sicily falls under Fatimid rule.

**910—24** Ordoño II of León: abortive attacks on the Caliphate.

**911** Treaty between Byzantium and Russia. Himerius' naval expedition against the Arabs off Samos a failure.

**c. 900** Iron industry on Bauchi plateau, Nigeria. Beginning of Ogiso dynasty of Benin.
**c. 900—c. 1400** Kalomo culture in Zambia.
**?c. 900—1911** Hausa dynasty of Daura, Nigeria.

**c. ante 901—2** Trade treaty between Ethiopia and Yemen.
**902—8** Dai Abu Abdallah gradually takes parts of N Africa.

**903—9** Ziyadat-Allah III, last Aghlabid.

**904** Dai Abu Abdallah takes Sétif.
**904—5** Shayban, last Tulunnid ruler of Egypt.

**905—6** Precarious Abbasid hold on Egypt: former officers of Ibn Tulun strive for independence.
**905** Dai Abu Abdallah takes Tobna and Belezina.

**908** Tahert destroyed by Dai Abu Abdullah.

**909** Abdallah al-Hasan al-Shii and Said b. Husayn, a Shiite claiming descent from Fatima, daughter of Muhammad, overthrow Aghlabid dynasty: Said proclaimed Imam Ubaydallah al-Mahdi: Fatimid dynasty established: capital Qayrawan.
**909—73** Fatimid dynasty in N Africa
**910** Ubaydallah enters Raqqada.

**911** al-Shii killed by Ubaydallah: seizes all N Africa from Morocco to Libya. Tahert destroyed Dai Abu Abdallah executed for treason. Kotama rebels against Ubaydallah.

| THE NEAR EAST | THE FAR EAST | RELIGION & CULTURE |
|---|---|---|
| | c. ante 900 Department for economic affairs, staffed by experts, in existence in China.<br>c. 900 Salt tax the most productive item in the Chinese budget. Kitan, apparently Mongols, become dominant in NE Mongolia: vassals in W China, Korea and Mongolia. | ante 900 Abdallah al-Husayn al-Shii proclaims himself the precursor of the Mahdi among the Kitamah Berbers: origin of Fatimite Shiism. St Menas town destroyed.<br>c. 900 First paper mill in Egypt.<br>900–3 Benedict IV, Pope.<br>c. 900–50 Abu Ubaydah Muslim of Valencia: proponent of the sphericity of the earth. |
| 902–8 al-Muktafi, Caliph. | | 901–66 Abu Ali al-Qali, grammarian. |
| 903 Ismail b. Ahmad takes Khorasan from Saffarids: Samanid dynasty recognized by Caliphate: capital, Bokhara. | | 903 Oct.–Dec., Leo V, Pope.<br>903–4 Christopher, antipope.<br><br>904–11 Sergius III, Pope. |
| | | 905–59 Constantine Porphyrogenitus, writer and historian. |
| 907–49 Parantaka I, first important Chola ruler: campaigns against Pandyas: defeated by Rashtrakutas. | 907 Emperor and his entourage killed by Chuan-chung: later Liang dynasty established: end of Tang dynasty.<br>907–60 Five short dynasties in N China, and ten independent regimes in S China under military governors.<br>907–1125 N China partly under Liao dynasty. | 907 Schism in the eastern Church: Patriarch Nicholas of Constantinople dep.: Euthymios installed. |
| 908 17 Dec., al-Murtada Caliph for one day: deposed and killed.<br>908–32 al-Muqtadir, Abbasid Caliph. | | |
| c. 910–40 Mahipala, ruler of Pratihara Empire. | | 909 Limburg Cathedral begun.<br>909–88 St Dunstan, Archbishop of Canterbury.<br>910 al-Junayd, orthodox Sufi, d. in Baghdad. Abbey of Cluny founded by William, Duke of Aquitaine: beginning of reform of Benedictine Order.<br>?910–84 St Ethelwold.<br>911 Rollo, or Robert, Duke of Normandy, baptized.<br>911–3 Anastasius III, Pope.<br>911 Rollo, or Robert, Duke of Normandy, baptized.<br>911–3 Anastasius III, Pope. |

| WESTERN, NORTHERN & CENTRAL EUROPE | SPAIN, ITALY & EASTERN EUROPE | AFRICA & EGYPT |
|---|---|---|
| **912** Treaty between Oleg of Novgorod and Byzantium. **912–3** The Hungarians pillage Swabia and Franconia. | **912** Following numerous rebellions, Abd al-Rahman III succ. only to Córdoba and its environs (–929): first Muslim ruler of Spain to assume title of Caliph. Abd al-Rahman III takes Ecija. **912–3** Alexander II, Eastern Roman Emperor. **912–6** Sicilian Muslims rebel against Fatimids. | c. **912** or **915** al-Mahdia built as Fatimid capital. |
| **913** Eadwulf, King of Northumbria, d. **913–5** Constantine III of Scots campaigns as far as Corbridge to resist Danes. | **913** Abd al-Rahman III takes Elvira and Jaen: Archidona and Seville surrender. Simeon of Bulgaria attacks Constantinople. **913–59** Constantine VII Porphyrogenitos, Eastern Roman Emperor (with the Augusta Helena). | **913–4** Abortive Fatimid attempt on Egypt. |
| **914–1014** Continuous Viking attempts to conquer Ireland. | **914** Simeon of Bulgaria takes Adrianople. **914–23** Ordoño II, King of Galicia: establishes Christian Kingdom of León: capital at León. Ordoño II, King of León, devastates Muslim area to the south. | **914** Ubaydallah seizes Alexandria. |
| **915–24** Berengar, Holy Roman Emperor. | **915** Byzantines defeat Fatimids at Garigliano. | c. **915** Sofala already trading with S Arabia. al-Masudi visits (? ) Comoro Is. or Madagascar. |
|  |  | **916** Ubaydallah raids Egyptian Delta and also Malta, Sardinia, Corsica, and Balearic Is. |
| **917** The Hungarians pillage Alsace-Lorraine. Edward the Elder occupies Danelaw from S of R. Mersey to the Humber, including East Anglia: Danes disunited. | **917** Cretan pirate Leo of Tripoli overwhelmingly defeated by the Byzantines off Lemnos. Abd al-Rahman III takes Reggio. Sicily reverts to the Fatimids. Ordoño II captures an Arab general, and nails his head beside a wild boar's head at S. Estaban de Gormaz. Simeon defeats the Byzantines at Anchialos: demands the imperial crown. **917–26** Arab attacks on S Italy. |  |
| **918** The Hungarians destroy Bremen. **919** The Hungarians raid Lorraine. **919–36** Henry I the Fowler, King of Germany. | **918** Arabs destroy Reggio. **919** Romanus I Lecapenus makes himself Emperor (–944). | **919–20** Second Fatimid invasion of Egypt fails. |
| **921** Edward the Elder receives homage of King of Scots at Bakewell. | **920** Abd al-Rahman III recovers S. Estaban: defeats Ordoño II and Sancho the Great of Navarre at Val de Junqueras. **921–6** Hungarian raids on Italy. | **920** Ubaydallah moves to new capital al-Mahdia, on the Tunisian coast. **920–1050** Zenith of the Sarakole Empire of Ghana. **921** Fatimids occupy Audaghost. Abu Yazid rebels. |
| **922** Battle of Soissons: Charles the Simple (d. 929) defeated and deposed deposed: succ. Robert of Neustria (–923). **923–36** Hugh the Great makes his brother-in-law Raoul King of France, while continuing to exercise real power. **924** The Hungarians ravage the Rhone valley. Nine years' truce follows. | **922–6** Rudolf II of Burgundy, King of Italy. **923–70** Fernando Gonzalez, Count of Castile. **924** Simeon of Bulgaria and Romanus Lecapenus meet at Constantinople: truce arranged. | **922** Fatimids take most of Morocco. |

| THE NEAR EAST | THE FAR EAST | RELIGION & CULTURE |
|---|---|---|
| | 912–c. 922 Harshavarman I, King of Cambodia. | 912 Notker Balbulus d.: author of *Gesta Karoli Magni.* <br> c. 912 Ibn Khurdadhbih d.: former head of the Caliphal Post Office and intelligence service, and author of first known postal directory. |
| 913 Ismail b. Ahmad d.: succ. Nasr (−943): apogee of Bokhara. | c. 913 Wang unifies Korea under a single dynasty (−1392). | 913–4 Lando, Pope. |
| | | 914–28 John X, Pope. |
| c. 916 Kanauj captured by Indra III Rashtrakuta: chaos in N India. | 916 Abu Zayd describes Kedah as centre of trade in aloes, Brazil wood, camphor, ebony, ivory, sandal, spices, tin and other things. | 915/6 al-Jubbai, Mutazilite theologian, d. <br> c. 915 7 Building of Abbey of Cluny begun. <br> 915–65 al-Mutanabbi, poet. <br> c. 915–17 Cluny Abbey church began. |
| 920 War between Byzantium and the Arabs renewed. | | 920 Council of Constantinople to reconcile differences. |
| 921 Ahmad b. Fadhlan b. Hammad sent by al-Muqtadir as ambassador to the Bulgars: writer of a (lost) account of Russia. | | |
| | 923–36 Later Tang dynasty in N China. | 922 al-Hallaj, Persian mystical pantheist, put to death in Baghdad. al-Tabari, historian, d. <br> c. 922–73 Liutprand, historian. |

| WESTERN, NORTHERN & CENTRAL EUROPE | SPAIN, ITALY & EASTERN EUROPE | AFRICA & EGYPT |
|---|---|---|
| | **924** Abd al-Rahman III demolishes Pamplona, capital of Navarre. | |
| **925–39** Athelstan, King of England: York and Northumbria conquered. | **925** Simeon declares himself Tsar of Bulgaria. | |
| **926** The Hungarians invade Lorraine and Champagne. | **926–47** Hugh of Arles, King of Italy. | |
| **927** Athelstan unites Scots and Britons against Danes at Penrith. Robert I, Duke of Normandy, abdicates: succ. as 2nd Duke, William I Longsword (–942) **927–35** Herbert de Vermandois rebels in France. | **927** Simeon d.: Peter, Tsar of Bulgaria, (–968). Taranto destroyed by the Arabs. | |
| | **928** The Byzantines take Theodosiopolis. | |
| **929** 28 Sept., Wenceslaus, King of Bohemia, murdered by his brother, Boleslaus I. | **929** 16 Jan., Abd al-Rahman III proclaims himself Caliph (–961). **929–1035** Umayyad Caliphs of Córdoba. | |
| **931** Witanagemot meets at Luton. | | **931** Abd al-Rahman III of Córdoba takes Ceuta from the Fatimids: later secures much of the coast. |
| | **932** Abd al-Rahman III campaigns in N Spain: Toledo captured: army of 100,000 defeated at Simancas: flees to Córdoba: crucifies 300 officers for cowardice. | |
| **933** 15 March, Henry the Fowler defeats the Hungarians at Riade. **934** Henry I takes Schleswig. Witanagemot meets at Winchester. Athelstan attacks Scotland by land and sea. **934–41** Rebellions against Otto I. **935** The Hungarians invade Burgundy and N Italy. | **933** Byzantines under John Curcuas take Melitene. **934 or 5** Genoa sacked by the Fatimid fleet. | **933** Fatimids occupy Sijilmasa. **934–46** Abd al-Qasim Muhammad al-Qaim, second Fatimid Imam. **935–69** Ikhshidid dynasty in Egypt. **935–46** Muhammad b. Tughj, first Ikhshidid. **935** Fatimids campaign against Sijilmasa. **c. 940** al-Masudi visits Egypt. |
| **936–54** Louis IV, King of France. **936–62** Otto I the Great, King of Germany (later Emperor). **936–86** Harold Bluetooth, King of Denmark. **937** Norwegians, Scots and men from Strathclyde defeated by Athelstan at Brunanburgh. The Hungarians raid as far as Berry and Rome. | **937** Navarre recognizes suzerainty of Córdoba. | |
| **940–6** Edmund I, the Magnificent, King of England. | **939** Ramiro III of León and Queen Regent Tota of Navarre defeat Abd al-Rahman III at Alhandega: Queen Tota visits court of Córdoba with her son, Sancho the Fat. **c. 940** Córdoba said to have ½ m. inhabitants; 700 mosques; 300 public baths; palace with 400 rooms; | |

| THE NEAR EAST | THE FAR EAST | RELIGION & CULTURE |
|---|---|---|

THE FAR EAST

**925** Foreign merchants forbidden to trade in China.
**c. 925** New Zealand first known to the ancestors of the Maori: called *Tiritiri o te Moana*.
**c. 925—?c. 928** Isanavarman II, King of Cambodia.

**927** Kitan destroy Po-hai, bringing Tungus tribes, including Jurchen, under obedience.
**927—36** Ming Ti, Later Tang Emperor.

RELIGION & CULTURE

**?925—92** St Oswald.
**926** The Bulgarian Church becomes autocephalous.
**926—42** St Odo, second Abbot of Cluny.

THE NEAR EAST

**928—1042** Ziyarid dynasty of Tabaristan founded by Mardawij b. Ziyar.
**929—91** Shi'ite Hamdanid dynasty of Mosul.

**930** Qârmatians carry off the Black Stone from Mecca.

**932—4** al-Qahir, Caliph.
**932—1055** Buwayhid (or Daylamite) dynasty of Fars.

**934** Buwayhids occupy province of Shiraz.
**934—40** al-Radi, Abbasid Caliph.

**935—6** Buwayhids occupy Khuzistan and Kerman: Shiraz becomes Buwayhid capital.

THE FAR EAST

**c. 928—41** Jayavarman IV, King of Cambodia.

**c. 929** Kingdom of E Java, under Sindok, gains in power and importance: title, King of Mataram (—947). Ugrasena, ruler of part of Bali.

RELIGION & CULTURE

**928—9** Leo VI, Pope.

**929—31** Stephen VIII, Pope.

**930** Eckhard of St Gall: *Walter of Aquitaine* (epic).
**931** Edict in Baghdad requiring test of all medical practitioners: 860 receive *ijazahs* (certificates).
**931—5** John XI, Pope.
**932—1020** Firdausi, Persian poet.
Karaouine Mosque at Fez rebuilt.

**933** Text of the Koran finally fixed.

**935/6** Abu al-Hasan Ali al-Ashari of Baghdad d.: orthodox theologian and opponent of Mutazilites: founder of scholastic theology in Islam.
**936—9** Leo VII, Pope.
**936** St Leonard's Hospital, York, opened.

THE FAR EAST

**936** Kitan gain allegiance of Turkish general Shih Ching-tang: set on Chinese throne as a Kitan feudatory.
**936—46** Later Chin dynasty supersedes Later Tang.
**937—1125** Liao (Kitan) dynasty in N China.

**939** Vietnamese drive Chinese out of Vietnam.

RELIGION & CULTURE

**post 938** Constantine Porphyrogenitus: *The Book of the Ceremonies*.
**939—42** Stephen IX, Pope.

THE NEAR EAST

**940—4** al-Muttaqi, Abbasid Caliph.
**940—70** Krishna III, Rashtrakuta ruler.

RELIGION & CULTURE

**940** Chinese classics ordered to be printed by Feng Tao (882—954).

| WESTERN, NORTHERN & CENTRAL EUROPE | SPAIN, ITALY & EASTERN EUROPE | AFRICA & EGYPT |
|---|---|---|
| | bodyguard of 3750 'Slavs'; 113,000 houses; twenty-one suburbs; seventy libraries. **941** Igor, son of Rurik, leads fleet against Byzantium: destroyed by Greek fire. | |
| **942** 17 Dec., William I, 2nd Duke of Normandy, assassinated. **942–54** Malcolm I, King of Scots. **942–96** Richard I, the Fearless, 3rd Duke of Normandy. | | |
| **943** Igor sends raiding expedition into Transcaucasia. | | |
| | **944** Sons of Romanus Lecapenus force him to abdicate. Prince Igor prepares attack against Byzantium but is bought off. | **944** Abu Yazid takes al-Mahdia and Tunis |
| **945** Edmund of England devastates Cumbria: leased to Malcolm I of Scots. Treaty between Igor, Prince of Russia, together with other Russian princes, with Transcaucasian ruler. Drevlians revolt against taxes imposed by Igor of Russia, and kill him. Succ. as regent, his wife, Olga, who raises army and compels Drevlians to pay tribute. His son Sviatoslav, on reaching full age, makes war throughout western Europe, from the Danube, Dnieper and Volga to the Black Sea and the Caspian. **946** 26 May, Edmund I of England murdered. **946–55** Edred, King of England. | **945** Sons of Lecapenus deposed by Constantine Porphyrogenitus. **945–50** Lothair III, King of Italy. | c. **945** Arabs trading in Madagascar. Malagasy raid Waq-Waq near Sofala.

**946** Abu Yazid defeated. **946–52** Abu Abbas Ismail, Fatimid ruler: consolidates Fatimid power: takes title al-Mansur. **946–66** Abu al-Misk Kafur, an Ethiopian eunuch, real ruler of Egypt. **946–60** Abu al-Qasim Unujur, nominal ruler. **947** Abu Yazid d. al-Mansuria founded by Fatimid al-Mansur. |
| | **948–65** al-Hasan b. Ali b. Abi al-Husayn al–Kalbi, Muslim governor of Sicily. | |
| | **950** Berengar II and Adalbert crowned Kings of Italy as vassals of Otto I. | **950** Nubians raid upper Egypt. c. **950** Algiers, Roman Icosium, refounded as al-Jazair Bani Mazranna (whence corruption Algiers). Clans federate in Mogadishu against Somali pressure. Mogadishu trading with Sofala. |
| | **951** Otto I campaigns against Berengar II. | |

| THE NEAR EAST | THE FAR EAST | RELIGION & CULTURE |
|---|---|---|
| | | 940–97/8 Abu al-Wafa Muhammad al-Buzjani al-Hasib, astronomer and mathematician. |
| 941 Egypt regains Syria. Byzantines retake Dara and Nisibis, reaching Aleppo.<br>942 Egypt takes Mecca and Medina.<br>c. 942–97 Mularaja, King of Gujarat. | 941–68 Rajendravarman, King of Cambodia. | c. ante 942 *Alf Layla wa Laylah* (A Thousand Nights and a Night) collected in Iraq.<br>942 Evangelization of Hungary begun. Hosios Loukas Monastery begun.<br>942–6 Marinus II, Pope.<br>942–58 Odo, Abp of Canterbury.<br>943 Sinan b. Thabit, translator of learned works, d.<br>fl. 943–77 Ibn Hawqal, geographer: *Kitab Surat al-Ardh*. |
| | c. 943 Kedah replaces Canton as principal eastern entrepôt for Chinese trade. | |
| 944 John Curcuas captures the miraculous image of the Saviour from Edessa. Hamdanids seize N Syria, including Aleppo and Homs, from the Ikhshidites.<br>944–6 al-Mustakfi, Caliph.<br>944–67 Sayf al-Dawlah Abu al-Hasan Ali, Hamdanid ruler.<br>945 Dec., Ahmad b. Buwayh made *amir al-umara* (chief *amir*) with title Muizz al-Dawlah: makes Buwayhids effective rulers of the Caliphate (−1055). | | post 944 Constantine Porphyrogenitus: *Book of the Themes*.<br><br>945 al-Hasan b. Ahmad al-Hamdani, geographer, d. |
| 946–74 al-Muti, Abbasid Caliph. | 946–7 Kitan ruler occupies Chang-an and almost all China. | 946 Ibrahim b. Thabit, translator of learned works, d.<br>946–55 Agapetus II, Pope. |
| 947–67 Annual Hamdanid raids into Byzantine territory. | 947 War between Liao (Kitan) and the Chinese: victorious Chinese instal Sha-to dynasty.<br>947–50 Later Han dynasty in China. | 948 Einsiedeln monastery church completed.<br>c. 948–51 Constantine VII Porphyrogenitus: *On the administration of the Empire*.<br>ante 950 First Persian version of the *Thousand Nights and a Night*. |
| 949–83 Adud al-Dawlah, Buwayhid: first Muslim ruler to assume title Shahanshah. | | |
| c. 950–99 Dhanga, most powerful of the Chandel dynasty. | c. 950 Cambodian expedition against Champa. | 950 Muhammad b. Muhammad b. Tarkhan Abu Nasr al-Farabi d.: philosopher, translator, mathematician and musicologist.<br>fl. c. 950 al-Istakhri, geographer. |
| 951 The Black Stone restored to Mecca. | 951–9 Later Chou dynasty in China. | 951 At request of Abd al-Rahman III, a monk sent from Constantinople to expound Dioscorides' work on medicinal herbs. |

| WESTERN, NORTHERN & CENTRAL EUROPE | SPAIN, ITALY & EASTERN EUROPE | AFRICA & EGYPT |
|---|---|---|
| | | 952–75 Abu Tamim Maadd al-Muizz, Fatimid Imam: zenith of Fatimid power in NW Africa. |
| 953–5 German rebellions against Otto I. 954–62 Indulf, King of Scots and Picts. c. post 954 Indulf takes Edinburgh. 954–86 Lothair, King of France. 955 10 Aug., Otto I defeats the Hungarians at Lechfeld; and, 16 Oct., the Slavs at Mecklenburg. 955–9 Edwy, the Fair, King of England. | | 955 Egyptian fleet, built at Maqs, near Bulaq, raids Spain. |
| 956 Hugh the Great d. | | 956 Aswan temporarily occupied by the Nubians. Egyptian expedition tak Kasr Ibrim. |
| | 957 Grand Princess Olga of Russia visits Byzantium. 957–66 Sancho I, King of León. | c. 957 Kilwa founded by Ali b. al-Husain b. Ali. |
| | | 958 All Morocco in Fatimid hands. |
| 959–75 Edgar, the Pacific, usurper King of Mercia: and, 1 Oct., King of England. | 959–63 Romanos II, Eastern Roman Emperor, (with the Augusta Theophano). 960–1 Nicephorus Phocas reconquers Crete. | 960–6 Ali, ruler of Egypt. |
| | 961–3 Otto I campaigns against Berengar in Italy. 961–76 al-Hakam II, Caliph of Córdoba. | |
| 962 –7 Dubh, King of Scots. 962–92 Mieszko, King of Poland. | 962 2 Feb., Otto I crowned by Pope John XII as founder of 'The Holy Roman Empire of the German Nation'. | |
| 963 Mieszko, King of Poland, acknowledges imperial suzerainty: standing army of 13,000 established. 963–73 Otto I, Holy Roman Emperor. | 963 Otto I takes Berengar prisoner. 963–9 Nicephorus II Phocas, Eastern Roman Emperor (with the Augusta Theophano). | |
| 965 The English invade Gwynedd (Wales). | 965 Rebellion in Lombardy. Nicephorus Phocas retakes Cyprus. | |
| | 966–72 Otto I campaigns against Byzantines in Apulia. | 966–8 Abu al-Misk Kafur, an Ethiopian eunuch, ruler of Egypt. |
| 967–71 Cuilean, King of Scots. 967–72 Poland at war with Germany Germany. | 967 Alliance between Byzantium and Sviatoslav of Kiev against the Bulgars. Nicephorus Phocas refuses tribute from the Bulgarians: conquers Thrace. 968 Peter of Bulgaria d.: succ. Boris II. 968–70 War in Italy against the Byzantines. | 968–9 Ahmad, last Ikhshidid ruler of Egypt. |

| THE NEAR EAST | THE FAR EAST | RELIGION & CULTURE |
|---|---|---|

955 Buddhism persecuted in China: 30,336 temples and monasteries secularized: only 2,700 and 61,200 monks left: strict regulations made against Buddhists.
955–63 John XII (Octavianus, son of Alberic): first pope to take a throne name.

fl. c. 956 Saljuq, Turkish chieftain: head of Turkoman Ghuzz (or Oghuz): horde settles in Bukhara region.

956 Abu al-Hasan Ali al-Masudi, 'the Herodotus of the Arabs', d.: first Arab historian to group material topically.

957 The Byzantines take Amida.

957 Olga of Russia (subsequently canonized as St. Helen) baptized.

958 The Byzantines take Samosata.
959 Byzantine force crosses the Tigris.

959–88 St Dunstan, Abp of Canterbury: English monasteries reformed and restored.

960 Turkestan, under Turkoman Prince Karakhan, converted to Islam: Saljuq among their leaders.  Sung dynasty founded by Chao Kuang-yin, who takes title of Tai Tsu.
960–1279 Sung dynasty in China.
960–1126 Northern Sung dynasty.
960–1178 Frequent embassies from Sri Vijaya to China, bearing tribute.

961 Emperor Nicephorus Phocas captures Aleppo from Hamdanids: shortly withdraws.  Alptigin made governor of Khurasan.

c. 961 Hamzah al-Isfahani, annalist and critic, d. in Isfahan.

962 Byzantines take Anazarbus and Aleppo.  Alptigin seizes Afghanistan: developed into Ghaznavid empire of Afghanistan and Punjab.

962 13 Feb., Otto I grants privileges to Rome.

963 Sung administration completely reformed: all civil administrative tasks taken from the army.

963 4 Dec., Roman Synod deposes John XII. Ayia Laura, Athos, founded.
963–5 Leo VIII, Pope.
963–84 Ethelwold, Bp of Winchester: translator of the Rule of St Benedict.
964 Nicephorus Phocas issues edict restricting foundation of monasteries and acquisition of greater ecclesiastical wealth.

964 Nicephorus Phocas raids Syria.

964–5 Benedict V, Pope.
965 Harold Bluetooth, King of Denmark baptized.

965 Nicephorus Phocas takes Tarsus and Cilicia.

965–72 John XIII, Pope.
966 Flodard of Reims, historian, d.

967–91 Saad al-Dawlah Abu al-Maali Sharif, Hamdanid ruler.

967–1068 Height of ascendancy of Fujiwara family in Japan.

967 Christianity introduced in Poland from Bohemia.  Abu al-Faraj al-Isbahani (or al-Isfahani) d.: author of Kitab al-Aghani, Book of the Songs.

968 Nicephorus Phocas takes Laodicaea, Hierapolis and Emesa.

968–1001 Jayavarman V, King of Cambodia.

| WESTERN, NORTHERN & CENTRAL EUROPE | SPAIN, ITALY & EASTERN EUROPE | AFRICA & EGYPT |
|---|---|---|

**969** Olga of Russia d.

**969** Nicephorus Phocas assassinated by his succ., John I Tzimisces (−976). Peace between Byzantium and the Bulgars. Anarchy in Bulgaria.

**969** Fatimids, under general Jawhar al-Sigilli, take al-Fustat: building of al-Misr al-Qahíra (modern Cairo) begun.
**969−75** al-Muizz, first Fatimid to adopt style of Caliph.
**969−1171** Fatimid dynasty in Egypt

**970** Fernán González, Count of Castile d., leaving enlarged territories.
**970−1035** Sancho the Great, King of Navarre.

**971−95** Kenneth II, King of Scots.

**971** Sviatoslav of Kiev invades Thrace: defeated by Bardas Skleros. John Tzimisces compels Sviatoslav to cede Bulgaria and the Crimea and to accept a treaty.

**972** Sviatoslav I d., dividing possessions between his three sons, Iaropolk, Oleg and Vladimir.
**972−1015** Vladimir, Prince of Kiev: possesses five wives and 800 concubines.
**973** 11 May, Edgar, King of England, anointed and crowned by St Dunstan at Bath. Edgar said to have been rowed across R. Dee by six kings.
**973−83** Otto II, Holy Roman Emperor.

**972** John Tzimisces forces Sviatoslav to capitulate at Silistria.

**972** Caliph al-Muizz enters Cairo.
**972−1167** Zairite dynasty.

**973** Cairo becomes the official capital of the Fatimids, Bulukin takes Fez and all Morocco.

**974** Rebellion in Rome.

**975** Famine in England.
**975−9** St Edward, the Martyr, King of England.

**ante 975** *Catapan* of Italy founded at Bari to defend southern coast against Islam.

**975−96** Abu Mansur Nizar al-Aziz, Fatimid Caliph: first to reside permanently in Cairo.
**976** Sijilmasa taken by the Maghrawi Berbers.

**976** John Tzimisces d. in Constantinople: succ. Basil II Bulgaroctonos (−1025): Palestinian and Syrian possessions lost.
**976 ff.** Subh, mother of Hisham II, twelve years old at accession, real power behind the throne: Muhammad b. Abi Amir, court chamberlain (*hajib*) steadily seizes power.
**976−9** Bardas Skleros's rebellion.
**976−1009** Hisham II, Caliph of Córdoba, first reign.
**977** Fatimids invade S Italy.
**977−1014** Samuel, Tsar of Bulgaria.
**977−86** Samuel reconquers Thessaly and Macedonia.

**c. 977−8** Ethiopia in control of Zaila.

**978** Aix-la-Chapelle sacked by Lothair of France: Otto II advances on Paris.
**979** 18 March, St Edward the Martyr murdered by his stepmother near Corfe Castle.
**979−1013** Ethelred II, the Unready, King of England, first reign.
**980** Renewed Danish piratical raids on England: Chester, Southampton and Thanet attacked. Vladimir, having beaten his brother, sole ruler of Kiev (−1015).

**979** Bani al-Hamuya raid Nubia: Ethiopia devastated.

| THE NEAR EAST | THE FAR EAST | RELIGION & CULTURE |
|---|---|---|
| **969** Antioch taken by Byzantine army under Nicephorus Phocas (−1084): and then Aleppo: treaty between Byzantium and Amir of Aleppo. Damascus occupied by a Fatimid lieutenant. | | |
| | | **970** al-Azhar mosque begun.<br>**fl. c. 970** Ikhwan al-Safa (Brethren of Purity): eclectic school of philosophers at Basrah and Baghdad. |
| | | **972–4** Benedict VI, Pope. |
| **973** Second Chalukya dynasty of Kalyani founded by Taila or Tailapa II: dethrones the last Rashtrakuta. | **973** Sung protectorate acquired over Annam: influence extended over Indonesia. | **973** July–Oct., Donus II, Pope.<br>Thabit b. Sinan, translator of learned works, d.<br>**973–1038** Abu al-Rayhan Muhammad b. Ahmad al-Biruni, philosopher and scientist: author of description of India.<br>**973–1057** Abu al-Ala al-Maarri, poet and philosopher.<br>**974–85** Boniface VII, antipope. |
| **974** John Tzimisces takes Emesa and Nisibis.<br>**974–91** al-Tai, Abbasid Caliph.<br>**975** John Tzimisces takes Baalbek, Damascus and Beirut. | | **975** Bishopric of Prague created.<br>**c. 975** al-Azhar mosque becomes a university.<br>**975–84** Benedict VII, Pope.<br>**c. 975–1000** Abbey of Cluny reconstructed. |
| **976** Nazareth and Caesarea submit voluntarily to John Tzimisces: army returns to Antioch.<br>**976–97** Subultigin, real founder of the Ghaznawid dynasty (−1186).<br>**976–1012** Kabus, Ziyarid ruler: patron of al-Biruni. | | **976** Suidas: *Lexicon*. al-Hakam d., leaving a library catalogued in forty-four volumes. |
| **977** Ghazna begins to expand.<br><br>**978–1030** Mahipala, ninth 'Pala' ruler. | **977** Intermarriage between Balinese and Javanese ruling families first recorded. | **977** Abu Bakr b. Umar, known as Ibn al-Qutiyah, Andalusian historian, d. Library founded in Shiraz by Adud al-Dawlah.<br>**978–9** Bimaristan, hospital, at Baghdad built by Adud al-Dawlah. |
| | **ante 980** Sung incorporate many small states into the Empire.<br>**980–1005** Earlier Le dynasty in Vietnam. | **980–1037** Abu Ali al-Husain b. Sina (Avicenna), philosopher, physician and polymath: author of the *Qanun,* guide to medical practice. |

| WESTERN, NORTHERN & CENTRAL EUROPE | SPAIN, ITALY & EASTERN EUROPE | AFRICA & EGYPT |
|---|---|---|
| **981–2** Danish raids on Devon and S Wales. | **981** Muhammad b. Abi Amir assumes title al-Mansur bi-Allah following successes on N African coast: annual campaigns against Castile, Catalonia and León: takes Zamorra. <br> **982** 15 July, Otto II defeated by the Arabs at C. Colonna. | |
| **983** Otto III succ. Otto II (−1002): his mother, Theophano, regent (−991). | **983** Samuel of Bulgaria retakes Thessaly: threatens Greece. | |
| **984** Henry the Quarrelsome attempts to usurp Otto III. | | **984–96** al-Mansur b. Bulukin succ. his father. |
| **985** Icelandic fleet of twenty-five ships under Eric the Red colonizes Greenland. <br> **985–1014** Sweyn, King of Denmark. | **985** Muhammad b. Abi Amir sacks Barcelona. | **985** al-Mansur mounts unsuccessful campaign against Fez and Sijilmasa. <br> **986–8** al-Mansur repels revolt of the Kotama. |
| **986–7** Louis V, King of France. <br> **986–1014** Svend, King of Denmark. | **986** Basil II defeated by Samuel of Bulgaria. Bulgars conquer Albania. | |
| **987** Hugh Capet, mayor of the palace, son of Hugh the Great, made King of France by the nobility (−996). <br> **987–1328** Capet dynasty in France. <br> **988** Danes attack Devon, Somerset and Wales. Vladimir of Kiev seizes the Chersonese. <br> **988–91** Struggle between Hugh Capet and Charles of Lorraine. | **987** Bardas Phocas and Bardas Skleros rebel: Constantinople besieged. Catalonia refuses to acknowledge Hugh Capet as overlord. <br><br> **988** Muhammad b. Abi Amir takes León. | **988** Fatimid conquest of Syria completed. |
| | **989** Bardas Phocas killed at Abydos. <br> **989–90** Samuel of Bulgaria takes lower Macedonia. | |
| **990–1029** William, Duke of Aquitaine. | | **c. 990** Audaghost taken by Emperor of Ghana: African governor installed |
| **991** Danes defeated at Maldon, Essex: then bought off by treaty (*danegeld*). Hugh Capet defeats pretender Charles of Lorraine at Laon. | | |
| **992–1025** Boleslaw I, the Brave, King of Poland: conqueror of all Pomerania from the Oder to the Vistula. <br> **993** Yorkshire attacked by Danes. The Slavs retake Brandenburg. | **992** Muhammad b. Abi Amir replaces Caliph's name by his own on public documents. Basil II grants the Venetians commercial privileges. | |
| **994** London besieged by Sweyn of Denmark and Olaf of Norway. Vikings invade Frisia and Hadeland. | **994–1035** Sancho the Great, King of Navarre. | |
| **995–7** Constantine IV, King of Scots. <br> **995–1000** Olaf Trygvasson, King of Norway. | **ante 995** Samuel of Bulgaria takes Durazzo: Serbs made subject to Bulgaria. | |

| THE NEAR EAST | THE FAR EAST | RELIGION & CULTURE |
|---|---|---|
| | **981** China recognizes Vietnam as an independent kingdom.<br>**982** Vietnamese expedition against Champa.<br>**982–1029** Mahinda V, King of Ceylon: confusion in the kingdom: relies on S Indian mercenaries. | |
| **983–9** Sharaf al-Dawlah, Buwayhid. | | **983** The canal pound lock invented by Chiao Wei-Yo. A father and his son massacred by a crowd at Kiev for refusing to sacrifice to idols.<br>**984** Ibn Nubatah, preacher at court of the Hamdanids in rhymed prose, d.<br>**984–5** John XIV, Pope. |
| **985–1014** Rajaraja I, the Great, Chola ruler: establishes domains firmly: extensive campaigns against Kerala, Ceylon and the Pandyas: naval expedition against Maldive Is.<br>**986/7** Sabuktigin, Amir of Ghazna, raids territory of Raja Jaipal of Bathindah. | | **984–1047** Périgueux Cathedral built.<br>c. **985** Conversions to Islam make progress in Nubia.<br>fl. **985–6** al-Maqdisi, geographer.<br>**985–96** John XV, Pope.<br><br>**987** Chichén-Itzá occupied by Itzás: Mayapán then built by the Toltecs. |
| **988/9** Raja Jaipal raids Ghazna. | **988** Hsi-Hsia state becomes tributary to the Sung. | **988** al-Nadim: *al-Fihrist,* catalogue of existing Arab writings published in Baghdad.<br>**988 or 9** Beginning of conversion of Russia to Christianity. |
| **989–1012** Baha al-Dawlah, Buwayhid. | | |
| | **990** Kitan take over Hsi-Hsia state.<br>c. **990** E Java attacks Sri Vijaya. | **990** Vladimir of Kiev, after baptism, m. Anne, sister of the Emperors Basil II and Constantine VIII: large numbers of the people of Kiev baptized: the state made officially Christian. See of Dubrovnik founded.<br>**990–1012** Mosque of al-Hakim, Cairo, built. |
| **991–1031** al-Qadir, Caliph. Raja Jaipal organizes league of Hindu kings against Ghazna.<br>**991–1001** Said al-Dawlah Abu al-Fadhail Said, Hamdanid ruler subject to Egypt.<br>**992** Sri Vijaya appeals to Chinese Emperor for aid against Java. Java also sends embassy to China. | **991–1006** Power of E Java increases: Bali and W coast of Borneo brought under control.<br>c. **991–1007** Dharmavamca, ruler of Java.<br><br>**992** Anuradhapura abandoned as capital of Ceylon: invasion of Colas. | **990–1014** Tower and portico of St Germain-des-Près built.<br>**990–1030** Fan-Kuan, Chinese artist.<br>c. **991–1007** Javanese scholars translate old Sanscrit texts into Old Javanese: beginning of Javanese literature.<br>**991–7** First church built in Kiev.<br>**991–6** Gallican opposition to Rome led by Gerbert, Bp of Reims. |
| c. **993–4** Delhi (probably) founded. | post **993** Further Sri Vijaya embassy to China. | **993** Wazir Sabur b. Ardashir builds library at Baghdad for 10,000 books.<br>c. **993 or 1002** Abu Bakr al-Khwarizmi d.: first Arab author to leave a collection of literary correspondence.<br>**994** Ali b. al-Abbas al-Majusi d.: author, physician and dietician. Odilo, Bp of Cluny.<br>**994–1064** Ali b. al-Hazm, historian and polymath, of Córdoba. |
| **995** Basil II campaigns in Syria. | | **995** Gerbert of Reims deposed. Durham Cathedral begun. |

| WESTERN, NORTHERN & CENTRAL EUROPE | SPAIN, ITALY & EASTERN EUROPE | AFRICA & EGYPT |
|---|---|---|

**995–1014** Sweyn, King of Denmark, also King of Sweden.
**995–9** Adelaide, his grandmother, regent for Otto III.
**996** Hugh Capet makes Robert II, the Pious, associate King of France (–1031).
**996–1027** Richard II, the Good, 4th Duke of Normandy.
**997–9** Renewed Danish attacks on S England.
**997–1005** Kenneth III, King of Scots.
**997–1038** (St) Stephen, King of Hungary.
**997** Danzig becomes capital of Duchy of Pommerellen.

**996** 21 May, Otto III crowned Emperor in Rome. Basil II revises tax laws by the *Alleleggnon.* Samuel of Bulgaria defeated by Nicephorus Ouranos on R. Sperchios.
**997–8** Otto III puts down rebellion in Rome and Italy.

**996–1021** Abu Ali Mansur al-Hakim, Fatimid ruler: a vicious fanatic: Jews and Christians persecuted.

**999** Otto III makes Rome his capital.
**999–1207** Alfonso V, King of León.

**11th c.** Riazan and Yaroslav already founded.
**11th–14th c.** Frequent trade from Greenland and Iceland in walrus hides, ivory (walrus and narwhal), eiderdown and furs.

**c. 11th c.** Supposed Shona settlers arrive in Rhodesia: theocratic state: trade in gold and ivory against imported beads, cloth and porcelain.

**1000** End of the world confidently expected: widespread famine caused by failure to cultivate crops. Ethelred II of England campaigns in Cumberland and in the Is. of Man. Sweyn of Denmark and Sweden takes Norway.
**c. 1000** The Ghuzz Turks enter Russia.
**1001** Ethelred II of England m. Emma, daughter of Richard I, Duke of Normandy.

**1000** Byzantium recovers Bulgarian territory on the R. Danube. Sancho of Navarre takes Aragon.
**c. 1000–50** Twenty petty states succeed Caliphate in Spain: known as *reyes de taifas* (party kings).

**c. 1000** Gao, capital of Songhai. Majority of Berbers in Audaghost region nominal Muslims.

**1001** Rebellion in Rome against both Emperor and Pope. St Stephen of Hungary crowned by the Pope. Basil II begins conquest of Bulgaria.

**1001** Treaty between Byzantium and the Fatimids.

**1002** 13 Nov., massacre of St Brice: many Danes killed in England.
**1002–24** Henry II, the Saint, Holy Roman Emperor.

**1003–4** Polish occupation of Bohemia.
**1003–14** Frequent Danish attacks on England.
**1003–16** Robert the Pious conquers Burgundy.
**1004–18** Henry II at war with Poland.

**1002** Muhammad b. Abi Amir d. returning from an expedition against Castile: succ. as chamberlain his son, Abd al-Malik al-Muzaffar (–1008). Basil II takes Serbia and Vodena.
**1002–15** Arduin, Marquess of Ivrea, pretender to the throne of Italy.
**1003** Basil II takes Vidin.

**1004** Henry II crowned King of Italy. The Arabs pillage Pisa. Samuel of Bulgaria defeated on R. Vardar.

| THE NEAR EAST | THE FAR EAST | RELIGION & CULTURE |
|---|---|---|
| | | **995—1000** Olaf Trygvasson introduces Christianity into Norway. |
| | | **996—9** Gregory V, Pope. |
| | | **996** Trondheim Palace built. |
| **997—1030** Mahmud of Ghazna, most distinguished of the Ghaznavid dynasty: makes annual raids on NW India. | | **997** Muhammad b. Abi Amir demolishes church of St James of Compostela. |
| | | **997—8** John XVI, antipope. |
| **999** Samanid dynasty overthrown by Mahmud of Ghazna. Basil II again in Syria: Emesa recovered. Armenia reunited with the Empire. | | **998—1061** Song Chi, historian. |
| | | **999** Leif, son of Eric the Red of Greenland, reaches Labrador coast. |
| | | **999—1003** Sylvester II (Gerbert of Reims), Pope: first French Pope: first to introduce Arabic numerals into European mathematics. |
| | **11th c.** Tungus take part of Korea. Petchenegue Turks pressed out of C Asia towards Russia. Turks in Transoxiana. Thaton sacked by the Burmese. | **11th c.,** first quarter, Murasaki Shikibu, Japanese author of *Genji Monogatari* (The Tale of Genji). Itza of Chichén-Hzá, Cocoms of Mayapan, and Xins of Uxmal, dynasties in Mexico. |
| | | **c. 11th—12th c.** Decline of Maya civilization: temples and agriculture abandoned. |
| **1000** Mahmud of Ghazna defeats Jayapala, Shahiya ruler. | **1000** Chinese state budget 22,200,000 strings of cash. | **1000** Archbishopric of Gniesno, Poland, founded. |
| **c. 1000** Chalukya country ravaged by Chola Rajaraja the Great. | | **c. 1000** Inca Empire at its apogee: twin capitals Quitu (Quito) and Cuzco, S Peru: elaborate court culture and developed agriculture. Some three thousand monks on Mt Athos, including Russians. |
| | | **c. 1000—10** *Chanson de Roland.* |
| **1001** Mahmud of Ghazna defeats Raja Jaipal near Peshawar: Jaipal commits suicide: succ. Anandpal: second league of Hindu rulers formed. | **1001—2** Udayadityavarman I, King of Cambodia: quarrel for the succession. | **c. 1000—50** School of Medicine at Salerno flourishing, with rival school at Naples. |
| **c. 1001** Mahmud of Ghazna given the title al-Ghazi. | **1001—11** King of Ligor (Tambralinga) invades Dvaravati: repulsed at Haripunjaya: m. a Khmer princess and founds kingdom of Cambodia. | **c. 1001** Thorfinn Karlsefni with 150 Greenlanders migrates to Vinland (? Newfoundland, Nova Scotia or New England). |
| **1001—24** Mahmud leads seventeen campaigns in India: Punjab, Lahore, Multan and parts of Sind and Persia annexed. | | |
| **1002** Mahmud campaigning in Seistan. | **1002—50** Suryavarman I, King of Cambodia. | **1002—71** al-Khatib al-Baghdadi, historian: will leaving his books for other Muslims. |
| | **1003** Sri Vijaya informs Chinese Emperor prayers are offered for his welfare. | **1003** John XVII, Pope. |
| | **c. 1003—6** Jayaviravarman, Cambodian usurper in Angkor. | **1003—71** Abu al-Walid Ahmad b. Zaydun, Andalusian poet. |
| **1004—6** Mahmud attacks Multan, on lower Indus R. | **c. 1004** Chinese state budget about 20 m. strings of cash: military expenditure about 25%. | **c. 1004/5** Vinland colony destroyed by Skraeling natives: colonists retire to Greenland. |
| | | **1004—9** John XVIII, Pope. |

| WESTERN, NORTHERN & CENTRAL EUROPE | SPAIN, ITALY & EASTERN EUROPE | AFRICA & EGYPT |
|---|---|---|

**1005** Truce between Germany and Poland.  Kenneth III of Scots killed at Monzievaird by his cousin and succ., Malcolm II (–1034).

**1005** Samuel retakes Durazzo and Skoplie.

**1006** Abu Rukna rebels in Egypt.

**1007** Renewed war between Germany and Poland.
**1007–9** Two-year truce between England and Danes.

**1007** Basil II recovers Lower Macedonia.

**1007–9** Qala founded by Banu Hamm
**1007–1152** Hammadid dynasty.

**1009** Danes attack London.

**1009** First Normans reach Sicily: shortly defeated by Russian soldiers in the Byzantine army.  Castile temporarily seizes Córdoba: Hisham II deposed in a palace revolution.
**1009, 1010** Muhammad II, Caliph of Córdoba.
**1009–10** Sulayman, Caliph of Córdoba, first reign.
**1010–3** Hisham II, restored, Caliph of Córdoba.

**c. 1009–10** Dia Kossoi of Kukia converted to Islam: transfers capital to Gao.

**1010** The Normans defeat the English at Ringmere.

**1011** The Arabs again pillage Pisa.

**1012–90** Zirid Kingdom of Granada.

**1013** Poland invades Russia.  Peace of Magdeburg between Poland and Henry II.  Autumn, Ethelred the Unready flees to Normandy; Sweyn, King of Denmark and Norway since 986, proclaimed King of England by right of conquest (–1014).
**1014** 3 Feb., Sweyn, of England, Denmark and Norway, d.: Ethelred II restored in England (–1016).
14 Feb., Henry II crowned Emperor. 23 Apr., battle of Clontarf: Vikings defeated.  Canute of Denmark and Norway proclaimed King of England: ceded East Anglia, Mercia and Northumbria by treaty.
**1015–8** Renewed war between Henry II and Poland.
**1016** 23 Apr., Edmund II, Ironside, King of England; 30 Nov., murdered at Oxford.  Dec., Canute, King of Denmark and Norway, King of all England (1035).

**1017** Canute organizes England in four earldoms.

**1013** Córdoba sacked in a revolt.
**1013–6** Sulayman, Caliph of Córdoba, second reign.

**1014** Bulgarian army annihilated at Cimbalugu: Samuel d.

**1015–6** Genoa and Pisa conquer Corsica and Tunisia from the Arabs.
**1016** Further Normans arrive in S Italy.  Pisa captures Sardinia from the Muslims.
**1016–8** Ali b. Hammud, governor of Ceuta and Tangier, proclaims himself Caliph of Córdoba.

| THE NEAR EAST | THE FAR EAST | RELIGION & CULTURE |
|---|---|---|
| | c. 1005–7 Suryavarman I takes Angkor. | 1005 Dar al-Hikmah (House of Wisdom), with library of 600,000 books, set up by Caliph al-Hakim in Cairo.<br>1005–12 St Alphege, Abp of Canterbury.<br>c. 1005–89 Abp Lanfranc, theologian. |
| | 1006 Sri Vijaya attacks E Java: capital captured: royal palace burnt: zenith of Sri Vijaya power. | |
| 1007 Maldives conquered by the Cholas. | | 1007 Uxmal founded by the Xins.<br>1007–71 St Peter Damian.<br>1007–72 Ou-yang Hsiu, Chinese historian: the first to draw up rules of literary censorship. |
| 1008 Mahmud of Ghazna raids Punjab, taking home vast booty.<br>1009 Mahmud takes fortress of Kangra: held until 1044. | 1009–1225 Ly dynasty in Vietnam. | 1008–14 al-Hakim persecutes Christians and Jews.<br>1009 Caliph al-Hakim destroys Church of the Holy Sepulchre. Ali b. Yunus, Egyptian astronomer, d.<br>c. 1009–10 Dia Kossoi of Kukia converted to Islam.<br>1009–12 Sergius IV, Pope. |
| 1010–26 Mahmud raids Mathura, Thanesar, Kanauj and Somnath: wealth of temples described by al-Biruni. | 1010 Airlangga, a Balinese married to a princess of E Java, accepts throne of E Java from notables: civil war ensues. | 1010 Basle Cathedral begun.<br><br>1011 Caliph rules Fatimid descent from the Prophet spurious.<br>1011–77 Shao Yung, philosopher and poet. |
| 1012–42 Rajendra Choladeva I, Chola ruler: initially joint ruler with his father: annexes S Chalukya provinces (modern Hyderabad): further campaigns against Kerala and Ceylon: major campaign against Sri Vijaya to free Indian trade with China. | 1012 War between Cambodia and Sri Vijaya. Champa drought-resistant rice introduced into Fukien province of China. | 1012 St Alphege, Abp of Canterbury, martyred by the Danes. Counts of Tusculum gain control of papal elections.<br>1012–24 Benedict VIII, Pope.<br><br>c. 1013 Abu al-Qasim Khalaf b. Abbas al-Zahrawi d.: physician, surgeon and writer.<br><br>1016 St. Olaf's Church, Troudheim, built. |
| | | 1017–72 Wu Yang-Hsiu, Chinese poet.<br>1017–73 Chou Tun-i, Chinese philosopher. |

| WESTERN, NORTHERN & CENTRAL EUROPE | SPAIN, ITALY & EASTERN EUROPE | AFRICA & EGYPT |
|---|---|---|
| **1018** Assembly of Oxford: Danes subjected to English law. Poland invades Russia, taking Kiev: Jaroslav, son-in-law of Boleslaw of Poland, installed as Grand Duke. Peace of Budziszyn: Germany recognizes independence of Poland.<br>**1019** Denmark and England formally united.<br>**1019–54** Jaroslav I, Grand Prince of Kiev: known as the Wise for his good administration. | **1018** Basil II completes conquest of Bulgaria. Melo's rebellion in Apulia put down.<br>**1018–23** Abd-al-Rahman IV, Caliph of Córdoba. | **1019** Akkar Fortress, Lebanon, already built. |
| | **1021–2** Henry II campaigns abortively against the Byzantines in S Italy. | **1021** al-Hakim declares himself divine. Druze sect organized: al-Hakim disappears mysteriously: succ. al-Zahir (–1035).<br>**1021–35** al-Zahir, Fatimid Caliph. |
| **1023** Emperor Henry II and Robert II of France meet at Ivry.<br><br>**1024–1138** Salian Dynasty of Holy Roman Emperors.<br>**1024–37** Conrad II, the Salic, Holy Roman Emperor.<br>**1025–34** Mieszko II, King of Poland. | **1023** Abd al-Rahman V, Caliph of Córdoba.<br>**1023–5** Muhammad II, Caliph of Córdoba.<br>**1023–91** Banu Abbad dynasty of Seville.<br><br>**1025** Ali b. Hammud takes Málaga: founds petty Hammudid dynasty (–1057).<br>**1025–8** Constantine VIII, Eastern Roman Emperor. | |
| | **c. 1026–99** El Cid Campeador, warrior and hero. | **1026** Zairite dynasty becomes independent of the Fatimids. |
| **1027** Poland cedes Slovak province to Hungary.<br>**1027–8** Richard III, 5th Duke of Normandy.<br>**1028** Poland and Hungary raid Germany as far as the Elbe.<br>**1028–35** Robert II, 'The Devil' or 'The Magnificent', 6th Duke of Normandy.<br>**1029** German invasion of Poland defeated.<br><br><br><br><br>**1030** Second German invasion of Poland frustrated. | **1027** Caliphate of Córdoba abolished by an *ad hoc* council of *wazirs*.<br>**1027–31** Hisham III, Caliph of Córdoba.<br><br>**1028–34** Romanos III Argyros, Eastern Roman Emperor, (with the Augusta Zoe).<br>**1029** Duke of Naples grants the Norman Renoulf the town of Aversa. Garcia, last Count of Castile, murdered on Leonese instigation: Castile taken by Sancho the Great of Navarre: León then over-run: his son Ferdinand made ruler of Castile. | |
| **1031** Canute visits Scotland: receives submission of three kings.<br>**1031–60** Henry I, King of France. | **1031** Following fall of Caliphate, Ferdinand of Castile expands his territory. Violent riot in Córdoba. | **1031** Kurds settled near Krak des Chevaliers. |

## THE NEAR EAST

**1018** 2 Dec., Raja Haradatta of Baran (or Bulandshahr) accepts Islam: surrenders to Mahmud of Ghazna with 10,000 men.
**1018–60** Raja Bhoja, ruler of Malwa: scholar and patron of learning.

**1019** Jan., Mahmud expels Pratihara dynasty of Kanauj: town plundered. Autumn, Mahmud enters Ganda Chandel: Hindu army runs way: 580 elephants taken to Ghazna.

**1021–2** Basil II campaigns against Armenia. Mahmud again enters Ganda Chandel: tribute paid.

**1023** Rajendra Chola, Tamil King, extends kingdom to the Ganges: attacks Mahipala, King of Bihar and Bengal.

**1024** Mahmud of Ghazna takes Somnath, with huge booty.

**1027** Mahmud campaigns against Jats in Multan.

**1030** Romanos III's campaign in Syria repelled. Apr., Mahmud of Ghazna d. Saljuq, founder of Turkish Saljuqid empire, d.
**1030–63** Tughril Bey, ruler of the Saljuqid dominions.
**1031** The Byzantines take Edessa.
**1031–75** al-Qaim, Caliph.

## THE FAR EAST

**1019** Airlangga formally crowned King of E Java.

**1021** Chinese state budget 150,800,000 strings of cash.
**1021–86** Wang Anshih, reformer of Chinese financial system.

**1025** Rajindracola, Chola prince, attacks Sri Vijaya: King captured: Palembang taken and looted: Sumatra and Malay peninsula taken and sacked: Acheh and Nicobar Is. seized: conquest not followed up.
**1026** Lhade, King of Tibet: computation of time in sixty year cycles introduced. Sri Vijaya acknowledges Chola kingdom as overlord.

**1028** Sri Vijaya sends embassy to China.
**1028–37** Airlangga, King of E Java, campaigns against his rivals: kingdom reunited.

**1030** Airlangga m. a princess from Sri Vijaya.

**1031** Hsi-Hsia state takes name of Toba.

## RELIGION & CULTURE

**1018–78** Michael Psellus, historian.

**1019** Synod of Goslar votes for celibacy of priests. al-Darazi, organizer of the Druze sect, d.
**1019–86** Ssuma-Kuang, historian and poet.
**1020–77** Chang Tsai, Chinese philosopher
**1021** Following al-Hakim's death, Christians again tolerated in the Holy Land.
**1021–31** Basilica of Aquileia built.
**1021–58** Solomon b. Gabirol, Spanish Jewish Neo-Platonist.
**c. 1022** The *Cathari* sect emerges in southern France.
**1022 or 32** Ibn al-Bawwab, calligrapher, d.
**1023** Holy Sepulchre and other Jerusalem churches restored and rebuilt.
**1023–34** Abbey of Mont St Michel built.

**1024** Synod of Pavia demands celibacy of higher clergy.
**1024–32** John XIX, Pope.

**1025** Abd al-Jabbar, Mutazili scholar, d. Ferdausi, poet, d.

**1026–7** 700 pilgrims, including Norman knights, visit the Holy Places. Canute visits Rome.

**1027** Synod of Tuluges: origin of the 'Truce of God'.

**1028–94** al-Bakri, geographer.

**1030** Miskawayh d.: compiler of distinguished Islamic history. Speyer Cathedral founded.

**1031–40** al-Biruni in India: his *Tahqiq-i-Hind* gives detailed description of his visit.

| WESTERN, NORTHERN & CENTRAL EUROPE | SPAIN, ITALY & EASTERN EUROPE | AFRICA & EGYPT |
|---|---|---|
| **1032** Millenium of the Crucifixion causes widespread expectance of end of the world: further famine. | **ante 1032** The aristocracy seize power in Venice.<br>**1032–85** Banu Dhu al-Nun dynasty in Toledo. | |
| **1034–40** Duncan I, King of Scots. Interregnum in Poland.<br>**1035** Bohemia accepts German suzerainty. William the Bastard (later, the Conqueror) inherits as 7th Duke of Normandy by his father's Will.<br>**1035–40** Harold I, Harefoot, King of England. | **1034–41** Michael IV, Eastern Roman Emperor, (with the Augusta Zoě).<br>**1035** County of Castile becomes a kingdom under Ferdinand I (−1065). Rebellion in Lombardy. Ramiro I becomes King of Aragon (−1063). | **1034** Bône pillaged by Genoese and Pisans.<br>**c. 1035** Military brotherhood of al-Murabitun (commonly Almoravids) founded by Yahya b. Ibrahim among Lemtuna of lower Senegal.<br>**1035–94** al-Mustansir, Fatimid Caliph. |
| **1037** Rebellion in Poland.<br>**1037–56** Henry III, the Black, Holy Roman Emperor. | **1037** Former ruler of León killed in battle. Castile now pre-eminent amongst Christian kingdoms of Spain. | |
| **1038** Conrad II annexes Burgundy. | | |
| **1039** Gruffydd of Gwynedd and Powis defeats English. Bohemia conquers Poland. Duncan, King of Scots, makes abortive raid on Durham.<br>**1040** 14 Aug., Duncan, King of Scots, murdered by MacBeth, Mormaer of Moray, succ. as King of Scots (−1057).<br>**1040–2** Canute II (Hardicanute), King of England.<br>**1040–58** Casimir I, the Restorer, King of Poland.<br>**1041** Bohemia accepts Henry III as suzerain. | **1039–1141** Banu Hud established in Saragossa.<br><br>**1040** Bulgarian rebellion.<br>**post 1040** George Maniakes recovers Syracuse.<br><br>**1041** 4 May, Byzantines defeated by Lombards and Normans at Monte Maggiore.<br>**1041–2** Michael V Kalaphates, Eastern Roman Emperor. | **c. 1040** Mannu dynasty of Tekrur. founded: beginning of Islamization of Tekrur. |
| **1042–7** Magnus, King of Denmark.<br>**1042–66** St Edward, the Confessor, King of England. | **1042** Renoulf of Aversa takes Gaeta. George Maniakes disgraced. The Augustae Zoe and Theodora, joint Eastern Roman Empresses.<br>**1042–55** Constantine IX Monomachos, Eastern Roman Emperor.<br>**1043** George Maniakes rebels: d. Russians under Prince Vladimir attack Constantinople: Russian fleet destroyed by Greek fire: army compelled to retreat. | **1042** Abdallah b. Yasin campaigns against Zenata, Goddala and Lemtuna<br><br>**c. 1043** Mandingo Empire of Jenne founded. |
| **1044** Henry III makes war on Hungary. Gruffydd of Gwynedd and Powis defeats Danes invading from Ireland. | | |
| **1045** Peter of Hungary restored: does homage to Henry III. Harold, son of Godwin, Earl of Wessex, made Earl of East Anglia. | **1045** Navarre takes Calahorra. | **c. 1045** Abdallah b. Yasin expelled b Zenata: settles at Sijilmasa: Yahya b. Umar in command of army: many local purges. |

| THE NEAR EAST | THE FAR EAST | RELIGION & CULTURE |
|---|---|---|
| | | 1032—45 Benedict IX, Pope.<br>1032—85 Cheng Hao, neo-Confucianist philosopher. |
| | 1034 Breach between Hsi-Hsia and Sung. | c. 1033—1109 St Anselm, theologian and philosopher, Abp of Canterbury. |
| 1035 2 July, Robert the Devil, 6th Duke of Normandy, d. at Nicaea. | | ante 1035 The spinning wheel in use in China. |
| c. post 1035 Varangians under Harold Hardrada, fighting Muslims in Syria and Asia Minor. | | 1035—1101 St Bruno, founder of the Carthusians.<br>1035—89 Hospice of Great St Bernard built. |
| | | 1036 Romanos III restores the Church of the Holy Sepulchre.<br>1036—1101 Su Tung-po, poet: with his father, Su Shih, and his brother Su Che, poets, known as the Three Sus.<br>1037 Construction of Cathedral of St Sophia begun in Kiev, and a monastery outside the town.<br>1037—67 Abbey of Jumièges built. |
| 1037 Tughril and Dawud, grandsons of Saljuq, take Marw and Nisapur: Balkh, Jurjan, Tabaristan, Khwarizm, Hamadhan, Rayy and Isfahan shortly added to their possessions.<br>1038 Nayapala, 'Pala' ruler, sends mission to Tibet. | 1038—1227 Hsi-Hsia state in N China, formed by Toba tribes. Hsi-Hsia ruler proclaims himself Emperor of China. | 1038 St John Gualbert founds Order of Vallombrosa.<br>Between 1038 and 1042—1123/4 Umar Khayyam, poet and astronomer. |
| | | 1040 The Truce of God promulgated in Aquitaine.<br>c. 1040—1106 Li Lung-mien, artist, painter of horses. |
| 1041—1187 Saljuqid Kingdom of Kerman. | | 1041 Council of Montriond: Truce of God organized: fighting forbidden between Wednesday evening and Monday morning. |
| | 1042 Airlangga divides E Java into two states, Kediri and Janggala: separate heirs appointed. | 1042 The Truce of God promulgated in Normandy. |
| | | 1043—58 Michael Caerularius, Patriarch of Constantinople. |
| 1044 Hindus recover Kangra.<br><br>1045 The Byzantines conquer Armenia. | 1044—77 Anawratha, King of Pagan: first eastern ruler to use elephants as cavalry: changes allegiance from Mahayana to Theravada Buddhism. Founder of first Buddhist empire.<br>1044—1287 Pagan dynasty in Burma. | 1044—6 Gregory VI, Pope.<br>1044—51 Robert of Jumièges, Bp of London: first Norman to be consecrated in England.<br>1045 — 52 Novgorod Cathedral built by Greek architects.<br>1045 Law School at Constantinople reorganised by Constantine IX. First attempts to use moveable type made in China. 1 May, Benedict IX sells Papacy to John Gratianus, Gregory VI. Silvester III, antipope. |

| WESTERN, NORTHERN & CENTRAL EUROPE | SPAIN, ITALY & EASTERN EUROPE | AFRICA & EGYPT |
|---|---|---|
| | **1046** Henry III crowned Emperor in Rome. Norman conquests in Italy recognized. | |
| **1047** Rebellion of nobles put down by Henry I and William of Normandy at Val-des-Dunes. Henry III recreates dukedoms of Bavaria, Carinthia and Swabia. Peace made with Bohemia, Poland and Pomerania.<br>**1047–60** Andrew I, King of Hungary.<br>**1047–66** Harald Hardrada, King of Norway.<br>**1048** William of Normandy takes Domfront and Alençon. | **1047** Robert Guiscard, Norman leader, in Italy. Leo Tornicios rebels. | **1048** First campaign of the Almoravids. al-Muizz b. Badis forbids use of Fatimid currency. |
| **1049** William of Normandy begins to take Maine.<br><br>**c. 1050** Oslo founded by Harald Hardrada. | **1049** Quarrel between the Normans in Italy and the Papacy.<br>**1049–53** The Petchenegues settle in Bulgaria.<br>**1050** MacBeth, King of Scots, visits Rome.<br>**1050–84** Michael, King of Serbia: made king by Gregory VII. | |
| **1051** Godwin, Earl of Wessex, exiled by Edward the Confessor. William, 7th Duke of Normandy, visits Edward the Confessor: receives promise of succession to English throne.<br>**1051–2** Henry I campaigns against Hungary.<br>**1052** Peace made between Edward the Confessor and Godwin, Earl of Wessex.<br>**1052–3** Conrad, Duke of Bavaria, rebels. | **1052** Pisan army destroys Palermo. | **1052** Banu Hilal and Banu Sulaym move westward from upper Egypt: Tripolitania and Tunisia ravaged. |
| **1053** 15 Apr., Godwin, Earl of Wessex d.: succ. Harold, Earl of East Anglia, his son. Peace made between Henry III and Hungary.<br>**1054** Normans defeat Henry I at Mortémer. MacBeth defeated at Dunsinane by Siward, Earl of Northumbria, and Malcolm. | **1053** Normans defeat the papal army: Beneventum taken: Leo IX captured.<br><br>**1054** Ferdinand of Castile defeats and kills Garcia of Navarre. | **1053** Banu Hilal defeat al-Muizz near Gabès. |
| **1055** Bohemia throws off German suzerainty. Siward, Earl of Northumbria, d.: succ. Tostig, son of Godwin, Earl of Wessex. Gruffydd ap Llewellyn, King of Gwynedd and Powis, unites Wales: Herefordshire sacked.<br>**1056** Gruffydd forced to do homage by Harold, Earl of Wessex, and Leofric, Earl of Mercia.<br>**1056–1106** Henry IV, Holy Roman Emperor: Empress Agnes, Regent (–1062).<br>**1057** 15 Aug., MacBeth, King of Scots, killed by Malcolm, later King of Scots.<br>**1057–8** Lulach, King of Scots.<br><br>**1058** Normans defeat Henry I at Varaville. | **1055** Henry III defeated by the Normans in Italy.<br>**1055–6** The Augusta Theodora, Eastern Roman Empress.<br><br><br>**1056** *Pataria* (popular movement) begins in Milan.<br>**1056–7** Michael VI Stratiatikos, Eastern Roman Emperor.<br>**1056–81** Time of tension and troubles in Byzantium.<br><br>**1057–9** Isaac I Comnenos, Eastern Roman Emperor.<br>**1058** Richard of Aversa made Prince of Capua. | **1055** Sijilmasa and Audaghost taken by Almoravids.<br><br><br>**1056–1147** Almoravid dynasty.<br>**1056–82** Almoravids take Morocco and central Algeria.<br><br><br>**1057** Banu Hilal take Qayrawan.<br><br>**1058±65** Earliest level of Mapungubwe culture, Rhodesia. |

| THE NEAR EAST | THE FAR EAST | RELIGION & CULTURE |
|---|---|---|
| | | **1046** 20 Dec., Synod of Sutri: Gregory VI and Silvester III deposed by Emperor Henry III: 24 Dec., Clement II elected at Rome (–1047).<br>**1046–9** Nasir-i-Khusraw, Ismaili missionary visits Egypt: writes description of the brilliance of the Fatimid court.<br>**1047** 9 Oct., Clement II d.: Benedict IX returns: Damasus II elected (–1048).<br>**c. 1047–8** Abdun, an adventurer, becomes Abuna of Ethiopia by means of forged documents. |
| | **1050** Attempt in China to combat inflation by coining additional money.<br>**1050–66** Udayadityavarman II, King of Cambodia.<br>**1051** Revolt in Cambodia put down. | **1048** Benedict IX finally resigns: 9 Aug., Damasus II d.: Leo IX elected (–1054): ecclesiastical reformer. Holy Sepulchre repaired by Constantine IX Monomachos. St Maria im Capitol, Cologne, consecrated.<br>**1049–1109** Hugh, Abbot of Cluny.<br><br>**c. 1050** Prambanan temples built in Java.<br>**c.1050–1137** Romanuja, Tamil Brahmin theologian.<br>**c. 1051–1107** Mi Fei, Chinese painter, calligrapher, collector and critic. |
| **1052** The Saljuqs devastate region of Kars.<br>**1052 or 3** Somesvara Chalukya defeats and kills Rajadhiraja, Chola King, at Koppam. | | **1052** Building of Westminster Abbey begun.<br>**1052–70** Stigand, Abp of Canterbury.<br><br>**1053** Dispute between Pope Leo IX and Michael Caerularius. |
| **1054** The Saljuqs invade Georgia and Armenia.<br>**1055** 18 Dec., Tughril Bey enters Baghdad with Saljuq horde: welcomed as a deliverer by Caliph al-Qaim: Buwayhid rule ended: beginning of Saljuq Turkish period. | **1055–1110** Vijayabahu, King of Ceylon: capital at Polonnaruwa: Rajarata freed from Colas. | **1054** Pope Victor II excommunicates Michael Caerularius: the Great Schism between the Eastern and Western Churches. Constance Cathedral founded.<br>**1055–7** Victor II, Pope.<br>**c. 1055–1137** Ramanuja, Hindu philosopher.<br>**1055–61** Hildesheim Cathedral built. |
| **1056** Tughril Bey made regent of the Caliphate with the title Sultan. | **1056** Anawratha conquers Thaton. | **1056** The Holy Sepulchre closed. |
| | | **1057–8** Stephen X, Pope. |
| **1058** al-Basasiri, former Turkish commandant of Baghdad, seizes the city. | | **1058** al-Mawardi, ethicist and political theorist, d. Michael Caerularius arrested by Isaac I: then d. |

| WESTERN, NORTHERN & CENTRAL EUROPE | SPAIN, ITALY & EASTERN EUROPE | AFRICA & EGYPT |
|---|---|---|

**1058–79** Boleslaw II, King of Poland.
**1058–93** Malcolm III, King of Scots.

**1059** 23 May, Philip I made co-ruler of France.

**1059** Council of Amalfi: alliance between Pope Nicholas II and Robert Guiscard. Emperor Isaac Comnenos abdicates in order to take Holy Orders.
**1059–67** Constantine X Ducas, Eastern Roman Emperor.
**1059–81** Ducas dynasty of Byzantium.

**1060–3** Bela I. King of Hungary.
**1060–1108** Philip I, King of France: Baldwin V of Flanders, Regent.

**1060** Messina captured by Normans under Roger, son of Count Tancred de Hauteville; Reggio taken by Robert Guiscard from the Byzantines. Beginning of Norman conquest of Sicily.
**1060–91** Robert Guiscard and his brother Roger conquer Sicily.

**1061** Malcolm of Scotland invades Northumberland.

**1061–1106** Yusuf b. Tashfin, Almoravid ruler of Morocco, and, later, Spain: title Amir al-Muslimin.

**1062** Harold, Earl of Wessex, campaigns against Gruffydd of Wales. Gruffydd assassinated: Wales made a vassal of England. Apr., Anno, Bp of Cologne, kidnaps Henry IV: governs with Adalbert, Abp of Bremen (−1065).
**1063** Maine annexed by William of Normandy. German expedition against Hungary.
**1063–74** Solomon, King of Hungary.
**1064** Ferdinand I of Castile takes Coimbra: makes it capital of Portugal

**1062** Robert Guiscard takes Brindisi.

**1062** Tunka Menin succ. his uncle, Tunka Bas, as King of Ghana. Yusuf Tashfin establishes control in Seneg. and western Sahara: refounds Algier

**1063** Almoravids take Fez.
**1063±65** Burials in Njoro cave, Ken all Ethiopian or Caucasoid.

**1065** Henry IV comes of age. Harold, Earl of Wessex, visits William of Normandy: said to have sworn oath of fidelity. Tostig expelled from Northumbria: succ. Morcar.
**1066** 5 Jan., King Edward the Confessor d.: 7 Jan., Harold II usurps English throne. May, Tostig, with mercenary fleet, harries S coast of England. Sept., Harald Hardrada of Norway invades England: 20 Sept., defeats Morcar, Earl of Northumbria at Fulford, near York: 25 Sept., battle of Stamford Bridge: Harold of England defeats Norwegians. 27 Sept., Normans under William, 7th Duke of Normandy, set sail for England: 28 Sept., land at Pevensey: Oct., Harold of England hears at York of Norman landing; 14 Oct., battle of Hastings: Harold II killed: William becomes King of England by right of conquest (−1087). Population of England under 1½ m.
**1067** Philip I of France comes of age. March, William I of England returns to Normandy: many local risings follow in England (−1068).

**1065** Ferdinand I campaigns as far as Valencia. Breach between the Papacy and the Normans in Sicily. Ferdinand I of Castile d.: territory divided among his three sons as Castile, León and Galicia.
**post 1066** Many Anglo-Saxons flee from Norman rule in England, and take military service in Byzantium.

**1065** Cairo devastated by plague.

**1067** Milan frees itself from episcopal rule. The Papacy and the Normans in Sicily reconciled.

**c. 1067** Empire of Kanem extends west to R. Niger, including most of Hausaland.

| THE NEAR EAST | THE FAR EAST | RELIGION & CULTURE |
|---|---|---|

**1058—9** Benedict X, antipope.
**c. 1058 or 9—post 1127** Foucher de Chartres.
**1058—1111** Abu Hamid al-Ghazzali, greatest theologian of Islam and mystic: father of Sufism: author of numerous works.
**1059—61** Nicholas, II, Pope. 13 Apr., Pope Nicholas decrees that future Papal elections will be by Cardinals only.

**1060** Tughril regains Baghdad: Basasiri executed.
**. 1060** Raja Bhoja of Malwa defeated by armies of Gujarat and Chedi.

**c. 1060—1150** Church of St Sernin, Toulouse, built: contains relics of the twelve Apostles.

**1061—4** Honorius II, antipope.
**1061—73** Alexander II, Pope.

**1062—6** The *Abbaye-aux-Dames* built at Caen.
**1062** Fort of al-Marqab, Syria, built.
**1062—95** St Wulfstan, Bp of Worcester.

**1063** Caesarea (Cappadocia) taken by Alp Arslan: occupies all Anatolia, Armenia, Geórgia and Phrygia.
**1063—72** Arslan, chief of the Saljuqs.
**1064** Armenians migrate into Cilicia.

**1063** Anatolian monks build monasteries at Mt Athos. Greece. St Mark's, Venice, rebuilt.
**1063—1118** Cathedral of Pisa built.

**1064—5** 7,000 to 12,000 pilgrims visit the Holy Places: majority lose their lives.
**c. 1064—79** *Abbaye-aux-Hommes* built at Caen.

**1065** Two revolts in Cambodia. Chinese state revenue 116,000,000 strings of cash.

**1065** *Prabodha-chandrodaya* (Rise of the Moon of Intellect), play, exposé of Vedantic philosophy.
**1065—7** The Nizamiyah Academy founded at Baghdad.

**1066** Harshavarman III, King of Cambodia.

**1066** Pope Alexander II approves William of Normandy's expedition to England.
**1066—71** Abbey of Monte Cassino rebuilt.

**1067** Turks massacre their African mercenaries.

| WESTERN, NORTHERN & CENTRAL EUROPE | SPAIN, ITALY. & EASTERN EUROPE | AFRICA & EGYPT |
|---|---|---|
| | **1067—71** Romanos IV Diogenes, Eastern Roman Emperor, (with the Augusta Eudokia Makrembolitessa). | |
| **1068** William I campaigns in W and N England. | **1068** Córdoba absorbed by Seville, henceforward chief of Spanish Muslim kingdoms. | |
| **1068—9** Malcolm III of Scots m. Margaret, d. of Edgar Atheling: subsequently canonized as St Margaret, Queen of Scotland. | **1068—91** al-Mutamid, King of Seville. | |
| **1069—70** William I puts down rising in Northumbria: Yorkshire and Durham laid waste: Danish army defeated. | | **1069—72** Famine in Egypt. |
| **1070** William I puts down Hereward the Wake's rising in the Is. of Ely. Northumberland invaded by Malcolm of Scotland. Danes expelled from England. | | **1070** Bougie founded. **1070** Marrakesh founded as capital ⊦ Abu Bakr b. Umar. |
| **1070—1** Otto, Duke of Bavaria, rebels. | | |
| **1071** Philip I of France defeated by the Flemings at Cassel. | **1071** Roger de Hauteville takes Palermo. Robert Guiscard takes Bari. Serbia becomes independent under Constantine Bodin. | |
| | **1071—8** Michael VII Ducas, Eastern Roman Emperor. | |
| **1072** Malcolm III of Scots acknowledges suzerainty of William I of England by treaty of Abernethy. Normans invade Ireland from Britain. | **1072** Normans take Palermo. Sancho of Castile makes war on his brothers: assassinated at siege of Zamora: succ. his brother Alfonso VI of León and I of Castile (1109). | |
| **1073** General rebellion in Saxony. | **1073** Robert Guiscard takes Amalfi. | **1073—6** Badr al-Jamali, previously a Armenian slave, made wazir and commander-in-chief in Egypt. |
| **1074** Peace of Gerstungen made by Henry IV with the Saxons: rebellion shortly renewed. | | |
| **1074—7** Geiza, King of Hungary. | | |
| **1075** 9 June, Henry IV defeats Saxons. Dimitri of Kiev recognizes papal suzerainty. Dynasty of Isle of Man established by Godfrey Crovan (—1265). | | |
| **1076** Zvonimir crowned King of Croatia. Philip I of France compels William the Conqueror to raise the siege of Dol. | **1076** Robert Guiscard takes Salerno. | |
| **1077** 15 March, Diet of Forchheim: Henry IV deposed: Rudolf of Swabia elected Emperor (—1080): civil war in Germany. | **1077** Henry IV does penance at Canossa: receives absolution from Gregory VII. | **1077** Ghana taken by the Almoravi⊦ Berbers replace Soninke dynasty. Atziz invades Egypt: defeated by Badr al-Jamali. |
| **1077—95** Vladislav I, King of Hungary. | | |
| | **1078** Michael VII Dukas Parapinakes forced to become a monk: succ. Nicephorus Botaniates (—1081). | **c. 1078—80** Sosso Kingdom of Kan⊦ founded. |
| | | **c. 1078—c. 1130** Muhammad b. Tu⊦ takes title of Mahdi: followers calle⊦ Almohads (al-Muwahhidun). |

| THE NEAR EAST | THE FAR EAST | RELIGION & CULTURE |
|---|---|---|
| | **1068** Cholas recover Kedah for Sri Vijaya. <br> **1068–85** Shen Tsung, Emperor of China: liberal reformer. | **1068** Royal library in Cairo looted. |
| | | **1069** Monasteries in Scetis raided by Lewati. |
| **1070** Arab Prince of Aleppo made a vassal of Alp Arslan: Jerusalem taken from the Fatimids by Turks under Atzig. <br> **1070–1117** Saljuq rule in Syria. <br> **1070–1118** Rajendra II Kulottunga, Chola ruler. <br> **1071** Battle of Manzikart: Alp Arslan takes Emperor Romanos IV Diogenes prisoner: Armenia conquered: all Anatolia now under Saljuqid rule. Saljuqs found the Sultanate of Rum or Iconium. <br> **1072** Alp Arslan taken prisoner by Oghuz Turks and put in an iron cage, in which he d. <br> **1072–4** Roussel de Bailleul, a Norman, attempts to set up a principality in Anatolia. <br> **1072–92** Malikshah, Saljuq Sultan: builder and encourager of trade. | | **1070–89** Lanfranc, Abp of Canterbury: administration of church reformed in England: first Primate of All England. <br><br><br><br><br><br><br><br><br> **1072** Civil courts in England forbidden to hear ecclesiastical cases. Building of Lincoln Cathedral begun. |
| | | **1073–85** Gregory VII (Hildebrand), Pope. |
| | **1074–81** Harivarman IV, King of Champa. | **1074** 9 March, Gregory VII excommunicates married priests. <br> **1074–5** Astronomical observatory established at Rayy: Umar Khayyam calculates Persian calendar, more accurate than Gregorian calendar. |
| **1075–94** al-Muqtadi, Caliph. | **1075** Periodic examinations for the mandarinate introduced in Vietnam. | **1075** Papal decree on lay investiture. *Dictatus Papae* sets out papal claims in relation to temporal sovereigns. |
| **1076–1126** Vikramaditya, Chalukya ruler of Kalyani. | **1076** Chinese expedition against Tonkin. | **1076** 14 Jan., Synod of Worms: German bishops claim to depose Pope Gregory VII: the Pope excommunicates and deposes Henry IV. |
| **1077** Saljuq Sultanate of Rum (eastern Asia Minor) established by Sulaiman b. Qutlumish: capital Nicaea (Izniq). Kulottunga sends embassy of seventy-two merchants to China. | **1077–84** Sawlu, King of Pagan. | **1077** First English Cluniac house established at Lewes. <br> **1077–1115** St Alban's Abbey built. <br> **1077–1166** Abd al-Qadir al-Jilani, founder of Qadiriyyah dervish order at Baghdad: subsequently spread throughout the Islamic world. |
| | **1078–1178** Frequent embassies from Sri Vijaya to China, primarily as trade missions. | **1078** Diocese of Sherborne transferred to Salisbury. <br> c. **1078** Adam of Bremen, German historian, d. <br> **1078–93** St Anselm, Abbot of Bec. <br> **1078 (or 1081)** New Cathedral begun at Compostela. <br> c. **1078**–c. **1130** Muhammad b. Tumert, founder of Almohad movement in Moroccan Atlas: teaches strictly orthodox and puritanical form of Islam. |

| WESTERN, NORTHERN & CENTRAL EUROPE | SPAIN, ITALY & EASTERN EUROPE | AFRICA & EGYPT |
|---|---|---|

**1079–1102** Wladislaw I, King of Poland.

**1080** 15 Oct., battle of Pegau: Henry IV defeated. Rudolf of Swabia killed.

**ante 1080** First Consuls of Lucca appointed.
**1080** Alliance between the Pope and the Normans in Sicily.

**1081** William I campaigns in Wales.
**1081–8** Hermann of Luxembourg, rival Holy Roman Emperor.

**1081** Nicephorus Botaniates retires to a monastery. Alexios Comnenos crowned emperor (–1118). Rodrigo Díaz de Bivar (El Cid) expelled from Castile. Henry IV marches into Italy. Robert Guiscard invades Balkans.
**1081–1185** Comnenian dynasty of Byzantium.

**1082–7** Odo, Bp of Bayeux, and Earl of Kent, imprisoned by William I, his half-brother.

**1082** The *Chrysobull,* or Imperial Charter: Alexios I grants Venice extraordinary commercial privileges for aid against the Normans. Alexios defeated by Robert Guiscard at Durazzo. Alfonso VI of León and Castile raids Cordoba and Seville, and reaches Tarifa.
**1083** 3 June, Henry IV takes Rome by storm. Normans defeated by Alexios at Larissa. Alfonso VI takes Madrid.
**1084** 31 March, Henry IV crowned Emperor by Pope Clement III. May, Rome sacked by the Normans: Gregory VII flees to Salerno. Bogomil revolt in Thrace.

**1085** Peace between Henry IV and Saxony.

**1085** Robert Guiscard d. in Cephalonia. End of Norman attacks on Byzantine territory. Alexios I expels the Normans from the Balkans. Alfonso of León and Castile takes Toledo.
**1085–91** Siege of Syracuse by Roger de Hauteville.

**c. 1085–97** Umme, ruler of Bornu-Kanem, converted to Islam: assume title of Sultan.

**1086** William the Conqueror has the *Domesday Book* compiled: all land in England assessed and made dependent on the king.

**1086** Yusuf b. Tashfin, Almoravid, invited to Spain by al-Mutamid of Seville: marches unopposed through S: 23 Oct., defeats Alfonso VI of Castile at al-Zallaqa, near Badajoz: 40,000 heads sent to N Africa as a trophy: Yusuf returns to Africa.

**1087** 30 May, Conrad, Duke of Lorraine, son of Henry IV, elected King of Germany: Nov., rebels. William I repels invasion of Normandy by Philip of France: 9 Sept., d.: succ. William II, Rufus, in England (–1100); Robert, as 8th Duke of Normandy (–1106).
**1088** Odo of Bayeux leads rebellion in England against William II: besieged at Pevensey, then at Rochester: banished from England.
**1089** Henry IV m. Adelaide, Princess of Kiev.

**1087** Genoa and Pisa attack al-Mahdia. End of Almoravid dynasty in Ghana.

**1089** Pope Urban II takes Rome from Henry IV.
**1089–91** Petchenegues invade Thrace.

| THE NEAR EAST | THE FAR EAST | RELIGION & CULTURE |
|---|---|---|
| | | c. 1079—93 Cathedral of Winchester rebuilt.<br>1079—1142 Pierre Abélard, French theologian and poet. |
| 1080 Antioch made to pay tribute to Prince of Mosul. | 1080—1112 Mahidharapura dynasty in Cambodia: Jayavarman VI, first ruler (—1107). | 1080 7 March, Pope Gregory VII again excommunicates Henry IV. William the Conqueror declines to do homage as a papal vassal.<br>c. 1080 Abba Sawiros, Muslim imposter, Abuna of Ethiopia: builds mosques: imprisoned by Emperor.<br>1080/1—1169/70 Abu Hamid Muhammad al-Manzini of Granada, geographer (visited Russia 1136). |
| | 1081—1113 Jaya Indravarman II, King of Champa. | 1080—1100 Clement III, antipope.<br>1081—90 Tower of London built.<br>1081—1151 Suger, Abbot of St Denis, monk and statesman. |
| | | 1082—95 Fécamp Abbey built. |
| | 1083 Revolt of the Mons. | 1083—1145 Anna Comnena, historian.<br>1083—1189 Ely Cathedral rebuilt. |
| 1084 Iconium (Quniyah) taken by the Saljuqs: made capital of Rum. Antioch also taken. | 1084—1112 Kyansittha, (elected) King of Pagan. | 1084 Grande-Chartreuse founded by St Bruno. Salerno Cathedral built by Robert Guiscard. |
| | | 1085 Mosque and mausoleum of Badr al-Jamali built in Cairo. 25 May, Pope Gregory VII d. at Salerno. 25 May, first mass said in mosque, later Church of El Cristo de la Luz, Toledo. |
| | | c. 1086 Attempt made to enforce monogamy in Ethiopia.<br>1086—7 Victor III, Pope.<br>1086—1165 Mi-Yuan, Chinese painter. |
| | | 1087 Wallada of Córdoba, poetess, d. |
| 1087 Nizam al-Mulk grants hereditary military fiefs: many small semi-independent states a consequence within the Caliphate. | | |
| | | 1088 Bologna University founded.<br>1088—99 Urban II, Pope.<br>1088—1130 Cluny Abbey Church rebuilt. |
| 1089—1125 David the Restorer, King of Georgia.<br>1089 Tripoli (Syria) becomes independent under Shi'ite Banu Ammar. Fatimids recover Levant coast from Ascalon to Byblos. | 1089 Hierarchy of state officials with nine ranks established in Vietnam. | 1089 Pope Urban II writes to bishops and nobility of Spain making the reconquista a crusade. Gloucester Abbey begun. Cathedral of the Assumption, Kiev, consecrated. |

| WESTERN, NORTHERN & CENTRAL EUROPE | SPAIN, ITALY & EASTERN EUROPE | AFRICA & EGYPT |
|---|---|---|
| **1090–1112** Inge I, King of Sweden. | **1090** Henry IV campaigns in Italy: Pope Urban II flees. Nov., Yusuf b. Tashfin takes Granada. Malta taken by Roger de Hauteville.<br>**1090–1** Petchenegues under Tzachas besiege Constantinople.<br>**1090–1147** The Almoravid dynasty in Spain. | |
| **1091** Treaty of Caen between William II of England, Robert of Normandy, and their brother Henry (later Henry I of England): joint expedition to repel invasion of England by Malcolm III of Scots: Malcolm compelled to acknowledge William II Rufus.<br><br>**1092** William II annexes Cumberland from Scotland. | **1091** 29 Apr., Alexios I annihilates the Petchenegues at Liburnion. Syracuse falls to Roger de Hauteville: end of Norman conquest of Sicily. Yusuf b. Tashfin takes Seville and other towns, except Toledo and Saragossa: al-Mutamid sent in chains to Morocco. Tarragona captured by Catalonia.<br>**1092** Henry IV leaves Italy. | |
| **1093** 13 Nov., Malcolm III of Scots killed at Alnwick: succ. Donald Bane (–1094). Robert, Earl of Corbeil, and Richard de Grenville, cousins of William II, take Glamorgan from Wales.<br>**1093–1106** Conrad of Franconia, son of Henry IV, rebels. | **1093** Franco-Spanish army takes Lisbon, Santarem and Cintra. Lombard League instituted: Urban II returns to Rome. | **1093** Embassy from Egypt to Ethiopia, headed by Coptic Patriarch, begging ruler to allow the Nile to rise. |
| **1094** May, Donald Bane, King of Scots, deposed: succ. Duncan II: 12 Nov., Duncan II killed at Mondynes: Donald Bane restored (–1097). War between William II of England and Robert of Normandy: ended by risings in England. | **1094** Rodrigo Díaz de Bivar, El Cid Campeador, takes Valencia from the Almoravids: held until 1099. | **1094–1101** al-Mustali, Fatimid Cali[<br>**1094–1121** Afdal b. al-Badr, effecti[ ruler of Egypt. |
| **1095** Robert de Mowbray, Earl of Northumberland's, conspiracy against William II Rufus put down.<br>**1095–1103** Eric I, King of Denmark.<br>**1095–1116** Koloman, King of Hungary.<br><br>**1096** Robert of Normandy sells Normandy to William II of England for 10,000 marks before departing on Crusade. | **1095** Teresa, daughter of Alfonso of León and Castile, m. Count Henry of Burgundy: given Portugal as her dowry, subject to Castile. Emperor Alexios Comnenos appeals to Pope Urban II for aid against Saljuq incursions. Council of Piacenza.<br>**1096** French and Spanish army takes Huesca. First Crusade sets off from France under Peter the Hermit (of Amiens) and Walter the Penniless: greater number killed by the Turks near Nicaea: second party under Godfrey of Bouillon and other nobles follows. | **1095–1130** Gojemasu, King of Kan[ builds Kano city. |
| **1097** War between William II Rufus and Philip I of France. Donald Bane, King of Scots, defeated and expelled to England by his nephew, Edgar, King of Scots (–8 Jan. 1106). | **1097** Spring, 150,000 Crusaders reach Constantinople. Henry IV returns to Italy. Portugal made a County. | |
| **1098–1103** Magnus Bareleg seizes Western Isles of Scotland, Orkney, Hebrides and Man. | **1098** Pope Urban II renews treaty with Normans in Sicily. | |

| THE NEAR EAST | THE FAR EAST | RELIGION & CULTURE |
|---|---|---|

**1089–1111** Harsha, King of Kashmir.

**1089** Council of Greek bishops at Constantinople: Pope Urban II's name restored to the diptychs.
**1089–1173** Hemachandra, political commentator.
**1090–1150** Zurich Cathedral built.

**1090** Assassin movement *(hashshashshun)* founded at Alamut, Persia, by al-Hasan b. al-Sabbah.

**1090–1153** St Bernard of Clairvaux, theologian and poet.

**1091** Baghdad becomes the Saljuq capital.

**1091/4–1162** Abu Marwan Abd al-Malik b. Abi al-Ala, known as Ibn Zuhr: physician, statesman and writer.
**1091** Rebuilding of Avila Cathedral begun. Catania Cathedral started.

**1092** Wazir Nizam al-Mulk murdered by an Assassin.
**1092–1107** Qilij Arslan, Saljuq Sultan of Quniyah (Iconium).

**1092** Vladislav, King of Hungary, permits priests to marry.
c. **1092**–c.**1143** William of Malmesbury, chronicler.
**1093–1109** St Anselm, Abp of Canterbury: scholar and author of *Cur Deus Homo.*
**1093–1133** Durham Cathedral built.

**1094** Tutush, son of Alp Arslan, founds Saljuq dynasty of Syria: takes Aleppo, Edessa and Mosul.
**1094–1117** Saljuq dynasty of Syria.
**1094–1118** al-Mustazhir, Abbasid Caliph.

**1094** William II Rufus begins quarrel with St Anselm. Cathedral of St Mark in Venice consecrated. Abu Ubaid Abdallah b. Abd al-Aziz al-Bakri, geographer and polymath, of Córdoba, d.

**1095** Qilij Arslan elected Sultan in Nicaea.
**1095–9** First Crusade.
**1095–1104** Duqaq, Saljuq ruler of Damascus.
**1095–1113** Ridwan b. Tutush, Saljuq ruler of Syria: capital at Aleppo.
**1095–1154** Mosul ruled by independent Atabegs.

**1095** Pope Urban II visits France: consecrates new Abbey Church at Cluny: Council of Clermont: 27 Nov., preaches first Crusade (–1099). Philip I of France excommunicated. Clergy forbidden to take oaths of fealty.

**1096–1141** Hugh of St Victor.

**1097** 19 June, Crusaders take Nicaea: Smyrna, Ephesus and Sardis fall. 1 July, battle of Dorylaeum (Eski-Shahr): Crusaders restore W Asia Minor to Alexios Comnenos. 21
**1097** 21 Oct.–**1098** 3 June, Crusaders besiege Antioch.
**1098** Crusaders capture al-Ruha, Armenia: first Latin state founded, with Baldwin as king; Tancred of S Italy takes Cilicia. 3 June, Crusaders take Antioch.

**1098** Bureau for housing and care of the aged and destitute established in China.

**1097** William II Rufus quarrels finally with St Anselm: St Anselm exiled to Rome, and then to Cluny (–1100). Westminster Hall built.

**1098** Abbey of Cîteaux founded. Order of Knights of St John of Jerusalem founded. *K'ao-ku-tu* (Pictures for the Study of Antiquity) published in China. Messina Cathedral begun.

| WESTERN & NORTHERN EUROPE | CENTRAL, SOUTHERN & EASTERN EUROPE | AFRICA & EGYPT |
|---|---|---|

**1099** David the Restorer, King of Georgia, expels the Turks from the Kingdom. Louis VI associate King of France with his father, Philip I. 6 Jan., Henry V elected king. Revolt at Beauvais. William II Rufus submits Maine.
**12th c.** Towns of Vladimir, Moscow, Tver and Tula founded: northern Russia steadily populated, partly by semi-nomads, many intermarrying with Finns. Kiev dynasty evolves practice of giving the throne to the senior male of the house of Rurik: practice continued until 1722.

**ante 1100** Trade guilds appear in Germany.
**1100** 2 Aug., William II shot by an arrow in the New Forest: crown of England seized by Henry I (–1135): 11 Nov., m. Matilda, daughter of Malcolm, King of Scots.

**1099** Arabs recover Valencia.
**c. 1099** Consuls instituted in Genoa.

**12th c.** Marabout cults become popular in N Africa. Ali b. al-Hasan, first Kilwa sultan to mint coins, otherwise unknown. Timbuktu originated as a Tuareg watering-place. Mzizima, now Dar es Salaam, Tanzania already occupied. Merca, Somalia, already occupied. Remains of Arab fort at Mailakapasy, Madagascar.

**c. ante 1100** Shona the dominant culture at Mapungubwe, Rhodesia.
**c. 1100** Dynasty of Habe Kings of Katsina founded (–present).

**1101** Robert of Normandy invades England: English rise in support of Henry I: Treaty of Alton: Robert reinstated as Duke of Normandy with an annuity.
**1102** Robert of Bellême's revolt put down by Henry I.
**1102–39** Roger, Bp of Salisbury, Chancellor and Justiciar of England: the Exchequer established.
**1103** Peace of Mayence. Magnus III of Norway invades Ireland: 24 Aug., killed.
**1104–34** Nicholas, King of Denmark.

**1101** Roger I de Hauteville of Sicily d.: succ. Roger II (–1154). French and Spanish army takes Barbastro.

**1102** Wladislaw of Poland d.: kingdom divided by his sons Zbigniew and Boleslaw III, the Wry-Mouthed (–1138). The Almoravids take Valencia.

**1104–34** Alfonso I of Aragon.

**1101** Dated epitaph at Sane of Abu Abdallah Muhammad, King of Songhai
**1101–30** al-Amir, Fatimid Caliph.

**1105** War between Henry I of England and Robert of Normandy.

**1106** 28 Sept., Henry I defeats Robert at Tinchebray: Robert imprisoned at Cardiff (–1134): Henry takes Normandy. End of investiture controversy in France.

**1107–1124** Alexander I, King of Scots.

**1105** Emperor Henry IV taken prisoner by his son, Henry V: abdicates. Colonization of eastern Germany begun.
**1106** 7 Aug., Henry IV d.
**1106–25** Henry V, Holy Roman Emperor. Lothair of Supplinburg, Duke of Saxony.
**1106–43** Ali b. Yusuf succ. his father Yusuf b. Tashfin as ruler of Morocco and Spain: Christians, Jews and liberal Muslims persecuted.

**1105** First dated Muslim inscription in E Africa at Barawa, Somalia.

**1106** Ibn Tashfin d.

**1107** Original Friday mosque built at Kizimkazi, Zanzibar, with dedicatory inscription in Persian style.

## THE NEAR EAST

## THE FAR EAST

## RELIGION & CULTURE

**1098** 28 June, Turks defeated near Antioch: Baldwin of Boulogne made Count of Edessa (Homs): Bohémond made Prince of Antioch. The Fatimids take Jerusalem.
**1099** Crusaders under Count Raymond of Toulouse take Syrian coast and Lebanon; 7 June, Jerusalem besieged; 15 July, Jerusalem taken; July, Ascalon taken: Godfrey de Bouillon made 'baron and defender of the Holy Sepulchre' (–1100).
**First half of 12th c.** Vishuvardhana establishes Hoysala dynasty: capital Dorasamudra, near Mysore: patron of Vaishnava philosopher Ramanuja.

**12th–16th cc.** Cult of the Tooth Relic of Buddha develops in Ceylon.

**1099–1118** Paschal II, Pope.
**end of 11th c.** Stavanger Cathedral built.

**12th c.** Inca reach highlands of S Peru. Jodo-Shinshu, Nichiren and Zen Buddhist sects emerge in Japan. Kalhana: *History of the Kingdom of Kashmir.* Popular acclaim makes first saints *(wali)* in Islam.

**12th or 13th c.** Manco Capac, Inca ruler.
Genoa and Salamanca Cathedrals begun. Dien Nham, Vietnamese poetess.
**1100** Theodoric, antipope.
**c. 1100** Paper making introduced into Morocco.
**c. 1100–50** Temple of Angkor Vat constructed. Kuo Hsi, Chinese artist.
**1100–54** Geoffrey of Monmouth, chronicler.
**1100–66** al-Idrisi, geographer b. at Ceuta: passes life at court of Roger II of Sicily.
**c. 1100–70** Mao-Yi, painter.
**c. 1100–80** John of Salisbury.
**post 1100** Roman law principal subject of study in Europe. Jayadeva: *Govinda.*

**c. ante 1100** Assassins convert Saljuq Prince of Aleppo, Ridwan b. Tutush.
**1100** Arabs expelled from Tiflis by David III of Georgia. Commercial agreement between Kingdom of Jerusalem and Venice. Pisa given rights in Jaffa: Caesarea and Acre made tributary to Jerusalem: Haifa taken: Godfrey d.: 25 Dec., Baldwin I crowned King of Jerusalem at Bethlehem (–1118).
**c. 1100–60** Govindachandra, ruler of Kanauj.

**1101–25** Hui Tsung, Sung Emperor: art collector: creator of Academy of Painting.

**1102** Fatimids defeated by Baldwin I at Ramleh: Caesarea taken. Tortosa taken by Raymond de St Gilles.

**1102** State health service established in China.

**1101–64** Héloise, *savante.*
**?1101–71** Henry of Blois, Bp.

**1102** Albert, antipope.

**1103–12** Tancred, regent of Antioch.

**1103–5** St Anselm again in exile at Rome.

**1104** Crusaders take Acre (Akka) and Byblos. Turks defeat Crusaders at Harran.
**1104–8** Bohémond of Antioch campaigns in Epirus against Byzantium.
**1105** Tancred defeats the Turks at Tizin: Aleppo threatened.

**1104** State bureau for the burial of the poor instituted in China.

**1104** Philip I of France absolved by the Pope.

**1105–11** Sylvester, antipope.

**1107** Qilij Arslan I takes Mosul.

**1107** Pope Paschal II visits France. St Anselm and Henry I of England reach compromise over investiture.

## WESTERN & NORTHERN EUROPE

1108–9 *Communes* formed at Beauvais and Noyon.
1108–37 Louis VI, sole King of France.
1108–24 Louis VI grants autonomy to many French towns, exempting them from feudal obligations.
1109–13 The Affair of Gisors: war between Louis VI and Henry I.

1112 Rebellion against Henry I in Normandy suppressed: Robert of Bellême imprisoned. Communal rebellion at Laon.
1112–8 Philip, King of Sweden.

1113 Treaty of Gisors.
1113–8 *Leges Henrici* compiled.
1113–25 Vladimir II, Grand Duke of Kiev.

1114 7 Jan., Emperor Henry V m. Matilda, daughter of Henry I of England.

1116–7 *Commune* established at Amiens.

1117–20 War between Henry I and William Clito, son of Robert of Normandy, having support from Anjou, Flanders and France.
1118 E Normandy rebels against Henry I.

1119 20 Aug., Louis VI of France and William Clito defeated by Henry I of England at Brémule. Robert, son of William of Normandy, instigated by Louis VI of France to take Normandy from Henry I of England: beaten at Gisors, but defeats Henry I at Brenneville: war ended by Peace of Gisors.
1119–27 Charles the Good, Count of Flanders.

## CENTRAL, SOUTHERN & EASTERN EUROPE

1108 Poland invades Bohemia. Alfonso of León and Castile defeated by the Almoravids at Uclés: Saragossa and Valencia lost. Alexios I takes Bohémond prisoner.

1109 Boleslaw III of Poland defeats Germans at Hundsfeld. Alfonso of León and Castile d.: succ. Urraca (–1126), d. of Alfonso VI: m. Alfonso I of Aragon.
1110 Henry V intervenes in Bohemia.
c. 1110 Lisbon taken by the Almoravids.
1110 or 1111 Louis VI forms a coalition against Henry I.
1111 13 Apr., Henry V crowned in Rome. Matilda of Tuscany makes him her heir. Alexios I grants Pisa commercial privileges. Almoravids take Saragossa.

1113–5 Pisa conquers Balearic Is.

1114 Western Germany rebels: Henry V defeated at Andernach. Almoravids besiege Barcelona: defeated at Martorell.
1115 11 Feb., imperial army under Henry V defeated by Lothair of Saxony at Welfesholz. Matilda of Tuscany d.
1115–31 Stephen I, King of Hungary.
1116 Henry V takes Tuscany.
1116 Vladimir founded.

1118 Saragossa retaken by Alfonso I of Aragon.
1118–23 Roger II campaigns in Sicily.
1118–43 John II Comnenos, Eastern Roman Emperor.

1119 Assembly of Mayence. War between Genoa and Pisa.

## AFRICA & EGYPT

c. 1110 Ibn Tumert, founder of Almohad movement, leaves to study in Damascus and Baghdad.
1110±80 Iron in use at Talaky, Madagascar.

1116–8 Baldwin I campaigns in Egypt.

1118 Baldwin I, King of Jerusalem, attacks Egypt: al-Farama burnt: d. of an accident.

| THE NEAR EAST | THE FAR EAST | RELIGION & CULTURE |
|---|---|---|

**1108** Tancred takes Laodicaea.

c. **1108** Jubbah (Argobbah) converted to Islam.

**1109** Crusaders take Tripoli (Syria). Tripoli made a County under the Count of Toulouse.

**1109** See of Ely created. St Anselm d.: see of Canterbury vacant for five years. **?1109—67** St Ailred of Rievaulx.

**1110** Beirut and Sidon taken by the Crusaders under Baldwin I. Maudud of Mosul attempts to take Tripoli.
c. **1110—41** Vishnuvardhana Hoysala (Bittideva or Bittiga), of Mysore, patron of learning and temple-building.

c. **1110** See of Greenland created.
**1110** Worms Cathedral built.
**1110—42** Castle of Krak des Chevaliers built.

**1111** 4 Feb., Treaty of Sutri: Henry V renounces investiture: Paschal II surrenders *regalia*: 12 Feb., Paschal imprisoned by Henry V.

**1112** Roger of Salerno succ. Tancred.

**1112—67** Alaungsithu, King of Pagan.

**1112** Sept., Henry V excommunicated by Synod of Vienne. St Bernard enters Cistercian Order at Cîteaux. Lateran Council: Privilege of Albano renounced.

**1113** The Turks advance on Lampsaca. Baldwin I defeated near Tiberias.
**1113—4** Alp Arslan al-Akhras, Saljuq ruler of Syria.
**1114—7** Sultan Shah, Saljuq ruler of Syria.

**1113—c. 1155** Suryavarman II, King of Cambodia: builder of temple mausoleum of Angkor Vat and other monuments.

**1113** Rule of the Canons of St Victor drawn up by Guillaume de Champeaux. Scone Abbey founded. Grand Priory of the Knights of Crato founded.

**1114** Juchen (or Jurchen), subjects of the Kitan, make themselves independent.

**1114** Abbey of Pontigny founded.
**1114—1202** Alain de Lille, poet.

**1115** Alliance between Crusaders and Atabeg of Damascus. Baldwin I conquers Moab. Battle of Tell Danith.

**1115** 25 June, St Bernard founds Clairvaux: Abbot until 1153.
c. **1115** See of Glasgow founded.

**1116** Battle of Philomelion: peace made between Byzantium and the Turks.
**1117—57** Sanjar, King of Khorasan.

**1118** John II campaigns in southern Asia Minor.
**1118—31** Baldwin II, King of Jerusalem.
**1118—35** al-Mustarshid, Caliph.

**1118** Order of Knights Templar founded in Palestine by Hugues des Payens.
**1118—9** Gelasius II, Pope.
**1118** 7 Apr., Pope Gelasius II excommunicates Henry V. Jedburgh Abbey founded.
**1118—21** Gregory VIII, antipope.
**1118—90** Saigyo, Japanese poet.
**1119—24** Calixtus II, Pope.

**1119** Roger of Salerno defeated and killed at Tell Aqribin by al-Ghazi.

c. **1119** Many wealthy persons in Canton in possession of eastern African slaves.

**1119—1520** Saragossa Cathedral built.

| WESTERN & NORTHERN EUROPE | CENTRAL, SOUTHERN & EASTERN EUROPE | AFRICA & EGYPT |
|---|---|---|
| **1119–56** Turloch More O'Connor, High King of Ireland. **1120** 25 Nov., shipwreck of the *White Ship*: Henry I of England's two sons drowned off Harfleur. Peace between Henry I and Louis VI. | | **c. 1120** Kilwa ousts Mogadishu from gold export monopoly at Sofala. Ibn Tumert preaching in Morocco. |
| | **1121** Saxony rebels. Assembly of Würzburg. **1122–6** Byzantium at war with Venice. | |
| **1123–5** William of Clito, again supported by coalition, rebels against Henry I: truce between Louis VI and Henry I. | **1123** Emperor John II defeats Serbia. | |
| **1124** Henry V aids Henry I of England in France. **1124–53** David I, King of Scots. | **1124** Emperor John II defeats Hungary. | |
| | **1125** 23 May, Henry V d.: succ. Lothair II the Saxon (−1138). | **1125** Ibn Tumert, preaching in the Atlas Mts, claims to be Mahdi. |
| **1126** 25 Dec., English barons swear fealty to Matilda as heir of Henry I. *Commune* established in Soissons. | **1126** Alfonso I of Aragon campaigns through Valencia, Murcia and Andalusia, reaching Motril. Alfonso VII crowned King of León and Castile (−1157). John II conquers Branitchevo in Serbia. **1126–39** Henry the Proud, Duke of Bavaria and other German possessions. | |
| **1127** 2 March, Charles the Good, Count of Flanders, murdered. 22 May, Empress Matilda m. Geoffrey V Plantagenet, Count of Anjou and Duke of Normandy. **c. 1127** *Communes* established at Bruges, Lille and St Omer. **1128** Aug., William Clito d. | **1127** 18 Dec., Conrad of Hohenstaufen proclaimed king in Germany and Italy: abortive campaign in Tuscany. Roger II unites Norman possessions in Sicily. **1128** Battle of São Mameda: Afonso I of Portugal makes himself independent of Castile. | |
| **1129–30** First *Pipe Roll* compiled in England. **1129–55** Swerker I, King of Sweden. **1130** Rising in Moray. **1130–3** City of London chartered. | **1130–54** Roger II. King of Sicily: most brilliant period of Sicilian culture: dressed as a Muslim: half-Muslim court: crowned, 25 Dec. | **c. 1129–31** Sulaiman, Sultan of Kilwa. **1130** Muhammad b. Tumert d.: succ by Abd al-Mumin b. Ali as leader of the Almohad movement (−1163): founder of the Almohad dynasty of Morocco and Spain (−1269): proclaimed *Amir al-Muminin* in the Atlas Mts. al-Amir, Fatimid caliph, killed by the Assassins: succ. al-Hafiz (−1149). |

| THE NEAR EAST | THE FAR EAST | RELIGION & CULTURE |
|---|---|---|
| | | 1120 Premonstratentian Order founded by St Norbert, Count of Xanten. |
| 1121—2 John II finally annihilates the Petchenegues. | | |
| | | 1122 Concordat of Worms: end of German conflict about investiture: Henry V absolved. Abélard's works on the Trinity condemned as heretical by the Council of Soissons. |
| | | 1122—56 Peter the Venerable, Abbot of Cluny. |
| | 1123—35 Emperor Taitsung subdues greater part of Mongolia. | 1123 March, first General Council of the Lateran: Concordat of Worms confirmed: decrees against simony and the marriage of priests. |
| | | 1123—36 William of Corbeil, Abp of Canterbury. |
| 1124 al-Hasan b. al-Sabbah d.: founder of the Assassin (hashshashun) movement: succ. Buzurg Amid. Crusaders take Tyre. | | 1124 Celestine II, antipope. |
| | | c. 1124 Church of the Pantocrator built in Constantinople. |
| 1125 Bursuqi, Atabeg of Mosul, takes Aleppo: defeated by Baldwin II at Aziz. | 1125 Jurchen seize Peking: end of Liao dynasty. | 1124—30 Honorius II, Pope. |
| | 1125—1211 Kara-Kitai state, remnant of the Liao, in N Turkestan (W Liao state). | 1125 al-Aqmar Mosque, Cairo, built. |
| | 1125—1234 Chin (Tartar or Mongol) dynasty in N China. | |
| 1126 Baldwin II advances as far as Damascus. | 1126 Jungchen capture N Sung capital and emperor: end of the N Sung dynasty. Southern Sung capital at Nanking, shortly moved to Hangchow. | 1126 Mozarabs of Granada banished to Morocco. Adelard of Bath translates al-Khwarizmi's tables into Latin. |
| | | 1126—51 Abp Raymond I of Toledo: maintains school for translation of Arabic works into Latin. |
| | 1126—1279 Southern Sung dynasty in China. | 1126—98 Abu al-Walid Muhammad b. Ahmad b. Rushd (Averroes), philosopher and physician, of Córdoba. |
| | | ante 1127 Guillaume d'Aquitaine: Chansons. |
| 1127—1262 Zangid dynasty of Mosul. | | post 1127 Foucher de Chartres: Historia Hierosolymita. Cathedral and eighteen churches built in Tyre. |
| 1127 Zangi, Atabeg of Mosul (—1146), seizes northern Mesopotamia. | | |
| 1128 Zangi takes Aleppo. | 1128 Suryavarman II of Cambodia campaigns against Dai Viet. | 1128 Abbey of Holyrood founded. |
| 1129—37 Leo I of Lesser Armenia expels the Byzantines from Cilicia. | | 1129—45 Cefalù Cathedral built. |
| | | 1130 Canterbury Cathedral consecrated. |
| 1130 Zangi takes Hama: attacks Antioch. Sanjar invades Transoxiana. John II begins reconquest of Paphalagonia. | | ?c. 1130 University of Oxford founded. |
| | | 1130—7 Anacletus II, antipope. |
| | | 1130—43 Innocent II, Pope. |
| | | c. 1130—48 fl. Marcabru, troubadour. |
| | | c. 1130—55 fl. Cercamon, troubadour. |
| | | 1130—80 Adam of St Victor, hymnographer. |
| | | 1130—1200 Chu Hsi, neo-Confucianist philosopher and historian. |

| WESTERN &<br>NORTHERN EUROPE | CENTRAL, SOUTHERN<br>& EASTERN EUROPE | AFRICA & EGYPT |
|---|---|---|

**1131** 8 Sept., English barons renew oath of fealty to Matilda as heir of Henry I. 25 Oct., Louis VII made co-ruler of France.

**1131–41** Bela II, King of Hungary.
**c. 1131–70** Daud b. Sulaiman, former governor of Sofala, Sultan of Kilwa.

**1132** Alfonso of Castile renews hostilities in Spain. Lothair in Italy: capital at Roha.
**1133** 4 June, Lothair crowned Emperor: granted Tuscany by Pope Innocent III. Pisa and Genoa partition Corsica: Sardinia taken by Pisa.
**1134** 7 Sept., Alfonso of Aragon defeated and killed by Arabs at Fraga. Albert the Bear granted Nordmark by Lothair.

**1135** 1 Dec., Henry I of England d.: throne seized by Stephen of Blois (–1154).

**1135** Alfonso VII of León and Castile takes title of Emperor. Treaty of Merseburg: King of Poland to do homage to the Emperor for Pomerania only. King of Denmark does homage to Emperor.
**1136** Lothair campaigns against the Normans in Italy: Apulia taken.

**1135** Treaty between Zairite al-Hasan b. Ali and Roger II of Sicily.
**1135–1204** Abu Imran Musa b. Maymun (Maimonides), Córdoba Jewish physician: resided chiefly in Cairo.

**1136** 1 Jan., rising in S Wales led by Gruffydd ap Cynan. Feb., treaty of Durham: David of Scotland acknowledges Stephen of England. Office of Steward made hereditary in Scotland: origin of Stewart family. Charter of Oxford.
**1137** Stephen of England defeats Geoffrey of Anjou. Gruffydd of Wales d.: succ. Owain the Great (–1170).
**1137–80** Louis VII, King of France.
**1137** Louis VII m. Eleanor of Aquitaine.
**1137–46** Eric III, King of Denmark.
**1138** Robert of Gloucester rebels with Scottish support. 22 Aug., David of Scotland defeated by Stephen of England at Battle of the Standard, near Northallerton.

**1137** 4 Dec., Lothair d. Pisa sacks Amalfi. Most remaining Mozarabs banished to Morocco. Attempted Norman invasion foiled at battle of Cape Dimas.
**1137–62** Ramon Berenguer IV of Barcelona, Regent of Aragon.

**1138** First coins bearing a date in Arabic numerals issued in Sicily by Roger II. Boleslaw of Poland d.: law of succession gives inheritance henceforward to the eldest male of the family: Poland divided into numerous principalities for the next two centuries.
**1138–59** Wladislaw II, Duke of Poland.
**1138–1254** Hohenstaufen dynasty of Holy Roman Emperors.
**1138–52** Conrad III, Holy Roman Emperor.
**1138** Henry the Proud of Saxony opposes Conrad's election: Saxony given to Albert the Bear.

**1137** Zagwa founds Zagwe dynasty of Ethiopia.

**1139** 30 Sept., Matilda lands at Arundel to dispute claim to English throne: civil war ensues: her husband, Geoffrey of Anjou, attacks Normandy.

**1139** Bavaria taken from Henry the Proud: granted to Leopold, Margrave of Austria. 20 Oct., Henry the Proud d.: succ. Henry the Lion.
**1139–85** Afonso, King of Portugal: acknowledges papal suzerainty.
**1140** Navarre recognizes suzerainty of Aragon. Roger II of Sicily takes Pope Innocent II prisoner: treaty of Mignano. Assizes of Ariano: law code for Sicily.
**1140–73** Vladislav II, King of Bohemia.

**1140** Unsuccessful embassy from Ethiopia to Egypt requesting more bishops.

| THE NEAR EAST | THE FAR EAST | RELIGION & CULTURE |
|---|---|---|
| 1131–43 Fulk I of Anjou, King of Jerusalem. | 1131 Dai Viet tributary to Cambodia. | 1131 Gilbertine Order founded by St Gilbert of Sempringham.<br>1131–2 Augustinian monastery built at Coimbra.<br>1132 Vézelay Abbey completed. Autun Cathedral finished.<br>c. 1132 Abbey of St Denis built.<br>1133 See of Carlisle created.<br>1133–1212 Huen Shonian, reformer of the Japanese Jodo sect.<br><br>1134–50 W façade of Chartres Cathedral built.<br>1134–92 Qadi al-Fadil, secretary to Saladin: library contains 100,000 books. |
| 1135 Zangi invades County of Tripoli.<br>1135–6 al-Rashid, Abbasid Caliph. | 1135–60 Jayabhaya, King of Kadiri, Java: orders composition of *Bharatayudda*. | 1135 Council of Pisa. Great Mosque of Tlemcen built.<br>1135–43 Henry of Blois, Bp of Winchester.<br>c. 1135–68 Sens Cathedral built.<br>1135–1200 St Hugh of Lincoln.<br>1135–1212 Samson, Abbot of Bury St Edmund's. |
| 1136–49 Raymond of Poitiers, Prince of Antioch.<br>1136–60 al-Muqtafi, Abbasid Caliph.<br>1136–1225 Dynasty of Atabegs of Azerbaijan. | | 1136 Abélard teaching at the University of Paris. Melrose Abbey founded. Hospital of St Cross, Winchester founded. |
| 1137 Fulk surrenders at Barin (Montferrand). Zangi pushed back by Emperor John II. | | 1137 See of Aberdeen created. Mayence Cathedral completed.<br>1137–44 Church of Abbey of St Denis built. |
| 1138 Saladin (al-Malik al-Nasir al-Sultan Salah al-Din Yusuf) b. at Takrit, Iraq. Emperor John II compels Raymond of Antioch to recognize his suzerainty. Atziz rebels in Khwarizm (Khiva). | 1138 Suryavarman II again campaigns against Dai Viet. | c. 1138 Pskov Cathedral begun.<br>1138 Victor III, antipope. Official charter of protection given by al-Muktafi to Nestorians. Abu Bakr Muhammad b. Yahya b. Bajjah, Spanish philosopher and polymath, d. at Fez. |
| 1139 Fulk of Jerusalem allies with Damascus against Zangi. | | 1139 Apr., 2nd Lateran Council.<br>1139–81 Verona Cathedral built.<br>1139–1192 Lu Hsiang-shan, Chinese philosopher. |
| 1140 Zangi compelled to raise the siege of Damascus. Samarqand rebels: put down by Sanjar after six months' siege.<br>c. 1140 Assassins capture fortresses in N Syria. | | 1140 The Royal Chapel at Palermo begun. Bayonne Cathedral begun.<br>1140–59 Peter Lombard teaching in Paris.<br>fl. 1140–1206 Saxo Grammaticus, historian.<br>c. 1140–1360 Archaic period of Benin art. |

| WESTERN & NORTHERN EUROPE | CENTRAL, SOUTHERN & EASTERN EUROPE | AFRICA & EGYPT |
|---|---|---|
| **1141** 2 Feb., Stephen taken prisoner at Lincoln. April, Matilda proclaimed Queen of England at Winchester. Dec., Stephen exchanged for Robert of Gloucester: 25 Dec., crowned. **1141–4** Geoffrey Plantagenet conquers Normandy. | **1141–61** Geiza, King of Hungary. | |
| **1142** War between Louis VII and Thibaud of Champagne. | **1142** Saxony restored to Henry the Lion. Bavaria granted to Henry Jasimirgott. Alliance between Conrad III and Byzantium. | |
| **1143** Treaty of Vitry between Louis VII and Thibaud. | **1143** Afonso Henriques forces recognition of Portugal as an independent kingdom by Castile. Civil revolt against the Pope in Rome: a *commune* constituted. Lübeck founded. **1143–6** Tashfin, Almoravid ruler of Spain. | **1143** Roger II of Sicily ravages African coast. |
| **1144** Hereditary monarchy replaces tanistry in Scotland. **1144–51** Geoffrey of Anjou, Duke of Normandy. | **1144** Alfonso VII takes Córdoba: Granada and Seville sacked. | **1144–6** Abd al-Mumin b. Ali takes principal Moroccan towns, defeating Almoravids. |
| | **1145** Arnold of Brescia becomes leader of the revolt in Rome. **1145–50** Almohad army in Spain: Abd al-Mumin acknowledged as suzerain. | |
| | **1146** Ibrahim, Almoravid ruler of Spain. **1146–7** Ishaq, Almoravid ruler of Spain. **1146** Wladislaw II of Poland deposed: succ. Boleslaw the Curly (−1173). | **1146** Normans take Tripoli (−1158) and Sfax (−1156). **1146–7** Siege of Marrakesh by Abd al-Mumin b. Ali: Marrakesh becomes Almohad capital. |
| **1147** Robert of Gloucester d. Matilda leaves England. Moscow first mentioned as a place. **1147–9** Louis VII of France takes part in Second Crusade: Suger, Abbot of St Denis, regent: ·Louis returns without his army. | **1147** Lisbon taken by Afonso Henriques: Stephen of Hastings, an Englishman, made its first bishop. Henry the Lion rebels: takes Mecklenburg: anarchy in Germany. Alfonso VII of Castile raids S coast of Spain, taking Almería (held until 1157). Afonso of Portugal retakes Santarem. Normans, under Roger II of Sicily, take Corfu and pillage Greece: Thebes and Corinth captured. | **1147** Ishaq b. Ali, last Almoravid, executed. |
| | **1148** Diet of Spier. Catalonia takes Tortosa. Emperor Manuel grants Venice additional commercial privileges. **1148–50** Guelph VI, brother of Henry the Proud, rebels. | **1148** Normans take al-Mahdia: all Tunisian coast subject to Roger II of Sicily (−1160). |
| | **1149** Catalonia takes Lérida. Louis VII, returning from Palestine, allies with Roger II of Sicily. Conrad III returns. Manuel retakes Corfu. Treaty between Emperors Conrad and Manuel against Roger II of Sicily. | **1149–54** al-Zafir, Fatimid Caliph. |

## THE NEAR EAST

**1141** Sanjar defeated by Kara Khitai: Kara Khitai occupies Merv and Nishapur.

**1142** Zangi defeats the Crusaders on he Orontes.

**1143** John II d. in Cilicia: succ. Manuel I Comnenos (—1180).
**1143—5** Conflict between Byzantium and Antioch: Raymond submits.
**1143—51** Byzantines expelled from Cilicia by Thorus II.
**1143—62** Baldwin III, King of Jerusalem.
**1143—72** Kumarapala, Saurashtra ruler of Gujarat.
**1144** Zangi takes the County of Edessa: takes al-Ruha from the Crusaders.

**1146** Nur al-Din Mahmud succ. Zangi as Atabeg of Mosul. Joscelin of Edessa retakes the city: then loses it to Nur al-Din.

**1147—9** Second Crusade led by Conrad III of Germany and Louis VII of France: Damascus besieged for four days: other actions abortive.
**1147** Emperor Conrad III defeated by the Turks at Dorylaeum. Eleanor of Aquitaine visits Jerusalem.

**1148** Crusaders besiege Damascus without success. Atziz of Khwarizm makes himself independent of the Saljuqs. Salghurid dynasty of Atabegs of Fars established in Fars: capital at Shiraz.
**1148—1215** Ghorid dynasty between Herat and Ghazna.
**1149** Nur al-Din takes Apamaea: Raymond of Poitiers defeated and killed.

## THE FAR EAST

**1141** Twenty-three geisha houses instituted for the entertainment of soldiers in China. S Sung forced to pay tribute to Jurchen.

**1143** Chinese expedition defeated by the Mongols.

**1145—9** Suryavarman II occupies Champa.

**1149** Jaya Harivarman I of Champa recovers kingdom from Cambodia.

## RELIGION & CULTURE

**1141** Council of Sens: Peter Abélard condemned. Hugh of St Victor, theologian, d.
**c. 1141** Ahmad b. Arif introduces Sufi thought into N Africa.
**1141—3** Peter the Venerable, Abbot of Cluny, sponsor of first Latin translation of the Koran.
**1142** Abélard d.

**1143** Order of Teutonic Military Knights founded. State hospitals re-organized in China. Paderborn Cathedral begun.
**?1143** William of Malmesbury, historian, d.
**1143—4** Celestine II, Pope.

**1144—5** Lucius II, Pope.

**1145** al-Khwarizmi, *Algebra*, translated by Robert of Chester. St Bernard preaching against the Cathari.
**c. 1145** First autopsy performed in China. Sculptures of the Royal Door at Chartres set up.
**1145—53** Eugenius III, Pope.
**1145—1217** Abu al-Husayn Muhammad b. Ahmad al-Jubayr, traveller and writer.
**1146** Assembly of Vézelay: St Bernard preaches the Second Crusade. Angers Cathedral and present Basilica of the Holy Sepulchre, Jerusalem, begun.
**c. 1146** Tomb of the Imam Yahya built at Mosul.

**1147** Cultivation of silk introduced into Sicily by the Normans. Geoffrey of Monmouth: *Historia Regum Britanniae*, St Stephen's Cathedral, Vienna, consecrated.
**c. 1147—1220** Giraldus Cambrensis, historian and topographer.

**1148** Council of Reims: Gilbert de la Porrée recants. Synod of Irish bishops at Inispatric reorganizes Irish Church. Anna Comnena: *The Alexiad*.
**1148—1222** Abbey at Alcobaça built.

**1149** Basilica of the Holy Sepulchre, Jerusalem, consecrated.

| WESTERN & NORTHERN EUROPE | CENTRAL, SOUTHERN & EASTERN EUROPE | AFRICA & EGYPT |
|---|---|---|
| **1150–60** Eric the Saint, King of Sweden.<br>Ghazna: populace murdered. Nur al- | **1150** Louis VII of France and Roger II of Sicily conspire to crusade against Byzantium. Most of Spain, except for Murcia, under Almohad control. populated from Polynesia: inhabitants<br>**1150–3** Aragon liberates all Spain N of the Ebro. | **c. 1150** Fortification of Kano completed by Yusa. |
| **1151** Geoffrey, Duke of Normandy, d.: succ. his son Henry, later Henry II of England.<br><br>**1152** Louis VII divorces Eleanor of Aquitaine: she marries (future) Henry II of England, Duke of Normandy, and Count of Anjou, Maine and Touraine: Henry renews war against Stephen. Matilda renounces her claim to England in favour of Stephen, conditionally on succession of her son, later Henry II, as heir.<br>**1153** 18 Aug., Eustace, son of Stephen d. Henry of Normandy and Anjou lands in England: 7 Nov., treaty of Wallingford: recognized as heir by Stephen and associated in work of government.<br>**1153–65** Malcolm IV, King of Scots.<br>**1154** 25 Oct., Stephen of England d.; succ. Henry II (–1189): 19 Dec., Henry II crowned. St Thomas Becket, Chancellor of England.<br>**1155** Pope Adrian IV awards Ireland to Henry II of England. | **1151** Albert the Bear inherits Brandenburg. Manuel makes Serbia a Byzantine Protectorate. Ancona occupied.<br>**1152** Conrad III d.: succ. Frederick I Barbarossa (–1190). Guelph VI acquires Tuscany and Spoleto.<br><br>**1153** Treaty of Constance between Frederick Barbarossa and Pope Eugenius II: alliance against Roger II of Sicily and Arnold of Brescia.<br><br>**1154** Roger II of Sicily d.: succ. William I (–1166). Frederick Barbarossa in Italy.<br>**1154–84** George III, King of Georgia.<br>**1155** 18 June, Frederick I Barbarossa crowned Emperor. Arnold of Brescia hanged. Emperor Manuel I attacks Normans in S Italy.<br>**1155 or 6** Cyprus sacked by Renard de Chatillon. | **c. 1151** Mai of Bornu, Dunama b. Umme, drowned on the pilgrimage to Mecca.<br><br>**1152** Abd al-Mumin b. Ali conquers Algeria. Siuna (now Sena), Mozambique, already a trading centr for Africans, Arabs and Indians.<br><br><br>**1153** Normans take Bône, Gabès an Jerba.<br><br><br><br>**1154–60** al-Faiz, Fatimid Caliph. |
| **1156** Moscow founded by Yuri Dolgoruki: palisaded defences built.<br><br><br>**1157** Henry II of England campaigns against Owain the Great of Wales; and against Malcolm IV of Scotland: Cumberland, Northumberland and Westmorland regained by England. Assembly of Besançon: Frederick Barbarossa breaks with the Papacy.<br>Eric of Sweden takes Finland.<br>**1157–74** Andrew Bogolioubski, Prince of Suzdal.<br>**1157–82** Waldemar I, the Great, King of Denmark.<br>**1158** Henry II of England takes Dehenbarth and Gwynedd: becomes overlord of Brittany. | **1156** Rebellion in Rome. Normans take Brindisi. Hungary recognizes Byzantine suzerainty. Frederick I Barbarossa restores Bavaria to Henry the Lion. Austria becomes an independent Duchy.<br><br><br><br><br><br><br><br><br>**1158** Frederick Barbarossa campaigns in Lombardy. Nov., Diet of Roncaglia: imperial rights defined in Italy. Peace made by Manuel I and William I of Sicily.<br>**1158–1214** Alfonso VIII, King of León and Castile. | **1156** Normans lose Sfax.<br><br><br><br><br><br><br><br><br><br><br><br>**1158** Abd al-Mumin b. Ali conquers Tunisia. |

| THE NEAR EAST | THE FAR EAST | RELIGION & CULTURE |
|---|---|---|
| | **1150** Suryavarman II again campaigns against Dai Viet.<br>**c. 1150±** New Zealand already populated from Polynesia: inhabitants hunting the moa, a bird from six to ten feet high. | **ante 1150** Works of Abu Hamid al-Ghazzali translated into Latin: influences medieval scholasticism: some ideas taken up by St Thomas Aquinas and by Pascal.<br>**c. 1150** *Cantar del mio Cid*, outstanding Spanish epic. Paper making introduced in Spain.<br>**1150—90** The Kutubya built at Marrakesh. Building of Rabat begun.<br>**1150—95** Bernard de Ventadour, poet.<br>**1150—1250** Langres Cathedral built.<br>**1151** 13 Jan., Suger d. Trondheim made an archbishopric. |
| **151** Ala al-Din Husain of Ghur sacks Ghazni: populace murdered. Nur al-Din, Zangid, conquers al-Ruha: Joscelin II taken prisoner. | | |
| | | **1152—3** Ailred of Rievaulx: *Genealogy of the Kings* of England.<br>**1152—4** First quarrel between Frederick Barbarossa and the Pope. |
| **153** Sanjar defeated and taken prisoner by Ghuzz nomads. Ascalon taken by Baldwin III of Jerusalem. | **1153—86** Parakrama Bahu I, King of Ceylon: warrior, statesman and builder. | **1153** St Bernard d. Rebuilding of Erfurt Cathedral begun. Mosque of Tinmel built.<br>**1153—4** Anastasius IV, Pope. |
| **154** Nur al-Din, Zangid, takes Damascus. | | **1154** al-Idrisi, *Kitab Rujar*.<br>**1154—9** Adrian IV, only English Pope: quarrel with the Empire renewed.<br>**1154—81** Ripon Cathedral built.<br>**c. 1155** Senlis Cathedral built. |
| | **c. 1155—?** Dharanindravarman II, King of Cambodia.<br>**1155** Chingis Khan, Mongol conqueror b. (−1227): conquests extend from N China to Persia, India and Russia: Mongol armies include many Turks. Court based on Karakorum.<br>**c. 1156—81** Taira family, under Taira Kiyomori, dominant in Japan. | **1155** Wace: *Roman de Brut*. Great Mosque of Konia built. Pipe Rolls begun.<br>**c. 1155—70** Thomas: *Tristan et Iseult*<br>**?c. 1155—?c. 1213** Geoffroi de Villehardouin, chronicler. |
| **156** Sept., Damascus pays tribute to the Crusaders. Atziz, founder of the Khwarazmian state d.: succ. Il-Arslan (−1172). | | **1156** Alliance between Pope Adrian IV and William I of Sicily. Concordat of Beneventum. Carmelite Order founded. Order of Knights of Alcántara instituted. |
| | | **1157** Cistercian Abbey of Belmont, Lebanon, founded (−1289). |
| **158** Manuel reconquers Cilicia. Peace made between Byzantium and Antioch, and Jerusalem. Baldwin III retakes Harim: Nur al-Din defeated at Butaha.<br>**158—69** Vallala-Sena, or Ballal Sen, ruler of part of Bengal: stated to have re-organized caste system. | | **1158** Order of Military Knights of Calatrava founded. |

| WESTERN & NORTHERN EUROPE | CENTRAL, SOUTHERN & EASTERN EUROPE | AFRICA & EGYPT |
|---|---|---|
| **1159** Henry II and Malcolm IV of Scotland attack Toulouse: defended by Louis VII. Scutage tax imposed in England in lieu of feudal military service.<br>**1160** Rising in Galloway put down by Malcolm IV.<br>**1160–2** Henry the Lion subjects the Wends. | **1159** Revolt in Milan put down.<br><br>**1160** Jan., Frederick Barbarossa takes Crema. Imperial Council held at Pavia. | **1160** Abd al-Mumin takes Libya: further campaigns in Morocco. Abd al-Mumin b. Ali conquers Tripolitania: Almohad empire now a its greatest extent.<br>**1160–71** al-Adid, Fatimid Caliph. |
| **1161–84** Magnus V, King of Norway. | **1161–2** Qilij Arslan pays state visit to Constantinople.<br><br>**1162** Milan sacked by Frederick Barbarossa: Pisa and Genoa ally against William of Sicily.<br>**1162–96** Alfonso II of Aragon: capital at Saragossa: known as Emperor of the Pyrenees.<br>**1163** Emperor Manuel makes Stephen Nemanya Prince of Serbia.<br><br>**1164** Venice forms League of Verona against Frederick Barbarossa. | **1161–9** Crusaders make four attem to invade Egypt.<br><br><br>**1163** Abd al-Mumin d. Rabat made the Almohad capital.<br>**1163–84** Abu Yaqub b. Abd al-Mumin, Almohad ruler.<br><br>**1164** Amaury I compels Saljuqs under Shirkuh to evacuate Egypt. Saladin takes part in campaign in Egypt. |
| **1165** Abortive invasion of Wales by Henry II. Alliance between Henry and Frederick Barbarossa.<br>**1165–1214** William the Lion, King of Scots. | **1165** May, Diet of Würzburg: supporters of Pope Alexander III persecuted. War between Byzantium and Hungary. | **1165** Alleged letter from 'Prester John' to Byzantium. |
| **1166** Henry II compels his Breton subjects to recognize his son as heir to the dukedom. Assize of Novel Disseisin instituted by Henry II of England. Assize of Clarendon institutes Grand Jury.<br>**1167** Aug., Norman force under Richard Godebeot arrives in Ireland. Battle of Zengmin. | **1166** Frederick Barbarossa campaigns in Italy. War between Henry the Lion and Albert the Bear.<br>**1166–89** William II, King of Sicily.<br><br>**1167** 28 May, Frederick Barbarossa defeats Romans at Tusculum: Rome taken. 1 Aug., Frederick crowned emperor. Dec., Lombard League formed: joins League of Verona: Frederick retires.<br>**1168** Alessandria, Piedmont, founded. Milan rebuilt. Henry the Lion and Albert the Bear reconciled: Henry m. Matilda, daughter of Henry II of England. | **1167** Amaury I takes Cairo (–1168<br><br><br>**1168** Amaury I compelled to leave Egypt: Nur al-Din takes Cairo. |
| **1169** 6 Jan., peace made between Henry II of England and Louis VII of France. 1 May, further Normans arrive in Ireland. Kiev sacked and burnt by Prince Andrew Bogolioubski: end of Kiev as a capital.<br>**1169–1243** Twenty-two different Grand Princes of Kiev: frequent civil wars. | **1169** Genoa given special trading privileges in the Byzantine empire. Alfonso II of Aragon takes offensive in Spain. | **1169–1252** Ayyubid dynasty in Egypt: Saladin (initially with title *Wazir*) first ruler (–1193).<br>African mercenaries in Egypt revolt put down by Turks under Saladin. |

| THE NEAR EAST | THE FAR EAST | RELIGION & CULTURE |
|---|---|---|
| **1159** The Franks and Byzantines besiege Aleppo: peace made with Nur al-Din. Manuel conquers Phrygia: pays state visit to Antioch as suzerain. | | **1159** John of Salisbury: *Policraticus.* <br> **1159—60** Peter Lombard, Bp of Paris. <br> **1159—64** Victor IV, antipope. <br> **1159—81** Alexander III, Pope. |
| **1160** Nur al-Din takes Renaud de Chatillon prisoner. Manuel takes Meander valley. Ghuzz Turkmans take Ghazna. <br> **1160—70** al-Mustanjid, Abbasid Caliph. | **1160** Tariff of Chinese taxes: salt 50%; wine 36%; tea 7%; customs 7%. | **1160** Abu Bakr al-Quzman, Córdoban wandering minstrel, d. Papal Synod of Toulouse. <br> **c. 1160** Béraud: *Tristan et Iseul.* <br> The *Niebelungenlied* composed. <br> **1160—1234** Izz al-Din b. al-Athir, historian. |
| **1161** Qilij Arslan recognizes Manuel as his suzerain. | **1161** Mongols defeated by Chin. <br> **c. 1161** Yesugei, father of Chingis Khan, d. | **1161** Emperor Manuel recognizes Pope Alexander III: plan for reunion of eastern and western church. <br> **1162** Poitiers Cathedral begun. |
| **1162—73** Amaury I, King of Jerusalem. | | **1162—70** Thomas Becket, Abp of Canterbury. <br> **1162—1231** Abd al-Latif al-Baghdadi, scholar and *wazir* of Egypt. |
| | | **1163** Quarrel between Henry II of England and Thomas Becket. Council of Tours. <br> **c. 1163—82** Nôtre-Dame, Paris, built. |
| **1164** Nur al-Din captures Bohémond III of Antioch and Raymond III of Tripoli. Nur al-Din takes Harim. | | **1164** Jan., Constitution of Clarendon: Henry II defines rights of the king over the church in England: 2 Nov., Henry II accuses Becket of dishonesty: Becket flees to France. Uppsala, Sweden, made an archbishopric. Church organized in Norway. <br> **1164—8** Paschal III, antipope. |
| | **1165** S Sung recognized as an equal state by Jurchen. <br> **1165 fl.** Yasovarman II, King of Cambodia: throne usurped by mandarin Tribhuvanadityavarman. | **1165** Henry II of England breaks off relations with Pope Alexander III: recognizes Paschal III, antipope. Thomas Becket leaves England. <br> **c. 1165—1240** Abu Bakr Muhammad b. Ali Muhyi al-Din b. Arabi, Spanish mystic. |
| **1166** Tancred takes Apamaea. Qilij Arslan I takes Melitene. | **1166—7** Jaya Indravarman IV usurps the throne of Champa. | |
| | **1167** Chinese government provides low interest loans to poor persons. <br> **1167—70** Narathu, King of Pagan. | |
| | | **1168** Portico of Cathedral of Santiago de Compostella begun. <br> **1168** Aztec said to be migrating eastward towards Anáhuac valley. <br> **1168—78** Calixtus III, antipope. |
| | | **1169** Mosaics constructed in the upper Church of the Nativity at Bethlehem. <br> **1169—85** Palermo Cathedral built. |

| WESTERN & NORTHERN EUROPE | CENTRAL, SOUTHERN & EASTERN EUROPE | AFRICA & EGYPT |
|---|---|---|

**1169–1328** Great Dukes of Vladimir, rulers of Russia.
**1170** 15 July, Prince Henry, Duke of Normandy, heir of Henry II of England, crowned king by Abp of York. 23 Aug., Norman force under Richard Strongbow, Earl of Pembroke, lands at Waterford; Sept., Dublin taken: Pembroke becomes King of Leinster.

**1171** Henry II of England lands at Waterford with 4,000 men: Pembroke confirmed: many Irish chiefs submit: Hugh de Lacy appointed Justiciar, or viceroy: Dublin, Wexford and Waterford annexed: general submission made: administration reorganized.
**1172** Queen Eleanor rebels in Aquitaine against Henry II. 11 June, future Richard I installed as Duke of Aquitaine at Poitiers.
**1173** First Parliament held in Scotland. Rebellion in France and Ireland against Henry II, led by his sons. Henry II arbitrates between Toulouse and Aragon: Toulouse becomes his vassal. Louis VII defeated at Verneuil.
**1174** 13 July, William I of Scots captured attacking Alnwick: acknowledges English suzerainty by treaty of Falaise. Louis VII defeated at Rouen. 30 Sept., treaty of Montlouis: peace between Henry II of England and Louis VII of France.
**1175** Treaty of Windsor: Kingdom of Connacht brought under tribute. Queen Eleanor's rebellion collapses.

**1170** The Lombard League supports Alexander III. Albert the Bear d.
**1170–80** War between Castile and León.

**1171** Alfonso II of Aragon takes Teruel. Emperor Manuel confiscates Venetian assets and goods in Byzantium.

**1172** Abortive attempt of Venice to attack Emperor Manuel. War between Byzantium and Serbia.

**1173** Emperor Manuel sets Bela III on the Hungarian throne (−1196).
**1173–7** Mieszko the Old, Duke of Poland, first reign.
**1173–89** Sobeslav II, Prince of Bohemia.

**1174–5** Frederick Barbarossa unsuccessfully besieges Alessandria: buys Corsica, Sardinia, Spoleto and Tuscany from Guelph VI.

**1175** 16 Apr., treaty of Montebello between Frederick Barbarossa and Lombard League. Peace treaty between Byzantium and Venice.

**c. 1170–88** Sulaiman Hasan b. Dau Sultan of Kilwa: builds fortifications and other stone buildings.

**1171** Last Fatimid d.: end of Shi'isr in Egypt. Turan Shah campaigns in Nubia. Red Sea and eastern Africa becomes a sphere of Egyptian trade influence.

**1172–3** Turan Shah's second campaign in Nubia.

**1174** Saladin declares Egypt independent.

**1176** 1 June, Pembroke d.: Leinster passes to the English Crown. Assize of Northampton: itinerant judges made the practice in England.

**1177** Council of Oxford: Henry II makes Prince John Lord of Ireland. Ulster conquered. Henry and Louis VII make peace at Nonancourt (treaty of Ivry).
**1177–1202** Sverrir, King of Norway.

**1178** Henry II of England and Louis VII of France plan a crusade. Court of the King's Bench instituted in England.

**1176** 29 May, Lombard League defeats Frederick Barbarossa heavily at Legnano. Nov., negotiations at Anagni between Frederick and Pope Alexander III.
**1177** 22 July, peace of Venice between Frederick Barbarossa and Pope Alexander III. Mieszko of Poland forced to abdicate: succ. Casimir II, the Just, Duke of Poland (−1194). Armies of Aragon and Castile take Cuenca. Alfonso VIII of Castile m. Eleanor, daughter of Henry II of England.

**1176** Building of Cairo Citadel and fortifications begun (−1193).
**c. 1176** Second dynasty of Benin founded by Oranmiyan.

## THE NEAR EAST

## THE FAR EAST

## RELIGION & CULTURE

**1170** Amalric defeats Nur al-Din, Zangid, near the Dead Sea; then defeats Saladin at Gaza.
**1170—80** al-Mustadi, Abbasid Caliph.

**1171** Saladin dethrones Amalric, King of Jerusalem.

**1172—1200** Takash, Saljuq ruler of Khwarizm.

**1173** Ghazna incorporated into Ghur by Sultan Ghiyas al-Din: government given to his brother, Muhammad Ghuri.
**1173—85** Baldwin IV, King of Jerusalem.

**1174** Saladin defeated by Baldwin IV at Montgisard. Turan Shah takes Yemen for Saladin, his brother. Saladin conquers Syria following battle of Qurun Hamah: Damascus taken.

**1175** May, Abbasid Caliph recognizes Saladin as ruler of W Arabia, Egypt, Maghrib, Nubia, Palestine and central Syria; title: Sultan.
**c. 1175** Chola ascendancy waning: power of feudatories increases: challenged by Yadava, Hoysala and Kakatiya dynasties.
**1175—6** Muhammad Ghuri attacks Multan and Uch.
**1175—1340** Muslim conquest of India.
**1176** Byzantine campaign against the Saljuq Sultanate of Iconium (Konia): 17 Sept., defeated by the Turks at Myriocephalon: Phrygia lost to Byzantium.
**1177** Manuel I campaigns in the Meander valley.
**1177—94** Sultan Tugril, Saljuq Sultan of Iraq.

**1178** Muhammad Ghuri attacks Gujarat: repelled by Bhimdev II of Anhilwara (Patan).

**1170—3** Naratheinkha, King of Pagan.

**1173—1210** Narapatisithu, King of Pagan.

**1177** Cham invasion of Cambodia.

**1178** Emperor of China appoints Chuan-Chou as permanent establishment for Sri Vijaya trade: further embassies forbidden, but continue to 1279.

**1170** 3 Dec., Becket returns to Canterbury. 25 Dec., Becket excommunicates all who had assisted at Prince Henry's coronation. 29 Dec., Becket murdered in Canterbury Cathedral. Pope Alexander III makes regulations for the canonization of saints: negotiates with Frederick Barbarossa at Veroli.
**1171** 25 Jan., Henry II's French possessions interdicted. Synod of Cashel: Irish church reformed: Roman authority asserted. First *madrassa*-type mosque built.

**1172** 21 May, Henry II reconciled with Pope Alexander III. Brunswick Cathedral begun.
**1172—95** Great Mosque of Seville built.
**1173** 23 Feb., St Thomas Becket canonized. Leaning Tower of Pisa built.
**c. 1173** Pierre Waldo founds sect of Waldenses at Lyons.

**1173** William of Tyre, author of the *History of the Kingdom of Jerusalem*, elected Abp of Tyre.

**1174** 12 July, Henry II of England does penance at Canterbury for death of St Thomas Becket. Tarragona Cathedral begun. Choir of Canterbury Cathedral built.
**1174—82** Cloisters of Monreale built.

**1175** Ahmad al-Rifai d.: founder of Rifaite dervish order.
**c. 1175—1212** Soissons Cathedral built.
**c. 1175—1253** Robert Grosseteste. English statesman and theologian.

**1177** Great Hospital begun at Angers.

**1178—9** Richard FitzNigel: *Dialogus de Scaccario* describes English financial administration.

**WESTERN &
NORTHERN EUROPE**

**CENTRAL, SOUTHERN
& EASTERN EUROPE**

**AFRICA & EGYPT**

**1179** 1 Nov., Philip II Augustus made co-ruler of France. Grand Assize of Windsor: feudal court powers checked in favour of royal courts. Louis VII visits Canterbury.

**1180** Ranulf de Glanville, Chief Justiciar of England: English judiciary reformed.
**1180–9** Philip II at war with Henry II of England.
**1180–1223** Philip II Augustus, King of France.
**1181** Henry II of England's sons rebel. Assize of Arms: all able-bodied men in England required to possess arms. Tver founded.
**1182–1202** Canute VI, King of Denmark.

**1183** Prince Henry, Duke of Normandy, and his brother, attack Richard of Aquitaine (later Richard I of England): 11 June, Prince Henry d.: end of rebellion.

**1184** Further rebellion of Henry II's sons. Assize of Woodstock *re* royal forests in England.

**1185** Philip Augustus acquires Amiens and Vermandois.

**1186** 19 Aug., Geoffrey, Duke of Brittany, son of Henry II, d.

**1187** Breach between Henry II of England and Philip Augustus of France: Philip takes Tournai. Rising in Moray.
**1187–8** Philip Augustus takes Berry.

**1188** Saladin tithe instituted in England.

**1179** Breach between Frederick Barbarossa and Henry the Lion. Swabia sold to Frederick Barbarossa by Guelph VI. Treaty of Cazorla demarcates areas of influence of Castile and Aragon.
**1180** Jan., Frederick Barbarossa at war with Henry the Lion: Henry's fiefs divided amongst other princes. Congress of Leczyca: Polish clergy and nobility granted numerous privileges.
**1180–3** Alexios II Comnenos, Eastern Roman Emperor.
**1181** Frederick Barbarossa and Henry the Lion reconciled: Henry given Brunswick.

**1182** Florence takes Empoli. Massacre of Latins in Constantinople: Alexios II Comnenos imprisoned and blinded.
**1183** Andronicus Comnenos acclaimed Emperor (–1185). Hungary takes Zara from Venice. Stephen Nemanya takes the Morava valley. Peace of Constance: Lombard League recognized by Frederick Barbarossa.
**1183–5** Andronicus I Comnenos, Eastern Roman Emperor.
**1184** Diet of Mayence: Frederick Barbarossa betroths his heir, Henry, to Constance, heiress to Kingdom of Sicily. Cyprus makes itself independent of Byzantium.
**1184–1212** Tamara, Queen of Georgia.

**1185** Treaty between Frederick Barbarossa and Milan. Treaty between Byzantium and Venice. Norman expedition against Byzantium: Aug., Thessalonica taken: populace massacred: Normans advance on Constantinople: Andronicus deposed: succ. Isaac II Angelus (–1195).
c. **1185** Treaty between Byzantium and Saladin: Byzantium to recognize Saladin in Palestine in return for recognition of imperial suzerainty. Isaac Angelus makes Cyprus independent of the empire.
**1185–1211** Sancho I, King of Portugal.
**1185–1284** Angelus dynasty in Constantinople.
**1186** 27 Jan., Henry VI m. Constance of Sicily. Bulgaria regains its independence: Second Bulgarian kingdom established.

**1188** Aug., Henry the Lion exiled. *Cortes* (council) instituted in León.

**1182** Crusaders raid Ailat and Aidhab.

**1184–99** Abu Yusuf b. Abu Yaqub, Almohad: known as al-Mansur. al-Mansur puts down abortive Almoravid *coup*.

## THE NEAR EAST

## THE FAR EAST

## RELIGION & CULTURE

**1179** Saladin raids Tyre.

**c. 1178** East Java superseding Sri Vijaya in commercial importance.

**1179** 3rd Lateran Council: papal and episcopal elections reformed.
**1179–80** Innocent III, antipope.
**1179–1229** Yaqut b. Abdallah al-Hamawi: *Mujam al-Buldan*, geographical dictionary.
**ante 1180** Ranulf de Glanville: *Tractatus de Legibus.*
**1180** Windmills first appear in Normandy and France. Wells and Beauvais Cathedrals begun.
**c. 1180–1234** Hia-Kuei, Chinese artist.

**1180** First consuls in history appointed by Genoa to Acre, and, later, Egypt. Truce between Baldwin IV and Saladin.
**1180–1225** al-Nasir, Caliph: attempts to restore authority of the Caliphate.

**1181–c. 1218** Jayavarman VII, King of Cambodia: fortifications of Angkor Thom built.

**1181** Alcázar of Seville begun.
**1181–5** Lucius III, Pope.
**1181–1235** Umar b. al-Farid, Sufi poet, of Cairo.

**1182** Saladin raids Nazareth, Tiberias and Beirut. Muhammad Ghuri conquers Sind.

**1183** Saladin takes Aleppo: Samaria sacked.

**1182** Jews expelled from France. Papal legate sent by Pope Lucius III to Constantinople.
**1182–1226** St Francis of Assisi.

**1183–1223** St Salvator, Bruges, built.

**1184** Saladin raids Galilee.

**1184** Damascus possesses twenty schools (*madrassah*), two free hospitals and numerous Dervish convents. Giralda tower built in Seville. Diet of Verona: negotiations between Pope Lucius III and Frederick Barbarossa fail.
**post 1184** Dervish monasteries introduced in Egypt.

**1185** Malik Dinar seizes Khorasan with Ghuzz aid. Muhammad Ghuri conquers Lahore and attacks Rajput Kingdoms on Ganges plain.

**1185** Following sea battle against Taira at Shimonoseki, Minamoto family paramount in Japan: beginning of the *samurai: hara-kiri* first mentioned: Makamura made the centre of administration.

**1185** A Latin church built in Constantinople. Quarrel between western Emperor and the Pope renewed.
**1185** Patriarch Heraclius of Jerusalem visits Henry II of England.
**1185–7** Urban III, Pope.

**1186** Muhammad Ghuri seizes Lahore from the Ghaznavids: all Punjab occupied. Saladin takes N Syria and Mosul.
**1186–95** Guy de Lusignan, King of Jerusalem.
**1187** 1 July, Saladin takes Tiberias. 3-4 July, battle of Horns of Hittin: Crusader army destroyed: Saladin takes Guy de Lusignan, King of Jerusalem, captive. 2 Oct., Jerusalem surrenders to Saladin.
**1188** Saladin ruler of all former Crusader territories, except Antioch, Tripoli and Tyre.

**1187–96** Nissanka Malla, King of Ceylon: great builder.

**1186** Breach between Frederick Barbarossa and Pope Urban III. Evangelization of Livonia begun.
**1186–1204** Evora Cathedral built.

**1187** Gregory VIII, Pope. Church in Wales placed under Abp of Canterbury. Gerard of Cremona, translator of Arabic works into Latin, d.
**1187** Lambert le Bègue, founder of Beguinages, d.
**1187–91** Clement III, Pope.

**1188** Reconciliation between Pope Gregory VIII and the Roman *commune.*

1188–1194
WESTERN &
NORTHERN EUROPE
CENTRAL, SOUTHERN
& EASTERN EUROPE
AFRICA & EGYPT

**1188** 18 Nov., alliance between Prince Richard of England and Philip Augustus of France: Richard does homage for Aquitaine.

**1189** 3 Apr., Peace of Strasbourg: reconciliation between Frederick Barbarossa and Clement III. Meeting at Colombiers between Henry II of England and Philip II Augustus of France. 6 July, Henry II of England d.: succ. Richard I, *Coeur de Lion* (–1199). 20 July, Richard I invested as Duke of Normandy at Rouen. 5 Dec., Richard I acknowledges Scottish independence: Berwick-on-Tweed and Roxburgh sold to William the Lion. Treaty of Canterbury abrogates treaty of Falaise. Commercial treaty between German and Novgorod merchants.

**1189** Richard I of England takes Cyprus. William II of Sicily d.: succ. Tancred of Lecce.
**1189–91** Conrad Otto I, Prince of Bohemia.

**1190** Stephen Nemanya takes Kossovo. Frederick Barbarossa d.: succ. Henry VI (–1197): makes peace with Henry the Lion. Tancred of Lecce rebels against Henry VI. 4 Oct., Richard I of England storms Messina. Treaty of Messina between Philip Augustus and Richard I of England.

**c. 1190** Kanem in control of Saharan trade routes.
**1190–1225** Lalibela, Emperor of Ethiopia: great church builder: capital at Lasta: considerable literary activity.

**1191** Philip of Alsace, Count of Flanders, d.: Flanders partitioned between France and Baldwin of Hainault.

**1191** 14 Apr., Henry VI crowned Emperor: abortive expedition against Sicily. General rebellion in Germany. Richard I takes Cyprus: sells it to the Knights Templar (–1426). 12 May, Richard I marries Berengaria of Navarre at Limassol.
**1191–2** Wenceslas II, Prince of Bohemia.

**c. 1191–1215** al-Hasan b. Sulaiman II, Sultan of Kilwa: ? builder of Husuni palace.

**1192** Agreement of Péronne between Philip Augustus and Baldwin of Hainault.

**1192** Guy de Lusignan purchases Cyprus from the Knights Templar: becomes King (–1194).

**1192** 21 Dec., Richard I of England taken prisoner by Leopold, Duke of Austria, while returning from Palestine.

**1193** Philip Augustus of France attacks Normandy. Prince John of England does him homage. Philip seizes English possessions in France.
**1193–9** Inconclusive fighting for English possessions in France between Philip of France and England.

**1193** German rebellion collapses.
**1193** 14 Feb.–**1194** 3 Feb., Richard I of England held prisoner by Emperor Henry VI.

**1194** 22 July, Richard of England defeats Philip Augustus of France at Fréteval: English possessions in France recovered. Limerick annexed. Richard I briefly in England.
**1194–1240** Llywelyn the Great, Prince of Gwynedd.

**1194** 3 Feb., Richard I set free. Tancred of Lecce d.: Henry VI conquers Sicily. Alfonso VIII of Castile formally challenges Almohad ruler Yaqub.
**1194–7** Amaury, King of Cyprus.
**1194–1202** Mieszko the Old, Duke of Poland restored.

## THE NEAR EAST

## THE FAR EAST

## RELIGION & CULTURE

**1188—9** Fadhail b. Naqid, Jewish Egyptian authority on ophthalmology, d.

**1189—93** Third Crusade: led by Frederick Barbarossa of Germany, Philip Augustus of France, and Richard I of England.
**1189** 27 Aug.—**1191** 12 July, Crusaders besiege Acre by land and sea: garrison surrenders.

**1189** Chingis Khan becomes leader of the Mongols.

**1189** The French clergy refuse to pay the Saladin tithe.

**1190** Frederick Barbarossa takes Iconium: d. in Cilicia. Hoysala kingdom of Mysore becomes independent.
**1190—2** Richard I of England in Palestine.

**1190** War between Cambodia and Champa: Cambodia takes Vijaya, capital of Champa: fails to maintain hold: country reunited under Jaya Indravarman V.
**1190—1222** Kertajaya, last king of Kadiri.

c. **1190** William of Tyre, historian of the Crusades, d.

**1190—1224** Ma-Yuan, Chinese painter.

**1191** Philip of France quarrels with Richard I of England, and returns home, leaving Richard to continue the struggle. Muhammad Ghuri mounts expedition against India: Hindu rulers form confederacy. First battle of Tarain: Muhammad Ghuri defeated by Rajputs under Prithviraja.
**1191—2** Vira Ballala, Hoysala ruler, extends dominions at expense of Yadavas of Devagiri.
**1192** 2 Nov., peace made between Crusaders and Saladin: Levant coast left to Latins: Saladin retains interior. Rashid al-Din Sinan, master of the Assassins d.: bore title of 'Old Man of the Mountain' in Crusader chronicles. Conrad of Montferrat elected King of Jerusalem. Second battle of Tarain: Muhammad Ghuri defeats Prithviraja: Delhi and Ajmer conquered: Qutb al-Din Aibak put in charge.
**1193** 3 March, Saladin d. in Damascus: succ. his sons al-Malik al-Afdal in Damascus; al-Aziz in Cairo; al-Zahir in Aleppo; and brother al-Adil at al-Karak. Qutb al-Din Aibak occupies Delhi: Kanauj taken: Bihar seized by Muhammad Khilji.
**1193—1229** Saladin's conquests in Syria slowly revert to the Crusaders.
**1194** Tughril defeated by Takash: Takash seizes secular power in Baghdad. Jaichant of Kanauj defeated by Muhammad Ghuri: end of Kingdom of Kanauj.

c. **1191** Windmills first appear in England.
**1191** Order of Teutonic Knights founded by the Pope. al-Suhrawardi, mystic, d.
**1191—8** Celestine III, Pope.

**1192** Minamoto Yoritomo named *Se-i tai-shogun* ('barbarian-subduing great general') by Japanese Emperor: origin of shogunate as a permanent office: state administration known as *Bakufu* ('camp office') (—*c.* 1339).

**1192** Rebuilding of Lincoln Cathedral begun.

**1193** Zen order founded in Japan by Eisai. W. front of Peterborough Abbey begun.
**1193—1280** Albert the Great, theologian and philosopher.
c. **1193—1253** St Clare, foundress of the Poor Clares.

**1194** Civil war in Mexico between the Cocoms with Chichén-Itza and Uxmal.
**1194—1260** Chartres Cathedral rebuilt.

| WESTERN & NORTHERN EUROPE | CENTRAL, SOUTHERN & EASTERN EUROPE | AFRICA & EGYPT |
|---|---|---|
| **1195** Famine in England. | **1195** Battle of Alarcos: Christians defeated: Toledo, Madrid and Guadalajara still held. Isaac II Angelus deposed, blinded and imprisoned by his brother, Alexios III (–1203). Henry VI takes Meissen. Henry the Lion d. Armenia and Cyprus recognize Henry VI as suzerain. | |
| **1196** Philip II of France takes parts of Normandy and Aquitaine from Richard I of England. William the Lion defeats Harold, Earl of Orkney. | **1196** Henry VI attempts to make the Imperial Crown hereditary. The Emperor Alexios III pays tribute to Henry VI.<br>**1196–1204** Emeric I, King of Hungary.<br>**1196–1213** Peter II, King of Aragon. | **1196–1217** Abu Muhammad Abd al-Haqq, Marinid ruler<br>**1196–1464** Marinid dynasty of Fez. |
| **1197** Richard I of England organizes a feudal coalition against Philip Augustus: Philip defeated by Baldwin of Flanders at Ypres. | **1197** Henry VI puts down rebellion in Sicily. 28 Sept., Henry VI d. General rebellion in Italy. Bohemia and Moravia separated.<br>**1197–1207** Kalojan, Tsar of Bulgaria.<br>**1197–1208** Philip and Otto IV, rival Holy Roman Emperors.<br>**1197–1230** Ottokar I of Bohemia. | |
| **1198** Renewed war between Richard I of England and Philip II of France: Philip's army destroyed at Gisors: loses Aire and St Omer. | **1198** 3 June, Philip, Duke of Swabia, elected King of Germany. 19 July, Otto IV of Brunswick elected King of Germany by the Guelph party. War between Pope Innocent III and Sicily: Innocent III takes Spoleto and Ancona: 17 May, Frederick II crowned King of Sicily. | **1198–9** al-Mansur Muhammad, Ayyubid ruler.<br><br>**1199–1222** al-Nasir, Almohad ruler.<br>**1199–1218** al-Adil I Saif al-Din, Ayyubid ruler. |
| **1199** Pope Innocent III mediates a truce between Philip Augustus and Richard I. 6 Apr., Richard I of England d. at siege of castle of Chalus: succ., his brother, John (–1216): Arthur, son of John's elder brother, Geoffrey of Britanny, claimant to the English throne, flees to French court.<br>**1199–1210** Swerker II, King of Sweden. | **1199** 28 May, Declaration of Spier: German princes affirm right to free election of king. | |
| **13th c.** Tartars seize Dnieper valley, cutting off Russian communications with Byzantium. Area of upper Volga basin, R. Oka and Kliazma becomes known as Great Russia. Lithuania converted to Christianity. | | **?13th c.** Kalundwe empire establishe |
| **1200** 22 May, peace of Le Goulet between Philip II of France and John of England: John m. Isabel of Angoulême. City of Riga founded. Llywelyn the Great takes Anglesey.<br>**1200–8** Building of Dublin Castle begun. Royal court established in Dublin. | **1200** Pope Innocent III pronounces in favour of Otto IV of Brunswick.<br>**c. 1200** Population of Constantinople 800,000 to 1 m. | **c. 1200** Nta (or Ntafo), ancestors of the Akan, begin to disperse from near Gonja (present Ghana). Benin constitution revised. Fulani begin to appear in Borgu, and amongst Hausa some entering Senegambia. Jews given special privileges in Morocco, which they have enjoyed ever since.<br>**post 1200** Kingdoms of Sine and Saloum founded by Sereres. Arabic begins to displace Berber in Morocco<br>**1200–35** Soumangouroun. |

## THE NEAR EAST

**1195–1231** St Anthony of Padus, missionary in N Africa.
**1195** Choir of Lichfield Cathedral and W front of St Alban's Abbey begun.
**c. 1195–9** Mosque of al-Hasan at Rabat built.

**1197** Tlemcen becomes a pilgrimage centre.
Amaury of Cyprus becomes King of Jerusalem.

**1199** End of the 'Pala' dynasty: place taken by Sena dynasty of Bengal.
**1199 or 1202** Muhammad Khilji conquers Bengal.

**13th c.** Yadava lay claim to Gujarat.

**1200–19** Muhammad, Khwarazmian ruler: empire extended over parts of Afghanistan and India.
**1200–20** Ala al-Din Muhammad succ. Takash.

## THE FAR EAST

**late 12th c.** Pali, Sanscrit and Mon discarded for inscriptions in Burma: Burmese alone used: considerable output of theological commentaries and grammatical works.

## RELIGION & CULTURE

**c. 1195–1259** Matthew Paris, chronicler.

**1197–1208 fl.** Unkei, Japanese sculptor.
**1197–1276** Madhva, Indian philosopher, theologian, teacher of Hindu theology and devotion.

**1198–1216** Innocent III, Pope.
**1198** Philip Augustus of France quarrels with Pope Innocent III.
Château Gaillard built. Abu Midyan al-Ghawth, introducer of Qadiriyyah Sufi order into Morocco, d.

**1199–1200** Alcazar of Seville built.

**c. late 12th c.** Offices of Ecclesiastical Censor and Commissioner of Ecclesiastical lands created in Burma.

**13th c.** The spinning wheel reaches western Europe. Aztecs reach central plateau of present Mexico: agriculture and religion with human sacrifice developes.
**c. 13th c.** The longbow brought into use in England. Moveable type used in Korea.
**1200** Pope Innocent III interdicts France.
**c. 1200** Naskhi script replaces Kufic in Arabic inscriptions. Incas begin to dominate Cuzco valley. Temple of Juggernaut-Puri built. Yucatán peninsula abandoned by Mayas.
**c. 1200–37** Bamberg Cathedral built.
**c. 1200–50** Nave of York Minster built. *Aucassin and Nicolette* written.
**c. 1200–c. 1428** Slow expansion of the Incas.
**post 1200** Vernacular literature begins to emerge in Europe.

| WESTERN & NORTHERN EUROPE | CENTRAL, SOUTHERN & EASTERN EUROPE | AFRICA & EGYPT |
|---|---|---|

**1201** Poitou rebels against John of England. Llywelyn does homage to John. Canute VI of Denmark takes Holstein.

**1202** John of England relieves siege of Eleanor of Aquitaine in castle of Mirebeau, Poitou, by Arthur of Brittany: Arthur taken prisoner. Breach between England and France: Pope Innocent III threatens Philip Augustus with excommunication.
**1202–4** Fourth Crusade: preached by Foulques, parish priest of Neuilly-sur-Marne.
**1202–41** Waldemar II, King of Denmark.
**1203** 3 Apr., Arthur of Britanny killed, probably murdered: many of John of England's supporters join Philip II of France. Waldemar II takes Lübeck. Innocent III threatens Philip Augustus with excommunication.
**1204** July, John of England invades Scotland: 4 Aug., peace made. March, Philip II of France takes Château Gaillard; then conquers Normandy, Maine, Anjou and Touraine: Poitou submits: Gascony alone left to England. Eleanor of Aquitaine d.

**1205** Pope Innocent III supports Court decree declaring English possessions in France unlawful: John of England submits.

**1206** John of England makes abortive attempt to regain Poitou. Truce between John and Philip Augustus. London granted the right to elect a mayor.

**1202** Zara taken for the Venetians.
**1202–6** Wladislaw Longshanks, Duke of Poland.

**1203** Almohads take Balearic Isles.

**1204** March, treaty between Crusaders and Venice for partition of Byzantine empire. 13 Apr., Crusaders take the city: Alexios IV and Isaac II killed. Alexios V proclaimed and then deposed: Baldwin, Count of Flanders, crowned emperor (–1205): Latin Emperors until 1261. Boniface of Montferrat becomes King of Thessalonica. Michael I Angelus founds Despotate of Epirus. Peter II of Aragon acknowledges the Pope as suzerain.
**1205** 6 Jan., Philip crowned at Aix-la-Chapelle. 15 Apr., Kalojan, King of Bulgaria, defeats Crusaders at Adrianople: Emperor Baldwin taken prisoner. Theodore I defeated at Adramyttion. Otho de la Roche founds Duchy of Athens.
**1205–35** Andrew II of Hungary.
**1206** 27 July, Philip of Swabia defeats Otto IV of Brunswick at Wassemberg. Treaty of Guadalajara between Aragon, Castile and Navarre.
**1206–16** Henry of Flanders, Latin Emperor of Constantinople.
**1206–27** Leszek the White, Prince of Cracow.
**1207** Boniface de Montferrat, King of Thessalonica, killed in a fight with the Bulgars: war with Epirus follows.

**1203** Soumangouroun takes Ghana.

**1204** Traditional date of foundation of sultanates of Pate and Vumba, Kenya.

**1208** Llywelyn takes Powys.

**1208** 21 June, Philip of Swabia murdered at Bamberg by Otto of Wittelsbach.

| THE NEAR EAST | THE FAR EAST | RELIGION & CULTURE |
|---|---|---|
| | | **1201** A Master of the Schools appointed at Oxford.<br>**1201–14** Choir of Rouen Cathedral rebuilt.<br>**1201–74** Nasir al-Din al-Tusi, head of the Il-Khanid library and observatory at Maraghah. Robert de Sorbon, founder of the University of the Sorbonne, Paris. |
| | | **1202** Retro-choir of Winchester Cathedral begun. Brethren of the Sword founded by Bp Albert of Riga. |
| **1203** Bundelkhand conquered. Paramardi, or Parmal, last Chandel ruler, defeated by Qutb al-Din Aibak. Ghiyas al-Din, Sultan of Ghur, d.: succ. his brother, Muhammad Ghuri. | **1203–20** Champa made a Cambodian province. | **1203** Lérida Cathedral begun.<br>**1203–70** Muwaffaq al-Din Abu al-Abbas Ahmad b. Abi Usaybiah, physician, botanist, and medical historian, at Damascus. |
| **1204** Crusaders take Nicomedia from Emperor Theodore, defeating him at Poimanenon. Dynasty of the Great Comneni founded at Trebizond. Ghuzz crushed by Sad, Atabeg of Fars.<br>**1204–61** Lascarid dynasty (Nicaean Empire). | **1204** S Sung campaign against N China a disaster. | |
| **1205** Revolt of the Khokhar put down by Muhammad Ghuri. | **1205** Philippine Is first mentioned in Chinese literature. | |
| **1206** March, Muhammad Khilji assassinated by an Ismaili: succ. Qutb al-Din Aibak enthroned at Lahore with title of Sultan: makes Delhi the capital: known as the Slave dynasty of Sultans of Delhi (−1526). | **1206** Temujin proclaimed Chingis Khan, or 'universal ruler' of the *Yeke Mongol ulus: Great Yasa,* or code of law, promulgated: royal bodyguard increased to 10,000. | **1206** St Francis retires from the world. St Dominic begins preaching against the Albigenses.<br>c. **1206–80** St Albert the Great, theologian and philosopher. |
| | **1207** Chingis Khan sends his son Jochi with an army against the Oirat, Buriyat, Turkish Kirghiz and Tumet: all subjugated as Jochi's appanage.<br>**1207–10** Chingis Khan besieges Erikaya. | **1207** Pope Innocent III and Philip of Swabia reconciled. Port of Liverpool founded.<br>**1207–8** John of England quarrels with the English clergy.<br>**1207–28** Stephen Langton, Abp of Canterbury.<br>**1207–35** St Elizabeth, Queen of Hungary.<br>**1207–73** Jalal al-Din al-Rumi, poet and philosopher: founder of Mawlawite dervish order: first of the 'dancing dervishes'.<br>**1208–1363** Magdeburg Cathedral built. |
| **1208** Theodore I Lascaris crowned Emperor at Nicaea: Nicaea becomes the centre of Byzantine resistance to the Latins. | | |

1208–1217

WESTERN &
NORTHERN EUROPE

CENTRAL, SOUTHERN
& EASTERN EUROPE

AFRICA & EGYPT

**1208** The Bulgars defeated at
Philippopolis by Henri de Hainault.

**1209** 4 Aug., Treaty between
England and Scotland. Oct., Welsh
princes do homage to John of
England at Woodstock.

**1209** 4 Oct., Otto IV crowned
Emperor (−1218).
**1209–29** Crusade against the
Albigenses led by Simon de Montfort.

**1209** Almohads defeat Banu Sulaim
Jebel Nefusa.

**1210** June, John of England and
Llywelyn of Wales at war. John
campaigns in Ireland.

**1210** Peter of Aragon renews war in
Spain. Otto IV invades S Italy.

**1211** 9 Dec., Diet of Nuremberg:
Frederick II elected King in Germany.
**1211–23** Afonso II of Portugal:
struggles against royal family and the
church.

**1212** 16 July, Battle of Las Navas de
Tolosa: Kings of Aragon, Castile,
Navarre and Portugal, led by Alfonso
VIII of Castile, defeat Almohad
Muhammad b. Nasir: 1,000 Muslims out
of 600,000 said to have survived: end of
Almohad rule in Spain. Frederick II
recognizes papal suzerainty. Bohemia
becomes an hereditary kingdom.

**1213** 3 June, truce between
England and Llywelyn. Pope
Innocent III offers Philip Augustus
the English Crown. John of
England acknowledges papal
suzerainty. Coalition formed by
John of England with Emperor Otto
IV, and Flanders, against Philip II of
France.

**1213** 12 Sept., Albigenses defeated at
Muret: Peter II of Aragon killed:
peace made by Raymond VI of
Toulouse. Gertrude, Queen of
Hungary, murdered by nobles.
**1213–76** James I of Aragon, 'the
Conqueror': *Cortes* of all three estates
developed: Barcelona becomes a
centre of Mediterranean trade: *Llibre
del Consolat de Mar* instituted to
protect Catalan trade: consuls
stationed in foreign ports.

**1214** 27 July, Philip II defeats
coalition army at Bouvines, Flanders:
Flanders taken by France. Truce of
Chinon. Treaty of Metz. Heavy
scutage tax levied in England: revolt
of northern barons spreads.
**1214–26** Louis VIII of France: co-
ruler with Philip Augustus (−1223).
**1214–49** Alexander II, King of
Scots.

**1214** Alfonso VIII of Castile d.:
succ. Enrique I (−1217).

**1215** 15 June, Stephen Langton, Abp
of Canterbury, persuades John to
make terms with English barons:
*Magna Carta* signed at Runnymede.

**1215** 8 Jan., Simon de Montfort
(elder) elected Lord of Languedoc at
Montpellier: awarded County of
Toulouse by Pope Innocent III.
**1215–50** Frederick II of
Hohenstaufen, ruler of Germany and
Sicily: Holy Roman Emperor from
1220; King of Jerusalem from 1225.
**1216–9** Peter de Courtenay, Latin
Emperor of Constantinople.

**1216** Jan., English barons begin
revolt: May, Louis of France reaches
London with French army; 19 Oct.,
John of England d. at Newark Castle:
succ. Henry III, aged nine (−1272):
regency under William the Marshal:
*Magna Carta* made the basis of policy.
**1216–72** Government of Ireland
organized on English lines.
**1217** French defeated at Lincoln.
24 Aug., French fleet defeated off
Sandwich.

**1217** Stephen Nemanya II crowned as
first King (Kral) of Serbia.

**1217** Battle of Wadi Sebu between
Almohads and Banu Marin.
**1217–21** Fifth Crusade.

| THE NEAR EAST | THE FAR EAST | RELIGION & CULTURE |
|---|---|---|
| | | **1208** Quarrel between John of England and Pope Innocent III on appointment of Abp of Canterbury: 23 March, England placed under an interdict. |
| | **1209** Khitan Turks submit to Chingis Khan. Chingis Khan rejects with contempt embassy of Emperor Wei Shao Wang, demanding tribute. Hsi-Hsia state submits to the Mongols. | **c. 1208** Choir of Southwark Cathedral begun. |
| **1210** Ala al-Din Muhammad seizes Persia, Bukhara and Samarqand. Qutb al-Din Aibak d.: succ. his son, Aram. | **1210** Erikaya falls: all Tangut submits to Chingis Khan. | **1209** First community established by St Francis. Nov., John of England personally excommunicated by Pope Innocent III. Townsfolk hang two Oxford students: some flee to Cambridge. |
| **1211** Aram deposed: succ. Iltutmish, son-in-law of Qutb al-Din Aibak. | **1210—34** Nadoungmya, King of Pagan. **1211** Chingis Khan attacks China across the Gobi desert. | **1210** Innocent III excommunicates Otto IV: threatens to depose him. Foundation of the Franciscans approved. Nave of Strasbourg Cathedral begun. |
| | | **1211** Reims and Riga Cathedral begun. Mausoleum of Imam al-Shafii, Cairo, built. |
| | | **1211—82** Shams al-Din Muhammad b. Khallikan, biographer and jurist, at Damascus. |
| | **1213** Chingis Khan annihilates Chinese army of 100,000. | **1212** England absolved by Pope Innocent III from allegiance to John. Second Order of Franciscans for women founded by St Clare (Chiara degli Scifi). **c. 1212** University of Palencia founded. |
| **1214** Ala al-Din Muhammad, Khwarazmshah, seizes Ghazna. | | **1213** 15 May, John of England submits to Pope Innocent III: acknowledges Pope as feudal overlord: interdict and excommunication lifted. St Francis visits Spain. Geoffrey de Villehardouin d.: author of *The Conquest of Constantinople*. **1213—c. 1296** Sharaf al-Din Muhammad, poet: author of *al-Burdah*. |
| | | **c. 1214—92** Roger Bacon, philosopher and scientist. |
| **1215** Khwarazmian embassy sent to Chingis Khan. Peace treaty between al-Adil and Frederick of Hohenstaufen. | **1215** Ceylon invaded by South Indians: state of chaos and small princedoms. Kingdom of Mogaung in N Burma founded by Thai migration. Mongols besiege Chung-tu. | **1215** 24 Aug., Pope Innocent III annuls *Magna Carta:* Abp Langton threatened with excommunication. 4th Lateran Council: Statutes of the University of Paris approved. Benedictine houses, hitherto autonomous, form provincial chapters. |
| **1216** Caliph al-Nasir seeks aid of Chingis Khan against the Saljuqs: Ala al-Din Muhammad flees. | **1216** Chingis Khan returns to Mongolia from China: administrative and tax reforms made. | **1216—27** Honorius III, Pope. Honorius III proclaims the Fifth Crusade. Foundation of the Order of Preachers (Dominicans) by St Dominic approved. |
| **1217** Mongol empire extended westwards to the Pamirs and R. Syr-darya. Castle of Athlit founded. | **1217** Mongols, under Mukali, campaign in China. Mongols conquer Manchuria and Korea. | **1217** Dominican houses established in Rome and in England. Lady Chapel of Hereford Cathedral begun. |

| WESTERN & NORTHERN EUROPE | CENTRAL, SOUTHERN & EASTERN EUROPE | AFRICA & EGYPT |
|---|---|---|
| **1217** 11 Sept., treaty of Lambeth: French agree to leave England. 23 Sept., *Magna Carta* formally confirmed at Merton. Raymond VI reconquers Toulouse. | **1217–52** Ferdinand III, King of Castile. | |
| **1217–63** Haakon IV, King of Norway. | | |
| **1218** March, Peace of Worcester between England and Wales. 25 June, Simon de Montfort killed attempting to regain Toulouse. | **1218** *Cortes* instituted in Catalonia. Zurich becomes a free imperial city. | **1218** Crusaders land in Egypt: Damietta besieged. |
| **c. 1218** Rostock founded. | **1218–41** John Asen II, King of Bulgaria. | **1218–38** al-Kamil Muhammad, Ayyubid ruler of Egypt. |
| **1219** Louis VIII of France campaigns against the Albigenses. Waldemar, King of Denmark, takes Estonia. William the Marshal d. | | **1219** Nov.–**1221** Aug., Crusaders occupy Damietta. |
| | | **1219** St Francis of Assisi visits Egypt: holds religious discussions with al-Kamil. |
| **1220** 28 Oct., Henry III of England crowned. | **1220** 20 Apr., Henry VII elected King of the Romans. Afonso II of Portugal holds inquiry into titles of land held by the church and the nobility: discovery of abuses leads to hostility to the throne. | **c. 1220** Ethiopia and Nubia invaded by Damdam. |
| **1221** Nizhni (Lower) Novgorod founded. | **1221** Frederick II pacifies Sicily. **1221–8** Robert de Courtenay, Latin Emperor of Constantinople. | **1221–59** Dunama Dubalemi, Mai of Kanem: empire of Kanem at its zenith. |
| **1222** Yaroslav of Novgorod defeats German invaders. | **1222** Theodore of Epirus takes possession of Kingdom of Thessalonica. Henry VII rebels in Italy against his father, Frederick II. Bohemia and Moravia united. | |
| **1223** Philip II Augustus of France d. Raymond VII reconquers Toulouse. Apr., Pope Honorius III declares Henry III of England of age to rule. Mongols defeat three Russian armies at R. Kalka and then withdraw. | **1223–46** Sancho II, King of Portugal. | |
| **1223–6** Louis VIII, sole King of France. | | |
| **1224** Louis VIII of France over-runs Poitou: checked in Aquitaine: 4 May, war declared on England. | | **c. 1224** Walata founded. |
| **1225** March, English take Gascony. | **1225** Diet of Cremona. Duke Conrad of Masovia invites Teutonic Knights to settle in E Prussia. | |
| **1226** Louis VIII campaigns in Languedoc: Toulouse conquered: then d.: succ. (St) Louis IX (–1270): Blanche of Castile, regent. | **1226** Frederick II takes Ancona and Spoleto. New Lombard League formed. | |

## THE NEAR EAST | THE FAR EAST | RELIGION & CULTURE

**THE NEAR EAST**

**1218** Treaty between Chingis Khan and Khwarazm.

**1219** Aug., commercial treaty between Theodore I Lascaris and Venice. Chingis Khan, with force of 150,000, seizes Khwarazmian empire: Bukhara captured.
**1219—23** Mongols over-run NW Iran, parts of Georgia, the Ukraine and Crimea.
**1220** Chingis Khan expels Khwarazmian dynasty. Ala-Din Muhammad, Khwarazmshah, d. of despair: succ. Jelal al-Din. Iltutmish establishes N frontier along R. Indus: campaign against the Rajputs.
**c. 1220** Treaty between Theodore I Lascaris and Venice.
**1220—37** Ala al-Din Kai Kobad I, Saljuqid ruler of Konia (Quniyah): Saljuqid state at its apogee.
**1221** Chingis Khan reduces former Khwarazmian territory as far as R. Indus: Jelal al-Din, Khwarazmshah, escapes.

**1222—54** John III Ducas Vatatzes, Emperor of Nicaea.

**c. 1225** Jelal al-Din, Khwarazmshah, again in control of Kerman, Shiraz, Khorasan and Mazandaran: occupies Azerbaijan and Georgia.
**1225—6** al-Zahir, Abbasid Caliph.
**1226—42** al-Mustansir, Abbasid Caliph.

**THE FAR EAST**

**c. 1218—43** Indravarman II, King of Cambodia.

**1220** Cambodia evacuates Champa.
**c. 1220** Indraditya installed as first Thai ruler of Sukhotai dynasty.

**1222** New Javanese kingdom founded by Singosari, replacing former dynasty: known as Singosari dynasty (—1292).

**1223** Kingdom of Muong Nai founded by Thais.

**1225** Great fire in Pagan: many temples destroyed. Sri Vijaya in possession of fifteen vassal states.

**1226—c. 1252** Jaya Paramesvaravarman, King of Champa.

**RELIGION & CULTURE**

**c. 1217—69** Abu Muhammad Abd al-Haqq b. Sabin, Spanish mystic.

**1218** Madrassa al-Adiliyya built in Damascus. St. Peter Nolasco founds *Order of Nôtre Dame de la Merci* to redeem Christian slaves in N Africa.

**1219** Franciscans set up houses in France and Spain.

**1220** Building of Brussels Cathedral begun. Shrine of St Thomas at Canterbury and Salisbury Cathedral Lady Chapel begun.
**1220—38** Frederick II legislates against heresy.
**c. 1220—88** Amiens Cathedral built.

**1221** 6 Aug., St Dominic d.
Abp Langton appointed Papal Legate.
Burgos Cathedral begun. Great Mosque of Constantine completed.
**1221—62** Salisbury Cathedral built.

**1222** Padua University founded.
*Constitutions* of Abp Langton promulgated at Osney Abbey, Oxford.
Great Hall, Winchester Castle, built.
**1222—82** Nichiren, Japanese preacher.

**1223** Franciscan rule of 1221 confirmed. Horizontal looms with treadles in use in Novgorod.
The Inquisition, with the duty of countering errors in Catholic doctrine, established by Pope Gregory IX.

**1224** University of Naples founded by charter from Frederick of Hohenstaufen.
10 Sept., Grey Friars (Franciscans) set up in England, Worcester Cathedral choir begun.
**1224 fl.** Abd al-Wahid al-Marrakushi, Moroccan historian residing in Spain.
**c. 1224—53** Robert Grosseteste, first Chancellor of Oxford University.
**c. 1224—1317** Sire Jean de Joinville, historian.
**1225** Officers training school set up in Vietnam. Münster and Visby Cathedrals begun.
**c. 1225** Toledo Cathedral begun.
**1225—80** Mosaics in the Baptistery of Florence Cathedral made.

**1226** 3 Oct., St Francis of Assisi d.
Rule of Carmelite Order confirmed.
**1226—74** St Thomas Aquinas, theologian, philosopher and poet.

| WESTERN & NORTHERN EUROPE | CENTRAL, SOUTHERN & EASTERN EUROPE | AFRICA & EGYPT |
|---|---|---|

**1227** Truce between France and England.

**1227** Leszek of Poland killed by a Pomeranian prince: struggle for succession ensues. Jochi, Khan of Kipchak, d.: succ. Batu (—1255): successors (—1405) known as the Golden Horde (of Mongols) and commonly called Tartars: capital at Batu Serai.

**1228** Reval founded.

**1228** Stephen I Simone d.
**1228—61** Baldwin II de Courtenay, Latin Emperor of Constantinople.

**1228—1574** Hafsid dynasty of Tunis
**1228—49** Abu Zakaria Yahya I, Hafsid ruler.

**1229** Alliance between Henry III of England and Count of Brittany. Treaty of Meaux (or of Paris) between Louis IX and Raymond VII ends war against the Albigenses.

**1229** Louis of Bavaria rebels. James I of Aragon takes Majorca. Pope Gregory IX invades Sicily. Frederick II restores imperial authority in Sicily.

**1229** Abu Zakaria takes Bougie and Algiers.

**1230** Treaty of Kruszwica: Teutonic Knights granted sole possession of territory between Pomerania and Courland. Henry III of England campaigns abortively in Brittany and as far as Bordeaux.
**c. 1230** Stralsund and Danzig founded.
**1230—1** Rothesay castle taken by a Norwegian adventurer.

**1231** 4 July, three year truce between Brittany, England and France.
**1231—8** Henry the Bearded of Silesia, Duke of Poland.

**1230** Frederick II makes peace with the Pope at St Germano: absolved by the Pope at Ceprano. Bulgarians under John Asen defeat Theodore of Epirus at Kloktinitza: Theodore taken prisoner: succ. Manuel. Arjona rebels against Arabs. Ferdinand III of Castile becomes King of León (—1252): crowns united. The *heller* first coined at Hall, Swabia.
**1230—53** Wenceslas I, King of Bohemia.
**1231** Canton of Uri becomes independent. Frederick II strikes gold coinage. James I of Aragon takes Minorca. Constitutions of Melfi regularize laws of Sicily.
**1231—7** Jean de Brienne, Regent of the Latin Empire of Constantinople.

**1232** Henry VII rebels in Germany.
**1232—1492** Nasrid dynasty of Granada.
**1232—73** Muhammad b. Yusuf b. Nasr, founder of the Nasrid dynasty of Granada.

**1233** Rising in England against Henry III's councillors.
**1234** Blois, Chartres and Sancerre ceded by Theobald of Champagne to the French Crown. Rising in Galloway.

**1235** Conquest of Connacht by Richard de Burgo: annexed to England.

**1233** James I of Aragon attacks Valencia.
**1234** Henry VII joins the Lombard League. Venice obtains large commercial privileges in Rhodes.
**1234—1512** Navarre governed by French dynasty.
**1235** Diet of Mayence. Frederick II deposes and imprisons Henry VII. Frederick declares war on Lombard League. John Asen of Bulgaria and John Vatatzes of Nicaea besiege Constantinople. James I of Aragon takes Ibiza.

**1234** Commercial treaty between Abu Zakaria and Pisa. Bougie made Hafsid capital.

**c. 1235—55** Sundiata Keita, King of Mali.
**c. 1235** Sundiata Keita defeats Soumangouroun.
**1235—1554** Abdalwadid dynasty of Tlemcen.

## THE NEAR EAST

**1227–8** Fortress of Sidon (Saida) built.
**1227–9** Sixth Crusade.

**1228** Half of Jelal al-Din's army destroyed by the Mongols near Isfahan.
**1228–9** Frederick II campaigns in Syria.
**1229** Iltutmish invested by the Caliph as Sultan-i-Azam. Treaty between al-Kamil and Frederick of Hohenstaufen: Jerusalem ceded to Crusaders and corridor to Acre; 17 March, Frederick enters Jerusalem.
**1229–41** Mongols raid India, gaining control of W Punjab.

**1231** Jelal al-Din, last Khwarazmshah, murdered by a Kurdish tribesman: organized resistance collapses: Mongols take N Persia, N Iraq and Armenia.
**1231–88** Erthogrul, first Ottoman Sultan: first of his line to be converted to Islam: granted Bithynia by the Saljuqids.

## THE FAR EAST

**1227** Hsi-Hsia state annihilated by Chingis Khan. 24 Aug., Chingis Khan d., aged 72: succ. Ogodai (–1241): Mongol Empire divided between Chingis's sons: Jochi, Khan of Kipchak, receives lands W of the Aral Sea: Jaghatai, E from R. Amu Darya towards China and Mongolia: Tolui, the Mongolian homeland: remainder to Ogodai.
**1227–48** Anusapati, ruler of Java.

**1229** Ogodai formally installed as Great Khan at Karakorum. Assam conquered by the Thais: Ahom Kingdom founded.

**1230** Mongol attack on E Kansu beaten off.
**1230–70** Chandrabhanu, ruler of Tambralinga, makes himself independent of Sri Vijaya: seizes Grahi.

**1232** Mongols destroy Chinese army of 150,000 at Kun-chou.
**1232–3** Mongols besiege Ta-liang.
**1232–1326** Dynasty of Sinhalese kings at Dambadeniya, and later at Kurunegala.
**1233** S Sung ally with the Mongols.

**1234–50** Kyaswar, King of Pagan.

## RELIGION & CULTURE

**1226–84** Abu al-Faraj b. al-Ibri (Barhebraeus), Syrian Jacobite Catholicos: last classical scholar in Syriac literature.
**1227–41** Gregory IX, Pope.
**1227** Pope Gregory IX excommunicates Frederick II. Cathedral of the Transfiguration, Nizhni-Novgorod, begun. 11 Aug., foundation stone of new cathedral at Toledo laid.

**1228** Pope Gregory IX deposes Frederick II: forbids teaching Aristotle's philosophy.
**1228–53** Double Church of St Francis built at Assisi.
**1229** Toulouse University founded. Paris University rebels against the King.
**1229–55** Tosa Tsunetaka, Japanese painter, founder of the Tosa school.

**1230** c. 1,300 students already at Oxford.
c. **1230** First mention in literature of the magnetic compass in a collection of Persian tales. Ibn Ali al-Marrakushi, geographer.
c. **1230–76** Guido Guinizelli, Italian poet.
**1230–94** Brunetto Latini, Italian poet.
c. **1230–1306** Jacopone da Todi, Italian poet.

**1231** 13 June, St Anthony of Padua d. Gregory IX: Bull *Parens Scientiarum*. Gregory IX publishes expurgated text of Aristotle. Rebuilding of Abbey of St Dénis, Paris, begun. Chancellor recognized by writ at Cambridge University.

**1232** 20 May, St Anthony of Padua canonized.
c. **1232** Qutb Minar built at Delhi.

**1233–1315** Ramón Llull, Catalan writer: *Book of Contemplation*.
**1234** 12 July, St Dominic canonized. Al-Mustansiriyah founded as a seminary and law school.

**1235** Lausanne Cathedral begun.
c. **1235–84** Siger de Brabant.

| WESTERN & NORTHERN EUROPE | CENTRAL, SOUTHERN & EASTERN EUROPE | AFRICA & EGYPT |
|---|---|---|
| **1236** Batu, nephew of Ogodai Khan, leads army of 120,000 horsemen into Russia: probably Turks with Mongol officers. Fresh rising in England against Henry III. <br> **1236–63** Alexander Nevsky, Grand Duke of Novgorod. | **1236** Frederick II campaigns against the Lombard League. Ferdinand III of Castile takes Córdoba. Mongols, with partly Turkish army, attack Bulgars. | **1236–7** Abu Zakaria makes commercial treaties with Genoa, Sicily and Venice. |
| **1237** Henry III of England accepts baronial control of finance. Mongols drive Bulgars into Russia. <br> **1237–8** Mongols over-run Russia: then retire to Don basin. <br><br> **1238** Moscow sacked by Mongol army. | **1237** Frederick II elects Conrad IV King of Germany: campaigns in Lombardy: Lombard League defeated at Cortenuova. <br> **1237–61** Baldwin II, sole Latin Emperor of Constantinople. <br> **1238** Enzio, son of Frederick II, made King of Sardinia. Frederick II abortively attacks Brescia. The Pope, Genoa and Venice ally against Frederick II. James I of Aragon takes Valencia. Christian Kingdom of Granada established. Cuman Khan Kotyan flees to Hungary with 200,000 persons: allowed to settle on condition of becoming subjects and Catholics. Mongols take Georgia. <br> **1238–41** Henry the Pious, Duke of Poland. | **1237** Embassy from Kanem to Tunis. <br><br><br> **1238** Mogadishu a flourishing trade centre: minaret of Friday mosque completed. <br> **1238–40** al-Adil II, Ayyubid ruler. |
| **1239** 7 Jan., Princess Eleanor of England m. Simon de Montfort (younger), Earl of Leicester. Viborg founded. <br> **1240** Mongols take Kiev, Cracow, Pest and Zagrev: reach Adriatic: Hungary conquered. Gun-powder introduced by the Mongols into Europe. Prince Alexander of Novgorod defeats Swedes near R. Neva: henceforward called Nevsky. <br> **1240–6** Dafydd ap Llywelyn, Prince of Snowdon. <br> **1240–63** Mendovg, ruler of Lithuania: protected by the Pope. <br> **1241** Hugh de Lusignan rebels. Russian princes accept investiture from the Mongols. <br> **post 1241** Office of justiciar left unfilled in England. | **1239** Pope Gregory IX excommunicates Frederick II: allies with Milan and Piacenza against him: Frederick fails to take Milan. <br> **1240** Frederick II invades Papal States: halted at Faenza. <br><br><br><br><br> **1241** 9 Apr., Mongols defeat Polish princes under Batu at Liegnitz: Henry of Poland killed: Bela IV of Hungary routed. Lithuania and E Poland conquered. Mongols ravage Poland: Sandomir, Cracow and Wroclaw sacked: Albania, Dalmatia and Serbia laid waste. Abps of Cologne and Mayence rebel. John Asen II of Bulgaria d.: John Vatatzes takes Bulgaria and Thrace from Bulgaria. | **1240** Empire of Ghana finally destroyed by Sundiata Keita: incorporated into Mali. <br> **1240–9** al-Salih Najm al-Din, Ayyubid ruler: m. Shajar al-Durr. |
| **1242** Henry III of England defeated by Louis IX at Taillebourg and Saintes: Hugh de Lusignan submits. James I of Aragon and Raymond VII of Toulouse ally against Louis IX. Alexander Nevsky beats Germans in battle fought on ice on L. Peipous. <br> **1243** Treaty of Bordeaux: five years peace between England and France: Henry III resigns claim to Poitou: Is. de Ré ceded to France. Peace of Lorris between France and Toulouse. | **1243–79** Boleslaw the Modest, Duke of Cracow. <br> **1243–55** Independent Pomeranian princes overthrown by Teutonic Knights. <br> **1243–76** Urus I, King of Serbia. | |

## THE NEAR EAST

**ante 1236** Iltutmish subdues Khalji Maliks of Bengal: retakes Gwalior: seizes Malwa and Sind. Iltutmish d.: succ. Rukn al-Din: shortly replaced by his sister, Raziyyat al-Din.
**1236–47** Balian d'Ibelin, Lord of Beirut.

**1237** Ala al-Din Kai Kobad I d.: Saljuqid empire breaks up into ten principalities.

**1238** Armenia conquered by the Mongols.

**1239** Château de Beaufort, Lebanon, built by Fulk of Jerusalem.

**1240** Armenian rulers restored as vassals of the Mongols. Raziyyat al-Din deposed: two successors deposed as failures.

**1241–2** Mongols occupy and wreck Lahore: raids on Sind and Multan.

**1242–58** al–Mustasim, Abbasid Caliph.

**1243** Mongols invade Saljuqid territory: Saljuqids flee at battle of Erzindjan.

## THE FAR EAST

**1241** 11 Dec., Ogodai Khan d.: his widow, Toregene, regent (–1243): Mongol warfare halted by election of a new Khan.

**1243** Guyuk elected Great Khan.

## RELIGION & CULTURE

**1236** Henry III of England: *Nolumus leges Angliae mutari,* against ecclesiastical courts. Great Mosque of Córdoba transformed into a Cathedral by Ferdinand III.
**c. 1236** First part of *Roman de la Rose* written by Guillaume de Lorris. Michael Scot, translator of Arabic works into Latin, d.
**1237** Brethren of the Sword unite with Teutonic Knights.
**c. 1242** N.transept of York Minster begun. Chapel of the Nine Altars in Durham Cathedral begun.

**1240** Bulgarian Church adopts the Byzantine rite. Gregory IX calls an Ecumenical Council: forbidden by Frederick II. *'Secret History of the Mongols'* written.
**1240–1302** Giovanni Cimabue, artist.

**1241** Frederick II takes those attending the Council prisoner.
Celestine IV, Pope.
**1241–3** Papacy vacant (*sede vacante*).

**c. 1243** University of Salamanca founded.
**1243–54** Innocent IV, Pope.

| WESTERN & NORTHERN EUROPE | CENTRAL, SOUTHERN & EASTERN EUROPE | AFRICA & EGYPT |
|---|---|---|
| **1244** English barons demand the right to appoint the Chancellor and the Justiciar.<br>**1245** First known strike of workers at Douai.<br>**1245–85** Charles d'Anjou, Count of Provence. | **1244** Pope Innocent IV flees to Genoa, and then to Lyons.<br>**1245** Sancho of Portugal dethroned by Pope Innocent IV: succ. Afonso III (–1279). | **1244** Almohads defeat Marinids near Fez. Abu Yahya Abu Bakr seizes Meknes. |
| **1246–82** Llywelyn ap Gruffydd, Prince of Snowdon, later Prince of Wales.<br><br><br><br>**1247** Frederick II attempts to take Lyons. | **1246** Frederick II seizes vacant duchies of Austria and Styria. Ferdinand of Castile allies with Granada. John Vatazes takes Thessalonica: Empire of Nicaea now comprises all Byzantine possessions except Constantinople. Christians take Jaén.<br>**1246–7** Henry Raspe, Landgrave of Thuringia, rival Holy Roman Emperor.<br>**1247** Ottokar of Bohemia seizes Austria and Styria.<br>**1247–56** William of Holland, rival Holy Roman Emperor. | |
| **1248** Gascony rebels: Simon de Montfort sent by Henry III of England as governor. | **1248** Frederick II defeated by Lombards near Parma: takes Romagna and Spoleto. Seville recovered by Ferdinand III of Castile. Afonso III moves Portuguese capital from Coimbra to Lisbon. Mongol embassy to Louis IX of France in Cyprus. Two Mongol envoys received in Rome by Pope Innocent IV. Genoa takes Rhodes.<br>**1248–50** Seventh Crusade. | **1248** Banu Marin take much of Morocco.<br>**post 1248** Many Andalusian Muslims migrate to Tunis, following capture of Seville. |
| **1249** Swedish rule in Finland extended by Birger Jarl. Truce renewed between England and France. Alphonse of Poitiers inherits the County of Toulouse. Alexander Nevsky last Prince of Kiev to be invested by the Mongols: thereafter a Mongol governorate.<br>**1249–86** Alexander III, King of Scots.<br>**c. 1250** Parliament of Paris instituted.<br>**1250–75** Waldemar I, King of Sweden: Birger Jarl, Regent (–1266). | **1249** Frederick II retires to Sicily. Castle of Mistra built by Guillaume de Villehardouin.<br><br><br><br><br>**1250** 13 Dec., Frederick II d.: succ. Conrad IV (–1254). *Cortes* instituted in Castile. | **1249** 29 June, Crusaders occupy Damietta.<br>**1249–50** Shajar al-Durr, widow of al-Salih, ruler of Egypt: title 'Queen of the Muslims': only woman Egyptian Muslim ruler.<br><br>**1250** al-Muazzam Turan Shah, Ayyubid ruler: nominal reign only: murdered by his mother, Shajar al Durr. Shajar al-Durr, last effective Ayyubid ruler, m. Izz al-Din Aibak, first Bahri Mamluk Sultan. Apr., Crusader army destroyed at al-Mansura: Louis IX taken prisoner: released following ransom and surrender of Damietta.<br>**c. 1250** Fakhr al-Din dynasty of Mogadishu founded by Abu Bakr b. Fakhr al-Din.<br>**1250–2** al-Ashraf Musa, last Ayyubid ruler: nominal reign only.<br>**1250–74** Ethiopia without an Abuna<br>**c. 1250–1300** Mannu dynasty of Futa Toro.<br>**1250–1382** Bahri Mamluk dynasty in Egypt. |
| **1251** May, Gascony subdued by Simon de Montfort (younger). Henry III of England claims overlordship of Scotland. | **1251** Afonso III of Portugal takes the Algarve. Conrad goes to Italy. | |

| THE NEAR EAST | THE FAR EAST | RELIGION & CULTURE |
|---|---|---|
| **1244** Jerusalem taken from Crusaders by a column of Khwarazm Turks. | | **1244** Persecution of Albigenses ended. |
| **1245–1389** Kurt dynasty of Herat. | | **1245** Rebuilding of Westminster Abbey begun. Council of Lyons: Frederick II condemned and deposed: Giovanni de Piano de Carpini sent on a mission to the Mongols (–1247). 14 Nov., Innocent IV: *Ordinem vestrum:* property of Franciscans seized. Siena Cathedral begun. |
| **1246–66** Nasir al-Din, Sultan of Delhi. | **1246** Guyuk enthroned as Great Khan of the Mongols (–1248). **1246–8** Mongol embassy to Tibet. | **1246** Hayles Abbey founded. |
| | **1247** Chandrabhanu makes vain attempt to seize Ceylon: colony of Javakas, or peninsular Malays, settle there: ruler, his son. State orphanages set up in China. **1248** Guyuk d.: Ogul Gaimysh, regent (–1251). **1248–68** Visnuvardhana, ruler of Java. | **1247** Carmelites become mendicant friars. **1248** Abdallah b. Ahmad b. al-Baytar d.: herbalist and botanist. **1248–c. 1350** Alhambra Palace, Granada built. Sainte Chapelle, Paris, completed. Bergen Cathedral and choir of Cologne Cathedral begun. |
| **1250–4** Louis IX of France in Syria: Acre, Haifa, Caesarea and Sidon fortified. | **1250–4** Uzana, King of Burma. | **1250** Dominicans (Order of Preachers) open first school of oriental studies in Europe at Toledo. **c. 1250** Mariner's compass and sand-glass developed in Italy. Warsaw and Léon Cathedrals begun. **c. 1250 fl.** Mu-chi, Chinese painter. **c. 1250–1300** Guido Cavalcanti, Italian poet and philosopher. **1250–1330** Zara Cathedral built. |
| | **1251–9** Mongke, Great Khan of the Mongols. | **1251** Pope Innocent IV returns to Italy. Qaysar b. Musafir Taasif, Egyptian engineer, d. |

| WESTERN & NORTHERN EUROPE | CENTRAL, SOUTHERN & EASTERN EUROPE | AFRICA & EGYPT |
|---|---|---|

**1252** Hanseatic market founded at Bruges.
**1252–63** Alexander Nevsky, Grand Duke of Novgorod, also Grand Duke of Vladimir.
**1252–70** Louis IX reforms administration and justice in France.
**1253** Simon de Montfort obtains Gascony for England. Truce between England and France renewed. Margaret of Hainault obtains Charles d'Anjou's support against William of Holland.

**1254** St Louis returns to France.

**1256** Harvest fails in England. William of Holland killed in battle against the Frisians.

**1257** Famine in England. Llywelyn ap Gruffydd proclaims himself Prince of Wales: unites Anglesey, Powis and Snowdon. The Welsh defeat Henry III of England.
**1257–1327** Twelve Mongol raids on Russia.

**1258** Gallowglasses arrive in Ulster. Spring, unseasonable frosts in England: famine recurs: barons, led by Simon de Montfort, resort to arms, and demand Great Council: 11 June, Provisions of Oxford set out programme of reform.

**1259** 1 Aug., peace made between England and Wales. Provisions of Westminster: further reforms in English administration. Treaty of Paris between St Louis and Henry III of England defines English territories in France: Henry III does homage.

---

**1252** The Florin first minted at Florence.
**1252–84** Alfonso X of Castile, 'the Learned'.

**1253** Pope Innocent promises the Crown of Sicily to Prince Edmund of England.
**1253** Louis II, Duke of Bavaria, made guardian and heir of Conradin, son of Conrad IV.

**1254** League of the Rhine instituted. Pope Innocent IV attempts to conquer Sicily; defeated at Foggia: Manfred recognizes Conradin, his nephew, as King. Alliances between Henry III and the Pope; and between Henry III and Alfonso of Castile. *Cortes* instituted in Portugal. First *Cortes* held at Leiria. Conrad IV d. *Interregnum* in the Empire (–1273).
**1255** Manfred attempts to obtain the Crown of Sicily from Pope Alexander IV. Theodore II defeats the Bulgarians at Rupel.

**1257** Alliance between Manfred and Genoa.
**1257–73** Diets of Frankfurt: Richard, Earl of Cornwall, and Alfonso X, son of Ferdinand of Castile, rival candidates for Holy Roman Empire. Alfonso prevented by Spanish nobility and the Pope: 17 May, Richard at Aix-la-Chapelle.
**1258** Manfred crowned King of Sicily at Palermo. Pope Alexander IV retracts grant of Sicily to Prince Edmund of England. Treaty of Corbeil between Louis IX and James I of Aragon: Pyrenean frontiers agreed.

**1259** Mongols again ravage Poland.

**1260** 12 July, Ottokar of Bohemia defeats Hungarians at Croissenbrun. 4 Sept., Battle of Montaperti: Florentine Guelphs wiped out by Tuscan Ghibellines. Lisbon becomes the capital of Portugal.

---

**1253** al-Mustansir, Hafsid, proclaims himself Caliph. Marinids defeat the Almohads near Fez.

**c. 1255–70** Mansa Ule, King of Mali.

**1256–7** Abu al-Qasim al-Azafi becomes ruler of Ceuta subject to the Almohads.

**1257** Izz al-Din Aibak murdered in his bath because Shajar al-Durr hears he is taking a second wife: she is then battered to death. Dunama Dubalemi sends embassy to Tunis.
**1257–9** Nur al-Din Ali, Bahri Mamluk Sultan.

**1258** Marinids in control of all Morocco except Tlemcen and Fez.

**c. 1260** Korau, King of Katsina: makes war on Kwararafa. Mansa Ule of Mali makes pilgrimage to Mecca.
**1260–77** al-Malik al-Zahir Baybars, Mamluk Sultan of Egypt.

## THE NEAR EAST

## THE FAR EAST

## RELIGION & CULTURE

**1252** Kubilai Khan attacks China in Szechwan and Yunnan.
**1252—8** Mongol armies reach Annamese frontier: political resident imposed.

**1252—9** St Thomas Aquinas teaching in Paris.

**1253** Hulagu Khan invites Caliph al-Mutasim to join in his campaign against the Assassins: no reply sent.

**1253** Ahoms, a Shan people, conquer Kamurapa and set up a kingdom, later Assam. Kubilai Khan conquers eastern Tibet. Mongols, under Kubilai Khan, occupy Nan-Chao: Thai kingdom set up in Yunnan. Kingdom of Sukhotai founded by Thais at expense of Khmer Empire.

**1253** The *Sorbonne* founded. University of Paris on strike.

**1254—8** Theodore II, Emperor of Nicaea.

**1254—87** Narathihapati, King of Pagan.

**1254—61** Alexander IV, Pope.
**1254** Quarrel between the University of Paris and the Pope.
**1254—1322** Chao Meng-fu (or Chung-mu), painter.
**1254—1324** Marco Polo, Venetian traveller and writer.
**1254—67** Utrecht Cathedral built.

**1255** Mongke Khan sends his brother Hulagu to attack W Asia.

**1255** Gold coins first issued in France. Hugh of Lincoln (Little St Hugh) murdered. Stockholm founded

**1256** Hulagu Khan seizes Alamut and other Assassin strongholds: rulers of present Afghanistan. Persia and S Russia do homage. Hulagu (—1265) founds Ilkhan dynasty of Persia.

**1256** 4 May, Order of Hermits of St Augustine founded.
**1256** fl. Khalifah b. Abi al-Mahasin, ophthalmologist.
**1256** Seville University founded.

**1257** Mongols attack Sung China from NW and S: Ho-chou besieged: Yunnan pacified.

**1257** St Bonaventure becomes General of the Franciscans. The University of Paris submits to the Pope. Gold pence first minted in England. Roger Bacon forbidden to lecture. Cracow rebuilt by German colonists.
**1257—60** S. Chiara, Assisi, built.

**1258** Jan., Hulagu begins siege of Baghdad; 10 Feb., city taken: Caliph offers unconditional surrender: population annihilated: city burnt.
**1258—61** John IV Lascaris, Emperor of Nicaea.
**1258 and 9** Balban campaigns against Hindus of the Doab.
**1259** Michael VIII Palaeologus crowned Emperor of Nicaea (—1282): defeats Latin army near Castoria.

**1258** Mongols penetrate Tonkin and pillage Hanoi. All SW China in Mongol hands.

**1258** Ali al-Shadhili, founder of Shadhilite dervish order, d.: chiefly followed in Morocco and Tunisia. S Transept of Nôtre-Dame, Paris, and W front of Strasbourg Cathedral begun.
**c. 1258** Badajoz Cathedral begun.

**1259** 11 Aug., Mongke Khan d.

**post 1259** Matthew Paris: *Chronica Maiora.*
**1259** Maraghah observatory built near Lake Urmiyah by Hulagu Khan.

**1260** Balban campaigns against the Meos: July, 12,000 insurgents put to death. Hulagu takes Aleppo, Hamah and Harim: returns to Persia: 3 Sept., Mongol army in Syria destroyed by Mamluks of Egypt at Ain Jalut: all Syria occupied by the Mamluks.

**1260** Kubilai Khan proclaimed supreme Khan of the Mongols: war between Kubilai Khan and rival Khan Arik Boge (—1264).

**c. 1260** al-Kuhin al-Attar, druggist and pharmacist in Cairo, d.
**1260** Nicholas Pisano's pulpit built in the baptistery at Pisa.
**1260—1435** Upsala Cathedral built.

1260–1267

WESTERN &
NORTHERN EUROPE

CENTRAL, SOUTHERN
& EASTERN EUROPE

AFRICA & EGYPT

**1261** Pope Alexander IV dispenses Henry III of England from Provisions of Oxford: Simon de Montfort retires to France.

**1261–1453** Palaeologi dynasty of Byzantium.
**1261** 25 July, Michael VIII Palaeologus' army enters Constantinople without a blow: Aug., Michael crowned in St Sophia: Baldwin II and Latin clergy flee. Commercial treaty of Nymphaeum between Michael VIII and Genoa. Ottokar of Bohemia obtains Styria.

**1261** al-Mutawakkil installed in Cairo as Caliph, but without temporal power, by Sultan Baybars: line of Caliphs continued in Cairo to 1517.

**1262** Skye raided brutally by Norwegians. Henry of England visits France: Prince Llywelyn of Wales attacks border with England: barons call on Simon de Montfort to aid them.
**1263** 23 Jan., Mise of Amiens: Louis IX of France mediates between barons and Henry III of England in his favour: civil war ensues in England: 14 May, Henry III defeated by barons under Simon de Montfort at Lewes: Henry III and future Edward I made prisoner. Norwegian expedition against Scotland: defeated at Largs: Haakon of Norway cedes Hebrides. Daniel, son of Alexander Nevsky, makes Moscow capital of his principality (–1315): Danilovich dynasty (–1598).
**1263–80** Magnus VI of Norway.
**1264** Treaty between Urban II and Charles d'Anjou.

**1262** 14 Sept., Alfonso X of Castile takes Cadiz. Guelphs, with papal aid, regain power in Tuscany. James I of Aragon's son Peter m. Manfred's daughter. Ottokar formally invested with Austria and Styria.

**1264** Venetian fleet defeats Genoese off Trapani.

**1264** Treaty between Sultan Baybars and Charles d'Anjou, King of Sicily. Commercial treaty between Pisa and Tunis.

**1265–72** Henry III of England partly retires from active politics: future Edward I real ruler of England.
**1265** 20 Jan. (–1266), Parliament summoned by Simon de Montfort at Westminster: representatives of boroughs and knights of the shire summoned. Prince Edward escapes from captivity: 4 Aug., defeats Simon de Montfort at Evesham: de Montfort killed.
**1266** Supporters of Simon de Montfort surrender to future Edward I at Kenilworth: *Dictum de Kenilworth* makes peace, confirming Magna Carta and other liberties. Treaty of Perth: Scotland recovers Norwegian Scottish possessions except Orkney and Shetland.
**1267** Treaty of Shrewsbury (or Montgomery): Henry III recognizes Llywelyn as Prince of Wales: 3,000 marks annual tribute to be paid to England. Statute of Marlborough: principal Provisions of Westminster re-enacted.

**1265** Byzantine army defeated by Kipchak Khan and Bulgarians. Charles d'Anjou visits Rome: relieves Papal States from Manfred.

**1265** Final date for hoard of more than 250 Chinese coins found at Kajengwa, Zanzibar.

**1266** 6 Jan., Charles d'Anjou crowned King of Naples and Sicily: 26 Feb., Charles d'Anjou defeats and kills Manfred at Benevento: conquers Kingdom of Sicily.

**1266** Almohads take Marrakesh

**1267** James I of Aragon attempts to take Sardinia. Portuguese claim to the Algarve agreed by Castile: present Portugal now united.

| THE NEAR EAST | THE FAR EAST | RELIGION & CULTURE |
|---|---|---|
| **1260–1304** Baghdad and Iraq under Il-Khans of Persia, with territory from the Caucasus to the Indian Ocean: capital at Tabriz. | | |
| **1261** Secret treaty between Hulagu Khan and Michael VIII of Byzantium. | **1261** Kubilai Khan announces intention of replacing Sung dynasty with his own, as the Yuan dynasty. | **1261–4** Urban IV, Pope. **1261** St Mary of the Mongols, Constantinople, built. Merton College, Oxford, founded. |
| | | **1262** Valencia Cathedral begun. |
| **1263** Baybars takes al-Karak: church of the Annunciation at Nazareth destroyed. **1263–71** Egyptians under Baybars raid Crusader towns in the Levant. | **1263** Javakas in Ceylon acknowledge Pandyan King as overlord. | |
| | | **1264** Urban IV makes *Corpus Christi* a feast of the universal church. |
| **1265** Baybars takes Caesarea and Arsuf. Hulagu Khan d. at Maraghah: succ. Abaqa (–1281). Mongols under Borak invade Persia: defeated by Abaqa near Herat. | | **1265–8** Clement IV, Pope. **1265–1321** Dante Alighieri, Italian poet. **1265** Nave of Lichfield Cathedral built. |
| **1266** 23 July, Baybars takes Safad: 2,000 Knights Templar executed in spite of amnesty granted on surrender. **1266–86** Ulugh Khan Ghiyas al-Din Balban, Sultan of Delhi. | **1266** Arik Boge d. | |
| | **1267** Kubilai Khan sends embassy to demand submission of Japan: prevented by storms at sea. **1267–72** Mongols besiege Siang-yang. | **c. 1267–1337** Giotto (di Bondone), artist, architect and sculptor. |

| WESTERN & NORTHERN EUROPE | CENTRAL, SOUTHERN & EASTERN EUROPE | AFRICA & EGYPT |
|---|---|---|
| | **1268** Conradin visits Rome: 23 Aug., defeated by Charles d'Anjou at Tagliocozzo: 29 Oct., beheaded in Naples. | **1268** Elaborate *Mihrab* of Arbaa Rukun mosque, Mogadishu, constructed: displays wealth of trade centre. |
| | **1269** Ottokar takes Carinthia and Carniola.<br>**1269–70** Charles d'Anjou pacifies his Italian estates. | **1269** Marinids take Marrakesh. |
| **1270–85** Philip III, King of France. | **1270** Charles d'Anjou takes Tuscany. Abortive expedition against Cyprus by Baybars. | **1270** Eighth Crusade: Louis IX of France attacks Tunis: army destroyed by plague: 25 Aug., Louis IX d.; Hafsids defeated by Charles d'Anjou: peace follows. Spanish occupy Larache.<br>**1270–85** Yekuno Amlak, founder of Solomonic dynasty of Ethiopia: capital, Ankober.<br>**c. 1270** War between Mali and Tekrur. |
| **12/1** Philip III acquires Poitou. | **1271** Charles d'Anjou takes Albania: allies with the Bulgars and Serbs. | **1271** Hafsid trade restored with Aragon, Pisa and Venice; and with Genoa (1272). |
| **1272** 16 Nov., Henry III of England d.: succ. Edward I (−1307). Llywelyn of Wales refuses tribute to England. | **1272** Urus I of Serbia conquers the upper Vardar valley.<br>**1272–90** Ladislaus, King of Hungary. | |
| | **1273** Genoa defeats Charles d'Anjou.<br>**1273–91** Rudolf I of Hungary elected King of Germany. | **1273** Marinids take Tangier. |
| **1274** 19 Aug., Edward I crowned at Westminster.<br>**1274–8** Commission of *Quo Warranto* inquires into English land titles.<br>**1274** Philip III makes Lyons a protectorate.<br>**1275** Llywelyn of Wales again refuses tribute. First Statute of Westminster grants the king the right to tax wool.<br>**1275–90** Magnus I, King of Sweden.<br>**1276** Edward I, with army supported by fleet, takes Anglesey. | **1274** Diet of Nuremburg: breach between Rudolph and Ottokar. Alliance between Rudolph and Charles d'Anjou.<br><br>**1275** Charles d'Anjou defeated by the Ghibellines at Roccavioni: evacuates Piedmont. Abps of the Rhineland league against Rudolf of Hapsburg. Alfonso X formally renounces title of Holy Roman Emperor.<br>**1276** 24 June, Rudolf outlaws Ottokar: 21 Nov., submits to Rudolf: permitted to retain Bohemia and Moravia.<br>**1276–82** Dragontine, Prince of Serbia.<br>**1276–85** Peter III of Aragon: m. daughter of Manfred, King of Sicily: basis of later Aragonese claims to Sicily. | **1274–5** Hostilities between Ethiopia and Ifat.<br>**1274 or 5** Abu al-Qasim al-Azafi gives allegiance to the Marinids.<br>**1274** Marinids take Sijilmasa.<br><br>**1275–6** Umar b. Dunya-huz, Sultan of Ifat, d. Egyptian campaigns in Nubia.<br>**c. 1275** Yoruba destroy Nupe kingdom.<br><br>**1276** New Fez (al-Fas al-Jadid) built by Marinids. Further Egyptian campaign in Nubia. |
| **1277** Treaty of Aberconway: Llywelyn compelled to cede all Wales except Gwynedd to Edward I.<br>**1277 ff.** Castles built by Edward I at Aberystwyth, Builth, Flint and Rhuddlan to contain Wales.<br><br>**1278** Edward I of England claims overlordship of Scotland. | **1277** Otto Visconti, Abp of Milan, granted *Signoria* of Milan. 22 July, Congress of Venice: independence of Venice confirmed: Pope and Emperor reconciled.<br><br><br>**1278** 26 Aug., Ottokar defeated and killed by Rudolf at Dürnkrut. Henry of Bavaria rebels. | **1277** Asma attacks Makhzumi sultanate of eastern Shoa.<br>**1277–9** Barakah, Bahri Mamluk Sultan.<br>**1277–9** Marinid campaign in Spain<br>**c. 1277–94** al-Hasan b. Talut, Sultan of Kilwa. |

# THE NEAR EAST

**1268** Baybars takes Jaffa and Antioch.

**1270** Lahore refortified: Mongols checked by Sunqar.
**1270–2** Future Edward 1 of England in Crusade in Palestine.

**1271** 24 March–8 Apr., Baybars successfully besieges Knights Hospitaller fort of Husn al-Akrad: other neighbouring castles taken.

**1272** Abaqa devastates Khwarazm and Transoxiana.

**1274** Assassin movement finally wiped out by Mamluk Sultan Baybars.

**1275–1466** Karamanli dynasty at Karaman, successor of Saljuqids of Konia.

**1277** Mongols defeated by Baybars at Abulistin. Charles d'Anjou demands the Crown of Jerusalem: takes Acre.

**1278–9** Abaqa makes abortive attempts to take Syria.

# THE FAR EAST

**1268–92** Kertanagara, last King of the Singosari dynasty.

**1270** Chandrabhanu again makes abortive attempt to seize Ceylon.
**1270–1340** Twenty-one successive Sakya-pa lamas, rulers of Tibet.

**1271** Kubilai Khan proclaims Yu dynasty: Yao Shu, new order, for centralized administration. Kingdom of Pagan ordered to pay tribute by Kubilai Khan: embassy refused audience by Narathihapati.
**1272–84** Yapahuva capital of Ceylon.

**1273** Kubilai Khan sends letter demanding tribute from Pagan: envoys executed by order of Narathihapati. Sung armies defeated by the Mongols.
**1274** Sung Emperor Tu-Tsung d.: replaced by four year old son: Empress Sie, regent. Kubilai Khan sends armada against Japan: beaten off after stubborn battle.

**1275** Mongols attack Mien, N Burma. Kertanagara plans unification of all Malaysia and Indonesia: all Java conquered.

**1276** Hangchow taken by the Mongols. Empress Sie and her son surrender to Kubilai Khan. War between Sung generals and Mongols (–1279).

**1277** Burmese armies invade Kingdom of Kaungai with 60,000 infantry, 2,000 elephants and some cavalry: opposed by 12,000 Mongol cavalry: elephants, wounded by Mongol archers, turn on Burmese: Burmese break in confusion.
**1278** Fresh Burmese army sent to fortresses of Ngazaunggyan and Kaungzin.

# RELIGION & CULTURE

**1268–71** Papacy vacant (*sede vacante*).
**c. 1268–76** Paper making introduced into Italy.
**c. 1268–1337** Cino da Pistoia, Italian poet.
**1269** The Pragmatic Sanction grants immunities to the French clergy. Mosque of Sultan Baybars, Cairo, built. Fakhr al-Din Mosque, Mogadishu, built.
**1270** First condemnation of Siger of Brabant. Eastern chapels of Hayles Abbey begun.

**1271** Observatory built at Kirsehir by the Saljuquids. Gök Medresse (Blue *madrassa*), Sivasi, built as a theological school.
**1271–6** Gregory X (Tebaldo Visconti), Pope.
**1272** Building of choir of Narbonne Cathedral begun. Emperor Michael makes Serbian and Bulgarian churches subject to Constantinople.
**1273** Limoges Cathedral begun.
**1273–1332** Abu al-Fida, historian and geographer: governor of Hamah.
**1273–1349** Sta Maria Novella built in Florence.
**1274** St Thomas Aquinas d. on his way to the Council of Lyons. Council of Lyons: Emperor Michael VIII accepts *filioque* clause, use of unleavened bread, and supreme authority of the Pope: known as Union of Lyons.
**c. 1275–1348** Giovanni Villani, Italian historian.
**c. 1275–1342** Marsilio of Padua, political philosopher.

**1276** College for the instruction of missionaries for the east instituted at Palma by Ramón Llull. Ahmad al-Badawi d. at Tanta, Egypt: founder of the Ahmadiyyah dervish order, principal order in Egypt: burial mosque built.
**1276** Innocent V, Pope. Adrian V, Pope.
**1276–7** John XXI, Pope.
**1277** Teachings of St Thomas Aquinas condemned in Paris and Canterbury. Siger de Brabant again condemned.
**1277–80** Nicholas III (Orsini), Pope.

**1278** Arsenite council held in Thessaly or Epirus.
Vale Royal Abbey begun.
**1278–91** Roger Bacon imprisoned.

| WESTERN & NORTHERN EUROPE | CENTRAL, SOUTHERN & EASTERN EUROPE | AFRICA & EGYPT |
|---|---|---|
| **1278** Statute of Gloucester: feudal jurisdiction limited by writs of *Quo Warranto*. | | |
| **1279** Edward I takes Ponthieu: 23 May, Philip III recognizes his claim to Ponthieu and Agenais. | **1279** Pope Nicholas III establishes his temporal power in Romagna and Tuscany. **1279–88** Leszek the Black, Duke of Cracow. **1279–1325** Denis 'the Farmer', King of Portugal: leader of improvements in agriculture: makes Portuguese the language of law and administration: patron of learning and the arts: Portuguese navy founded. | **1279** Salamah, Bahri Mamluk Sultan **1279–90** al-Malik al-Mansur Qalaun, Mamluk Sultan: trade with Barcelon Genoa and Venice greatly developed **1279–1370** Anarchy in N Africa. **1279** Spanish occupy Ceuta. |
| **1280–99** Eric II, King of Norway. **1280** Alliance between Visby and Lubeck against pirates. | **1280** Charles d'Anjou campaigns in Albania. | c. **1280** Oguola, Oba of Benin: wars with the Ibo. |
| **1281** Philip III makes Toul a protectorate. | **1281** Charles d'Anjou defeated at Berat. Charles d'Anjou makes a treaty with Venice. **1281–2** Philip of Aragon forms a coalition against Charles d'Anjou. | **1281** Commercial treaty between Egypt and Byzantium. Abdulwadids beseige Tlemcen. |
| **1282** Welsh revolt: Flint and Rhuddlan castles besieged by David, brother of Llywelyn: 11 Dec., Llywelyn killed. Riga joins alliance of Visby and Lubeck. | **1282** Rudolf of Austria invests his sons Adolf and Rudolf with Austria, Carinthia and Styria. Manfred, King of Sicily d.: Pope awards Sicily to Charles d'Anjou: the 'Sicilian Vespers': islanders appeal to Peter III of Aragon: Peter takes Sicily and Kingdom of Naples: war ensues with France and the Pope. Alfonso X deposed by the *Cortes* of Castile. **1282–1321** Milontine, King of Serbia: conquers the Seres region. **1282–1328** Andronicus II Palaeologus, Eastern Roman Emperor. | |
| **1283** Teutonic Order conquers Prussia. Jan., Edward I holds Councils at York and Canterbury. 1 Oct., David, brother of Llywelyn, hanged. | **1283** Charles d'Anjou prevented from disembarking in Sicily. Marinid campaign in Spain. | c. **1283** Walls of Benin built. |
| **1284** Philip the Fair m. Jeanne of Navarre. March, Statute of Wales issued at Rhuddlan: Edward I organizes Wales in counties on English model: Caernarvon, Conway and Harlech castles begun. | **1284** Genoa defeats Pisa off Meloria: beginning of decline of Pisa. **1284–95** Sancho IV, King of Castile: treaty with Aragon partitioning N Africa into spheres of interest: Morocco assigned to Castile. | |
| **1285** Statute of Westminster on public order. Statute of Watch and Ward initiates rudimentary police system in London. **1285–1314** Philip IV the Fair, King of France. **1286** Treaty of Paris between England and France. **1286–90** Margaret. the Maid of Norway, Queen of Scots. **1286–1319** Eric VI Menved, King of Denmark. | **1285** Nov., Peter III of Aragon d.: succ. Alfonso III (−1291). Charles d'Anjou d. **1286** Truce between Aragon and France. | **1285** Asma destroys Makhzumi sultanate. **1285–94** Yagbea Sion of Ethiopia: successful campaign against Zaila. c. **1285–1300** Sakura, King of Mali. c. **1286** Egyptian embassies to Nubian rulers. |

| THE NEAR EAST | THE FAR EAST | RELIGION & CULTURE |
|---|---|---|
| | **1278—82** Skirmishes between Thai raiders and Burmese. | **1278** The Dominicans formally adopt Thomism (the teaching of St Thomas Aquinas). |
| **1279—82** Rebellion in Bengal led by Tughril: suppressed by Balban. | **1279—1368** Yuan (Mongol) dynasty in China: Kubilai Khan, first emperor. All higher government posts and garrisons reserved for Mongols: Persian used as a *lingua franca*: intermarriage of Mongols with S Chinese forbidden. | **1279** Statute of Mortmain: church endowments curtailed in England. Nicholas III: Bull *Exiit qui seminat* on Franciscan property. *Madrassa al-Zahiriyyah*, Damascus, founded; |
| **1280** Abaqa defeated by Egyptian army at Homs. | **1280** Kubilai Khan orders Champa to be treated as a Mongol province: Mongol envoys seized. Magadu proclaims himself King of Martaban, with throne name Wareru. | **1280** *Madrassa* al-Saffarin, Fez, built. **1280** Sta Maria di sopra Minerva built in Rome. Belfry at Bruges built. **c. 1280** Spectacles invented in Tuscany. **1280—1349** William of Ockham, philosopher. |
| **1281—4** Ahmad, Ilkhan of Persia. | **1281** Mongol armada with 150,000 men sent against Japan: 14 Aug., completely destroyed by a typhoon after fifty-three days fighting. | **1281—5** Martin IV, Pope. **1281—4** Peterhouse, first Cambridge college, founded. **1281** Union of Lyons ended by Pope Martin IV. |
| **1282** 15 Apr., truce between Qalaun and Knights Templar of Antartus. **1282—1338** Bengal held as a governorate by Balban's descendants. | **1282** Mongols occupy Champa and Cambodia. | **1282** Andronicus II revokes union of eastern and western churches. Ibn Khallikan d.: first compiler of an Arab national biographical dictionary. |
| | **1283** War between Mongols and Champa: Mongols take Mu Cheng. Rama Kamheng succ. to throne of Sukhothai. Mongol army with Thai allies attack Burma: Ngazaunggan and Kaungzin fall: King Narathihapati flees from Pagan: embassy sent demanding surrender. | **1283** Siamese script invented. |
| **1284—91** Arghun succ. Ahmad as Ilkhan of Persia: enters into negotiations with the Pope and European courts to expel Egyptians from Syria. | **1284** Kertanagara seizes Bali. Bali proclaims itself independent. Thais in control of most of Malay peninsula. Burmese regroup at Tagaung: Mongols destroy Tagaung, but monsoon precludes follow-up: Upper Burma declared a Chinese province as Chiang-Mien. Narathihapati sends peace envoy to Mongols. Mongols conquer Annam and Cambodia. | **1284** Maristan (hospital), with a school and a mosque, built at Cairo by Qalaun. |
| **1285** 25 May, Qalaun takes fort of al-Marqab, near Tortosa. 18 July, truce between Qalaun and Princess of Tyre, ruler of Beirut. | **1285** Mongol army defeated by Champa. | **1285—7** Honorius IV, Pope. **c. 1285—1367** Exeter Cathedral built. |
| **1286** Balban d.: succ. Muizz al-Din Qaiqabad (—1290). Henry II of Cyprus, King of Jerusalem. | | **c. 1286** Ibn Said, geographer, d. |

| WESTERN & NORTHERN EUROPE | CENTRAL, SOUTHERN & EASTERN EUROPE | AFRICA & EGYPT |
|---|---|---|

**1286–1386** *Quoniam Attachiamenta*, or 'Auld Lawis', Scottish law code.
**1287–1345** Jacques van Artevelde, 'the brewer of Ghent'.

**1287** Council of Würzburg: Public Peace proclaimed by Rudolf I. Treaty of Oléron between Edward I of England and Alfonso III of Aragon. Nobles exact charter 'Privilege of the Union' from Alfonso III of Aragon. Mongols again invade Poland. Rabban Sauma, Turco-Chinese Nestorian monk, sent to Europe as Mongol ambassador: visits Rome, Genoa and Florence: meets Philip the Fair of France and Edward I of England.
**1287–1308** Guy II de la Roche, Duke of Athens.

**c. 1287** Egyptian campaign against Dongola.

**1288** 5 June, battle of Worringen: decides Limburg war of succession in favour of Brabant.

**1289** 6 Nov., treaty of Salisbury between England, Norway and Scotland. Mongol ambassador visits London.

**1289–90** Henry Probus, Duke of Cracow.

**1289** Further Egyptian campaign against Dongola.

**1290** 10 March, Treaty of Bingham-on-Tweed: marriage of infant Queen Margaret of Scotland and Prince of Wales agreed. 26 Sept., Queen Margaret of Scotland d.: interregnum (–1292): thirteen candidates for the throne. Is. of Man annexed by Edward I. Statute of *Quia Emptores:* subinfeudation forbidden.
**1290–1318** Birger, King of Sweden: Torkil Knutson, Regent (–1306).

**c. 1290** Principalities emerge in Rumania.
**1290–6** James of Aragon King of Sicily.
**1290–1301** Andrew III, King of Hungary.

**1290–3** al-Malik al-Ashraf Qalil, Mamluk Sultan of Egypt.
**1290** Marinids beseige Tlemcen.

**1291** 1 Aug., League of three communities, Uri, Schwyz and Nidwald coalesce: origin of the Swiss Confederation. Treaty of Tarascon between France and Aragon: Kingdom of Naples to be property of the House of Anjou, and Sicily awarded to Aragon. Rudolf of Hapsburg d.
**1291–1327** James II, King of Aragon.
**1292** 5 May, Adolph of Nassau elected King of Germany: 24 June, crowned Holy Roman Emperor (–1298). Fortress of Tarifa taken by Sancho IV.

**1291** Vivaldi brothers reach C Nun.
**c. 1291–1339** Fumomadi the Great Sultan of Pate: controls coast from Pate to Mogadishu.

**1292** 17 Nov., Edward I of England, as arbitrator, awards Crown of Scotland to John Baliol: Baliol acknowledges Edward as Lord Paramount.

**THE NEAR EAST** | **THE FAR EAST** | **RELIGION & CULTURE**

**1287** Armies of Kubilai Khan seize Pagan.
**1287–98** Kyawswar, puppet King of Pagan under the Mongols.
**1287** Mongols attack Vietnam: Hanoi falls: king escapes: Mongol supply fleet destroyed. Narathihapati compelled to swallow poison at Prome: succ. in Lower Burma by Kyawswar. Mongols seize Pagan after heavy losses inflicted by Burmese guerillas: Pagan sacked: Central Burma made a province of China as Chung-Mien: Mongols withdraw without leaving garrison or administration: Arakan, Pegu and Mon states declare themselves independent. Mon governor of Pegu declares himself king with throne name Tarabya: allies with Wareru of Martaban: both conquer Lower Burma: Tarabya then killed in a skirmish by Wareru.
**1287–1306** Wareru, King of Hanthawaddy (Pegu), founder of dynasty.
**1287–1539** Dynasty of Hanthawaddy (Pegu), Burma.

**1287** Cathedral of Tripoli, Lebanon, turned into a mosque; completed in 1294.

**1288 and 93** Marco Polo visits Kayal in Pandya Kingdom.
**1288–1326** Uthman, first Ottoman to use title Sultan: domains, earlier Bithynia, cradle of Ottoman dynasty in Asia (–1366).
**1289** Apr., Qalaun takes Tripoli (Syria) and al-Batrun: 7,000 Christians killed in Tripoli, and the town destroyed.

**1290** Muizz al-Din Qaiqabad murdered: last of slave Sultans of Delhi: Firuz Shah Jalal al-Din, a Khilji, placed on the throne: Khilji dynasty (–1320).

**1289** Kertanagara sends Mongol ambassadors back to Kubilai Khan with their faces mutilated. Kaidu, nephew of Guyuk Khan, siezes Karakorum: defeated but continues fighting (–1301).
**1290** Toqtai elected Khan of the Golden Horde of Mongols.

**c. 1288–9** Abu al-Hasan Ali b. al-Nafis, dean of Qalaun's hospital in Cairo, d. in Damascus: discovered circulation of the blood.
**1288–92** Nicholas IV, Pope.
**1288** Choir of Exeter Cathedral begun.
**1289** Montpellier University founded. Giovanni de Monte Corvino in Asia. Gloucester Hall (later Worcester College), Oxford, founded.
**1290** Privileges of French clergy confirmed by Philip III. University of Lisbon founded. Jews expelled from England.
**c. 1290–1330** Orvieto Cathedral built.
**c. 1290** Regular traffic in coal from Newcastle to London begun.

**1291** May, Acre taken from Crusaders by al-Ashraf; 18 May, Crusaders abandon Tyre; 14 July, Sidon; 21 July, Beirut; 3 Aug., Tortosa; Aug., Athlit: end of Crusader occupation of Syria.
**1291–5** Gaikhatu, Ilkhan of Persia.

**1291** Eleanor Crosses erected. Nave of York Minster begun.

**1292** c. 100,000 Mongols invade India: defeated at Sunam by Firoz Shah.

**1292** Kertanagara takes Malayu, and then all Sumatra: Sri Vijaya falls under his influence. Thais take control of Ligor. Thais united by Rama Kamheng.

**1292** Perlak, Sumatra, converted to Islam: conversion of Indonesia and Malaysia follows (–1600).
**1292** Glass and bead manufacture already flourishing at Murano, near Venice.

1292–1298

WESTERN &
NORTHERN EUROPE

CENTRAL, SOUTHERN
& EASTERN EUROPE

AFRICA & EGYPT

**1292** Dispute between English and French sailors at Bayonne leads to hostilities.

**1293** Is. of Man restored to Scotland. English and French merchant fleets fight off Mahé, Brittany. Gascony attacks France. Vladimir and Souzdal sacked by Mongols. Torkil Knutson takes Karelia: Viborg founded.

**1293–4** al-Nasir, Bahri Mamluk Sultan (first term). Sakura, King of Mali, makes the pilgrimage to Mecca

**1294** Wales revolts: speedily repressed by Edward I. Philip IV of France condemns Edward I to lose Gascony: June, England declares war on France. Alliance between England and Emperor Adolf.

**1294** Commercial treaty between England and Portugal.

**1294–6** Kitbugha, Bahri Mamluk Sultan.

**1295** 'Model Parliament' held at Westminster: commons (*communes*) again represented. 22 Jan., English defeat Welsh at Conway. 1 July, alliance between France and Scotland: Scotland declines to support England against France.

**1295** Frederick II of Sicily cedes his title to the Pope: given right to conquer Corsica and Sardinia in exchange. Agreement of Anagni between Pope Boniface VIII and James II of Aragon.
**1295–6** Przemyslaw, Duke of Cracow.
**1295–1312** Ferdinand IV, King of Castile.
**1295–1320** Michael IX co-Emperor of Byzantium with his father, Andronicus II.

**1295** Cairo devastated by plague.
**post 1295** Sultanate of Ifat expands.

**1296** March, Edward I sacks Berwick-on-Tweed. Apr., John Baliol renounces English suzerainty: Edward I invades Scotland: 27 Apr., Scots defeated at Dunbar: Edward campaigns as far as Elgin: Stone of Scone transported to Westminster. July, John Baliol surrenders to Edward I: interregnum (–1306): Earl of Surrey, Governor of Scotland. Thirty Sheriffdoms already in existence in Scotland.
**1297** English defeated at Furnes. Apr., peace between England and France: England loses most of Gascony. Philip IV takes Lille. May, William Wallace leads rebellion in Scotland: 11 Sept., English defeated at Stirling. 12 Oct., *Confirmatio Cartarum:* Edward I solemnly confirms *Magna Carta* and restricts right to raise taxes. First Irish Parliament at Dublin.
**1298** 31 Jan., truce between England and France at Tournai. Edward I campaigns in Scotland: 22 July, defeats Wallace at Falkirk: Perth and St Andrews burnt.

**1296** Sicily rebels against James II of Aragon: Frederick II made King by popular election (–1337). Milontine, King of Serbia, invades Albania.

**1297** Venice defeated by Genoa off Curzola.

**1298** 23 June, Emperor Adolf dethroned: 2 July, killed at battle of Göllheim: 27 July, Albert I of Hapsburg elected (–1308). Milontine's conquests recognized by Emperor Andronicus II.
**1298–1300** Aragon and Naples campaign against Frederick of Sicily.

**1296** Famine in Egypt: students sell books from Fadiliya library for food
**1296–8** Lajin, Bahri Mamluk Sultan

**1298–1308** al-Nasir, Bahri Mamluk Sultan (second term).

## THE NEAR EAST

## THE FAR EAST

## RELIGION & CULTURE

1292 Marco Polo, his father and uncle, visit Indonesia as ambassadors for the Mongols.
c. 1292 State of Tumasik (Old Singapore) emerges.

1293 Sir Geoffrey Langley returns from an embassy to the Ilkhan Gaikhatu.

1293 Mongols, with a fleet of 1,000 ships and 20,000 men, sent to invade Java: Kertanagara murdered: succ. Jayakatwang: Mongols land unchallenged: assist Vijaya to expel Jayakatwang: Vijaya then expels Mongols: dominions fragmented. Burma pays voluntary tribute to Mongols.
1293–1309 Raden Vijaya, or Kritarajasa, ruler of Javanese 'empire' of Majapahit.

1293 Christian missionaries reach China.

1294 Yadava Raja of Devagiri attacked by Ala al-Din Khilji: vast booty carried off. Paper money first printed in Tabriz, in Arabic and in Chinese characters.

1294 Wareru of Martaban receives recognition from the King of Sukhotai, his father-in-law, with the present of a white elephant. Wareru appoints customary law commission, which produces *Code of Wareru*. Kubilai Khan d.: Temur, Great Khan and Chinese Emperor (−1307).

1294 5 June, St Celestine V elected Pope: 13 Dec., abdicates. Congregation of Fraticelli formed.
1294–1303 Boniface VIII, Pope.
1294–1381 John of Ruysbruck, mystic.

1295 Baidu, then Ghazan Mahmud —1304), Ilkhans of Persia. Revenue and administration reformed by Ghazan: capital, Tabriz, splendidly equipped with public buildings.

1295 Malayu requests Chinese Emperor's protection. Ranga-Lawe rebels against Vijaya.
c. 1295 Malayu, Bali, Madura and Tanjongpura united with Majapahit by dynastic marriages: Jayanagara proclaimed heir to Vijaya.

1295 Mausoleum of Jalal al-Din al-Rumi, Konia, built.
1295–1359 Nicephorus Gregoras, Byzantine historian.

1296 July, Firuz Shah decapitated: succ. Ala al-Din Khilji. Mongol raid on Sultanate of Delhi.

1296 Rama Kamheng seizes Khmer possessions in Menam basin. Mangray founds Thai Kingdom of Lan Na: capital built at Chieng Mai. Wareru assassinated by a grandson of Tarabya: Martaban attacked by Thais of Sukhotai: fighting continues intermittently for a long period.

1296 Building of Florence Cathedral begun. Pope Boniface VIII: bulls *Clericis laicos* and *Ineffabilis amoris*: ecclesiastics forbidden to pay taxes to temporal rulers.
c. 1296 Salah al-Din b. Yusuf, ophthalmologist at Hamah.
1296–1304 Giotto: *Life of St Francis.*

1297 Ala al-Din sends army against Gujarat: Baghela Rajput territory seized, with large booty. Further Mongol raid on Sultanate of Delhi.

1297 Jan., Kyawswar sends his son to submit to Mongols at Tagaung; March, Kyawswar recognized as King of Burma, abolishing Chung-Mien province: Dec., Kyawswar dethroned: succ. Saw Hnit. Shans invade Upper Burma. Malik al-Salih, King of Perlak, d.: his epitaph, imported from Cambay, first Islamic inscription in Indonesia.

1298 Barcelona Cathedral begun. Giovanni de Monte Corvino at the Chinese court. Ramleh Cathedral converted into a mosque. Marco Polo: *Travels*
1298–1313 Signoria Palace built in Florence.

| WESTERN & NORTHERN EUROPE | CENTRAL, SOUTHERN & EASTERN EUROPE | AFRICA & EGYPT |
|---|---|---|

**1299** 19 June, Treaty of Montreuil between England, France and Flanders. Nov., Stirling Castle retaken by Scots.
**1299–1319** Haakon V, King of Norway.
**First half of 14th c.** Golden age of the Mongol horde: control exercised from the Carpathians to the Volga.
**14th–15th cc.** Seventeen principalities issuing coinage in present Russia among a total of twenty to thirty princes.

**1300** July–Aug., England at war with Scotland. Philip II takes Flanders. *Articuli super cartas*: Edward III accepts twenty articles on the charters further restricting taxation. Population of Scotland *c.* 400,000.
**c. 1300** Population of England *c.* 3m.
**1301** 7 Feb., Prince Edward, son of Edward I, created Prince of Wales and Earl of Chester. Philip IV acquires part of Bar.

**1302** Jan., truce between England and Scotland. Philip IV defeated at Courtrai by the Flemings. French currency devalued: Bishop of Pamiers declines to surrender church revenues: supported by Pope Boniface VIII: Philip IV of France summons States-General which declares in his favour.

**1303** 20 May, treaty of Paris: Gascony restored to England. Sept., Edward I again campaigns in Scotland. Edward I: *Carta mercatoria*, grants privileges to foreign merchants.
**1304** Philip IV defeats Flemings by sea at Zierickzee and by land at Mons-en-Pévèle. 20 July, English retake Stirling: William Wallace taken prisoner.
**1304–18** Michael II of Vladimir the most influential of Russian princes.

**1305** Treaty of Athis between Philip IV and Flemings: Flanders ceded to Robert of Bethune in exchange for Lille and Douai. 23 Aug., Wallace hanged in London.
**1306** 25 March, Robert Bruce crowned King of Scotland (–1329): 26 June, defeated by English at Methuen; and, 11 Aug., at Dalry.

**1299** 8 Dec., Emperor Albert and Philip IV ally against Pope Boniface VIII. Treaty between Venice and the Turks.

**1300–5** Wenceslaus (or Waclaw) of Bohemia, King of Poland: all Poland united except Masovia and Silesia.
**c. 1300** Printing and banknote factory set up in Genoa.

**1301** 14 Jan., Andrew III of Hungary d.: end of Arpad dynasty: replaced by Angevin dynasty: succ. Wenceslaus (–1306). Pope Boniface calls on Charles de Valois to pacify Ghibellines in Florence.
**1302** General peace signed *re* Sicily: Frederick left in possession. Ferdinand IV comes of age: allies with Aragon: active anti-Muslim policy. The Guelphs take power in Florence. Albert I asserts authority over Electors of Cologne, Mayence, Palatinate and Trier.

**1303** Emperor Andronicus hires Grand Catalan Company to fight the Turks.

**1305–7** The Grand Catalan Company besieges Constantinople.

**1306** Pope Clement V invests James III of Aragon with Corsica and Sardinia. Wenceslas III of Bohemia, last of the Przemysls d.: Rudolf, son of Albert I, invested.
**1306–33** Wladislaw the Dwarf, King of Poland.

**1299–1307** Marinids beseige Tlemcen.
**1299–1314** Wadem Arad, Emperor of Ethiopia.

**14th c.** Ibo moving into their present habitat. Kingdom of Kongo established.
**14th–15th cc.** Jenne developes as a centre for the gold trade.

**c. 1300** Ga migrating from Benin to Accra region. Yoruba, Bedde and Tekrur reaching present habitats. Fulani reaching Adamawa. Sena said be the residence of the King of Sofa

**1302** Commercial treaty between Egypt and Venice, al-Mansuria built Abu Yaqub.

**1303–7** Abu Zayan, Abulwadid.

**1306** Thirty man embassy sent to Spain from Ethiopia. Tetuan founded

| THE NEAR EAST | THE FAR EAST | RELIGION & CULTURE |
|---|---|---|
| **1299** Large Mongol force under Qutlugh Khwaja attacks Delhi: routed by Sultan Ala al-Din. 23 Dec., Egyptian army defeated by the Mongols at Homs. | **1299** Pagan burnt by Shan usurpers. | **c. 1299** Brass-casting introduced from Benin into life. |
| **14th c.** Kashmir converted to Islam. Coffee introduced into S Arabia. | **14th c.** Coin replaces rice as medium of exchange in Japan. | **14th c.** *Kebra Negast* (Book of the Glory of the Kings of Ethiopia) compiled. Autopsies permitted in Bologna. Production of Ming blue-and white porcelain begins. Meteora monasteries develop. Coptic *Book of the Chrism* written. Qa'at al-Irsan, Cairo, built.<br>**14th to 15th cc.** Chichimecs over-run Toltecs and holy city of Teotihuacán. |
| **1300** Mongols occupy Damascus and N Syria: March, Mongols evacuate Damascus: regained by Egyptians. Ottoman capital transferred to Afyon Karahissar. | **1300** June, Mongols declare Kumara Kassapa King of Burma.<br>**c. 1300** Siamese Kingdom in Menam valley: tribute demanded from small settlements in Malaysia. | **c. 1300** Duns Scotus teaching at Oxford. Chapter House, York, built.<br>**c. 1300–49** Richard Rolle, mystic.<br>**c. 1300–99** Franco Sacchetti, Italian writer. |
| **1301** Ranthambhor taken by Delhi. | **1301** Jan., Mongol army invades C Burma: Myinsaing besieged: Mongols bribed to retreat: Saw Hnit recognized as King of Burma. | **1301–74** Ni Tsan, painter.<br>**1301** Bull *Super cathedram* forbids friars to preach unasked in parish churches. al-Umari, geographer, b. |
| **1302** Knights Templar expelled from Arwad (Aradus), last Crusader stronghold in Syria, by al-Malik al-Nasir Muhammad.<br>**1302 ff.** al-Nasir campaigns against Armenia: Christians and Jews persecuted in Egypt and Syria.<br>**1302–11** Malik Kafur campaigns in S India. | | **1302** Boniface VIII: bull *Unam Sanctam* on papal supremacy. |
| **1303** Chitor taken by Delhi: held until 1311. Mongol expedition checked at Marj al-Suffar, S of Damascus. | **1303** Mongols withdraw completely from Burma. | **1303** Pope Boniface VIII's arrest attempted by Philip IV: excommunicated. Mosque of Qalaun, Cairo, completed. Mosque of Baybars II built. León Cathedral completed. Rome University founded.<br>**1303–4** Benedict XI, Pope.<br>**1304** School of al-Nasiriyah built by al-Nasir in Cairo.<br>**1304–8** Duns Scotus teaching in Paris.<br>**1304–74** Francesco Petrarca (Petrarch), Italian poet.<br>**1304–77** Muhammad b. Abdallah b. Battuta, of Tangier: greatest of Arab travellers. |
| **1304–16** Oljeitu, Ilkhan of Persia. | | |
| **1305** Delhi annexes Ujjain, Mandu, Dhar and Chanderi. | | **1305** Bernard de Got, Bp of Bordeaux, elected Pope as Clement V (–1314). |
| **1306** Mongols cease to harry India, returning because of troubles in Transoxiana. | **1306–10** Hkun Law, King of Hanthawaddy. | **1306** Philip IV expels the Jews from France: all property confiscated. Bulls *Clericis laicos* and *Unam sanctam* revoked. Pope Clement V holds inquiry into the Inquisition. Abd al-Mumin al-Dimyati d.: Cairene authority on horses and veterinary medicine. |

| WESTERN & NORTHERN EUROPE | CENTRAL, SOUTHERN & EASTERN EUROPE | AFRICA & EGYPT |
|---|---|---|
| **1307** 10 May, Robert Bruce defeats Earl of Pembroke at Loudoun Hill. 10 and 13 May, Edward I defeated by Robert Bruce in Ayr. 7 July, Edward I of England d.: succ. Edward II (−1327): Piers Gaveston, favourite. 25 Dec., Earl of Buchan defeated by Robert Bruce at Staines. | **1307** Philip IV arrests the Knights Templar: confiscates their property. The Cortes of Castile gains control of taxation. May, Albert I defeated at Lucka by Frederick of Meissen. Rudolf of Bohemia d.: Henry of Carinthia elected king (−1310). Albert I invades Bohemia. **1307–13** The Angevins of Naples seize the Morea. The Grand Company of Catalans campaigns in Greece. | **1307–32** Kankan Mansa Musa, ruler of Mali: seizes Songhai. **1307** 12 May, Abu Yaqub, Marinid, assassinated before Tlemcen: end of siege. **1307–8** Abu Thabit, Marinid. **1307–18** Abu Hammu Musa, Abdulwadid. |
| **1308** Apr., English barons compel exile of Piers Gaveston. Assembly of Tours. Edward II of England m. Isabel of France. | **1308** 1 May, Albert of Austria assassinated while advancing on Switzerland. Otto of Wittelsbach abdicates the throne of Hungary: succ. Carobert or Robert Charles of Anjou (−1342). **1308–13** Henry VII of Luxembourg, Holy Roman Emperor. | **1308–9** Baybars II, Bahri Mamluk Sultan. **1308–10** Abu al-Rabi, Marinid. |
| **1309** July, Gaveston permitted to return to England. | **1309** Grand Master of the Teutonic Knights moves to Marienburg, Prussia. 3 June, Henry VII recognizes Swiss League. Union of Aragon and Valencia made permanent. **1310** The Knights Hospitaller take Rhodes. Ferdinand IV takes Gibraltar. 31 Aug., John, Count of Luxembourg, made King of Bohemia (−1346). | **1309–40** al-Nasir, Bahri Mamluk Sultan (third term): trade with Barcelona, Marseilles, Pisa and Venice at Alexandria, Damietta and Rosetta **1309** Marinids retake Ceuta. **1310–31** Abu Said Uthman, Marinid. **c. 1310–33** al-Hasan b. Sulaiman II, Sultan of Kilwa. |
| **1310** English invade Scotland. Parliament of Kilkenny. Teutonic Knights take Danzig and Pomerellen. March, twenty-one Lords Ordainers appointed by English Parliament. **1311** Frequent border forays from Scotland into England. Barons revolt in England: Gaveston exiled. Ordinances issued by Lords Ordainers: power transferred from Edward II to barons. Treaty of Périgueux between England and France. **1312** 19 July, Gaveston executed. English invade Scotland. Scots sack Durham. | **1311** Catalans defeat French Duchy of Athens and Thebes near R. Cephisus: Catalan control established (−1379). Henry VII crowned King of the Lombards. The Guelphs revolt. Matteo Visconti seizes Milan.

**1312** 29 June, Henry VII crowned Holy Roman Emperor in Rome: fails to take Florence: allies with Frederick II of Sicily. **1312–50** Alfonso XI, King of Castile. | **1311** Aqueduct built by al-Nasir to bring water from the Nile to the Citadel of Cairo. |
| **1313** 13 Jan., Scots take Perth. Oct., Edward II reconciled with barons. Robert Bruce takes Isle of Man. Bad harvest in England. | **1313** 24 Aug., Emperor Henry VII d. | **c. 1313** Mossi Kingdom of Ourbri founded. |
| **1314** 17 June, Edward II, with army, crosses Scots border: 24 June, defeated by Robert Bruce at Bannockburn: Scotland again independent. Sept., Edward II confirms Ordinances of the Lords Ordainers. Jacques de Molay, last Templar Grand Master, and three other knights, beheaded: de Molay warns Philip IV of France and Pope Clement V that they will both shortly appear before the divine judgement seat: both shortly d. **1314–16** Louis X, King of France. **1315** Edward, brother of Robert Bruce, lands with 6,000 men at Larne. | **1314–22** Frederick III of Austria, rival Holy Roman Emperor. **1314–47** Louis IV of Bavaria, Holy Roman Emperor. | **1314–44** Amda Sion the Great of Ethiopia.

**1315–23** Nubia usurped by Kanz al-Daula. |

| THE NEAR EAST | THE FAR EAST | RELIGION & CULTURE |
|---|---|---|
| **1307** Ilkhan capital moved to Sultaniye. Ala al-Din III, last Saljuqid Sultan, killed by the Mongols. | **1307–11** Khaishan, Great Khan and Chinese Emperor. | **1307** Pope Clement V meets Philip IV at Poitiers: Philip demands condemnation of Pope Boniface VIII. Central tower of Lincoln Cathedral built. Lisbon University transferred to Coimbra. |
| | | **1308** Duns Scotus, theologian and philosopher, d. Giovanni de Monte Corvino, Abp of Peking (–1333). Second meeting of Pope Clement V and Philip IV at Poitiers. Coimbra University founded. |
| **1309** Ramachandra, last independent ruler of the Deccan, submits to Malik Kafur.<br><br>**1310** Delhi exacts tribute from Warangal: Malwa subjected. | **1309** Thihathu crowns himself King of Burma. Vijaya of Majapahit d.: succ. Jayanagara (–1328). **1309–27** Nandi leads rebellion against Jayanagara in E Java. **1310–24** Saw O, King of Hanthawaddy. | **1309** Le Sieur de Joinville: *Livre saint Louis*. Doge's Palace, Venice, rebuilt. **1309–54** Asti Cathedral built.<br><br>c. **1310–70** Fazio degli Uberti, Italian poet. |
| **1311** Feb., Hoysala ruler, Ballala III, surrenders to al-Malik Kafur: Mabur looted: Oct., al-Malik Kafur returns to Delhi. | **1311–20** Buyantu, Great Khan and Chinese Emperor. | **1311–12** Council of Vienne: chairs of Arabic and Mongol ordered to be created at Paris, Louvain and Salamanca. **1311–75** Leu-Ki, Chinese poet. **1311** The Iron Crown first used for the imperial coronation. |
| | **1312** Queen-Dowager of Pagan formally recognizes Thihathu as king. **1312–64** Thihathu, founder of Pinya dynasty. **1312** Champa state made feudatory to Vietnam. | **1312** Council of Vienne: Bull *Vox in excelso*: Order of Knights Templar suppressed. Portuguese Order of Christ founded: endowed with estates of former Knights Templar. Tekla Haimanot, Ethiopian saint and missionary, d. Gerona Cathedral begun. c. **1312** Dante: *Inferno*. |
| **1313–93** Muzaffarid dynasty in S Persia. | | ante **1312** Debra Libanos monastery, Ethiopia, founded. **1313** Constitution *Exivi de paradiso* on Franciscan property. **1313–74** Lisan al-Din b. al–Khatib, historian and poet, at Córdoba. **1313–75** Giovanni Boccaccio, poet and writer. **1314** Constitution *Romani principes*. Bull *Pastoralis cura*. Dante: *Purgatorio*. |
| | c. **1315** Mangray d.: succ. Grama, followed very shortly by his son Sen Phu (–1334). | |

| WESTERN & NORTHERN EUROPE | CENTRAL, SOUTHERN & EASTERN EUROPE | AFRICA & EGYPT |
|---|---|---|

**1315** Feb., barons make themselves administrators of royal revenues in England: Hugh Despenser, father and son, royal favourites, removed from the Council. Louis X of France grants charters to French provinces.
**1315—26** Yuri, Grand Prince of Vladimir.
**1315—42** Gedymin, ruler of Lithuania: introduces civilization and religious tolerance.
**1316** 1 May, Edward Bruce crowned King of Ireland. Parliament of Lincoln forces Edward II to accept Thomas of Lancaster as counsellor.
**1316—22** Philip V, King of France.

**1315** 15 Nov., Leopold of Austria, leading force to seize Switzerland, defeated at Monte Catini: pact of Brunnen ends war. 9 Dec., new treaty between Swiss confederates.

**1316** Louis IV of Bavaria confirms privileges of Swiss Cantons.

**1316** Yahya b. Azafi makes Ceuta independent of the Marinids (—1326).

**1317** Philip V of France crowned.

**1317** Pope John XXII excommunicates the Visconti: attempts to seize Imperial temporal rights in Italy.
**1318** Naples again administers Morea.

**1318** Thomas of Lancaster rebels: treaty of Leek between Edward II and baronial factions. Parliament held at York. Hugh Despenser, royal favourite. 14 Oct., Edward Bruce defeated and killed at Faughart. Scots take Berwick-on-Tweed.
**1319** Scots take Mytton.
**1319—26** Christopher II, King of Denmark.
**1319—63** Magnus II Smek, King of Norway and Sweden.
**1320** Parliament of Dublin: English rule in Ireland fully restored. Declaration of Arbroath: Scots inform Pope they will never accept English rule. 'Black' Parliament at Scone: seventy persons tried for conspiring to commit treason. Christopher II of Denmark renounces many prerogatives in favour of the Estates. 5 May, peace of Paris between Flanders and France. Kiev taken by Gedymin of Lithuania.
**1320—2** Cathari submit at Albi, Carcassonne and Cordes.
**1320—80** Bertrand du Guesclin, warrior and, later, Lord High Constable of France.
**1321** July, English barons insist on the exile of Hugh Despenser.
**1322** Feb., Despensers return. 16 March, Edward II defeats Thomas of Lancaster at Boroughbridge: Lancaster beheaded. 2 May, Parliament of York declares that legislation requires consent of both King and Parliament. Scots take Byland.
**1322—8** Charles IV, King of France.
**1323** Truce between England and Scotland for thirteen years. Robert Bruce recognized as King of Scotland by the Pope.
**1323—8** Jacquerie in Flanders.

**1318—36** Ibn Tashfin, Abdulwadid.

**1319** Naples gives Genoa protection from the Visconti. Castilian army checked before Granada. Wladislaw solemnly crowned King of Poland.

**1320—8** Andronicus II, sole Eastern Roman Emperor.

**1321** Miloutine, King of Serbia, d.: succ. Urus III.
**1322** 28 Sept., battle of Muhldorf: Louis IV defeats and takes prisoner Frederick of Austria.
**1322—86** Catalan Duchy of Athens.

**post 1321** Ifat invades Ethiopia.

**c. 1322—6** Magha, ruler of Mali: Timbuktu burnt by Mossi: Gao lost to Songhai.

**1323** Louis of Bavaria sends army into Italy to compel Robert of Naples to raise the siege of Milan. Poland and Lithuania partition Galicia. James I of Aragon takes Sardinia from Pisa.

| THE NEAR EAST | THE FAR EAST | RELIGION & CULTURE |
|---|---|---|
| | 1315—23 Sawyn, founder of Sagaing dynasty: son of Thihathu, King of Pinya.<br>1315—64 Dynasty of Sagaing, Burma. | |
| ante 1316 Ala al-Din loses Gujarat Chitor and Devagri.<br>1316 Jan., Ala al-Din d. at Delhi: infant son enthroned: Malik Kafur in control for thirty-five days, then beheaded: Qutb al-Din Mubarak Khan, a debauchee, enthroned.<br>1316—35 Abu Said, last Ilkhan of Persia. | | 1316—34 John XXII, Pope, at Avignon.<br>1316—91 Papal Palace built at Avignon. Constitution *Ex debito* regulates Annates.<br>1316—1401 Ibn Arafa, jurisconsult, at Qayrawan. |
| 1318 Qutb al-Din leads expedition against Deogiri. Qutb al-Din killed by his creature, Khusru Khan: Khusru succ. (—1320). | | 1317 Pope John XXII issues bull *Quoniam nulla (Clementinae constitutiones).*<br>1318 Waldenses teaching in Bohemia and Poland. Building of St Ouen begun at Rouen. Mosque built by al-Nasir in the Citadel of Cairo with materials from Acre Cathedral.<br>1318—39 Church of St Ouen, Rouen, built. |
| 1320 Ghazi Malik elected Sultan of Delhi: takes throne-name Ghiyas al-Din Tughluq Shah. | 1320—3 Sudhipala, Great Khan and Chinese Emperor. | 1320—84 John Wycliffe, ecclesiastical reformer and translator of the Bible.<br>c. 1320—91 Hafiz, Persian poet.<br>c. 1320 Lady Chapel of Lincoln Cathedral begun.<br>1320—64 Cracow Cathedral rebuilt. |
| | | 1321 Dante: *La Divina Commedia.* Ely Lady Chapel begun. Octagon of Ely Cathedral begun. Cologne Cathedral Choir completed.<br>1321—38 Pope John XXII interdicts Frederic of Sicily. |
| | 1322 Fr Odorico di Pordenone visits Java.<br>1322 or 4 Sen Phu makes good his claim to Thai throne of Chieng Mai. | 1322 Decretal *Quia nonnunquam* reopens conflict on Franciscan poverty. |
| | 1323—8 Yesun Temur, Great Khan and Chinese Emperor.<br>1323—36 Tarabyagyi, King of Sagaing. | 1323 Pope John XXII orders Louis of Bavaria to abdicate.<br>c. 1323—82 Nicole Oresme, astronomer.<br>1323—1404 William of Wykeham, Bp and statesman. |

| WESTERN & NORTHERN EUROPE | CENTRAL, SOUTHERN & EASTERN EUROPE | AFRICA & EGYPT |
|---|---|---|
| **1324** Charles IV takes possession of Gascony. | **1324** 5 Jan., Frankfurt Appellation against the Pope. 22 May, Louis IV's Appellation against the Pope. The Arabs take Baza from Castile. James II of Aragon conquers Sardinia. Louis of Bavaria makes peace with the Hapsburgs.<br>**1325–7** Bertrand du Pouget takes Modena, Parma and Reggio.<br>**1325–30** Frederick III of Austria, joint Holy Roman Emperor.<br>**1325–57** Afonso IV, King of Portugal. | **1324** Kankan Mansa Musa's pilgrimage to Mecca.<br><br><br><br>**c. 1325** Haqq al-Din, Sultan of Ifat, again campaigns in Ethiopia.<br>**1325** Timbuktu occupied by the Mandingo, Gao taken by Ghana. |
| **1326** 24 Sept., Queen Isabel of England and Roger Mortimer head rebellion against Edward II: 26 Oct., elder Despenser hanged; 16 Nov., Edward II taken prisoner; 20 Nov., younger Despenser hanged. Scots Parliament held at Cambuskenneth: burghs represented for the first time.<br>**1326–41** Ivan I, Prince of Moscow: makes Moscow the administrative centre.<br>**1327** 7 Jan., Edward II abdicates: succ. Edward III (–1377). June–Aug., Scots campaign against England. 21 Sept., Edward II murdered at Berkeley Castle at instigation of Queen Isabel and Roger Mortimer.<br>**1328** 4 May, treaty of Northampton: England recognizes Robert Bruce as King of Scotland. Oct., Roger Mortimer made Earl of March. Ivan of Moscow invested by Mongol Uzbeg Khan with title of Grand Prince of Vladimir and all Russia: *Book of Laws* codified.<br>**1328–50** Philip VI, King of France.<br>**1328–1480** Grand Dukes of Muscovy, rulers of Russia.<br>**1328–1498** Dynasty of Valois in France.<br>**1329** 7 June, King Robert Bruce d.: succ. David II (–1371). First formal unction and coronation of a Scottish king authorized by Pope John XXII. Edward III of England does homage at Amiens to Philip VI of France for Guyenne and Ponthieu.<br>**1330** 1 May, Convention of Vincennes regulates homage and status of Aquitaine. 29 Nov., Mortimer hanged: Isabel, Queen-Mother of England, exiled.<br><br>**1331** 30 March, Edward III ratifies Treaty of St Germain *re* Aquitaine. 31 March, Edward III does homage to Philip VI of France. Danes defeated by Gerard the Great of Holstein at Danewerk. | **1327** Louis IV of Bavaria becomes King of the Lombards: Galeazzo Visconti of Milan submits.<br><br><br><br><br>**1328** 17 Jan., Louis IV crowned Emperor in Rome. Louis Gonzaga, first of the Gonzaga dynasty of Mantua. Rome taken by John Orsini. Assembly of Pisa. Andronicus III of Byzantium (–1341) seizes the throne from his grandfather, Andronicus II (d. 1332).<br><br><br><br>**1329** Louis IV returns to Germany.<br><br><br><br><br>**1330** 13 Jan., Frederick of Austria d.: 6 Aug., treaty of Haguenau: Louis IV recognized by the Hapsburgs. Serbs defeat the Bulgars at Köstendal.<br>**1330–2** War between Poland and the Teutonic Knights.<br>**1331** John of Bohemia becomes head of the Guelph coalition. Urus III deposed: succ. Stephen III Dushan as King of Serbia (–1355): Stephen III takes Thessalonica. Poland invaded by the Teutonic Knights: defeated at Plowce. | **1328** Amda Sion takes Haqq al-Din prisoner: Ethiopia annexes Ifat and Fatajar.<br><br><br><br><br><br>**c. 1330** Leone Vivaldi reaches Mogadishu: refused passage to Ethiopia.<br><br><br><br>**1331–2** Ibn Battuta visits Zaila, Mogadishu, Mombasa and Kilwa.<br>**c. 1331** Embassy from Mali to Fez. |

| THE NEAR EAST | THE FAR EAST | RELIGION & CULTURE |
|---|---|---|
| | **1324–31** Saw Zein, King of Hanthawaddy.<br>**1324–43** Uzana, King of Pinya. | **1324** 23 March, Pope John XXII excommunicates and deposes Louis of Bavaria. Burgos Cathedral consecrated. Perpignan Cathedral begun. Mosque of Gao built by Ishaq al-Saheli. |
| **1325** Ghiyas al-Din Tughluq Shah murdered: succ. his son Muhammad b. Tughluq (–1351). | **1325** Chinese rise against the Mongols.<br>**1325 or 1328** Chieng Sen founded by Sen Phu. | **1325** Tenochtitlán city, Mexico, founded. University of Paris raises its ban against Thomism.<br>**c. 1325** Frescoes in lower church of St Francis at Assisi painted by Lorenzetti.<br>**? c. 1325–1408** John Gower, poet.<br>**c. 1325–1475** Church of St Mary Redcliffe at Bristol built.<br>**post 1325** Rowel spurs become common in the West. |
| **1326** Tarmashirin, Khan of the Chagatai Mongols, invades Khorasan. Sultan Uthman I d. at Bursa.<br>**1326–59** Urkhan, Ottoman Sultan: first Ottoman to strike coinage: mosques, hospitals and schools built at capital, Bursa: Janissaries founded. | **1326** Champa regain freedom from Vietnam. | **1326** Cathedral of the Assumption built in the Kremlin. Moscow becomes the seat of the Patriarch in place of Kiev. |
| **1327** Rebellion against Muhammad b. Tughluq in the Deccan.<br>**1327–30** Court of Delhi temporarily moved to Daulatabad, but found to be unsuitable. | | **1327** Meister Eckhart, philosopher, d.<br>**c. 1327–1426** Hubert van Eyck, Flemish artist.<br>**1327** Jingereber Mosque, Timbuktu, built. |
| **1328** Rebellion against Muhammad b. Tughluq in Multan and Sind.<br>**1328–9** Tarmashirin invades India: raids to near Delhi. | **1328** Asikipa, Kushala and then Togh Temur (–1332) successively Great Khans and Chinese Emperors. Jayanagara murdered at instigation of Gajah Mada: regency under Princess Tribu (–1350). | **1328** 18 Apr., Emperor Louis IV proclaims Pope John XXII deposed for heresy and *lèse-majesté*.<br>**1328–30** Nicholas V, antipope, in Rome.<br>**c. 1328** Royal Mausoleum, Gao, built. |
| **1329–32** Muhammad b. Tughluq issues debased currency of brass and copper for silver: value destroyed by easy forgery. | **1329** 7.6 m. persons in China said to be starving: total population estimated at 45 m., with 1 m. Mongols.<br>**1329–50** Tribhuvana, ruler of Majapahit. | **1329** Gilbert of Ockham: *Quaestiones de auctoritate. Compendium errorum.* John Eckhart condemned. Retro-choir of Wells Cathedral begun. |
| **1330** The port of Hormuz founded. | | **1330** Ettal Abbey founded. Murals of Braga Cathedral begun. Hall of the Blackheads and Castle, Riga, built.<br>**c. 1330–c. 1400** William Langland, poet. |
| **1331–2** Embassy sent from Delhi to Cairo. | **1331** Saw E, King of Hanthawaddy.<br>**1331–?** Binnya E Law, King of Hanthawaddy, followed by various claimants of uncertain date. Hojo family depose Japanese Emperor Go-Diago: returns after two years with military backing: last Hojo regent, his family and 800 retainers, commit *hara-kiri.* | **1331** 16 Nov., the Holy Roman Rota, supreme court of the Catholic Church, constituted. S transept of Gloucester Abbey begun. |

| WESTERN & NORTHERN EUROPE | CENTRAL, SOUTHERN & EASTERN EUROPE | AFRICA & EGYPT |
|---|---|---|

**1332** Edward, son of John Baliol, leads English army into Scotland: 12 Aug., defeats David II at Duplin Moor Moor: 24 Sept., crowned: 23 Nov., treaty of Roxburgh, recognizing English suzerainty: 16 Dec., flees to England. Robert d'Artois exiled. Sweden takes Schonen from Denmark.
**1333** 19 July, Edward III defeats Scots at Halidon Hill.

**1334** David II of Scotland flees to Château Gaillard, France (−1341). 12 June, treaty of Newcastle: Baliol submits to Edward III: cedes Berwick-on-Tweed. Edward III makes military service obligatory in England.
**1335** Edward III invades Scotland.

**1336** Philip VI invades Is. of Wight and Channel Is. Edward III campaigns in Scotland. Dispute between Edward III and Flanders: Edward bans export of wool to Flanders: staple moved from Bruges to Antwerp.

**1337** Oct., Edward III of England claims French throne: '100 Years War' begins (−1453): Nov., Count of Flanders defeated at Cadsand.
**1338** June, Portsmouth burnt by French; July, Edward III seeks alliances in Flanders and Germany. Ghent rebels against the Count of Flanders.
**1339** Edward III initiates textile industry at Bristol. Oct., Edward III abortively attacks France from Flanders.

**1340** 25 Jan., Edward III of England proclaims himself King of France at Ghent. Philip VI seizes English towns ir Guyenne and Flanders: 24 June, French fleet annihilated by English off Sluys: 25 Sept., truce of Esplechin between England and France. John of Gaunt b.
**1340–75** Waldemar IV, King of Denmark.

**1332** Coalition in Italy against John of Bohemia. John of Bohemia returns to Germany. 7 Nov., Lucerne joins Swiss Confederation.

**1333** Gibraltar retaken by the Arabs.
**1333–70** Casimir III, the Great, King of Poland.

**1334** Stephen III Dushan conquers eastern Macedonia: truce with Andronicus III. Jews in Poland freed from all civil and commercial disabilities.

**1335** Louis IV grants Carinthia to the Hapsburgs.
**1335–6** Negotiations between Pope Benedict XII and Louis of Bavaria break down.
**1336** Byzantines retake Lesbos from Genoa.
**1336–87** Peter the Ceremonious, King of Aragon.

**1337** 5 Sept., treaty of Coblentz: Louis IV of Bavaria allies with Edward III of England against France.

**1339** Treaty between Casimir of Poland and Louis of Hungary: Louis appointed heir to Polish throne, subject to respect for Polish law and custom. Venice takes Treviso.

**1340** Alfonso XI allies with Portugal and Aragon: 5 Apr., Marinid and Hafsid fleets defeat Spanish off Gibraltar. 30 Oct., Muslims defeated near R. Salado.

c. **1332–6** Mossi burn Timbuktu. Songhai loses Gao.

c. **1333–56** Daud b. al-Hasan, Sultan of Kilwa.

**1336–1433** Timbuktu subject to Mali.

**1338** Timbuktu sacked by Mossi.

c. **1339–92** Umar b. Muhammad Sultan of Pate: claims to control coast from Mogadishu to Kerimba Is

**1340–1** Abu Bakr, Bahri Mamluk Sultan.

| THE NEAR EAST | THE FAR EAST | RELIGION & CULTURE |
|---|---|---|
| | **1331—51** Gajah Mada campaigns to compel Java and all the archipelago to unite as Nusantara: East Java, Madura and Bali taken.<br>**1331—64** Gajah Mada, Prime Minister of Majapahit.<br>**1332** Rinchen Pal, Chinese Emperor. | **1332** Theological dispute between Pope John XXII and the University of Paris. Ahmad al-Nuwayri, encyclopaedist, of Cairo, d.<br>**1332—1406** Abd al-Rahman b. Khaldun of Tunis, historian: originator of theory of historical development. |
| **1333** Giovanni di Monte Corvino d.<br>**1333—46** Ibn Battuta in India. | **1333** Arakan raid Burma as far as Thayetmo. | **1333** Philip VI of France supports the University of Paris against Pope John XXII. Königsberg Cathedral begun.<br>**1333—48** John Stratford, Abp of Canterbury.<br>**1334** Napoleon Orsini's conspiracy: Pope John XXII d. The Campanile at Florence begun by Giotto di Bondone. Tower of Salisbury Cathedral begun.<br>**1334—42** Benedict XII, Pope, in Avignon. |
| **1334** Pandyan Kingdom of Madurai revolts successfully against Delhi.<br>**1334—5** Mabar (Coromandal) revolts successfully against Delhi: governor, Ahsan Shah, issues currency in his own name.<br>**1335** Muhammad b. Tughluq leads fruitless expedition against Mabar. Famine in Delhi region.<br>**1335—51** Puppet Il-Khans in Persia. | | **1335** First compound crank recorded in France. Pluralism forbidden. |
| **1336—1411** Jalayr Mongol dynasty in Iraq.<br>**1336—1646** Hindu Empire of Vijayanagar.<br>**1336 fl.** State of Vijayanagar slowly built up by brothers Harihara and Bukka: Harihara, Raja (1336—1354—5).<br>**1336** City of Vijayanagar founded.<br>**9th Apr.**, Timur-i-leng (Tamberlane) b. at Kesh, Transoxiana, of Turkish origins.<br>**1337** Nagarkot (Kangra) annexed by Delhi. | **1336—40** Shwetaungtet, King of Sagaing. | **1336** The *Fraticelli* condemned. Reform of Order of St Benedict begun.<br>**c. 1336** 'King Arthur's Table' at Winchester constructed.<br>**1336** Teylan Mosque, Tripoli, Lebanon, built.<br><br>**1337** Ockham's works condemned by the University of Paris. New choir of Gloucester Abbey begun. |
| **1338** Fakhr al-Din rebels against Muhammad b. Tughluq: Bengal becomes independent (—1576). | **1338—68** Toghan Temur, nominal Great Khan, and Chinese Emperor. | **c. 1338—1406** Jean Froissart, chronicler.<br>**c. 1338—1418** Tao-yen, Chinese monk and philosopher: compiler of encyclopaedia *Yung-lo ta-tien*. |
| **1339 ff.** Muslim dynasty in Kashmir. | **1339—1573** Muromachi period of Japanese history: Shogun Ashikaga Takauji establishes capital at Muromachi: frequent full scale civil war between rival *Shoguns*: emperors reduced to nonentity. | **1339** Grenoble University founded. Map of Africa made by Angelino Dulcert in Mallorca. |
| **1340** Sultanate of Delhi at its greatest extent, with twenty-four provinces. | **1340—50** Kyaswar, King of Sagaing. | **1340** Beginning of persecution of *Cathari* in Bosnia. Bakr b. al-Mundhir al-Baytar d.: author of treatise on veterinary medicine. Troitzkaya monastery founded. Great Mosque of Mazagan built.<br>**c. 1340—1400** Geoffrey Chaucer, poet.<br>**1340—84** Gerard Groote, founder of the Brethren of the Common Life.<br>**c. 1340** The Luttrell Psalter. |

| WESTERN & NORTHERN EUROPE | CENTRAL, SOUTHERN & EASTERN EUROPE | AFRICA & EGYPT |
|---|---|---|
| **1341** 15 Jan., Edward III removes all sheriffs. 30 Apr., John, Duke of Brittany d.: war of succession between Charles de Blois and John de Montfort. Philip VI awards Brittany to Charles de Blois.<br>**1341–53** Simeon, Grand Prince of Moscow.<br>**1342** Edward III of England supports Jean de Montfort in Brittany: Aug., defeated at Morlaix. | **1341** 15 March, Louis IV of Bavaria allies with Philip VI of France. Charles of Luxembourg made Regent of Bohemia.<br>**1341–65** John V, Emperor of Byzantium, first reign: Anne of Savoy, regent (–1347).<br>**1342** Emperor John V purchases the support of Stephen III Dushan.<br>**1342–9** Revolt of Zealots at Salonika.<br>**1342–82** Louis II the Great, King of Hungary. | **1341–2** Qujuq, Bahri Mamluk Sulta<br>c. **1341–60** Sulaiman, King of Mali kingdom re-established.<br><br>**1342** Ahmad, Bahri Mamluk Sultan<br>**1342–5** Ismail, Bahri Mamluk Sulta |
| **1343** Treaty of Malestroit between Edward III and Philip VI. German merchants granted trading privileges at Bergen by Norway.<br>**1343–4** Philip VI purchases Dauphiné from Humbert II. | **1343** Holy League between the Pope, Cyprus, the Knights of Rhodes and Venice. Treaty of Kalisz between Poland and the Teutonic Knights settles boundary questions. Pope Clement VI demands abdication of Louis IV.<br>**1343–4** Peter the Ceremonious conquers Roussillon and the Balearic Is.<br>**1343–82** Jeanne I, Queen of Naples. | |
| **1344** Philip VI makes his son Duke of Orléans. Lord Derby campaigns successfully in Guyenne. | **1344** The Holy League expels Turkish pirates from the Greek Is. Diet of Frankfurt: German Electors refuse papal interference in elections of the King of Germany: support for Louis IV withdrawn: Charles of Luxembourg preferred. Alfonso XI captures Algeciras. | **1344–72** Saifa Harud, Emperor of Ethiopia. |
| **1345** Louis IV takes Frisia, Hainault, Holland and Zeeland. Ghent rebels against James van Artevelde: 24 July, murdered. 21 Oct., Lord Derby defeats French at Auberoche.<br>**1346** Henry of Lancaster campaigns successfully in Aquitaine: 26 Aug., Edward III defeats French at Crécy: first use of cannons in a European battle. Lord Derby takes Poitiers. 27 Oct., Scots defeated at Neville's Cross by army led by Queen Philippa of England: David II taken prisoner. Valdemar of Denmark sells Estonia to the Teutonic Knights. The Black Death begins.<br>**1346–7** English besiege Calais for eleven months: Calais falls: held by English until 1558.<br>**1347** 19 June, English defeat French at La Roche: 3 Aug., Calais surrenders: 28 Sept., truce between England and France. Swedish law codified. Hanseatic merchants organized at Bruges. | **1345** Jeanne of Naples has her husband murdered.<br>**1345–77** Olgierd, ruler of Lithuania.<br><br>**1346** Easter Day, general assembly of Serbian clergy and nobility at Skoplje: Stephen III Dushan elected Emperor: independent Serbian patriarchate inaugurated: code of law promulgated. 11 July, Charles IV of Luxembourg elected Holy Roman Emperor (–1378): receives papal recognition. Pope Clement VI deposes Louis IV of Bavaria.<br><br>**1347** Breach between Stephen Dushan and John VI Cantacuzene. John VI takes Constantinople: duly crowned (–1355). 11 Oct., Louis IV of Bavaria d. Nicholas di Rienzi, dictator of Rome. Polish Diet convened at Wislica: Statute of Wislica defines Polish laws.<br>**1347–50** Louis of Hungary attempts conquest of Naples. | **1345–6** al-Kamil Shaaban, Bahri Mamluk Sultan.<br><br><br>**1346** Jac Ferrer's expedition to Rio d'Oro.<br>**1346–7** al-Muzaffar Hajji, Bahri Mamluk Sultan.<br><br><br><br>**1347–51** al-Hasan, Bahri Mamluk Sultan (first term).<br>**1347** Marinids take Bougie, Constantine and Tunis from the Hafsids. |
| **1348** 23 Apr., Order of the Garter instituted by Edward III. | **1348** Peter IV of Aragon defeats the Aragonese nobility at Epila: 'Privilege of the Union' revoked. Genoa attacks the Byzantine fleet in the Bosporus without success. Despotate of Mistra founded. *Siete Partidas,* encyclopaedia of Spanish law, promulgated. | **1348–55** Egypt devastated by plag c. 900,000 d. in Cairo.<br>**1348–57** Abu Ainan, Marinid. |

| THE NEAR EAST | THE FAR EAST | RELIGION & CULTURE |
|---|---|---|
| | **1341–51** Bhuvanaika Bahu IV, King in Ceylon: capital at Gampola: other rulers at Udarata (Kandy), Kotte and Jaffna. | **1341** Edward III in conflict with Abp Stratford: reconciled by Parliament. 8 Apr., Petrarch crowned Poet Laureate in Rome. **c. 1341** Mosque of al-Hasan, Salé, built. |
| **1342** Muhammad b. Tughluq receives honorary investment from the Caliph in Egypt. | | **1342–52** Clement VI, Pope, in Avignon. |
| **1343** City of Vijayanagar completed. | **1343–50** Ngarsishia, King of Pinya. | **1343** 27 Jan., Pope Clement VI: Bull *Unigenitus Dei*: each fiftieth year to be kept as a Jubilee Year, Gold florins first minted in England. |
| **1344** The Holy League takes Smyrna. **1344–50** The Deccan and Malwa reorganized administratively: disorder ensues as far as Gujarat: sultan fails to restore order. | | **1344** Prague Cathedral begun: made an archepiscopal see. |
| | | **1345–1430** Perugia Cathedral built. |
| **1346** Shah Mirza seizes throne of Kashmir from Hindu ruler, marrying his widow. | | **1346** Valladolid University founded. Mosque of Misbahiya, Fez, built. |
| **1347–58** Ala al-Din Hasan Shah al-Wali al-Bahmani, first Bahmani Sultan of the Deccan: capital at Gulbarga. | | **1347** Chester Bridge built. |
| **1348** The Black Death starts in Asia, gradually spreading into the Mediterranean and all Europe (–1353). | | **1348** Prague University founded. Giovanni Villani, Florentine historian, d. **1348–53** Giovanni Boccaccio: *Il Decamerone*. **c. 1348–1400** Wadi al-Natrun monasteries almost depopulated by Black Death. **c. 1348** Banks established by Florence in France, England, Italy and Constantinople. |

| WESTERN &<br>NORTHERN EUROPE | CENTRAL, SOUTHERN<br>& EASTERN EUROPE | AFRICA & EGYPT |
|---|---|---|
| **1349** Philip VI purchases Montpellier and Dauphiné. | **1348** Stephen III Dushan takes Janina. Pope Clement VI buys Avignon.<br>**1349** Günther of Schwarzburg, elected rival Holy Roman Emperor: then d. Diet of Skoplje: Stephen Dushan promulgates code of law.<br>**1349—52** Casimir of Poland takes Galicia.<br>**1349—87** Charles the Bad, King of Navarre. | **1349** Ibn Battuta returns to Tangier from his travels. |
| **1350** 29 Aug., English defeat Spanish fleet off Winchelsea. Rienzi imprisoned by Charles IV.<br>**1350—64** John II, King of France. | **1350** 14 Feb., Treaty of Bautzen: Wittelsbachs recognize Charles IV: granted Brandenburg and Tyrol. Stephen III Dushan repels Byzantine attack in Macedonia.<br>**1350—5** War between Genoa and Venice.<br>**1350—69** Peter I, King of Castile, 'the Cruel': intense struggle for the succession: royal family executed ruthlessly. | |
| **1351** Statute of Labourers, intended to check rise of wages, in England. | **1351** Stephen III Dushan besieges Thessalonica. Swabian League formed. Zurich joins Swiss Confederation. | **1351—4** al-Salih, Bahri Mamluk Sultan. |
| **1352** English Statute of Treasons defines the offence. Charles IV sends Rienzi as a prisoner to the Pope. English take Guisnes: defeat French in Brittany. | **1352** 14 Jan., peace made between Louis of Hungary and Jeanne of Naples. Glarus and Zug join Swiss Confederation. Austria at war with Zurich. Orkhan defeats Stephen III Dushan at Demotika. | **1352—3** Ibn Battuta visits Western Africa. |
| **1353** Edward III: *Ordinatio stapularum:* wool staple moved from Bruges to England. Simeon the Proud of Russia d. from the Black Death together with many of his subjects.<br>**1353—9** Ivan II of Russia: real power in the hands of Metropolitan Alexis Plechtcheiev. | **1353** Berne joins Swiss Confederation.<br>**1353—7** Cardinal Albornoz, legate, re-establishes authority in the Papal States.<br>**1353—90** Rupert I, Elector Palatine. | **1353—76** Idris, King of Kanem. |
| **1354** Alliance between France and Scotland. | **1354** Fresh Lombard League established. Pope Innocent VI sends Rienzi to Rome: dictatorship re-established: 8 Oct., murdered. Charles IV visits Italy: the Visconti made Imperial Legates. Ottomans attack fortress of Gallipoli: walls collapse from an earthquake: Europe opened to Ottomans: Turks seize and fortify empty cities.<br>**1354—7** Matthew Cantacuzene, Eastern European Emperor, as associate with his father. | **1354—61** al-Hasan, Bahri Mamluk Sultan (second term). |
| **1355** Aug., English defeated by Scots at Nesbit. | **1355** John VI Cantacuzene compelled to abdicate by John V. 5 Apr., Charles IV crowned Emperor in Rome: opposed by Czech nobility. | |

| THE NEAR EAST | THE FAR EAST | RELIGION & CULTURE |
|---|---|---|
| | c. 1349 State of Tumasik said to be engaging in piracy. | 1349 Persecution of Jews in Germany. 29 Sept., Richard Rolle, mystic, d. St Brigid of Sweden settles in Rome. Pope Clement VI condemns the Flagellants. |
| | 1350 Thai prince founds Kingdom of Ayuthia in Menam valley: becomes known as the Kingdom of Shan, eventually Siam (Thailand). Nawrahtaminye, King of Sagaing, followed by Tarabyange. The 'Blood Bath of Bubat': Gajah Mada attempts to gain Sunda by stratagem. Malacca founded by refugees from Java. c. 1350 *Tainui, Te Arawa, Aotea, Takitimu* and *Tokomaru* canoes from Polynesia bring ancestors of many modern Maori tribes to New Zealand. 1350–9 Kyawswange, King of Pinya. 1350–89 Rajasanagara or Hyam Wuruk, King of Majapahit. | 1350 St Vincent Ferrer, OP, preacher. |
| 1351 Amir Qazghan of Transoxiana besieges Herat: Kurt made vassal. Bahmani, having conquered the Deccan, in possession of Goa and Dabhol. March, Muhammad b. Tughluq d.: 23 March, succ. Firuz Shah Tughluq (–1388), enthroned by the army. | 1351 Dykes on the Yellow River burst: 175,000 men employed to repair them: revolts in many parts of China. | 1351 English Statute of Provisions forbids papal provisions and reservations. 1351–1427 Cho Denshu, Japanese artist. |
| | 1352 S Chinese first admitted to official positions under the Mongols. Kuo Tzu-hsing leads rising against Mongols in S Honan. 1352–64 Minbyank, King of Sagaing. | 1352 Antwerp Cathedral begun. Ranulph Higden: *Polychronicon*. 1352–62 Innocent VI, Pope, in Avignon. |
| 1353–4 Firuz Shah leads fruitless campaign against Bengal. | 1353 Kuo links his movement with Chu Yuan-chang: contacts with secret White Lotus Society. Kingdom of Lan Chang founded in Laos. 1353–85 Binnya U, King of the Mons, King of Hanthawaddy. | 1353 Edward III: Statute *De praemunire:* English clergy forbidden to appeal to Rome, Cloisters of Windsor Castle built. Boccaccio: *Decamerone*. |
| 1354/5–77 Bukka, Raya of Vijayanagar: constant wars against the Bahmani. | | |
| | 1355 Kuo d.: Chu takes over his army. | 1355–1417 Tsong Kapa, founder of the Yellow Lamas. |

| WESTERN & NORTHERN EUROPE | CENTRAL, SOUTHERN & EASTERN EUROPE | AFRICA & EGYPT |
|---|---|---|
| **1355** The Black Prince (Edward, Prince of Wales), appointed Lieutenant in Gascony: allied with Kingdom of Navarre: disembarks English army at Bordeaux. | **1355** Congress at Buda: Louis of Hungary makes further promises respecting the Polish throne. Stephen III Dushan attempts to take Constantinople: then d.: Serbian realm collapses: succ. Urus IV (−1370). | |
| **1356** Feb., English raid on Scotland. The Black Prince raids from Bordeaux up the Loire: 19 Sept., defeats John II of France at Poitiers: John II and his son Philip taken prisoner: France ruled by the Dauphin (−1357). French States-General meets: reforms demanded by Etienne Marcel. | **1356** 26 Dec., Charles IV issues Golden Bull: remains constitution of Holy Roman Empire until 1806. War between Hungary and Venice. Peace made between Austria and Zurich. | |
| **1357** 23 May, two year truce between England and France concluded at Bordeaux. 3 Oct., David II of Scotland liberated by Treaty of Berwick. Council of Scone. French States-General vote standing army of 30,000. Rebellion in Paris led by Etienne Marcel and Robert le Coq (−1358). | **1357** Cardinal Albornoz issues *Constitutiones Aegidianae*: remains code of law of the Papal States until 1816. Polish statute of *Privilegia Judaeorum* defines Jewish privileges. **1357—67** Pedro I, the Cruel, King of Portugal. | **1357** Abu Inan campaigns against Constantine and Tunis. |
| **1358** Jan., preliminary treaty of peace between England and France. Etienne Marcel allies with the *Jacquerie*, rising of peasants against the war with England: Charles the Bad puts down the *Jacquerie*: takes Paris: rebellion against Etienne Marcel, who d. | **1358** Venice cedes Dalmatia to Hungary. Austria twice defeated by Zurich: peace made by Austria with Swiss Confederation. **1358—67** Cardinal Albornoz's second term as legate in the Papal States. | **1358—9** Muhammad, Marinid. **1358—89** Abu Hammu Musa II, Abdulwadid. |
| **1359** 24 March, French Estates-General rejects treaty of London, restoring to Edward III all Henry II's French dominions. Nov., Edward III invades France. Edward III grants English merchants in the Netherlands self-government. John of Gaunt m. Blanche of Lancaster: becomes Duke of Lancaster *iure uxoris*. **1359—62** Dimitri II, Grand Duke of Moscow. | | |
| **1360** 11 Jan., treaty of Guillon between England and Burgundy. 8 May, treaty of Brétigny: John of France ransomed for 3m. *écus* of gold: France abandons claims to Guyenne, Ponthieu, Guines and Calais to England. 24 Oct., treaty of Calais: Duchy of Aquitaine restored to England. Waldemar IV of Denmark regains Schonen from Sweden. | **1360—1** The Turks take Philippopolis and Adrianople. | **1360—74** Mari Diata II, King of Mali. |
| **1361** Waldemar IV takes Visby, Gothland. Burgundy reunited with the French Crown. **1361—7** Lionel, Duke of Clarence, lieutenant of Ireland. | **1361** Peter I of Cyprus takes Adalia and Korikos. Adrianople (now Edirne) made the Ottoman capital: Ottoman power begins to shift from Asia Minor to Europe: Demotika and Seres taken. | **1361—3** Muhammad, Bahri Mamluk Sultan. |
| **1362** Brittany conquered by Jean de Montfort. English wool staple transferred to Calais. Edward III of England grants to his son, the Black Prince, the Duchy of Aquitaine: capital at Bordeaux. Hanseatic towns, with Sweden and the Teutonic Knights, at war with Denmark: defeated by Waldemar IV off Helsingborg. | | |

| THE NEAR EAST | THE FAR EAST | RELIGION & CULTURE |
|---|---|---|
| | **1355-68** Chu conducts many small campaigns, gradually taking China from the Mongols. | |
| | **1356** Ayuthia and Chengmai attack Mons in Lower Burma: all Tenasserim coast taken: King Binnya U of Lower Burma moves capital to Pegu.<br>**1359-64** Narathu, King of Pinya. | **1356** Mosque of Sultan Hasan in Cairo: provides accommodation for four orthodox schools of law. |
| | | **1357** The Waldenses murder two inquisitors in Provence. |
| **1358-73** Muhammad b. Ala al-Din, Bahmani Sultan: wars against Vijayanagar and Warangel: believed to have killed ½m. Hindus. | | **fl. c. 1358-78** William of Cologne, German artist.<br>**1358-1408** Shogun Yoshimitsu, patron of the arts.<br>**1358** Murcia Cathedral begun. |
| **1359** Firuz Shah campaigns abortively in Bengal: successful raid on Puri, Orissa.<br>**1359-89** Murad I, Ottoman Sultan. | | **1359** Nave of Vienna Cathedral begun. |
| **1360** Independent kingdom of Khwarazm founded by Husain Sufi.<br>**March**, Timur-i-leng takes control of Kesh, Transoxiana. | | **1360** Pope Innocent VI reforms the Order of Preachers (Dominicans). Crusade against the Cathari in Bosnia.<br>**1360-1402** The Alcazar built at Seville.<br>**c. 1360-1500** 'Precocious' period of Benin art. |
| **1361** Timur-i-leng becomes viceroy of Transoxiana. | | **1361** Pavia University founded.<br>**post 1361** The choir of York Minster reconstructed: Lady Chapel begun. |
| **1362-3** Firuz Shah's expeditions against Sind a disaster. | | **1362** William Langland: *Piers Plowman*. English used for first time in Parliament by Edward III: English ordered in the law courts. Sultan al-Hasan Mosque built in Cairo.<br>**1362-70** Urban V, Pope, in Avignon to October 1367. |

| WESTERN & NORTHERN EUROPE | CENTRAL, SOUTHERN & EASTERN EUROPE | AFRICA & EGYPT |
|---|---|---|
| **1362** Dimitri Donskoi succ. to Russian throne aged 13 (–1389): Metropolitan Alexis real power during his minority.<br>**1363** Magnus, King of Sweden, deposed by Albert of Mecklenburg: succ. Albert (–1389). | **1363** Rudolf of Austria obtains the Tyrol. Battle near Adrianople: Slavs and Hungarians defeated by Ottomans. Casimir the Great of Poland arbitrator in dispute between Emperor Charles IV and Louis, King of Hungary. | **1363–76** al-Ashraf Shaaban, Bahri Mamluk Sultan. |
| **1364** 29 Sept., Jean de Montfort defeats and kills Charles de Blois at Auray. 16 May, Du Guesclin overcomes Jean de Grailly, commander of the troops of John the Bad, King of Navarre, at Cocherel.<br>**1364–80** Charles V, King of France. | **1364** 10 Feb., formal family agreement between the houses of Luxembourg and Hapsburg at Brünn. Crete rebels against Venice.<br>**1364–5** The Swiss Confederation occupies Zug. | **1364** Alleged first visits of the Dieppois to Guinea and Senegal.<br>**1364–5** Famine in Egypt. |
| **1365** Treaty of Brittany: Brittany awarded to de Montfort family: house of Blois awarded Penthièvre and Limoges. 4 June, Charles IV crowned at Arles as King of Burgundy: allies with France: makes the Dauphin his vicar. Treaty of St Denis: end of war between France and Navarre.<br>**1366** Feb., Parliament of Kilkenny: many reforms made in favour of English colonists. | **1365** Genoa occupies Soldaia and Balaclava. Henry of Trastamare rebels against Pedro the Cruel.<br><br>**1366** Amadeus of Savoy campaigns against the Turks in Gallipoli. Macedonia separated from Serbia. Following war with Russia, Volhynia taken by Poland.<br>**1366–9** France troubled by roaming bands of armed landless peasants: sent by Charles to Spain under du Guesclin to serve Henry of Trastamare, in rebellion against his brother Pedro the Cruel, King of Castile: Henry crowned at Burgos: Pedro flees to the Black Prince at Bordeaux. | **1365** Peter I of Cyprus pillages Alexandria.<br><br>**1366** Riots between Mamluks in Cairo. |
| **1367** May, Dublin Parliament orders absentee landlords to reside in Ireland. Nov. 19, Hanse confederation formed at Cologne against Waldemar of Denmark.<br><br>**1368** The Cologne league takes Copenhagen. The Black Prince condemned by the Parliament of Paris *in absentia*: Armagnac rises against him. | **1367** The Black Prince joins in war against Castile: 3 Apr., defeats Pedro the Cruel at Nájera: captures Bertrand du Guesclin.<br>**1367–83** Ferdinand I, King of Portugal. | **1367** Further riots in Cairo. |
| **1369** Peace between England an Scotland for fourteen years. | **1369** Venice repels Hungarian invasion. Peter I of Cyprus assassinated: succ. Peter II. | c. **1369–1437** Etsu Ede, King of Nupe.<br>**1369–93** Abu al-Abbas Ahmad II, Hafsid. |

**THE NEAR EAST**    **THE FAR EAST**    **RELIGION & CULTURE**

**1363—5** Timur-i-leng makes Transoxiana virtually independent.

**1363** 4 Aug., Pope Urban V extends right of reservation to all monasteries and bishoprics. Gui de Chauliac: *Chirurgie.*
**1363—5** François Borel, inquisitor, drives the Waldenses across the Alps.
**1363—1428** Jean Charlier de Gerson, theologian.
**1364** Cracow University founded.
**1364—1442** Taqi al-Din Ahmad al-Maqrizi, historian of Egypt.

**1364—1555** Kings of Ava (Shan-Burmese dynasty), Burma. Uzana, King of Pinya: assassinated by Thadominbya, founder of the Ava dynasty. King of Pinya allies with Maw Shans against Sagaing, abandoning them in battle: Maw Shans take Sagaing and Pinya, and all Upper and Central Burma: Thai Empire established throughout almost all Indo-China: Maw Shans suddenly abandon possessions, returning to the N of Burma: new Burmese dynasty set up at Ava by Thadominbya. Gajah Mada d.: Majapahit gaining considerable share in spice trade. Council of five ministers appointed to rule Majapahit by Hyam Wuruk: elaborate civil service. Minbyauk, King of Sagaing, assassinated by Thadominbya, King of Ava.

**1365** Abu Said, last Ilkhan of Persia, d.: Ilkhan dominions dissolve.

**1365** Statute of *Praemunire* renewed. Charles IV visits Avignon. University of Vienna instituted.
Propança: *Nagarakertama,* historical panegyric of Kingdom of Majapahit.

**1366** Ottoman capital transferred to Adrianople (Edrine) from Bursa.

**1366** 25 Jan., Henry Suso, mystic, d. England refuses to pay taxes to the Pope. Durham Cathedral kitchen built.

**1367** Peter I of Cyprus pillages the Syrian coast.

**1367** Pope Urban V leaves Avignon for Rome: 16 Oct., solemn entry. William of Wykeham made Lord Chancellor (—1376) and Bishop of Winchester. New College, Oxford, founded by William of Wykeham.
post **1368** Observant Franciscans founded.

**1368** Sikander Shah builds Adina Mosque at Pandua, with 400 small domes.

**1368** Chu Yuan-chang proclaimed first Emperor of the Ming dynasty: capital at Peking: widespread reform of government.
**1368—1401** Swasawke, King of Ava.
**1368—1644** Ming dynasty in China.

**1369** Timur-i-leng proclaimed ruler at Samarqand.

**1369** Monastery of St Tekla Haimanot built. Geoffrey Chaucer: *Boke of the Duchesse.*

| WESTERN & NORTHERN EUROPE | CENTRAL, SOUTHERN & EASTERN EUROPE | AFRICA & EGYPT |
|---|---|---|

**1369** Following complaints against the Black Prince, Charles V summons him to court: he refuses: Du Guesclin sent against him: English steadily reduced by guerrilla tactics, until only Bayonne, Brest, Bordeaux, Calais and Cherbourg are left to them.
**1370** 19 Sept., the Black Prince sacks Limoges. Sept., French defeat English near Paris: Dec, and in Gascony and Maine. Hanse towns make treaty of Stralsund with Denmark and Norway. Owain ap Thomas proclaims himself Prince of Wales.
**1371** English defeat Flemings off Bourgneuf. Franco-Scottish treaty renewed. Mongols in Russia in confusion following succession dispute.
**1371–3** Charles V reconquers Poitou, l'Aunis and Saintonge.
**1371–90** Robert II, King of Scots: first king of the house of Stewart.
**1372** 23 June, English defeated off La Rochelle by France and Castile. 7 Aug., English take Poitiers: Brittany occupied. Sept., French take Angoulême and La Rochelle. Treaty of Vincennes between France and Scotland. Owain of Wales allied with France: June, takes Guernsey. Two clerical proctors from each diocese added to commons in Irish Parliament.
**1373** England imposes Tunnage and Poundage upon foreign traders. Treaty of friendship between England and Portugal. England invades France from Calais to Bordeaux.

**1375** 27 June, truce of Bruges between England and France: English confined to Bayonne, Bordeaux and Calais. Waldemar IV of Denmark d.: quarrels *re* succession follow. Sixty Irish representatives attend English Parliament. Dimitri of Moscow defeats Tartars of Kazan: imposes tribute. Peace between Tver and Moscow: Prince of Tver recognized as 'younger brother' of Prince of Moscow.
**1376** Apr.–July, the 'Good Parliament': Commons make first impeachments before Lords. 8 June, the Black Prince d.
**1376–87** Olaf V, King of Denmark.
**1376–1417** Art Oge MacMurrough, King of Leinster.

**1369** Pedro the Cruel of Castile killed by Henry of Trastamare (succ. –1379). John of Gaunt proclaims himself King of Castile, but is not recognized. Throne also claimed by Ferdinand I of Portugal.

**1370** 17 Feb., Teutonic Knights defeat Lithuanians at Rudau. 3 Nov., Casimir the Great of Poland d.: throne bequeathed to Louis of Hungary (–1382).
**1370–1** Sultan Murad I conquers Bulgaria.

**1371** Sultan Murad I defeats the Serbs on the Maritza.

**1372** Jeanne of Naples renounces her rights in Sicily: 27 Aug., Sicily occupied by Frederick III of Aragon. Lazarus reunifies northern Serbia.

**1373** Treaty of Fürstenwalde: Charles IV obtains Brandenburg.
**1373–4** Sultan Murad I occupies western Thrace.

**1374** Emperor John V recognizes Sultan Murad as suzerain. Pact of Koszyce: Polish nobility granted freedom from all duties and services to the state. Peace made between Aragon and Castile.
**1374–7** Charles IV obtains part of Mecklenburg.
**1375** 'War of the Hooded Men': Switzerland invaded by English, French and Welsh mercenaries. Nish taken by the Ottomans.

**1376** 6 July, Wenceslaus, son of Charles IV, elected King of the Romans. Swabian League reorganized.
**1376–9** Andronicus IV usurps the throne from his father, John V.

**1372–82** Neonya Mariam of Ethiopia: further troubles with Ifat.

**1374–81** Musa II, King of Mali.

**1376–81** Ala al-Din Ali, Bahri Mamluk Sultan.

| THE NEAR EAST | THE FAR EAST | RELIGION & CULTURE |
|---|---|---|
| | | **1369** John V Palaeologus visits Rome: recognizes Papal Supremacy. **1369—1444** Leonardo Bruno, biographer. |
| **1370** 10 Apr., Timur-i-leng proclaimed king in Balkh. **1370—1** Khan Jehan, chief minister of Firoz Shah d. **1370—81** Ghiyath al-Din, King of Herat. | | **1370** Brigittine Order recognized. 17 Apr., Pope Urban V returns to Avignon; d. 19 Dec. **1370—8** Gregory XI, Pope: reigning partly in Avignon and partly in Rome. **1370—1430** Andrea Rublyov, iconographer. **? 1370—? 1450** John Lydgate, poet. |
| **1371** Timur-i-leng takes Khiva from Khwarazm, followed by Kath. | **1371** Kings of Ava and Pegu meet to demarcate the frontier. Maw Shans submit to Ava as vassals. Champa invade Red River Valley: Hanoi pillaged. | **1371** London Charterhouse begun. |
| **1373—8** Mujahid b. Muhammad, Bahmani Sultan. | **1373—93** Maw Shans recommence raiding Burmese territory. | **1373** Froissart: *Chronicles.* |
| | | **1374** Last persecution of the Cathari at Toulouse. |
| **1375** End of the Kingdom of Lesser Armenia. | **1375—6** Timur-i-leng campaigns against Qamar al-Din. | **1375** First Aztec ruler elected. Nave of Westminster Abbey begun. |
| | | **1376** Stephen Tvrtko makes Catharism the official religion of Bosnia. |

## WESTERN & NORTHERN EUROPE

## CENTRAL, SOUTHERN & EASTERN EUROPE

## AFRICA & EGYPT

**1377** 22 June, Edward III of England d.: succ. his grandson, Richard II (−1399). English Parliament institutes poll tax.

**1378** Charles V seizes Charles the Bad's possessions in Normandy. England acquires Brest and Cherbourg. Owain of Wales killed. Scots recover Berwick-on-Tweed. Dimitri of Moscow defeats Tartars on the R. Voja.

**1379** Brittany rises against Charles V. English recover Berwick-on-Tweed. Rebellion in Flanders.

**1380** Nov., graduated poll tax increased in England. English Parliament, by Statute of Absentees, requires absentee Irish landlords to return under pain of confiscation of two-thirds of their property. Du Guesclin d. at siege of Châteauneuf-Randon. Charles V of France d.: creator of French *Parlement:* founder of the *Bibliothèque Royale,* now the *Bibliothèque Nationale.* Olaf V, King of Denmark, becomes King of Norway (−1387). Dimitri of Moscow defeats Mongols at Kulikov on R. Don: regarded as a national hero as the first Russian to defeat the Mongols: Moscow then taken by Mongols through treachery and sacked.
**1380–1422** Charles VI, King of France.
**1381** The Peasants' Revolt in Essex and Kent, led by Wat Tyler: spreads to St Albans, Bury St Edmunds and Cambridge: John of Gaunt's Palace burnt in the Strand: 14 June, Simon Sudbury, Abp of Canterbury, beheaded.
**1382** 26 Aug., Moscow burnt by the Mongols. 27 Nov., Flemings and French defeat Ghent citizens at Roosebeke. Maillotin rising in Paris and Rouen.

**1377** 21 May, Swabian League defeats Ulrich of Württemburg at Reutlingen. Jagellon, Duke of Lithuania.

**1378** Peace between Florence and the Papal States. The Ciompi rebel in Florence. Unrest in Rome. Red Russia incorporated into Hungary.
**1378–81** War of Chioggia: Venice defeats Genoa.
**1378–1400** Wenceslaus IV of Luxembourg, Holy Roman Emperor.

**1379** 25 Sept., treaty of Neuberg: Hapsburg possessions partitioned between Albert III and Leopold III. Henry II of Trastamare d. Navarrese invasion ends Catalan dominion in Greece. Andronicus IV Palaeologos deposed.
**1379–90** John V Palaeologos, Eastern Roman Emperor restored with Turkish aid.
**1379–90** John I, King of Castile.
**1380** English army sent to Portugal to join in war against Castile: fleet of Castile and France defeated off Ireland. Sultan Murad I takes Monastir. Charles of Durazzo rebels.

**1381** 17 June, Swabian and Rhenish Leagues ally. Charles of Durazzo takes Naples. Peace of Turin between Byzantium and Genoa.

**1382** Jeanne of Naples d.: succ. Charles III of Durazzo (−1386): contested by Louis d'Anjou. 11 Sept., Louis I of Hungary and Poland d.: Hungary and Poland separated: succ. in Hungary his daughter Maria (−1385): *interregnum* in Poland (−1384).
**1382–1402** Morea in the hands of the Company of Navarre.
**1383** Genoa pillages Cyprus: Famagusta occupied.

**1381–2** al-Salih Hajji, Bahri Mamluk Sultan (first term).

**1382–1516** Burji Mamluk dynasty in Egypt.
**1382–99** al-Zahir Sayf al-Din Barquq first Burji Mamluk Sultan of Egypt.
**1382–1411** David I of Ethiopia.

## THE NEAR EAST

**1377—1404** Harihara II, Raya of
Vijayanagar: period of peace and
consolidation.

**1378** Daud, Bahmani Sultan:
murdered by a slave.
**1378—97** Muhammad II, Bahmani
Sultan.

**1379** Timur-i-leng takes Urgenj: all
Khwarazm annexed to Transoxiana.

**1380—93** Timur-i-leng campaigns in
Afghanistan, Persia and Kurdistan.

**1381** Timur-i-leng takes Herat and
Khurasan.
**1381—2** Timur-i-leng campaigning in
Persia.

**1383** Timur-i-leng again campaigns in
Persia and Afghanistan: Kandahar
taken.

## THE FAR EAST

**1377** Malayu independent: king
obtains title of King of Sri Vijaya
from Chinese Emperor.

## RELIGION & CULTURE

**1377** Court of the Lions begun in the
Alhambra. Cloisters built in Gloucester
Abbey. Ulm Cathedral begun.
Concordat between Rome and England.
**1377—8** John Wycliffe tried and
acquitted.
**1378** Pope Gregory XI d.: Urban VI
(—1389) elected in Rome: Clement VII
(—1394) elected at Fondi: Great
Schism begun. Winchester College
founded.
**1378—84** John Wycliffe attacking
ecclesiastical abuses, the Papacy and the
Mass.
**1378—1411** Nave of Canterbury
Cathedral rebuilt.
**1378—1455** Lorenzo Ghiberti, sculptor.
**1379** Feast of the Visitation of the
B.V.M. instituted by Pope Urban VI.
Antipope Clement VII removes to
Avignon after being defeated in Italy.
Great Mosque, Bursa, begun.
**1379—98** Hôtel de Ville at Bruges
built by Pierre van Ost.
**c. 1379—1446** Filippo Brunnelleschi,
architect and sculptor.
**1379—1471** St Thomas a Kempis,
mystical writer.
**1380** 29 Apr., St Catherine of Siena d.
*Societas magna Alemaniae* founded by
Joseph Hompys, New College begun.
Choir of York Minster and nave of
Palma Cathedral, Majorca, begun.
**1380—1420** Kabir, Indian philosopher.
**c. 1380—1451** Lin Leang, Chinese
painter.
**1380—1459** Giovanni Francesco Poggio
Bracciolini, historian.
**c. 1380—c. 1460** Fernão Lopes,
chronicler.
**c. 1380** Meister Wilhelm, Cologne
master painter, do. Forty Muslim
missionaries working in Kano.

**1381** The University of Paris requests
an ecumenical council to resolve the
papal schism.

**1382** 'Black Madonna' brought to
Czestochowa.
**1382—4** Wycliffe's translation of the
Bible (by various hands): first
consecutive English prose work.

| WESTERN & NORTHERN EUROPE | CENTRAL, SOUTHERN & EASTERN EUROPE | AFRICA & EGYPT |
|---|---|---|

**1383** John I of Castile proclaims himself King of Portugal *iure uxoris:* Portuguese revolt: John of Aviz acclaimed regent as John I (−1385).

**1384** Feb., war between England and Scotland. Philip of Burgundy becomes Count of Flanders, Artois and Franche Comté *iure uxoris.* Louis d'Anjou d. Rebellion in Liège.

**1384** March, Polish burghers formally given the right to sit in council with the clergy and nobles.
**1384−6** Hedvig, Queen of Poland.

**1385** 1 May, war between England and France renewed. Peace of Tournai between Philip of Burgundy and Flanders. Richard II of England raids Scotland.

**1385** Gian Galeazzo Visconti in sole power in Milan. Breach between Pope Urban VI and Charles of Durazzo. Swabian and Rhenish Leagues ally with Swiss Confederation. Sultan Murad I takes Sofia. Battle of Aljubarrota secures House of Aviz on the Portuguese throne against Castile.
**1385−1433** John I, King of Portugal.

**1386** Oct., Council of Eleven appointed by English Parliament. John of Gaunt returns to Castile to press his wife's claim to the throne: a military failure: daughter Philippa of Lancaster m. John I of Portugal: daughter Constance m. Henry, Prince of Asturias, heir to Castile.

**1386** 27 Feb., Charles III of Durazzo d.: quarrel for succession between Louis II of Anjou (−1400) and Ladislas, Charles III's son. 4 March, Jagellon, Grand Duke of Lithuania, crowned King of Poland as Wladislaw II (−1434): powers of Polish nobility increased: Kiev reconstituted as a state. July, Swiss defeat and kill Leopold III of Austria at Sempach. Formal treaty of alliance between England and Portugal 'for ever': oldest treaty at present in existence. Sultan Murad I takes Nish.
**1386−1572** Jagellon dynasty in Poland.

**1386** Haqq al-Din of Ifat killed in battle with David I of Ethiopia.

**1387** Parliament accuses Richard II's favourites of treason and incompetence. Louis d'Orléans m. Valentina Visconti. 3 Aug., Margaret the Great, Queen of Denmark (−1412): Queen of Norway from 1388 and of Sweden from 1389.

**1387** Murad takes Salonica. Balkan League formed by Lazarus of Serbia against the Ottomans. 31 March, Sigismund of Luxembourg becomes King of Hungary *iure uxoris* (−1437).
**1387−95** John I, King of Aragon.

**1388** 3 Feb.−4 June, the 'Merciless Parliament': Burley, Tresilian, and other royal favourites hanged. 19 Aug., English defeated Scots at Otterburn.

**1388** Swabian and Rhenish Leagues defeated at Döffingen and Worms.

**1388±60** Second stage of Mapungub culture, Rhodesia.

**1389** 24 Feb., Danes defeat Albert of Sweden at Falköping: Sweden joined with Denmark. Three year truce of Boulogne between England, France and Scotland.
**1389−1425** Vassili II Grand Prince of Moscow and Vladimir.
**1389−1439** Eric of Pomerania, King of Norway.

**1389** 15 June, Battle of Kossovo Polie: Serb army destroyed: Turco-Serb alliance follows: Sultan Murad killed: succ. Bayazid (−1401): conquest of Karaman and Konia follows: with Anatolia, Cappadocia and other parts of Cappadocia.

**1389−91** al-Salih Hajji, Bahri Mamlu Sultan (last Bahri Mamluk ruler).

**1390−1** Franco-Scottish treaty renewed.
**1390−1406** Robert III, King of Scots.

**1390−1** John VII usurps the Byzantine throne for several months.
**1390−2** Crusade of Henry of Lancaster in Lithuania.
**1390−1406** Henry III, King of Castile.
**1391** Sultan Bayazid claims all Byzantine possessions: besieges Constantinople: invades Thessaly: conquers Serbia, Adalia, and Philadelphia: Sigismund of Hungary raises Crusading army against the Turks.

**1390−1410** Kanajeji, King of Kano: introduces quilted armour and iron helmets.
**1390−1517** Burji Mamluk dynasty.

**1391** English Statute of Provisors re-enacted. Statute of Mortmain enacted.

| THE NEAR EAST | THE FAR EAST | RELIGION & CULTURE |
|---|---|---|
| | | **1384** Mosque of Sultan Barquq built in Cairo. |
| **1385–6** Azerbaijan pillaged by Toqtamish. | **1385–1423** Razadarit, King of Hanthawaddy. <br> **1385–1425** Forty Years War between Ava and Pegu. | **1385** Batalha Abbey begun. Bodiam Castle begun. Geoffrey Chaucer: *Troilus and Criseyde.* |
| **1386** Timur-i-leng takes western Persia, and then Georgia and Armenia. Azerbaijan annexed by Timur-i-leng. | **1386** Further abortive expedition from Ava against Pegu: army repulsed. | **1386** Heidelburg University founded. <br> **1386 fl.** Donatello (Donato di Betto Bardi), sculptor. <br> **c. 1386–1440** Jan van Eyck, painter. <br> **1386–1466** Donatello (Donato di Betto Bardi), sculptor. |
| **1387** Qiptchaq rebellion in Transoxiana put down by Timur-i-leng. Nov., Timur-i-leng takes Hamadan, Isfahan and Shiraz. Toqtamish campaigns against Timur-i-leng in Persia. | **1387** Chinese begin to build fortifications in S China against Japanese pirates (–1467). | **1387** Milan Cathedral, only Gothic cathedral in Italy, begun. See of Vilno founded: evangelization of Lithuania begun. Winchester College begun. <br> **1387–1400** Geoffrey Chaucer: *The Canterbury Tales.* <br> **1387–1455** Fra Giovanni da Fiesole Angelico, artist. |
| **1388** Timur-i-leng assumes title of Sultan. Sept., Firuz Shah d.: no obvious successor. Faruqi dynasty of Khandesh founded (–1601). Toqtamish attacks Transoxiana. <br> **1389** c. Jan., Timur-i-leng defeats Toqtamish north of the R. Sir Darya. <br> **1389–90** Timur-i-leng campaigns in Mughulistan. | **1388** Pegu army enters Ava territory: inconclusive battle: patched-up peace until 1401. <br><br> **1389** Ayam Wuruk of Majapahit d.: chaos in Mujapahit: Vikramarvaddhana ruler (–1429). | **1388** Lollards persecuted in England. Cologne University founded. Dominican convent, Batalha, begun. Oviedo Cathedral rebuilt. <br><br> **1389** Pope Urban VI orders each thirty-third year to be kept as a Year of Jubilee. Convent of the Assumption, Moscow, built. <br> **1389–1404** Boniface IX, Pope, at Rome. |
| | **c. 1390** Parameswara, future ruler of Malacca, lands on Tumasik Is. (Singapore). | **1390** Elgin Cathedral burnt by Alexander, the Wolf of Badenoch. <br> **c. 1390** Wycliffe's writings spread to Bohemia. |
| **1391** Timur-i-leng campaigns in Turkestan: 19 June, defeats Toqtamish near Orenburg. Zafar Khan appointed governor of Gujarat. | | **1391** Gerson requests Charles VI to intervene to end the Great Schism. |

| WESTERN & NORTHERN EUROPE | CENTRAL, SOUTHERN & EASTERN EUROPE | AFRICA & EGYPT |
|---|---|---|
| | **1391** Jews massacred in Castile. **1391—1423** Manuel II Palaeologos, Eastern Roman Emperor. | |
| **1392** Charles VI of France becomes insane. Commercial treaty between Hanse towns and Novgorod. Aliens forbidden to sell by retail in England. | **1392** Sultan Bayazid sends fleet to Black Sea against Emperor Manuel. Bayazid completes conquest of Serbia. **1392—4** Louis d'Orléans, brother of Charles VI, campaigns in Italy. | |
| **1393** Statute of *Praemunire* re-enacted. | **1393** Convention of Sempach (Women's Charter) redefines Swiss Confederation. Turks take Trnvo, capital of Bulgaria, and all Bulgaria. | **1393—1433** Abu Faris, Hafsid. |
| **1394** Rebellion in Ireland: 29 Sept., Richard II of England crosses to Ireland (—1395): treaties made with Irish rebels. | **1394** Wenceslas of Bohemia taken prisoner by rebels led by Jobst of Moravia. Sultan Bayazid I invades Wallachia. **1394—1460** Prince Henry of Portugal, called 'the Navigator'. | c. **1394** Venice sends masons, painters and artisans to Ethopia. **1394—8** Omar, King of Kanem. |
| **1395** General amnesty granted in Ireland. Timur-i-leng turns back at the R. Don from attacking Russia. Overland trade between Russia and England ended. | **1395** Gian Galeazzo Visconti becomes Duke of Milan. Albert III of Hapsburg d.: his possessions partitioned. **1395—1410** Martin I, King of Aragon. | |
| **1396** Battle of the Clans, at North Inch of Perth, fought by thirty champions from each side. 4 Nov., Richard II of England m. Isabella of France: further twenty-eight year truce between England and France. | **1396** Poland seizes Bessarabia. Bayazid campaigns in Greece. Sigismund of Hungary's army defeated at Nicopolis by Bayazid. Charles VI becomes suzerain of Genoa. | |
| **1397** 20 July, Union of Kalmar between Denmark, Norway and Sweden. Duke of Gloucester banished to Calais by Richard II: 9 Sept., d. mysteriously. 21 Sept., Earl of Arundel executed; his brother, Abp of Canterbury, banished. | **1397** Sultan Bayazid I invades Morea. **1397—9** French army under Marshal Boucicaut sent to aid garrison of Constantinople. | **1397** Rebellion in Kano. |
| **1398** 31 Jan., Parliament of Shrewsbury grants life income to Richard II. The Teutonic Knights take Visby: end of piracy in the Baltic. **1398—1402** Charles VI of France besieges Benedict XIII in Avignon. | | **1398—1405** al-Nasir al-Din Faraj, Burji Mamluk ruler (first term). |
| **1399** 3 Feb., John of Gaunt d.: possessions seized by Richard II. Second visit of Richard II to Ireland. 30 Sept., Richard II abdicates: succ. Henry IV, son of John of Gaunt (—1413). Annual Parliaments demanded in Scotland. | **1399** Milan seizes Pisa. Witold of Lithuania badly defeated by the Mongols at Vorskla: peace of Salm between Witold and the Teutonic Knights. **1399—1400** Emperor Manuel II visits Venice, France and England to seek aid against the Turks. **1399—1402** John VII, associate Eastern Roman Emperor. | |

# THE NEAR EAST

# THE FAR EAST

# RELIGION & CULTURE

**1392–6** Timur-i-leng campaigning in Persia. Sultan Bayazid I fails to take Konia (Quniyah).

**1393–1416** Sikander, Sultan of Kashmir: uses sword to propagate Islam. Bayazid takes Konia. Timur-i-leng campaigns in Iraq: Oct., Baghdad taken without resistance.

**1394** Khwaja Jahan made Governor of Jaunpur by Sultan of Delhi. Timur-i-leng takes all Mesopotamia.
**1394–7** Mahmud and Nusrat Shah contest Sultanate of Delhi.

**1395** Timur-i-leng destroys Sarai and Astrakhan: trade route between Russia and China closed.

**1397** Shams al-Din, Bahmani Sultan: deposed, and imprisoned or blinded. Ghiyas al-Din, Bahmani Sultan: blinded and deposed. Army under Pir Muhammad, grandson of Timur-i-leng, takes Uch.
**1397–1422** Firuz, Bahmani Sultan.
**1398** May, Pir Muhammad takes Multan. Autumn, Timur-i-leng crosses Indus with 90,000 cavalry: defeats Mahmud Tughluq: Delhi occupied: Timur proclaimed ruler: following resistance of citizens, Delhi sacked: plunder carried off to Samarqand: Gujarat, Malwa and Jaunpur revolt from Delhi.
**1398–1414** No regular government in Delhi.
**1399** 1 Jan., Timur-i-leng leaves Delhi. Mubarak Shah Sharqi, son of Khwaja Jahan, sets himself up as independent ruler of Jaunpur (–1402). Harihara II, ruler of Vijayanagar, invades Bahmani kingdom: army taken by surprise, and routed by Firoz Shah.
**1399–1400** Timur-i-leng sends force into Kashgaria.

**1392** Ni Taijo, or Litan, founds new dynasty in Korea: capital established at Seoul.

**1393** Wars in Annam: Chinese send armies: fleet inaugurated as protection against Japan: Cheng Ho, first admiral of the Chinese fleet. Maw Shans defeated crushingly by Ava: raids end.

**1398** Chu Yuan-chang d.: succ. Hui Ti (1399–1402).

**1392** Erfurt University founded.

**1394** University of Paris again demands end of the Great Schism.
**1394–1409** Benedict XIII, Pope at Avignon.

**1395** Castile, England and France make vain efforts to end the Great Schism. Gerson becomes Chancellor of the University of Paris.
**1395–1472** Card. John Bessarion, Scholar.
**1396** The canal pound lock first found in Europe.
**1396–9** Great Mosque, Bursa, built.

**c. 1397** Wilton Diptych painted.
**1397–1475** Paulo Uccello, artist.
**1397** Canterbury Cathedral cloisters begun. Richard II attends pageant at York.

**1398–1481** Francesco Filelfo, humanist.

**1399** Rebuilding of Westminster Hall completed.
**1399–1419** Towers of Strasbourg Cathedral built.
**1399–1482** Luca della Robbia, sculptor.
**end of 14th c.** Pauline monastery. Czestochowa, built.

| WESTERN & NORTHERN EUROPE | CENTRAL, SOUTHERN & EASTERN EUROPE | AFRICA & EGYPT |
|---|---|---|
| **15th c.** Bristol fishermen fishing off Iceland and Greenland. Kiev and surrounding country repopulated from Lithuania. | | **c. early 15th c.** Ngoni settled in Natal. Karanga settled in Rhodesia. Great Enclosure built at Zimbabwe. Congolese kingdoms in process of formation.<br>**c. 15th c.** Kingdom of Nikki established.<br>**c. 15th—18th c.** Lwoo moving from S Sudan to present habitats.<br>**c. ante 1400** Tutsi arrive in Rwanda and Burundi.<br>**c. 1400** Peoples of Sierra Leone reach present habitat. Fante occupy Gold Coast. |
| **1400** Jan., Henry IV annihilates supporters of Richard II at Cirencester. 14 Feb., Richard II murdered.<br>**1400—9** Revolt in Wales led by Owain Glyndwr (Owen Glendower). Emperor Manuel II visits England. | **1400** 20—21 Aug., Diet of Oberlahnstein: Emperor Wenceslas deposed: Rupert III of Bavaria elected (—1410).<br>**1400—14** Ladislas, King of Naples. | |
| | **1401** 18 Jan., Compact of Wilno: Witold recognized as Grand Duke of Lithuania. Treaty of Radom: Poland and Lithuania united. Rupert III fails to be crowned Emperor in Italy.<br>**1401—3** Interregnum in Ottoman dominions. | |
| **1402** Scots invade England: 22 June, defeated at Nesbit Moor: 14 Sept., defeated by Percies at Homildon Hill. | **1402** 3 Sept., Gian Galeazzo Visconti of Milan d.: struggle for succession ensues. | **1402** Jean de Bethencourt's expedition to the Canary Is. |
| **1403** 21 July, Percies defeated at Shrewsbury by Henry IV. | **1403** Umbria added to the Papal States. Valais and Tessin join Swiss Confederation.<br>**1403—21** Muhammad I, joint claimant with Sulaiman to Ottoman dominions (—1410); and joint claimant with Musa (1410—13). | |
| **1404** Margaret of Denmark takes Holstein. Owen Glendower allies with France. Philip of Burgundy d.: succ. John the Fearless (—1419).<br><br>**1405** Abp Scrope of York and Earl of Nottingham rebel: 6 June, executed. | **1404** Ladislas of Naples recognized by the Pope. Treaty of Raciaz between Poland and the Teutonic Knights.<br>**1404—5** Venice takes Padua, Verona and Vicenza.<br>**1405** 14 Sept., League of Marbach formed against Rupert of Bavaria. | **1405—6** al-Mansur Izz al-Din Abd al-Aziz, Burji Mamluk Sultan.<br>**1405** Lanzarote taken by Jean de Bethencourt. |

## THE NEAR & FAR EAST

**15th c.** Kedah subject to Malacca. Silver and copper currency begins to be common in Japan: gold and silver mined and exported.
**15th—16th c.** Japanese foreign trade greatly increased and prosperous.

**1400** Timur-i-leng devastates Georgia: Aug., marches on Turks in Asia Minor: takes Sivas from the Ottomans: Oct., attacks Syria: Aleppo, Hama, Homs, Baalbek taken: Damascus abandoned.
**c. 1400** Parameswara arrives at Malacca: friendship with Ming China facilitates setting up of trading state.
**c. 1400—1511** Malay Kingdom of Malacca.
**1401** Feb., Timur-i-leng takes Damascus: makes George VI of Georgia tributary. Rebellion in Iraq put down: 10 July, general massacre in Baghdad. Kingdom of Malwa founded by Shihab al-Din Ghuri (—1405). Zafar Khan makes himself independent ruler of Gujarat, with title of Sultan Muzaffar Shah. Whole Malay peninsula acknowledges Siam as overlord. Arakan raids Ava territory: Ava invades Arakan: son-in-law of Minkhaung placed on throne: King of Arakan flees to Bengal: Pegu then invades Ava: peace made at Prome: Ava gains port dues at Bassein. Tarabya, King of Ava.
**1401—6** Civil war in Mujapahit.
**1401—22** Minkhaung, King of Ava.
**1402** June, Timur-i-leng campaigns in Asia Minor: 20 July, Ottoman army defeated at Ankara: Sultan Bayazid I taken prisoner: Bursa pillaged: 2—16 Dec., Smyrna besieged and taken from Knights of Rhodes. Ibrahim succ. as ruler of Jaunpur (—1438).
**1403** 6 March, Bayazid d.: Timur-i-leng retires to central Asia: Sulaiman succ. Bayazid (—1411). Timur-i-leng again devastates Georgia. Chinese fleet under Yin Ching, visits Malacca.
**1403—4** Tatar Khan usurps his father, Zafar Khan of Gujarat: poisoned by his father.
**1403—24** Yung-lo, Ming emperor, succ. his brother after fighting for the throne: capital at Peking now permanent.
**1404** Harihara II, Raya of Vijayanagar, d.: succ. Virupaksa quickly ousted by Bukka II (—c. 1406).

**1405** 19 Feb., Timur-i-leng d. at Otrar: buried at Samarqand: his empire, from China to Asia Minor, dissolves.

## THE AMERICAS

**15th c.** Peoples of the W Indies still living in the New Stone Age.

## RELIGION & CULTURE

**15th c.** Jositsu, Japanese artist. The quadrant invented. Controversy on The Three Births or Two Births of Christ in Ethiopia. Muslim town in existence at Anpanasina, Madagascar.

**1400** 25 Oct., Geoffrey Chaucer d.: *The Canterbury Tales* left unfinished. Antwerp Cathedral begun. Khan al-Khalil, Cairo, founded. York Minster, east window constructed.
**1400—10** Mausoleum and convent of Sultan, Barquq, Cairo, built.
**c. 1400—70** Ramanand, Indian philosopher.
**c. 1400—74** Guillaume Dufay, composer.
**1400—68** Jan Gutenberg, printer.
**1400—75** Bartolomeo Colleoni, freebooter.
**1401** *De heritico comburendo*, statute against Lollard heresies in England.
**1401—55** Hôtel de Ville built at Brussels.
**1401—64** Cardinal Nicholas de Cusa, theologian.

**1402** John Huss, Rector of the University University of Prague. Seville Cathedral begun: largest Gothic church in the world.

**1403** John Huss preaches Lollard doctrines in Bohemia. Jews expelled from France.
**1403—14** Eski Gamii, Edirne, built.

**1404—6** Innocent VII, Pope, at Rome.
**1404—72** Leone Battista Alberti, architect.

**1405** Rising in University of Paris against Pope Benedict XIII. John Thornton: glass in York Minster.

1405–1412

WESTERN &
NORTHERN EUROPE

CENTRAL, SOUTHERN
& EASTERN EUROPE

AFRICA & EGYPT

|  |  |  |
|---|---|---|
|  | **1405** Golden Horde breaks up into small hordes. Sigismund of Hungary defeated by Waldenses in Bosnia. |  |
| **1406** 28 Feb., treaty of Aberdaron; Glendower, Mortimer and Percies conspire to partition England. Feb.–Dec., Parliament carries out financial and constitutional reforms in England.<br>**1406–20** Robert, Duke of Albany, Regent of Scotland.<br>**1406–37** James I, King of Scots: captured by the English and kept prisoner (–1424).<br>**1407** John the Fearless murders Louis d'Orléans. Oct., Parliament of Gloucester reasserts parliamentary control over money bills. Henry IV charters first Merchant Adventurers.<br>**1407–8** Franco-Scottish treaty renewed.<br>**1407–35** Civil war in France between the Armagnacs and Bourguignons.<br>**1408** 29 Feb., Earl of Northumberland in rebellion: killed at Bramham Moor. Nijni-Novgorod burnt and sacked by the Mongols. | **1406** Florence takes Pisa.<br>**1406–54** John II of Castile.<br><br><br>**1407** Sigismund of Hungary occupies Bosnia: Waldenses put down.<br><br><br><br>**1408** Ladislas of Naples makes himself master of Rome. | **1406–12** al-Nasir Nasir al-Din Faraj, Burji Mamluk Sultan (second term). |
|  | **1409** Martin I of Aragon becomes King of Sicily *iure uxoris.* Venice at war with Sigismund of Hungary: Dalmatia recovered. |  |
| **1410** Last recorded ship visiting Greenland from the Baltic. | **1410** Martin I of Aragon and Sicily d.: civil war ensues in Aragon: Bianca, regent of Sicily (–1412). 15 July, Germans defeated at Grünwald (Tannenberg) by allied army of Lithuanians, Poles and Russians.<br>**1410–37** Sigismund of Hungary, Holy Roman Emperor.<br>**1410–11** Jobst of Moravia, rival Holy Roman Emperor. | **1410** Abu Faris, Hafsid, takes Algiers |
| **1411** Nov., Burgundians and English defeated Orléanists at St Cloud. Margaret of Denmark defeated by Germans at Eggebeck. Henry of Monmouth attempts to depose his father, Henry IV, without success. | **1411** 1 Feb., Peace of Thorn between Jagellon and the Teutonic Knights. 31 Oct., peace between Castile and Portugal.<br>**1411-12** Appenzell and St Gall join the Swiss Confederation. |  |
| **1412** Guyenne sold to England. Henry IV of England sides with Orléanists.<br>**1412–39** Eric of Pomerania, King of Denmark, Norway and Sweden. | **1412** Compromise of Caspe: separate *Cortes* of Aragon, Catalonia, and Valencia, elect Ferdinand of Antequera and Trastamare King of Aragon (–1416), already regent for boy King John II of Castile. Treaty of Lubovia between Jagellon and Emperor Sigismund. Ladislas of Naples expels Gregory XII: makes peace with John XXIII. | **1412** Caliph al-Adil al-Mustain, Burji Mamluk Sultan.<br>**1412–21** al-Muayyad Shaykhu, Burji Mamluk Sultan.<br>**c. 1412–21** al-Malik al-Adil Muhammad b. Sulaiman, Sultan of Kilwa. |

| THE NEAR & FAR EAST | THE AMERICAS | RELIGION & CULTURE |
|---|---|---|

**THE NEAR & FAR EAST**

**1405** Cheng Ho, with Chinese fleet, visits Indo-China and reaches Arabia: accords recognition to Parameswara at Malacca.
**1405–35** Hushang Shah, ruler of Malwa: capital moved to Mandu.
**1406** Firoz Shah again defeats Vijayanagar army. Fresh hostilities begun by Pegu against Ava. Ava destroys two northern Shan kingdoms. Chinese army attacks Vietnam.
**c. 1406** Bukka II of Vijayanagar dethroned: succ. Devaraya I (−1422).

**1407** Zafar Khan (Muzaffar Shah), Sultan of Gujarat, d. Shah Rukh emerges as successor to the Timurid empire (−1447): capital at Herat: golden age of Persian art and literature. Ava invades Mon territory by land and sea.
**1407–27** Chinese briefly in control of Vietnam.

**1408** Sawbwa of Hsenwei, Maw Shan state, attacks Ava: Sawbwa killed in single combat: Chinese reinforcements prevent capture of Hsenwei.
**1409** Indecisive battle between Ava and Pegu. Cheng Ho again visits Malacca: city proclaimed a market and a kingdom.
**1409–11** Embassy from Persia visits China.
**1410** Ava invades Irawaddy delta without success: Arakan seized.

**1411** Canals repaired in China to evade Japanese attacks on shipping. Parameswara, ruler of Malacca, pays state visit to Peking. Chinese expedition invades W Ceylon: ruler of Rayigama carried off.
**1411–41** Ahmad Shah, Sultan of Gujarat: capital, Ahmadabad: constant fighting with neighbouring principalities: on good terms with Bahmanids.
**1412** Mons attack Prome: defeated: abortive attack on Ava by Sawbwa of Hsenwei.
**1412–67** Parakrama Bahu VI, King of Kotte, Ceylon: recognized by Chinese emperor.

**RELIGION & CULTURE**

**1405–64** Aeneas Sylvius Piccolomini, later Pope Pius II, humanist.

**1406–9** Gregory XII, Pope, at Rome.
**1406–69** Fra Filippo Lippi, artist.

**1407** Central tower of York Minster rebuilt following collapse.

**1408** 29 June, Council of Cardinals meets to end Great Schism.

**1409** Council of Pisa: Gregory XII (Rome) and Benedict XIII (Avignon) both deposed: Alexander V elected: opposed by deposed Popes. Leipzig University founded.
**1409–10** Alexander V, Pope, at Rome.

**1410** Struggle between Abp of Prague and John Huss: latter supported by popular rebellion.
**1410–15** John XXIII, Pope, at Rome.

**1411** Papal Legate sent to excommunicate John Huss. Thomas Hoccleve: *De regimine principum.*
**1411–26** Guildhall built in London.
**1411–69** Abu al-Mahasin b. Taghri-Birdi, historian of Egypt.

**1412** St Andrew's University founded.
**1412–31** St Joan of Arc.

| WESTERN & NORTHERN EUROPE | CENTRAL, SOUTHERN & EASTERN EUROPE | AFRICA & EGYPT |
|---|---|---|
| | **1412–47** Philip-Maria, Duke of Milan: last Visconti duke. | |
| **1413** 21 March, Henry IV of England d.: succ. Henry V (–1422). Henry Beaufort, Chancellor of England. Lollard rebellion in England. Estates-General meets in Paris. Rising of Cabochians. Orléanists expel Burgundians from Paris. **1413–47** John Talbot, Lord Furnival, several times viceroy of Ireland. | **1413** 2 Oct., Act of Horodlo confirms union between Lithuania and Poland. Ottoman rival Sultan Musa defeated and killed by his brother, Muhammad I: policy of friendship with Byzantium. | |
| **1414** Conferences of Leicester and Ypres: John the Fearless and Henry V arrange partition of France: Henry V demands all lands held by the Plantagenets. | **1414** War between Poland and the Teutonic Knights. **1414–55** Jeanne II, Queen of Naples. | **1414–29** Yeshaq of Ethiopia: continues war with Zaila. |
| **1415** 11 Aug., Henry V leads expedition against France: 22 Sept., Harfleur taken: 25 Oct., French defeated at Agincourt: English army 6,000, French 12,000: 7,000 French casualties, 500 English: Henry V withdraws to England. Peace of Arras: Armagnacs and Burgundians reconciled. | **1415** Sigismund defeats Frederick of Austria: grants Electorate of Brandenburg to Frederick VI of Nuremberg. Hussite League formed in Bohemia: Catholics expelled from Prague. Following Imperial order, Swiss take Aargau from the Hapsburgs. Manuel II visits Morea. | **1415** Portuguese take Ceuta. Spaniards take Tenerife. Yeshaq occupies Zaila. **c. 1415** Embassy from Malindi to China. |
| **1416** 15 Aug., treaty of Canterbury between Emperor Sigismund and Henry V of England. 8 Oct., treaty of Calais between Emperor Sigismund, Burgundy and England. Henry V of England recognized as King of France by John the Fearless. | **1416** Ferdinand of Aragon d.: succ. Alfonso V the Magnanimous as King of Aragon and Sicily. Amadeo VIII, Count of Savoy, made a Duke by Emperor Sigismund. John I of Castile comes of age. Venetian fleet defeats Turks off Gallipoli. | **c. 1416** Walasma dynasty revived as Sultans of Adal. |
| **1417** Henry V leads second expedition against France: 21 Sept., Caen taken: Normandy occupied: Rouen besieged (–Jan. 1419). | **1417** Despotate of Mistra recovers Morea from the Latins. | **1417–19** Chinese fleet under Cheng Ho visits Mogadishu, Barawa and Malindi. |
| **1418** The Burgundians take Paris. The Armagnacs massacred. Henry V of England attempts to conquer Normandy. | **1418** The Portuguese take Madeira. | **1418** Canary Is, ceded to Castile. |
| **1419** 19 Jan., Rouen surrenders to Henry V of England. 29 July, Peace of Melun between the Dauphin and Burgundy. 10 Sept., John the Fearless of Burgundy assassinated: succ. Philip II the Good (–1467). Alliance between Philip and Henry V of England. | **1419–36** War between the Empire and the Hussites in Bohemia. | |
| **1420** 21 May, Treaty of Troyes: Charles VI recognizes Henry V as his heir and as Regent of France. | **1420** The Emperor Sigismund becomes King of Bohemia. 1 Nov., defeated by Hussites at Vysehrad. | |

**1413** Ladislas of Naples expels John XXIII from Rome.

**1414** Parameswara, ruler of Malacca, m. a Muslim princess of Pasai, N Sumatra, and becomes a Muslim: takes name of Muhammad Iskandar Shah: visits Peking: Malacca becomes principal centre of diffusion of Islam in Malaya. Ava invades Lower Burma: Chinese army reaches Ava: retreat following death of Chinese champion in single combat.

**1414** Council of Constance: John Huss arrested. Statute against the Lollards passed by English Parliament. Song School founded at Durham. Jews again expelled from Spain.

**1414–21** Tajul Mulk, Wazir of Delhi conducts campaigns in nearby territories.
**1414–22** Khizr Khan, Sayyid of Delhi.
**1414–31** Jalal al-Din, ruler of Bengal: period of conversion to Islam.
**1414–50** Affairs of the city of Delhi and fluctuating territory administered by 'Sayyids' answerable to Mongols.
**1415** Internal Chinese merchant traffic carried by canal.

**1415** John XXIII attempts to transfer Council of Constance to Italy: 2 March, John XXIII abdicates: Papacy vacant (*sede vacante*) to 1417. 6 July, John Huss burnt as a heretic. Prince Henry 'the Navigator' establishes school of navigation, cartography, science and shipbuildings at Sagres. Thomas à Kempis: *Of The Imitation of Christ*.
**1416** 30 May, Jerome of Prague, a Hussite, burnt as a heretic.
**1416–92** Piero della Francesco, artist.

**1417** Embassy from Shah Rukh to Peking reopens trade with Ming Empire.
**1417–27** Vietnamese war of liberation against China.

**1417** John, Lord Cobham, burnt as a Lollard heretic. Orban Camii, Bursa, built.
**1417–31** Martin V (Colonna), Pope.
**1418** Ahmad al-Qalqashandi d.: author of work on Fatimid civil and military administration. Pope Martin V dissolves the Council of Constance. Catholicism re-established in Prague.

**1419** Muhammad Iskandar Shah of Malacca visits Peking.

**1419** Rostock University founded. Green Mosque, Bursa, built.

**1420** Firuz Shah Bahmani defeated at Pangal. Nicolo Conti, Italian traveller, visits and describes Vijayanagar.

**1420** Pope Martin V proclaims a Crusade against the Hussites: Hussites publish Four Articles of Faith. Temple of Heaven built in Peking.

| WESTERN & NORTHERN EUROPE | CENTRAL, SOUTHERN & EASTERN EUROPE | AFRICA & EGYPT |
|---|---|---|

**1420** 2 June, Henry V m. Catherine of France: Dauphin continues war: 1 Dec., Henry V enters Paris.
**1420—4** Murdoch, Duke of Albany, Regent of Scotland.
**1421** The Dauphin defeats and kills the Duke of Clarence at Baugé. Philip the Good purchases the county of Namur.

**1422** 31 Aug., Henry V d.: succ. Henry VI, aged nine months (—1461): John, Duke of Bedford, Regent of France; Humphrey, Duke of Gloucester, Protector in England. 21 Oct., Charles VI of France d.: succ. Charles VII (—1461): Charles in possession of Auvergne, Berry, Dauphiné, Orléans, and Touraine: capital at Bourges: remainder of France subject to England.

**1423—9** France, with Scots support, at war with England.
**1423** 1 Aug., English beat French at Crévant. Franco-Scottish treaty renewed.
**1424** 17 Aug., English beat French and Scots at Verneuil. Truce between Charles VII and Philip the Good. Oct., Duke of Gloucester invades Hainault. James I of Scotland released from captivity: the Regent Murdoch executed.
**1425** 2 Aug., English take Le Mans. Brittany sides with Charles VII. Rivalry between the Duke of Gloucester and the Beaufort family.
**1425—62** Vassili II the Blind, Grand Prince of Moscow: struggles for the succession.
**1426** 19 Jan., English defeated by Philip the Good. All Scottish tenants-in-chief required to attend Parliament in person.

**1427** Alliance between England and Burgundy. French defeat English at Montargis.

**1428** 3 July, treaty of Delft: Burgundy acquires Hainault, Holland and Zeeland. Franco-Scottish treaty renewed. Bicameral Parliament emerges in Scotland.
**1428—9** English besiege Orléans.
**1429** 1-3 May, Joan of Arc raises English siege of Orléans.

**1420** Venice takes Belluno and Friuli. Peace of Melno between Poland and the Teutonic Knights.

**1421** Czech rebellion headed by Taborites.. 2 Oct., Sigismund defeated at Saaz: Diet of Caslar votes deposition of Sigismund. Florence obtains Livorno (Leghorn).
**1421—9** Giovanni dei Medici, Gonfaloniere of Florence.
**1421—51** Murad II, Ottoman Sultan: policy of hostility to Byzantium: pretender recognized by Byzantines.
**1422** Aug., Sultan Murad II besieges Constantinople: repelled by the inhabitants. Treaty between Poland and Teutonic Knights at L. Melno. Diet of Nuremberg. Korybut made Regent of Bohemia. Sigismund defeated by Hussites.

**1423** Civil war in Germany. Prague revolts against the Taborites. Anarchy in Bohemia. Adrianople made capital by Murad II. Salonica sold to Venice. Ottomans take Morea.
**1424** Union of Brisgau against Sigismund. Portugal settles the Canary Is. Edict of Wielun against the Hussites in Poland.
**1424—6** Cyprus taken by Sultan Barsbay.

**1425** The Pope, Florence and Venice ally against Milan.
**1425—48** John VIII Palaeologos, Eastern Roman Emperor.
**1425—79** John, King of Navarre.

**1426** Procopius the Great becomes leader of the Taborites. Mamluks of Egypt raid Cyprus.

**1427** Diet of Frankfurt. The Taborites become masters of Prague. Murad II restores Ottoman authority in Serbia.

**1428** Procopius the Great devastates Moravia and Silesia.

**1429—33** Cosimo dei Medici, Gonfaloniere of Florence.

**1421** al-Muzaffar Ahmad, Burji Mamluk Sultan. al-Zahir Sayf al-Din Tatar, Burji Mamluk Sultan.
**1421—2** al-Salih Nasir al-Din Muhammad, Burji Mamluk Sultan.
**1421—2** Cheng Ho revisits Mogadishu and Malindi.
**c. 1421—42** Sulaiman b. Muhamma Sultan of Kilwa: Friday Mosque restored.
**ante 1428**
**1422—38** al-Ashraf Sayf al-Din Barsbay, Burji Mamluk Sultan.

**1427** King of Cyprus recognizes Egypt as overlord. Ethiopian emba to Aragon.
**1427—1550** Wattasid dynasty at Fe

**1428±60** Third stage of Mapungub culture.
**ante 1428** Yeshaq of Ethiopia conquers Enarya.

## THE NEAR & FAR EAST  THE AMERICAS  RELIGION & CULTURE

**1420–67** Zain al-Abidin, Sultan of Kashmir: policy of religious toleration: later venerated as a saint.

**1421** Byzantines attack Turks in Gallipoli. Shah Rukh campaigns in Azerbaijan. Cheng Ho visits Bengal.

**1422** Firuz Shah, Bahmani Sultan, deposed and strangled by his brother and succ. Ahmad Shah (–1435): capital moved to Bidar. Devaraya I of Vijanagar d.: succ. Ramachandra shortly dethroned: succ. Vijaya (–1425/6): Devaraya II sharer in his administration.
**1422–3** War between Bahmanis and Vijayanagar.
**1422–6** Thihathu, King of Ava.
**1422–34** Mubarak Shah, Sayyid of Delhi: takes title of Sultan.
**c. 1423** Severe famine in the Deccan.
**1423–6** Binnyadhamaraza, King of Hanthawaddy.

**1424–5** Bahmanis acquire Warangal: frontiers now reach the sea.
**1424–7** Murad retakes Anatolia.
**1424–44** Sri Maharajah Muhammad Shah, ruler of Malacca; 1424 visits Peking.

**1425/6–46** Devaraya II, Raya of Vijayanagar: Kondavidu seized.

**1426** Minhlange, King of Ava: poisoned by Shin Bohmai, Shan Queen.
**1426–7** Chief of Kalekyetaungnyo made King of Ava by Shin Bohmai.
**1426–35** Hsuan Tsung, Ming Emperor, with throne name of Hsuan-te.
**1426–46** Binnya Ran, King of Hanthawaddy.
**1427–40** Mohnyinthado, King of Ava: m. Shin Bohmai as junior queen: founder (by chief queen) of Burmese dynasty of Ava.
**1427–1772** Le dynasty in Vietnam.

**1428** Chinese evacuate Vietnam.

**1429** (? ) Suhita, ruler of Majapahit.

**1420–34** Filippo Brunelleschi builds the cupola of Florence Cathedral: lantern added 1461.
**c. 1420** Brace-and-bit invented in Flanders.
**1421** Hussite synod held in Prague: Utraquist Church organized. Taborites emerge as opponents of the Hussites. Catterick bridge built. Berne Minster begun.

**1422** Jews expelled from England.
**c. 1422** Thomas Walsingham, historian, d.
**c. 1422–35** Cá d'Oro built at Venice.
**1422–91** William Caxton, printer, editor, translator and publisher.
**1422–1516** Giovanni Bellini, artist.
**1422–50** Agnes Sorel, beauty.

**1423** Council of Padua opens: transferred to Siena. SW tower of Canterbury Cathedral begun.
**c. 1423–57** Andrea del Castagno, architect.
**1424** Pope Martin V dissolves Council of Padua.
**1424–7** Mosque, mausoleum and *madrassa* of Murad II, Bursa, built.

**1426–1503** Giovanni Pontano, Italian poet.
**1426** Platonic Academy, Florence, founded. Louvain University founded.

**1427** Benedictine Priory established in Constantinople.

**1429** Solovetzki monastery founded.

| WESTERN &<br>NORTHERN EUROPE | CENTRAL, SOUTHERN<br>& EASTERN EUROPE | AFRICA & EGYPT |
|---|---|---|
| **1429** 17 July, Charles VII crowned king at Reims. 6 Nov., Henry VI crowned at Westminster. Joan of Arc fails to take Paris. English beat French at Rouvray. Order of the Golden Fleece instituted by Philip of Burgundy. | | |
| **1430** 23 May, Joan of Arc captured at Compiègne by Burgundians: Nov., sold to the English. Burgundy acquires Brabant and Limburg. | **1430** Witold of Lithuania d. Renewed struggle between Poland and the Teutonic Knights. Murad II takes Salonica and Janina. | |
| **1431** 30 May, Joan of Arc burnt at Rouen. 17 Dec., Henry VI of England crowned King of France in Paris. Rebellion in Sweden against Eric of Pomerania. | **1431** The Hussites defeat Germans at Domazlice. <br>**1431–3** German peasantry revolts near Worms. | **1431** Azores Is. discovered by Portuguese. |
| **1432** Armistice between the Hanse towns and Eric of Pomerania. | | |
| | **1433** 31 May, Sigismund crowned Emperor. Diet of Basle: *Reformatio Sigismundi.* Constitution of Cracow grants right of *Habeas Corpus* to Polish nobility. <br>**1433–4** Cosimo dei Medici exiled from Florence: the Albizzi in power. <br>**1433–8** Edward I, King of Portugal: Portuguese law revised and codified: estates in default of a male heir to revert to the Crown. | **1433** Tuareg take Timbuktu (−1438 <br>**1433–4** Gil Eanes reaches C. Bogador. |
| **1434** Rising against England in Normandy. | **1434** Civil war in Bohemia: Taborites defeated at Lipany: Procopius killed. Rebellion in Rome: Pope Eugenius IV flees to Florence. <br>**1434–44** Wladislaw III, King of Poland. <br>**1434–64** Cosimo dei Medici again Gonfaloniere of Florence. | **1434** Gil Eanes reaches Cameroun. <br>**1434–68** Zara Yaqub of Ethiopia: civil and religious reformer: Solomonic dynasty reaches a high peak in power and culture. |
| **1435** 17 July, peace of Vordingborg: Hanse town privileges confirmed: Denmark cedes Schleswig to Holstein. 15 Sept., John, Duke of Bedford d. at Rouen. Peace of Arras: Charles VII gains support of Duke of Burgundy: retakes Ile de France. <br>**1436** 13 Apr., Charles VII regains Paris. Rebellion put down in Sweden. Sigismund recognized as King of Bohemia. | **1435** 2 Feb., Jeanne II of Naples d.: Naples governed by an elected council. Alfonso V of Aragon defeated and taken prisoner. Perpetual Peace signed between Poland and the Teutonic Knights. <br><br>**1436** Alfonso V of Aragon set free: campaigns in Italy. <br>**1436–1517** Cardinal Ximénes, Spanish statesman. | **1435–87** Abu Umar Uthman, Hafsid |
| **1437** James I of Scots assassinated: succ. James II (−1460). | **1437** Venice obtains Dalmatian Coast from Sigismund. Coalition of nobles agains Charles VII. 9 Dec., Sigismund d.: succ. 1438 Albert II of Hapsburg as King of Bohemia and Hungary (−1439). | **1437** 16 Oct., Portuguese expedition against Ceuta destroyed: Ceuta abandoned. |
| **1438** 1 July, nine year truce between England and Scotland. <br>**1438–41** Trade war between the Hanse towns and Holland. | **1438** 18 March, Albert II elected King of Germany. Diet of Nuremberg undertakes reform of the Empire. <br>**1438–81** Afonso V, King of Portugal: succ. aged five: disputed regency leads to strife. | **1438** al-Aziz Jamal al-Din Yusuf, Burji Mamluk Sultan. <br>**1438–53** al-Zahir Sayf al-Din Jaqmaq, Burji Mamluk Sultan. |

| THE NEAR & FAR EAST | THE AMERICAS | RELIGION & CULTURE |
|---|---|---|
| **1429** Shah Rukh's second campaign in Azerbaijan. | | |
| | | **1430–46** Pazzi Chapel built by Brunelleschi in Florence.<br>**c. 1430–94** Hans Memling, Flemish artist.<br>**c. 1430–95** Jean de Ockeghem, composer.<br>**c. 1430** Sherborne Abbey Choir begun.<br>**1431** Caen and Poitiers Universities founded. |
| **1431** Cheng Ho visits Bengal.<br>**1431–2** Chinese fleet visits Jiddah. | | **1431–47** Eugenius IV, Pope.<br>**1431–7** Council of Basle.<br>**1431–47** Eugenius IV, Pope: orders transfer Council of Basle to Bologna, to negotiate with Byzantines. |
| | | **1431–?85** François Villon, poet.<br>**1431–1506** Andrea Mantegna, artist.<br>**1432** The Council of Basle declines to move: meetings held with Hussites.<br>**1432–84** Luigi Pulci, Italian poet.<br>**1432–98** Antonio Pollaiuolo, artist.<br>**1433** Czech delegates visit Council of Basle. Further meetings result in Compact of Prague: the Four Articles recognized. Tattershall Castle begun.<br>**1433–99** Marsilio Ficino, humanist. |
| **1432–6** Mahmud Ghuri, ruler of Malwa. | | |
| **1434** Shah Rukh sends a third expedition to Azerbaijan. Sayyid Mubarak Shah assassinated: succ. Muhammad Shah (−1444/5). | | **1434** College of Cardinals reformed. |
| **1435–57** Ala al-Din II, Bahmani Sultan: further war with Vijayanagar. | | **1435** Meetings at Brno between the Council of Basle and the Utraquists. Council abolishes Annates, fees for the *pallium,* and other taxes. Eugenius IV orders liberation of slaves in the Canary Is.<br>**1435–88** Andrea del Verocchio, artist and sculptor.<br>**1436** 5 July, Compact of Iihlava (Iglau): Utraquists reconciled. Council of Basle divided on reform of the Holy See. First ecclesiastical seminary opened in Florence. Krittivasa, translator of the *Ramayana*, b. |
| **1436** Sultan Mahmud Ghuri poisoned by his *wazir*, Mahmud Khan, founder of Khilji dyansty of Malwa: ruler to 1469.<br>**1436–49** Ying Tsung, Ming Emperor: enthroned aged eight. | | **1437** Dispute between the Council of Basle and the Pope on unity with the Byzantines: Council transferred to Ferrara (−1438).<br>Zawiya of Maulay Idris, Fez, built.<br>Thomas Damett, composer, d. |
| | **post c. 1438** Inca civilization spreads throughout Peru, Bolivia, S. Argentina, Chile and Ecuador: imperial administration maintained from Peru.<br>**1438–71** Pachacuti, Inca ruler. | **1437–1541** Church of St Maclou built at Rouen.<br>**1438** *The Pragmatic Sanction* regulates relation between the French clergy and the Holy See: beginning of Gallicanism. |

| WESTERN, NORTHERN & CENTRAL EUROPE | SPAIN, ITALY & EASTERN EUROPE | AFRICA & EGYPT |
|---|---|---|
| | **1438—1806** Holy Roman Emperors of the House of Hapsburg. | **1438** Sonni Ali Songhai pillages Timbuktu. |
| **1439** 28 Sept., truce of Calais between Burgundy and England. Standing army first made lawful in France. Rebellion in Denmark and Norway: Eric deposed: succ. Christopher of Bavaria (−1448). **1439—40** Peace negotiations between England and France break down. | **1439** 27 Oct., Albert II d. fighting the Turks. Serbia made a Turkish province. | |
| **1440** Rebellion of the Praguerie in Paris, led by the Dauphin, put down. | **1440** Murad II attempts to take Belgrade. **1440—57** Vladislav Posthumus, King of Hungary and Bohemia. **1440—93** Frederick III, Holy Roman Emperor. | **c. 1440** Ewuare the Great, Oba of Benin: great traveller and warrior. Rozvi King Mutota launches campaign to set up an empire: takes title Mwene Mutapa (commonly Monomotapa). **1440** João Fernandes visits Sahara: witnesses salt and gold trades. |
| **1441** Peace of Copenhagen between the Hanse towns and Holland. Philip the Good acquires Luxembourg. | **1441** Second Ottoman siege of Byzantium. John of Castile proclaims himself King of Navarre. | |
| **1442** Charles of Orléans and Philip the Good rebel against Charles VII. | **1442** Zurich allies with Frederick III against the Swiss Confederation. John Hunyadi expels the Turks from Transylvania. Alfonso V of Aragon takes Naples. | |
| **1443** Commercial treaty between Castile and the Hanse towns. Copenhagen made the Danish court residence. | **1443** Alfonso V of Aragon recognized by the Pope as King of Naples: moves court to Naples: Queen left as regent in Aragon. Poland takes part of Silesia. John Hunyadi takes Nish, Pirot and Sofia from the Turks. Serbia and Albania rebel against the Turks. | |
| **1444** 28 May, treaty of Tours between England and France: peace for two years. Henry VI betrothed to Margaret of Anjou. | **1444** June, treaty of Szegedin between Poland and Turkey. Nov., Poland again at war with Turkey: Poles almost exterminated at Varna: Wladislaw III killed. **1444—7** Interregnum in Poland. | |
| **1445** 22 Apr., Henry VI m. Margaret of Anjou. Permanent cavalry force first instituted in France. Maine ceded by England to France by secret treaty. | **1445** Civil war in Aragon: nobles defeated at Olmedo. Portugal settles the Azores. Vassili II taken prisoner by Khan of Kazan, Ulu Mahmet: shortly released. | **1445** Ethiopia at war with Mogadish and Adal. Portuguese build trading fort at Arguin. |
| | **1446** Pope Eugenius promises imperial crown to Frederick III. John Hunyadi, Regent of Hungary (−1453). Murad II invades Morea: made a vassal state. | |
| **1447** 23 Feb., Humphrey, Duke of Gloucester, d., leaving his books to Oxford University. | **1447—92** Casimir IV, King of Poland. | **1447** Malfante, a Genoese, reaches Touat. |
| **1448** Franco-Scottish treaty renewed. War between England and Scotland. French retake Anjou and Maine. | **1448** Frederick of Brandenburg seizes Berlin, making it his capital. | **1448** Dinis Dias reaches Sierra Leon |

| THE NEAR & FAR EAST | THE AMERICAS | RELIGION & CULTURE |
|---|---|---|

<table>
<tr><td></td><td></td><td>1439 Metropolitan Isidore attends Council of Florence on behalf of Russian Church. 16 May, Council of Basle proclaims conciliar decrees dogma: 25 June, deposes Eugenius IV: 6 July, union with Byzantine Church proclaimed: not accepted by Byzantines: 4 Sept., Eugenius IV excommunicates the Council: its decrees condemned. Council of Ferrara moved to Florence.</td></tr>
<tr><td>1440—3 Minyekyawswa, King of Ava.<br>1440—1518 Kabir, a leader of the Bhakti movement.</td><td>post 1440 Accession of Moctezuma I of Mexico.</td><td>1440—9 Felix V, antipope.<br>1440—86 The Paston Letters.<br>c. 1440—94 Matteo Maria Boiardo, poet.<br>1440 City of (Old) Goa founded. Sidi Yahya, Mosque, Timbuktu, built. The caravel invented. Hospital of the Knights. Rhodes, begun.</td></tr>
<tr><td>1441 Thohanbwa, leader of Maw Shans, attempts to re-establish Kingdom of Nan-Chao: raids Ava and attacks Yunnan: Thohanbwa taken prisoner to Ava.</td><td>c. 1441 Cocom power collapses in Mexico.</td><td>1441 Metropolitan Isidore deposed for having agreed to unity with Rome at the Council of Florence. King Henry VI founds Eton College, and King's College, Cambridge.<br>1442—58 Western towers of Burgos Cathedral built.</td></tr>
<tr><td>1443 Abd al-Rezzaq, Afghani ambassador to Calicut, visits Vijayanagar.<br>1443—69 Narapati, King of Ava.</td><td></td><td>1443 Council of Jerusalem, attended by eastern Patriarchs: Council of Florence condemned. Final session of the Council of Basle. Council of Florence removed to the Lateran.</td></tr>
<tr><td>1444 Devaraya II advances boundary of Vijayanagar to Rajahmundry, and, later, Kerala, except Calicut.<br>1444—5 Alam Shah, Sayyid of Delhi (—1451). Sri Parameswara Deva Shah, ruler of Malacca.<br>ante 1445 Office of Bendehara created in Malacca: Sriwa Raja, first Bendehara (—1445): office combines duties of chief minister, Lord Chancellor, and Commander-in-chief. Siamese army defeated in abortive expedition against Malacca.<br>1445—c. 1456 Sultan Muzaffar Shah, ruler of Malacca: Tun Ali, Bendehara.<br>1446 Chinese army besieges Ava demanding surrender of Thohanbwa: Thohanbwa commits suicide.<br>1446—50 Binnya Waru, King of Hanthawaddy.<br>c. 1447 First Dalai Lama appointed ruler of Tibet. 2 March, Shah Rukh d.: succ. Olugh-beg (—1449).<br>1447—51 Bhre Tumapel (?), ruler of Majapahit.<br>1447—65 Mallikarjuna, Raya of Vijayanagar.</td><td></td><td>1444 Diet of Prague. Utraquism becomes the official religion in Bohemia.<br>1444—60 Palazzo Medici, Florence, built.<br>1444—1514 Donato Lazzari Bramante (Lazzari Urbino), architect. Catania University founded.<br>1445 Lateran Council dissolved.<br>1445—90 Shogun Yoshimasa, patron of the arts.<br>c. 1445—c. 1499 Martin Schongauer, German artist and engraver.<br>1445—1510 Sandro Botticelli, artist.<br><br>1446 Abps of Cologne and Trier deposed by Pope Eugenius IV for opposing Frederick III.<br>c. 1446—1506 Christopher Columbus.<br>1446—1524 P. Vannuchi Perugini, artist.<br>1447—55 Nicholas V, Pope.</td></tr>
<tr><td></td><td></td><td>1448 Russian synod separates from Constantinople for having agreed to unity with Rome.</td></tr>
</table>

| WESTERN & NORTHERN EUROPE | CENTRAL, SOUTHERN & EASTERN EUROPE | AFRICA & EGYPT |
|---|---|---|

**1448** Christopher of Bavaria d.: Christian, Count of Oldenburg, succ. as King of Denmark (—1481): succ. as King of Sweden Charles VIII (—1457).

**1449** Further war between England and France: France recovers Normandy, except for the Channel Is.

**1448** John Hunyadi defeated by Sultan Murad II at Kossovo. Agreement between Casimir IV of Poland and the Duke of Moscow. George of Podiebrad seizes power in Bohemia (—1471).
**1448—53** Constantine XI, Byzantine Emperor.
**1449** Civil War in S Germany. Battle of Alfarrobeira: Duke of Braganza regent of Portugal. Murad II campaigns abortively in Albania.

**1450** 15 Apr., French wipe out English army at Formigny. Commons impeach Duke of Suffolk: May, Suffolk flees to France: 2 May, intercepted and summarily beheaded. May-July, Jack Cade's abortive rebellion in London. 1 Aug., Christian of Denmark becomes King of Norway. 12 Aug., French take Cherbourg.
**1451** Jacques Coeur, French banker, arrested.
**1451—3** French recover all English possessions in France with the exception of Calais.
**1451—7** Hanse towns make trade war against Burgundy and Flanders.
**1452** 23 Oct., English retake Bordeaux. The Duke of York again rebels.

**1450** 26 Feb., Francesco Sforza, Duke of Milan (—1466).

**1451** Murad II d., succ. Muhammad II (—1481).

**1452** 19 March, Emperor Frederick III crowned: last emperor to be crowned by the Pope. George Podiebrad, Regent of Bohemia (—1458). Uprising in Constantinople against unity with Roman Church.

**c. 1450** Empire of Kanem re-organized.
**c. 1450—80** Matope, second Monomotapa, establishes authority Rhodesian plateau and S of R. Zambesi.

**1452** Ethiopian embassies to Aragon and Lisbon.

**1453** 17 July, English defeated by the French at Castillon.  Aug., Henry VI of England becomes insane. 19 Oct., English surrender Bordeaux to France: end of 'Hundred Years' War': England left with Calais and Channel Is. only. Battle of Stamford Bridge between the Percies and the Nevilles.

**1454** 27 March, Duke of York appointed Protector of England.

**1453** 20 Apr., Genoese defeat Turkish fleet off Constantinople. Apr. — 29 May, Constantinople besieged by Sultan Muhammad II. 29 May, Constantinople, after an energetic defence, taken by Muhammad II: shadow Byzantine Empire continued in Trebizond (—1461). Constantine IX killed in battle. Ottoman capital transferred from Adrianople to Istanbul.
**1454** 9 Apr., treaty of Lodi between Milan and Venice. Prussian League appeals to Poland against the Teutonic Knights: Poles defeated at Chojnice. Statute of Nieszawa, *'Magna Carta'* for Polish nobility.
**1454—74** Henry IV, King of Castile.

**1453** al-Mansur Fakhr al-Din Uthma Burji Mamluk Sultan.
**1453—60** al-Ashraf Sayf al-Din Inal, Burji Mamluk Sultan.

**1455** Henry VI recovers: Duke of York raises army: 22 May, Duke of York defeats royal army at St Albans: beginning of Wars of the Roses: 12 Nov., Duke of York again made Protector. Earl of Devon pillages Exeter Cathedral.
**1456** 25 Feb., Duke of York removed from Protectorship.

**1455** Alfonso V of Aragon attempts to organize a Crusade against the Turks. Knights of Rhodes decline to pay tribute to the Ottomans.

**1456** July, John Hunyadi compels Muhammad II to raise the siege of Belgrade. Ottomans take Thrace and Athens. 8 Aug., John Hunyadi d.. Vlad III expels Ottomans under Muhammad II from Wallachia (1466).

**1455—6** R. Gambia explored.

| THE NEAR & FAR EAST | THE AMERICAS | RELIGION & CULTURE |
|---|---|---|

**1448** Concordat of Vienna between Pope Nicholas V and Emperor Frederick III. Frederick III expels the rump Council of Basle: it moves to Lausanne. Eton College Chapel built. Queens' College, Cambridge, begun.

**1449** 27 Oct., Olugh-beg murdered by his son Abd al-Latif. Kapilesvara, ruler of Orissa, takes Rajahmundry and Kondavidu. Ying Tsung captured in campaign against the Mongols: a prisoner for ten years: Ching Tsung, a baby, enthroned: rule by court cliques.

**1449** 7 Apr., Felix V, antipope, abdicates. 25 Apr., Council of Lausanne disbands. York Guildhall begun.

**1449–62** Graz Cathedral built.

**1449–92** Lorenzo dei Medici, poet, statesman, and patron of the arts.

**1449–94** Domenico Ghirlandaio, sculptor.

**1450** 9 May, Abd al-Latif murdered: fresh struggle for succession amongst Timurids.

**1450–1** Abdallah, Timurid, seizes Samarqand.

**1450–3** Binnya Kyan, King of Hanthawaddy.

**1450** Vatican Library founded by Pope Nicholas V. Moravian Brethren (now Moravian Church) instituted. Gutenburg opens printing-shop at Mayence. Gloucester Abbey Tower built.

**c. 1450–1505** Francesco Bello, poet.

**c. 1450–1521** Joaquin des Pres, composer.

**c. 1450–c. 1525** Vittorio Carpaccio, artist.

**1451** Alam Shah abdicates: succ. Buhlul Lodi, first Afghan Sultan of Delhi (–c. 1476).

**1451–3** Bhre Pamotan (?), ruler of Majapahit.

**1451–1526** Dynasty of Lodi Sultans of Delhi.

**1452** Abu Said, Timurid, seizes throne of Samarqand.

**1452–7** Babur Mirza, Timurid, ruler of Herat.

**1451** Glasgow University founded.

**1451–2** Cardinal Nicholas of Cues visits Germany to reform secular clergy.

**1451–1512** Amerigo Vespucci, navigator.

**1452–1519** Leonardo da Vinci, artist and sculptor.

**1452** First sugar refinery built in Madeira. Rumeli Hisar (castle) built.

**1453** Leik Munhtaw, King of Hanthawaddy.

**1453–72** Lady Shin Saw Bu, Queen Regnant of Hanthawaddy.

**1453** John Dunstable, composer, d.

**1453–5** John Gutenberg uses first moveable printing press in Europe at Mayence to print Bible.

**1453–1515** Afonso d'Albuquerque, navigator and Portuguese Viceroy of Goa.

**1454** Tower of Hôtel de Ville, Brussels, built.

**1454–5** Attempt in Rome to organize a Crusade against the Turks.

**1454–1513** Bernardi Betti Pinturicchio, artist.

**1455** Palazzo Venezia, Rome, built. First wine crop reported from Madeira.

**1455–8** Calixtus III (Borgia), Pope.

**1455–1509** Philippe de Commynes, diplomatist and chronicler.

**1455–1522** Johann Reuchlin, grammarian.

**1456** Siamese again attack Malacca: retreat after Malaccan show of force: **1456 ff.,** Malaccan empire built up, extending from Malay border with Siam and Rokan, Siak, Kampar and Indragiri districts of Sumatra.

**1456** 7 July, trial of John of Arc set aside. The Dauphin takes refuge in Burgundy. Breach of relations between the Pope and Alfonso V of Aragon.

**1457** 24 June, Charles VIII of Sweden deposed: succ. Christian I of Denmark and Norway (−1464).

**1458** Possessions of Duke d'Alençon confiscated. Charles VII takes Luxembourg.

**1459** Sept.—Oct., Yorkist rising suppressed by Henry VI: battle of Blore Heath.
**1459—1525** Jacob II Fugger, banker.

**1457** 6 June, Poland takes Marienburg. 23 Nov., Vladislav Posthumus of Hungary and Bohemia d. Skander-beg defeats the Turks at Alessio.
**1457—1504** Stephen the Great of Moldavia.
**1458** 24 Jan., Matthias Corvinus, son of John Hunyadi, elected King of Hungary (−1490). 2 March, George Podiebrad (regent since 1444) elected King of Bohemia (−1471). John, King of Navarre, becomes King of Aragon and Sicily as John II (−1479): Ferdinand I, King of Naples (−1494), illegitimate son of Alfonso V of Aragon. June, Ottomans take Athens.
**1459** Frederick III attempts to seize the throne of Hungary: Matthias Corvinus invades Austria. The Turks take Serbia.

**1460** 10 July, Duke of York defeats Henry VI at Northampton: Henry taken prisoner. 30 Dec., Queen Margaret of England defeats Yorkists near Wakefield: Duke of York killed: 31 Dec., Earl of Salisbury beheaded. Parliament of Ireland declared independent.
**1460—88** James III, King of Scots.

**1460** 13 Nov., Prince Henry 'the Navigator' d. John of Anjou defeats Ferdinand I of Naples at Sarno. George Podiebrad takes Silesia. Rebellion in Catalonia against Aragon. First Chamber of Commerce opened at Antwerp. Ottomans end Despotate of Morea.

**1460** Cape Verde Is. discovered.
**1460—1** al-Muayyad Shihab al-Din Ahmad, Burji Mamluk Sultan.
**1460—±90** Earliest occupation of the circle at Engaruka.
**1460** Blessed Anthony Noyrot, OP, martyred at Tunis.

**1461** 2 Feb., Edward, Duke of York (later Edward IV) defeats Lancastrians at Mortimer's Cross. 17 Feb., Queen Margaret defeats army of Earl of Warwick at St Albans. 4 March, Henry VI deposed: succ. Edward IV (−1470). 29 March, Edward IV defeats Henry VI at Towton Moor, near Tadcaster: Henry VI and Queen Margaret flee to Scotland. 28 June, Edward IV crowned at Westminster.
**1461—83** Louis IX, King of France.
**1462** John II of Aragon cedes Roussillon and Cerdagne to Louis XI. 28 June, Queen Margaret of England allies wtih France.

**1461** Swiss Confederation takes Thurgovia from Tyrol. Ottomans take Trebizond: last vestige of Byzantine Empire removed. Charles of Viana, heir to Aragon, poisoned. War between Frederick III and Albert VI.
**1461—2** Truce between Muhammad II and Skander-beg.

**1461—7** al-Zahir Sayf al-Din Khushqadam, Burji Mamluk Sultan.

**1462** Aug., Gibraltar taken by Castile. Pope Pius II takes the Marches and Romagna from Sigismund Malatesta. The Turks take Mytilene.

**1462** Bissagos Is. discovered.

| THE NEAR & FAR EAST | THE AMERICAS | RELIGION & CULTURE |
|---|---|---|

**1456–66** Bhre Vengker (? ), ruler of Majapahit.
**c. 1456–77** Sultan Mansur Shak, ruler of Malacca.
**c. 1456–98** Tun Perak, Bendehara of Malacca.
**1457** 19 July, Abu Said seizes Herat.
**1457–61** Humayun, Bahmani Sultan.

**1457** University of Freiburg founded.
**c. 1457–1504** Filippino Lippi, artist.

**1458** The Pitti Palace, Florence, begun. Cluniac monasteries reformed. Mosque of Ayyub, Istanbul, built.
**1458–64** Pius II (Aeneas Silvius Piccolomini), Pope.
**1458–1508** Wu Wei, Chinese artist.
**1458–1530** Jacopo Sannazaro, Italian poet.
**1458–1558** Jules-César Scaliger, scholar.

**1459** Arakan prosperous from Bengal and Malacca trade: seizes Chittagong.

**1459** Congress of Mantua fails to organize a crusade.
Basle University founded.
**1459–1535** St John Fisher, Cardinal, theologian.

**1459–64** Ying Tsung restored.
**1459–74** Rukn al-Din Barbak, an Ethiopian slave, King of Bengal.

**1459–74** Tomb and Lesser Golden Mosque of Gaur built.
**1459–1506** Martin Behaim, German cosmographer.

**1459–97** Le Thanh Tong, ruler of Vietnam: reformer, patron of learning and poet: Champa mostly conquered: central Vietnam colonized.
**1459–1511** Mahmud Bigarha, Sultan of Gujaret: the most eminent of his dynasty: conquers much surrounding territory.
**1460** Uriya takes Warangal.

**1460** 18 June, Pope Pius II, *Execrabilis* forbids appeals from the Pope to a Council.
**c. 1460–1524** Hans Holbein the Elder, German artist.
**c. 1460–c.1520** William Dunbar, Scots poet.
**c. 1460–1529** John Skelton, poet.
**c. 1460–1540** Thomas Linacre, physician and scholar.
**1460–83** St George's Chapel, Windsor, built.
**1460–1528** Bernhardin Strigel, German artist.
**1460–1529** Andrea Sansovino, sculptor and architect.
**1460–1523** Gerard David, Flemish artist.
**1461** Louis XI annuls the Pragmatic Sanction of Bourges.

**1461–3** Nizam, Bahmani Sultan.

**1462** System of civil service examinations reformed in Vietnam.

**1462** Pope Pius II annuls the *Compactata* of Iihlava: the Chalice forbidden to the laity. Pius II formally condemns W African slave trade. Topkapi Sarayi, Sultan's Palace, Istanbul, begun.

1462—1470

WESTERN &
NORTHERN EUROPE

CENTRAL, SOUTHERN
& EASTERN EUROPE

AFRICA & EGYPT

**1462–3** Queen Margaret's army, under Pierre de Brezé, abortively raids England.
**1462–1505** Ivan III (the Great), Grand Duke of Muscovy (Tsar from 1480).
**1462–1598** Dynasty of Rurik, rulers of Russia.
**1463** Aug., Queen Margaret retires to Flanders, and then France. Burgundian towns on the Somme surrendered to Louis XI.

**1463** The Sforza take Genoa. Sigismund Malatesta takes Rimini. Peace between Frederick IV and Matthias Corvinus: Albert of Austria d.: Frederick IV takes his possessions. Muhammad II invades Bosnia.
**1463–79** War between Venice and the Ottomans.

**1463–99** Mohamman Rumfa, King of Kano.

**1464** 1 May, Edward IV marries Elizabeth Woodville secretly. 1 June, peace between England and Scotland. Christian I of Denmark deposed from throne of Sweden: Charles VIII of Sweden restored (–1465). *Ligue du Bien public* formed by principal nobles against Louis XI by Charles the Bold.
**1465** Jan., Edward IV granted tunnage and poundage by Parliament. Angel-noble first coined in England. 16 July, Louis XI defeated by Burgundians at Montléry. 29 Oct., peace of St Maur faced with demands of the *Ligue*, Louis XI makes concessions: the *Ligue* dissolved.

**1464–9** Piero I dei Medici, Gonfaloniere of Florence.

**1465** Kettil Karlson Wasa, and then Jöns Bengtston Oxenstjerna (–1466), successively administrators of Kingdom of Sweden. 5 July, Henry IV the Impotent of Castile and León deposed by assembly of nobles and ecclesiastics at Avila.
**1465–6** Ottomans take Herzogovina.
**1465–1508** Albert the Wise, Duke of Bavaria.

**1464–92** Sonni Ali the Great (Ber), King of Songhai.

**1465** Sonni Ali campaigns against nearby peoples.

**1466** Charles the Bold destroys Dinant. Parliamentary records instituted in Scotland. Alliance between Louis XI of France and the Earl of Warwick.
**1466–7** Erik Axelsson Tott, administrator of the Kingdom of Sweden.
**1467** Rebellion in Liège.
**1467–70** Charles VIII restored in Sweden.
**1467–77** Charles the Bold, Duke of Burgundy.
**1468** 14 Feb., Earl of Desmond beheaded for alleged treason at Drogheda. French Estates-General meet at Tours. Rebellion led by Duke of Brittany put down. Charles the Bold takes Liège.

**1466** The Pitti conspire against the Medici in Florence. Austria rebels against Frederick III. Treaty of Thorn: Teutonic Knights evacuate W Prussia: granted E Prussia as a fief of Poland: Poland gains Pomerania, Thorn and Danzig.

**1467–8** Bohemia rebels against George Podiebrad.

**1468** Castilian nobles compel Henry IV of Castile and León (the Impotent) to recognize his sister Isabel as his heir. Skander-beg d.: Albania falls to the Ottomans.

**1466** 12 June, Portugese royal government formally set up by charter in C. Verde and Guinea.

**1467** al-Zahir Sayf al-Din Yalbay, Burji Mamluk Sultan.
**1467–8** al-ZahirTimurbugha, Burji Mamluk Sultan.

**1468** Sonni Ali expels Tuareg from Timbuktu.
**1468–78** Baeda Mariam of Ethiopia: provinces re-organized: capital peripatetic.
**1468–93** Timbuktu under Songhai.
**1468–95** al-Ashraf Sayf al-Din Qait-bay, Burji Mamluk Sultan.
**1469** Portuguese take Anfa.

**1469** Charles the Bold purchases Upper Alsace from Sigismund of Austria. Edward IV taken by Earl of Warwick at Northampton: imprisoned at Middleham.

**1469** 19 Oct., Isabel of Castile m. Ferdinand of Aragon. Matthias Corvinus proclaims himself King of Bohemia.
**1469–78** Giuliano I dei Medici governor of Florence with his brother Lorenzo the Magnificent (sole ruler 1478–92).

**1470** Oct., Edward IV flees to Flanders: 9 Oct., Henry VI restored by Earl of Warwick (–1471). Assembly of Notables meets at Tours.

**1470** Negropontus taken by the Ottomans from the Venetians.

**1470** Benedetto Dei visits Timbuktu.
**c.1470** Ngazargarmu founded as capital of Bornu.
**1470–1524** Muhammad al-Shaikh al-Portugali, Wattasid.

| THE NEAR & FAR EAST | THE AMERICAS | RELIGION & CULTURE |
|---|---|---|

**1463** Uriya raid Kanchi.
**1463–82** Muhammad III, Bahmani Sultan.

**1463** 22 Oct., Pope Pius II proclaims a Crusade against the Ottomans.
**post 1463** The *Cathari* in Bosnia gradually disappear.
**1463–94** Pico della Mirandola, philosopher and theologian.
**1463–70** Mosque of Muhammad the Conqueror, Istanbul, built.
**1464–71** Paul II (Barbo), Pope.
**1464–1534** Philippe de Villiers de l'Isle-Adam, Grand Master of the Knights of St John of Jerusalem.

**1464** Hurricane, followed by pestilence, devastates Yucatán peninsular.

**1465–85** Virupaksa, Raya of Vijayanagar:territory expanded.

**1465–1536** Hector Boethius (or Boece), Scots historian.
**c.1465–c.1536** Gil Vicente, Portugese dramatist.
**1465–1547** Conrad Peutinger, antiquary.

**1466–78** Bhre Pandan Salar (?), ruler of Majapahit.

**1466** George Podiebrad of Bohemia deposed and excommunicated by Pope Paul II.
**1466–1536** Desiderius Erasmus, Dutch humanist.

**1467** Paraktama Baku VI d.: Kingdom split up into Udarata, Kotte and many small princes.

**1468** Pope Paul II arrests and tortures members of the Roman Academy: the Academy dissolved. See of Vienna created.
**1468–1560** Andrea Doria, admiral.
**c. 1468** Muhammad al-Kati, historian, b.

**1469** 17 Feb., Abu Said put to death by Uzun Hasan, Turcoman leader.
**1469–78** Uzun Hasan, ruler of Persia.
**1469–81** Thihathura, King of Ava.
**1469–1501** Ghiyas al-Din, Sultan of Malwa.
**1469–1539** Chaitanya, Bhakti movement leader.
**1470–4** Russian merchant Athanasius Nikitin travelling in Bahmani dominions.

**1469–1527** Niccolò Machiavelli, political writer and historian.
**1469–1539** Baba Nanak, founder of the Sikh sect.

**1470** 19 Apr., Paul II ordains each twenty-fifth year as a Year of Jubilee. First Church built in Madeira.
**1470–1523** Tang Yin, Chinese artist.
**c.1470–1529** Mathias Grünewald, German artist.
**1470–1547** Cardinal Pietro Bembo, historian and poet.

| WESTERN & NORTHERN EUROPE | CENTRAL, SOUTHERN & EASTERN EUROPE | AFRICA AND EGYPT |
|---|---|---|
| **1471** Spring, Edward IV returns to England: 14 Apr., defeats and kills Earl of Warwick and Yorkist army at Barnet: 4 May, defeats Queen Margaret at Tewkesbury: Edward, Prince of Wales, killed: 21 May, restored to the throne (–1483): Henry VI d. (? murdered) in the Tower of London. Louis XI takes Picardy from Charles the Bold. Charles the Bold besieges Beauvais.<br>**c.1471–80** Danish seamen visit Greenland with partly Portuguese crew: Labrador or Newfoundland reached.<br>**1471–97** Steno I, Administrator of the Kingdom of Sweden. | **1471** 22 May, George Podiebrad of Bohemia d.  27 May, Vladislav II elected (–1516): Matthias Corvinus retires to put down rebellion in Hungary. | **1471** Portuguese take Tangier, Arzila and Larache. João de Santarem and Pedro d'Escobar reach R. Niger estuary. Chechaouen founded.<br>**1471–6** Gao besieges Jenné. |
| **1472** Ivan III of Russia m. Zoë Sophia Paleologus, niece of the last Emperor of Byzantium: adopts two-headed eagle in his arms.<br>**1472–7** In a series of manoeuvres and battles, Louis XI puts an end to the power of the feudal nobles in France. | **472** Rebellion in Roussillon. John II of Aragon retakes Barcelona. War between Hungary and Poland. | **1472** Fernão da Po discovers the island now named after him.<br>**1472–1504** Ali Ghadji, King of Kane capital, Ngazargarmu. |
| **1473** 29 Sept., Charles the Bold fails to obtain royal title from Frederick III in Trèves. Charles the Bold takes Guelderland and Zutphen: invades Lorraine. | **1473** Venetians attempt to take Cyprus. | **1473** Songhai frees itself from Mali.<br>**1473–4** Ethiopia twice defeated by Adal. |
| **1474** Peace of Utrecht between Edward IV and the Hanse towns. Treaty between Edward IV and Charles the Bold. Roussillon becomes part of France. | **1474** June, the 'Perpetual Arrangement': the Swiss Confederation recognized by Austria. Oct., Swiss declare war on Charles the Bold of Burgundy. Alsace rebels against Burgundy: Union of Constance between the Swiss and Alsace. Cologne rebels against Charles the Bold: he besieges Neuss. Pope Sixtus IV conquers Umbria. Sultan Muhammad II invades Wallachia.<br>**1474–9** War of succession in Aragon.<br>**1474–1504** Isabel, Queen of Castile, wife of Ferdinand II (the Catholic), later King of Aragon. | |
| **1475** Edward IV makes war on France: 29 Aug., peace of Picquigny: Edward bought off by a ransom payment and an annuity. Charles the Bold invades Lorraine: Nancy taken. | **1475** The Ottomans take Caffa: Khan of Crimea made subject: Stephen the Great of Moldavia expels Turks from Wallachia. | **1475** 25 Nov., Ruy de Sequeira reaches St Catherine: 21 Dec., São Tomé.<br>**c.1475** Warri founded. |
| **1476** Charles the Bold defeated by the Swiss at Grandson and Morat. Lorraine rebels. Lorenzo dei Medici seizes the property of Pazzi. | **1476** Stephen the Great of Moldavia takes over Wallachia. | **1476–1524** Spain occupies Canary I |

| THE NEAR & FAR EAST | THE AMERICAS | RELIGION & CULTURE |
|---|---|---|

**1471** Chams defeated by Vietnam: Champa state shortly crumbles.

**1471—93** Reign of Topa-Inca Yupanqui, Inca ruler.

**1471—84** Sixtus IV (della Rovere), Pope.
**1471—1528** Albrecht Dürer, German artist, etcher and engraver.

**1472** Muhammad Shah Bahmani recovers Goa.
**1472—92** Dhammazedi, elected King of Hanthawaddy: m. predecessor's daughter.
**1472—92** Dhammazedi, King of Pegu: Theravada Buddhism established and purified: legal reforms carried out: high point in Burmese culture.
**1473** Muhammad Shah Bahmani takes Belgaum.
**1473 or 1474** Famine in the Deccan.

**1474** Kedah state becomes Muslim.

**1472** Newfoundland reached by Dietrich Pining, a Dane.

**1472** Mosque of Qait-Bay built. St Andrew's made an archbishopric. Monte della Pietà, pawnshop, opened in Salimbeni Castle, Siena.
**1472—1522** Pietro Torrigiano, Italian sculptor.

**1473—1529** Wang Yang-Ming, philosopher and general.
**1473—1543** Nicholas Copernicus, Polish astronomer.
**1473—84** Sistine Chapel constructed.
**1474** First book printed in Poland.
**1474—1533** Lodovico Ariosto, poet and playwrite.
**1474** First printing shop set up in Valencia, Spain. Building of Magdalen College, Oxford, begun. St George's Chapel, Windsor, begun. Mosque and mausoleum of Qait Bay, Cairo, completed.

**1475—1541** Gednndub, second Dalai Lama ruler of Tibet.

**1475** Diego d'Almagro, conquistador in Peru.

**1475** Buda University founded. Pope Sixtus IV opens the Vatican Library to the public.
**1475—9** Uspensky Cathedral built in the Kremlin by Aristotle Fioravanti of Florence.
**1475—1517** Fra Bartolemmeo di San Marco, artist.
**1475—1525** Giovanni Rucellai, Italian poet.
**c.1475—1530** Thomas, Cardinal Wolsey, statesman and ecclesiastic.
**1475—1535** St (Sir) Thomas More, Lord High Chancellor of England, historical and political writer, and martyr.
**c.1475—1560** Clément Jannequin, composer.
**1475—1564** Michelangelo Buonarotti, artist, architect and sculptor.
**1476** Uppsala University founded. William Caxton sets up first printing press in England in precincts of Westminster Abbey.
**1476—1514** Church of St Satiro, with *trompe d'oeil* apse, built by Bramante in Milan.

1477—1483
WESTERN &
NORTHERN EUROPE

CENTRAL, SOUTHERN
& EASTERN EUROPE

AFRICA & EGYPT

**1477—1513** Gerald, 'Great Earl' of Kildare, ruler of Ireland.

**1477** 5 Jan., Swiss victorious at Nancy: Charles the Bold killed. Louis XI annexes Burgundy: René restored in Lorraine. 19 Aug., Maximillian of Austria m. Margaret of Burgundy. Pope Sixtus IV interdicts Florence. Matthias Corvinus invades Austria.

**1477** Revolt in the Canary Is. put down.

**1478** Court of the Star Chamber instituted in England. Nijni Novgorod taken by Ivan III: market closed and transferred to Moscow.

**1478** Apr., the Pazzi conspire against the Medici: 2 May, Giuliano dei Medici murdered. Pope Sixtus IV excommunicates Lorenzo dei Medici: makes war on Florence. Peace of St Jean de Luz between France and Castile.

**1478—94** Eskender, Emperor of Ethiopia.

**1479** 7 Aug., Maximilian defeats the French at Guinegatte.

**1479** Ferdinand II (the Catholic) succ. John II of Aragon without opposition (—1516): crowns of Aragon and Castile united: separate administration continued (—1512). Revolt in Milan: Lodovico Maria Sforza, *Il Moro*, takes power (—1499). Treaty of Constantinople between Venice and the Ottomans: Venice cedes Lemnos and part of Albania. Peace of Olmütz between Hungary and Poland. The Ottomans invade Styria.

**1479** Mossi takes Walata.

**1480** 10 July, René of Lorraine d.: Louis XI inherits Bar and Anjou. Abortive expedition against Russia by Mongols halts on R. Ugra. Ivan III (the Great) proclaims himself Tsar of Russia. John Lloyd of Bristol sent to discover Brazil: reaches N Atlantic islands.

**1480** 6 March, treaty of Toledo: Portugal cedes Canary Is. to Spain: Spain recognises Portugese conquests in Morocco. *Consejo Real* (Royal Council) reformed in Aragon: nobles deprived of right to vote but allowed to attend: voting membership confined to *Istrados* (learned men) summoned by the Crown. Pope Sixtus IV and the Medici reconciled. 28 July, Turks take Otranto: 12,000 inhabitants murdered.

**ante 1480** Changa, later Changamire, and Torwa, begin to make themselves independent of Monomotapa.
**c. 1480—90** Nyuhuma, Monomotapa

**1481** Louis XI takes Franche Comté, Provence and Maine.
**1481—1513** Hans, King of Denmark and Norway.

**1481** 22 Dec., Convention of Stanz: Freiburg and Solothurn join Swiss Confederation. Matthias Corvinus invades Austria. The Turks expelled from Otranto. Granada renews hostilities against Castile. John II of Portugal (—1495): Duke of Braganza executed: power of Portugese nobles sharply curbed: eighty put to death with or without trial.

**1481** John Tintam and William Fabia first English interlopers on W African coast. Jem, brother of Ottoman Bayazid II, given refuge by Qait Bay.

**1482** Khan of Crimea takes Kiev: cathedral of St Sophia pillaged. English temporarily occupy Edinburgh: recover Berwick. Mary of Burgundy d.: 23 Dec., treaty of Arras: Max Maximilian acquires Franche Comté, Luxembourg and the Netherlands.
**1483** 9 Apr., Edward IV d.: succ. Edward V: Richard, Duke of Gloucester named Protector. 23 June, Edward V and his brother, Duke of York, murdered in the Tower of London: 26 June, Richard usurps throne as Richard III (—1485): Henry Tudor, Earl of Richmond, emerges as Lancastrian claimant. 30 Aug., Louis XI of France d.: succ. Charles VIII (—1498). College of Arms established in London.
**1483—97** Perkin Warbeck's rebellion in Ireland.

**1482** Ferdinand of Aragon takes al-Hammah, gateway to Granada.
**1482—4** Venice provokes war in Italy.

**1482** Elmina Fort, Gold Coast, built by the Portugese.

**1483** Mossi raid Walata: routed by Sonni Ali.

| THE NEAR & FAR EAST | THE AMERICAS | RELIGION & CULTURE |
|---|---|---|

**1477—88** Sultan Ala al-Din Shah, ruler of Malacca.

**1477** Universities of Mainz and Tübingen founded.
**1477—1510** Giorgione da Castelfranco, artist.
**1477—1576** Titian, otherwise Tiziano Vecellio, artist.

**1478** Holy Office, or Inquisition, instituted in Castile.
**1478—1533** Frascatorius, authority on contagious diseases.
**1478—1549** Giovanni Giorgio Trissino, Italian poet.

**1479—1529** Baldassare Castiglione, author.

**1480** Import of foreign books into Spain freed from customs duties. Vaulted roof of Divinity School, Oxford, built. The Parachute invented by Leonardo da
**c. 1480** The screw-jack invented.
**1480—1540** Gerard Hoorenbault, Flemish artist.
**c. 1480—1562** Adrian Willaert, composer.

**1481—1512** Bayazid II, Ottoman Sultan.
**1481** Muhammad Shah Bahmani takes Kondapalli: assumes title of Ghazi: campaigns against Vijayanagar: raids Kanchi.
**1481—1502** Minkhaung, King of Ava.

**1481** Verrochio's statue of Colleoni erected in Venice. Sistine Chapel decorated. Ethiopian Embassy received at the Vatican. Sixtus IV forbids sale of arms in W Africa.

**1482** Muhammad Shah Bahmani d. of drunken excesses: succ. Mahmud (—1518): provincial governors make themselves independent.

**1482** Concordat between the Holy See and Spain. Postal system organized in England by Edward IV, with relays of horses every twenty miles.

**1483** 17 Oct., Inquisition in Spain put under joint direction of church and state
**1483—1520** Raphael of Urbino, artist and architect.
**1483—1530** Francesco Guiccardini, Italian historian.
**1483—1546** Martin Luther, Protestant reformer.
**1483—1546** Francisco de Vitoria, theologian and international jurist.

| WESTERN & NORTHERN EUROPE | CENTRAL, SOUTHERN & EASTERN EUROPE | AFRICA & EGYPT |
|---|---|---|
| **1483–1501** Hans, King of Denmark and Norway, also King of Sweden.<br>**1484** 31 March, Edward Prince of Wales, d.: buried at Sheriff Hutton. Franco-Scottish treaty renewed, truce between England and Scotland. The Estates-General meet at Tours. | **1484** 7 Aug., peace of Bagnolo between Ferrara and Venice: Venice gains the Polesina. The Colonna family rebel in Rome.<br>**1484 or 1485** John II of Portugal declines Columbus's proposal to explore western route to the Indies. | c. **1484–1504** Ozolua, Oba of Benin. |
| **1485** 7 Aug., Henry Tudor, Earl of Richmond, lands at Milford Haven: 22 Aug., defeats Richard III at Market Bosworth: Richard III killed. Henry VII King by right of conquest (–1509): 30 Oct., crowned. Ivan III takes Tver.<br>**1485–8** 'The Foolish War': rebellion of the Dukes of Brittany and Orléans put down in France.<br>**1485–1508** Walls of the Kremlin built.<br>**1485–1603** Tudor dynasty in England.<br>**1486** 17 Jan., truce between England and France. 18 Jan., Henry VII of England m. Elizabeth of York. | **1485** 22 May., Matthias Corvinus takes Vienna. Rebellion against Ferdinand of Naples supported by Pope Innocent VIII. Ferdinand of Aragon takes Navarre. Stephen the Great of Moldavia seeks alliance with Casimir Jagellon against the Ottomans. Hernán Cortés b.<br>**c.1485** Isabel of Castile refers Columbus's plan for exploration of the western route to the Indies to a committee (–1492).<br><br>**1486** 16 Feb., Maximilian I of Austria elected King of the Romans. Peace between the Pope and Naples. Rebellion led by the Orsini harshly put down in Rome.<br>**1486–1525** Frederick, the Wise, Elector of Saxony. | **1485** S Tomé colonized by Portuguese.<br>**c.1485–6** João Afonso d'Aveiro visits Benin: returns with ambassador to Lisbon.<br><br>**1486** Wolof ruler of Bemoim visits Lisbon: presents John II with 100 slaves. |
| **1487** Ivan III takes Kazan. 17 Apr., commercial treaty of Novgorod with the Hanse towns. 5 May, Yorkist rebellion; 24 May, Lambert Simnel, pretender, crowned in Dublin: lands in Lancashire: 16 June, defeated at Stoke-on-Trent: imprisoned in the Tower. Nov., Henry VII of England reforms the Court of the Star Chamber.<br>**1488** Maximilian I removes the commercial privileges of Bruges to Antwerp. Crusade in the Alps against the Waldenses. Battle of St Aubin du Cormier ends the 'Foolish War'.<br>**1488–1513** James IV, King of Scots. Truce between England and Scotland renewed.<br>**1489** 10 Feb., treaty of Redon between Brittany and England. 14 Feb., treaty of Dordrecht between England and the Empire. 27 March, commercial treaty between England and Spain. Massacre of Waldenses in Dauphiné. First act against enclosure of common land in England. | **1487** Ferdinand of Aragon takes Málaga.<br>**1487–94** Grand-Masterships of Spanish military orders vested in the Crown.<br><br><br><br><br>**1489** Cyprus occupied by Venice.<br>**1489–91** Embassy from Kongo to Portugal. | **1487** Portuguese establish factory at Wadan.<br><br>**1488** Apr., Bartholemeu Dias sights Cape of Good Hope.<br>**1488–90 or 91** Pedro da Covilhão visits Red Sea and eastern Africa, returning to Cairo.<br>**1488–1518** Sultan of Adal pursues policy of neutrality towards Ethiopia. |
| **1490** Rebellion in Cornwall. | **1490** 6 Apr., Matthias Corvinus d.: succ. Vladislav II of Bohemia (–1516). 15 July, Vladislav II of Bohemia elected King of Hungary (–1516). Attack on Granada fails. Frederick III retakes Austria. Maximilian I of Austria m. Anne, Duchess of Brittany. | c.**1490–4** Changamire makes himself fully independent of Monomotapa: Changamire dynasty founded. |

**THE NEAR & FAR EAST** | **THE AMERICAS** | **RELIGION & CULTURE**

**1484 or 1490** Imad al-Mulk makes Berar independent of the Bahmani: Imad Shahi dynasty founded (−c.1619).
**1484–1508** Parakrama Bahu VIII of Kotte: agrees (1505) to pay tribute to Portugal.
**1485** Virupaksa II of Vijayanagar murdered by his son: murdered by his younger brother: power seized by Saluva Narasimha, a usurper (−1490–1).

**1486** Walls of Toungoo fortified by Minkyinyo: recognized as sovereign by Ava, Pegu and Chengmai.
**1486–1531** Minkyinyo, King of Burma.
**1486–1752** Toungoo dynasty, Burma.

**1488** Pedro da Covilhã visits Aden, Hormuz and Calicut.
**1488–1511** Sultan Mahmud Shah, ruler of Malacca (d. 1528): Malacca at its zenith.

**1489** Sultan Buhlul Lodi d.: Nizam Khan, his son, elected successor: takes throne-name Sultan Sikandar Ghazi (−1517): Agra, chief residence. Yusuf Adil Khan, governor of Bijapur, revolts against the Bahmani: alleged to be son of Ottoman Murad II: Sultan of Bijapur (−1510), founder of Adil-Shahi dynasty (−1686).
**1490** Malik Ahmad, governor of Junnar, revolts against the Bahmani: defeats Mahmud Bahmani: founds city of Ahmadnagar: assumes throne-name of Ahmad Nizam Shah: founder of Nizam Shah dynasty.
**1490–1** Narasimha, usurper of Vijayanagar, d.: succ. Immadi Narasimha, an infant: Narasa Nayaka, regent.

**1487** 20,000 persons sacrificed to god Huitzilopochtli on site of present cathedral of Mexico City.

**1484** Innocent VIII: Bull *Summis desiderantis affectibus* against witchcraft. College of Arms, London, incorporated.
**1484–8** Mosque of Bayazid II, Edirne, built.
**1484–92** Innocent VIII (Cybo), Pope.
**1484–1531** Ulrich Zwingli, reformer.

**1485** First printing of the Koran in Arabic made by Alessandro de Paginini in Venice. Holy Office, or Inquisition, instituted in Aragon. Sir Thomas Malory: *Morte d'Arthur.*
**1485–1555** Bp Hugh Latimer, Anglican reformer and divine.
**c.1485–1561** Matteo Bandello, writer.
**c.1485–1561** Jean Duvet, French engraver.
**1485–1514** Funchal Cathedral built.
**1485–1546** Juliano Giamberti Sangallo, architect.

**1486–9** Girolamo de Savonarola, OP, preaching in Italy.
**1486–1500** Cardinal Morton, Abp of Canterbury.
**1486–1533** Chaitanya, Bengali school teacher, spreads Hindu devotional *Vaishnava* movement.
**1486–1570** Jacopo Sansovino, sculptor and architect.
**1486** Freiburg-im-Breisgau University founded.

**1488** Pavia Cathedral begun. Duke Humphrey's Library opened at Oxford.
**1488–1530** Andrea del Sarto, artist.
**1488–1568** Miles Coverdale, translator of the Bible.
**c. 1488–1535** John Houghton, martyr, last Prior of the London Charterhouse.

**1489–1544** Francesco Maria Molza, Italian poet.
**1489–1556** Abp Thomas Cranmer, theologian and liturgist.

**1490** Savonarola elected Prior of St Mark's in Florence. Tower of Magdalen College, Oxford, begun.
**c. 1490–1536** William Tyndale, translator of the Bible.
**1490–1547** Vittoria Colonna, Italian poetess.
**c. 1490–1553** François Rabelais, satirist.

| WESTERN & NORTHERN EUROPE | CENTRAL, SOUTHERN & EASTERN EUROPE | AFRICA & EGYPT |
|---|---|---|

**1491** France occupies Brittany. Anne of Brittany's marriage with Maximilian I annulled: 6 Dec., she m. Charles VIII of France. 21 Dec., truce of Coldstream between England and Scotland renewed for five years.
**1491–2** Franco-Scottish treaty renewed.
**1492** Henry VII of England besieges Boulogne: 3 Nov., bought off by Treaty of Etaples.

**1493** 19 Jan., peace of Barcelona: Rousillon and Cerdagne ceded to Ferdinand of Castile by Charles VIII of France. 23 May, Treaty of Senlis: Charles VIII of France cedes Franche Comté and Artois to Austria. Commercial war between England and Flanders.
**1494** 13 Oct., Sir Edward Poynings takes office as Viceroy of Ireland. 6 Nov., Ivan III closes Hanse mart at Novgorod. Sante Cruz de Tenerife founded.
**1494** 1 Dec. **–1495** 'Poynings' Parliament': royal supremacy enforced in Ireland: acts of 'pretended Parliament of 1460 annulled: 'Poynings' Law' restricts powers of Dublin Parliament.

**1495** Perkin Warbeck, and his Irish allies, surrender at Waterford: Warbeck moves to Scotland.
**1495–7** James IV of Scotland invades England on behalf of Perkin Warbeck.

**1496** 24 Feb., *Magnus Intercursus* ends trade war between England and Flanders. 18 July, England joins the Holy League. Sept., Scotland invades England (–1497). Poynings leaves Ireland: virtual home rule in Ireland restored.

**1491** 7 Nov., treaty of Pressburg: Bohemia and Hungary recognize the Hapsburg right of succession to both thrones. Christian encampment outside Granada destroyed by fire: new town, Santa Fé, built in stone by Isabel of Castile.

**1492** 2 Jan., Granada capitulates to Ferdinand of Aragon. Jews expelled from Castile and Aragon: numbers estimated from 165,000 to 800,000 emigrate. Jan., Isabel of Castile appoints Columbus Admiral, Viceroy and Governor of all lands he may discover. Treaty of friendship between Bavaria and the Swabian League.
**1492–4** Piero II dei Medici, ruler of Florence.
**1492–1501** John Albert, King of Poland.
**1492–1506** Alexander, King of Lithuania.
**1493** Diet of Piotrkow gives new constitution to Poland.
**1493–1519** Maximilian I, Holy Roman Emperor.

**1494** 7 June, treaty of Tordesillas between Spain and Portugal delimits their areas of influence in the New World. 1 Sept., Charles VIII invades Italy. Nov., Piero II dei Medici deposed: Florence ruled by a council. 31 Dec., Charles VIII of France enters Rome, after a triumphal march through Italy. Emperor Maximilian recognizes Perkin Warbeck as King of England. Title of the 'Catholic Monarchs' conferred by the Pope on Ferdinand and Isabel.
**1494–7** John Albert Jagellon attempts to conquer Moldavia.
**1495** 22 Feb., Charles VIII takes Naples. 31 March, Holy League, the Holy See, the Empire, Milan, Spain and Venice formed against Charles VIII. Nov., Charles VIII retreats from Italy. Jews expelled from Portugal. Diet of Worms: Berthold of Henneberg produces plan to reform the Empire: Perpetual Peace proclaimed: Imperial Chamber made a court of appeal: general tax imposed.
**1495–1521** Manuel I of Portugal, 'the Fortunate'.
**1496** 21 Oct., Philip, son of Maximilian, m. Joanna, heiress presumptive of Spain. Regular military service organized in Spain.

**1491** Portugese expedition to Angola Kongo embassy (sent 1489) returns with missionaries and artisans: King Nzinga a Nkuwa baptized as Afonso I.

**1492** Cairo devastated by plague: 12,000 persons said to have died in one day.
**c.1492-3–1541-2** Muhammadu Koran, first Muslim King of Katsina.

**1493–1535** Askia Muhammad of Songhai: adopts title Askia: re-organizes Songhai empire.

**1494–8** Naod, Emperor of Ethiopia.
**1494** Pedro da Covilhã reaches Ethiopia: detained at court (–1525).
**c. 1494–1502** War between Monomotapa and Changamire.

**1495–8** al-Nasir Muhammad, Burji Mamluk Sultan.
**1495–9** al-Fudail, Sultan of Kilwa.

**1496** Spain takes Melilla.

| THE NEAR & FAR EAST | THE AMERICAS | RELIGION & CULTURE |
|---|---|---|
| | | **1491–1544** Teofilo Folengo ('Merlino Coccaio'), Italian poet.<br>**1491–1551** Martin Bucer, reformer.<br>**1491–1556** St Ignatius of Loyola, founder of the Jesuits. |
| **1492–1526** Binnya Ran, King of Hanthawaddy. | **1492** 3 Aug–**1493** 15 March, Columbus's first voyage: reaches Bahamas, Cuba and Hispaniola.<br>**1492** 12 Oct., Columbus sets foot on San Salvador, now Watling Is.: cruises along N Cuba and Hispaniola (now Haiti and Dominican Republic). | **1492–1503** Alexander VI (Borgia), Pope. |
| **1493–1519** Ala al-Din Husain Shah, ruler of Bengal, of Ethiopian origin. | **?** c.**1493** Sugar first introduced into the Caribbean.<br>**1493–6** Columbus's second transatlantic voyage: settlement made at Hispaniola: first clergy sent to New World.<br>**1493–1527** Huayna Capac, Inca ruler. | **1493** 4 May, Alexander VI: *Inter cetera divina* divides discoveries between Portugal and Spain.<br>**1493–1569** Bernardo Tasso, Italian poet. |
| **1494** Sultan Sikandar of Delhi campaigns against rebels in Jaunpur. | **1494** Columbus visits Jamaica and Cuba.<br>c.**1494** Robert Thorner and Hugh Eliot, Bristol merchants, reach Newfoundland. | **1494–1534** Antonio da Correggio, artist.<br>**1494–1568** Jean Parisot de la Vallette, Grand Master of the Knights of Malta. |
| | | **1495** Aberdeen University founded. Savonarola ignores summons to Rome.<br>**1495–1517** Francisco, Cardinal Ximénes, Abp of Toledo, reformer of Spanish Church and statesman.<br>Leonardo da Vinci: *The Last Supper.*<br>c.**1495–1545** John Taverner, composer.<br>**1495–1544** Clement Marot, poet.<br>**1495–1550** St John of God, mystic. |
| **1496** Hieronomo de Santo Stefano, Genoese merchant, first known European to reach Pegu. | | **1496** Forced conversion of Jews and Muslims in Portugal: many expelled. All substantial Scottish landowners required to send their sons to school and university. Rebuilding of Peterborough Abbey begun. |

1497–1503
WESTERN &
NORTHERN EUROPE

CENTRAL, SOUTHERN
& EASTERN EUROPE

AFRICA & EGYPT

| WESTERN & NORTHERN EUROPE | CENTRAL, SOUTHERN & EASTERN EUROPE | AFRICA & EGYPT |
|---|---|---|
| **1497** July–Sept., Perkin Warbeck raises rebellion in Cornwall: imprisoned in the Tower. 30 Sept., truce between England and Scotland. 28 Oct., Hans II of Denmark defeats Swedes at Brunksberg: King of Sweden (–1501).<br>**1498** 7 Apr., Charles VIII d.: succ. Louis XII (–1515). Henry VII returns the wool staple to Antwerp: treaty of Westminster with Hanse towns. | **1497** *Cortes* of Portugal consulted before sending of Vasco da Gama to India: advise against voyage.<br><br>**1498** Grisons join Swiss Confederation.<br>**1498–1512** Niccolo Màchiavelli Secretary of the Government in Florence. | **1497** Askia Muhammad makes pilgrimage to Mecca. 22 Nov., Vasco da Gama reaches the Cape.<br><br>**1498** 2 March, Vasco da Gama reaches Mozambique; 7 Apr., Mombasa; 14 Apr., Malindi.<br>**1498–9** al-Zahir Qansawh, Burji Mamluk Sultan. |
| **1499** Louis XII makes alliances with Venice and Florence: 16 March, treaty of Lucerne with the Swiss. Henry VII orders execution of Perkin Warbeck (23 Nov.) and Earl of Warwick (28 Nov.). Louis XII m. Anne of Brittany.<br>**16th c.** Industrial boom in Europe accompanied by severe inflation as a result of import of gold and silver from C and S America.<br>**1500** Ivan III takes the left bank of the Dnieper from Poland. | **1499** 9 Sept., Vasco da Gama back in Lisbon. Oct., Louis XII, with Swiss and Venetian mercenaries, takes Milan and Genoa.<br>**1499–1501** Caesar Borgia, natural son of Pope Alexander VI, conquers Romagna.<br><br>**1500** 2 Aug., Diet of Augsburg: Council of Regency for imperial administration established. 10 Apr., Ludovico of Milan defeated and taken prisoner at Novara. 11 Nov., treaty of Granada: France and Spain agree on partition of Italy. Unsuccessful revolt of Milan against the French: Genoa voluntarily submits to Louis XII. Maximilian inherits Gorizia. | **1499–1500** al-Ashraf Jan-balat, Burji Mamluk Sultan.<br>**1499** Vasco da Gama bombards Mogadishu.<br><br>**1500** Cabral visits Mozambique, Sofala and Kilwa.<br>**c. 1500** Luba empire founded. Ngola dynasty of Ndongo founded. Mapungubwe abandoned. First Bito dynasties in Uganda. Muzaffarids replace Fakhr al-Din dynasty in Mogadishu. Maize introduced into Africa from Brazil.<br>**c. post 1500** Wolof Kingdoms emerge in Senegambia.<br>**1500–16** al-Ashraf Qansawh al-Ghawri, Burji Mamluk Sultan.<br>**1500–1800** Peoples of Congolese origin move into Zambia and Rhodesia. |
| **1501–3** Steno I again administrator of Kingdom of Sweden. | **1501** July-Aug., Louis XII of France and Ferdinand of Aragon conquer Naples: 13 Oct., peace of Trento: Emperor recognizes French conquests in Upper Italy. The Turks take Durazzo. Basle and Schaffhausen join the Swiss Confederation.<br>**1501–6** Alexander, King of Poland. | **1501** Ascension Is. discovered. |
| **1502** 2 Apr., Arthur, Prince of Wales, betrothed of Katherine of Aragon, d. Anglo-Scottish treaty of friendship: 8 Aug., James IV of Scotland m. Margaret, elder daughter of Henry VII. War between France and Spain. | **1502** 12 Feb., Muslims in Granada given choice between conversion to Christianity or exile.<br>**1502–12** Piero Soderini, Gonfaloniere of Florence. | **1502** Kilwa pays tribute to Portugal. St Helena discovered. |
| **1503** English Statute of Retainers. | **1503** Breach of relations between Aragon and France: French expelled from Naples: 29 Dec., battle of R. Garigliano. *Casa de Contratación* (Board of Trade) established at Seville for Spanish overseas possessions and trade with America. | |

| THE NEAR & FAR EAST | THE AMERICAS | RELIGION & CULTURE |
|---|---|---|
| | **1497** Bartolomé Columbus appointed to rule Hispaniola. John Cabot, from Bristol, reaches Newfoundland, and probably Nova Scotia and New England. | **1497** Savonarola excommunicated. Jesus College Cambridge founded. c.**1497–1535** Francesco Berni, Italian poet. **1497–1543** Hans Holbein the Younger, German artist. **1497–1560** Philipp Schwarzerd Melanchthon, theologian. |
| **1498** 20 May, Vasco da Gama anchors near Calicut (–29 Aug.): welcomed by Zamorin. **1498–1500** Tun Puteh, Bendehara of Malacca. | **1498** John Cabot leads six ships *via* Iceland and Greenland, to Labrador and perhaps Chesapeake Bay. **1498–1500** Columbus's third voyage: reaches Trinidad and Venezuela. | **1498** 23 May, Savonarola burnt as a heretic. Charles VIII requests a general council. Henry VII's Tower, Windsor built. Turin Cathedral begun. **1498–1552** André Osiander, theologian. |
| **1499** Deogiri, or Daulatabad, surrenders to Ahmad Nizam Shah. | | **1499** Muslims in Spain required to conform to Christianity: Arabic books and MSS burnt. Convento dos Jerónimos de Bealem founded **1499–1562** St Peter of Alcantara, founder of the Dischalced Franciscans. |
| **16th c.** Gold mining already begun in Pakang, Malaya. | | **16th c.** Buddhist monk Taranatha: *History of Tibet.* |
| **1500** Ghigas al-Din of Malwa abdicates in favour of his son, Nasir al-Din. Portuguese obtain Cranganore. c. **1500** Chinese population estimated at 15.28 m. Population of Philippine Is. c.½ m. **1500–10** Tun Mutahir, Bendehara of Malacca. **1500–1600** Some 800 Portuguese vessels reach India. | **1500** 22 Apr., Pedro Alvares Cabral discovers coast of modern Brazil: 23 Apr., takes possession for Portugal. Voyage of Gaspar Corte Real to Newfoundland. Francisco Bobadillo sent to Hispaniola as governor: Columbus recalled in chains. | **1500** The Pope celebrates the Jubilee Year: general tithe imposed: Crusade against the Turks proclaimed. c. **1500** Baktashi dervish order founded: principally in European and Asian Turkey. Qadiriyyah order introduced amongst the Somali. **1500–41** Giovanni Guidiccioni, Italian poet. **1500–55** Bp Nicholas Ridley, theologian. **1500–71** Benevenuto Cellini, goldsmith and sculptor. c.**1500–72/3** Christopher Tye, composer. |
| **1501** Nasir al-Din of Malwa poisons his father. | **1501** First African slaves imported into Hispaniola. Portugese expedition explores Brazilian coast. Second voyage of Gaspar Corte Real to Newfoundland: vanishes without trace. Subsequent Portuguese vessels sent to fish off Newfoundland. | **1501–5** Mosque of Bayazid II, Istanbul, built. |
| **1502** Vasco da Gama reaches Calicut again: rupture with Zamorin: turns on Arab shipping. Yusuf Adil Shah makes Shi'ism the state religion in Bijapur. **1502–24** Ismail, Shah of Persia, founder of Safavid dynasty (–1736): Ithna-ashari Khoja Shi'ism declared the state religion. **1502–27** Shwenankyawtshin, King of Ava. | **1502** Accession of Moctezuma II of Mexico. **1502–4** Columbus's fourth transatlantic voyage: coast of C America explored. | **1502** Wittenberg University founded. Censorship of books, and licences to print or sell, introduced in Spain. fl. c. **1502–10** Ludovico di Varthema, Italian traveller and writer. **1502** Gibraltar Cathedral built. Valencia University founded. |
| **1503** Narasa Nayaka d.: succ. as regent of Vijayanagar, Vira Narasimha: murders Raya Immadi and seizes power (–1509). Ludovico di Varthema of Bologna, first Christian known to visit Mecca; reaches Pegu: describes his astonishment at local wealth. | **1503** Portugese expedition under Gonçalo Coelho explores Brazilian coast. | **1503** Pius III (Todeschini-Piccolomini) Pope. *Madrassa* of al-Ghuri, Cairo, built. **1503–13** Julius II (della Rovere), Pope. **1503–19** Henry VII's Chapel at Westminster built. **1503–36** Garcilaso de la Vega, Spanish poet. |

1503–1510
WESTERN &
NORTHERN EUROPE

CENTRAL, SOUTHERN
& EASTERN EUROPE

AFRICA & EGYPT

**1504** 31 Jan., and 31 March, treaties of Lyons: France cedes Naples to Aragon (−1713). 22 Sept., treaty of Blois between Louis XII and Maximilian. Raid of Eskdale puts down Scottish border troubles. Battle of Knocktoe: Kildare takes Galway. Ivan III bans issue of coinage by princes in Russia.
**1505** Estates-General meet at Tours: Claude of France m. Francis of Angoulême. Rising of workers at Lyons.
**1505–33** Vassili III of Russia: territory expanded and re-organized.

**1506** 30 Apr., *Malus Intercursus* between England and the Netherlands. French Estates-General meets at Tours.

**1504** Stephen the Great of Moldavia d.: succ. Bogdan submits to the Ottomans: Moldavia absorbed in Turkey until 1658, Wallachia until 1716. Senate instituted in Poland. 26 Nov., Isabel of Castile d.: succ. Joanna declared unfit to rule because of mental incapacity: Philip of Burgundy regent of Castile.

**1506** 20 May, Columbus d. 25 Sept., Philip of Burgundy d.: Ferdinand of Aragon regent of Castile: recognizes Charles, Joanna's eldest son, as heir to Aragon. 6 Dec., militia instituted in Florence by Macchiavelli. Mob massacres Jews in Lisbon.
**1506–48** Sigismund I, King of Poland.

**1507** 12 March, Caesar Borgia d. 10–28 Apr., Genoa rebels against France: 28 Apr., French rule restored. Apr.–May, Diet of Constance: Imperial Chamber and tax roll established.

**1508** 6 Feb., Maximilian I of Austria assumes imperial title without being crowned. 10 Dec., League of Cambrai between Holy See, Maximilian I of Austria, Louis XII of France and Ferdinand of Spain, against Venice.
**1508** Funchal made a city.

**1504** Portuguese forbid trade S of R Congo.
**1504–34** Amara Dunkas, first Funj King of Sennar.
**1504–50** Esigie, Oba of Benin.

**1505** Francisco d'Almeida sacks Kilwa and Mombasa: Fort Santiago built at Kilwa: Portugese seize monopoly of Indian Ocean carrying trade; Portuguese fort built at Sofala. Spaniards take Mers el-Kebir; Portuguese take Agadir.
**c. 1505–30** Zaria converted to Islam.
**1506** Portuguese explore Madagascar. Barawa taken. Tristan da Cunha Is. discovered.
**1506–43** Imam Ahmad b. Ibrahim al-Ghazi, nicknamed Gran (left-handed).
**1506–43** Nzinga Mvemba Afonso I of Kongo: rapid superficial westernization.
**1507** Portuguese Fort at Sofala completed.

**1508** Vasco Gomes d'Abreu complete church, fort, factory and hospital at Mozambique. Annual expeditions from Portugal to Kongo begin: friction develops.
**1508–40** Lebna Dengel of Ethiopia.

**1509** 21 Apr., Henry VII of England d.: succ. Henry VIII (−1547). 11 June, Henry VIII m. Katherine of Aragon.

**1509** 23 March, Pope Julius II joins League of Cambrai: 27 Apr., excommunicates Venice: 14 May, Louis XII defeats Venice at Agnadello: the Pope reoccupies Romagna: Ferdinand of Aragon takes Otranto and Brindisi.

**1509** Oran taken by Cardinal Ximénes: held until 1708. Portuguese factory established in Malindi.

**1510** Parliament grants Henry VIII tunnage and poundage, and duties on wool, for life. 17 Aug., Dudley and Empson, Henry VII's tax-gatherers, executed. Newfoundland fish being sold in the market at Rouen.

**1510** 24 Feb., excommunication of Venice lifted: league between Pope Julius II and Venice against France. Poles defeat Tatar raid at Wiesnowiec. Louis XII and Maximilian I summon a Council at Pisa.

**1510** Spain takes Bougie, Tunis and Tripoli. Francisco d'Almeida killed in fight at Table Bay.
**1510–1659** Dynasty of Sharifs of the Banu Saad in Morocco.

## THE NEAR & FAR EAST

## THE AMERICAS

## RELIGION & CULTURE

**1504** Portuguese viceroy appointed at Cochin. Babur (Zahir al-Din Muɪ.ammad), hereditary ruler of Farghana, seizes Kabul.

**1504** Hernán Cortés arrives in Cuba.
**c. 1504 ff.** Breton and Norman fishermen begin fishing off Newfoundland.

**1503–42** Sir Thomas Wyatt, poet and courtier.
**1503–56** Giovanni della Casa, Italian poet.
**1504** Russian Synod condemns rationalist heretics.
**1504–73** Giovanni Battista (Cinzio) Giraldo, Italian writer.

**1505** Nov., Lourenço d'Almeida, driven off course from the Maldives, anchors off Colombo. Disastrous earthquake in India and Persia.
**1505–9** Dom Francisco d'Almeida, first Portuguese Viceroy of the Indies.

**1505** Martin Luther enters an Augustinian convent. (Royal) College of Surgeons established in Scotland.
**1505–69** Rej of Naglowice, Polish translator of the *Psalms*.
**c. 1505–85** Thomas Tallis, composer.
**1505–8** Archangel Cathedral, Moscow, built.

**1506** Jean Denyn of Honfleur visits Newfoundland.

**1506** Reconstruction of St Peter's, Rome, begun by Bramante.
**c. 1506–52** John Leland, antiquary.
**1506–52** St Francis Xavier, missionary, and Apostle of the Indies.
**c. 1506–59** Niccolò Tartaglia, Italian mathematician.
**1506–73** Ercole Bentivoglio, poet.
**1506–82** George Buchanan, Scottish historian.

**1507** Portuguese under Albuquerque attempt to take Hormuz; Mahmud of Gujarat allies with Egypt against Portuguese: Egyptian fleet, built at Suez, arrives and joins with Indian vessels under Malik Ayaz. Maw Shans again invade Ava.
**1508** Jan., Egypto-Indian fleet defeats Portuguese squadron off Chaul. Ahmad Nizam Shah of Ahmadnagar d.: succ. Burhan Nizam Shah (–1553). Shah Ismail of Persia occupies Baghdad (–1516).

**1507** The name America first appears on a German map.

**1508** Thomas Aubert of Dieppe visits Newfoundland.

**1507** Pope Julius II promulgates indulgences for rebuilding of St Peter's. Printing introduced in Scotland.
**1507–66** Annibale Carlo, Italian poet.

**1508** Papal Bull gives King of Spain 'royal patronage of the Indies', *de facto* supreme control of the Church in America. New Cathedral built at Salamanca. Luther appointed Professor of Theology at Wittenburg. Alcalá University founded by Cardinal Ximénes de Cisneros. Juan de Montalvo: *Amadis of Gaul.*
**1508–80** Andrea Palladio, architect.
**1509** Erasmus: *In Praise of Folly.* Watch invented by Peter Henle of Nuremberg.
**1509–64** Jean Calvin (Cauvin), Protestant reformer.
**1509–88** Bernardo Telesio, Italian poet.
**1509–90** Ambroise Paré, inventor of artificial limbs.

**1509** Krishadevaraya of Vijayanagar defeats Sultan Mahmud of Bidar: Yusuf Adil Khan defeated and killed. Egypto-Gujarati fleet annihilated by Portuguese off Diu in Kathiawar. Rana Sanga, King of Mewar, rebels against Delhi: allied with Babur. Diego Lopes de Sequeira arrives at Malacca with four or five Portuguese ships: Malaccan attempt to seize Portuguese ships fails: Sequeira withdraws, burning two ships.
**1509–29** Krishnadevaraya, Raya of Vijayanagar.
**1510** Feb., Albuquerque takes Goa from Bijapur by surprise attack: Aug., retaken by Yusuf Adil Shah, who shortly d.: Goa then recovered by Portuguese. Krishnadevaraya of Vijayanagar besieges Raichur: moves on Gulbarga and Bidar. Shah Ismail

**1509** Diego Columbus, governor of Hispaniola. Ponce de León, governor of Puerto Rico. Alonso de Ojeda's expedition against N Colombia: Diego de Nicuesa's expedition to C America: both routed by Indians. Sebastian Cabot, son of John Cabot, penetrates the Hudson Strait.

**1510** First slaves from Guinea reach Haiti.

**1510** Cathedral of Goa founded.
**1510–11** Luther in Rome.
**1510–14** Erasmus holds chair of Greek at Cambridge.
**1510–54** Francesco Coppetta, Italian poet;
**1510–56** Thomas, Lord Vaux, poet.
**1510–68** Luigi Tansillo, Italian poet.

| WESTERN & NORTHERN EUROPE | CENTRAL, SOUTHERN & EASTERN EUROPE | AFRICA & EGYPT |
|---|---|---|
| | | **1510–17** Abu Abdallah Muhammad, Sharif of Morocco. |
| **1511** Russians besiege Smolensk.<br>**1511–22** War between Poland and Russia.<br>**1511–29** Thomas Wolsey paramount influence in English politics. | **1511** 4 Oct., Pope Julius II forms Holy League, of Aragon, England and Venice, to expel the French from Italy. | **1511** Spanish expansion in Morocco checked. Portuguese abandon Socotra |
| **1512–13** England at war with France. | **1512** 11 Apr., battle of Ravenna: French driven out of Italy. July, Castile and Aragon formally united: Ferdinand takes title of King of Spain: creates Palace Guard, nucleus of future standing army: conquers Navarre.<br>**1512–13** Cardinal Giovanni dei Medici (later Pope Leo X), Gonfaloniere of Florence.<br>**1512–20** Salim I, Ottoman Sultan. | **1512** Askia Muhammad the Great of Songhai takes Katsina, Kano and Zaria. Portuguese fort at Kilwa dismantled. Dry-stone building reported in Monomotapa's territory. Simão da Silva sent as resident Portuguese ambassador to Kongo. |
| **1513** Scots invade England as allies of France: 9 Sept., defeated at Flodden: James IV killed: succ. James V (−1542). Russians again besiege Smolensk.<br>**1513–33** Christian II, King of Denmark. | **1513** The French again invade Milan: 6 June, battle of Novara: the French beaten: the English invade N France: 16 Aug., victorious at Guinegatte (Battle of the Spurs): the Swiss invade France as far as Dijon. Appenzell joins the Swiss Confederation. Rebellion of peasants in Breisgau.<br>**1513–16** Giuliano II dei Medici, Gonfaloniere of Florence. | **1513** 565 slaves sent from Guinea to Portugal.<br>c. **1513** Bourbon (now Réunion) and Cirne (now Mauritius) discovered both uninhabited. |
| **1514** 4 Aug., alliance between Emperor Maximilian I and Tsar Vassili III made at Gmünden. 6 Aug., Peace of London between England and France: Louis XII marries Mary, younger sister of Henry VIII (later Duchess of Suffolk). Tithes being paid in Brittany on Newfoundland fishing. Russia takes Smolensk from Poland. Russians defeated by Poles at Orsza.<br>**1514–24** John, Duke of Albany, Regent of Scotland. | **1514** Peasants revolt in Hungary. | **1514** 978 slaves sent from Guinea to Portugal. Antonio Fernandes explores Sofala hinterland. King of Kongo complains of extent of slave trade with Portugal. Portuguese take Mazagan. Abu Yusuf Aruj b. Yaqub, commonly Barbarossa, takes Djidjelli |
| **1515** 1 Jan., Louis XII of France d.: succ. Francis I (−1547). Further act against land enclosure in England.<br>**1515–89** Dynasty of Valois-Angoulême in France. | **1515** July–Aug., treaties between the Empire, Hungary and Poland determine succession. Francis I of France attacks Milan: 13 and 14 Sept., Milanese army cut to pieces at Marignano: Milan and Genoa taken. 14 Dec., treaty of Bologna: peace between Pope Leo X and Francis I: Leo X surrenders Parma and Piacenza. 29 Nov., Perpetual Peace signed between France and Switzerland. Navarre incorporated into Spain. | **1515** 1,423 slaves sent from Guinea to Portugal.<br>c. **1515–61** Muhammadu Kantu, first King of Kebbi: rebels against Songhai.<br>**1515–1830** Turkish domination of Algeria and Tunisia. |

## THE NEAR & FAR EAST

of Persia defeats Usbeg Shaibani.
**1510–11** Paduka Tuan, Bendehara of Malacca.
**1510–15** Afonso d'Albuquerque, Portuguese Viceroy of the Indies.
**1510–34** Ismail b. Yusuf, Sultan of Bijapur: reign spent fighting his neighbours.
**1511** Babur takes Samarqand with aid from Persia. Patih Yunus, first Sultan of Demak, conquers Japara. Afonso d'Albuquerque attacks Malacca with 18 ships and over 1,000 men: 15 Aug., town seized after hard fighting and systematically sacked: Sultan and family flee: Portuguese build fortress churches and civic buildings. Albuquerque sends embassies to Siam and Pegu.
**1511–17** Krishnadevaraya expands Vijayanagar territory southwards.
**1512** Nasir al-Din of Malwa d.: succ. Mahmud II (–1531). Portuguese obtain Chaul.
**c.1512** Abd al-Jamil, with his son Mansuo, joint Sultans of Pahang.
**c. 1512–15** Tomé Pirès reports complex trade communications of Malacca, reaching Egypt and E Africa, Near East, India and China.

**1513** Salim I takes Armenia. Albuquerque abortively attempts to take Aden. Javanese fleet of 100 defeated in the Strait of Malacca. Portuguese obtain Calicut.
**c. 1513** Mahmud, last Sultan of Malacca, sets up new state of Johore, with capital at Bintang, in order to attack Portuguese shipping and to take over Malaccan trade.
**1514** Aug., Shah Ismail of Persia defeated by Ottoman Salim I at Chaldiran: Tabriz and Mesopotamia taken.

**1515** Ottomans occupy part of Armenia. Albuquerque takes Hormuz: fortress built: occupied until 1622.
**1515–24** Johore attacks on Malacca.
**c. 1515–30** Ali Mughjaat Shah founds sultanate of Acheh.

## THE AMERICAS

**1511** *Audiencia* (Crown Court) set up in Santo Domingo. Abortive Spanish expedition to Mexico.
**1511–19** Aguilar, Spanish castaway, cared for by friendly Indians in Mexico.

**1513** Vasco Nuñez de Balboa crosses Panama and sights Pacific Ocean: takes possession of ocean and all surrounding lands by raising flag of Castile.

**1514** Ponce de León discovers Florida.

**1515** Governor Diego Velásquez makes Cuba the main centre of Spanish operations in America.
**post 1515** Brief gold boom in Cuba and Puerto Rico.
**1515 or 1516** Pestilence in Yucatán peninsula.

## RELIGION & CULTURE

**1511** Council of Pisa opened: shortly transferred to Milan. Tsar Vassili III appoints a Patriarch of Moscow on his own authority. First bishops appointed in America: two in Hispaniola, one in Puerto Rico.
**1511–71** Giorgio Vasari, Italian artist, architect and writer.

**1512** Council of Milan disbands. Luther becomes Augustinian Prior at Wittenberg. Polyglot Bible published. Michelangelo completes decoration of Sistine Chapel.
**1512–17** 5th Lateran Council.

**1513** First warships built in England.
**1513–21** Leo X (dei Medici), Pope.

**1514** Johann Tetzel first sells indulgences. Earliest issue known of Arabic press at Fano, Italy.
**1514–30** Thomas Wolsey, Abp of York.
**1514–64** Andreas Vesalius, anatomist.
**1514–72** John Knox, Scots reformer.
The Psalms printed in Geez in Rome.

**1515** Thomas Wolsey made a Cardinal. Château of Chenonceau built.
**1515–68** Roger Ascham, educationist and writer.
**1515–82** St Teresa of Avila, Spanish mystic, religious reformer and writer.
**1515–95** St Philip Neri, religious reformer.
**c. 1515–85** John Feckenham, last Abbot of Westminster.

| WESTERN & NORTHERN EUROPE | CENTRAL, SOUTHERN & EASTERN EUROPE | AFRICA & EGYPT |
|---|---|---|
| **1516** 3 Dec., peace of Brussels between the Empire and France: Verona ceded to Venice: Empire retains Tyrol. 18 Aug., concordat of Boulogne between France and the Vatican. | **1516** 23 Jan., Ferdinand of Aragon d.: succ. Charles I of Hapsburg (−1556): Castile and Aragon united under a single ruler. 13 Aug., treaty of Noyon between France and Austria. Mongols raid Poland, carrying off 50,000 prisoners and much booty. Manuel I of Portugal absorbs grand masterships of military orders into the Crown. **1516–19** Lorenzo II dei Medici, Gonfaloniere of Florence. | **1516** Aruj (Barbarossa) takes Algiers. Ethiopia at war with Adal. **1516–17** al-Ashraf Tuman-bay, last Burji Mamluk Sultan. **1516–17** Salim I takes Syria and Egypt. |
| **1517** Franco-Scottish alliance renewed. Court of the Star Chamber reorganized. | **1517** Charles I visits Spain to receive oaths of fealty from different *Cortes*. English merchants in Andalusia granted privileges. | **1517** 22 Jan., Ottoman Turks, led by Sultan Salim, defeat Sultan Tuman-bay outside Cairo: city seized: 14 Apr., Tuman-Bay hanged: Egypt henceforward subject to Turkey: Caliph al-Mutawakkil deported to Istanbul (Constantinople): Khair-Bey, first Viceroy. Zaila burnt by Portuguese. **1517–1798** Turkish domination of Egypt: 100 different pashas of Egypt. |
| **1518** 2 Oct., Peace of London between the Empire, England, France, the Pope and Spain. Christian of Denmark conquers Sweden. | | **1518** Aruj (Barbarossa) killed. Khair al-Din I Barbarossa offers Algiers to the Ottomans: confirmed with title of Beylerbey. Berbera burnt by Portuguese. **1518 (or 1520)** 'Leo Africanus' captured and presented as a slave to Pope Leo X, who frees and baptizes him. |
| | **1519** 12 Jan., Maximilian I d.: Francis I of France and Henry VIII of England candidates for the imperial throne: 28 June, Charles I of Spain elected as Emperor Charles V (−1556). Mongols again raid Poland. **1519–23** Cardinal Giulio dei Medici (later Pope Clement VII), Gonfaloniere of Florence. | **1519** Abortive Spanish attack on Algiers. |
| **1520** 26-9 May, Charles V visits Henry VIII at Canterbury and Dover. 4–24 June, Field of Cloth of Gold: meeting between Francis I of France and Henry VIII of England. 10 July, Henry VIII of England meets Emperor Charles V at Gravelines: 14 July, secret treaty concluded at Calais. 7 Nov., 'Blood Bath of Stockhold'. Embassy from the Pope to Moscow. **1520–2** Thomas, Earl of Surrey, Viceroy of Ireland. **1521** 25 Aug., secret treaty between Emperor Charles V and England at Bruges against France: war between Charles V and France (−1526): Charles V takes Tournai: 19 Nov., the Sforza take Milan from France. Earl of Strafford beheaded. The Tatars burn the suburbs of Moscow. | **1520** 6 Feb., Württemberg sold by Swabian League to Charles V. Charles V leaves Spain for Germany: a Fleming, future Pope Adrian VI, appointed Regent of Spain: riots and repudiation of the regent ensue: 29 July, Junta of Avila. Salim I, Ottoman Sultan, d.: succ. Sulayman the Magnificent (−1566): Ibrahim, Vizier of Turkey. **1521** 28 Apr., Ferdinand, brother of Charles V, granted Austria. 28 May, Pope Leo X and Charles V ally against France. Oct., Spanish rebels against Charles V crushed at Vilhalar. Peace treaty between Venice and Turkey renewed: Venice granted capitulations. French besiege Pamplona in an attempt to regain Spanish Navarre. | **1520** Funj defeat Turks at Hannak. Khair al-Din Barbarossa defeated by Hafsids. Capital of Adal moved to Harar. **1520–6** Massawa occupied by the Portuguese. **1521** Khair al-Din Barbarossa takes Collo. Lamu pays tribute to Portugal in Venetian currency. |

## THE NEAR & FAR EAST

**1516** Jan-Birdi al-Ghazali, Governor of *wilayah* of Damascus, deserts Egypt for the Ottomans. 24 Aug., battle of Marj Dabiq: Ottomans defeat Qansawh al-Ghawri: Aleppo taken; Oct., Damascus taken; conquest of Syria by Ottoman Turks completed.

**1517** Sikandar Lodi d.: following quarrel for the succession, Ibrahim Shah Lodi succ. (−1526): Gwalior taken. Fernão Pirés de Andrade, Portuguese, visits Canton: first modern European to reach China. Force from Johore sets up stronghold on R. Muar, from which to raid Malacca.
**1517 and 1519** Babur makes reconnaissance raids on India.
**1517−1697** 133 different Ottoman governors of Damascus.
**1518** Rising in Kiangsi crushed by Wang Yang-Ming. Golconda separates from Bahmani sultanate under Quli Qutb Shah (1543): Qutb Shahi dynasty (−1611): capital moved from Warangal to Golconda.
**1518−26** Four puppet Bahmani Sultans: real power in the hands of Qasim Barid, a Turk.
**1519** Ala al-Din Shah d.: succ. Nusrat Shah: Great Golden Mosque and Kadam Rasul built. Portuguese trading station opened at Martaban: trade greatly stimulated. First firearms introduced into China by the Portuguese.

**1520** State of Majapahit finally collapses. Jan-Birdi al-Ghazali proclaims himself independent as al-Malik al-Ashraf of Damascus: Khair Bey, former Mamluk governor of Aleppo, proclaims Aleppo independent under him: both immediately put down by Sulayman I. 19 May, Krishnadevaraya recovers fortress of Raichur from Bijapur.

**1521** Magalhães (Magellan) visits Brunei and Molucca Is. 16 March, Magalhães discovers Philippine Is.: killed in a skirmish at Mactan. Spaniards massacred at Cebú.
**1521−66** Shih Tsung, Ming Emperor.

## THE AMERICAS

**1516** Juan Díaz de Solis discovers R. Plate estuary: killed and eaten on landing by Indians.

**1517** Expedition under Francisco Hernández de Córdoba explores Mexican coast.

**1518** Spanish expedition to Mexico led by Juan de Grijalva.

**1519** Good Friday, Cortés lands in Mexico with fleet of eleven, 550 men and sixteen horses: Villa Rica de la Vera Cruz founded: council elects Cortés Governor and Commander of New Spain. 20 Sept., Fernão de Magalhães begins circumnavigation of the world. Sebastian Cabot visits W Indies.
**1519−22** Mexico conquered by Hernan Cortés.
**1520** 30 June, Cortés withdraws to Tlaxcola, following disastrous retreat. Oct., Magalhães (Magellan) navigates the Strait named after him. Magellan gives Pacific Ocean its name. Moctezuma, ruler of Mexico killed accidentally: succ. Cuitlahuac d. of smallpox after eighty days: succ. Cuauhtemoc.
**1520−50** Spanish *conquistadores* take most of S America (excluding Brazil) and much of present southern US.
**1521** 6 March, Magalhães discovers Ladrone Is. May, Cortés renews attack on Mexico. 13 Aug., Cortés takes and razes Tenochtitlán, Mexican capital: ruler Cuauhtemoc captured: new Mexico City built on the site. João Alvares Fernandes appointed Governor of N American discoveries. Portuguese establish garrison at Pernambuco against French pirates.

## RELIGION & CULTURE

**1516** N. Macchiavelli: *The Prince*. Thomas More: *Utopia*. Erasmus: edition of the *New Testament*. The Oratory of Divine Love founded. Zwingli, a priest of Zurich, first attacks the adoration of relics, monastic abuses and the luxury of the Vatican.
**1516−87** John Foxe, Protestant martyrologist.
**1516−90** Algiers Kasbah built.

**1517** 31 Oct., Luther nails his Ninety-Five Theses to the cathedral door in Wittenberg. Protests by the Parliament and the University of Paris against the Concordat of Boulogne. Franciscan mission set up in Goa.
**?1517−47** Henry Howard, Earl of Surrey, poet.
**1517−86** Luis de Morales, Spanish artist.

**1518** Luther summoned to Rome: appeals to a Council: 12 Oct., interrogated by Cardinal Cajetan at Augsburg. Cardinal Wolsey appointed Papal Legate *a latere* in England.
**1518 94** Tintoretto (Jacopo Robusti) artist.

**1519** 10 Aug., Luther condemned at Cologne. Zwingli prevents the preaching of indulgences in Zurich.
**1519−72** Admiral Gaspard de Coligny, French Protestant leader.
**1519−79** Thomas Gresham, financier.

**1520** 15 June, Pope Leo X: Bull *Exsurge* excommunicates Luther: 10 Dec., Luther burns the bull.
**1520−69** Pieter Breughel (elder), Flemish painter.
**1520** Tower of Belem completed. Sultan Selim Mosque, Istanbul, built.

**1521** 27 Jan., Diet of Worms opened: 17-18 Apr., Luther examined by Papal Nuncio: 26 May, edict of Worms outlaws Luther and his disciples. 20 May, Ignatius Loyola wounded: experiences conversion. Aug., Henry VIII of England publishes *Golden Book* refuting Luther, *Babylonish Captivity of the Church*. Anabaptist movement begins in Wittenberg.

1521–1527
WESTERN &
NORTHERN EUROPE

CENTRAL, SOUTHERN
& EASTERN EUROPE

AFRICA & EGYPT

**1521–44** Intermittent war between
France and Spain.
**1521–57** John III, King of Portugal.

**1522** May, England attacks France in
Picardy. Franco-Scottish alliance
renewed. The Spanish attack Bayonne.
Treaty between Lithuania and
Russia: Russia obtains Smolensk.
Five year truce between Poland and
Russia.
**1523** 20 Jan., Christian II of
Denmark deposed: succ. Frederick
I (−1533). 7 June, Gustavus I Vasa
elected King of Sweden (−1560).
Charles de Bourbon, Constable of
France, deserts to Charles V. House
of Commons rebuffs Wolsey's
demand for extra taxation.

**1522** Dec., the Ottomans take Rhodes.
The French beaten by German and
Spanish army at Bicocca: expelled
from duchy of Milan.

**1523** Russian embassy visits Rome.

**1522** Mamluks revolt in Fayoum
and W Delta.
**fl. 1522–1872** Sultanate of Baghirmi

**1524** Aug., Imperial army repulsed
at Marseilles: pursued by Francis I.
Charles de Bourbon invades Provence.

**1524** 25 Apr., battle of R. Sesia:
Chevalier Bayard killed. 26 Oct.,
the French retake Milan: Francis of
Angoulême restored (−1525).
Catholic Assembly held in Ratisbon.
Peasant revolt in S Germany, Alsace,
and Thuringia, by Thomas Münzer.
Spanish Royal and Supreme Council
of the Indies created.

**1524** Abortive rebellion in Egypt.

**1525** 30 Aug., peace between Henry
VIII and France. Lübeck seizes
Visby.

**1525** 24 Feb., Battle of Pavia: German,
Italian and Spanish army defeats
Francis I of France: taken prisoner:
kept in captivity in Madrid for a year.
Prussia made a duchy. Catholic League
formed at Dessau. Münzer's peasant
rebellion put down. Portuguese *Cortes*
agrees to meet each tenth year.
Muslims in Spain again given choice
of conversion to Christianity or exile.
Permanent commission of the *Cortes*
instituted in Castile.
**1525–32** John the Steadfast, Elector
of Saxony.
**1526** 15 Jan., Treaty of Madrid: Francis
I released. 27 Feb., Lutheran rulers of
Gotha and Hesse make defensive
alliance. 22 May, League of Cognac:
the Pope, Florence, France, Milan and
Venice coalesce against Charles V.
29 Aug., Louis II of Hungary defeated
and killed by Ottomans at Mohacs:
succ., 23 Oct., by Ferdinand I of
Austria as King of Bohemia (−1564):
and, 16 Dec., by John Szapolya as
King of Hungary (−1527).

**1525** Ibrahim Pasha, Grand Vizier
of Turkey, re-organizes Egyptian
administration. Banu Saad take
Marrakesh. Khair al-Din Barbarossa
extends Turkish dominions. Ahmad
Gran begins to make Hubat a centre
of power.

**1526** King of Kongo again complains
of extent of Portuguese slave trade.
**1526–46** Muhammad Idris, Sultan
of Bornu.

**1527** 30 April, treaty of Amiens:
Francis I and Henry VIII ally against
Charles V: French reach Naples.
Henry VIII first raises the question
of annulment of his marriage.

**1527** 1 Jan., Austrian administration
re-organized. Jan., Ferdinand III
elected King of Hungary. 6 May, Rome
sacked by imperial troops under Charles
de Bourbon: Charles killed. May,
future Philip II of Spain b. 6 June.
Florence ruled by a Council (−1530).
Aug., Ferdinand III defeats John
Szapolya at Tokay. Mongols routed
at Kaniow: 80,000 Polish prisoners
recovered.

**1527** Ahmad Gran defeats Ethiopian
army in Adal.

| THE NEAR & FAR EAST | THE AMERICAS | RELIGION & CULTURE |
|---|---|---|
| | c. 1521–5 Portuguese, under João Alvares Fagundes, found colony at C. Breton. | 1521 Henrique, son of Afonso I of Kongo, appointed Vicar Apostolic of Kongo. First conversions of Filipinos to Christianity. |
| 1522 Antonio de Brito builds Portuguese fort at Ternate. | 1522 Cortés appointed Governor and Captain-General of New Spain (Mexico), (–1535). | 1522 2 Feb., Pope Leo X gives Henry VIII of England title of Defender of the Faith *(Fidei Defensor)*: borne by all subsequent English sovereigns. Sept., Luther's *New Testament*, first edn. 1522–3 Adrian VI (Florent), Pope: only Dutch Pope, and last non-Italian. |
| 1523 On invitation of governor, Babur invades Punjab: retires following Usbeq pressure on Balkh. Attempts by Portuguese to obtain a foothold in Sumatra foiled by conquest of Pasai and Pedir by Acheh. Johore raid on Malacca. | 1523 Cristóbal de Olid's expedition to Honduras. French interlopers seize Spanish vessels in the Caribbean. 1523–30 Pedro de Alvaro conquers Guatemala. | 1523 Diet of Nuremberg demands a Council of the Church within one year. Pope Adrian VI promises reforms. First school for Indians started at Texcoco, Mexico, by Franciscan Fr Pedro de Grante. Granada Cathedral begun. 1523–34 Clement VII (dei Medici), Pope. 1523–54 Gaspara Stampa, Italian poet. |
| 1524 Portuguese fort at Colombo dismantled. Johore raid on Malacca. Ava frontier forts occupied by Maw Shans. 1524–76 Tahmasp, Shah of Persia. | 1524 Giovanni Verrazano reaches Newfoundland and Belle Isle: apparently the first to realize that America is a continent, and not a series of islands. | 1524 Heretics expelled from Lyons. c. 1524 Château of Chambord built. Anabaptism spreads in Switzerland. c. 1524–60 Joachim du Bellay, poet and antiquary. c. 1524–80 Luis de Camoens, Portuguese poet. 1524–85 Pierre de Ronsard, poet. |
| 1525 Afghan nobles in Delhi invite Sultan Ibrahim of Kabul to take the throne. | | 1525 William Tyndale: translation of the *New Testament*. Import of Lutheran books forbidden in Scotland. c. 1525 Chiu Ying, Chinese artist. 1525–94 Giovanni Pierluigi da Palestrina, Italian composer. ?1525–1605 John Stow, antiquary. |
| 1526 Babur invades India: 21 Apr., defeats and kills Ibrahim Shah at Panipat: first artillery used in N India: Delhi and Agra occupied. After capturing Johore stronghold on R. Muar, Portuguese sack Bintang: Sultan Mahmud flees to Kampar, Sumatra. 1526–39 Takayutpi, King of Hanthawaddy. ate 1526–1537 Feb., Bahadur Shah, Sultan of Gujarat. | 1526 All Spanish vessels ordered to voyage in groups because of pirates. | 1526 June, Diet of Spires. Evangelical constitution promulgated in Hesse. Luther's Liturgy published. Anabaptists increase in S Germany. Order of Friars Minor Capuchin founded by Matteo di Bassi. 1526–90 Wang Shih-chen, Chinese dramatist. |
| 1527 Rana Sanga of Mewar opposes Babur: 16 March, defeated and routed at Khanna, near Agra. Shah Khan enters Babur's service. Shah Tahmasp defeated by Uzbeq Turks. Shwenankyawtshia, King of Ava, assassinated by Shan Chief Thohanbwa. Maw Shans sack Ava: end of Shan-Burmese dynasty of Ava. 1527–55 Burma ruled by Shan chiefs: Toungoo becomes centre of Burmese nationalism. | 1527–46 Series of Spanish expeditions to Mexico led by Francisco de Montejo. *Audiencia* set up in Mexico. John Rut visits Puerto Rico and S Domingo from England. Huayna Capac, Inca ruler of Peru, d.: divides Kingdom between his sons, Huáscar at Cuzco, and Atahualpa at Quito: Huáscar overcome by Atahualpa. | 1527 Luther m. a nun. Diet of Oldensee: Lutheranism becomes state religion of Denmark. Diet of Västeras: Sweden follows suit. Theologians at Valladolid grant approval to Erasmus's writings. Marburg University founded. 1527–72 Pellegrino Pellegrini, artist. |

1528–1533

WESTERN &
NORTHERN EUROPE

CENTRAL, SOUTHERN
& EASTERN EUROPE

AFRICA & EGYPT

| WESTERN & NORTHERN EUROPE | CENTRAL, SOUTHERN & EASTERN EUROPE | AFRICA & EGYPT |
|---|---|---|
| **1528** 21 Jan., England declares war on the Empire. July, James V of Scotland given full powers, aged sixteen. | **1528** 24 Feb., treaty between John Szapolya and the Ottomans. 30 Aug., French defeated at Aversa. 12 Sept., Genoa becomes a republic under Spanish protection. 23 Oct., treaty between John Szapolya and France. Franco-Ottoman commercial treaty. | **1528** Rising against Portuguese in Eastern Africa: Portuguese sack Mombasa. |
| **1529** 17 Oct., Cardinal Wolsey dismissed by Henry VIII: 25 Oct., Sir Thomas More succ. as Lord Chancellor (−1535). **1529–36** Reformation Parliament in England. | **1529** 22 Apr., treaty of Saragossa between Spain and Portugal on respectives spheres of influence in the East: Spain surrenders Molucca Is. 29 June, treaty of Barcelona between Charles V and the Pope. Battle of Landriano: French lose N Italy: 5 Aug., Peace of Cambrai: Francis I pays indemnity to Charles V, but retains France and Burgundy: Charles V holds all Italy: 28 Aug., England accedes to the treaty. 27 Sept.–14 Oct., Ottomans besiege Vienna: army of 120,000 against 16,000 defenders. Ottomans pillage environs. Civil war between Catholic and Protestant Cantons in Switzerland: Catholics defeated. Negotiations between Charles V and Persia. | **1529** Treaty between Navarre and Morocco. Khair al-Din Barbarossa retakes Algiers: new port constructed state administration re-organized. **1529–42** War between Ahmad Gran and Ethiopia. |
| **1530** 29 Nov., Cardinal Wolsey d. | **1530** 24 Feb., Charles V crowned Emperor at Bologna. 31 Dec., Protestant League of Schmalkalden formed. Knights of St John of Jerusalem take Malta. **1530–7** Florence a republic: Alexander dei Medici, Head of State (Duke from 1532). | **1530** William Hawkins of Plymouth trading in Liberia. **c. 1530** 4,000–5,000 slaves shipped annually from Kongo. |
| **1531** Poor law in England forbids able-bodied beggars. | **1531** 5 Jan., Ferdinand of Austria made King of the Romans. 31 Jan., truce between Ferdinand I and John Szapolya. 11 Oct., Catholic Cantons of Switzerland crush the Protestant Cantons at Keppel: Zwingli killed. 24 Oct., Bavaria joins League of Schmalkalden by treaty of Saalfeld: followed by S German Free Cities and Strasbourg. Alliance between Francis I and John Szapolya. | **1531** Ahmad Gran occupies Dawaro and Shoa. Portuguese open market at Sena. **c. 1531–91** Tsoede (Edegi), first Etsuzhi of Nupe |
| **1532** 16 May, Sir Thomas More resigns the Lord Chancellorship. 20 Nov., treaty of Boulogne. Administrative union between Brittany and France. College of Justice instituted in Scotland. Christian II, former King of Denmark, attempts to take Norway: made prisoner: Frederick I of Denmark becomes King of Norway (−1533). **1533** 25 Jan., Henry VIII secretly m. Anne Boleyn. 12 Apr., Thomas Cromwell appointed Secretary of State in England. 23 May, Abp Cranmer pronounces decree of divorce of King Henry VIII from Katherine of Aragon. 28 May, Abp Cranmer pronounces Henry VIII's marriage to Anne Boleyn valid. | **1532** 26 May, treaty of Scheyern between Bavaria, France, Hesse and Saxony against Frederick I of Austria. June, Ottoman campaign in Hungary: defeated at Güns: 25 June, peace of Nuremberg. French embassy sent to Turkey. **1532–47** John Frederick, the Magnanimous, Elector of Saxony. **1533** 2 June, Peace treaty between Austria and Turkey. Turkish embassy visits France. | **1533** Ahmad Gran takes Amhara, Lasta and other parts of Ethiopia. Embassy from France to Morocco. |

| THE NEAR & FAR EAST | THE AMERICAS | RELIGION & CULTURE |
|---|---|---|

**? 1528–64** Ala al-Din Riayat Shah, Sultan of Johore: ? capital at Johore Lama.

**1528** Francisco Pizarro appointed Governor and Captain-General of Peru. Pánfilo de Nárvaez leads abortive expedition to Florida. First French voyage to W Indies.

**1528** Pope Clement VII holds inquiry into Henry VIII's marriage. Ignatius de Loyola joins University of Paris. William Tyndale: *Obedience of a Christian Man.* Juan de Zumárraga appointed first bishop in Mexico.
**1528–88** Paulo Veronese, artist.
**1529** Second Diet of Spires, disavowed by Charles V. Luther and Zwingli dispute at Marburg: fail to agree on eucharistic doctrine. Anabaptism spreads in the Netherlands. Pope Clement VII declares himself against annulment of Henry VIII's marriage.

**1529** 29 Jan., Babur takes Chanderi by storm; Afghan chiefs of Bihar and Bengal defeated. Krishnadevaraya of Vijayanagar d.: succ. Achyutaraya (−1542).

**1530** Dec., Babur d.: empire consists of Badakhsham, Afghanistan, Punjab, Delhi, Bihar and other territories: succ. Humayun. Uzbeq Turks besiege Herat (−1531). Portuguese officials in Malacca reported as corrupt. Jean Parmentier, first French sea-captain to visit Indonesia, reaches Sumatra. Portuguese obtain Damão.
**1530–4** Tabinshwehti conquers Irawaddy delta, capturing Bassein.
**1531–2** Bahadur of Gujarat seizes Malwa.
**1531–51** Tabinshwehti, King of Burma.

**1530** French destroy Portuguese post at Pernambuco: retaken by Martim Afonso de Souza. Pizarro sets out from Panama to conquer Incas with 180 men and 27 horses.
**c. 1530** Inca Empire stretches from S Colombia to N Argentina and Chile.
**1530–2** Portuguese under Martim Afonso de Souza explore Brazilian coast.

**post 1531–1650** Peru and Mexico leading exporters of gold and silver.

**1530** 20 June, Diet of Augsburg opened: 25 June, Confession of Augsburg: 22 Sept., final breach between Catholics and Lutherans. Barnabite Order founded. *Collège de France* founded.
**c. post 1530** First church built at Warri, Nigeria.
**c. 1530–67** Philippe Verdelot, composer.
**c. 1530–1600** Peter Brueghel Elder, artist.
**1530– post 1578** Jan Kochanowski, 'Prince of Polish Poets.'
**1531** Feb., Henry VIII proclaimed Supreme Head of the Church in England. 9 Dec., appearance of the Virgin of Guadeloupe on Tepeyac hill, near Mexico City. Granada University founded.
**1531–1601** Scipione Ammirato, Italian historian.

**1532** Citadel of Jerusalem completed.

**1532** 16 Nov., Pizarro's expedition reaches Cajamarca, capital of Inca ruler Atahualpa: many thousand Indians slaughtered: Atahualpa taken prisoner. São Vicente (now Santos), Brazil, founded: Brazil organized in twelve captaincies.

**1532** Payment of Annates to Rome by English bishops suspended. English clergy submit to Henry VIII. Calvin starts to preach reform in Paris. Jaén Cathedral built.
**c. 1532–94** Roland de Lassus (Ordando di Lasso) composer.

**1533** Almagro arrives at Cajamarca with reinforcements for Pizarro: Atahualpa executed: Nov., Pizarro enters Cuzco and seizes large booty of gold. Cartagena, Colombia, founded.

**1533** 30 Mar., Thomas Cranmer, Abp of Canterbury. 11 July, Henry VIII excommunicated by Pope Clement VII. Cardinal le Veneur persuades the Pope that titles to land in N America belong to its discoverers.
**1533–92** Michel Eyquem de Montaigne, essayist.

| WESTERN & NORTHERN EUROPE | CENTRAL, SOUTHERN & EASTERN EUROPE | AFRICA & EGYPT |
|---|---|---|

**1533** 7 Sept., Princess Elizabeth (future Queen Elizabeth) b. to Anne Boleyn. Pope Clement VII meets Francis I of France at Marseilles.
**1533—7** Civil war in Denmark.
**1533—59** Christian III, King of Denmark and Norway.
**1533—84** Ivan IV the Terrible, Tsar of Russia: succ. aged three.
**1534** Denmark and the Hanse towns at war. Ghent rebels against Charles V.
**1534—5** Rising in Ireland, led by Thomas, Lord Offaly.

**1534** Treaty of Augsburg between France and League of Schmalkalden. Anabaptists, led by Mathys and John of Leiden, seize power in Münster.

**1534—51** Nail, King of the Funj.
**1534—1705** Tunis ruled by Deys.

**1535** June, naval battle of Svendborg: Christian III sacks Lübeck and forces it to make peace: end of Hanseatic League as a power.

**1535** 1 Nov., Francesco II Sforza, Duke of Milan, d.: 2 Nov., Milan occupied by Charles V (−1540). War between France and the Empire renewed. Münster taken: Anabaptists massacred. Geneva declares itself a republic. France granted capitulations by Sulayman I.

**1535** Charles V in person takes Tunis: Turkish garrison escapes to Algiers. Military agreement between Algiers and France. Ahmad Gran seizes Tigrai: Ethiopia appeals to Portugal for help.
**c. 1535** Portuguese begin to build at Tete.
**c. 1535—80** Yamta-ra-Wala the Great founds Amirate of Biu.

**1536** Feb.—Apr., Savoy and Piedmont taken by France. 17 May, Abp Cranmer annuls marriage of Henry VIII and Anne Boleyn. 19 May, Anne Boleyn beheaded. 20 May, Henry VIII m. Jane Seymour. 2 July, Thomas Cromwell made Lord Privy Seal, and vicar-general and viceregent of the king in spiritual matters. July, Charles V invades Provence: beseiges Marseilles. 14 July, treaty of Lyons: France and Portugal ally against Spain. Sept., Charles V expelled from France by Marshal de Montmorency. England and Wales united administratively. Parishes in England made responsible for the poor.
**1536—7** Reformation Parliament in Ireland.
**1536—8** Francis I and Charles V again at war.
**1537** 14 Oct., Queen Jane Seymour d. following childbirth.

**1536** Vaud added to Switzerland by conquest.

**1537—74** Cosimo I dei Medici, Duke of Florence (Grand Duke from 1569).

**1536** Khair al-Din Barbarossa recalled to Constantinople to become commander-in-chief to Turkish navy: succ. in Algiers Hasan Agha.
**c. 1536** Zaria town founded.

| THE NEAR & FAR EAST | THE AMERICAS | RELIGION & CULTURE |
|---|---|---|

**1533—84** St Charles Borromeo, Cardinal Abp of Milan.

**1534** Sulayman the Magnificent invades Persia: Tabriz taken: campaign indecisive. Bahadur of Gujarat storms Chitor.
**1534—5** Mallu b. Yusuf, Sultan of Bijapur: blinded after 6 months reign.
**1534—82** Oda Nobunaga, Japanese general and statesman: favourable to Jesuit missionaries: first Japanese to have a reputation in Europe.
**1534—5—6** Abortive attacks by Tabinshwehti on Pegu.
**1535** Bahadur of Gujarat defeated by Humayun Padshah: forced to take refuge in Malwa: Humayun forced to retreat by trouble on Afghan border: Bahadur regains Gujarat. Portuguese enclave with fort set up at Diu. Portuguese first reach Vietnam.
**1535—57** Ibrahim I b. Ismail, Sultan of Bijapur: Sunni rite restored as state religion: makes state visit to Vijayanagar.

**1536—40** António Galvão, Governor of the South (Malacca).
**1536—98** Toyotomi Hideyoshi, Japanese soldier-statesman.

**1534** Pedro de Alvarado's expedition to Ecuador. Quito, Ecuador, founded. Jacques Cartier reaches Gulf of St Lawrence: first contacts between Europeans and 'Red Indians'.

**1535** Jan., Lima, Peru, founded by Pizarro. Conquest of Inca Empire complete. Antonio de Mendoza supersedes Cortés as Viceroy of New Spain (—1550). Pedro de Mendoza sent by Charles V to R. Plate: city of S. María del Buen Aire, now Buenos Aires, founded. *Audiencia* set up in Panama. Jacques Cartier's second voyage: travels up R. St Lawrence to Quebec region and beyond to near present Ottawa: founds settlement at Montreal.
**1535—7** Diego de Almagro's expedition into northern Argentina and Chile.
**1536** Popayán, Colombia, founded by Sebastian de Belelcazar.

**1534** 23 March, Pope Clement VII declares Henry VIII's marriage to Anne Boleyn invalid. 15 Aug., Ignatius Loyola and his companions take first vows of the Society of Jesus in Montmartre. Henry VIII has himself recognized as Supreme Head of the Church in England by Act of Supremacy: Peter's Pence abolished in England: clergy required to submit to the King.
**1534—49** Paul III (Farnese), Pope.

**1535** Jan., papal authority abjured by most English bishops. 21 Jan., Thomas Cromwell appointed visitor-general of English monasteries. 22 June, Cardinal Fisher of Rochester beheaded; 6 July, Sir Thomas More beheaded, both for refusal to abjure papal authority. Schools for Indians in Mexico started by Bp de Zumárraga.
**c. 1535—1611** Tomás Luis de Victoria, Spanish composer.

**1536** 27 March, first Helvetian Confession issued. 29 March, Lutheran *Concordia* issued at Wittenberg. Oct., revolt of the Pilgrimage of Grace in Lincolnshire and Yorkshire: led by Robert Aske: suppressed following free pardon. 'Injunctions' in England. Cromwell orders destruction of sacred images and relics. About 400 smaller monasteries in England dissolved by Act of Parliament. The Ten Articles of Religion promulgated. Calvin leaves Paris for Geneva: *Institutio religionis Christianae* published.

**1537** Feb., Bahadur of Gujarat visits Portuguese Viceroy on board ship: fearing capture, jumps overboard: dies by being knocked on the head by a sailor. Humayun moves against Sher Khan: Sher Khan captures Gaur and escapes with booty. Gujarat annexed by the Mughuls.

**1537** Asunción, Paraguay, founded. Cali, Colombia, founded by Belelcazar. Civil war between Pizarro and Almagro in Peru.

**1537** Ignatius Loyola ordained. *Concilium de emendanda Ecclesia* appointed by Pope Paul III. University of Lisbon transferred to Coimbra. First printing press established in Mexico by Bp de Zumárraga. Pope Paul III excommunicates all Catholics engaging in the slave trade; voids all contracts made by Catholics who have deprived Africans of liberty or goods.

| WESTERN & NORTHERN EUROPE | CENTRAL, SOUTHERN & EASTERN EUROPE | AFRICA & EGYPT |
|---|---|---|
| | **1538** 24 Feb., treaty of Grosswardein between Ferdinand I of Austria and John Szapolya. 10 June, Catholic Princes in Germany form League of Nuremberg. The Pope mediates ten year truce between France and Charles V: 17-June, truce of Nice signed. Holy League formed by Pope Paul IV, Charles V and Venice: Sept., Venice defeats Ottoman fleet off Prevesa. | **1538—49** David, Pasha of Egypt. |
| **1539** 6 Jan., Henry m. Anne of Cleves. <br> **1539—40** Rebellion in Ghent. <br> **1539—41** Strike of printers in Paris and Lyons. | **1539** 1 Feb., treaty of Toledo between the Empire and France. March, truce between Venice and Turkey. Congress of the League of Schmalkalden at Frankfurt: 19 Apr., truce of Frankfurt between Charles V and German Protestants. <br> **1539—92** Commercial struggle between Brandenburg and Pomerania. | |
| **1540** 13 July, Henry VIII's marriage with Anne of Cleves annulled by Abp Cranmer. 29 July, Thomas Cromwell executed. 8 Aug., Henry VIII m. Catherine Howard. <br> **1540—8** Sir Anthony St Leger, Viceroy of Ireland. <br> **1540—60** *Rada* (private council) organized by Metropolitan Macarios to advise Ivan IV. <br> **1540—71** John Sigismund, Prince of Transylvania. | **1540** 22 July, John Szapolya d. Ferdinand I besieges Buda. Philip II of Austria made Duke of Milan (— 1598). | **1540** Hafsid dominions disintegrati Turkish raids on eastern African coa **c. 1540** New fortress begun in Mozambique. <br> **post 1540** French privateers active off Guinea. <br> **1540—59** Galawdewos, Emperor of Ethiopia. <br> **c. 1540—75** Andriamanelo, first Merina ruler in Madagascar. |
| **1541** June, Irish Parliament votes Henry VIII King of Ireland. Montmorency disgraced. | **1541** 26 Aug., Ottomans take Buda: part of Hungary made an Ottoman province.(—1688). 29 Dec., treaty of Gyalu: John Szapolya's widow cedes remainder of Hungary to Ferdinand I of Austria: under Austrian suzerainty to 1918. Charles V mounts expedition against Algiers: fleet destroyed in a gale. Charles V invests Philip II with the government of Spain. Diet and meetings at Ratisbon. | **1541** 400 Portuguese under Cristov da Gama reach Massawa to aid Ethiopia against Ahmad Gran. <br> **1541—73** Ahmad b. al-Hasan, Hafs |
| **1542** 13 Feb., Catherine Howard beheaded. Aug., Henry VIII attacks Scotland: defeated at Hadden Rig: 24 Nov., Scots defeated at Solway Moss. 14 Dec., James V of Scotland d.: succ. his daughter, Mary (—1567), aged six days: Earl of Arran, Regent of Scotland. Siege of Perpignan raised. Alliance between Charles V and Henry VIII. | **1542—4** Francis I again at war with Charles V. | **1542** Occupied provinces in Ethiop rise against Ahmad Gran: indecisive battle at Anasa: da Gama captured and murdered: Oct., Emperor Galawdewos and Portuguese take offensive. |

| THE NEAR & FAR EAST | THE AMERICAS | RELIGION & CULTURE |
|---|---|---|

**1537–73** Anarchy in Gujarat.
**1537–80** Ali b. Ibrahim, Sultan of Bijapur.

**1538** Aug., Sher Khan besieges Chunar and Jaunpur: takes Bihar and other territory. Hindal, brother of Humayun, proclaims himself ruler of Agra. Tabinshwehti takes Pegu: king flees to Prome: Mons flee to Martaban: armies of Prome and Pegu defeated by Bayinnaung: fleets of Prome, Pegu and Ava defeated by Tabinshwehti: Martaban besieged for seven months. Egyptian expedition against Portuguese in Diu.

**1538** Apr., battle of Las Salinas: Pizarro defeats and kills Almagro. Bogotá, Colombia, founded. Sucre, Bolivia, founded.

**1537** Danish Church Order promulgated by Christian III defines Lutheran Church organization in Denmark.
**1537–1612** Giovanni Battista Guarini, Italian poet and playwright.
**1538** The Bible ordered to be set up in English parish churches: church registers of baptisms, marriages and burials ordered to be kept. St Thomas Becket's shrine at Canterbury destroyed. Reformers persecuted in France. Henry VIII formally excommunicated by Pope Paul III. Mercator publishes map of the world.
c. **1538** *Sejarah Melayu*, court history of Malacca, composed: final redaction c. 1612.
**1538–41** Calvin exiled from Geneva to Strasbourg.

**1539** Sher Khan defeats Humayun: Humayun flees to Lahore.
**1539–50** Hanthawaddy under Burmese rule.

**1539** Hernando de Soto in Florida: defeats Indians in battle: leaving garrison, explores Oklahoma and Texas.

**1539** Apr., second Act of Dissolution of the monasteries in England: larger monasteries dissolved. May, Statute of the Six Articles: commits English church to Catholic doctrine. Brandenburg and Saxony become Lutheran. St Ignatius of Loyola founds Society of Jesus (SJ) in Rome.
**1539–83** Sir Humphrey Gilbert, explorer.

**1540** May, Sher Khan defeats Humayun near Kanauj. Combined Malay fleet, from Johore, Perak and Siak, defeat Acheh fleet of 160 vessels. Malay traders settle in Macassar. Faifi, Vietnam, established as Portuguese trading centre.
**1540–45** Nominal reign of Sher Khan.
**1540–51** Kashmir ruled by an invader, Mirza Haidar.

**1540** Jan., Pedro de Valdivia authorized to conquer Chile. Gonzalo Pizarro appointed governor of Quito.

**1540** 23 March, Waltham Abbey, last remaining monastery in England, dissolved. 27 Sept., Pope Paul III approves Society of Jesus. Six new bishoprics established in England. Calvin recalled to Geneva. Philip of Hesse commits bigamy: controversy ensues among German Protestants. John Leland visits N England.
c. **1540** First dredgers built in the Netherlands.

**1540–1609** Joseph Justus Scaliger, scholar.
**1540–1614** Pierre de Bourdeille Brantôme, memoir writer.

**1541** Martaban taken by Tabinshwehti.

**1541** 12 Feb., Santiago de Chile founded by Pedro de Valdivia. June, Pizarro assassinated in Lima, Peru. Hernando de Soto d. of fever after discovering Mississippi. Buenos Aires evacuated because of hostility of local Indians. Capital of Guatemala ruined by an earthquake. French settlement made in Canada on the Cap Rouge R., nine miles above Quebec, by Jacques Cartier.

**1541** 20 Nov., Calvin reorganizes church in Geneva with Presbyterian constitution. Mennonites begin preaching in the Netherlands. John Knox begins teaching Calvinistic doctrines in Scotland.
**1541–2** St Francis Xavier visits Mozambique. Malindi and Socotra.

**1542** 23 Nov., Akbar b. at Umarkot. A Portuguese vessel, blown off course, visits Japan, Timor and New Guinea. Arakan army destroyed by Bayinnaung: Prome taken by Tabinshwehti: Shans routed: Tabinshwehti crowned at Pagan. Expedition from Mexico to the Philippines under Villalobos.

**1542** Dutch begin to trade in W Indies. Cartier's colony abandoned: new colony set up by Jean-François de la Rocque, Sieur de Roberval, proves abortive. New Laws of the Indies promulgated. *Audiencia* set up in Lima.

**1542** 6 May, St Francis Xavier arrives in Goa as Papal Nuncio in the Indies. Cardinal Carafa organizes the Inquisition in Rome. Jesuits start work in Goa.

**1542–91** St John of the Cross, Spanish mystic and poet.
**1542–1621** St Robert Bellarmine, theologian.

| WESTERN & NORTHERN EUROPE | CENTRAL, SOUTHERN & EASTERN EUROPE | AFRICA & EGYPT |
|---|---|---|
| **1542** Conn O'Neill created Earl of Tyrone. | | |
| **1543** Feb., alliance of Charles V and Henry VIII against Francis I. 1 July, peace of Greenwich between England and Scotland: Prince Edward (later Edward VI) to marry Mary, Queen of Scots. 12 July, Henry VIII m. Katherine Parr. 11 Dec., Scots Parliament declines to ratify treaty of Greenwich. Charles V takes Guelderland and Zutphen from the Duke of Cleves: joined to the Netherlands. Franco-Turkish fleet takes Nice. | | **1543** 21 Feb., Ahmad Gran killed in battle with Portuguese. 100 Portuguese families settle at Frémonat. Wazir Abbas tries to form Muslim state in Ethiopia. |
| **1544** 13 Apr., French beat Imperial army at Cérisoles. Charles V and Henry VIII attack in N France: Charles V takes St Dizier: 9 Sept., treaty of Crépy between Charles V and Francis I: Henry VIII besieges Montreuil: 14 Sept., takes Boulogne: returns to England through lack of money. May, English invade Scotland: Edinburgh and Leith taken. Coinage debased in England. Gustavus I Vasa makes the Swedish crown hereditary in his family. Serfs freed in French royal domains. | | **1544** Portuguese factory opened at Quelimane. **1544–52** Hasan Pasha, son of Khair Din Barbarossa, Beylerbey of Algiers (first term). |
| **1544–5** English ravage southern Scotland. | | |
| **1545** 25 Feb., English defeated by Scots at Ancrum Moor. Sept., English invasion of Scotland renewed. | **1545** Treaty of Adrianople between the Empire and Ottoman Turkey. | **1545** Galawdewos defeats Wazir Abbas. **1545–7** Galla invade Dawaro, expanding northwards. |
| **1546** 7 June, Treaty of Ardres completes end of war between England, France, and Charles V: Boulogne to be held by England for eight years. Navy Board established in England. | **1546** Maurice of Saxony allies with Charles V: war made on the League of Schmalkalden. Alliance between Pope Paul III and Charles V against Protestant powers. | **1546–63** Dunama, Mai of Bornu. |
| **1547** 16 Jan., Ivan IV solemnly crowned as Tsar: first Tsar to be crowned. 28 Jan., Henry VIII of England d.: succ. Edward VI (–1553): 31 Jan., Sir Edward Seymour made Governor of the King's person: 16 Feb., made Duke of Somerset: 12 March, Protector of the Realm (–1549). 31 March, Francis I of | **1547** 24 Apr., Battle of Mühlberg: Charles V defeats the League of Schmalkalden. 19 May, Maurice made Elector of Saxony (–1553). 19 June, truce between the Empire and the Ottomans for five years. Rebellion in Bohemia put down by Ferdinand I. | |

| THE NEAR & FAR EAST | THE AMERICAS | RELIGION & CULTURE |
|---|---|---|
| **1542—c. 1570** Sadasiva Raya of Vijayanagar: real ruler Ramaraja. **1542—1616** Tokugawa Ieyasu, Japanese soldier-statesman. **1543** Ramaraja allies with Ahmadnagar and Golconda against Bijapur. Jamshid, his son and succ., murders Quli Qutb Shahi of Golconda. Abortive invasion of Arakan by Tabinshwehti. | **1543** *Audiencia* set up in Guatemala. | **1543** Nicholas Copernicus: *On the Revolution of the Celestial Spheres.* **1543—1623** William Byrd, composer. |
| **1544** Fakhr al-Din I, Prince of Lebanon d. Humayun takes refuge at court of Shah Tahmasp: becomes Shi'a: granted military aid to take Qandahar. | | **1544** St Francis Xavier visits Ceylon. Konigsberg University founded. **1544—95** Torquato Tasso, Italian poet. **1544—1603** William Gilbert, scientist: first systematic writer on magnetism. |
| **1545** Qandahar taken by Humayun: retained by him in spite of promise to give to the Shah: attack then made on Kabul in hands of Kamran, Humayun's brother. Sher Khan killed at siege of Kalanjar, Bandelkhand: succ. Jalal Khan with throne name of Islam Shah (—1553). Portuguese acquire share of trade of Bantam: 3½m. pounds of pepper exported annually to China and India. Portuguese conclude treaty with Brunei. Vietnam divided into north and south between warring factions. | **1545** Potosi Mt. silver deposits discovered in Bolivia. | **1545** 13 Dec., Council of Trent convened (—1563). Massacre of Waldenses at Avignon. The Palatinate becomes Lutheran. St Francis Xavier in Malacca. **1545—1618** Giulio Caccini, Italian composer. **1545—1613** Sir Thomas Bodley, diplomatist and bibliophile. |
| | **1546** Spanish gain control of Yucatán peninsula: Tayasal remains independent (—1697). | **1546** 18 Feb., Luther d. 29 May, Cardinal Beaton murdered. John Knox leads Scottish revolt against Rome. Pope Paul III in conflict with the Council of Trent. The Inquisition instituted in Naples. *Index expurgatorius* (Index of forbidden books) first published in Spain. St Francis Xavier visits Amboina. **1546—1601** Tycho Brahe, Danish astronomer. |
| **1547** Ottoman Turks under Piri Reis occupy Aden. Fleet from Acheh, N Sumatra, passes through Malacca Strait unmolested: sets up base at Perlis to attack Portuguese shipping. **1547—8** Ilkass, brother of Shah Tahmasp, rebels. | **1547** Potosi, Bolivian mining town, founded to exploit richest silver mine in the world. Pedro de Valdivia appointed governor of Cuba. | **1547** Statute of the Six Articles repealed at instance of Protector Somerset: chantries dissolved: Somerset House built from the proceeds. John Knox exiled to France. Council of Trent transferred to Bologna. **1547—9** Thirty-nine saints canonized by the Russian church. **1547—1616** Miguel Cervantes, novelist. |

| WESTERN & NORTHERN EUROPE | CENTRAL, SOUTHERN & EASTERN EUROPE | AFRICA & EGYPT |
|---|---|---|

France d.: succ. Henry II (−1559): Montmorency returns to power. 10 Sept., English defeat Scots at Pinkie.
**1547–1609** Olden-Barneveldt, Grand Pensionary of Holland.
**1548** 26 June, Netherlands administration made independent of the Empire. Mary, Queen of Scots, betrothed to the Dauphin (later Francis II): sent to France. Rebellion in Cornwall: Exeter besieged.

**1548–72** Sigismund II Augustus, King of Poland.

**1548–56** Abu Abdullah Muhammad al-Mahdi, Sharif of Morocco.

**1549** June–Sept., risings in Cornwall, Devon, Norfolk and Yorkshire against *Book of Common Prayer:* parishioners of Sampford Courtenay, Devon, in anger, describe it as 'a child's Christmas play'. 9 Aug., England at war with France. 13 Oct., Duke of Somerset dismissed from being Protector of the Realm: succ. John Dudley, Earl of Warwick (later Duke of Northumberland). Commission appointed in England to inquire into enclosures. Commercial courts instituted at Lyons and Toulouse.
**1550** Peace made between England and France: Boulogne restored to France. *Zemski Sobor,* assembly of boyars and clergy, summoned by Ivan IV to revise law code: provincial administration reformed. Helsinki (Helsingfors) founded.
**1550–1** Northumberland attempts to persuade future Mary I to abjure the Catholic Church.

**c. 1550** Ottomans take Ibrim and territory between 1st and 3rd Cataracts. António Caído, trader, adviser to Monomotapa. 1,500 slaves sent annually from Guinea to Portugal.
**c. 1550–78** Orhogbua, Oba of Benin, Portuguese educated Christian.
**c. 1550–1612** Lunda empire founded by Kibinda Ilunge.
**c. 1550–c. 1825** Inyanga, Rhodesia, in continuous occupation.

**1551** Parliament of Paris declines to allow the Jesuits in France. English currency reformed.

**1551** 9 March, Philip II made sole heir of Charles V by the Hapsburgs. 19 July, treaty of Karlsburg affirms Ferdinand I of Austria's rights in Hungary and Transylvania. Henry II of France at war with the Pope in Italy. League of Dresden formed by Maurice of Saxony. Lisbon population c. 100,000, of whom 10,000 slaves: sixty or seventy slave-markets.

**1551** Ottoman Turks take Tripoli (Libya). First resident English merchants settle in Morocco.

| THE NEAR & FAR EAST | THE AMERICAS | RELIGION & CULTURE |
|---|---|---|

**1548** Tabinshwehti invades Siam: Portuguese mercenaries fighting on both sides: Siam forced to sue for peace.

**1548** La Paz, Bolivia, founded. Zacatas mines, Mexico, discovered by the Spaniards. *Audiencia* set up in New Galicia (Guadalajara).

**1548** 13 Feb., Council of Trent suspended by Pope Paul III: 18 Feb., Charles V disavows the Council. 15 May, *Interim* vote of the Diet of Augsburg: the chalice to be given to the laity: priests allowed to marry pending a decision of an ecumenical Council. Jesuit College of St Paul founded in Malacca. St Ignatius Loyola: *The Spiritual Exercises.*
**1548–9** New Testament in Geez printed in Rome.
**1548–1600** Giordano Bruno, Italian poet.
**c. 1548–1614** El Greco (Domenico Theotocopouli), Cretan Greek artist settled in Toledo (1577).

**ost 1549** Ming China engaged constantly in war with Mongols.

**1549** *Audiencia* set up in Bogotá. Captain-General established at Bahia, now Salvador, to govern Brazil. Large Jesuit contingent sent. Tomé de Souza, first Portuguese Captain-General of Brazil.

**1549** June, *Consensus Tigurinus:* Calvinists and Zwinglians agree on eucharistic doctrine. 9 June, first Act of Uniformity enacted in England: first *Book of Common Prayer* instituted. 13 Sept., Pope Paul III disbands Council of Bologna. St Peter Canisius, SJ, begins working in Germany. St Francis Xavier visits Japan: conversions of estimated some 300,000 to Christianity by the Jesuits: population estimated 15–20m. Bologna University founded.

**550** Jamshid of Golconda d.: ucc. Ibrahim (–1580). Burhan 'izam Shah of Ahmadnagar allies 'ith Hindu Raya of Vijayanagar. ueen of Japara besieges Malacca. 'ongols reach Peking.
**550–1** Smim Sawhtut rebels gainst Burmese rule: proclaims imself ruler of Hanthawaddy.

**1550** Cattle first introduced into S America at Asunción.

**1550** Jesuit College founded in Rome. *Tserkovny Sóbor* (Assembly of the Clergy) summoned by Ivan IV to draw up code of canon law *(Stoglav).*
**c. 1550** Wang To-kun (?): *Shui-hu-chuan* (The Story of the River Bank).
**1550–5** Julius III (Ciocchi dal Monti), Pope.
**1550–91** Jakob Handl, German composer.
**c. 1550–1602** Emilio di Cavalieri, Italian composer.
**1550–1617** John Napier, inventor of logarithms.
**1550–1650** Coal production increased fourteen-fold in England.

**551** Ottoman Turks under Piri .eis occupy Muscat. Johore attack n Malacca. Smim Htaw, brother f King Takayutpi, King of 'anthawaddy: defeated by Bayinnaung f Toungoo. Tabinshwehti ssassinated: empire collapses: Pegu, oungoo and Prome declare 'emselves independent: delta onquered by Bayinnaung, who 'akes himself king: Toungoo, rome and Pegu recaptured.
**551–81** Bayinnaung, King of 'urma.

**1551** Antonio de Mendoza transferred as governor to Peru (–1552).

**1551** 1 March, Council of Trent reopened by Pope Julius III: disavowed by Henry II of France. John Knox made a Royal Chaplain in England. First bishop appointed in Bahia. Universities of Lima and Mexico founded. Palestrina made choir master in St Peter's, Rome.
**1551–1623** William Camden, antiquary.

1551–1556

WESTERN &
NORTHERN EUROPE

CENTRAL, SOUTHERN
& EASTERN EUROPE

AFRICA & EGYPT

| WESTERN & NORTHERN EUROPE | CENTRAL, SOUTHERN & EASTERN EUROPE | AFRICA & EGYPT |
|---|---|---|
| **1552** 15 Jan., treaty of Chambord: German Protestants cede Metz, Toul and Verdun to France: French occupy Lorraine and Luxembourg: hostilities renewed by Charles V against France: Metz besieged. 22 Jan., Duke of Somerset beheaded. Ivan IV besieges and takes Kazan. | **1552** May, Maurice of Saxony occupies Augsburg and Tyrol: defeats Charles V at Innsbruck. Truce between France and the Pope. Rhodes taken by the Ottomans. | **1552–7** Salah Rais, Beylerbey of Algiers. |
| **1553** 2 Jan., Francis of Guise relieves Metz. 6 July, Edward VI of England d.: succ. Lady Jane Grey proclaimed as Queen Jane, following Henry VIII's will: 19 July, Mary I proclaimed, with popular support (−1558).<br>**1553–4** Sir Hugh Willoughby explores Nova Zembla and Lapland, then d. with his crew. Richard Chancellor reaches Russia *via* Archangel. | **1553** 9 July, battle of Sievershausen: Albert of Brandenburg defeated by Maurice of Saxony: Maurice killed. The French take Corsica. | **1553** Capt. Windham, first Englishm to visit Benin. |
| **1554** 26 Jan., Sir Thomas Wyatt's (or Wyat's) rebellion at Rochester: 11 Apr., executed. 12 Feb., Lady Jane Grey executed. 12 Apr., Mary of Lorraine, Regent of Scotland (−1559). 25 July, Mary I of England m. Philip of Spain (later Philip VI).<br>**1554–7** War between Ivan the Terrible and Gustavus I Vasa for Finland. | **1554** French beat Imperial army at Reuty: battle of Mariano: French lose Tuscany. | **1554** Abortive Songhai expedition against Katsina. Fez taken by Shari of Morocco. Abortive Portuguese order for construction of fort and mission at Mombasa. |
| **1555** Richard Chancellor again visits Archangel. Muscovy Company chartered. Charles V abdicates in the Netherlands in favour of his son, Philip II. Willoughby's voyage to the White Sea. | **1555** July– Sept., Diet of Augsburg allows freedom of religion to Catholics and to Protestants. Calvin puts down attempted rebellion in Geneva by a reign of terror. Treaty of commerce between France and Turkey. | **1555** Frémonat founded by Fr. An de Oviedo. |
| **1556** Ivan IV takes Astrakhan. Second *Zemski Sobor* summoned for a war against Poland. Clanmalier, Leix, Offaly and Slievemargy, planted with English colonists.<br>**1556–71** Sir Henry Sidney, Viceroy of Ireland. | **1556** 16 Jan., Charles V abdicates, retiring to monastery of St Just, Estramadura: succ. as Emperor his brother, Ferdinand I (−1564): succ., as King of Spain and the Netherlands, Philip II (−1598). 5 Feb., Truce of Vauxcelles between France and Austria. The Spaniards in Naples renew war against the Pope with French aid. Sigismund II of Poland intervenes in quarrel between Livonia and Abp of Riga. | **1556** Turks take Tripoli from the Knights of Malta. Diogo I of Kongo defeated by Ngola. Ngola sends embassy to Portugal requesting missionaries. |

| THE NEAR & FAR EAST | THE AMERICAS | RELIGION & CULTURE |
|---|---|---|

**1551—1740** Hanthawaddy under Burmese Toungoo dynasty.

**1552** Pachuca mines, Mexico, opened. Portuguese introduce sugar cultivation into Brazil.

**1552** Jan., second *Book of Common Prayer* issued in England: second Act of Uniformity. Forty-Two Articles follow. Aug., treaty of Passau: Lutherans granted freedom of religion: Charles V revokes the *Interim*. St Francis Xavier reaches China: 27 Nov. or 2 Dec., d. *Collegium Germanicum* founded in Rome. Scottish *Catechism* published.
**c. 1552—99** Edmund Spenser, poet.
**c. 1552—1616** Richard Hakluyt, compiler of works on voyages.
**c. 1552—1618** Sir Walter Raleigh, explorer and writer.
**1552—1623** Fra Paolo (Pietro) Sarpi, Venetian patriot, theologian, church reformer and natural scientist.
**1552—1634** Sir Edward Coke, jurist.
**1552—1637** Gabriello Chiabrera, Italian poet.

**1553** Islam Shah d.: succ. Muhammad Adil Shah (—June 1555). Humayun blinds his brother, Kamran.

**1553** Valdivia defeated in battle by Araucanian Indian leader Lautaro and executed. First wheat crop in Chile.

**1553** Aug.—Sept., English bishops not recognized by Rome arrested: bishops in Roman orders restored. Protestant translation of the Bible into Polish published at Brzese.
**1553—1600** Richard Hooker, Anglican divine.
**1553—1606** John Lyly, dramatist.

**1554** Bayinnaung makes abortive attack of Ava.

**1554** 30 Nov., England formally reconciled to the Roman church: all Acts of Parliament contrary thereto repealed, dissolution of the monasteries excepted: anti-heresy laws revived: *Book of Common Prayer* abolished.
**1554—86** Sir Philip Sidney, poet.
**1554—1624** Szymonowicz, Polish poet.

**1555** Humayun invades India: July, Delhi and Agra taken: Muhammad Adil Shah deposed. Peace treaty of Amasia between Persia and Turkey. Ava taken.
**1555—6** Famine in N India.
**1555—7** Bayinnaung conducts brief and successful campaigns against Shan states in N and E.
**1556** Jan., Humayun d. in Delhi by falling from his library stairs: succ. in India his son Akbar, aged thirteen (—1605): his son Muhammad Khan ruler of Kabul. 14 Feb., Akbar formally enthroned at Kalanaur, Gurdaspur District. 5 Nov., second battle of Panipat: Hemu, usurper of Delhi, defeated: killed by Akbar.

**1555** Grapes first produced in Chile.
**1555—60** Abortive French Huguenot colony in bay of Rio de Janeiro.

**1555** May, John Knox returns to Scotland. 16 Oct., Bps Latimer and Ridley burnt as heretics at Oxford. Marcellus II (Cervini), Pope.
**1555—9** Paul IV (Carafa), Pope.
**1555—1628** François de Malherbe, poet.
**1555—1636** Tung Chi-chang, Chinese artist.
**1556** 21 March, Abp Cranmer burnt as a heretic at Oxford. 22 March, Cardinal Pole made Abp of Canterbury. 31 July, St Ignatius Loyola d. Jesuit colleges opened in Belgium, and at Prague and Ingolstadt. John Knox expelled from Scotland.
**1556—1617** Tang Hsien Tsu, Chinese dramatist.
**1556—1629** Carlo Moderno, architect.

| WESTERN & NORTHERN EUROPE | CENTRAL, SOUTHERN & EASTERN EUROPE | AFRICA & EGYPT |
|---|---|---|

**1557** 7 June, English army invades Artois and Picardy: 10 Aug., French defeated at St Quentin by English and Spanish. Bankruptcy in France and Spain. Financial crisis in Antwerp.

**1557** The French, under the Duc de Guise, campaign abortively in Italy. Philip II at war with the Pope.
**1557–78** Sebastian, King of Portugal.

**1557** Bp André de Oviedo, SJ, at Frémonat. Turks seize Massawa and Arkiko: monks at Debra Damo massacred: Tigre rises, driving Turks back. Portuguese take Zaila.

**1558** 20 Jan., French take Calais from England, last surviving English continental possession. 24 Apr., Mary, Queen of Scots, m. the Dauphin. 13 July, Count of Egmont totally defeats French at Gravelines. 17 Nov., Mary I of England d.: succ. Elizabeth I (–1603). Cardinal Pole d. 20 Nov., William Cecil, Lord Burghley (1571) made Secretary of State by Queen Elizabeth I (–1598).
**1558–98** Struggle between Russia, Sweden, Poland and Sweden for possession of Livonia: Poland emerges with parts of Livonia and Lithuania.
**1559** 10 July, Henry II of France killed accidentally: succ. Francis II (–1560), a minor: house of Lorraine in power in France. 21 Oct., rebellion in Scotland against Mary of Lorraine: deposed from regency. Shane O'Neill, Lord of Tyrone: title of Earl declined: uncompromising opponent of English rule in Ireland.
**1559–88** Frederick II, King of Denmark.
**1559–98** Struggles between Catholics and Protestants in France.
**1559–1641** Maximilien, Duc de Sully, statesman.

**1558** 14 March, Ferdinand I formally assumes title of Emperor. 21 Sept., Charles V d.

**1559** 3 Apr., treaty of Cateau-Cambrésis: between Henry II of France and Philip II of Spain: France keeps Saluzzo: Philip II regains Savoy and Piedmont: Duke of Savoy restored: m. Margaret, sister of Henry II.
**1559–84** Escorial Palace and Monastery built.

**1558** Thirty-five galleys and twenty-five brigantines engaged in piracy from Algiers. Mozambique replaces Sofala as Portuguese eastern African capital.

**1559** Philip II of Spain sends fleet of Germans, Italians and Spaniards against Algiers: utterly destroyed by the Turks. Harar attacks Ethiopia: Emperor Galawdewos killed in battle: succ. Minas (–1563).

**1560** 12 Jan.–1 Feb., Second Reformation Parliament in Dublin: Acts of Supremacy and of Uniformity passed. 27 Feb., treaty of Berwick between England and Scottish Protestants. 6 July, treaty of Leith (or Edinburgh): French troops to withdraw from Scotland: Council of Regents instituted: treaty disavowed by Mary, Queen of Scots. 5 Dec., Francis II of France d.: succ. Charles IX (–1574): Catherine dei Medici, Queen-Mother, Regent (–1563). English currency reformed. Swedes invade Esthonia. Ivan IV of Russia devastates Livonia.
**1560–8** Eric XIV, King of Sweden.
**1561** Mary, Queen of Scots, returns to Scotland. Recoinage carried out in England: debased coins withdrawn. Estates-General meet at Orléans and Poissy. Ivan the Terrible annihilates the Teutonic Knights: Courland made

**1560** Madrid made the capital of Spain.
**1560–85** Palazzo degli Uffizi built in Florence.

**c. 1560** First Jesuit missions in Mozambique.
**c. 1560–1605** Farima, first Mani King of Loko.

**1561** Philip II makes Madrid capital of Spain. Patriarch of Constantinople recognizes title of Ivan IV as Tsar.

**1561** Anglo-French fleet trading off W-Africa.

| THE NEAR & FAR EAST | THE AMERICAS | RELIGION & CULTURE |
|---|---|---|

**1557** Sur pretenders to throne of Delhi surrender.
**1557—79** Ali Adil Shah, Sultan of Bijapur: reverts to Shi'ism.
**1557—80** Dharmapala, King of Kotte: baptized as Dom João, a puppet under the Portuguese.
**1558** Armies of Vijayanagar and Bijapur ravage Ahmadnagar. Bayinnaung conquers Chengmai: King made a vassal: all Shan chiefs on Burma-China border submit: Rajah of Manipur sends tribute.
**1558—60** Gwalior and Ajmer recovered by Delhi.

**1557—72** Mem de Sá, Captain-General of Brazil.

**1558** Guanajuato mines, Mexico, opened.

**1557** 11 Sept.—28 Nov., disputations at Worms fail to reconcile Catholics and Protestants in Germany. 3 Dec., first 'Covenant' signed in Scotland. Goa made an archbishopric: Malacca and Cochin bishoprics.
**1557—1602** Thomas Morley, composer.
**1558** Death penalty imposed in Spain for importing or printing books without permit. Diet of Frankfurt fails to unite German Protestants. John Knox: *A First Blast of the Trumpet against the Monstrous Regiment of Women.* University of Jena founded.
**1558—94** Thomas Kyd, dramatist.

**1559** Bayazid, rebel son of Sulayman the Magnificent, takes refuge in Persia. Laos and Siam ally against Bayinnaung.
**1559—60** Anthony Jenkinson visits Bokhara and Persia as ambassador of the Tsar.

**1559** Mercury made a royal monopoly in Spanish America.

**1559** 1 Jan., the 'Beggars' Summons' requires Scottish friars to do charitable works. 17 Apr., Act of Supremacy of 1534 restored in England, with slight amendments: all but one Catholic bishop refuse to take oath of supremacy: deprived of office. 27 Apr., Act of Uniformity requires use of 1552 *Book of Common Prayer* in England. May, first Calvinist synod held in Paris. 11 May, religious houses looted in Perth. Jesuit university founded at Evora. Jesuit college founded in Munich. University of Geneva founded. Abp Carranza of Toledo, Primate of Spain, tried by the Inquisition: found 'suspect'.
**1559—65** St Pius V (dei Medici), Pope.
**1559—73** Frederick III, Elector Palatine: Calvinism made the state religion in place of Lutheranism.
**1559—1614** Isaac Casaubon, theologian.

**1560** Akbar dismisses Bairam Khan, his protector: 'petticoat' government (—1562).

**1560** Spanish convoy system instituted because of piracy. French evicted by Portuguese from Rio de Janeiro Bay: French take Recife temporarily: then occupy N Maranhão (—1615).

**1560** Aug., Scots Parliament abolishes papal authority in Scotland: sacraments reduced to two: Mass made a penal offence, with death for the third conviction. General Assembly of the Kirk first meets in Scotland. The Inquisition set up in Goa. Fr Villela, SJ, creates a Christian community in Japan. Jesuits start work in Mozambique.
**1560—1613** Carlo Gesualdo, Prince of Venosa, Italian composer.
**1560—1609** Jacob Harmensen Arminius, Dutch Protestant, founder of the Arminians.

**1561** Jan., Bairam Khan murdered in Gujarat. Akbar m. a princess of Ajmer. Bayazid and four of his sons handed over to Ottomans by Shah Tahmasp for 400,000 gold pieces.

**1561** Olives first produced in Chile.

**1561** Jesuits arrive in Philippine Is. John Knox: *Book of Discipline.* Protestant synod meets at Poitiers. French clergy meet at Poissy.
**1561—1628** Francis Bacon, philosopher and essayist.

1561–1566

WESTERN &
NORTHERN EUROPE

CENTRAL, SOUTHERN
& EASTERN EUROPE

AFRICA & EGYPT

a duchy: Sweden takes Estonia:
Poland takes Livonia.
**1561–8** Seven years war between
Denmark and Sweden.
**1562** 3 Jan., massacre of Vassy:
Duke of Guise kills 650 Huguenots
engaged in worship: Protestant
rebellion follows: beginning of wars
of religion in France. Rouen
besieged: 19 Dec., Huguenots
defeated at Dreux. 21 Sept., treaty
of Hampton Court between Elizabeth
I and the Huguenots: Le Havre ceded
to England.
**1562–3** First Huguenot war in
France.
**1563** 24 Feb., Duke of Guise
murdered. Catholics besiege Orléans.
19 March, peace of Amboise ends
war with Huguenots: Orléans
surrenders. 28 July, France regains
possession of Le Havre. Statute of
Apprentices in England: poor law
reformed: Statute of Artificers.
Agitation against the Spanish in the
Netherlands. The Fuggers go
bankrupt. *Corps de gardes* (royal
bodyguard) formed in France.
**1564** 12 Apr., peace of Troyes
between England and France. 31
May, Swedes defeated by Denmark
and Lübeck off Gothland. Office
of Superintendent of Finances
created in France. Ivan the Terrible
creates the *opritchina*, civil servants
replacing hereditary boyars: 3,470
boyars and other functionaries
killed.
**1564–6** Administration of justice
reformed in France.

**1565** 29 July, Mary, Queen of Scots
m. Henry, Lord Darnley.

**1566** 9 March, David Riccio murdered
in Holyroodhouse. Future James I
and VI b. Rebellion put down in
Ulster. English settlement by Sir
Walter Raleigh in Munster. Calvinists
riot in Antwerp: cathedral, churches
and monasteries sacked. Funchal sacked
by French adventurer Montluc.

**1562** 2 Nov., treaty of Fossans
between France and Savoy. 30 Nov.,
Maximilian II, son of Ferdinand I,
elected King of the Romans and
Bohemia (–1576). Treaty of Prague
between Emperor Ferdinand I and
Turkey.

**1563** Treaty between Brandenburg
and Poland regulates succession in
Brandenburg.

**1564** Trade war begun between
Spain and England: privateering rife.
**1564–5** The Turks besiege Malta.
**1564–76** Maximilian II, Holy Roman
Emperor.

**1565** Spanish fleet takes Malta: May–
Sept., Malta unsuccessfully besieged
by the Turks. Moriscos rebel in
Andalusia.

**1566** Turks invade Hungary: siege of
Sziget (or Szigetvar): 5–6 Sept., town
burnt: Sulayman the Magnificent d.
the same night: succ. Selim II (–1574).
The Ottomans take Chios from Genoa.
Valetta founded.
**1566–79** Muhammad Soqolly, Grand
Vizier of Turkey.

**post 1562** Annual voyages from
England to W Africa by 'interlopers'.
**1562–91** Turkish raids on the
eastern African coast.

**1563** Galla control a third of
Ethiopia. Fr Gouveia, SJ,
recommends Portugal to annexe
Ndongo in order to convert it to
Christianity.
**1563–97** Sarsa Dengel, Emperor
of Ethiopia.

**1564** French consulate established
at Algiers.
**c. 1564** Abdallah b. Dunama, Mai
of Bornu.

## THE NEAR & FAR EAST THE AMERICA RELIGION & CULTURE

**1561—3** Anthony Jenkinson in Persia as ambassador of England.

**1562** May, Shams al-Din Atga Khan, *Wazir* of Delhi, murdered. Adham Khan executed. Fortress of Mirtha taken by Delhi.
**1562—4** Akbar makes administrative reforms.

**1562** Sir John Hawkins's first voyage to the W Indies. Abortive French Huguenot settlement in Florida.

**1562** 17 Jan., Huguenots in France formally recognized by Edict of St Germain: permitted to worship outside towns. 18 Jan., Council of Trent recalled. The Thirty-Nine Articles of Religion agreed by Convocation in England.
c. **1562—1628** John Bull, composer.
**1562—1635** Lope de Vega, Spanish dramatist: alleged to have written 1800 plays: c. 700 authenticated.

**1563** Bayinnaung attacks Siam: Ayuthia surrendered after brief siege: King of Siam taken prisoner with immense booty of religious *objets d'art*.

**1563** 19 March, Edict of Amboise grants a measure of toleration to Huguenots. 14 Dec., Council of Trent disbanded. Jesuits take over Dillingen · University. Joseph Caro: *Shulchan Aruch* (guide to Jewish religion).
**1563—1626** John Dowland, composer.

**1564—1631** Cardinal Frederigo Borromeo, founder of the Ambrosian Library.
**1564** 24 Nov., Pope Pius IV publishes *Index of Prohibited Books*. Catholicism re-established in Bavaria. Bull *Benedictus Deus* confirms the Council of Trent. Building of Tuileries Palace begun.
**1564—93** Christopher Marlowe, dramatist.
**1564—1616** William Shakespeare, poet and dramatist.
**1564—1637** Pieter Breughel (younger), artist.
**1564—1642** Galileo Galilei, astronomer and scientist.

**1564** Ahmadnagar, Bidar, Bijapur and Golconda form league against Vijayanagar: headquarters set up at Talikota. Akbar henceforth rules alone. Portuguese mission at Amboina destroyed by Sultan Hairun of Ternate. Acheh sacks Johore Lama; Sultan Ala al-Din taken prisoner: succ. Muzaffar Shah (—c. 1569): new capital at Bukit Seluyut.
**1564—79** Eight expeditions sent by Bayinnaung to pacify Chengmai.

**1564** Hawkins's second voyage to the W Indies.

**1565** 23 Jan., Vijayanagar army defeated by allies: Ramaraja of Vijayanagar killed: supremacy of Islam in the Deccan now assured: city of Vijayanagar razed. Miguel Lopez de Legazpi's expedition to the Philippines: 27 Apr., Cebú burnt: 8 May, construction of Spanish fort begun at St Miguel. Fortress of Agra begun. Philippine Is. occupied by Spain. Kotte, Ceylon, razed by order of Portuguese Viceroy of Goa.
**1565—7** Akbar suppresses rebellions among the Uzbegs: put his cousin to death.

**1565** St Augustine, Florida, founded by Spanish colonists.
**1565—1815** Regular Spanish trade convoys between Mexico and the Philippine Is.

**1565** Philip II issues religious *Compromise* with the reformers in the Netherlands: opposed by William of Orange and leading Protestant citizens. Abd al-Wahhab al-Sharani, mystic and writer, d. in Egypt. The graphite pencil invented by Konrad Gesner. Jesuits set up schools in Poland.
**1565—1635** Alessandro Tassoni, Italian poet.
c. **1565—1637** Peter Breughel Younger, artist.

**1566** March, second Helvetian Confession issued. *Catechismus Romanus* (Catechism of the Council of Trent) issued: composed by St Charles Borromeo.
**1566—72** St Pius V (Ghislieri), Pope.
**1566—1607** St Maddalena de Pazzi, Carmelite.

| WESTERN & NORTHERN EUROPE | CENTRAL, SOUTHERN & EASTERN EUROPE | AFRICA & EGYPT |
|---|---|---|

**1567** 10 Feb., Darnley murdered. 15 May, Mary, Queen of Scots m. 4th Earl of Bothwell. 17 June, Mary, Queen of Scots, imprisoned at Loch Leven. 24 July, Mary, Queen of Scots, abdicates: 29 July, James VI crowned (−1625: later James I of England). Aug.− 1570 James, Earl of Moray, Regent of Scotland. Aug., Duke of Alba conducts a reign of terror against Protestants in the Spanish Netherlands. 29 Sept., conspiracy of Meaux: Huguenots renew civil war in France: second Huguenot war (−1568). Ivan the Terrible grants the Muscovy Company freedom of trade in his dominions.

**1567** Philip II of Spain forbids foreigners and heretics to trade in the Spanish dominions: end of peaceful trade between England and Spain: Muslims again banned.

**1567** Galla devastate Harar.

**1568** 23 March, peace of Longjumeau ends second Huguenot war. 13 May, Mary, Queen of Scots, defeated at Langside, in an attempt to regain throne: flees to England: kept in captivity for nineteen years by Queen Elizabeth I. Aug., Huguenots rebel: third Huguenot war (−1570). 30 Sept., Eric XIV of Sweden deposed: succ. John III (−1592).

**1568** 17 Feb., Maximilian II cedes parts of Hungary to Sultan Salim II. Duke of Alba establishes a 'tribunal of troubles' in Antwerp. Count of Egmont and Admiral Hoorn beheaded. Maximilian II protests to Philip II against Alba's excesses.
**1568−70** Rising of Alpujarras in Spain: Muslims deported from Granada and settled up and down Spain: 12,000 families of northern peasants moved to Granada.

**ante 1568** Bakuba migrating to present habitat: settling finally c. 1600. Jaga invade Kongo.
**c. 1568** Turks raid Cambo, E Africa.

**1569** 13 March, Huguenots defeated at Jarnac: Prince de Condé executed. Rising in N of England: Mass said again: 800 rebels executed. Fitzmaurice's rebellion in Ireland (−1574).
**1569−73** First Desmond revolt in Ireland.

**1569** 1 July, Diet of Lublin centralises government of Poland and Lithuania: future diets to meet in Warsaw.

**1569** Francisco Barreto leads abortive expedition against Monomotapa. English consulate established at Algiers. Portuguese fort begun in Mombasa. Cambo accepts Turkish protection. Pate rebels. Revolt in Harar: Talha elected sultan.
**1569−86** Dakin, King of the Funj, great administrator.

**1570** 23 Jan., Earl of Moray, Regent of Scotland, murdered. 27 Jan.− 1571, Matthew, Earl of Lennox, Regent of Scotland. 8 Aug., peace of St Germain: amnesty granted to Huguenots: ends third Huguenot war. Nijni Novgorod sacked by Ivan the Terrible. Peace of Stettin between Denmark and Sweden.

**1570** The Turks occupy Cyprus. The Pope, Spain and Venice ally against them.

**1570** Zimba ravage country near R. Zambezi.
**c. 1570** Galla still advancing. reaching Amhara and Begemder.
**c. 1570−1706** Katsina at war with Kano for control of Saharan trade terminus.

**1571** 5 Sept.−1572 John, Earl of Mar, Regent of Scotland. Ridolfi's plot to put Mary, Queen of Scots on the English throne: 30 Sept., Duke of Norfolk attainted and beheaded. Printers in Paris and Lyons on strike. Khan of the Crimea attacks Moscow: suburbs burnt. Act of Parliament in England forbids publication of Bull *Regnans in excelsis*: attempts at reconciliation with Rome made

**1571** 30 July, treaty between Brandenburg and Pomerania regulating mutual succession. 7 Oct., Venetian and Spanish fleet under Don John of Austria defeats Turks at naval battle of Lepanto: end of Turkish mastery of the sea in the Mediterranean.
**1571−6** Stephen Bathory, Prince of Transylvania.

**1571** Portuguese campaign in Kongo against Jaga: virtual military occupation (−1576).
**1571−3** Francisco Barreto's expedition against Manica.
**1571−1603** Idris Alooma, Mai of Bornu: introduces firearms: many campaigns.

| THE NEAR & FAR EAST | THE AMERICAS | RELIGION & CULTURE |
|---|---|---|
| **1567** 20 Oct.–1568 23 Feb., Akbar besieges and takes Chitor. | **1567** City of Rio de Janeiro founded. Hawkins's third voyage to the W Indies, accompanied by Sir Francis Drake. | **1567–1620** Thomas Campion, composer. **1567–1622** St François de Sales, theologian. **1567–1643** Claudio Monteverdi, Italian composer. **1567–1635** Samuel de Champlain, founder of Quebec. |
| **1568** Yemen taken by Sinan Pasha for Ottoman Turkey. Malacca besieged by Acheh with 15,000 men. King of Siam returns to Ayuthia by a ruse: Bayinnaung again invades Siam with (sic) 546,000 men, including Portuguese musketeers and artillery: Siamese defend city with Portuguese mercenaries: city taken after ten months following treachery: abortive expedition against Laos follows. **1569** June, Legazpi takes possession of the Philippine Is. for Spain. Aug., Salim, later Emperor Jehangir, b. Akbar takes Rajputana: fortress of Kalanjar captured. **c. 1569–70** Abd al-Jalil, Sultan of Johore. | **1568** Oct.–Dec., Portuguese fleet blockades Spaniards in Cebú. <br><br> **1569–81** Francisco de Toledo, governor of Peru. | **1568** St John of the Cross founds the Order of Discalced Carmelites. College for English Catholics opened at Douai by William Allen, to train priests for conversion of England. Brunswick becomes Protestant. **1568–1639** Tommaso Campanella, Italian poet. **1568–1639** Sir Henry Wotton, poet. **1569** 1 July, Union of Lublin: Lithuania and Ukraine accept to be Uniates, accepting Latin doctrines while conserving Orthodox rites. Education in Bavaria brought under Catholic control. Selemainiye Camii, Edirne, built. **c. 1569–1642** Jan Breughel, Flemish artist. |
| **1570** 6 June, Spaniards take Luzon. Regime of *encomiendas* and *encomenderos* instituted. Alliance between Bijapur and Ahmadnagar against the Portuguese: joined by rulers of Calicut and Achin: Goa besieged for ten months: held by 700 Portuguese successfully. Sultan Hairun of Ternate murdered while visiting Portuguese: succ. Baabullah (–1584) vows vengeance. **c. 1570–3** Ranga, Raya of Vijayanagar. **c. 1570–97** Ali Jalla Riayat Shah, Sultan of Johore. **1571** Captain of the Fortress of Malacca re-named Governor of the South. Manila burnt by its inhabitants: 3 June, Spanish city of Manila founded by Legazpi. | **1570** Drake's first privateering voyage. <br><br><br><br><br><br><br><br><br><br><br><br><br><br><br> **1571** Last Inca, Tupac Amaru, captured and executed. Inquisition set up in Mexico. | **1570** 25 Feb., Elizabeth of England excommunicated and deprived of title by Bull *Regnans in excelsis*. 14 Apr., Consensus of Sendomir: Calvinists, Lutherans and Moravians unite in Poland. 19 July, Pope Pius V promulgates revised *Roman Missal*: excommunicates anyone who should presume to alter it. Inquisition installed at Lima. **1570 ff.** *Prophesyings*, Puritan groups for Bible-study, spread in England: illegal conventicles, led by Independents, increase. **c. 1570– c. 1632** Thomas Dekker. dramatist and pamphlet writer. **1571** Sept., Archbishops appointed in St Andrews and Glasgow. The Thirty-Nine Articles of Religion confirmed by Parliament. Sokollu Mehmet Pasha Camii, Istanbul, built. **1571–1630** Johannes Kepler, astronomer. |

| WESTERN & NORTHERN EUROPE | CENTRAL, SOUTHERN & EASTERN EUROPE | AFRICA & EGYPT |
|---|---|---|
| treason: import of Papal Bulls forbidden. Royal Exchange opened in London. | | |
| **1572** July, Lord Burghley appointed Lord High Treasurer of England. 18 July, William (the Silent) of Orange elected Stadholder: war for liberation of Dutch provinces begins. 24 Aug., Massacre of St Bartholomew's Day in Paris: fourth Huguenot war (– 1574). Rising in the Netherlands. Nov.– 1578 March, James, Earl of Morton, Regent of Scotland. | **1572** 7 July, Sigismund II of Poland d.: end of Jagellon dynasty: *interregnum* until 1574. Philip II imposes additional taxation, including a capital levy, upon the Netherlands. | **1572** Epidemic in Algiers kills one third of the population. Portuguese Augustinians open school at Elmina. **c. 1572** Jaga routed. |
| **1573** 9 May, Henry, Duke of Anjou, brother of Charles IX of France, elected King of Poland. 6 July, Pacification of Boulogne ends fourth Huguenot war. Haarlem taken by the Spaniards: Duke of Alba recalled to Spain. | **1573** 7 March, peace of Constantinople between the Ottomans and Venice. | **1573** Francisco Barreto's second expedition: d.at Sena. Don John of Austria attacks Tunis. **1573–5** Abu Abdallah Muhammad II Sharif of Morocco. |
| **1574** 30 May, Charles IX of France d.: succ. Henry III, (–1589), King of Poland:June, flees from Poland. **1574–6** Fifth Huguenot war in France: abortive sieges of Sancerre and La Rochelle. | **1574–95** Murad III, Ottoman Sultan. | **1574** Abortive Portuguese expedition against Ceuta and Tangier. Vasco Fernandes Homem's expedition to Manica. Mozambique razed by African tribesmen. Tunis taken by th Turks. |
| **1575** 19 Oct., battle of Dormans: Huguenots defeated by Henry of Guise. | **1575** 15 July, Henry III of France formally deposed from Polish throne. 14 Dec., Stephen Bathory, Prince of Transylvania, elected King of Poland with Turkish support (–1586). Spain again bankrupt. | **1575–1610** Ralamba, Merina ruler, increases his dominions. |
| **1576** 6 May, Edict of Beaulieu: 7 May, Peace of Monsieur (or of Loches): end of fifth Huguenot war: Huguenots allowed freedom of religion, save in Paris. 4 Nov., the 'Spanish Fury': Antwerp sacked by unpaid and mutinous troops. Order restored by Don John of Austria: compelled to allow all traditional liberties: 8 Nov., Pacification of Ghent unites Dutch against Spain. League for the Defence of the Catholic Faith formed in France: Henry III declared Head of the League at Blois. **1576–8** Don John of Austria, Governor of the Spanish Netherlands. **1577** 12 Feb., Don John publishes Perpetual Edict to pacify Netherlands: | **1576–1612** Rudolf II, Holy Roman Emperor. | **1576** Tribesmen destroy Portuguese fort at Accra. **1577** Ethiopians take Harar: end of Harar sultanate: new sultanate set up in Aussa (–1672). |

| THE NEAR & FAR EAST | THE AMERICAS | RELIGION & CULTURE |
|---|---|---|
| **1572** July, Akbar begins conquest of Gujarat. | **1572** Francis Drake captures Spanish fleet off Panama Isthmus. | **1572** 24 Nov., John Knox d. Augustinians start work in Goa. Episcopacy restored in Scotland. **1572—85** Gregory XIII (Buoncompagni), Pope. **1572—1626** William Crashaw, poet. **1572—1641** St Jeanne-Françoise-Marie de Chantal. |
| **1573** Revolt led by Mirzas in Akbar's army in Gujarat: 31 Aug., Akbar reaches Ahmadabad, covering 600 m. in nine days: 2 Sept., defeats rebels and annexes Gujarat: 4 Oct., Akbar back in Fathpur-Sikri: makes further administrative reforms: builds city as capital (—1588). Akbar receives Antonio Cabral, ambassador of the Portuguese Viceroy of Goa, at Surat. Juan de Salcedo takes Camarines and Cantanduanes Is. **c. 1573—85** Venkata I, Raya of Vijayanagar. **1573—1619** Shen Tsung (Wan Li), Ming Emperor. **1574** 29 Nov., Limahong, Chinese pirate, attacks Philippines: driven from Manila: founds settlement in Pangasinan. Akbar attacked by Daud Khan, Afghan King of Bengal: drives Daud from Patna and Hajipur. Ahmadnagar seizes Berar. Indonesians destroy Portuguese fortress of Ternate. Javanese fleet from Japara makes abortive attack on Malacca. **1575** March, Limahong besieged: 4 Aug., escapes with his fleet. **1575—6** Akbar makes further administrative reforms: record department organized. | **1574** Drake's second privateering voyage. | **1573—1631** John Donne, poet and divine. **c. 1573—1637** Benjamin Jonson, poet and dramatist. **c. 1573—c. 1652** Inigo Jones, architect. **1573—1656** Thomas Tomkins, composer.

**1574** First Catholic priest from Douai landed in England. Jesuits start work in Transylvania. **1574—1645** Feng Meng-Lung, Chinese novelist.

**1575** Pope Gregory XIII approves the foundation of the Oratorians by St Philip Neri. Akbar builds Ibadat Khana at Fathpur-Sikri: discussion held with Muslim divines (—1579). **c. 1575—1623** Thomas Weelkes, composer. **c. 1575—1626** Samuel Purchas, compiler of voyages. |
| **1576** July, Daud Khan again defeated: Bengal annexed by Akbar: Mewar added to his empire. **1576—8** Ismail II, Shah of Persia. | **1576** 40,000 African slaves in S America. **1576—8** Three voyages of Martin Frobisher reach Baffin Is. and Hudson Strait. | **1576** Observatory built for Tycho Brahe on Hveen Is., Denmark. May-June, Lutheran Articles of Torgau drawn up. Warsaw University founded. First permanent theatre opened in London. Macao made a bishopric. Valletta, Malta, Cathedral built. **1576 and 1577** Akbar holds religious discussions with Fr Julian Pereira. **1576—1631** Enrico Caterino Davila, Italian novelist. **1576—1660** St Vincent de Paul. |
| **1577—8** Akbar reorganizes the mint. | | **1577** Pope Gregory XIII orders Palestrina to revise plainchant. Greek College |

| WESTERN & NORTHERN EUROPE | CENTRAL, SOUTHERN & EASTERN EUROPE | AFRICA & EGYPT |
|---|---|---|

rejected by William of Orange: Estates-General declare Don John 'enemy of the fatherland'. March, sixth Huguenot war in France: 17 Sept., concluded by the Peace of Bergerac: Edict of Poitiers follows. 13 Dec.– 1580 ? 30 Sept., Sir Francis Drake circumnavigates the world in the *Golden Hind.*

**1578** 12 March, James VI, aged twelve, declared of age to rule in Scotland. 13 Aug., Francis, Duke of Anjou, declared 'Defender of Dutch Liberties': attempts to conquer southern provinces. 1 Oct., Don John of Austria d.: succ. Alexander Farnese (later Duke of Parma and Piacenza) as Governor of the Spanish Netherlands (–1581).

**1578–9** Henrique (Cardinal Henry) King of Portugal.

**1578** June, Portuguese fleet of 500 ships and 17,000 ment sent against Morocco: 4 Aug., defeated utterly at Alcazar-Kabir: Sebastian of Portugal and 8,000 men killed: only 100 return to Portugal. Ethiopians defeat Turks: fortress of Dabarwa taken.
**1578–85** Sir Francis Drake intermittently harrying Portuguese shipping off W Africa.
**1578–1603** Abu al-Abbas Ahmad I, Sharif of Morocco: supplied with arms by Elizabeth I of England.

**1579** 25 Jan., the United Provinces (modern Holland) proclaim themselves independent by Union of Utrecht: federal republic formed. May, Ordinance of Blois limits nobility in France. 17 May, peace of Arras: Netherlands southern provinces submit to Philip II of Spain. Eastland Company set up to trade between England and Scandinavia. Spanish contingent attempts to land in Ireland.
**1579–70** Measures for the 'reduction' of Ireland passed by Irish Parliament.
**1579–83** Second Desmond revolt suppressed.
**1580** Seventh Huguenot war in France: Henry of Navarre takes Cahors: 26 Nov., peace made at Fleix. Commercial treaty between England and the Ottomans. England granted capitulations by Ottoman Sultan Murad III.

**1579** Poland makes war on Russia: Polock taken.

**1580** Cardinal Henry d.: Philip II of Spain takes Portugal: Portugal subject to Crown of Spain until 1640.

**1579** War between Ngola and Portuguese.
**1580** Portuguese offensive against Ngola: army largely African.
**?c. 1580** fl. Fumo Liongo, Sultan of Ozi, hero of Swahili epic.
**c. 1580–90** Makua revolt in Mozambique.

**1581** 26 July, Federal Republic of the United Provinces (of Holland) formally renounces allegiance to Philip II of Spain. Negotiations for marriage of Queen Elizabeth I of England to Francis of Anjou pursued. 30 Nov., Alexander Farnese regains Tournai. Ivan the Terrible murders the Crown Prince. Conquest of Siberia begun. Levant (or Turkey) Co. formed. Commercial treaty between

**1581** Palais de France built in Pera, Constantinople.

## THE NEAR & FAR EAST

## THE AMERICAS

## RELIGION & CULTURE

instituted in Rome. 28 May, *Formula Concordiae*, definitive Lutheran confession of faith. First Dominican mission to Mozambique. Akbar grants the fourth Sikh *guru* the site of the Golden Temple, Amritsar. First Douai priest executed in England.

**1577–82** Abp Grindal of Canterbury suspended by Queen Elizabeth for declining to take action against Puritanism.

**1577–87** About 250 Catholic priests executed in England.

**1577–1640** Peter Paul Rubens, artist.

**1578** Chinese population 60.6 m. Portuguese fort built at Tidore. Brunei taken by Spaniards from Philippine Is.

**1578–87** Muhammad Khudabanda, Shah of Persia.

**c. 1578** Oda Nobunaga, a lord of central Japan, becomes leading figure by exploitation of muskets.

**1578** Marquis de la Roche appointed Governor of New France, comprising Canada, Hochelaga, Saguenay, Labrador, Newfoundland, Acadia, Norumbega and Sable Is.: attempt at colonization a failure.

**1578** The Catacombs rediscovered in Rome. Veronese begins decoration of the Palace of the Doges in Venice. Ingolstadt seminary founded. Douai College moved to Reims. Pendelis monastery founded.

**c. 1578** Muskets first used in Japan.

**1578–1651** William Harvey, physician and scientist.

**c. 1579** Portuguese trading settlement made at Hugli, Bengal.

**1579** 1 May, English College established in Rome. Sept., Akbar sends to Goa requesting two priests to instruct him in the Gospel: Frs Rodolfo Aquaviva and Antonio Montserrate, SJ, sent. Akbar pronounces 'Infallibility Decree', making his decisions on Islam binding. Scottish Bible, a version of the Geneva Bible, approved. Fausto Sozzini (Socinus) founds Socinian sect in Poland.

**1579–82** Akbar holds discussions with non-Muslim divines in palace of Fathpur-Sikri.

**1579–1644** Cardinal Guido Bentivoglio, historian.

**1579–1625** John Fletcher, dramatist.

**1580** Jan., rebellion against Akbar in Bengal as a result of Akbar's religious tolerance. Dom João Dharmapala, King of Kotte, Ceylon, makes King of Portugal his heir. Ali b. Ibrahim of Bijapur assassinated: succ. Ibrahim II, his nephew (–1626).

**1580–91** Rajasinha I, King of Kandy, Ceylon: power seized from Portuguese in a limited area.

**1580–1611** Muhammad Quli, ruler of Golconda.

**1581** Feb., Akbar leads campaign against his brother Muhammad Hakim of Kabul: Aug., enters Kabul with little resistance: Muhammad Hakim left in power (–1585). Spanish expedition to Borneo. Tumet attack China. Bayinnaung d.: Burmese Empire at a peak of cultural and commercial activity: succ. Nandabayin: his uncle, governor of Ava, conspires to rebel: Ava easily

**1580** Buenos Aires refounded by Juan de Garay: 500 cattle and 1,000 horses imported: beginning of S American stock industry. First Dutch settlement in Guiana.

**1580** Edmund Campion and Robert Parsons, SJ, commence work in England. Over 100 priests from Douai working in England. Kilish Ali Pasha Mosque, Pera, built.

**post 1580** Use of beaver wool for hats in Paris stimulates trade with N America.

**? 1580–? 1625** John Webster, dramatist.

**1580–1666** Frans Hals, Dutch artist.

**1580–1632** George Calvert, Lord Baltimore, colonial founder.

**1581** 28 Jan., James VI signs the 'King's Covenant' of 'Negative Confession', abjuring Popery: signed also by his court. General Assembly finally establishes Presbyterianism in Scotland. Penalties against English Recusants increased, Protestants banned in Hapsburg possessions.

**1581–2** Edmund Campion executed. Pope Gregory XIII attempts to reconcile Russian church.

**1581–1610** Fr Matteo Ricci, SJ, in China.

1581–1587
WESTERN &
NORTHERN EUROPE

CENTRAL, SOUTHERN
& EASTERN EUROPE

AFRICA & EGYPT

France and Turkey: France granted
right to protect Christians in the
Ottoman Empire.
**1582** 15 Jan., peace of Jam-Zapolski:
Russia cut off from access to the
Baltic by Poland. 22 Aug., Raid of
Ruthven: James VI seized by pro-
English party in Scotland.

**1582** Alexander Farnese takes
Oudenarde. Spain prevents French
attempt to take the Azores. Philip II
confirms Portuguese autonomy under
the Spanish Crown. Venetian
constitution reformed.

**1583** 7 Feb., Francis of Anjou puts
down revolt in Antwerp. James VI
escapes captivity by aid of French
ambassadors. Throckmorton's plot,
to place Mary, Queen of Scots, on
the English throne, discovered.

**1583–4** War between Catholics and
Calvinists for possession of
archbishopric of Cologne: Calvinists
defeated.
**1583–98** Casa Lonja (Exchange)
built in Seville.

**1584** May, Scottish Parliament passes
the 'Black Acts': James VI made Head
of the Kirk. 10 July, William of
Orange assassinated: succ. as
Stadholder, Maurice (1585–1625).
31 Dec., League of Joinville formed
by the Guises and Philip II of Spain
against the Huguenots. Ivan IV d.:
succ. Feodor, a feeble-minded Tsar
(–1598). Yermak, a Don Cossack,
defeats the Mongols near the Tobol:
Siberia added to Russia.
**1585** 17 Aug., Farnese retakes
Antwerp and S Netherlands: rebels
supported by English supplies and
volunteers: Dec., Earl of Leicester
sent to support United Provinces
with 7,000 men. 2 Feb., treaty of
Joinville between the Guise and
Philip II of Spain. Feb., Henry III
of France declines the throne of
the Netherlands. Act for better
government of London and
Westminster. The Composition of
Connacht.
**1585–98** Eighth and last Huguenot
war in France: known also as the
War of the three Henrys (Henry III,
Henry IV, and Henry of Guise).
**1586** Aug., Anthony Babington's
plot discovered. 22 Sept., minor
engagement at Zutphen: 17 Oct.,
Sir Philip Sidney, poet, courtier and
soldier, d. of wounds. 14–15 Oct.,
Mary, Queen of Scots, tried for
treason. Anglo-Scottish treaty of
mutual defence. Articles for the
plantation of Desmond lands in
Munster approved.
**1587** 8 Feb., Mary, Queen of Scots,
beheaded at Fotheringay Castle.

**1585** Cartagena sacked by Sir Francis
Drake.

**1585** Portuguese badly defeated by
Ngola. Amir Ali Bey, Turkish
corsair, rouses eastern African
coast against Portuguese.

**1586** 13 Dec., Stephen Bathory, King
of Poland, d. Preparations for an
invincible Armada against England
begun in Spain.

**1586** Sarsa Dengel leads expedition
against Enarya.

**1587** Apr., Sir Francis Drake pillages
Cadiz and the Spanish coast: many

**1587** Zimba horde sacks Kilwa:
three-quarters of population of 4,000

| THE NEAR & FAR EAST | THE AMERICAS | RELIGION & CULTURE |
|---|---|---|

**THE NEAR & FAR EAST**

conquered; Siam rebels: punitive expedition fails.
**1581—99** Nandabayin, King of Burma.
**1582** Portuguese ships assist in defence of Johore against attack by Acheh.
**1582—90** Toyotomi Hideyoshi, after several brilliant campaigns, subjects all Japan: 100 years peace ensues: administration and currency reformed: huge castle built at Osaka: fiction of imperial authority vigorously maintained.

**1583** Akbar builds fort of Allahabad.

**1584** Supreme Court instituted in the Philippines. 4,000 Chinese settle in Manila.

**c. 1585** Venkata I, Raya of Vijayanagar: capital moved to Chandragiri: subsequent rulers mere local chiefs.
**1585, 1586** Nandabayin leads further abortive expeditions against Siam.

**1586** Yusufzi and other Afghans rebel in Khyber Pass region: army sent by Akbar defeated. Kashmir annexed by Akbar.

**1587** Malacca attacked by Johore. Turks defeat Persians near Baghdad.

**THE AMERICAS**

**1583** Sir Humphrey Gilbert establishes colony in Newfoundland: lost at sea on return voyage.

**1585—8** NW Atlantic explored by John Davis as far as the Arctic.
**1585** English colony established by Sir Richard Grenville at Roanoke, Virginia: Ralph Lane left in charge: colony disappears without trace.

**1586** Sir Francis Drake raids Spanish W. I.

**1587** John White establishes second colony at Roanoke: settlement a failure.

**RELIGION & CULTURE**

**1581—1656** James Ussher, divine.
**1581—1660** St Vincent de Paul.

**1582** Oct., Pope Gregory XIII institutes Gregorian Calendar: accepted initially in Catholic countries only. Akbar renounces Islam, and proclaims *Din Ilahi* (religion of God): issues regulations hostile to Islam. Universities of Edinburgh and of Würzburg founded.
**1582—1646** François de Meynard, poet.
**1582—1652** Gregorio Allegri, Italian composer.
**1583** Jesuits withdraw from Fathpur-Sikri. Jesuits open church at Galata, Istanbul: granted further permission to open church at Smyrna.
**1583—1604** John Whitgift, Abp of Canterbury: strict discipline maintained among the clergy: Puritan clergy deprived.
**1583—1625** Orlando Gibbons, composer.
**1583—1645** Hugo Grotius (van Groot), Dutch writer and statesman.
**1583—1648** Edward, Lord Herbert of Cherbury, historian and philosopher.
**1584** Nov., English Parliament passes additional laws against Catholics. Seminary for Maronite students established in Rome by Gregory XIII.
**1584—1616** Francis Beaumont, dramatist.

**1585** March, further Acts of Parliament against Catholics in England: virtual Inquisition established. 9 Sept., Pope Sixtus V declares Henry of Navarre disqualified from French throne because of his Protestant allegiance. All Protestant privileges revoked by Henry III of France.
**1585—90** Sixtus V (Peretti), Pope.
**1585—1638** Cornelius Jansen, originator of Jansenism.
**1585—1672** Heinrich Schütz, German composer.

**1586** College of Cardinals reorganized: number fixed at seventy. The potato introduced into Europe.
**c. 1586** Over ¼ m. Filipinos already baptized.
**1586—1647** Nicholas Stone, sculptor.
**1586—1652** Pietro della Valle, Italian traveller and writer.

**1587** Vatican Press established.

1587–1592
WESTERN &
NORTHERN EUROPE

CENTRAL, SOUTHERN
& EASTERN EUROPE

AFRICA & EGYPT

20 Nov., Henry of Navarre beats French Catholic army at Coutras. Bill to reform Church of England refused by Queen Elizabeth: Peter Wentworth imprisoned for demanding right of free speech in the Commons.

**1588** 12 May, rising of League supporters in Paris: 'Day of the Barricades': Henry III flees to Blois. July, the 'Invincible Armada' reaches the English Channel with 130 ships and 30,000 men: 27 July, at Calais: forced out by fireships: 18 July, engagement off Calais: Spanish retreat *via* N Sea and Ireland: gales wreck many ships: Sept., only 65 vessels and 10,000 men return. Oct., French Estates-General meet in Blois. 23 Dec., Henry of Guise assassinated. 24 Dec., Cardinal de Guise murdered.
**1588–98** Boris Godunov, Regent of Russia.
**1588–1648** Christian IV, King of Denmark.
**1589** 3 Apr., reconciliation between Henry III of France and Henry of Navarre. Pope Sixtus V deposes Henry III of France: 2 Aug., Henry III assassinated: the Catholic League sets up Cardinal de Bourbon as Charles X: Henry of Navarre assumes title as Henry IV: war ensues (−1594): Henry IV takes Dieppe: 20 Sept., battle of Arques. James VI of Scotland m. Anne of Denmark.
**1589–1793** Dynasty of Navarre in France.
**1590** 14 March, Henry IV defeats the Catholic League, and again near Evreux: besieges Paris: Sept., siege raised by Alexander Farnese: Henry IV besieges Rouen (−1592) with reinforcements from Brandenburg.

**1591** 15 May, Dimitri, only brother of Tsar Feodor, assassinated. Edict of Mantes. The Catholic League engages in a reign of terror in Paris. Rebellion in Aragon put down.

**1592–1604** Sigismund III of Poland also King of Sweden.

ships and stores destroyed. 9 Aug., Sigismund III Vasa elected King of Poland (−1632).
**1587–1668** Vasa dynasty in Poland.

**1589** 5 Jan., Catherine dei Medici d. Anthony, pretender to the Portuguese throne, sent thither by Elizabeth I of England: campaign turns into a rout.

**1590** Rising in Aragon. Treaty of Constantinople between Turkey and Persia.

**1591** 3 Feb., League of Torgau formed by German Protestant states. *c.* 29 Aug., Sir Richard Grenville defies the Spanish Fleet off the Azores in the *Revenge*.

**1592** 3 Dec., Alexander Farnese d.

killed and eaten. Portuguese fleet puts down rebellion on E coast.

**1588** Zimba reach Mombasa: Amir Ali Bey attacks Mombasa by sea: Tomé de Sousa repels Turks: fails to prevent sack by Zimba: Zimba attack Malindi: annihilated by force of Portuguese and Segeju.
*c.* **1588** Portuguese factories at Cache Lagos, Warri, New and Old Calabar an Cameroons R.

**1589** Morocco cedes Arzila to Spain.

**1590** Moroccan army under Judar Pasha invades and seizes Songhai. Wallo Galla at war with Aussa. Portuguese defeated by allied army o Jaga, Kongo, Matamba and Ndongo.

**1591** Sir James Lancaster, first Englishman to water at Comoro Is. and in Zanzibar.
**1591–1748** Moroccan Pashas of Timbuktu nominally subject to Marrakesh: 150 in 157 years.
**ante 1592** Portuguese factory set up in Zanzibar. Portuguese force from Sena and Tete routed by Zimba.

| THE NEAR & FAR EAST | THE AMERICAS | RELIGION & CULTURE |
|---|---|---|

Portuguese destroy Johore Lama: new capital of Johore built at Batu Sawar. Portuguese treaty with Acheh.
1587–90 Turks invade Persia.
1587–1629 Abbas I, the Great, Shah of Persia: new capital built at Isfahan.
1588 Demak conquered by Mataram.

of Christians in Japan. Dominicans arrive in Philippine Is.
1587–91 Rialto Bridge built in Venice.
1587 Portuguese fort of Mirani, Muscat, built.

1588 Jesuits arrive in Paraguay: *reducciones* (mission towns) soon established for Indian converts.

1588 Palace of Udaipur built. The Bible published in Welsh. Luis de Molina, SJ, attacks Thomism: controversy between Dominicans and Jesuits.
1588–1648 Antoine Le Nain, French artist.
1588–1679 Thomas Hobbes, materialist philosopher.

1589 Capital of Golconda moved to Bhagnagar, shortly renamed Hyderabad. Revolts against Spaniards in Philippine Is.: government reforms follow.

1589 Ecumenical Patriarch of Constantinople confers dignity of Patriarch of all Russia upon Job, former Abp of Novgorod. Academy of Kiev founded.

1590 Tabriz ceded to Turkey by Persia. Akbar takes southern Sind. Akbar sends embassies to Khandesh, Ahmadnagar, Golconda and Bijapur: Khandesh promises obedience: others refuse. Nandabayin's expedition against Siam again abortive.
1590–3 Manila fortified.
1590–1635 Fakhr al-Din al-Mani II, Prince of Lebanon.
c. 1590–1811 Regular trade in Chinese goods between the Philippines and Mexico.
1591 Usurper Konappa Bandara makes himself King of Kandy by force as Vimala Dharma Suriya I.
1591–1750 Sind subject to the Mughuls.

1591 Santos burnt by Thomas Cavendish.

1590 Urban VII (Castagna), Pope. Great Mosque of Isfahan built.
1590–1 Gregory XIV (Sfrondrati), Pope.
1590–2 Second Jesuit mission at Fathpur-Sikri.
1590–1607 Borghese Palace, Rome, built.

1591 Innocent IX (Facchinetti), Pope. Trinity College, Dublin, founded. Donskoi Monastery begun.
1591–9 Edmund Spenser, poet laureate of England.
1591–1674 Robert Herrick, poet.

1592 Orissa taken for Akbar by Man Singh. Rajasinha I, former King of Kandy, d. of blood poisoning. Nandabayin's expedition against Siam fails: Siamese occupy Tenasserim coast. Vietnam temporarily re-united.
1592–8 Japan invades Korea with 200,000 men: Seoul and other cities taken: country devastated: King of Korea made subject to Japan (–1790).

1592 Congregation for Affairs of the Faith established: beginning of modern missionary activity. Definitive edition of the Vulgate published. Site of Pompeii rediscovered. 'Golden Act' in Scotland: Presbyterianism finally established.
1592–1605 Clement VIII (Aldobrandini), Pope.
1592–1655 Pierre Gassendi, philosopher.
1592–1660 Jacques Sarazin, sculptor.

| WESTERN &<br>NORTHERN EUROPE | CENTRAL, SOUTHERN<br>& EASTERN EUROPE | AFRICA & EGYPT |
|---|---|---|
| | **1593** Michael the Brave takes Wallachia from the Ottomans: becomes Prince of Wallachia.<br>**1593–1601** Austria and Turkey at war in Hungary.<br>**1593** Lord Essex destroys shipping in Cadiz harbour. | **1593** Portuguese again routed by Zimba. 1,200 slaves sent across Sahara to join Moroccan army.<br>**1593–6** Fort Jesus, Mombasa, built. |
| **1594** 27 Feb., Henry IV crowned at Chartres: 22 March, enters Paris.<br>**1594–1603** The Tyrone War in Ireland. | **1594** Philip II closes port of Lisbon to Dutch merchants: stimulates Dutch enterprise in the East. The Ottomans take Raab. | **1594** End of Songhai Empire. Portuguese establish customs house in Mombasa. |
| **1595** 17 Jan., Henry IV of France makes war on Spain. 6 June, battle of Fontaine-Française: Henry IV takes Boulogne from Spain.<br>**1595–9** (Future) Charles IX administrator of Sweden. | **1595** 28 Oct., Ottomans defeated by Sigismund Bathory at Giurgevo.<br>**1595–1603** Muhammad III, Ottoman Sultan. Much power in the Ottoman Empire wielded by the *harim* (–1687). | **1595** First Dutch voyage to the Gold Coast. |
| **1596** Apr., Spain takes Calais. 30 June – 1 July, English sack Cadiz. Treaty of Greenwich: England, France and the United Provinces ally against Spain. 17 Dec., riots in Edinburgh: Scottish law courts moved to Linlithgow. Special Exchequer Commission appointed in Scotland.<br>**1596–7** Assembly of notables in Rouen.<br>**1597** 1 Jan., James VI regains control of Edinburgh. Spain takes Amiens: 25 Sept., retaken by Henry IV. Abortive Spanish naval expeditions against England. English Parliament orders erection of workhouses: 'sturdy beggars' forbidden. | **1596** 23–6 Oct., Ottoman victory at Keresztes. Spanish decree proclaims national bankruptcy.<br><br>**1597–1651** Maximilian I, Duke of Bavaria (Elector from 1623). | **1597–1603** Yaqub, Emperor of Ethiopia. |
| **1598** 2 May, Treaty of Vervins between France and Spain. 4 Aug., William Cecil, Lord Burghley d. 15 Aug., battle of the Yellow Ford: Irish defeat English force. Rebellion in Ireland. Spanish troops assist rebels (–1602). Boris Godunov elected Tsar (–1605).<br>**1598–1605** Dynasty of Godunov in Russia.<br>**1599** 15 Apr., Earl of Essex lands 16,000 infantry and 1,300 cavalry in Dublin: 8 Sept., truce made with Ireland. Second abortive Spanish *Armada* sent against Britain: destroyed by a storm. East India Co. set up in England. Confederation of Vilno.<br>**1599–1658** Oliver Cromwell, soldier and statesman. | **1598** 13 Apr., Pope Clement VIII seizes Duchy of Ferrara. 25 Sept., Sigismund of Poland defeated by Charles IX at Stangebro in an attempt to conquer Sweden.<br>**1598–1621** Philip III, King of Spain and of Portugal: Duke of Lerma, chief minister (–1618). | **1598** Dutch establish four factories in W Africa.<br>c. **1598** Portuguese make al-Hasan b.Ahmad, King of Malindi, their puppet King of Mombasa. |

## THE NEAR & FAR EAST

**1593** Akbar sends armies against S India. Jan., Chinese intervene against Japanese in Korea: following Korean victories at sea, Japanese retreat: 70 Japanese vessels sunk by reversible *Kwi-son*, armoured 'tortoise-boat'. Rebellion of Mons in Burma: Siamese join them, besieging Pegu: Siam retreat, but hold Moulmein and Martaban: Nandabayin's son, governor of Prome rebels: rebellion put down by Siamese, who take Chengmai.

**1594** Baluchistan and Makran taken for Akbar. Abortive Portuguese attempt to instal Dona Caterina on the throne of Kandy.
**1594—1604** Chinese campaigns in Annam, Burma and Thailand, with a view to colonization.
**1595** War between Ahmadnagar and Bijapur. Qandahar surrendered to Akbar by its Persian governor. First Dutch expedition to India and Java.
**1595—8** Famine in N India and Kashmir, accompanied by plague.
**1595—1634** Fakhr al-Din, Amir of the Lebanon.
**1596** Berar ceded to Akbar. 5 June, first Dutch vessels reach Sumatra; 23 June, Bantam, Java: Cornelis de Houtman in charge as chief merchant: subsequently visits Jakarta. First Dutch treaty in Indonesia, with Prince of Bantam.

**1597** Persians defeat Uzbeqs near Herat. Japan again invades Korea. Philip II of Spain proclaimed King of Ceylon.
**1597—1613** Ala al-Din Riayat Shah II, Sultan of Johore.

**1598** Sir Anthony, and Sir Robert, Sherley visit Persia. Japanese forced to abandon Korea: many raids on coast of central China. Toyotomi Hideyoshi d.: Tokugawa Ieyasu appointed regent for his five year old son, Hideyori: Japan steadily made subservient to Ieyasu. Five Dutch expeditions to the E Indies.

**1599** June, Cornelis de Houtman killed in an attack on his ship in Acheh harbour. Akbar occupies Burhanpur, capital of Khandesh. Salim, son of Akbar, rebels. Three Dutch expeditions to the E Indies. Moro pirates attack Philippine Is. Arakan fleet seizes Syriam; Toungoo besieges Pegu: city found to be

## THE AMERICAS

**1594** Sir Walter Raleigh's first voyage to Guiana.

**1595** Sir Walter Raleigh explores mouths of Rs Amazon and Orinoco.

**1597** Sir Walter Raleigh's second voyage to Guiana.

## RELIGION & CULTURE

**1593** Feb., Act of Parliament against Puritans. 15 July, Henry IV of France abjures Protestantism. Assembly of Uppsala makes Lutheranism the state religion in Sweden. *Qanun* of Ibn Sina (Avicenna), translated from Arabic into Latin, printed in Rome: used by European physicians during the 17th c..
**1593 or 1594** Richard Hooker: *The Laws of Ecclesiastical Polity.*
**1593—1633** George Herbert, poet.
**1593—1646** Count Fulvio Testi, Italian poet.
**1593—1648** Louis Le Nain, French artist.
**1593—1683** Izaak Walton, biographer.
**1594** Parliament of Paris bans Jesuits.
**1594—1665** Nicolas Poussin, French artist.

**1595** 17 Sept., Henry IV of France absolved by Pope Clement VIII. Jesuit mission becomes permanent in Lahore. Bishopric of São Salvador created.

c. **1596** Augustinian missions set up in Mombasa, Lamu and Faza. The air thermometer invented by Galileo.
**1596—1650** René Descartes, philosopher and mathematician.
**1596** Cagliari University founded.
**1596—1665** Jan van Bolland, SJ, founder of the Bollandists.
**1596—1655** Abd al-Rahman al-Sadi, historian, at Timbuktu.

**1597** Valve water closet made by Sir John Harington. Feb., eighteen Japanese Christians, and six Spanish Franciscans, crucified at Nagasaki. Yeni Camii (Yeni Valide) mosque begun in Istanbul.

**1598** 12 Jan., Edict of Nantes: Huguenots granted toleration. Pope Clement VIII forbids the Chalice to the laity in the Hapsburg domains.
c. **1598—1612** Augustinian mission in Zanzibar.
**1598—1662** Zurburan, Spanish artist.
**1598—1680** Giovanni Lorenzo Bernini, artist. architect and sculptor.

**1599** James VI of Scotland: *Basilikon Doron*: assert divine right of Kings: condemns Presbyterianism.
**1599—1641** Sir Anthony van Dyck, Flemish artist.
**1599—1660** Velázquez, Spanish artist.
**1599—1677** Francesco Borromini, architect.

| WESTERN EUROPE | NORTHERN, CENTRAL & SOUTHERN EUROPE | AFRICA |
|---|---|---|

**17th c.** Frequent Portuguese campaign in present Angola and Kinshasa. Lwoo chieftainship set up in present Alur region. Lozi Kingdom founded.

**1600** Jan., further rising in Tyrone. 5 Aug., the Gowrie Conspiracy: alleged to be a plot against James VI. 31 Dec., (English) East India Co chartered. Bank of Amsterdam instituted. The Spanish beat the Dutch and the English at Nieuport. Maurice of Nassau attempts to invade Belgium. Henry IV of France m. Mary dei Medici. Cámara de Indias (Chamber of the Indies) created in Spain to control American possessions.

**1600** Sweden invades Polish Province of Livonia. Feb., Charles IX beheads pro-Polish leaders at Linköping.

**c. 1600** Coptic ceases to be spoken: still used as a liturgical language. Many peoples in W, C and E Africa reach their present habitats. Lunda empire founded. First Sakalava dynasty founded.
**post 1600** Galla moving southward, reaching Kenya coast.

**1601** Brief hostilities between France and Savoy: 17 Jan., treaty of Lyons between France and Savoy: France cedes her trans-Alpine possessions: recovers Bresse, Bugey and Valromey, and district of Gex. 25 Feb., Earl of Essex beheaded for attempted rebellion. 15 July, Spain besieges Ostend (−1604). Thirty-three Spanish vessels and 4,000 men sent to Ireland to help Tyrone and O'Donnell: 23 Sept., land at Kinsale. 24 Dec., Irish and Spaniards routed by English at battle of Kinsale. Overseers of the Poor instituted in England.
**1602** 2 Jan., Spaniards surrender at Kinsale. 20 March, Dutch East India Co. (*Vereenigde Oostindische Compagnie*) founded.

**1601** Severe famine in Russia. The Dutch destroy a Spanish fleet off Gibraltar.
**1601–6** Valladolid, capital of Spain.

**1601** Army mutiny in Egypt. De **Bry** vists Benin.
**c. 1602** Dutch make settlement at C. Mount, Sierra Leone.
**1603–29** Zaidan, Sharif of Morocco.

**1602** Alliance between France and the Swiss Confederation renewed. Dec., Duke of Savoy fails to take Switzerland. Persia and Spain declare abortive war on Turkey.

**1602** First French visit to Madagascar.

**1603** 24 March, Queen Elizabeth d.: succ. James VI of Scotland as James I (−1625). 30 March, The O'Neill submits: end of Tyrone war.
**1603–1714** Stewart dynasty in England.

**1603** Henry IV arranges an alliance between Grisons and Venice.
**1603–4** The pretender Dimitri attempts to usurp Boris Godunov.
**1603–17** Ahmad I, Ottoman Sultan.

**1603** Keira dynasty of Darfur founded.
**1603–4** Za Dengel, Emperor of Ethiopia.
**1603–24** Fr Paris, SJ, in Ethiopia: missionary activity in Tigre.

undefended: spoil divided between
Arakan and Toungoo: city then
burnt; Siamese besiege Toungoo:
Siamese forced to retreat by Arakan.
Philip de Brito y Nicote left as
governor of Syriam.
**17th c.** Kedah exporting pepper.

**1600** Apr.– 1601 Jan., Akbar
besieges Asirgarh. Aug., Ahmadnagar
falls to Akbar. Sept., treaty between
Dutch and Amboina: Dutch allowed
to build fortress: granted monopoly
of spice trade in return for protection.
21 Oct., Ieyasu defeats rebellion of
territorial lords at Sekigahara. 14
Dec., Spanish destroy Dutch fleet
in Manila harbour. De Brito makes
himself King of Syriam: recognized
by Goa and Portugal: authority
covers Lower Burma. Will Adams,
with twenty-four Dutch survivors
of a ship-wreck, first Englishman
to visit Japan: settles as a diplomatic
agent. Two Dutch expeditions to the
E Indies. Moro pirates again attack
Philippine Is.
**c. 1600** Population of India estimated
at c.100 m.
**1601** 17 Jan., Asirgarh falls to Akbar:
Ahmadnagar, Berar and Khandesh
re-organized as provinces. 25 Dec.,
Dutch fleet defeats Portuguese off
Bantam. Akbar sends embassy to
Goa. Four Dutch expeditions to
the E Indies. First strike, of textile
workers, on record in China.
**1601–3** First English voyage to
India under Sir James Lancaster.

**1602** Dutch make contact with King
of Kandy, Ceylon. Banda grants the
Dutch a monopoly of the nutmeg
trade: Dutch shortly murdered.
Demak and Mataram at war.
**1602–27** Persian campaigns against
Turkey.
**c. 1602** The Manchu begin to attack
Chinese cities in Manchuria.

**1603** 3 Oct., 25,000 Chinese revolt
in Manila: put down by Spanish with
Filipino aid. 21 Oct., Persians retake
Tabriz. Turks defeated near L.
Urmia. Reconciliation between
Akbar and Salim. Dutch capture
Portuguese carrack from China in
Johore R. Tokugawa Ieyasu
appointed Shogun. Goa blockaded by
the Dutch.

**1600** Pierre Chauvin granted ten year
monopoly of Canadian fur trade, on
condition of transporting fifty
colonists to America annually:
monopoly a failure. Brazil the chief
world producer of sugar.
**c. 1600** C. 200,000 Indians E of the
Mississippi: not more than ½m.
Indians N of Mexico.

**1602** Pierre Chauvin d.: succ. in the
monopoly, Sieur de Chaste, sails with
Samuel de Champlain.
**1602–6** Capt. Charles Leigh's tobacco
settlement in Guiana.

**1603** Champlain's first visit to
America: St Lawrence R. explored.

**1600** Scots College founded in Rome.
Giordano Bruno burnt in Rome. Royal
Palace, Naples, begun.
**c. 1600–43** Anne Hutchinson, religious
enthusiast and 'Antinomian' leader in
New England.
**1600–81** Pedro Calderón, Spanish
dramatist.
**1600–82** Claude de Lorraine, French
artist.

**1601** Disputation between Jesuits and
Protestants at Ratisbon.
**1601–10** Fr Matteo Ricci, SJ, at the
Chinese court: highly esteemed as an
astronomer.
**1601–67** Alonso Cano, artist, architect
and sculptor.
**1601** Gobelins tapestry manufacture
established at Reims.

**1602** First Russian Missal published:
alleged to contain many errors.
Protestants persecuted in Austria,
Bohemia and Hungary. St Francis de
Sales teaching in Paris.
**1602–74** Philippe de Champaigne.
**1602–76** Pietro Francesco Cavalli,
Italian composer.
**1602–76** Abraham Bosse.
**1602–86** Otto von Guericke, scientist:
inventor of the air pump.
**1603** Sept., Henry IV permits the Jesuits
to return to France. 17 July, James I
announces toleration for Roman Catholic
in England: Parliament angered. James I
of England requests an Ecumenical
Council.
**1603–5** Venice issues decrees against
ecclesiastical privileges.
**1603–17** Dolmabahçe Palace, Pera,
built.

| WESTERN EUROPE | NORTHERN, CENTRAL & SOUTHERN EUROPE | AFRICA |
|---|---|---|
| **1604** Feb., Act of Oblivion forgives all previous crimes in Ireland. The Spanish take Ostend. 28 Aug., peace treaty between James I of England and Spain: undertakes not to support the Dutch or trade with of Indies. Quarrel between James I of England and the Commons on a disputed election. (First) French East India Co founded. **1605** 5 Nov., Gunpowder Plot discovered. Irish ordered to abjure the Church of Rome. **1605–6** Duke of Bouillon rebels in France. | **1604** 21 Jan., Boris Godunov defeats the pretender Dimitri. 20 March, Charles IX, former Regent, King of Sweden (–1611). Tomsk founded. *Conselho da India* established in Spain. Poland defeats Sweden at Weisenstein. Protestants rise in Hungary under Stephen Bocskay. **1604–13** Time of Troubles in Russia. **1605** Apr.– 1606 Stephen Bocskay, Prince of Transylvania. 23 April, Boris Godunov d.: son Feodor proclaimed Tsar: 20 June, assassinated: *interregnum* in Russia (–1613): Pretender Dimitri enters Moscow. Poland defeats Sweden at Kirchholm. | **1604–32** Susenyos, Emperor of Ethiopia. **1604–5** Ibrahim Pasha, governor of Egypt: harsh rule provokes military revolt. **1604** 17 June-25 Aug., Dutch blockade Mozambique Is. **1605** Egyptian troops kill Ibrahim Pasha. |
| **1606** Henry IV puts down the Duke of Bouillon's rebellion: Sédan occupied. | **1606** Apr., rebellion against Rudolf V of Austria. 17 May, pretender Dimitri assassinated. 23 June, treaty of Vienna between Austria and Hungary: Bocskay acknowledged: religious toleration granted. 11 Nov., treaty of Sitva-Torek between Austria and Turkey. Vassili Chouiski proclaims himself Tsar. **1606–7** Dispute between Pope Paul V and Venice arbitrated by Henry IV of France. | **1606–11** Adlan, King of the Funj: court distinguished by numerous holy men. |
| **1607** 14 Sept., Earls of Tyrone and Tyrconnell and others flee from Ireland: estates in Ulster confiscated: granted to Protestant Scottish and English settlers (Plantation of Ulster, to 1610). Navarre formally united to France. English House of Commons rejects union with Scotland. | **1607** Spain again bankrupt. Sigismund III defeats rebellion in Poland. | **1607** Dutch abortively besiege Mozambique. Muhammad Pasha, governor of Egypt. |
| **1608** June, treaty of mutual defence between England and the United Provinces. | **1608** 27 Apr., Protestants disrupt Diet of Ratisbon. 26 June, Emperor Rudolf V of Austria abdicates: succ. his brother Matthias (–1619). A second pretender named Dimitri claims the Russian throne. **1608–19** John Sigismund, Elector of Brandenburg. | **1608** July-Aug., Dutch again besiege Mozambique. 1 Aug., Portuguese make treaty with Monomotapa. |
| **1609** 9 Apr., Twelve Year truce between Spain and the United Provinces: United Provinces formally recognized. 17 July, Twelve Year | **1609** Compromise of Dortmund regulates succession to Duchy of Cleves. Sigismund III Vasa of Poland besieges Smolensk. | **1609** Rising in Egypt. 80,000 Moriscos said to have arrived in Tunis. Treaty between Monomotapa Gatsi Rusere and Portuguese. |

| THE EAST | THE AMERICAS | RELIGION & CULTURE |
|---|---|---|

**1604** Nov., Salim arrested, and then released.

**1604** Champlain plants first settlement on Dochet Is., St Croix R.: Port Royal (Annapolis) founded.
Dutch fleet attacks Bahia.
**c. 1604—84** Roger Williams, founder of Rhode Is.

**1604** 14—16 Jan., Hampton Court Conference: James I reaches terms with the Church of England.
**1604—19** Arminians attack Calvinist doctrine of predestination in the United Provinces.
**1604—88** Johan Rudolf Glauber, German chemist, inventor of Glauber Salts.

**1605** 22 Sept., Prince of Gowa declares allegiance to Islam. 27 Oct., Akbar d., possibly of poison: succ. Salim, with throne name Nur al-Din Muhammad Jahangir Padshah Ghazi, commonly Jahangir: 13 Nov., enthroned at Agra. Tokugawa Ieyasa abdicates shogunate in favour of his son, Hidetada (—1622). Amboina accepts suzerainty of Dutch EIC. Portuguese leave Molucca Is. Kings of Ava and of Siam d. campaigning against Toungoo.
**1605—28** Anankpetlun, King of Burma.

**1605** Sixty-seven English settlers killed by Caribs on St Lucia.
**1605—6** Champlain surveys New France (New England) as far as Rhode Is. Site of future New Amsterdam (New York) visited.

**1605** First Jesuits arrive in America at Asunción. Leo XI (dei Medici). Pope. Alexeyevski Monastery, Tomsk, founded.
**1605 — 21** Paul V (Borghese), Pope.
**1605—38** Adrian Brouwer, Dutch artist.
**1605—74** Giacomo Carissimi, Italian composer.
**1605—82** Sir Thomas Browne, writer.
**1605—91** Albert Cuyp, Dutch artist.
**1605—89** Jean Baptiste Tavernier, explorer.

**1606** Apr., Prince Khusru rebels against Jahangir: Jahangir takes ruthless vengeance on his supporters. Jesuits obtain influence over Jahangir. Spanish occupy deserted fort of Tidore. Expedition from Philippines against Molucca Is. Dutch-Johore treaty against Malacca signed. Dutch attack Malacca. Dutch open trade at Banjermasin, Borneo. First known discovery of Australia: Willem Jansz, Dutch captain of *Duyfken*, explores New Guinea and Gulf of Carpentaria.
**1606—45** Hargobind, sixth Sikh *guru*, transforms Sikh sect into a military order.

**1606** 10 Apr., London Company chartered to plant a colony in America between Lat 34° and 41°; Plymouth Co. chartered to plant colony between Lat. 38° and 45°.

**1606** Office of Moderator of the General Assembly of the Church of Scotland made permanent. Further anti-Catholic legislation in England.
**1606—84** Pierre Corneille, dramatist.
**1606—87** Edmund Waller, poet.
**1606—89** Rembrandt Harmens Rijn, Dutch artist.

**1607** Sept., Jahangir sends embassy to Goa. Alliance between Dutch and Sultan of Ternate.
**1607—36** Iskander Shah Mahkota Alam, Sultan of Acheh: policy of fierce rivalry with Johore and Malacca: Acheh includes Pahang, Kedah and Perak.
**1607—40** Dutch seek to cut off trade from the Portuguese in Malacca.

**1607** 13 May, Jamestown, Virginia, founded. Monopoly of fur trade in New France ended: Sieur de Poutrincourt continues Champlain's work.
**1607—8** Anáhuac basin, Mexico, partly drained.

**1607—77** Matthieu le Nain, French sculptor.

**1608** Aug., Capt. William Hawkins arrives at Surat with letter from James I of England to Jahangir: converses with the Emperor in Turki: granted right to trade. Treaty between Fakhr al-Din II of Lebanon and Ferdinand, Duke of Tuscany. Anankpetlun of Toungoo takes Prome.
**1608—46** Imam Kuli, ruler of Bokhara.

**1608** July, Champlain founds settlement at Quebec.

**1608** 19 May, Evangelical Union between German Calvinists and Lutherans formed at Anhausen.
**1608—47** Evangelista Torricelli, scientist.
**1608—74** John Milton, poet.

**1609** Dutch trading settlement made at Pulicat, north of Madras. Dutch begin trading in Japan.
**1609—10** Dutch blockade Manila.

**1609** Champlain joins war party of Montagnais and Algonquin Indians: explores Lake Champlain and Lake St George. 209 English immigrants

**1609** 9 July, freedom of conscience proclaimed in Bohemia. 10 July, Catholic Counter-League formed in Munich. 25 Sept., Reform of Port Royal. Prelates

| WESTERN EUROPE | NORTHERN, CENTRAL & SOUTHERN EUROPE | AFRICA |
|---|---|---|
| Alliance of the United Provinces with England and France. Charter of (English) East India Co. renewed. | **1609–11** *c.* 500,000 Moors expelled from Spain: transported on government provided vessels to Africa. | |
| **1610** 14 May, Henry IV of France assassinated: succ. Louis XIII (–1643): Mary dei Medici, Regent (–1614). 9 June, Arabella Stuart m. secretly Lord William Seymour (later 2nd Duke of Somerset): imprisoned in the Tower. Commission of 'fire and sword' issued against Clan MacGregor. **1610–11** James I of England in conflict with Parliament. **1611** Baronets instituted by James I of England: patent fee £1000. | **1610** 12 Feb., Henry IV of France allies with the German Evangelical Union. Sigismund, King of Poland, persuades a group of boyars to make his son Ladislas Tsar: Polish garrison installed in the Kremlin. Poles defeat Russians at Kluszyno. **1611** March, Polish troops besieged in the Kremlin: Sigismund of Poland takes Smolensk; the Swedes take Nijni Novgorod. 4 Apr., war between Denmark and Sweden. 8 Nov., Charles IX of Sweden d.: succ. Gustavus II Adolphus (–1632). Treaty of alliance between Austria and Spain. **1611–56** John George I, Elector of Saxony. | **1610–13** Desultory hostilities between Monomotapa and Portuguese *c.* **1610** Tananarive becomes the Merina capital. **1610–37** Yusuf, Dey of Tunis, organizer of piracy. **1610–13** Abu Mahalli, claiming to be Mahdi, seizes Marrakesh. **1611–16** Badi Sid el Qom, King of Sennar: repudiates alleged suzerainty of Ethiopia. |
| **1612** 24 May, Lord Burghley d. 22 Aug., peace treaty between France and Spain. 18 Oct., Louis XIII betrothed to Anne of Austria. 5 Nov., Henry, Prince of Wales, d. | **1612** Aug., army of national liberation, led by the butcher Minine, marches on Moscow: Oct., Poles capitulate. | **1612** *c.* 10,000 slaves shipped annually from Angola. **post 1612** Pemba made subject to King of Malindi. |
| **1613** 14 Feb., Elizabeth, daughter of James I of England, m. the Elector Palatine. **1613–15** Chichester's Parliament in Ireland: Ulster and other plantations confirmed. | **1613** 20 Jan., peace of Knaeroed ends war between Denmark and Sweden. 21 Feb., *Zemski Sobor* elects Michael Romanov as Tsar: grand-nephew of Ivan IV, aged 17 (–1645). **1613–22** *Zemski Sobor* in almost continuous session. **1613–29** Gabriel Bathory, Prince of Transylvania. | |
| **1614** 19 Feb., the Prince de Condé rebels in France. 15 May, peace of St Menehould between France and | **1614** 12 Nov., treaty of Xanten partitions Jülich and Cleves between Brandenburg and Neuburg. Tsar | **1614** Portuguese bombard al-Hasan, Sultan of Mombasa, in his palace: Sultan visits Goa to protest. |

## THE EAST

**1609—17** Pieter Both, first Governor-General of Netherlands India: governors-general appointed until 1946.
**1609—36** Iskandar Muda, Sultan of Acheh.

**1610** Johore treaty with Malacca. Anankpetlun recovers Toungoo. Toungoo attacked by de Brito: palace and fortifications burnt.

**1611** Jahangir m. Mihr al-Nisa, a Persian: obtains great influence behind the throne: coinage struck in her name. English factory established at Masuliputam. Hendrik Brouwer, driven off course, discovers Abrolhos, W Australia.

**1612** Nov., naval battle between *Dragon,* Capt. Best, and *Osiander* pinnace, with four Portuguese galleons and twenty-five or six frigates. Peace treaty between Persia and Turkey. End of Usman Khan's rebellion in Bengal. Shahjahan m. Mumtaz Mahal. English East India Co. granted right to trade at Surat.
**1612—15** Marcellus de Boschuwer, Dutch envoy to Kandy.
**1613** Right of English to trade at Surat confirmed by a *farman:* Surat becomes the first Presidency of the EIC. Portuguese seize four imperial ships: Jahangir demands compensation: war ensues. Batu Sawar, capital of Johore, destroyed by Acheh: Acheh obtains control of all NW of Indonesia. Anankpetlun besieges Syriam for three months: city taken by tunneling under the walls: de Brito impaled alive. English begin trading in Japan. Christian population of Malacca estimated at 7,400.
**1613—18** Fakhr al-Din II of Lebanon expelled to Florence.
**1613—45** Tjakrakusuma Ngabdurrahman (Sultan Agung) ruler of Mataram.
**1613—23** Abdallah Ma'ayat Shah, Sultan of Johore.
**1614** Mewar submits to Jahangir.

## THE AMERICAS

killed in Grenada. Robert Harcourt attempts to colonize Guiana. Samuel de Champlain, with a party of Hurons and Algonquins, has brush with Iroquois near Ticonderoga. Henry Hudson explores Hudson R. for the Dutch. Virginia granted a new charter.
**1609—10** Sir Thomas Roe establishes small settlement in Guiana: followed by others in 1611 and 1614.
**1610** Champlain assists Indian allies capture an Iroquois camp: St Lawrence R. cleared of Iroquois raiders: opens trade for Algonquins of Ottawa and Hurons of Georgian Bay.
**1610—13** Trade of New France increases rapidly: fur trade of all the Great Lake region tapped.

**1611—16** Sir Thomas Dale, Governor of Virginia.

**1612** 15 Oct., Samuel Champlain Governor of New France (—20 July 1629). Tobacco growing begun in Virginia by John Rolfe. Settlement in Bermuda from Virginia.

**1613** Champlain obtains new fur monopoly. Samuel Argall of Virginia seizes French colony at Port Royal and ships people back to France on spurious grounds that they were encroaching in Virginia.

## RELIGION & CULTURE

restored in Scotland. *Accademia dei Lincei* founded at Rome. Congregation of female Jesuits founded. Ambrosian Library, Milan, founded.
**1609—74** Edward Hyde, Earl of Clarendon, statesman and historian.
**1609—76** Sir Matthew Hale, jurist.
**1609—16** Mosque of Sultan Ahmad, Istanbul, built.

**1610** The telescope invented by Galileo.
**1610—85** Adriaan van Ostade, Dutch artist.
**1610—94** David Teniers, Flemish artist.
**1610—25** Rosenborg Palace, Copenhagen, built.
**1610—88** Charles du Cange, Latin lexicographer.

**1611** Authorized Version. or King James's Bible, published. Astronomical telescope invented by Kepler. Frs Pierre Biard and Ennemond Massé, SJ, first missionaries in Acadia. Meeting of Huguenots at Saumur.

**1612** Two Unitarians burnt at the stake: last heretics to be burnt in England. Scottish Parliament allows restoration of bishops. Japanese edict forbids Christianity. Basilica of St Peter, Rome, completed.
**c. 1612—49** Richard Crashaw, poet.
**1612—94** Antoine Arnauld, Jansenist divine.

**1613** Cannon foundry at Brenchley, Kent, manufacturing for export: 200 men employed. Thomas de Jesu, Carmelite friar, proposes a *Congregation for the Propagation of the Faith.* The Oratorians start work in France.
**c. 1613** The foot rule invented.
**1613—18** The Bodleian Library, Oxford, built.
**1613—80** François, Duc de la Rochefoucauld, writer on morals.
**1613—82** Ku Yen-Wu, Chinese encyclopaedist.
**1613—1700** André le Nôtre, landscape gardener.

**1614** All foreign missionaries ordered to leave Japan for good: churches to be demolished. Logarithms invented

| WESTERN EUROPE | NORTHERN, CENTRAL & SOUTHERN EUROPE | AFRICA |
|---|---|---|
| Condé. The Addled Parliament. Louis XIII of France attains his majority: regency continues until 1617.<br>**1614—5** French Estates-General.<br>**1615** 23 Feb., Estates-General of France prorogued: last session until 1789. 9 Aug., Condé rebels again (—1616). 27 Sept., Arabella Stuart d. | Michael defeats the Cossacks at Rostokino. Danish East India Co. founded. Savoy and Spain at war.<br><br>**1615** Duke of Savoy invades Milan. | **1614—41** Struggle for the succession in Kongo.<br><br>**1615** Sultan of Mombasa murdered by Nyika tribesmen at Portuguese instigation: succ. Yusuf b. al-Hasan, sent to Goa for education. |
| **1616** 3 May, treaty of Loudoun: Condé's rebellion ended. 1 Sept., Condé arrested. 25 Nov., Richelieu first appointed Secretary of State (—Apr. 1617). | **1616** Agreement of Gratz: Archdukes Albert and Maximilian forego their claims to the Empire in favour of Ferdinand (II) of Hapsburg. | **1616—45** Rubat b. Badi, King of Sennar. |
| **1617** 7 March, Sir Francis Bacon appointed Lord Keeper. 24 Apr., Concino Concini, Marshal d'Ancre, favourite of Mary dei Medici, murdered. | **1617** 27 Feb., treaty of Stolbovo between Russia and Sweden: southern shore of Gulf of Finland ceded to Swedes in return for Nijni Novgorod. 6 June, 29 July, Austria and Spanish Hapsburgs agree on mutual succession. 29 June, Archduke Ferdinand (II) crowned King of Bohemia. 9 Oct., treaty of Pavia between Savoy and Spain defines Savoy-Milan frontier.<br>**1617—18** Mustafa I (an imbecile), Ottoman Sultan. | |
| **1618** 7 June, Sir Francis Bacon made Lord Chancellor. 23 Aug., Johan van Oldenbarneveldt and Hugo Grotius arrested. 29 Oct., Sir Walter Raleigh beheaded. Company of Merchant Adventurers Trading into Africa founded in London. | **1618** Feb., peace of Madrid between Austria and Venice. 23 May, 'Defenestration' of Prague. 24 Dec., Poland makes truces with Sweden and with Turkey. Duke of Lerma disgraced in Spain. Rebellion against Ferdinand (II) in Bohemia. Prussia granted Brandenburg as a fief of Poland. *Cortes* of Castile recommends programme of retrenchment and reform. Fort of Jenisseisk, Siberia, constructed.<br>**1618—20** 'Conspiracy of Venice': Duke of Osuna, Viceroy of Naples, attempts to prevent alliance between Holland and Venice.<br>**1618—22** Uthman II, Ottoman Sultan. | **1618** Source of the Blue Nile discovered by Pedro Paez. Portuguese campaign against Ndongo. Morocco relinquishes control of Timbuktu: Pashas henceforward elected by soldiery.<br>**c. 1618** Fort James built by English at Bathurst, Gambia. |

| THE EAST | THE AMERICAS | RELIGION & CULTURE |
|---|---|---|

**THE EAST**

**1615** William Edwards brings Jahangir a letter from James I. Sea battle between Acheh and Malacca

**1615—17** Arakan repulses Portuguese raid with Dutch help. Anankpetlun takes Martaban, some Siamese territory, and Chengmai.

**1615—18** Sir Thomas Roe sent as ambassador to Jahangir.

**1616** Steele, an English merchant, opens trade with Persia by sea from Surat. Ahmadnagar fort surrenders to Khurram, brother of Jahangir: given title of Shahjahan. Nurhachu, a Manchu, proclaims himself Emperor of China of the Tai Ching dynasty. Maturan defeats Pasuruan. Sea battle between Acheh and Malacca. Johore attack on Malacca: shipping burnt in the harbour: three months siege of fort abortive. Castle of Osaka taken by Ieyasu: his power over Japan now complete. Tokugawa Ieyasu d.: persecution of Christianity in Japan made more rigorous. Commercial treaty between the Dutch and Japan.

**1616—17** Connock, English merchant, visits Persia.

**1616—18** Abortive Turkish campaigns against Persia.

**1616—24** Plague in Panjab.

**1617** 14 Apr., Dutch-Spanish naval battle off Playa Honda, Philippine Is. 24 Dec., Bantamese warriors force their way into fortress of Batavia.

**c. 1617** Batu Sawar abandoned.

**1618** Aug., attack on Batavia from Mataram beaten off with difficulty. The Manchu conquer the greater part of Manchuria.

**1618—19** Spanish embassy to Persia led by Don Garcia de Silva y Figueroa.

**1618—23** Jan Pieterzoon Coen, Governor-General of Netherlands EI.

**THE AMERICAS**

**1615** Champlain exploring Huron country.

**1615—27** Champlain tries to maintain monopoly of fur trade in order to pay for new colonists and fortification of Quebec.

**RELIGION & CULTURE**

by John Napier. Groningen University founded.

**1614—28** Salzburg Cathedral built.

**1614—78** Jean François Paul de Gondi, Cardinal de Retz, writer.

**1615** Three Recollect Fathers and a lay brother arrive in Quebec: evangelization of Indians begun. Theological Academy founded at Kiev. First Convocation of the Church of Ireland: 104 Articles of Religion promulgated. Jesuits start work in Vietnam.

**1615—91** Richard Baxter, divine and hymnographer.

**1616** Galileo forbidden to teach by Inquisition.

**1617** Practice of Catholicism forbidden in Sweden.

**1617—81** Gerard Terborch, Dutch artist.

**1617—82** Bartholomé Estaban Murillo, Spanish artist.

**1617—92** Elias Ashmole, antiquarian.

**1618** 27 Aug., Five Articles of Perth passed: victory for Scottish Episcopalians: Synod of Doordrecht: victory of Gomarian Calvinists over the Arminians. Benedictine Congregation of St Maur constituted: special attention given to Patristic studies. Council of Russian bishops held to discuss the Missal.

**1618—54** Richard Lovelace, poet.

**1618—80** Sir Peter Lely. artist.

**1618—67** Abraham Cowley, poet.

| WESTERN EUROPE | NORTHERN, CENTRAL & SOUTHERN EUROPE | AFRICA |
|---|---|---|
| **1619** 13 March, Johan van Oldenbarneveldt executed. | **1619** 20 March, Emperor Matthias d. 26 Aug., Ferdinand (II) deposed from the throne of Bohemia: Frederick V of the Palatinate elected: action real beginning of the Thirty Years Wars (–1648). 28 Aug., Ferdinand II elected Emperor (–1637). Philaret (Feodor) installed as Patriarch of Russia: becomes virtual ruler of Russia: programme of thorough reform initiated. Treaty of Dailino between Russia and Poland. Philip III pays state visit to Portugal. Bank of Hamburg founded. Treaty between French EIC and the Bank of Amsterdam. | **1619** Pestilence kills 330,000 persons in Egypt. **1619** –21 Abortive Portuguese attem to find silver mines in Chicoa, Mozambique. |
| **1620** Béarn united with France. Huguenots rebel: 10 Feb., battle of Ponts de Cé: 10 Aug., treaty of Angers. Maurice of Nassau obtains the right to appoint the Grand Pensionary of Holland. | **1620** 3 July, agreement of Ulm between Evangelical Union and Catholic League. Sigismund Vasa defeated by the Ottomans at Cecora. | |
| **1621** War between Spain and the United Provinces renewed: 25 Apr., treaty of Madrid. Louis XIII of France fails to take Montauban from the Protestants. Parliament impeaches Sir Giles Mompesson: Francis Bacon, Lord Chancellor, accused of bribery and corruption: deprived of office. Dutch West India Co. chartered. Bank of Nuremberg founded. | **1621** 22 Jan., Frederick V of Bohemia outlawed. War between Poland and Sweden: Gustavus Adolphus takes Riga. **1621–65** Philip IV of Spain: weak and vicious: Count-Duke of Olivares real power. | **1621** Dutch station established at Gorée. **c. 1622** Some 3,000 slaves sent annually from Guinea to Portugal. |
| **1622** Jan., Cardinal Richelieu restored to the Royal Council. 18 Oct., treaty of Montpellier: Louis XIII makes peace with the Huguenots: Edict of Nantes confirmed: Montauban and La Rochelle left in Huguenot possession. Treaty between France and Bavaria. Spinola takes Bergen-op-Zoom. | **1622** 16 Jan., Articles of Milan. Patriarch Philaret d. *Zemski Sobor* revived. Uthman II, Ottoman Sultan, massacred by the Janissaries: succ. Mustafa I again (–1623). Count Tilly defeats armies of Baden, Halberstadt and Mansfeld. | **1622** English bombard Algiers. Susenyos of Ethiopia submits to the Holy See. Wallo Galla raid Amhara. Anglo-Dutch fleet blockades Mozambique. |
| **1623** 7 Feb., treaty of Paris: alliance between France, Savoy and Venice. | **1623** 7 March – 30 Aug., Charles, Prince of Wales, with Duke of Buckingham, visits Madrid: fails to secure Spanish princess as a bride. Diet of Ratisbon: Bavaria made an Electorate: Maximilian I, Elector (–1651). Ottoman Sultan Mustafa I d.: succ. Murad IV (–1640). | **c. 1623** Xhosa and Tembu reach Umzimvutu R. |
| **1624** 10 March, England at war with France: Parliament votes large subsidy. Monopolies declared illegal in England. 20 June, treaty of Compiègne between France and the United Provinces. Earl of Middlesex, Lord Treasurer, impeached. **1624–42** Cardinal Richelieu Chief Minister in France. | **1624** 11 May, treaty of Düsseldorf between Brandenburg and Neuburg. Following treaty of Paris, France occupies Valtellina. | **1624** Eight Jesuit missions on the Zambezi R. **c. 1624** Ajuran and Madaule Somali migrate from El Wak region. End of Muzaffarid dynasty of Mogadishu. |

| THE EAST | THE AMERICAS | RELIGION & CULTURE |
|---|---|---|

**THE EAST**

**1619** 30 May, Dutch take Jacarta town. Berar annexed by Bijapur. Acheh attacks Kedah: Kedah pepper plantations destroyed. Tuban made a vassal of Mataram. Dutch establish themselves at Sunda Kalapa, renamed Jacarta: fort built, and, 12 March, called Batavia. Wei Chung-hsien, a eunuch, all-powerful in China.

**1620** 28 Dec., English merchantmen defeat Portuguese off Jask, Persia. Fortress of Kangra surrenders to Jahangir. Danes set up factory at Tranquebar.

**1621** Manchu capital established at Liaoyang. Local rebellions in Philippine Is.

**1622** Jan., Prince Khusru d. June, Shah Abbas retakes Qandahar (– 1638). Shah Abbas of Persia, with aid of English squadron, retakes Hormuz from the Portuguese. Shahjahan rebels against his father. Sultan Agung makes Queen of Banjermasin, Borneo, a vassal of Mataram.
**1622–51** Tokugawa Iyemitsu, Shogun.
**1623** Dutch factory established at Bandar Abbas. Shahjahan's army defeated at Balochpur. Johore capital of Lingga destroyed by Acheh. English cease trading with Japan. 'Massacre of Amboina': eight Englishmen executed for alleged plot to seize the fort with Japanese mercenaries.
**1623–38** Baghdad occupied by Shah Abbas of Persia.
**1623–77** Abd al-Jalih Shah II, Sultan of Johore.
**1624** Sultan Agung conquers Madura Is.

**THE AMERICAS**

**1619** 30 July, House of Burgesses of Virginia, first American parliamentary institution, meets at Jamestown. Population of Virginia c.2,000. First iron forge in America built by John Berkeley at Falling Creek, Virginia.
**1619–20** Amazon Co. formed by Roger North.

**1620** 22 Dec., *Mayflower* reaches America: New Plymouth founded. First African slaves imported into America at Jamestown.

**1621** Charter for Nova Scotia granted.

**1623** St Kitts settled from England.
**1623–38** The Dutch seize 500 Portuguese and Spanish vessels off the Americas.

**1624** Dutch Fort Orange established on R. Hudson. Dutch West Indies Co's fleet seizes Bahia but unable to hold it. Dutch settle at New Amsterdam, Manhattan Is., later New York. London Co charter revoked: Virginia made a Crown Colony.
**1624–5** Barbados Is. settled from England.

**RELIGION & CULTURE**

**1619** Arminian conflict ends in the United Provinces. Gotenburg founded. Imperial Château of Schonbrünn begun.
**1619–37** Ben Jonson, English poet laureate.
**1619–55** Savinien Cyrano de Bergerac, dramatist.
**1619–90** Charles Le Brun, French artist.
**1619–83** Jean-Baptiste Colbert, French statesman.

**1620** 19 June, Protestants massacred at Valtellina.
**1620–1706** John Evelyn, diarist.
c. **1620–30** The slide rule invented.
**1620–1705** Ninon de Lenclos, beauty.
**1620–82** Jean Picard, astronomer.
**1621** 14 May, Evangelical Union in Germany disbands. 16 Nov., Gregory XV: bull *Aeterni Patris,* on Papal elections. Strasbourg University founded.
**1621–3** Gregory XV (Ludovisi), Pope.
**1621–78** Andrew Marvell, poet.
**1621–86** Louis II, Prince de Condé, general.
**1621–95** Jean de la Fontaine, fable-writer and poet.
**1622** 6 Jan., Pope Gregory XV founds the *Sacred Congregation for the Propagation of the Faith:* 22 June, Bull *Inscrutabili divinae* sets out duties of congregation in promoting missions: beginning of modern missionary activity Richelieu made a Cardinal. St Ignatius de Loyola and St Francis Xavier canonized.
**1622–1673** Jean-Baptiste Poquelin de Molière, dramatist.
**1623–44** Urban VIII (Barberini), Pope.
**1623–62** Blaise Pascal, philosopher.
**1623–69** Jesuit training college for missionaries at Sao Salvador, Angola.

**1624** Order of Lazarists founded. Catholic mission sent to Tibet.
**1624–91** George Fox, Quaker preacher and diarist.
**1624–1709** Père François de la Chaise, SJ.

| WESTERN EUROPE | NORTHERN, CENTRAL & SOUTHERN EUROPE | AFRICA |
|---|---|---|

**1625** 27 March, James I of England and VI of Scotland d.: succ. Charles I (−1649): 11 May, m. Henrietta Maria of France. 23 Apr., Maurice of Nassau d.: succ. Frederick Henry as Stadholder. 10 June, Spinola takes Breda. 15 Sept., Huguenots under Soubise defeated: Soubise flees to England. 9 Dec., treaty of the Hague: England and the United Provinces ally with Denmark against the Emperor: subsidy provided. Charles I granted tunnage and poundage by Parliament for one year.
**1626** 5 Feb., peace of La Rochelle ends Huguenot rebellion. 6 Feb.– 15 June, Charles I's second Parliament: following Buckingham's impeachment, dissolves Parliament: continues levying tunnage and poundage: Forced Loan collected. Cardinal Richelieu appointed Grand Master of the Navigation and Commerce of France. Nobility forbidden to duel in France. Edict of Nantes orders destruction of fortified castles in France. Assembly of Notables held in Rouen.
**1627** 20 March, treaty between France and Spain. Protestants fortify La Rochelle: Oct., siege ordered by Richelieu. Nov., Buckingham's expedition to the Is. de Ré abandoned. Charles I offers Ireland the 'Graces': toleration afforded to Catholics.
**1627–32** England and France at war.

**1628** 1 June, Petition of Right presented to Charles I by Parliament: Remonstrance: Parliament protests against unlawful taxation. 23 Aug., Duke of Buckingham murdered. 28 Oct., Huguenots at La Rochelle capitulate: flee to southern France: Duke of Rohan continues fighting.

**1629** Jan.– 2 March, Charles I quarrels with Parliament: 2 March, the Speaker held in his chair for the passage of three resolutions: Parliament dissolved. 24 Apr., peace of Susa between England and France. 28 June, Edict of Grace of Alais (or Alès) ends war with Huguenots: followers of Duke de Rohan surrender. Edict of Nîmes grants Huguenots freedom of religion and equality with Catholics.
**1629–40** Charles I rules without Parliament. *c.* 60,000 persons emigrate, of whom 20,000 to New England.

**1625** 7 Apr., Wallenstein given command of Imperial armies. Gustavus Adolphus takes Dorpat. New treaty between Austria and Turkey.

**1626** 5 March, treaty of Moncon: France and Spain guarantee independence of Grisons. 25 Apr., Ernst of Mansfeld defeated by Count Tilly at Dessau: Pomerania occupied. 27 Aug., Count Tilly defeats Christian IV of Denmark at Lutter.
**1626–8** Protestant peasants rebel in Austria.

**1627** 26 Dec., Duke of Mantua d.: war for succession between the Empire and France (−1631). Tilly and Wallenstein take Jutland, Holstein and Silesia: the Danes expelled from Germany. Imperial ordinance makes the throne of Bohemia hereditary.

**1628** 26 Jan., Wallenstein granted Duchy of Mecklenburg. 21 Apr., Wallenstein made Admiral of the Baltic. 9 June, Dukes of Mecklenburg outlawed. Aug., Wallenstein fails in an attempt to take Stralsund.

**1629** 22 May, treaty of Lübeck between Denmark and the Emperor. 16 June, Wallenstein made Duke of Mecklenburg. 26 Sept., truce of Altmark between Sigismund Vasa of Poland and Gustavus Adolphus of Sweden: Poland cedes Livonia and parts of Prussia. The Dutch obtain right to trade at Archangel.

**1625** Abomey conquered by Tacoodounu, chief of the Fons: Kingdom of Dahomey established.
**1625–1911** Kasanje empire in present Kinshasa one of the principal African states.

**1626** Yusuf b. al-Hasan enthroned as sultan in Mombasa as a Christian with name Dom Hieronimo Chingulia: sen letter of obedience to the Pope.
**1626–32** Bp Alphonso Mendez, SJ, in Ethiopia.

**1627** Incipient revolt in Kilwa.
**1627–41** Bou Regreg an independent republic.

**1628** Eleven Jesuit missions in Ethiopia: many imperial ordinances against the Ethiopian church. French set up factory at Ste Luce, Madagascar. French obtain coral monopoly in Algiers.

*c.* **1629** First attempts to cultivate maize, manioc (cassava), sweet potatoes, pawpaw, guavas, coconuts and groundnuts in small farms near Luanda.

## THE EAST

## THE AMERICAS

## RELIGION & CULTURE

**1625** Peace made between Jahangir and Shahjahan. English factory founded at Armagaon, first English fortified station in India. Sultan Agung takes Surabaya.

**1625** Abortive English attempt to occupy Tobago. French take St Christopher.

**1625** Further Jesuits reach Quebec. St Vincent de Paul founds *Congrégation des Prêtres de la Mission*. Pope Urban VIII obtains the Duchy of Urbino.
**1625–1709** Thomas Corneille, dramatist. 3 Jan., Monti dei Paschi, first modern bank, opened in Siena.

**1626** Jahangir taken prisoner by Mahabat Khan.
**1626–43** Abahai, Manchu ruler.
**1626–56** Muhammad b. Ibrahim II, Sultan of Bijapur.

**1626** Dutch purchase Manhattan Is. Seignory first granted by the Hundred Associates of Nôtre Dame des Anges in Quebec.

**1626** Irish College founded in Rome. New St Peter's, Rome, consecrated Ahmad Baba, writer, d.at Timbuktu.
**1626–96** Marie de Rabutin-Chantal, Marquise de Sévigné, letter-writer.
**1626–97** Francesco Redi, scientist.
**1626–1700** Armand de Rancé, reformer of the Trappists.

**1627** 8 Nov., Jahangir d. Nov., Dawar Baksh made titular emperor. Shahjahan orders the death of all his male relatives. Sir Dodmore Cotton's embassy to Shah Abbas.
**1627–9** J.P.Coen again Governor-General.
**1627–58** Shahjahan, Great Mughul.
**1627–77** Fifty year war between N and S Vietnam.

**1627** Cardinal Richelieu sets up Company of New France, or the Hundred Associates, to encourage N Atlantic trade and colonization: Catholic colonists alone permitted. Scottish colonists, sent by Sir William Alexander, set up at Port Royal, Acadia. Roger North and Robert Harcourt attempt to form settlement in Guiana.
**1627–40** Tortuga centre of buccaneers.
**1628** David Kirke, with three ships of Scottish colonists, sails to Quebec and demands its surrender: refused by Champlain: eighteen vessels of the Hundred Associates captured by Kirke. Nevis Is. settled from England. Salem, Massachusetts, founded.
**1628–40** c. 20,000 Puritans emigrate from England to N America.

**1627** Company of the Holy Sacrament founded. *Propaganda* College founded in Rome.
**1627–32** Roman Breviary revised.
**1629–82** Jacob-Isaac Ruysdael, artist.
**1627–91** Robert Boyle, scientist: discoverer of Boyle's law.
**1627–95** Dorothy Osborne, Lady Temple, letter writer.
**1627–1704** Bp Jacques Bénigne Bossuet, theologian and preacher.

**1628** Feb., Shahjahan enthroned –1635): Peacock Throne constructed. Revolt of Jujhar Singh, Bundela chief. Khan Jahan Lodi, governor of the Deccan, rebels. Acheh again attacks Malacca. Rajasinha II, King of Kandy.
**1628–9** Minyedaikpa, King of Burma.

**1628** Declaration of submission to the Thirty-Nine Articles drawn up by Abp Laud. William Harvey: *De motu cordis et sanguine* describes the circulation of blood.
**1628–38** Palace of Delhi built.
**1628–82** Jakob Isaac van Ruisdael, Dutch artist.
**1628–88** John Bunyan, religious writer.
**1628–94** Marcello Malpighi, biologist.
**1628–99** Sir William Temple, essayist and statesman.

**1629** 4 June, wreck of the *Batavia*, under Capt. François Pelsart, off Abrolhos Is.: first reluctant settlement in Australia: 125 castaways murdered by Jerome Cornelis. Johore, Patani and the Portuguese from Malacca crush Acheh in naval battle off Malacca. Minyedaikpa seizes the throne by killing his father Anankpetlun: executed by his uncle Tharlun Min, who takes the throne.
**1629–42** Shah Safi I, Shah of Persia.
**1629–48** Tharlun, King of Burma.

**1629** Massachusetts Bay Co. chartered. David, Lewis and Thomas Kirke compel Champlain to surrender Quebec: Champlain taken prisoner to England. Spaniards devastate St Kitts and Nevis. 400 persons settle in Massachusetts. English colonization of C. Breton begun.

**1629–95** Christiaan Huygens, physicist.

## WESTERN EUROPE

## NORTHERN, CENTRAL & SOUTHERN EUROPE

## AFRICA

**1630** 31 March, Richelieu seizes Pignerol. 10 Nov., rising in Dijon (Day of Dupes). Mary dei Medici banished to Compiègne.

**1630** July, Electors meet at Ratisbon to protest against the Emperor and Wallenstein. 6 July, Gustavus Adolphus attacks Pomerania: Stettin besieged. 18 July, the Spaniards take Mantua. Louis XIII conquers Savoy: 20 July, Salucca taken. 13 Aug., Wallenstein dismissed. 13 Oct., treaty of Ratisbon. 5 Nov., peace of Madrid between England and Spain.

**1630** Many Capuchins go to Cairo to evangelize Ethiopia.
*c.* **1630–60** Oti Akenten, Asantehen
*c.* **1630–80** Apogee of Bakuba culture: marked development in administration and agriculture.

**1631** 31 May, agreement of Fontainebleau. Baltimore, Ireland, sacked by Barbary corsairs. Gaston of Orléans rebels. Mary dei Medici flees to the United Provinces. The *Gazette de France* founded by Théophraste Renaudet.

**1631** 23 Jan., treaty of Bärwald. 20 May, Count Tilly takes Magdeburg: massacre follows. 11 Sept., Sweden allies with Brandenburg. 17 Sept., Gustavus Adolphus defeats Count Tilly at Breitenfeld. Nov., the Elector of Saxony conquers Bohemia: 15 Nov., Prague falls. Rebellion on coast of Bay of Biscay: *junta* formed at Guernica.

**1631** Aug., Muslim rebellion in Mombasa: *c.* 250 African, Goan and Portuguese martyred following murder of the governor: rising affect whole coast. Musa Pasha, Viceroy o Egypt, suspended by grandees: Egyp ruled for twenty-five years by an elected viceroy: Faqariyyah most influential section of grandees.

**1632** 6 Jan., treaty of Vic makes Lorraine a French protectorate. Sept., Richelieu puts down rebellion of Gaston d'Orléans. 20 Oct., Montmorency beheaded for rebellion. Treaty of St Germain-en-Laye: ends hostilities between England and France: Quebec restored to France: Pignerol recognised as a French possession.
**1632-4** Sir Thomas Wentworth (later Earl of Strafford) Viceroy of Ireland.

**1632** 15 Apr., Gustavus Adolphus defeats Count Tilly on R. Lech. 17 May, Swedish army enters Munich. 3-4 Sept., battle of Nuremberg between Gustavus Adolphus and Wallenstein. 15-16 Nov., battle of Lützen: Wallenstein beaten: Gustavus Adolphus d.: succ. Christina as Queen of Sweden (–1654). Unsuccessful attempt of Russia to regain Smolensk from the Poles. Fort of Yakutsk, Siberia, constructed.
**1632–44** Oxenstierna, Chancellor of Sweden.
**1632–48** Wladislaw IV, King of Poland.

**1632** 8 Jan., abortive Portuguese attempt to recover Mombasa: 16 Ma Sultan Yusuf abandons Mombasa an takes to piracy: 5 Aug., Portuguese re-enter Mombasa. Emperor Suseny breaks with Rome. 17 Sept., Susenyos d.: succ. Fasilidas (–1667) Jesuits expelled: Catholic missionari banned under pain of death.

**1633** Charles I visits Scotland: 168 Acts of Parliament passed in one day: 18 June, crowned at Edinburgh.

**1633** 23 Apr., Oxenstierna constitutes the League of Heilbronn, South German, Swedish and French Protestants. 12 Oct., Wallenstein defeats Swedish army in Silesia. French treaty with Duchy of Parma against Spain.

**1633–5** War between Dembo and Portuguese.
*c.* **1633** Gondar built as the imperial capital of Ethiopia.

**1634** 20 Oct., Charles I raises Ship Money in London without Parliamentary authorization. Powers of Court of High Commission in Scotland increased.

**1634** 25 Feb., Wallenstein assassinated at Eger. 6 Sept., imperial troops win battle of Nordlingen. Wladislaw IV beats the Russians: peace treaty of Polianow between Poland and Russia: Poland allowed to keep Smolensk on condition of renouncing claim to Russian throne: Poland acquires Courland and Livonia. New constitution in Poland.

**1635** 28 Apr., treaty of Compiègne between France and Sweden. 19 May, France declares war on Spain and the Empire. 4 Aug., Charles I extends collection of Ship Money to all England. Oct., treaty of St Germain. Commission for Defective Titles established in Ireland.

**1635** 30 May, treaty of Prague between the Empire and Saxony: end of the union of Heilbronn: Saxony acquires Lusatia. 11 July, treaty of Rivoli. 12 Sept., twenty year treaty of Stuhmsdorf between Poland and Sweden. Spanish army defeated at Grisons by Duc de Rohan.

**1635** Anglo-Moroccan treaty. Engli expedition against Algiers.

| THE EAST | THE AMERICAS | RELIGION & CULTURE |
|---|---|---|

**1630** Shahjahan raises siege of Parenda, Ahmadnagar. Turks take Hamadan from Persia: fail to take Baghdad. Portuguese force under de Sà cut to pieces at Vellavaya, Uva, Ceylon.
**1630–2** Famine in the Deccan and Gujarat.
**1630–3** Peter Mundy, English merchant, in Patna.
**1631** June, Mumtaz Mahal d. Bijapur besieged but siege raised by Shahjahan for lack of supplies. Fath Khan holds fortress of Daulatabad against Shahjahan's forces: surrenders: end of Nizam Shahi Kingdom of Ahmadnagar.

**1632** June 24–Sept. 24, Portuguese besieged by Qasim Khan at Hugli: Sept., taken: 400 prisoners taken to Agra: offered choice between Islam or death: Christians persecuted to 1635: Hindus persecuted also.

**1633** Native imamate established in Yemen (−1871). Shahjahan visits Panjab and Kashmir. Tharlun Min moves capital to Pegu.

**1634** Tharlun Min moves capital from Pegu to Ava. Batavian government recognizes formal overlordship of Mataram.

**1635** Feb., Fakhr al-Din II of Lebanon taken prisoner to Istanbul and beheaded. Turks take Erivan from Persia. Dutch East India Co opens factory at Syriam.
**1635–6** Shahjahan campaigns in the Deccan: Golconda surrenders: Bijapur conquered and over-run.
**1635–78** Johan Maetsuycker, Governor-General of the E Indies.

---

**1630** Abortive English settlement at mouth of R. Amazon. 900 settlers reach Salem: eight towns, including Boston, founded.
**1630–40** Dutch seize several Caribbean islands.
**1630–54** Dutch hold Olinda, and Recife, port of Pernambuco: attempt to conquer Brazil begun.

**1631** First representative assembly meets in Massachusetts.

**1632** June, French under Guillaume de Caën return to Quebec. Antigua and Barbuda settled from England. Citizens of Watertown, Massachusetts, refuse to pay defence tax. Nova Scotia, or Acadia, restored to France: Isaac de Razilly, governor. Montserrat Is. settled from England.

**1634** Maryland founded by Lord Baltimore: leaders Catholic, remainder Protestant: toleration stipulated. 6,000 slaves in Barbados. Massachusetts assembly assumes full legislative powers. Post and mission established by French at Trois Rivières. Plague in New France.

**1635** Plymouth Co charter revoked. Dec., Samuel de Champlain d.

---

**1630** Congregation of English Ladies instituted at Munich. 13 Jan., Pope Urban VIII dissolves the female Jesuits.
c. **1630–77** Matthew Locke, composer.
**1630–77** Gabriel Metsu, Dutch artist.
**1630– c. 1681** Pieter de Hooch, Dutch artist.

**1631** 20 Feb.– 12 Apr., Convention of German Protestants held at Leipzig.
**1631–1700** John Dryden, poet and dramatist.
**1631–1712** Sir Thomas Osborne, statesman.

**1632** July, Catholic worship and evangelical work restored in Quebec by Frs Paul le Jeune and Anne de Noüe, SJ. Tax of one-twentieth imposed to support clergy in Virginia. Construction of Taj Mahal begun at Agra to receive Mumtaz Mahal's remains: completed 1653.
**1632–73** Spinoza, Dutch philosopher. Vermeer of Delft, Dutch artist.
**1632–87** Jean Baptiste Lully, French composer.
**1632–95** Anthony à Wood, antiquary.
**1632–1704** John Locke, philosopher.
**1632–1723** Antony van Leeuwenhoek, scientist. Sir Christopher Wren, architect.
**1633** Saint-Cyran becomes spiritual director at Port-Royal. Galileo compelled by the Inquisition to recant his 'errors and heresies'.
**1633–45** William Laud, Abp of Canterbury.
**1633–1703** Samuel Pepys, diarist and Secretary of the Navy.
**1634** Tobacco forbidden by Russian clergy on pain of death: law subsequently changed to a tax. St Vincent de Paul and Louise de Marillac found the Sisters of Mercy. The Thirty-Nine Articles of Religion imposed in Ireland: undergraduates at Trinity College, Dublin, required to subscribe. Urbain Grandier, parish priest of Loudu executed for sorcery. The Oberammergau *Passion Play* first performed. Hidari Jingaro, Japanese sculptor, d.
**1635** 10 Feb., the *Académie Française* founded by Cardinal Richelieu. Museum of Natural History founded in Paris. May, Scottish *Book of Canons* issued by Charles I. Boston Latin School opened Seminary opened in Quebec for Red Indians.
**1635–82** Johann Joachim Becher, scientist.
**1635–1703** Robert Hooke, scientist.
**1635–1719** Françoise d'Aubigné, Marquise de Maintenon, letter-writer.

| WESTERN EUROPE | NORTHERN, CENTRAL & SOUTHERN EUROPE | AFRICA |
|---|---|---|
| **1636** 9 Oct., Charles I issues third writ for Ship Money: John Hampden refuses payment. New monopolies created and additional taxation raised in England. French invade Picardy. | **1636** 7 Aug., the Spanish take Corbie. 4 Oct., Sweden defeats Saxony at Wittstock. Nov., the Spanish lose Corbie. 22 Dec., Ferdinand III elected King of the Romans. Rising against Spain in Portugal. Duchy of Parma devastated by Spanish troops. | **1636** Francisco de Seixas de Cabreir Governor of Mombasa: punitive expeditions against many EA coasta towns.<br>**1636—43** Algiers at war with France |
| **1637** 10 Oct., Franco-Dutch army takes Breda from the Spaniards. | **1637** 15 Feb., Emperor Ferdinand II d. succ. Ferdinand III (—1657). Russian Cossacks take fortress of Azov. | **1637** Portuguese scheme for colonization of Mozambique abandoned. Portuguese surrender Elmina, Gold Coast, to the Dutch. |
| | **1638** 5 March, treaty of Hamburg between France and Sweden. 4 Oct., Charles Emanuel II, Duke of Savoy (—1675). 19 Dec., Brisach, Alsace, taken by Bernard of Saxe-Weimar. **1638—9** French gain French Roussillon and short-lived footholds in Irún and Catalonia. | **1638** French build St Louis, Senega Dutch occupy Mauritius.<br>**c. 1638** English fort built at Cormantin. |
| **1639** 24 May, engagement of Turriff, beginning of war between Scotland and Charles I: June, hostilities cease pending meeting of Scottish Parliament and General Assembly. 18 June, Pacification of Berwick. 21 Oct., Dutch destroy Spanish fleet of 70 ships and 10,000 men off the Downs. Last Writ of Ship Money issued by Charles I. Alsace purchased by Richelieu.<br>**1639—41** Last Irish Parliament until 1689 to include Roman Catholics.<br>**1640** 13 Apr.—5 May, the Short Parliament: Charles I fails to achieve co-operation. Scots occupy N of England. 2 June, Scottish Parliament meets: clergy expelled: Covenant made obligatory: Triennial Act passed. Arras and Turin besieged by the French: 9 Aug., Arras falls. 20 Aug., Scots invade England: Newcastle, and all Northumberland and Durham occupied. | **1639** Russians reach sea of Okhotsk.<br><br>**1640** 12 May, Catalonia proclaims itself itself a republic under French protection. French occupy Barcelona and Tarragona. 1 Dec., rising against Spain in Portugal concluded after three hours: 2 Dec., Duke of Braganza acclaimed King of Portugal as John IV (—1656). Abortive risings in parts of Spain. Treaty between Holland and Portugal, suspending hostilities for ten years. | **1639** Dutch blockade mouth of R. Zaire.<br>**1640** All Portuguese missionaries expelled from Ethiopia.<br><br>**c. 1640—70** Sulaiman Solong, Sulta of Darfur. |

## THE EAST

**1636** 6 May, Shahjahan makes treaty with Bijapur: made a tributary. 14 July, Aurangzeb, aged fourteen, appointed Viceroy of the Deccan (—1644). Moro pirates again attack Philippine Is. Rajasinha II of Ceylon asks for Dutch aid against the Portuguese. Persians retake Erivan. Dutch trading post set up in S Vietnam.

**1637** Aurangzeb m. a Persian. Ahmadnagar formally annexed by Shahjahan. Embassy from Holstein to Persia. Manchus and Mongols unite to conquer Korea. Rising at Shimabara, Japan: 30,000 men, women and children fight bitterly defending castle of Hara for three months; many Christians included. Dutch make treaty with Johore against Malacca. Dutch trading post set up at Pho Hien, N. Vietnam.

**1638** 28 March, Portuguese army under Diego Melo de Castra annihilated by Rajasinha II at Gaunoruva, Ceylon: Rajasinha II signs treaty with the Dutch. Apr., Hara castle falls. Portuguese suspected of complicity in revolt, and ordered to leave: all Japanese forbidden to leave the country under pain of death: country completely closed to foreigners: Chinese and Dutch trade tolerated at Nagasaki only. Ottoman Sultan Murad IV retakes Baghdad. Shahjahan recovers Qandahar. Manchu army reaches near to Peking, but retires. Treaty between Rajasinha II of Ceylon and the Dutch at Pulicat, S India: Rajasinha recognized as king of the whole island: Dutch given sole trading rights.

**1639** Peace made between Persia and Turkey. Site of Madras granted to an English factor, Francis Day. 20,000 Chinese massacred in the Philippine Is. Japan expels Portuguese from carrying trade in the Far East. Goa blockaded by the Dutch.

**1640** Aug., Dutch, with 4,000 men besiege Malacca (—1641). Portuguese send peace delegation to Nagasaki: all but thirteen beheaded, and their vessel burnt: survivors sent back to Macao. Widespread droughts in N China. Dutch seize cinnamon-growing districts of Galle and Negombo, Ceylon.

## THE AMERICAS

**1636** 11 June, Charles Jacques Huault de Montmaguy, Governor of New France (—1648). Providence, Rhode Is., founded by Roger Williams: separation of church and state, with other radical views emphasized. **1636—9** More than twelve seignories, lay and clerical, granted in New France.

**1637** Thomas Gage, OP, visits Porto Bello, and describes Spanish convoy trading system with Panama and Peru. Plague in New France.

**1638** Plague in New France: missionaries blamed by Red Indian medicine men.

**1639** Christian Indian village founded at Sillery, near Quebec. Fundamental Orders of Connecticut, first written American made constitution, drawn up at Hartford: bicameral legislature.

**1640** Tortuga taken by France. **c. 1640** Population of New England c. 30,000.

## RELIGION & CULTURE

**1636** Harvard College (later University) founded. Utrecht University founded. **1636—7** Mania for the flower trade reaches its peak in Holland. **1636—72** Adrian Vandervelde, Dutch artist. **1636—1711** Nicolas Boileau, dramatist.

**1637** Charles I imposes use of new *Prayer Book* in Scotland: rebellion in Scotland: thousands sign covenant. University of Uppsala reformed. Huguenot synod in France holds that slavery is not condemned by the law of God. Society of hermits instituted at Port-Royal. **1637—80** Jan Swammerdamm, zoologist. **1637—1707** Diderik Buxtehude, Danish composer. **1637—1711** Thomas Ken, hymnographer. **1638** 27 Feb.—9 March, Scottish General Assembly renews National Covenant of 1581. Trinitarian Order reformed. Galileo measures the density of air. **1638—74** Thomas Traherne, poet and writer. **1638—1709** Meindert Hobbema, Dutch artist.

**1639** Aug., General Assembly of Church of Scotland abolishes bishops. First printing press set up in America at Cambridge, Massachusetts. Pope Urban VIII excommunicates all Catholics who engage in the slave trade. Ursuline and Augustinian nuns start work in Quebec: first hospital opened. **1639—99** Jean Racine, dramatist and poet.

**1640** The Jesuits forbid the teaching of Cartesianism in their institutions. Abo and Genoa universities founded. **1640—?1715** Pu Sung-lin, author of Chinese short stories. **1640—89** Afra Behn, poetness.

| WESTERN EUROPE | NORTHERN, CENTRAL & SOUTHERN EUROPE | AFRICA |
|---|---|---|

**1640** 28 Aug., Petition of Twelve Peers for new Parliament: 3 Nov., Long Parliament meets: Earl of Strafford impeached. 16 Oct., Anglo–Scottish truce. Dec., Abp Laud impeached and imprisoned. 11 Dec., Root and Branch Petition of Parliament. French currency reformed: the *louis d'or* first issued. French win battles of Casal and Ivrée.

**1640** Ottoman Sultan Murad IV d.: succ. Ibrahim (−1648).
**1640–8** Frederick William, Elector of Brandenburg.
**1640–1910** Dynasty of Braganza in Portugal.

**1641** 12 May, Strafford beheaded. Aug., treaty of friendship and commerce between France and Sweden. Oct., rebellion in Ireland: Catholics rise against Protestant masters. 23 Oct., abortive Irish attempt to seize Dublin. Nov., Irish defeat English at Drogheda. Irish under Rory O'More defeat English at Julianstown. 22 Nov., the Grand Remonstrance, drawn up by John Pym: attack made on Church of England: passes Commons by eleven votes. Dec., Parliament passes Militia Act, taking control of all military appointments. Pym refuses Chancellorship of the Exchequer. Courts of Star Chamber and High Commission, and Councils of the North and Wales, abolished by Parliament. Treaty of Ripon between England and Scotland. Count de Soissons revolts against Louis XIII. Protestants own 3m. acres out of 3.5m. acres of cultivable land in Ulster.

**1641** 1 Feb., Portugal allies with France against Spain. Azov taken by the Zaporogues: given to Tsar Michael: Turkish attack repulsed. 22 June, truce between Portugal and the United Provinces. Lisbon made a free port: trade greatly benefitted.

**1641** Dutch attempt to take Angola. Jaga state of Kakonda established. 13,000–16,000 slaves exported annually from Angola.

**1642** 4 Jan., Charles I attempts to arrest Pym, Hampden, and three other members of the Commons for treason. 11 July, London rises against Charles I. Aug., Irish Parliament meets. 22 Aug., Charles I raises Royal Standard at Nottingham: beginning of English Civil War. 10 Sept., Earl of Essex put in supreme command of Parliamentary forces. 23 Oct., battle of Edgehill: Essex retreats: Charles I retires on Oxford. Oct., Catholic Confederacy founded at Kilkenny as a bicameral legislature (−1649): supports Royalist cause. 4 March, Cardinal Richelieu d.: Cardinal Mazarin becomes chief minister in France (−1661). French army takes Roussillon: Perpignan surrenders. 'Adventurers' Act' forbids the pardon of Irish rebels. Condé wins battle of Bléneau: defeated by Turenne at Gien: battle of the Faubourg St. Antoine between forces of Condé and Turenne: Paris opened to Turenne by the French Princess Royal: Condé retires to the Netherlands.

**1642** 2 Nov., Sweden defeats Imperial Army at Breitenfeld. Swedish army defeats Imperial army at Cologne. Half of Aragon in French hands: Spanish defeated at Lérida. Olivares dismissed. Azov restored to Turkey by Russia.

**1642** Dutch take fort at Axim from the Portuguese; attack English, taking all forts except Cape Castle. Ethiopian embassy to Yemen.

THE EAST                                    THE AMERICAS                          RELIGION & CULTURE

**c. ante 1641** New Johore capital at
Makam Tauhid.
**1641** Jan., Portuguese surrender
Malacca to Dutch.
**1641–66** Trade revival in Johore.

**1641** Portuguese settlers revolt
against Dutch on Brazilian coast.
**1641–2** Iroquois raids on French
reach scale of war.

**1641** Oct., massacre of Protestants in
Ulster.
**1641–1712** Nehemiah Grew, botanist:
discoverer of the sexuality of plants.

**1642** 13 Dec., Abel Tasman, with
*Heemskerck* and *Zeehaen,* first sights
S Island, New Zealand: west coast
charted and named Staten Landt, and,
later Nieuw Zeeland. Tasmania
discovered. Friendly Is., Fiji and
Solomon Is. visited on return to
Batavia. Statutes of Batavia codified.
**fl. c. 1642–5** Ranga II, Raya of
Vijayanagar.
**1642–66** Shah Abbas II of Persia.

**1642** La Ville Marie de Montréal,
(modern Montreal), founded by Paul
de Chomedey, Sieur de Maisonneuve.
**1642, 1643, 1644** Iroquois attack
Montreal and St Lawrence–Ottawa
trade route.
**1642–70** Many Cavaliers emigrate
from England to America.

**1642** 10 June, Presbyterian Church of
Ireland first organized at Carrickfergus.
22 Dec., Pope Urban VIII: *Universa per
Orbem* reduces Catholic feast days to
thirty-two. Pope Urban VIII: Bull *In
eminente* condemns Cornelius Jansen's
*Augustinus.* Congregation of St
Sulpice founded by Canon Olier.
Sulpicians arrive in Montreal. The first
calculating machine invented.
**1642–1707** Vincenzo da Filicaja,
Italian poet.
**1642–1727** Sir Isaac Newton,
astronomer.

| WESTERN EUROPE | NORTHERN, CENTRAL & SOUTHERN EUROPE | AFRICA |
|---|---|---|
| **1643** 14 May, Louis XIII of France d.: succ. Louis XIV, aged five: Anne of Austria, Queen-Mother, Regent. 19 May, French under Condé defeat 20,000 Spaniards at Rocroi. 24 June, Parliamentary force under John Hampden defeated at Chalgrove: Hampden killed. 25 July, Parliament abolishes bishops and the House of Lords. 15 Sept., Irish rebellion ended by 'First Cessation'. 20 Sept., indecisive battle between Charles I and Parliamentary forces at Newbury. 25 Sept., Solemn League and Covenant between Parliament and Scotland: Scottish army to assist Parliament in return for establishment of Presbyterian Church in England. 3 Dec., John Pym d. | **1643** March, peace between the Empire and the Ottomans renewed. Oxenstierna invades Denmark. | |
| **1644** Jan., Scots army under Leslie crosses border: joins Fairfax and Cromwell near York: 2 July, royalists defeated at Marston Moor: 2 Sept., Parliamentary army defeated at Lostwithiel: Essex surrenders. 1 Sept Sept., Montrose defeats Elcho at Tippermuir: occupies Perth: 13 Sept., sacks Aberdeen. | **1644** Jan., Sweden declares war on Denmark. Condé defeats Imperial army at Fribourg. Lérida recaptured by Spain. 23 Nov., peace conference opened at Münster; and, 4 Dec., at Osnabruck. | **1644** Pemba at war with Faza. Dutch at war with Nzinga. Monomotapa acknowledges Portuguese suzerainty; |
| **1645** 10 Jan., Abp Laud beheaded. 21 Jan., Sir Thomas Fairfax made commander of Parliamentary forces. Feb., Montrose defeats Campbells at Inverlochy. 3 Apr., Parliament passes 'Self-Denying Ordinance': all members, including peers, relinquish their commissions: Sir Thomas Fairfax and Oliver Cromwell train New Model Army. Apr., Montrose takes Dundee. 14 June, New Model Army under Cromwell defeats royalists at Naseby.  Aug., Montrose defeats Parliamentary forces at Kilsyth: in possession of all Lowlands. 25 Aug., treaty of Glamorgan grants concessions to Irish Catholics. 12 Sept., Montrose defeated at Philiphaugh by David Leven. Papal Nuncio Rinuccini arrives in Ireland, with funds to support royalists. | **1645** 7 March, Sweden defeats Imperial force at Jankau. 23 Aug., peace of Brömsebro between Denmark and Sweden: Denmark cedes possessions in Sweden. Condé defeats Imperial army at Nordlingen. **1645–69** Turks conquer Crete. **1645–76** Alexis I, Tsar of Russia, at age of sixteen: indecisive ruler of great piety. | **1645** Badi Dign, King of Sennar. First slaves exported from Mozambique to Brazil. |
| **1646** Charles I offers 'Ormond Peace' to Ireland: anti-Catholic penalties to be removed: land titles confirmed: Charles I excommunicated with all those favouring peace. 5 May, Charles I surrenders to Scottish army at Newark. 5 June, Owen Roe defeats English-Scottish army at Benburh, Tyrone. July, Montrose disbands his army: retires to Norway. Dunkirk taken by Condé. | **1646** France and Sweden devastate Bavaria. **1646–7** Rising against Spain in Sicily put down. | **1646** Rising in Cacheu. |

| THE EAST | THE AMERICAS | RELIGION & CULTURE |
|---|---|---|
| **1643** New Zealand visited by de Surville. | **1643** Indian massacre in New York. <br> **1643—98** Confederation of colonies of New England. | **1643** 25 Sept., Presbyterianism instituted in England by Assembly of Westminster. Edition of the *Acta Sanctorum* begun by J. Bolland, SJ. Torricelli measures the weight of air. <br><br> **1643—1715** Bp Gilbert Burnet, historian. |
| **1644—1912** Ch'ing (Manchu) dynasty in China. 24 Apr., Peking falls to General Li Tzu-Cheng: last Ming Emperor commits suicide: Li Tzu-cheng proclaimed Emperor. 6 June, General Wu San-kui seizes Peking, following alliance with the Manchus: Li Tzu-cheng flees, followed by Wu: Manchu take Peking. <br> **1644—62** Fu Lin, with throne name Shun-chih, first Manchu emperor. <br> **1644** Aurangzeb resigns his viceroyalty. Eight year truce between the Dutch and Portuguese in Ceylon: agreement of mutual protection against Rajasinha II follows. <br> **1645** 16 Feb., Aurangzeb made Governor of Gujarat (—1647). 30 Nov., severe earthquake partly destroys Manila. Dutch acquire monopoly of silk trade with Persia. Mongols make fifth Dalai Lama supreme ruler of Tibet. Ranga II confirms grant of Madras to Francis Day. Manchu take Nanking from a Ming prince: S China gradually conquered: many officials, scholars and landowners commit suicide. Chinese compelled by Manchu law to wear pigtails and Manchu clothing. Marriages between Chinese and Manchus prohibited: Manchu made legally the master race. Peace made between Bantam and Batavia. <br> **1645—77** Prabu Amangkurat I (Sunan Tegalwangi), Sultan of Mataram. <br> **1646** Prince Murad Bakhsh and Ali Mardan Khan campaign successfully in Badakhshan and Balkh. Peace treaty between Batavia and Mataram. Marion de Fresne visits New Zealand. | **1644** Sugar growing introduced into the Antilles Is. <br><br><br> **1645** Company of the Hundred Associates assign fur trade to *Compagnie des Habitants*. <br><br> **1646** French negotiate peace with Mohawk Indians. Fr Isaac Jogues killed by the Mohawks: Mohawks raid Ottawa, and Montreal to Trois Rivières. Bahamas occupied by England. | **1644** The barometer invented by Torricelli. <br> **1644—55** Innocent X Pamfili, Pope. <br><br><br> **1644—1737** Antonio Stradivari, violin maker. <br> **1645—96** Jean de la Bruyère, French moralist. <br><br> **1646** Synod of Puritan churches in Massachusetts promulgates 'Cambridge Platform'. <br> **1646—1716** Gottfried Wilhelm Leibniz, philosopher. <br> **1646—1708** Jules Hardouin-Mansard, architect: builder of many celebrated buildings in Paris and Versailles. <br> **1646—8** Confession of Westminster. |

## WESTERN EUROPE

## NORTHERN, CENTRAL & SOUTHERN EUROPE

## AFRICA

**1647** 3 Feb., Scottish army sells Charles I to Parliament for £400,000: taken to Holmby House, Northants. June, Charles I taken to Newmarket: thence to Hampton Court. Army Grand Council demands a new Parliament. 28 July, Dublin surrenders to English Parliament forces. Aug., Fairfax takes London: Levellers' mutiny suppressed by Cromwell. 11 Nov., Charles I escapes from Hampton Court: flees to Carisbrooke Castle, Is. of Wight: 26 Dec., signs treaty with Scottish army, who change sides. 13 Nov., English Parliamentary army defeats Irish army at Knocknanoss.
**1647** 14 March–**1650** William II of Orange, Stadholder.
**1648** 30 Jan., peace between Spain and the United Provinces. July, Scottish army crosses into England in support of Charles I. 17 Aug., Cromwell defeats Scots at Preston in a three day battle. 6 Dec., Pride's Purge of the Commons: remainder known as Rump Parliament. Fronde troubles begin in France: Anne of Austria flees to St. Germain: Paris blockaded by Condé. Condé beats the Spanish army at Lens.

**1649** 20 Jan., Charles I's trial opens in Westminster Hall: 30 Jan., beheaded in Whitehall. The monarchy abolished: House of Lords again abolished. 30 March, agreement of Reuil: end of first phase of the Fronde. 29 May, England declared a Commonwealth: Oliver Cromwell, Protector of England (–1658). 23 June, Charles II signs the Covenant. 15 Aug., Cromwell arrives in Ireland with 20,000 men. 11 Sept., Drogheda sacked by Cromwell; 11 Oct., Wexford: all defendants put to death: Cromwell campaigns in Ireland with brutality: the Mass forbidden. Second phase of Fronde rebellion: Turenne rebels.
**1649–50** Dispute between William II and Holland.
**1650** 18 Jan., Condé arrested. March, Kilkenny surrenders to Cromwell. 9 May, Cromwell repelled by Irish at Clonmel.

**1647** 14 March, Bavaria, France and Sweden sign treaty of neutrality at Ulm. General rebellion in the Kingdom of Naples.

**1648** Turenne beats the Imperial army at Summershausen. 26 July, the Swedes take Prague. 24 Oct., treaty of Westphalia between the Empire, France and Sweden concludes Thirty Years War: France obtains Alsace: Sweden obtains the estuaries of Rs Oder, Elbe and Weser: independence guaranteed for all German states, Switzerland and the United Provinces. Insurrection in Galicia: Crimean Tartars recognized by Poles. Rising in Moscow against oppressive bureaucracy. Out of 292 boyars attending the *Zemski Sobor*, 141 illiterate. Dejnev discovers the Bering Sea. Ottoman Sultan Ibrahim I assassinated: succ. Muhammad IV (–1687).
**1648–9** *Zemski Sobor* adopts *Oulojenie*, new legal code.
**1648–68** John II Casimir, King of Poland.
**1649** Sale of baptized slaves forbidden in Russia. Cossack rebellion in Poland defeated at Zborovo.

**1650** 26 June, peace of Nuremberg between the Empire and Sweden. Poles defeated by Tartars at Pilawice: reign of terror follows in Ukraine.

**1647–74** Carmelite mission in Madagascar.
**1647** Rising put down in Cacheu. Ha⌐ made an independent sultanate by Al Daud. Ethiopian embassy to Yemen.

**1648** The Portuguese eject the Dutch from Angola.
**1648–55** Ceuta besieged by Ahmad Gailan, rebel Moroccan chieftain.

c. **1650** Jenne one of the principal markets of the Muslim world. Yoruba seize Dahomey. Portuguese begin to export slaves from Mozambic annually.

## THE EAST

**1647** Jan., Aurangzeb appointed governor of Balkh and Badakhshan (—1649). Madras district taken by Golconda: English rights confirmed. Moghuls evacuate Balkh. English East India Co. establishes factory at Syriam. Abortive Dutch attack on Cavite, Philippine Is.

**1648** Shahjahan moves Moghul capital from Agra to Delhi.
**1648—61** Pindale, King of Burma.

**1649** Uzbegs threaten to invade N India: Aurangzeb transferred to be governor of Multan: 11 Feb., Qandahar falls to the Persians: May, Aurangzeb fails to take Qandahar: 5 Sept., abortive siege raised. Ruler of Bijapur takes fortress of Jingi: successful operations against Goa. New treaty between Rajasinha II and Dutch, repeating the provisions of 1638.

**1650** Omani Arabs expel Portuguese from Muscat. Persia recovers Qandahar. Russians establish fort on R. Amur, Turkestan.

## THE AMERICAS

**1647** Council set up in New France, of the governor, the Jesuit superior, and the lieutenant-governor of Montreal: syndics, or representatives, elected to appear before the council.

**1648** 20 Aug., Louis d'Aillebouet de Coulonge, Governor of New France (—1651). Iroquois raids resumed on French settlements.

**1649** Company of Brazil founded.
**1649—50** Huron tribe virtually wiped out by Iroquois.

**1650** 18,000 slaves in Barbados. Anguilla Is. settled from England. Anglo-Dutch frontier defined in N America.

## RELIGION & CULTURE

**1647** 'Ye Ould Deluder Law' enacted in Massachusetts: state school system inaugurated.
**1647—80** John Wilmot, Earl of Rochester, poet.
**1647—90** St Margaret Mary Alacoque.
**1647—1706** Pierre Bayle, encyclopaedist.

**1648** Royal Academy of Sculpture and Painting founded in Paris. Society of Friends (Quakers) founded by George Fox.
**1648—55** Royal Palace, Amsterdam, built.
**1648—1718** Jeanne Marie Guyon, quietist writer.
**1648—1721** Grinling Gibbons, woodcarver and sculptor.
**1648—1723** Sir Godfrey Kneller, artist.

**1649** Maryland assembly passes Toleration Act. First English translation of the Koran made.
**1649—1708** Dr. John Blow, composer.

**1650—3** Code of Canon Law (*Nomocanon*) revised in Russia.

| WESTERN EUROPE | NORTHERN, CENTRAL & SOUTHERN EUROPE | AFRICA |
|---|---|---|

**WESTERN EUROPE**

**1650** June, Charles II lands in Scotland. 3 Sept., Cromwell defeats Scots at Dunbar. 6 Nov., William II d.: no Stadholder appointed. 19 Dec., Edinburgh surrenders to Cromwell.

**1651** 1 Jan., Charles II crowned King of Scots at Scone. Feb., Mazarin exiled: Condé set free: Turenne joins the royalists. 1 Sept., General Monk sacks Dundee. 3 Sept., Cromwell defeats Charles II at Worcester: Charles escapes to France. 9 Oct., Navigation Act: foreign imports to be brought into England on English vessels only. 27 Oct., Limerick surrenders to Cromwell.

**1652** 25 Feb., Dunottar Castle, last Royalist stronghold in Scotland, falls. Feb., English Act of Pardon and Oblivion, reconciliation of English Royalists. May, Galway surrenders to English Parliamentary army: end of Royalist resistance in Ireland. 26 May, Cromwell leaves Ireland: Ireton left in charge. 30 June, England declares war on the United Provinces. July, Dutch warships sail up the R. Thames: 28 July, battle off Portland Bill: coast of Holland blockaded. Aug., Cromwell's Act of Settlement for Ireland. Sept., the Spanish take Dunkirk. 21 Oct., Louis XIV retakes Paris from the Fronde. Nov., the Fronde allies with Spain.
**c. 1652** Irish population reduced by war to c. ½m.
**1652–4** England at war with Holland.
**1653** 20 Apr., Rump Parliament dissolved by Cromwell. June–July, Cromwellian 'Transplantation' into northern Ireland. 4 July–12 Dec., Barebones, or Little, Parliament. End of the Fronde: Cardinal de Retz imprisoned: Mazarin returns to Paris: 3 Aug., Bordeaux capitulates. 9 Aug., Dutch fleet defeated by English off Texel. Sept., Cromwellian Act of Satisfaction: further Protestants granted estates in Ireland, following Catholic dispossessions. 16 Dec., Instrument of Government issued by Cromwell: installed in Westminster Abbey as Lord Protector: Council of State inaugurated: freedom of worship guaranteed to all except Anglicans and Catholics. Ireland declared part of the English Protectorate: represented in the Commons by thirty members: free trade with England and its colonies.
**1654** 5 Apr., treaty of Westminster ends Anglo-Dutch war: Holland accepts Navigation Act. 12 Apr., Ireland and Scotland united with England by Ordinance of Union: land taken from Irish Catholics and given to English settlers.

**NORTHERN, CENTRAL & SOUTHERN EUROPE**

**1650** Turenne, at the head of a Spanish army defeated at Rethel by French loyalist troops: Condé raises a small army in Germany at his own expense: Turenne given leadership: Condé takes service with Spain.
**1651–2** Spanish besiege Barcelona for fifteen months: French gradually withdraw.
**1651–79** Ferdinand Maria, Elector of Bavaria.

**1652** Feb., alliance of Hildesheim between N German Protestants and Sweden. 20 July, Electorate of Saxony partitioned into four areas. 11 Oct., Catalan rebellion put down: Barcelona recovered. Nikon elevated to Patriarchate of Moscow: given title equal to the Tsar: correction of translation of the Liturgy and strict discipline of the clergy follows.

**1653** 10 March, Anglo-Portuguese commercial treaty. 24 May, Ferdinand IV elected King of the Romans (–1654). Last meeting of the *Zemski Sobor*: autocracy the rule in Russia until the 20th c.

**1654** 6 June, Queen Christina of Sweden abdicates in favour of Charles X (–1660). 9 July, Ferdinand IV d. 10 July, Anglo-Portuguese treaty renewed. Russia invades Lithuania. Little Russia annexed.

**AFRICA**

**c. mid 17th c.** Jie, Karamojong, Lange and Teso expanding. Kabaka Kaberega of Buganda attacks Bunyoro doubles size of kingdom.

**1651** Dutch blockade Bou Regreg against pirates.
**c. 1651** Delegation from Mombasa request aid from Oman to expel Portuguese.

**1652** Omani raid on EA coast as far as Zanzibar. Jan van Riebeeck founds Cape Colony. First Swedish voyages to Gold Coast: trading lodges set up at Takoradi, Cape Coast, Osu and Accra, later Christiansborg Castle.

**1653** Kwararafa besiege Katsina. Armed Dutch expedition against Hottentots.

| THE EAST | THE AMERICAS | RELIGION & CULTURE |
|---|---|---|
| | **c. 1650** Settlement of N and S Carolina and of Georgia begun.<br>**1650 ff** Many buccaneers operating from Hispaniola and Jamaica. | |
| **1651–80** Tokugawa Iyetsuna, Shogun.<br>**1651–83** Abulfatah Agung, Sultan of Bantam: policy of modernization. | **1651** 14 Oct., Jean de L'ouzon, Governor of New France (−1658). | **1651** Baptist Conference held in Lincolnshire. Société des Missions Etrangères (SME) (Paris Evangelical Mission) founded. Reform of religious music in Russia: monophony mandatory: sale of *vodka* forbidden on Sundays and festivals. Yellow Temple, Peking, begun.<br>**1651–1715** Abp François de Salignac de la Mothe Fénelon, writer and controversialist.<br>**1651–1716** John, Lord Somers, writer. |
| **1652** May–July, Qandahar again abortively besieged by Aurangzeb. | | **1652** The air pump invented by Otto von Guericke. 9 March, probable cipher date of the *Hamziya*, earliest known dated Swahili poem.<br>**1652–66** Nikon, Patriarch of Moscow.<br>**1652–1715** William Dampier, explorer and writer. |
| **1653** Apr.–Sept., third siege of Qandahar, under Prince Dara Shikoh, a failure. Aurangzeb again appointed Viceroy of the Deccan. Chinese confirm authority of Dalai Lama, who visits Peking.<br>**1653–5** War between Batavia and Macassar. | **1653** 100 colonists arrive in Montreal. French Canadian population 600 to 700. | **1653** Pope Innocent X again condemns Jansenism. Blaise Pascal joins Jansenists at Port-Royal. St Vincent de Paul founds the Saltpetrière Hospital.<br>**1653–1713** Arcangelo Corelli, Italian composer. |
| | **1654** Party of young Frenchwomen arrive in New France as brides for colonists. Acadia seized by New Englanders with assistance from Cromwell. Dutch expelled by the Portuguese from Brazil. | **1654** Ejectors appointed to remove incapable Anglican clergy. Franciscans build church in Jaffa.<br>**1654–1705** Jacques Bernoulli, mathematician.<br>**1654–1743** André Hercule, Cardinal de Fleury, French statesman. |

| WESTERN EUROPE | NORTHERN, CENTRAL & SOUTHERN EUROPE | AFRICA |
|---|---|---|

**1654** 7 July, Louis XIV of France crowned. 3 Sept., first Protectorate Parliament opened; 11 Sept., republicans excluded. 14 Sept., Anglo-Danish commercial treaty. Rising in Scotland crushed.

**1655** 22 Jan., Protectorate Parliament dissolved. Aug., Cromwell divides England into eleven districts under Major-Generals. 24 Oct., Anglo-French commercial treaty. Council of State established to govern Scotland. Royalist rising in W of England crushed by Cromwell.

**1655–72** Jan de Witt, Grand Pensionary of Holland.

**1656** June, Anglo-Swedish commercial treaty. Russia invades Swedish Baltic territory. 5 Sept., England allies with France against Spain. 17 Sept., second Protectorate Parliament opened: votes £400,000 in return for removal of Major-Generals.

**1655** Charles X of Sweden invades Poland: 30 Aug., Warsaw taken; and, 8 Oct., Cracow: abortively proclaims himself King of Poland.

**1655–7** Admiral Blake campaigns in the Mediterranean.

**1655** Plague in Angola: population said to have been halved. Tunisian corsair fleet destroyed by Blake. English bombard Algiers.

**1656** 17 Jan., treaty between Brandenburg and Sweden: Prussia made a Swedish fief. Feb., Spain declares war on England. 28-30 July, Swedes and Brandenburgers defeat Poles at Warsaw: treaties of Königsberg and Marienburg partition Poland between them. 3 Nov., treaty of Vilna between Poland and Russia. 20 Nov., treaty of Labian between Brandenburg and Sweden: Sweden cedes Prussian territory. John IV of Portugal d.: succ. Afonso VI (−1668),, a subnormal paralytic: Queen-Mother regent (−1662). War of religion in Switzerland.

**1656–61** Muhammad Keuprulu, Grand Vizier of Turkey.

**1657** 23 March, treaty of Paris: England and France ally against Spain. 31 March, Humble Petition and Advice: Cromwell offered throne of England: refuses. 25 May, second Humble Petition and Advice: new House of Lords constituted: Cromwell's power strengthened. 26 June, Additional Petition and Advice gives Parliament greater powers. 3 Oct., French take Mardyke.

**1657** 2 Apr., Emperor Ferdinand III d.: succ. Leopold I (−1705). 20 Apr., English fleet destroys Spanish off Santa Cruz. June, Charles X abandons Poland. 19 Sept., treaty of Wehlau: Poland abandons sovereignty over Prussia to Brandenburg. 6 Nov., alliance between Brandenburg and Sweden against Poland. The Turks take Lemnos and Tenedos.

**1657** Danes drive Swedes out of all their Gold Coast trading lodges. Cape Dutch expand into Liesbeeck valley: slaves imported from Madagascar and Java.

**1658** 4 Feb., Cromwell dissolves Parliament. 13 June, battle of the Dunes: Anglo-French army defeats Spaniards: 25 June, Dunkirk taken; 24 Aug., Gravelines taken. 3 Sept., Oliver Cromwell d.: succ. his son, Richard (−1659).

**1658** 8 March, treaty of Roskill between Denmark and Sweden. Aug-Nov., Charles X of Sweden besieges Copenhagen. 16 Aug., League of the Rhine formed. Cossack revolt: rebels beaten by Russia at Konotop.

**1658** Army revolt in Cairo. Dutch abandon Mauritius.

**1658–70** Algiers ruled by Aghas with council.

| THE EAST | THE AMERICAS | RELIGION & CULTURE |
|---|---|---|

**1654** New settlement made by Dutch in Guiana and some small islands: sugar planting begun in W Indies.

**1655** Sivaji, a Maratha robber chieftain, murders the Raja of Jaoli: first appearance of the Marathas in history. Battle of Kumara between China and Russia.

**1655** Jamaica and the Cayman Is. taken by England from Spain.

**1655** 3 Nov., Queen Christina of Sweden becomes a Catholic. 24 Nov., use of the *Book of Common Prayer* banned by Cromwell. Synod of French clergy condemns Jansenism: Port-Royal members dispersed. Protestants massacred in Savoy. French mission starts amongst the Onondagas. Axum Cathedral founded.
**1655—67** Alexander VII (Chigi), Pope.

**1656** Aurangzeb, with minister Murshid Quli Khan, reforms Deccan administration: Feb., Golconda besieged (−30 March): raised in return for an indemnity: Mir Jumla made *wazir* of the empire. 12 May, Colombo surrendered by the Portuguese to the Dutch; Jaffua falls later; Dutch forts built at Batticoloa and Trincomalee.
**1656—73** Ali II b. Muhammad, Sultan of Bijapur.

**1656** Boston Library founded. Spinoza excommunicated by the Jews of Amsterdam. B. Pascal: *Les Provinciales,* attacks the Jesuits.
**1656—1723** Guillaume, Cardinal Dubois, French statesman.
**1656—67** Piazza di S. Pietro, Rome, constructed by Bernini.

**1657** Aurangzeb campaigns in Bijapur: March, Bidar taken: 1 Aug., Kalyani capitulates: Shahjahan intervenes: peace made for an indemnity. Sept., Shahjahan falls: his sons, Dara Shikoh, Shuja, Aurangzeb, and Murad Bakhsh, begin to dispute the succession: all four regional governors: eldest, Dara Shikoh, favoured by Shahjahan: Shuja enthrones himself in Bengal: 5 Dec., Murad Bakhsh enthrones himself in Ahmadabad. English close factory in Syriam.
**1658** Feb., Aurangzeb begins to assume imperial prerogatives: Shuja defeated at Bahadurpur by Sulaiman Shikoh, son of Dara Shikoh: Apr., effects junction with Murad's army at Malwa: agrees with Murad to partition the empire: Shahjahan sends force against Aurangzeb and Murad under Sulaiman, son of Dara Shikoh: 25 Apr., utterly defeated at Dharmat. 29 May, further army under Dara Shikoh defeated by Aurangzeb and Murad at Samugarh. 8 June, fort of Agra surrenders to Aurangzeb: Shahjahan made prisoner for life: 25 June, Murad Bakhsh taken prisoner. 21 July, Aurangzeb enthroned informally (−1707).

**1657** John Washington, ancestor of George Washington, arrives in America.

**1657** Patriarch Nikon of Russia retires to Monastery of the New Jerusalem. Cromwell founds Durham University (closed 1660). The pendulum clock invented.
**1657—1757** Bernard le Bovier de Fontenelle, writer.
c. **1657—1716** Ogata Korin, Japanese painter.

**1658** 11 July, Pierre de Voyer, Vicomte d'Argenson, Governor of New France (−1661).

**1658** Hajji Khalfah, encyclopaedist, d. at Istanbul. Academy of Sciences founded in Paris. Socinians expelled from Poland. The spring-balance invented.

**1659** 7 May, the Long Parliament recalled. 21 May, treaty of the Hague: England, France and the United Provinces ally at the Hague to compel Denmark and Sweden to make peace. 25 May, Richard Cromwell abdicates. 12 Oct., the Long Parliament dissolved by the army. Nov., General Monk holds a Convention in Scotland. 16 Dec., Long Parliament again recalled.

**1660** 3 Feb., General Monk arrives with army in London: 16 March, Parliament declares itself dissolved. 4 Apr., Declaration of Breda: Charles II of England and Scotland offers total amnesty: 25 May, lands at Dover: 29 May, reaches London. 15 Apr.–29 Dec., Convention Parliament, principally royalists. 7 Nov., Council of Trade instituted in England. 1 Dec., Council for Foreign Plantations instituted in England. Louis XIV of France m. Maria Teresa of Spain. English Navigation Act of 1651 re-enacted.
**1660–7** Sir Edward Hyde (later Earl of Clarendon), Lord Chancellor of England.
**1660–73** James, Duke of York, Lord High Admiral of England.
**1660–85** Charles II, King of England.
**1660–97** Charles XI, King of Sweden.
**1661** 9 March, Cardinal Mazarin d.: Louis XIV governs personally with former ministers. 23 Apr., Charles II crowned.
**1661** 8 May–**1667** 'Cavalier Parliament'.
**1661–81** Canal du Midi built in France, joining the Atlantic to the Mediterranean.
**1661–83** Jean Baptiste Colbert, Controller-General of Finance in France.
**1662** 6 Feb., treaty of Montmartre: Lorraine ceded to France. 19 May, Press Act imposes censorship in England: Act of Uniformity makes Book of Common Prayer (slightly revised) compulsory to England; Conventicles Act, against nonconformists: over 1,000 Puritan clergy resign their livings. 21 May, Charles II of England m. Catherine of Braganza: Tangier and Bombay ceded by Portugal as dowry, with 2m. *cruzados*: England undertakes to defend Portugal by land and sea: British army dispatched to Portugal: threat of Spanish invasion countered. 23 June, alliance between England and Portugal.

**1659** 7 Nov., treaty of the Pyrenees between France and Spain. France retains Cerdagne and Rousillon: claim to Catalonia abandoned. The Elector of Brandenburg expels Sweden from Prussia and Pomerania.

**1660** 3 May, peace of Oliva ends war between Austria, Brandenburg, Poland and Sweden. 6 June, treaty of Copenhagen between Denmark and Sweden. 13 Oct., the Diet of Copenhagen make the Danish monarchy hereditary. The Ottomans attack Transylvania.

**1661** 10 Jan., Frederick III of Denmark obtains exclusive prerogative over the Danish constitution. 21 June, peace of Kardis between Sweden and Russia. Muhammad Keuprulu, Grand Vizier of Turkey d.: succ. Ahmad, his son (–1676): invasion of Transylvania and Hungary follows. Rising against taxation in Oporto.
**1661–8** Oder-Spree canal built.

**1662** Afonso VI declares himself of age: favourite Conde de Castelo Melhor real ruler (–1667).

**1659** St Louis, Senegal, founded.

**1660** Further Omani raid on EA coast.
**1660–78** Bushmen raiding Dutch Cape settlements.
**c. 1660–97** Obiri Veboa, Asantehene.

**1661** 14 Feb.,–24 March, Omani temporarily hold Mombasa. French expedition against Algiers.

**1662** Jan van Riebeeck moves from Cape to Malacca.
**c. 1662 or 1663** English build Cape Coast Castle.

| THE EAST | THE AMERICAS | RELIGION & CULTURE |
|---|---|---|

**1658** Yung-Li, last Ming Emperor, takes refuge in Ava: Chinese army takes to brigandage and rapine.
**1659** 7 Jan., Aurangzeb routs Sulaiman Shikoh at Khajwah. 12-14 Apr., Dara Shikoh's army routed at Pass of Deorai. May, Aurangzeb formally enthroned in Delhi: takes title Alamgir: coins issued: taxes nominally remitted. 30 Aug., Dara Shikoh beheaded. Punitive expedition mounted under Afzal Khan to put down Sivaji: Afzal killed treacherously. Coxinga, a pirate, pillages Nanking.
**1660** May, Sulaiman Shikoh defeated and killed by the Arakanese. Shayista Khan sent against Sivaji: Sivaji penetrates his quarters and kills his son. Ruler of Macassar signs treaty with the Dutch to stop trading in the Spice Is.: treaty not kept. War between Batavia and Macassar.

**1659** More than 100 colonists arrive in French N America.

**1660 ff** 4,000–5,000 slaves reached Barbados annually at £17 each.

**1659** François Xavier de Laval-Montmorency appointed first Vicar Apostolic of Quebec. The universal joint invented. Royal Library, Berlin, founded.
**1659–60** Last Huguenot Synod at Loudun. *Discipline* of French Calvinists published.
**1659–95** Henry Purcell, composer.
**1659–1725** Alessandro Scarlatti, composer.
**1660** Assembly of the French clergy requires the Jansenists to sign a *Formulary.*
**1660–90** Quarrels in Russia between *Raskolniki* (schismatics) and orthodox.
**1660–1731** Daniel Defoe, novelist and journalist.
**1660–1734** Georg Ernst Stahl, scientist.

**1661** Dec., Cooch Behar annexed by Aurangzeb. Murad Bakhsh executed. Wu San-kui completes conquest of W China: delivers up last Ming prince to the Manchu. Coxinga retires to Formosa.
**1661–72** Pye, King of Burma.

**1661** 31 Aug., Pierre Dubois, Baron d'Avaugour, Governor of New France (–1663).
**1661–2** Redonde Is. settled from England.
**1661–75** Virginian Assembly sits without permitting elections.

**1661** Bishops restored in Scotland. Palace of Versailles begun by Le Van. New Testament translated into Algonquin by John Eliot.
**1661–1736** Nicholas Hawksmoor, architect.

**1662** March, Garhgaon, capital of Cooch Behar, taken for Aurangzeb. May, Sulaiman Shikoh murdered at Gwalior. Chinese population 100m.

**1662** Connecticut granted a charter. Honduras first settled from England.

**1662** 19 May, Act of Uniformity requires use of *Book of Common Prayer* and consent of Anglican clergy to the *Thirty-Nine Articles.* Puritanism forbidden. 15 July, Royal Society founded. Over 1,500 Quakers imprisoned in England for refusal to conform: very many other nonconformists persecuted and imprisoned.
**1662–1742** Richard Bentley, scholar.

| WESTERN EUROPE | NORTHERN, CENTRAL & SOUTHERN EUROPE | AFRICA |
|---|---|---|

**1662** Sept., Act for the Settlement of Ireland. 27 Sept., Charles II sells Dunkirk to France for 2½m. *livres.*
**1663** 16 Feb., Louis XIV takes Venaissin. 10 June, Royal African Co. chartered. Aug., the French occupy Lorraine. Act of Explanation in Ireland: Cromwellians forced to surrender usurped lands: many injustices occur. Franco-Danish treaty of alliance.

**1663** March, League of the Rhine renewed. 18 Apr., the Ottomans declare war on Austria. June, Ahmad Keuprulu again attacks Hungary. Spaniards attack Portugal: 8 June, defeated at Ameixal. 3 Aug., Frederick III of Denmark joins the League of the Rhine. Rising in Moscow on account of the cost of living.

**1663** First English settlement built in Sierra Leone. School for Dutch and Hottentots opened in Cape Town.

**1664** Colbert reforms French taxation: inland duties abolished. Triennial Act enacted: English Parliament required to meet each third year. French East India Co. founded and West Indian Co. organized, by Colbert.

**1664** 1 Aug., battle of St Gotthard: Ottomans defeated. 10 Aug., treaty of Eisenburg between the Emperor and the Ottomans. Poland takes Novgorod-Sieversk.

**1664–6** War between English and Dutch in W Africa.
**1664–1710** Dutch re-occupy Mauritius.
**1664–present day** Sharifs of Morocco, Filali branch.

**1665** March, England and Holland at war (–1667). 3 June, Dutch defeated in Southwold Bay. Nov., Dutch blockade the Thames. June–Sept., Great Plague in London. Building of naval arsenal begun at Brest. English Navigation Act renewed.

**1665** Spain again attacks Portugal: defeated by Anglo-Portuguese force at Montesclaros. Don Cossacks raiding the Urals and as far as the Caspian Sea.
**1665–1700** Charles II of Spain, an imbecile: Queen-Mother Mariana, regent: German Jesuit Nithard, inquisitor-general real power.

**1665** 29 Oct., battle of Mbwila: Portuguese now paramount in present Angola. Bourbon (Réunion) occupied by France. French expedition against Algiers.
**1665–1911** Sultanate of Wadai.

**1666** Jan., Louis XIV bans complaints to the Parliament of Paris. 26 Jan., England and France at war. 11 Feb., alliance between Denmark and the United Provinces. 11-14 June, Albemarle defeated by de Ruyter off Dunkirk. 4 Aug., de Ruyter defeated by Albemarle off North Foreland. 2-6 Sept., Great Fire of London. Nov., Pentlands rising in Scotland. Irish Cattle Bill forbids export of cattle to England. Colbert made Secretary of the French Navy.
**1667** 31 March, secret treaty between Charles II and Louis XIV. 13 June, Admiral de Ruyter enters R. Medway, attacking Chatham, and destroying several English warships. 31 July, Peace of Breda between England and Holland. 30 Aug., Clarendon dismissed and banished. 30 Aug., Cabal (Clifford, Ashley, Buckingham, Arlington and Lauderdale) Ministry in England (–1673). Protectionist tariff in France.

**1666** 16 Feb., alliance between Brandenburg and the United Provinces. 25 Oct., Quadruple Alliance between Brandenburg, Brunswick, Denmark and the United Provinces. Elector of Brandenburg makes E Prussia free from Poland. Afonso VI of Portugal m. Marie Françoise of Savoy. George Lubomirski's rebellion put down.
**1666–7** Poland and Turkey at war.
**1666–71** Don and Volga Cossacks in rebellion.
**1667** 20 Jan., armistice of Androussovo: boundaries between Poland and Russia demarcated. 9 June, Oldenburg annexed to Denmark. Aug., League of the Rhine dissolved.

**1666–7** Cape Town Castle built.

**1667** 31 July, England receives Cape Coast Castle from the Dutch. Indians begin to arrive at the Cape.
**1667–82** Yohannes I of Ethiopia: many ecclesiastical reforms: first royal library and chancery built at Gondar.

| THE EAST | THE AMERICAS | RELIGION & CULTURE |
|---|---|---|

**1663** Dutch take Malabar.
**1663–1722** Sheng Tsu (with name of ruling period Kang-Hsi), Ching Emperor.

**1663** 15 Sept., Augustin de Saffray, Sieur de Mézy, Governor of New France (–1665). Rhode Island granted a charter. Company of One Hundred Associates surrenders its charter: governor of New France given an *intendant* as officer in charge of justice, police and finance. Charter granted for N and S Carolina and Georgia: Fundamental Constitution drawn up by John Locke. Population of New France *c.* 2,500.

**1663** The guinea first minted.

**1664** Prince Muazzam made governor of the Deccan: captures Purandar: June, Sivaji forced to cede twenty-three forts and become a Moghul vassal. Sivaji plunders Surat: town defended by Sir George Oxinden. First French and Russian embassies to Persia. Raja of Cooch Behar restored.
**1664–94** Shayista Khan, Governor of Bengal.

**1664** 29 Aug., New Amsterdam taken from Dutch by three English warships: renamed New York.

**1664** July, Conventicles Act forbids Puritan meetings in England. Trappist Order founded.
**1664–1726** Sir John Vanbrugh, architect.

**1665** 12 Sept., Daniel Rémy, Sieur de Courcelles, Governor of New France (–1672). Superior Council of New France reconstituted: governor, *intendant,* bishop and five *habitants* nominated by the king. *Coutume de Paris,* common law of N France, established as the law of New France. Carignan Regiment, of 1200 officers and men, sent to New France: Marquis de Tracy commander-in-chief: campaign against Mohawks brings about ten years of freedom from raids. De Ruyter beaten off Barbados.
**post 1665** Industry and agriculture greatly stimulated in New France.

**1665** Pope Alexander VII: Bull *Regiminis Apostolici* requires Jansenists to sign a *Formulary. London Gazette* first published. Five Mile Act restricts Puritan ministers in England. *Journal des Savants* founded.
**1665–1731** Bartolommeo Cristofori, inventor of the piano.

**1666** 1 Feb., Shahjahan d. a natural death. Sivaji forced to surrender: Dec., escapes. Chittagong ceded by King of Arakan to Bengal.
**1666–8** Cornelis Speelman sent on expedition against Macassar.
**1666–86** Johore at war with Jambi.
**1666–94** Sulaiman I, (Sofi II), Shah of Persia.

**1666** Newton discovers the decomposition of light: uses infinitesimal calculus (not published until 1692). Patriarch Nikon of Moscow formally deposed by a council of Russian bishops. Great Schism (*Raskol*) in the Russian Orthodox Church.

**1667** Sivaji appointed a Raja. Sultan of Tidore recognizes overlordship of Dutch EIC.

**1667** Acadia returned to France by Treaty of Breda.

**1667–9** Clement IX (Rospigliosi), Pope.
**1667–1745** (Dean) Jonathan Swift, satirist.
**1667–1748** Jean Bernoulli, mathematician.
**1667** Gobelins factory made a royal monopoly.

| WESTERN EUROPE | NORTHERN, CENTRAL & SOUTHERN EUROPE | AFRICA |
|---|---|---|

**1667–8** France and Spain at war in the Netherlands. Louis XIV seizes Brabant, Flanders and Franche Comté from Spain: England, Holland and Sweden join Spain against him.
**1668** 23 Jan., England and Holland ally against France in treaty of the Hague. Feb., France takes Franche Comté. 2 May, Treaty of Aix-la-Chapelle: Louis XIV cedes his gains to Spain except twelve fortresses in Flanders.

**1668** 13 Feb., Treaty of amity between France and Spain. Spain formally recognizes Portuguese independence. Apr., Sweden accedes to Anglo-Dutch treaty. 19 Sept., John Casimir of Poland abdicates to retire to a monastery: interregnum to 1669. Afonso VI of Portugal deposed by his brother Peter II (−1706): Afonso's marriage annulled: Marie-Françoise m. Peter II.

**1668** England creates Tangier a borough. Council of Gondar requires all resident Franks to adhere to Ethiopian Church: Muslims required to live in separate villages.

**1669** 31 Dec., secret treaty between France and Brandenburg.

**1669** 25 Feb., Don John of Austria rebels in Spain. 19 June, Michael Wisniowiecki elected King of Poland (−1673). 27 Sept., Candia taken by the Ottomans: Venetians expelled from Crete. Don John of Austria seizes Madrid with Catalan army: Nithard dismissed: Don John, Viceroy of Aragon.

**1670** 1 June, secret treaty of Dover: Charles II agrees to give France a free hand in Holland in return for subsidy. Aug., France occupies Lorraine. 26 Aug., new penal code published in France. French Levant Co. formed. Hudson's Bay Co., formed to make good the English claim in northern America. English Navigation Act excludes Ireland.

**1670** Jan., Triple Alliance guarantees Spain the possession of the Spanish Netherlands. 17 Feb., Franco-Bavarian treaty. Emperor Leopold I puts down a rebellion of Hungarian nobility. Don Cossacks on the Volga: take Astrakhan and Tsaritsin: defeated near Simbirsk by Prince Bariatinski.
**1670–1** Rebellion of Stenka Razine in Russia.
**1670–99** Christian V, King of Denmark.
**1671** Feb., treaty of assistance between Brandenburg and the United Provinces. Apr., Hungarian rebels executed. 11 July, treaty of Hildesheim. 1 Nov., secret treaty of neutrality between the Empire and France.

**1670** Timbuktu over-run by Bambara Kwararafa sack Kano and attack Katsina. Omani raid E.A. as far as Mozambique: town sacked and burnt. Algiers ruled by Deys and Pasha-Deys (−1830).
**c. 1670–5** Dutch fort built at Sekondi.
**c. 1670–82** Musa b. Sulaiman, Sultan of Darfur.
**1670–96** Cape Colony exporting grain to Batavia.

**1671** 2 Feb., secret treaty between Louis XIV and the Emperor renewed. 17 Dec., treaty between Spain and the United Provinces. Dutch East India Co. dissolved.

**1671** French fort built at Whydah. Madagascar declared a French royal property. Vansleb sent by Louis XIV to visit churches in the Nile Valley.

**1672** 2 Jan., Stop of the Exchequer announced in England: many businesses bankrupted. 24 Feb., William of Orange, Captain and Admiral-General of the Netherlands. 28 March, England at war with Holland; 6 Apr., France at war with Holland (−1678). 6 May, alliance between Holland and Brandenburg effective. 14 Apr., Franco-Swedish alliance. 3 July, the French take Utrecht. 7 June, battle of Sole Bay. 4 July, William of Orange made Stadholder. 21 Aug., de Witt brothers murdered. Louis XIV invades Holland: occupies Franche-Comté: French army sent into Catalonia: rising fomented in Sicily (−1678). Dutch open dykes to prevent French invasion. Irish population 800,000 Catholics, 300,000 Protestants: Catholics own 4.5m. acres, Protestants 8.5m. acres: Protestant ascendancy now assured.

**1672** 23 June, alliance between the Emperor and Brandenburg. 25 July, alliance between the Empire and the United Provinces. Turkey attacks Poland: 18 Oct., treaty of Buczacz: Kamienic, all Ukraine and Podolia ceded to Turkey: treaty not ratified by Poland.
**1672–81** War between Russia and Turkey.

**1672** English bombard Algiers. English fort built at Sierra Leone. Cape peninsula formally bought from the Hottentots.
**1672–1750** R. Africa Co.
**post 1672** Moroccan slave raids to the S.
**1672–1727** Maulai Ismail b.Muhammad Sharif of Morocco.

**THE EAST**  **THE AMERICAS**  **RELIGION & CULTURE**

**1668** King of Macassar surrenders:
18 Nov., signs treaty of Bongaja:
Dutch governor installed in Macassar:
fortress of Rotterdam erected.
Sultanate of Acheh collapses.
**1668–9** Sivaji re-organizes his
government: Maratha power grows
steadily.

**1669** Jat peasants rebel in Mathura
district: suppressed after a battle.
Dutch traders murdered at
Banjermasin, Borneo.
**1669–77** Gerald Aungier, Governor
of Bombay.

**1670** Sivaji resumes hostilities:
extorts protection money in
Khandesh: Oct., again plunders
Surat, for three days.
**1670–80** Great Tower of Nizwa,
Muscat, built.

**1670** Population of Virginia *c.*
40,000. Charleston founded. Anglo-
Spanish treaty recognizes English
title to Jamaica and all other *de
facto* possessions in America. England
promises to stop buccaneering.

**1671** Some 400 French settlers in
Acadia.

**1672** Satnami Hindu sect rebels
against Aurangzeb at Narnaul,
Patiala: defeated and put to death.
Rising of Yusufzais at Ali Masjid
against governor of Kabul. English
trading post set up at Pho Hien.
**1672–3** Narawara, King of Burma.

**1672** 12 Sept., Louis de Buade,
Comte de Palluan et de Frontenac,
Governor of New France (–1682).
(British) Virgin Is. acquired by
England.
**1672–4** New York again in Dutch
hands.

**1668** 'Peace of the Church' between
Pope Clement IX and the Jansenists.
*Académie de France* founded in Rome.
**1668–1733** François Couperin (le
Grand), French composer.
**1668–1744** Giovanni Battista Vico,
Italian philosopher.
**1668–1779** William Warburton,
theologian.
**1668–94** Chapel of the Holy Shroud,
Turin, built.
**1669** 1 Feb., fresh declaration limits
the extent of the Edict of Nantes.
Aurangzeb issues orders to destroy
Hindu schools and temples. Phosphorus
discovered.

**1670** The *Invalides*, Paris, begun. The
mercury thermometer invented by
Rinieri.
**1670–6** Clement X (Altieri), Pope.
**1670–89** John Dryden, English poet
laureate.
**1670–1729** William Congreve,
dramatist.
**1670–c. 1745–6** Dionysius of
Fourna, author of the *Painter's Manual.*

**1671** Newton builds reflecting
telescope. Lully founds the *Académie
de Musique* in Paris.
**1671–1713** Antony Ashley Cooper,
Earl of Shaftesbury, philosopher.
**1671–1741** Jean Baptiste Rousseau,
French poet.
**1671–1757** Colley Cibber, poet
laureate, dramatist and actor.
**1672** 25 March, *Declaration of
Indulgence* published for English
Catholics and nonconformists.
The Tsar proclaimed Protector of all
Greek Orthodox Christians. Council in
Jerusalem confirms Russian liturgical
reforms.
**1672–1719** Joseph Addison, essayist
and poet.
**1672–1729** Sir Richard Steele,
essayist and playwrite.
**1672–1750** Lodovico Antonio
Muratori, historian and editor.

## WESTERN EUROPE

## NORTHERN, CENTRAL & SOUTHERN EUROPE

## AFRICA

**1673** 30 June, the French take Maestricht. William of Orange arranges coalition of the United Provinces, Denmark, and Spain, against France.
**1673–8** Earl of Danby, secretary of state: English finances re-organized.

**1673** 6 June, treaty of Vossem between Brandenburg and France. 30 Aug., the Emperor allies with Lorraine and the United Provinces against France. 16 Sept., the Emperor declares war on France. 11 Nov., John Sobieski defeats Ahmad Keuprulu at Khoczim.

**1673** French Senegal Co. for slave trade founded. Richard Baxter, *Christian Directory*, denounces slave-hunting.

**1674** 19 Feb., treaty of Westminster: England withdraws from war with Holland. The Empire, the Pope and Spain ally against France. 10 July, alliance between Denmark and the United Provinces. 11 Aug., battle of Seneffe.

**1674** 24 May, German Diet declares war on France. 1 Nov., imperial forces invade Alsace. Dec., Sweden invades Brandenburg and Prussia. Sweden at war with Denmark.
**1674–1696** John III Sobieski, King of Poland.

**1674** Sultan of Morocco attempts to take Ceuta from Spain. French evacuate Madagascar.

**1675** 27 July, Turenne killed by a spent bullet at battle of Salzbach. The French take Liège, Dinant, and Limburg: Trêves lost.

**1675** 9 Jan., battle of Turckheim. 11 June, John Sobieski defeats the Turks at Lwow. Franco-Polish alliance of Jaworow. 25 June, Elector of Brandenburg defeats Swedes at Rathenau; and, 28 June, Fehrbellin. Sept., Brandenburg and Denmark ally against Sweden.

**?c. post 1675** Masai begin to enter present Kenya.

**1676** 17 Feb., secret alliance between England and France. 29 Apr., de Ruyter d.

**1676** 6 Jan., battle of the Lipari Is. 22 Apr., French Admiral Duquesne defeats Dutch fleet under Dutch Admiral Ruyter at Stromboli. 1 June, naval battle off Oeland. Denmark invades Scania. 2 June, battle of Aosta. Sept., Imperial army takes Philippsburg. Oct., Ahmad Keuprulu d.: succ. as Grand Vizier by Kara Mustafa. 27 Oct., peace of Zurawno between Poland and Turkey: Podolia partitioned. 3 Dec., Charles XI of Sweden defeats the Danes at Lund.
**1676–82** Feodor III Tsar of Russia: a sickly monarch, d. aged twenty.

**1677** Feb., Lord Shaftesbury arrested. 15 Nov., William of Orange m. Mary, d. of Duke of York. France takes St Omer, Cambrai and Valenciennes.

**1677** Apr., treaty between the Empire and Poland. 11 Apr., William of Orange defeated at Cassel. June, naval battle of Fimern. July, naval battle of Kjöge. The Danes defeated at Landskrona. 17 Nov., the French take Freiburg-im-Breisgau. 27 Dec., Stettin capitulates. Don John of Austria makes himself the real power in Spain.
**1677–9** Elector of Brandenburg takes parts of Pomerania and Rügen: pursues Swedes to Riga.
**1677–82** Count Tököly leads Hungarian rebellion against Austria.

**1677** Slave children under twelve required to attend school in Cape Colony. Moroccan capital moved to Meknès.

**1678** 10 Jan., Anglo-Dutch treaty of the Hague. March, France takes Ghent and Ypres. Treaties of Nijmegen: 10 Aug., between France and the United Provinces; 17 Sept., between France and Spain: France gains Franche-Comté and various Dutch towns.

**1678** Count Tököly revolts again in Hungary: occupies Slovakia. Alliance between France and Hungary. The Turks take Tchiguirin from Russia.
**1678–9** Sweden invades Prussia: expelled by the Elector of Brandenburg.

**1678** French take Arguin from the Dutch. Portuguese send punitive expedition against Lamu, Manda, Pate and Siu.

| THE EAST | THE AMERICAS | RELIGION & CULTURE |
|---|---|---|

**THE EAST**

**1673** Johore capital at Batu Sewar destroyed by Jambi. English attempt to re-open trade with Japan: refused because Charles II had married daughter of King of Portugal. Wu San-Kui proclaims himself Emperor: the Manchu march against him.
**1673—86** Sikandar, Sultan of Bijapur
**1673—98** Minyekyawdin, King of Burma.
**1674** June, Sivaji enthrones himself as an independent raja. French trading settlement founded at Pondᵍcherry. Rising of Afridis: Aurangzeb engages in operations against them and Yusufzais near Peshawar (—1675). Trunajaya, Prince of Madura, rebels against the Dutch in Batavia.
**1675** Tegh Bahadur, ninth Sikh guru, executed for refusing to accept Islam.
**1675—1708** Gavind Singh, tenth and last Sikh *guru*, founder of Sikh military power.

**1676** Sivaji campaigns in Bijapur and Golconda.
**1676 or 1677** Muhammad Sultan, eldest son of Aurangzeb, executed.

**1677** Mataram recognizes Dutch suzerainty.
**c. 1677—85** Ibrahim Shah, Sultan of Johore: capital at Bintang (Rhio).
**1677—98** Amir Khan, governor of Kabul: peace ensues in Afghanistan.
**1677—1703** Amangkurat II, Sultan of Mataram.

**1678** Raja Jaswant Singh of Marwar (Jodhpur) d.: Aurangzeb takes opportunity to act against Rajas and Hindus. Trunajaya's rebellion put down: Kadiri conquered by the Dutch.

**THE AMERICAS**

**1674** Monopoly of the French West India Co. ended in New France. Dutch take Martinique.

**1675—6** War with Indians in New England.

**1676** Nathaniel Bacon's rebellion in Virginia: landless class rise against royal governor: Jamestown burnt. Population of New France *c.* 8,500.

**1678** English colony established in Honduras. Turks Is. settled from England.
**1678—84** Maranhão Co., Brazil.

**RELIGION & CULTURE**

**1673** 22 March, Test Act: Roman Catholics excluded from offices under the Crown in England: Duke of York compelled to resign as Lord High Admiral. Declaration of Indulgence revoked.
**1673—1707** Jeremiah Clarke, composer.
**1673—1716** Blessed Louis Grignion de Montfort, missionary.
**1674** Bp François de Laval, Vicar Apostolic, made first Bp of Quebec.
**•1674—1738** Charles, second Viscount Townshend ('Turnip Townshend'), politician and agriculturalist.
**1674—1748** Isaac Watts, poet.
**1674—1754** James Gibbs, architect.
**1675** Leibniz invents differential calculus. Royal Observatory established at Greenwich. Office of Astronomer Royal established in England.
**1675—91** 20,000 persons burn themselves in protest against alleged unorthodoxy of the Russian church.
**1675—1710** St Paul's Cathedral, London, rebuilt: begun by Sir Christopher Wren.
**1676** Olaus Römer first calculates the speed of light. Repeating clocks and watches invented by Barlow.
**1676—89** Innocent XI (Odescalchi), Pope.
**1676—1748** Pietro Giannone, Italian historian.
**1676—1764** Benito Jerónimo Feijoo y Montenegro, Spanish essayist.

**1677** Innsbruck University founded.
**1677—1746** Guillaume Coustou, sculptor.
**1677—1756** Jacques Cassini, astronomer.
**1677—1726** Claud Sicard, SJ, first modern investigator to reach Aswan.

**1678** 21 May, Bossuet condemns R. Simon: *Histoire critique du Vieux Testament.* Aug., Titus Oates falsely alleges a Roman Catholic plot: Catholics persecuted in England: excluded from Parliament. Nov., new Test Act. Turin Academy of Sciences founded.
**c. 1678—1743** Antonio Vivaldi, composer.

| WESTERN EUROPE | NORTHERN, CENTRAL & SOUTHERN EUROPE | AFRICA |
|---|---|---|
| **1679** 28 Feb., Duke of York banished to Brussels. March, new Parliament elected in England: Earl of Danby impeached. Names 'Whig' and 'Tory' first used. 27 May, Act of *Habeas Corpus* in England. Halifax becomes chief minister. 22 June, Scottish rebels beaten by Monmouth at Bothwell Bridge.<br>**1679—1720** Anthony Heinsius, Grand Pensionary of Holland. | **1679** 5 Feb., treaty of Nijmegen between France and the Empire: Freiburg-im-Breisgau and Breisach given up by France. 29 June, treaty of St Germain between Brandenburg and Sweden: all Swedish conquests ceded. 2 Sept., treaty of Fontainebleau between Denmark and Sweden: Danish conquests ceded. 25 Sept., second treaty of St Germain. 26 Sept., treaty of Lund. Don John of Austria d.: Queen-Mother Mariana again in power in Spain.<br>**1679—1726** Maximilian II, Elector of Bavaria. | **1679** Omani fleet temporarily compels Portuguese to withdraw from Pate. French Senegal Co. refounded. |
| **1680** Colbert made Secretary for Foreign Affairs in France. May, Exclusion Bill, to exclude the succession of the Duke of York, passes Commons: rejected by the Lords. Penny post inaugurated in London. | **1680** Rebellion against the Empire in Bohemia. Brandenburg seizes the Archbishopric of Magdeburg. Charles XI m. Ulrica-Eleanora of Denmark.<br>**1680—2** Charles XI makes Sweden an absolute monarchy. | **c. 1680** Ga migration from Accra plain to Anecho, Dahomey. Akwamu take over Accra plain. Ewe state of Anlo already established. |
| **1681** Jan., Parliament dissolved. 19-28 March, Parliament of Oxford: no further Parliament summoned by Charles II. 28-30 Sept., Strasbourg occupied by France. Nov., new treaty on subsidies between France and England. | **1681** 11 Jan., secret defensive alliance between France and Brandenburg. 8 July, Duke of Mantua sells Casale to France. Treaties of Bakche-Serai between Russia and Turkey, and with Poland recognize Russian possession of the right bank of the Dnieper and of Kiev. Louis XIV again campaigns in Flanders and Luxembourg: French army again sent to Catalonia. | **c. 1681** Civil war in Monomotapa's territory. |
| **1682** 28 Feb., the Empire allies with the United Provinces at the Hague. Green Ribbon Club plot. | **1682** 22 Jan., treaty between Brandenburg and France. Feb., alliance between Brandenburg and Denmark. 27 Apr., Feodor III of Russia d.: revolt of the Streltsy (royal guards): Ivan, aged sixteen, proclaimed Tsar (—1689); Peter proclaimed co—Tsar (—1725) with Tsarina Sophia as regent (—1689): further troubles from the Streltsy: Tsarina under influence of Prince Vassili Golitsyne, a cultivated nobleman. 2 May, Spain adheres to treaty of the Hague. Treaty between Hungary and Turkey. Dec., breach between Austria and Turkey.<br>**1682—8** Count Tököly, King of Hungary, as a Turkish vassal. | **1682** Algiers bombarded by French fleet for alleged acts of piracy.<br>**1682—3** Expeditions from Cape to Namaqaland in search of copper.<br>**1682—1706** Iyasu I the Great of Ethiopia.<br>**c. 1682—1722** Ahmad Bakr b. Musa, Sultan of the Fur: spreads Islam: mosques and schools set up: El Fasher founded. |
| **1683** June, Rye House Plot, to assassinate Charles II and Duke of York, discovered: 21 July, Lord Russell; and, 7 Dec., Algernon Sydney, executed. Duke of Monmouth exiled to Holland. 30 July, Queen Maria Teresa of France d.: Louis XIV shortly m. Madame de Maintenon (? 1684). 26 Oct., Louis XIV declares war on Spain: invades Belgium. 10 Dec., Louis XIV accepts Anglo-Dutch mediation.<br>**1683—4** Revision of borough charters in England. | **1683** 31 March, John Sobieski promises Austria Polish aid against Turkey. 14 July—12 Sept., Ottomans besiege Vienna. 12 Sept., Charles of Lorraine routs Turks at Kahlenburg. 28 Oct., Ottomans defeated at Parkau by Austria and Poland: Turks driven from Hungary. 11 Nov., Ottomans again routed at Stettin: end of Ottoman expansion in Europe. Marie-Françoise of Portugal d.<br>**1683—98** War between Turkey and Austria: and with Poland to 1699. | **1683** R. Africa Co. bankrupt. |

## THE EAST

**1679** Aurangzeb re-imposes *jizya* (poll-tax) on all non-Muslims: in residence at Ajmer (−1681): orders destruction of shrines in Rajputana, Udaipur, Chitor and Jaipur: war against the Rajputs (−1681).

**1680** French trading post set up at Pho Hien, Vietnam.
**1680** 15 Apr., Sivaji d.
**1680−1709** Tokugawa Tsunayoshi, Shogun, patron of the arts, and animal lover, especially of dogs.
**c. 1680** Bugis groups from Celebes Is. found settlements in N Borneo, N Java, Malacca Straits, and W Malaya: important settlements at Selangor and Klang.
**1681** 1 Jan., Akbar, son of Aurangzeb, rebels: joins Rajputs: deserted by them when Aurangzeb intervenes. June, treaty between Aurangzeb and Mewar cedes some districts: war with Marwar continues to 1709. Aurangzeb visits the Deccan: Nov., reaches Burhanpur. Wu Shih-fan, succ. of Wu San-kui defeated: end of opposition to Manchu rule. Jats again rebel.
**1682** Aurangzeb moves to Aurangabad.
**1682−4** War of succession in Bantam.

**1683** Aurangzeb moves to Ahmadnagar: operations against the Marathas. Capture of Formosa completes Manchu dominance of China. Ternate recognizes Dutch suzerainty. Mahratta raiders attack Goa: dispersed by a Mughul army.

## THE AMERICAS

**1679** 18 Sept., New Hampshire separated from Massachusetts. Western Hispaniola ceded by Spain to France. New France population *c.* 9,400.

**1680** Fourth Iroquois war. Portuguese encroach on Spanish territory at present Colonia, Uruguay: expelled by Spanish.
**1680−1726** 2,130,000 slaves imported into British colonies in America and W Indies.
**1680−8** R Africa Co. delivers 46,396 slaves in the W Indies.

**1682** July, Philadelphia, Pennsylvania, laid out. 9 Oct., Joseph Antoine Lefebre de la Barre, Governor of New France (−1685). Pennsylvania founded by William Penn with *c.* 100 Quakers: 'Great Charter' enacted as constitution. *Compagnie du Nord* formed by La Chesnaye to expel English from Hudson Bay.

**1684** Germantown, Pennsylvania, founded by German colonists.

## RELIGION & CULTURE

**1679** Philip van Dyck, Dutch artist.

**1680** Protestant synod forbidden in France. *Comédie Française* instituted. Kiangshi porcelain kilns reopened: new colour processes originated.

**1681** March and Nov., Assemblies of the Clergy held in France: additional disabilities for Huguenots, including ban on foreign study: *dragonnades*, armed force, used to compel Huguenots to retract. Protestants in Hungary granted toleration.

**1682** Newton discovers the law of gravity. 19 March, Declaration of Four Articles in France: 11 Apr., Gallicanism condemned by Pope Innocent XI. Duelling abolished in Uppsala University.

**1683−1753** Gottfried Silbermann, organ-builder.
**1683−1757** René Antoine Ferehault de Réaumur, scientist.
**1683−1760** Christoph Graupner, German composer.
**1683−1764** Jean Philippe Rameau, French composer.

| WESTERN EUROPE | NORTHERN, CENTRAL & SOUTHERN EUROPE | AFRICA |
|---|---|---|
| **1684** Feb., Congress of the Hague. 29 Apr., French ultimatum to the United Provinces. 29 June, agreement between France and the United Provinces. Louis XIV accepts truce: 4 June, Luxembourg added to France. | **1684** 5 March, Holy League formed at Linz between Austria, Poland and Venice against Turkey: the League invades Hungary and takes Pest. May, Genoa bombarded by French fleet. 15 Aug., twenty year Truce of Ratisbon between France and the Empire. | **1684** English abandon Tangier after destroying fortifications. **1684–1750** R. Africa Co. re-formed. |
| **1685** 6 Feb., Charles II of England d.: converted to Catholicism on his death bed: succ., James II (–1688). James II dispenses many Roman Catholics, enabling them to hold public office: Parliament declines to repeal Test Act: dissolved. June-July, rebellion of Duke of Monmouth; 6 July defeated at Sedgemoor: 15 July, beheaded; 'Bloody Assize' in west of England held by Lord Chief Justice Jeffreys: *c.* 150 sentenced to death: 800 transported as slaves to Barbados. | **1685** Neuhäusel taken from the Ottomans. | **1685** French Guinea Co. for slave trade founded. **c. 1685** Successful wine-growing started in Cape Colony. |
| **1686** Treaty of neutrality between England and France concerning claims in N America. Louis XIV devastates Vaudois: Geneva forbidden to receive refugees. | **1686** March, alliance between Brandenburg and the Empire. 9 July, Austria takes Buda. League of Augsburg formed between the Empire, the Palatinate, Saxony, Spain and Sweden. Treaty of perpetual peace signed by Prince Vassili Golitsyne with King John Sobieski of Poland: Russia joins Holy League of 1684: brings Russia into concert of Europe, including the Empire and Venice, against Turkey. Army reformed by Golitsyne. | **1686** Pate rebels against Portuguese: sultan taken captive to Goa. |
| **1687** 12 July, James II dissolves Parliament. **1687–91** Earl of Tyrconnell, Viceroy of Ireland. | **1687** Aug., Venice takes Corinth: besieges Athens. 12 Aug., Ottomans defeated by Austria at Mohacs. Russian army checked by Ottomans in Crimea. Janissaries revolt: Muhammad IV deposed: succ. Sulayman II (–1691). 31 Oct., Diet of Pressburg makes succession hereditary in House of Hapsburg. Peter II of Portugal m. Maria Sophia, d. of Elector Palatine. | **1687** Rif tribesmen attack Melilla. |
| **1688** 10 June, male heir born to James II of England, James Francis Edward, Prince of Wales. 30 June, seven peers invite William of Orange to assume the throne of England. 27 Sept., Louis XIV takes Avignon. 5 Nov., William of Orange lands at Torbay. 26 Nov., Louis XIV invades the United Provinces. 11 Dec., James II presumed to have abdicated. 23 Dec Dec., James II flees from England. 28 Dec., William III and Mary enter London: known as the 'Glorious Revolution of 1688'. **1688–90** French expedition to replace James II on the English throne a failure. | **1688** 6 Sept., Belgrade taken by Austria. Oct., Louis XIV invades Germany: 22 Oct., convention of Magdeburg against Louis XIV: 24 Oct., takes Heidelberg. **1688–97** War of the League of Augsburg: William III of Orange raises all Europe, except Denmark and Turkey, against France. **1688–1713** Frederick III, Elector of Brandenburg. | **1688** French expedition against Algiers. Omani temporarily occupy Pate. **1688–9** French Huguenot settlers arrive at the Cape. Systematic breeding of negroes for the supply of the Moroccan army begun. |
| **1689** Feb., 'Convention Parliament' meets. 12 Feb., Declaration of Rights defines relation between English monarchy and Parliament. | **1689** Jan.–June, French campaign in the Palatinate. | **1689** French treaty with Algiers. Port Natal bought from a Bantu chief for £1,700, but not occupied. |

| THE EAST | THE AMERICAS | RELIGION & CULTURE |
|---|---|---|
| **1684** Bantam recognizes Dutch suzerainty. | **1684** Massachusetts charter annulled. Iroquois crushed by 800 Canadian militia, supported by marines and Indians. | **1684—1721** Antoine Watteau, French artist.<br>**1684—1745** Jean-Baptiste Vanloo, artist. |
| **1685** Aurangzeb moves to Sholapur: campaigns against Golconda. English fail in an attempt to seize and fortify Chittagong. Chinese destroy Russian settlement on R. Amur, Turkestan.<br>**c. 1685—99** Mahmud Shah, Sultan of Johore: capital at Kota Tinggi. | **1685** 1 Aug., Jacques René de Boisay, Marquis de Denonville, Governor of New France (—12 Oct.). 12 Oct., Comte de Palluan et de Frontenac, Governor of New France: second term (—1699). Hudson's Bay Co., seizes Fort Bourbon: war follows. | **1685** 18 Oct., Edict of Fontainebleau revokes the Edict of Nantes: many Huguenots flee to England, the United Provinces, and Brandenburg. 8 Nov., Edict of Potsdam concerning Huguenot refugees. July, Court of Ecclesiastical Commission instituted.<br>**1685—1732** John Gay, dramatist.<br>**1685—1750** Johann Sebastian Bach, German composer.<br>**1685—1753** Bp George Berkleley, philosopher.<br>**1685—1757** Domenico Scarlatti, composer.<br>**1685—1759** George Frederick Handel, composer. |
| **1686** Oct., Bijapur annexed by **Aurangzeb**: Chandarnagar founded. **King** Sikandar imprisoned for life. | **1686** French expedition against Hudson's Bay Co.: English posts at Moose, Rupert, and on James Bay taken: Fort Nelson (or York Factory) alone left to English. | **1686—1758** Alexander Ramsay, poet.<br>**1686—1761** William Law, non-juror and and theologian.<br>**1686** St Cyr Academy founded.<br>**1686—1736** Gabriel Daniel Fahrenheit, inventor of the thermometer called after him. |
| **1687** March, Muazzam, son of Aurangzeb, imprisoned. Oct., Golconda taken by Aurangzeb: King Abd al-Razzaq receives seventy wounds, but recovers: end of Qutb-Shahi dynasty. | **1687** Outbreak of measles and smallpox precludes French expedition against Iroquois. | **1687** The Parthenon blown up accidentally by a Turkish bomb.<br>**1687** 2 Apr., James II issues Declaration of Indulgence, suspending all penal laws against Catholics and nonconformists. Unconverted Huguenots banished from France. Sir Isaac Newton: *Principia Mathematica.*<br>**1687—1762** Francesco Geminiani, Italian composer.<br>**1687—1768** Yusuf Saman al-Samani (Assemani), Lebanese scholar: author of *Bibliotheca Orientalis.* |
| **1688** English leaders abandon Bengal. Siam breaks off contacts with the W.<br>**1688—9** Aurangzeb forbids the compilation of official annals and histories written by private individuals.<br>**1688—1707** Jats again in rebellion. | **1688** Pennsylvania Quakers condemn slavery. | **1688** 4 May, second Declaration of Indulgence: Abp of Canterbury and six other bishops protest: 29—30 June, bishops tried and acquitted.<br>**1688—1744** Alexander Pope, poet.<br>**1688—1750** Apostola Zeno, Italian dramatist.<br>**1688—1760** Giuseppe Castiglione (ps. Lang Shih-ning), Italian missionary, introducer of some western techniques into Chinese painting.<br>**1688—1722** Emmanuel Swedenborg, theosophist. |
| **1689** Raja Sambhaji, Sivaji's successor, caught: executed, with others, with great brutality. | **1689** 5 Aug., violent attack on Montreal by Iroquois: island held, but small settlements ravaged. | **1689** Eleven bishops, including Abp of Canterbury, refuse to pay allegiance to William III and Mary II: known as Non-jurors. |

| WESTERN EUROPE | NORTHERN, CENTRAL & SOUTHERN EUROPE | AFRICA |
|---|---|---|

**WESTERN EUROPE**

**1689** 13 Feb., William III (−1702) and Mary II (−1694) formally proclaimed King and Queen-regnant of England. Rebellion in Ireland: 12 March, James II lands: 3 Apr., takes Dublin: 20 Apr.−1 Aug., siege of Londonderry. 21 Apr., William III and Mary II crowned. 11 Apr., Scottish Parliament sets out conditions accepting William III and Mary II as sovereigns. 15 Apr., France declares war on Spain. 7 May, 'Patriot Parliament' summoned by James II in Dublin: majority of Catholics. 11 May, battle of Bantry. 12 May, England and Holland join Grand Alliance. 17 May, William III declares war on France. 24 May, Indemnity Act, Mutiny Act, and Toleration Act. 27 July, William III defeats Scottish loyalists at Killiecrankie: Fort William built. 1 Aug., siege of Londonderry ended by Col. Wolseley: Ulster lost to Patriots. Aug., alliance between England and the Netherlands. 13 Aug., Marshal Schomberg lands at Bangor with 20,000 men. 20 Dec., England accedes to the treaty of Vienna.
**1689–91** The 'Williamite War' in Ireland.
**1690** June, indecisive battle between English and French fleets off Beachy Head. William III of England disembarks in Ireland with 36,000 men, chiefly Danes, Huguenots and Germans: 11 July, defeats James II at Battle of the Boyne: James II returns to France. 3 Oct., Irish rebels capitulate at Limerick. Scottish Protestant farmers given land in Ulster. 7,000 French regulars under Marshal Lauzun arrive to aid Patriots in Ireland.
**1690–1730** Some 120,000 Irish 'Wild Geese' take service in foreign armies.
**1691** 12 July, final defeat of Irish army at Aughrim. 4 Sept.−3 Oct., second siege of Limerick. 3 Oct., Limerick surrenders to William III's forces: French fleet and army arrives too late. Commission appointed in England to examine government accounts.
**1692** 4 Feb., treaty between William III and Ireland. 13 Feb., Macdonalds massacred at Glencoe. 29 May-3 June, English fleet defeats French at La Hogue: French lose a quarter of their fleet. 3 Aug., Marshal de Luxembourg defeats William III at Steinkirk. Irish Parliament summoned, exclusively Protestant: all Catholics excluded from office (−1829).
**1693** 14 March, William III refuses assent to Bill for Triennial Parliaments.

**NORTHERN, CENTRAL & SOUTHERN EUROPE**

**1689** 9 Sept., Peter I (the Great) takes power in Russia from the Regent Sophia (−1725). Queen-Mother Mariana of Spain d. Russia at war with Turkey. Louis XIV again makes war in Flanders and Catalonia: French troops occupy Catalonia to 1697, including Barcelona.

**1690** 6 June, Spain joins the Grand Alliance. 18 Aug., Piedmont beaten at Fleurus. 8 Oct., the Turks retake Belgrade. 20 Oct., Savoy joins the Grand Alliance.

**1691** 19 July, Ottomans defeated by Louis of Baden with imperial troops at Szlankamen: Mustafa Keuprulu killed. French take Nice, and invade Piedmont.

**1692** 5 June, Grosswardein taken by Louis of Baden. Hanover made an Electorate.

**1693** 22 May, French sack Heidelberg. 27−28 June, battle of Cape St Vincent.

**AFRICA**

**1690** Solemn visit of Emperor Iyasu I to the Ark of the Covenant in Axum.

**1691** Morocco retakes Arzila.

**1692** Faqariyyah hegemony restored in Cairo. Abuna Synnada replaces Abuna Marcos as head of Ethiopian Church: synod held to resolve Christological differences. English take St Louis and Gorée.

**1693** French embassy to Morocco. French expel English from St Louis and Gorée.

| THE EAST | THE AMERICAS | RELIGION & CULTURE |
|---|---|---|

**1689** Treaty of Nerchinsk defines Chinese-Russian boundary.
**1689—1700** Raja Ram succ. Raja Sambhaji as Maratha ruler.
**1689—1743** Syriam port, Burma, used as repair depot for British ships.

**1689—91** Alexander VIII (Ottoboni), Pope.
**1689** John Locke: *Treatise on Civil Government*, condemns slavery.
**1689—1755** Charles Louis de Secondat, Baron de Montesquieu, sociologist.
**1689—1761** Samuel Richardson, novelist.
**1689—1762** Lady Mary Wortley—Montagu, letter-writer.
**1689—1752** Shah Abd al-Latif, Indian mystical poet.

**1690** 24 Aug., Calcutta founded as an English trading settlement by Job Charnock. English factory established at Calcutta. Manchu defeat Galdan, who had attempted to set up a Mongol state in Manchuria.
**1690—1701** Fausto Cruzat y Góngora, Governor of the Philippines: 'Ordinances of Good Government' reform administration.

**1690** Jan., Louis de Frontenac launches three guerrilla raids against Indians on New England and New York border: other raids follow. Late summer, New York militia gathers at Albany to repel French: action prevented by smallpox. Oct., New England militia and fleet attack Quebec: 19 Oct., withdrawn after a bombardment as a result of smallpox. First attempt to dig Lachine canal. English fleet of thirty-four ships under Sir William Phipps defeated off Quebec by de Frontenac.
**1690—3** Near famine in New France: military duties impede agriculture.

**1690** John Locke: *Essay concerning Human understanding*. Huyghens evolves theory of undulation of light. Presbyterianism formally established in Scotland. First newspaper published in Boston. The *célérifère*, primitive bicycle, invented. The diving bell invented. Peking and Nanking made bishoprics.

**1691** Aurangzeb levies tribute from Tanjere and Trichinopoly.

**1691** New charter granted to Massachusetts as a Crown Colony.

**1691—1700** Innocent XII (Pignatelli), Pope.
**1691—1781** Bp Richard Challoner, Roman Catholic Vicar Apostolic (from 1741), and reviser and for the Bible into English.

**1692** Christianity authorized by Imperial edict in China. Lloyd's Coffee House becomes a centre for marine insurance.
**1692—1715** Nahum Tate, an Irishman, English poet laureate and versifier of the Psalms.

**1693** New charter granted to English East India Co.

**1693** Jan., French mount large raid against Mohawks. Gold rush to Minas Gerais, Brazil, begins.

**1693** *Dictionary* of the French Academy published. French church reconciled with the Pope. Halley constructs astronomical tables. College of William and Mary, Virginia, founded.

## WESTERN EUROPE

## NORTHERN, CENTRAL & SOUTHERN EUROPE

## AFRICA

**1693** 29 July, Marshal de Luxembourg defeats William III at Neerwinden. National Debt established in England. East India Co. rechartered.

**1693** Changamire conquers much of Monomotapa's territory.

**1694** June, Jean Bart defeats the Dutch fleet. 27 July, Bank of England founded by William Paterson, a Scot. 3 Dec., Triennial Act provides for triennial Parliaments. 28 Dec., Mary II of England d.

**1694** Ottomans repel Venetian attack on Chios.
**1694–1733** Frederick Augustus I, the Strong, Elector of Saxony.

**1694** Exceptionally low Nile flood: famine and pestilence in Egypt.
**1694–1720** Abortive Moroccan blockade of Ceuta.

**1695** 1 Sept., William III takes Namur. Window tax introduced in England. Office holders under the Crown excluded from the English Parliament. Bank of Scotland established. Penal code against Irish Catholics instituted.

**1695** Russian army and fleet unsuccessfully attacks Turkish fort of Azov. Prince George of Darmstadt brings German army into Spain: leads resistance to French in Catalonia.
**1695–1703** Mustafa II, Ottoman Sultan.

**1695** Changamire defeats Portuguese: then d.

**1696** Jan., English currency reformed. Feb., Jacobite plot discovered in England. May, financial crisis in England. Board of Trade and Plantations instituted in England. *Habeas Corpus* Act suspended.

**1696** 17 June, John Sobieski d. 28 June, Azov taken by Peter the Great of Russia: new fleet built. 6 Oct., treaty of Turin between France and Savoy: Savoy leaves the Grand Alliance: recovers Pinerolo from France. Duke of Savoy invades Milan: 7 Oct., treaty of Vigevano.
**1696–1706** Russian conquest of Kamchatka.

**1696** March, Saif b. Sultan, Sultan of Oman, besieges Fort Jesus, Mombasa fleet and army of 3,000 against 2,500 defenders. Portuguese gain access to silver mine in Chicoa. First Captain-General of Bissau appointed.

**1697** 9 May, Congress of Ryswyck opens; 6 June, the French take Ath; treaties signed, 21 Sept. and 30 Oct.: Catalonia and Luxembourg restored to Spain: Louis XIV retains Strasbourg: recognizes William III as King of England. Irish Parliament ratifies treaty of Limerick.

**1697** March–**1698** Sept., Tsar Peter visits German court; spends several months in Netherlands: works as a labourer at naval dockyard near Amsterdam: visits England and Vienna: fails to obtain treaty with Austria against Turkey: visits Augustus II of Poland. 27 June, Augustus II of Saxony elected King of Poland (–1733). 11 Sept., Prince Eugene defeats Ottomans at Zenta.
**1697–1718** Charles XII, King of Sweden.

**1697** Jan., Portuguese in Fort Jesus reduced to twenty by plague: Sept., small relieving force gains entry. *S. Antônio de Tanna*, frigate, sinks in front of Fort Jesus. Turkish governor Egypt deposed by Janissaries.
**1697–1712 or 1717** Osei Tutu, Asantehene: beginning of expansion of Ashanti empire.
**1697–1724** André Bruë exploring Senegal.

**1698** 19 July, Franco-Swedish alliance. 11 Oct., Hague agreement on Spanish succession: Spanish possessions to be divided between the Electoral Prince of Bavaria, the Dauphin and the Archduke Charles. New English East India Co. chartered. First Eddystone lighthouse built.

**1698** Sept., Tsar Peter returns to Moscow: puts down revolt of the Streltsy; 24 Oct., 330 rebels executed in Red Square: some executed by Peter in person. Prince George of Darmstadt made Viceroy of Catalonia (–1701).
**1698–1727** George Louis, Elector of Hanover.

**1698** Dec., Fort Jesus, with eleven survivors, falls to Omani. Janissaries cause disturbances in Cairo. Treaty between France and Algiers: Algiers renounces Holy War. Yoruba conquer Great Ardra.

**1699** English legislation destroys Irish woollen industry.

**1699** 26 Jan., treaty of Karlowitz ends War of the Holy League against Turkey: Austria gains Croatia, Hungary, Slavonia and Transylvania: Poland gains Podolia and Ukraine: Morea awarded to Venice. 6 Feb., Electoral Prince of Bavaria d. Privy Chancery instituted in Russia: mayors appointed in all towns for juridical and fiscal functions: country divided into eight governorates, of Moscow, St Petersbourg, Kiev, Smolensk, Archangel, Kazan, Azov and Siberia: standing army established. One ton and a half of gold, first large consignment, arrives in Lisbon from Brazil.
**1699–1730** Frederick IV of Denmark.

**1699** Omani seize Zanzibar. Slaves exported from Guinea required to be previously baptized. Dr Poncet and Fr Brèvedent reach Ethiopia.
**1699–1700 or 1701** Ashanti at war with Denkyera.
c. **1699** Galla raids reach environs of Malindi.

| THE EAST | THE AMERICAS | RELIGION & CULTURE |
|---|---|---|

**1694** Apr., Muazzam released: made governor of Kabul: Prince Akbar, with Persian aid, attempts to invade India: compelled to retire by Muazzam.
**1694—1722** Husain, Shah of Persia.

**1695** Aurangzeb visited by Dr Gemelli-Careri, Italian lawyer.

**1696** English factory at Calcutta fortified. Manchu again defeat Galdan. Coffee growing introduced into Java from India.

**1697** English post at Hanoi closed.

**1698—1702** Quarrels between the EIC and the New English Co.
**1698—1714** Sanay, King of Burma.

**1699** Sultan Mahmud Shah of Johore assassinated. William Dampier visits Australia.
**1699—1718** Abd al-Jalil Riayat Shah III, former Bendahara, founder of new dynasty in Johore (−1812): capital at Panchor, and, later, Rhio.
**late 17th and early 18th cc.** Many schools founded in Japan for Samurai youth: learning greatly promoted.

---

**1695** Iroquois resume raiding.

**1696** Large French force under Governor Frontenac defeat Iroquois.
**1696—7** Naval action between English and French in Hudson's Bay: French win, gaining Fort Nelson.

**1697** Last capital of the Itza destroyed in Mexico. Spanish take Tayasal.

**1698—1708** 104,668 slaves delivered in the W Indies.

**1699** 14 Sept., Louis Hector de Callières, Governor of New France (−1705). Pierre d'Iberville founds Biloxi at the mouth of the Mississipi: beginning of Louisiana. William III compels Scots to abandon trading colony of Darien, on isthmus of Panama.

---

**1694** Halle University founded. Bank of England established.
**1694—1773** Philip Dormer Stanhope, Earl of Chesterfield, letter writer.
**1694—1778** François Marie Arouet de Voltaire, poet, dramatist, novelist, philosopher.
**1695** Press censorship abolished in England. Breslau University founded. Fénélon made Abp of Cambrai: holds controversy with Boileau.
**1695—7** P. Bayle: *Dictionnaire historique et critique.*

**1696** Berlin Academy of Arts created. Latin introduced into the curriculum of the ecclesiastical Academy of Moscow. Schools set up in every parish in Scotland. Schonbrünn rebuilt.
**1696—1770** Giovanni Battista Tiepolo, artist.
**1696—1787** St Alphonso de Liguori, founder of the Redemptorists.

**1697—1763** Abbé Antoine François Prévost d'Exiles, novelist.
**1697—1764** William Hogarth, artist and engraver.
**1697—1768** Antonio Canale, known as Canaletto, artist.
**1697—1780** Madame du Deffand, letter-writer.
**1697—1782** Jean-Baptiste Bourguignon d'Anville, French cartographer.

**1698** Christians persecuted in Indo-China.
**1698—1782** Pietro Metastasio (Trapassi), Italian poet and playwright.
**1698—1782** Jacques-Ange Gabriel, architect.

**1699** Persecution of Huguenots in France relaxed. Pope Innocent XII condemns works by Fénelon. Calendar reformed in Russia. Paris *Académie des Sciences* reorganized.
**1699—1783** Francisco Vieira de Matos, Portuguese artist.
**1699—1779** Jean Baptiste Siméon Chardin, French artist.
**1699—1753** Bertrand François Mahé de la Bourdonnais, colonial governor.

| WESTERN & NORTHERN EUROPE | CENTRAL & SOUTHERN EUROPE | AFRICA |
|---|---|---|

**AFRICA**

**18th c.** Lunda copper trade expands. Khami, Rhodesia, built.

**c. 1700** Yoruba kingdom in decay. Franciscans in Bissau protest against the slave trade. Dhlo-Dhlo, Rhodesia, built. Royal bodyguard established in Buganda. Omani governor installed in Zanzibar: Omani power gradually extended on E coast. Kasbah Mosque, Rabat, reconstructed by English renegade Ahmad al-Inglisi.

**WESTERN & NORTHERN EUROPE**

**1700** 6 Apr., alliance between Brandenburg and Denmark. 18 Aug., treaty of Travendaal between Denmark and Sweden. 30 Nov., Charles XII of Sweden defeats Peter the Great at Narva. 4 Dec., Louis XIV takes over the government of the Spanish Netherlands.
**c. 1700** Following Williamite settlement, about seven-eighths of Ireland in Protestant hands. Irish population of 1½m. increased to 4½m. by 1799.

**CENTRAL & SOUTHERN EUROPE**

**1700** 2 Feb., alliance between Brandenburg and Poland. 25 March, final partition treaty of the Spanish dominions. 23 June, treaty of Constantinople between Russia and Turkey: Turkey cedes Azov and Kuban. 9 Aug., Russia invades Livonia. 3 Oct., Charles II of Spain makes Philip of Anjou his sole heir. 1 Nov., Charles II of Spain d.: succ. Philip V.

**1701** Feb., France occupies S Spanish Netherlands. 4 June, alliance between Denmark, the Empire and the United Provinces. 12 June, Act of Settlement makes Sophia, wife of the Elector of Hanover, and her (Protestant) descendants heirs to the English throne. 18 July, Charles XII of Sweden defeats Peter the Great at Riga. 7 Sept., coalition treaty of the Hague against France and Spain. 17 Sept., James II of England d. Louis XIV recognizes James III (Old Pretender) as King of England.

**1701** 18 Jan., Frederick III of Brandenburg crowned as Frederick I of Prussia (−1713). 4 Apr., treaty between France and Savoy. June–July, Charles XII of Sweden takes Livonia and Courland: invades Poland.
**1701–14** War of the Spanish Succession: France at war with the Empire, England, Holland, Portugal and Savoy: only allies Spain and Bavaria.

**1701** War between Morocco and Turk
**1701–91** Mascara the residence of the Beys of Algiers.

**1702** 8 March, William III d.: succ. Anne (−1714) as Queen of England: no Stadholder appointed until 1711. 15 June, the Coalition declares war on France and Spain. French victorious at Friedlingen.
**1702–4** Camisard rebellion of Huguenots in the Cévennes.
**1703** 27 May, St Petersbourg founded. Aug., the Coalition takes Huy. Peter the Great takes Swedish fort of Nienschantz, at the mouth of the R. Neva: southern coast of Baltic and Narva occupied. Charles XII takes Elbing, Posen, and Thorn.

**1702** 8 May, Charles XII of Sweden takes Warsaw; 19 July, defeats Poles and Saxons at Klissow: Augustus II flees to Saxony: Charles seizes Cracow. Allied naval expedition against Cadiz fails. Spanish silver fleet captured at Vigo.

**1703** 1 May, Peter the Great defeated by Charles XII at Pultusk. Hungary rebels with French support. 16 May, Portugal joins the Coalition. Charles III proclaimed King of Spain in Vienna. Fleet of 188 allied vessels and 10,000 men sail for Lisbon. Marlborough occupies Cologne. 27 May, foundation of Fortress of Sts Peter and Paul, St Petersbourg, laid. 4 Nov., Savoy allies with the Empire. 27 Dec., Methuen Treaty: Anglo-Portuguese treaty renewed with fresh provisions: Portugal imports British woollens: English begin to drink port. Revolt of the Janissaries: Ahmad III dethrones Mustafa II: proclaimed Ottoman Sultan (−1730).

**1702** Xhosa cross Kei R. and hunt beyond Fish R.

**1703** Iyasu I leads expedition against the Galla.

**1704** Apr., Tory ministry formed by Harley and St John. Peter the Great takes Dorpat: fortifies Kronstadt. Gavelkind Act prevents Irish Catholics from buying or acquiring property other than by inheritance.

**1704** 15 Feb., Frederick Augustus II of Saxony deposed from the Polish throne. 1 March, English arrive in Lisbon. Savoy occupied by the French. 15 July, Stanislaw Leszczynski, King of Poland, first reign (−1709), at instigation of Charles XII.

**1704** Many buildings destroyed by earthquake in Gondar. French burn Benguela.

## THE EAST & AUSTRALASIA

**18th c.** Tribute paid by Kedah to
Siam in gold and silver fashioned
into ornamental plants and leaves.
**Early 18th c.** Fort al-Hazm, Muscat,
built.
**1700** British factory at Calcutta
renamed Fort William: made
Presidency of Bengal. Raja Ram d.:
succ. his widow, Tara Bai. Dutch post
at Hanoi closed.
**c. 1700** Population of Madras *c.*
300,000.
**c. 1700—7** Banjarmassin, Borneo,
has EIC factory and fort.

**1703—4** Plague in the Deccan.
**1703—5** Amangkurat III (Sunan Mas),
Sultan of Mataram.

**1704** Akbar, son of Aurangzeb, d.
**1704—8** Vassals of Sultan of
Mataram revolt: first Javanese war
of succession.

## THE AMERICAS

**18th c.** Mexico still the greatest
silver producer in the world.

**c. ante 1700** Gold and diamonds
discovered in Brazil.
**1700** Feb., Company of the Colony
with board of directors including
three members of the Superior
Council set up in New France.
**1700—60** Immigrants into New
France not exceeding 4,000, mainly
soldiers and artisans: approx. 1,000
convicts on minor charges.

**1701** Council of French and Indians
held in Montreal to make peace
treaty: Iroquois withdraw,
remaining neutral.

**1702** War between English and
French in N America: Massachusetts
Governor Joseph Dudley aims at
conquering French possessions: stirs
up Indians against French: French
raid Deerfield.

**1703** Smallpox outbreak in N America.

**1704** Company of the Colony in New
France bankrupt: severe inflation in
the colony. Fox tribe encouraged to
settle near Detroit. New Englanders
fail in attack on Port Royal.

## RELIGION & CULTURE

**1700** 1 Jan., Russia adopts the Julian
Calendar: conservatism of clergy
precludes introduction of Gregorian
Calendar. Patriarch Adrian of Moscow
d.: Peter the Great refuses to appoint
another patriarch, placing patriarchate
in the hands of mixed commission of
clergy and laity. *Akademie der
Wissenschaften zu Berlin* (Berlin
Academy) founded.
**1700—21** Clement XI (Albani), Pope.
**c. 1700** Vernacular letters begin to be
sent to the Vatican in place of Latin.
Antonian heresy first reported in Kongo.
**1701** Catechism made compulsory for
all slaves in Guinea.
Society for the Propagation of the
Gospel in Foreign Parts (SPG) founded
in England. School of Navigation
opened in Moscow, directed by an
Englishman. Yale College (later
University) founded.
**1701—54** Wu Ching Tzu, Chinese
novelist.

**1702** First Arabic press set up at
Aleppo. First English daily newspaper,
the *Daily Courant*, published.
**1702—14** Castle Howard, near York,
built by Vanbrugh.
**1702—85** Pietro Falca Longhi, artist.

**1703** *Compagnie du St Esprit,* first
French missionary society, founded.
Roman Catholic bishops, vicars-general
and regular clergy banished from
Ireland: priests tolerated if they take a
simple oath of allegiance. 'Schools of
arithmetic' started in Moscow.
*Vyedomosti* first daily newspaper
published in Moscow.
**1703—27** Sir Isaac Newton, President
of the Royal Society.
**1703—58** Jonathan Edwards, American
theologian and philosopher.
**1703—62** Shah Wali-ullah of Delhi,
Muslim theologian: translator of the
Koran into Persian: begins reform
movement.
**c. 1703—87** Muhammad b. Abd al-
Wahhab, founder of the Wahhabi sect
in the Hijaz.
**1703—91** John Wesley, divine and
founder of Methodism.
**1704** Protestant dissenters in Ireland
excluded from office by Test Act.
Pope Clement XI condemns 'Chinese
ceremonies'. *Weekly Review*, first
American newspaper, first published
at Boston.

| WESTERN & NORTHERN EUROPE | CENTRAL & SOUTHERN EUROPE | AFRICA |
|---|---|---|

**1704** 4 Aug., Admiral Sir George Rooke takes Gibraltar. 13 Aug., Marlborough and Prince Eugène defeat French at Blenheim. 20 Sept., Marlborough and Prince Eugène defeat French at Hochstedt, compelling them to leave Germany. First houses built in St Petersbourg.

**1705** 25 Oct., Whig majority in English Parliament. Conscription introduced in Russia: promotion by merit, not by birth. Army gradually increased to 300,000 plus irregulars: fleet to forty-eight vessels of the line, 800 galleys and 28,000 men.

**1705** 9 Oct., Charles III proclaims himself King of Spain at Barcelona: recognized in Aragon, Catalonia and Valencia. 14 Oct., further allied force lands in Barcelona: city taken by storm: Prince George of Darmstadt killed. The French take Nice and Piedmont. *Streltsy* garrison revolts in Astrakhan: put down by a division.
**1705–11** Joseph I, Holy Roman Emperor.

**1705–1922** Tunis ruled by Husainid dynasty of Beys from Crete.

**1706** 23 May, Marlborough defeats French at Ramillies: occupies Brussels and Antwerp. May, Philip V escapes to France. 16 July, treaty of Union between England and Scotland agreed. 3 Dec., Sunderland made Secretary of State. Swedes defeated by Russian General Menchikov in pitched battle. Rebellion of Don Cossacks. Irish exports of £0.55m. rise to £5m. by 1796.

**1706** 13 Feb., Saxons and Russians defeated by Charles XII of Sweden at Fraustadt. 22 May, English raise French siege of Barcelona. 28 June, Charles III takes Madrid with English and Portuguese support. 3 Aug., Philip V retakes Madrid. 7 Sept., Prince Eugène defeats French at Turin. 24 Sept., Saxony and Sweden make peace at Alt Ranstädt: Frederick Augustus of Saxony renounces claim to Polish throne.
**1706–50** John V, King of Portugal.

**1706** Iyasu of Ethiopia murdered: succ. Takla Haimanot I (–1708).
**1706–11** Janissaries cause trouble in Cairo.

**1707** 16 Jan., treaty of Union of Great Britain agreed by Scottish Parliament. 1 May, Parliament of Great Britain (including England and Scotland) meets for the first time: Act of Union effective. Sixteen elected Scottish peers added to House of Lords (–1963) under Act of Union.

**1707** 4 Jan., Louis of Baden d. Prussia gains Neuchâtel and Tecklenburg. 25 Apr., battle of Almansa: allies routed by Duke of Berwick for Philip V: 24 May, Saragossa retaken. Aug., coalition unsuccessfully besieges Toulon: takes Kingdom of Naples. Peter the Great defeats Swedish general Loewenhaupt in Poland: 1 Sept., Charles XII allies with the Empire: takes Vilno: allies with Cossacks. Nov., Valencia and Lérida lost by the coalition. Vauban disgraced on account of *La Dîme Royale*. Formal union between Aragon and Castile.

**1708** Feb., all Whig government formed in England. March, abortive attempt of fleet under James III and VII, with French aid, to reach Scotland. Aug.–Sept., the coalition besieges and takes Lille. 28 Oct., Prince George of Denmark, consort of Anne of England, d. Oct., the Swedes defeated at Dobroie and Liessnaia. A pretender to the Russian throne, Ivan, crystallizes opposition to Peter the Great.
**1708–78** William Pitt the Elder (later Earl of Chatham), statesman.

**1708** 11 July, battle of Oudenarde: French compelled to withdraw from Belgium and Italy. Aug., English take Sardinia. Sept., English take Minorca.

**1708** Spain loses Oran and Mers el-Kebir. Takla Haimanot I murdered: succ. Theophilus (–1711): beginning of a period of palace revolution in Ethiopia.

**1709** 8 July, Charles XII of Sweden defeated by Peter the Great at Poltava: flees to Turkey: Russia annexes Esthonia and Livonia.

**1709** 30 July, Marlborough and Prince Eugène capture Tournai. Aug., Frederick Augustus II of Saxony expels Stanislaw Leszczynski from Poland: resumes Polish throne (–1733).

| THE EAST & AUSTRALASIA | THE AMERICAS | RELIGION & CULTURE |
|---|---|---|

*Vossische Zeitung* published in Berlin.

**1705** Fort of Wakinkera taken for Aurangzeb.
**1705—19** Pakubuwana I (Sunan Puger), Sultan of Mataram.

**1705** 15 Sept., Philippe de Rigaud, Marquis de Vaudreuil, Governor of New France (—1726). Autumn, treaty of neutrality between New England and New France proposed. Shipbuilding begun in Quebec. St John's, Newfoundland, captured by St-Ovide, Governor of Placentia. Failure of crops and famine in New France.
**post 1705** Wheat and flour surplus in New France exported: timber begins to be exported.
**1706** Management of Company of the Colony ceded to Messrs Aubert, Neret and Gayot, of France, for twelve years. Population of New France 16,417.

**1705** Pope Clement XI: Bull *Vineam Domini*, condemns Jansenism. Moscow University founded. Blenheim Palace, near Oxford, begun by Vanbrugh. Thomas Newcomen invents 'atmospheric steam-engine', first practical use of steam power for pumps.
**1705—39** José da Silva, Portuguese composer.
**1705—65** Carle Vanloo, artist.

**1706** Excavation of Herculaneum and Pompeii begun.
**1706—90** Benjamin Franklin, American statesman and scientist.

**1707** 4 March, Aurangzeb d. 10 June, Muazzam and Azam, sons of Aurangzeb contest throne at battle of Jajan: Muazzam (Shah Alam) becomes Emperor with style Bahadur Shah. Ajit Singh, Sikh leader, takes Jodhpur. Sultan of Johore hands over power to his brother, Raja Muda. British traders murdered at Banjermasin, Borneo. Coffee plants distributed to local chiefs near Batavia.

**1707** English attack Port Royal: possibility of treaty of neutrality ended.

**1707** Denis Papin invents the first steam boat: destroyed by a mob. Fénelon banished from the court of France.
**1707—54** Henry Fielding, novelist.
**1707—78** Carl Linnaeus, naturalist.
**1707—88** George Louis Leclerc, Comte de Buffon, naturalist. Charles Wesley, hymn writer and evangelist.
**1707—93** Carlo Goldoni, Italian dramatist.

**1708** EIC and New English Co. united as the United Co. of Merchants of England trading to the East Indies (commonly EIC): organized in three Presidencies, Bombay, Madras and Bengal. Govind Singh murdered at Nander: Sikhs, led by Banda, attack Sirhind: Bahadur Shah defeats him and Ajit Singh. Peter the Great of Russia sends embassy to Persia. French trade treaty with Persia.

**1708** New Englanders destroy Port Royal.

**1708** 13 July, P. Quesnel condemned by Pope Clement XI. Château of Mont-bijou, Berlin begun.

**1709** Jan., Kambaksh, son of Aurangzeb, defeated near Hyderabad by Bahadur Shah. Persian garrison of Qandahar massacred. Tin deposits found at Bangka, Indonesia.

**1709** Abortive New York militia attack on Montreal. Mass emigration of Germans from the Palatinate to Pennsylvania.

**1709** 23 Oct., Louis XIV expels devotees from Port Royal. The pianoforte invented.

| WESTERN & NORTHERN EUROPE | CENTRAL & SOUTHERN EUROPE | AFRICA |
|---|---|---|

**1709** 11 Sept., Marlborough and Prince Eugène defeat French at battle of Malplaquet. 20 Oct., the coalition takes Mons from the French. 29 Oct., first treaty of La Barrière. Whigs impeach Dr Sacheverell. Rebellion of Bachkirs. First Russian prisoners sent to Siberia.

**1710** 31 March and 4 May, alliance of the Hague: Swedish possessions in Germany made neutral. 6 Apr., the Duchess of Marlborough banned from court. 14 June, Sunderland dismissed. July, Russia takes Riga. 8 Aug., Whig government falls: Tory ministry under Harley and St John. 13 Oct., the English take Port Royal. Oct., Peter the Great demands expulsion of Charles XII from Turkey. Turkey declares war on Russia: Peter the Great demands keys of the Holy Sepulchre and protection of all Christians in the Ottoman Empire: Russian ambassador Tolstoi imprisoned by the Ottomans. 17 Oct., Dr Sacheverell tried. 25 Nov., new Parliament with a Tory majority. (English) South Sea Co. formed.

**1711** 16 Apr., the Dauphin, heir of Louis XIV, d. 23 May, Harley created Earl of Oxford. 31 Dec., Marlborough dismissed by Queen Anne. Having repudiated his first wife, Peter the Great m. a courtesan, Catherine Alexeievna. Senate created in Russia under a Procurator-General.

**1711–51** William IV of Orange-Nassau, Stadholder of Frisia.

**1712** 17 Jan., Walpole imprisoned in the Tower of London. 29 Jan., Congress of Utrecht opened. 18 Feb., Duke of Burgundy, heir apparent of Louis XIV, d. 8 March, Duke of Brittany, next heir apparent of Louis XIV, d. 7 July, St John made Viscount Bolingbroke. 17 July, armistice between Britain and France. 24 July, French defeat Prince Eugène at Denain: armistice between France and the United Provinces. Sweden defeated by Danes and Russians in the Baltic and Scandinavia. Execution of alleged witches ended in England. Newspaper Stamp Act in England.

**1713** 11 Apr., peace of Utrecht between Britain, France, Holland, Portugal and Savoy ends War of Spanish Succession: Louis XIV cedes to England French possessions in Canada: Philip V of Spain keeps all Spanish colonies: Austria obtains Netherlands, Milan, Naples and Sardinia: Duke of Savoy receives Sicily: Elector of Brandenburg recognized as King of Prussia: receives Neuchâtel and Upper Guelderland: Britain ceded Gibraltar and Minorca.

**1710** 27 July, English defeat French at Almenara. 20 Aug., English victory at Saragossa. 28 Sept., Charles III again takes Madrid: Philip V obtains reinforcements from France: Charles III retreats to Barcelona. 9 Dec., English defeated at Brihuega. 10 Dec., battle of Villaviciosa: French defeat Austrians: confirms Philip V on the throne of Spain (−1746).

**1711** 29 Jan., treaty of Szatmar between the Empire and Hungary. 17 Apr., Emperor Joseph d.: succ. Charles III of Spain as Charles VI. 28 July, Turks defeat Russians on R. Pruth: armistice of Falciu follows immediately: Azov ceded.

**1712** 17 Nov., armistice between France and Portugal. Peace of Adrianople between Russia and Turkey: war again follows. St Petersbourg made the capital of Russia.

**1713** 21 March, Asiento Treaty: Spain grants England slave trading privileges. 19 Apr., Charles VI promulgates the Pragmatic Sanction, enabling females to succeed to Austrian possessions: the succession to the Empire not affected. Philip V promulgates Salic law in Spain, forbidding female succession: renounces his right of succession to the French throne. Charles (III) VI's troops evacuated from Catalonia on British vessels.

**1710** Treaty between France and Tunis. Dutch abandon Mauritius.

**c. 1710** Arab fort built at Zanzibar: garrison installed at Kilwa.

**1711** 18 June, Janissaries massacred in battle outside Cairo.

**1711–16** Yostos I of Ethiopia, only Emperor not of Solomonic blood.

**1711–1835** Karamanli dynasty of Tripoli, independent of Turkey.

**c. 1712–55** Bambara Kingdom of Segu founded.

| THE EAST & AUSTRALASIA | THE AMERICAS | RELIGION & CULTURE |
|---|---|---|
| **1709** EIC establish a dockyard at Syriam.<br>**1709–13** Tokugawa Iyenobu, Shogun. | **1709–10** Fighting between settlers on New York State border. | **1709** Abraham Darby, Shropshire ironmaster, devises furnace for smelting pig-iron with coke: coal thus becomes important. First British Copyright Act. First European porcelain made at Meissen.<br>**1709–84** Samuel Johnson, lexicographer and essayist. |
| **1710** Sikhs rebel against Bahadur Shah. Chinese population 116 m. | **1710** Captaincy of São Paulo, Brazil, created. Subercase captured by English: renamed Annapolis Royal. | **1710–36** Giovanni Battista Pergolesi,<br>**1710–70** Marie-Anne de Camargo, dancer.<br>**1710–78** Thomas Augustine Arne, composer.<br>**1710–79** William Boyce, composer. |
| | **1711** Land laws revised in New France: grantees receive land without payment, subject to annual dues: penalties for non-cultivation. Abortive English expedition against Quebec led by Sir Hovenden Walker. | **1711** Royal Academy of Arts founded in London: Sir Godfrey Kneller, first President. Madrid National Library founded.<br>**1711–76** David Hume, philosopher and historian.<br>**1711–79** Richard Grenville, 2nd Earl Temple, politician. |
| **1712** Bahadur Shah d. | **1712** Massacre of Fox tribesmen near Wisconsin. Population of Jamaica c. 3,500 white, 42,000 black. | **1712** Religious war in Switzerland: 11 Aug., ended by treaty of Arrau.<br>**1712–70** George Grenville, statesman.<br>**1712–78** Jean-Jacques Rousseau, philosopher.<br>**1712–93** Francesco Guardi, artist. |
| **1713** Following war of succession, Jahandar Shah enthroned: murdered after eleven months: succ. Farrukhsiyar.<br>**1713–16** Tokugawa Iyetsugo, Shogun.<br>**1713–27** Murshid Quli Khan (Jafar Khan), governor of Bengal. | **1713** Treaty of Utrecht, in spite of ineffective English actions against the French, stipulates return of Hudson Bay to Hudson's Bay Co., and Newfoundland to England: British sovereignty over Iroquois acknowledged. Britain henceforward dominant in N America. French lose Acadia to the British. Nova Scotia and Newfoundland become English possessions. New France population 18,119. | **1713** 6 July, Schism Act in England. 8 Sept., Pope Clement XI: Bull *Unigenitus* condemns P. Quesnel: *Moral Reflections*, as Jansenist. Royal Spanish Academy founded.<br>**1713–68** Lawrence Sterne, novelist.<br>**1713–81** John Needham, scientist.<br>**1713–84** Allan Ramsay, Scottish artist.<br>**1713–84** Dénis Diderot, encyclopaedist. |

| WESTERN & NORTHERN EUROPE | CENTRAL & SOUTHERN EUROPE | AFRICA |
|---|---|---|
| **1713** Russian fleet takes Helsingfors, capital of Finland. | **1713** Catalonia strives for recognition as an independent republic: besieged by Britain for thirteen months. New peace treaty of Adrianople between Russia and Turkey mediated by Britain and Holland: France supports Turkey against Russian expansionism in the Mediterranean.<br>**1713--40** Frederick William I, King of Prussia. | |
| **1714** 27 July, Earl of Orford dismissed: 30 July, Duke of Shrewsbury, Lord Treasurer. 1 Aug., Queen Anne d.: succ., George I, Elector of Hanover (−1727): Hanoverian dynasty in England (−1914). Sept., Whig ministry formed by Townshend including Halifax, Orford, Sunderland and Walpole. Russian fleet defeats Swedes at Hangoud: Aland Is. captured. First Commissioners of Police appointed in Scotland. All hereditary property in Russia declared indivisible and inalienable. | **1714** 6 March, treaty of Rastadt between the Empire and France: Philip V cedes Flanders, Milan, Naples and Sardinia to the Empire; Sicily ceded to Savoy. Sept., Barcelona falls to the Duke of Berwick and Alba: dissidence continues: measures taken to assimilate Catalonia to Spain: Catalan language banned from official use. 7 Sept., peace of Baden between the Empire and France: France retains Alsace. Queen of Spain d.: 16 Sept., Philip V m. Isabel Farnese of Parma. 9 Dec., war breaks out again against Turkey: Austria, Russia and Venice ally. | **1714** French Senegal Co. sets up factories in Guinea. |
| **1715** 28 March, Lord Bolingbroke flees to France. 3 Apr., treaty between France and Sweden. 16 July, Lord Oxford imprisoned: *Habeas Corpus* Act suspended: Parliament passes Riot Act. 1 Sept., Louis XIV d.: succ. Louis XV, his great-grandson, aged five (−1774): Duke of Orléans, Regent of France (--1723): Cardinal Dubois, Chief Minister. 6 Sept., Jacobite rising in Scotland begun by the 11th Earl of Mar at Braemar: led by the Old Pretender, *soi−disant* James III. 12−14 Sept., Jacobite forces surrender at Preston. 11 Oct., Walpole appointed Chancellor of the Exchequer. 13 Nov., Jacobites defeated at Sheriffmuir. 15 Nov., Barrier treaty between Austria and the United Provinces: Austria gains Spanish Netherlands. Tsarevitch Alexis flees Russia to court of Naples. Charles XII of Sweden attacks Norway. | **1715** Jan., Luxembourg and Limburg occupied by the Empire. 6 Feb., treaty of Madrid between Portugal and Spain. 1 May, alliance of Denmark, Hanover, Prussia and Saxony declares war on Sweden. 2 May, Bremen and Verden ceded to Hanover by Denmark. 24 Dec., Prussia takes Stralsund from Sweden. Turks reoccupy Peloponnese. | **1715** First Boer commandos organized against Bushmen. First tax on wine at the Cape.<br>**c. 1715** Zamfara independent of Kebbi: penetration of Zamfara by Gobir begins. |
| **1716** 2 Jan.−4 Feb., the Old Pretender in Scotland: gains little support: 4 Feb., flees Scotland with Earl of Mar. 7 May, Triennial Act replaced by Septennial Act in Britain (−1911). 6 Apr. and 25 May, treaties of Westminster: mutual defence alliances between Austria and Britain. 28 Nov., defensive alliance between Britain and the United Provinces against France. 15 Dec., Townshend dismissed. | **1716** Apr., Austria and Venice make offensive alliance against Turkey: 13 Apr., war declared: Ottomans take Belgrade. Aug., Prince Eugène defeats Ottomans at Peterwardein. Peter the Great arbitrates in Poland: Oct., occupies Mecklenburg. Nov., Prince Eugène occupies the Banate; Ottomans besiege Corfu. | **1716** Treaty between Britain and Tunis.<br>**1716−21** David III of Ethiopia. |
| **1717** 4 Jan., triple alliance between Britain, France and the United Provinces. Omsk, Siberia, founded. | **1717** 18 Aug., Prince Eugène takes Belgrade. Aug.−Oct., Spain takes Sardinia from the Empire. | **1717** Prussia sells her African possessions to Holland. |

| THE EAST & AUSTRALASIA | THE AMERICAS | RELIGION & CULTURE |
|---|---|---|
| | | 1713–86 Count Gasparo Gozzi, Italian poet and essayist.<br>1713–96 Abbé Guillaume Thomas François de Raynal, writer.<br>1713–80 Jacques-Germain Soufflot, architect. |
| 1714–17 J. Surman's embassy to Delhi: EIC granted free trade in Bengal: Surat dues commuted: EIC mints currency in Bombay.<br>1714–20 Balaji Visvanath, *peshwa* (second minister) of the Marathas: re-organizes Maratha domains.<br>1714–33 Taninganway Min, King of Toungoo dynasty: reign famous for works of literary merit: U Kala, first historian of Burma; Padetha Raza, poet and first Burmese playwright. | 1714 French evacuate Fort Bourbon (York Factory) and Placentia in favour of Britain. Spanish Honduras founded. Twenty-five shops in Montreal producing textiles.<br>post 1714 British Newfoundland fishery mainly conducted by residents.<br>1714–16 First Fox War: Fox tribe attempt to prevent French trading directly with the Sioux.<br>1714–63 French shore fishery greatly developed at points of French Newfoundland and around Gulf of St Lawrence. | 1714 15 Feb., Louis XIV compels the Parliament of Paris to register the Bull *Unigenitus*: Abp of Paris declines to accept it: 28 March, condemned by the Pope. 28 Feb., Peter the Great institutes public education in Russia. Spanish Academy of Science founded. Mercury thermometer invented by Fahrenheit.<br>1714–70 George Whitefield, preacher.<br>1714–82 Richard Wilson, artist.<br>1714–85 Jean-Baptiste Pigalle, French sculptor.<br>1714–87 Christoph Willibald Gluck, German composer.<br>1714–88 Carl Philipp Emanuel Bach, German composer. |
| 1715 Second embassy sent by Peter the Great to Persia. Disturbances in W Mongolia: Tsewang Rabdan, Khan of Olot, rises against the Chinese: China conquers all Mongolia and parts of E Turkestan: Tibet taken: new Dalai Lama installed as Chinese vassal. | 1715 French war party defeated by Fox tribe.<br>post 1715 French fishing off Newfoundland chiefly conducted from France. | 1715–47 Luc de Clapiers, Marquis de Vauvenargues, moralist.<br>1715–71 Claude Adrien Helvétius, philosopher.<br>1715–80 Etienne Bonnot de Condillac, philosopher.<br>1715–83 James Nares, composer.<br>1715–89 Victor Riqueti, Marquis de Mirabeau, economist. |
| 1716 Building of Fort William, Calcutta, completed.<br>1716–23 Abortive attempt to grow coffee in Ceylon.<br>1716–45 Tokugawa Yoshimune, Shogun. | 1716 French defeat Fox tribe at their camp at Butte des Morts. | 1716 Shogun Yoshimune relaxes ban on import of works in Western languages into Japan: works in Dutch imported: Japanese translations made of medical and military works. Lisbon made a Patriarchate. The General Bank, joint-stock bank founded by John Law in Paris.<br>1716–17 Peter I of Russia again visits Europe.<br>1716–81 Giovanni Battista Beccaria, physicist.<br>1716–91 Thomas Gray, poet.<br>1716–97 Yuan Mei, author of Chinese short stories. |
| 1717 Peter the Great of Russia attempts to seize Khiva. | | |

| WESTERN & NORTHERN EUROPE | CENTRAL & SOUTHERN EUROPE | AFRICA |
|---|---|---|

**1717** 10 Apr., Walpole resigns: succ. Stanhope. George I reconciled with Bolingbroke. May, Tsar Peter I visits Paris. 17 Aug., Convention of Amsterdam: France, Prussia and Russia agree to maintain treaties of Baden and Utrecht. *Compagnie Commerciale* set up to exploit French American possessions: taken over by the *Compagnie des Indes*.

**1718** March, Earl of Sunderland reconstructs British ministry: Stanhope, Secretary of State. 26 June, Tsarevitch Alexis executed. 2 Aug., Quadruple Alliance between Britain, the Empire, France and the United Provinces against Spain. 26 Aug., Cardinal Dubois made Secretary of State for Foreign Affairs in France. 4 Dec., Law's bank becomes the Royal Bank of France. 11 Dec., Charles XII of Sweden killed at Frederikshall: succ. his sister, Ulrica Eleanor (–1720). Nine ministeries created in Russia as colleges with nine members each. Poll tax introduced.

**1718–51** William IV of Orange–Nassau, Stadholder of Groningen.

**1719** 7 Apr., the South Sea Co. charged with the amortization of the British National Debt. Abortive Jacobite rising under Earl Marischal in Lewis. 13 Apr.–10 June, abortive Spanish invasion of Scotland. 26 May, Law consolidates all French overseas trading companies in *La Grande Compagnie des Indes*. July, Peter the Great invades Sweden. 4 Nov., truce between Denmark and Sweden. House of Commons rejects Peerage Bill to abolish House of Lords. Declaratory Act abolishes appellate jurisdiction of Irish House of Lords, and affirms right of English Parliament to bind Ireland by its Acts.

**1720** 5 Jan., Law made Controller-General in France. 21 Jan., treaty of Stockholm between Prussia and Sweden. 4 Apr., Ulrica Eleanor of Sweden abdicates in favour of her husband, Frederick I of Hesse-Cassel (–1751). June, Townshend and Walpole return to office. 9 June, treaty of Stockholm between Denmark and Sweden. 3 July, riots in Paris. 15 July, treaty of Frederiksborg between Denmark and Sweden. Sept.–Dec., shares of South Sea Co. rise from £100 to £1,000: 'South Sea Bubble' bursts. 1 Nov., Royal Bank of France goes bankrupt as a result of over-issue of paper money. Russia and Turkey renew Treaty of Pruth, declaring 'perpetual peace'. *Ukase* regulating conduct of the Senate in Russia. More than 85,000 persons die of plague at Marseilles.

**1717** Ottomans defeated at battle of Matapan by Portugal. Casa de Contratación moved from Seville to Cadiz. Salt tax replaces all other taxes in Valencia.

**1718** 21 July, Austria and Venice, with British mediation, make peace treaty of Passarowitz with Turkey: Turks cede Belgrade: Hungary entirely liberated. Spain attacks Sicily: Sicily allies with Britain and France: French over-run Basque provinces and Catalonia: British storm Vigo and Pontevedra: devastate Galicia: British fleet destroys Spanish off Sicily.

**1719** 5 Jan., alliance of Vienna between Britain, the Empire, Hanover, Poland and Saxony against Prussia and Russia. 9 Jan., France declares war on Spain. 27 May, Emperor Charles VI founds Oriental Co.: Trieste made a free port. 18 June, the French take Fuentarabia. 8 Aug., treaty between Britain and Prussia. 19 Aug., the French take St Sebastian. 23 Sept., Liechtenstein becomes an independent principality. 23 Oct., the French take Urgel. 20 Nov., peace between Hanover and Sweden: Hanover purchases Bremen and Verden.

**1720** 26 Jan., Philip V joins Quadruple Alliance: renounces Sardinia and all Italian possessions.

**1720** Treaty between Spain and Tunis.

| THE EAST & AUSTRALASIA | THE AMERICAS | RELIGION & CULTURE |
|---|---|---|
| **1717** Bugis from Selangor aid Raja Kechil in attack on Johore: origin of Bugis power as Yam-tuan-Muda in Johore. Sultan of Johore deposed by usurper, Raja Kechil (Abd al-Jalil Rahmat Shah (−1721). **1717−23** Second Javanese war of succession. | **1717** Viceroyalty of New Granada created to rule N region of S America. **1717−18** French take posts from Fox tribe: Fox tribe attacks Illinois tribe. | **1717** Four Jansenist Bishops appeal from Pope Clement XI to a General Council. Union Grand Lodge of English Freemasons founded. **1717−35** Monastery-Palace of Mafra built by John V of Portugal. **1717−83** Leonhard Euler, Swiss mathematician. Jean le Rond d'Alembert, philosopher and mathematician. **1717−79** David Garrick, actor. |
| | **1718** Messrs Aubert, Neret and Gayot merge with monopoly Company of the West (−1742). New Orleans founded by Bienville: Illinois country annexed to Louisiana. | **1718** Society of Antiquaries of London founded. Lady Mary Wortley-Montagu publicizes vaccination against smallpox. |
| **1719** Farrukhsiyar murdered: 18 Feb.−27 Aug., three 'phantom emperors': succ. Muhammad Shah (−1748) Murshid Quli Khan adds Bihar to governorate of Bengal. **1719−25** Amangkurat IV, Sultan of Mataram. | **1719** Population of New France 22,530. | **1719** Protestant dissenters tolerated in Ireland. |
| **1720** Afghan raid into Persia. Balaji Visvanath d.: succ. Baji Rao: office of *peshwa* becomes hereditary (−1818): Maratha army re-organized. Tibet conquered by China. Javanese coffee crop 12m. lbs. | **1720** Louisbourg fort built. Captaincy of Minas Gerais, Brazil created. | **1720−93** Gilbert White, naturalist. **1720−1806** Count Carlo Gozzi, Italian dramatist. **1720** Portuguese clergy expelled from Bombay **1720−78** Giovanni Battista Piranesi, architect. |

| WESTERN & NORTHERN EUROPE | CENTRAL & SOUTHERN EUROPE | AFRICA |
|---|---|---|
| **1721** Jan., inquiry into the South Sea Co. 26 Jan., inquiry into Law's financial management in France. 3 Apr.–Feb. 1742, Sir Robert Walpole, First Lord of the Treasury and Chancellor of the Exchequer: first effective British Prime Minister. 14 May, George I promises to restore Gibraltar to Spain. 13 June, triple alliance between Britain, France and Spain. 10 Sept., peace of Nystadt ends Russo-Swedish wars: Russia takes Livonia, Esthonia, Ingria, Carelia and eastern Finland: Poland retains Courland. Walpole arranges for Bank of England and East India Co. to take over shares of South Sea Co. Sale of slaves forbidden in Russia, except as complete families. **1722** 16 June, Marlborough d. Austrian EIC established at Ostend. Oct., *Habeas Corpus* Act suspended. English Workhouse Test Act passed. Peter the Great revises the dynastic law, giving the Tsar the right to nominate his successor: issues 'Table of Ranks' for armed services and court: end of boyars. **1722–5** William IV of Orange–Nassau, Stadholder of Drent and Guelderland. | **1722** Hungary accepts the Pragmatic Sanction. | **1721** French annex Mauritius, re-named Ile de France. **1721–30** Asma Giorgis 'Bacaffa' of Ethiopia: great warrior, traveller and builder. |
| **1723** 13 Feb., Louis XV attains his majority. 10 Aug., Dubois d.: Duke of Bourbon chief minister: proposed Spanish marriage for Louis XV rejected. Frederick of Sweden attempts to make himself independent of the Diet. | **1723** 12 Oct., treaty of Charlottenburg between Britain and Prussia. | **1723** Sultan Ibrahim of Kilwa requests Portuguese aid to expel Omani Arabs from E.A. c. **1723** Agadja, King of Abomey, invades Kingdom of Allada. |
| **1724** 18 July, French Ordinance against beggary. | **1724** 10 Jan., Philip V of Spain abdicates: succ. his son, Louis. 31 Aug., Louis of Spain d.: Philip V returns to the throne (–1746). **1724–38** Diplomatic relations broken off between Portugal and France. | **1724** Corps of Amazons formed in Dahomey: Great Ardra taken. |
| **1725** 8 Feb., Peter the Great d.; grandson Alexis passed over in favour of Peter's widow, Catherine I (–1727). 15 Aug., Louis XV m. Maria Leszczynska, daughter of deposed King Stanislaus of Poland. Scottish Highlands disarmed by General Wade: roads system built. Armed forces absorb two-thirds of Russian budget. Behring discovers Behring straits. | **1725** 1 May, treaty of Vienna between Spain and the Empire: Emperor formally abandons claim to Spanish throne: promises support in recovery of Gibraltar and Minorca: trading concessions and mutual defence agreed. 23 Sept., treaty of Herrenhausen, guaranteeing mutual integrity between Britain, France and Prussia. Ripperda, chief minister in Spain. | **1725** Treaty between Austria and Tunis. **1725–92** Algerian fleet and commerce decline. c. **1725** Kilindi dynasty of Vuga founded in Usambara Mts by Mbega. *Jihad* begun in Futa Toro: Karamoko Alfa Ba takes title of *Almamy*. |

## THE EAST & AUSTRALASIA

**1721** Afghans raid Khorasan. Earthquake destroys Tabriz.
**c. 1721** Daing Parani and Bugis army depose Sultan of Johore: succ., Sulaiman (–1760).
**1721–77** Bugis kings, subject to Johore, exercising effective power over it, with title Yam-tuan-Muda.

**1722** Russia takes Derbend. Afghans defeat Persians at Gulnabad: Isfahan surrendered to Mahmud.
**1722–3** Turks invade Georgia: Tiflis taken.
**1722–4** Asaf Jah (Chin Qilich Khan), Mughul wazir.
**1722–8** Daing Merewah, King of Bugis, subject to Johore.

**1723** Resht and Baku taken from Persia by Russia. 12 Sept., Russo-Persian treaty signed at St Petersbourg. French EIC re-organized. Afghans massacre thousands of persons in Isfahan.

**1724** 22 Feb., Russo-Turkish treaty of Constantinople, partitioning Persia. Turks take Hamadan and Erivan. Afghans massacre Safavid princes. Asaf Jah resigns: founds Nizam dynasty in the Deccan. Shiraz taken by the Afghans. Saadat Khan made ruler of Oudh: founds dynasty.
**1724–6** Kedah at war with Minangkebans and Bugis: Bugis candidate on throne of Kedah.
**1724–7** War between Persia and Turkey.
**1725** Turks take Tabriz: all western Persia in Turkish hands. Ashraf succ. Mahmud as ruler of Afghanistan: holds Isfahan, Shiraz and SE Persia.
**1725–49** Pakubuwana II, Sultan of Mataram.

## THE AMERICAS

**1721** Parishes reorganized in New France.

**1722–4** Abenaki Indians fighting New England: aided secretly by the French.

**1725** Pierre Gaultier de Varennes, Sieur de la Vérendrye, opens up fur trade N of L. Superior.

## RELIGION & CULTURE

**1721** Patriarchate of Moscow replaced by the Holy Synod, clerics with a lay procurator-general appointed by the Tsar: church henceforward subordinated to the state. First Masonic Lodge inaugurated in France.
**1721–4** Innocent XIII (Conti), Pope.
**1721–6** St Martin in the Fields built by J. Gibbs.
**1721–5** The Spanish Steps, Rome, constructed.
**1721–71** Tobias George Smollett, novelist.
**1721–85** Khwadja Mir Daud, Urdu mystical poet.

**1722** Lama Temple, Peking, built. New Cathedral built in Cadiz. Imperial Library, Vienna, constructed.
**1722–71** Christopher Smart, poet.
**1722–1795** Robert Bakewell, stock-breeder and agriculturalist.
**1722–96** Chien Lung, Chinese artist and architect.
**1722–1803** Samuel Adams, American revolutionary leader.
**1723–36** Following ecclesiastical disputes, Christianity banned in China.
**1723–77** Tai Chen, Chinese philosopher and scientist.
**1723–80** Sir William Blackstone, jurist.
**1723–90** Adam Smith, economist and writer.
**1723–92** Sir Joshua Reynolds, artist.
**1723–96** Sir William Chambers, architect.
**1724** 14 May, French declaration against the Huguenots. The *Bourse* founded in Paris.
**1724–30** Benedict XIII (Orsini), Pope.
**1724–1803** Gottlieb Friedrich Klopstock, poet.
**1724–1804** Immanuel Kant, philosopher.

**1725** College of Nobles founded in Madrid. Academy of Science founded in St Petersbourg.
**1725–98** Giovanni Jacopo Casanova de Seingault, writer and adventurer.
**1725–1805** Jean Baptiste Greuze, French artist.
**1725–1815** Nicholas Desmarest, geologist.

| WESTERN & NORTHERN EUROPE | CENTRAL & SOUTHERN EUROPE | AFRICA |
|---|---|---|
| **1726** Feb., Supreme Secret Council of six persons placed over Senate by Catherine I of Russia. 12 June, Cardinal Fleury, chief Minister of France (−1743). | **1726** 14 May, Ripperda disgraced: Patiño in power (−1736). 6 Aug., treaty between Austria and Russia against Turkey. 12 Oct., treaty of Wusterhausen between Austria and Prussia. <br> **1726–45** Charles Albert, Elector of Bavaria. | **1726** Mahé, Seychelles Is., founded by Bertrand Mahé de la Bourdonnais. |
| **1727** 12 June, George I of England d.: succ. George II (−1760). Catherine I d.: succ. Peter II, aged eleven (−1730): power in hands of brothers, Princes Dolgorouki. Russia occupies Courland. Franchise withdrawn from Irish Roman Catholics. <br> **1727–37** Chauvelin, French Foreign Secretary. <br> **1727–60** Irish Parliament sits without elections for thirty-three years. <br> **1728** 28 Dec., Britain declares war on Spain. | **1727** Feb., Britain and Spain at war: abortive Spanish siege of Gibraltar. 14 March, Sweden accedes to the treaty of Herrenhausen. 16 Apr., Denmark accedes to the treaty of Herrenhausen. 12 Nov., Union of Mannheim formed. Peace treaty between Persia and Turkey signed at Constantinople: alliance made against Russia. | **1727** First Mazrui governor *ad int.* of Mombasa. Sultan of Pate requests Portuguese aid to expel Omani Arabs. |
| | **1728** 10 Jan., alliance between Poland and Prussia. 6 March, convention of Prado terminates war between Britain and Spain. 23 Dec., treaty of Berlin between the Empire and Prussia. | **1728** Treaty between Britain and Morocco: British slaves in Morocco liberated. Tunis makes treaties with France and Holland. Portuguese re-occupy Pate and Mombasa. |
| **1729** 21 Nov., the United Provinces accede to the treaty of Seville. | **1729** 9 Nov., treaty of Seville between Britain and Spain: ends alliance between Spain and Austria. Corsica achieves independence from Genoa. | **1729** Portuguese finally expelled from Pate and Mombasa. Dahomey made tributary to Oyo. |
| **1730** 30 Jan., Peter II d. of smallpox: end of the male line of Romanovs: 11 Feb., succ. Anna (−1740), daughter of Ivan V, Duchess of Courland: Dolgorouki brothers exiled: many Germans appointed to high positions: Supreme Secret Council suppressed: replaced by a cabinet. 15 May, Walpole and Townshend quarrel: Townshend resigns. <br> **1730–46** Christian VI, King of Denmark. | **1730** 4 Aug., Frederick, Crown Prince of Prussia, imprisoned at Kustrin by his father following attempt to flee to Britain. 30 Sept., Victor Amadeus II, Duke of Savoy, d.: succ. Charles Emmanuel I (−1773). Further treaty between Persia and Turkey. Ahmad III of Turkey deposed: succ. Mahmud I (−1754). | **1730** Ground-nut cultivation first described in Gambia. Empress Mentuab regent of Ethiopia (−1755). <br> **?c. 1730** Yao make first contacts with Arab traders on the coast. Trekking into the interior of the Cape begins. |
| | **1731** 20 Jan., Duke of Parma d.: succ. Prince Charles of Spain (−1788): sails to Parma with Spanish army escorted by British fleet. 22 July, treaty of Vienna between Britain, the Empire, Spain and the United Provinces: Pragmatic Sanction guaranteed: Parma and Piacenza recognized as Spanish territory. | **1731–42** Opoku Ware, Asantehene. <br> **c. 1731–43** War between Bornu and Kano. |
| | **1732** 11 Jan., German Diet confirms the Pragmatic Sanction: Bavaria and the Palatinate abstain. 13 Sept., agreement of Löwenwold between the Empire, Prussia and Russia. | **1732** Spanish fleet regains Oran. |

| THE EAST & AUSTRALASIA | THE AMERICAS | RELIGION & CULTURE |
|---|---|---|

**1726** War in Persia between Afghans and Turks: Turks defeated.

**1727** Nadir Quli, with 5,000 Afshars and Kurds, joins Shah Tahmasp: Meshed and Herat taken. Murshid Quli Khan, governor of Bengal d.: succ. his son, Shuja al-Daula (−1738): Orissa province added to Bengal. Treaty of Nerchinsk revised: Russians allowed to set up a legation, commercial agency and a church in Peking.

**1728** Bugis invade Perak.
**1728−40** French exports to India increase ten-fold; British twenty-fold.
**1728−45** Daing Chelak, King of Bugis, subject to Johore.

**1729** Afghans severely defeated by Persians at R. Mehmandost; and at Murchakhar: Isfahan recovered. French East India Co. establish a dockyard at Syriam. Legation set up in Peking for Uighurs (Muslims), with a mosque. Chinese population 127m.
**1730** Afghans defeated at Zarghan: driven back to Qandahar: Ashraf killed.

**1731** Renewed war between Turkey and Persia.

**1732** Peace treaty between Persia and Turkey signed at Hamadan: many cities of western Persia ceded: Nadir Quli takes Shah Tahmasp prisoner: Abbas III, an infant, made Shah (−1736).

**1726** 2 Sept., Charles, Marquis de Beauharnois, Governor of New France (−1749). English fur traders limited to two days stay at Montreal to preserve French fur trade. English post set up at Oswego, S of L. Ontario. Spaniards build fortified post on site of present Montevideo.
**1727** French fortify Niagara, to balance Oswego. Second Fox War: Fox tribe harry French.

**1728** Fort Beauharnois founded in Sioux country: French expedition against Fox tribe abortive. Caracas Co. founded. Diamonds found at Minas Gerais, Brazil.

**1730** American colonies begin to issue paper currency. Fox band massacred. New France population 33,682.

**1731** French build Fort St Frédéric at Crown Point. Hudson's Bay Co. construct Prince of Wales's Fort on R. Churchill to compete with French expansion. French defeat Natchez tribe. La Vérendrye undertakes to seek 'Western Sea' in return for monopoly of trade beyond Kaministiquia.

**1732** Royal Charter granted to General James Oglethorpe and others for Georgia. La Vérendrye passes through Lake of the Woods: builds Fort St Charles.
**1732−99** George Washington, first President of US.

**1726** First circulating library instituted by Allan Ramsay in Edinburgh.
**1726−9** Voltaire in England.
**1726−97** James Hutton, geologist.
**1726−1814** Charles Burney, composer.

**1727** Slavery first publicly denounced by English Quakers. Lloyd's founded.
**1727−81** Anne-Robert Jacques Turgot, Baron de l'Aulne, political economist.
**1727−88** Thomas Gainsborough, artist.

**1728** Imperial (now Leningrad) Academy founded.
**1728−74** Oliver Goldsmith, dramatist, poet and essayist.
**1728−79** Anton Raphael Mengs, German artist. James Cook, navigator.
**1728−92** Robert Adam, architect.
**1729−81** Gotthold Ephraim Lessing, philosopher.
**1729−97** Edmund Burke, statesman, political philosopher and essayist.
**1729−99** Lazaro Spallanzani, scientist.
**1729−1811** Louis Antoine de Bougainville, navigator.
**1730** John V of Portugal obtains right from the Vatican to appoint to bishoprics. Townshend begins crop rotation. Réaumur's thermometer invented.
**1730−40** Clement XII (Corsini), Pope.
**1730−57** Colley Cibber, English poet laureate.
**1730−94** James Bruce of Kinnaird, traveller.
**1730−95** Josiah Wedgwood, pioneer of fine pottery.

**1731** 31 Oct., Protestants expelled from archbishopric of Salzburg. Hadley invents naval quadrant. First American subscription library started by Benjamin Franklin.
**1731−94** Girolamo Tiraboschi, Italian historian.
**1731−1800** William Cowper, poet.
**1731−1802** Erasmus Darwin, scientist.
**1731−1810** Henry Cavendish, chemist.
**1732−91** al-Sayyid Murtada al-Zabidi, Indian Muslim lexicographer and commentator at Cairo.
**1732−99** Pierre Augustin Caron de Beaumarchais, dramatist.
**1732−1804** Jacques Necker, economist and statesman.
**1732−1806** Jean Honoré Fragonard, French artist.
**1732−1809** Franz Josef Haydn, Austrian composer.

| WESTERN & NORTHERN EUROPE | CENTRAL & SOUTHERN EUROPE | AFRICA |
|---|---|---|
| **1733** 29 Nov., treaty of neutrality between France and the United Provinces. British Molasses Act attempts to suppress trade between W Indies and British N America. | **1733** 1 Feb., Frederick Augustus (II) of Poland d.: Stanislaw Leszczynski re-elected (−1735). July, agreement between Austria, Saxony and Russia. 26 Sept., treaty of Turin between France and Piedmont. 5 Oct., Frederick Augustus (III) of Saxony elected King of Poland (−1763). 7 Nov., treaty of the Escorial: first 'Family Compact' between France and Spain, to regulate succession in Poland. 15 Nov., treaty between France and Bavaria. Conscription instituted in Prussia. **1733—4** War of Polish succession: Austria and Russia ally against Stanislaw Leszczynski: Stanislaw flees to Dantzig: France attempts to restore him. | |
| **1734** Treaty of commerce between Britain and Russia. | **1734** 1 Jan., the Empire declares war on France. 30 June, Russia takes Dantzig: Stanislaw banished from Poland. Marshal de Coigny defeats Austrian armies at Parma and Guastalla: Milan recovered for France: Spain, following victory at Bilonto, takes Kingdom of Naples. | **1734** Sultan of Bornu becomes overlord of Kano. **1734—44** Bertrand Mahé de la Bourdonnais, governor of Ile de France: sugar industry established. |
| **1735** 5 Aug., Russo-Swedish alliance renewed. | **1735** 3 Oct., peace of Vienna: Charles III takes Naples and Sicily (−1759): Austria takes Parma and Piacenza. Stanislaw of Poland granted Lorraine: Tuscany to Duke of Lorraine on Grand Duke's demise. 1 Dec., truce between the Empire, Sardinia and Spain. Russia at war with Turkey. The Turks retake Nish and Vidin from Russia: Crimea cleared of Russians. | **1735 or 1744** Ethiopia at war with the Funj. **c. 1735—50** Yorina Bussa, founder of Amirate of Borgu. |
| **1736** 7 Sept., Porteous riots in Edinburgh. | **1736** 26 Jan., Stanislaw Leszczynski formally abdicates the Polish throne. 12 Feb., Maria Theresa of Hapsburg m. Francis Stephen of Hapsburg—Lorraine. 13 Apr., convention between Austria and France, shortly joined by Spain and Savoy. 15 Apr., Baron Theodore of Neuhoff, Westphalia, elected King of Corsica with English aid (−Nov. 1738). May, war between Austria and Russia. Russians take Nish and Azov from Turkey: Crimea invaded. 17 Oct., second Russo-Turkish treaty: treaty between Persia and Turkey. **1736—7** Further Russo-Turkish war. **1737** The Turks retake Nish and Vidin: Russians expelled from Crimea. Treaty of Niemirow between Russia and Turkey. | **1736—43** Egypt ruled by triumvirate. |

## THE EAST & AUSTRALASIA

**1733** Nadir Quli campaigns against the Turks. Manipur gains control of W bank of the Irawaddy.
**1733—52** Mahadhammaraza Dipadi, King of Burma.

**1734** Russia surrenders her conquests in Persia. Filipino villages armed against Moro pirates.

**1735** Nadir Quli defeats Turks at Bagharand. Russians cede Baku and Derbend. Russian colonial settlers found town of Orenburg, in W Kazak region.

**1736** Shah Abbas III d.: Nadir Quli seizes Persian throne (—1747): end of Safavid dynasty: Afsharid dynasty (—1795): Shi'ism ceases to be state religion of Persia.
**1736—9** Fighting between Mongols (now called Kalmuks) and Chinese.
**1736—96** Chien-lung period in China.

**1737** Marathas, already in possession of Gujarat, Malwa and Bundelkhand, make demonstration in force in suburbs of Delhi.
**c. 1737** al-Shaykh Zahir al-Al Umar, governor of Lebanon, takes Tiberias.
**1737—8** Nadir Shah campaigns in Afghanistan.

## THE AMERICAS

**1733** State of Georgia founded for debtors and criminals from Fleet prison, London. French again defeat Fox tribesmen at Butte des Morts.

**1734** 8,000 Protestants migrate from Salzburg to Georgia. 163,000 *arpents* in cultivation in New France, yielding c. 1m. bushels of cereals. Fort Maurepas built on Rod River, off L. Winnipeg. Fifty-two sawmills operating in New France. French expedition against Fox tribe.
**1734—1820** Daniel Boone, American pioneer.
**1735** Freedom of the press established in New England by Zenger case.

**1736** Sioux attack French on Massacre Is. French expedition against Fox tribe defeated.
**1736—40** Open warfare between French and Chickasaw tribe, backed by S Carolina British traders.

**1737** Last ships from S America trading in convoy system.

## RELIGION & CULTURE

**1733** John Kay, Lancashire weaver, devises 'flying shuttle'. Jethro Tull invents horse-drawn seed drill. Non-Catholics excluded from public office in Poland. Charter schools founded in Ireland for Protestants only. First Masonic Lodge opened in Germany.
**1733—1801** Jacques Antoine, architect.
**1733—1804** Joseph Priestley, chemist.
**1733—1813** Christoph Martin Wieland, poet.

**1734** Spanish Academy of Medicine founded. The Moravian Brethren reorganized by Zinzendorf.
**1734—1802** George Romney, artist.
**1734—c. 1833** al-Zayyani, historian.

**1734—8** Royal Library built at the Hague.
**1735** The marine chronometer invented. Academy of Fine Art founded in Stockholm.
**1735—82** Johann Christian Bach, German composer.
**1735—93** Cesare Beccaria, Italian legist.

**1736—1813** Joseph Lewis Lagrange, mathematician.
**1736—1819** James Watt, inventor.

**1737** Göttingen University founded. Plays in England made subject to Lord Chamberlain's censorship.
**1737—41** First Moravian mission on Gold Coast.
**1737—94** Edward Gibbon, historian.
**1737—98** Luigi Galvani, scientist.
**1737—1809** Thomas Paine, political writer.
**1737—1814** Jacques Henri Bernardin de Saint-Pierre, novelist.
**1737—1823** Joseph Nollekens, sculptor.
**1737/8—1815** Ahmad al-Tijani, founder of Tijaniyyah Sufi order.

| WESTERN & NORTHERN EUROPE | CENTRAL & SOUTHERN EUROPE | AFRICA |
|---|---|---|
| **1738** Oct., Franco-Swedish alliance. 18 Nov., France recognizes Pragmatic Sanction. | **1738** 27 May, the Turks retake Otchakov from Russia. War of Polish succession between Austria and France: Russia intervenes to aid Austria: 18 Nov., ended by treaty of Vienna. | |
| **1739** English courts reverse opinion of law officers of the Crown that slaves become free by being in England or by being baptized. | **1739** The Turks besiege Belgrade. Russia recovers Iassy. Treaties made at Belgrade, 18 and 23 Sept.: Belgrade ceded to Turkey: Russia loses right of navigation in the Black Sea: allowed to send an embassy to Constantinople. 19 Oct., 'War of Jenkins' Ear' between Britain and Spain (−1740): Nov., British take Portobello: British fail to take Cartagena: abortive Spanish siege of Gibraltar. | **1739–46** Muhammad b. Uthman al-Mazrui, governor of Mombasa: family effective rulers of Mombasa to 1837. **1739–52** Abu al-Qasim, Sultan of Darfur: unsuccessful war against Wadai. |
| **1740** 28 Oct., Anna of Russia d.; succ. her grand-nephew Ivan VI, great-grandson of Ivan V, still a babe in arms: Biron initially regent: supplanted by parents of Ivan VI, Anton of Brunswick and his wife Anna. **1740–4** Marquis de Pombal, Portuguese Minister in London. | **1740** 8 May, Ottoman Mahmud I makes treaty with Louis XV of France, putting all Christian visitors to the Ottoman dominions under French protection. 9 July, treaty of alliance between Sweden and Turkey: Sweden provides Turkey with a man-of-war and 30,000 guns. 16 Dec., Frederick II of Prussia attacks Silesia. **1740–2** *Interregnum* in Holy Roman Empire. **1740** Maria Theresa of Hapsburg, Archduchess of Milan, and Queen of Bohemia and Hungary (−1780). **1740–86** Frederick II, the Great, King of Prussia. **1740–1817** Thaddeus Kosciusko, Polish patriot. | **c. 1740** Lunda kingdom of Kazembe established. |
| **1741** May–June, elections in England. Aug., Sweden declares war on Russia. 5 Dec., Elizabeth, second daughter of Peter the Great, with support of Preobrajenski Regiment, overthrows Ivan VI in *coup d'état*: Duke and Duchess of Brunswick exiled with Ivan VI: all other Germans executed or deported to Siberia: seizes throne (−1762). | **1741–8** War of the Austrian Succession: Charles VI leaves all his possessions to his daughter, Maria Theresa: will contested severally by Poland, Prussia, Spain and Bavaria: Duke of Bavaria supported by France: England, Holland and Russia support Maria Theresa. 18 Apr., Frederick II of Prussia defeats Austria at Mollwitz: takes Silesia. 28 May, treaty between Bavaria and Spain. 5 June, Franco-Prussian treaty against Austria. 24 June, alliance between Britain and Austria. July, alliance between Bavaria and France. 15 Aug., France invades Austria, Bohemia and S Germany with Bavarian and Saxon allies. 10 Sept., France and her allies take Linz. 25 Sept., France and her allies take Prague: forced to retreat. Oct., secret armistice of Klein Schnellendorf between Austria and Prussia. Oct., agreement between Maria Theresa and Hungary. | |
| **1742** 2 Feb., Walpole resigns: succ. Lord Wilmington, with Lord Carteret as Secretary of State. 15 March, alliance between France and Denmark. | **1742** 23 Jan., Austria retakes Linz. 24 Jan., Charles VII Albert of Bavaria elected Holy Roman Emperor (−1745). 23 Feb., Austria takes Munich. 11 June, armistice of Breslau between Austria and Prussia. | |

| THE EAST & AUSTRALASIA | THE AMERICAS | RELIGION & CULTURE |
|---|---|---|
| **1738** Nov., Nadir Shah crosses R. Indus into India. Shuja al-Daula d.: succ. Sarfaraz (–1740). Baji Rao takes possession of Malwa.<br>**1738–56** Banjarmassin fort and factory reopened by EIC.<br>**1739** Nadir Shah passes through Ghazna, Kabul and Lahore without obstruction: defeats Muhammad Shah at Karnal: enters Delhi with Muhammad Shah: following rising, thousands slaughtered in Delhi: 26 May, Muhammad cedes to Persia all territory W of the Indus, including all Afghanistan: Nadir Shah retires to Persia with immense booty, including the Peacock Throne. Kalmuks cede half of their territory to China: Ili region retained: later, fighting continues. Kings of Kandy replaced by new S Indian dynasty from Madura.<br>**1740** Sarfaraz removed from governorate of Bengal: succ. Ali Vardi (–1756). Baji Rao d.: succ. Balaji Rao after Maratha opposition. Rohillas take Rohilkhand. Nadir Shah campaigns against Bokhara: Abu al-Faiz Khan submits: Khiva taken. Abortive rebellion in Pegu. Massacre of Chinese in Batavia.<br>**1740–1** Maratha attacks on the Carnatic: Nawab Dost Ali killed: Trichinopoly taken.<br>**1740–3** War between Batavia and Mataram.<br>**1740–7** Smim Haw Buddhaketi, ruler of Hanthawaddy.<br>**1740 or 1742** Sultan of Perak attends installation of Bugis prince as Sultan of Selangor.<br>**1741** Chinese population 143 m. Famine in Vietnam.<br>**1741–2** Nadir Shah campaigns abortively in Daghestan. | **1738** Fox tribe pacified.<br><br>**1739** German newspaper begins publication at Germantown, Pennsylvania. New France populatic 42,701: increase chiefly due to natural growth.<br><br>**1740** The Havana Co. founded. Fort Dauphin built at junction of L. Winnipegosis and L. Manitoba.<br><br>**1741** Fort Bourbon at Cedar Lake on White River built. Capt. Christopher Middleton exploring banks of R. Churchill. One in every four *habitants* of New France living in Quebec, Montreal or Trois Rivières. | **1738** Spanish Academy of History founded.<br>**1738–1815** John Singleton Copley, American artist.<br>**1738–1822** Sir William Herschel, astronomer.<br>**1739** Academy of Science founded in Stockholm.<br>**1739–1809** John Augustus Eberhard, German philosopher.<br><br>**1740** Frederick II of Prussia abolishes torture: grants freedom of worship and the press. University of Pennsylvania founded.<br>**1740–58** Benedict XIV (Lambertini), Pope.<br>**1740–95** James Boswell, biographer and diarist.<br><br>**1741** Pope Benedict XIV condemns slavery in Brazil: condemns policies of the Jesuits in China.<br>**1741–1801** Johann Kaspar Lavater, poet and physiognomist.<br>**1741–1807** Angelica Kaufmann, Swiss artist.<br>**1741–1816** Count Alessandro Verri, Italian poet.<br>**1741–1816** Giovanni Paisiello, Italian composer.<br>**1741–1820** Arthur Young, writer on agriculture. |
| **1742** J.F. Dupleix appointed governor of Pondicherry. Trichinopoly retaken by the Nizam. Calcutta fortified with a ditch in fear of a Maratha invasion. | **1742** La Vérendrye's sons François and Louis-Joseph explore Dakotas and cross R. Missouri, sighting Black Hills. | **1742** Jews expelled from Russia.<br>**1742–3** R. Scientific Society founded in Copenhagen.<br>**1742–1819** Gerhard von Blucher, Prussian field-marshal. |

| WESTERN & NORTHERN EUROPE | CENTRAL & SOUTHERN EUROPE | AFRICA |
|---|---|---|

**1742–57** Count Bestoujev-Rioumine, principal Russian adviser on foreign affairs.

**1743** 29 Jan., Cardinal Fleury d. 2 July, Wilmington d.: succ. Hon. Henry Pelham as Prime Minister. 17 Aug., peace of Abo between Russia and Sweden: Russia ceded southern Finland. Russian population 14m.
**1743–57** Count d'Argenson, Secretary of State for War in France.

**1744** 15 March, Louis XV declares war on Austria and Britain: plan to invade England fails through stormy weather: Piedmont and the United Provinces invaded. 14 Nov., Carteret dismissed: British cabinet reconstructed under Pelham.
**1744–7** Marquis d'Argenson, French Secretary of State for Foreign Affairs.

**1745** 11 May, battle of Fontenoy: French defeat Duke of Cumberland: French enter Brussels. 25 July, the Young Pretender lands at Moidart. 25 Aug., Peter III of Russia m. Sophia-Frederica-Augusta of Anhalt-Zerbst. 17 Sept., the Young Pretender takes Edinburgh; 21 Sept., defeats English at Prestonpans. 4 Dec., Young Pretender enters Derby; 6 Dec., retreat begun. Penal Laws suspended in Ireland. Madame de Pompadour becomes royal favourite. Scottish clans put down by Duke of Cumberland.
**1746** 17 Jan., the Young Pretender defeats English at Falkirk: 16 Apr., defeated and routed by Duke of Cumberland at Culloden: 20 Sept., escapes to France: 'Butcher' Cumberland suppresses Scottish clans. 10-12 Feb., Earl of Bath, Prime Minister: 14 Feb., Pelham's ministry reconstructed (–1754): William Pitt (later Earl of Chatham) included. 21 Feb., the French take Brussels. 11 Oct., France defeats Austria at Rocoux: takes Austrian Netherlands.
**1746–66** Frederick V, King of Denmark.
**1747** Feb., Austria and Sardinia abortively attack Provence. 17 Apr., France and the United Provinces at war. 10 May, pro-Orange revolution in Holland: William IV of Orange-Nassau made Stadholder of all the United Provinces. 29 May, alliance of Stockholm between Prussia and Sweden.

**1742** 28 July, treaty of Berlin between Austria and Prussia: Prussia gains Silesia and Glatz. 29 Nov., alliance between Britain and Prussia. 12 Dec., France evacuates Prague.
**1743** 27 June, George II of England defeats French at Dettingen: last occasion of British monarch leading troops in battle in person. 13 Sept., treaty of Worms between Austria, itain and Sardinia. 25 Oct., second imily Compact': defensive and offensive treaty between France and Spain.

**1744** 25 May, Prussia gains E Friesland. 5 June, Franco-Prussian alliance. 15 Aug., Frederick II of Prussia attacks Saxony: enters Bohemia. 16 Sept., Frederick II takes Prague: shortly driven out.
**1744–9** Marquis de Pombal, Spanish minister in Vienna.

**1745** 8 Jan., Austria and Saxony join the Quadruple Alliance. 22 Apr., peace treaty of Füssen between Austria and Bavaria. 4 June, Frederick II of Prussia defeats Austria at Hohenfriedberg. 13 Sept., Francis Stephen of Hapsburg-Lorraine, Holy Roman Emperor (–1765). 15 Dec., Frederick II of Prussia victorious at Kesselsdorf. 25 Dec., treaty of Dresden between Prussia and Saxony: Prussia retains Silesia: recognizes Pragmatic Sanction. Convention of Aranjuez between France, Genoa and Spain.
**1745–77** Maximilian III, Elector of Bavaria.
**1746** 7 March, Austrian and Sardinian army take Asti. 21 Apr., treaty between France and Saxony. 2 June, Austria and Russia ally against Prussia. 10 Aug., Ferdinand VI succ. Philip V of Spain (–1759): m. Maria of Braganza.

**1744** Ethiopia at war with Sennar: defeated by Funj with Fur allies. Mombasa proclaims independence from Oman.
**1744–54** Janissary commander Ibrahim, ruler of Egypt.

**1745** Oman re-asserts suzerainty in Mombasa.

**1746** Plague of locusts at the Cape.

**1747–8** Funj at war with Musabaat. Dahomey finally conquered by Yoruba. The Mazrui seize Pemba.

| THE EAST & AUSTRALASIA | THE AMERICAS | RELIGION & CULTURE |
|---|---|---|
| **1742** Bugis invade Perak. | **1742** H.M.S. *Canada*, sixty-gun vessel, last naval vessel to be built at Quebec. | |
| **1743** 11 Nov., Mataram becomes a vassal of the Dutch.<br>**1743–4** Rebellions put down in Persia.<br>**1743–5** War between Persia and Turkey.<br>**1743** Tay Son proclaims himself 'Great General Protector of the People' in Vietnam. | **1743–1826** Thomas Jefferson, American statesman. | **1743** American Philosophical Society founded by Benjamin Franklin.<br>**1743–94** Jean Antoine Nicolas de Caritât, Marquis de Condorcet, sociologist. Antoine Laurent Lavoisier, father of experimental chemistry.<br>**1743–95** Count Alessandro Cagliostro, alchemist and impostor.<br>**1743–1805** Luigi Boccherini, Italian composer. William Paley, Anglican theologian. |
| **1744** Population of Bombay *c.* 70,000; Calcutta *c.* 100,000. | **1744** Peace made between Chickasaw tribe and French. La Vérendrye deprived of his fur trading licence for failing to find 'Western Sea'. French now diverting fur trade to Montreal from Hudson's Bay. | **1744** First 'General Conference' of Methodists.<br>**1744–1803** Johann Gottfried von Herder, critic and poet.<br>**1744–1829** Jean Lamarck, biologist.<br>c. **1744** Rubber first used in Europe. |
| **1745** Persians defeat Turks near Kars: peace treaty made. Treaty between Johore and Dutch in Malacca. Dutch fort at Pulau Dinding rebuilt.<br>**1745–60** Tokungawa Iyeshige, Shogun.<br>**1745–77** Daing Kemboja, King of Bugis, subject to Johore. | **1745** Second British expedition exploring N of Churchill R. French seize Canso and raid Annapolis, Nova Scotia. English seize Louisbourg.<br>**1745–1813** Benjamin Rush, American physician, politician and educationist. | **1745** Robert Bakewell improves sheep by systematic breeding. Steam heating invented by W. Cooke. Church of St Sulpice, Paris, completed.<br>**1745–1827** Alessandro Volta, physicist.<br>**1745–7** Palace of Sans Souci, Potsdam, constructed. |
| **1746** June, indecisive sea battle off Coromandel coast between British and French. 21 Sept., French take Madras: quarrel ensues between Dupleix and La Bourdonnais. | **1746** Nov., French destroy British post at Saratoga. Mohawks raid as far as Montreal: French destroy Massachusetts settlement of Northfield in reprisal. Outbreak of typhus prevents French fleet attacking British. | **1746–1813** James Wyatt, architect.<br>**1746–1818** Gaspard Monge, mathematician.<br>**1746–1827** Johann Friedrich Pestalozzi, educational reformer.<br>**1746–1828** Francisco José de Goya y Lucientes (commonly Goya), Spanish artist.<br>**1746–1830** Stéphanie Félicité de Genlis, author. |
| **1747** Rebellion in Lower Burma becomes a Mon rebellion. Nadir Shah assassinated: succ. Adil Shah (–1748). Ahmad Khan elected Shah of Afghanistan as Ahmad Shah (–1773): Kabul becomes the capital. Sulayman Agha (later Pasha) Abu Layla, first Circassian Mamluk governor of Baghdad. | **1747** French fleet, attempting to recapture Louisbourg, defeated by British. Land fighting indecisive. | **1747** Beet sugar discovered by Andreas Marggraf at Berlin.<br>**1747–55** S. Johnson: *Dictionary of the English Language*.<br>**1747–56** Great Imperial Palace of Tsarkoye Selo built.<br>**1747–92** (John) Paul Jones, American admiral. |

| WESTERN & NORTHERN EUROPE | CENTRAL & SOUTHERN EUROPE | AFRICA |
|---|---|---|
| **1747** 2 July, French defeat British and Dutch army under Duke of Cumberland at Lauffeld: take Bergen-op-Zoom. 9 Dec., convention of St Petersburg between Britain, Holland and Russia.<br>**1748** 28 Oct., treaty of Aix-la-Chapelle ends war of Austrian Succession: Maria Theresa m. Francis of Lorraine, who is proclaimed Emperor: Prussia gains Silesia. | | |
| **1749** 30 Apr., truce of Aix-la-Chapelle between France and the maritime powers.<br>**1749–91** Comte de Mirabeau, statesman.<br>**1749–1806** Charles James Fox, statesman and orator. | **1749** 5 Oct., Anglo-Spanish treaty of Aquisgran: British commercial privileges confirmed by Spain. | **c. 1749–54** Dan Juma, founder of Amirate of Gumel. |
| **1750** Co. of Merchants Trading to Africa established by Parliament. | **1750–77** Joseph I, King of Portugal. Marquis de Pombal, chief minister.<br>**1750–61** Keith, outlawed Earl Marischal of Scotland, governor of Neuchâtel. | **c. 1750** Wallo Gallo begin to be converted to Islam. |
| **1751** 20 March, Frederick Louis, Prince of Wales d. June, British cabinet reconstructed: George Grenville, Lord President of the Council. 22 Oct., William V of Orange-Nassau, Stadholder of the United Provinces (−1795).<br>**1751–3** Irish Parliament asserts right over money bills.<br>**1751–71** Adolf Frederick II of Holstein-Gottorp, Bp of Lubeck, King of Sweden. | | **1751–71** Ryk Tulbagh, governor of Cape Colony. |
| | **1752** 14 June, treaty of Aranjuez: Portugal and Spain exchange mutual guarantees. Treaty between Austria, Parma, Portugal, and Tuscany confirms *status quo* in Italy. | **1752** First SPG missionaries reach Cape Coast Castle. Administration of Mozambique made separate from Goa. |
| **1753** France goes bankrupt. Conference of London on Indian questions. | **1753** Corsica rises against Genoese rule: five regents installed (−1769). | **1753** Cape laws relating to slavery codified. |

| THE EAST & AUSTRALASIA | THE AMERICAS | RELIGION & CULTURE |
|---|---|---|

**1747** Dutch in Batavia attempt to open trade relations with Mexico.
**1747—57** Binnya Dala, ruler of Hanthawaddy.
**1747—1830** Iraq under a Circassian Mamluk oligarchy.
**1748** Adil Shah dethroned: succ: Shah Rukh: then imprisoned: struggle for power ensues. Muhammad Shah of Delhi d.: succ. Ahmad Shah. Ahmad Shah Abdali of Afghanistan marches on the Punjab: repulsed at Sirhind. British recover Madras by treaty of Aix-la-Chapelle.
**1749** Ahmad Shah of Afghanistan attempts to take Lahore: bribed to retire.
**1749—55** Third Javanese war of succession.
**1749—88** Pakubuwana III, Sultan of Mataram.

**1750** al-Shaykh Zahir al—Al Umar takes Akka: treaty made with Ali Bey of Egypt. Karim Khan occupies S Persia: takes title *Vakil* (Regent) for puppet Shah Ismail: capital at Shiraz: undisputed ruler (−1779). Ahmad Shah of Afghanistan takes Herat and Meshed. Balaji Rao makes Poona the Maratha capital as head of a confederacy of chiefs. Mon embassy visits Pondicherry: welcomed by Dupleix: Ava taken by Binnya Dala with French support.
**1751** Sept., French besiege Trichinopoly; Robert Clive seizes Arcot with 210 men: Nov., Trichinopoly relieved. Dec., Ahmad Shah of Afghanistan campaigns in Punjab: Multan and Punjab ceded. Orissa annexed by Raghuji Bhonsla of Berar. Ahmad Shah of Afghanistan besieges Nishapur.

**1752** June, French surrender to British at Is. of Srirangam. Mons conquer Upper Burma: Alaungpaya rebels against Mons: proclaims himself king with capital at Shwebo: Alaungpaya successfully prevents Mon attack on Shwebo: gains control of great part of Upper Burma.
**1752—3** Burmese capital at Shwebo.
**1752—60** Alaungpaya, founder of Alaungpaya dynasty of Burma.
**1752—1885** Alaungpaya dynasty of Burma.
**1753** Dupleix again besieges Trichinopoly. Six month war in Delhi over the appointment of a *wazir*. Alaungpaya takes Ava without fighting: gains Shan states: Mon counter-attack routed.

**1748** Treaty of Aix-la-Chapelle returns Louisbourg to the French. Anglo-American fur trade supreme on upper Ohio R. and its tributaries. French occupy mouth of St John R., in spite of English protests.

**1749** 15 Aug., Jacques Pierre de Taffanel, Marquis de la Jonquière, Governor of New France (−1752). French build Fort Beauséjour to protect Louisbourg by land. British settle 3,000 British and German settlers at Halifax and Lunenburg, Nova Scotia: first settlements to be maintained by British taxation. French claim upper Ohio valley in force.
**1750** Francisco de Miranda b. in Caracas. British build Fort Lawrence, Nova Scotia. French begin intensive exploitation of posts on Rs. Assinieboine and Saskatchewan: Fort Paskoyac founded. Population of Acadia *c.* 11,000. Population of the thirteen British North American colonies *c.* 1½m.
**1750—3** Rising of Indians in Brazil against Jesuits.

**1752** July, Marquis Duquesne de Menneville Governor of New France (−1755).

**1753** Fort Le Boeuf built by the French on the Allegheny R., with garrison of 300. Dec., George Washington, from Virginia, challenges Fort Le Bouef: Washington defeated:

**1748** Princeton University founded.
**1748—1825** Jacques Louis David, French artist.
**1748—1832** Jeremy Bentham, political economist.

**1749** Benjamin Huntsmann invents cast steel.
**1749—1801** Domenico Cimarosa, Italian composer.
**1749—1803** Count Vittorio Alfieri, poet and playwright.
**1749—1817** Abraham Gottleb Werner, geologist.
**1749—1832** Johann Wolfgang von Goethe, poet, dramatist and philosopher.
**1749—1823** Edward Jenner, scientist.
**1750** Twenty-four Roman Catholic bishops quietly tolerated in Ireland.
**1750—3** Voltaire in Berlin.
**1750—1810** William Windham, statesman.
**1750—1836** Marie-Laetitia Buonaparte, 'Madame Mère', mother of Napoleon.

**1751** First volume of the French *Encyclopaedia*, compiled by Diderot and d'Alembert, published. The Portuguese government forbids the burning of heretics.
**1751—1816** Richard Brinsley Sheridan, dramatist.

**1752** 9 Feb., the French *Encyclopaedia* condemned in France as harmful to royal authority and religion. Affair of confession tickets. 2-14 Sept., Britain changes to the Gregorian Calendar. The lightning conductor invented by Benjamin Franklin. Spanish Academy of Fine Arts founded.
**1752—1832** Muzio Clementi, Italian composer.
**1752—1835** John Nash, architect.
**1752—1840** Frances d'Arblay (née Burney), novelist.
**1753** Concordats between Portugal and the Vatican, and between Spain and the Vatican: crown patronage strengthened. British Museum founded. Strawberry Hill begun by Horace Walpole.

| WESTERN & NORTHERN EUROPE | CENTRAL & SOUTHERN EUROPE | AFRICA |
| --- | --- | --- |

**1754** 6 March, Pelham d.: Duke of Newcastle, Prime Minister (−1756).

**1754–7** Uthman III, Ottoman Sultan.
**1754–1808** Janissaries and court eunuchs in virtual control of Turkish Empire.

**1755** Apr., Admiral Edward Boscawen cuts off French squadron bound for N America. 8 July, Britain and France break off diplomatic relations. Sept., subsidy agreement between Britain and Russia. 20 Nov., George Grenville, Legge and William Pitt dismissed from the cabinet.

**1755** 6 July, treaty between Hanover and Saxony. Aug., alliance between Austria and Britain ended. 1 Nov., earthquake in Lisbon destroys four-fifths of the city: dead estimated from 8,000 to 80,000: Pombal emerges as dictator of Portugal.

**1755–69** Ioas of Ethiopia: Empress Mentuab regent: court dominated by Galla: monarchy in state of collapse.

**1756** 16 Jan., Anglo-Prussian alliance of Westminster. 1 May, alliance of Versailles between Austria and France reverses previous French policy. 15 May, Britain and France at war. 12 July, treaty between France and Sweden. 12 July, alliance between Denmark and Sweden against Britain. Nov., Newcastle's ministry falls: Duke of Devonshire, Prime Minister: 4 Dec., William Pitt, Prime Minister (−June 1757).

**1756** 26 June, French seize Minorca from Britain. 29 Aug., Frederick II invades Saxony: beginning of Seven Years War (−1763). 1 Oct., Frederick II of Prussia defeats Austria at Lobowitz. 15 Oct., Saxony capitulates to Frederick II at Pirna. Wine Company of Upper Douro created to encourage port wine industry.

**1757** 2 Feb., alliance between Austria and Russia. 14 March, Admiral Byng shot for cowardice. 21 March, alliance between France and Sweden. 5 Apr., Pitt's ministry falls: 29 June, Newcastle again Prime Minister with William Pitt as Secretary of State: known as the 'Coalition Ministry' (−1761). 1 May, second treaty of Versailles between Austria and France provides for partition of Prussia. Nov., new agreement between Britain and Prussia.

**1757** Apr.–May, Frederick II invades Bohemia: 6 May, takes Prague. 15 July, Russia takes Memel. 18 June, Austria defeats Frederick II at Kolin. 26 July, Britain defeated by France at Hastenbeck. 11 Aug., the French take Hanover. 23 Aug., the French take Werden. 30 Aug., Russia defeats Prussia at Gross Jägersdorf. 8 Sept., British capitulate by agreement of Kloster-Seven. 5 Nov., Frederick II defeats Austria and France at Rossbach. 5 Dec., Frederick II defeats Austria at Leuthen. Riots in Oporto put down with severity.
**1757–74** Mustafa III, Ottoman Sultan.

**1758** 11 Apr., convention of London between Britain and Prussia: subsidies agreed.

**1758** 23 June, France defeated at Crefeld. Russia takes Königsberg: 25 Aug., defeated by Frederick II at Zorndorf.

## THE EAST & AUSTRALASIA

## THE AMERICAS

## RELIGION & CULTURE

**1754** Aug., Dupleix recalled: succ. M. Godeheu: siege of Trichinopoly raised: French and British agree to restore *status quo ante*. Ahmad Shah (Moghul) deposed and blinded: succ. Alamgir II: *Wazir* Imad al-Mulk real ruler. Peace between the Kalmuks and China: raids by both sides follow. Chinese population 184.5 m. Moro piracy in the Philippines at its peak.

**1755** 13 Feb., Javanese war of succession ended by treaty: Mataram divided into Surakarta and Jogyakarta: Dutch EIC henceforward the greatest power in Java: about 3½m. under control. Danish trading settlement founded at Serampore, near Calcutta. Alaungpaya campaigns against Mons in Lower Burma: Dagon taken, and re-named Rangoon. Further treaty between Dutch and Johore, followed by Dutch attack on Bugis. Decisive Chinese victory over the Kalmuks.

**1755—92** Abdurrahman Amangkubuwana I (Mangkubumi), Sultan of Jogyakarta.

**1756** 21 Apr., Ali Vardi Khan, governor of Bengal d.: succ. his grandson, Siraj al-Daula: seizes English factory at Kasimbazar: 16 June, besieges Calcutta: British evacuate non-combatants: 'Black Hole' of Calcutta. Alaungpaya takes Syriam: French ambassador de Bruno executed: permission given to English for settlement at Negrais and a factory at Bassein in return for arms: trade centre agreed at Rangoon. Malacca attacked by Bugis.

**1757** Jan., Delhi sacked by Ahmad Shah of Afghanistan: city pillaged. 2 Jan., Clive takes Calcutta; 9 Feb., makes peace with Siraj al-Daula. March, Clive recovers Chandernagar. 22 June, Clive leaves Calcutta: 23 June, battle of Plassey: Siraj al-Daula flees: 28 June, Clive instals Mir Jafar as Nawab at Murshidabad: normal trade resumed. 1 July, Siraj al-Daula executed. Alaungpaya takes Pegu: all Burma now in his hands.

**1758** French reinforced by Comte de Lally, as both governor and commander-in-chief: 2 June, takes Fort St David, near Pondicherry:

constructs Fort Necessity: French take Washington prisoner, but allow him to retire. Revolt of Indians in Paraguay.

**1753—4** Bad harvests in New France.

**1754** 19 June, Albany Conference, first inter-colonial conference in America: attended by representatives of seven colonies: Benjamin Franklin proposes a federation: rejected.

**1755** 10 July, Pierre de Rigaud, Marquis de Vaudreuil-Cavagnal, Governor of New France (—8 Sept. 1760). Sept.—Oct., Acadians deported from Annapolis to Grand Pré by British and New England militia: number about 11,000. All Indians in Brazil declared free: clergy forbidden to exercise civil authority. French army defeated in Virginia. French in New France reinforced by 3,000 men. English reinforced with 2,000 men. Emancipation of Indians in Brazil stimulates demand for African slaves. British reinforcements in America twenty battalions of 20,000 men in addition to American militia, rangers and rifle companies.

**1755—1835** John Marshall, American jurist.

**1756** French reinforcements sent to New France under Marquis de Montcalm: friction between French Canadians and French follows. Aug., Oswego captured.

**1757** Feb., Canadian force attacks Fort William Henry on Lake St Sacrement: subsequently captured by Montcalm. The Santo Domingo Co. founded.

**1757—1804** Alexander Hamilton, American statesman and first Secretary for the Treasury.

**1758** June, British fleet reaches Louisbourg. 8 June, Brigadier James Wolfe in action at Gabarus Bay. 27 July, Louisbourg surrenders to British.

**1753—1808** Hubert Robert, artist.
**1753—1814** Benjamin Thompson, Lord Kelvin, scientist.

**1754** Columbia University, New York, founded as King's College.
**1754—1806** Utamaro, Japanese printer.
**1754—1821** Joseph de Maistre, philosopher.
**1754—1828** Vincenzo Monti, Italian poet.
**1754—1832** George Crabbe, poet.
**1754—1838** Charles-Maurice de Talleyrand-Périgord, Prince de Talleyrand, statesman.
**1755** Bp Hayter, sermon against slavery. Lazarist mission set up in Damascus. College (now University) of Pennsylvania founded. University of Moscow, first Russian University, founded. Nuru Osmaniye mosque, Istanbul, built.
**1755—1826** John Flaxman, sculptor.
**1755—1831** Sarah Siddons, actress.
**1755—1846** Thomas Grenville, diplomat and bibliophile.

**1756** Oct., papal encyclical ends affair of confession tickets in France. Catholic Committee founded in Ireland.
**1756—91** Wolfgang Amadeus Chrysostom Mozart, composer.
**1756—1823** Sir Henry Raeburn, Scots artist.
**1756—1827** Thomas Rowlandson, caricaturist.
**1756—1836** John Loudon McAdam, pioneer of modern road-making.

**1757—1822** Antonio Canova, artist and sculptor.
**1757—1827** William Blake, poet, painter and engraver.
**1757—1834** Thomas Telford, civil engineer.
**1757—1824** Hercule, Cardinal Consalvi, diplomat.
**1757—1834** Marie-Joseph, Marquis de la Fayette, politician and general.

**1758—69** Clement XIII (Rezzonico), Pope.
**1758—1810** John Hoppner, artist.

| WESTERN & NORTHERN EUROPE | CENTRAL & SOUTHERN EUROPE | AFRICA |
|---|---|---|
| **1758** June–Sept., British blockade French ports: Cherbourg fired: attempted landing abortive. 9 Oct., Duc de Choiseul appointed French Secretary of State for Foreign Affairs. | **1758** Sept., attempt on Pombal's life. 14 Oct., Austrians victorious at Hochkirch. | |
| **1759** 20 Nov., British fleet defeats French off Quiberon Bay. **1759–60** Dec.–Apr., abortive peace negotiations at the Hague. **1759–1833** William Wilberforce, advocate of the abolition of slavery. | **1759** 13 Apr., French victory at Bergen, near Frankfurt. 1 Aug., France defeated at Minden. 12 Aug., Frederick II defeated by Austria and Russia at Kunersdorf. 21 Nov., Prussia capitulates at Maxen. **1759–88** Charles III, former King of the Two Sicilies, King of Spain. | |
| **1760** 25 Oct., George II of England d.: succ. George III (–1820). | **1760** 23 June, Prussia defeated at Landshut. 15 Aug., Frederick II defeats Austria at Liegnitz. 3 Nov., Frederick II defeats Austria at Torgau. Torgau. 9-10 Oct., Russia and Austria occupy Berlin: treasury and arsenal pillaged. | **c. 1760** Oyo invades Borgu, and is defeated. |
| **1761** 27 Jan., Choiseul becomes Secretary of State for War. March, John Wilkes first enters Parliament. 25 March, Earl of Bute, Secretary of State. 31 March, France proposes peace with Britain. 7 June, British take Belle-Ile. 5 Oct., Pitt resigns, leaving Newcastle in sole control (–1762). 15 Oct., Choiseul made Secretary of State for the Navy. | **1761** 15 Aug., third 'Family Compact' between France, Spain, Naples and Parma. 1 Oct., Austria takes Schweidnitz. 16 Dec., Russia takes Kolberg. Portuguese College of Nobles instituted. Royal board of censorship replaces Inquisition in Portugal. Russia invades Pomerania. Trade treaty between Prussia and Turkey. | |
| **1762** 5 Jan., Elizabeth of Russia d.: succ. Peter III (–1762) (Charles Peter Ulric, Duke of Holstein-Gottorp, aged fourteen, last descendant of Peter the Great). 18 Jan., slavery formally abolished in Russia: act of the Tsar not promulgated. Apr., Britain withdraws subsidy to Prussia. 26 May, Earl of Bute, Prime Minister (–1763). | **1762** 2 Jan., Spain at war with Portugal: 4 Jan., Britain intervenes: Spanish withdraw. 5 May, peace made between Prussia and Russia. 22 May, peace made between Prussia and Sweden. 21 July, Frederick II of Prussia defeats Austria at Burkersdorf. 16 Aug., Brunswick takes Göttingen. Battle of Reichenbach. 25 Aug., Spain takes Almeida. 9 Oct., Frederick II retakes Schweidnitz. | |

## THE EAST & AUSTRALASIA

Oct., besieges Madras (–March 1759). Marathas seize Punjab: Lahore taken. Nasir Khan rebels against Ahmad Shah of Afghanistan in Baluchistan. Bugis recognize Johore Sultan and Dutch monopoly of tin trade by treaty. Manipur conquered by Alaungpaya.
1758–1775 EIC factory at Tatta, Sind.
1759 March, Lally raises siege of Madras. Col. Forde defeats French near Vizagapatam: takes Masulipatam. Ahmad Shah of Afghanistan re-occupies the Punjab. Alamgir II murdered: succ. Shah Alam II. Suspecting treachery, Alaungpaya destroys English settlement at Negrais. Government of Goa transferred to Panjim: peace made with the Mahrattas.

1760 Jan., Sir Eyre Coote defeats Lally at Wandiwash: Pondicherrry besieged. Clive leaves Calcutta. Ahmad Shah of Afghanistan defeats Marathas near Delhi. 3 Feb., Marathas defeat Nizam at Udgir: then seize Delhi: 23-4 Oct., Ahmad Shah of Afghanistan crosses R. Jumna to attack Delhi. Madho Rao succ. as Maratha *peshwa*. Apr., Alaungpaya campaigns against Siam: d. preparing to assault Ayuthia. army withdraws to Burma, his death being kept secret.
1760–1 Abd al-Jalil Muadham Shah, Sultan of Johore.
1760–3 Naungdawgi, King of Burma.
1760–84 Bugis again in effective control of Johore.
1760–86 Tokugawa Iyeharu, Shogun.
1761 13 Jan., third battle of Panipat: Marathas routed by Ahmad Shah of Afghanistan: Ahmad's army mutinies: retires to Kabul. 16 Jan., Sir Eyre Coote takes Pondicherry. British factory in Bandar Abbas closed. Carsten Niebuhr exploring in the Yemen.
1761–70 Najib al-Daula in practice ruler of Delhi.
?1761–70 Ahmad Riayet Shah, Sultan of Johore.
1761–90 Sikhs spread over Punjab in numerous war bands: annual assembly, Sarbat Khalsa, held at Amritsar.
1762 Feb., Ahmad Shah of Afghanistan defeats Sikhs. 5 Oct., British take Manila: Philippine Is. surrender. Sultan of Sulu grants EIC Balambangan Is. EIC withdraws factory from Bassein. British embassy to Acheh abortive.

## THE AMERICAS

1758 Montcalm, with 3,500 men, holds British attack at Carillon (Ticonderoga). Americans capture Oswego and Fort Frontenac.

1759 26 June, British fleet reaches Quebec: siege begins: 12 Sept., British scale Heights of Abraham in night attack: Wolfe and Montcalm killed: 13 Sept., French retire on Montreal: Quebec capitulates. First British governor appointed for Newfoundland.
1759–88 Charles III of Spain initiates administrative reforms in S America.

1760 British and Americans take Montreal: end of French rule in Canada: military governors set up by British at Montreal, Trois Rivières and Quebec. 200,000 slaves in Virginia: negroes constitute 30% of population in the thirteen British American colonies.
1760–3 5,000 to 6,000 New Englanders move into Nova Scotia.

1761 Dominica settled by Britain.

1762 13 Aug., British take Havana. Treaty of Paris cedes all of New France as far as the Mississippi: renamed Province of Quebec. Spain gains Louisiana. French raid Newfoundland: St John's captured: expelled at end of year except for St Pierre and Miquelon Is. Grenada and St Vincent acquired by Britain.

## RELIGION & CULTURE

1758–1823 Pierre-Paul Prud'hon, artist.
1758–1843 Noah Webster, American lexicographer.

1759 8 March, the *Encyclopaedia* again condemned in Paris. Jesuits s expelled from Portugal and Spain. University of Evora suppressed. First English canal built by James Brindley for Duke of Bridgewater: the 'Duke's Canal', near Manchester. *Annual Register* first published: Edmund Burke. editor (–1788).
1759–96 Robert Burns, Scots poet.
1759–1834 William Wyndham Grenville, statesman.
1759–1805 Jonann Christoph Friedrich von Schiller, German poet.
1760 Bp Warburton preaches against the slave trade. Gas lighting first used. Jesuits expelled from Angola and Mozambique. Trondheim Academy of Sciences founded.
1760–1825 Claude Henri de Rouvroy, Comte de Saint-Simon, philosopher.
1760–1842 Maria Luigi Zenebio Carlo Salvatore Cherubini, Italian composer.
1760–1846 Thomas Clarkson, abolitionist of slavery.
1760–1849 Hokusai, Japanese painter.

1761 Salamanca University refuses to establish a department of mathematics as 'fraught with dishonour'.
1761–1807 John Opie, artist.
1761–1821 John Rennie, architect.
1761–1809 Sir John Moore, general.

1762 Parliament of Paris orders suppression of the Jesuits.
J. J. Rousseau: *Le contrat social.*
1762–8 *Le Petit Trianon* built by J. A. Gabriel.
1762–1814 Johann Gottlieb Fichte, philosopher.
1762–1827 D'Arcy Wentworth, largest landowner in N.S.W.
1762–1830 António Fonseca, Portuguese composer.

| WESTERN & NORTHERN EUROPE | CENTRAL & SOUTHERN EUROPE | AFRICA |
|---|---|---|

**1762** June, the *North Briton* first published by John Wilkes. 17 July, Peter III assassinated: succ. Catherine II (–1796). Oct., preliminary peace moves between Britain, France and Spain.
**1763** 10 Feb., peace of Paris ends Seven Years War between Britain, France, Portugal and Spain: England ceded Minorca: France cedes Senegal, N American, India and W Indian possessions to England, and Louisiana to Spain. 7 Apr.–16 July 1765, George Grenville, Prime Minister of Britain. 23 Apr., No. 45 of the *North Briton* published, with biting criticism of the King's Speech: John Wilkes accused of libel.
**1764** 19 Jan., John Wilkes expelled from the Commons. 15 Apr., Madame de Pompadour d. Plot to restore Ivan VI of Russia: Ivan VI murdered. British Sugar Act attempts to halt illicit trade.
**1764–1845** (2nd) Earl Grey, statesman and reformer.

**1762** 29 Oct., battle of Freiberg. 1 Nov., French capitulate at Cassel: right bank of the Rhine evacuated. 24 Nov., truce between Austria, Prussia and Saxony.
**1763** 17 Jan., Frederick August III of Poland d.: *interregnum* to 1764. 15 Feb., peace of Hubertsberg between Austria and Prussia: Silesia ceded.

**1763–9** Senegambia made a British Crown Colony.
**c. 1763–80** Kyambugu, ruler of Buganda: first record of trade with east coast.

**1764** 11 Apr., Prusso-Russian treaty on Poland. 7 Sept., Stanislaw II Poniatowski elected King of Poland (–1795).

**1765** 23 March, Stamp Act passed levelling duties on British North American colonies. 16 July–1766, Marquess of Rockingham, Prime Minister. Dec., the Dauphin d.: Louis, his son (later Louis XVII), heir to France. Catherine II confirms privileges of Russian nobility.

**1765** Bank of Berlin instituted.
**1765–90** Joseph II, Holy Roman Emperor: Maria Theresa of Austria, his mother, co-regent.

**1766** 23 Feb., Lorraine definitively annexed to France. 11 March, Stamp Act repealed. Declaratory Act asserts right to tax British North American colonies. 12 July, William Pitt, Prime Minister: Aug., elevated as Earl of Chatham. Cossack rebellion put down.
**1766–1808** Christian VII, King of Denmark and Norway.
**1767** Dec.–1770 Duke of Grafton, Prime Minister. Denmark acquires Schleswig-Holstein.
**1767–8** Legislative Commission appointed by Catherine II: issues *Nakaze* (Instruction), setting out fundamental rights, causing a sensation in Europe: assumes right to protect Orthodox in Poland.
**1767–74** Marquess Townshend, Viceroy of Ireland.
**1768** 28 March, John Wilkes elected for Middlesex. 8 June, Wilkes imprisoned for libel.

**1766** 'Esquilache' revolt in Spain.

**1768** 15 May, treaty of Versailles: Corsica ceded to Genoa by France. Oct., Turkey declares war on Russia in interests of Poland (–1774).

**1767** Treaty between Morocco and Spain.

**1768–76** Babba Zaki, King of Kano: royal guard of musketeers established
**c. 1768** Yao on L. Malawi trading with Kilwa.

# THE EAST & AUSTRALASIA        THE AMERICAS        RELIGION & CULTURE

**1763** Haidar Ali, an adventurer, seizes Kanara, Mysore. Four battles between Mir Kasim and the EIC. English factory founded at Bushire. Pondicherrry restored to the French as an open town.
**1763-76** Hsinbyushin, King of Burma.
**1763-83** Burmese capital at Ava.

**1764** 22 Oct., EIC defeat Mir Kasim at Baksar: British now in complete control of Bengal. Ahmad Shah of Afghanistan visits Lahore: recalled to Afghanistan to quell civil war. Sikhs occupy Lahore. Clive appointed Governor and Commander-in-Chief of Bengal. Haidar Ali seizes throne of Mysore. Philippine Is. returned to Spain by Britain. Second British embassy to Acheh abortive.

**1765** 3 May, Clive returns to Calcutta: Shah Alam confers right to raise taxation and dispense justice in Bengal on the EIC. Muhammad b. Saud, founding ancestor of the Saudi Arabian dynasty, d.: supporter of Muhammad b. Abd al-Wahhab. Chinese attack on Burma: decisively repelled.

**1766** Jan., Burmese attack Siam: decisive battle outside Ayuthia. 12 Nov., Nizam Ali of Hyderabad cedes Northern Circars, Madras, to EIC. Treaty between Dutch and King Kirti Siri of Kandy, increasing Dutch area of control in Ceylon. Chinese army defeated in Upper Burma.

**1767** Feb., Clive retires. Aug., Burma invades Siam. Patiala Sikh state founded by Amar Singh. Ahmad Shah of Afghanistan abandons central Punjab, retaining Peshawar. Chinese army invades Burma, reaching thirty miles N of Ava. Burmese take Ayuthia: booty taken back to Ava.

**1768** Nepal conquered by the Gurkhas. French open dockyard at Rangoon. Chinese army retreats to Yunnan.

**1763** 7 Oct., royal proclamation establishes boundaries of Province of Quebec. Indian confederacy led by Chief Pontiac attacks Virginia: peace restored by military. Brazilian capital moved from Bahia to Rio de Janeiro. Coalition of Indian tribes defeated by British Americans at Bushy Run. British Government enacts 'Proclamation Line', making the Appalachians the boundary of the American colonists.
**1764** 10 Aug., military government of Province of Quebec ended; 13 Aug., James Murray sworn first governor: Roman Catholics denied public office in spite of protests: English legal system partially instituted. Britain doubles tax on continental goods shipped to America. Parliament forbids issue of paper money by colonies. Tax placed on West Indian sugar entering British North American colonies. 140,000 negroes in Jamaica.
**1765** 23 March, Stamp Act taxes newspapers, legal and other documents in British colonies: rioting follows in Massachusetts, New York, N Carolina and Virginia. Sons of Liberty organization established. José de Galvéz sent as Visitor-General to Mexico: government reorganized and reformed.

**1766** Duties imposed on commodities entering British North America, including tea, paper and paint. Britain occupies the Falkland Is. Murray withdrawn from Quebec: Col. Guy Carleton governor *ad int.*

**1767** Jesuits banished from America. Townshend Act: imports of tea, paper, glass and painters' colours taxed in the American colonies.

**1768** 26 Oct., Col. G. Carleton confirmed as Governor of Quebec: new policy of concession to Canadians.

**1763** Primary education made compulsory in Prussia.
**1763-1804** George Morland, artist.
**1763-1817** Aimée Dubucq de Rivery, mother of Sultan Mahmud II.
**1763-1814** Marie-Joseph Tascher de la Pagerie, later Vicomtesse de Beauharnais, later Empress Joséphine.
**1763-1820** Joseph Fouché, French Minister of Police.
**1763-1850** Amir Bashir, Prince of the Lebanon.
**1764** Ecclesiastical mortmain abolished by Catherine II: 900,000 peasants freed in Russia. Winter Palace built in St Petersbourg.
James Watt invents condenser and air-pump, making improved steam engine.
**1764-90** The Pantheon built at Paris.
**1764-1850** Johann Gottfried Schadow, German sculptor.
**1764-1842** Church of La Madeleine, Paris, built.
**1765** Law Officers of the British Crown rule N American Roman Catholics are not subject to English penal laws and disabilities. National Theatre founded in Warsaw. Economic Societies of Friends of the Country founded in Basque territories. Hargreaves invents the 'Spinning Jenny'.
**1765-1805** Francisco Vieira, Portuguese artist.
**1765-1816** Philip Quaque, first Ghanaian Anglican deacon.
**1765-1838** Thomas Attwood, composer.
**1766** Hydrogen discovered by Cavendish.
**1766-1817** Anne Louise Germaine (Necker), Baronne de Staël-Holstein, novelist.
**1766-1834** Thomas Robert Malthus, economist.
**1766-1837** Samuel Wesley, composer.
**1766-1844** John Dalton, scientist.
**1766-1835** William Cobbett, political journalist.
**1767** 27 Feb., the Jesuits expelled from Spain: 10,000 shipped to Italy from Spain and the Indies: May, expelled from France. Emperor Joseph II requires papal orders to be submitted to him before publication.
**1767-1835** Karl Wilhelm von Humboldt, philologist.
**1767-1845** August Wilhelm von Schlegel, poet, translator and critic.
**1767-1849** Maria Edgeworth, novelist.
**1768** Catherine II secularizes Russian church property.
**1768-1834** Friedrich Daniel Ernst Schliermacher, theologian and philosopher.

| WESTERN & NORTHERN EUROPE | CENTRAL & SOUTHERN EUROPE | AFRICA |
|---|---|---|

**1768** Irish Octennial Act passed.

**1769** 21 Jan.–1772 21 Jan., *Letters of Junius* appear in the London *Public Advertiser*, discrediting Grafton ministry: possibly by Sir Philip Francis. 3 Feb., Wilkes again expelled from the House of Commons: 16 Feb., 16 March and 13 Apr., again re-elected: rejected each time by the House of Commons. French EIC dissolved.
**1769–74** Madame du Barry, mistress of Louis XV.
**1769–1822** Henry Robert, Viscount Castlereagh, statesman.

**1770** 28 Jan., Duke of Grafton resigns: March, Lord North (later Earl of Guilford), Prime Minister (–1782). 16 May, marriage between the Dauphin and Marie-Antoinette of Austria. 24 Dec., Choiseul dismissed. Wilkes elected Lord Mayor of London.
**1770–2** Struensee, chief minister, reforms government in Denmark.

**1771** 20 Jan., Parliament of Paris exiled. 23 Feb., administration of justice reformed in France. Troops repel rising of serfs from the Oura mines. Serious outbreak of plague in Moscow. Maupeou, chief minister of France.
**1771–92** Gustav III, King of Sweden.

**1772** Apr., the Bonnets seize power in Sweden. 19 Aug., Gustav III of Sweden regains power by *coup d'état*. 28 Oct., Struensee executed. Royal Marriage Act in England. Patriot Party formed in Irish Parliament, aimed at obtaining a 'free' constitution. Lord Mansfield rules that the status of slavery is unknown in the law of England.

**1773** Feb., Franco-Swedish alliance renewed. Trial and acquittal of Robert Clive. East India Co. Regulating Act.

**1768** Russo-Polish treaty guarantees integrity of Poland.
**1769** Aug., Frederick II of Prussia and Emperor Joseph II meet at Niesse, Silesia. 13 Aug., Napoleon Buonaparte b. (–1821). Russia occupies Rumania.

**1770** 5-6 July, Russian fleet defeats Turks off Tsheshme, near Chios: complete Turkish Mediterranean fleet destroyed. Sept., meeting between Frederick II and Joseph II at Neustadt.

**1771** The Russians reoccupy the Crimea: July, alliance between Austria and Turkey. Russians take Bender and penetrate Bulgaria. Serfdom abolished in Savoy.

**1772** 5 Aug., first partition of Poland: Austria takes E Galicia and Lodomeria; Prussia: W Prussia, except for Danzig, and Ermland; Russia: territory E of Rs Dvina and Dnieper. Russian armies advance in Bulgaria. Cossack privileges abolished: revolt put down. Negotiations for peace between Russia and Turkey begun.

**1773** 19 Apr., Polish Diet compelled to endorse partition.

**1769** Ali Bey, Turkish viceroy of Egypt, declares Egypt independent: makes treaty with Russia against Turkey. Venice sends punitive expedition against Tunisian pirates.
**1769–70** Abortive Portuguese expedition to recover Mombasa.
**1769–72** James Bruce of Kinnaird in Ethiopia.
**1769–1777** Takla Haimanot II of Ethiopia.
**1769–1855** Period of *masafent*, or regional kings, in Ethiopia.

**1770** Ali Bey, governor of Egypt, seizes Syria and Hijaz.
**c. 1770** Ashanti seize Gomba.
**1770** Bizerta bombarded by the French fleet.

**1771** Emperor of Ethiopia fights three battles against Ras Michael Sehul at Sarbakuse.
**1771–85** J. van Plettenburg, Governor of the Cape.

**1772** Ali Bey superseded in Egypt by Abu al-Dhahab.

**1773** Abu al-Dhahab becomes viceroy of Egypt: struggle amongst Mamluks for power (–1798).

## THE EAST & AUSTRALASIA

**1769** Treaty of mutual assistance between EIC in Madras and Haidar Ali of Mysore. Burma made a dependency of China by Manchu general Ming Jui. First Supervisors of revenue appointed by the EIC in Bengal. Captain James Cook reaches New Zealand in *Endeavour*: accompanied by (Sir) Joseph Banks and Daniel Solander, botanists. Population of Maoris estimated at 100,000: probably 200,000. Chinese army again invades Burma: Chinese, after serious defeat at Kaungton, sue for peace.

**1770** Famine in Bengal: one-third of the rural population die. British factory in Bushire moved to Basra. Army of Ali Bey takes Mecca: Sharif of Mecca recognizes him as Sultan of Egypt. Capt. James Cook, in *Endeavour*, maps E coast of Australia: accompanied by (Sir) Joseph Banks: Tahiti visited: landing made at Stingray Harbour (later Botany Bay): Great Barrier Reef described: New Holland (later New South Wales) claimed for Britain. Siam at war with Burma. Bugis under Raja Haji invade Kedah: capital temporarily occupied. Abortive rebellion in Manipur against Burma.

**1770—6** Simón de Anda y Salazar, Governor of the Philippines: successful economic reforms.

**?1770—1812** Mahmud Shah, Sultan of Johore.

**1771** Marathas persuade Shah Alam to accept their protection over Delhi: Kora and Allahabad ceded to them. Damascus and other Syrian cities taken by Ali Bey's army under Abu al-Dhahab: Abu al-Dhahab then deserts Ali Bey and negotiates with the Porte. Talks between Francis Light and the Sultan of Kedah: British protection against Siam sought. Bugis from Selangor invade Kedah: sultan takes refuge in Perlis. Tay Son revolution in Vietnam (—1802).

**1772** Jan.—**1782** Mirza Najaf Khan, effective ruler of Delhi.

**1772** Apr., Ali Bey flees from Egypt to Acre. al-Shaykh Zahir al-Umar al-Al occupies Sidon: defeated by governor of Syria. Warren Hastings appointed Governor of Bengal Presidency: instructed to reform administration. Edward Monckton sent by EIC to negotiate with Sultan of Kedah: third embassy to Acheh: both abortive.

**1773** Sept., treaty of Benares: Allahabad and Kora ceded by Marathas to EIC.

## THE AMERICAS

**1769** St John Is. made a separate colony. California occupied by Spaniards.

**1770** 5 March, 'Boston Massacre': three persons killed by troops in a mêlée. 'Battle of Golden Hill': friction between townsfolk and soldiery in New York. Townshend Act repealed, except for tea duty. Volcano Izalco appears in El Salvador. Carleton returns to England (—1774).

**c. 1770** Boston foreign trade employing 600 vessels annually.

**1771—9** Antonio María Bucareli, Viceroy of New Spain.

**1772** 28 Feb., Boston Assembly threaten to secede from Britain unless colonists' rights are protected: Lord North removes all taxes except that on tea. Committee of Correspondence set up in Massachusetts. HMS *Gaspee*, customs vessel, attacked by citizens after running ashore near Providence, Rhode Is.

**1773** Lord North grants monopoly of tea trade with American colonies to the East India Co.

## RELIGION & CULTURE

**1768—1848** François René, Vicomte de Chateaubriand, writer.

**1769** Inquisition reformed in Portugal. Richard Arkwright patents Spinning Frame.

**1769—70** First steam truck invented.

**1769—74** Clement XIV (Ganganelli), Pope.

**1769—1821** John Crome, artist.

**1769—1830** Sir Thomas Lawrence, artist.

**1769—1838** William Smith, engineer and geologist: 'father' of English geology.

**1769—1859** Friedrich Heinrich Alexander von Humboldt, naturalist and traveller.

**1770—1827** Ludvig van Beethoven, German composer. George Canning, statesman, journalist and poet.

**1770—1831** Georg Wilhelm Friedrich Hegel, philosopher.

**1770—1833** Ram Moha Roy, Indian scholar and reformer.

**1770—1837** François Gérard, French artist.

**1770—1850** William Wordsworth, poet.

**1770—1845** Elizabeth Vassal Fox, Lady Holland, political hostess.

**1770—1844** Bertel Thorvaldsen, Danish sculptor.

**1770—1861** Adam Czartoryski, Polish statesman.

**1771** Bogland Act begins to afford relief to Irish Catholics. *Encyclopaedia Britannica* first published. Monge invents analytical geometry. Spanish edict requires modernization of textbooks: professors to be appointed by competition.

**1771—1806** Mungo Park, explorer.

**1771—1832** Sir Walter Scott, novelist and poet.

**1771—1851** John Lingard, historian.

**1771—1855** Dorothy Wordsworth, diarist.

**1771—1858** Robert Owen, English social reformer.

**1772** Coimbra University reformed. Nitrogen discovered by Rutherford.

**1772—1823** David Ricardo, economist.

**1772—1829** Karl Wilhelm Friedrich Schlegel, poet, critic and scholar.

**1772—1834** Samuel Taylor Coleridge, poet, critic and philosopher.

**1773** 21 July, Society of Jesus suppressed by the Pope. Grand Orient Lodge established in France.

| WESTERN & NORTHERN EUROPE | CENTRAL & SOUTHERN EUROPE | AFRICA |
|---|---|---|
| **1773** Pougatchev, a pretender posing as Peter III of Russia, raises an army: fails to take Orenburg: put down by army under Bibikov. | **1773** 16 Oct., Oldenburg ceded by Denmark to Russia. Russia checked in Moldavia. | **1773** Successful rising in Kilwa against additional taxation. |
| **1774** 10 May, Louis XV d.: succ. his grandson, Louis XVI (−1793): Malesherbes, Turgot and Maurepas, ministers: programme of moderate reform begun. 12 Nov., Parliament of Paris restored. Pougatchev executed in Red Square, Moscow. **1774–6** Potemkin, favourite of Catherine II. | **1774** 21 July, treaty of Kutchuk-Kainardji between Russia and Turkey: Russia obtains right to navigate in the Black Sea and freedom of passage of the Dardanelles; commercial privileges; freedom for Russians to make pilgrimages to the Holy Sepulchre; right to protect Christians in Ottoman Empire; right to build a church at Pera. **1774–89** Abd al-Hamid I, Ottoman Sultan. | **1774** All Christian slaves liberated in Morocco. |
| **1775** Apr.–May, famine in Paris: 'Flour War'. Wilkes re-elected to Parliament. Henry Grattan enters Irish Parliament. Sietah, republic of the Zaporogues, steppe nomads, put down by Potemkin. Local government reorganized in Russia. **1775–1847** Daniel O'Connell, Irish statesman and patriot. | **1775** 7 May, Turkey cedes Bukovina to Austria. 19 March, treaty of commerce between Poland and Prussia. | **1775** Slaves in Algiers henceforward held solely by the state. Spanish army sent to relieve Ceuta and Melilla. **c. post 1775** Masai expand, reaching Ngong Hills. |
| **1776** 5 Jan., the *corvée* and corporations abolished in France. | | **1776** 14 Sept., treaty between Sultan of Kilwa and French slave-trader J.V. Morice for supply of 1,000 slaves annually for 100 years. |

| THE EAST & AUSTRALASIA | THE AMERICAS | RELIGION & CULTURE |
|---|---|---|

**1773** Regulating Act creates post of Governor-General of Fort William in Bengal with council of four: given authority over Presidencies of Bombay and Madras: Supreme Court set up: Warren Hastings, first Governor-General. Ali Bey d. British factory at Bushire reopened. Ahmad Shah of Afghanistan d.: succ. Taimur Shah (–1793): Sikh power grows in Punjab. Taimur puts down rebellion in Samarqand. Abortive Mon rebellion in Lower Burma: many Mons flee to Siam. EIC settlement made on Balambangan Is.

**1774** Feb., Rohilla war: Rohillas defeated at Miranpur Katra: Rohilkhand incorporated into Oudh. Popular rising in Shantung province, China. 2 Nov., Clive commits suicide. N attacks S Vietnam.

**1775** March, treaty of Surat: Raghunath cedes Salsette and Bassein to EIC. Burma invades Siam: withdraws following news of death of King Hsinbyushin.
**1775–6** Karim Khan takes Basra for Persia.
**1775–1802** Popular rising in Honan, organized by the Society of the White Lotus: other provinces follow.
**c. 1775** Balambangan Is. settlement destroyed by pirates.
**1775–1804** Jazar, Amir of Lebanon.

**1776** Treaty of Surat revised by treaty of Purandhar.

**1773** 16 Dec., the 'Boston Tea-Party': Samuel Adams and his followers empty 343 chests of tea into Boston harbour. Quebec Act: boundaries of Quebec enlarged to include Labrador and NW: Roman Catholic faith recognized as lawful: tithes to be paid to RC clergy: civil law to be Canadian, but penal law British: council instituted, with power to legislate but not to raise taxation. St John Is. granted a colonial assembly. Virginia burgesses set up first intercolonial committee. Antigua, second capital of Guatemala, ruined by an earthquake.
**1774** 28 March, four Acts of Parliament passed to coerce Boston: Quebec Act extends Canadian boundary. 29 May, correspondence and intercolonial committees propose cessation of all trade with England. 1 June appointed as a day of prayer and fasting by Virginia legislature: burgesses dismissed by governor. 1 Aug., first Provincial Convention held in Virginia: beginning of revolutionary legislatures in America. 21 Sept.–26 Oct., 'Continental Congress' held by American colonists in Philadelphia: first assembly of colonists in British North America: Georgia alone unrepresented: Samuel Adams of Boston demands complete independence: fifty-one delegates draw up petition of colonial rights. American Continental Congress invites Canadians to join revolting colonies. Boston Port Act. Quebec Revenue Act.
**1775** 18 Apr., troops from Boston determine to seize unlawful military stores at Concord: 19 Apr., skirmish at Lexington: siege of Boston follows and general uprising. 10 May, second Continental Congress meets in Philadelphia: American Continental Army organized: George Washington put in command: Ticonderoga fortress taken. June, military law proclaimed in Quebec Province. 16-17 June, battle of Bunker Hill: British ose 1,054 men in successful frontal attack: Americans lose 441: beginning of American War of Independence (–1783). Aug., Benedict Arnold attacks Montreal and Quebec: 31 Dec., night attack by Americans repulsed: 400 taken prisoner. Ethan Allen and 'Green Mountain Boys' seize Ticonderoga and Crown Point; Benedict Arnold of Connecticut briefly holds St Jean. Population of Nova Scotia 17,000–18,000, chiefly New England farmers.
**1776** March, American patriots take Boston. Washington assembles 8,000 troops in New York;

**1773** 21 July, Society of Jesus suppressed by the Pope. Grand Orient Lodge established in France.
**1773** First cast-iron bridge constructed at Coalbrookdale.
**1773–1829** Thomas Young, scientist and polymath.
**1773–1836** James Mill, historian.
**1773–1857** Sir George Cayley, Bt, aeronautical pioneer.
**1773–1850** Louis-Philippe, Duc d'Orléans, later King of France.

**1774** Toleration of non-Catholics granted in Hungary. John Wesley: *Thoughts on Slavery.* Society of Friends decrees expulsion of a friend for engaging in slave trade. Priestley discovers oxygen.
**1774–1843** Robert Southey, poet.
**1774–1848** Pietro Giordani, Italian writer.
**1774–1856** Josef von Hammer-Purgstall, Austrian orientalist.

**1775** The water closet invented. Economic Societies of Friends of the Country spread to Madrid. Girard invents the turbine. Sacristy of St Peter's Rome built. Watt builds first steam-engine.
**1775–99** Pius VI (Braschi), Pope.
**1775–1817** Jane Austen, novelist.
**1775–1826** Conrad Malte-Brun, Danish geographer.
**1775–1831** Pietro Coletta, Italian historian.
**1775–1834** Charles Lamb, essayist and poet.
**1775–1836** André Marie Ampère, physicist.
**1775–1851** John William Mallord Turner, artist.
**1775–1854** Friedrich Wilhelm Joseph von Schelling, philosopher.
**1775–1864** Walter Savage Landor, poet.

**1776** Society of Friends makes manumission obligatory for any slaves owned by Friends.

1776–1780

WESTERN &
NORTHERN EUROPE

CENTRAL &
SOUTHERN EUROPE

AFRICA

**1776** 12 May, Malesherbes resigns:
Turgot dismissed. June, Necker,
assistant to Controller-General of
Finance in France. 11 Aug., *corvée*
and corporations restored in France.
First trade union founded in England.
Resolution in House of Commons
that slavery is contrary to the law of
God lost.

**1776** Abd al-Qadir, Terobe Fulani,
overthrows Denianke dynasty of Futa
Toro: leads *jihad* against neighbours.
Annual caravan said to be crossing
from Kilwa to Angola.
**c. 1776** First direct contracts between
Dutch and Xhosa on Zeekee R.

**1777** 28 May, defensive alliance be-
tween France and Switzerland.
June, Necker, Director-General of
Finance in France (–1781).

**1777** Joseph I of Portugal d.: succ.
Maria I (–1792) and her consort
Peter (–1786) jointly: Pombal
removed from power. Swiss
constitution revised. School of War
founded in Paris.
**1777–99** Charles Theodore, Elector
of Bavaria.

**1777** Rising of al-Azhar students
against misappropriation of Waqf
funds by Beys.

**1778** 6 Feb., commercial, defensive
and offensive treaty between France
and US. 11 May, William Pitt, Earl
of Chatham, d. 17 June, France and
Britain at war. Irish Volunteers
raised: some 80,000 enlist, chiefly
Protestants.

**1778** 3 Jan., convention between
Austria and the Palatinate on partition
of Bavaria. 3 July, Prussia declares
war on Austria on Bavarian behalf:
invades Bohemia.

**1778** Fernando Po ceded to Spain.
Dutch and Xhosa demarcate
boundary on Fish R.

**1779** Serfdom abolished in French
royal demesnes. English government
grants concessions to Irish trade:
most Restrictive Acts repealed.

**1779** 12 Apr., Franco-Spanish alliance
of Aranjuez against England. 13 May,
peace of Teschen: Prussia gains right
of reversion of Ansbach and Bayreuth:
Austria takes Inn Quarter. 16 June,
Spain joins the French in war against
England: Gibraltar besieged (–1780).

**1779** Cape Patriots demand a written
constitution from Holland.
**1779–84** Takla Giorgis of Ethiopia.

**1780** 10 March, Catherine II of Russia
declares armed neutrality to prevent
Britain searching neutral shipping:
subsequently confirmed by Austria,
Denmark, Prussia, Spain and Sweden.

**1780** Feb., Rodney raises the siege of
Gibraltar. June, Catherine II and
Joseph II meet.

**1780** Treaty of Aranjuez of friendship
and commerce between Morocco and
Spain.

| THE EAST & AUSTRALASIA | THE AMERICAS | RELIGION & CULTURE |
|---|---|---|

**1776** Rebellions in Siam: Hsinbyushin d.: Burmese withdraw, leaving Siam again independent.
**1776—82** Singu, King of Burma.

**1776** British number 35,000: Washington retires to New Jersey: patriot force dwindles to 3,300. March, Pennsylvanian suffrage extended to all male taxpayers: similar action follows in other states. American rebels expelled from Canada. 5 May, Quebec relieved by British fleet: Americans withdraw. June, civil government restored in Quebec Province. 4 July, American Declaration of Independence, drawn up by Thomas Jefferson. Sept., Congress authorizes long-term enlistments in army. Nov., Americans defeated in Nova Scotia. Spanish Viceroyalty of Río de la Plata created: Upper Peru (later Bolivia) transferred from Peru. Buenos Aires separated from Viceroyalty of Peru. Entail of estates abolished in Virginia.

**1776** Adam Smith: *The Wealth of Nations.* Academy of Fine Art founded in Palazzo de Brera, Milan. Muhammad b.al-Abbas Saghanughu, Dyula scholar, d.
**1776—88** E. Gibbon: *Decline and Fall of the Roman Empire.*
**1776—1831** Barthold Niebuhr, Roman historian.
**1776--1837** John Constable, artist.
**1776—1856** Amedro Avogadro, physicist.
c. **1776** Islam introduced into Dahomey by Yoruba.

**1777—84** Raja Haji, Bugis underking in Johore. Tay Son gains control of S Vietnam.

**1777** Jan, Quebec Legislative Council meets: provision made for operation of Quebec Act. 24 Aug., Washington raises patriot army to 11,000 near Philadelphia: 3 Oct., defeated by British at Germantown. 19 Sept., brush between English and American patriots at Freeman's Farm. 17 Oct., British army from Canada against Americans led by Major-General John Burgoyne: decisively defeated at Saratoga. 15 Nov., Articles of Confederation, first US constitution.

**1777** *Journal de Paris*, first French newspaper, begins publication.
**1777—1837** Francis Howard Greenway, architect of Sydney.
**1777—1844** Thomas Campbell, Scots poet.
**1777—1859** Henry Hallam, historian.
**1777—1832** Casimir Pierre Périer, French statesman.
**1777—1849** Madame Récamier, hostess.

**1778** Chinese population 243m.
**1778—93** Many Moro raids on the Philippines.

**1778** Apr., Livins, Chief Justice of Quebec, arbitrarily dismissed for giving a judgement contrary to the governor's opinion: no replacement appointed for eight years. 27 June, Lieut. General Frederick Haldimand replaces Carleton as Governor of Quebec. Capt. Cook discovers Sandwich Is. (later Hawaii). José de San Martín b. in Argentina. British take Savannah. States of Connecticut, Delaware, Pennsylvania, Rhode Is., and Virginia prohibit import of slaves.
**1778—82** Continuous fighting on Quebec border with American states.
**1778—88** Spanish trade with S America said to have declined 70%.

**1778** Savins Bank estalished in Paris. Gardiner's Relief Act for Irish Roman Catholics. Relief Act for Catholics in England.
**1778—1827** Ugo Foscolo, Italian poet.
**1778—1829** Sir Humphrey Davy, chemist.
**1778—1830** William Hazlitt, essayist.
**1778—1842** John Varley, artist.
**1778—1840** George Bryan Brummell, 'Beau Brummell'.
**1778—1843** John Murray, publisher.
**1778—1846** Louis Buonaparte, brother of Napoleon and father of Napoleon III.

**1779** Committee set up in London to consider setting up 'a Colony of Disgracefuls at some distant part of the earth': New South Wales recommended by Sir Joseph Banks. 13 Jan., Convention of Wadgaon. Feb., force under Col. Leslie reaches Surat from Bengal. Karim Khan d.: struggle for power ensues (−1782).
**1779—82** EIC at war with the Marathas. Taimur of Afghanistan campaigns in Sind.
**1780** July—Sept., Haidar Ali of Mysore seizes the Carnatic.

**1779** British take interior of Georgia and S Carolina. 16 June, Spain declares war on Britain in favour of US.

**1779** Samuel Crompton invents the spinning mule. Royal Academy of Sciences founded in Lisbon.
**1779—1850** Adam Gottlob Ohlenschläger, Danish poet.
**1779—1851** Lorenz Oken, biologist and naturalist.

**1780** May, British under General Cornwallis take Charleston: more than 60,000 refugees leave for Canada, West Indies and England.

**1780—2** *Bengal Gazette*, first newspaper in India.

| WESTERN & NORTHERN EUROPE | CENTRAL & SOUTHERN EUROPE | AFRICA |
|---|---|---|
| **1780** 2-8 June, Gordon riots in London against Catholic Relief Act of 1778. 20 Nov., Britain declares war on the United Provinces. Office of Secretary for the Colonies and Board of Trade abolished in England. Irish Test Act for Protestant dissenters abolished. State supervision of industry abolished in Russia.<br>**1780–3** England blockades French, Spanish and neutral ports in Europe: French fleet cuts English communications with America.<br>**1781** 19 May, Necker dismissed. | **1780** June, Austro-Russian agreement of Mohilev. 29 Nov., Maria Theresa d.: her *thaler* of 1780 continues to be minted for use in Arabia and N Africa: Emperor Joseph II, Archduke of Austria. | **1780–2** Desultory war between British and Dutch in WA.<br>**c. 1780** Awallini dynasty of Haggaro founded.<br>**c. 1780–1800** Some 10,000 slaves exported from Mozambique to S America. |
|  | **1781** May, Frederick II joins Armed-Neutrality League. Serfdom abolished in Austria. Freedom of the press introduced. | **1781** Uthman dan Fodio becomes tutor to royal family of Gobir. Oyo at war with Dahomey. |
| **1782** Feb., Volunteer Convention held at Dungannon. 9 March, Lord North resigns: Marquess of Rockingham, Prime Minister. May, Irish Parliamentary independence granted. 1 July, Rockingham d.: succ. as Prime Minister, Earl of Shelburne (–1784): William Pitt the Younger, Chancellor of the Exchequer. Customs tariff in Russia limiting the import of manufactured goods. | **1782** 5 Feb., Spain recovers Minorca from Britain. July, Portugal joins Armed Neutrality League. | **1782** Spain abandons Fernando Po. |
| **1783** 24 Apr., Shelburne resigns: Coalition Ministry under Duke of Portland, with Charles James Fox and Lord North. 17 July, Parliament of Besançon demands the Estates-General be convened. 3 Sept., treaty of Versailles: England recognizes independence of USA: France recovers Indian and W Indian possessions, Gorée and Senegal: Spain regains Minorca. 10 Nov., Convention of Irish Volunteers in Dublin. 17 Dec., Fox's India Bill defeated in the Lords. 19 Dec., Portland resigns: William Pitt the Younger, Prime Minister, aged twenty-four (–1801). Quakers petition Parliament for abolition of slave trade. The *corvée* abolished in the Empire. Peasant revolt in Bohemia. | **1783** Sicily joins Armed Neutrality League. The Russians occupy the Crimea. | **1783** US at war with Algiers: pays tribute to the pirates.<br>**1783, 1784** Spain bombards Algiers. |
| **1784** 20 May, peace of Versailles between England and the United Provinces. Foster's Corn Law in Ireland makes it an important corn-growing country. | **1784** Emperor Joseph II abolishes the Transylvanian constitution: German made the official language in all his possessions. | **1784** Abortive attempt by Saif b. Ahmad al-Busaidi, pretender to Oman and Muscat, to stir up rebellion in EA<br>**1784–8** Iyasu III of Ethiopia. |

## THE EAST & AUSTRALASIA

**1780** Ahmad al-Jazzar made governor of Syria and Lebanon (−1804).

**1781** 1 July, Sir Eyre Coote defeats Haidar Ali at Porto Novo: conquest of Mysore follows. 13 Nov., EIC take Dutch settlement at Negapatam, Madras. Ali Murad seizes Shiraz. Government Tobacco monopoly established in the Philippines.

**1782** 11 Jan., Dutch surrender Trincomalee, Ceylon, to EIC. 12 Feb., battle of Sadras, near Madras, between British and French. 17 May, treaty of Salbai: Salsette retained by EIC: end of Mahratta war. 6 July, naval engagement of Cuddalore between British and French. 7 Dec., Haidur Ali of Mysore d.: succ. Tipu Sahib. Suffren defeats English in the Indian Ocean. Singu, King of Burma, assassinated: succ. Maung-Maung deposed after seven days; succ. Bodapaya (−1819). Trincomalee captured, first by English and then by French. Suffren refits French fleet at Acheh. Burmese retake Arakan. Struggle for succession in Ava: Bodawpaya eventually emerges as successful. Bangkok founded.
**1782–5** Ali Murad, ruler of Persia: capital transferred to Isfahan: Zend dynasty (−1794).
**1783** 9 Apr., British surrender Bedmore to Tipu Sahib. Mir Fath Ali Khan becomes virtually independent of Afghanistan in Sind. French use Mergui, Burma, and Trincomalee, Ceylon, for refitting fleet.
**1783–1823** Burmese capital at Amarapura.

**1784** 11 May, EIC sign peace treaty of Mangalore with Tipu Sahib. 13 Aug., Pitt's India Act: EIC placed under government Board of Control

## THE AMERICAS

**1780** 16 Aug., British defeat Americans at Camden. Holland sides with US: 20 Nov., Britain declares war on Holland. Nov., Tupac Amaru, Inca heir, rebels: controls S Peru, most of Bolivia and some of Argentina.

**1781** March, Articles of Confederation agreed in US. 19 Oct., British under Lord Cornwallis capitulate at Yorktown. British defeat Americans under Nathaniel Greene at Guilford Courthouse. Tupac Amaru captured and executed with his family and staff.

**1782** British abandon ports in southern US. Admiral George Rodney defeats French at naval battle of the Saints, WI.

**1783** 24 July, Simon Bolivar b. Florida retained by Spain. More than 30,000 American British loyalists migrate to Nova Scotia. Midshipman Magra (later Matra) recommends American settlement by US loyalists in Australia.

**1784** 10,000 settlers arrive in Kentucky. *Habeas Corpus* Act passed in Quebec. Bank of New York founded.

## RELIGION & CULTURE

**1780–1845** Elizabeth Fry, prison reformer.
**1780–1867** Jean Auguste Dominique Ingres, French artist.
**c. 1780** The screwdriver invented.
**1780–1839** Lady Hester Lucy Stanhope, eccentric.
**1780–1849** James Justinian Morier, diplomatist and author.
**1780–1851** John James Audubon, ornithologist.

**1781** Sunday Schools first opened in England. William Herschel discovers the planet *Uranus*. Muslim *Madrassah* founded in Calcutta.
**1781–2** Tijaniyyah Order founded.
**1781–5** Numerous monasteries abolished in Austria.
**1781–1848** George Stephenson, engineer and inventor.
**1782** Pope Pius VI visits Vienna and Munich. Gardiner's second Catholic Relief Act in Ireland.
**1782–1840** Niccolo Paganini, Italian composer and violinist.
**1782–1842** John Sell Cotman, artist.
**1782–1854** Hugues Felicité Robert de Lamennais, philosopher and political writer.
**1782–1871** Daniel François Esprit Auber, French composer.
**1782–1837** John Field, Irish composer.
**1782–1857** Etienne Quatremère, orientalist.

**1783** 2 Nov., Montgolfier, inventor of the balloon, has first ascent made by Rozier and Arlande. Emperor Joseph II visits Rome: concordat signed *re* Lombardy. Lavoisier achieves analysis of water.
**1783–1826** Bp Reginald Heber, poet.
**1783–1842** Marie-Henri Beyle (de Stendhal), novelist.
**1783–1854** Gabriele Rossetti, Italian poet.
**1783–1859** Washington Irving, American writer.

**1784** 'Meeting for Sufferings' publishes *The Case of our fellow creatures. the oppressed Africans.* Asiatic Society of Bengal founded.

| WESTERN & NORTHERN EUROPE | CENTRAL & SOUTHERN EUROPE | AFRICA |
|---|---|---|

**1784—5** 'Orde's Commercial Resolutions' offer Ireland unrestricted rights to trade except in S Africa, S America and India: eventually withdrawn.
**1784—1801** British colonies managed by a committee of the Privy Council.

**1785** 8 and 10 Oct., treaties of Fontainebleau: Barrier Treaty of 1715 abrogated. Pitt proposes to abolish many rotten boroughs. Charters of the nobility and for towns declare their respective powers in Russia.
**1785—6** Affair of the Queen's Necklace in France: Marie Antoinette's reputation destroyed.

**1785** 23 July, the Fürstenbund, league of German princes, establishe by Frederick II against Joseph II.

**1785** US ships *Maria* and *Dauphin* seized by Algerian pirates near Gibraltar. Bizerta again bombarded b the French fleet.

**1786** 26 Sept., Anglo-French treaty of commerce and navigation: known as the Eden treaty. Commissioners for the reduction of the National Debt appointed in England. Pitt reforms government finances: taxation simplified. Impeachment of Warren Hastings decided upon.

**1786** 25 May, Peter III of Portugal d.: Maria I reigns alone (−1807). 17 Aug., Frederick II, the Great, of Prussia d.: succ. Frederick William II (−1797). Treaty between Spain and Turkey ends piracy in W Mediterranean. Turks again declare war on Russia, supported by Gustav III of Sweden.
**1786—9** Emperor Joseph II institutes a cadastral survey.

**1786** Ottoman fleet sent to restore Turkish authority in Egypt. Treaty between Morocco and USA.

**1787** 22 Feb.— 12 May, Assembly of the Notables in France: Calonne's proposals for reform rejected. 27 July, Parliament of Paris exiled. 17 Aug., riots in Paris. 13 Sept., Prussia intervenes in the United Provinces to support William V.

**1787** 11 Jan., commercial treaty between France and Russia. 8 Aug., Austria and Russia at war with Turkey (−1792). Census in Spain: 3,148 towns and villages in the hands of the Church: 2,067 monasteries; 1,122 convents; 62,000 religious; and 71,000 adherents. 17 cities, 2,358 townships, 8,818 villages, in the hands of the nobility.

**1787** British settle captured slaves in Granville Town. Plague kills 17,000 in Algiers.
**1787—1810** Andrianampoinimerina, King of the Merina: expands kingdom in Madagascar.

**1788** 9 Jan., Association for Promoting the Discovery of the Interior Parts of Africa founded in London. Feb., trial of Warren Hastings begun (−1795). 15 Apr., alliance between Britain and the United Provinces. 9-10 May, riots in Rennes. 11 June, riots in Dijon. 19 June, riots in Pau. 8 Aug., Louis XVI calls meeting of the French Estates-General for 1789. 16 Aug., France declared bankrupt. 28 Aug., Necker recalled to the French Ministry of Finance. 6 Nov.−12 Dec., second assembly of notables in Paris. George III of England first exhibits symptoms of *porphyria*: is alleged insane. William Pitt, William Wyndham Grenville, and William Wilberforce demand abolition of slave trade in Parliament. Serfdom abolished by Denmark. Russians under Potemkin take Otchakov. Gustave III of Sweden obliged to leave Russia to put down a rising of his nobles.
**1788—90** War between Russia and Sweden.

**1788** Feb., Austria declares war on Turkey. 6 Oct., Polish Diet meets to revise constitution.
**1788—1808** Charles IV, King of Spain.

**1788** Galla state of Begemder founded.

## THE EAST & AUSTRALASIA

(–1858): intervention in native affairs forbidden. Trincomalee returned to the Dutch. EIC embassies to Acheh and Rhio, both abortive. Bugis attack Malacca. Dutch seize Rhio. Dutch drive out Bugis from Johore.
**1784–95** Dutch rule at Rhio.

**1785** Mahadji Sindia made regent of the empire. Royal Co. of the Philippines founded, a failure.
**1785 ff.** Wars between Siam and Burma.
**1785–6** Sir John Macpherson, Governor-General of Bengal *ad int.*
**1785–9** Jafar, ruler of Persia.

**1786** 11 Aug., EIC settlement at Penang inaugurated: Francis Light first superintendent. US trading vessel *Hope* visits Batavia. English trading base established at Penang.
**1786–93** Marquess Cornwallis, Governor-General of Bengal: first term.
**1786–1838** Tokugawa Iyenari, Shogun.
**1787** 10 May, Warren Hastings impeached by Edmund Burke. Sindia defeated at Lalsout, in Rajpatana. Shah Alam blinded by Ghulam Qadir: Ghulam subsequently executed. Sultan Mahmud's attempt to form alliance of Malay States against British and Dutch a failure. Burmese expedition against Siam defeated.

**1788** 26 Jan., Capt. Arthur Phillip, with party of seamen, soldiers and convicts, lands in Sydney Cove and establishes colony. Two French ships under Comte de la Pérouse visit Sydney for two months: both ships subsequently lost at sea. Colony at Norfolk Is. founded. Port Jackson, New Zealand, founded as a penal settlement. Population of Penang *c.* 1,000, chiefly Malays.
**1788–92** Capt. Arthur Phillip, Governor of New South Wales.
**1788–1820** Pakubuwana IV, Prince of Surakarta (formerly Mataram).
**1788–1840** Bashir al-Shihabi, Amir of Lebanon.

## THE AMERICAS

**1785** 10 Sept., commercial treaty between US and Prussia. Land Ordinance makes provision for land for schools in US. Ordinance forbids expansion of slavery into NW America.

**1786** Jefferson obtains bill from Virginia legislature ensuring religious freedom. Delegates of five states meet at Annapolis: Alexander Hamilton persuades delegates to call for further meeting to consider constitution. Haldimand retires; 23 Oct., Carleton Governor-in-Chief of British N America, as Lord Dorchester.

**1787** May, Convention meets to consider constitution: Washington, President. 17 Sept., Federal Constitution of the United States passed. US Northwest Ordinance provides for expansion N of Ohio. Alexander Mackenzie exploring near L. Athabaska.

**1788** 30 Apr., George Washington sworn first President of US (–1797). Rising against Portuguese in Brazil led by Tiradentes (pseudonym of Joaquim José da Silva Xavier).
**1788–90** New York capital of US.

## RELIGION & CULTURE

**1784–1849** Peter de Wint, artist.
**1784–1859** Ludwig Spohr, German composer.
**1784–1859** James Henry Leigh Hunt, poet and essayist.
**1784–1865** Henry John Temple, Viscount Palmerston, statesman.
**1784–7** Academy of Sciences, St Petersbourg, built.
**1785** Emperor Joseph II forbids pilgrimages and processions. First Channel crossing by balloon. First steam cotton mill built in Nottingham. Edmund Cartwright patents Power Loom: Salsana invents seismograph.
**1785–1841** Sir David Wilkie, artist.
**1785–1859** Thomas de Quincey, essayist.
**1785–63** Jacob Grimm, story teller.
**1785–1870** Achille Victor, Duc de Broglie, political writer.
**1785–1873** Alessandro Manzoni, Italian poet and novelist.
**1786** Emperor Joseph II sets up state seminaries: trial for witchcraft forbidden. First ascent of Mont Blanc. Coal gas first used to make light. The threshing machine invented.
**1786–1826** Karl Maria Friedrich Ernst, Baron von Weber, German composer.
**1786–1859** William Grimm, story teller.
**1786–1880** Stratford Canning, Viscount Stratford de Redcliffe, diplomatist.
**1787** Association for Abolition of Slavery founded in England. Rt. Rev. Charles Inglis made Bp of Nova Scotia: first Anglican Bp in Canada.
**1787–1849** William Etty, artist.
**1787–1854** Georg Simon Ohm, physicist.
**1787–1855** Mary Russell Mitford, novelist and dramatist.
**1787–1874** Francois Pierre Guillaume de Guizot, historian and statesman.
**1788** 1 Jan., the *Times* first published. First steam boat built.
**1788–1824** George Gordon, Lord Byron, poet.
**1788–1827** Augustin Fresnel, scientist.
**1788–1860** Arthur Schopenhauer, philosopher.
**1788–1827** Hugh Clapperton, explorer.
**1788–1850** Sir Robert Peel, Tory Prime Minister.
**1788–1856** William Hamilton, philosopher.

## WESTERN & NORTHERN EUROPE

## CENTRAL & SOUTHERN EUROPE

## AFRICA

**1789** 5 May, Estates-General opened at Versailles. 20 May, French clergy renounce their financial privileges: 23 May, nobility follow suit. 19 June, the Third Estate constitutes itself the National Assembly: Louis XVI orders its closure. 20 June, the Oath on the Tennis Court. 23 June, Louis XVI rejects resolutions by the Third Estate. 27 June, Louis XVI orders the nobility and clergy to sit with the Third Estate. June, Whig Club formed in Ireland. 9 July, the National Assembly declares itself a constituent assembly. 11 July, Necker dismissed. 14 July, the Bastille prison opened by the Paris mob. 4 Aug., the National Assembly decrees equality of taxation, abolition of feudal rights and privileges, and the sale of offices. 23 Aug., National Assembly decrees freedom of religion; and 24 Aug., freedom of the press. 28 Aug., Necker recalled. Declaration of the Rights of Man. 6 Oct., Paris mob marches on Versailles, and forces Louis XVI to return to Paris with the royal family. Oct., William Wyndham Grenville drafts new constitution for Canada on British model.
**1789 ff.** French Revolution.

**1790** 15 Jan., France divided into eighty-three *Départements*. 13 Feb., National Assembly decrees the abolition of monastic vows; 15 Feb., all feudal rights; 17 March, the sale of national property; 22 May, making the nation sole arbiter of war and peace; 9 June, civil list of the King and Queen; suppressing titles, liveries and armorial bearings. 14 July, Feast of the Federation in the Champ-de-Mars. 14 Aug., peace made between Sweden and Russia. 4 Sept., Necker dismissed. 2 Dec., Austria retakes Brussels: end of Belgian independence. 26 Dec., Louis XVI accepts civil constitution of the clergy. Theobald Wolfe Tone elected Secretary of the Irish Catholic Committee. Forth and Clyde Canal opened. Tories win elections in Britain. Trade unions forbidden.
**1791** 28 Feb., Paris mob destroys ramparts of the Château de Vincennes. 4 Apr., church of St Geneviève made the Panthéon: Mirabeau buried there. 31 May, the guillotine introduced. 20 or 21 June, Louis XVI and the royal family flee Paris; 22 June, King arrested at Varennes; 25 June, King and royal family brought back to Paris. 9 July, National Assembly orders all émigrés to return to France within two months.

**1789** 7 Apr., Selim III, Ottoman Sultan (−1807): Turkish army and fleet re-organized. 31 July, Suvorov defeats the Turks at Foczani; Oct., takes Belgrade. 13 Dec., Austrian Netherlands proclaim their independence as Belgium: capital Brussels.

**1790** 9 Jan., Convention of Berlin between Britain, Prussia and the United Provinces *re* Belgium. 3 March, alliance between Prussia and Turkey. 29 March, alliance between Prussia and Poland. 27 July, treaty of Reichenbach between Austria and Prussia. 3 Nov., Treaty of Alliance between Prussia and Turkey. Russians defeat Turks on Lower Danube. Casa de Contratación abolished in Spain.
**1790–2** Leopold II, Holy Roman Emperor.

**1791** 21 March, Anglo-Prussian agreement against Russia. 3 May, new constitution adopted in Poland. 11 June, agreement between Austria and Prussia. 6 July, Emperor Leopold II calls on all crowned heads to coalesce against the revolution. 4 Aug., Austro-Turkish treaty signed at Sistova. 11 Aug., Russo-Turkish peace treaty signed at Galatz. 27 Aug., the Emperor and the King of Prussia make agreement of Pilnitz to rescue Louis XVI.

**1789** Smallpox epidemic at Cape Coast. St Louis, Senegal, sends *cahier* of grievances to French Estates General. Xhosa cross Fish R.: allowed to remain 'without prejudice to the ownership of Europeans'.
**1789–94** Hezekias of Ethiopia.

**1790–2** Yazid b. Muhammad, Sharif of Morocco: persecutes Christians, Jews and even Muslims.
**c. 1790** Buganda greatly expands frontiers, incorporating Buddu. Lunda empire at its apogee as a trading power.

| THE EAST & AUSTRALASIA | THE AMERICAS | RELIGION & CULTURE |
|---|---|---|

**1789** 29 Dec., Tipu Sahib attacks Travancore.
**1789–94** Lutf Ali Khan, ruler of Persia.

**1789** Negro slave rebellion in Saint-Domingue. US census shows population of 4m.
**1789–94** Count Revillagigedo, Viceroy of New Spain: administrative reformer.

**1789–1848** Ibrahim Pasha, Turkish general.
**1789–1851** Fenimore Cooper, novelist.
**1789–1859** Sir James Stephen, civil servant.

**1790** 1 June, EIC treaty with Marathas. 4 July, EIC allies with the Nizam of Hyderabad.
**1790–1** Chinese conquer Nepal.

**1790** Dec., Congress meets in Philadelphia: Departments of State, War and Treasury created: Bill of Rights enacted. Population of Kentucky and Tennessee over 100,000.
**1790–4** War between US and Indians.
**1790–5** Vancouver explores the Pacific coast.
**1790–1800** Philadelphia capital of US.

**1790** First Life boat built. The dental drill invented. Edmund Burke: *Reflections on the Revolution in France*. *Jardin des Plantes* instituted in Paris.
**1790–1832** Jean François Champollion, first modern scientific Egyptologist.
**1790–1869** Alphonse Prat de Lamartine, historian and poet.
**c. post 1790** Tijaniyyah order spreads rapidly in Mauritania.

**1791** Jan., first contingent of the 'Rum Corps', correctly N.S.W. Corps, arrives at Sydney. Cornwallis takes Mangalore. Taimur of Afghanistan puts down rebellion in Peshawar. First superintendent of police appointed in Calcutta: police system gradually established throughout India. Treaty between EIC and Kedah, ceding Penang to EIC. Kedah mounts attack on EIC settlement at Penang: frustrated by Francis Light attacking first.

**1791** 22 Aug., negro rising in San Domingo. Revolt of slaves in Haiti led by Toussaint l'Ouverture. 15 Dec., first ten amendments to US Constitution voted. Kentucky and Vermont made States. Washington, D.C., founded. Indians raid American settlements S of Ohio: American force under General Arthur St Clair defeated. Excise law imposes tax on home-made whisky in US.

**1791** 13 Apr., the Pope condemns the French civil constitution of the clergy. Thomas Paine: *The Rights of Man*.
**1791–1831** Casimir Brodzinski, Polish poet.
**1791–1857** Karl Czerny, Austrian composer.
**1791–1863** Giuseppe Gioacchino Belli, Italian poet.
**1791–1864** Giacomo Meyerbeer, German composer.
**1791–1867** Michael Faraday, chemist and physicist.

## WESTERN & NORTHERN EUROPE

**1791** 15 July, Louis XVI suspended by the National Assembly. 13 Sept., Louis XVI accepts new constitution. 30 Sept., National Assembly closed, being replaced, 1 Oct., by Legislative Assembly. Oct., Society of United Irishmen formed in Belfast by Wolfe Tone. 28 Oct., 8 and 11 Nov., National Assembly takes various measures against the *émigrés.* Canadian Constitutional Act passed by British Parliament.

**1792** 28 Apr., hostilities near Lille. 8 June, National Assembly decrees establishment of a camp near Paris: 10 June, vetoed by Louis XVI: 20 June, mobs rise against Louis XVI. 19 June, French victorious at Menin; 20 June, at Courtrai and Ypres. 11 July, National Assembly decrees that France is in danger. 10; 12 Aug., Louis XVI suspended and imprisoned with his family in the Temple. 10 Aug., decree of National Assembly calling a national Convention; 15 Aug., decree against the Girondins. 2 Sept., Paris mob assassinates persons detained in prison for political reasons. 14 Sept., French retreat to Châlons-sur-Marne. 20 Sept., French defeat the Prussians at Valmy. 21 Sept., last session of the National Assembly: the Convention inaugurated: declares royalty abolished and proclaims republic: year I of the First Republic officially begins on 22 Sept. (–1804). 10 Oct., Convention decree forbids the use of *Monsieur* and *Madame,* replacing them with *citoyen* and *citoyenne.* 22 Oct., Prussians evacuate French territory. 6 Nov., French victorious at Jemappes: conquer Austrian Netherlands. 8, 12 Nov., French take Tournai, Ghent and Charleroi. 13-30 Nov., French take most of present Belgium. 5 Dec., Louis XVI's trial before the Convention begins. Catholic Relief Act in Ireland grants minor concessions. 499 petitions to British Parliament against slavery.
**1792–1878** Lord John Russell (later Earl Russell) statesmen and reformer.

**1793** Jan., Hobart's Catholic Relief Act removes most Catholic disabilities in Ireland other than holding public office. 17 Jan., Louis XVI condemned to death; 21 Jan., guillotined. 21 Jan., emigré princes declare the Dauphin King of France. 1 Feb., the Convention declares war on England and Holland. 7 March, the Convention declares war on Spain. 28 March, civil war in La Vendée. 28 March, Revolutionary Tribunal formed in Paris.

## CENTRAL & SOUTHERN EUROPE

**1791** Treaty of Sistova: Austria makes separate peace with the Turks. Turks defeated by Russians by land and sea.

**1792** 9 Jan., Russo-Turkish treaty of Iassy: Russia gains control of the Crimea. Turkey begins to build a fleet. 7 Feb., Austria and Prussia ally against France. 12 March, second partition of Poland agreed between Prussia and Russia. 20 Apr., Emperor Francis II of Austria declares war on France. 19 May, Russia invades Poland. 17 July, Poles under Kosciusko defeated by Russia: constitution of 1791 abrogated. 24 July, Prussia declares war on France. Aug., Austria and Prussia invade France. 11 Sept., Comte d'Artois joins the Prussian army with 6,000 cavalry. 29 Sept., Prussians retreat. 19 Oct., France takes Mayence. 21, 27 Nov., Savoy made part of France. 21 Dec., French army in control from the Saar and the Moselle as far as Consaarbrück. Godoy comes to power as prime minister in Spain. Maria of Portugal becomes insane: her son John regent (–1816).
**1792–1806** Francis II, Holy Roman Emperor.
**1792–1809** Gustav IV Adolf, King of Sweden.

**1793** 23 Jan., secret Prusso-Russian treaty partitioning Poland. Feb., coalition against France of Austria, Britain, Prussia, Sardinia, the Two Sicilies, Spain, the States of the Church, and the United Provinces. 25 March, Prusso-Russian treaty published: Prussia acquires Thorn, Danzig, and provinces of Posen, Kalisz, and Plock: Russia takes palatinates of Kiev, Minsk, Braclaw, and most of Volhynia. Turkish army reformed.

## AFRICA

**1792** 1,190 negroes settled in Sierra Leone from Nova Scotia. Oyo Empire at its greatest extent. 'Patriots' take control of Bourbon and Ile de France.

**1793** Further American ships seized by Algiers.
**1793–4** James Watt and Matthew Winterbottom exploring in W Africa.

| THE EAST & AUSTRALASIA | THE AMERICAS | RELIGION & CULTURE |
|---|---|---|

**1791** First wheat grown in Australia by James Ruse. Burmese defeat Siamese in Tenasserim.

**1791–1868** (Dean) Henry Hart Milman, historian and poet.

**1792** 5 Feb., Tipu Sahib defeated at Seringapatam: obliged to cede half of Mysore to EIC. Oct., Capt. Phillip resigns and leaves Sydney: Lieutenant-Governors King and Grose *ad int.* Ranjit Singh succeeds to leadership of the Sikhs, aged twelve. Australians settle at Dusky Sound, New Zealand: whalers follow, hunting cachalot.
**1792–1810** Abdurrahman Amangkubuwana II (Sultan Sepuh), Sultan of Jogyakarta.
**1792–1839** Ranjit Singh, ruler of the Sikhs.

**1792** 21 Apr., Tiradentes beheaded. Col. J.A. Simcoe appointed Governor of Upper Canada (–1796): first legislature for Upper Canada meets. Many loyalists from US migrate to Upper Canada. American Capt. Robert Gray enters mouth of R. Columbia. Kentucky becomes a US State. Population of Lower Canada 145,000 French, 10,000 English: Legislative Assembly thirty-four French, sixteen English: English hold slight majorities in legislative and executive councils. Capt. George Vancouver charts coast N from Strait of Juan de Fuca.
**1792–1808** (Sir) John Wentworth, Governor of Nova Scotia.

**1792** Jan., the *Northern Star* first published in Belfast. Muhammad b. Abd al-Wahhab, puritanical Muslim reformer in Najd, d. The White House, Washington, begun by James Hoban. Wooden signal telegraph invented in France.
**1792–1822** Percy Bysshe Shelley, poet.
**1792–1830** The Capitol, Washington, built by William Thornton.
**1792–1866** Rev. John Keble, divine and poet.
**1792–1868** Gioacchino Antonio Rossini, Italian composer.
**1792–1871** Sir John Frederick William Herschel, astronomer.
**1792–1878** George Cuikshank, caricaturist and illustrator.
**1792–1879** Baldomero Espartero, Spanish soldier and dictator.
**1792–1878** George Cruikshank,
**1792–1834** Edward Irving, 'Irvingite'.
**1792–1848** Capt. Frederick Marryat, R.N., author.

**1793** A group of young Scots transported to Sydney for advocating reform of Parliament and universal suffrage: known as the 'Scottish Martyrs'.
**1793** May, the Cornwallis Code reforms administration of the EIC: organizes 'Permanent Settlement' of Bengal. EIC Charter renewed. Taimur Shah of Afghanistan d., leaving twenty-three sons: succ. Zaman Shah (–1803). British seize French settlements in India.

**1793** 23 Apr., Washington proclaims US neutrality in war between England and France. Alexander Mackenzie crosses Rocky Mts, descending Fraser R.

**1793** 1 Aug., the decimal system adopted in France. Henri Mezière: *Les Français libres à leurs frères Canadiens:* first exposition of French Canadian nationalism. Right Rev. Jacob Mountain, appointed first Anglican Bp of Quebec. English law first grants recognition to insurance companies and friendly societies. Board of Agriculture instituted in England.
**1793–1859** David Cox, artist.

**WESTERN &
NORTHERN EUROPE**

**CENTRAL &
SOUTHERN EUROPE**

**AFRICA**

**1793** 6 Apr., Committee of Public Safety formed in Paris (−1795). 31 May−2 June, the Mountain triumphs over the Gironde: twenty-nine deputies and two ministers hostile to the Mountain arrested. 14 July, Marat assassinated by Charlotte Corday. 27 Aug., English take Toulon. 9 Oct., Lyons taken by French from insurgents. 16 Oct., Marie Antoinette condemned to death and guillotined. 17 Oct., French defeat Prince of Coburg at Wattignies. 31 Oct., twenty-one Girondin deputies guillotined. 31 Oct.−8 Dec., the Duc d'Orléans and other notables guillotined. 10 Nov., the cult of Reason established in Paris. 19 Dec., Toulon retaken by the French: Napoleon Buonaparte takes part as an artillery captain. Hearth tax abolished in Ireland.

**1794** 4 Feb., the Convention proclaims all blacks to be free, and orders the immediate abolition of slavery in the French colonies without compensation. 15 Feb., the Convention adopts the *Tricolor* as the French national flag. 24 March, Danton and other Hébertists guillotined. 19 Apr., England, Holland and Prussia sign treaty of the Hague against France. 30 Apr., Landrecies taken by the Coalition. 7 May, Robespierre has the existence of the Supreme Being proclaimed. 15 June− 31 July, French victorious at Fleurus, Ypres, Ostend, Mons, Tournai, Ghent, Brussels, Namur, Nieuport and Antwerp. July, atrocities committed in various French departments; 27 and 28 July, fall of Robespierre and the Mountain; Robespierre guillotined with sixty-nine supporters: end of Reign of Terror. 22 Sept.−7 Oct., French occupy parts of Belgium. 25 Dec., the French invade Holland. Feb.− June, the English occupy Corsica.

**1795** 19 Jan., the French occupy Amsterdam; 30 Jan., the Dutch fleet, caught in the ice, taken by French hussars. 7 Feb., Prince of Orange orders all Dutch overseas possessions to surrender authority to Britain. 15 Feb., first pacification of La Vendée. 19 Feb., peace treaty between France and Tuscany. 1 Apr., Paris suburbs rise against the Convention. 23 Apr., Warren Hastings acquitted by the House of Lords. 16 May, Treaty of Peace and Alliance between France and Holland. 8 June, death of the Dauphin, son of Louis XVI, announced: Comte de Provence assumes title of Louis XVIII. 21 Sept., 'Battle of the Diamond': affray between Catholics and Protestants in Armagh: first Orange Lodge founded.

**1794** March, Poles rise under Kosciusko; 6 June, defeated by Prussia and Russia at Rawka; 2 July, invaders reach Warsaw: siege until 6 Sept. 19 July, Geneva revolts in favour of France. 1 Aug., French take Fuenterrabia; 4 Aug., St Sebastian. 6 Aug., Russians take Vilno. 15 Sept., Russians under Suvorov defeat Polish army at Brzesc. 22 Sept., French occupy Aix-la-Chapelle. 9 Oct., Russians under Suvorov defeat Poles under Kosciusko at Maciejowice. 7 Nov., Russians take Warsaw.

**1795** 3 Jan., third treaty of partition of Poland between Austria and Russia. 5 Apr., peace of Basle between France and Prussia. 17 July, French occupy Bilbao and Vitoria. 22 July, peace treaty between France and Spain signed at Basle. 6 Sept., French take Düsseldorf. 20 Sept., Mannheim falls to the French. 11 and 29 Oct., Austrians defeat French at Hochst and Mayence. 24 Oct., third partition of Poland announced: Austria takes Cracow and Lublin: Prussia takes Warsaw and central Poland: Russia takes remainder of Lithuania and Volhynia. 25 Nov., Stanislaw II Poniatowski formally abdicates Polish throne.

**1794** Ile de France ignores French abolition of slavery.

**1795−7** Mungo Park reaches Segu and R. Niger.
**1795−1803** First British occupation of the Cape.

## THE EAST & AUSTRALASIA THE AMERICAS RELIGION & CULTURE

**1793** Abortive British mission to China.
**1793–7** Breeding of Merino sheep begun in Australia by John Macarthur.
**1793–8** Sir John Shore, Governor-General of Bengal.
**1793–1872** William Charles Wentworth, Australian explorer, landowner and politician.

**1793–1873** William Charles Macready, actor manager.

**1794** Mahadji Sindra, Maratha leader, d. Britain takes Seychelles Is. from France. Aga Muhammad Khan overthrows Lutf Ali Khan: end of Zend dynasty: Qajar dynasty of Persia founded (–1924). Arakan rebels: Burmese pursue rebels into British territory in Bengal.

**1794** 22 Feb., the English take Martinique, followed by St Lucia, and, temporarily, Guadaloupe. 20 Aug., US General Wayne decisively defeats Indians at Fallen Timbers. 'Whisky Rebellion' in US. Jay's treaty: outstanding differences between Britain and US settled.
**1794–5** Etienne Boré makes New Orleans a major centre of the sugar industry. York (Toronto) made capital of Upper Canada. American expedition against Indian tribes at Fallen Timbers. Anti-British riots in Canada against Militia Act: countered by Alien and Sedition Act.

**1794** Ball bearings invented. Benares Sanskrit College established. *Ecole Polytechnique* instituted in Paris. Cotton ginning machines invented by Eli Whitney. Spanish translation of Rousseau, *Declaration of the Rights of Man,* printed secretly in Bogotá by Antonio Nariño.
**1794–1854** John Gibson Lockhart, Scots biographer.
**1794–1865** Charles Cavendish Fulke Greville, diarist.
**1794–1871** George Grote, historian.

**1795** 5 Dec., Dutch in Batavia proclaim their continued allegiance to the Hague. Johore ejects Dutch with help of Ilanun of Borneo. British take over defence of Malacca with consent of Dutch government in exile in England. Bugis leader claims title of Yam-tuan-Muda and exercises power in Johore. British mission to Burma under Captain Michael Symes: attempt to negotiate commercial treaty fails: agency of East India Co. agreed at Rangoon. Marathas attack Hyderabad: March, Nizam defeated at Kharda. English seize Trincomalee from the Dutch.
**1795–1800** Capt. John Hunter, Governor of N.S.W.

**1795** Treaty of Greenville: Indians cede lands forming present state of Ohio. Slave revolt in Jamaica. France acquires eastern Hispaniola.
**1795–1801** John Adams, President of US.
**1795–1850** Antonio López de Santa Anna.

**1795** *Conservatoire de Musique* established in Paris. *Institut de France* established. Maynooth Seminary founded, endowed from public funds. London Missionary Society founded. Lazarist School for Boys founded in Damascus.
**1795–1821** John Keats, poet.
**1795–1842** Thomas Arnold, historian and educationist.
**1795–1856** Jacques Nicholas Augustin Thierry, historian.
**1795–1860** Sir Charles Barry, architect.
**1795–1881** Thomas Carlyle, essayist and historian.
**1795–1886** Leopold von Ranke, historian.

| WESTERN & NORTHERN EUROPE | CENTRAL & SOUTHERN EUROPE | AFRICA |
|---|---|---|

**1795** 23 Sept., Constitution of the Year III proclaimed in Paris. 2 Oct., English take Ile d'Yeu. 5 Oct., rising in Paris crushed by General Buonaparte. 26 Oct., Convention closed. 28 Oct., Legislative Councils opened in Paris. 1 Nov., the Directory formed, with Senate, Council of fifty-five, and an executive Directory of five members: in power to 1799. Abortive Catholic Relief Bill in Ireland.

**1796** 1 Jan., Ministry of Police inaugurated in Paris. 1 March, Dutch EIC dissolved. 29 March, rebellion in La Vendée ended. 11 Apr.–10 May, Buonaparte wins a number of engagements in Italy. 5 Aug., Franco-Prussian Treaty of Berlin. 15 Dec., French fleet with 15,000 men to attack Ireland under General Hoche embarks at Brest: 22 Dec., wrecked or turned back in Bantry Bay. Catherine II of Russia d.: succ. Paul I (–1801): restricts succession of Russian throne to male primogeniture: Cabinet again re-established as colleges: former forms of administration in Poland and Sweden restored: powers of nobility restricted: ½m. persons made serfs. Insurrection Act of extreme severity passed in Ireland.

**1796** 23 Feb., Buonaparte nominated to command French army in Italy. 19 Aug., treaty of San Ildefonso: offensive and defensive alliance between France and Spain against England. 8 Oct., Spain declares war on England. 10 Oct., Peace Treaty between France and the Two Sicilies. 22 Oct., English driven out of Corsica. Montenegro proclaims its independence. Russian army occupies Transcaucasia.

**1796** US treaties with Tunis, and Tripoli.

**1797** March to Oct., Ulster disarmed. 15 Apr., preliminary peace treaty between France and Austria. 15 Apr.–16 June, mutinies in the fleet at Spithead and the Nore. June, Franco-Dutch fleet, with 14,000 men, embarks at Texel to attack Ireland. 4 Sept., Directory carries out *coup d'état* against opposition in the Senate and Council of Fifty-Five. 11 Oct., Franco-Dutch fleet defeated at Camperdown by Admiral Duncan.

**1797** 14-16 Jan., battle of Rivoli; 29 Jan., Trento occupied by the French; 2 Feb., Mantua taken; 9 Feb., Ancona taken; 19 Feb., treaty between Pope Pius VI and France. 20-23 Apr., armistice on the Rhine. 17 Oct., Treaty of Campo-Formio between Austria and France. 9 Dec., Congress of Rastadt opened. British forces sent to aid Portugal against France and Spain.
**1797–1840** Frederick William III, King of Prussia.

**1797** US treaty with Algiers.
**1797–1814** Semakokiro, Kabaka of Uganda: regular trade with east coast.

**1798** 9 Jan., last Irish Parliament meets. 22 Jan., Batavian Republic established in Holland (–1806). 19 May, French expedition leaves for Egypt. 26 May–30 June, rebellion in Co. Wexford. 21 June, General Lake defeats Wexford rebels at Vinegar Hill. 17 July, Act of Amnesty for Irish rebels. 22 Aug., 1,000 French land at Killala Bay, Ireland, under General Humbert: shortly defeated. 5 Sept., military conscription made compulsory in France. 19 Nov., Wolfe Tone d. 23 Dec., Russo-Turkish treaty against France; 24 Dec., Anglo-Russian treaty.

**1798** 28 Jan., France invades Switzerland. 15 Feb., Roman Republic proclaimed. 26 March, Geneva annexed to France. 29 March, Switzerland reorganized as the Helvetic Republic. 10-13 June, French take Malta. 19 Aug., alliance between France and the Helvetic Republic. 9 Sept., Turkey declares war on France. Nov., British take Minorca. 6 Dec., Naples and Sardinia declare war on France. 8 and 10 Dec., French occupy Turin. 15 Dec., French enter Rome.

**1798** 1-3 July, French take Alexandria. 21 July, battle of the Pyramids: Napoleon Buonaparte takes Cairo: 1 Aug., Nelson destroys French fleet in Aboukir Bay. Francisco Lacerda's expedition begun across Africa.

**1799** 12 July, 'Combinations' (political associations of labourers) forbidden in England.

**1799** 23 Jan., French occupy Naples: Parthenopean Republic proclaimed.

**1799** 24 July, Napoleon Buonaparte defeats Turks at Aboukir: 22 Aug., secretly leaves Egypt: Kléber left in command.

| THE EAST & AUSTRALASIA | THE AMERICAS | RELIGION & CULTURE |
|---|---|---|

**1795–1800** Nana Fadnavis, leading Maratha politician.
**1795–1807** Raja Ali, Bugis under-king in Johore.
**1795–1818** British establish joint Anglo-Dutch administration in Malacca.

**1796** Feb., EIC in Madras signs treaty with King Rajadhirajasinha of Kandy: British take over all previous Dutch rights: 16 Feb., Colombo surrenders to British: Galle and Matara follow. Russia abortively invades Persia. Aga Muhammad Khan formally crowned as Shah. Shah Rukh d., following torture. Zaman Shah of Afghanistan campaigns abortively in the Punjab.
Chinese population 275.6m.
**1796–1821** Jen Tsung, Chinese Emperor, with throne-name Chia Ching.

**1796** 1 June, Tennessee becomes a US State. Riots in Quebec against *corvée*. Pro-French feeling subsequently slowly dwindles, being replaced by French Canadian nationalism. Spain at war with England: value of exports from Buenos Aires falls from 5½m. in 1796 to 335,000 *pesos* in 1797. Dutch settlement in Guiana.
**1796–1808** Boom in Canadian fur trade.

**1796** E. Jenner first makes vaccine against smallpox from cows.
Glasgow Missionary Society founded.
Jews granted civil rights in Amsterdam.
**1796–1832** Sadi Carnot, French military engineer and scientist.
**1796–1875** Jean Baptiste Camille Corot, French artist.
**1796–1859** William Prescott, historian.

**1797** Jan., Zaman Shah enters Lahore. June, Committee of Investigation appointed to report on revenue and other matters in Ceylon. Treaty between EIC and Oudh: fort of Allahabad ceded to EIC. Aga Muhammad Shah assassinated: succ. Fath Ali Shah (–1834). Rajadhirajasinha, King of Ceylon, d.: succ. Sri Vikrama Rajasinha. Penang headquarters for British expedition to attack Spanish shipping in the Philippines.
**1798** 1 Sept., treaty between EIC and Nizam of Hyderabad: French officers removed from Hyderabad army. Marathas attack Madras and Bombay. Oct., Frederic North appointed Governor of Ceylon (–1805): judiciary, revenue and education organized, but much follows on Dutch precedents. Sir Alfred Clarke, Governor-General of Bengal *ad int.* British occupy Perim Is. Bass Strait discovered by George Bass and Matthew Flinders.
**1798–1805** Earl of Mornington, subsequently Marquess Wellesley, Governor-General of Bengal.
**1798–1843** Ahmad Taj al-Din, Sultan of Kedah.
**1799** Feb.–16 Apr., Buonaparte takes El Arish, Jaffa, Gaza and Mt Tabor: besieges Acre: following plague, withdraws to Egypt (20 May).

**1797** 27 Apr., General Robert Prescott, Governor-in-chief of Canada (–1807). French squadron off Newfoundland and Nova Scotia: no damage done. Trinidad taken by the British from Spain.
First plough patented in US.

**1798** US naval vessels engage and defeat French warships. US Alien and Sedition Laws. Honduras taken by Britain.

**1799** 14 Dec., George Washington d. St John Island renamed Prince Edward Is. Immigration of Scottish and Irish Catholic peasantry begins.

**1797** May, further abortive Catholic Relief Bill in Ireland. 22 Oct., Jacques Garnerin makes the first drop by parachute in Paris.
**1797–1828** Franz Peter Schubert, Austrian composer.
**1797–1848** Gaetano Donizetti, Italian composer.
**1797–1863** Alfred, Comte de Vigny, novelist and poet.
**1797–1875** Charles Lyell, geologist.
**1797–1877** Louis Adolphe Thiers, historian and politician.
**1798–1837** Giacomo Leopardi, Italian poet and philosopher.
**1798–1855** Adam Mickiewicz, Polish poet.
**1798–1857** Auguste Comte, philosopher.
**1798–1863** Eugène Delacroix, French artist.
**1798–1874** Jules Michelet, historian.

**1799–1837** Alexander Pushkin, poet.
**1799–1845** Thomas Hood, poet and writer.

| WESTERN & NORTHERN EUROPE | CENTRAL & SOUTHERN EUROPE | AFRICA |
|---|---|---|

**1799** 27 Aug.–6 Oct., abortive Anglo-Russian expedition in Holland. 8 Oct., Buonaparte reaches Fréjus; 9 Nov., *coup d'état* in Paris: Buonaparte given command of all French armies: the Directory transferred to St Cloud: Council of Fifty-Five driven from the Chamber by armed force. 10 Nov., Buonaparte, Ducos and Sieyès named consuls by the Senate: Buonaparte, as First Consul, *de facto* ruler of France: Consulate to 1804. 24 Dec., Constitution of the Year VIII proclaimed in Paris: First Consul assisted by two consultative consuls, Senate of 60, Tribune of 100, and legislative body of 300 members. Final session of Irish Parliament. Pitt introduces income tax in England: taxes also on bricks, hats, manufactures, powder for wigs, and windows.

**1800** 17 Jan., treaty of Luçon: final submission of rebels in La Vendée to Buonaparte. 11 Feb., Bank of France established. 17 Feb., French administration centralized. May-June, France renews hostilities against the coalition. 20 June, new treaty between Austria and England at Vienna. 28 July, preliminary treaty between France and Austria: Ulm, Ingolstadt and Philippsburg ceded to France. 1 Aug., Act of Union (of 5 May) between Great Britain and Ireland becomes law: includes union between Churches of England and Ireland. 30 Sept., commercial treaty between France and the United States. 16 Dec., Paul I of Russia leaves the coalition, and allies with Denmark, Prussia and Sweden against England. Dec., Austro-French armistice. Treaty of alliance between Russia and Turkey against France. Georgia annexed by Russia.

**1801** 9 Feb., Peace of Lunéville between France and Austria. 14 March, Pitt resigns on grounds of George III's refusal to agree Catholic emancipation: succ. Henry Addington (later Viscount Sidmouth). 23 March, Paul of Russia murdered; succ. Alexander I (–1825). 2 Apr., Danish fleet defeated by Nelson off Copenhagen. Anglo-Russian relations restored. 5 July, French defeat English in naval engagement off Algeciras. 8 Oct., Congress of Amiens opens, to discuss peace between France and England. Peace treaty between Russia and France; and between Russia and Britain.

**1799** 12 March, Directory declares war on Austria: second coalition, of Austria, Britain, parts of the Empire, Naples, Portugal, Turkey, the Barbary States, and Russia formed. 17-19 June, battles of Trebia ruin French domination of Italy and Lombardy. George XII of Georgia bequeaths Georgia to Paul I of Russia by his Will.
**1799–1825** Maximilian IV, Elector of Bavaria (King from 1806).

**1800** 2 and 4 June, French occupy Milan: Cisalpine Republic proclaimed. 14 June, French victorious at Marengo. 5 Sept., Malta capitulates to the English. 3 Dec., French victory over Austria at Hohenlinden.

**1801** 3 and 8 June, French occupy Vicenza and Verona. 22 Feb., Spain enters war as ally of France against Portugal: Portugal supported by England. 18 March, treaty between France and Naples. 21 March, Franco-Spanish treaty. 29 Sept., peace of Badajoz between France and Spain. 1 Oct., treaty of St Ildefonso between France and Spain: Louisiana ceded to France. Franco-Spanish ultimatum to Portugal: Spain invades Portugal: withdraws after three weeks.

**1799** Commercial treaty between Morocco and Spain. US defaults in treaty payments to Algiers, Tripoli and Tunis.

**1800** F. Hornemann d. after visiting Bilma, Kuka, Katsina and the Nupe. 24 Jan., treaty of El Arish between Kléber and English under Sir Sidney Smith. 20 March, following English denunciation of treaty of El Arish, fresh hostilities in Egypt: Kléber overcomes Egyptian rebels: is assassinated (14 June).
**c. 1800–50** Export of slaves from Mozambique to S America rises to over 15,000 and up to 25,000 annually.

**1801** 21 March, French defeated by British and Turks at Alexandria; 3 Sept., French evacuate. Muhammad Ali arrives in Egypt with local levies from Kavalla. Bey of Tripoli insists on payment of US debt: Four Years War ensues.

## THE EAST & AUSTRALASIA

**1799** 6 May, Tipu Sultan killed in storming of Seringapatam: Hindu royal family restored in Mysore: EIC annexes Kanara, Coimbatore and Seringapatam. EIC also takes over administration of Surat. 31 Dec., Dutch East India Co. dissolved: property taken over by the state. Zaman Shah appoints Ranjit Singh Raja of Lahore. Burmese force pursuing Arakanese rebels encounters and defeats small British force.
**1799—1878** Rev. John Dunmore Lang, Australian preacher and politician: advocate of a federated, republican, Australia.

**1800** EIC takes over part of Oudh. Nana Fadnavis d.: Daulat Rao Sindia and Jaswant Rao contest Maratha leadership. Indian population c. 130m. Sir John Malcolm's first mission to Persia. Zaman Shah of Afghanistan blinded and deposed: succ. Mahmud Shah (−1805). Sir George Leith, Lieut.-Governor of Penang, obtains cession of part of mainland Kedah: named Province Wellesley. Population of Penang 12,000, chiefly Malays, but also Chinese and Indians. British begin to import Indian opium into China.
**1800—6** Captain Philip King, Governor of N.S.W.
**c. 1800** Battambang and Siam-reap annexed by Siam. Japanese population c. 29m.: kept constant by infanticide of unwanted children.
**post 1800** American, British and French whalers fishing off New Zealand.

**1801** Wahhabi sack Karbala. EIC takes over the Carnatic and Tanjore. John Malcolm's first embassy to Persia: makes commercial and political treaties for EIC. Ranjit Singh defeats the Bhangis. Governor King of N.S.W. complains that the colony is swamped with political prisoners.
**1801—2** Mahmud Shah of Afghanistan puts down Ghilzai rebellion.

## THE AMERICAS

**1799** General Peter Hunter, Governor of Upper Canada: large grants of lands to senior officials and friends.

**19th c.** Coffee planting increases in Brazil.
**1800** Oct., France purchases Louisiana from Spain.
**c. 1800** c. 776,000 negroes in Spanish America and 300,000 in Jamaica.
**post 1800** Iron industry begun in Pittsburgh.

**1801** 4 March, Thomas Jefferson (Rep.) becomes President of US (−1809): first to be sworn in Washington, D.C., now the capital. Toussaint l'Ouverture in control of Santo Domingo as well as Haiti.
**1801—35** John Marshall, Chief Justice of US.

## RELIGION & CULTURE

**1799—1850** Honoré de Balzac, novelist.
**1799—1854** Almeida Garrett, Portuguese novelist, epic poet, lyricist and dramatist.
**1799—1856** Heinrich Heine, German poet.
**1799—1875** George Finlay, historian.
**1799—1874** Comtesse de Ségur, woman of letters.
**1799—1890** John Joseph Ignatius Döllinger, theologian and historian.

**ante 1800** Latin still the language of science.
**1800** Robert Owen begins pioneer reforms at New Lanark. Volta invents the electric pile. Last surviving Jesuit in Canada d.: huge Jesuit estates passed to Crown: used to finance education.
**1800—23** Pius VII (Chiaramonti), Pope.
**1800—59** Thomas Babington, Lord Macaulay, Whig historian and essayist.
**1800—68** Ramon Maria Narvaez, Spanish soldier and dictator.
**1800—75** Jacques Paul Migne, publisher of the works of the Fathers.
**1800—82** Edward Bouverie Pusey, Anglican theologian.
**1800—82** Friedrich Wöhler, chemist.
**1800—84** Jean-Baptiste Dumas, novelist.
**1800—91** Helmuth Carl Bernhard, Count von Moltke, German soldier and strategist. George Bancroft, American historian and statesman.
**c. 1800** The screw lathe invented.

**1801** 15 July, concordat restores French relations with the Vatican: Catholic Church fully restored in France. 24 Dec., road steam locomotive, carrying passengers, invented by Richard Trevithick. Royal Institute for the Advancement of Learning established in Canada. Johannes van der Kemp, first LMS missionary, reaches Cape Town.
**1801—3** Lord Elgin brings the 'Elgin Marbles' from the Pantheon to England.
**1801—52** Vincenzo Gioberti, Italian philosopher.
**1801—76** Edward William Lane, orientalist and Arabic lexicographer.
**1801—85** Anthony Ashley-Cooper, Earl of Shaftesbury, statesman and reformer.

| WESTERN & NORTHERN EUROPE | CENTRAL & SOUTHERN EUROPE | AFRICA |
|---|---|---|

**1801** 8 Oct., treaty of Paris: Franco-Turkish relations restored: Egypt given back to Turkey. First Secretary of State for the Colonies and War appointed in England.

**1802** 27 March, Peace of Amiens between England and France. 19 May, Legion of Honour instituted in France. 26 Apr., general amnesty proclaimed in France for all *emigrés*. 2 Aug., French Senate proclaims Buonaparte First Consul for life (−1804). Council of the Russian Empire created. First Act passed in Britain to protect child labour.

**1802** 26 Jan., Buonaparte becomes President of the Italian Republic. Aug.–Sept., Buonaparte annexes Elba, Parma, Piacenza and Piedmont.

**1802** John Trutor and William Somerville explore Bechuanaland. **c. 1802–67** Kimweri the Great, Sultan of Vuga.

**1803** Apr., Buonaparte occupies parts of Holland in attempt to control Straits of Dover. 18 May, Britain renews war with France: blockade of France renewed. 23 July, abortive insurrection in Ireland led by Robert Emmet: 19 Sept., executed. Oct., Russia and the Ottoman Empire make peace with France. 2 Dec., French encamp at Boulogne with a view to invading England.

**1803** 2 Feb., Act of Mediation: new constitution given to Switzerland by Buonaparte: six additional cantons admitted. 23 Feb., Diet of Ratisbon reorganizes German constitution. March, British decline to evacuate Malta. British seize Dutch colonies. May, France occupies Hanover. 27 Sept., alliance between France and Switzerland. Tsar Alexander I occupies Georgia.

**1803** Feb.–1806 Jan., Batavian Republic rules the Cape. Uthman dan Fodio summoned from retirement to Gobir. Xhosa claim territory between Fish R. and Sunday R. Commando against Hottentots and Kaffirs. **1803–4** American naval operations against Tripoli.

**1804** 15 Feb., arrest of Georges Cadoudal, and Generals Pichegru and Moreau, for conspiring against Buonaparte. 7 May, the *Code Civile* (or *Code Napoléon*) promulgated. 10 May–Feb. 1806, William Pitt (the Younger) Prime Minister. 18 May, Napoleon Buonaparte proclaimed Emperor by the Legislature (−1814): the French empire declared hereditary: new constitution promulgated. 19 May, eighteen French generals made Marshals of France. 24 May, defensive alliance between France and Russia.

**1804** 15 March, Duc d'Enghien abducted from Baden, and 21 March, executed after trial in Paris. 8 Aug., Francis II, Holy Roman Emperor, takes title of Emperor of Austria (−1835). 6 Nov., Austro-Russian convention. 12 Dec., Britain at war with Spain.

**1804** Muhammad Ali expels Mamluks from Cairo. 21 Feb., Uthman dan Fodio's *Hijra* or Flight: beginning of *jihad* in present N Nigeria: Uthman ruler of Sokoto (−1817). Battle of Tsuntua: 200 scholars killed.

## THE EAST & AUSTRALASIA | THE AMERICAS | RELIGION & CULTURE

1801—90 John Henry, Cardinal Newman, theologian, apologist and poet.

1802 23 Oct., Maharajah Holkar of Indore defeats Peshwa Baji Rao II of Poona and Daulat Rao Sindia of Gwalior at Poona: Amrit Rao made Peshwa. 31 Dec., treaty of Bassein by Britain and Marathas: Baji Rao II restored under British protection as Peshwa: British now supreme in Deccan. Persian embassy to Bombay. Mir Fath Ali Khan of Sind d.: Sind partitioned into four amirates. Ranjit Singh obtains control of Amritsar. British embassy sent to Burma with a regiment: agreed that a British agent should reside at Rangoon. Ceylon made a British Crown Colony: governors henceforward appointed by the Crown, but also answerable to EIC: peace of Amiens confirms British possessions. White Lotus rising finally suppressed: 20,000 beheaded in city of Wuchang.
1802—3 Australian coast surveyed by Matthew Flinders.
1803 Jan., British declare war on Sinhalese at Kandy: town speedily evacuated: puppet Muttu Swamu made king. 24 June, British force in Ceylon trapped by Sinhalese: officers and men shot: Muttu Swamu executed by order of Sri Vikrama Rajasinha. 3 Aug., British declare war on Daulat Rao Sindia of Gwalior: second Mahratta war. 23 Sept., Arthur Wellesley (later Duke of Wellington) defeats Sindia of Gwalior at Assaye. 30 Dec., treaty of Surji Arjungaon: Sindia of Gwalior submits to the British. Treaty of Deogaon with Bhonsla raja. Delhi occupied by Lord Luke. Lord Wellesley forbids sacrifice of children on Saugor Is., R. Hugli. Wahhabi take Mecca. First settlement made in Tasmania. Sydney firm begins hunting seals off Dusky Sound, New Zealand. Sept., 11,000 seal skins exported from Sydney.
1804 16 Apr., EIC declare war on Holkar of Indore. 13-17 Nov., Holkar defeated at Dig. Wahhabi take Medina. Hobart founded by Lieut. Bowen.

1802 French expedition against Toussaint l'Ouverture: French suffer numerous losses, but succeed in capturing him.

1803 30 Apr., France sells Louisiana to US for $15m. Meriwether Lewis and William Clark explore the Pacific coast of USA: basis laid for Missouri Fur Co. British Guiana ceded to Britain. Tobago and St Lucia acquired by Britain. State of Ohio formed. Canadian Judicature Act: imperial Parliament gives Canada power over 'the Indian territory'. *Marbury* v. *Madison* establishes right of US Supreme Court to review laws passed by Congress and by State legislatures.

1804 Dessalines succ. Toussaint l'Ouverture: Saint-Domingue declared independent as Haiti.

1802 1 May, French system of public instruction reformed: *Lycées* created. The *Edinburgh Review* founded. Cobbett begins publication of the *Political Register*.
1802—28 Richard Parkes Bonington, artist.
1802—61 Jean Baptiste Henri de Lacordaire, preacher and journalist.
1802—73 Sir Edwin Landseer, artist.
1802—85 Vicomte Victor-Marie Hugo, novelist and poet.
1802—29 Henry Abel, Norwegian mathematician.
1802—65 Nicholas Patrick Stephen, Cardinal Wiseman, 1st Abp of Westminster.
1802—78 Felix Antoine Philibert Dupanloup, Bp of Orléans, polemicist.
1803 Sunday School Union instituted.
1803—64 Robert Smith Surtees, sporting novelist.
1803—69 Hector Berlioz, French composer.
1803—70 Aléxandre Dumas (père), novelist.
1803—70 Prosper Mérimée, novelist.
1803—73 Edward Bulwer-Lytton, Lord Lytton, novelist and statesman.
1803—73 Justus von Liebig, chemist.
1803—75 Robert Stephen Hawker, poet.
1803—81 George Borrow, traveller and writer.
1803—82 Ralph Waldo Emerson, American poet, writer and Transcendentalist.
1803—36 Richard Hurrell Froude, Anglican theologian.
1803—89 António da Costa Cabral, Portuguese statesman.
1804 British and Foreign Bible Society founded. Kharkov University founded. Père Lachaise cemetery opened. Kazan University founded.
1804—49 Johann Strauss (senior), Austrian composer.
1804—57 Mikhail Ivanovitch Glinka, Russian composer.
1804—65 Richard Cobden, Liberal politician and free-trader.
1804—69 Charles-Augustin Sainte-Beuve, poet and historian.
1804—76 George Sand (ps. of Baronne Amandine Lucile Aurore Dudevant), novelist.
1804—81 Benjamin Disraeli, Earl of Beaconsfield, statesman and novelist.
1804—57 Daniele Manin, Italian patriot.
1804—68 Nathaniel Hawthorne, American novelist.

| WESTERN & NORTHERN EUROPE | CENTRAL & SOUTHERN EUROPE | AFRICA |
| --- | --- | --- |

**1804** 16 Aug., Napoleon distributes Crosses of the Legion of Honour to French troops encamped at Boulogne, preparatory to the invasion of England. 24 Aug., Russia breaks off relations with France. 2 Dec., Coronation of Napoleon and Josephine in Nôtre Dame. 3 Dec., alliance between Russia and Sweden.
**1804—1814** First Empire in France.
**1805** Jan., alliance between Russia and Sweden. 18 March, Napoleon becomes King of Italy: Eugène Beauharnais, viceroy. 8 Apr., treaty of St Petersbourg: third coalition between Britain and Russia against France. May, Napoleon again attempts to get control of the Straits of Dover. 22 July, naval action off Cape Finisterre. 27 Aug., Napoleon breaks up camp at Boulogne, having abandoned project of invading England. Alexander I of Russia decrees that landowners may liberate their slaves: decree almost without effect.

**1805** 4 June, Napoleon takes Genoa. Ligurian League united with France. 9 Aug., Austria joins the coalition. 11 Sept., Austria invades Bavaria. 21 Sept., treaty of Paris between France and Naples: Naples declared neutral. 25 Sept., the Grand Army crosses the Rhine. 8 Oct., Austrians defeated at Werlingen. 9 Oct., French occupy Augsburg; 10 Oct., Munich; 14 Oct., Memmingen; 17-20 Oct., Ulm; 21 Oct., English fleet defeats combined French and Spanish fleet at Trafalgar: Nelson killed. 29-31 Oct., French cross Adige Pass, and occupy Salzburg. 13 Nov., French occupy Vienna; 14 Nov., Trent; 15 Nov., Pressburg; 19 Nov., Bryün. 2 Dec., French victory at Austerlitz: Russians lose 21,000 men. Turkey recognizes Napoleon as Emperor. 15 Dec., treaty of Schönbrunn between France and Prussia. 26 Dec., treaty of Presburg between Austria and France, followed by agreements with Bavaria, Prussia and Württemberg. Bavaria and Württemberg become kingdoms; Baden a Grand Duchy. 27 Dec., Napoleon dethrones Ferdinand III of Sicily.

**1805** 12 May, Muhammad Ali installed as Viceroy of Egypt (—1848). July, British return to the Cape.
**1805—1952** Egypt under the House of Muhammad Ali.

**1806** 23 Jan., Pitt d.: Feb., succ. William Wyndham, Lord Grenville: 'Ministry of All the Talents'. 15 Feb., treaty of Paris: France and Prussia ally against Britain. Apr., Britain blockades France. 20 July, preliminary arrangements made for peace between France and Russia. 6 Oct., fourth coalition against France announced.
**1806 f.** Speranski, confidant of Paul I, real power in Russia and follower of Napoleonic ideas of legalized autocracy.

**1806** 8 Feb., France invades Kingdom of Naples. 30 March, Italy divided into fiefs held by Buonaparte family and friends. Joseph Buonaparte, King of the Two Sicilies. May, Godoy pays Napoleon 24m. francs: Portugal to be partitioned. 5 June, Louis Buonaparte proclaimed King of Holland (—1810): 12 July, Confederation of the Rhine created under French protection. 6 Aug., Francis II abdicates as Holy Roman Emperor, taking title of Emperor of Austria (—1835). 14 Oct., rising in Prussian Poland in favour of France. French victorious at Jéna; 16 Oct., Erfurt capitulates; 17 Oct., engagement at Halle; 18 Oct., Leipzig occupied; 24 Oct., Potsdam occupied; 25 Oct., Berlin and Brandenburg occupied. 29 Oct., French take Stettin; 1 Nov., Kustrin; occupation of Hesse-Cassel; 6-7 Nov., Lubeck taken; 10 Nov., Hanover and Posen taken. 21 Nov., 'Continental System' inaugurated by Napoleon. 28 Nov., duchies of Mecklenburg occupied: Russia declares war on France. 11 Dec., peace treaty between France and

**1806** Mungo Park assassinated.
**1806** Jan.—21 March 1877, second British occupation of the Cape.
**1806—7** Ashanti-Fante war.
**1806—56** Sayyid Said bin Sultan, ruler of Oman and Muscat, and of Zanzibar.

| THE EAST & AUSTRALASIA | THE AMERICAS | RELIGION & CULTURE |
|---|---|---|

1804—85 Sir Julius Benedict, composer.

**1805** Apr., Russian vessel off Nagasaki asked to leave and not return: Japanese decline contact with foreigners. July, Marquess Cornwallis, Governor-General of Bengal: second term. 5 Oct., Cornwallis d.: succ. Sir George Barlow (—1807). 23 Nov., EIC treaty with Sindia revised. Wahhabi invade Syria and Iraq: territory extends from Palmyra to the border of Oman. Mahmud Shah of Afghanistan deposed: succ. Shuja al-Mulk (—1809). EIC makes Penang a Presidency, with more than fifty officials: first governor P. Dundas; Thomas Raffles an assistant secretary.
**1805—11** Sir Thomas Maitland, Governor of Ceylon: administration re-organized.

**1805** New Indian confederacy formed by Shawnee chief, Tecumseh: his brother, proclaiming himself a prophet, preaches anti-white doctrines to Indians. American expedition of Lewis and Clark explores lower Columbia from inland.

1805—59 Alexis Clerel de Tocqueville, historian.
1805—82 William Harrison Ainsworth, novelist.
1805—72 Giuseppe Mazzini, Italian patriot.
1805—75 Hans Christian Andersen, Danish poet and writer.
1805—80 Ellen Tree, actress.
1805—91 Vicomte Ferdinand de Lesseps, canal promoter.

**1806** French embassy to Persia. Shah Alam II d.: succ. Akbar II (—1837).
**1806—8** Captain William Bligh, Governor of N.S.W.: policy of strict discipline and repression of abuses.
**1806—15** Rise of the Pindaris in C India.

**1806** Apr., US forbids British imports. 27 June, unauthorized expedition, led by Commodore Sir Home Popham, attacks Río de la Plata: Buenos Aires captured: $1m. prize money sent home: British shortly evicted by the inhabitants: provisional *junta* formed. Benito Juárez b. at Oaxaca, Mexico. Dessalines shot: chaos in Haiti. Aaron Burr acquitted of treason against US. Francisco de Miranda lands in Venezuela: attempt to provoke revolution abortive.

1806 13 Feb., breach between France and the Vatican. The *Arc de Triomphe* begun in Paris.
1806—61 Elizabeth Barrett Browning, poetess.
1806—73 John Stuart Mill, philosopher and economist.
1806—73 Franz-Xavier Winterhalter, artist.
1806—75 Dom Prosper Guéranger, OSB, Abbot of Solesmes, liturgist.
1806—82 Frederic Le Play, economist.

## WESTERN & NORTHERN EUROPE

## CENTRAL & SOUTHERN EUROPE

## AFRICA

Saxony: Saxony made a kingdom: joins Confederation of the Rhine.
**1806–12** War between Russia and Turkey.

**1807** 5 Jan., French take Breslau. 7 March, Grenville cabinet resigns following George III's refusal to grant Catholic emancipation: succ., Duke of Portland (−1809), with Canning and Castlereagh. 25 March, slave trade abolished in all British possessions. 2-5 Sept., British bombard Copenhagen: Danish fleet seized. 16 Oct., treaty of Alliance between France and Denmark. 17 Oct., first French expedition against Portugal. 27 Oct., secret treaty of Fontainebleau between France and Spain. 30 Oct., treaty of alliance between Denmark and France. 11 Nov., treaty between France and Holland. 30 Nov., the French take Lisbon. Daniel O'Connell becomes leader of the Catholic Association in Ireland.

**1807** 14 Jan., Napoleon enters Warsaw. 7-8 Feb., Napoleon defeats Prussians and Russians at Eylau. 23 Apr., convention of Bartenstein between Prussia and Russia. 7 May, Franco-Prussian treaty of Finkenstein. 20 May, French take Danzig. 25 May, Selim III deposed by the Janissaries: succ. Mustafa IV (−1808): military reforms abolished. 14 June, French victorious at Friedland; 16 June, take Königsberg; 25 June, Napoleon meets Alexander of Russia at Tilsit. 7 July, peace treaty of Tilsit between France and Russia, and, 9 July, France and Prussia: Prussia loses possessions west of R. Elbe: Warsaw made a Grand Duchy. Nov., French army under Junot marches through Spain and attacks Portugal: 13 Nov., Portuguese royal family withdraw to Brazil with 2,000 persons. Portugal ruled by French military governors. 1 Dec., war between Britain and Prussia. 8 Dec., Kingdom of Westphalia created for Jerome, brother of Napoleon (−1813): 10 Dec., Kingdom of Etruria created for Joseph, brother of Napoleon.

**1807** March, British occupy Alexandria briefly. Mombasa instals a puppet sultan in Pate. Slave trade stopped at the Cape: Earl of Caledon, first British civil governor. Slave trade abolished by Britain (effective 1 March 1808).

**1808** 21 Feb., Russia invades Finland. 1 March, Napoleon creates a new Imperial nobility. 8 Sept., Convention of Paris between France and Prussia: 27 Sept.–14 Oct., Alexander I of Russia and Napoleon meet at Erfurt: Russia committed to war against Sweden: all of Finland taken by Russia. Scottish judicial system reformed.

**1808** Jan., war between Austria and Britain. 2 Feb., the French enter Rome. March, 100,000 French take possession of N Spain: Murat marches on Madrid: Spanish royal family flee to America: Charles IV of Spain abdicates: succ. Ferdinand: forced by Napoleon to abdicate in favour of his father: 20 March, Charles IV then abdicates in favour of Napoleon. 2 May, popular rising in Madrid: *juntas* formed in many towns. 20 July, Joseph Buonaparte makes solemn entry into Madrid as King of Spain) (−1813). 28 July, Mustafa IV deposed by Mahmud II (−1839): policy of reform and modernization ensues. 1 Aug., Sir Arthur Wellesley (later Duke of Wellington), disembarks with British force in Portugal. Aug., 160,000 French troops in Spain. 13 Aug., Madrid retaken by the Spaniards. 21 Aug., battle of Vimeiro. 30 Aug., Cintra capitulates. Sept., Central *Junta* constituted at Aranjuez as government of Spain. 5 Nov., Convention of Berlin. 10 Nov., French take Burgos; 12 Nov., battle of Espinosa; 23 Nov., of Tudela. 4 Dec., French take Madrid. Dec., George Karageorge recognized as hereditary Prince of Serbia (−1813).

**1808** Uthman dan Fodio takes Bornu brother Abdullahi Amir of Gwandu. Sierra Leone made a Crown Colony.

**1809** 9 Apr., fifth coalition against France announced. 6 June, Gustav IV Adolf of Sweden forced to abdicate: succ. Charles XIII (−1818).

**1809** 5 Jan., peace treaty between Britain and Turkey. Stratford Canning (later Lord Stratford de Redcliffe), sent to Turkey.

**1809** Fante attack Accra and Elmina. Hottentots put under colonial law.

**THE EAST & AUSTRALASIA**     **THE AMERICAS**          **RELIGION & CULTURE**

---

**1807** May, treaty of Finkenstein between France and Persia.
**1807—8** French military mission to Persia under General Gardanne: Persian army reorganized. French ceded Is. of Kharak, Persia.
**1807—13** Lord (later Earl of) Minto, Governor-General of Bengal.

**1807** May, General Whitelocke sent with reinforcements to Buenos Aires: reaches Montevideo, finding 6,000 English refugees from Buenos Aires; June, further reinforcements sent, making 10,000 men. 5 July, British attack Buenos Aires: repulsed by inhabitants: 400 British killed, 650 wounded, 1925 taken prisoner: British evacuate remainder to Montevideo. 24 Oct., Sir James H. Craig, Governor-in-Chief of Canada (—1812). 22 Dec., Jefferson embargoes American navigation. H.M.S. *Leopard* gratuitously attacks U.S.S. *Chesapeake* off Virginia. Steam boat service organized by Fulton on Hudson River. Following closure of Baltic, Canadian timber trade begins to flourish: Ottawa valley occupied.
**1807—70** Robert E. Lee, American Confederate General.

**1807** Vaccination against smallpox first made compulsory by Bavaria.
**1807—82** Giuseppe Garibaldi, Italian patriot.
**1807—82** Henry Wadsworth Longfellow, American poet.
**1807—80** Louis Félicien de Sauley, archaeologist and numismatist.
**1807—81** Jane Elizabeth Digby, commonly Lady Ellenborough, traveller and romantic.
**1807—83** Abd-elKader, Algerian resistance leader.

---

**1808** 26 Jan., the 'Rum Corps' depose Governor Bligh and the Judge-Advocate: no governor of N.S.W. until 1810. Sir John Malcolm's embassy to Persia. Rebellion put down by Shah Shuja al-Mulk of Afghanistan. Jaswant Rao Holkar becomes insane.
**1808—9** Sir Harford Jones's mission to Persia.

**1808** 1 Jan., import of slaves into USA forbidden. Jan., Dom João, Regent of Portugal, takes refuge in Brazil with 2,000 followers; March, court established in Rio de Janeiro. Town councils in Spanish America repudiate French repudiation of Spanish throne. American Fur Co. formed by John Jacob Astor.
**1808—10** Revolutionary movements start in Mexico, and spread throughout S America.
**1808—18** Alexandre Pétiou, 'President of the Republic of (S) Haiti'.
**1808—20** General Henri Christophe, ruler of N Haiti.

**1808** Scottish judicial system reformed; Pope Pius VII declines to invest bishops nominated by Napoleon. First printing press established in Brazil. The Holy Sepulchre, Jerusalem, destroyed by fire: shortly rebuilt.
**1808—42** Espronceda, Spanish poet.
**1808—70** Michael William Balfe, composer.
**1808—72** Giuseppe Mazzini, Italian writer and patriot.
**1808—92** Henry Edward, Cardinal Manning, ecclesiastic and statesman.

---

**1809** 12 March, Anglo-Persian defensive and offensive treaty made by Sir Harford Jones.

**1809** 9 Jan., US Non-Intercourse Act against British commerce.

**1809** 12 June, Napoleon excommunicated. National Society formed to promote Church of England schools. *Quarterly Review* founded.

| WESTERN & NORTHERN EUROPE | CENTRAL & SOUTHERN EUROPE | AFRICA |
|---|---|---|

**1809** 28 July—23 Dec., abortive British expedition to Walcheren Is. 17 Sept., peace of Frederikshamn between Russia and Sweden: Russia gains Finland. Oct. Duke of Portland resigns: Spencer Perceval, Prime Minister (—1812). 16 Dec., Napoleon divorces Josephine de Beauharnais. Secret treaty between Britain and Turkey. Landowners in Russia forbidden to send their alves to Siberia.

**1809** 16 Jan., Sir John Moore killed at Corunna. 21 Feb., French take Saragossa. 28 March, French take Medelin; 29 March, Oporto. 10 Apr., Austria at war with France. War between Russia and Turkey renewed. 16 Apr., battle of Sicily; 20 Apr., battle of Abensburg; 22 Apr., battle of Eckmühl; 23 Apr., Ratisbon taken. 1 May, Napoleon annexes Papal States: Pope Pius VII taken prisoner to Savona. 3 May, Russia declares war on Austria. 10—18 May, French evacuate Portugal. 12 May, Wellington takes Porto. 13 May, Vienna occupied. 21-22 May, battle of Aspern. 14 June, battle of Raad. July, Count Metternich made Chief Minister in Austria (—1848). 4 July, French cross the Danube; 5 July, battle of Enzensdorp; 5-6 July, battle of Wagram. 28 July, battle of Talavera. 14 Oct., treaty of Vienna: western Galicia added to Grand Duchy of Warsaw: Russia retains eastern Galicia: France holds Trieste and Illyria: Salzburg and Inn awarded to Austria. Napoleon in command in Spain with some 300,000 men.

**1809—11** Henry Salt's expedition to Ethiopia.

**1810** 1 Jan., Council of the Russian Empire re-organized: ministers replace former colleges. 6 Jan., peace treaty between France and Sweden. 4 Feb., Alexander I of Russia declines to allow Napoleon to take his sister in marriage. 2 Apr., Napoleon marries Marie-Louise of Austria. 9 July, France annexes Holland. 21 Aug., Marshal Bernadotte adopted as heir by Charles XIII of Sweden. 17 Nov., Sweden declares war on Britain.

**1810** 2 Feb., French occupy Seville. 5 Feb., French occupy Malaga. 13 May, French take Lérida. Sept., Constituent *Cortes* of 105 deputies summoned in Spain by Regency Council. Krupp factory opened at Essen.

**1810** 7-8 July, English take Bourbon Is. 3 Dec., English take Ile de France (shortly renamed Mauritius). **1810—14** Shaikh Ahmad Loba, Massina Fulani, conquers Massina. **1810—28** Radama I, Merina ruler: opens Madagascar to European influences. **c. 1810** Abiodun, Alafin of Oyo, d.: Yoruba Kingdom breaks up. Ilorin becomes an independent state.

**1811** 5 Feb., Regency Act: Prince of Wales appointed Regent for George III, stricken with *porphyria*.(—1820). March, Luddite rising in Nottingham-shire smashes weaving machines (—1815). 20 March, King of Rome, heir to Napoleon b. Dec., secret agreement between Britain and Russia to break Continental System.

**1811** 22 Jan., Napoleon annexes North Sea coast. 10 Feb., Russia takes Belgrade: Turkish army captured. 20 Feb., Austria bankrupt. 5 March, French checked at Lines of Torres Vedras. 10 March, French take Badajoz. May, French withdraw from Portugal. 28 June, French take Tarragona. 17 Oct., Prusso-Russian military convention. 25 Oct., battle of Sagonta.

**1811** 1 March, Muhammad Ali massacres Mamluks in Cairo. Further war between Ashanti and Fante. Fulani over-run Oyo.

| THE EAST & AUSTRALASIA | THE AMERICAS | RELIGION & CULTURE |
|---|---|---|

**1809** 25 Apr., EIC signs treaty with Ranjit Singh, Sikh ruler of Lahore. June, treaty between England and Shah Shuja al-Mulk of Afghanistan. Mahmud Shah of Afghanistan restored (−1829): Fath Khan, *Sirdar,* real power. French expelled from Persian court. Following ill treatment by Europeans, Maoris kill and eat crew of the *Boyd.* Intermittent war between Maoris and Europeans.
**1809−24** Rama II, King of Siam: cautious beginning made in contacts with the W.

**1809** French evicted from Dominica: first republic of Dominica proclaimed.
**1809−17** James Madison (Rep.), President of US.

**1809** The electric telegraph invented by Samuel Sömmering.
**1809−47** Jakob Ludwig Mendelssohn−Bartholdy, German composer.
**1809−49** Julius Slowack, Polish poet and philosopher. Edgar Allan Poe, novelist.
**1809−50** Giuseppe Giusti, Italian poet.
**1809−52** Nicolai Gogol, Russian novelist.
**1809−61** Leopold O'Donnell, Duke of Tetuan, Spanish politician and general.
**1809−65** Pierre Joseph Proudhon, political writer.
**1809−82** Charles Darwin, explorer, naturalist and scientist.
**1809−83** Edward Fitzgerald, translator of Umar Khayyam and dramatist.
**1809−91** Samuel Ajayi Crowther, first Yoruba to become an Anglican bishop. Georges Eugène, Baron Haussmann, planner of modern Paris. Alexander William Kinglake, traveller and historian.
**1809−92** Alfred, Lord Tennyson, poet.
**1809−93** Marie-Edmé Patrice Maurice de MacMahon, Duke of Magenta, French statesman and Marshal of France.
**1809−94** Oliver Wendell Holmes, American author.
**1809−98** William Ewart Gladstone, statesman and polymath.

**1810** Dec.−**1821** Col. Lachlan Macquarie, Governor of N.S.W.: 73rd Highlanders Regiment accompanies him.
**1810** Sir John Malcom's third mission to Persia. Two Filipinos sent as representatives to Spanish *Cortes.* Population of N.S.W. 10,000.

**1810** 19 Apr., *Junta* set up to govern Venezuela in Caracas: delegation, including Bolívar, sent to London and Paris to request recognition. 25 May, provisional *junta* of the Provinces of Río de la Plata, governing for Ferdinand VII, proclaimed at Buenos Aires: Cornelio Saavedra, President. *Juntas* formed in many Spanish American towns loyal to Ferdinand VII of Spain: temporary self-government then leads to eventual independence. Mexican parish priest, Fr Miguel Hidalgo y Costilla, urges Indian peasants to revolt: mob attacks Spaniards: Fr Miguel unable to control his followers: shortly executed: succ. Fr. José María Morelos. Francisco de Miranda returns to Venezuela: proclaimed commander-in-chief and dictator. US population *c.* 7m.

**1810** University of Berlin founded. Great Mosque of Jaffa built.
**1810−49** Frédéric François Chopin, Polish composer.
**1810−56** Robert Schumann, German composer.
**1810−57** Alfred de Musset, dramatist and poet.
**1810−61** Camillo, Count Cavour, Italian statesman.
**1810−76** Samuel Sebastian Wesley, composer. Félicien David, composer.
**1810−77** Herculano, Portuguese poet, historian and novelist.
**1810−95** Sir Henry Rawlinson, orientalist.
**1810−65** Abraham Lincoln, American President and statesman.
**1810−80** Ole Bull, Norwegian violinist.
**1810−92** Alexander Raugabe, Greek statesman and writer.

**1811** 18 Sept., British expedition under Lord Minto takes Java: Thomas Raffles appointed Lieutenant-Governor (−1816). Mysore transferred to the EIC. Jaswant Rao Holkar d. Chin Byan, Arakanese refugee in Bengal, collects force of refugees and Indians with weapons obtained from the British: occupies Arakan, and proclaims himself king: defeated by Burmese army and returns with force to British territory.
**1811−18** Muhammad Ali of Egypt makes war on the Wahhabi at the request of the Porte.

**1811** 2 Feb., US renews Non-Intercourse Act. June, Paraguay declared independent. Dr José Gaspar Rodríguez de Francia, President (−1840). 5 July, Venezuela proclaimed independent: civil war ensues: Simon Bolívar, commander-in-chief. July, Michilimackinac taken by Canadians: western Indian tribes won to British. Aug., Americans surrender Fort Detroit and Michigan country. Sept., *junta* at Buenos Aires replaced by a triumvirate. Major-General Isaac Brock, administrator and C.-in-C. of Upper Canada.

**1811** Two-thirds of Welsh Protestants secede from the Church of England. The carpet sweeper invented. Oslo University founded.
**1811−17** Waterloo Bridge built by Sir John Rennie.
**1811−63** William Makepeace Thackeray, novelist.
**1811−70** Charles Dickens, novelist.
**1811−72** Théophile Gautier, dramatist, poet and novelist.
**1811−78** Sir George Gilbert Scott, architect.
**1811−86** Franz Liszt, Hungarian composer.
**1811−89** John Bright, statesman and orator.

1811–1813

WESTERN &
NORTHERN EUROPE

CENTRAL &
SOUTHERN EUROPE

AFRICA

**1812** 24 Jan., treaty of Paris between France and Prussia. 4 March, treaty of alliance between France and Austria. 9 Apr., Russo-Swedish secret treaty of Abo. May, formal diplomatic relations broken off between France and Russia. 11 May, Spencer Perceval shot dead in the lobby of the House of Commons: 9 June, Earl of Liverpool, Prime Minister (–1827)(Conservative). 18 July, Britain, Russia and Sweden ally at Örebro. 1 Aug., treaty of St Petersburg between England and Russia. 17 Aug., French take Smolensk; 17-18 Aug., battle of Polotsk: French army begins to disintegrate through sickness and desertion. 7 Sept., battle of Borodino: French again victorious: Russians evacuate Moscow and withdraw: Moscow fired, only one-fifth of the houses remaining. 23 Oct., French retreat from Moscow begins: Moscow evacuated. 12 Nov., battle of Wiazma. 14-16 Nov., French evacuate Smolensk. 26-28 Nov., French conduct fighting retreat at Beresina river. 10-11 Dec., French evacuate Vilno; and 16 Dec., Kovno. 30 Dec., remains of Napoleon's army cross R. Niemen, having lost 300,000 men either dead or taken prisoner. Convention of Tauroggen between Prussia and Russia. Irish Catholic Association suppressed. Large scale ship-building begun on the Clyde.
**1812–22** Viscount Castlereagh (later Marquess of Londonderry), Foreign Secretary of the UK.
**1813** 8 Sept., French surrender San Sebastian to English. 9 Sept., Treaty of Töplitz: Austria, Prussia and Russia ally against France. 8 Oct., Wellington invades southern France. 16 Nov., French evacuate Amsterdam. 17 Nov., Netherlands declares herself independent. 1 Dec., William I of Orange-Nassau made King of the Netherlands. 5 Dec., Stettin capitulates. 11 Dec., Treaty of Valençay. 11 Dec., six allied divisions cross Rhine: beginning of allied invasion of France: 24 Dec., French evacuate Holland.

**1812** 19 Jan., Wellington victorious at Ciudad Rodrigo. 19 March, Constitution of Cadiz, new Spanish constitution promulgated by Constituent *Cortes*. 6 Apr., British victorious at Badajoz. 28 May, peace treaty of Bucharest between Russia and Turkey: Russia gains Bessarabia. 2 June, secret convention between Austria and Russia. 23-24 June, Napoleon crosses R. Niemen and advances into Russia. 22 July, British take Salamanca. Battle of Arapiles; 28 July, French enter Vitebsk.

**1813** 31 Jan., armistice between Austria and Russia. 9 Feb., Russia occupies Warsaw, and then all Poland: end of the Grand Duchy of Poland. 28 Feb., Prusso-Russian alliance of Kalisch. 1 March, sixth coalition formed against France. Treaty of alliance between Prussia and Russia. 12 March, French evacuate Hamburg. 16 March, Prussia declares war on France. 18 March, Russia takes Hamburg. 2 May, battle of Lutzen. 30 May, French re-occupy Hamburg. 4 June, armistice of Plesswitz. 21 June, battle of Vitoria. 14, 15 and 27 June, treaties of Reichenbach. 12 July, Congress of Prague opens. 12 Aug., Austria declares war on France. 26-27 Aug., battle of Dresden. 8 Oct., treaty of Ried: Bavaria joins allies. 16-18 Oct., battle of Leipzig. 30 Oct., battle of Hanau.

**1812** Muhammad Ali sends embassy to the Fuaj. Xhosa driven back behind Fish R.
**1812–16** Radama I increases his territory.
**1812–46** Sahela Selassie, King of Shoa.

**1813** Mazrui attempt to seize Lamu: defeated at Shela.
**1813–14** J.L. Burckhardt exploring Upper Egypt and Nubia.

| THE EAST & AUSTRALASIA | THE AMERICAS | RELIGION & CULTURE |
|---|---|---|

**1812** Petra reached by J.L. Burckhardt: visits Mecca and Medina. Pindaris and Pathans raid Mirzapur.

**1811** *The Tonquin*, owner J.J. Astor, rounds Cape Horn: Astoria founded. American expedition against Shawnee Indians.
**1811–4** José Miguel Carrera, dictator of Chile.
**1812** 26 March, disastrous earthquake in Venezuela: 20,000 dead in Caracas region. 14 Apr., Louisiana made a US State. 18 June, war declared by President Madison on Britain: New England and NE states remain neutral; known as the 'War of 1812' (–1814). 15 July, Sir George Prevost, Governor-in-Chief of Canada (–1816). 31 July, Caracas retaken by Spanish royalists: Francisco de Miranda taken prisoner and deported to Spain: Bolívar allowed to leave for Columbia. 2,000 militia embodied as volunteers in Lower Canada.

**1811–99** Robert Wilhelm von Bunsen, chemist.

**1812** 23 Feb., Napoleon annuls the Concordat. June, Pope Pius VII brought to Fontainebleau as prisoner. Toleration Act repeals Five Mile Act and Conventicle Act in England. Church Missionary Society (CMS) instituted. Baptist Union of Great Britain formed. Hydraulic jack invented.
**1812–52** Augustus Welby Northmore Pugin, architect.
**1812–58** Sigismund Krasinski, Polish poet.
**1812–88** Edward Lear, writer of comic verse.
**1812–89** Robert Browning, poet.
**1812–1904** Samuel Smiles, biographer and writer.
**1812–84** Paul Abadie, architect.
**1812–87** Alfred Krupp, arms manufacturer.
**1812–96** Harriet Beecher Stowe, American authoress.

**1813** EIC Charter renewed. Treaty of Gulistan between Russia and Persia: Persian vessels excluded from the Caspian. Rising in N China by secret 'Society of Heaven's Law'. Raffles deprives Javanese princes of remaining powers. Blue Mountains, N.S.W., first crossed by Gregory Blaxland, William Lawson and William Charles Wentworth.
**1813–23** Earl of Moira (later Marquess of Hastings), Governor-General of Bengal.

**1813** Aug., Bolívar, with republican army, retakes Caracas. Oct., Bolívar acclaimed liberator of Venezuela. Nov., Fr. José Morelos in control of S Mexico: convenes congress to proclaim Mexican independence. Paraguay proclaims herself independent of Spain and of Río de la Plata: José Gaspar Rodríguez Francia, first President. American naval force burns parts of York (Toronto): Lake Erie and Detroit taken.

**1813** 25 Jan., Concordat of Fontainebleau between Napoleon and Pope Pius VII. Muhammad Ali initiates policy of sending Egyptians to study in Europe. The fire extinguisher invented. Puffing Billy and Wylam Dilly, steam locomotives built by William Hedley. First educational grant made by EIC. The Inquisition suppressed in Spain.
**1813–43** Robert Southey, English poet laureate.
**1813–55** Soren Kierkegaard, Danish philosopher.
**1813–73** Dr David Livingstone, explorer, traveller and writer.
**1813–83** Wilhelm Richard Wagner, German composer.
**1813–86** Edward Cardwell, Lord Cardwell, Liberal politician.
**1813–98** Sir Henry Bessemer, engineer.
**1813–1901** Giuseppe Verdi, Italian composer.

| WESTERN & NORTHERN EUROPE | CENTRAL & SOUTHERN EUROPE | AFRICA |
|---|---|---|

**1813** 11 Nov., French surrender Dresden. 26 Dec., Austria invades Switzerland.

**1814** 1 Jan., French surrender Danzig. 3 Jan., Austrians occupy Montbéliard. 4 Jan., Russians occupy Haguenau. 14 Jan., treaty of Kiel between Denmark and Sweden: Denmark cedes Norway. 17 Jan., allies take Langres: 19 Jan., Dijon: 21 Jan., Châlon-sur-Saône. 17 Jan., Napoleon retakes St Dizier. 5 Feb., Congress of Chatillon, between Austria, England, Prussia and Russia opened. Châlons-sur-Marne occupied; 17 Feb., Troyes occupied. 1 March, treaty of Chaumont between Allies. 2 March, allies take Soissons. 12 March, Duc d'Angoulême enters Bordeaux. 13-14 March, Napoleon retakes Reims. 24 March, Austrians occupy Lyons. 31 March, Paris surrenders to allies: Louis XVIII re-established on throne (−1815). 1 Apr., provisional government set up at Paris by the Senate. 5 Apr., Convention of Chevilly. 6 Apr., Napoleon abdicates. 10 Apr., battle of Toulouse. 11 Apr., new constitution in Norway. 20 Apr., Napoleon leaves Fontainebleau for Elba. Louis XVIII enters London in state: 23 Apr., Conventions signed in Paris by allies and the Count d'Artois for France. 24 Apr., Louis XVIII disembarks at Calais. 27 Apr., Treaty of Paris: Napoleon made King of Elba. 4 Nov., new constitution in Sweden. Holland makes the slave trade illegal.

**1815** 26 Feb., Napoleon leaves Elba. 1 March, Napoleon disembarks near Cannes: beginning of the Hundred Days. 10 March, Napoleon reaches Lyons. 20 March, Louis XVIII flees from Paris: Napoleon enters. 7 June, Napoleon opens legislature in Paris. 18 June, battle of Waterloo. 21 June, Napoleon returns to Paris; and, 22 June, abdicates again. 25-26 June, risings and massacres in Marseilles. 28 June, state of siege in Paris. 29 June, Napoleon leaves Paris. 3 July, Convention of St Cloud. 8 July, Louis XVIII restored in Paris (−1824): Bourbon dynasty again (−1830). July-Sept., 'White Terror' in France against the former officials of the imperial regime, chiefly in the S (ended only in 1816). 8 Aug., Napoleon exiled to St Helena. 26 Sept., Holy Alliance signed in Paris between the Emperors of Austria and Russia, and the King of Holland. 20 Nov., Treaty of Paris between France, Austria, Britain, Prussia and Russia. 20 Nov., Britain, Portugal, Prussia and Russia guarantee perpetual neutrality and inviolability of Switzerland.

**1814** Ferdinand VII of Spain returns from captivity in France: 4 May, constitution annulled: Inquisition restored. 15 July, Convention of the Straits: the Dardanelles and Black Sea closed to war vessels of all nations whenever Turkey is at peace. 9 Sept., new federal constitution ratified in Switzerland. 12 Sept., Geneva, La Valais and Neuchâtel join Swiss Confederation. 1 Nov., Congress of Vienna opened. Nov., rebellion in Serbia. Rebellion in Pamplona in favour of constitution.

**1815** 3 Jan., alliance between Austria, Britain and France. 6 Apr., Murat occupies Florence. 2-3 May, battle of Tolentino. 31 May, Treaty of Vienna: final coalition of Austria, England, Holland, Prussia and Russia against Napoleon. 9 June, Congress of Vienna closes. 26 Aug., Holy Alliance between Austria, Prussia and Russia. 5 Nov., Britain obtains protectorate over Ionian Is: High Commissioner resident at Corfu (−1864) introduces cricket to the island.

**1814** Abdallah b. Ahmad al-Mazrui declares Mombasa independent. 13 Aug., the Cape becomes a British Colony: Lord Charles Somerset, Governor (−1827). 26 Oct

**1815** 13 Oct., Napoleon arrives in St Helena. US peace treaties with Algiers and Tripoli. French re-occupy Bourbon. Namiembali, first King of Mangbetu dynasty, greatly expands kingdom.

| THE EAST & AUSTRALASIA | THE AMERICAS | RELIGION & CULTURE |
|---|---|---|

**1814** Hung Hsiu-chuan b. Chinese population 374.6m. 26 Oct., EIC at war with Gurkhas in Nepal. 23 Nov., treaty between England and Persia. Rebellion in Philippine Is.
**1814–15** Pindaris and Pathans plunder Hyderabad and Madras Presidency.

**1814** Jan., Bolívar made Dictator of Venezuela. July, indecisive battle between British and US troops at Lundy's Lane. Sept., Spain reconquers Venezuela: Bolivar goes into exile in Haiti. 24 Dec., treaty of Ghent between Britain and US ends 'War of 1812'. Americans try in vain to cut the St Lawrence route. British occupy Maine. Chief Justice Sewell impeached by Canadian Assembly for plotting to unite Lower Canada with New England. New Mexican constitution promulgated by Fr. Morelos. Ferdinand VII of Spain imposes reactionary regime in S America. Spain regains Santo Domingo (Dominica) (–1821).
**1814–17** Spanish power restored in Chile. José de San Martín, Governor of Cuyo.
**1814–40** Dr Francia, dictator of Paraguay.

**1814** 25 Dec., Rev. Samuel Marsden first to preach in New Zealand: lay industrial CMS missionaries set up at the Bay of Islands. Pope Pius VII restores the Society of Jesus, the Inquisition and the Congregation of the Index. The Blucher locomotive built by George Stephenson. First street lighting in London by gas. Machine press first used to print the *Times.*
**1814–70** Juan Prim, Marquis de los Castillejos, Spanish general and Liberal statesman.
**1814–73** Joseph Sheridan Le Fanu, novelist.
**1814–75** Jean François Millet, French artist.
**1814–78** Julius Robert Mayer, physicist.
**1814–79** Eugène Emmanuel Viollet-le-Duc, French architect.
**1814–84** Charles Reade, novelist.

**1815** Second Kandyan war: 2 March, British governor receives submission of Kandyan chiefs. 9 March, Kandyan Convention signed: all provinces of Ceylon formally ceded to Britain: end of Kingdom of Kandy. Apr., Gurkhas lose Jaitak and Almora. July, envoy of Gaekwar of Baroda murdered by Marathas at Pandurpur. Sept., Trimbakji, favourite of the Peshwa, imprisoned for complicity in the envoy's murder. Abortive attack by Daulat Rao Sindia on Bhopal.
**1815–90** Sir Henry Parkes, Australian politician.

**1815** Andrew Jackson defeats British under Edward Pakenham at New Orleans. 16 Dec., Brazil proclaimed by Dom João an Empire equal with Portugal. 22 Dec., Fr Morelos executed in Mexico City. Settlement of British war veterans on Rideau R.
**1815–42** Corn laws protect Canadian wheat exports.

**1815** 24 Apr., Tooth Relic of the Buddha formally installed in the Dalada Maligava, Kandy. *The New Zealander's First Book,* first Maori dictionary, by Thomas Kendall, published.
**1815–16** The Davy safety lamp invented.
**1815–82** Anthony Trollope, novelist.
**1815–84** Giovanni Prati, Italian poet.
**1815–86** Sir Thomas Erskine May, constitutional lawyer and historian.
**1815–98** Otto Eduard Leopold, Prince von Bismarck, German statesman.
**1815–71** Ali Pasha, Turkish reformer.
**1815–91** George Leveson-Gower, Earl Granville, statesman.
**1815–91** Ernest Meissonier, artist.

## WESTERN & NORTHERN EUROPE

## CENTRAL & SOUTHERN EUROPE

## AFRICA

**1815** 27 Nov., new constitution in Poland: Tsar of Russia made hereditary ruler, with Diet. Scottish judicial system again reformed. Robinson's Corn Law forbids import of corn into England unless price exceeds £4 a quarter. Russia obtains almost all the ancient Kingdom of Poland; Prussia takes Posen region; Austria takes Galicia.
**1815–25** Araktcheiev the *eminence grise* in Russia.
**1816** 8 May, divorce abolished in France. Britain abolishes income tax, reduces armaments and restores gold standard.

**1816** 13 March, treaty between France and Switzerland. 5 May, first constitution in Germany granted by Karl August of Saxe-Weimar. 5 Nov., German Diet meets at Frankfurt. Conspiracy against Ferdinand VII of Spain discovered in Madrid.
**1816–26** John VI, King of Portugal.

**1816** Anglo-Dutch fleet under Lord Exmouth destroys port and fleet of Algiers.

**1817** 28 Feb., treaty of Paris between France and Portugal. 17 Sept., trade treaty between Britain and Spain: West Indies trade opened to Britain. Partial famine in Ireland.

**1817** 13 July, George Karageorge, assassinated by Milosh Obrenovitch; 18 Oct., German student demonstration at Wartburg. 6 Nov., Milosh I Obrenovitch, Prince of Serbia (–1839). Revolutionary conspiracy in Lisbon put down harshly. Rising in Catalonia. Serbia granted autonomy by Turkey.

**1817** Privateering forbidden by Morocco. Uthman dan Fodio d.: Muhammad Bello, Sultan of Sokoto (–1837), warrior and author. British treaty with Ashanti, and with Radama I.

**1818** 30 Sept., Congress of Aix-la-Chapelle: allies evacuate France. British Board of Agriculture abolished. Slave trade made illegal by France.

**1818** 26 May, new constitution in Bavaria. 29 Aug., new constitution in Baden. Alexander I of Russia opens Diet of Warsaw: ancient forms of government restored in Poland.

**1818** Muhammad Ali of Egypt made Wali of Ethiopia. French expand sphere of influence in Senegal. Cloves introduced into Zanzibar.
**1818–20** Sultan of Fezzan raises taxes on 4,000 slaves passing annually through his territory.

| THE EAST & AUSTRALASIA | THE AMERICAS | RELIGION & CULTURE |
|---|---|---|

**1816** March. EIC peace treaty with Gurkhas: resident installed at Khatmandu. Raghuji Bhonsla II of Nagpur d.: treaty absorbs Nagpur into EIC sphere. 1 June, an Irishman sells his wife in Hobart, Tasmania, for a gallon of rum and twenty ewes. 19 Aug., Java and adjoining possessions restored to Holland. Nov., Siamese require Sultan of Kedah to invade Perak to collect tribute. Fath Khan occupies Herat. Chandra Kanta Singh, King of Assam, flees to Bhutan: asks Burmese aid: restored: following Burmese withdrawal, dethroned. Abortive British mission to China. First free immigrants reach Tasmania. Egyptians under Ibrahim Pasha begin operations against Wahhabis.
**1816–17** Pindaris driven back to Nemawar.

**1817** July, treaty of Poona: Peshwa formally renounces headship of Maratha confederation. 5 Nov., Peshwa attacks Poona, and then Nagpur and Indore: third Mahratta War begun. Burmese nominee established on the throne of Assam. Kedah forces deposition of Sultan of Perak: Raja Muda appointed subject to Kedah. J.T. Bigge sent by British government to report on conditions in Australia. First bank opened in Sydney.
**1817–18** EIC punitive expedition against the Pindaris. Treaties made by EIC with nineteen Rajput states, including Jaipur, Jodhpur and Udaipur. Rebellion against the British in Ceylon: Tooth Relic removed secretly from Kandy, and then falls into British hands: end of ineffective struggle.
**1818** 6 Jan., Treaty of Mundosir: EIC annexes Indore. 21 Dec., Mahrattas severely defeated. Fath Khan blinded: Mahmud Shah, and his son Kamran, confined to Herat: remainder of Afghanistan divided by the Sadozai brothers: Dost Muhammad Khan takes Ghazna. Mughul canal system repaired. Egyptians crush Wahhabi: capital of Diriyah razed.

**1816** March, Bolívar returns to Venezuela: hailed 'Supreme Chief of the Republic'. 9 July, Tucumán Congress: Río de la Plata Provinces proclaim independence: Juan Martín Pueyrredón, Supreme Director (–1819): congress established in Buenos Aires. 12 July, Sir John Sherbrooke, Governor-in-Chief of Canada (–1818). 11 Dec., Indiana becomes a US State. Dec., Bolívar returns to Venezuela with army equipped in Haiti: seizes Orinoco estuary: independence of Venezuela proclaimed with Angostura (re-named Ciudad Bolívar) as capital: congress summoned.

**1817** Jan., Montevideo taken by Portuguese troops. Jan., Army of the Andes, led by José de San Martín, crosses Andes from Argentina into Chile. 12 Feb., San Martín routs Spanish army at Chacabuco: 15 Feb., elected governor of Chile: rejects honour in favour of Bernardo O'Higgins, Chilean hero. 4 March, James Monroe (Rep.) sworn President of US (–1825). 10 Dec., Mississippi becomes a US State. Rush-Bagot Agreement: Great Lakes disarmed. Ferdinand VII buys Russian warships to mount expeditio against rebels in S America. Bolívar receives volunteer reinforcements from England.
**1817–25** Erie Canal (Clinton's Ditch) built, linking Great Lakes with R. Hudson.

**1818** 12 Feb., Chile proclaimed independent by San Martín. March, San Martín defeated by Spanish at Cancha Rayada. 5 Apr., Spanish royalist forces defeated by José de San Martin at Maipú, Chile: Bernardo O'Higgins, President. 30 July, Duke of Richmond and Lennox, Governor-in-Chief of Canada (–1819). 20 Oct., frontier between Canada and US delimited. 3 Dec., Illinois created a US State.

**1816** Elgin Marbles acquired by the British Museum. The stethoscope invented. School of Engineering founded in Cairo. First Malayan school opened in Penang.
**1816–55** Charlotte Brontë, novelist.
**1816–62** Arthur Gobineau, historian and novelist.
**1816–75** Sir William Sterndale Bennett, composer.
**1816–92** Ernst Werner von Siemens, electrician.
**1816–99** Philo Remington, American inventor.

**1817** Sacred Congregation for the Propagation of the Faith reformed. Gallican project for a concordat with Rome. Prussian Evangelical Church founded by Frederick William III. Liège University founded.
**1817–93** Benjamin Jowett, scholar.
**1817–94** Sir Henry Layard, explorer and writer.
**1817–98** Sir Sayyid Ahmad Khan of Delhi, Indian political leader.
**1817–1904** George Frederick Watts, artist and sculptor.
**1817–75** Pierre Larousse, encyclopaedist.
**1817–79** John Thaddeus Delane, editor of the *Times* (1841-77).
**1817–88** Pascal-Stanislaus Mancini, Italian politician.
**1817–1903** Theodore Mommsen, historian.

**1818–48** Emily Brontë, novelist.
**1818–59** St Jean-Marie Vianney, Curé d'Ars.
**1818–66** John Mason Neale, hymnographer.
**1818–83** Karl Marx, political philosopher. Ivan Turgeniev, Russian novelist.
**1818–86** William Edward Forster, Liberal politician.
**1818–89** James Prescott Joule, scientist.
**1818–89** Louis Faidherbe, colonial governor.

1818–1821

WESTERN &
NORTHERN EUROPE

CENTRAL &
SOUTHERN EUROPE

AFRICA

| | | |
|---|---|---|
| **1819** 16 Aug., 'Peterloo Massacre' at Manchester. Children forbidden to labour in mills in England under age nine: limit of twelve-hour day for other young workers. | **1819** 1 Jan., rising in Cadiz of 18,000 troops ordered for service in America: return to the 1812 constitution demanded: troops allowed not to sail: similar risings in other Spanish cities follow: provisional *Junta* accepted by Ferdinand VII. 23 March, Kotzebue assassinated by Sand, a student. May-Nov., conference of Vienna. Aug.-Sept., conference of Carlsbad. Württemberg given a constitution. Rising in Valencia. **1819–61** Prince Albert of Saxe-Coburg-Gotha, husband of Queen Victoria. | **1819** Cape troops campaign against the Ndhlambi. Muhammad Ali tours Nubia. First British consul appointed to Kumasi. |
| **1820** 29 Jan., George III of England d.: succ. George IV (−1830). 13 Feb., Duc de Berry murdered. 2-3 June, riots in Paris. July-Nov., Queen Caroline's divorce Bill before Parliament. Preobajensky Guards mutiny. Cato Street conspiracy. | **1820** 5 Jan., Spanish revolution against the monarchy begins (−7 March). 2 July, rebellion in Naples and Palermo. 28 Aug., revolution in Portugal: garrison of Oporto rebels: joined by Lisbon garrison: provisional *junta* established. 27 Oct.−17 Dec., congress of Troppau. 19 Nov., right of intervention promulgated. Debates of Polish Diet made secret. | **c. 1820** War between Sakalava and Merina. Zulu *impis* organized by Dingiswayo, King of the Abetetwa. **1820–1** Egyptian conquest of the Sudan by Ismail Kamil Pasha. About 5,000 British take up 100-acre farms in Cape Colony. |
| **1821** 20 March, riots in Grenoble. George IV visits Ireland. 29 July, George IV crowned: does not receive Communion: Queen Caroline excluded. | **1821** 26 Jan.−12 May, Congress of Laybach. 7 March, Austria defeats Naples at Rieti. 13 March, Victor Emmanuel I abdicates: succ. Charles Felix abdicates after one day: succ. Charles Albert of Savoy (−21 March). 23 March, rebellion in Turin: provisional government. 25 March, the Morea revolts against Turkey. 8 Apr., Austria defeats Piedmont at Novara. | **1821** 5 May, Napoleon d. in St Helena. Muhammad Ali introduces cotton into Egypt. **1821–5** Oudney, Denham and Clapperton exploring Nigeria. **1821–81** The Sudan under Egyptian administration. **1821** Sierra Leone, Gambia and the Gold Coast united as British West Africa. |

## THE EAST & AUSTRALASIA

**1818** Raja Jafar signs agreement with W. Farquhar giving EIC freedom to trade in Johore. Malacca restored to the Dutch.
**1818, 1819** Penang sends trade representations to Bangkok.
**1818–1819** Ranjit Singh takes Multan.

**1819** 6 Feb., Raffles signs treaty with Sultan of Johore, giving EIC right to build a factory: Sultan receives annual pension of $5,000. Feb., Raffles signs treaty of alliance with Acheh, without positive result. 2 June, the Peshwa surrenders to Sir John Malcolm: Poona and Mahratta dominions incorporated into Bombay Presidency. The Sikhs take Kashmir. Bagyidaw becomes King of Burma (—1837): schemes of public works abandoned: frontier troubles with British. Maoris first use muskets.

**1820** Piracy on W coast of India between Kolhapur and Goa put down. EIC treaty with Sind renewed. Water again flows in Delhi Canal. First Maori chiefs sent to visit England. Singapore port revenue already meeting cost of administration. New Spanish Constitution proclaimed in Philippines: four deputies sent to the *Cortes*.
**1820 ff.** Steady Chinese immigration into Sungei Ujong, Selangor and Perak.

**1821** Sultan of Kedah refuses Siamese order to visit Bangkok: Siamese army invades Kedah: sultan seeks protection of EIC: Governor Philips of Penang refuses to surrender sultan. Unofficial agent of Penang sent to Bangkok. Population of N.S.W. 40,000: farmland increased five-fold since 1810.
**1821 f.** Roads built in Ceylon by compulsory labour.

## THE AMERICAS

**1818** Lord Cochrane (later 10th Earl of Dundonald) organizes Chilean, and then Peruvian, navies. Jean Pierre Boyer succ. Aléxandre Pétiou in S Haiti. Free Port Act preserves position of Nova Scotian and New Brunswick shipping in W Indies. Agreement between Canada and US on fishing rights: 20 Oct., boundary between Canada and US defined: Oregon placed under joint occupation for ten years. Canadian Assembly for the first time votes whole revenue of government. Population of Canada c. 796,000.
**1819** 2 March, Alabama becomes a US State. 7 Aug., Bolívar takes Bogotá. c. 5,000 English, Irish and Scots in Bolívar's army. 17 Dec., Republic of Gran Colombia (Venezuela, Ecuador and New Granada) proclaimed: Bolívar, President. Spain formally cedes Florida to US. *McCulloch* v. *Maryland* establishes that US Constitution implicitly holds governmental prerogatives even if unstated. *Caudillos* and *gauchos* in control of most of Argentina. Lachine Canal Co. formed. Canadian Assembly refuses vote on expenditure without detailed investigation: annual strife thereafter between Governor-in-chief and Assembly. Lord Cochrane (later Earl of Dundonald) made commander of Chilean navy: progressive liberation of Peruvian coast begun.
**1820** 2 March, Missouri compromise: Missouri admitted as a State of US: Maine divided off from Massachusetts: slavery forbidden N of Lat 30° 30´ in Louisiana. 19 June, Earl of Dalhousie, Governor-in-Chief of Canada (—1831). Nov. armistice between Bolívar and Spanish royalists. Government land obtainable in US at $1.25 an acre. Chilean army of liberation sails from Valparaiso to Peru. *Gauchos* spread anarchy in Argentina: government forces defeated at Cépeda. Boyer unites all Haiti.
**1820 ff.** Trade develops on Santa Fé trail.
**1820–4** Controversy over aliens in Canada.
**1821** 24 June, Bolívar army defeats Spanish force at Carabobo. 9 July, José de San Martín leads army of liberation into Lima: 28 July, Peru proclaimed independent in San Martín's absence. 15 Sept., 'absolute independence' of Central America declared in Guatemala City: ruled by *junta*. 27 Sept., Agustin de Iturbide emerges as leader of Mexican army of independence: enters Mexico City in triumph.

## RELIGION & CULTURE

**1818–93** Charles François Gounod, French composer.
**1818–94** James Anthony Froude, historian.
**1818–86** Marco Minghetti, Italian statesman.
**1818–97** Jacob Burckhardt, Swiss historian.

**1819** May-July, severe censorship of books, newspapers and periodicals imposed upon Poland.
**1819–51** Dr. John Philip, LMS superintendent missionary in S Africa: work started among Bushmen.
**1819–75** Charles Kingsley, novelist.
**1819–80** Jacques Offenbach, French composer. 'George Eliot' (Mary Ann Evans), novelist.
**1819–83** Butrus al-Bustani, Lebanese scholar, writer and teacher.
**1819–91** James Russell Lowell, American author.
**1819–92** Walt Whitman, American poet.
**1819–95** Franz von Suppé, Austrian composer.
**1819–1900** John Ruskin, writer.
**1819–1901** Francesco Crispi, Italian statesman.

**1820** Joseph Smith claims to have seen visions which led to the foundation of the Mormon Church. Vichy Spa opened.
**1820–49** Anne Brontë. novelist.
**1820–91** William Tecumseh Sherman, American general.
**1820–95** Friedrich Engels, political philosopher.
**1820–1903** Herbert Spencer, philosopher.
**1820–1910** Florence Nightingale, pioneer of modern nursing.
**1820–1914** Sir John Tenniel, illustrator and cartoonist.
**1820–1900** Sir George Grote, musicologist.
**1820–50** Mirza Ali Muhammad, the 'Bab', founder of the Bahai.

**1821** 17 May, the *Opera* opened in Paris. Benjamin Lundy founds anti-slavery journal *The Genius of Universal Emancipation*. McGill University founded. The *Manchester Guardian* founded. *Ecole des Chartes,* Paris, founded.
**1821–5** Stockton and Darlington railway built.
**1821–67** Charles Pierre Beaudelaire, poet.

1821–1823

WESTERN &
NORTHERN EUROPE

CENTRAL &
SOUTHERN EUROPE

AFRICA

**1821** 18 Oct., Charles Felix, King of Sardinia, restored in Savoy, Turin and Piedmont (−1831). John VI returns to Portugal. New *Cortes* elected in Portugal: new Regency Council appointed. National Patriotic Society founded in Warsaw.

**1822** 12 Aug., Castlereagh commits suicide: George Canning, Foreign Secretary (−1827). George IV visits Scotland. Russian landowners again allowed to deport their slaves to Siberia. Protective tariffs set up in Russia. Further famine in Ireland. Insurrection Act in Ireland.

**1822** 13 Jan., Greece proclaims her independence from Turkey. Apr., Turks massacre Greeks in Chios. May, the Turks take Janina. Albania submits. 30 June, Spanish rebels take Ferdinand VII prisoner. 20 Oct.−14 Dec., Congress of Verona: discussion of Greek and Spanish questions. Spanish *Cortes* meets: debates in disorder: risings in many parts of Spain. New constitution promulgated by *Cortes* in Portugal: accepted by John VI.

**1822** Oct. or Nov., rising in Sudan: Ismail Pasha and retinue massacred. Liberia founded as a colony for freed slaves from US. Rising in Luanda. Omani suzerainty forcefully asserted in E.A. English the official language in Cape Colony.
**1822–30** Khartoum town built.

**1823** Reforms of Corn Law and Penal Code in Britain. Catholic Association of Ireland formed by Daniel O'Connell to procure emancipation.

**1823** Jan., Holy Alliance demands restoration of order in Spain. 7 Apr., 100,000 French 'Sons of St Louis' invade Spain. 23 May, French take Madrid. 5 June, Dom Miguel takes Lisbon. 31 Aug., French take Fort Trocadero near Cadiz: Ferdinand VII restored: French remain in Spain until 1828. Provincial Diets established in Prussia.
**1823–33** Calomarde, minister of justice in Spain: regime of extreme conservative oppression.

**1823** Shaka attacks Natal. First recorded caravan from Zanzibar, led by Musa Mzuri, an Indian, reaches L. Tanganyika.
**c. 1823** Makololo migrate to L. Ngami.
**1823–31** Ashanti at war with British

| THE EAST & AUSTRALASIA | THE AMERICAS | RELIGION & CULTURE |
|---|---|---|

**THE EAST & AUSTRALASIA**

**1821–3** War between Persia and Turkey.

**1821–4** Minor outbreaks of rioting in Ceylon.

**1821–5** General Sir Thomas Brisbane, Governor of N.S.W.

**1821–post 1830** Civil wars between Maori tribes.

**1821–50** Tao-Kuang period in China.

**1822** EIC revenue department reformed. John Macarthur given two gold medals for Merino wool from Australia. Governor-General of India sends John Crawfurd as ambassador to Siam. Sultan of Selangor liberates Perak from Siam: tribute paid henceforth by Perak to Selangor.

**1823** Jan.–Aug., Hon. John Adam, Governor-General of Bengal *ad int.* June, army mutiny in Manila.

**1823–8** Lord Amherst (later Earl Amherst). Governor-General of Bengal.

**1823–37** Burmese capital at Ava.

**THE AMERICAS**

**1821** Sept., British proclaim Honduras a Crown Colony. *Cohens* v. *Virginia* establishes right of US Supreme Court to review decisions of State courts. First Anglo-American settlement in Texas under Stephen F. Austin. Dominican patriots again proclaim independence as Spanish Haiti. Dom João leaves Brazil for Portugal: Dom Pedro, Regent of Brazil.

**1821–4** Bernardino Rivadavia, President of Argentina: administration organized.

**1822** 1 Jan., following Guatemalan request, Iturbide sends force from Mexico to take over Central America. 24 May, General Sucre takes Quito, Ecuador, with army sent by Bolívar. 21 July, Agustín de Iturbide crowned Emperor of Mexico. 26-7 July, conference at Guayaquil, Colombia, between Bolívar and San Martín: 28 July, San Martín returns to Peru, and then goes into exile in France. Aug., Iturbide imprisons fifty members of Mexican Congress. 7 Sept., Brazil becomes independent under Peter I; 12 Oct., proclaimed the Empire of Brazil. 1 Dec., Dom Pedro crowned Emperor of Brazil (–1831): José Bonifacio, Prime Minister. Dec., General Antonio López de Santa Anna rebels against Iturbide. S American republics recognized by Britain. Abortive attempt to unite the two Canadas. President Boyer of Haiti marches on Santo Domingo: whole island united (–1844). Rocky Mountain Fur Co. founded.

**1823** Feb., Ramón Freire leads successful rebellion in S Chile: O'Higgins exiles himself to Peru. Feb Santa Anna and Guadalupe Victoria issue federalist republican plan for Mexico. Iturbide deposed and exiled: Republic of Central America restored. July, constituent assembly meets in Guatemala City: independence of the 'United Provinces of C. America' proclaimed. 2 Dec., President Monroe of US sends message containing 'Monroe Doctrine' to Congress: American continent closed to further colonial settlement by European powers: European powers excluded from all interference with American republics: US will not intervene in European affairs: US respect existing European colonial rights. British Canada Trade Act provides for division of customs duties between Upper and Lower Canada. Expedition up R. Missouri against the Arikara Indians. José Antonio Páez expels Spanish from Puerto Cabello, Venezuela. First British consuls appointed to S American republics.

**RELIGION & CULTURE**

**1821–80** Gustave Flaubert, novelist.

**1821–81** Feodor Dostoievsky, Russian novelist. Auguste Mariette, Egyptologist.

**1821–90** Sir Richard Francis Burton, traveller, writer and anthropologist.

**1821–1901** Albert, Duc de Broglie, historian and political writer.

**1822** Society for the Propagation of the Faith founded. Abd al-Rahman b. Hasan al-Jabarti, historian and astronomer, d.

**c. 1822** Bulaq Press established in Cairo.

**1822–84** Gregor Mendel, geneticist.

**1822–88** Matthew Arnold, historian and poet. Sir Henry Maine, jurist.

**1822–90** César August Franck, Belgian composer.

**1822–95** Louis Pasteur, scientist.

**1822–96** Thomas Hughes, novelist. Edmond de Goncourt, novelist jointly with his brother Jules (1830–79).

**1822–1911** Francis Galton, scientist.

**1822–94** Giovanni Batista Rossi, archaeologist.

**1823** William Wilberforce forms the *British and Foreign Anti-Slavery Society.* First school opened in Singapore.

**1823–9** Leo XII (della Genga), Pope.

**1823–83** Sir William Siemens, electrician and metallurgist.

**1823–92** Edward Augustus Freeman, historian. Victor Antoine Edouard Lalo, French composer. Ernest Renan, historian and philosopher.

**1823–96** Coventry Kersey Dighton Patmore, poet.

**1823–1901** Charlotte Mary Yonge, novelist.

| WESTERN & NORTHERN EUROPE | CENTRAL & SOUTHERN EUROPE | AFRICA |
|---|---|---|
| **1824** March, Anglo-Dutch Treaty: Holland cedes to Britain Malacca and all its dependencies; withdraws objections to Singapore; Britain cedes Bencoolen to the Dutch, who retain monopoly of spice trade. June, convention of St Petersbourg between Russia and Turkey concerning Greece. 16 Sept., Louis XVIII of France d.: succ. Charles X (–1830). Anti-combination Act repealed: trade unions become lawful in England. Scottish judicial system further reformed. | **1824** Feb., Muhammad Ali of Egypt sent to put down Greek rebellion by the Porte. 19 Apr., battle of Missolonghi between Greece and Turkey: Lord Byron d. of fever. | **1824** Conscription introduced in Egypt. Ashanti army surrounds British: Sir C. McCarthy commits suicide. Sokoto at war with Bornu. First fort built at Khartoum. **1824–6** British Protectorate over Mombasa. |
| **1825** 21 March, French law gives indemnities to émigrés. 8 Oct., riots in Rouen. 19 Nov., Alexander I of Russia d.: 1 Dec., Grand-Duke Constantine proclaims his brother, Grand Duke Nicolas, Tsar at Warsaw: Constantine himself proclaimed in St Petersbourg. 12 Dec., Grand Duke Constantine formally renounces Tsardom; 14 Dec., ceremony arranged for confirmation of Grand Duke Nicolas as Tsar: troops rise in support of Constantine and are put down by force. Suppression Act ends the Catholic Association of Ireland. Economic crisis in Britain (–1827). | **1825** 4 Jan., Ferdinand I of Naples d.: succ. Francis I (–1830). Feb., Egyptian army arrives in Morea: Pylos taken. July, Greeks ask for British protection. Magyar made the official language in Hungary. **1825–48** Ludwig I, King of Bavaria. | **1825** Assembly of notables inaugurated in Khartoum. Mutiny in Bissau. Advisory Council for government set up in Cape Town. |
| **1826** 6 Dec., Nicolas I of Russia appoints commission to examine the administration. **1826–47** James Stephen at the Colonial Office (Permanent Secretary from 1836). | **1826** 10 March, John VI of Portugal d.: Crown of Portugal devised by his heir, Peter of Brazil, to his daughter, Maria II (–1853), aged seven: Dom Miguel, regent (–1828). 4 Apr., Anglo-Russian protocol on Greece made at St Petersbourg. 23 Apr., Ibrahim Pasha takes Missolonghi. 26 Apr., Portuguese *Cortes* made to accept a constitution. 16 June, Mahmud II of Turkey massacres the Janissaries: 6,000 killed: ordinance suppresses both the Janissaries and the Baktashi fraternity: surviving Janissaries exiled. 26 Aug.–5 June, 1827, Ibrahim Pasha besieges Athens. Oct., treaty of Akerman: Russia obtains autonomy for Moldavia and Wallachia from the Turks. | **1826** First Sudanese officers commissioned in Egyptian army. Shilluk raided for slaves. British rout Ashanti at Dodawa. Three Griqua states established in SA. Major Laing reaches Timbuktu, then assassinated. |
| **1827** 17 Feb., Lord Liverpool collapses. Apr.–Sept., George Canning, Prime Minister. | **1827** Apr., constitution agreed in Greece. 14 Apr., John Capodistrias elected President of Greece (–1831). | **1827** 4 Oct., France opens hostilities against the Dey of Algiers. Britain takes over Fernando Po. |

# THE EAST & AUSTRALASIA

**1824** Jan., following failure to demarcate frontier, British declare war on Burma: May, British fleet enters Rangoon: Burmese evacuate all citizens: Burmese decisively defeated at Rangoon. British take Prome. British reach Yandabo, fifty miles from Ava: Burmese accept British terms: Arakan, Assam and Tenasserim ceded to British: recognize Cachar, Jaintia and Manipur as British territory: Burmese pay indemnity of £1m.: British Resident to be stationed at Ava: commercial treaty to be agreed. Aug., second treaty between EIC and Sultan of Johore. Oct., mutiny of Indian troops at Barrackpur. First Chinese mining settlement at Lukut, Selangor. British obtain full control over Singapore Is. Singapore population 10,000 to 11,000: less than one half Malays: one third Chinese. Nominated Legislative Council of seven advisory members appointed in N.S.W.
**post 1824** Coffee industry develops rapidly in Ceylon.
**1825** Gokcha seized from Persia by Russia. Rising of Muslims in Chinese Turkestan.
**1825—** June **1826** Mission of Capt. Henry Burney to Raja of Ligor, Siam, to prevent Siamese intervention in Malaya: treaty signed.
**1825—30** Dipa Negara, a prince of Jogyakarta, rebels against the Dutch.
**1825—31** General Sir Ralph Darling, Governor of N.S.W.

**1826** Feb., treaty of Yandabo between Britain and Burma: frontiers delimited. Sept., British embassy to Burma led by John Crawfurd: frontier agreed at R. Chindwin. June, Anglo-Siamese Treaty, or Treaty of Bangkok. Russia at war with Persia: Erivan (Armenia) taken: Tabriz seized: Shah of Persia sues for peace, ceding his Armenian provinces. Dost Muhammad Khan takes Kabul: proclaims himself Amir (−1863). Malacca and Singapore become dependencies of the Presidency of Penang. First Anglo-Burmese war. Treaty between EIC and Perak. 'The Great Black War': settlers and aborigines fight in Tasmania. *Hobart Town Gazette* requests protection for young seals.
**1827** Russia takes Erivan and Tabriz.

# THE AMERICAS

**1824** Aug., army of liberation under Bolívar enters Peruvian highlands: 6 Aug., indecisive battle at Junín. 9 Dec., Bolívar's army under General Sucre defeats Spanish royalists at Ayacucho, Peru. Oct., Federalist Constitution adopted in Mexico. Iturbide returns to Mexico and is shot. Brazilian constitution promulgated. *Gibbons* v. *Ogden*: US Supreme Court establishes right to regulate inter-state commerce.
**1824—7** Average of 25,000 slaves imported into Brazil.
**1824—9** Welland Canal cut.

**1825** 28 Feb., Anglo-Russian treaty defines respective boundaries in N America. 6 Aug., Bolivia, in highlands of upper Peru, declared an independent republic as the 'Republic of Bolívar'. Rising of patriots in Uruguay; 25 Aug., Uruguay becomes independent of Brazil. Portugal recognizes independence of Brazil. France recognizes independence of Haiti. British commercial treaties with Argentina, Colombia and Mexico.
**1825—8** Argentina and Brazil at war.
**1825—29** Guadalupe Victoria, President of Mexico. John Quincy Adams (Rep.), President of US.

**1826** Texas declared independent. Radical *Colonial Advocate* press broken up by Canadian conservatives. Slavery ended in Chile. Last Spanish garrison evicted. Britain accorded special economic privileges by Brazil: Brazil agrees to abolish slave trade within three years. 22 June—15 July, abortive congress of S American republics called by Bolívar to propose a league of nations.
**1826—34** Rideau Canal cut.

**1827** Trade Union founded by Quebec printers.

# RELIGION & CULTURE

**1824** French episcopate gains control of primary education. Anglican bishoprics of Barbados and Jamaica established. J.F. Champollion, *Précis du système hiéroglyphique,* deciphers Rosetta Stone. First technical school established in Berlin. *Westminster Review* founded. Muhammad Ali Mosque, Cairo, begun.
**1824—84** Bedrich Smetana, Czech composer.
**1824—89** William Wilkie Collins, novelist.
**1824—95** Aléxandre Dumas, *fils,* novelist.
**1824—96** Anton Bruckner, Austrian composer.

**1825** 27 Sept., Stockton and Darlington Railway, first English railway, opened. The water turbine invented.
**1825—64** Ferdinand Lassalle, Socialist writer.
**1825—89** Sir Frederick Arthur Gore Ouseley, composer.
**1825—90** Castello Blanco, Portuguese novelist.
**1825—95** Thomas Henry Huxley, biologist.
**1825—99** Edward Frankland, chemist. Johann Strauss, the younger, composer.
**1825—1900** Richard Doddridge Blackmore, novelist.
**1825—1901** Bp William Stubbs, historian.
**1826** Smithsonian Institution, Washington, endowed by James Smithson (1765-1829).
The photographic camera invented.
**1826—77** Walter Bagehot, political scientist and economist.
**1826—98** Gustave Moreau, French artist.
**1826—35** Beylical Palace, Constantine, built.

**1827** School of Medicine founded in Cairo. Ohm's law *re* electric current discovered.

| WESTERN & NORTHERN EUROPE | CENTRAL & SOUTHERN EUROPE | AFRICA |
|---|---|---|
| **1827** 6 July, treaty of London: Britain, France and Russia agree to support Greek independence. 8th Aug., Canning d. 5 Sept.–1828, Viscount Goderich, Prime Minister. | **1827** 20 Oct., Turkish fleet defeated at Navarino by allied fleets of Britain, France and Russia. Federation of Pure Royalists issues manifesto in Catalonia against Ferdinand VII: risings follow: put down with severity: Don Carlos, the king's brother, candidate for the throne: origin of Carlism. | **1827** Sayyid Said of Oman receives submission of Mazrui in Mombasa. Administration of justice reformed in Cape Colony. |
| **1828** 25 Jan., Duke of Wellington, Prime Minister (–1830). Test and Corporation Acts repealed in Britain: Corn Laws revised: sliding scale introduced. | **1828** 27 Apr., war between Russia and Turkey (–1829). 23 June, Dom Miguel proclaims himself King of Portugal (–1834). 17 Aug., French expedition leaves for Morea. Customs Union (*Zollverein*) between Prussia and Hesse-Darmstadt. Russian troops occupy Danubian provinces as far as Adrianople: Turkish strongholds taken in Transcaucasia, including Erzerum. | **1828** Freedom of the press guaranteed in Cape Colony. Shaka murdered: succ. Dingaan. **1828–43** British Gold Coast settlements ruled by Committee of Merchants. **1828–61** Ranavalona I, Queen of the Merina. |
| **1829** Apr., Roman Catholic Relief Act ends penalties against Roman Catholics in England: Irish Catholic Emancipation Act. 29 Sept., policing of London reformed by Robert Peel: police known as 'Peelers' or 'Bobbies': other cities follow example of Metropolitan Police, setting up local forces. | **1829** May, the Tsar visits Poland. 14 Sept., treaty of Adrianople between Russia and Turkey: Russians keep Danubian conquests: the Straits to be open to international commerce: Greek independence recognized: autonomy of Moldavia, Wallachia and Serbia recognized under protection of Russia. **1829–31** Numerous risings of liberals in Portugal: many emigrate to the Azores and England. | **1829** Advisory Council set up in Cair Abortive French expedition against Madagascar. |
| **1830** 4 Feb., conference of London: Britain, France and Russia formally recognize Greek independence under British protection. 26 June, George IV of England d.: succ. William IV (–1837). 26 July, Charles X of France issues four *ordonnances*. 27 July, beginning of rising in Paris against Charles X. 27-9 July, the 'Three Glorious Days': Paris in a state of siege: rebels seize Arsenal, Hôtel de Ville and palaces: 30 July, National Guard resumes control: 31 July, the Duc d'Orléans proclaimed lieutenant-governor of France. 2 Aug., Charles X of France and his eldest son abdicate; 3 Aug., Chambers assemble: Charles X and his family leave for England: 7 Aug., Chamber of Deputies declares the throne vacant, and appoints Louis-Philippe, Duc d'Orléans, King: 9 Aug., Louis-Philippe takes oath. | **1830** 3 Feb., Greek frontier with Turkey fixed by protocol. 5 Feb., Milosh Obrenovitch elected hereditary Prince of Serbia. 29 Feb., Pragmatic Sanction of King Ferdinand VII of Spain. 25 May, following incident with the Dey, French fleet leaves Toulon for Algiers. 8 Nov., Francis I of Naples d.: succ. Ferdinand II (Bomba)(–1848). 29 Nov., risings against the Russians in Poland. Polish Diet opened by Nicolas I of Russia in person. **1830–73** Campaign of Germanization in Prussian Poland. | **1830** 14 June, French troops disembark on Algerian coast; 19 June battle of Staouéli. 4 July, French take Algiers; and, later, Bône, Bougie and Oran. Egba establish Abeokuta. Oyo rebuilt: Ibadan made the Yorub military headquarters. Luba army annihilated. 17 Nov., French expedition against Blida. **c. 1830** Moshesh (Moshoeshoe) unites Basuto confederacy. |

| THE EAST & AUSTRALASIA | THE AMERICAS | RELIGION & CULTURE |
|---|---|---|

**1827** Sir Moses Montefiore, Jewish philanthropist, visits Jerusalem: finds 2,000 Jewish residents.

**1827—64** John Hanning Speke, explorer.
**1827—1910** William Holman Hunt, artist.
**1827—1912** Joseph Lister (later Lord Lister), surgeon.
**1827—92** James Augustus Grant, explorer.
**1827—1908** Casimir-Adrien Barbier de Meynard, orientalist.

**1828** 22 Feb., treaty of Turkmanchai between Persia and Russia: Persia cedes part of Armenia, including Erivan. March, Hon. W. Butterworth Bayley, Governor-General of Bengal *ad int.* South Indian coolies first recruited to work on Sinhalese coffee plantations. Captain Charles Sturt explores courses of the Rs Macquarie, Darling, and related streams (—1831). NSW Legislative Council increased to fifteen members.
**1828—33** Lord William Bentinck, Governor-General of India.

**1828** 27 Aug., preliminary peace between Brazil and Argentina: independence of Uruguay recognized. UK Select Committee reports on Canada. Upper Canada Assembly makes citizens of all persons resident in Upper Canada for seven years prior to 1 March 1828. 47,450 slaves landed in Rio de Janeiro.

**1828** University of London opened. *al-Waqai al-Misriyah*, first Egyptian newspaper, founded. Thomas Arnold appointed headmaster of Rugby School. *Brahmo Socmaj* movement started by Ram Mohan Roy in India.
**1828—82** Dante Gabriel Rossetti, poet.
**1828—85** Edmond About, novelist.
**1828—93** Hippolyte Adolphe Taine, historian.
**1828—95** George Augustus Sala, novelist.
**1828—97** Margaret Oliphant, novelist.
**1828—1905** Jules Verne, novelist.
**1828—1906** Hendrik Ibsen, dramatist.
**1828—1909** George Meredith, novelist and poet.
**1828—1910** Count Leo Tolstoy, novelist.
**1828—1923** John, Viscount Morley, biographer, writer and statesman.

**1829** June, Swan River Settlement (later Western Australia) founded: Capt. Stirling, first Lieutenant-Governor: future city of Perth founded. Lord William Bentinck begins to promote spread of the English language in India: English made the language of all higher courts. Mahmud Shah of Afghanistan d.: succ. Kamran acknowledges suzerainty of Persia.

**1829** Spanish expedition from Havana to regain Mexico: repelled by General Santa Anna. Oil first discovered in USA. Vicente Guerrero, briefly President of Mexico: succ. Anastasio Bustamante (—1832). Andrés Santa Cruz seizes power in Bolivia (—1839). Slavery abolished in Mexico. Many anti-clerical laws. 57,100 slaves imported into Brazil.
**1829—37** Andrew Jackson (Dem.), President of US.
**1829—52** Juan Manuel de Rosas, dictator of Argentina.
**1830** 17 Dec., Simón Bolívar d. Reciprocity Treaty between UK and US allows US to trade in W Indies, and admits British colonial shipping to US ports. Four Orders-in-Council regulate slavery in Trinidad, St Lucia, Demerara and Berbice. 25,000 Americans settled in Texas. Population of New York c. 200,000. Constitution adopted in Uruguay. Ecuador becomes a republic. 32,200 slaves imported into Brazil.
**1830 ff.** American migrants reach California.
**1830—46** José Antonio Páez, principal figure in Venezuelan politics.
**1830—48** British extend control in Honduras.
**1830—58** Present Colombia designated New Granada.
**1830—61** Chile dominated by Conservatives.
**1830—1915** Porfirio Díaz, Mexican dictator.

**1829** 2 Feb., York Minster set on fire by a madman. 11 Apr., first buses in Paris. Braille invented. First railways constructed in Austria, France and USA. George Stephenson invents 'The Rocket' engine.
**1829—30** Pius VIII (Castiglioni), Pope.
**1829—90** Henry Parry Liddon, divine.
**1829—96** Sir John Everett Millais, artist. August Kekulé, chemist.
**1829—1902** Samuel Rawson Gardiner, historian.
**1829—1916** Charles Melchior, Marquis de Vogüé, diplomatist and archaeologist.

**1830** Campaign against *thags* (thugs) begun by Col. Sleeman. *Sati* (suttee) forbidden. Dawud, last Circassian governor of Baghdad, d.: builder of schools. Major Henry Burney sent as first British Resident at the court of Ava. Penang reduced in status from a Presidency to a Residency, directly dependent upon India: Malacca and Singapore also become Residencies. Population of Singapore 16,634.
**1830—5** Many roads built in the Philippines.
**1830—60** Whaling industry builds up off Tasmania.
**c. 1830** Sugar cultivation introduced into Malaya.
**c. 1830—40** Chinese immigrating into Malaya at 2,000—3,000 annually.

**1830** 15 Sept., Liverpool to Manchester railway opened. The *Book of Mormon* published: Mormon Church organized. The lawn mower and the sewing machine invented. Codrington College, Barbados, completed. Mico Training School opened at Kingston, Jamaica. American School for Girls founded in Beirut. *Godey's Lady's Book* (journal) first published in US. Ram Mohan Roy visits England.
**1830—89** Numa Dénis Fustel de Coulanges, historian.
**1830—94** Anton Rubinstein, Russian composer.
**1830—94** Christina Georgina Rossetti, poetess.
**1830—96** Frederick Leighton, Lord Leighton, artist.
**1830—1903** Camille Pissarro, French artist. Robert, 3rd Marquess of Salisbury, Conservative statesman.
**1830—1914** Frédéric Joseph Etienne Mistral, Provençal poet.

1830–1833

WESTERN &
NORTHERN EUROPE

CENTRAL &
SOUTHERN EUROPE

AFRICA

**1830** 25 Aug., rising in Belgium. 18
Oct., riots in Paris and Vincennes.
16 Nov., Wellington resigns: Earl
Grey, Prime Minister (−1834)(Whig).
18 Nov., Belgium proclaimed
independent by provisional
government (−1831). Bad harvest in
England: 'Labourers' Revolt' severely
suppressed. Death penalty abolished
for many offences in England.

**1831** 20 Jan., protocol of London
declares neutrality of Belgium. 3 Feb.,
Duc de Nemours, third son of Louis-
Philippe of France, elected King of
the Belgians: election not ratified by
his father. 1 March, Lord John
Russell introduces Reform Bill into
the Commons: passed by one vote.
General election follows with
increased Whig majority. 4 June,
Leopold I, of Saxe-Coburg-Gotha,
elected King of Belgium (−1865). 1
Aug., Holland invades Belgium.
21 Nov., rising in Lyons. National
Education system introduced in
Ireland: English the sole language of
instruction. Revolt in Novgorod
region of Russia.

**1831** Feb., risings in Modena, Parma
and Romagna put down by Austria.
Polish Diet proclaims a republic: 25
Feb., Polish army forced to retire at
Grochow. 27 Apr., Charles Felix of
Savoy, Piedmont and Sardinia d.:
succ. Charles Albert (−1849). 26
May, Poles defeated at Ostrolenka.
11 July, French expedition against
Portugal: fleet enters the Tagus. 8
Sept., Russians take Warsaw:
colonial régime ensues. 9 Oct., John
Capodistrias assassinated. 20 Dec.,
Augustine Capodistrias, President of
provisional government in Greece
(−1832).

**1831** Treaty between Ashanti and
Britain. Matabele at war with Griquas
and Korana.

**1831–2** Abortive Egyptian
expedition against Hadendowa.

**1832** 22 March, cholera outbreak in
Paris. Apr., abortive rising in La
Vendée led by Duchesse de Berry.
30 Apr., riot in Marseilles. 9 May,
Grey resigns: succ., Duke of
Wellington, for one week: 17 May,
Grey returns to office. 23 May,
rising in W of France; and, 5 and 6
June, at Paris. 4 June, Reform Bill
passed by House of Lords. July,
Scottish Parliamentary Reform Bill
passed. 30 Nov., Antwerp besieged
by the French at request of Belgium.
23 Dec., the French take Antwerp
from the Dutch for Belgium. King
of Rome, son of Napoleon, d.

**1832** Feb., Ancona occupied by the
French: battle of Konia: Russia
occupies the Dardanelles. 14 Feb.,
Russians proclaim new organic law
in Poland, instituting tyranny. 26
Feb., Polish constitution abolished.
7 May, Prince Otto of Bavaria elected
King of Greece. Liberals from the
Azores land in Oporto: civil war in
Portugal. Palace revolution in Spain
counters Carlism.

**1832** Portuguese colonies re-organized.
French expand trading stations in W
Africa. Embassy from Zanzibar to
Madagascar.

**1832–4** R. Lander explores R. Niger.

c. **1832–6** Frontier wars between
Egyt and Kwara, Ethiopia.

**1832–43** Abd-el-Kader fighting the
French in Algeria.

**1833** 29 Jan., first reformed Parliament
opened in UK. 28 Aug., EIC monopoly
of trade between Europe and China and
India abolished.

**1833** 5 July, battle of Cape St Vincent.
8 July, treaty of Hounkiar-Iskelessi
between Russia and Turkey: Russian
fleet visits the Bosporus. July,
liberals seize Lisbon: Miguelist fleet
destroyed: Sept., María of Portugal
returns to Lisbon. 10-12 Sept.,
conference of Münchengrätz between
Austria, Prussia and Russia. 29 Sept.,
Ferdinand VII of Spain d.: succ.
Isabella II (−1868): her mother María
Cristina regent (−1840). Nov.,
Carlist rising in Basque region,
Catalonia and Valencia.

**1833** 4 May, Turco-Egyptian treaty
of Kontaiah: Egyptian independence
of Turkey recognized. Sudan
government centralized. Moshesh on
friendly terms with Boers. New
constitution in Cape Colony.

| THE EAST & AUSTRALASIA | THE AMERICAS | RELIGION & CULTURE |
|---|---|---|

**THE AMERICAS**

1830—1960 Forty-five presidents in Ecuador.

**RELIGION & CULTURE**

c. 1830 Conical tower and Great Outer Wall built at Zimbabwe.
1830—1905 Elisée Reclus, geographer.

**THE EAST & AUSTRALASIA**

1831 Sayyid Ahmad of Bareilly d. fighting a *jihad* against the Sikhs in Swat. EIC annexes Mysore by treaty. Rising against the Siamese in Kedah: Siam reconquers Kedah without difficulty. Aborigines in Tasmania made to surrender. Free grants of land abolished in Australia: replaced by auction.
1831—6 Sir Thomas Mitchell's exploration in Victoria: land quickly taken up by settlers (squatters).
1831—7 General Sir Richard Bourke, Governor of NSW.
1831—8 EIC establishes virtual protectorate over Sind.
1831—40 Syria and Lebanon occupied by Egypt: governor, Ibrahim Pasha.
1831—41 50,000 settlers arrive in Australia, paid for by £1.1m. derived from land sales.
1832 Khurasan taken by Russia. Resident of Singapore becomes a Governor of the Straits Settlements; Penang and Malacca to have Resident Councillors. Naning incorporated into Malacca following brief war.

**THE AMERICAS**

1831 4 Feb., Lord Aylmer, Governor-in-Chief of Canada (—1835). First civil list for the life-time of the sovereign voted in Upper Canada. Nat Turner's rebellion: sixty to seventy slaves involved. General Scott and US naval force sent to Charleston to prevent S Carolina's attempt to ignore federal unity. Dom Pedro of Brazil abdicates in favour of his son, Pedro II (—1889): regency until 1841.
1831—4 Revolts and minor civil wars in Brazil.

1832 New charter for Bank of US vetoed by President Jackson. Canadians killed by troops in an election riot. General Santa Anna seizes power in Mexico: leaves control to Valentín Gómez Farías.

**RELIGION & CULTURE**

1831 27 Dec., voyage of the *Beagle*, with Charles Darwin as geologist (—1836). Michael Faraday discovers electromagnetic induction. The dynamo and the transformer invented. The *Liberator* founded in Boston by William Lloyd Garrison to combat slavery. Indians on upper Columbia request missions. Scots College in Sydney begun by Rev. J.D. Lang. First newspaper, *Surabaya Courant*, appears in Dutch EI. Great fire in Pera quarter, Constantinople.
1831—46 Gregory XVI (Capellari), Pope.
1831—79 James Clerk Maxwell, physicist.
1831—95 Henry Moore, artist.
1831—1907 Joseph Joachim, Hungarian composer.

1832 9 June, Pope Gregory XVI: encyclical *Mirari vos*. First grant, of £20,000, for public education in England.
1832—8 The National Gallery, London, built by W. Wilkins.
1832—83 Edouard Manet, French artist.
1832—97 Léon Gautier, historian.
1832—98 Charles Lutwidge Dodgson, (Lewis Carroll), mathematician and children's writer.
1832—1902 George Alfred Henty, author of boys' books.
1832—1914 Walter Theodore Watts-Dunton, poet and novelist.
1832—1916 Echegaray, Spanish dramatist and Nobel prize-winner.

**THE EAST & AUSTRALASIA**

1833 Lord William Bentinck, Governor-General of Bengal. EIC Charter renewed. Shah Shuja al-Mulk attempts to regain Afghanistan. Ranjit Singh takes Ladakh. Indian Law Commission established. Wahhabis restored for a short period. James Busby, first British Resident, appointed in New Zealand.

**THE AMERICAS**

1833 Lower Canada Assembly refuses supply: deadlock follows. Britain annexes the Falkland Is. Constitution proclaimed in Chile confirms hegemony of landowners: landless and illiterates excluded from suffrage.

**RELIGION & CULTURE**

1833 14 July, John Keble's sermon *National Apostasy* inaugurates Oxford Movement. Greek Church becomes independent of Constantinople. New York *Sun* begins publication under Benjamin Day. The *Knickerbocker* first published in US. Society of St Vincent de Paul founded.
1833—70 Adam Lindsay Gordon, Australian poet.
1833—87 Alexander Porfirievitch Borodin, Russian composer.
1833—96 Alfred Nobel, scientist.
1833—97 Johannes Brahms, German composer.
1833—98 Sir Edward Burne-Jones, artist.
1833—83 Gustave Doré, artist.

| WESTERN & NORTHERN EUROPE | CENTRAL & SOUTHERN EUROPE | AFRICA |
|---|---|---|

**1834** 19 March, the 'Tolpuddle Martyrs'. 9-12 Apr., riots in Lyons. July, Grey resigns: Lord Melbourne, Prime Minister. 1 Aug., slavery ended throughout British possessions. 14 Aug., Poor Law Amendment Act. Nov., Melbourne resigns: provisional government follows. Dec.—8 Apr. 1835, Sir Robert Peel, Prime Minister. Robert Owen fails to form 'Grand National Trades Union'.

**1834** Feb., Mazzini attempts to take Savoy. 22 Apr., Quadruple Alliance between Britain, France, Portugal and Spain: pretender Dom Miguel to be expelled: Don Carlos raises revolt in Navarre: civil war to 1839. 26 May, Dom Miguel capitulates by Convention of Evora-Monte: María II restored (—1853). Spanish Royal and Supreme Council of the Indies abolished.

**1834** French military government re organized in Algeria. British restore Fernando Po to Spain. Angola ignores Portuguese abolition of slave trade. 12,000 Xhosa attack Cape Colony. Slaves emancipated at the Cape. First exploration parties prepare for Great Trek. Kassala foun by Egyptians.

**1835** 18 Apr., Peel resigns: Lord Melbourne returns to office (—1841). 9 Sept., Municipal Corporation Act reforms English local government.

**1835** Liberal risings in many parts of Spain.
**1835—48** Ferdinand I, Emperor of Austria.

**1835** 26 Nov., French expedition against Mascara, Algeria. Egyptians defeat Ethiopians at Kwara. Coffee growing introduced into Gold Coast. Rozwi state broken up. Oct., Great Trek begins. Ngoni begin to migrate northward.

**1836** 3 Aug., Tithe Commutation Act in England. 29 Oct., Louis Napoleon (later Napoleon III) fails in attempt to seize Strasbourg: exiled. 6 Nov., Charles X of France d. in exile. Agitation against Corn Laws begins in England.
**1836—48** Chartist Movement in England.

**1836** Portuguese Treasury burnt down. Sept., constitution of 1822 restored. Slavery abolished in Portuguese colonies. Mendizábal chief minister in Spain: Church property confiscated to reduce national debt. Palace revolt at La Granja, Spain: compromise charter for constitution published.

**1836** 5 Jan., French expedition agai Tlemcen. 9 Nov., French expedition against Constantine. Egyptian expedition against Kwara. Great Tre much of Transvaal and OFS reached Potgeiter and Maritz set up republic. Treaty between Britain and Matabele Plague depopulates Mogadishu.

**1837** 20 June, William IV of England d.: succ. Victoria (—1901): succ. as King of Hanover, Ernest Augustus. New Zealand Association founded by Edward Gibbon Wakefield: distinguished membership headed by Lord Durham. Lord John Russell lays Ten Resolutions on reform of government in Canada before Parliament.

**1837** *Cortes* approves new liberal Spanish constitution. Constitution of Hanover suppressed.

**1837** Egyptian administration reformed. Regular steam-ship servic London—Alexandria and Suez— Bombay begun. Ethiopians defeat Egyptians at Wad Kaltabu. Sayyid Said exiles leading Mazrui to Bandar Abbas. Piet Retief joins Great Trek. Zhosa cede half Natal to Britain. 30 May, Treaty of Tafna.

## THE EAST & AUSTRALASIA

**1834** May, Dost Muhammad Khan loses Peshawar to the Sikhs. Fath Ali Shah d.: succ. Muhammad Shah (–1848). Shah Shuja al-Mulk defeated by Dost Muhammad Khan near Samarqand. Raja of Coorg deposed for cruelty. Cachar annexed by EIC. T.B. Macaulay joins council in India. Rebellion against the Ottoman Turks in Palestine and Syria. First tea plants in India ordered from China. Lord William Bentinck's title changed to Governor-General of India (–1835). Population of Ceylon 1.16m.: revenue £3.7m.: 1,105 schools with 13,891 pupils.
**1834–8** British Military Mission to Persia.
**1835** March, Sir Charles Metcalfe, Governor-General of India *ad int* (–1836). Macaulay's minute on Indian education. Transit duties abolished in India. Last coinage minted in name of Shah Alam: thereafter EIC currency alone minted. Eastern coast of Australia up to Queensland sparsely settled. Ill mounted police in all Australia. Charles Philip Hippolytus de Thierry proclaims himself 'sovereign chief of New Zealand': thirty-five Maori chiefs sign Declaration of Independence. Capt. Thomas McDonnell appointed as a second British Resident at Hokianga, New Zealand.

**1836** Dec., Colony of S Australia founded. Population of Singapore 29,984, of whom less than half Chinese.
**1836–42** Lord (later Earl of) Auckland, Governor-General of India.

**1837** Apr., Melbourne founded. Sept., Alexander Burnes sent by EIC on a commercial mission to Kabul. Nov., Persians besiege Herat. Peshawar defended by Ranjit Singh against Dost Muhammad Khan. Aden Colony annexed by Britain. Akbar II, Mughul Emperor, d.: succ. Bahadur Shah II (–1857).

## THE AMERICAS

**1834** Apr., Santa Anna ousts Gómez Farías: governs in person until Jan. 1835. William Lyon Mackenzie presents report on Upper Canada grievances: congressional government demanded. Permanent Central Committee advocating revolution set up in Montreal. Provincial legislatures created in Brazil.

**1835** 2 Apr., Earl Amherst, Governor-in-Chief of Canada (–Aug.). 24 Aug., Earl of Gosford, Governor-in-Chief of Canada (–1838): instructed to head Royal Commission on difficulties of government in Lower Canada. Oct., Mexican Congress ends federal constitution. Americans in Texas rise against Mexico. Andrés Santa Cruz, dictator of Bolivia, unites Peru with Bolivia by force (–1839): styled 'Protector' of the Peruvian-Bolivian Confederation.
**1835–45** War of secession in Rio Grande do Sul, Brazil.

**1836** 2 March, Texas proclaimed independent (–1845): David Burnet, President. 6 March, General Santa Anna's army kills 150 Texan militia to the last man. 21 Apr., Texan militia under Sam Houston wipes out Mexican column: Santa Anna captured. 15 June, Arkansas becomes a US State. Dec., centralized constitution promulgated in Mexico. Direct nominating conventions become the general practice in US. Ten hour day instituted in US shipyards. Deadlock in Barbados Assembly between representatives and the governor on apprentices.
**1836–9** Chile at war with Peru.
**1837** Jan., Anastasio Bustamante, President of Mexico (–1841). 26 Jan. Michigan becomes a US State. Nov., ill-prepared revolutionary movement halted by military in Upper Canada. 7 Dec., attempt by William Lyon Mackenzie to capture Quebec foiled. Elijah P. Lovejoy murdered by mob at Alton, Illinois, for advocating abolition of slavery.

## RELIGION & CULTURE

**1834** Pedal tricycle invented in Scotland. Palace of Westminster gutted by fire, except for Westminster Hall.
**1834–66** Ramkrishna Paramahamsa, Indian mystic.
**1834–96** William Morris, artist, designer and poet.
**1834–1902** Lord Acton, historian.
**1834–1903** James Abbott McNeill Whistler, American artist.
**1834–1913** August Weismann, geneticist.
**1834–1917** Edgar Hilaire Germaine Degas, French artist.
**1834–1924** Sabine Baring-Gould, novelist and hymnographer.
**1834–1900** Gottlieb Daimler, inventor of the motor car.

**1835** Buckingham Palace completed by John Nash. *New York Herald* founded by Gordon Bennett. Christianity proscribed in Madagascar. American Mission Press moved from Malta to Beirut. Religious orders expelled from Goa.
**1835–81** Modest Petrovich Moussórgsky, Russian composer.
**1835–82** William Stanley Jevons, logician.
**1835–1901** Fukuzawa Yukichi, founder of Keio University, Japan.
**1835–1902** Samuel Butler, novelist and philosopher.
**1835–1910** Mark Twain (ps. of Samuel Clemens), American novelist.
**1835–1913** Alfred Austin, poet.
**1835–1921** Charles Camille Saint-Saens, French composer.
**1835–1922** Albert Venn Dicey, jurist.
**1836** Jesuits return to Argentina. The Bible translated into Mandingo. Mosque and school built at Dongola.
**1836–65** Isabella Beeton, writer on cookery.
**1836–91** Léo Delibes, French composer.
**1836–1904** Ignace Henri Jean Théodore Fantin-Latour, French artist.
**1836–1908** Sir Henry Campbell-Bannerman, Liberal Prime Minister.
**1836–1911** Sir William Schwenk Gilbert, dramatist, and collaborator with Sir Arthur Sullivan.
**1836–1912** Sir Lawrence Alma-Tadema, artist.
**1836–1914** Joseph Chamberlain, statesman.
**1836–1921** Alfred Grandidier, explorer.
**1837** Struggle between state and Catholic Church begun in Prussia. Morse invents the telegraph in New York. Durham University re-chartered. Steel first used to face ploughshares in US. Athens University founded. James R. Wellsted, description of S Arabia.
**1837–83** John Richard Green, historian.

| WESTERN & NORTHERN EUROPE | CENTRAL & SOUTHERN EUROPE | AFRICA |
|---|---|---|
| **1837** First railways in France. Orange Order, with 125,000 adherents, banned in Ireland.<br>**1837–42** Period of industrial depression in England. | | **1837** Sanusiyah confraternity founded by the Algerian Shaykh al-Sanusi: spreads widely in Libya: foundation of short-lived Sanusi dynasty. 13 Oct., the French take Constantine. |
| **1838** 24 Sept., Cobden founds Anti-Corn Law League. 8 May, People's Charter drawn up: riots ensue throughout England. 8 Aug., Charter formally adopted by mass meeting of working men. Irish Tithe Act and Poor Relief Act. Anglo-Turkish commercial treaty. | **1838** March, riots in Lisbon: Apr., new bicameral constitution in Portugal, with both chambers elected. France evacuates Ancona. Austria evacuates Bologna. Convention of Dresden brings about monetary unity in Germany. | **1838** Muhammad Ali visits Sudan. Bonët-Willaumez exploring W Africa. Governor of Angola removed for slave trade. Egyptians raid Qalabat: panic in Gondar. Sir George Napier tries to halt Great Trek. French expand in Algeria. |
| **1839** 1 and 2 Jan., riots at La Rochelle. 10 Jan.-5 July, Lady Flora Hastings's scandal. 9 March, French treaty with Mexico. 19 Apr., treaty of London re Belgium. Luxembourg independent as a Grand Duchy. 12 May, riots in Paris. July, House of Commons rejects the People's Charter.<br>**1839–40** Cunard Line founded. | **1839** 9 March, child labour prohibited in Prussia. Mahmud II attacks Muhammad Ali of Egypt: 24 June, defeated at Nezib: 27 July, European powers impose peace. 1 July, Mahmud II of Turkey d.: succ. Abd al-Majid I (−1861). 31 Aug., Convention of Vergara ends Carlist war: Don Carlos withdraws to France with 8,000 followers. 3 Nov., Abd al-Majid I, Ottoman Sultan, proclaims *Tanzimat*: rescript of fundamental laws of Turkish constitution: all citizens guaranteed equality without difference of religion: conscription introduced: tax system regularized. | **1839** 1 July, Turkish fleet surrenders in Alexandria harbour. 28 Oct., French reach Portes-aux-Fer, Algeria. Dingaan acknowledges Boer claims in Natal.<br>**c. 1839 ff.** Frequent caravans from Zanzibar into EA interior. |
| **1840** 10 Feb., Queen Victoria m. Prince Albert of Saxe-Coburg-Gotha. 10 Jan., penny post introduced in Britain by Rowland Hill. | **1840** 7 June, Frederick William III of Prussia d.: succ. Frederick William IV (−1861). | **1840** 3-6 Feb., heroic defence of the fort of Mazagran. |

| THE EAST & AUSTRALASIA | THE AMERICAS | RELIGION & CULTURE |
|---|---|---|

**THE EAST & AUSTRALASIA**

**1837** HMS *Rattlesnake* visits New Zealand to protect Bay of Islands settlers against the Maoris. Filipino representation in Spanish *Cortes* ended. Capt. George Grey explores W Australian coast. Hung Hsiu-chuan proclaims himself 'Christ's younger brother': initiates Kingdom of Tai Ping (universal peace).
**1837—8** Famine in N India.
**1837—46** Tharawaddy, King of Burma.
**1837—59** Burmese capital at Amarapura.
**1838** 16 July, Tripartite Treaty between EIC, Persia and Shah Shuja al-Mulk: 23 July, Ranjit Singh adheres. 1 Aug., slavery abolished in India. Aug., Persia raises siege of Herat. 1 Oct., Lord Auckland declares war on Afghanistan: first Afghan war. Dec., Capt. Hobson appointed British Consul in New Zealand. First US consul in New Zealand appointed. EIC occupies Bukkur. Nearly 40 *lakhs* of rupees spent on famine relief in Bengal. New Zealand trade expanding: Bay of Islands visited by 56 US ships, 30 Australian and New Zealand, 23 English and 21 French. European population of New Zealand *c.* 2,000. Vigilance committee, Kororareka Association, founded in New Zealand.
**1838—43** N.S.W. and Tasmania explored by Strzlecki.
**1838—46** Sir George Gipps, Governor of N.S.W.
**1838—53** Tokugawa Iyeyoshi, Shogun.
**1839** Apr., EIC takes Qandahar. June, Ranjit Singh d.: anarchy follows: succ. his son Kharak Singh. July, EIC takes Ghazna. 7 Aug., EIC forces enter Kabul: Shah Shuja al-Mulk restored. EIC occupies Karachi. Grand Trunk Road from Delhi to Calcutta begun. Ibrahim Pasha proclaims equality before the law of members of all religious denominations in Syria and Lebanon. Ottoman army crushed at Nizzib, Syria, by rebels. Land boom at Melbourne. Chartists transported to Tasmania. British Government orders an end to transportation to Australia. Land purchased by E.G. Wakefield and others in New Zealand. Nanto-Bordelaise Co. founded to promote French colonization in New Zealand. Import of opium banned by China.
**1839—40** Abortive Russian expedition against Khiva.
**1840** Jan., Capt. Hobson arrives in New Zealand with a view to making treaties with Maori chiefs.

**THE AMERICAS**

**1837** Republic of Texas recognized by US. First civil list for the life-time of the sovereign voted in New Brunswick. *Les Fils de la Liberté* movement set up in Montreal. Political unrest throughout summer in Canada: Roman Catholic hierarchy in opposition to democrats.
**1837—41** Martin van Buren (Dem.), President of US.
**1838** 29 May, Earl of Durham, Governor-in-Chief of Canada (—Dec. 1838). 11 Oct., French intervene in La Plata, Argentina: Martin-Garcia Is. taken. 27 Nov., French intervene in Mexico: take St Jean d'Ulloa. Dec., republic proclaimed in Lower Canada: put down by troops. French squadron lands at Veracruz, Mexico: 'Pastry Cook' War: French repelled by Santa Anna. Republic of C. America dissolves. Guatemala, Honduras, El Salvador, Nicaragua and Costa Rica become independent. West Indian Prisons Act. Apprenticeship system abolished.
**1838—43** Yucatán peninsula secedes from Mexico.
**1838—65** Rafael Carrera the dominant figure in Guatemalan politics.
**1839** Jan., Chilean army defeats Santa Cruz at battle of Yungay: Santa Cruz flees: Agustín Gamarra, President of Peru, attempts to annex Bolivia. 11 Jan., earthquake in Martinique. 17 Jan., Sir John Colborne, Governor-in-Chief of Canada (—Oct.). 19 Oct., C.P. Thomson (later Lord Sydenham), Governor-in-Chief of Canada (—1842). First federal appropriation for agriculture in US. Spain recognizes independence of Mexico.
**1840** 10 Feb., following Durham Report on Canadian constitution, Upper and Lower Canada united:

**RELIGION & CULTURE**

**1837—1903** Grover Stephen Cleveland. American President.
**1837—1909** Algernon Charles Swinburne, poet.
**1838** Protestant Church of Syria founded. The screw propeller invented. French Catholic mission established in New Zealand. The term socialist first used in France. The *Times of India* founded as the *Bombay Times*. Regular steam ship services between Britain and US begun. Kremlin Palace built.
**1838—75** Georges Bizet, French composer.
**1838—82** Léon Gambetta, French statesman.
**1838—1900** Henry Sidgwick, economist.
**1838—1903** William Edward Hartpole Lecky, historian.
**1838—1916** Ernst Mach, physicist.
c. **1838—1908** Mirza Ghulam Ahmad, founder of Ahmadiyyah (Qadiani) movement.
**1838—1929** Emile Loubet, French statesman.
**1839** Pope Gregory XVI, Bull *In supremo* condemns slavery and the slave trade. *Oeuvres des Noirs* founded by Fr F.M.P. Libermann in Haiti. The bicycle invented. W.H. Fox Talbot invents photographic negative. L. Daguerre invents the daguerrotype. Jews in Meshed, Persia, forcibly converted to Islam.
**1839—72** Methodist mission in Kumasi.
**1839—94** Walter Horatio Pater, novelist and critic.
**1839—97** Jamal al-Din al-Afghani, Egyptian religious teacher and first Islamic modernist.
**1839—1906** Paul Cézanne, French artist.
**1839—1914** C.S. Peirce, American philosopher.
**1839—1922** James, Viscount Bryce, historian and statesman.
**1839—1934** Charles Lindley Wood, 2nd Viscount Halifax, statesman and worker for Christian unity.
**1839—89** Carlo Pellegrini, ('Ape'), cartoonist.
**1840** Grammar Schools Act reorganizes elementary education in England.
6 May, first postage stamp, issued by Britain.

| WESTERN & NORTHERN EUROPE | CENTRAL & SOUTHERN EUROPE | AFRICA |
|---|---|---|
| **1840** 12 May, French law enacted to enable return of the remains of Napoleon to **France.** 7 July, treaty of London between Austria, Britain, Prussia, Turkey and Russia. French treaty with Texas. Aug., Louis Napoleon attempts abortive rising in Boulogne. 7 Oct., William I of Holland abdicates: succ. William II (–1849). 30 Nov., remains of Napoleon arrive at Cherbourg: buried solemnly in Les Invalides. Irish Municipal Reform Act. New Zealand Co. given a Royal Charter. | **1840** 12 Oct., Queen María Cristina resigns Regency of Spain: succ. Espartero. Elections in Portugal favour return to constitutional charter of 1826. | **1840** 15 March, French occupy Cherchel, Algeria; battles at Meskiana (21 March), Selson (24 March), and Afroun (27 March). 17 May, French occupy Médéah; 8 June, Milianah. Egyptian possessions in Sudan extended. Beke explores Gojjam. Sayyid Said moves his court from Oman to Zanzibar. Government of India acquires bases in Tadjoura and Zaila. Dingaan d. Dec., Pretorius at war with Pondo. French obtain territory in Madagascar. Beecroft explores R. Benin and R. Niger. **1840–1** Chiefs in Madagascar accept French treaties of protection. **c. 1840** Imbangala and Ovimbundu caravans fighting. |
| **1841** 13 July, second treaty of London: Convention of the Straits guarantees Turkish independence: Dardanelles and the Bosporus closed to warships. 28 Aug., Sir Robert Peel succ. Lord Melbourne as Prime Minister (–1846). O'Connell begins to demand independence for Ireland. | **1841** Basque rising. **1841–58** Stratford Canning, later Viscount Stratford de Redcliffe, British Ambassador in Istanbul. | **1841** Jan., Marshal Bugeaud appointed Governor of Algeria. 5 May France annexed Is. of Nossi-bé and Nossi-Komba, off Madagascar. Pashalik of Egypt made hereditary in Muhammad Ali's family. Palm-oil industry started in Dahomey. British Consulate moved from Muscat to Zanzibar. British mission to Shoa. France obtains Mayotte, Comoro Is. |
| **1842** 11 June, first French railway legislation: nine main lines, seven of them starting from Paris. Aug., Chartist riots in England. New sliding scale introduced for Corn Laws in England. Mines Act forbids women and children to work in mines in England. Young Ireland Party founded. | **1842** 14 Sept., Michael III Obrenovitch deposed in Serbia. Barcelona rebels, demanding new Constituent *Cortes*: city bombarded by Espartero. Costa Cabral marches on Lisbon: constitutional charter of 1826 restored: Costa Cabral, dictator (–1846). | **1842** Aug., France occupies Mayotte, Comoro Is. Migration from Sierra Leone to Abeokuta. French treaties with Guinea, Ivory Coast and Gabon chiefs. **1842–3** Wars between Boers and British in Natal. |

# THE EAST & AUSTRALASIA

**1840** 5 Feb., gathering of Maoris at Waitangi; 6 Feb., treaty of Waitangi signed, followed later by other chiefs, granting sovereignty over New Zealand to Queen Victoria. 21 May, Capt. Hobson proclaims British sovereignty over New Zealand 'with himself as Lieutenant-Governor' (technically subject to NSW until 1841): capital at Waitemata. 12-13 Sept., French bombard Beirut; 26 Sept., French take Saida (former Sidon). 10 Oct., Beirut occupied by the British. 27 Oct., Amir Bashir, Prince of Lebanon, submits. Nov., Muhammad Ali of Egypt evacuates troops from Syria. Dost Muhammad Khan surrenders to EIC. The Agha Khan rebels in Yezd: then flees to India. Kharak Singh murdered: succ. Nao Nihal Singh: killed accidentally after one day: succ. Sher Singh. British bombard ports in SE China as a result of ban on opium. Chinese introduce cultivation of pepper into Johore. Australian wool competitive with wool on the German home market. Edward John Eyre traverses Great Australian Bight to S Australia: reaches Adelaide on whaler, *Mississippi*. No more convicts settled in Australia: Norfolk Is. and Tasmania still open. First bank opened in New Zealand.
**c. 1840** Long Ja'afar, District Officer, invites Chinese to mine tin in Larut. Tin mining begun at Kanching, Selangor. Russian naval station established at Ashurada, Caspian Sea.
**1841** 2 Nov., general revolt in Kabul: Alexander Burnes murdered: second Afghan war begins. First metalled roads built in Ceylon. British enter Yangtze estuary and Nanking in force. 26 Aug., Amoy captured by Admiral Parker and General Gough; 30 Aug., evacuated. Gold first discovered near Bathurst, Australia. Plymouth Co., offshoot of New Zealand Co., founds settlement at New Plymouth.
**1841 ff.** Disturbances between Druzes and Maronites in Lebanon.
**1841–4** Depression in Australia due to fall in wool price: many banks fail, including Bank of Australia.
**1842** 2 Jan., EIC sign treaty of evacuation from Afghanistan. 6 Jan., 16,000 men march out of Kabul. 13 Jan., Dr Brydon reaches Jalalabad as only survivor of EIC army of 16,000: remainder killed by Afghans and the winter. Feb., Lord Ellenborough arrives in India. 5 Apr., Shah Shuja al-Mulk murdered.

# THE AMERICAS

responsible government not granted: single legislature and administration: separate legal and educational systems respected: English only official language: Kingston made the capital: large programme of public works undertaken. July, violent riots in Mexico City put down by Santa Anna. Emigration to Canada encouraged. First steamship enters Valparaiso harbour.
**1840–60** Many Germans emigrate to Chile.
First steamship enters Valparaiso harbour.
**1840–60** Many Germans emigrate to Chile.

**1841** William Henry Harrison (Whig), President of US: d. 4 Apr.; succ. his Vice-President, Henry Tyler (Whig) (–1845). July, Santa Anna stages military revolt in Mexico. Oct., Santa Anna Provisional President of Mexico. Gamarra killed in battle. Exploitation of guano in Peru made a government monopoly. John Bidwell leads emigrants to Oregon.
**1841–7** José Ballivián, President of Bolivia: order restored.
**1841–62** Carlos Antonio Lopez, President of Paraguay.

**1842** 12 Jan., Sir Charles Bagot, Governor-in-Chief of Canada (–1843). 9 Aug., Webber-Ashburton Treaty between UK and US setties NE boundary between Canada and US. Aug., France occupies Tahiti, and the Marquises Is., Polynesia. US declares that it will not tolerate the annexation of the Sandwich Is. by any other power.

# RELIGION & CULTURE

**1840** The Church in possession of half the land in use in Mexico. Mechanical reapers introduced in US.
**1840–50** Decade of 'railway mania' in Britain.
**1840–1860** Houses of Parliament rebuilt by Sir Charles Barry.
**1840–93** Peter Ilyitch Tchaikovsky, Russian composer.
**1840–97** Alphonse Daudet, novelist and poet.
**1840–99** Alfred Sisley, artist.
**1840–1901** Sir John Stainer, composer.
**1840–1902** Emile Zola, novelist.
**1840–1917** François Auguste Rodin, French sculptor.
**1840–1921** Austin Dobson, poet and essayist.
**1840–1922** Wilfrid Scawen Blunt, poet. Giovanni Verga, Italian novelist.
**1840–1926** Claude Oscar Monet, French artist.
**1840–1928** Thomas Hardy, novelist.

**1841** *Punch* first published. Vulcanized rubber invented.
**1841–94** Aléxis Emmanuel Chabrier, French composer.
**1841–6** Mrs. Caroline Chisholm campaigns to provide proper care and shelter for immigrant girls in Australia.
**1841–1904** Anton Dvorak, Bohemian composer.
**1841–1904** Sir Henry Morton Stanley, traveller and journalist.
**1841–1919** Pierre Auguste Renoir, French artist.
**1841–1922** Felipe Pedrell, Spanish composer.
**1841–1924** Sir Walter Parratt, composer.
**1842** Anaesthetics invented. Jesuits return to Canada. Vicariate Apostolic of the Two Guineas established.
**1842–98** Stephane Mallarmé, poet.
**1842–99** Sophus Lie, mathematician.
**1842–1900** Sir Arthur Seymour Sullivan, composer.
**1842–1905** José Maria de Heredia, French poet.

| WESTERN & NORTHERN EUROPE | CENTRAL & SOUTHERN EUROPE | AFRICA |
|---|---|---|

**1842** End of slavery decreed in Russia: decree remains a dead letter.

**1842–58** Stratford Canning (Lord Stratford de Redcliffe), British Ambassador to Turkey.

**1843** 2 and 3 May, French railways from Paris to Rouen, and Paris to Orléans, opened. 2 Sept., Queen Victoria makes state visit to Paris. 8 Oct., Daniel O'Connell forbidden to hold a mass meeting at Clontarf: subsequently prosecuted for conspiracy. Agitation in Ireland for repeal of Act of Union.

**1843** 27 June, Alexander I Kara Georgevitch, Prince of Serbia (−1859). July, Espartero flees to London: 8 Nov., Queen Isabella declared of age at thirteen: Queen María Cristina returns: Generals Narvaez and Serrano in real power in Spain. Sept., revolution in Greece: National Assembly called by King Otto.

**1843** 16 May, Duc d'Aumale defeats Abd-el-Kader: Smala, Algeria, taken. Greek and Italian traders begin to set up in Khartoum. Sanusi sect started in Libya. British Crown resumes direct control of Gold Coast settlements. French make further treaties on W coast. Natal proclaimed a British Colony: Basutoland annexed. Orléansville built. Sidi Bel Abbès founded.

**1844** 1 Jan., Corn Laws replaced in England by Corn Importation Act. 19 July, Bank Charter Act reforms Bank of England. 12 Sept., Louis-Philippe of France pays state visit to Queen Victoria. 24 Oct., French Treaty of Commerce with China. Factory Act forbids children in England to work more than six and one half hours a day.

**1844** 2 March, new constitution in Greece. Nov., Holstein Estates declare Duchies of Schleswig and Holstein independent. 214 persons shot at different times for political offences in Spain.

**1844** Sudanese administration centralized. France at war with Morocco. 6 March, 'The Bond of 1844': treaty between British, Fante and others. French Consulate opened in Zanzibar. Boers from Natal set up at Potchefstroom. Administration of Cape Colony and Natal combined. 19 July, Maulai Abd al-Rahman of Morocco attacks French in Algeria: repelled: French take Oudja oasis from Morocco. 6 Aug., French bombard Tangier. 14 Aug., battle of Isly: Bugeaud defeats Abd-el-Kader. 15 Aug French bombard Mogador. 20 Sept., Convention of Tangier ends hostilities between France and Morocco. Oct., French campaign in Algeria against the Kabyles.
**1844–5** Many local risings in Portuguese Guinea.
**c. 1844** Arab trading centre set up at Unyanyembe, near Tabora.

**1845** Orange Order permitted to revive in Ireland.
**1845–8** The Great Famine in Ireland: population reduced from some 8m. to 6½m.

**1845** New constitution in Spain. Swiss Catholic cantons form *Sonderbund*. Russian penal code imposed in Poland.

**1845** June, revolt of the Kabyles. 22 Sept., 450 Frenchmen massacred in an ambush at Sidi Brahim, Algeria. Further French and Portuguese treaties in W Africa. Queen Ranavalona declares all foreigners subject to local laws: Anglo-French ultimatum: Tamatave bombarded.

## THE EAST & AUSTRALASIA

**1842** 16 Sept., EIC retake Kabul: Fath Yang recognized as King. 12 Oct., EIC forces evacuate Afghanistan: Fath Yang retires to India. Sir Charles Napier put in command in Sind: some minor skirmishes. Treaty between Russia and Khiva. China capitulates to Britain: Hong Kong ceded and becomes British Colony: indemnity paid: Capitulations granted to foreign powers: Chinese customs supervised by foreign consuls. Sultan restored in Kedah: Perlis founded. Assisted immigration to Australia begun. W.C. Wentworth demands that further convict labour be sent to to Australia. Sydney chartered as a city. British take Labuan. British take Hong Kong.
**1842–3** Financial crisis in Australia.
**1842–4** Lord (later Earl of) Ellenborough, Governor-General of India.
**1843** 15 Feb., British Residency in Hyderabad attacked by forces of the Amirs of Sind: Napier defeats Amirs at Miani: Sind annexed. Sher Singh murdered: succ. Dulip Singh, with Rani Jindan as regent. Mixed Commission adjudicates Perso-Turkish boundary. Slavery abolished in India. Shanghai made an open port.

**1844** Russia occupies coast of the Aral Sea. Treaties made by China with France and USA: missionaries allowed to work in treaty ports. Land controversy in Australia.
**1844–5** Maori revolt against the British.
**1844–8** Sir Henry Hardinge (later Viscount Hardinge), Governor-General of India.

**1845** 11 Dec., Sikhs cross R. Sutlej: Sikh war with EIC begins. Dost Muhammad Khan re-emerges as real power in Afghanistan. Danish settlements in India sold to the British. New Zealand Co. granted a development loan.

## THE AMERICAS

**1842** Geological Survey of Canada organized.
**1842–52** Argentina at war with Uruguay and Brazil.

**1843** 30 March, Sir Charles T. Metcalfe, Governor-in-Chief of Canada (–1845). The 'Great Emigration': 200 families settle in Oregon. Montreal made the capital of Canada. Boyer driven into exile by urban mulattoes in Haiti: Santo Domingo proclaimed a separate republic.
**1843–1915** Twenty-two dictators succeed each other in period of chaos in Haiti.
**1843–52** Rosas besieges Montevideo.
**1844** 2 Jan., Santa Anna elected President of Mexico. Dec., Santa Anna deposed: José Joaquín Herrera, President of Mexico. Commercial treaty between China and US. Haiti negroes expelled from Santo Domingo: locals proclaim it independent Republic of Dominica. Iron ore found in Wisconsin and Michigan. Population of Costa Rica 80,000.
**1844–1864** Pedro Santana and Buenaventura Báez dominant political figures in Dominican Republic.

**1845** 1 March, US formally annexes Texas: made a state of the Union: 3 March, Florida made a US State. Anglo-French fleet blockades Río de la Plata (–1847-8). Britain declares she will seize all Brazilian slaves found at sea: shipments of slaves increase.

## RELIGION & CULTURE

**1842–1906** Albert Sorel, historian.
**1842–1910** William James, American philosopher.
**1842–1912** Jules Emile Frédéric Massenet, French composer.
**1842–1919** John William Strutt, Lord Rayleigh, scientist.
**1842–1924** Alfred Marshall, political economist.
**1842–1908** François Coppée, French poet.

**1843** The *Economist* first published.
**1843–50** William Wordsworth, English poet laureate.
**1843–1901** Bp Mandell Creighton, historian.
**1843–1907** Edvard Hagerup Grieg, Norwegian composer.
**1843–1910** Robert Koch, pathologist.
**1843–1914** Sir William Anson, jurist.
**1843–1920** Pérez Galdós, Spanish novelist.
**1843–1926** Charles Montagu Doughty traveller, writer and poet.
**1844** Apostolic Prefecture of Madagascar established.
**1844–96** Paul Verlaine, poet.
**1844–1900** Friedrich Wilhelm Nietsche, German philosopher.
**1844–1908** Nicolas Andreievitch Rimsky-Korsakov, Russian composer.
**1844–1912** Andrew Lang, poet and writer.
**1844–1924** Anatole France (ps. of Jacques Antoine Anatole Thibault), novelist. Sir John Frederick Bridge, composer.
**1844–1929** Karl Benz, inventor of the motor car.
**1844–1930** Robert Seymour Bridges, poet.
**1844–1937** Charles Marie Jean Albert Widor, French composer.
**1844–89** Gerard Manley Hopkins, poet.

**1844–1923** Sarah Bernhardt, actress.

**1845** Grant-in-aid system increases educational facilities in India. John Henry Newman converted to Catholicism. CMS Grammar School opened at Freetown. First schools opened in Cameroun. The pneumatic tyre invented. Berlin Zoo founded.

| WESTERN & NORTHERN EUROPE | CENTRAL & SOUTHERN EUROPE | AFRICA |
|---|---|---|

|  |  | **c. 1845** Zwangendaba d.: Ngoni fragment, some migrating to future Malawi and Tanzania. |

**1846** 16 Apr., attempt made on Louis-Philippe's life in Paris. 23 May, Corn Laws repealed in Britain. Peel resigns: 30 June, Lord John Russell (later Earl Russell), Prime Minister (−1852): Lord Palmerston, Foreign Secretary. 8 July, Christian VIII of Denmark refuses to recognize independence of Schleswig and Holstein. 15 Sept., France makes treaty of commerce and navigation with Chile.

**1846** 25 May, Louis Napoleon escapes from the fortress of Ham. Aug., 'Spanish Marriages' affair over marriage of Queen Isabella of Spain and her sister: Oct., double wedding celebrated. Sept., 'Intellectual Diet of the German People' held by German professors at Frankfurt. Rising in Galicia: Costa Cabral· dismissed: Oct., Saldanha comes to power in Portugal through palace *coup*. 6 Nov., Austria annexes Cracow. Dec., anti-Austrian demonstration in Milan. Rising of Polish gentlemen in Austrian Galicia: free government installed in Cracow.

**1846** Massawa and Suakin leased by Egypt to Turkey. French defeat rebels in Algeria. War between Cape and the Xhosa. Beginning of segregation in Natal. French expand in Madagascar.
**1846−7** 100,000 Bantu in Cape Colony: eight reserves created.
**1846−56** Livingstone's first journeys.

**1847** Ten Hours Act limits working day in England.
**1847−8** Industrial depression in England.

**1847** 3 Feb.−June, united *Landtag* held in Prussia. 22 Feb., Portuguese army defeats rebels. May, Russia makes Poland a province. July, the Swiss Diet dissolves the *Sonderbund*. 2 Sept., Espartero recalled to Spain. 21 Oct.−29 Nov., civil war (*Sonderbund* war) in Switzerland. Dec., beginning of *Risorgimento* in Italy. Agricultural and economic crisis in Europe.

**1847** Apr., abortive Anglo-French operations against the Hovas in Madagascar. 23 Nov., Abd-el-Kader submits to the French in Algeria. Duc d'Aumale, Governor-General of Algeria. French campaigns in Kabylia. Liberia proclaimed independent. Da Silva Porto explores Barotseland. First Spahis recruited.
**c. 1847** Future Emperor Theodore gathers a band of malcontents, overrunning Gondar.

**1848** 20 Jan., Christian VIII of Denmark d.: succ. Frederick VII (−1863). 23-5 Feb., riots against Louis-Philippe in Paris and the provinces. 24 Feb., provisional government formed in Paris. 25 Feb., Louis-Philippe abdicates: Tuileries palace pillaged: violent riots in Paris. Second Republic proclaimed (−1852). 23 March, Schleswig and Holstein separate from Denmark. 9 Apr., Denmark occupies Schleswig and Holstein. 10 Apr., Chartists hold monster rally in Hyde Park before presenting a petition to Parliament.

**1848** 12 Jan., revolution starts in Sicily. 10 Feb., new constitution in Naples. 17 Feb.−12 Sept., new constitution agreed in Switzerland. 17 Feb., new constitution in Tuscany. 13-15 March, revolution in Vienna: Metternich resigns. 15 March, Pope Pius IX grants constitution to Papal States. 22 March, Venice proclaims herself independent. 26 March, Charles Albert of Savoy, Sardinia and Piedmont declares war on Austria. 11 Apr., Hungary proclaims democratic constitution.

**1848** Tunisian embassy to London without notification of the Porte. First Senegalese deputy sent to French Assembly. Sultan of Pate deposed for asserting independence from Oman. Britain annexes territory between Orange and Vaal rivers. New constitution in Cape Colony. Ibrahim, Khedive of Egypt, regent during Muhammad Ali's imbecillity.

| THE EAST & AUSTRALASIA | THE AMERICAS | RELIGION & CULTURE |
|---|---|---|

**1845** Capt. Sturt explores central Australia: reaches Stony Desert. Second rising of Muslims in Chinese Turkestan.
**1845–53** George Grey, Governor of New Zealand: Maoris pacified.
**1845–1906** William Farrer, agronomist: Australian Government Wheat Experimentalist.

**1846** 28 Jan., EIC defeats Sikhs at Aliwal. 10 Feb., Sikh army routed at Sobraon. 9 March, treaty of Lahore: end of Sikh war: British Resident established in Lahore: Kashmir ceded to Golab Singh. Rajput Rana family seize premiership of Nepal: king a cipher to 1949. Britain acquires Labuan: James Brooke, first governor. Masters and Servants Act in Australia. Constitution with two legislative houses, and municipal councils, proposed for New Zealand. US Commodore Biddle attempts to open trade with Japan: repulsed. British mission allowed to settle at Okinawa.
**1846–50** Sir Charles Augustus Fitzroy, Governor of NSW.
**1846–53** Pagan, King of Burma.
**1846–67** Emperor Komei, 121st Emperor of Japan: breaks total seclusion with the aid of advisers: members of Satshuma, Choshu, Tosa and Hizen clans from W Japan work with Kyoto nobles and Osaka merchants.
**1847** 15 Apr., French expedition to Cochin-China. Treaty of Erzerum demarcates Perso–Turkish boundary. Sikh troops used to quell a rebellion in Kashmir.
**1847–81** Ili region in China slowly conquered by Russia.

**1848** Apr., Sikhs under Diwan Mulraj rebel in Multan: second Sikh war begins. Riots and disturbances in Ceylon following imposition of new taxes. Irish rebels transported to Tasmania. Otago, New Zealand, founded. Rising in Hunan Province, China.
**1848–56** Earl (later Marquess) of Dalhousie, Governor-General of India. Gregory and Mueller explore northern interior of Australia.
**1848–96** Nasir al-Din, Shah of Persia.

**1845** Copper and iron rush in the Marquette Range. 3,000 persons emigrate up the Oregon trail. *c.* 20,000 slaves imported into Brazil. Population of California *c.* 11,000–12,000.
**1845–9** James Knox Polk (Dem.), President of US.
**1845–51** Ramón Castilla, President of Peru.

**1846** 24 Apr., Earl Cathcart, Governor of Canada (–1847). 13 May, US and Mexico at war (–1847): Mexico loses California, New Mexico, Arizona, Nevada, Utah, and part of Colorado. 15 June, Canadian frontier with US in Oregon defined by Treaty of Washington. July, US occupies California with fleet in support. Aug., Santa Anna recruits Mexican army. Dec., Gómez Farías, President of Mexico. 28 Dec., Iowa becomes a US State. Bidlack treaty: US guarantees Colombia sovereignty over Panama isthmus. French restored as an official language in Canada.
**1846–61** Venezuela controlled by brothers José Tadeo and José Gregorio Monagas.

**1847** 30 Jan., Earl of Elgin, Governor-in-Chief of Canada (–1854). Feb., indecisive battle of Buena Vista between Mexico and US: both sides claim victory. March, Gómez Farías deposed by Santa Anna: replaced by a nonentity. March, US captures Vera Cruz, Mexico. 14 Sept., US forces enter Mexico City. Canadian grain market collapses as a result of competition with the Baltic and Russia. Many immigrants reach Canada from Ireland.
**1848** 2 Feb., treaty of Guadalupe Hidalgo ends Mexican–US war: Mexico receives $15m.: US acquires Arizona, California, Nevada, New Mexico, and Utah, with parts of Colorado and Wyoming: possession of Texas confirmed. 29 May, Wisconsin becomes a US State. Responsible government established in Canada. Costa Rican Constitution agreed. Free-Soil Party emerges during campaign for US Presidency.
**1848–9** Gold discovered in California: San Francisco becomes a metropolis.

**1845** Queen's College founded in Dublin, Cork and Galway. First 'Clipper' built in Boston.
*c.* **1845** Porcelain false teeth invented in USA.
**1845–1924** Gabriel Urbain Fauré, French composer.
**1845–1933** George Saintsbury, critic.
**1845–1902** Benjamin Constant, painter.
**1845–1923** Wilhelm Conrad Röntgen, physicist.
**1846** Pupil-teacher system instituted in England. The planet Neptune discovered by the French astronomer Le Verrier. Vicariate of C. Africa and the Galla created.
**1846–78** Pius IX (Mastai Ferretti), Pope.
**1846–91** Charles Stewart Parnell, Irish politician.
**1846–1908** Edmondo de Amicis, Italian novelist and writer.
**1846–1914** Paul Déroulède, poet and dramatist.
**1846–1916** Henry Sienkiewicz, Polish writer and novelist. Gaston Camille Charles Maspéro, Egyptologist.
**1846–1920** Paul Fabergé, Russian goldsmith.
**1846–1924** Francis Herbert Bradley, philosopher.

**1846–1900** Alexandre Albert de Serpa Pinto, explorer.

**1847** Jesuits expelled from Argentina. *Il Risorgimento,* newspaper, founded by Cavour. United Presbyterian Church formed.
**1847–1924** Angel Guimerà, Catalonian dramatist.
**1847–1929** Archibald, 5th Earl of Rosebery, Liberal politician.
**1847–1931** Thomas Alma Edison, American inventor.
**1847–1933** Annie Besant, theosophist.
**1847–1922** Alexander Graham Bell, inventor.
**1848** Feb., Karl Marx and Frederick Engels issue *Communist Manifesto.* Congregations of the Holy Ghost and of the Sacred Heart of Mary amalgamated. France forbids slavery in all colonies. Christian Socialist Movement begins in England. The breech-loading rifle invented.
**1848–87** Richard Jefferies, novelist.
**1848–1903** Paul Gauguin, artist and sculptor.
**1848–1907** Joris Karl Huysmans, French novelist.

| WESTERN & NORTHERN EUROPE | CENTRAL & SOUTHERN EUROPE | AFRICA |

**1848** 27 Apr., slavery finally abolished in French colonies. 4 May, Constituent Assembly meets in Paris: 900 members include representatives from Algeria and the colonies. 10 May, Constituent Assembly in Paris appoints an executive committee of five members.. June–Aug., Smith O'Brien's abortive rising in Ireland. 23–6 June, serious riots in Paris. 26 Aug., armistice of Malmö between Denmark and Germany. 12 Nov., new French constitution proclaimed: President elected for four years, and 750 deputies for three years. 10 Dec., Louis-Napoleon elected President of France (–1851). Educational reforms in Russia.

**1848** 13 Apr., national committee formed in Prague. May, German Federation occupies Schleswig and Holstein. 15 May, Emperor promises a constituent assembly in Austria. Second revolution in Vienna. 18 May, Parliament of Frankfurt meets. 22 May, massacre of liberals in Sicily. Constituent Assembly meets in Prussia. 2 June, Pan-Slav Congress meets in Prague. 17 June, Czech rebellion put down in Prague. 30 June, Archduke John made regent of the Empire. 7 July, Venice joined to Piedmont. 5 Aug., Austria seizes Milan. 9 Aug., armistice between Austria and Charles Albert. 28 Aug.– 3 Sept., workers' Parliament in Frankfurt. 7 Sept., feudalism abolished in Austria. 11 Sept., Louis Kossuth becomes dictator in Hungary. 3 Oct., Hungarian Diet dissolved. 6 Oct., third revolution in Vienna. 31 Oct., Prince Windischgrätz takes Vienna. 2 Nov., reactionary cabinet formed in Prussia. 24 Nov., Pope Pius IX flees to Gaëta, disguised as a footman. 2 Dec., Ferdinand I of Austria abdicates: succ. Francis-Joseph (–1916). 5 Dec., constitution granted in Prussia. 15 Dec., Prince Windischgrätz invades Hungary.
**1848–58** 500 miles of railway laid in Spain.
**1848–64** Maximilian II, King of Bavaria.

**1849** 17 March, William II of Holland d.: succ. William III (–1890). 26 May, French Constituent Assembly dissolved: legislative Assembly assumes office. 5 June, new constitution approved in Denmark. 10 June, Marshal Bugeaud d. 13 June, riots in Paris; 15 June, riots in Lyons. 29 June, Navigation Acts repealed by Britain. Queen Victoria visits Ireland. Encumbered Estates Act provides for sale of ruined estates in Ireland.

**1849** 5 Jan., Windischgrätz occupies Budapest. 23 Jan., Prussia proposes a German union, without Austria. 9 Feb., Giuseppe Mazzini proclaims republic in Rome. 4 March, constitution granted in Austria. 12 March, Charles Albert denounces truce with Austria. 23 March, Austria victorious at Novara: Charles Albert of Piedmont, Sardinia and Savoy abdicates: succ. Victor Emmanuel II (–1878). 27 March, constitution agreed by German National Assembly. 28 March, Frederick William IV elected Emperor by Parliament of Frankfurt. 7 Apr., Hungarians defeat Windischgrätz at Gödöllö: Budapest recaptured. 14 Apr., Hungary proclaims herself independent. 25 Apr., French force to restore the Pope lands in the Papal States. 27 Apr., Frederick William IV declines imperial crown. Apr.–May, King of Naples recovers Sicily. 9 May, Prussia puts down rebellion in Dresden. 11 May, Garibaldi enters Rome. 12 May, rebellion in Baden. 26 May, League of the Three Kings formed (Hanover, Prussia and Saxony). 2, 3 July, French occupy Rome to restore Pope Pius IX. 28 July, Austria restores Grand Duke of Tuscany.

**1849** Beecroft's mission to Dahomey to end slave trade rebuffed. Courts of Equity established in Nigeria. Libreville, Gabon, founded for freed slaves. Hamburg traders begin to operate in Zanzibar. Warden zone for Basuto frontier established.
**1849–53** J. Beecroft, British Consul for Bights of Benin and Biafra.
**1849–54** Abbas I, Khedive of Egypt.

## THE EAST & AUSTRALASIA THE AMERICAS RELIGION & CULTURE

**1848—51** José Joaquin Herrera, President of Mexico.

**1848—1914** Sir Charles Hubert Hastings Parry, composer.
**1848—1916** Helmuth, Count von Moltke, German general.
**1848—1930** Arthur James Balfour, statesman and philosopher.
**1848—1935** Hugo de Vries, botanist.

**1849** 13 Jan., Lord Gough defeats Sikhs at Chillianwalla. 21 Feb., Lord Gough finally defeats Sikhs in Gujarat. 12 March, remainder of Sikhs surrender at Rawalpindi. March, EIC, by treaty with Maharajah of Lahore, annexes the Punjab. Turks re-establish a *wali* (governor) in Yemen. Russia occupies mouth of R. Sir Darya. First railway agreements made in India. Anti-Transportation League active in Australia.
**1849—1928** Sayyid Amir Ali, first Indian member of the Judicial Committee of the Privy Council.

**1849** Apr., Tory riot in Montreal: Lord Elgin rescued by Toronto cavalry after giving assent to Rebellion Losses Bill: Parliament buildings burnt. Oct., Montreal Tories demand annexation by US. Dec., conference of British American League in Kingston: idea of federation of Canada mooted. Guarantee Act facilitates construction of railways in Canada. Court of Chancery reformed in Canada. Hudson's Bay Co. ceases to have monopoly of fur trade. Colony of Vancouver Is. founded by Hudson's Bay Co.
**1849—50** Zachary Taylor (Whig), President of US.
**1849—52** First railway built in Chile.
**1849—56** Trade in sugar, cotton, cattle, and coffee doubled in Brazil.
**1849—58** Liberals in power in Colombia: intense struggle between church and state.
**1849 ff.** Capital of Canada moved each four years between Toronto and Quebec.
**1849—59** Faustin I (Faustin Soulouque), Emperor of Haiti.

**1849** Tischendorf's edition of the Greek New Testament. Sir Henry Layard excavates Nineveh: *c.* 25,000 tablets and fragments found: transpires to be Ashurbanipal's library: state documents, and literary, religious and scientific works.
**1849—1905** Muhammad Abduh, mufti of Egypt and religious reformer.
**1849—1912** William Thomas Stead, journalist.
**1849—1928** Sir Edmund William Gosse, critic, essayist and poet.
**1849—1929** Prince Bernhard von Bülow, German statesman.

1849–1852

WESTERN &
NORTHERN EUROPE

CENTRAL &
SOUTHERN EUROPE

AFRICA

**1849** 6 Aug., peace of Milan between Austria and Victor Emmanuel II. 13 Aug., Hungarian rebels surrender to Russia at Vilagos. 27 Aug., Austria rejects Prussian proposal of German union. 25 Oct., Saxony declines to join German union: Hanover follows suit. 14 Dec., Archduke John resigns the regency of the Empire.

**1850** 31 May, new electoral law in France. June, Tenant Right League formed in Ireland. 2 Aug., convention of London between Britain, Denmark, France, Russia and Sweden, guarantees Danish integrity. 17 Aug., Denmark sells Gold Coast possessions to Britain. 26 Aug., Louis-Philippe d. in England. Irish Franchise Act increases number of Irish voters.

**1850** 15 Jan., Don Pacifico incident: Britain blockades Piraeus following alleged assault on British subject. 5 Feb., new constitution in Prussia. 20 March, German Parliament meets at Erfurt (−29 Apr.). 12 Apr., Pope Pius IX returns to Rome with French troops. 2 July, peace of Berlin between Denmark and Prussia: Prussia withdraws from Schleswig and Holstein. 1 Sept., Hesse-Cassel rises: Elector supported by Austria: Prussia backs rebels. 20 Sept., Prussia occupies Hesse-Cassel. 11 Oct., Austria, Bavaria, Saxony and Württemberg ally against Prussia. Count Camillo Cavour becomes chief minister in Piedmont. 26 Oct., Austro-Russian agreement against Prussia. 29 Nov., convention of Olmütz: Prussia gives way to Austria.

**1850** Feb., new constitution in Cape with elective upper house. Damaraland explored. Gold Coast separated from Sierra Leone. Hajj Umar attacks Segu, Kaarta and Massina from Futa Jalon. Executive and Legislative Councils set up in Gold Coast. Barth's expedition reaches Bornu, Kano and Kuka. Sayyid Said sends troops against Gazi.
**1850–3** Anglo-Kaffir war.

**1851** 22 Feb., Lord John Russell resigns following Parliamentary defeat: Lord Stanley fails to form government: Russell returns on same day. 27 Feb., commercial treaty between Britain and Sardinia. 12 Dec., following much unrest and agitation, *coup d'état* in France: Louis Napoleon empowered for ten years: 20 Dec., new French constitution drawn up. 19 Dec., Palmerston resigns: 26 Dec., Lord Granville, Foreign Secretary.

**1851** 15 Jan., Otto von Bismarck nominated Prussian representative in the German Diet. 15 May, Saldanha rebels in Portugal: Lisbon seized. 20 Aug., ministerial responsibility abolished in Austria. 7 Sept., *Zollverein* instituted in Germany: commercial treaty between Hanover and Prussia. Narvaez resigns. Bravo Murillo, Prime Minister of Spain: Dec., Murillo falls. 31 Dec., Austrian constitution abolished.

**1851** May-June, expedition of General Saint-Arnaud against Little Kabylia. Oct., Egyptian State Railway begun under Robert Stephenson. Moshesh greatly enlarges Basuto territory. 26 Nov., French fleet bombards Moroccan ports of Salé and Rabat in revenge for acts of piracy. Abortive British attack on Lagos: city freed. Barth and Overweg explore L. Chad. Cotonou founded.

**1852** 14 Jan., new constitution promulgated in France. 22 Jan., Orléans family banished from France. 22 Feb., Lord John Russell resigns: 27 Feb.–18 Dec., Conservative ministry under Earl of Derby: Disraeli, Chancellor.

**1852** 2 Jan., Austria opens negotiations with South German states for a customs union. 21 March, Montenegro declares itself independent under Danilo I. 20 Apr., convention of Darmstadt.

**1852** French take Laghouat and Ourgla. Treaty between Britain and Lagos. First Legislative Assembly meets in Gold Coast. Treaty between Britain and Begemder. Sand River Convention; Transvaal recognized by Britain.

1850 Indian town committees permitted to levy local indirect taxation. Indian tea industry expands rapidly. Australian Constitution Act: NSW and Victoria separated: S Australia and Tasmania obtain representative government: first Governor-General appointed. Jolo annexed to the Philippines. Canterbury, New Zealand, founded. Copper extraction at Burra Burra, Australia, begun. Malay tin industry largely in Chinese hands: Malay labour rarely available. Chinese population 414.4m. Population of Malaya about 300,000.
1850–5 Dost Muhammad Khan recovers Afghan Turkestan. Sir Charles Augustus Fitzroy, first Governor-General of Australia.
c. 1850 Tallow industry developed in Australia, consuming 2½m. sheep a year. Western banks open in Singapore.

1851 4 Feb., gold found in Summer Hill Creek, Australia. Victoria proclaimed a separate colony. British government offers Australian colonies self-government: welcomed by W.C. Wentworth. Turcomans destroy Russian naval station on Ashurada Is. Governor of Rangoon tightens precautions against smuggling: two British captains found guilty of fraud: captains then demand £1,920 from the Burmese. Following British seizure of Burmese vessel, Burmese fire on British squadron: British demand £100,000 compensation.
1851–61 Wen Tsung, Chinese Emperor, with throne name Hsien-feng.

1852 Second Anglo-Burmese war: British take Martaban and Rangoon; May, Bassein; June, Pegu; Oct., Prome. Oct., Admiral Putyatin leaves Russia with four ships to negotiate a commercial treaty with Japan.

1850 19 Apr., Clayton-Bulwer Treaty between Britain and US: US agrees to joint control of any canal constructed in Panama: Britain renounces all rights in C America: construction of Panama railway begun. Clayton-Bulwer Treaty regulates boundaries and British rights in British Honduras. 9 July, Zachary Taylor, President of US, d.: succ., his Vice-President, Millard Fillmore (Whig)(–1853). 9 Sept., California becomes a US State: slave trade forbidden in District of Columbia. Widespread legal reform in Canada: primogeniture abolished: seignorial tenure ended. Slave trade banned by Brazil. First telegraph line in Chile. Utah organized as a US territory: refused statehood on account of Mormon practice of polygamy. About 20,000 escaped slaves living free in northern US. US population over 23m.: 3.2m. slaves.
1850–60 2.45m. immigrants in US, chiefly to N and W. 200,000 miles of railway built, chiefly in the N.

1851 Treaty between Brazil and Uruguay: part of border transferred to Brazil. Responsible government granted in Prince Edward Is.
1851–2 Cholera epidemic in Jamaica.

1852 3 Feb., Juan de Rosas overthrown by battle of Caseros in Argentina: army supported by 3,000 Brazilians: Brazilians henceforward dominant in Uruguay.

1850 15 March, education law reformed in France. 28 May, France demands recognition of her rights in the Holy Places. 29 Sept., Catholic Hierarchy restored in England. The Bab, founder of the Bahai sect of Islam, executed in Tabriz. Auguste Mariette begins excavation of Memphis. Rudolf Clausius discovers second law of thermodynamics. R.W. Bunsen invents Bunsen burner. Paraffin first manufactured at Alfreton, Derbyshire. Reuter's Agency founded. The ophthalmoscope invented. First telegraph cable laid between Dover and Calais.
1850–92 Alfred, Lord Tennyson, English poet laureate.
1850–93 Guy de Maupassant, author. Silva Porto, Portuguese artist.
1850–94 Robert Louis Stevenson, essayist and novelist.
1850–1906 Sir Frederic William Maitland, historian.
1850–1916 Lord Kitchener, soldier and statesman.
1850–1923 Pierre Loti (Julien Viaud), novelist.
1850–1933 Augustine Birrell, essayist.
1850–1937 Thomas Masaryk, Czech statesman.
1851 16 March, concordat between Spain and the Vatican: Catholicism recognized as the sole faith in Spain: church in control of the press and education. 1 May–15 Oct., Great Exhibition held in Crystal Palace, London. 1 Aug., Ecclesiastical Titles Act forbids territorial titles to Roman Catholic bishops in England. Oct., the Tsar demands recognition of Russian right to protect the Orthodox in the Holy Places. Jewish schools recognized in England. The rotary press invented.
1851–1920 Mrs. Humphrey Ward (Mary Arnold), novelist.
1851–1922 Leslie Ward ('Spy'), cartoonist.
1851–1929 Ferdinand Foch, French Marshal.
1851–1940 Sir Oliver Joseph Lodge, scientist.
1852 26-7 July, first Co-operative Societies Congress held in London. Convocation of Canterbury restored. First man carrying glider launched by Sir George Cayley. Safety matches invented in Sweden.

## WESTERN & NORTHERN EUROPE

**1852** 8 May, Austria, Britain, France, Prussia, Russia and Sweden guarantee integrity of Denmark by treaty of London. 14 Sept., Duke of Wellington d. 7 Nov., Louis-Napoleon proclaimed Emperor of the French (as Napoleon III): ratified by plebiscite, 20-21 Nov. 2 Dec., the Second Empire solemnly proclaimed in Paris (–1870). 16 Dec., Disraeli's budget defeated. 18 Dec., Lord Derby resigns: 28 Dec., coalition ministry under Earl of Aberdeen (–1855): Gladstone, Chancellor. 200,200 Irish emigrate to USA: similar numbers in following sixty years.

**1853** 30 Jan., Napoleon III m. Eugénie de Montijo. 9-21 Feb., Russia proposes partition of Turkey to UK. 18 Apr., Gladstone's first budget: indirect taxation greatly reduced. Charity Commission established.

## CENTRAL & SOUTHERN EUROPE

**1852** 6 May, constitution abolished in Tuscany. 4 Nov., Cavour made Prime Minister in Piedmont.

**1853** 19 Feb., commercial treaty between Austria and Prussia. 29 Feb., Russian embassy sent to Istanbul. 3 March, peace between Montenegro and Turkey. 4 March, the *Zollverein* renewed. 4 Apr., Hanover and Oldenburg join *Zollverein*. 27 May, Russia and Turkey break off diplomatic relations. 2 June, British and French fleets sent to the Dardanelles. 3 July, Russia occupies Danubian provinces of Turkey. 28 Aug., German navy sold by auction. 23 Oct., hostilities begin between Russia and Turkey. 15 Nov., María of Portugal d.: succ. Peter V (–1861): regency until 1855: period of quiet reform. 30 Nov., war between Russia and Turkey: Russia demands protectorate over all Turkish Christian subjects. Turkish fleet destroyed at Sinope.
**1853–6** The Crimean War.

## AFRICA

**1853** Leopold of Belgium visits Egypt. British consulate established in Lagos. Ras Kassa (later Emperor Theodore) conquers Gojjam, Begemder, Tigrai and Shoa. New constitution in Cape Colony.
**1853–6** Livingstone's trans-Africa expedition.
**1853–95** Kigeri IV Rwabugiri, Mwami of Rwanda: responsible for present boundaries.

**1854** 12 March, treaty of alliance between Britain, France and Turkey against Russia. 27 and 28 March, Britain and France declare war on Russia. 10 Apr., Anglo-French treaty on the Near East. June, Colonial Office and War Office separated. 14 Oct., treaty between Britain and Japan. 18 Oct., Ostend Manifesto urges US occupation of Cuba.

**1854** 1 Jan., commercial treaty between Austria and the *Zollverein*. 9 Apr., Four Power Protocol against Russia. 20 Apr., Austria and Prussia make defensive alliance against Russia. 26 May, Allies occupy Piraeus: Greece blockaded for having attacked Turkey: Greece declares herself neutral. June, the Allies disembark at Varna. 3 June, Austrian ultimatum to Russia. 14 June, treaty between Austria and Turkey: Austria to occupy Danubian principalities. Petition for new constitution in Spain: state of siege proclaimed in Madrid: 28 June, revolution in Madrid led by Carlist General O'Donnell: other provinces

**ante 1854** Ovimbundu traders crossing Africa to Mozambique.
**1854** Abbas I of Egypt murdered: succ. Muhammad Said (–1863). Ferdinand de Lesseps granted concession to build Suez Canal. al-Hajj Omar preaches Holy War: takes Bambouk. Convention of Bloemfontein: Orange Free State constituted. First Cape Parliament meets.
**1854–61** Colonel Faidherbe, governor of Senegal.

## THE EAST & AUSTRALASIA

**1852** Constitution for New Zealand agreed: six provisional councils and bicameral legislature: property franchise excludes almost all Maoris. *c.* 700 Maoris attending government schools: curriculum includes practical subjects. Orders in Council authorizing the revival of transportation revoked. Tai Ping movement captures Hankow.
**1852–78** Unrest in Australia caused by gangs of bushrangers.

**1853** Aug., American squadron at Nagasaki with letter from President Fillmore, demanding that Japan should trade with USA and other concessions: includes two steamships: commander Commodore Perry: Abe Masahiro, chief counsellor of the shogunate, consults great lords and scholars: some answer that trade should be opened so that Japan can master western technology. Pagan deposed: Mindon enthroned as King of Burma (–1878): Pegu made a British province. Period of intense formal literary activity at Burmese court. 11 Dec., EIC annexes Nagpur. British Legislative Council Act sets up Indian legislature. Indian Civil Service opened to competitive examination. EIC Charter renewed. First Indian cotton mill established in Bombay. Tai Ping movement captures Nanking, and makes it the capital. Transportation of convicts to Australia ceases. 40,000 gold diggers in the Eureka, Gravel Pits, and Canadian Leads near Ballarat: subsequently one of the greatest goldfields in the world.
**1853–5** Tai Ping movement advances towards Tientsin: attempt to capture Peking abortive.
**1853–8** Tokugawa Iyesadá, Shogun.
**1854** Jan., Russian squadron, ignored in 1853, returns to Nagasaki: Japanese prepare defences, and procrastinate. Feb., Commodore Perry returns with US squadron. 31 March, at Yokohama, treaty of Kanagawa between Japan and US: ports of Hakodate and Shimoda opened to US. Oct., Admiral Sterling, RN, obtains written agreement from Japanese allowing British vessels to obtain supplies at Nagasaki and Hakodate. Apr., Maori gathering of *c.* 1,000 assembles at Mawanapon, to discuss problems of European immigration and sale of land.

## THE AMERICAS

**1852** 20 Feb., Justo José de Urquiza takes Buenos Aires by force: quarrels with provincial legislature: withdraws, governing Argentina from Paraná (–1860): Rosas exiled. Siege of Montevideo lifted by Urquiza. Urquiza holds constituent congress at Santa Fé.

**1853** May, Argentinian constitution promulgated at Paraná. 24 Sept., French annex New Caledonia. Slave trade completely ended by Brazil. William Walker declares independent republic in Mexican Lower California and Sonora.
**1853–5** Santa Anna again in power in Mexico.
**1853–7** Franklin Pearce (Dem.), President of US.

**1854** Guerrilla bands, organized by Juan Álvarez, become active in S Mexico: March, Liberal *Plan de Ayutla* issued. 31 March, US treaty with Japan. 2 May, Britain declares Monroe doctrine inacceptable to European countries. 30 May, Kansas and Nebraska become US territories: Missouri compromise repealed by Congress. 16 Oct., Abraham Lincoln makes Free-Soil speech at Peoria. 19 Dec., Sir Edmund W. Head, Governor-in-Chief of Canada (–1861). The Ostend Manifesto: three Democrat ministers propose US annexation of Cuba. Republican Party founded in US.

## RELIGION & CULTURE

**1852** First dirigible airship built, and flown by Gifford. The gyroscope invented.
**1852–83** Arnold Toynbee, economist.
**1852–1921** Hans Huber, Swiss composer.
**1852–1924** Sir Charles Villers Stanford, composer. Lin Shu, Chinese translator of European short stories and novels.
**1852–1928** Henry Herbert Asquith, later Earl of Oxford and Asquith, Liberal statesman.
**1852–1931** Joseph Joffre, French Marshal.
**1852–1905** Pierre Savorgnan de Brazza, French explorer.
**1853** 3 March, Catholic hierarchy restored in Holland. Capitation grants provided for rural schools in England. Vaccination against smallpox made compulsory in England. First railway constructed in Canada. Sir Richard Burton visits Mecca in disguise.
**1853–90** Vincent Willem van Gogh, Dutch artist.
**1853–1902** Cecil Rhodes, statesman.
**1853–1917** Leander Starr Jameson, S African politician.
**1853–1921** Yen Fu, first Chinese translator of European philosophical and scientific books.
**1853–1931** Hall Caine, novelist.
**1853–1932** Bp Charles Gore, Anglican theologian.
**1853–1942** Sir William Flinders Petrie, archaeologist.

**1854** Newman's abortive attempt to set up a Catholic university in Ireland. 8 Dec., Pope Pius IX proclaims the Immaculate Conception to be an article of faith. The safety lift invented. John Snow shows cholera to be a water-borne infection. Aluminium first isolated. Place de la Concorde laid out.
**1854–1900** Oscar O'Flahertie Wilde, poet and dramatist.
**1854–91** Jean Nicolas Arthur Rimbaud, poet.
**1854–1912** Henri Poincaré, statesman.
**1854–1921** Engelbert Humperdinck, German composer.
**1854–1925** Alfred, Lord Milner, statesman.

1854–1856

WESTERN &
NORTHERN EUROPE

CENTRAL &
SOUTHERN EUROPE

AFRICA

join rebellion: Espartero joins
O'Donnell: Queen Maria Cristina's
palace sacked: exiled for life. 8 July,
Austria joins the Four Power Protocol.
30 July, Russians retire in Bessarabia.
8 Aug., English and French troops
disembark at Varna. Austria, Britain
and France state Four Point peace
conditions in Vienna. 22 Aug.,
Austria occupies Danubian
principalities. 7 Sept., the Allies
abandon Varna. 14 Sept., English,
French, Sardinian and Turkish forces
disembark at Eupatoria. 20 Sept.,
Russians defeated at Alma. 12 Oct.,
Upper House reconstructed in Prussia.
17 Oct., Sebastopol besieged (−1855).
25 Oct., English defeat Russians at
Balaclava: charge of the Light Brigade.
5 Nov., Battle of Inkermann. 2 Dec.,
Britain and France guarantee Austrian
Italian possessions for the duration of
the war.

**1855** 7 Jan., Russia accepts protocol
of 8 July 1854 as basis for
negotiation with Allies. 6 Feb.–1858
Viscount Palmerston, Prime Minister
(Lib.). 18 Feb., Nicolas I of Russia
d.: succ. Alexander II (−1881). 15
June, newspaper stamp duty
abolished in Britain. 21 Nov.,
Sweden joins the Allies.

**1855** 26 Jan., Piedmont and Sardinia
join the Allies against Russia. 9-19
Apr., Allies checked at Sebastopol.
May, liberal institutions abolished in
Hanover. 18 June, second battle at
Malakoff: Allies checked. 16 Aug.,
battle of Traktir. 8 Sept., Sebastopol
taken by the Allies after eleven
months siege. Malakoff taken. 27
Nov., Russians take Kars. 29 Dec.,
Austrian ultimatum to Russia. *Cortes*
passes new constitutional charter in
Spain.
**1855–7** *c.* 8,000 die in Lisbon of
cholera and yellow fever.

**1855** Egyptian post set up at Fashoda
to check slave trade. French build
fort at Medina against al-Hajj Omar.
7 Feb., Ras Kassa crowned as Emperor
Theodore II of Ethiopia (−1868).
Livingstone discovers Victoria Falls.
Cape Colony adopts free trade. New
constitution in Transvaal.
**1855–92** Soninki-Marabout wars in
Gambia.

**1856** 29 Jan., the Victoria Cross
instituted by Queen Victoria. 16
March, the Prince Imperial, son of
Napoleon III, b. 19 March,
Alexander II of Russia agrees to
peace: announces interior reforms in
Russia: serfage abolished. 25 Feb.–
30 March, congress of Paris. 30 March,
treaty of Paris: Russia abandons Kars
for Sebastopol; abandons possessions

**1856** 18 Feb., the *Hatt-i-humaioun*
promulgated, guaranteeing equality to
all Turkish subjects: civil powers of
Christian churches abolished: religious
freedom granted: prison reforms and
end of torture promised. 27 May,
Alexander II grants amnesty to rebels
in Poland. July, Espartero resigns.
3 Sept., rebellion in Neuchâtel.

**1856** Cairo-Alexandria railway
completed. Sayyid Said of Zanzibar
d.: succ. Sayyid Majid (−1870) in
Zanzibar only. Pretoria made capital
of Transvaal. South African Republic
set up: Marthinius Pretorius, first
President. Natal chartered as a
Crown Colony. Indian indentured
labour sent for from Natal.

## THE EAST & AUSTRALASIA

**1854** Nov., Russian squadron again visits Osaka: alarm amongst the Japanese: Russians sail away: Russian vessel *Diana* sunk in whirlpool caused by earthquake: Japanese believe this due to the wrath of the gods. 29 Nov., meeting of 10,000 gold diggers at Bakery Hill, Australia: Chartists and Irish confront police; 3 Dec., troops sent in: amnesty eventually granted. Sir Charles Wood's despatch on Indian education. 800 mile telegraph line opened from Calcutta to Agra. Burmese embassy sent to Calcutta, requesting return of Pegu. Riots in Singapore between Hokkien and Cantonese Chinese. NSW Legislative Assembly votes to declare war on Russia. European population of New Zealand about 32,500: nearly 12,000 in capital, Auckland.

**1855** Feb., Russo-Japanese treaty signed at Shimoda: southern Kurile Is. go to Japan, N Kurile Is. to Russia: Sakhalin to remain unpartitioned: Nagasaki, Shimoda and Hakodate to be open to Russians: Russians granted extra-territorial rights. Japanese treaty with Dutch: steamship bought by Japanese government: shipyards under Dutch inaugurated. 30 March, treaty of Peshawar: EIC and Afghanistan ally against Persia. Anglo-Persian diplomatic relations broken off. Abortive British attempt to obtain commercial treaty with Burma. Dutch establish authority in NW Borneo. First jute-spinning machine set up near Serampore. Pastoral Protection Society founded in Australia. All Australian colonies except W Australia granted responsible government. Yellow River changes its course, entering the sea at Tientsin: disaster to Honan and Anhui regions.
**1855—68** Peasant risings of Nien Fei in Honan and Anhui provinces.
**1855—73** Muslim revolt in Yunnan province, China: said to have cost 1m. lives.
**1855—1909** British Consular jurisdiction maintained over British subjects in Siam.
**1856** 13 Feb., EIC annexes Oudh. Persia occupies Herat: EIC force sent to Persian Gulf compels Persians to make peace. General Service Enlistment Act in India requires recruits to serve wherever needed: causes caste and religious resentment in Indian army: story that cartridges are greased with cow and pig fat spreads rapidly.

## THE AMERICAS

**1854** Pennsylvania Rock Oil Co. founded.
**1854—62** Ramón Castilla, President of Peru.

**1855** Aug., Santa Anna leaves Mexico for Colombia, never to return to power. Nov., Liberals, headed by Álvarez, take Mexico City: Álvarez made President: jurisdiction of eccesiastical and military courts immediately curtailed. Dec., Ignacio Comonfort, President of Mexico. William Walker leads expedition into Nicaragua. Huron Ship Canal opened. Responsible government granted in Newfoundland. Gold discovered in Fraser R., Canada: rush begins: area proclaimed under the jurisdiction of Vancouver Is.
**1855—76** Period of *La Reforma* in Mexico.

**1856** Committee to examine future of of Hudson's Bay Co. set up by Colonial Office. Western Union Telegraph Co. founded.

## RELIGION & CULTURE

**1854—1925** Sir Paul Gavrilovitch Vinagradoff, jurist.
**1854—1932** John Philip Sousa, American composer.
**1854—1935** Edward Carson, Irish statesman.
**1854—1941** Sir James George Frazer, anthropologist.

**1855** 29 May, monasteries and orders dissolved in Piedmont. 18 Aug., concordat between Austria and the Vatican: clergy gain control of education, censorship and matrimonial courts. Henry Bessemer invents process enabling mass production of steel. Electric telegraph constructed from England to Balaclava. Printing-telegraph invented. The hypodermic syringe invented. Balmoral Castle completed.
**1855—94** Marie Corelli, novelist.
**1855—1928** Stanley Weyman, novelist.
**1855—1932** Paget Jackson Toynbee, translator.
**1855—1934** Sir Arthur Wing Pinero, dramatist.
**1855—1935** Michurin, Russian geneticist.

**1856** Jesuits suppressed in Mexico: much church land sold compulsorily. Academy of Moral and Political Sciences established in Madrid. Aniline dyes first produced by W.H. Perkins.
**1856—7** Experimental voyages of French refrigerator ship, *La Frigorifique,* bring Argentine meat to Europe.
**1856—1915** Keir Hardie, Labour politician.
**1856—1921** Theobald von Bethman-Hollweg, German statesman.

| WESTERN & NORTHERN EUROPE | CENTRAL & SOUTHERN EUROPE | AFRICA |
|---|---|---|
| at the mouth of the Danube; loses the right to station warships in the Black Sea; renounces right to protect Christian subjects of the Ottoman sultan. 15 Apr., Austria, Britain and France guarantee Turkish integrity by second treaty. 16 Apr., Declaration of Paris on naval war. 17 July, English law on limited liability companies. 26 July, French commercial legislation revised. | **1856** 15 Sept., O'Donnell in power in Spain: 1845 constitution restored: 1 Oct., O'Donnell falls: Narvaez recalled (–1857). 2 Dec., Franco-Spanish frontier defined by treaty. Saldanha dismissed: Liberal ministry in Portugal under Loulé. | **1856–7** Arab traders reach Urua (N Katanga). **c. 1856–65** Tippu Tib trading with the Luba. |
| **1857** 14 June, commercial treaty between France and Russia. 25 June, Prince Albert created Prince Consort. 28 Aug., Matrimonial Causes Act enables civil divorce in England. 12 Oct., serious financial crisis begins in Britain. 20 Nov., Alexander II of Russia sets up secret committee for amelioration of the position of the serfs: no provision made for redemption or for land. | **1857** 22 March, diplomatic relations severed between Austria and Sardinia. 1 Aug., Garibaldi founds Italian National Association for unification of Italy. Sept., Napoleon III and the Tsar meet in Stuttgart. 25 Oct., Narvaez falls: O'Donnell in power again in Spain (–1862): 'Liberal Union' coalition government. Vienna currency convention creates monetary unity in Austria and the *Zollverein*. Earthquake in Basilicata region, Italy. | **1857** French conquer Grand Kabylia. al-Hajj Omar besieges Medina. Pretorius invades OFS: peace made by Paul Kruger. *Charles et Georges,* French slaver, captured by Portuguese off Mozambique: French protest. **1857–9** R.F. Burton and J.H. Speke reach L. Tanganyika from Bagamoyo. |
| **1858** 14 Jan., attempt on Napoleon III's life by Orsini. 19 Feb., Lord Palmerston resigns. 25 Feb.–1859, Earl of Derby, Prime Minister (Con.). 2 July, imperial serfs liberated in Russia. 21 July, Napoleon III and Cavour meet at Plombières: unification of Italy planned. 23 July, Jewish Disabilities Act ends disabilities of Jews in England. 26 Aug., commercial treaty between England and Japan. 1 Nov., EIC territories pass into control of the Crown. | **1858** 13 May, the Turks defeated by Montenegro at Grahovo. Feb.–July, war between Turkey and Montenegro. July, O'Donnell restored in Spain. 7 Oct., Frèderick William IV of Prussia declared insane: William, Prince Regent. 8 Nov., independence of Montenegro recognized by great powers: boundaries fixed. 23 Dec., Alexander Karageorgevitch deposed in Serbia: Milosh Obrenovitch restored. **1858–60** Algeria governed directly from Paris. | **1858** J.H. Speke reaches southern end of L. Victoria. Msiri sets up trading station for ivory, copper and slaves in Katanga. Basuto, Batalpin, Bushmen and Koranas invade Transvaal: 29 Sept., treaty of Aliwal North: Basuto boundary redrawn. **1858–64** Livingstone's Zambezi expedition. |

## THE EAST & AUSTRALASIA

**1856** Sayyid Thuwaini succ. Sayyid Said as Sultan of Oman and Muscat. Chinese arrest British ship for smuggling. Tasmania granted self-government. Townsend Harris arrives as US consul at Shimoda. '1856 Compact' regularizes financial relations of provincial and central government in New Zealand.
**1856—8** Viscount (later Earl) Canning, Governor-General of India (Viceroy 1858—62).

**1857** March, Indian regiment disbanded at Barrackpur. 10 May, Indian troops mutiny at Meerut: beginning of Indian Mutiny: officers shot: 11 May, Delhi taken by rebels: troops mutiny in many other cities. June, US convention with Japanese grants US citizens extra-territorial rights and open ports at Shimoda and Hakodate. 11 June, Allahabad taken from the rebels. 27 June, British surrender at Cawnpore: Massacre of Cawnpore: British prisoners murdered in spite of promise of safe-conduct, including 125 women and children. 1 July, Lucknow besieged. 7 July—25 Sept., Gen. Havelock fights eight pitched battles to relieve Lucknow. 20 Sept., Delhi retaken by British: Bahadur Shah II, last Mughul Emperor deposed and exiled to Rangoon. 25 Sept., Lucknow temporarily relieved: shortly again besieged. 6 Nov., Cawnpore retaken. 13 Nov., final relief of Lucknow. Telegraph line reaches Lahore and Peshawar. Port Philip separated from NSW. Cotton planting encouraged by Rev. J.D. Lang. 'Lorcha War' between China, Britain and France. Mining begun at Ampang, Klang Valley, near Kuala Lumpur.
**1857—61** Persia campaigns against the Turcomans. Mandalay built as new capital of Burma.
**1858** 8 July, peace proclaimed in India. 1 Nov., British Government of India Act: Secretary of State appointed: EIC powers taken over by British government: Lord Canning adds Viceroy to his existing title (—1862). Britain occupies Perim Is. Rebellion of peasants against the Ottomans in N Lebanon. Ii Nassuke, lord of Hikone, chief adviser of Shogunate: makes treaties for Japan with France, Russia, UK and USA in defiance of the Emperor. Te Wherewhero elected king by the Maoris.

## THE AMERICAS

**1857** 5 Feb., Liberal constitution promulgated in Mexico: civil war ensues: conservatives hold Mexico City: Benito Juárez, Liberal leader, retires to the country: Comonfort re-elected President. Oct., Sinn Fein (Irish Republican Brotherhood) founded in New York. William Walker surrenders and returns to USA. Ottawa (Bytown) made the capital of Canada by personal choice of Queen Victoria. First railway built in Argentina. Supreme Court declares that Congress has no power to exclude slavery from any US territory (Dred Scott case).
**1857—61** James Buchanan (Dem.), President of US.

**1858** Jan., two Presidents and two governments in Mexico: Félix Zuloaga in Mexico City, shortly followed by Miguel Mirámon: Benito Juárez rules outlying states. May, Benito Juárez makes Veracruz his capital. 12 May, Minnesota becomes a US State. Seneca Oil Co. founded. First French consul appointed in Quebec.
**1858—61** Present Colombia designated the Granadine Confederation.

## RELIGION & CULTURE

**1856—1924** Woodrow Wilson, American President.
**1856—1925** William Ferguson Massey, New Zealand politician. Sir Henry Rider Haggard, novelist. John Singer Sargent, American artist.
**1856—1927** Matilde Serao, Italian novelist.
**1856—1937** Frank Billings Kellogg, American statesman.
**1856—1939** Sigmund Freud, Austrian psychologist.
**1856—1940** Joseph John Thompson, physicist.
**1856—1950** George Bernard Shaw, dramatist.
**1857** Trans-Atlantic cable completed. Westerton v. Liddell trial on charge of ritual. National Portrait Gallery founded. Bombay, Calcutta and Madras universities founded. British Museum Reading Room opened. Juan Vicente Goméz, Venezuelan dictator, b. Egyptian Museum founded.
**1857—94** Heinrich Hertz, physicist.
**1857—1924** Joseph Conrad (Korzeniowski), novelist.
**1857—1927** Wilhelm Johannsen, botanist.
**1857—1930** William Howard Taft, American President. George Gissing, novelist.
**1857—1932** Paul Doumer, French statesman and President. Ronald Ross pathologist and discoverer of the actiology of malaria.
**1857—1934** Sir Edward Elgar, composer.
**1857—1936** Sir Charles Harding Firth, historian.
**1857—1941** Robert, Lord Baden-Powell, founder of the Boy Scouts. Sir John Lavery, artist.

**1858** Appearances of the Blessed Virgin Mary at Lourdes. *Hadiqat al-Akhbar,* first Syrian newspaper, founded. Universities (Scotland) Act passed. Bp Ignace Bourget of Montreal attacks the *Institut Canadien,* rationalist free-thinking society.
**1858—1914** Fr Charles-Eugène, Vicomte de Foucald, soldier, priest, explorer, linguist and apostle of the Sahara.
**1858—1917** Emile Durkheim, sociologist.

1858–1860

WESTERN &
NORTHERN EUROPE
          CENTRAL &
SOUTHERN EUROPE
          AFRICA

**1858** Property qualification for British Members of Parliament abolished. Sinn Fein founded in Ireland.
**1858–68** 10,000 miles of railway laid in Spain.

**1859** 19 Jan., alliance between France and Piedmont. 3 May, France declares war on Austria to safeguard Italy. 10 June, Lord Derby resigns. 18 June–1865, Viscount Palmerston, Prime Minister (Lib.). 8 July, Oscar I of Sweden d.: succ. Charles XV (–1872).

**1859** 19 Apr., Austria demands disarmament of Piedmont. 27 Apr., revolution in Tuscany. 28 Apr., revolution in Modena. 29 Apr., Austria attacks Piedmont. 1 May, revolution in Parma. 20 May, French defeat Austrians at Montebello; and, 31 May, at Palestro. 22 May, Ferdinand II of Sicily d.: succ. Francis II (–1861). 4 June, French defeat Austrians at Magenta; 8 June, enter Milan; 24 June, defeat Austrians at Solferino. 8 July, armistice between Austria and France. 11 July, preliminary peace of Villafranca between Austria and France: Parma and Lombardy to be ceded to Piedmont: Tuscany and Modena restored: Venice remains Austrian. 12 July, Cavour resigns. 15-16 Sept., assembly of Frankfurt: German National Association to promote German unity founded. 10 Nov., treaty of Zurich confirms preliminary treaty of Villafranca.

**1859** Construction of Suez Canal begun. Further French treaties in W Africa. Sayyid Majid of Zanzibar sign trade treaty with Hanseatic towns. French treaties with Madagascar. Dopper Kerk leaves DRC. Consul Plowden murdered: John Bell shot protecting Emperor Theodore.

**1860** 23 Jan., Cobden commercial treaty between Britain and France.

**1860** 20 Jan., Cavour returns to office. 5 March, *Reichsrat* (council of Austrian Empire) increased in number. 11-15 March, Emilia, Modena, Parma, Romagna and Tuscany vote for union with Piedmont. 24 March, treaty of Turin: Savoy and Nice ceded to France by Piedmont. 2 Apr., first Italian Parliament meets at Turin. 4 Apr., revolution in Sicily. 11 May, Garibaldi's expedition with the 1,000. 27 May, Garibaldi takes Palermo. Aug., Austria requests to join the *Zollverein*. 13 Aug., Danilo of Montenegro assassinated: succ. Nicolas (–1918). 7 Sept., Garibaldi takes Naples: Francis II flees. 8 Sept., rising in Papal States.

**1860** War between Morocco and Spain: Spain gains Santa Cruz de Mar Pequeña: Ceuta and Melilla made free ports. Treaty of peace between France and al-Hajj Omar. Mbarak b. Rashid al-Mazrui, Wali of Gazi: frequently in rebellion against Zanzibar. British Kaffraria made a Crown Colony. Cape Parliament demands secession from Britain.
**1860–90** Slave trade develops in N and E Congo.

# THE EAST & AUSTRALASIA

# THE AMERICAS

# RELIGION & CULTURE

**1858** China cedes part of N Manchuria to Russia. S Australia passes Real Property Act requiring registration of land: system later imitated in UK, USA, British Empire and parts of Europe.
**1858–63** Civil war in Pahang.
**1858–66** Tokugawa Iyemochi, Shogun.

**1858–1919** Ruggiero Leoncavallo, Italian composer.
**1858–1923** Andrew Bonar Law, British statesman.
**1858–1924** Giacomo Puccini, Italian composer.
**1858–1938** Aylmer Maude, writer and translator of Tolstoy.
**1858–1943** John Burns, trade union leader. Beatrice Webb, economist.
**1858–1945** Frederick, Lord Lugard, colonial statesman.
**1858–1947** Max Planck, physicist.
**1858–1949** Edith Oenone Somerville, novelist.

**1859** Dec., Queensland made a colony and separated from NSW. Circassia taken by Prince Bariatinski: inhabitants dispersed in Russia and Ottoman Empire. First jute power loom set up in India. Bengal Tenancy Act.
**1859–85** Burmese capital at Mandalay.
**1859** 17 Feb., French take Saigon (-22 March). Dec., Queensland made a colony and separated from NSW. Circassia taken by Prince Bariatinski: inhabitants dispersed in Russia and Ottoman Empire. First jute power loom set up in India. Bengal Tenancy Act.
**1859–85** Burmese capital at Mandalay.

**1859** 14 Feb., Oregon becomes a US State. 29 Aug., oil first successfully drilled at Oil Creek, Pennsylvania: oil industry subsequently spreads to eastern states, Canada, Illinois, Alberta and California. 16 Oct., John Brown raids Harper's Ferry in fanatical attempt to liberate and arm freed slaves. Gold Rush to Pike's Peake Country. Silver found in Colorado. Urquiza defeats force from Buenos Aires at Cépeda: Buenos Aires accepts 1853 constitution. *Laws of Reform* issued by Juárez in Mexico.

**1859** First electric light plant built in New York. Sinai MS of New Testament found by L.F.K. von Tischendorf. Cottage hospitals instituted.
**1859–1906** Pierre Curie, scientist.
**1859–1914** Jean Jaurès, French politician and publicist.
**1859–1919** Theodore Roosevelt, American President.
**1859–1924** Cecil James Sharp, composer and collector of English folk music.
**1859–1925** Marquess Curzon of Kedleston, statesman.
**1859–1927** Jerome Klapka Jerome, dramatist and humorous novelist.
**1859–1930** Sir Arthur Conan Doyle, novelist and spiritualist.
**1859–1932** Kenneth Grahame, children's writer.
**1859–1933** Sir John Fortescue, military historian.
**1859–1936** Alfred Edward Housman, poet.
**1859–1939** Henry Havelock Ellis, writer and psychologist.
**1859–1940** George Lansbury, Labour politician.
**1859–1941** Henri Louis Bergson, philosopher.
**1859–1947** Sidney James Webb, Lord Passfield, economist and political writer.

**1860** Jan., Ii Naosuke assassinated. July, French expedition to Syria, to protect the Maronite Christians against the Druzes. Indian Penal Code comes into force. 11,000 Christians massacred by the Ottomans in Lebanon: French troops intervene. Treaty defines Dutch and Portuguese boundary in Timor. British expedition against Peking: Emperor flees: Treaty of Tientsin cedes Kowloon to Britain and gives British numerous privileges. Population of Singapore 80,792, of whom 50,000 Chinese. Vladivostock founded by Russia. Usuri province ceded by China to Russia.

**1860** 6 Nov., Abraham Lincoln (Rep.) elected President of US (–1865). Dec., Mexican Liberal armies take Mexico City. 20 Dec., S Carolina secedes from US: Mississippi and five others follow. William Walker captured and executed by Honduran army. Civil war in Colombia. Juárez takes Mexico City: becomes President of Mexico.
**1860–95** García Moreno, dominant figure in politics of Ecuador: conservative and clerical.
**1860–70** Number of factories in US increases by 80%: value of manufactures by 100%.

**1860** English Church Union founded. Russian Orthodox Monastery built in Jerusalem. The Bulgarian Church separates from Constantinople.
**1860–1904** Theodor Herzl, founder of political Zionism. Anton Chekhov, Russian dramatist.
**1860–1907** Francis Joseph Thompson, poet.
**1860–1909** Isaac Albeniz, Spanish composer.
**1860–1911** Gustav Mahler, Austrian composer.
**1860–1934** Raymond Poincaré, French statesman and President.
**1860–1937** Sir James Matthew Barrie, dramatist and novelist.

1860–1862

WESTERN &
NORTHERN EUROPE

CENTRAL &
SOUTHERN EUROPE

AFRICA

**1860** 11 Sept., King Victor Emmanuel invades Papal States. 18 Sept., Papal army defeated at Castelfidardo. 26 Sept., Milosh I of Serbia d.: Michael III Obrenovitch restored (−1868). 20 Oct., Austrian constitution amended by October Diploma. 21-22 Oct., Naples and Sicily vote for Italian unification. 4-5 Nov., the Legations and Umbria vote for Italian unification.

**1861** 3 March, serfs abolished in Russia: 47m. peasants affected. 10 Apr., Russia grants Finland a constitution. 13 May, Britain proclaims herself neutral in the American war. 16 Sept., Post Office Savings Bank opened in Britain. 14 Dec., Prince Consort d.

**1861** 2 Jan., Frederick William IV of Prussia d.: succ. William I (−1888), later Emperor. 14 Feb., Francis II of Naples capitulates at Gaeta. 26 Feb., the 'February Patent': Austrian constitution centralized. 27 Feb., Warsaw massacre: Russian troops fire on demonstration against Russian rule. 11 March, German Commercial Law Code promulgated. 17 March, Victor Emmanuel II proclaimed King of Italy (−1878). June, German Progressive Party founded. 6 June, Cavour d. 25 June, Abd al-Majid of Turkey d.: succ. Abd al-Aziz (−1876). 1 Nov., Peter V of Portugal d. of typhus: succ. Luis I (−1889). 23 Dec., principalities of Moldavia and Wallachia united as Rumania: Alexander John I Cuza, first prince (−1863). Secret society 'Young Russia' founded by Tchernychevski: deported (1862) to Siberia, after being pilloried in St Petersbourg.

**1861** British bombard Porto Novo. British Protectorate of Lagos proclaimed. 'Northern' Arabs expelled by British from Zanzibar.
**1861–3** Radama II, King of Merina: 12 Sept., treaty with France.

**1862** Feb., France obtains Roquebrune and Mentone by purchase from Monaco. 2 Aug., commercial treaty between France and Prussia.

**1862** 29 Aug., Garibaldi attempts to take Rome: taken prisoner by royalists at Aspromonte. 22 Sept., Bismarck appointed Prime Minister of Prussia. 13 Oct., Bismarck makes 'blood and iron' speech: governs without a budget until 1866. 22 Oct., Otto of Greece deposed. 23 Oct., provisional government in Greece under A.G. Bulgaris.

**1862** Baikie visits Bida, Kano and Zaria. R.F. Burton visits Benin. France buys Obock for 10,000 Maria Theresa dollars. Egyptian expedition against Ethiopia halted by smallpox epidemic. Emperor Theodore requests alliance with Queen Victoria against Muslims: refused: British Consul and other Europeans imprisoned.
**c. 1862** Chamber of Commerce established in Khartoum.

| THE EAST & AUSTRALASIA | THE AMERICAS | RELIGION & CULTURE |
|---|---|---|

**THE EAST & AUSTRALASIA**

**1860–1** Burke and Wills cross Australia to Gulf of Carpentaria.
**1860–4** War between Europeans and Maoris in New Zealand.

**1861** 2 Sept., commercial treaty between China and Prussia. Famine in N India. British Indian Councils Act. Ceylon Volunteer Ordinance forms detachments of infantry, gunners and sappers. Lebanon granted local autonomy within the Ottoman Empire.
**1861–2** France at war with Vietnam following murder of French and Spanish missionaries. 1 July, Saigon taken. John McDouall's explorations in central Australia: crossing from Adelaide to Van Diemen's Gulf made: telegraph line from Adelaide to Darwin made possible (1872).

**1862** 5 June, treaty of Hué between France and Vietnam: France acquires southern half. Outbreak of Larut wars, between rival Chinese tin-mining groups. Siamese fleet at Trenggann: fort shelled. Anglo-Burmese Commercial Treaty signed. Rule compelling Japanese lords (*daimyo*) to reside at Shogunate in alternate years abolished. Emperor instructs Shogun to expel all foreigners from Japan in the following year: Shogun warns foreigners but says no action will be taken. Much unrest on the part of xenophobic fanatics. Persian ambassador shot in Bombay.

**THE AMERICAS**

**1861** 29 Jan., Kansas becomes a US State. Feb., seven seceding states meet at Montgomery, Alabama: Confederate States of America formed: Jefferson Davis elected provisional president: four other states join subsequently. 12 Apr., Confederates attack Fort Sumter, Charleston Harbour: beginning of American Civil War (–1865). July, Tomás Cipriano de Mosquera seizes power in Bogotá as provisional president (–1867): Liberal anti-clerical government. July, Juárez orders suspension of service of foreign debt: Britain and France sever relations with Mexico. 21 July, agreement between Britain, France and Spain on Mexican debts: French establish Emperor Maximilian as ruler of Mexico (–1864). Confederates defeat Union force at Bull Run, N Virginia: other victories follow. 28 Nov., Lord Monck, Governor-in-Chief of Canada (–1869). Granadine Confederation becomes the United States of Colombia. Santo Domingo cedes her independence to Spain.
**1861–3** José Antonio Páez, dictator of Venezuela.
**1861–5** Dominica ruled temporarily as a Spanish colony. American Civil War: twenty-three loyalist states' population c. 22m.: eleven Confederate states with population c. 9m., including 3½m. negroes: northern railways 22,000 miles; southern 9,000.

**1862** Jan., French expeditionary force lands at Veracruz. Apr., battle of Shiloh: Union and Confederates both withdraw in disorder. 5 May, French defeated by Mexicans at Puebla. 4 July, Union forces take Vicksburg: Confederate forces broken in two. 29 Aug.– 1 Sept., second battle of Bull Run: Union forces driven back. 17 Sept., Union forces defeat Confederates at Antietam: prevents Confederates entering the north. 22 Sept., Lincoln declares all US slaves free with effect from 1 Jan. 1863. July, *Alabama* incident: Britain fails to stop new ship sailing to aid Confederates.

**RELIGION & CULTURE**

**1860–1941** Ignacy Jan Paderewski, Polish composer, pianist and statesman.
**1860–1942** Walter Richard Sickert, artist. Philip Wilson Steer, artist.
**1860–1948** Sir Charles William Chadwick Oman, historian.
**1860–1954** (Dean) William Ralph Inge, theologian and journalist.
**1860** John Joseph Pershing, American general, b.

**1861** Royal Academy of Music founded. Germ theory of disease evolved by Louis Pasteur. First iron-clad warship built. William Gifford Palgrave exploring in Arabia. American College for Girls opened in Cairo.
**1861–4** Abortive UMCA mission to Shire.
**1861–1926** William Bateson, botanist.
**1861–1927** John Bagnell Bury, historian.
**1861–1928** Douglas, Earl Haig, soldier.
**1861–1930** Fridtjof Nansen, Norwegian explorer.
**1861–1931** Nellie Melba, Australian singer.
**1861–1936** Edmund, Lord Allenby, soldier.
**1861–1941** Sir Rabindranath Tagore, Indian poet.
**1861–1947** Alfred North Whitehead, philosopher and mathematician.
**1861–1955** Horace Annesley Vachell, novelist.
**1861–74** Paris Opera House built.

**1862** J.W. Colenso, Bp of Maritzburg, S Africa, denies authority of the Pentateuch. World Exhibition in London. Acetylene discovered. Foucault measures the speed of light. Morrill Land-Grant College Act provides for endowment of colleges of agriculture and industry in US. Bibliothèque Nationale, Algiers, founded.
**1862–1918** Claude Débussy, French composer.
**1862–1919** Louis Botha, South African statesman and soldier.
**1862–1923** Auguste Maurice Barrès, political writer and novelist.
**1862–1925** Arthur Christopher Benson, essayist and novelist.

| WESTERN & NORTHERN EUROPE | CENTRAL & SOUTHERN EUROPE | AFRICA |
| --- | --- | --- |

**1863** 30 March, Schleswig incorporated in Denmark. June, Franco-Italian commercial treaty. Nov., Thiers forms Third Party against Napoleon III. 15 Nov., Frederick VII of Denmark d.: succ. Christian IX (−1906). 18 Nov., new constitution in Denmark. 24 Dec., German troops enter Holstein.

**1863** 22 Jan, Poland rebels against Russia. 8 Feb., Prussia allies with Russia to suppress Poland. Feb., O'Donnell resigns. March, Russia divides Poland into ten provinces: 30,000 Poles killed: 150,000 exiled to Siberia. 30 March, Prince George of Denmark elected King of Greece (−1913). 16 Aug.–1 Sept., abortive meeting of German princes at Frankfurt to reform Confederation. 14 Nov., Ionian Is. ceded to Greece by Britain. *Zemlia i Volia* (Land and Liberty) secret society founded in Russia. German Workers Association founded by F. Lassalle.

**1863** Sultan Abdul Aziz of Turkey visits Egypt. Baker expedition meets Speke at Gondokoro. al-Hajj Omar takes Timbuktu: capital set up at Hamdillahi. Dakar founded. Menelik, King of Shoa. Napoleon III refuses Emperor Theodore's request for aid. Holy Ghost Fathers established in Zanzibar.
**1863–79** Ismail Pasha, Khedive of Egypt.

**1864** 13 Jan., provincial councils established in Russia by Zemstvo Law. 16 Jan., Austria and Prussia send ultimatum to Denmark on Schleswig. 18 Apr., Germany invades Denmark: Danes defeated at Duppel. 25 Apr.– 25 June, abortive London Conference on Denmark. 25 May, Loi Emile-Ollivier: French workers granted the right to strike. Protestant riots in Belfast. International Workers' Association instituted in London.

**1864** 22 Aug., Geneva Convention: Red Cross Society founded. Sept., Narvaez becomes Prime Minister of Spain (−1865). 15 Sept., treaty between France and Italy: France withdraws troops from Rome: Italy renounces claim to Rome: Florence made capital (−1870). 30 Oct., peace of Vienna: Denmark cedes Schleswig, Holstein and Lauenburg to Germany. 28 Nov., new constitution in Greece.
**1864–86** Ludwig II, King of Bavaria.

**1864** Sudanese troops mutiny at El Obeid. Sharif Abd al-Rahman of Morocco (1859–73) decrees absolute equality for Jews in Morocco. al-Hajj Omar killed: succ. Ahmadu Sefu (−1884).

## THE EAST & AUSTRALASIA

**1862–4** (8th) Earl of Elgin, Governor-General and Viceroy of India.
**1862–74** Mu Tsung, Chinese emperor, with throne name Tung-chih: Empress Tzu Hsi regent.

**1863** June, Choshu shore batteries in Shimonoseki Strait fire on Dutch, French and US vessels: France and US retaliate: obstruction continues: Kagoshima bombarded by British. 3 June, disastrous earthquake in Manila. Dost Muhammad Khan captures Herat. Dost Muhammad Khan d.: civil war ensues in Afghanistan between his sixteen sons: Amir Shir Ali Khan succ. (–1879). French protectorate over Cambodia. Tobacco growing begun in Sumatra. New Zealand Settlements Act confiscates Maori lands. 35,000 European immigrants into New Zealand in gold rush in Otago. Turkey recognises constitution for Armenia.
**1864** Sept., combined Dutch, French, UK and US fleet demolish Choshu batteries: Japan agrees to open Strait of Shimonoseki. Nanking recaptured from the Tai Ping. First telegraph line opened in Persia. First Indian, Satyendra Nath Tagore, enters Indian Civil Service.
**1864–5** Muslim rising in Kansu province, China.
**1864–9** Sir John Lawrence, Governor-General and Viceroy of India.

## THE AMERICAS

**1862** Canadian Militia Act provides for a force of 50,000 men. Government land obtainable in US by settling. British Honduras formally annexed by Britain. Pacific Railway Bill unites the Union Pacific and Central Pacific Railroads.
**1862–6** Peru at war with Spain.
**1862–8** Bartolomé Mitre, President of Argentina: central administration organized.
**1862–70** Francisco Solano Lopez, son of his predecessor, President of Paraguay.
**1862–85** Period of tension and unrest in Peru.

**1863** 2-4 May, Confederates defeat Union force at Chancellorsville. 5 June, French, with British and Spanish allies, take Mexico City: Archduke Maximilian of Austria proclaimed Emperor (–1867): Juárez retreats to the N. 20 June, W Virginia becomes a US State. 1-3 July, battle of Gettysburg: Union forces victorious after prolonged contest. 4 July, Union forces take Vicksburg. 24-25 Nov., Union force victorious at Chattanooga. First US National Banking Act.
**1863–93** Conservatives in power in Nicaragua.

**1864** 10 Apr., Archduke Maximilian of Austria accepts throne of Mexico from Napoleon III. 1 Sept., Confederates evacuate Atlanta. 10 Oct., conference in Quebec opened to discuss Canadian federation: delegations from Canada, New Brunswick, Prince Edward Is., Nova Scotia and Newfoundland. 31 Oct., Nevada becomes a US State. 22 Dec., Union force under General Sherman takes Savannah. Spain seizes guano islands off Peru: Bolivia, Chile and Ecuador join Peru in war against Spain: Spanish shell Valparaiso and Callao: war thereafter abortive (–1879). Second US National Banking Act.
**1864–70** Paraguay at war with Argentina, Brazil and Uruguay: population of Paraguay reduced by war from 525,000 to 221,000, of whom only 28,746 males.
**1864–71** Mariano Melgarejo, 'the scourge of God', President of Bolivia.

## RELIGION & CULTURE

**1862–1926** Edward Granville Browne, father of Persian studies in Britain, orientalist.
**1862–1932** Aristide Briand, French statesman.
**1862–1933** Edward, Lord Grey of Fallodon, statesman.
**1862–1934** Frederick Delius, composer.
**1862–1935** Henri Pirenne, Belgian historian.
**1862–1936** Sir Edward German, composer. Montague Rhodes James, scholar.
**1862–1938** Sir Henry Newbolt, poet.
**1862–1949** Count (Maurice) Maeterlinck, Belgian dramatist, poet and philosopher.
**1862–1960** Eden Philpotts, novelist and dramatist.
**1863** Bp Colenso deprived for heresy by the S African Anglican bishops. Boulaq Museum, later the Egyptian Museum, founded. First electric lighthouse constructed. National Academy of New York founded. The Football Association founded in England.
**1863–1923** Joaquín Sorolla, Spanish artist.
**1863–1933** 'Anthony Hope' (Sir Anthony Hope Hawkins), novelist.
**1863–1937** Sir Arthur Somervell, composer.
**1863–1938** Gabriele d'Annunzio, Italian poet and novelist.
**1863–1944** Sir Arthur Quiller-Couch, novelist.
**1863–1945** David, Earl Lloyd-George, Liberal statesman.
**1864** 22 Aug., Geneva Convention starts Red Cross Society. 8 Dec., Pope Pius IX: *Quanta Cura* and *Syllabus Errorum*. Privy Council rules Bp Colenso's deprivation *ultra vires*. Louis Pasteur invents pasteurisation. Metropolitan Railway, London, opened (first underground railway). UMCA mission established in Zanzibar. Universities of Belgrade and Bucharest founded.
**1864–91** Henri de Toulouse-Lautrec, French artist.
**1864–1926** Israel Zangwill, novelist.
**1864–1936** Miguel de Unamuno, Basque poet, philosopher and essayist.
**1864–1949** Richard Strauss, Austrian composer.
**1864–1952** William Morris Hughes, Australian politician and Prime Minister.

| WESTERN & NORTHERN EUROPE | CENTRAL & SOUTHERN EUROPE | AFRICA |
|---|---|---|

**1865** 30 May, commercial treaty between Britain and the *Zollverein*. 15 Sept., Fenian leaders arrested in Ireland. Oct., Bismarck meets Napoleon III at Biarritz: Napoleon III recognizes Prussian hegemony in Germany and united Italy. 18 Oct., Lord Palmerston d.: succ. Lord John Russell (–1866). Colonial Laws Validity Act grants varying partial autonomy to British colonies. First voluntary arbitration accepted in building trade at Wolverhampton. Annexation of Algeria proclaimed in Paris. New constitution in Sweden. **1865–1909** Leopold II, King of Belgium.

**1865** 29 June, Narvaez dismissed: O'Donnell, Prime Minister of Spain (–1867). 14 Aug., convention of Gastein: Holstein ceded to Austria: Schleswig, Kiel and Lauenburg to Prussia. 20 Sept., Austrian constitution annulled (–1867). Dec., Transylvania incorporated into Hungary. 31 Dec., commercial treaty between Italy and Prussia.

**1865** Sudanese cotton industry greatl[y] expanded. Theodore II makes unsuccessful attempt to take Shoa from Menelik. British Kaffraria incorporated into Cape. OFS-Basuto war. Cetewayo acknowledged leader of the Zulu.

**1866** 17 Jan., Habeas Corpus Act suspended in Ireland. May-Aug., banking crisis in Britain. 22 June, new constitution in Sweden. 26 June, Lord John Russell resigns following defeat on Reform Bill. 6 July, Earl of Derby, Prime Minister (Con.)(–1868). 28 July, new constitution in Denmark. 5 Aug., Napoleon III demands the left bank of the Rhine. 20 Aug., Napoleon III demands Luxembourg and Belgium. Abortive attempt on the life of Tsar Alexander II by a student, Karakozov.

**1866** 23 Feb., Alexander of Rumania deposed: succ. Charles of Hohenzollern as Carol I (–1914). 8 Apr., offensive and defensive alliance between Italy and Prussia against Austria. 8 June, Prussia annexes Holstein. 12 June, secret treaty between Austria and France: France to be neutral provided Venice can be handed over to Italy. 14 June, German Federal Diet votes to mobilise against Prussia in Holstein: Prussia declares German Confederation. ended. 15-16 June, Prussia invades Hanover, Hesse and Saxony. 20 June, Italy declares war on Austria. 24 June, Austria defeats Italy at Custozza. 29 June, Prussia defeats Hanover at Langensalza. 3 July, Prussia defeats Austria at Sadowa. 4 July, Venice ceded by Austria. 20 July, Austria destroys Italian fleet off Lissa. 26 July, preliminary peace of Nikolsburg between Austria and Prussia. 12 Aug., armistice between Austria and Italy. 23 Aug., peace of Prague confirms preliminary peace of Nikolsburg. 2 Sept., Crete rebels against Turkey: unites with Greece. 3 Oct., treaty of Vienna ends war between Austria and Italy. Nov., National Liberal Party founded in N Germany. Abortive attempt at revolution in Spain led by Prim.

**1866** Ismail, ruler of Egypt, granted title of Khedive.

**1867** 13 Feb., Fenian outrage in Kerry. 5 March, Fenian risings attempted in Ireland. 1 Apr., control of (Malay) Straits Settlements passed from the India Office to the Colonial Office.

**1867** 17 Feb.–12 June, Dual Monarchy worked out in the Hungarian Diet as a compromise with Austria. 18 Feb., Hungarian constitution of 1848 restored.

**1867** Sir Samuel Baker's expedition to Gondokoro. Menelik proclaims himself independent as King of Shoa. Dec., British expedition of 68,000 under Sir Robert Napier against Emperor Theodore arrives at Zulla.

| THE EAST & AUSTRALASIA | THE AMERICAS | RELIGION & CULTURE |
|---|---|---|

**1865** Tashkent occupied by Russia, capital of Khanate of Kokand. Peace made in New Zealand with Maoris under Wiremu Tamihana. Transportation of convicts to Australia abolished.
**1865–1909** Vladivostok a free port.

**1864–82** Buenaventura Báez dominant figure in Dominican Republican politics.
**1865** 9 Apr., General Robert E. Lee, Confederate Commander-in-Chief, surrenders to Union force at Appomatox. 14 Apr., Abraham Lincoln assassinated: succ. Andrew Johnson (Rep.)(–1869). Oct., US demands withdrawal of French troops from Mexico. 18 Dec., Thirteenth Amendment to US constitution abolishes status of slavery. Pedro II refuses to allow papal bull banning Freemasonry to be published in Brazil. US denounces Rush-Bagot convention of 1817. Santo Domingo again independent. Serious riots in Jamaica.

**1865** Freemasonry banned by the Vatican. Salvation Army founded by William Booth. E.B. Pusey: *Eirenicon* attempts to find basis for reunion between Anglicans and Rome. American College founded in Asyut.
**1865–1922** Alfred Harmsworth, Viscount Harmsworth, newspaper proprietor.
**1865–1923** Warren Gamaliel Harding, American President.
**1865–1936** Rudyard Kipling, poet, novelist and writer of short stories.
**1865–1937** Erich Ludendorff, German soldier.
**1865–1939** Henri Brémond, essayist. William Butler Yeats, Irish poet, critic and dramatist.
**1865–1940** Herbert A.L. Fisher, historian and politician.
**1865–1947** Baroness (Emmuska) Orczy novelist.
**1865–1957** Jean Sibelius, Finnish composer.

**1866** Amir of Bokhara declares *jihad* against Russia, without success. Kanaung, Crown Prince of Burma, assassinated by Princes Myingun and Myingondaing while presiding in High Court: rebellion follows. Cheshu clan of Honshu Is. raise army of samurai, peasants and townsmen in European style. King Norodom of Cambodia transfers capital to Pnom-Penh. *c.* 1m. die in famine in Orissa.
**1866–7** Tokugawa Yoshinobu (Kei–Ki), Shogun.
**1866 ff.** Rising of Yakub Beg in Turkestan: said to have cost 10m. lives: Ili conquered.
**1866–73** Civil war in Selangor.

**1866** Reciprocity Treaty between Canada and US ended. Fourteenth Amendment clarifies status of negroes as US citizens: rejected by Southern legislatures. The *Great Eastern* lays the first successful cable from Newfoundland to Ireland. Tennessee rejoins the US. Granges, or Patrons of Husbandry, farmers' associations, formed in US. Vancouver Is. joined with British Columbia as Colony of British Columbia: capital, Victoria. Sinn Fein Brotherhood carrying out raids in Canada and New Brunswick: tension between Canada and US.

**1866** Antiseptic surgery introduced by Joseph Lister. The torpedo invented. Dynamite invented by Alfred Nobel. The dynamo invented. (Royal) Aeronautical Society founded: Dr. T.T. Barnardo opens first home for lost children in Stepney. Syrian Protestant College, later American University of Beirut, founded. Ku Klux Klan founded. Dom Gregor Mendel, OSB, publishes paper describing 'Mendelianism
**1866–1914** Romain Rolland, writer and dramatist.
**1866–1924** Leon Bakst, artist and theatrical costume designer. Ferruccio Benevenuto Busoni, Italian composer.
**1866–1925** Sun Yat-sen, Chinese reformer and statesman.
**1866–1937** James Ramsay MacDonald, Labour politician.
**1866–1946** Edward Phillips Oppenheim, novelist. Herbert George Wells, novelist.
**1866–1954** Jacinto Benavente, Spanish dramatist.
**1866–1957** George Gilbert Murray, scholar and political writer.
**1866–1962** Benedetto Croce, Italian philosopher.

**1867** Nov., Shogun Kei-ki (last Shogun), following pressure, abdicates his powers to the Emperor. Franco-Siamese treaty recognizes French rights over Cambodia.

**1867** 1 March, Nebraska becomes US State. 30 March, US purchases Alaska from Russia for $7m. 15 May, French troops withdrawn from Mexico.

**1867** First Pan-Anglican Synod (or Lambeth Conference) held. First Vatican Council summoned by Pope Pius IX. Alexander II forbids Poles to have relations with the Vatican. The refrigerator invented.

| WESTERN & NORTHERN EUROPE | CENTRAL & SOUTHERN EUROPE | AFRICA |
|---|---|---|
| **1867** 6 June, attempt made on the Tsar's life in Paris by Berezowski, a Pole. 11 May, London Conference guarantees neutrality of Luxembourg. 15 Aug., Parliamentary Reform Act in UK extends suffrage. 18 Sept., Fenian outrage in Manchester. Nov., House of Commons votes £2m. for British prisoners in Ethiopia. 13 Dec., Fenian outrage in London: twelve killed. | **1867** 17 Apr., North German Confederation, led by Prussia, formed. 8 July, N German Confederation makes customs treaties with S German states. 22 Oct., Garibaldi starts march on Rome. 28 Oct., French army lands at Civitavécchia. 3 Nov., Garibaldi defeated at Mentana and taken prisoner. 5 Nov., O'Donnell, Prime Minister of Spain, d. | **1867** Gold reported at Tati and in Mashonaland. |
| **1868** 25 Feb., Lord Derby resigns: succ. Benjamin Disraeli. 28 Feb.–8 Dec., Benjamin Disraeli, Prime Minister. 11 May, freedom of the press and assembly permitted in France. 9 Dec., following electoral victory, William Ewart Gladstone forms Liberal government (–1874). First Trades Union Congress. Royal | **1868** 10 June, Michael III of Serbia murdered: succ. Milan IV (–1889). 17 Sept., Spanish navy, and then army, rise: 30 Sept., Queen Isabella flees to France: declared deposed: regency under Francisco Serrano (–1870). 11 Dec., Turkey sends ultimatum to Greece demanding evacuation of Crete. First International founded in Spain with twenty-one members in Madrid. | **1868** French obtain Cotonou. French treaties in Cameroun. Jan., British expedition under Sir Robert Napier disembarks at Annesley Bay: marche 420m. inland by April. March, British prisoners in Ethiopia freed. 13 Apr., Napier takes Magdala: 18 June, last man of Napier expedition leaves Africa. Emperor Theodore commits suicide. **1868–89** Yohannes IV, Emperor of Ethiopia. |
| **1869** 24 June, Corn Importation Act repealed. 12 July, parliamentary system adopted in France. | **1869** 6 Feb., Greece agrees to evacuate Crete. Feb., Constituent *Cortes* assembles in Spain: new charter provides for limited monarchy and bicameral elective parliament: Prim, Prime Minister. 10 May, alliance between Austria, France and Italy. 1 June, new Spanish constitution promulgated. Portugal makes all slaves *libertos,* with right to wages before liberation. German Social Democratic Party founded. | **1869** 17 Nov., Suez Canal opened by Empress Eugénie. Tunis bankrupt: Britain, France and Italy take control. Msiri proclaims himself King of Garaganza. Italy purchases Assab. Djibouti replaces Obock as French coaling station. Diamond 'Star of S Africa' found: diamond rush begins. **1869–74** Gustave Nachtigal exploring W Africa and Sudan. **c. 1869–70** Tippu Tib trading with Bemba, Lungu and Kazembe with caravan of 4,000. |

## THE EAST & AUSTRALASIA

**1867** Cambodia annexed by France, followed by penetration in Haiphong and Hanoi. Second Anglo-Burmese Commercial Treaty. The Shogunate abolished in Japan. Tea first planted in Ceylon.
**1867—73** Sir Harry Ord, first colonial Governor of Singapore.
**1867—1912** Meiji, 122nd Emperor of Japan.

**1868** Jan., fighting between supporters of ex-Shogun and imperial forces at Toba-Fushimi: end of Shogunate: castle of Yedo surrendered to Emperor. Apr., Emperor Meiji proclaims new, open, attitude to the west in the 'Charter Oath': many Japanese sent abroad to study full range of western sciences and techniques. Autumn, Emperor of Japan visits Yedo, now re-named Tokyo: Shogun's castle made the Imperial Palace: government by court oligarchy. Shir Ali emerges as victor in Afghan civil war: recognized as Amir. Punjab and Oudh Tenancy Acts. Bokhara made tributary to Russia. Samarqand acquired by Russia.
**1868—9** Famine in Rajputana and Bundelkhand.
**1868** Last imperial troops withdrawn from New Zealand. 2017 South Sea Islanders settled in Queensland.
**1868—97** Japanese imports of raw materials increase fivefold: exports of finished goods twenty-fold: nine-tenths of external trade in hands of foreign agents.
**1869** Jan., Amir Shir Ali Khan victorious at Zermat: March, visits India: received by Lord Mayo. Sept., Persian mission to Kabul. 21 Sept., new constitution proclaimed in Manila: republicanism spreads rapidly. Midhat Pasha made governor of Baghdad: author of first Iraqi constitution. Britain obtains Russian recognition of Shir Ali of Afghanistan's possessions. Slavery abolished in Indonesia. All Japanese lords surrender their fiefs to the Emperor: feudalism abolished. Japan sends delegation of amity to China. Secret ballot introduced in New Zealand.
**1869—72** Earl of Mayo, Governor-General and Viceroy of India.

## THE AMERICAS

**1867** 19 June, Emperor Maximilian executed by Juárez: Juárez re-elected President (—1872). 1 July— 5 Nov. 1873, Sir J.A. Macdonald, Canadian Prime Minister. 1 July, UK British North American Act establishes confederation as Kingdom of Canada: includes Canada, Nova Scotia and New Brunswick: remainder of British North America yet to be brought in. Lord Monck first Governor-General of Canada (—1869). Aug., first Canadian national General Election. Henry Barnard appointed first US Commissioner for Education. French troops evacuate Mexico. US Reconstruction Act.

**1868** Feb., President Andrew Johnson impeached before the Senate: found not guilty by one vote. Eight hour day established in US for public works. Arkansas, Alabama, Louisiana, Florida and N and S Carolina rejoin the US. Nova Scotia delegation to London asking to leave Canadian federation: refused by Duke of Buckingham and Chandos, Colonial Secretary. Contingent of French Canadians sent to Rome as Papal Zouaves.
**1868—72** José Balta, President of Peru: numerous railways built.
**1868—74** Domingo Faustina Sarmiento, President of Argentina: period of rapid development.
**1868—78** The Ten Years War in Cuba.

**1869** 2 Feb., Sir John Young (later Lord Lisgar), Governor-General of Canada (—1872). 4 March, General Ulysses S. Grant sworn President of US (—1877). 9 March, UK buys territories of Hudson's Bay Co. for Canada. 10 May, Pacific Railway completed at Promontory Point, Utah. Noble Order of Knights of Labour founded in US as broadly based trade union. Fifteenth Amendment grants franchise to freedmen. US paid $15.5m. as compensation for the *Alabama* incident. Prohibition Party first organized in US. Wyoming State the first to institute women's suffrage. First census in Argentina: population 1.8m., of whom 400,000 in Buenos Aires.

## RELIGION & CULTURE

**1867** May-Oct., Universal Exhibition in Paris.
**1867—1931** Enoch Arnold Bennett, novelist.
**1867—1933** John Galsworthy, novelist and dramatist.
**1867—1934** Marie Curie, scientist.
**1867—1935** Joseph Pilsudski, Polish statesman.
**1867—1936** Luigi Pirandello, Italian playwright.
**1867—1939** Arthur Rackham, artist and illustrator.
**1867—1942** Léon Daudet, novelist and critic.
**1867—1947** Stanley Baldwin, later Earl Baldwin, Conservative Prime Minister.
**1867—1953** Princess Mary of Teck. Queen Mary.
**1868** 1 Jan., *O Primeiro de Janeiro,* leading Oporto newspaper, founded: uproar in Portugal against sales tax: Oporto merchants refuse to trade until it is lifted. Cornell University founded. Royal Historical Society founded. Compulsory church rates abolished in England and Wales. Jamiyyat al-Maarif (publishing house) founded in Cairo.
**1868—1916** Enrique Granados, Spanish composer.
**1868—1918** Edmond Eugène Alexis Rostand, dramatist and poet.
**1868—1926** Gertrude Margaret Bell, oriental traveller and archaeologist.
**1868—1927** Gaston Leroux, novelist.
**1868—1936** Maxim Gorki, novelist.
**1868—1938** Edward Verrall Lucas, essayist.
**1868—1947** James Louis Garvin, journalist.
**1868—1952** Charles-Marie Maurras, poet and writer.
**1868—1963** William E. Burghardt du Bois, father of Pan-Africanism.

**1869** 1 March, Church of Ireland disestablished. 8 Dec., first Vatican Council (—1870). Harvard College made a University. College for Women, later Girton College, Cambridge, founded. Russian language made compulsory in Poland for official correspondence and in universities. Ball-bearings, celluloid, margarine and the washing-machine invented.
**1869—70** Joseph Halévy discovers Himyaritic inscriptions.
**1869—96** José Rizal, Filipino patriot.
**1869—1940** Neville Chamberlain, Conservative Prime Minister.
**1869—1941** Sir Henry Walford Davies, composer.
**1869—1943** Laurence Binyon, dramatist and poet.

1869—1871

WESTERN &
NORTHERN EUROPE

CENTRAL &
SOUTHERN EUROPE

AFRICA

**1870** 12 Jan., E. Ollivier forms ministry in France. 20 Apr., French Senate given legislative powers. 4 June, British Civil Service reformed: competitive examinations instituted, except for Foreign Office. 25 June, Isabel II of Spain abdicates formally in Paris. 28 June, municipal government reformed in Russia. 2 July, Leopold, Prince of Hohenzollern, accepts Spanish throne. 12 July, Leopold's acceptance withdrawn by Prussia. 13 July, French ultimatum to Prussia: 'Ems telegram' follows. 19 July, France declares war on Prussia. 1 Aug., Irish Land Act to protect peasant tenants. 4-18 Aug., French defeated by Prussians in several actions. 9 Aug., Married Women's Property Act in England passed. 1 Sept., Germans defeat French at Sédan: French capitulate: Napoleon III taken prisoner. 4 Sept., French Committee of Public Defence formed by General Trochu (—1871): Third Republic proclaimed (—1940). 19 Sept.—28 June 1871, Germans besiege Paris: Germans opposed in many other actions.

**1871** 18 Jan, William I proclaimed German Emperor at Versailles (—1888). 29 Jan., Paris capitulates: armistice of Versailles. 8 Feb., National Assembly elected in France; 17 Feb., provisional government formed under Adolphe Thiers (—1873). 26 Feb., preliminary peace of Versailles. 13 March, London Conference ends neutrality of Black Sea under Treaty of Paris, 1856. 18- March—28 May, insurrection of the Commune in Paris. 8 May, general convention on arbitration between UK and USA. 21—8 May, the 'Bloody Week' in Paris. 29 June, British Trade Unions legalized. 20 July, purchase of commissions forbidden in England by act of royal prerogative.

**1870** May, Prim, dictator of Spain: shortly retires. 20 Sept., Rome occupied by Italian patriots: the Pope becomes the prisoner of the Vatican (—1931). 2 Oct., Rome made capital of Italy. 3 Oct., Baden requests membership of N German Federation. 15 and 23 Nov., N German Federation allies with Württemberg and Bavaria. 16 Nov., Amadeo, Duke of Aosta, elected King of Spain (—1873). First International in Spain has 153 chapters with 15,000 members, two thirds in Barcelona. 13 Dec., German Centre (Catholic) Party formed. 30 Dec., Prim assassinated.

**1871** 16 Apr., constitution of German Empire promulgated. 10 May, treaty of Frankfurt between France and Germany: France cedes Alsace and Lorraine: pays indemnity: agrees to army of occupation pending payment. 13 May, Italian Law of Guarantees declares the Pope inviolable: confirms his possession of the Vatican.
**1871—9** Frontes, Prime Minister of Portugal.

**1870** Egyptian army re-organized. Décret Crémieux makes all Algerian Jews French citizens. Estimated 2,000 slave merchants between Ubangi and Bahr al-Ghazal. Egypt occupies Zaila and N Somalia. Diggers' Republic proclaimed at Klipdrift.

**1871** Unrest in Cairo. Gondokoro annexed for Egypt. 10 Nov., Livingstone and Stanley meet at Ujiji Cecil John Rhodes treks from Natal to Kimberley. Basutoland annexed to Cape Colony.

## THE EAST & AUSTRALASIA   THE AMERICAS   RELIGION & CULTURE

**1869–1944** Sir Edwin Landseer Lutyens, architect. Stephen Leacock, Canadian essayist and humorist. Sir Henry Wood, conductor.
**1869–1948** (Mahatma) Mohandas Karamchand Gandhi, Indian statesman.
**1869–1949** Albert Frederick Pollard, historian.
**1869–1951** Algernon Blackwood, novelist. André Paul Guillaume Gide, novelist and dramatist.
**1869–1954** Henri Matisse, French artist.
**1869–1959** Frank Lloyd Wright, American architect.

**1870** Western Australia given representative government. Cobb and Co. control all coaching service of NSW, Queensland and Victoria: 6,000 horses used daily: coaches travel 28,000 miles a week. Overland telegraph line combined with submarine cable joins Australia with London: distance from Adelaide to London 12,500 miles. Japanese population *c.* 34m. Extensive modernization in progress in every sphere of activity.
**1870–1** Makran boundary between India and Persia demarcated.
**1870–3** Civil war brings in Chinese at Kanching and Kuala Lumpur.
**1870–80** Private enterprise in Dutch EI takes the place of government control of agriculture. Sugar becomes the principal Javanese export.
**1870–90** Dutch immigration into Indonesia.
**c. 1870** Indian labourers begin to migrate abroad on indenture system for five to seven years: Indians reach British Guiana, Burma, Ceylon, Malaya, Mauritius, Natal and Trinidad, and later Kenya.

**1871** 6 May, Yakub Khan, son of Amir Shir Ali Khan, seizes Herat: July, surrenders: Sept., appointed Governor of Herat by his father. British set up Irrawaddy Flotilla Co., providing steamer service in Burmese interior. Telegraph system established. First Sino-Japanese treaty.

**1870** May, John O'Neill organizes two Fenian attacks on Quebec from Vermont: turned back by Canadian militia. 5 Sept., Manitoba and NW Territory annexed to Canada. Virginia, Texas, Mississippi and Georgia rejoin the US. Treaty of Washington between UK and US settles outstanding questions on Canada. Iron found in the Vermilion Range. Toronto Typographical Society wins strike for nine hour day.
**1870–6** Brazil occupies Paraguay.
**1870–82** Tomás Guardia, dictator of Costa Rica.
**1870–88** Antonio Guzmán Blanco, either president or principal political figure in Venezuela.
**1870–1910** More than 20m. immigrants enter US.
**1870–1954** Thirty-nine presidents in Paraguay.

**1871** 20 July, British Columbia becomes a province of Canada. Last British regulars withdrawn from Canada. Rio Branco law in Brazil frees state and Crown slaves and all future children of slaves: 1.7m. slaves freed. Yellow fever epidemic in Buenos Aires: 13,614 die in five months. Leeward Is. federated. Abortive Fenian raid on Canada.
**1871–80** 338,269 Canadians migrate to US.
**1871–85** Justo Rufino Barros the dominant figure in Guatemalan politics.

**1870** 18 July, Constitution *Pastor aeternus*: infallibility of the Pope when defining faith or morals defined. 30 July, Austria withdraws from concordat with the Vatican. 2 Dec., the Pope excommunicates King Victor Emmanuel II. W.E. Forster's Elementary Education Act establishes secular board schools in England. Keble College, Oxford, founded. Excavation of Troy begun by Heinrich Schliemann. Committee to produce the Revised Version of the Bible appointed. H.M. Stanley commissioned by *New York Herald* to search for Livingstone. Department of Public Instruction inaugurated in Ceylon.
**1870–1917** Giovanni Cena, Italian novelist and poet.
**1870–1924** Nikolai Lenin, Russian statesman.
**1870–1937** Elie Halévy, historian.
**1870–1945** Lord Alfred Douglas, poet.
**1870–1948** Franz Lehár, Hungarian composer.
**1870–1950** Jan Christian Smuts, S. African statesman and soldier.
**1870–1953** Hilaire Belloc, historian, poet and essayist.
**1870–1963** Herbert, Viscount Samuel, Liberal statesman.
**1871** 16 June, repeal of the English University Test Act. 8 July, beginning of *Kulturkampf* in Prussia against Roman Catholic Church. Abp of Munich excommunicates J.J.I. Döllinger for refusing to accept decrees of Vatican Council. First Old Catholic Congress meets in Munich. English Ecclesiastical Titles Act repealed. Decrees in Portugal separate church and state, expel religious orders, secularize education: new universities created in Lisbon and Oporto. Teaching of modern languages forbidden in Russian universities: ancient languages alone permitted. Epidemic of smallpox in England.
**1871–1909** John Millington Synge, Irish dramatist.
**1871–1915** Alexander Nicolaievitch Scriabin, Russian composer.

| WESTERN & NORTHERN EUROPE | CENTRAL & SOUTHERN EUROPE | AFRICA |
|---|---|---|

**1871** 14 Aug., Local Government Board replaces General Board of Health in UK. 31 Aug., Thiers elected President of France (−1873).

**1872** 18 July, British Secret Ballot Act. 28 July, conscription becomes law in France. 18 Sept., Charles XV of Sweden d.: succ. Oscar II (−1907). 5 Nov., commercial treaty between Britain and France. Licensing Act restricts opening hours of public houses in England.
**1872–94** Constitutional dispute in Denmark.

**1872** Jan., First International banned in Spain. 26 Apr., Carlos of Spain, resident in France, declares himself King of Spain: calls for general rising in Spain against Amadeo: second Carlist war ensues (−1876). 4 May, Carlists defeated: Don Carlos escapes to France. July, attempt to assassinate Amadeo of Spain. 7 Sept., meeting between the Emperors of Austria, Germany and Russia in Berlin. 14 Sept., Geneva award on *Alabama* incident: US awarded $15.5m. damages. 9 Dec., local government reformed in Germany, following creation of twenty-five peers.

**1872** British take over Dutch forts on Gold Coast. Asantehene threatens Britain with war. Disastrous hurricane destroys plantations in Zanzibar, Pemba and Mafia. Cape Colony granted responsible government. Griqualand West annexed to Cape Colony.

**1873** 9 Jan., Napoleon III d. in England. 13 March, Liberals defeated on Irish University Bill: cabinet reshuffled by Gladstone following Disraeli's refusal of office. March, administration of law reformed in England: Supreme Court established with different divisions: Court of Appeal instituted. 6 May, military convention between Germany and Russia. 24 May, Thiers resigns: Marshal MacMahon, President of France (−1879). 15 Sept., German armies withdraw from France. Home Rule League founded in Ireland by Isaac Butt.

**1873** 11 Feb., Amadeo I abdicates in Spain: republic declared by *Cortes:* anarchy ensues: four presidents in one year. 23 Apr., monarchist demonstrations in Madrid. 8 Sept., Emilio Castelar comes to power in Spain. 22 Oct., alliance of the Emperors of Austria, Germany and Russia. Nov., Buda and Pest united as Budapest, as Hungarian capital. 300,000 Anarchists in 270 centres in Spain.

**1873** Mixed courts established in Egypt. Post offices opened in Sudan. Hospital established in Khartoum. Ashanti defeat British at Assin Nyankumasi: 26 Nov., British advance on Kumasi: Ashanti retreat. 30 Apr., Livingstone d. Cetewayo crowned King of the Zulu.

## THE EAST & AUSTRALASIA        THE AMERICAS        RELIGION & CULTURE

**1872** 20 Jan., Cavite insurrection in Philippine Is. 8 Feb., Earl of Mayo, Viceroy of India, murdered. Sistan boundary Arbitration Commission. Half of Bombay corporation elected by ratepayers. Last recorded lion killed in India. Peace made in New Zealand with Maoris under Wiremu Kingi. First Burmese diplomatic mission to England: treaty of friendship signed with Italy: commercial treaty signed with France. Compulsory mass education instituted in Japan. Full scale Chinese war in Larut.
**1872–6** Lord Northbrook, Governor General and Viceroy of India.

**1872** 25 June, Earl of Dufferin (later Marquess of Dufferin and Ava), Governor-General of Canada (−1878). 18 July, Juárez d.: succ. Sebastián Lerdo de Tejada as President. John D. Rockefeller gains control of Cleveland oil refineries, and subsequently in New York, Philadelphia and Pittsburgh. Automatic binders for reapers introduced in US.

**1871–1922** Marcel Proust, novelist.
**1871–1925** Friedrich Ebert, German Socialist President.
**1871–1936** David, Earl Beatty, admiral.
**1871–1937** Ernest Rutherford, scientist.
**1871–1940** Sir Edward Denison Ross, orientalist. William Henry Davies, poet and writer.
**1871–1943** Sir William Holdsworth, jurist.
**1871–1955** Cordell Hull, American statesman.
**1872** Jesuits expelled from Germany. First General Assembly of Protestants held in France since 1659. Scottish Education Department created. Polish forbidden in secondary schools. Marx: *Das Capital* first made available in Russian. Fifth Great Synod of Buddhism held in Mandalay. International Bureau of Weights and Measures founded.
**1872–98** Aubrey Beardsley, illustrator.
**1872–1928** Roald Amundsen, Norwegian explorer.
**1872–1929** Serge Diaghilev, Russian ballet dancer.
**1872–1932** Lord Birkenhead (F.E. Smith), jurist and orator.
**1872–1933** Calvin Coolidge, American President.
**1872–1936** Louis Blériot, French aviator.
**1872–1944** Heath Robinson, cartoonist.
**1872–1945** Roger, Lord Keyes, admiral. Sir William Rothenstein, artist.
**1872–1949** John Hammond, economist, historian and journalist.
**1872–1950** Léon Blum, French statesman.
**1872–1952** Sir Max Beerbohm, critic and novelist.
**1872–1956** Pío Baroja, Basque poet.
**1872–1958** Ralph Vaughan Williams, composer.

**1873** Khiva acquired by Russia. Russia accepts Shir Ali's possession of Badakhshan. 20 Nov., Hanoi taken by the French.
**1873** or **1874** First Ceylon tea exported to England: tea growing subsequently ousts coffee growing.
**1873–4** Famine in Bengal and Bihar.
**1873–5** Sir Andrew Clarke, Governor of Singapore.
**1873–1904** War between Dutch EI and Acheh.

**1873** 7 Nov.–**1878** 16 Oct., A. Mackenzie, Canadian Prime Minister. Economic panic and depression in US. Secret alliance between Peru and Bolivia against Chilean border encroachments in mining area. Silver demonetized by US Congress. Royal Canadian Mounted Police founded.

**1873** 11-14 May, 'May Laws' subject clergy to state control in Prussia. 14 May, minor seminaries supressed in Germany. Dec., papal nuncio expelled from Switzerland. Universities secularized in Austria. Anti-Christian laws repealed in Japan. Italian government abolishes monasteries in Rome: theological faculties of universities closed. British National Federation of Employers founded. The typewriter invented by C.L. Sholes and Glidden. Colour photography invented. First oil well drilled in Baku.
**1873–5** D.L. Moody and I.D. Sankey hold revivalist meetings in England.
**1873–1914** Charles Péguy, poet.
**1873–1936** Clara Butt, singer.
**1873–1938** Fedor Chaliapin, singer. Sir Landon Ronald, composer.
**1873–1939** Ford Madox Ford, poet and novelist.

1873–1875
WESTERN &
NORTHERN EUROPE

CENTRAL &
SOUTHERN EUROPE

AFRICA

**1874** 13 Jan., conscription adopted in Russia, with other military reforms. 2 Feb.–1880, Disraeli, Prime Minister. Isaac Butt, with fifty-nine Irish followers, enters Parliament. 18 Apr., Dr Livingstone buried in Westminster Abbey. July, Iceland granted self-government by Denmark. 30 Aug., British Factory Act institutes working week of fifty-six hours. Employment of children as chimney sweeps forbidden. Plimsoll Line regulation for merchant ships. Peaceful picketing in industrial disputes legalized.

**1874** Jan., *Cortes* dismissed by Pavía, Captain-General of Castile: cabinet of generals formed. 2 Jan., Castelar resigns in Spain: 3 Jan., Marshal Francisco Serrano becomes dictator. May, further anti-clerical laws in Germany. Socialist Working-Men's Party formed in Germany. 29 May, new constitution for Switzerland. 4 Oct., Count Arnim, former German ambassador in Paris, prosecuted. 31 Dec., following *coup d'état,* Alfonso XII, King of Spain (–1885).

**1874** 31 Jan., British defeat Ashanti at Amoafo: 4 Feb., Sir Garnet Wolseley enters Kumasi: 14 March, makes peace treaty with Asantehene. Feb., Gordon arrives in Egypt: March, takes up post of Governor of the Equatorial Nile Basin in Sudan. Sudan Railway inaugurated. Yohannes IV of Ethiopia requests Russian aid against Muslims: receives no reply.
**1874–7** H.M. Stanley exploring the Congo.
**1874–81** Campaign for confederation of SA.

**1875** 30 Jan., republican constitution in France passed by a single vote. 23 Feb., law on organization of French Republic: the President to be elected by the Senate and Chamber of Deputies. 8 Apr., Britain and Russia intervene in Germany to prevent war against France. 13 Aug., Artisans' Dwellings Act, Agricultural Holdings Act and Land Transfer Act, passed in England. Aug., Carnavon conversations on South African federation. 25 Nov., Britain buys 176,602 Suez Canal shares from the Khedive for £4m.
**c. 1875** Union of Southern Russian Workers founded.

**1875** 10 May, the Tsar visits Berlin. July–Aug., risings against Turkey in Bosnia and Herzogovina.
**1875–81** Cánovas del Castillo, Prime Minister of Spain.

**1875** French campaign against Ahmadu Shehu. Ashanti attack Juaben. Tippu Tib settles at Kasongo becoming virtual ruler of region. Three Egyptian expeditions against Ethiopia: Harar taken.

## THE EAST & AUSTRALASIA    THE AMERICAS    RELIGION & CULTURE

**1874** Jan., Pangkor meeting between Governor of Singapore and Perak notables: Chinese Engagement, under which Chinese agree to keep the peace: Pangkor Engagement settles problems of Malay chiefs. Resident installed in Perak. 15 March, Treaty of Hué between France and the Empire of Annam: country opened to French trade: Tonkin made a French protectorate. Apr., British treaty with Sungei Ujong: British Assistant Resident installed: Sempang put directly under British rule. Japan attacks Ryuku Is. and Formosa. Direct mail-boat service begun between Spain and the Philippines. Japanese expedition against Formosa following alleged ill-treatment of Japanese sailors.
**1874 ff** S Chinese, Filipinos, Javanese and Singalese recruited as labour for S Australian sugar plantations.

**1874** Boundary treaty between Bolivia and Chile. Canadian Elections Act introduces ballot: all voting throughout country to be done on a single day.
**1874–89** 600,000 immigrants enter Brazil.
**1874–90** Period of expansion in Argentina.

**1873–1943** Serge Rachmaninov, Russian composer.
**1873–1952** Count Carlo Sforza, Italian political writer and philosopher.
**1873–1954** Colette (Madame Henri de Jouvenel), novelist. Sir John Simon, politician.
**1873–1956** Walter John de la Mare, novelist and poet.
**1874** 7 Aug., Public Worship Regulation Act in England. Pius IX forbids Italian Catholics to take part in political life. W.E. Gladstone attacks papal infallibility. Old Catholics agree to use vernacular and to allow priests to marry. Watch Tower, or Jehovah's Witnesses, founded in USA. Catholic University of Beirut founded. International Postal Union formed in Berne. Canadian R. Military College established at Kingston.
**1874–1908** Mustafa Kamil, Egyptian nationalist.
**1874–1922** Sir Ernest Henry Shackleton, explorer.
**1874–1934** Gustave Theodore Holst, composer.
**1874–1936** Gilbert Keith Chesterton, writer and controversialist.
**1874–1937** Guglielmo Marconi, inventor of radio telegraphy.
**1874–1945** Maurice Baring, novelist and poet.
**1874–1946** Gertrude Stein, American novelist.
**1874–1948** Nicholas Berdyaev, Russian religious thinker.
**1874–1950** William Mackenzie King, Canadian statesman.
**1874–1951** Arnold Schönberg, composer.
**1874–1961** Sir Ernest Barker, historian and philosopher.
**1874–1965** Winston Spencer Churchill, statesman and Conservative Prime Minister.
**1874–1965** William Somerset Maugham, novelist.

**1875** Aug., Prince of Wales (later Edward VII) visits India. 1 Nov., James Birch, British Resident, Perak, assassinated. British embassy to Mandalay successfully demands cession of Karenni states. Russia exchanges Kurile Is. with Japan for Sakhalin.
**1875–1909** Te Tsung Chinese Emperor, with throne-name Kuang-hsu: Empress Tzu Hsi regent (–1889).

**1875** First US factory to use Bessemer steel-making process built by Andrew Carnegie: beginning of a steel empire. Peru seizes Chilean nitrate works at Tarapacá. Argentina still importing grain.

**1875** May, religious orders expelled from Germany. *Arya Samaj* movement started by Swami Dayananda. Theosophical Society founded by Madame Blavatsky in New York. Anglo-Arabic College founded at Aligarh. (Royal) Geographical Society of Egypt founded. The submarine invented.
**1875–77** Charles Doughty travelling in Arabia.
**1875–1912** Samuel Coleridge-Taylor, composer.
**1875–1926** Rainer Maria Rilke, poet.
**1875–1932** Edgar Wallace, novelist and dramatist.
**1875–1937** Maurice-Joseph Ravel, French composer.
**1875–1940** John Buchan, Lord Tweedsmuir, biographer and novelist. Sir Donald Francis Tovey, composer.

| WESTERN & NORTHERN EUROPE | CENTRAL & SOUTHERN EUROPE | AFRICA |
|---|---|---|

**1876** 28 March, Cave report on Egyptian finances published. Sept., International Geographical Conference at Brussels founds International African Association. Russian legal system enforced in Poland. Demonstration of students threatened in St Petersbourg: 3,000 workers expected: 200 arrive. Socialist People's Party formed in Russia.

**1876** Jan., new constitution in Spain: suffrage based on property qualification: bicameral legislature, largely elected: king given power to dissolve *Cortes:* required to call it again within three months. 31 Jan., Sultan agrees to reforms in Turkey: rejected by rebels. 28 Feb., Carlist forces withdraw from Spain: Carlos VII flees. 9-16 March, Bulgarians massacred by Turks. 10 May, liberal ministry formed in Istanbul by Midhat Pasha. 13 May, Berlin Memorandum on reform in Turkey sent by Austria, Germany and Russia: Britain refuses approval. 30 May, Abd al-Aziz of Turkey murdered: succ. Murad V (−31 Aug.). 30 June, Serbia declares war on Turkey. 2 July, Montenegro declares war on Turkey. 31 Aug., Murad V of Turkey deposed for insanity: succ. Abd al-Hamid II (−1909). 1 Sept., Turks defeat Serbs at Alexinatz. 31 Oct., Turkey agrees to six week armistice following ultimatum from Russia. 12 Dec.−20 Jan., Istanbul Conference, called by UK, on Turkish problems. 23 Dec., constitution granted to Turkey by Abd al-Hamid II. Republican Party created in Portugal. German Conservation Party formed.
**1876−87** Agostino Depretis, Prime Minister of Italy.

**1876** Oct., British and French Dual Control of Egyptian finances instituted. British punitive expedition on R. Niger. Zanzibar forbids slave caravans: riots in Mombasa. Blantyre founded.

**1877** 1 Jan., Queen Victoria proclaimed Empress of India. 31 March, London Protocol of Great Powers insists on Turkish reforms. 16 May, President MacMahon dismisses Jules Simon: Monarchist ministry under Duc de Broglie (−Nov.). 13 Dec., General Rochebouet resigns: succ. Jules Dufaure.

**1877** 15 Jan., treaty between Austria and Russia. 18 Jan., Abd al-Hamid refuses Istanbul conference proposals; 20 Jan., conference breaks up without result. 5 Feb., Midhat Pasha dismissed. 28 Feb., peace made between Serbia and Turkey. March, fresh attempts to mediate between Russia and Turkey. 17 March, Turkish Parliament first meets. 12 Apr., Abd al-Aziz refuses London Protocol. 24 Apr., Russia declares war on Turkey: invades Rumania. 25 Apr., new Turkish constitution accepted by Turkish Parliament. May, Turkish Parliament suppressed by Abd al-Hamid II: direct rule until 1908. 18 Nov., Russians take Kars. 10 Dec., Turks surrender to Russians at Plevna. 12 Dec., Turkey unsuccessfully requests mediation from the Powers. 14 Dec., Serbia again declares war on Turkey.

**1877** 31 March, Sir Bartle Frere, High Commissioner in SA, with instructions to work for federation. 17 Oct., Stanley reaches Boma, Congo, having taken 999 days from Zanzibar. Police, water supply and street lighting organized in Zanzibar. Eastern Telegraph Co. links Zanzibar to Aden. Menelik confirmed in his title by Yohannes IV. Serpa Pinto explores country between Angola and Victoria Falls, and thence to Pretoria and Durban. Brito Capêlo and Ivens explore country between Angola and upper Congo.
**1877−8** First Kaffir War.
**1877−85** General Gordon, Governor General of the Sudan.

## THE EAST & AUSTRALASIA          THE AMERICAS                    RELIGION & CULTURE

**1875–1946** Mikhail Ivanovich Kalinin, Russian statesman.
**1875–1956** Edmund Clerihew Bentley, humorist, novelist and journalist.
**1875–1962** Fritz Kreisler, Austrian composer and violinist.
**1875–1965** Albert Schweitzer, theologian, missionary, and musician.

**1876** 26 Feb., Korea declared an independent state by China. Treaty of Jacobabad: Khan of Kalat occupies Quetta: becomes British military base. Gaekwar of Baroda deposed for allegedly attempting to poison the British Resident. Khanate of Kokand made Russian province of Ferghana. Japan forces Korea to open Fusan to Japanese settlement and trade. Japan annexes Ryuku Is. All those implicated in assassination of Birch arrested: three persons executed, others exiled to the Seychelles. Abortive attempt to bring Japanese immigrants to Australia.
**c. 1876** Chinese immigrate into S Australia and Queensland in substantial numbers.
**1876–8** Famine in India: *c.* 5 m. die: Famine Commission appointed.
**1876–80** Earl of Lytton, Governor-General and Viceroy of India.

**1876** Aug., Colorado becomes a US State. Nov., Porfirio Diaz takes Mexico City with rebel army from US: President Lerdo exiled. Supreme Court of Canada established. Electoral reforms in Brazil reduce emperor's powers.
**1876–9** Hilarión Daza, President of Bolivia.
**1876–1911** Porfirio Diaz, dictator of Mexico.

**1876** Elementary education made compulsory in England. Presbyterian Church of England formed. Henry Wickham, an Englishman, smuggles rubber plants from Brazil to Kew Gardens: plants subsequently sent to Ceylon: origin of far eastern rubber plantations. Indian Association formed. Johns Hopkins University founded. Alexander Graham Bell invents the telephone. Cathode rays discovered. Basilica of Lourdes consecrated. American Library Association founded.
**1876–1938** Sir Muhammad Iqbal, Indian theologian.
**1876–1946** Manuel de Falla, Spanish composer.
**1876–1952** 'Ian Hay' (Major-General John Hay Beith), novelist.
**1876–1962** George Macaulay Trevelyan, historian.
**1876–8** Kursaal, with concert hall for 6,000, erected at Ostend.
**1876–1952** Albert Mansbridge, founder of the Workers' Educational Association.

**1877** Midhat Pasha's Iraqi constitution abolished by Abd al-Hamid. Chinese general Tso Tsung-tang (1812–85) puts down Yakub Beg's insurrection. Samurai revolt in Kyushu led by Saigo Takamori abortive. Rubber plants first introduced into Malaya.
**1877–89** Hugh Low, Resident in Perak: administration a model for British Residents.

**1877** 2 March, Rutherford B. Hayes elected President of US, following controversy, by one vote (–1881). Dock workers strike in Quebec. Popular primary education and other reforms initiated in Uruguay.

**1877** Education from six to nine made compulsory in Italy. *Truth* (journal) first published. The microphone and the phonograph invented by T.A. Edison. First public telephone installed. The cream separator invented by G. Laval. National Muhammadan Association founded by Amir Ali in Calcutta. All England Lawn Tennis championships instituted at Wimbledon. Library Association founded in UK. Royal Institute of Chemistry formed. Society for the Preservation of Ancient Monuments founded.
**1877–1940** Lev Trotsky, Russian politician.
**1877–1946** Harley Granville-Barker, actor and dramatist. Sir James Jeans, astronomer.
**1877–1947** James Agate, dramatic critic.
**1877–85** Ryks Museum built in Amsterdam.

| WESTERN & NORTHERN EUROPE | CENTRAL & SOUTHERN EUROPE | AFRICA |
|---|---|---|

**1878** 1 May, Universal Exhibition opened in Paris. Aug.–1879 Dec., seventeen Russian revolutionaries executed. 19 Nov., de Broglie resigns: succ. General Rochebouet. 25 Nov., Comité d'Etudes du Haut-Congo formed. H.M. Stanley agrees to serve Léopold II for five years. Irish National Land League founded.

**1878** 9 Jan., Victor Emmanuel I of Italy d.: succ. Humbert (–1900). Turkey capitulates to Russia at Shipka Pass. 20 Jan., Russians take Adrianople. 23 Jan., British fleet arrives at Istanbul but shortly withdrawn. 31 Jan., armistice between Russia and Turkey at Adrianople. 2 Feb., Greece declares war on Turkey. 15 Feb., British fleet again at Istanbul. 3 March, Preliminary treaty of San Stefano between Russia and Turkey: independence of Montenegro, Rumania and Serbia recognized; principality of Bulgaria created; Russia awarded Danube estuary, and Batum and Kars in the Caucasus. 25 March, Austria declines to agree to treaty of San Stefano. 27 March, British troops sent to Malta. 11 May and 2 June, attempts to assassinate Emperor of Germany. 4 June, Turkey cedes Cyprus to Britain. 13 June–13 July, Congress of Berlin: England, France and Germany unite to defend the Ottoman Empire: Treaty of San Stefano abrogated: Bulgaria divided, half being made a principality, Eastern Roumelia made autonomous, both under Ottoman suzerainty; Bosnia and Herzogovina awarded to Austria; Britain gains Cyprus; Russia left with Danube estuary, Batum and Kars. 13 July, Serbia made an independent principality. 2 Oct., following risings, reforms promised in Turkey. 18 Oct., anti-Socialist law in Germany (–1890). Nationalist Socialist Party founded in Warsaw: suppressed shortly by Russia. Many minor revolts in Russia. Portugal institutes labour code for colonies: forced labour abolished.

**1878** 18 March, Walvis Bay annexed by Britain. 18 Aug., ministerial government in Egypt: Nubar Pasha, premier: Dual Control suspended. British ultimatum to Zulus. Civil war among Barotse.

**1879** 30 Jan., Marshal MacMahon resigns: Jules Grévy, President of France. 24 Nov.–9 Dec., W.E. Gladstone's Midlothian campaign. 27 Nov., French parliament moved from Versailles to Paris. 1 Dec., the Imperial train blown up on the way back from Crimea: Tsar escapes, having taken the preceding train. 4 Dec., 'Executive Committee', following various incidents, publishes sentence of death on Alexander II of Russia. Bad harvest and cattle disease in Britain.

**1879** 22 Feb., constitution granted in Bulgaria. 29 Apr., Alexander I, of Battenberg, elected Prince of Bulgaria (–1886). 12 July, protectionist laws passed in Germany. Aug., Count Taaffe forms ministry in Austria (–1893). 7 Oct., Dual Alliance between Austria and Germany.
**1879–81** Sixty new peers created in Portugal to pack upper chamber.

**1879** United Africa Co. founded by Sir George Goldie. Cocoa introduced into Gold Coast. Rubber first exported from Angola. Yohannes IV refuses Gordon's frontier proposals. 12 Jan.– 1 Sept., Zulu War: 22 Jan., British massacred at Isandhlwana: 28 Aug., Cetewayo captured. 18 Feb., Nubar Pasha's ministry falls in Cairo: succ., Apr., Sharif Pasha. 1 June, the Prince Imperial killed in Zululand. 29 June, Khedive Ismail of Egypt deposed: succ. Muhammad Tewfiq (–1892). 4 Sept., Dual Control reimposed in Egypt.

| THE EAST & AUSTRALASIA | THE AMERICAS | RELIGION & CULTURE |
|---|---|---|

**1878** Britain and Russia send missions to Kabul: British envoy refused: declaration of war follows. Oct., Britain invades Afghanistan: 19 Oct., Amir Yakub abdicates, surrendering to Britain: Second Afghan War. Calcutta and Madras set up corporations on Bombay model. Vernacular Press Act imposes restrictions in India. First Trade Union Act in New Zealand. Petah Tikvah, first Zionist settlement in Palestine, founded.
**1878—85** Theebaw, a Buddhist monk, King of Burma.

**1878** Prohibition Act in Canada controls sale and consumption of spirits. Catastrophic rains in Peru. 18 Oct.—1891 6 June, Sir J.A. Macdonald, Canadian Prime Minister. 25 Nov., Marquess of Lorne (later Duke of Argyll), Governor-General of Canada (−1883).

**1878** 7 Feb., Pope Pius IX d.: succ. Leo XIII (Pecci), 'the working man's Pope'. Roman Catholic hierarchy restored in Scotland. Flemish adopted as the official language in Flanders. Cleopatra's Needle re-erected in London. The electric lamp invented by Edison and Swan. First electric street lighting in London. Charles Brush invents the arc lamp. Repeating rifle invented by Mannlicher. Modern microscope first made by Zeiss of Jena.
**1878—1929** Gustave Stresemann, German statesman.
**1878—1931** Sir William Orpen, artist.
**1878—1952** Sir Desmond MacCarthy, critic.
**1878—1955** Emile Cammaerts, Belgian essayist, poet and theologian.
**1878—1959** Sir Alfred Munnings, artist.

**1879** 8 Jan., British occupy Qandahar. 21 Feb., Shir Ali d.: succ. Yakub: 26 May, treaty of Gandamak between Afghanistan and Britain: British Resident established in Kabul: Britain assigned Khyber Pass districts. 24 July, Sir Louis Cavagnari reaches Kabul as British envoy. 3 Sept., Cavagnari and staff murdered in legation in Kabul. 6 Oct., British defeat Afghans at Charasia. 12 Oct., British enter Kabul. 23 Dec., Afghans defeated by the British outside Kabul. Cotton duties abolished in India. Financial crisis in New Zealand: serious unemployment. Manhood suffrage introduced in New Zealand.

**1879** Feb., Chilean naval squadron attacks nitrate port of Antofagasta, Bolivia, chiefly inhabited by Chileans: war ensues: Chile seizes Bolivian coast: Peru supports Bolivia. Chile occupies Iquique, Peru. Chile occupies Antofagasta, Bolivia. Canada imposes tariffs to protective levels against American goods.
**1879—83** Chile at war with Peru and Bolivia.

**1879** 1 June, primary education laicised in Belgium. Law against French Jesuits. 4 Aug., Pope Leo XIII: encyclical *Aeterni Patris* defends Thomism. First Church of Christ Scientist founded by Mary Baker Eddy in Boston. Teaching of Magyar made compulsory in Hungarian schools. First London telephone exchange set up. Lady Anne Blunt explores Najd. Royal University of Ireland established. Scandium discovered.
**c. 1879** Sheep-shearing machine invented in Australia.
**1879—1936** Ottorino Respighi, Italian composer.
**1879—1941** Frank Bridge, composer. Sir Herbert Hamilton Harty, composer.
**1879—1953** Joseph Vissarionovitch Djougachvili, known as Stalin, Russian politician.

1879–1881

WESTERN &
NORTHERN EUROPE

CENTRAL &
SOUTHERN EUROPE

AFRICA

**1880** 17 Feb., dining-room of the Winter Palace blown up: Imperial family not affected: sixty soldiers killed. 28 Apr.–1885, Gladstone, Prime Minister (Lib.). 3 May, C. Bradlaugh, M.P., declines to take Commons oath, insisting on 'affirming'. 14 July, first official celebration of the Fourteenth July in France. 2 Aug., Relief of Distress (Ireland) Act. Sept., Jules Ferry, Prime Minister of France (–1881). Dec., Capt. C.C. Boycott 'boycotted' by peasants in Co. Mayo for refusing to accept rents fixed by them. *Okhrana* (secret police) instituted to replace 'Third Section' in Russia.

**1880** 26 Nov., Montenegro occupies Dulcigno. 20 Apr., Germans convict Schnaebelé, French frontier official, for spying.

**1880** St Louis, Rufisque and Gorée made *communes de pleine exercice*. 30 Apr., Léopold II proclaimed sovereign of the Congo at Vivi. Menelik defeats Galla and prepares to take Harar. 16 Oct., Britain and Transvaal at war: 30 Dec., Paul Kruger proclaimed President.

**1881** 31 Jan.–2 Feb., Irish MPs obstruct Irish Coercion Bill: House sits for forty-one hours. 2 March, Habeas Corpus Act suspended in Ireland. 13 March, Alexander II of Russia murdered: succ. Alexander III (–1894). 19 Apr., Disraeli (Lord Beaconsfield) d.: Marquess of Salisbury, leader of the opposition. 16 Aug., Irish Land Act secures fair rents, fixiture of tenure and free sale. Irish population 5.5 m. 13 Oct., Parnell imprisoned for incitement to intimidation. 14 Nov., Jules Ferry falls: Léon Gambetta forms 'Grand Ministry' (–1882).
**1881–2** Pogroms against Jews in Russia organized by C.P. Pobedonostsev, Procurator of the Holy Synod.

**1881** 26 March, Rumania proclaimed a kingdom. 18 June, League of the Three Emperors, Austria, Germany and Russia, renewed. 28 June, alliance between Austria and Serbia. 3 July, Turco-Greek convention: Greece ceded Thessaly and port of Epirus. 13 July, new constitution in Bulgaria.
**1881–84** Coalition government in Spain under Sagasta.

**1881** Apr., French troops and navy occupy Tunisia with little opposition: 13 May, Treaty of Bardo: Regency of Tunis made a French Protectorate. May, Bou Amama rising in Algeria. 19 June, Muhammad Abduh of Dongola proclaims himself Mahdi in the Sudan (–1885). 9 Sept., nationalist rising in Egypt. Oct., end of resistance against French in Tunisia. British mission to Ashanti. Many IAA posts opened in the Congo (–1885). Menelik's expedition against Arusi. 28 Jan., Boers repulse Britain at Laing's Neck; and 27 Feb., Majuba Hill: treaty of Pretoria: Britain recognizes Boer republic.

## THE EAST & AUSTRALASIA          THE AMERICAS          RELIGION & CULTURE

**1879—1955** Albert Einstein, scientist.
**1879—1957** Sir Patrick Abercrombie, architect.
**1879—1961** Augustus Edwin John, artist.
**1879—1962** John Ireland, composer.
**1879—1963** Lord Beveridge, economist. Sir Maurice Powicke, historian.
**1879—1964** William Aitken, Lord Beaverbrook, newspaper proprietor.

**1880** July, Amir Abd al-Rahman recognized as Amir of Kabul (—1901): British reserve right to control foreign policy. 27 July, Afghans defeat British at Maiwand. 7 Aug., Afghans take Qandahar. 31 Aug., British retake Qandahar. Ili region returned to China.
**1880—4** Marquess of Ripon, Governor-General and Viceroy of India.
c. **1880—1900** British and French companies obtain mining concessions in Malaya.

**1880** Aug., Tahiti and the Society Is. annexed by France. Sept., beginning of construction of the Panama Canal. Chilean army occupies Lima, Tacna and Arica.

**1880—2** Rafael Núñez, President of Columbia: Conservative government: church restored.
**1880—4** Manuel González made President of Mexico at instance of Porfirio Diáz.

**1880** March, Jesuits suppressed in France: other religious associations required to regularize themselves. 29 June, papal nuncio expelled from Brussels. 15 Oct., restoration of Cologne Cathedral completed. Owens College refounded as Manchester University. Parcel post introduced in England. First electric street lights in New York. The blowlamp invented. Pasteur discovers the streptococcus. The typhus bacillus discovered by Ebert. First Test Match between England and Australia.
**1880—1932** Giles Lytton Strachey, biographer.
**1880—1950** Siti binti Saad, Swahili poetess.
**1880—1958** Alfred Noyes, poet.
**1880—1959** Sir Jacob Epstein, sculptor.
**1880—1960** Sir Giles Gilbert Scott, architect.
**1880—1962** Richard Henry Tawney, historian.
**1880—1964** Douglas MacArthur, American general.

**1881** 27 Apr., British evacuate Afghanistan. Russia defeats Turkomans: Merv taken. Russia conquers Ili region, Turkestan. State of Mysore restored to its Raja. Census shows Indian population of 253m. Peace made in New Zealand and Maoris under the Maori king. Empress of Japan announces that a national representative assembly will be instituted in 1890. Kaishinto (Progressive Party) formed in Japan by Okuma Shigenobu to oppose ruling oligarchy, and in opposition to Jiyuto (Liberty Party): both minority parties. Richon-le-Zion founded.

**1881** 15 Feb., Gambier Is. annexed by France. James Abram Garfield (Rep.), President of US; 19 Sept., assassinated; succ., his Vice-President, Chester Alan Arthur (Rep.)(—1885). Samuel Gompers organizes Federation of Organized Trade and Labour Unions of US and Canada. Tierra del Fuego partitioned between Argentina and Chile.
**1881—4** Chile occupies Lima.
**1881—5** 392,802 Canadians migrate to US.

**1881** Royal Commission on Ecclesiastical Courts in England. The Revised Version of the New Testament published. Czech faculties established in the University of Prague. Natural History Museum, S Kensington, opened. American Federation of Labour founded.
**1881—1938** Lascelles Abercrombie, English poet.
**1881—1938** Mustafa Kemal Atatürk, Turkish statesman.
**1881—1939** Ethel M. Dell, romantic novelist.
**1881—1944** Abp William Temple, theologian.
**1881—1945** Béla Bartók, Hungarian composer
**1881—1951** Ernest Bevin, Labour statesman.
**1881—1955** Sir Alexander Fleming, pathologist.
**1881—1958** Juan Ramón Jiménez, Spanish poet.
**1881—1973** Pablo Picasso, Spanish artist.
**1881—1975** Pelham Grenville Wodehouse, novelist.

| WESTERN & NORTHERN EUROPE | CENTRAL & SOUTHERN EUROPE | AFRICA |
|---|---|---|
| **1882** 27 Jan., Gambetta falls: succ. Charles Freycinet. 2 May, 'Kilmainham treaty' of amnesty in Ireland. 6 May, Lord Frederick Cavendish, Chief Secretary for Ireland, and T.H. Burke, his secretary, murdered in Phoenis Park, Dublin. 6 June, Hague Convention makes three-mile limit for territorial waters. July, Prevention of Crimes Bill for Ireland: juries suspended. 7 Aug., Freycinet falls: succ. Duclerc. 31 Dec., Gambetta killed by an accident. House of Commons resolution recommends transfer of all administrative responsibility in W Africa to the 'natives' except 'probably' in Sierra Leone. Municipal Corporations Act. Student unrest in Russia. | **1882** 22 Jan., electoral law reformed in Italy. 6 March, Serbia made a kingdom. 20 May, Italy joins alliance of Austria and Germany (Triple Alliance). Von der Goltz mission to Istanbul. Workers' Association founded in Spain. | **1882** 11 July, British and French bombard Alexandria: 13 Sept., British defeat Egyptians at Tel el-Kebir: 15 Sept., British take Cairo. First French Resident installed at Cotonou. Britain refuses Cameroun kings and chiefs request for a protectorate. Italy establishes colony of Eritrea. Menelik campaigns in Gojjam: Jimma made vassal. |
| **1883** 30 Jan., Clement Fallières forms ministry in France. 21 Feb., Jules Ferry returns to power in France (–1885). 18 Aug., Corrupt and Illegal Practices Act on British elections. 24 Aug., Comte de Chambord, last French Bourbon, d. 31 Aug., machinery of justice re-organized in France. 19 Oct., *Conseil supérieur des colonies* instituted in France. Inspectorate of Labour created in Russia to promote reforms. Russian Marxist Party founded. Further student unrest in Russia. | **1883** 1 May, Bismarck introduces insurance scheme in Germany against sickness. 30 Sept., Bulgarian constitution of 1879 restored. 30 Oct., secret alliance between Austria, Germany and Rumania. | **1883** 13 June, French bombard Tamatave. **1883–6** French expedition against the Hovas of Madagascar, following their attack on the French protected areas. **1883–90** Nubar Pasha, premier of Egypt. **1883–1907** Sir Evelyn Baring (later Lord Cromer), British Agent in Egypt. |
| **1884** Jan., poll tax abolished in Russia. 28 June–2 Aug., London conference on Egypt. Norwegian constitution revised. Imperial Federation League founded. 4 Aug., French constitution partially revised by Congress of Versailles. 10 Dec., Redistribution Bill inaugurates universal male suffrage in Britain over age twenty-one: extended to Ireland. | **1884** 17 March, League of the Three Emperors of 1881 renewed. 15 Nov.–1885 24 Feb., Berlin Conference on Africa: free trade on R. Congo: slavery and the slave trade abolished. Cánovas de Castillo again in power in Spain. | **1884** Gordon reaches Khartoum with orders to evacuate Egyptians. 13 Oct., Mahdi takes Omdurman. Germany occupies Togoland. H.M. Stanley leaves Congo, having set up forty posts and made 400 treaties. Anglo-Ethiopian alliance against the Mahdi. Gobad and Tadjoura ceded to France. Protectorate of British Somaliland established. German Protectorate proclaimed in SWA. |

# THE EAST & AUSTRALASIA

**1882** Russian armies reach Afghan border. Virtual free trade reached in India. Trade treaty between Korea and USA. First cargo of frozen meat exported from New Zealand to UK. First Yemeni Jews migrate to Palestine. Hovevei Zion (Lovers of Zion), Russian Zionists, arrive in Palestine.

**1883** June, Melbourne—Sydney railway completed. 25 Aug., Treaty of Hué: Vietnam placed under French protectorate. The *Famine Code* enacted in India. Trade treaties between Korea and Germany, and with UK. Paper currency office established by British in Rangoon. Volcano of Krakatau destroyed by its own eruption. New Guinea annexed by Queensland (Australia). Burmese embassy sent to Europe. Oil production begun in Sumatra.
**1883—4** French at war with Tonkin and with China.

**1884** 1 Jan., slavery and debt-bondage abolished in Perak. 11 May, First treaty of Tientsin between France and China. 18 June, France annexes Cambodia. Korea makes trade treaties with Italy and Russia. Russians occupy Merv. War between France and China.
**1884—8** Earl of Dufferin (later Marquess of Dufferin and Ava), Governor-General and Viceroy of India.

# THE AMERICAS

**1882** Assiniboia, Saskatchewan and Alberta added to Canada, with representatives in House of Commons. St Kitts and Nevis federated. Nickel mining begun at Sudbury, Canada. Congress forbids Chinese immigration: first US legislation on immigration. Anaconda Copper Mine opened. Standard Oil Co. formed.
**1882—99** Ulises Heureaux, dictator of Dominica.

**1883** 23 Oct., Marquess of Lansdowne, Governor-General of Canada (—1888). Peace between Chile and Peru: Peru cedes Arica and coast to the S: Bolivia loses Antofagasta and all coast: Chile undertakes to construct railway from coast to La Paz. Pendleton Civil Service Act. Northern Pacific Railway completed. Royal Commission advocates union for Leeward and Windward Is. Royal commission on Finance and taxation in W Indies.
**1883—1914** Nitrate boom in Chile.

**1883—1914** Nitrate boom in Chile.

**1884** US begins to enter S American markets. Cotton-seed oil trust set up in US. Catastrophic rains in Peru. Constitutional reform in Jamaica.
**1884—5** Civil war in Colombia.
**1884—94** Núñez again President of Colombia.

# RELIGION & CULTURE

**1882** Pope Leo XIII condemns Irish 'National Tribute' to Parnell. The Jews expelled from Russia. Prussia resumes relations with the Vatican. Education made compulsory, free, and non-sectarian, in France. Society for Psychical Research founded. Primrose League founded. London Chamber of Commerce inaugurated. Channel Tunnel first proposed. Royal Society of Canada founded by Marquess of Lorne to promote humanities and sciences. Regent St Polytechnic opened. Edison constructs first electricity generating and distributing station in New York. First petrol engine constructed by Gottlieb Daimler. Berlin Philharmonic Orchestra founded.
**1882—94** Eduard Glaser discovers Himyaritic inscriptions in Arabia.
**1882—1937** John Drinkwater, poet and dramatist.
**1882—1940** Eric Rowland Gill, sculptor, engraver and type designer.
**1882—1941** James Joyce, Irish novelist. Virginia Woolf, novelist.
**1882—1944** Jean Giraudoux, dramatist and essayist.
**1882—1945** Sir Arthur Eddington, scientist.
**1882—1956** Alan Alexander Milne, novelist, dramatist and journalist.
**1882—1963** Georges Braque, French artist and sculptor.
**1882—1964** Jack Hobbs, cricketer.
**1882—** Eamon de Valera, Irish statesman.
**1883** Social Democratic Federation formed. R. College of Music founded. Metropolitan Opera House founded in New York. First skyscraper built in Chicago. The Boys Brigade founded. Vatican Archives opened to *bona fide* scholars. Beit al-Ajaib, Zanzibar. built.
**1883—1945** Pierre Laval, French politician. Benito Mussolini, Italian politician.
**1883—1946** John Maynard Keynes, Lord Keynes, economist and writer.
**1883—1950** Archibald, Earl Wavell, soldier.
**1883—1953** Sir Arnold Edward Bax, composer.
**1883—1955** Ortega y Gasset, Spanish writer. Maurice Utrillo, French artist.
**1883—1967** Clement, Earl Atlee, Labour Prime Minister.
**1884** Socialist League formed. The dirigible balloon invented by the Renard brothers. The maxim gun invented by Hiram Maxim. The fountain pen invented. The steam turbine invented.
**1884—1915** James Elroy Flecker, poet and dramatist. Georges Duhamel, French author.
**1884—1920** Amadeo Modigliani, artist.

| WESTERN & NORTHERN EUROPE | CENTRAL & SOUTHERN EUROPE | AFRICA |
|---|---|---|

**1884** Dec., preliminary commercial convention between France and Timbuktu. Anglo-Portuguese Treaty recognizes Portuguese rights N of the Congo.
**1884–6** Spain acquires Río de Oro.

**1885** 31 March, Ferry falls. 7 Apr., Brisson-Freycinet ministry in France. 9 June, Gladstone resigns. 24 July– 1886, 3rd Marquess of Salisbury, Prime Minister. 1 Aug., constitution of Congo Free State proclaimed in Brussels. 14 Aug., office of Secretary of State for Scotland created. Irish Land Bill passed. Aug., Belgian Labour Party founded. Nov., Redistribution of Seats Act passed in UK. 28 Dec., Jules Grévy re-elected President of France. First meeting of the Colonial Defence Committee. Strike of 8,000 textile workers at Orekhevo-Zonieva, near Moscow: put down by Cossack troops.

**1885** 26 Feb., Berlin Act creates Congo Free State. 18 Sept., Eastern Roumelia joined to Bulgaria. 13 Nov., Serbia invades Bulgaria. 17 Nov., Bulgaria defeats Serbia at Slivnitza: Austria intervenes. 25 Nov., Alfonso XII of Spain d.: regency follows on account of the pregnancy of Queen María Cristina de las Mercedes. 27 Nov., Bulgaria takes Pirot. Polish Proletariat Party suppressed by Russia.

**1885** 9 Jan., Spain proclaims protectorate over Spanish Guinea. 25 Feb., Germany annexes German East Africa. 26 Jan., Mahdi takes Khartoum: Gordon killed. 22 June, Mahdi d.: succ. Khalifa Abdallahi b. Muhammad: dervishes in control of all Sudan. 5 June, British Protectorate established over 'Niger Districts'. 3 July, St Louis–Dakar railway opened in Senegal. Sept., Bechuanaland proclaimed a Crown Colony. 17 Dec., Treaty between France and the Hova.
**1885–1911** Germany gradually penetrates Kamerun.

**1886** 8 Jan., Freycinet ministry reshuffled in Paris. 27 Jan., Lord Salisbury resigns: 1 Feb., Gladstone forms his third Liberal government. 7 June, Gladstone's Home Rule Bill for Ireland defeated by 343 to 313 votes. 23 June, France banishes Buonaparte and Orléans families. 26 July, following general election, Conservative government under Lord Salisbury (–1892). 15 Dec., Freycinet falls: René Goblet, premier of France. Scottish Home Rule Association formed.

**1886** 3 March, peace of Bucharest between Bulgaria and Serbia. 20 Apr., Prussian Colonization of the Eastern Marches Act to provide land for German settlement in Poland. 8 May–June, Greece blockaded by the Powers, to prevent her intervention in E Roumelia. 17 May, Alfonso XIII born King of Spain (–1931): Queen María Cristina de las Mercedes, Regent (–1902). 20-21 Aug., military *coup* in Sofia. 7 Sept., Alexander of Bulgaria abdicates: Stambulov, Montkurov and Karavellov, regents (–1887). Polish League formed.
**1886–91** Sagasta, prime minister of Spain.
**1886–1913** Otto, King of Bavaria, incurably insane: regent, Luitpold (–1912).

**1886** 13 Jan., Colony of Lagos instituted. 3 June, Anglican and Roman Catholic converts martyred in Buganda. 29 June, Savorgnan de Brazza, Commissioner-General for Gabon and French Congo. *Force Publique* established in CFS. 1 Nov., Anglo-German agreement on spheres of interest in E Africa. Yohannes IV declares war on the Mahdi. Italian expedition against Harar defeated. German-Portuguese treaty recognizes German rights in SWA, and between Mozambique and German East Africa. French Protectorate established in Comoro Is.
**1886–8** Galliéni's expeditions against Samory and Bambara.

**1887** 12 Feb., agreement between Britain and Italy on the Mediterranean. 1 March, five students hanged for treason in Russia. 24 March, agreement between Britain and Austria on the Mediterranean. 4 Apr., first Colonial Conference in London. 4 May, agreement between Britain and Spain on the Mediterranean. 16 May, Goblet ministry falls. 18 May, Maurice Rouvier forms ministry in France.

**1887** 11 Jan., Bismarck urges larger army for Germany. 20 Feb., Triple Alliance between Austria, Germany and Italy. 18 June, Reinsurance Treaty between Germany and Russia following Austrian refusal to renew League of the Three Emperors. 7 July, Ferdinand I of Saxony elected Prince of Bulgaria (–1918). 31 July, Francesco Crispi, Prime Minister of Italy (–1891).

**1887** Jan., Ethiopians defeat Italians at Sagati: Galla rising: June, Mahdists burn Gondar: another Mahdist expedition repelled: Menelik takes Harar. Feb., Tippu Tib made Governor of Stanley Falls District, CFS. 22 May, Britain signs convention with Egypt to withdraw within three years. 21 June, Britain completes annexation of Zululand. Cecil Rhodes acquires control of de Beers.

## THE EAST & AUSTRALASIA    THE AMERICAS    RELIGION & CULTURE

1885 Jan., new Franco-Burmese commercial treaty signed. 30 March, Russians occupy Panjdeh Oasis. Apr., Second treaty of Tientsin between France and China. 20 July, Saigon—Mytho railway opened in Cochin-China. Sept., Russo-Afghan Boundary Commission. Dec., first meeting of the Indian National Congress in Bombay. Railway operating from Taiping to R. Larut. Cabinet and Privy Council instituted in Japan: Kuroda Kiyotaka, first prime minister. Korea declared a joint sphere of interest by China and Japan. Inter-state negotiations in Australia for federation. Federal Council of Australasia Act enacted.
post 1885 Numerous settlers leave New Zealand.
1885–6 British commercial mission to Tibet agreed but does not take place.
1886 Aug., dispute between British and Burma over Burmese High Court judgement in Bombay Burma Trading Corporation case. 17 Nov., British expeditionary force enters Burma: 29 Nov., King Theebaw surrenders to British and is exiled: Burma annexed by Britain. Trade treaty between Korea and France. Mission from India to Tibet. Burma Oil Co. established. New Zealand legislature transferred from Auckland to Wellington. Kuala Lumpur Railway opened.
1886–1900 Intermittent Burmese guerrilla activity against the British.
1886–1948 Burma under British suzerainty.

1887 July, Anglo-Russian agreement on Afghanistan. 1 Oct., Baluchistan annexed to India. Anglo-Afghan treaty defines border with India. Railway opened between Rangoon and Prome. Dordrecht Oil Co. founded to exploit oil in Indonesia.
1887–90 Sir Charles Crosthwaite, Chief Commissioner for Burma: period of severe repression.

1885 March-Nov., rebellion in Saskatchewan: leader, Louis Riel, hanged for treason. 7 Nov., Canadian Pacific Railway completed. Linseed oil trust set up in US. Knights of Labour start first strikes in US.
1885–9 Grover Cleveland (Dem.), President of US, first term.

1886 Slavery abolished in Cuba. Republic of Colombia proclaimed. Knights of Labour count 700,000 members.

1887 US obtain right to use Pearl Harbour, Hawaii, as a naval station. US Inter-State Commerce Act. Hatch Act sets up agricultural experimental stations in US. Manufacture of aluminium begun in US. Lead, sugar and whisky trusts set up in US. Fifty-seven refrigerator ships in service between Argentina and Britain. Argentina exports 237,000 tons of grain.

1884–1929 Hugo von Hofmannsthal, Austrian poet.
1884–1941 Sir Hugh Seymour Walpole, novelist.
1884–1946 Alfred Damon Runyon, American novelist.
1884–1952 Gilbert Frankau, novelist.
1884–1954 Francis Brett Young, novelist.
1884–1964 Sean O'Casey, dramatist.
1885 5 Jan., five CMS converts martyred in Buganda. Breach between polygamous and monogamous Mormons. Pasteur invents inoculation against rabies. Internal combustion engine invented by Gottlieb Daimler. First single cylinder motor car constructed by Karl Benz. Incandescent gas mantle patented. Fingerprints shown to be individual and permanent. J.A. Froude. visiting New Zealand, observes a 'certain republican quality of manners'. About twenty-eight newspapers, Dutch and Malay, appearing in Indonesia.
1885–1930 David Herbert Lawrence, novelist.
1885–1940 Humbert Wolfe, poet and critic.
1885–1945 George Smith Patton, American general.
1885–1959 Sir Henry Tizard, scientist.
1885–1962 Niels Behr, Danish physicist.

1886 The Statue of Liberty erected in New York Harbour. Severn Tunnel completed. Héroult invents electrolytic process for making aluminium. Hertz discovers electromagnetic waves. The buoy invented. Oil production begun in Java. English Historical Review founded with Mandell Creighton as editor. Newspaper El Día founded in Uruguay by José Batlle y Ordóñez, reformer.
1886–1914 Alain Fournier, novelist.
1886–1960 Sir Lewis Bernstein Namier, historian.
1886–1965 Karl Barth, German theologian.

1887 The linotype machine invented. 'Esperanto' language invented. Artificial silk invented.
1887–1915 H.G. Moseley, atomic scientist. Rupert Brooke, poet.
1887–1958 Rose Macaulay, novelist and poet.
1887–1960 Ernö von Dohnányi, Hungarian composer.
1887–1965 Charles Edward Jeanneret, 'Le Corbusier', French architect.

| WESTERN & NORTHERN EUROPE | CENTRAL & SOUTHERN EUROPE | AFRICA |
|---|---|---|
| **1887** 21 June, Queen Victoria celebrates her Golden Jubilee. 13 Nov., Irish 'Bloody Sunday' in London. 2 Dec., Jules Grévy, President of France, resigns, following scandals. 3 Dec., Sadi Carnot elected President of France (−1894). Independent Labour Party formed in Britain. **1888** 15 Apr., C. Floquet forms ministry in France (−1889). 9 Aug., County Councils established in UK by Local Government Act. 13 Aug., Imperial Defence Act passed. Scottish Labour Party founded by Keir Hardie. **1888—91** Russia obtains substantial loans from France. | **1887** 7 Sept., Polish forbidden in primary schools: general strike of school children follows. 12 Dec., Austria, Italy and UK sign treaty on Near East. **1888** 28 Jan., military agreement between Germany and Italy. 9 March, Emperor William I of Germany d.: succ. Frederick III. 15 June, Emperor Frederick III of Germany d.: succ. William II (−1918). 6 Aug., Corinth Canal opened. 6 Oct., Turkey grants German concession to begin Baghdad railway. 20 Oct., Suez Canal Convention of Constantinople declares canal open to all nations in war as in peace. Anarchists in Spain join syndicalist National Confederation of Labour. | **1887—94** Menelik subdues Galla and Sidama. **1887—96** Civil war in Ashanti. **1888** French Protectorate over Futa, Guinea. British treaty with Oyo. Bushiri's rebellion in German East Africa. Matabele accept British Protectorate. Rhodes gains control of Kimberley. **c. 1888—1933** Njoya, King of Foumbau, inventor of Bamoun script. |
| **1889** Feb., Pierre Tirard forms government in France (−1890). 31 March, Naval Defence Act, to enlarge British Navy. 8 Apr., General Boulanger leaves France, fearing trial for treason. June, Brussels Conference on colonial problems. 19 Aug.—14 Sept., London Dock strike: Cardinal Manning mediates. London County Council established (−1965). The Second International founded at the first International Socialist Congress in Paris. | **1889** 30 Jan., Archduke Rudolf, Crown Prince of Austria, commits suicide at Mayerling. 6 March, Milan IV of Serbia abdicates: succ. Alexander I Obrenovitch (−1903). 19 Oct., Louis I of Portugal d.: succ. Charles I (−1908). Emperor William II of Germany visits Istanbul. Baghdad Railway begun. | **1889** 10 March, Yohannes IV killed at battle of Metemna: Menelik proclaimed Emperor. 2 May, Ethiopia and Italy sign treaty of Ucciali: Italy claims it implies a protectorate. Budget surplus restored in Egypt. French Protectorate over Ivory Coast. Léopold II declares all 'vacant' land in CFS state property. 6 Sept., Kabaka Mwanga of Buganda deposed: succ. Kiwewa: 18 Oct., Muslims expel missionaries from Buganda: Kiwewa deposed: succ. Kalema. Dec., British Protectorate proclaimed in Nyasaland. Salisbury, Rhodesia, founded. Serpa Pinto crosses Africa from Mozambique. |
| **1890** 1 July, Anglo-German Convention: Britain cedes Heligoland in return for Zanzibar and Pemba. 2 July, Brussels Act: colonial conference forbids slave trade and sale of hard liquor to primitive peoples. 23 Nov., William III of Holland d.: succ. Wilhelmina (−1948)(d. 1962). 23 Nov., Luxembourg separated from Holland. Finland, hitherto a Grand Duchy with its own Diet and Senate, incorporated into Russia. | **1890** 15-28 March, international congress for the protection of workers in Berlin. 20 March, Bismarck dismissed by William II: succ. Count Caprivi (−1894). 25 March, Germany denounces Russo-German Reinsurance Treaty. 29 July, first industrial courts established in Germany to adjudicate wages. 17 Aug., Tsar Alexander III and Emperor William II meet at Narva. Cánovas de Castillo again Prime Minister of Spain. | **1890** 1 Aug., Sultan of Zanzibar signs Anti-Slavery Decree. 4 Nov., British Protectorate over Zanzibar proclaimed. 12 Nov., Cardinal Lavigérie's 'Algiers Toast' attempts to improve relations between Church and State. Dec., Asantehene refuses British protectorate. 18 Dec., F. Lugard occupies Uganda for IBEA. British ultimatum to Portugal on possession of Rhodesia. Italy re-organizes Colony of Eritrea. |

## THE EAST & AUSTRALASIA   THE AMERICAS   RELIGION & CULTURE

1887–1975 Sir Julian Huxley, scientist.
1887–1976 Bernard Law Montgomery, Viscount Montgomery, soldier.
1887–1975 Chiang Kai-Shek, Chinese statesman.

1888 Tibet attacks Sikkim. Irish form one-fifth of Australian population: chiefly concentrated in NSW.
1888–94 Marquess of Lansdowne, Governor-General and Viceroy of India.

1888 11 June, Lord Stanley of Preston, Governor-General of Canada (–1893). Brazilian Parliament frees all slaves in Brazil.
1888–94 Period of disorder and short-lived presidents in Venezuela.
1888–98 1¼ m. immigrants enter Brazil, chiefly Italians and Portuguese coffee industry rapidly developed, followed by rubber.

1888 *Institut Pasteur* established. Fabian Society formed. *Financial Times* first published. Pneumatic bicycle tyre invented by J. B. Dunlop. George Eastman invents Kodak box camera. Alternating current electric motor invented. Nansen's expedition to Greenland. Canadian Jesuits given $400,000 for estates lost in 1800. Ethiopian mission to Russia to join in celebration of 900th anniversary of introduction of Christianity. Tell el-Amarna Tablets discovered.
1888–1915 Julian Henry Francis Grenfell, poet.
1888–1935 Thomas Edward Lawrence ('T.E. Shaw'), historian, archaeologist and war writer.
1888–1946 John Logie Baird, inventor of television.
1888–1948 Georges Bernanos, novelist.
1888–1957 Mgr. Ronald Arbuthnott Knox, theologian, translator, poet and writer.
1888–1965 Thomas Stearns Eliot, author and poet.

1889 11 Feb., New constitution in Japan, following Imperial German model. Plural voting abolished in New Zealand. W.G. Spence initiates trade union to include every type of mining in Australia: subsequently organizes Shearers' Union. Raub Australian Gold Mining Ltd. established in Pahang. Imperial Bank of Persia established.
1889 ff. Trouble between Australian sheep-owners and Shearers' Union.

1889 15 Nov., Pedro II of Brazil forced to abdicate by military *coup d'état*: Manoel Deodoro da Fonseca, *de facto* dictator (–1891): United States of Brazil proclaimed. First Pan-American Conference held in Washington. Match trust set up in US. Trinidad and Tobago united. Population of Brazil *c.* 14m.
1889–93 Benjamin Harrison (Rep.), President of US.

1889 International Exhibition in Paris: the Eiffel Tower built. Hull House, Chicago, founded by Jane Addams. Catholic University of Washington founded. Celluloid film first produced. Cordite invented.
1889–1944 Philip Guedalla, biographer.
1889–1945 Adolf Hitler, German dictator.
1889–1946 Christopher Richard Wynne Nevinson, artist.
Paul Nash, artist and designer.
1889–1952 Sir Stafford Cripps, Labour politician.
1889–1953 Edwin Hubble, astronomer.
1889–1963 Jean Cocteau, French author.
1889–1975 Arnold Joseph Toynbee, historian.
1889–1977 Charles Chaplin, actor.

1890 Dec., general election in New Zealand won by Liberals: struggle between Conservative upper house and Liberal lower house follows. First Imperial Diet opened in Japan, with two houses: ministers responsible to Emperor alone. Rescript on education promulgated by Emperor. New criminal code in force in Japan: new civil code drafted. Strikes in Australia of seamen and sheep-shearers.

1890 US Anti-Trust Act. Tobacco trust set up in US. Farmers' Alliances reach 2m. members in US: form Populist Party. Mesabi, richest iron range in the world, discovered. 5,848 miles of railway in Argentina. Apr., national rising in Argentina: cabinet resigns: fighting follows (–July): radical government established (–1930).
1890–1 Financial crisis in Argentina.

1890 Court of the Arches judgement against Bp King of Lincoln for ritual practices upheld by Privy Council. First Labour May Day celebrations, held in Germany. Free elementary education instituted in England. First English electric power station built at Deptford. Forth Bridge completed. The *École Biblique* founded in Jerusalem. Daughters of the American Revolution founded. First steel framed buildings erected in Chicago.

1890–1893

WESTERN &
NORTHERN EUROPE

CENTRAL &
SOUTHERN EUROPE

AFRICA

**1890** Universal suffrage at age of twenty-four granted in Spain.

**c. 1890** Rinderpest destroys many cattle in EA, followed by serious outbreaks of smallpox among Masai, Kikuyu and Kamba.
**1890–4** French conquests of *Afrique Occidentale Française.*

**1891** 24 March and 15 Apr., agreements between Britain and Italy on Abyssinia. 23 July, official French naval visit to Kronstadt. 27 Aug., alliance between France and Russia. Oct., 'Newcastle Programme' adopted by British Liberal Party. 7 Oct., Charles Stewart Parnell d. Congested Districts' Board established in Ireland. Land Purchase Act in Ireland.

**1891** Jan., rising in Oporto: Portuguese republican party outlawed. 31 Jan., Crispi resigns: succ. Marquis di Rudini (–1892). 9 Apr., Pan-German League founded. 6 May, Triple Alliance renewed for twelve years. 21 May, Serbian constitution of 1869 restored.

**1891** Feb., Anglo-Egyptian expedition from Suakin routs Uthman Digna. 9 Feb., Emperor Menelik denounces Italian claims to a protectorate. Portuguese form Mozambique Co. Sisal first introduced into German East Africa. Dood's campaign in Senegal. Department of Native Affairs set up in Senegal.
**1891–4** War between Arabs and Belgians in CFS.

**1892** 11 Aug., following general election, Gladstone forms Liberal government (–1894). 17 Aug., secret military agreement between France and Russia. Sept.–1903, Witte Finance Minister in Russia: responsible for successful financial reforms and encouragement of industry. Panama Canal scandal in France following fraudulent share issue.

**1892** 1 Feb., Germany makes commercial treaties with Austria, Belgium, Spain and Switzerland. 26 March, Labour Dept. formed in Germany. May, Giovanni Giolitti forms ministry in Italy (–1893). 14 June, Portugal declares herself bankrupt: some reforms made by Ferreira Dias. 12 Dec., Pan-Slav Congress in Cracow. Corinth Canal opened.

**1892** June, Chagga defeat Germans near Moshi. 23 July, Tafari Makonnen, future Emperor Haile Selassie I, b. 1 Aug., Ndebele raid Mashona. Oct., Emin Pasha murdered in CFS. 3 Dec., French Protectorate over Dahomey proclaimed.
**1892–4** General war in Kasai.
**1892–1914** Abbas II Hilmi, Khedive of Egypt.

**1893** 13 Jan., Independent Labour Party founded in Britain. 8-21 March, Ferdinand de Lesseps and associates fined following Panama scandal trial. Apr., general strike in Belgium. June, commercial treaty between France and Russia. 15 June, sentences on de Lesseps and others set aside.

**1893** 13 July, German army enlarged: military service reduced to two years. 10 Dec., Giolitti falls: Crispi returns to office. 27 Dec., Franco-Russian military agreement ratified by Russia. Germany makes commercial treaties with Rumania, Serbia and Spain. Rising of Young Czechs in Prague.

**1893** 10 March, IBEA hands over Uganda to British Government. French Colonies of Guinea and Ivory Coast formally established. 10 May, Natal granted self-government. Nov., L.S. Jameson crushes Matabele revolt and occupies Bulawayo. 13 Nov., Swaziland annexed by Transvaal. Rabeh, former slave, makes war on Bornu: proclaimed sultan (–1900).

## THE EAST & AUSTRALASIA

**1890** Trade treaty between Tibet and British India. Australian Federation Conference held in Melbourne. W Australia given responsible government. Royal Dutch Oil Co. founded to exploit Sumatran oil. Maritime strike in Australia: spreads to New Zealand. Monetary economy spread throughout Burma.
**c. 1890** Town Sanitary Boards developed in Malaya.
**1890—1900** Japanese population rises from 40m. to 44m.
**1890 ff** Japanese diplomatic activity secures favourable revision of foreign treaties.
**1891** July—1892 Apr., twenty-one banks in Melbourne, and twenty in Sydney, go bankrupt. Strikes in Australia put down. Labour Party wins thirty-seven seats in NSW Parliament. First Labour Electoral Leagues formed in Australia. National Australasian Federation Convention: 'Commonwealth of Australia' adopted as title. Burma Corporation established for mining. Burmese railway extended to Mandalay.

**1892** Imperial Legislative Council in India reformed: 60 members: 28 nominated by Viceroy: 9 local government representatives: 32 non-officials, of whom 27 elected. Indian Councils Act: powers of councils enlarged in India: questions allowed and discussion on annual budget. Trade treaty between Korea and Austria. Land laws simplified in New Zealand.
**1892—1906** Richard John Seddon, Prime Minister of New Zealand.
**1892 ff.** Canals built in India to irrigate waste or desert land.

**1893** Jan., Turks begin massacres in Armenia. Durand mission to Afghanistan: Durand line agreed as frontier between Afghanistan and India. Australasian Federal Council held in Hobart. Municipal councils introduced in the Philippines. Women enfranchised in New Zealand. Thirty-seven registered trade unions in New Zealand.

## THE AMERICAS

**1891** Jan., civil war in Chile: Jorge Montt, provisional president. 24 Feb., Republican constitution promulgated in Brazil. Deodoro da Fonseca, first President. 16 June—1892 24 Nov., Sir J.J.C. Abbott, Canadian Prime Minister. 23 Nov., naval rising in Brazil: Deodoro da Fonseca expelled from office: Florians Peixoto, President. US Forest Reserve Act sets aside 150m. acres: further 85m. acres in Alaska and NW set aside for study. New constitution in Brazil on US model. Catastrophic rains in Peru.
**1891—1920** One hundred changes of government in Chile.
**1892** 5 Dec.—1894 12 Dec., Sir J.S.D. Thompson, Canadian Prime Minister. *Unión Liberal* organized in Mexico. Knights of Labour movement collapses. Rubber trust set up in US.

**1893** Feb., US makes Hawaii a Protectorate. 18 Sept., Earl of Aberdeen, Governor-General of Canada (—1898). Brazilian Navy revolts: civil war for eight months.
**1893—7** Grover Cleveland (Dem.), President of US, second term.
**1893—1909** José Santos Zelaya, Liberal, President of Nicaragua: brutish and tyrannical government.

## RELIGION & CULTURE

**1890—1938** Karel Capek, Czech author and dramatist.
**1890—1946** Harry L. Hopkins, American statesman.
**1890—1970** Charles de Gaulle, soldier and President of France.
**1890—** Sir Harold Spencer Jones, astronomer.
**1890** Imperial Palace, Addis Ababa, begun.

**1891** 15 May, Leo XIII: Encyclical *Rerum Novarum*, on labour conditions. General and Particular Baptists in England unite.
**1891—1904** Trans-Siberian Railway built.
**1891—1953** Sergei Prokofiev, Russian composer.
**1891—1963** David Low, cartoonist.
**1891—1974** Ann Bridge (ps. of Lady O'Malley), novelist.
**1891—1975** Sir Arthur Bliss, composer.

**1892** 2 Feb., Pope Leo XIII: *Inter sollicitudines*. Community of the Resurrection founded by Bp Charles Gore. Electrons discovered by Lorentz. The electric oven invented by Moissan. Chicago University founded.
**1892—1919** Sir John William Alcock, airman.
**1892—1933** Stella Benson, novelist.
**1892—1934** Engelbert Dolfuss, Chancellor of Austria.
**1892—1944** Wendell Wilkie, American statesman.
**1892—1953** Ugo Betti, Italian dramatist.
**1892—1959** Sir Stanley Spencer, artist.
**1892—1961** Sumner Welles, American statesman.
**1892—1962** Richard Aldington, biographer, novelist and poet.
**1892—1962** Victoria Sackville-West, poet, novelist and biographer.
**1892—** General Josip Broz Tito, President of Jugoslavia.
**1893** The cinematograph invented by Marey. The zip fastener invented by W.L.Judson. The carburettor invented. World Exhibition held in Chicago. University of Wales founded. Imperial Institute, S Kensington, founded.
**1893—6** Nansen's expedition to the North Pole.
**1893—1935** Huey Pierce Long, American politician.

| WESTERN & NORTHERN EUROPE | CENTRAL & SOUTHERN EUROPE | AFRICA |
|---|---|---|

**1893** 1 Sept., Gladstone's second Irish Home Rule Bill passes Commons: 8 Sept., rejected by Lords by 419 to 41. 13-29 Oct., Russian naval visit to Toulon. 9 Dec., an anarchist, A.Vaillant explodes bomb in French Chamber of Deputies.
**1893–5** Customs war between France and Switzerland.
**1894** 3 March, Parliamentary Liberal Party split over Irish Home Rule Bill: Gladstone resigns: Earl of Rosebery, Prime Minister (–1895). Apr., Sir Henry Vernon Harcourt introduces death duties in annual budget. 24 June, President Carnot of France assassinated in Lyons: succ. Jean Casimir-Périer (–1895). July, Anglo-Japanese convention. 1 Nov., Alexander III of Russia d.: succ. Nicolas II (–1917). 22 Dec., Alfred Dreyfus condemned for treason. Scottish Grand Committee established in British Parliament.

**1894** 10 Feb., commercial treaty between Germany and Russia. 11 July, Italian laws against anarchists and Socialists passed. 26 Oct., Count Caprivi resigns: Prince Hohenlohe, German Chancellor (–1900).
**1894–7** Greeks rise in Crete against Turks.

**1893–4** Special police operations carried out by Spanish army in Melilla.

**1894** Jan., C.J. Rhodes wins Cape elections. 3 March, treaty between Britain and Toro: 11 Apr., Uganda declared a British Protectorate. 5 May, Anglo-Italian agreement assigns Harar to Italy. 22 June, Dahomey proclaimed a French Colony. 17 July, Italians take Kassala from the Dervishes: CFS clash with Dervishes. Oct., risings in German EA. 10 Nov.–1896 Jan., French conquest of Madagascar. Menelik campaigns against Walamo in person. Gold discovered in Transvaal. Bulawayo begins to develop rapidly. Coal first located at Wankie, S Rhodesia. SA Glen Grey Act inaugurates new native policy. Britain annexes Pondoland.
**1894–1900** French exploration and occupation of Chad.

**1895** 13 Jan., President Casimir-Périer resigns. 17 Jan., François Félix Faure elected President of France: ministry formed by Alexandre Ribot. 11 June, Liberals defeated in Parliament: 25 June, Conservative Unionist government under Lord Salisbury (–1902). 1-8 Aug., Emperor William II and Lord Salisbury hold discussions at Cowes on partition of Turkey. Nov., Léon Bourgeois forms Radical government in France.
**1895–1903** Joseph Chamberlain, Colonial Secretary. *Confédération Générale du Travail* of French trade unions formed.

**1895** 15 June, Stambulov, Prime Minister of Bulgaria, murdered. 19 June, Kiel Canal opened. 1 Oct., Armenians massacred in Istanbul. 17 Oct., Abd al-Hamid II of Turkey agrees to reforms: Armenian massacres continue: UK squadron sent to Dardanelles. 7 Nov., Russia proposes to seize Istanbul, but desists. Cánovas de Castillo again Prime Minister of Spain. National League replaces the Polish League.

**1895** March, Ashanti embassy sent to London. 25 March, Italian troops enter Ethiopia. 2 May, BSA Co. territory S of R. Zambezi organized as S Rhodesia. 15 June, *Afrique Occidentale Française* (*AOF*), French West African Federation, established. 1 July, British East African Protectorate, including present Kenya, Uganda and Zanzibar, proclaimed. 4 July, mutiny in CFS *Force Publique*. 26 Aug., British bombard Zanzibar town: Sayyid Hamid installed as Sultan. 1 Oct., French Protectorate established in Madagascar. 12 Dec., Busoga incorporated into Uganda. 29 Dec., Jameson raid. Slave trade forbidden in Kamerun. 'Kaffir Boom' in mining shares spreads to London, Berlin and Paris. French expedition to Madagascar: Tananarive (Hova capital) taken.
**1895–9** Risings in Mozambique.
**1895–1908** Mustafa Pasha Fahmi, premier of Egypt.
**1895–1912** British gradually occupy Northern Frontier District of Kenya.

**1896** 5 Jan., Anglo-French agreement on Siam. Apr., F. Médine forms government in France.

**1896** Feb., Crete revolts against Turkey. 5 March, Crispi dismissed: Marquis Rudini again Prime Minister of Italy.

**1896** 2 Jan., Jameson surrenders at Doornkop: 3 Jan., William II of Germany sends 'Kruger telegram'.

| THE EAST & AUSTRALASIA | THE AMERICAS | RELIGION & CULTURE |
|---|---|---|

**1893** Australian Federation Conference held at Sydney. Gold rush in Western Australia.

**1893–1946** Hermann Goering, German politician.
**1893–1950** Harold Joseph Laski, political scientist.
**1893–1951** Ivor Novello, composer.

**1894** May, China puts down rebellion in Korea at request of king. 10 June, Japan occupies Seoul and Korean treaty ports: war between China and Japan follows. 25 July, Japan sinks Chinese troopship: Japanese capture Port Arthur, Liaotung peninsula, and Wei-hai-wei. 23 July, Japanese seize royal palace in Seoul: 27 July, Korea declares war on China. New Zealand Advances to Settlers Act finds capital for would-be farmers. New Zealand Industrial and Arbitration Act: first compulsory industrial system of arbitration in the world: Conciliation Boards elected by masters and workers. Bank of New Zealand Share Guarantee Act nationalizes Bank of New Zealand. First internal loan floated in China.
**1894–6** Armenians massacred by the Turks.
**1894–9** (9th) Earl of Elgin, Governor-General and Viceroy of India.
**1894–1906** No strikės in New Zealand.

**1894** Pullman Strike in US. Mexican budget balanced for the first time. Colonial Conference held in Ottawa. 21 Dec.–1896 27 Apr., Sir Mackenzie Bowell, Canadian Prime Minister.
**1894–8** Joaquín Crespo, President of Venezuela.
**1894–9** Policarpo Bonilla, President of Honduras.

**1894** Lord Halifax holds first conversations on reunion between the Church of England and Rome. Anti-diptheria serum invented.
**1894–1930** Peter Warlock (ps. of Philip Heseltine), composer.
**1894–1958** Charles Morgan, novelist and dramatist.
**1894–1963** Aldous Leonard Huxley, novelist and poet. James Thurber, American humorous writer.
**1894–** Rudolph Hess, German Nazi politician.
**1894–1971** Nikita Khrushchev, Russian politician.
**1894–** Harold MacMillan, Conservative Prime Minister.

**1895** 17 Apr., peace treaty of Shimonoseki between China and Japan: Japan keeps Formosa, Pescadores, Port Arthur and Liaotung peninsula, and receives indemnity: Korea made independent. 8 May, 'Triple Intervention', by France, Germany and Russia, compels Japan to restore Liaotung peninsula and Port Arthur to China. 8 Oct., Queen of Korea assassinated. Written constitution instituted for Johore. Two more railways opened in Malaya. Chinese scholar Kang Yo-wei asks for reforms. Rising in Kansu. Chitral campaign on border of India and Afghanistan.

**1895** 16 Dec., President Cleveland sends message to Congress hinting at war with Britain over British Guiana and Venezuela frontier: arbitration by US follows. Economic depression in Cuba, enhanced by US sugar tariff: rebellion led by José Martí (–1898). Hydro-electric plant installed at Niagara Falls. Athabaska, Franklin, Mackenzie, Ungava and Yukon given seats in Canadian Parliament. Spain recognizes Honduras. Population of Argentina 3.95m.: 1m. foreigners.
**1895–6** Dispute between Britain and Venezuela on boundary of British Guiana: settled by international arbitration.
**1895–1944** Liberals in power in Ecuador: twenty-eight presidents.

**1895** World Student Christian Federation founded. National Trust founded. London School of Economics founded. *American Historical Review* founded. The safety razor invented. The cinema camera invented by the brothers Lumière. X-rays discovered by W.Röntgen. G. Marconi invents wireless telegraphy. Promenade Concerts founded by Sir Henry Wood.
**1895–1964** Sir Milton Margai, Sierra Leone statesman.
**1895–1975** Nikolai Bulganin, Russian politician.
**1895–** John George Diefenbaker, Canadian politician.
**1895–** Christian Archibald Herter, American politician.
**1895–** Paul Hindemith, Swiss composer.
**1895–** Henry Williamson, author.
**1895–1974** General Juan Domingo Perón, Argentinian statesman.

**1896** Feb., King of Korea escapes to Russian Legation.

**1896** 4 Jan., following Mormon abandonment of polygamy, Utah becomes a US State.

**1896** The *Daily Mail* founded. Nobel prizes instituted. Radio-activity discovered by Henri Becquerel.

## WESTERN & NORTHERN EUROPE

## CENTRAL & SOUTHERN EUROPE

## AFRICA

**1896** 3 June, treaty of alliance between China and Russia. July, further Irish Land Act. Oct., Tsar Nicolas II and the Tsarina visit Paris, and then London. 1,000 people killed in a panic at Nicholas II's coronation.

**1896** Apr., Abd al-Hamid promises reforms in Macedonia. 1 July, Civil Law Code enacted in Germany. 3 July, Abd al-Hamid agrees to self-government in Crete. 26 Aug., Armenians raid Ottoman Bank, Istanbul: one-day massacre. Aug., Austro-Russian agreement on the Balkans. 24 Oct., Russo-German Reinsurance Treaty published by Bismarck.

**1896** 21 Feb., rebellion against French in Madagascar. 1 March, Ethiopians defeat Italians decisively at Adowa: Italy forced to sue for peace. 16 March, Anglo-Egyptian force sent to the Sudan: 23 Sept., Dongola taken. 20 May, French Somaliland proclaimed a French possession. 16 Aug., British Protectorate over Ashanti proclaimed. 18 Aug., France annexes Madagascar. 26 Oct., treaty of Addis Ababa: Italian claim to protectorate withdrawn. German post established in Usumbura, Rwanda.
**1896—1900** Resistance against French in Madagascar.
**1896—1901** Uganda railway built from Mombasa to Kampala.

**1897** 28 Apr., agreement of St Petersbourg between Austria and Russia on the Balkans. June-July, Colonial Conference in London. 22 June, Queen Victoria celebrates her Diamond Jubilee. Aug., the Tsar again visits France: Franco-Russian treaty announced. 18 Sept., agreement between Britain and France on Tunisia. Nov., French government inquiry begun into the Dreyfus case.

**1897** 18 March, Crete unites with Greece. 18 Apr., Turkey declares war on Greece. 12 May, Turkey defeats Greece in Thessaly: armistice follows shortly. 5 June, Alfred von Tirpitz becomes Secretary for the German Navy. 20 Oct., Prince von Bülow appointed German Foreign Secretary. 5 Nov., agreement between Austria and Italy on Albania. 16 Dec., peace treaty of Istanbul between Greece and Turkey. Cánovas de Castillo assassinated: Sagasta again Prime Minister of Spain.

**1897** 4 Jan., British Consul-General Phillips, with large party, massacred attempting to reach Benin. 27 Jan., British occupy Benin; and, 16 Feb., Ilorin. 28 Feb., French depose Queen of the Hovas, Madagascar: island annexed by France. Apr., legal status of slavery abolished in Zanzibar. 14 May, Anglo-Ethiopian treaty on Somali boundaries. 6 July, Kabaka Mwanga of Buganda rebels against British: replaced by infant son, Daudi Chwa. 19 Sept., Kitchener reaches Fashoda: Marchand required to withdraw. 25 Dec., Italy cedes Kassala to Egypt. Ashanti Goldfields Corporation commences operations in Gold Coast. Congolese troops mutiny at Uvira. Natal makes it a criminal offence for a white man to marry an Indian. First demand for a white Legislative Council in S Rhodesia made by Bulawayo Literary and Debating Society. Railway construction begun on Gold Coast.
**1897—8** German operations against Hehe under Mkwawa: Mkwawa commits suicide.
**1897—1900** Ethiopia annexes much Somali territory in various expeditions.
**1897—1901** Sudanese mutiny in Uganda.

**1898** 11 Jan., M.C. Esterhazy acquitted of forging a document in the Dreyfus case: Emile Zola publishes *J'accuse*. Feb., Joseph Chamberlain proposes Anglo-German alliance. 13 May, Joseph Chamberlain's Birmingham speech advocating friendship with Germany and US against Russia. June, Brisson forms ministry in France. Luigi Pelloux forms ministry in Italy.

**1898** Feb., international commission appointed for control of Greek finances. 28 March, first German Naval Act passed. 30 Apr., German Navy League founded by von Tirpitz. Apr.—May, riots in Italy. 10 Sept., Empress Elizabeth of Austria assassinated at Geneva. 26 Nov., Turkey evacuates Crete.

**1898** Jan., British operations against Ngoni in N Rhodesia. 10 July, General Marchand occupies Fashoda. 30 Aug., secret Anglo-German agreement on Portuguese African territories. 2 Sept., Anglo-Egyptian force takes Omdurman: end of Mahdist revolt. Legislative Council with official and elected members in S Rhodesia. Anglo-Portuguese expedition against Yao chief Mataka.

## THE EAST & AUSTRALASIA

**1896** 1 July, Federation of Malay States (Negri Sembilan, Pahang, Perak and Selangor) inaugurated: capital, Kuala Lumpur, Selangor: Resident-General for Federation answerable to Governor of Singapore. Nasir al-Din, Shah of Persia, assassinated: succ. Muzaffar al-Din (–1906). Perso-Baluch Boundary Commission. Plague and famine in India. 20 Aug., general rebellion begun in Philippine Is. 30 Sept., secret treaty between China and Russia on Manchuria. First rubber plantation in Malaya. 42,000 Maoris in New Zealand.
**1896–1914** Butter production in New Zealand rises by nearly 500%; cheese by over 1,000%.
**1897** July, first Conference of Rulers of the Federated Malay States at Kuala Kangsar. Aug., peace restored in the Philippines by treaty between Spain and rebels. 20 Oct., King of Korea proclaims himself Emperor. German Vice-Consulate opened in Bushire. General rising of Pathans on India border: quelled by Sir Bruce Lockhart. Anglo-Siamese agreement on frontiers of Siam and Malaya. Australian Federal Council meets in Hobart. Australian Federal Convention held in Adelaide.

**1898** 1 May, naval battle between Spain and USA off Manila: Filipinos rise in favour of US: 23 June, Filipino revolutionary government proclaimed: 13 Aug., US troops take Manila. Belgian administration of Persian customs begun. Burmese railway extended. Kang Yo-wei again asks Chinese Emperor for reforms: army, communications, education, law and trade reorganized in China: reforms terminated by imprisonment of Emperor (–1909)

## THE AMERICAS

**1896** 1 May–8 July, Sir Charles Tupper, Canadian Prime Minister. 11 July–1911 6 Oct., Sir Wilfrid Laurier, Canadian Prime Minister. Severe economic recession in US: many businesses collapse. Gold struck on R. Klondike, Canada. Royal commission on sugar in the W Indies.

**1897** More than half of population of Havana Province (101,000) d. in concentration camps.
**1897–1901** William McKinley (Rep.), President of US.

**1898** 15 Feb., USN *Maine* blown up in Havana Harbour by persons unknown. 24 Apr., US declares war on Spain. 1 May, US fleet destroys Spanish fleet at Manila. 3 July, US defeats Spain at Santiago. 25 July, US invades Puerto Rico. 12 Nov., Earl of Minto, Governor-General of Canada (–1904). 10 Dec., treaty of Paris between Spain and US: Spain cedes Puerto Rico, Guam and the Philippines to US: Cuba temporarily in US custody.

## RELIGION & CULTURE

**1896** First electric submarine constructed in France. First modern Olympic Games held in Athens. Oil production begun in Borneo. Theodor Herzl: *The Jewish State* (pamphlet).
**1896–1913** Alfred Austin, English poet laureate.
**1896–** John Dos Passos, American author.
**1896–** Trygve Haivdan Lie, Norwegian statesman.
**1896–** Sir Oswald Mosley, British Fascist politician.
**1896–1974** Dom David Knowles, OSB, historian.

**1897** *Revue de Sociologie* founded by Durkheim. Wireless Telegraph Co. formed by Marconi. Tate Gallery opened in London. International Jewish Congress held at Basle: Zionism formally established. First aircraft flight made by Clément Ader. Helium discovered by Ramsay. Malarial bacillus discovered by Sir Ronald Ross. Monotype type-setting machine invented.
**1897–1960** Aneurin Bevan, Labour politician.
**1897–1967** Sir John Cockcroft, atomic physicist.
**1897–1977** Anthony Eden, Earl of Avon, British Prime Minister.
**1897–1975** Ian Fraser, Lord Fraser of Lonsdale, worker for the blind and statesman.
**1897–** Pope Paul VI.
**1897–1976** Stuart Cloete, South African novelist.
**1897–1974** Haj Amin al-Husaini, Mufti of Jerusalem.
**1897–1975** Thorton Wilder, novelist.

**1898** Bilingualism established in Belgium. The airship invented by Count Ferdinand von Zeppelin. Irish Agrarian League founded. *Action Française* (newspaper) founded. Radium and polonium discovered by Pierre and Marie Curie. Paris *Métro* begun.
**1898–1936** García Lorca, Spanish poet and dramatist.
**1898–1937** George Gershwin, American composer.
**1898–** Golda Meir, Prime Minister of Israel.

## WESTERN & NORTHERN EUROPE

## CENTRAL & SOUTHERN EUROPE

## AFRICA

**1898** 30 July, Théophile Delcassé becomes Foreign Secretary of France (−1905). 12 Aug., County Councils established in Ireland by Irish Local Government Act. 30 Aug., Col. Henry admits forging a document in the Dreyfus case. Secret Anglo-German agreement on Portuguese colonies. 26 Nov., commercial treaty between France and Italy. 10 Dec., treaty of Paris: Spain cedes Philippines to USA. Imperial Department of Tropical Agriculture established.
**1898 ff.** Frequent outbreaks of pillage by peasants in Russia.
**1899** 15 Feb., Russia terminates liberties of Finland. 16 Feb., President Faure of France d.: 18 Feb., succ. Émile Loubet (−1906). 13 May−29 July, first Peace Conference at the Hague: Geneva Convention extended to poison gas, naval warfare and explosive bullets: permanent Court of Arbitration agreed. 22 June, René Waldeck-Rousseau forms government in France. 9 Aug., London Borough Councils set up. Franco-Russian alliance modified secretly. Aug.−Sept., Dreyfus re-tried. 9 Sept., Dreyfus found guilty 'with extenuated circumstances'. 19 Sept., Dreyfus granted a presidential pardon. 14 Oct., secret treaty of Windsor between Britain and Portugal renews treaties of 1642 and 1661. 14 Nov and 2 Dec., agreements between Germany, UK and USA on Samoa. 19-25 Nov., William II of Germany and von Bülow visit Britain: Anglo-German alliance discussed. UK Enabling Act allows loans to colonies at low rates.
**1900** 27 Feb., (British) Labour Party founded: Ramsay MacDonald, first secretary. 16 Oct., Conservatives win Khaki election in Britain. Anglo-German agreement on the Yangtze. Town Council (Scotland) Act reforms Scottish local government.

**1899** March, Prince George of Greece appointed High Commissioner in Crete. 11 Dec., Germany rejects alliance with Britain.

**1900** 14 July, second German Navy Act. 29 July, Humbert of Italy assassinated: succ. Victor Emmanuel III (−1946). 6 Oct., Kruger flees to Europe: refused audience by Kaiser. 17 Oct., Prince Bernhard von Bülow appointed Chancellor of Germany (−1909). 14-16 Dec., secret agreement between France and Italy on Morocco and Tripolitania.

**1899** 19 Jan., Anglo-Egyptian Condominium instituted in the Sudan (−1956). 21 March, Anglo-French convention ends Fashoda crisis. Sept., Muhammad b. Abdallah (the 'Mad Mullah') proclaims himself Mahdi in Somalia: raids British and Italian Somaliland (−1920). 12 Oct.−1902 31 May, Boer War. Nov., Boers take Ladysmith; 11 Dec., repulse British at Magersfontein; 15 Dec., at Colenso.

**1900** 1 Jan., British Protectorate of N Nigeria established: Sir F.D. Lugard, High Commissioner (−1907): policy of Indirect Rule, later main theme of British colonial government, inaugurated. 10 Jan., Lord Roberts, C.-in-C. in SA, with Lord Kitchener as Chief of Staff. 28 Feb., Redvers Buller relieves Ladysmith. 13 March, Roberts takes Bloemfontein. 17 May, relief of Mafeking. 24 May, Britain annexes OFS. 26 June, British Toro and Buganda agreements. 31 Aug., Johannesburg occupied. Aug. (−1902) Boers steadily gathered into concentration camps. 5 Sept., Chad proclaimed a French military protectorate. 25 Oct., Britain annexes Transvaal. French extend territory in Algeria.
**1900−4** Four British expeditions against the 'Mad Mullah' in Somaliland.

| THE EAST & AUSTRALASIA | THE AMERICAS | RELIGION & CULTURE |
|---|---|---|

by Empress Tzu Hsi: reformers killed. Russia leases Port Arthur and tip of Liaotung peninsula from China: railway built from Harbin to Port Arthur and Dalny (Dairen), ice-free ports. Australian Federal Conventions held in Sydney and Melbourne. Trades and Labour Conference set up in New Zealand to promote Labour Party. Uninterrupted ninety-hour session in the New Zealand Parliament on old age pensions. Wilhelm II visits Jerusalem.
**1898—1909** Empress Tzu Hsi in control of China: reactionary rule.
**1899** 21 Jan., Filipino congress at Malolos proclaims constitution of Filipino Republic. 4 Feb., US at war with Filipino Republic (—1902). 22 Feb., Manila burnt. Famine in India: Scott-Moncrieff Commission to extend irrigation. Japanese in Indonesia granted equality of status with Europeans. Farmers' Union formed in New Zealand.
**1899—1905** Lord (later Marquess of) Curzon, Viceroy of India.

**1898** 200,000 Spanish troops in Cuba. Hawaii annexed by US. Erdman Act for the arbitration of railwaymen's disputes in US.
**1898 and 1899** Serious hurricanes in the W Indies.
**1898—1902** Cuba under US military government. Manoel de Campos Salles, President of Brazil.
**1898—1920** Manuel Estrada Cabrera, dictator of Guatemala.

**1899** 23 May, Cipriano Castro seizes Venezuela by force: president until 1908. US arbitrates on border between Argentina and Chile. José Manuel Pando, President of Bolivia (—1904): capital transferred from Sucre to La Paz. Canadian contingent of 1,000 joins British in Boer war. Banana companies join to form United Fruit Co. of Boston. Population of Cuba 1.57m.

**1899** Pope Leo XIII: *Testem benevolentiae,* condemns false opinions, including 'Americanism'. Board of Education established for England and Wales. John Rylands Library opened in Manchester. Schools of Tropical Medicine set up in Liverpool and London. International Women's Congress held in London. Aspirin invented. Sound first recorded magnetically.
**1899—1960** Nevil Shute, novelist.
**1899—** Erich Kästner, German author.
**1899—1974** Eric Linklater; novelist.

**1900** July, Commonwealth of Australia Constitution Act. Boxer rising: Chinese government diverts rising against foreigners: international army sent to capture Peking: China compelled to pay indemnities (—1940s). Japanese troops play conspicuous part in rescuing legations during Boxer Rising. Japanese imperial ordinance requires Ministries of War and Navy to be filled by generals and admirals on active list: beginning of military domination of Japan. *c.* 25,000 miles of railways in India.
**1900—10** Japanese population rises from 44m. to 50m.

**1900** 14 March, US adopts gold standard. New Liberal Party founded in Mexico. Brazil producing most of the world's rubber. US the largest buyer of Brazilian products. 278 refrigerator ships in service between Argentina and Britain. 10,269 miles of railway in Argentina. Population of Mexico 13.6m., of whom one-sixth literate.

**1900** José Enrique Rodó: *Ariel* stimulates anti-US feeling among S American intellectuals. Scottish Free Church joins United Presbyterian Church. 2 July, first flight by Zeppelin airship. Max Planck evolves *quantum* theory. Uranium first isolated by W. Crookes. General Federation of Trade Unions founded. Universal Exhibition in Paris. Magnetic tape invented. Browning revolver invented. The *Daily Express* founded. Institute of Medical Research set up in Kuala Lumpur. Abbey of the Dormition, Jerusalem, begun.
**1900—44** Antoine de Saint-Exupéry, novelist.
**1900—** Alan Busch, musician.
**1900—** Earl Mountbatten, British admiral and statesman.
**1900—** Adlai Stevenson, American politician (Dem.).
**1900—** Earl Mountbatten of Burma, British admiral and statesman.

| WESTERN & NORTHERN EUROPE | CENTRAL & SOUTHERN EUROPE | AFRICA |
|---|---|---|

**1901** 19–30 Jan., Kaiser Wilhelm II visits England: abortive negotiations for an alliance follow (–27 Dec.). 22 Jan., Queen Victoria d.: succ. Edward VII (–1910). 27 Feb., Russian Minister of Education Bogolepov assassinated. 22 July, Taff Vale case: Law Lords hold that the Taff Vale Railway Co. may sue for loss of receipts caused by a strike. Sept., further visit of the Tsar and Tsarina to France to confirm treaty. 8 Sept., Hendrik Verwoerd b. near Rotterdam. Social Revolutionary Party formed in Russia.

**1901** Catalan separatists (regionalists) elected to Spanish *Cortes*. Labour riots in Spain.

**1901** 1 Apr., status of slavery abolish abolished in Nigeria. 20 July, Morocco grants France control of frontier police. Aug., Ankole included in Uganda. 25 Sept., Ashanti Kingdom annexed to Gold Coast Colony. Kitchener uses scorched earth policy against Boers.

**1902** 15 Apr., Russian Minister of the Interior Sipiaguine assassinated: revolt of peasants put down by Plehve. 2 June, R.Waldeck-Rousseau, Prime Minister of France, resigns: succ. by anti-clerical ministry led by E.Combes. 30 June-11 Aug., Colonial Conference in London institutes imperial preference. 12 July, Lord Salisbury retires: Arthur James Balfour (later Earl of Balfour), Prime Minister (–1905). 18 Dec., Education Act extends primary education in England and Wales. President of France visits Russia and Denmark.

**1902** May, Alfonso XIII of Spain declared of age. 10 May, Portugal bankrupt. 28 June, Triple Alliance renewed. 30 June, secret Franco-Italian treaty of neutrality. 25 Dec., Germany introduces protectionist tariff.

**1902** Jan., first political meeting of white settlers in Kenya forms Colonists' Association. Feb., Bauchi taken by British: Bornu submits. 1 Apr., Eastern Province of Uganda transferred to Kenya. 31 May, Peace of Vereeniging ends Boer War: Britain promises representative government and £3m. for restocking farms. Cecil Rhodes d. 27 Sept., Kenya Crown Land Ordinance inaugurates white settlement of the Highlands. Dec., Aswan Dam opened.

**1903** Irish Land Act. May, Edward VII of England pays official visit to France. Sir Roger Casement's report on atrocities in CFS published. 6-9 July, President Émile Loubet of France visits London. Oct., Women's Social and Political Union founded by Mrs. Emmeline Pankhurst. Icelandic constitution amended: responsible government granted by Denmark.

**1903** 21 Feb., Austro-Russian negotiations with Turkey on Macedonia. 5 May, Turkey grants Germany Baghdad Railway concession. 11 June, Alexander of Serbia murdered with his wife: succ. Peter Kara Georgevitch (–1921). 7 July, general rising in Macedonia. 31 Aug., Edward VII visits Vienna. 29 Sept., Emperors of Austria and Russia meet at Mürzsteg: 1-3 Oct., agreement reached on Macedonia.

**1903** Feb., Joseph Chamberlain, Colonial Secretary, visits SA: policy of conciliating Boers. 3 Feb., Kano submits to Britain. 15 March, British occupation of N Nigeria completed. June, Lord Delamere settles permanently in Kenya: forms Kenya Planters and Farmers Association. Afrikaner Bond becomes the South African Party. Sultan of Morocco borrows £800,000 from Britain, France and Spain. J.Biker, Governor of Portuguese Guinea, exposes contract labour scandal in Angola.
**1903–10** CFS railway system built.
**1903–11** Kamerun railway built.

## THE EAST & AUSTRALASIA

**1901** 1 Jan., Commonwealth of Australia comes formally into being. May, Duke of Cornwall (later King George V) opens first Australian Federal Parliament. 4 July, William H. Taft, first US civil governor of the Philippines, inaugurated (–1904). 7 Sept., Peace of Peking between China and the Great Powers. 1 Oct., Abd al-Rahman, Amir of Afghanistan, d.: succ. Habiballah Khan (–1919). Sixty-year oil concession granted by Persia to D'Arcy, founder of Anglo-Persian Oil Co. Population of India c. 294m. Following official discouragement, Chinese in Australia dwindle to 32,000. Cook Is. annexed by New Zealand. Socialist Party formed in New Zealand. Japanese 'Black Dragon Society', or 'Society of the River Amur', extreme nationalist anti-Russian group, founded. Population of Singapore 228,555, of whom 164,000 Chinese.
**1901–3** Lord Hopetoun (later Marquess of Linlithgow), first Governor-General of Australia. Edmund Barton, first Federal Prime Minister of Australia.
**1902** 30 Jan., Anglo-Japanese alliance. 8 Apr., Russo-Chinese convention on Manchuria. 20 Apr., Filipino General Zamora surrenders to US troops. Lord Kitchener appointed Commander-in-Chief in India. Empress Tzu Hsi returns to Peking. Australian Manufacturers' Encouragement Act sets up steel industry.
**1902–5** Lord Forster, Governor-General of Australia.

**1903** First elections for city councils in Dutch EI. Papua Act: Papua transferred from Britain to Australia. King Edward VII holds *durbar* as Emperor in Delhi. Tukoji Rao Holkar of Indore deposed for murder. Berar taken over by Britain on 'perpetual lease'.
**1903–4** Colonel F.E. Younghusband's mission to Tibet. Alfred Deakin, Federal Prime Minister of Australia (first term). Lord Tennyson, Governor-General of Australia.
**1903–5** Second Sistan Boundary Arbitration Commission.

## THE AMERICAS

**1901** June, constitution adopted by Cuban Congress, with certain powers reserved to US (Platt Amendment). 14 Sept., President William McKinley assassinated: succ., his Vice-President, Theodore Roosevelt (Rep.)(–1909). 18 Nov., Anglo-US (Hay-Paunceforte) treaty provides for construction of Panama Canal, and ending of British treaty rights in the area. US Steel Corporation founded by J.P.Morgan with capital of $1,400m. Mexico becomes a principal exporter of petroleum: 10,000 barrels exported. Canadian population 5.37m.

**1902** 19 Dec., Britain, Germany and Italy blockade Venezuelan coast to procure payment of debts. Reclamation Act provides for large-scale irrigation projects in US. Catastrophic earthquake in Martinique, destroying town of St Pierre. Argentina and Chile agree on frontier.
**1902–6** Francisco de Paulo Rodrigues Alves, President of Brazil. Estrada Palma, President of Cuba.

**1903** 19 Jan., first radio message transmitted from US to England. 3 Nov., US warship *Nashville* arrives at Colón, Colombia. President Theodore Roosevelt requests permission of Colombia to construct Panama Canal: concession refused: 6 Nov., uprising in Panama City: independent republic proclaimed: Panama independent of Colombia as a US protectorate. Elkins Act requires US railways to publish rates. Trades and Labour Congress re-organized in Canada. Part of Bolivia ceded to Brazil.
**1903–7** José Batlle, President of Uruguay: democratic constitutionalist on Swiss model.

## RELIGION & CULTURE

**1901** G.Marconi transmits first trans-Atlantic radio message. Nobel prizes first given. Adrenalin first manufactured. Jewish National Fund established.
**1901–66** Walt Disney, cinema dramatist.
**1901–** Margaret Mead, social anthropologist.
**1901–** Edmund Rubbra, composer.

**1902** 18 Dec., English Education Act: denominational schools brought into state system. Armenian Church persecuted in Russia. Order of Merit instituted by King Edward VII. The *Times Literary Supplement* founded. Hormones discovered by W. Bayliss and E. Starling. Peking University founded. Gordon Memorial College (now Khartoum University) opened.
**1902–** R.A.Butler, Lord Butler, politician.
**1902–** Lord David Cecil, author.
**1902–** Henry Cabot Lodge, American politician.
**1902–** John Steinbeck, novelist.
**1902–** William Walton, composer.
**1903** 18 March, religious orders dissolved in France. Nov., congress of Russian socialists held in London: breach between Bolsheviks and Mencheviks. Dec., Pope Pius X condemns A.Loisy for heresy. 17 Dec., first powered aircraft flown by Wright brothers at Kitty Hawk, North Carolina. First Ford motor factories established. First taxis appear in London. 20 m.p.h. speed limit introduced for cars in Britain. Krupp's arms factory founded at Essen. Electrocardiography invented. Lord Curzon reforms Indian education: educational controversy with Congress (–1904). Free places granted in New Zealand secondary schools.
**1903–14** St Pius X (Sarto), Pope.
**1903–66** Evelyn Waugh, novelist.
**1903–73** Louis S.B.Leakey, prehistoric archaeologist.

1903–1906

WESTERN &
NORTHERN EUROPE

CENTRAL &
SOUTHERN EUROPE

AFRICA

**1904** 8 Apr., *Entente Cordiale* between Britain and France. 28 July, Russian Minister of the Interior Plehve assassinated. 21 Oct., Dogger Bank incident between Russia and Britain. Crown Prince Alexis of Russia, a haemophiliac, b. Russian Trans-Siberian Railway completed. First Algerians arrive in France to work in Marseilles sugar refineries.

**1904** Apr., President Loubet visits Rome. Turco-Bulgarian agreement on Macedonia. 28 July, German commercial treaties with Austro-Hungary, Belgium, Sweden and Switzerland. Sept., general strike in Italy. 3 Oct., Franco-Spanish agreement on Morocco.

**1904** 22 Feb.–1908 2 Feb., Dr. L.S. Jameson, Prime Minister of Cape Colony. Feb., Chinese coolie labour recruited for Transvaal. Apr., special regime created for Tangier. 18 May, Perdicaris incident: British and US fleets sent to Tangier. 3 Oct.–1908, rising of Herero and Hottentots in German SWA. 18 Oct., French territory of Haut-Sénégal-Niger constituted. Dar es Salaam to Morogoro railway built. German Agricultural Exhibition in Dar es Salaam. First power gin built in Kampala. Famine in N Nigeria. **1904–5** Royal Commission of Inquiry sent to CFS.

**1905** 17 Feb., Grand Duke Serge, Governor of Moscow, assassinated in the Kremlin. 30 Apr., Franco-British military convention. 14 June, mutiny of the crew of the *Potemkin* in Odessa harbour. 27 Sept., Norway becomes independent of Sweden. 2-18 Oct., newspaper strike in Russia, followed by railway strike for two days: *soviet* (committee) of workers formed in St Petersbourg. 17 Oct., official manifesto promising civil liberty and parliamentary institutions published in Russia. 16 Nov., Witte appointed Prime Minister of Russia. 18 Nov., Haakon VII elected King of Norway (–1957). 28 Nov., Sinn Fein Party founded in Dublin. 5 Dec., all 230 members of the St Petersbourg Soviet arrested. 5 Dec.–1908, Sir Henry Campbell-Bannerman, Prime Minister. 15 Dec., abortive rising of workers in Moscow put down by a bombardment.

**1905** 30 March, Greeks revolt against Turks in Crete. 23-24 July, treaty of Björkö between Emperors of Germany and Russia. German commercial treaties with Bulgaria and Ethiopia. **1905–7** Tariff war between Austria and Serbia.

**1905** Botha forms *Het Volk* organization to agitate for responsible government in Transvaal. 31 March, Emperor William II visits Tangier. 19 May, Acting Provincial Commissioner in Ankole speared to death. May, Transvaal granted constitution: regarded by Botha as inadequate. Sept., Bp Cassian Spiess murdered in Maji-Maji uprising. Nov. Royal Commission of Inquiry in CFS excuses Léopold II. Risings in French Guinea. French Mauritania re-organized. Nandi Field Force raised to control Nandi tribe. Bank of Ethic founded. **1905–7** Maji-Maji rebellion in German EA: southern area chiefly affected.

**1906** 12 Jan., Liberal landslide in British general election: Sir Henry Campbell-Bannerman, Prime Minister (–1908). 5 May, Witte resigns: succ. Goremykin. 6 May, Russian constitution published. 10 May, first meeting of the Duma. 9 July, Duma finds doors closed to prevent its assembly. Goremykin resigns: Stolypin succ. as Prime Minister.

**1906** 1 Jan., Count Helmuth von Moltke appointed Chief of German General Staff. 16 Jan.–7 Apr., Algeciras Conference: Spain and France agree on spheres of interest in Morocco. 30 May, Giovanni Giolitti, Prime Minister of Italy (–1909). 5 June, third German Navy Act. 15 Aug., Edward VII holds conversations with the Kaiser at Cronberg.

**1906** 1 May, Colony and Protectorate of S Nigeria instituted. 4 July, Britain, France and Italy guarantee independence of Ethiopia. Dinshaway incident: affray between British shooting party and Egyptian villagers. Risings of Abinsi and Satiru, Nigeria. Winston Churchill visits EA Protectorate. **1906–10** Saad Zaghlul, Egyptian Minister of Education.

| THE EAST & AUSTRALASIA | THE AMERICAS | RELIGION & CULTURE |
|---|---|---|

**1903–** Lennox Berkeley, composer.
**1903–** Sir Alexander Frederic (Alec) Douglas-Home, Conservative politician.

**1904** 6 Feb.–1905, Russo-Japanese war: Japan fearful of Russian hegemony in Manchuria and Korea: 8/9 Feb., three Russian warships sunk: 10 Feb., Japan officially declares war; Dec., Port Arthur falls to the Japanese. 7 Sept., treaty between UK and Tibet: British trade mission established at Gyantse (–1947). Lord Curzon appointed for a second term. Some modest reforms attempted in China. Korea forced to accept Japanese financial and diplomatic advisers. Malaya producing 40,000 tons of tin annually, half of world output. John Christian Watson, Federal Prime Minister of Australia.
**1904–5** George Houston Reid, Federal Prime Minister of Australia.
**1904–8** Lord Northcote, Governor-General of Australia.
**1905** 1 Jan., Russia surrenders Port Arthur to Japan. 1-9 March, Japanese defeat Russians on land at Mukden. 21 March, Anglo-Afghan treaty. May, Russian Baltic fleet arrives off Japan; 27 May, battle of Tsushima, Japanese totally destroy Russian fleet: Japan loses three torpedo boats. Aug., Lord Curzon resigns following quarrel with Lord Kitchener. 12 Aug., Anglo-Japanese treaty of alliance renewed. 5 Sept., Treaty of Portsmouth (New Hampshire, USA) between Japan and Russia: Japan gains Korea and Russian railway systems and territories on mainland China S of Ghangchun, and half Sakhalin Is. 18 Nov., Korea made a Japanese protectorate. Indian National Congress gains support of mass of middle class in India. Ceylon Social Reform Society, Ceylonese nationalist group, formed.
**1905–8** Alfred Deakin, Federal Prime Minister of Australia (second term).
**1905–10** Earl of Minto, Governor-General and Viceroy of India.
**1906** 5 Aug., Persian constitution promulgated. Oct., first National Assembly opened in Teheran. All India Moslem League founded in India by the Agha Khan: representative government demanded with separate electorates for Muslims. Anglo-Turkish dispute on Gulf of Aqaba. 274 registered trade unions in New Zealand.

**1904** 4 July, construction of Panama Canal begun. 10 Dec., Earl Grey, Governor-General of Canada (–1911). President Theodore Roosevelt enunciates 'Roosevelt Corollary' in message to Congress: Monroe Doctrine to be understood that ill-doing or disorder in the W hemisphere may force US to take police action. US establishes receivership for debts of Santo Domingo. Arica, Chile, made a free port for Bolivia: Chile undertakes to build railway from Arica to La Paz.
**1904–7** Abortive civil war in Uruguay.
**1904–9** Rafael Reyes, President and Conservative dictator of Colombia.

**1905** Industrial Workers of the World organization founded in US.
**1905–30** US intervenes in Dominican Republic to prevent European countries from collecting debts by armed force.

**1906** Hepburn Act gives US Inter-State Commerce Commission to regulate railway charges. US Pure Food and Drugs Act. Earthquake in Costa Rica. Earthquake at Valparaiso. Following revolution in Cuba, US installs Charles Magoon as governor (–1909).
**1906–9** Affonso Penna, President of Brazil.

**1904** 8 March, Jesuits permitted to return to Germany. 17 May, breach between France and the Vatican. 7 July, religious orders in France forbidden to teach. 18 Nov., E.Combes introduces bill to separate Church and State in France. Workers' Educational Association founded in England. The *Daily Mirror* founded. Rolls-Royce Co. founded. Universities Act remodels Indian universities: post-graduate studies initiated in Calcutta.
**1904–** Nnamdi Azikiwe, Nigerian statesman.
**1904–** Ralph Bunche, US diplomatist.
**1904–** Christopher William Bradshaw Isherwood, writer.
**1904–** Graham Greene, novelist.
**1904–** Alexei Nikolaevich Kosygin, Russian politician.
**1905** 3 March, religious reforms in Russia promised by Tsar Nicolas II. 9 Dec., French law decrees separation of Church and State. Baptist World Alliance founded in London. A.Einstein evolves theory of relativity. The zip fastener invented. First motor buses in London. Automobile Association founded. Singapore Medical School founded.
**1905–61** Dag Hammarskjöld, Swedish statesman.
**1905–** Patrick, Lord Devlin, jurist.
**1905–** Arthur Koestler, novelist.
**1905–** C.P. Snow, Lord Snow, novelist.
**1905–10** Deutsch-Axum-Expedition excavates Axum.

**1906** Feb., Pope Pius X: encyclical *Vehementer nos* condemns separation of Church and State in France. CFS–Vatican agreement that each mission will provide a school. Italian *Confederazione Generale del Lavoro* founded. Drainage of Zuider Zee begun. Simplon tunnel opened.
**1906–63** Hugh Todd Naylor Gaitskell, Labour politician.

| WESTERN & NORTHERN EUROPE | CENTRAL & SOUTHERN EUROPE | AFRICA |
|---|---|---|

**1906** 12 July, Dreyfus found innocent after a further trial. 12 Aug., thirty persons killed by mob in Prime Minister Stolypin's house. Oct., Georges Clemenceau, Prime Minister of France (−1909). 9 Nov., Imperial Russian decree granting communal land for use of rich peasants. 13 Dec., Trade Disputes Act reverses Taff Vale judgement. Anglo-Italian agreement on Ethiopia.
**1906−13** Armand Fallières, President of France.
**1907** Feb.−Apr., Edward VII visits Paris, Madrid and Rome. 5 March, second Duma meets. 14 June, female suffrage introduced in Norway. 15 June−18 Oct., peace conference at the Hague. 16 June, second Duma dissolved. June, 200,000 roubles taken by Social Democrats from State Bank at Tiflis: organized by Djougachvili, later known as Stalin. 31 Aug., Anglo-Russian agreement on Asia: Russia joins the *Entente*. 14 Nov., third Duma meets (−1912). 8 Dec., Oscar II of Sweden d.: succ. Gustav V (− (−1950).

**1906** 13 Dec., Reichstag dissolved following opposition to colonial war budget. Committee of Union and Progress founded at Salonica by the 'Young Turks'.
**1906−8** João Franco, dictator of Portugal.

**1907** 1 Jan., universal suffrage introduced in Austria. March, Rumania puts down revolt in Moldavia. 16 May, Anglo-Spanish agreement on the Mediterranean. July, Triple Alliance renewed for six years. 3-6 Aug., Emperors of Germany and Russia meet at Swinemünde. Franco dismisses the Portuguese *Cortes*.

**1906−12** Baron F. von Rechenburg, Governor of German EA: first governor to speak Swahili: develops a 'plantation colony'.

**1907** 22 March, French physician murdered at Marrakesh. 23 May, Legislative Council instituted in Mozambique. 4 Aug., French bombard Casablanca: Casablanca and Rabat occupied. Aug., first Kenya Legislative Council meets. 21 Sept., rising in German SWA suppressed. 7 Dec., first National Congress in Egypt. Emperor Menelik of Ethiopia paralysed: Lijj Iyasu nominated as successor: Ras Tasamma, regent. Mahatma Gandhi organizes first passive resistance among Transvaal Indians. Unofficial majority in S Rhodesian Legislative Council.
**1907−14** Lagos harbour improved for ocean-going vessels.

**1908** 8 Apr., Sir Henry Campbell-Bannerman resigns: succ. Herbert Henry Asquith (−1916). June, Edward VII of England visits France, Sweden and Russia. 20 Aug.−9 Sept., Belgian Parliament votes annexation of CFS. 28 Oct., *Daily Telegraph* publishes interview with William II. Old Age Pensions introduced in Britain.

**1908** 28 Jan., revolution in Portugal foiled: martial law proclaimed: 1 Feb., Charles of Portugal and his eldest son assassinated: succ. Manuel II (−1910): Franco dismissed. March, Prussian Expropriation Act deprives many Poles of their lands. 14 June, fourth German Navy Act. 24 July, Turkish constitution restored: Parliament resuscitated, following Young Turk rising (6 July). 5 Oct., Ferdinand I proclaimed Tsar of Bulgaria (−1918). Austria annexes Bosnia and Herzogovina. 12 Oct., Crete united with Greece. 10-11 Nov., Reichstag debate on *Daily Telegraph* interview worsens Anglo-German relations. 2 Dec., rebellion in Bohemia. 17 Dec., Turkish Parliament meets, with Young Turk majority.

**1908** March, Lord Delamere leads settler demonstration outside Government House, Nairobi, protesting against labour policy. 9 Apr., Comoro Is. annexed to Madagascar. 26 June, *Afrique Equatoriale Française* established, comprising all French CA colonies. 20 Aug., Léopold II hands over CFS to Belgium. 25 Sept., Casablanca incident: German deserters from French Foreign Legion taken by force from German consular official. J.C.Smuts proposes union of SA and S Rhodesia. Slavery abolished in S Tomé and Principé.
**1908−9** Convention in Durban and then Cape Town drafts constitution for a Union of SA.

**1909** 12 March, British Navy Bill. 29 Apr., Lloyd George presents 'People's Budget'. 24 July, Clemenceau resigns: Aristide Briand Prime Minister of France (−1911). 30 Nov., Lloyd George's 'People's Budget' rejected by the House of Lords: 2 Dec., Parliament dissolved. 17 Dec., Léopold II of Belgium d.: succ. Albert I (−1934).

**1909** 9 Feb., Franco-German agreement on Morocco. 28 Feb., Austro-Turkish agreement on Bosnia. 24 Apr., Abd al-Hamid II deposed and deported: succ. Muhammad V (−1918): real power in hands of Young Turk triumvirate: Enver Pasha, Prime Minister. 14 July, Bülow dismissed: succ. as Chancellor of

**1909** Jan., Native Courts proclamation in Uganda institutes Indirect Rule. 25 March, press censorship in Egypt to curb nationalists. Apr., Prince Albert of Belgium visits Belgian Congo: Jules Renkin, Minister for Belgian Congo, tours for four months. French occupy Wadai, Chad.

| THE EAST & AUSTRALASIA | THE AMERICAS | RELIGION & CULTURE |
|---|---|---|

**1906** Federated Malay States have 1600 miles of metalled roads and 270 miles unmetalled.
**1906—11** J.G.Ward, Prime Minister of New Zealand.

**1906—75** Dmitri Shostakovich, composer.

**1907** Anglo-Russian Convention recognizes China as suzerain of Tibet. Secret Russo-Japanese convention partitions Manchuria into spheres of influence. Korea made virtually a Japanese colony. Anglo-Russian agreement on spheres of influence in Persia. Lord Morley nominates two Indians to the India Council. Indian National Congress meets in Surat: clash between moderates and extremists. Amir Habibullah of Afghanistan visits India. Tata Iron and Steel Co. established at Jamshedpur, Bihar. First successful borings for oil made in Persia. New Zealand gains dominion status.
**1907—8** Movement to start Australian Navy.
**1907—9** Muhammad Ali, Shah of Persia.
**1908** 1 May, Hijaz Railway reaches Medina from Damascus. 23 June, *coup d'état* in Persia: Shah crushes National Assembly: revolution in Tabriz. 14 Nov., Emperor Te Tsung assassinated; 15 Nov., Empress Tzu Hsi d. Bal Gangadhar Tilak, Indian nationalist leader, imprisoned for six years for incitement to violence. *Budi Utomo*, intellectual nationalist movement, founded in Java. Dalai Lama visits Peking. Opinion shocked in Japan by parade in Tokyo of socialists and anarcho-syndicalists: repressive police action follows. Universal adult suffrage introduced in Australia.
**1908—9** Andrew Fisher, Federal Prime Minister of Australia (first term).
**1908—11** Lord Dudley, Governor-General of Australia.
**1909** March, Anglo-Siamese Treaty signed in Bangkok. July, Persian nationalists take Teheran: 16 July, Muhammad Ali Shah deposed: succ. Sultan Ahmad Shah (—1924). 25 Oct., Prince Ito of Japan murdered by a Korean: Japanese dictatorship follows in Korea. Indian Councils Act, commonly known as Morley-Minto reforms.

**1908** W.E.B.du Bois founds National Association for Advancement of Coloured Peoples (NAACP).
**1908—12** Augusto Leguía, President of Peru.
**1908—15** Orderly government wholly breaks down in Haiti.
**1908—18** Central American Court, for adjudicating disputes in that area.
**1908—35** Juan Vicente Gómez, dictator of Venezuela.

**1909** State of Delaware forbids employment of children under fourteen: other states follow.
**1909—11** Civil war in Honduras.
**1909—13** José Miguel Gómez, President of Cuba. William Howard Taft (Rep.), President of US.

**1907** 26 March, law on freedom of worship in France. 6 Sept., Pope Pius X: Encyclical *Pascendi Gregis* against Modernism. Boy Scouts founded. Shell Co. founded. School strike in Prussian Poland against Germanization. Education Dept. instituted in Zanzibar: Roman script used for writing Swahili in place of Arabic script. Colour photography invented by A.Lumière.
**1907—65** Louis MacNeice, author.
**1907—73** Wystan Hugh Auden, poet.
**1907—** Christopher Fry, dramatist.
**1907—** Alberto Moravia, Italian novelist.
**1907—** Eric Shipton, mountaineer.
**1907—** Sir Basil Spence, architect.
**1907—** Sir Frank Whittle, aeronautical engineer.

**1908** Ecclesiastical property in France distributed to administrative districts and secular works of charity. Federal Council of Churches founded in USA. Berlin Copyright Convention. National University of Ireland replaces Royal University of Ireland. National University, Cairo, founded. Olympic Games held in London. Pasteur Institute, Brazzaville, founded.
**1908—42** J.L. Garvin, editor of *The Observer*.
**1908—64** Ian Lancaster Fleming, novelist.
**1908—** Simone de Beauvoir, French author.
**1908—** Donald Bradman, cricketer.
**1908—** Sir Vivian Ernest Fuchs, explorer.
**1908—** Nelson Rockefeller, US Vice-President.

**1909** Apr., Beatification of Joan of Arc. 25 July, first aircraft crossing of the Channel made by Louis Blériot. The Girl Guides founded. R.E.Peary reaches the North Pole. The 'T' Ford constructed by Henry Ford. W.Cadbury: *Labour in Portuguese West Africa* causes boycott of São Tomé cocoa to be instituted. Swiss National Park founded.

1909–1912

WESTERN &
NORTHERN EUROPE

CENTRAL &
SOUTHERN EUROPE

AFRICA

| WESTERN & NORTHERN EUROPE | CENTRAL & SOUTHERN EUROPE | AFRICA |
|---|---|---|
| | Germany T. von Bethmann-Hollweg (–1917). 26 July–26 Sept., general strike in Barcelona with riots on account of troops being sent to Melilla. 2 Dec., Baron Sonnino Prime Minister of Italy (–1910). | **1909** Somalis reach R. Tana. Berber attacks on Melilla. A.M.Jivanjee, first Indian appointed to Kenya Legislative Council. |
| **1910** 15 Jan., Liberals return to power in Britain with reduced majority. Feb., Sir Edward (later Lord) Carson becomes leader of the Irish Unionist Party. 10 Feb., Swedish constitution revised. 28 Apr., Lloyd George's budget passed. 6 May, Edward VII d.: succ. George V (–1936). 6 July, Parliament Act, reducing powers of the House of Lords, passed. Dec., following elections, Liberals in Britain gain slight majority. | **1910** March, Luigi Luzzatti Prime Minister of Italy (–1911). Apr., Albanian revolt in Turkish army put down. July, treaty of commerce between Austria and Serbia. Aug., Republicans win Portuguese elections. 28 Aug., Montenegro proclaimed a kingdom under Nicholas I. 5 Oct., Manuel II of Portugal deposed: Democratic Republic proclaimed: Teófilo Braga, provisional President. 18 Oct., Eleutherios Venizelos Prime Minister of Greece (–1915). 4-5 Nov., Emperors of Germany and Russia meet at Potsdam. 9 Nov., financial agreement between Austria, Germany and Turkey on the Baghdad railway. | **1910** 20 Feb., Butros Ghali, only Coptic premier of Egypt, murdered. 24 May, L.S.Jameson founds Unionist Party in SA. 1 July, South Africa becomes a Dominion. Saad Zaghlul, Egyptian Minister of Justice. Convention of Associations set up by Kenya settlers. **1910–11** Portuguese operations against Kasanje and Mahungo: Lunda province occupied. |
| **1911** 4 May, first National Health Insurance Bill introduced in Britain by D.Lloyd George. 15 May, Parliament Act passed in Britain. 28 June, Joseph Cailloux, Prime Minister of France. Aug., dock strike in Britain. 31 Aug., military convention between France and Russia. 18 Sept., Stolypin assassinated; 19 Sept., Vladimir Kobovtsoff succ. as Prime Minister of Russia. 23 Oct., Winston Churchill becomes First Lord of the Admiralty. 4 Nov., Franco-German Convention on the French Congo, ceding part to Germany, in return for French freedom of action in Morocco. 21 Nov., suffragette riots in London. Communal peasant property in villages suppressed in Russia: distributed amongst 3m. peasant proprietors. General Joffre becomes Chief of Staff in France. | **1911** 24 Feb., German Army Act. 26 May, Germany grants constitution to Alsace-Lorraine. 18 Aug., Portuguese Constituent *Cortes* approves new constitution. 19 Aug., German-Russian agreement on the Baghdad railway. 29 Sept., Italy declares war on Turkey in order to seize Tripoli. 12 Dec., Canalejas, Spanish Prime Minister, assassinated. **1911–15** Dr Manuel de Arriaga, President of Portugal. | **1911** Apr., France takes Fez. June, Spain occupies Larache and Alcazarquivir. 1 July, German gunboat *Panther* arrives at Agadir: international tension created. 28 Sept., Italy and Turkey at war over Tripolitania. 5 Nov., Italy annexes Tripolitania and Cyrenaica. Ras Tasamma d.: Lijj Iyasu rules Ethiopia with a council. 'Police' and 'Government' chiefs instituted in Rwanda. **1911–14** Lord Kitchener, British Agent and Consul-General in Egypt. **1911–60** Sayyid Khalifa b. Harub, Sultan of Zanzibar, following abdication of Sayyid Ali because of increasing British influence. Zanzibar controlled by a British Resident (–1963). |
| **1912** 14 Jan., Raymond Poincaré, Prime Minister of France and Foreign Secretary (–1913). | **1912** 8-11 Feb., R.B.Haldane (later Lord Haldane), British Secretary of State for War, visits Berlin. | **1912** 30 March, French Protectorate of Morocco proclaimed: accepted by Maulai Hafiz of Morocco. |

## THE EAST & AUSTRALASIA

## THE AMERICAS

## RELIGION & CULTURE

**1909** Anglo-Persian Oil Co. founded. Federal Council established for Federated Malay States: includes four nominated unofficial members: Resident-General becomes Chief Secretary. Chinese force enters Tibet. Russia occupies Tabriz. First ship of Australian Navy ordered.
**1909–10** Alfred Deakin, Federal Prime Minister of Australia (third term).
**1909–11** Two year old Pu Yi Chinese Emperor, with throne-name Hsuan-tung.
**1910** Feb., Dalai Lama flees to Darjeeling. 4 July, Russo-Japanese agreement on Manchuria and Korea. 22 Aug., Japan annexes Korea (–1945). Lord (later Viscount) Hardinge, Governor-General and Viceroy of India. Zenith of rubber boom in Malaya. New constitution in Ceylon: legislative council instituted, with official majority of one. Trengganu and Perlis, Malaya, accept British protection. National Assembly, with nominated Upper House, and elected Lower House, convened in China. Risings in Yunnan province. First Labour Party formed in New Zealand.
**c. 1910** Burmese national feeling begins to re-form around Buddhism: U Thila and Ledi Sayadaw, prominent monks and holy men.
**1911** July, ex-Shah makes abortive effort to return. Disturbances on railway in W China, followed by revolt in Wuchang: 10 Nov., General Yuan Shih-kai made Prime Minister: revolutionaries demand a republic. 12 Dec., Delhi Durbar held by King George V. 18 Dec., republic refused in China: constitutional monarchy agreed. 29 Dec., revolutionaries in China set up provisional government at Nanking: Sun Yat-sen, President. American Financial Mission to Persia. The Dalai Lama returns to Lhasa. Hutuktu of Urga, Outer Mongolia, declares himself independent of China: Chinese expelled. *Sarekat Dagang Islam* movement founded in Java. Anglo-Japanese treaty of alliance again renewed, for ten years. Alleged anarchist plot to kill Japanese emperor: intense indignation against socialists. Commonwealth of Australia assumes control over Northern Territory of S Australia.
**1911–14** Lord Denman, Governor-General of Australia.
**1912** 12 Feb., Manchu government formally renounces throne of China: provisional republic of China declared.

**1910** 7 June, Francisco Madero, Liberal leader, enters Mexico City: Francisco de la Barra, President *ad int.* Sept., Emiliano Zapata conducting guerrilla operations in Mexico. R. Canadian Navy formed. Brazil producing nine-tenths of the world's rubber, and three-fourths of the world's coffee. US mining 500m. tons of coal a year.
**1910–30** Conservatives in power in Colombia.

**1911** 24 May, Porfirio Díaz driven from power in Mexico by mob. 10 Oct.–1920 July 10, Sir R.L. Borden, Canadian Prime Minister. 13 Oct., H.R.H. the Duke of Connaught Governor-General of Canada (–1916). 6 Nov., Francisco Madero, a Liberal, President of Mexico. Canadian population 7.2m. 13m. barrels of oil exported from Mexico. National Bank nationalized in Uruguay.
**1911–15** José Batlle y Ordóñez, second term as President of Uruguay: welfare state brought into being.

**1912** Light and power nationalized in Uruguay.

**c. 1909** Sixty-seven Catholic mission stations in German EA with 30,000 converts: seventy-three Protestant stations with 11,000 converts.
**1909–19** Nyabingi spirit cult gives trouble in Uganda.
**1909–** Senator Barry Goldwater, US politician.
**1909–** Dean Rusk, US politician.
**1909–** Stephen Spender, poet.
**1909–74** U Thant, Secretary-General of the UN.

**1910** Knossos, Crete, excavated by (Sir) Arthur Evans. Hanns Visscher, first Nigerian Director of Education, appointed. National University of Mexico re-established. Congo Museum, Tervueren, opened. Coptic Museum, Cairo, founded.
**c. 1910** Plastics invented.
**1910–** Pietro Annigoni, Italian painter.
**1910–** Jean Anouilh, French dramatist.
**1910–** John Hunt, Lord Hunt, mountaineer.

**1911** 21 Apr., Church and State separated in Portugal. 15 Dec., Roald Amundsen reaches S Pole. World Missionary Conference of Protestant churches held in Edinburgh: beginning of modern ecumenical movement. Copyright Act requires copies of all UK publications to be deposited in six copyright libraries in Britain.
**1911–** Hubert Humphrey, American politician.
**1911–74** Georges Pompidou, French President.

**1912** *Book of Common Prayer* of the Episcopal Church of Scotland revised.

| WESTERN &<br>NORTHERN EUROPE | CENTRAL &<br>SOUTHERN EUROPE | AFRICA |
|---|---|---|

**1912** 16 Jan. and 10 June, Commons pass Home Rule Bill for Ireland: 30 Jan. and 24 July, rejected by Lords. 26 Feb., miners begin strike in Britain. 15 Apr., the *Titanic* disaster. 23 May, dockers strike in London. 11 June, transport workers strike in Britain. 16 July, naval convention between France and Russia. 9-16 Aug., Poincaré visits St Petersbourg. 12 Aug., decree defines French citizenship in W Africa. Sept., Anglo-French naval convention. 18 Sept., anti-Home Rule demonstrations at Enniskillen. 28 Sept., Solemn Covenant signed by 200,000 Ulstermen to oppose Home Rule for Ireland. 20 Dec., peace conference in London between Turkey and her enemies. Strikers in Lena gold fields, Siberia, massacred. Fourth Duma elected.

**1912** 29 Feb., alliance between Bulgaria and Serbia. 18 Apr.–1 May, Turkey closes the Dardanelles. 4 May, Italy occupies Rhodes. 29 May, Bulgaria and Greece ally against Turkey. 17 Oct.–3 Dec., first Balkan War. 18 Oct., treaty of Lausanne between Italy and Turkey. 21 Oct., abortive monarchist rising in Portugal. 23-24 Oct., Serbia defeats the Turks at Koumanovo. 24 Oct., Bulgaria defeats Turks at Kirk-Kilisse; and, 3 Nov., Bourgas. 28 Oct., treaty of Ouchy between Italy and Turkey. 8 Nov., Greece takes Salonica from the Turks. 3 Dec., armistice between Turkey and her enemies. 5 Dec., Triple Alliance renewed.
**1912–13** Ludwig, Regent of Bavaria.

**1912** 28 Apr., General Lyautey made Resident-General of Morocco. June, J.C.Smuts becomes Finance Minister in SA. 18 Oct., first Peace of Lausanne: Libya and Tripolitania ceded by Turkey to Italy. 27 Nov., Franco Spanish convention defines respective zones in Morocco: Spanish zone to be governed by a Khalifa. 20 Dec., Botha cabinet reconstituted in SA: J.C.Smuts Finance and Defence Minister. Rising in Abeokuta. African National Council organized in SA. Tanga railway reaches Moshi.

**1913** 17 Jan., Poincaré elected French President (–1920). 21 Jan., Aristide Briand, Prime Minister of France (–1922). 22 Jan., peace treaty of London between Turkey and her enemies: *coup d'état* by the Young Turks: negotiations broken off. 28 March, conscription introduced in Belgium. 24 June–7 July, Poincaré visits England. 30 June, Germany enlarges her army. 7 Aug., French Army Act requires three years service. 5 Dec., Britain forbids sending arms to Ireland.

**1913** 3 Feb.–23 Apr., second Balkan War. 18 March, George I of Greece murdered. 26 March, Bulgaria takes Adrianople. 19 May–10 Aug., third Balkan War: Bulgaria at war with Greece, Serbia and Rumania: Turkey attacks Bulgaria. 30 May, Turkey agrees to Treaty of London. 1 June, treaty between Greece and Serbia. 17 July, Bulgaria sues for peace. 10 Aug., Treaty of Bucharest: Bulgaria required to disarm. 29 Sept., Peace Treaty between Bulgaria and Turkey.
**1913–18** Ludwig III, King of Bavaria.

**1913** 1 July, Zanzibar Protectorate put under control of the Colonial Office. 12 Dec., Emperor Menelik d.: Ras Mikael effective ruler of Ethiopia: Lijj Iyasu, Emperor (–1916). Maulai al-Mahdi, Khalifa in Spanish Moroccan Protectorate, takes up residence in Tetuan. Indirect Rule established in Gambia. Cape Federation of Industries founded. Cotton becomes Uganda's principal industry.
**1913–18** Bakongo rising against Portuguese.

**1914** 10 March, suffragettes riot in London. 10 May, Liberal Unionists unite with Conservatives in Britain. 15 June, Anglo-German agreement on Baghdad railway. 15-23 July, President Poincaré of France visits Russia. 26 July, rising against Britain in Dublin. 30 July, UK offers to mediate between Austria and Serbia. Jean Jaurès assassinated. 31 July, general mobilization in Russia. 2 Aug., German ultimatum sent to Belgium. 2 Aug., France mobilises. Germans enter Luxembourg and Lorraine. 3 Aug., Germany invades Belgium.

**1914** 10 March, Salandra, Prime Minister of Italy. 23 June, Kiel Canal enlargement opened. 28 June, Archduke Franz Ferdinand, Crown Prince of Austria, assassinated with his wife at Sarajevo by a Serb. 5-6 July, Germany promises Austria support in the event of hostilities with Serbia. 23 July, Austrian ultimatum to Peter I of Serbia, demanding suzerainty of his kingdom. 28 July, Austria declares war on Serbia. 28 or 29 July, Austria bombards Belgrade, Serbia. 31 July, Germany sends ultimatum to Russia, and to France.

**1914** 1 Jan., N and S Nigeria amalgamated. June, SA Indian Relief Act: Smuts-Gandhi agreement on Indian problems. 4 Aug., German cruisers bombard Bône and Philippeville. 8 Aug., British bombard Dar es Salaam. 8-10 Aug., Togo occupied by Anglo-French force. Aug., German troops penetrate Belgian Congo. SA campaign in German SWA begins. Aug.–Oct., Nigerian and French troops take Kamerun. 2 Sept., Convention of Lomé partitions Togo into British and French sectors. 27 Sept., allies occupy German SWA.

## THE EAST & AUSTRALASIA

**1912** 29 March, Russia bombards shrine of Imam Riza at Meshed. July, Emperor Meiji of Japan d.; succ. Taisho (–1926). Oct., Yuan Shih-kai elected President of China: separation of Tibet from China, demanded by Britain, rejected. Russia recognizes independence of Outer Mongolia by secret treaty. Delhi declared official capital of India. Lord Hardinge ignores his attempted assassination on his state entry into Delhi. Islington Commission on Public Services in India: G.K.Gokhale, nationalist leader, a member. Malayan Labour Code enacted: employers on estates obliged to provide scnools for workers' children. 80% of Malayan tin production under Chinese management. Executive Council instituted in Johore. Liberal land policy in New Zealand results in purchase and subdivision of 200 properties comprising 1,300,000 acres: enables 17,000 persons to be settled.
**1912–25** William Massey, Prime Minister of New Zealand.
**1912–27** Many attempts by generals to carve out independent states in China.
**1912–28** Reform Party in power in New Zealand without ever winning half of the votes of the electorate.
**1913** Lord Hardinge makes speech championing the cause of SA Indians. Russo-Chinese treaty recognizes autonomy of Outer Mongolia, but as part of the Chinese realm. Malayan Collieries Ltd. established. Social Democrat Party formed in New Zealand.
**1913–14** Joseph Cook, Federal Prime Minister of Australia.

**1914** 10 Jan., Chinese National Assembly dissolved: Yuan Shi-kai governs alone. 1 May, new constitution in China. 8-10 Aug., Samoa taken from Germany by the allies. 20 Aug.–7 Nov., Japanese besiege and take German possession of Kiao-Tcheou, China. 23 Aug., Japan declares war on Germany with allies: seizes German fort at Tsingtau, and German interests in Shantung: 'Twenty-One Demands' made of China, extending Japanese rights in S Manchuria: China agrees to treaties ceding to Japan all German interests, and privileges in S Manchuria and E Inner Mongolia.

## THE AMERICAS

**1912** Socialist Labour Party organized in Chile. Electoral reforms in Argentina. 20,400 miles of railway in Argentina.
**1912–33** Roosevelt Corollary applied to Nicaragua following disorders: US Marines train *guardia nacional.*

**1913** 22 Feb., Francisco Madero, President of Mexico, assassinated: succ. Gen. Victoriano Huerta. All W Indian colonies agree to preference for British goods.
**1913–14** General disorder in Mexico: many local dictators.
**1913–21** Mario García Menocal, President of Cuba. Woodrow Wilson (Dem.), President of US.

**1914** Apr., Álvaro Obregón, dictator of three-quarters of Mexico. 21-22 Apr., US fleet shells and takes Veracruz, Mexico. 5 July, Huerta re-elected President of Mexico. 15 July, Huerta resigns: succ. Venustiano Carranza (Constitutionalist). 1 Aug., Universal Negro Improvement Association and African Committees formed in Jamaica by Marcus Garvey. 3 Aug., first ship passes through Panama Canal. 4 Aug., US proclaims herself neutral. 15 Aug., Panama Canal opened.

## RELIGION & CULTURE

**1912** Remains of 'Piltdown Man' 'discovered' by C.Dawson: later found to be a hoax. R.F.Scott reaches the S Pole. 1 March, first parachute drop from an aircraft made in USA by Capt. Albert Louis.
**1912–13** Abortive attempt to disestablish Welsh Church.

**1913** Niels Bohr discovers atomic structure. Conveyor belt assembly technique invented by Henry Ford. Hospital at Lambaréné founded by Albert Schweitzer. *The New Statesman and Nation* founded.
**1913–30** Robert Bridges, English poet laureate.
**1913–61** Albert Camus, novelist and dramatist.
**1913–70** Iain Norman MacLeod, Conservative statesman.
**1913–76** Benjamin Britten, composer.
**1913–** Richard Nixon, American President (Rep.).
**1913–14** Artificial fertilisers invented.
**1914** First traffic lights installed, at Cleveland, Ohio. Women's Medical Service instituted in India. Basilica of the Sacred Heart, Paris, completed.
**1914–22** Benedict XV (della Chiesa), Pope.
**1914–53** Dylan Marlais Thomas, poet.
**1914–** John Masters, writer.

## WESTERN & NORTHERN EUROPE

**1914** 4 Aug., Britain declares war on Germany. 6 Aug., first British troops disembark in Belgium. 12 Aug., Britain and France declare war on Austro-Hungary. 14 Aug., French troops enter Belgium at Belgian request. 20 Aug., Germans enter Brussels. 21-23 Aug., battle of Charleroi. British retreat from Mons. 26 Aug., British defeated at Le Cateau. 31 Aug., Germans occupy Compiègne. 1 Sept., general retreat of British and French armies to R. Seine. 3 Sept., French government transferred to Bordeaux. 4 Sept., Pact of London: Britain, France and Russia agree not to seek a separate peace. 6-12 Sept., battle of the Marne: Germans retreat. 13-17 Sept., battle of the Aisne. 24-25 Sept., battle of the Somme. 1-26 Oct., battle of Arras. 25 Oct.—13 Nov., first battle of Ypres: Germans defeated. 23 Nov., British Navy bombards Zeebrugge. 10 Dec., French government returns to Paris. 16 Dec., Germans bombard coast of Yorkshire, England.

**1915** Jan, Fourth Duma recalled, for three sessions only. 24 Jan., British fleet defeats the Germans off the Dogger Bank. 16 Feb., British and French air forces bomb Zeebrugge. 26 Feb., French attack in Champagne. 1 March, Britain begins blockade of Germany. 10-20 March, battle of Neuve Chapelle. 20 Apr.—24 May, second battle of Ypres. 22 Apr.—17 May, German offensive in Flanders: 24 Apr., poison gas first used by the Germans. 26 Apr., secret treaty of London between the allies and Italy. May—June, allied offensive in Artois. 7 May, *Lusitania* sunk off the Irish coast by a German submarine, killing 1,145 civilians and crew: rouses US to go to war with Germany. 26 May, coalition government formed in Britain under H.H.Asquith. 20 June—July, German offensive against Verdun. 19 July, Duma again recalled. Sept.—Oct., allied offensive in Champagne.

## CENTRAL & SOUTHERN EUROPE

**1914** 31 July, Austria orders general mobilisation. 1 Aug., Germany declares war on Russia. 2 Aug., Germany allies with Turkey and Italy. 3 Aug., Germany declares war on France. Italy announces her neutrality. Germany allies with Rumania. 5 Aug., Austria declares war on Russia. 7 Aug., Spain declares herself neutral. 12-24 Aug., Austrian offensive in Serbia. 15-29 Aug., Russians invade East Prussia. 26 to 29 Aug., Russians defeated by Germany at Tannenberg. 14 Sept., Erich von Falkenhayn becomes German C.-in-C. 25 Sept.—30 Oct., Russians defeat Germans at Augustowo. 27 Sept., Russia invades Hungary. 29 Oct., Enver Pasha made C.-in-C. in Turkey. 29 Oct., Turkey attacks French and Russian vessels in the Black Sea: closes the Dardanelles to commerce. 30 Oct., Anglo-French fleet blockades the Dardanelles. 1 Nov., Paul von Hindenburg made German C.-in-C. on eastern front. 5 Nov., Britain declares war on Turkey: Cyprus annexed. 7 Nov., Austrian offensive against Serbia: Serbs retreat. 12 Nov., Turkey declares war on Britain, France and Russia. 15 Nov.—5 Dec., Russians defeated at Łódź. 25 Nov., Russians occupy Czernowitz. Polish National Council issues manifesto demanding reunification. 2-15 Dec., Serbs defeat Austrians at Roudniak. *Mancomunitat,* federation of four Catalan provinces, given special areas of autonomy in Spain. Portugal declares herself neutral.

**1915** 3 Jan., Russians defeat Turks at Ardahan; 3-4 Jan., further Russian successes against the Turks. 10 Jan., Russians masters of all Bukovina. 25 Jan., Germany introduces bread rationing. 14 Feb., Russians evacuate E Prussia. 18 Feb., German blockade of Britain begins: submarine warfare begun. 6 March, Gounaris, Prime Minister of Greece (—23 Aug.). 18 March, allied fleets penetrate the Dardanelles in spite of mines. 29 March, Turks evacuate Batum. 25-29 Apr., allied landings at Gallipoli. 4 May, Italy withdraws from the Triple Alliance. 6 May, Austrians and Germans take Tarnow. 23 May, Italy declares war on Austria. 24 May, Italians take part of the Tirol, including Caporetto. 27 May, Italians take Adige. 29 May, Dr Joaquim Teófilo Braga, President of Portugal (—Aug.). July, Austro-German advance across Rs Bug and Vistula. 4-27 July, Italians advance against the Austrians.

## AFRICA

**1914** Sept.—Dec., abortive pro-German rising in Transvaal. 13 Nov., pro-German rising crushed at Winburg, SA. Nov., Anglo-Indian force of 8,000 ambushed by General Lettow-Vorbeck near Tanga. 2 Dec., Germans repel Belgian attack on Rwanda. 17 Dec., Egypt proclaimed a British Protectorate: 18 Dec., Khedive Abbas II deposed: succ. Husain Kemal (—1917). French occupy Tibesti.
**1914—19** Sir F.D.Lugard, Governor-General of Nigeria.

**1915** 23 Jan.—3 Feb., rising in Nyasaland led by John Chilembwe. 4 Feb., Turks driven back from Suez Canal. 24 March, Sanusi revolt in S Tunisia. 9 July, Germans in SWA surrender to Botha. Local risings against recruitment in French West Africa. S Africans campaign in German EA.
**1915—16** Germans defeat Belgian attacks on Kisenyi.

## THE EAST & AUSTRALASIA  THE AMERICAS  RELIGION & CULTURE

**1914** 7 Nov., Anglo-Indian force takes Zubayr and Basra from the Turks. 30 Nov., Australians take German New Guinea. Japanese navy: 17 capital ships and 20 cruisers: products of Japanese shipyards and factories greatly in demand by allies. Yuan Shi-kai concentrates all power in his hands as President of China. Cement production begun in India. Membership of Johore Council of State broadened. Coalition government formed in New Zealand. 80,000 Europeans in Dutch EI.
**1914–15** Andrew Fisher, Federal Prime Minister of Australia (third term).
**1914–18** Over 100,000 New Zealanders enrolled in allied armies: *c.* 17,000 killed.
**1914–20** Sir R.C.Munro Ferguson (later Lord Novar), Governor-General of Australia.

**1914** Oct., 33,000 men of the Canadian Expeditionary Force sail to England. 15 Oct., US Clayton Anti-Trust Act. Nov., Carranza holds conference at Aguascalientes, Mexico, in an attempt to prevent civil war: anarchy ensues. 8 Dec., British defeat German fleet at battle of the Falkland Is. Canadian dollar leaves gold standard.

**1915** Jan., Kurds take Tabriz, Persia; 30 Jan., Russia retakes Tabriz. 12-14 Apr., abortive Turkish attack on Basra. 28 May–5 June, riots and disturbances in Ceylon. 3 June, British take Amara. 28 Sept., British take Kut al-Amara. Oct., Turko-German mission received in Kabul: fruitlessly attempts to drag Afghanistan into the war. 19 Oct., Japan accedes to treaty of London (4 Sept. 1914). 5 Nov., Yuan Shih-kai elected Emperor of China. 22 Nov., indecisive Turko-British battle at Ctesiphon. Mohandas Karachand Gandhi returns to India. Pro-German *Ghadr* conspiracy led by Har Dayal in the Punjab. Mrs Annie Besant creates Home Rule League in India. Russia occupies Urumia. Population of Ceylon 4.1m.: revenue £51.5m.: 4,303 schools with 384,533 pupils. Board of Trade set up in New Zealand to control prices and profits.

**1915** Jan., Vilbrun Guillaume Sam attempts to seize power in Haiti. March, Carranza returns to Mexico City. 28 July, Vilbrun Guillaume Sam murdered by a mob. Following public disorders, US applies Roosevelt Corollary by occupying Haiti with marines (–1934): Sudre Dartiguenave installed as president (–1922). La Follette Seamen's Act.

**1915** Sir Hugh Lane's controversial bequest to London and Dublin National Galleries. First fighter aircraft constructed by H.Junkers. Women's Institutes founded in UK. 'New Youth' (*Hsin Ching-nien*) journal founded, expressing Chinese student revolutionary progressivism supported by professors. G.K. Gokhale, Indian nationalist leader, d. Cowley motor car first produced at Oxford.

**1915–**  Humphrey Searle, composer.

| WESTERN &<br>NORTHERN EUROPE | CENTRAL &<br>SOUTHERN EUROPE | AFRICA |
|---|---|---|

**1915** 3 Sept., Duma suspended *sine die*. 8 Sept., Tsar Nicolas II takes personal command of the Russian forces. 18 Sept., Russians evacuate Vilno. 25 Sept.–4 Oct., successful British offensive: battle of Loos. 25 Sept.–25 Oct., successful French offensives on the W front. 11 Oct., Nurse Cavell shot in Brussels by the Germans as a spy. 15-20 Oct., allies declare war on Bulgaria. 6 Dec., Council of War at Chantilly: General Joseph Joffre French C.-in-C. 19 Dec., Sir Douglas Haig replaces Sir John French as British C.-in-C. on the western front.

**1916** 4 Jan., German offensive with poison gas in Champagne: Germans checked by wind blowing gas back onto them. 24 Jan., German offensive in Belgium. 28 Jan., German offensive in Artois. 20-22 Feb., German offensive at Ypres and in Alsace. 21 Feb.–28 Apr., Battle of Verdun: Germans and French retain previous positions following indecisive struggle. 25 Feb., General Philippe Pétain appointed to command at Verdun. 23 Apr., Easter Monday, rising in Dublin: Irish Republic proclaimed. 16 May, Sykes-Picot agreement on partition of Turkey. 24 May, conscription comes into force in Britain. 31 May, British fleet defeat Germans in battle of Jutland. 6 June, Lord Kitchener presumed drowned. 7 June, Verdun taken by the French. 23 June, new German offensive against Verdun. 1 July, French renew attack on Verdun (–15 Dec.): French successful. British army amounts to 5 m. men: Franco-British offensive on the R. Somme (–18 Nov.): considerable advance made: Germans lose many men and much material. 1 July–23 Oct., SA brigade heroically defends Delville Wood, Somme. 1 Nov., Duma recalled. 10 Nov., Stürmer becomes premier of Russia. 3 Dec., Robert Nivelle becomes French C.-in-C. 7 Dec.–1922 David Lloyd George (later Earl Lloyd-George), Prime Minister. 10 Dec., War Cabinet instituted in Britain. 16 Dec., Duma prorogued. 17 Dec., Rasputin assassinated. 27 Dec., Prince Golitsyn replaces Stürmer as premier of Russia. 30 Dec., allies decline Austro-German peace offer.

**1915** Aug., Germans advance in Poland. 5 Aug., Russians evacuate Warsaw. 7 Aug., Dr Bernardino Lúiz Machado Guimarãis, President of Portugal (–1919). 20 Aug., Italy declares war on Turkey. 23 Aug., Venizelos again Prime Minister of Greece (–5 Oct.). 26 Aug., Germans take Brest-Litovsk. 5 Oct., Zaimis, Prime Minister of Greece (–6 Nov.). Allies disembark at Salonica. 6-9 Oct., Austro-German offensive against Serbia. 8 Oct., Belgrade occupied by Austria and Germany. 29 Oct., Aristide Briand, Prime Minister of France. Nov., general retreat of the Serbs. 6 Nov., Sophocles Skouloudis, Prime Minister of Greece. 24-29 Nov., battle of Kossovo. 19-20 Dec., allies evacuate Gallipoli.

**1916** 6-9 Jan., allies evacuate Gallipoli. Feb., Austria conquers Albania. March, Germany declares war on Portugal. 24 March, *Spartakusbund* formed in Germany. 15 May, battle of Trentino begins: Austrians force Italians to retreat. June, Russian offensive in Galicia. 6-24 June, allies blockade Greece. 17 June, Russians take Czernowitz. 21 June, Italian counter-offensive in Trentino. 24 June, Austrian retreat in Trentino. 30 June, Russians halt offensive on E front, after many successes: German armies broken in Galicia. 4 Aug. *ff.*, Austro-Bulgarian offensive against Greece (–24 Aug.): halted by the allies. 17 Aug., Rumania joins the allies. 27 Aug., Italy formally declares war on Germany. 28 Aug., Rumania joins the allies. Hindenburg made Chief of German General Staff. 28 Aug., Turkey declares war on Russia. Sept., allied offensive on eastern front. 1 Sept., allied naval demonstration off the Piraeus. 11 Oct., Greek fleet surrenders following allied ultimatum. 15 Oct., allies take Athens. 18 Oct., Venizelos, Prime Minister of Greece, with separatist government at Salonica. 5 Nov., Austria and Germany promise to revive Poland as a state. 21 Nov., Emperor Francis Joseph of Austria d.: succ. Charles I (–1918). 26 Nov., Venizelos declares war on Germany. 1 Dec., French sailors massacred by the Greeks in Athens. 6 Dec., Germans take Bucharest.

**1916** 31 Jan., Sir Horace Byatt appointed Civil Administrator of British-occupied German EA. 18 Feb., Germans surrender to Nigerians and French in Kamerun. March-Aug., SA offensive under General Smuts takes German EA up to Central Railway. 6 March, part of Kamerun detached and administered with Nigeria as Cameroon. 3 Apr., remainder of Kamerun renamed Cameroun: incorporated into *AEF*. 20 Apr.–27 June, Belgians take Rwanda and Burundi from Germany. 24 Sept., Lijj Iyasu formally deposed for adopting Islam: Menelik's daughter Zawditu (Judith), Empress of Ethiopia: Ras Tafari Makonnen (subsequently Emperor Haile Selassie I) Regent and heir to the throne. 1 Dec., Fr Charles de Foucauld murdered at Tamanrasset. Risings against French in W Africa. Sayyid Idris al-Sanusi becomes Amir of Cyrenaica.

## THE EAST & AUSTRALASIA THE AMERICAS RELIGION & CULTURE

**1915–23** William Morris Hughes, Federal Prime Minister of Australia.

**1916** 16 Feb., Russians take Erzerum, Armenia, and then other towns. 2 March, Russians take Bitlis; 19 March, Isfahan. 22 March, Yuan Tche-Kai abdicates: succ. Li Yuan-hung. 18 Apr., Russians take Trebizond. 24 Apr., Townshend surrenders at Kut al-Amara. 13 June, Mecca taken from the Turks by the Arabs. 1 July, Turks take Kermanshah. 7 Aug., Turks take Bitlis; 10 Aug., Hamadan. 4 Nov., Sharif Husain proclaims himself King of the Hijaz at Mecca. 13 Dec., British offensive opens in Mesopotamia. 20 Dec., Australians repel Turks in an attack on the Suez Canal: El Arish captured. B.G. Tilak joins Mrs Annie Besant's Home Rule League: makes agreement with Muslims known as Lucknow Pact. Indian industrial commission appointed.
**1916–21** Lord Chelmsford, Governor-General and Viceroy of India.

**1916** 11 Nov., Duke of Devonshire Governor-General of Canada (–1921). Bryan-Chamorro treaty ratified: Nicaragua grants US right to build a transisthmian canal. Port facilities nationalized in Montevideo.
**1916–17** New constitution drawn up in Mexico.
**1916–24** US Marines sent to restore order in Dominican Republic.
**1916–30** Hipólito Irigoyen, first radical President of Argentina, elected: welfare legislation enacted.

**1916** Daylight Saving introduces 'Summer Time' in Britain. National Savings Movement founded in UK. School of Oriental and African Studies, London, founded. National Central Library founded. Lady Hardinge Medical College opened in New Delhi. The tank invented. Jazz 'craze' starts in USA.
**1916–** Edward Heath, British Prime Minister (Con.).
**1916–** James Harold Wilson, British Prime Minister (Lab.).

1917

WESTERN &
NORTHERN EUROPE

CENTRAL &
SOUTHERN EUROPE

AFRICA

**1917** 2 Feb., bread rationed in England. 4 Feb., Germans retreat on W front, pursued by allies. 25 Feb. OS, February Revolution: further strikes in Russia: first factory *soviets* elected. 27 Feb., garrison of St Petersbourg declares itself against the Tsar: Fortress of Saints Peter and Paul taken by the revolutionaries: the Duma dissolved by the Tsar. 16 March, Tsar Nicolas II abdicates, with the Tsarevitch and royal archdukes renouncing succession. 19 March, Aléxandre Ribot, Prime Minister of France. 31 March, Austria makes peace offer to France. Apr., Imperial War Conference. 3 Apr., Lenin arrives in Petrograd from Switzerland. 9 Apr., allied offensives in Artois; and, 16 Apr., in Champagne. 9-10 Apr., Canadians victorious at Vimy. 23-26 Apr., battle of Arras. 3-5 May, further battle of Arras. 5-9 May, battle of Chemin-des-Dames. 11-20 May, further battle at Arras. 3-21 June, Pan-Russian Congress of Soviets: 781 delegates present, of whom only 100 Bolsheviks. 10 June, riots in Dublin. 15 June, Philippe Pétain becomes French C.-in-C. 20 June, serious mutinies throughout French army. 26 June, first US troops disembark in France. July, successful Russian offensive; general allied offensive on W front. 4 July, first American troops reach Paris. 7 July, Kerensky succeeds Prince Lvov as Russian Prime Minister. 22 July, Joseph Pilsudski imprisoned for refusing oath of allegiance to Germany: 5,000 Polish followers interned. 31 July–16 Aug., Anglo-French offensive in Flanders: battle of Passchéndaele. Aug., Germany occupies Riga. 1 Aug., Romanov family deported to Tobolsk, Siberia. Sept.–Nov., successful allied offensive on W front. 12 Sept., Paul Painlevé, Prime Minister of France. 25 Sept., Trotsky elected President of the Soviet. 12 Oct., revolutionary military committee created: places all remainder of the Petrograd garrison at Lenin's orders. 25 Oct., marines and Lett soldiers seize the State Bank and the Palais Marie in Petrograd; afternoon, Lenin appears for the first time before the Congress of Soviets. 25/26 Oct., *Aurora* shells the Winter Palace. 26 Oct., Congress of Soviets votes that all lands be divided amongst the peasants: demands immediate peace with Germany and Austria.

**1917** Jan., Portuguese army of 25,000 sent to France. Germany proclaims all-out submarine warfare. 3 Feb., Germany and US break off relations. 12 Apr., Austria proposes peace to Germany. 17 Apr., German offensive against Russia and Rumania. 3 June, Albania proclaimed independent subject to Italian protection. 12 June, King Constantine of Greece abdicates: succ. Alexander I (–1920). 7 July, Bethman-Hollweg dismissed: Georg Michaelis, Chancellor of Germany. 19 July, peace motion passed by Reichstag. 19 July *ff.* German offensive breaks up Russian armies in Galicia. 19 July–2 Aug., German fleet mutinies. 3 Sept., Russians evacuate Riga. 11 Oct., Britain guarantees France the restoration of Alsace-Lorraine. 24 Oct., Austrians defeat Italians at Caporetto: Italian front crumbles: Austrians halted on R. Piave. 26 Oct., Michaelis dismissed: Count von Hertling, Chancellor of Germany. 28 Oct.– 2 Nov., British and French contingents sent to support Italians. 30 Oct., Vittorio Orlando, Italian Prime Minister. 6-7 Nov., Conference of Rapallo: allied support promised to Italy. 11 Nov., Italians retreat to R. Piave. Dec., military revolt in Portugal: Sidónio Pais, army commander, becomes dictator. 3 Dec., hostilities cease in Italy; and, 5 Dec., on Rumanian and Russian fronts. 7 Dec., Rumania almost totally occupied by Germans: King Ferdinand agrees to an armistice. 15 Dec., Armistice of Brest-Litovsk signed by Russia with Austria and Germany. 22 Dec., peace conference between Germany and Russia begins at Brest-Litovsk. Labour unrest on Spanish railways: revolutionary general strike ensues.

**1917** 11 Feb., Empress Zawditu crowned in Addis Ababa. May, a republic openly canvassed in SA. Anglo-American Diamond Corporation formed. 28/9 June, midnight, Sir Edmund Allenby takes up command in Cairo. Aug., French Togo incorporated into AOF. 18 Aug., French forbid female slavery in Cameroun. Many small actions in German EA. Nov., Lettow-Vorbeck crosses R. Ruvuma into Mozambique.

**1917–22** Fuad, Sultan of Egypt: King from 1922 as Fuad I (–1936).

## THE EAST & AUSTRALASIA

**1917** 24 Feb., Anglo-Indian offensive in Mesopotamia, leading to capture of Kut al-Amara from the Turks. 11 March, Baghdad taken from the Turks. 26-28 March, British defeat Turks at Gaza. 13 Apr., Turks retreat in Mesopotamia. 18-19 Apr., British repulsed by Turks at Gaza. 21 Apr., Samarra taken from the Turks. July, China and Siam join the allies. 20 Aug., Edwin Montagu announces policy of gradual development of self-government for India. 30 Aug., Turks take Merivan. 28 Sept., British take Ramadiah. 7 Nov., the British take Gaza. 17 Nov., the British take Jaffa. 9 Dec., Turks capitulate in Jerusalem to British under General Allenby. Young Men's Buddhist Association (YMBA) of Burma protests at non-inclusion of Burma in proposed reforms of Indian constitution. Ceylon Reform League founded. State butchers' shops set up in Auckland, New Zealand, to control meat prices. **1917–18** Edwin Montagu, Secretary of State for India, tours India during cold season. **1917 ff.** *Sarekat Islam* becomes hostile to Dutch in Indonesia.

## THE AMERICAS

**1917** 5 Feb., new constitution promulgated in Mexico. 6 Apr., following German sinking of eight US vessels, US declares war on Germany. Apr., all S American states and Cuba join the allies. Conscription introduced in Canada. Wheat Board set up in Canada. Canadian Northern Railway taken over by government. Federico A. Tinoco seizes Presidency of Costa Rica by force (−1919). New constitution in Uruguay. Guatemala City, third capital of Guatemala, ruined by an earthquake. Literacy test imposed on immigrants into US.

## RELIGION & CULTURE

**1917** 9 Aug., Pope Benedict XV offers to mediate to bring about peace. Patriarch Tikhon elected by the Russian Orthodox Council of Moscow. Agnes Maude Royden, first woman Congregationalist minister, appointed in London. Vernacular replaces literary Chinese in 'literary revolution'. **1917–63** John Fitzgerald Kennedy, American President (Dem.).

1917–1918
WESTERN &
NORTHERN EUROPE

CENTRAL &
SOUTHERN EUROPE

AFRICA

**1917** 27 Oct., Congress of Soviets adopts ministry of 'commissars of the people': Lenin, President; Rykov, Interior; Trotsky, Foreign Affairs; Lounatcharski, Education; Stalin, Nationalities (minorities). Nov., Generals Kornilov and Denikin raise anti-communist army amongst Don Cossacks: joined by numerous other officers and units: known as the 'Voluntary Army'. 2 Nov., Balfour declaration on Zionism promises support for a Jewish national home in Palestine. 7 Nov. (OS 26 Oct.), October Revolution in Russia. Lenin and Trotsky seize power: fighting ceases on E front. 12-14 Nov., general elections in Russia: republican socialists gain 20m. out of 36m. votes; Bolsheviks 9m. 16 Nov., Georges Clemenceau, Prime Minister of France. 20-30 Nov., British offensive near Cambrai: Hindenburg Line broken. 5 Dec., Finland proclaimed independent. 7 Dec., Extraordinary Commission set up by Lenin to combat counter-revolution, speculation and sabotage: known as *Cheka*, secret police. 13 Dec., preliminaries of armistice between Germany and Russia agreed near Dvinsk.

**1918** Jan., suffrage given in UK to all women over thirty. 5 Jan., Russian Constituent Assembly holds its only session: Bolsheviks under Lenin seize control. 8 Jan., Soviet government repudiates all debts contracted by the Tsarist government. 18 Jan., Russia proclaimed the Union of Socialist Soviet Republics (USSR). 28 Jan., Bolsheviks take Helsinki. Feb.–May, Germany continues hostilities in Russia. 19 Feb., all land nationalized in Russia, followed by industrial enterprises. March, Russian Communist Party (Bolshevik) formally constituted: system of cells in factories instituted: *Orgbureau* (office of organization) and *Politbureau* (office of politics) initiated. 3 March, Treaty of Brest-Litovsk signed between Austria, Germany and Russia. 8 March, Trotsky relieved of Ministry of Foreign Affairs in order to take up struggle against 'White' armies: anarchy in much of Russia ending only in 1920. 11 March, seat of Russian government transferred from Petrograd to Moscow. 15 March, Treaty of Brest-Litovsk ratified by Congress of Soviets. 21 March–4 Apr., Battle of Picardy: grave allied disasters: allies retreat.

**1918** 16 Jan., strike in Vienna. 28 Jan.–3 Feb., strike in Berlin. 9 Feb., Ukraine, as a new state, signs peace treaty with Austria and Germany. 31 March, Charles I of Austria proposes a separate peace to the allies. 7 May, peace treaty signed by Rumania with Austria and Germany. 15-23 June, battle of the Piave: Austrians checked. 29 Sept., Bulgaria capitulates. 3 Oct., Prince Max of Baden, Chancellor of Germany. 4 Oct., King Ferdinand of Bulgaria abdicates in favour of his son, Boris III. 18 Oct., Turkey asks for an armistice. 20 Oct., Germany ceases submarine warfare. 28 Oct., allies break Austro-Hungarian front at Vittorio Veneto. 30 Oct., allies sign armistice with Turkey. Czechoslovakia proclaimed a state in Prague. 31 Oct., revolution in Austria and Hungary. 3 Nov., allies grant Austria an armistice at Padua. German fleet mutinies. Revolution in Kiel. 8 Nov., Republic of Bavaria proclaimed in Munich. 9 Nov., revolution in Berlin: republic proclaimed: Friedrich Ebert, Chancellor. 10 Nov., Kaiser William II flees to Holland. Charles of Austria abdicates. 11 Nov., Joseph Pilsudski sets up independent Polish government in Warsaw.

**1918** 3 Nov., Saad Zaghlul demands independence for Egypt. 14 Nov., Lettow-Vorbeck's column surrenders at Fife, N Rhodesia. Fort Hare College founded. N Rhodesian Legislative Assembly elected by 589 white voters. 27 Nov., Britain refuses to receive delegation (*Wafd*) of Egyptian nationalists. Blaise Diagne appointed Commissioner-General for Recruitment of Black Troops in (French) Africa.
**1918–19** Major famine in Busoga and neighbouring regions.

THE EAST & AUSTRALASIA     THE AMERICAS          RELIGION & CULTURE

**1918** 24 Feb., Turks take Trebizond. 12 March, Turks take Baku. 21 March, Australians take Jericho. 7 Apr., Japan occupies Vladivostok. May, Azerbaijan proclaims itself an independent republic: capital at Baku. 18 May, People's Council, embryonic parliament, officially inaugurated in Dutch EI, with advisory powers only. 14 June, Turkish offensive in Palestine checked. 1-8 July, Manchu dynasty temporarily restored in China: Feng Kuo-chang then President. 6 July, Montagu-Chelmsford report published: policy of administrative devolution to provinces: three Indian members appointed to Viceregal council of seven: central bicameral legislature with 106 elected and forty nominated members: Council of State with unofficial majority. Governors and Councils instituted in United Provinces, Punjab, Bihar and Orissa. Aug., serious riots in Japan through rice shortage. 2 Aug., Japanese advance in Siberia. 4 Sept.–1922, Hsu Shih-chang, President of China at Peking: opposition government under Sun Yat-sen at Canton: country in the hands of generals: Japan dominant in Manchuria. 18 Sept., Anglo-French offensive in Palestine.

**1918** 8 Jan., Woodrow Wilson submits his Fourteen Points for peace to Congress. March, 80,000 US troops leave for France. Apr., 118,000 US troops leave for France. May, ¼m. US troops leave for France. Exploitation of oil in L. Maracaibo basin begun by British, Dutch and US companies in Venezuela. OBU (One Big Union), radical industrial trade union, set up at convention in Calgary, Canada. Rioting against conscription in Quebec. Catastrophic rains in Peru.

**1918** 5 Feb., Church and State formally separated in Russia. H.A.L. Fisher's Education Act reforms education in England and Wales. Asdic sonar apparatus invented. Daylight Saving introduced in USA. **1918–70** Gamal Abd al-Nasr (Nasser), Egyptian President and statesman. **1918–** Billy Graham, American revivalist preacher.

**1918** 23 March, Germans shell Paris.
Lithuania proclaimed independent.
26 March, Conference of Doullens
on the allied high command.
Marshal Foch made allied C.-in-C. in
France. Apr.–Dec., General
Skoropadski takes title of Hetman
and rules Ukraine. Czech and Slovak
refugees from Russian prison camps
form an anti-Bolshevik front on the
Volga: Apr., Kazan taken: Pan-
Russian government formed at
Omsk: taken over by Admiral
Koltchak (13 Dec.). 9 Apr., Latvia
proclaimed independent; and, 10
Apr., Estonia. 9-29 Apr., Battle of
the Lys: allies pushed back in
Belgium. 23 Apr., German
submarine fleet bottled up by the
British at Zeebrugge. 28 June,
British offensive at Nieppe. 1 July,
Americans advance at Vaux. 3 July,
Australians take Hamel. 5 July,
Count von Mirbach, German
Ambassador to Russia, assassinated.
10 July, first constitution of Soviet
Socialist Federative Russia
promulgated. 14 July, rationing
introduced in Britain. 15-17 July,
final German offensive on W front
gains little ground. 16 July, Nicolas
II of Russia and his family
assassinated. Aug., general allied
offensive on W front. 28 Aug.–10
Sept., Germans retreat to Hindenburg
line. Sept., general allied offensive
with numerous gains on W front.
5 Sept., 'reign of terror' begins in
Russia. Oct.–Nov., more than 7m.
people (more than all the war
casualties) die of 'Spanish' influenza.
Oct., allied offensive successful in
Belgium, France and Italy. 1¾m.
US troops in France: 1m. take part
in battle to break Hindenburg line.
3-4 Oct., Germany requests an
armistice. 4 Nov., renewed allied
offensive against Germany, now
deprived of all her allies. 11 Nov.,
allies grant armistice to Germany at
Compiègne. 30 Nov., Iceland
becomes independent of Denmark.
Dec., French troops and navy
disembark at Odessa: decline to
fight Reds. 8 Dec., Bolsheviks take
Estonia; 20 Dec., Lithuania; 22 Dec.,
Latvia. 13 Dec., President Wilson
arrives in Paris. 14 Dec., Lloyd
George's coalition wins general
election: Sinn Fein gains seventy
seats: refuse to sit in Parliament.
**1919** 19 Jan.–June, Peace
Conference of Paris: Germany
refused admittance by the allies.
Jan., first *Dáil Eireann* elected: 21
Jan., Irish Free State proclaimed.

**1918** 13 Nov., Russia denounces
treaty of Brest-Litovsk. 14 Nov.,
German fleet surrenders to British
Navy. Thomas Masaryk elected
President of Czechoslovakia. 28 Nov.,
William II of Germany abdicates. 29
Nov., Montenegro united with Serbia.
1 Dec., Kingdom of Yugoslavia
proclaimed. 14 Dec., Sidónio Pais,
President of Portugal, assassinated.
**1918–22** Muhammad VI Wahid al-
Din, last Ottoman Sultan.

**1919** 5 Jan., National Socialist (Nazi)
Party founded in Germany. 6-11 Jan.,
'Red Week' in Berlin. 17 Jan., Ignacy
Paderewski, also a distinguished
pianist, President of Poland (18 May).

**1919** March–Apr., SA African
National Union organizes meetings,
with burning of passes. 8 March,
Saad Zaghlul and other nationalists
deported from Egypt: riots ensue.

THE EAST & AUSTRALASIA    THE AMERICAS        RELIGION & CULTURE

**1918** 20 Sept., allies occupy Nablus.
21 Sept., allies occupy area S of
Lake Tiberias.  Oct., allied advance
in Syria: 1 Oct., Damascus taken;
7 Oct., Sidon; 8 Oct., Beirut; 13 Oct.,
Tripoli; 15 Oct., Homs.  1 Nov.,
British and French occupy Istanbul.
Gandhi becomes prominent in
Indian politics.  5m. die of influenza
in India.  Conference on the reform
of the Ceylon constitution.
Japanese expedition to Siberia to
prevent military supplies falling
into unfriendly hands.  Minimum
wage first fixed in New Zealand.
**post 1918** Japanese iron ore
extraction companies working in
Johore, Trengganu and Kelentan,
Malaya.
**1918–19** Franchise and Elections
Committee tours India during cold
season.

**1919** 20 Feb., Amir Habiballah Khan
of Afghanistan assassinated: succ.
Nasrullah Khan: 27 Feb., overthrown
by Amanullah Khan (−1929).  13
Apr., prohibited meeting broken up

**1919** 25 Sept., President Wilson
paralysed by a stroke: government in
USA alleged to be carried on by his
wife.  Grand Trunk Railway taken
over by Canadian government.

**1919** 14-15 June, first aircraft crossing
of the Atlantic made by J.W.Alcock
and A.W.Brown.  Welsh Church
disestablished.  The Church Assembly
instituted in England.

| WESTERN & NORTHERN EUROPE | CENTRAL & SOUTHERN EUROPE | AFRICA |
|---|---|---|

**1919** 25 Jan., conference of Paris agrees to League of Nations. 5 Feb., first session of League of Nations, in Paris. 14 Feb., League of Nations Covenant adopted.  March–Apr., White Army under Admiral Koltchak advance into Ural Mts.; Nov., driven from Omsk by Red Army; Whites put under protection of Czechs, in command of Trans-Siberian Railway. Admiral Koltchak shot by Reds 21 Jan. 1920. 5 Apr., De Valera elected President of Executive of Sinn Fein. 6 Apr., Finland proclaimed a republic. 7-14 May, coal miners strike in N France. 20 June, German Fleet scuppered in Scapa Flow. 28 June, Treaty of Versailles signed between the allies and Germany. 12 July, blockade of Germany ended. 10 Sept., treaty of St Germain between allies and Austria. 10 Sept., treaty of Neuilly between allies and Bulgaria. General Yudenitch, with British aid, forms government in Estonia: Oct., reaches within fifteen miles of Petrograd before being repulsed. 9 Dec., US delegates walk out of conference of Paris. Voluntary Army takes Kharkov and Kiev.
**1919–21** Terror in Ireland caused by IRA and 'Black-and-Tans'.

**1919** 11 Feb., Ebert elected President of Germany. 22 Feb.–1 Aug., Communists in power in Hungary under Béla Kun. 23 Feb., Benito Mussolini founds Fascist movement (*Fasci del Combattimento*). 21 Mar.–1 Aug., Soviet Republic in Hungary. 3 Apr., Hapsburg family exiled from Austria. 7 Apr., abortive Soviet Republic proclaimed in Munich. 21 June, Francesco Nitti, Prime Minister of Italy. 11 Aug., Weimar Constitution proclaimed in Germany. 12 Sept., Fiume taken from Yugoslavia by Gabriele d'Annunzio. Nov., Catalan regionalists petition Madrid for complete autonomy: similar petition sent to Conference of Paris. General strike in Barcelona spreads to rest of Spain. Four successive governments in Portugal.
**1919–23** Dr. António José de Almeida, President of Portugal.

**1919** 7 Apr., Saad Zaghlul released: proceeds to Conference of Paris. 10 July, Anglo-French agreement on partition of Togo. 28 Aug., Botha d.: 3 Sept., Smuts, Prime Minister of SA (–1924). Dec.–1920 Dec., Lord Milner heads commission on Egyptian constitution. Campaign for responsible government led by Sir Charles Coghlan in S Rhodesia.
**1919–22** Sir Edward Northey, Governor of Kenya.

**1920** 10 Jan., Treaty of Versailles and the League of Nations Pact come into force. 16 Jan., Aristide Briand, Prime Minister of France. 17 Jan., Paul Deschanel, President of France (–16 Sept.). 24 Jan., Reparations Commission constituted. March, Voluntary Army under command of Wrangel. 23 Apr., Poland invades Ukraine (–June). 6 May, the Poles take Kiev. 4 June, treaty of the Trianon between the allies and Hungary. 6 July, Russian counter-offensive against Poland. 10 Aug., Treaty of Sèvres: Turkey stripped of all her possessions by the allies other than a European region and Asia Minor. 5 Sept., military agreement between France and Belgium. 23 Sept., Aléxandre Millerand, President of France (–1924). 24 Sept., Leygues, Prime Minister of France. Nov., Wrangel's army retires to S Crimea:

**1920** 11 Feb., Danzig becomes a free city under the League. 15 Feb., the League takes control of the Saar. 1 March, Admiral Nicholas Horthy, Regent of Hungary. 16 March, Istanbul occupied by the allies: revolutionaries and nationalists declared outlaws by the sultan. 5 Apr.–14 May, the Ruhr provisionally occupied. Apr., San Remo conference. July, Spa conference on reparations. 10 Aug., Turkey signs treaty of Sèvres. 14 Aug., treaty between Czechoslovakia and Yugoslavia: origin of the Little Entente. 14-16 Aug., Russians defeated by Poles at Warsaw. 17 Aug., Rumania joins the Little Entente. 24 Aug., Greece occupies Adrianople. 12 Oct., armistice between Russia and Poland. 25 Oct., Alexander I of Greece d.: Constantine restored (–1922). 27 Oct., League of Nations headquarters established at Geneva.

**1920** Feb., first aircraft flight from London to the Cape across the Sahara. 30 May, *Union Générale des Ouvriers du Congo* organized in Elizabethville. July, East African Protectorate becomes Kenya Colony and Protectorate. German EA renamed Tanganyika. Sept., SA Party and Unionist Party merge. 4 Dec., administration of *AOF* reformed. National Congress of British West Africa formed in Accra. Partial indirect rule instituted in Belgian Congo. Diamang (*Companhia de Diamantes de Angola*) starts operations. Kikuyu Association formed in Kenya. Uganda Legislative Council instituted. Destour Party (DP) formed in Tunisia to obtain independence.
**1920–6** Abdelkrim's rebellion in Rif Mts.
**c. 1920** *Parti Communiste Algérien* (*PCA*) founded.

## THE EAST & AUSTRALASIA | THE AMERICAS | RELIGION & CULTURE

by troops under General Dyer in Amritsar: 379 killed: over 1,200 wounded: martial law proclaimed. 3 May, Third Afghan War breaks out: Kabul bombed by RAF: 31 May, Amir asks for armistice. 4 May, 'Movement of May 4th' begun: students of National University, Peking, demonstrate against government. 15 May, Greek army disembarks at Smyrna. 19 May, Mustafa Kemal (later Ataturk) moves secretly to Samsun, on the Black Sea: beginning of actions leading to Turkish Republic. 28 May, Armenia proclaims itself independent. 8 Aug., peace treaty of Rawalpindi between Afghanistan and Britain. 9 Aug., Anglo-Persian agreement. Oct., government commission of inquiry censures General Dyer. YMBA lobby British Parliament. Following failure, General Council of Burmese Association (GCBA) formed: boycott of British goods instituted. Ceylon National Congress, modelled on Indian National Congress founded. Japan, at Conference of Paris, obtains former German possessions in Far East. Japanese disappointed at failure at the Conference of Paris to get a declaration of racial equality inserted into the League of Nations Covenant. First aircraft flight from England to Australia by Keith and Ross Smith. New Zealand given League of Nations Mandate to govern W Samoa. British evacuate Baku and Tiflis. Following Treaty of Versailles, Australia granted former German Pacific possessions.
**1920** 8 March, Faysal I (later King of Iraq), proclaimed King of Syria (−25 July); Abdallah proclaimed King of Iraq. 23 Apr., Grand National Assembly, summoned by Mustafa Kemal, meets at Ankara. 27 Apr., Bolsheviks take Baku. May, Bolsheviks invade Persia. 11 May, Turkish National Assembly meets in Ankara. 23 May, Communist Party of the Indies founded in Dutch EI. 27 June, treaty between Afghanistan and Persia. July, Greek army occupies Brusa. 6 July, Britain evacuates Batum. 24 July, French occupy Damascus. 1 Aug., Gandhi begins civil disobedience campaign in India. 20 Oct., treaty of Ankara between France and Turkey. Dec., the Bolsheviks take Erivan. 3 Dec., Turks dictate peace terms to Armenians at Gümrü. 20 Dec., first strike in University of Rangoon, immediately following its incorporation.

**1919** Serious strikes in Vancouver and Winnipeg. Building workers strike in Winnipeg. International Labour Organization instituted.

**1920** 16 Jan., prohibition comes into force in US; US Senate refuses to join League of Nations. 19 March, US Senate rejects Treaty of Versailles. May, Carranza murdered: Álvaro Obregón takes Mexico City with 40,000 men: Adolfo de la Huerta, President *ad int.* 10 July− 1921 29 Dec., Arthur Meighen, Canadian Prime Minister. 26 Aug., female suffrage introduced in US. Dec., Álvaro Obregón, President of Mexico (−1924): revolutionary government. High protective tariffs established in US. New petroleum law in Venezuela: foreign companies required to pay substantial taxes: oil reserves protected. New constitution in Peru, first to provide elected president and congress. Communist Party organized in Chile. Canadian Wheat Board abolished.
**1920−1** Agricultural prices collapse in Canada.

**1919** Rutherford first splits the atom. Beirut Museum founded. Church of All the Nations, Gethsemane, begun.
**1919−** Sir Edmund Hillary, New Zealand mountaineer.
**1919−** Ian Douglas Smith, Rhodesian politician.

**1920** 30 Apr., use of religion in Turkey for political ends made punishable by death. 16 May, St Joan of Arc canonized. 20-23 May, unofficial conversations between Anglicans and Roman Catholics at Malines: continued at intervals until 1926. Royal Institute of International Affairs, London, founded. 'Peking Man' discovered. First public broadcasting stations opened in UK and USA. Witwatersrand University founded. Aligarh College becomes Aligarh University. Thompson sub-machine gun invented. Jewish Agency established.

| WESTERN & NORTHERN EUROPE | CENTRAL & SOUTHERN EUROPE | AFRICA |
|---|---|---|

joined by twenty-six naval units, which embark 135,000 White Russian refugees: *émigré* Russian colonies formed in many parts of Europe. 15 Nov.–18 Dec., first meeting of the League of Nations Assembly: Mandates over former German and Turkish possessions formally allocated: International Court of Justice instituted. 12 Dec., Cork burnt: martial law proclaimed. 14 Dec., treaty between Russia and Finland. 15–22 Dec., Reparations Conference at Brussels: Germany required to pay £13,450m. over forty-two years. 23 Dec., Government of Ireland Act separates the six northern counties, with separate legislatures for north and south.

**1920 and 1921** Many small risings of Russian peasants against the Bolsheviks. Period of bad harvests: 5m. persons said to have died.

**1921** 24-9 Jan., 'Reparations' Conference in Paris. 19 Feb., Alliance between France and Poland. 21-6 Feb., allied conference in London on the Near East. 27 Feb.–7 March, further 'Reparations' conference in London. 7-17 March, naval mutiny at Kronstadt ruthlessly put down by Trotsky. 15 March, *NEP* (New Economic Party) of state socialization announced by Lenin. 16 March, commercial agreement between Britain and Russia. Apr.–June, miners strike in Britain. 1 May, reparations fixed at 132,000m. gold francs: 52% to be paid to France. 5 May, allies send ultimatum to Germany on reparations: accepted, 10 May. 7 June, first Parliament meets in N Ireland. 22 June, Northern Irish Parliament opened at Stormont. Oct., London conference between Lloyd George and Sinn Fein leaders. 6 Dec., Anglo-Irish Treaty signed: Irish Free State recognized as a Dominion. Dec., France agrees to German moratorium on reparations.

**1920** 18 Nov., Queen Olga, Regent of Greece (–15 Dec.). Seven successive governments in Portugal.

**1921** 2 Jan., treaty of Rapallo between Italy and Yugoslavia. 3 March, alliance between Poland and Rumania. 23 Apr., alliance between Czechoslavakia and Rumania. 8 March, France occupies Duisburg, Ruhrort and Düsseldorf. 8 March, Dato, Prime Minister of Spain, murdered. 17 March, new Polish constitution promulgated. 18 March, treaty of Riga: Russia recognizes Polish boundaries. 27 March, and 20 Oct., Emperor Charles abortively attempts to regain the throne of Hungary. 14 May, twenty-nine Fascists elected at Italian general election. 7 June, alliance between Rumania and Yugoslavia. 16 Aug., Peter I of Yugoslavia d.: succ. Alexander I. Oct., revolution in Portugal. Five successive governments in Portugal. 26 Oct., Germany agrees to partition of Silesia with Poland.

**1921** Feb., Britain proposes abolition of protectorate in Egypt. 15 March, Rwanda and Burundi ceded to Belgium. 1 Sept., Europeans in Dar es Salaam protest against proposal for closer union with Kenya. Oct., Cape Town conference on union of Rhodesias with SA. 13 Dec., Niger made a French Colony. Dec., Taxpayer Protection League formed in Kenya. Young Kikuyu Association formed in Kenya. Meeting in Nairobi on Indian rights in Kenya. Smuts-Churchill agreement guarantees British Simonstown naval base. Council of Advice, with equal numbers of Afrikaners and Germans, set up in SWA. Lijj Iyasu caught and imprisoned.

| THE EAST & AUSTRALASIA | THE AMERICAS | RELIGION & CULTURE |
|---|---|---|

**1920** Rebellion against the British in the Lower Euphrates, and at Karbala and Najaf: direct rule by Britain ensues to 1927. Indian National Congress under Gandhi's leadership: non-violent non-co-operation movement begun against government: movement supported by Muslims. Financial control in China proposed to be exercised by international banking consortium: rejected by China. Prince of Wales (later King Edward VIII) visits Australia.

**1920—36** Period of isolationism in Canada.
**1920—38** Arturo Alessandri Palma, dominant figure in Chilean politics.

**1921** 3 Jan., first Parliament opened in India. Feb., Reza Khan, Persian Cossack officer, seizes Teheran with 3,000 men: made Minister of War. Feb., Trans-Jordan separated from Syria: Abdallah, first Amir (−1946). 20 Feb., Anglo-Persian Agreement annulled: Perso-Russian Agreement signed. 28 Feb., treaty between Afghanistan and Russia. March, following elections, Duke of Connaught inaugurates new Indian constitution. 11 March, Franco-Turkish treaty: France cedes Cilicia. 16 March, treaty between Russia and Turkey. May-July, Alawi rebellion in Syria. 20 May, treaty between China and Germany. Aug., Moplah outbreak in Malabar. 24 Aug.−16 Sept., battle of Sakkaria: Turks prevent Greeks from taking Ankara. Autumn, Prince of Wales (later Edward VIII) visits India: attempted boycott leads to violence. Oct., Communists forced to withdraw from *Sarekat Islam* in Dutch EI. 4 Nov., Takashi Hara, Prime Minister of Japan, murdered. 11 Dec., President of INC arrested. Abd al-Aziz b. Saud (known as Ibn Saud) ends Rashid dynasty of Hail. Government of India Act: India made fiscally autonomous. First Tamil political party, *Tamil Mahajana Sabha*, founded in Ceylon. Population of India 318m. Malayan population 2.9m. Burmese form Council of National Education: YMBA schools join, with title of National Schools. Austrian, German and Russian Capitulations abolished in China. Anti-Jewish riots in Palestine.

**1921** Jan., General Enoch Crowder sent to Cuba as economic adviser: virtually in financial control (−1923). 11 Aug., Lord Byng of Vimy, Governor-General of Canada (−1926). 24-29 Aug., US makes separate peace treaties with Austria, Germany and Hungary. 29 Oct.−March 1922, Washington Conference on naval disarmament. 13 Dec., Washington Treaty on the Pacific. 29 Dec., Washington Treaty limits naval armaments. 29 Dec.−25 Sept. 1926, W.L.Mackenzie King, Canadian Prime Minister. Congress imposes first quantitative restriction on immigrants into US. Canadian population 8,788,483.
**1921−3** Warren Gamaliel Harding (Rep.), President of US.
**1921−5** Alfredo Zayas, President of Cuba.
**1921−30** Augusto Leguía, dictator of Peru.

**1921** France sends an ambassador to the Vatican. British Broadcasting Company founded. British Legion founded. Simon Kimbangu organizes Kimbangist sect in Belgian Congo: 14 Sept., imprisoned. University College founded in Ceylon. Palestine Foundation Fund established. Catholic University of Milan founded.

1921–1923

WESTERN &
NORTHERN EUROPE

CENTRAL &
SOUTHERN EUROPE

AFRICA

**1922** 7 Jan., Anglo-Irish treaty approved by the Dáil. 12 Jan., Poincaré, Prime Minister of France. 22 Jan., first meeting of the Hague Court. 15 June–19 July, Hague Conference on reparations. 28 June, the Four Courts, Dublin, besieged. British Labour Party refuses affiliation to the CP. 6 July, Union of Soviet Socialist Republics (USSR) formally established. 9 Sept., William Cosgrave elected President of the Irish Free State. 10 Sept., commercial treaty between Britain and Russia. 19 Oct., Lloyd George falls: 23 Oct., Bonar Law forms Conservative government (–1923). 17 Nov., general election in Britain: Conservative victory: Liberal Party eclipsed by Labour. 6 Dec., Irish Free State formally proclaimed. 7 Dec., Northern Irish Parliament votes for separation. 26 Dec., Reparations Commission declares Germany in 'deliberate default'. Stalin elected Secretary-General of the Russian CP. Agrarian Code decreed in Russia.

**1923** 10 Jan., Lithuania takes Memel. March, Lenin retires: succ., as head of Russian CP, Joseph Stalin (–1953). 1 Apr., conscription for eighteen months enacted in France. 20 May, Bonar Law resigns: 22 May–1924, Stanley Baldwin (later Earl Baldwin of Bewdley), Prime Minister. 19 June, Anglo-American agreement on war debts. 27 June, letter by Pius XI against occupation of the Ruhr received badly by the French Chamber. Sept., Trotsky forms an opposition party of democratic workers. 6 Dec., Conservatives lose general election in UK. New constitution of USSR gives supreme authority to the Congress of Soviets of the Union: bicameral legislature.

**1922** 6 Apr.–19 May, Genoa Conference reaches an *impasse* on Russian debts. 16 Apr., Treaty of Rapallo between Germany and Russia: agreement on exchange of arms and industrial equipment. 16 June, Poland recovers Polish Silesia. 1 Aug., general strike in Italy. 12 Sept., Constantine of Greece abdicates: succ. George II. 24 Oct., Ebert re-elected President of Germany. Dec., Germany again defaults in payment of reparations. 28 Oct., Mussolini's march on Rome: 30 Oct., Fascist government formed. 1 Dec., Pilsudski resigns Polish presidency. *Estat Català*, extremist political party formed in Catalonia.

**1923** 11 Jan., France occupies the Ruhr: Germans retort with passive resistance (–23 Sept.). 10 July, Mussolini abolishes non-Fascist parties in Italy. 24 July, Treaty of Lausanne: settlement between Greece and Turkey. 6 Aug., Gustav Stresemann, Chancellor of Germany. 13-27 Aug., Italy occupies Corfu. 13 Sept., General Primo de Rivera (nephew of Primo de Rivera who proclaimed restoration in 1874) makes a *coup d'etát* in Spain: *Cortes* and government disbanded: military dictatorship set up (–1925). 23 Sept., Stresemann orders the end of passive resistance in Germany. 1 Oct., abortive Black Reichswehr *coup*. 8-9 Nov., Hitler's Munich *Putsch* fails. 30 Nov., Wilhelm Marx, Chancellor of Germany. *Accio Catalana*, Catalan political party, formed.

**1923–5** Manuel Teixeira Gomes, President of Portugal.

**1922** Jan.–Feb., strikes in the Rand. 21 Feb., British Protectorate in Egypt ended. 6 March, Communist Council of Action gains control in the Rand: 15 March, strike repressed. 16 March, Britain formally recognizes Kingdom of Egypt. 6 Sept., Wood-Winterton report received in Kenya: rejects restrictions on Indian immigration and segregation, except in 'White Highlands'. 6 Nov., referendum on responsible government in S Rhodesia: minority vote for union with SA. First elections to enlarged Legislative Council in Nigeria. Gold discovered S and E of L. Victoria. Status of slavery abolished in Tanganyika.

**1923** 15 March, Fuad I proclaimed King of Egypt; 19 Apr., new constitution proclaimed. Wafd Party victorious in general election. 1 Apr., British introduce poll tax in Tanganyika. Apr., alliance between Nationalist and Labour Parties, the 'Pact', in SA. 1 Sept., S Rhodesia formally annexed as a Crown Colony. 1 Oct., S Rhodesia granted responsible government: Sir Charles Coghlan, first Prime Minister (–1927). SA Urban Areas Act closes towns to influx of Bantu.

**1923–5** Voluntary repatriation of Indians from SA encouraged: 5,250 return home.

**1923–8** Discussions on 'Closer Union' in EA.

| THE EAST & AUSTRALASIA | THE AMERICAS | RELIGION & CULTURE |
|---|---|---|

**1921** Li Ta-chao and Mao Tse-tung found nucleus of Communist Party in Peking. Sun Yat-sen elected generalissimo in S China. Crown Prince of Japan visits France and UK. 56,000 Maoris in New Zealand.
**1921–4** Process of Indianization in army and civil service begun.
**1921–6** Earl (later Marquess) of Reading, Governor-General and Viceroy of India. Emperor Taisho of Japan suffers mental instability: son, Crown Prince Hirohito, regent.
**1921–33** Faysal I, King of Iraq.
**1922** 6 Feb., Nine Power Treaty guarantees Chinese independence: Japan renounces Shantung. Anglo-Japanese alliance allowed to lapse. 18 March, Gandhi sentenced to six years imprisonment. 26 Aug., Truks defeat Greeks at Hafioum-Kara-Hissar. 13 Sept., Turkey takes Smyrna (Izmir) from Greece. Oct., Japan evacuates Vladivostok. 10 Oct., armistice between Greece and Turkey. 2 Nov., Mustafa Kemal (later Ataturk) takes power in Turkey: Muhammad VI deposed from temporal power. Ceylon Labour Union founded. Constitution of Dutch Indies revised: People's Council gains unofficial majority. Government Meat Board set up in New Zealand.
**1922–3** Inchcape Retrenchment Committee in India.
**1922–5** American Financial Mission to Persia.

**1922** 1 Feb., Washington Conference restricts submarine warfare and use of poison gas. 6 Feb., Washington naval agreement between Britain, Japan and USA. 1 Apr.–15 Aug., coat strike in US. 20 Sept., US introduces protectionist tariff: restricts Canadian trade. Standard Oil Co. obtains concessions in Bolivia.
**1922–30** Louis Borno, President of Haiti.

**1922** Nov., Tutankhamun's tomb discovered at Luxor. Property of churches and monasteries confiscated in Russia. Insulin discovered by Drs Banting and Best. Dr Marie Stopes starts actively advocating contraception. Asmara Cathedral built.
**1922–39** Pius XI (Ratti), Pope.
**1922–** Kingsley Amis, novelist.
**1922–** Julius Kambarage Nyerere, President of Tanzania.

**1923** 10 Feb., treaty of alliance between Afghanistan and Turkey. 25 May, Transjordan made independent under Amir Abdallah. 1 Sept., earthquake ruins Yokohama and half of Tokyo (then third largest city in the world): c. 100,000 dead. 13 Sept., Ankara proclaimed capital of Turkey. 29 Sept., British Mandate over Palestine formally in force. 29 Oct., Turkish Republic proclaimed at Ankara: Mustafa Kemal, first President. Reza Khan becomes Prime Minister of Persia. Sultan Ahmad Shah leaves Persia. Britain grants Burma dyarchy: finance, defence and external affairs reserved: Burmese hold portfolios of agriculture, education, forests and public health: legislature of 103 members, seventy-nine elected and twenty-four appointed by governor (including fourteen officials). Franco-British treaty includes L. Huleh in Palestine.

**1923** Jan., 'Christ the King' movement in Mexico, against the government. 2 Aug., President Harding d.; succ., his Vice-President, Calvin Coolidge (Rep.)(–1929). Halibut Fisheries Treaty between Canada and US: first treaty signed by a Dominion without the presence of a UK representative.

**1923** 1 March, Gregorian Calendar introduced in Greece. 13 Dec., new agreement between France and the Vatican. Royal Fine Art Commission instituted in UK. Labour and Socialist International founded. The autogyro invented. Abd al-Salam Bennouna, 'father of Moroccan nationalism', opens free school in Tetuan.

**1924** 21 Jan., Lenin d.; Trotsky sent to the Caucasus 'for reasons of health'. 23 Jan., Ramsay MacDonald forms first Labour government in UK with Liberal support (–4 Nov.). 1 Feb., Britain recognizes USSR. 10 June, President Millerand forced to resign. 13 June, Gaston Doumergue elected President of France. 15 June, Edouard Herriot, Prime Minister of France. 16 July–16 Aug., Conference of London: Dawes Plan accepted for reparations. 25 Oct., Zinoviev letter published in London: Third International allegedly urges Britons to revolution. 28 Oct., France grants *de jure* recognition to USSR. 29 Oct., general election in Britain gives Conservatives an overall majority of 211. 6 Nov., 1929, Stanley Baldwin, Prime Minister.
**1924–31** Gaston Doumergue, President of France.
**1925** 1 Jan., Christiana, capital of Norway, renamed Oslo. 16 Jan., Trotsky dismissed. Apr., student strike in France. 3 Apr., Britain returns to the gold standard. 10 Apr., Paul Painlevé, Prime Minister of France. 27 Nov., Aristide Briand, Prime Minister of France. Dec., 14th Congress of the Communist Party in Russia. British Dominions Office separated from Colonial Office. Conscription introduced in Russia, two years with the colours, three on reserve.

**1926** 11 March, Fianna Fáil Party founded by Eamon de Valera. 29 Apr., French agreement with US on war debts. 1 May– 19 Nov., coal miners on strike in UK. 3-12 May, general strike in UK. 12 July, French agreement with Britain on war debts. 23 July, Poincaré, Prime Minister of France.

**1924** 25 Jan., treaty of alliance between Czechoslovakia and France. 27 Jan., treaty of Rome between Italy and Yugoslavia: Fiume returned to Italy. 1 Apr., Adolf Hitler sentenced to five years imprisonment. 24 May, republic proclaimed in Greece. 10 June, Giacomo Matteotti, a Socialist deputy, murdered in Italy: anti-Fascist opposition sternly put down: opposition leaves Chamber. 6 Aug., treaty of Lausanne. Dec., Ahmad Zogu (later known as King Zog) seizes power in Albania. 20 Dec., Hitler released.

**1925** 3 Jan., Fascism made the sole party in Italy. 25 Apr., Marshal Hindenburg becomes President of the German Republic. 1 May, Cyprus declared a Crown Colony. 4 May–17 June, Geneva arms conference. 1 July, France evacuates the Ruhr. 16 Oct., Treaty of Locarno, between Britain, France, Germany and Italy: agreement on German frontiers and demilitarisation of the left bank of the Rhine. 27 Oct., treaty of mutual aid between Czechoslovakia and France. Anglo-Italian treaty recognizes Ethiopia as an Italian sphere of influence: Ras Tafari's protest against it published by League of Nations. Adolf Hitler publishes Nazi programme in *Mein Kampf.* Mancomunitat abolished. Partly civilian cabinet introduced by General Primo de Rivera in Spain.
**1925–6** Dr Bernardino Lúiz Machado Guimarãis – 2nd term, President of Portugal.

**1926** 31 Jan.–22 Aug., Theodore Pangalos, dictator of Greece. 12 May, Pilsudski takes Warsaw by *coup de main*: Ignacy Moscicki, President: Pilsudski, War Minister, and virtual dictator (–1935). 18 May, preparatory conference on disarmament opens. 28 May, Gomes da Costa seizes power in Portugal.

**1924** 1 Apr., N Rhodesia taken over by the Crown. 25 June, Britain declines Egyptian demand for evacuation of the Sudan. 30 June, general election in SA: 'Pact' ministry under J.B.M.Hertzog (–1933). 19 Nov., Sir Lee Stack murdered in Cairo. Kilimanjaro Native Planters' Union, of Chagga coffee growers, founded. N.Leys: *Kenya* causes a sensation among Kenya settlers. SA Indians deprived of municipal franchise. Hottentots rebel against dog tax: more than 100 persons killed. New constitution in Sierra Leone. British Mandated Territory of the Cameroons administered henceforward as part of Nigeria. Legislative Assembly established in Tangier.

**1925** 7 July, SA Senate rejects colour-bar bill. 26 Aug., Marshal Pétain takes command of French army in Morocco. 6 Dec., Italian agreement with Egypt on Cyrenaica. Anglo-Italian Convention cedes part of Jubaland and port of Kismayu from Kenya to Somalia. Kikuyu Central Association replaces Young Kikuyu Association. Lord Delamere holds Tukuyu Conference of settlers from EA, Nyasaland and N Rhodesia. Afrikaans recognized as an official language on a par with English in SA. Indian residence in SA segregated by Areas Reservation Act. First demands for union of the Rhodesias and Nyasaland. New constitution in Gold Coast. Sudan Defence Force formed.
**1925–31** Sir Donald Cameron, Governor of Tanganyika.

**1926** 27 May, Rif war in Morocco ends: Abdelkrim surrenders to France. June, non-European Conference of ANC and SA Indian National Congress held at Kimberley. SA Immorality Act forbids carnal connection between persons of differing colour. Progressive Party organized in S Rhodesia.

## THE EAST & AUSTRALASIA          THE AMERICAS          RELIGION & CULTURE

**1923** First strike in Ceylon. Tariff Board set up in India. Sultan of Kedah accepts British protection. Dairy Board set up in New Zealand.
**1923–9** Stanley Melbourne Bruce (later Viscount Bruce), Federal Prime Minister of Australia.
**1924** 21 Jan., Kuomintang Congress in Canton: Communists and Russian advisers accepted. 3 Feb., treaty of friendship between Germany and Persia. 19 Feb., Shah Ahmad of Persia deposed: Reza Khan, Regent. March, attempt to establish a republic in Persia. 24 Apr., new constitution promulgated in Turkey. 11-15 July, communal riots between Hindus and Muslims in India. 28 Sept., General Sarrail replaces Marshal Weygand as High commissioner in Syria. Oct., Ibn Saud occupies Mecca. 5 Nov., civil war begins in China. Dec., Ibn Saud occupies Medina and Jeddah. Excise on cotton suspended in India. New constitution in Ceylon: representative government conceded, but based on franchise of 4% of the population. Sun Yat-sen re-elected in order to campaign against N China.
**1925** 20 Jan., treaty between Japan and Russia. Treaty of Peking between Britain and China. 28 Feb.–18 Apr., Kurdish rebellion in Turkey. 12 March, Sun Yat-sen d.: succ. Hu Han-min. 4 Apr., Japan evacuates Sakhalin. 30 May, anti-foreign riot in Shanghai: British troops fire on crowd. 18 July, rebellion in the Jabal al-Duruz (Jebel Druze), Lebanon and Syria (–June 1927). 18-20 Oct., French bombard Damascus. 31 Oct., Reza Khan usurps Qajar dynasty of Persia as Shah Reza, first of the Pahlevi dynasty. Britain obtains concession for the Iraq Petroleum Co. for seventy-five years. Women enfranchised in India. Excise on cotton abolished in India. New Zealand attempts to reform government in W Samoa.
**1925–30** Lord Stonehaven, Governor-General of Australia.

**1926** 8 Jan., Ibn Saud proclaimed King of Hijaz: name changed to Saudi Arabia. 23 May, Lebanon proclaimed a republic. 5 June, agreement between Britain and Turkey on Mosul. Sept., Chiang Kai-shek takes Hankow. 25 Dec., Emperor Taisho of Japan, d.: son, Emperor Hirohito, succ. (–present),

**1924** 1 Jan., Japanese immigration into the US forbidden. 1 Dec., Plutarco Elías Calles, President of Mexico (–1928). *Alianza Popular Revolucionaria Americana* (*APRA*) founded by Peruvian Socialist Haya de la Torre: primarily pro-Indian movement.

**1925** Dec., freehold of oil companies in Mexico abolished: replaced by fifty-year leases. Commercial agreement between Canada and the W Indies. Catastrophic rains in Peru.
**1925–33** Gerardo Machado, President of Cuba.

**1926** June, constitutional crisis in Canada: Parliament dissolved after initial refusal by Governor-General: Liberals gain in general election. June, serious charges of corruption of Canadian customs made in regard to liquor. 29 June–25 Sept., A. Meighen again Canadian Prime Minister.

**1924** 18 Jan., Pope Pius XI: encyclical *Maximam gravissimamque* authorizes French bishops to set up diocesan organizations. 3 March, the Caliphate formally abolished by Turkey. Insecticide invented. British Empire Exhibition held at Wembley. State University of Milan founded. Basilica of the Transfiguration, Mount Tabor, consecrated.

**1925** Feb., French ambassador to the Vatican withdrawn. 25 Feb., new Turkish enactment iterates law against use of religion for political ends. Wearing a *fez* forbidden in Turkey, and all forms of religious dress. 19-29 Aug., Ecumenical Conference of Protestant Churches in Stockholm. Oct., Education Conference in Dar es Salaam: beginning of standardization of Swahili. St Thérèse of Lisieux canonized. Patriarch Tikhon of Moscow d.: replaced by Metropolitan Peter, with title of 'Guardian of the Patriarchal Throne'. Anti-religious propaganda made systematic in Russia. Violent controversy on education between government and clergy in Mexico. Methodists, Congregationalists and part of the Presbyterian Church unite in the United Reformed Church of Canada. University of Louvain establishes medical and agricultural institutes in Congo. First traffic lights installed in London. Millikan discovers cosmic rays. 'Galilee Man' discovered.
**1926** 28 Feb., Papal Encyclical *Rerum Ecclesias gestarum* on indigenous clergy and evolution of missions into dioceses: looks forward to decolonization. 2 July, legislation against the Church in Mexico. *Action Française* condemned by the Pope. Protestant missionary conference at Le Zoute, Belgium. Reading University founded.

| WESTERN & NORTHERN EUROPE | CENTRAL & SOUTHERN EUROPE | AFRICA |
|---|---|---|
| **1926** 19 Oct.–18 Nov., Imperial Conference in London: Britain and the Dominions declared autonomous communities of equal status. | **1926** 9 July, General António de Fragosa Carmona seizes power in Portugal: President until 1951. 22 Aug., George Kondylis re-established in power in Greece. 8 Sept., Germany admitted to the League of Nations. 27 Nov., pact of Tirana between Albania and Italy. Patriotic Union formed in Spain. | **1926** 1 Aug., Muhammad Bennouna, Ahmad Balafrej, with six others, determine to work for Moroccan independence. 7 Dec., first meeting of Tanganyika Legislative Council. Ras Tafari takes personal command of Ethiopian army. Native Authority Ordinance formalizes Indirect Rule in Tanganyika. Srinivasa Sastri appointed first Indian Agent-General in SA. |
| **1927** May, opposition in Russia complains to Politbureau of Stalin's 'personal' rule 27 May, Britain severs diplomatic relations with Russia. 28 July, British Trade Union Act. 22-23 Aug., riots in Paris. Five Year Plan for 1928/9 to 1932/3 published in Russia. | **1927** 29 Jan., Wilhelm Marx re-elected Chancellor of Germany. 31 Jan., military control ended in Germany. 3-13 Feb., risings in Oporto and in Lisbon against Carmona government. 21 Apr., treaty between Italy and Hungary. 2-23 May, World Economic Conference at Geneva. 13 May, Black Friday: German economic system collapses. 15-16 July, Socialist riots in Vienna. 20 July, Ferdinand I of Rumania d.: succ. Michael I. 22 Aug., allied military control ended in Hungary. 30 Nov., USSR proposes immediate disarmament at Geneva: rejected as a Communist trick. National Assembly, or pseudo-*Cortes*, formed in Spain. | **1927** 23 Aug., Nahas Pasha becomes leader of the Wafd Party. 27 Aug., Sir C. Coghlan d.: H.U.Moffat succ. as Prime Minister of S Rhodesia. 2 Sept., domestic slavery abolished in Sierra Leone. Nov., conference of Indian Associations of EA in Nairobi: Isher Dass becomes leader of Indian non-cooperation. Nov., Indian Government Agency set up in Cape Town. Clove Growers Association formed in Zanzibar. Cameroun railway system completed. |
| **1928** Jan., Trotsky deported to Central Asia: Stalin steadily emerges as sole ruler. 7 May, all women over twenty-one enfranchised in Britain. 27 Aug., Kellog-Briand Pact signed in Paris by sixty-five governments. 22 Dec., Young Commission on reparations begins work. | **1928** 27 Apr., Dr António de Oliveira Salazar, Portuguese finance minister (–1940): balances budget for first time for seventy-five years. 28 June, Hermann Müller, Chancellor of Germany. Aug., Venizelos again Prime Minister of Greece. 1 Sept., Ahmad Zogu becomes King Zog I of Albania. | **1928** 19 July, *coup d'état* in Egypt: Parliament dissolved for three years: freedom of the press suspended. 2 Aug., Italy signs twenty year treaty of friendship with Ethiopia. *Coup d'état* in Ethiopia: Ras Tafari takes control: 17 Oct., crowned as Negus by Empress Zawditu. |

## THE EAST & AUSTRALASIA

with throne-name Showa: maintains tradition of impartiality and aloofness in politics. Treaty of perpetual peace between Persia and Turkey. Turkish legal system reformed: civil code on Swiss model introduced: Latin alphabet replaces Arabic alphabet. Treaty between Afghanistan and Germany, and Security Pact with Russia. All-India Women's Conference founded. Government of S China moved to Hankow. Family allowances introduced in New Zealand.
**1926–31** Lord Irwin (later Earl of Halifax), Governor-General and Viceroy of India.
**1927** 21 March, Chiang Kai–shek takes Shanghai. 15 Apr., Nanking made the Chinese seat of government. 20 May, Britain recognizes Saudi Arabia. 2 Sept., Turkey made a one-party state. 1 Oct., non-aggression pact between Persia and Russia. Nov., Simon Commission (–1929), with no Indian members, arouses resentment in India: faces demonstrations and boycotts. 14 Dec., Britain undertakes to recognize independence of Iraq: treaty of alliance made for twenty-five years. 14 Dec., China and Russia break off relations. New judicial system in Persia, on French model. Trans-Persian Railway begun. Parliamentary Commission, led by Earl of Donoughmore, visits Ceylon: new constitution follows: adult franchise, but foreign affairs, justice and finance reserved. Federal Council of Federated Malay States re-organized: official members thirteen; unofficial eleven. Malayan Communist Party (MCP) founded. Dutch EI constitution revised. Communist risings in Java and Sumatra. Prosperity at its peak in Dutch EI: 52,000 Indonesians make pilgrimage to Mecca. Mao Tse-tung organizes CP in Hunan. Banking crisis in Japan: many ruined by failure of smaller banks. Duke of York (later King George VI) visits Australia. Canberra becomes the Australian federal capital.
**1927–8** INC hold Congress in Madras: independence announced as goal.
**1928** 19 Apr., Japanese occupy Shantung. 10 May, capitulations abolished in Persia. 6 Oct., Chiang Kai-shek, President of China. Muddiman Committee appointed to examine working of reforms in India. All-parties Conference in India: Nehru Report produced. Gandhi returns to politics.

## THE AMERICAS

**1926** 31 July, priests in Mexico go on strike: government schools burnt: banditry and murder until end of strike in 1929. 25 Sept.–1930 Aug. 6, Mackenzie King, again Canadian Prime Minister. 2 Oct., Viscount (later Marquess of) Willingdon, Governor-General of Canada (–1931). Brazil withdraws from League of Nations. West Indian Conference convened by L.S.Amery.

**1927** 20 June–4 Aug., abortive Naval Disarmament Conference in Washington. 17 Dec., F.B.Kellogg, US Secretary of State, proposes pact for the renunciation of war. Vincent Massey appointed Canadian Minister to Washington: first Canadian diplomatic appointment.
**1927–33** US occupies Nicaragua.

**1928** July, Alvaro Obregón elected President of Mexico: shot after two weeks. Dec., Portes Gil, provisional President of Mexico. Record wheat crop in Canada. 166,783 immigrants into Canada. Population of Paraguay 800,000.

## RELIGION & CULTURE

**1926** Television invented by J.L.Baird. Rocket guided missiles invented. Dervish Orders suppressed in Turkey.
**1926–**  H.M. Queen Elizabeth II.

**1927** 20-21 May, Charles Lindbergh makes first solo aircraft crossing of the Atlantic. Protestant World Conference on Faith and Order held at Lausanne. (Sir) Leonard Woolley excavates Ur. British Broadcasting Company becomes the British Broadcasting Corporation. 'Talkies' (talking moving pictures) replace 'movies' in US: portrait (or caricature) of American life spread world wide. Dr. Aggrey, African educationist d. Earthquake damages Basilica of the Holy Sepulchre, Jerusalem. Gardens in England and Wales first opened to the public to support Queen's Institute of District Nursing.

**1928** 5 Apr., Turkish law formally separates church and state. 1 Nov., the Roman Alphabet adopted by Turkey. Ecumenical Missionary Conference held in Jerusalem. Revised *Book of Common Prayer* rejected by the House of Commons.

| WESTERN & NORTHERN EUROPE | CENTRAL & SOUTHERN EUROPE | AFRICA |
|---|---|---|
| **1928—31** Land collectivized in USSR. | **1928** 23 Sept., treaty of friendship between Greece and Italy. 15 Nov., Italian constitution amended to include Fascist Grand Council. Amanullah of Afghanistan visits Europe. | **1928** Portuguese—SA treaty regulating labour transport and recruitment. SA Communist Party re-organized, with increasingly Bantu membership. |
| **1929** 31 Jan., Trotsky finally exiled from Russia. 30 May, general election in UK won by Labour: 5 June, government formed by Ramsay MacDonald (−1931). 28 June, all agricultural products requisitioned in Russia. 27 July, Briand, Prime Minister of France. 6-31 Aug., Hague Conference on the 'Young Plan': Germany accepts: allies agree to evacuation of the Rhineland. 5 Sept., Briand proposes a federal union of Europe. 3 Oct., Anglo-Russian diplomatic relations resumed. 3 Nov., Tardieu, Prime Minister of France. **1929—30** Warren Fisher Committee on training of the Colonial Service. | **1929** 5 Jan., Alexander I of Yugoslavia assumes dictatorial power. 9 Feb., Eastern Pact between Estonia, Latvia, Poland, Rumania and USSR, renounces war. 27 June, German Protection of Republic Act repealed. 3 Oct., Stresemann d. 13 Nov., Bank for International Settlements founded in Switzerland. | **1929** Jan., Hilton Young report on Kenya land and racial questions: reiterates 'paramountcy' of native interests. 31 Oct., Egyptian constitution restored. Muslim Brotherhood founded by Hasan al-Banna at Ismailia. Tanganyika African Association (TAA) formed. Kikuyu Central Association agitates on land rights and female circumcision. Uganda government departments instructed if possible to appoint Africans: Indian officers to be appointed only on a temporary basis. |
| **1930** 2-20 Jan., new Hague Conference on the 'Young Plan'. 6 Jan., liquidation of *kulaks* announced by Stalin: collective farms compulsory. 2 March, Stalin urges collectivist farm organizers to be moderate in their zeal. 15 March, Stalin announces that members of collective farms may possess a cow and poultry as individuals. 29 March, 'Young Plan' ratified by France. Apr., Stalin grants privileges to collective farmers, including freedom from taxation. 22 Apr., naval Treaty of London between Britain, France, Italy, Japan and US. 27 June, arbitration treaty between Scandinavian countries. 1 Oct.—14 Nov., Imperial Conference in London leads to Statute of Westminster. 12 Nov.—1931 19 Jan., round-table conference on India in London. | **1930** 28 Jan., General Primo de Rivera resigns: succ. General Damaso Berenguer, as Prime Minister of Spain. 6 Feb., treaty of friendship between Austria and Italy. 18 Feb. 24 March, Geneva conference on tariffs. 30 March, right wing coalition government in Germany under Heinrich Brüning. 8 June, Crown Prince Charles elected as King of Rumania. 30 June, France finally evacuates the Ruhr. 30 July, National Union Party formed in Portugal to replace other political parties. 25 Aug.—28 Nov., right wing government in Poland under Marshal Pilsudski. 30 Oct., treaty of friendship between Greece and Turkey. 17-28 Nov., Geneva Economic Conference. | **1930** March, Ras Gugsa, brother of Empress Zawditu, revolts: 31 March, defeated and killed: 2 Apr., Empress d.: 3 Apr., Ras Tafari proclaimed Emperor of Ethiopia with throne-name Haile Selassie I. 19 May, white women granted vote in SA. Quota Act reduces Jewish immigration into SA. Education made compulsory for European children in Rhodesia. Court of Cassation established in Egypt. Motor rally from the Mediterranean to the Niger. **1930—75** Haile Selassie I, Emperor of Ethiopia. |

| THE EAST & AUSTRALASIA | THE AMERICAS | RELIGION & CULTURE |
|---|---|---|

**1928** Chang Tso-lin, war-lord of Manchuria, assassinated near Mukden by Japanese army officers. Russia again penetrates Ili region.
**1928—30** Sir J.G.Ward, Prime Minister of New Zealand.
**1929** 7 Jan., Amanullah of Afghanistan abdicates: succ. Inayatullah for three days: Habiballah, a brigand, occupies Kabul. 27 Feb., Turkey joins the Eastern Pact. 3 Apr., Persia joins the Eastern Pact. 12 Apr., Indian Trade Disputes Act and Public Safety Act. 15 Oct., Nadir Khan elected King of Afghanistan. Dec., Lord Irwin declares dominion status to be the object of British policy in India: round table conference announced: Gandhi demands scheme for immediate independence: refused. 29 Dec., Sukarno and leading followers of newly founded National Party of Indonesia arrested. All-India Muslim Conference unites Indian Muslims. Sarda Act raises age of marriage in India. Riots in W Samoa. Japanese troops withdrawn from China. Kuomintang strength 653,000 members. 0.15% of Chinese population. Anti-Jewish riots in Palestine.

**1929—31** James Scullin, Federal Prime Minister of Australia.
**1930** Feb., French garrison massacred at Yen Bay. 12 March, Gandhi begins civil disobedience movement ( 1931). 28 March, Turkish government formally renames Constantinople as Istanbul, and Angora as Ankara. 22 May, France promulgates a new constitution for Syria. 24 June, Simon Report on India published: recommends provincial self-government only: further unrest ensues. 30 June, Britain recognizes full independence of Iraq. 1 Oct., British evacuate Wei-hai-wei. Female adult suffrage instituted in Turkey for municipal elections. Sir Muhammad Iqbal proposes separate federation of Muslim provinces in India. Earthquake destroys much of Pegu. Rebellion in lower Burma led by Saya San (—1932): 10,000 rebels killed; 9,000 imprisoned; Saya San and 127 others hanged. Treaty between Perlis, Malaya, and Britain, regularizing protectorate. Immigration Ordinance halts free immigration into Malaya, imposing a quota system: Chinese principally affected. G.W.Forbes, Prime Minister of New Zealand.
**1930—2** Some 2,000 women imprisoned in India for political reasons.

**1929** 7 June, Young Plan on reparations published in US. 24 Oct., Wall St collapses: financial crisis in US: gradually spreads to the rest of the world: 12m. shares change hands on Wall St Stock Exchange. Congress imposes annual limit of 150,000 on immigrants into US. Sánchez Cerro seizes power in Peru. Further W Indian Conference held. *Partido Nacional Revolucionario* formed as the official party in Mexico.
**1929—32** Ortiz Rubio, President of Mexico.
**1929—33** Herbert C. Hoover (Rep.), President of US.

**1930** Aug., Conservatives win Canadian general election. 7 Aug.—1935 23 Oct., R.B.Bennett, Canadian Prime Minister. Sept., military *coup d'état* in Argentina: conservatives return to office. All Venezuela's external debt and most of internal debt paid off. Hudson Bay Railway completed.
**1930—41** Stenio Vincent, President of Haiti.
**1930—43** Conservative oligarchy in Argentina.
**1930—44** Maximiliano Hernández Martínez, President of El Salvador.
**1930—45** Getulio Vargas, President of Brazil.
**1930—46** Liberals in power in Colombia.
**1930—61** Rafael Leonidas Trujillo, dictator of the Dominican Republic.

**1928** Electric razor patented. Talking films come into commercial use. Penicillin discovered. Mogadishu Cathedral completed.

**1929** 11 Feb., Lateran Treaty between Italy and the Vatican: the Vatican State created: the Pope compensated for territorial losses of 1870: concordat signed. 21 June, agreement signed between Church and State in Mexico. 8-29 Aug., the *Graf Zeppelin* airship flies round the world. Scottish Presbyterian Churches unite to form the Church of Scotland. The iron lung invented. Palestine Archaeological Museum (Rockefeller Museum) built in Jerusalem.

**1930** 7 Oct., airship R101 crashes. Perspex glass invented. Youth Hostels Association founded in UK. Conakry Cathedral built.
**1930—** General Joseph Mobutu Sese, President of Zaire.

1930–1932

WESTERN &
NORTHERN EUROPE

CENTRAL &
SOUTHERN EUROPE

AFRICA

**1931** 27 Jan., Pierre Laval, Prime Minister of France. 19 March, French plan to combat unemployment published. 13 May, Paul Doumer, President of France (−1932). 11 Aug., London Protocol on Hoover's plan. 24 Aug., Ramsay MacDonald resigns: 25 Aug., forms National (coalition) government. 20 Sept., London Conference on reparations. 27 Oct., general election in UK: National Government 558, opposition 56: Ramsay MacDonald forms new ministry (−1935).

**1931** 21 March–3 Aug., abortive attempt at Austro-German customs union. 12 Apr., municipal elections in Spain: overwhelming republican victories in cities. 14 Apr., Maciá proclaims Catalonia independent of Spain. Alfonso XIII leaves Spain, but without abdicating. May, general disorder, strikes, burning of churches, ensue. 28 June, Constituent *Cortes* elected in Spain: new constitution, with single-chamber *cortes*: church disestablished: religious orders forbidden to teach: universal suffrage at age of twenty-three. Sept., new constitution in Yugoslavia. 13 Sept., abortive Fascist Heimwehr *coup* in Austria. 17 Sept., Germany suspends international payments. 30 Sept., League of Nations calls on Japan to evacuate Manchuria. 9 Dec., Alcalá Zamora, Prime Minister of Spain. 9 Dec., Spanish Republican Constitution proclaimed.
**1931–5** Twenty-eight different cabinets in Spain.

**1931** Jan., Earl of Clarendon appointed Governor-General of SA, first to be appointed on advice of SA ministers. 22 Apr., treaty of friendship between Egypt and Iraq. 5 May, Moroccan workers demonstrate for eight hour day and equality of wages. 1 July, Benguela-Katanga railway opened: completes first trans-African railway. 13 Nov., Lord Delamere d. New constitution in Ethiopia: unitary state with Senate and House of Representatives. Bank of Ethiopia established. European suffrage in SA freed from financial and educational restrictions. SA Natives' Urban Areas Amendment Act further restricts African residence rights. Diamonds discovered in Sierra Leone.

**1932** 22 Jan., second USSR Five Year Plan announced. 21 Feb., André Tardieu, Prime Minister of France. March, Kreuger scandal in Sweden. 1 March, Britain fixes exchange rates. 9 March, De Valera, President of Ireland. 6 May, President Doumer of France assassinated: 10 May, Albert Lebrun, President (−1940). 4 June, Herriot, Prime Minister of France. 29 Nov., non-aggression pact between France and USSR signed in Moscow. 15 Dec., France declines to pay debts to US. 18 Dec., Paul-Boncour, Prime Minister of France. British Union of Fascists formed by Sir Oswald Mosley.

**1932** 2 Feb.–1934, Disarmament Conference in Geneva. 10 Apr., Hindenburg defeats Hitler in German presidential election: Nazis steadily gain strength. 20 May, Engelbert Dollfuss, Chancellor of Austria (−1934). 16 June–9 July, Reparations Conference at Lausanne. 5 July, Dr. Salazar, Prime Minister of Portugal (−1968). 13 July, pact of friendship between Britain and France at Lausanne. 31 July, inconclusive election in Germany, with Nazi lead without a majority. 10-13 Aug., military rising in Seville led by General José Sanjurjo. 5-20 Sept., Stresa Conference on disarmament. 4 Nov., Tsaldaris, Prime Minister of Greece. 4 Dec., following further inconclusive elections in Germany, ministry formed by Kurt von Schleicher.

**1932** Jan.–Feb., conference between India and SA fails to solve SA Indian problems. Feb., Standing Economic Committee instituted in Kenya, with parity between officials and non-officials. Apr., SWA Legislature granted extended powers: German made an official language. Muslim Brotherhood headquarters moved to Cairo. Emperor Haile Selassie announces total abolition of slavery to be completed by 1952.

## THE EAST & AUSTRALASIA    THE AMERICAS    RELIGION & CULTURE

**1930 ff.** Australia mapped by aircraft by Donald Mackay.
**1931** 17 Feb.–4 March, conversations between Lord Irwin nd Gandhi. Feb., Bertram Thomas rosses Rub al-Khali (Empty Quarter). March, Gandhi–Irwin truce announced: ivil disobedience called off: INC agrees to recognize round table conference: political prisoners released. 5 May, provisional constitution adopted in Nanking. 24 June, Soviet-Afghan treaty. 7th Sept.– 1 Dec., second round table Conference on India: Gandhi attends: conference fails to reach agreement on minorities. 18 Sept., Japanese Kwantung army seizes Mukden and then Chanchung: beginning of occupation of Manchuria: Lytton Commission condemns action without result. 11 Dec., Japan leaves the gold standard. Bertram Thomas crosses Rub al-Khali (Empty Quarter). Malayan population 3.8m. First elections under new constitution in Ceylon: notables chiefly elected on non-party basis. Simon Commission appointed to recommend reforms in Burma. Indonesian People's Party founded by Dr Sutomo: members forbidden to seek seats in People's Council.
**1931–6** Sir Isaac Alfred Isaacs, Governor-General of Australia. Earl (later Marquess) of Willingdon, Viceroy of India.
**1931–40** Joseph A.Lyons, Federal Prime Minister of Australia.
**1932** 2 Jan., Republic of Manchukuo proclaimed. 28 Jan., Japan occupies Shanghai. 9 March, Pu Yi, former Emperor of China, made President of Manchukuo. 18 July, Turkey joins the League of Nations. 4 Aug., communal representation fixed in Indian provinces. 24 Sept., Poona Pact secures general and special representation for scheduled or depressed classes. 3 Oct., Iraq admitted to the League of Nations: British Mandate formally terminated. 29 Nov., Persia cancels 1901 Anglo-Persian Oil Concession. H.St.J.B. Philby crosses the Empty Quarter. Governor and Council established in Frontier Province of India. Agricultural population of China 73.3%.

**1931** 4 Apr., Earl of Bessborough, Governor-General of Canada (–1935). 20 June, President Hoover proposes a year's moratorium on war debts. Criminal cases in Canada no longer appealable to Judicial Committee of the Privy Council. Earthquake of Managua.
**1931–44** Jorge Ubico, dictator of Guatemala.

**1932** 9 July–Oct., uprising in São Paulo, Brazil. 21 July–20 Aug., Imperial Economic Conference in Ottawa: mutual agreement reached on tariffs. 8 Nov., Franklin Delano Roosevelt elected US President with majority of 7m.: remains President to 1945. 11 Nov., US refuses France a moratorium on war debts. 12m. unemployed in US: national income of 1929, $80,000m., reduced to $40,000m. Hawley-Smoot tariff further restricts Canadian trade with US. Canadian Radio Commission established. Social Credit movement started by William Aberhart in Alberta. Co-operative Commonwealth Federation organized by United Farmers Association in Canada. Royal Commission to study closer union between Leeward Is., Trinidad and the Windward Is. West Indian National League formed. Catastrophic rains in Peru.
**1932–4** Abelardo Rodriguez, President of Mexico.
**1932–5** Bolivia at war with Uruguay: Gran Chaco War.
**1932–48** Tiburcio Carías Andino, President of Honduras.

**1931** 15 May, Pope Pius XI: Encyclical *Quadragesimo anno*. 5 July, struggle between the Church and Fascism in Italy: Pope Pius XI: Encyclical *Non abbiamo bisogno*. C.D.Anderson discovers positive electrons. First Nok culture portrait heads discovered. Serdang Agricultural Training School inaugurated.
**Auguste Picard the first man to ascend into the stratosphere.**

**1932** Jan., the Jesuits suppressed in Spain. 26 May, drainage of Zuider Zee completed. 3 Oct., quarrel between Church and State in Mexico renewed. Five Year Plan to promote atheism promulgated in Russia: all places of worship to be closed by 1 May 1937. Wesleyans and Primitive Methodists in England unite to form the Methodist Church. 'Basic English' invented. Laws for the purification of the language adopted in Turkey: many Persian and Arabic terms replaced by Turkish neologisms.

**1933** 31 Jan., Edouard Daladier, Prime Minister of France. 3 Feb., Anglo-Persian agreement on oil. 16 March, British Disarmament Plan put forward. 27 Apr., trade agreement between Britain and Germany. 12 June–27 Aug., World Monetary and Economic Conference in London. 23 Oct., Albert Sarraut, Prime Minister of France. 22 Nov., Camille Chautemps, Prime Minister of France. Dec., the 'Stavisky affair' in France. Famine in Russia following collectivisation of farms.

**1933** 2-12 Jan., left wing revolt in Catalonia. 30 Jan., Hitler made Chancellor of Germany. 16 Feb., permanent council of the Little Entente created. 27 Feb., the Reichstag building burnt down. 6-16 March, Poland occupies Danzig. 19 March, Mussolini proposes a Four Power Pact between Britain, France, Germany and Italy. 26 March, new constitution in Portugal confirmed by plebiscite. 2 May, trade unions suppressed in Germany. 14 July, Germany becomes a one-party state under the Nazis. 15 July, Four Power Pact signed in Rome. 14 Oct., Germany walks out of the Disarmament Conference, and leaves the League of Nations. 12 Nov., Nazis take 95% of votes in German elections. 19 Nov., elections in Spain show swing to conservatism. *Falange Española*, Spanish Fascist party, founded.

**1933** 7 Jan., SA abandons the gold standard. 30 March, Hertzog and Smuts form National Coalition Party of 144: opposition 6. Development plan drawn up for Spanish Morocco. Uganda Indians restricted to special trading centres. SA Communist Party collapses. **1933–46** Léon Mba exiled from Cameroun for sedition.

**1934** 30 Jan., Daladier again Prime Minister of France. 9 Feb., Paul Doumergue, Prime Minister of France. 16 Feb., trade pact between Britain and USSR. 17 Feb., Albert I of Belgium d.: succ. Léopold III (–1950). 12 Sept., Baltic Entente constituted. 18 Sept., USSR joins the League of Nations. 9 Oct., Alexander I of Yugoslavia and Foreign Minister Barthou of France assassinated in Marseilles. 23 Oct.–19 Dec., abortive London Naval Disarmament Conference. Nov., Charles de Gaulle: *L'armée de métier* published. 9 Nov., Pierre Flandin, Prime Minister of France. 1 Dec., purge of CP begins in Russia.

**1934** 26 Jan., German-Polish ten year non-agression pact. 1-16 Feb., civil war in Austria against Socialists. 5 Feb., Italian Corporations Act passed. 9 Feb., Balkan Pact between Greece, Rumania, Turkey and Yugoslavia. June, Disarmament Conference adjourned. 14-15 June, Hitler and Mussolini meet in Venice. 15 June, Germany suspends all cash payments on foreign debts until 1 July. 30 June, Ernst Roehm and other opponents of Hitler murdered in Nazi 'purge'. 25 July, Dollfuss assassinated: 30 July, succ. Kurt Schuschnigg. 1 Aug., Hindenburg d.: 19 Aug., Hitler appointed Führer. 6 Oct., risings in Catalonia and the Asturias: vigorously put down.

**1934** 12 June, SA National Status Act: Cape Parliament retains right to secede from Commonwealth. United Party in S Rhodesia under Godfrey Huggins gains crushing victory at elections. 22 Nov., Wal-Wal incident: British claim provocation by Italians: 5 Dec., hostilities between Ethiopia and Italy.

## THE EAST & AUSTRALASIA

**1933** 23 Feb.–12 March, Japan invades Ho-Pei: area north of the Great Wall occupied. March, constitutional reform in India. 27 March, Japan leaves the League of Nations. 8 Nov., Nadir Shah of Afghanistan assassinated: succ. his son, Muhammad Zahir Shah. First Five Year Plan for industrialization promulgated in Turkey. Railways nationalized. Ibn Saud grants concession to Aramco (Arabian American Oil Co.). The word 'Pakistan' coined by Choudhri Rahmat Ali. Violent controversy in Burma over proposal for separation from India. New Zealand Legion, semi-Fascist organization set up. Reserve Bank of New Zealand set up. New Zealand National Mortgage Corporation established.
**1933–9** Ghazi, King of Iraq.
**1933–40** Sukarno interned, thus made a national hero.

**1934** 11 Feb., treaty of friendship between Britain, India and Yemen attempts to regularize British position in Aden. 1 March, Pu Yi proclaimed Emperor Kang Te of Manchukuo. 7 Apr., Gandhi suspends civil disobedience campaign. May–June, six weeks' war between Saudi Arabia and Yemen. 2 Oct., Royal Indian Navy established. 29 Dec., Japan renounces Washington Treaty. Full female suffrage granted in Turkey. International Congress of Women held in Istanbul. Muslim League re-organized by Muhammad Ali Jinnah. Commission on Banking in Ceylon. After quarrel with Chiang Kai-shek, CP makes 'Long March' to N China: new state set up in N Shensi: Yen-an, capital.

## THE AMERICAS

**1933** Jan., President Roosevelt enunciates 'Good Neighbour' policy of US: many professional men and women sent to aid C and S America. 2 Jan., US troops withdraw from Nicaragua. 14 Feb., bank crisis in US. 4 March, Roosevelt inaugurated: New Deal policies announced. 6-9 March, all banks closed in US. 9 March, Roosevelt granted dictatorial powers over credit and currency by Congress. Apr., Sánchez Cerro assassinated: succ. Marshal Oscar Benavîdes (–1939). 12 Apr., the dollar devalued. 25 Apr., Canada leaves gold standard. 30 Apr., US leaves gold standard. 18 May, Tennessee Valley Authority (TVA) created to develop its resources. 16 June, US National Industrial Recovery Act. 12 Aug., uprising in Cuba. Sept., Sergeant Fulgencio Batista seizes power in Cuba: Ramón Grau San Martín appointed President. 5 Oct., Twentieth Amendment to US Constitution: presidents to be inaugurated on 20 Jan.; Congress to assemble on 3 Jan. 5 Dec., Twenty-First Amendment to the US Constitution repeals the Eighteenth Amendment: prohibition ended. 18 Dec., Government of Newfoundland collapses: Commission appointed by UK. US Agricultural Adjustment Act. ½m. to 600,000 unemployed in Canada. Trans-Canada Air Route, for defence and transcontinental service, established. Roca-Runciman Treaty between Argentina and Britain: Britain to continue importing Argentine beef: US denounces treaty as anti-US.
**1933–7** Juan Bautista Sacasa, President of Nicaragua.
**1933–54** General Anastasio Somoza, head of *guardia nacional*, dictator of Nicaragua.
**1934** 24 March, US promises Philippines independence in 1945. 16 July, new constitution in Brazil with corporative provisions: 17 July, Vargas elected President. New constitution in Uruguay.
**1934–40** Lázaro Cardenas, President of Mexico.

## RELIGION & CULTURE

**1933** 1 April kept as an official anti-Semitic day in Germany: beginning of systematic persecution of German Jews. July, German Evangelical Church instituted. 20 July, concordat between Germany and the Vatican. July–Aug., massacre of Assyrian Christians in Iraq. 5 Sept., first attacks on the churches by the Nazis in Germany. First concentration camps for Jews opened in Germany. Islamic law forbidding depiction of human beings and animals formally rescinded in Turkey. British Museum buys Codex Sinaiticus from USSR for £300,000. Pro-Cathedral built in Addis Ababa.

**1934** Neutrons discovered by James Chadwick. The cat's-eye reflector invented. Hendon Police College founded. Garesa Museum, Mogadishu, opened. Jewish *Youth Aliyah* established, to rescue Jewish children from Nazi Germany.

**1934–** General Yakubu Gowon, President of Nigeria.

1934–1936

WESTERN &
NORTHERN EUROPE

CENTRAL &
SOUTHERN EUROPE

AFRICA

**1934** US, Hungary, Bulgaria, Czechoslovakia and Rumania recognize USSR.

**1935** 1 Jan., 1615 collective farms in Russia, as against 5m. persons with private land. 7 Jan., Franco-Italian agreement on boundaries in EA. 3 Feb., Franco-British *rapprochement* in London. 2 May, Franco-Soviet mutual assistance pact. 6 May, King George V's Silver Jubilee. 31 May, Bouisson, Prime Minister of France. 4 June, Pierre Laval, Prime Minister of France. 6 June–1937, S. Baldwin, Prime Minister. 18 June, Anglo-German Naval Agreement. Aug., Stakhanovite movement introduced in Russia. 14 Nov., National Government wins general election in Britain with 428 seats over 184. 9 Dec., Hoare-Laval proposals for Ethiopia announced in London. 19 Dec., Sir S. Hoare resigns: 23 Dec., Anthony Eden, Foreign Secretary.

**1935** Jan., Portuguese National Assembly and Corporative Chamber meet for the first time. 4-7 Jan., Premier Laval of France visits Mussolini in Rome: 6 Jan., agreement signed. 13 Jan, Saar plebiscite: majority opt for reunification with Germany (restored 7 March). 16 March, Germany reintroduces conscription: military clauses of Versailles treaty repudiated. 11 Apr., Stresa conference between Britain, France and Italy. 23 Apr., new constitution in Poland. 12 May, Pilsudski d.: Marshal Smigly-Rydz, virtual dictator of Poland. 19 May, Nazis gain in elections in Czechoslovakia. 17 Oct., Schuschnigg defeats Nazis in bloodless *coup d'état* in Austria. 3 Nov., George II of Greece restored by plebiscite. 18 Nov., League of Nations agrees on sanctions against Italy. 18 Dec., Edouard Benes, President of Czechoslovakia. Non-aggression pact signed between Czechoslovakia and USSR.

**1935** 1 Feb., Italy sends troops to Eritrea and Somalia. March, Ethiopia requests protection of League of Nations against Italy. May, Lusaka inaugurated as capital of N Rhodesia. 20-31 May, African strikes and riots on Copper Belt. 3 Oct., Italy invades Ethiopia, using aircraft and poison gas: 6 Oct., Adowa occupies: 8 Nov., Makalle and Tigre occupied. 12 Dec., Egyptian nationalists demand restoration of 1923 constitution. Grey Shirt movement in SA in imitation of Nazi Brown Shirts.

**1936** 15 Jan., Japan leaves London Naval Conference (begun Dec. 1935). 20 Jan., King George V d.: succ. Edward VIII. 22 Jan., Albert Sarraut, Prime Minister of France. 25 March, Naval Convention of London between Britain, France and USA. 26 Apr–3 May, general election in France returns a Popular Front majority. May, the *franc* devalued. 19 June, Irish Republican Army (IRA) proclaimed illegal. 9 Sept., Spanish Non-Intervention Committee of European powers holds first meeting in London. 25 Sept., the *franc* again devalued. Oct., Léopold III reiterates Belgian neutrality. 1 Oct., USSR joins London Naval Convention. 10 Dec., Edward VIII abdicates: succ. George VI (–1952). 12 Dec., Irish constitution amended. New constitution promulgated in USSR: Central Committee replaced by Supreme Soviet.

**1936** Feb.–June, 269 murders in Spain; 170 churches, 69 political clubs, 10 newspaper offices burnt; 113 general and 228 partial strikes. 16 Feb., elections in Spain: Popular Front, of anarchists, communists, republicans, socialists and syndicalists form coalition: constitution of 1931 re-established. 7 March, Germany re-occupies the Rhineland: Locarno agreements repudiated. 19 March, economic agreements between Albania and Italy. 23 March, Pact of Rome between Austria, Hungary and Italy. 10 May, Manuel Azaña, Prime Minister of Spain. 11 July, agreement between Austria and Germany acknowledging Austrian independence. 15 July, sanctions against Italy discontinued. 18 July, General Francisco Franco rebels against the Republican government in Spain: beginning of Spanish Civil War. 20 July, conference of Montreux on the Straits. 24 July, *Junta de Defensa Nacional*, Spanish nationalist government, set up in Burgos.

**1936** 31 March–2 Apr., Ethiopians defeated at Marchew. 7 Apr., SA Native Representation Act allows Africans to elect three Europeans to Parliament. SA Lands Act: Bantu given 37.5m. acres as reserves out of total of 302m. 28 Apr., Farouk, King of Egypt (–1952). 2 May, following advice of Council of Ministers, Emperor Haile Selassie leaves Ethiopia to keep international negotiations open. 5 May, Italians take Addis Ababa: 9 May, Ethiopia formally annexed by Italy: Victor Emmanuel III proclaimed Emperor: Ethiopian guerrilla resistance continues under Ras Imru and the Black Lions. 17 July, rising of Spanish army in Melilla and Morocco against Popular Front led by General Francisco Franco: rapidly spreads to Spain. 26 Aug., British end occupation of Egypt except for Canal Zone: twenty year Anglo-Egyptian treaty allows Britain to station 10,000 men in Egypt. Dec., Ras Imru surrenders: underground resistance persists.

## THE EAST & AUSTRALASIA THE AMERICAS RELIGION & CULTURE

**1935** 21 March, Persia renamed Iran. 4 Aug., British Government of India Act makes new constitution. Surnames made compulsory in Turkey. Lanka Sama Samaja Party (LSSP) founded in Ceylon. Do-Bama Asi-ayon ('We, the Burmese') Confederation formed. Labour wins New Zealand general election: in power to 1949.

**1936** 26 Feb., military cabinet formed in Japan. 8 Apr., treaty of mutual assistance between Mongolia and Russia. 15 July, Indonesian Government Officials party requests autonomy for Dutch EI. 11 Aug., Chiang Kai-shek enters Canton: China virtually united. 29 Oct., General Sidqi takes power in Iraq. 12 Dec., Chiang Kai-shek declares war on Japan. Labour laws promulgated in Turkey: strikes and lock-outs forbidden: arbitration provided. New Zealand elected to Council of League of Nations. Bureau of Industry set up in New Zealand.
**1936–9** Arab revolt in Palestine, led by Mufti of Jerusalem.
**1936–43** Marquess of Linlithgow, Viceroy of India.
**1936–44** Lord Gowrie (later Earl of Gowrie), Governor-General of Australia.

**1935** June, Calles quietly expelled from Mexico. 12 June, armistice between Bolivia and Paraguay ends Chaco War. 14 Aug., Social Security Act in US. 20 Aug., Ibarra, President of Ecuador, deposed: succ. Pons. Oct., general election in Canada: Liberals return to power. 23 Oct.–1948, Mackenzie King again Canadian Prime Minister. Nov., mutinies crushed in Rio de Janeiro and Pernambuco. 2 Nov., Lord Tweedsmuir, Governor-General of Canada (–1940). 17 Dec., Juan Vicente Gómez, dictator of Venezuela, d.: mob violence ensues in Caracas: military take control: succ. Contreras. US Wagner Act sets up Labour Relations Board. Reciprocal trade treaty between Canada and US. 'New Deal' programme in Canada: Trade and Industry Commission Act, Minimum Wages Act, Limitation of Hours of Work Act, Weekly Rest Act, Unemployment Insurance Act, and Natural Products Marketing Act passed. Bank of Canada established as a central bank. Canadian Wheat Board set up to sell annual wheat crop. Social Credit movement wins provincial elections in Alberta. Wave of strikes in Mexico. Constitutional reform in British Honduras. Progressive League founded in Barbados.
**1936** 3 Nov., F.D.Roosevelt re-elected President of USA by 528 votes against 3. US Farm Relief Act. Rearmament begun in Canada. Commercial flights across the Atlantic become regular. Canadian Broadcasting Corporation established. City of Santo Domingo re-named Ciudad Trujillo. Manpower and Citizens' Association founded in British Guiana. Constitutional reform in Windward and in Leeward Is.

**1935** 14 Jan., oil pipe-line from Iraq to the Mediterranean inaugurated. 15 Sept., Nuremberg racial laws in Germany outlaw Jews. Cardinal Fisher and Sir Thomas More canonized. The British Council founded. University of Teheran founded. Exhibition of Chinese Art in London. Astrid, Queen of the Belgians, killed in a motor accident.

**1936** Le Corbusier, on invitation of Brazilian government, visits Brazil to advise on lay-out of new university city. Faculty of philology and historical research instituted at Ankara. Ford Foundation instituted. Radar invented.
**1936–65** Patrice Lumumba, Congolese politician.

1936–1938

WESTERN &
NORTHERN EUROPE

CENTRAL &
SOUTHERN EUROPE

AFRICA

**1936** 4 Aug., General Metaxas seizes power in Greece. 14 Aug., Spanish nationalists take Badajoz. Sept., Spanish nationalists take Irún and San Sebastián. 1 Oct., General Francisco Franco Bahamonde, Head of the Spanish State (-1975). 1 Nov., Rome-Berlin Axis proclaimed by Mussolini. 6 Nov., Spanish nationalists checked by republicans before Madrid: siege of Madrid begins: Spanish republican government moves to Valencia. 18 Nov., Germany and Italy recognize Spanish nationalist government. 25 Nov., Anti-Komintern Pact between Germany and Japan.

**1936** Blum-Violette reforms in Algeria.

**1937** 2 Jan., agreement between Britain and Italy on Spain and the Mediterranean. 23-30 Jan., treason trial in Moscow. 28 May, Stanley Baldwin retires: succ. Neville Chamberlain (−1940). 30 June, the *franc* again devalued. 17 July, naval agreements between Britain and Germany, and Britain and USSR. 3-24 Nov., Brussels Nine Power Conference on the war between Japan and China. 29 Dec., Irish Free State renamed Eire. 21 June, Camille Chautemps again Prime Minister of France.

**1937** 7 Jan., agreement between Poland and Danzig. 8 Feb., General Franco takes Málaga with Italian support. 15-18 Feb., Balkan Conference in Athens. 18 March, Italian detachment supporting S Spanish nationalists routed on R. Guadalajara. 27 Apr., Spanish nationalists destroy Guernica. 31 May, German fleet supporting Spanish nationalists bombards Almería. 19 June, Spanish nationalists take Bilbao. 26 Aug., Spanish nationalists take Santander. 17 Oct., riots in Sudetenland. 20 Oct., Spanish nationalists take Gijón; 22 Oct., Oviedo. 6 Nov., Italy joins Anti-Komintern Pact. 17-21 Nov., Lord Halifax visits Hitler: beginning of 'appeasement' policy. 11 Dec., Italy withdraws from the League of Nations.

**1937** Feb., grenades thrown at Italian Viceroy in Addis Ababa: three day Black Shirt reign of terror: sporadic resistance continues. March, *Parti du Peuple Algérien (PPA)* founded. 16 March, Mussolini visits Libya. 2 Apr., SA prohibits political activity by foreigners in SWA. 8 May, Montreux Convention abolishes capitulations in Egypt. 26 May, Egypt joins League of Nations. Sir Patrick Duncan, first SA born Governor-General, appointed. Economic crisis in Morocco. Moroccan Unity Party founded.

**1938** 20 Feb., Anthony Eden resigns: 25 Feb., Lord Halifax, British Foreign Secretary. 2-15 March, treason trial in Russia. 13 March, Léon Blum, Prime Minister of France. 10 Apr., Daladier, Prime Minister of France. 16 Apr., Anglo-Italian Pact: Italy now agrees to withdraw troops from Spain: Italian sovereignty in Ethiopia recognized. 25 Apr., agreement between Britain and Eire. May, the *franc* again devalued. 4 May, Douglas Hyde, a Protestant, elected first President of Eire. 17 May, agreement between Britain and Turkey. 21 Nov.−12 Dec., political strike in France. 6 Dec., Franco-German agreement made in Paris.

**1938** 15 Feb., Franco takes Teruel. 11 March, German army seizes Austria: 13 March, Austria declared part of the German *Reich*. 15 Apr., General Franco takes the Ebro estuary. 3-9 May, Hitler visits Mussolini in Rome. 25 July, Sir Walter Runciman visits Prague: reports favourably on German demands. Aug.–Sept., crisis between Germany and other powers over the Sudetenland. 15 Sept., Chamberlain visits Hitler at Berchtesgaden; 22-23 Sept., at Gödesberg. 29-30 Sept., Munich agreement between Chamberlain, Daladier, Hitler and Mussolini: Sudetenland transferred to Germany. 1-10 Oct., Germany occupies Sudetenland. 25 Oct., Mussolini declares Libya part of Italy. 14 Dec., Italian Chamber of Deputies replaced by Chamber of

**1938** 9 Apr., civil disobedience campaign in Tunisia organized by Habib Bourguiba. May-June, census of SA urban Africans to enforce segregation. SA begins preparations for war. Bledisloe Commission on closer co-operation between Rhodesias and Nyasaland. Tanganyika League formed in Nairobi to resist return of the territory to Germany.
c. **1938** *UPA (Union Populaire Algérienne)* founded by Ferhat Abbas.

**1937** 24 Jan., agreement between France and Turkey on Alexandretta. 20 Feb., elections in India: INC gains majority. 1 Apr., Burma becomes a separate entity in the British Empire: House of Representatives of 132 members, all elected: Upper House of 36 members, of whom 18 appointed, and 18 elected by lower house. 8 July, Pact of Saadabad between Afghanistan, Iraq, Iran and Turkey: defensive agreement. July, fighting between Chinese and Japanese troops near Peking: leads to war with China (–1945): Aug., Japanese besiege Shanghai; Nov., city taken; Dec., Nanking taken. 7 July, partition plan for Palestine published. 11 Aug., General Sidqi assassinated. 1 Oct., Higher Arab Committee proscribed in Palestine. 16 Dec., convention between France and Syria. Sinhala Maha Sabha Party founded in Ceylon by Solomon West Ridgeway Bandaranaike.
**1937**–Feb. **1939** Dr Ba Maw, Prime Minister of Burma.
**1938** Jan., Japan takes Shantung province of China: Chiang Kai-shek flees to Chungking. 12 May, Germany recognizes Manchukuo. 17 May, British White Paper on Palestine, proposing partition and independence within ten years. 3 July–11 Aug., border fighting between Japan and Russia in Manchukuo. 21 Oct., Japanese take Canton; 25 Oct., Hankow. 10 Nov., Mustafa Kemal d.: succ. Ismet İnönü. Second Turkish Five Year Plan. Bank of Ceylon instituted. New Zealand Social Security Act increases pensions and family allowances: national health service introduced.
**1938**–54 Factory output doubled in New Zealand.

**1937** May, 17,000 oil operatives in Mexico strike for higher wages. 1 May, US Neutrality Act. 13 July, military *coup* in Bolivia. 6 Aug., Russo–US trade pact. 10 Nov., new constitution in Brazil. Reform of Supreme Court of US defeated. Canadian Attorney-General given power to lock the premises of any organization deemed by him to be subversive. Trans-Canada Air Lines Corporation formed. Ottawa Agreement with UK renewed. Railways, largely foreign owned, nationalized in Mexico. Some 10,000 to 20,000 Haitians killed in Dominica.
**1937**–54 General Anastasio Somoza, President of Nicaragua.

**1938** 18 March, British and US oil companies ordered by Mexican government to give employees substantial rises: companies refuse: all expelled: oil nationalized. 11 May, abortive Nazi rising in Brazil. 5 Sept., abortive Nazi plot in Chile. Oct., state of war declared in Brazil for fear of a Communist rising. 10 Oct., treaty between Bolivia and Paraguay gives Paraguay most of Gran Chaco. 24 Oct., US Fair Labour Standards Act provides 'a ceiling over hours and a floor under wages'. 9-26 Dec., Pan-American Conference of Lima. Reciprocal trade treaty between Canada and US extended. Earthquake in southern Chile. Royal Commission on the W Indies. People's National Party founded in Jamaica. Labour Congress held in British Guiana.

**1937** 18 March, Pope Pius XI: Encyclical *Mit brennender Sorge* on Nazism successfully smuggled into Germany. May-Sept, World Exhibition in Paris. Admitted by Yaroslavski, President of the Godless League, that one-third of Russians were still Christians, of whom two-thirds in the countryside. *Pithecanthropus* skull discovered in Java (Java Man). The Chaillot Palace built in Paris. Nylon invented. The 'jet' engine invented.

**1938** 8-14 Nov., violent persecution of Jews in Germany. 10 Nov., anti-Jewish legislation in Italy. National Institute of Economic and Social Research founded in London. Women's Voluntary Service founded. *Institut Français* (later *Fondamental*) *d'Afrique Noire* founded in Dakar. The biro pen invented. Stalin: *Abridged History of the Bolshevik Party* published.

## 1938–1940

### WESTERN & NORTHERN EUROPE     CENTRAL & SOUTHERN EUROPE     AFRICA

*Fasci* and Corporations. 22 Dec., Italy denounces all agreements with France. President Carmona of Portugal confirmed by plebiscite.

**1939** 27 Feb., France recognizes General Franco's government. 28 Feb., UK recognizes General Franco's government. 19 March, Britain guarantees independence to Rumania. 31 March, Britain and France guarantee independence of Poland. 13 Apr., Britain and France guarantee independence of Greece and Rumania. 16 Apr., abortive Russian proposal of alliance with France and Britain. May, conscription introduced in Britain. 12 May, Treaty between Turkey and UK. 23 June, treaty between France and UK. July, Franco-British military mission to Moscow. 3 Sept., Britain and France declare war on Germany: Italy remains neutral. 5 Sept., Winston Churchill and Anthony Eden join the British Cabinet. 30 Sept., USSR invades Finland. 2 Oct., French agreement with exiled Czech government; 6 Oct., with Poland; 19 Oct., with Britain and Turkey; 12 Dec., with Britain. 14 Oct., Germans sink HMS *Royal Oak* in Scapa Flow.

**1940** 8 Jan., food rationing begun in Britain. Feb., Colonial Development Fund approved by Parliament. 12 March, peace treaty between Finland and USSR. 21 March, Daladier resigns. 23 March, Paul Reynaud forms French government. 9 Apr., Germany invades Denmark and Norway. 9 Apr., Vidkun Quisling, puppet Prime Minister of Norway. 19 Apr., allies land in Norway. 10 May, Neville Chamberlain resigns: Winston Churchill, Prime Minister (–1945). Germany invades Belgium, Holland and Luxembourg. Britain occupies Iceland. Switzerland mobilises. 13 May, Churchill's 'blood, toil, tears and sweat' speech. 15 May, Holland surrenders. 28 May, Belgium surrenders. 28 May, Franco-British agreement. 28 May–3 June, British army evacuated at Dunkirk: troops of many other nations reach Britain. 9 June, Norway surrenders. 14 June, German army enters Paris. 16 June, Pétain, Prime Minister of France: requests an armistice with Germany. 18 June, General de Gaulle calls on France to continue resistance to Germany. 22 June, armistice between France and Germany. 24 June, armistice between France and Italy.

**1939** 10 Jan., Chamberlain and Halifax visit Mussolini. 13 Jan., Hungary joins Anti-Komintern Pact. 26 Jan., General Franco takes Barcelona. 15 March, Hitler occupies Czechoslovakia. 22 March, Memel ceded to Germany. 28 March, General Franco takes Madrid: end of Spanish civil war. 7 Apr., Good Friday, Mussolini seizes Albania. Spain joins Anti-Komintern Pact. 8 May, Spain leaves League of Nations. 22 May, ten year military alliance between Germany and Italy. 23 Aug., German–USSR non-aggression pact makes war inevitable. 1 Sept., Germany invades Poland. 9-30 Sept., French offensive in the Saar. 17 Sept., USSR invades Poland. 27 Sept., Poland capitulates; 30 Sept., partitioned between Germany and USSR. 14 Dec., Russia expelled by League of Nations.

**1940** 10 June, Italy declares war on Britain and France: seizure of Nice and Savoy follows. 2 July, Germany occupies Bessarabia and Bukovina. 6 Sept., Carol of Rumania abdicates: succ. Michael. 27 Sept., Tripartite Pact between Germany, Italy and Japan. 28 Sept., Italy attacks Greece; 29 Sept., British troops land in Greece. 8 Oct., Germany occupies Rumania.

**1939** 20 July, convention of British non-officials at Iringa backs closer union in EA. 4 Sept., Hertzog attempts to declare SA neutral: defeated by 80 votes to 67: 5 Sept., Smuts forms coalition. Continental Ethiopian resistance holds down fifty-six Italian battalions. Nigerian Regiment raises fifteen battalions. *PPA* dissolved.

**1939–45** Large numbers of African troops recruited in British and French territories for active service: treated by Germans with especial cruelty.

**1940** 14 June, Spain occupies Tangier. 3 July, British sink French fleets at Mers el-Kebir and Oran. 4 July, Italy invades the Sudan. 21 July, Smuts broadcasts to Britain and USA on an 'international society of free nations'. 4-17 Aug., Italy takes British Somaliland. 26 Aug., Niger and Chad declare in favour of de Gaulle. 27 Aug., Cameroun taken over by Free French; 28 Aug., French Congo follows suit. Sept., small British force working with Ethiopian guerrillas. 3 Sept., Italians reach Sidi Barrani in offensive on British positions in Egypt. 23-25 Sept., Anglo-French expedition to take Dakar fails. 8 Nov., Gabon taken over by Free French. 9 Dec., British under Wavell attack Italians; 12 Dec., Sidi Barrani taken; 15 Dec., drive Italians out of Libya: offensive until 8 Feb. 1941. 16 Dec., Italians driven from El Wak, British Somaliland.

598

| THE EAST & AUSTRALASIA | THE AMERICAS | RELIGION & CULTURE |
|---|---|---|

**1938–41** Pedro Aguirre Cerda, President of Chile, with Popular Front government.

**1939** 10 Feb., Japan occupies Hainan. 4 Apr., Ghazi I of Iraq d.: succ. Faysal II (–1958). May–Sept., fighting between Japanese and Russians on borders of Manchukuo and Outer Mongolia. 23 June, France cedes Alexandretta to Turkey. Aug., Japanese puppet government under Wang Tsing-wei set up in Nanking. 17 Oct., Viceroy re-affirms dominion status as goal for India, with action to be taken after war. 19 Oct., pact between Britain and Turkey. U Pu, Prime Minister of Burma, followed shortly by U Saw. Nehru visits Ceylon. United Socialist Party (USP) founded in Ceylon. British White Paper on future of Palestine.
**1939–54** New Zealand enjoys bulk purchase agreement with UK for agricultural products.

**1939** 20 March, US ambassador recalled from Berlin. 15 Apr., Roosevelt makes fruitless peace plea to Hitler. 9 Sept., Canadian Parliament votes to join war against Germany. 3 Nov., US Neutrality Act amended to end arms embargo: 'cash and carry' allowed. 13 Dec., battle of the R. Plate, off Montevideo. US–Panama treaty (1936) ratified by US Senate: Panama ceases to be a US Protectorate. Wartime Prices and Trade Board set up in Canada. Prairie Farm Assistance Act to assist drought areas in Canada. Hatch Act reforms US civil service. Dominica obtains separate constitution. Catastrophic rains in Peru.
**1939–45** Manuel Prado, President of Peru.

**1939** The 'Oxford Group' under Frank Buchman changes its name to Moral Rearmament (MRA). DDT invented by Paul Müller.
**1939–58** Pius XII (Pacelli), Pope.

**1940** May, following preaching of pacifism by Gandhi, 40,000 INC members imprisoned. Viceregal Council expanded to fifteen, with eleven Indian members. June, treaty of friendship between Japan and Siam. 1 June, Gandhi affirms that 'we do not seek our independence out of British ruin'. 8 Aug., Indian Congress Party declines to serve on War Advisory Committee. Sept., Japan occupies all N French Indo-China. Pakistan named as official aim of Muslim League in India. Ministers in Ceylon engage in foreign affairs, hitherto reserved to governor: ministerial delegation visits Delhi. Japan holding all China except western provinces. New Zealand abolishes Legislative Council: Parliament now unicameral.
**1940–1** Japan victorious over China: Japanese puppet governments set up in Canton, Nanking and Peking. R.G.Menzies, Federal Prime Minister of Australia.

**1940** 26 March, general election in Canada: Liberals again returned. 21 June, Earl of Athlone, Governor-General of Canada (–1946). Aug., Prime Minister King of Canada and President Roosevelt meet at Ogdensburg: Permanent Joint Defence Board created. 3 Sept., US sells Britain fifty destroyers: Britain leases naval bases to US from Newfoundland to British Guiana. 5 Nov., F.D.Roosevelt re-elected for a third term. 20 Nov., British and US agree on partial standardization of weapons. Conscription introduced in US. First Canadian troops sent to Britain. Canadians take over garrison duties in W Indies. Fulgencio Batista assumes power as President in Cuba (–1944). National Resources Mobilization Act in Canada authorizes selective service for home defence and civil employment: no conscription for overseas service. Havana Conference: W Indian National Emergency Committee demands federation. ¾m. peasant families given land grants in Mexico: co-operatives started for sale of produce. Population of Mexico 19.8m.
**1940–6** Manuel Avila Camacho, President of Mexico.

**1940** 3 Oct., anti-Jewish laws enacted in France. Penicillin developed as an antibiotic in St Mary's Hospital, Paddington. Society for Freedom in Science founded. Fabian Colonial Bureau founded. Kimberley (Australia) Research Station set up to irrigate 17,0000 square miles. 14,000 Poles foully massacred at Katyn, Poland.

1940–1941

WESTERN &
NORTHERN EUROPE

CENTRAL &
SOUTHERN EUROPE

AFRICA

**1940** 28 June, Britain recognizes General de Gaulle as head of the Free French Forces (*FFL*). 2 July, puppet French government of Unoccupied France installed at Vichy. 11 July, Pétain becomes Head of State in France (−1944). 2 Aug., General de Gaulle condemned to death for contumaciousness. 3-6 Aug., Estonia, Latvia and Lithuania become Soviet republics. 8 Aug.−5 Oct., battle of Britain: RAF defeats German Air Force. 7 Sept.−31 Oct., Germans bomb London: the 'Blitz'. 10 Nov., interview between Goering and Laval. 13 Dec., Flandin premier of France in place of Laval. 22 Dec., Anthony Eden becomes British Foreign Secretary. First Colonial Development and Welfare Act.

**1941** Jan., National Consultative Committee set up in France. 9 Feb., Darlan replaces Flandin as French premier. 11 Apr., US occupies Greenland. 10-11 May, House of Commons destroyed in German air raid. June, Workers' Charter published in France. 22 June, Hitler attakcs USSR. July, Franco-Japanese agreement. 11 July, battle of Bialystok-Minsk: Germans take 300,000 Russians prisoner. 20 July, Germans take Smolensk: Russians abandon Reval. 30 July, breach between France and USSR. Aug., General J.C.Smuts made a British Field-Marshal. Sept.-Oct., 600,000 Russians taken prisoner in battles of Kiev and Viazma-Briansk: Orel, Kharkov and Odessa fall to Germans. 9 Sept., Germans besiege Leningrad. 23 Sept., *Comité National Français* (*CNF*) set up in London. 16 Oct., Germans occupy Kalinine (Tver): diplomatic missions leave Moscow for Kuibychev (Samara): Stalin remains in Moscow. Nov.−1942 March, Russo-German front stabilized by winter. 16 Nov.−5 Dec., battle for Moscow.

**1941** 10 Jan., battle of the Straits of Sicily. 21 Jan., attempted *coup* in Rumania.   2 March, Germany invades Bulgaria. 25 March, Yugoslavia joins the Tripartite Pact. 27 March, Peter II seizes direct control in Yugoslavia. 28 March, battle of Cape Matapan. 5 Apr., Russo-Yugoslav Pact.   6 Apr., German troops enter Yugoslavia shortly after signature of non-aggression pact between Germany and Yugoslavia: occupation of Albania, Macedonia and Greece follows. 10 Apr., Croatia proclaims itself independent. 18 Apr., Yugoslavia surrenders. 27 Apr., Athens taken. 11 May, Rudolf Hess flies from Germany to Scotland to propose peace. 11-12 May, Hitler and Darlan meet at Berchtesgaden. 20-21 May, Germans occupy Crete. 18 June, Treaty of Friendship between Germany and Turkey: safeguards Turkish neutrality. 28 Aug., Boris III of Bulgaria d.: succ. Simeon II. 11 Dec., Germany and Italy declare war on USA. 19 Dec., Hitler takes personal command of the German forces.

**1941** 19 Jan., British offensive begins in East Africa: Kassala recovered. 20 Jan., Emperor Haile Selassie re-enters Ethiopia. 22 Jan., British take Tobruk. 30 Jan., pro-British rising in Ethiopia. Feb., riot following pro-Nazi meeting in Johannesburg. 7 Feb., British take Benghazi. 9 Feb., German troops cross to N Africa under command of Marshal Erwin Rommel. 26 Feb., British take Mogadishu. 17 March, British take Berbera. 31 March, German counter-offensive in N Africa begins. 2 Apr., British take Asmara. 5 Apr., following campaign, British take Addis Ababa; 6 Apr., Massawa. 7 Apr., British evacuate Benghazi in planned withdrawal. 12 Apr., Germans retake Bardia. 20 May, Ethiopia independent: British Military Administration: Sir Philip Mitchell, Chief Political Officer. 27 Sept., Italians capitulate at Gondar: end of Italian operations in Ethiopia. 18 Nov., British renew offensive in Libya.   19 Dec., Rommel begins withdrawal from Libya: 24 Dec., British regain Benghazi and Cyrenaica.

**1941** Jan., Indonesian nationalists press demands for autonomy. 28 Jan., end of hostilities between France and Siam. March, 'Thirty Comrades', led by Thakin Aung San, leave Burma secretly for intensive military training by Japanese. 5 Apr., Japanese air raid on Colombo by carrier-based bombers. 9 Apr., Japanese raid on Trincomalee harbour, Ceylon. 13 Apr., Japan and Russia sign a five-year neutrality pact. 2 May, Rashid Ali pro-Axis *coup* leads in Baghdad. 9 May, treaty between France and Siam. 31 May, Rashid Ali's rebellion put down by Britain. 8 June, British and Free French invade Syria. French Mandates over Syria and Lebanon relinquished. 2 July, China breaks off relations with Germany and Italy. July, Japan occupies all French Indo-China. 25 Aug., Britain and USSR occupy Iran. 16 Sept., Reza Shah Pahlavi abdicates: succ. Muhammad Reza Shah. 7 Dec., Japan annihilates US fleet at Pearl Harbour, simultaneously attacking Hawaii, Hong Kong, Malaya, Singapore, and the Philippines. 17 Dec., the allies occupy Timor. 19 Dec., Japanese occupy Hong Kong; 22 Dec., Philippines. Indian delegation visits Ceylon. 90,000 Indian troops involved in fall of Singapore. Burmese request for dominion status abruptly refused by Winston Churchill U Saw, Prime Minister of Burma, interned. Indian population 389m.; Muslims form 24% or 92m.; other minorites 42m. Arthur Fadden, Federal Prime Minister of Australia.
**1941—5** John Curtin, Federal Prime Minister of Australia.

**1941** 11 March, Lend-Lease Act passed in US. Apr., President Roosevelt makes Hyde Park Declaration: Canada enabled to exchange war supplies with US. 11 Aug., Churchill and Roosevelt meet in mid-Atlantic: 14 Aug., Atlantic Charter signed. 7 Dec., President Roosevelt declares the defence of Turkey necesary to the security of USA. Constitutional reform in Trinidad. US Army approx. 1½m.
**1941—5** 15m. men and women serve in US armed forces: 300,000 aircraft built, 86,000 tanks, 71,000 ships. Isaias Medina Angarita, President of Venezuela.
**1941—6** Elie Lescot, President of Haiti.

**1941** 2 June, additional anti-Jewish legislation in France. Orthodox Patriarchs take part in election of Patriarch Alexis as Patriarch of Moscow and of All Russia. Double Summer Time instituted in UK.

1942–1943

WESTERN &
NORTHERN EUROPE

CENTRAL &
SOUTHERN EUROPE

AFRICA

**1942** 10 Jan., German offensive in Crimea. 27-28 March, allied raid on St Nazaire. 18 Apr., Laval back in power. 12 May, Russian offensive begins near Kharkov: shortly broken. 26 May, twenty-year alliance between Britain and Russia. 25 June, General Dwight D. Eisenhower appointed C.-in-C., US Forces in Europe. 28 June, German offensive begins on a wide front: Koursk-Kharkov front pierced: R. Don passed: Rostov taken. 2 July, Germans enter Sebastopol. 28 July–2 Feb. 1943 Siege of Stalingrad. Belgians deported to Germany for forced labour. 12-15 Aug., Moscow Conference between Britain, USA and USSR. 19 Aug., allied raid on Dieppe. 6 Nov., Russians recover Kiev. 8 Nov., US breaks off diplomatic relations with Vichy France. 11 Nov., 'Unoccupied France' occupied by the Germans. 17 Nov., Pétain hands over power to Laval. 20 Nov., Sir William Beveridge's Report on Social Security published. 27 Nov., French fleet blown up by the Germans at Toulon. Dec., Leningrad relieved.

**1942** 4 Feb., George II ends dictatorship in Greece. 27 May, Heydrick, German Gestapo leader in Czechoslovakia, murdered. 30 May, Cologne raided by 1,000 bombers. 10 June, Lidice, Czechoslovakia, wiped out by the Germans. 30 Aug., Germany annexes Luxembourg. 9-11 Nov., Hitler and Laval meet in Berchtesgaden. 12 Dec., alliance between Czechoslovakia and USSR. Portugal and Spain form 'Iberian Bloc'.

**1942** 31 Jan., Anglo-Ethiopian military convention: Emperor resumes administration with British advisers at his request. 5 May–5 Nov., British occupy Madagascar. 7 May, Bizerta and Tunis liberated. June, racialist laws made by Vichy regime in Algeria. 9-28 June, British withdraw to El Alamein. 19 Aug., Alexander takes command of army in Middle East: Montgomery in command of Eighth Army. 23 Oct., Eighth Army begins battle of El Alamein. Nov., Moncef Bey forms nationalist government in Tunisia. 8 Nov., Allied First Army under General Dwight D. Eisenhower lands in Algeria. 13 Nov., Tobruk taken. 14 Nov., Germans disembark in Tunisia. 20 Nov., British take Benghazi. 30 Nov., British occupy Réunion. 14 Dec., Madagascar handed over to the *CNF* by the allies. 21 Dec., Algiers taken. 24 Dec., Admiral Darlan assassinated by a Frenchman in Algiers.

**1943** 16 Jan., Britain refuses to recognize the Spanish annexation of Tangier. 2 Feb., Germans capitulate before Stalingrad: 91,000 Germans taken prisoner, including twenty-four generals and one field-marshal. 2-28 Feb., Caucasus liberated. 7 March, Stalin assumes title of Marshal. 15 May, *Comité National de la Résistance* constituted in France. 5 Aug., Russia retakes Orel. 5 Sept., Russia retakes Stalino: Donetz basin liberated. 25 Sept., Russia retakes Smolensk. 19-30 Oct., Moscow Conference. 6 Nov., Russia retakes Kiev. 9 Nov., de Gaulle sole President of *CFLN*. North of Scotland Hydro-Electric Board created.

**1943** 5 Feb., Count Ciano, Foreign Minister, dismissed by Mussolini. 17 March, *Cortes*, part elected, part nominated and part *ex officio*, inaugurated in Spain. 4 July, General Sikorski, Free Polish leader, killed in an aircraft at Gibraltar. 10 July, the allies disembark in Sicily: Syracuse taken. 23 July, Palermo taken. 25 July, Mussolini falls: Marshal Badoglio forms Italian government. 28 July, the Fascist Party dissolved. 5 Aug., Catania taken. 15 Aug., beginning of allied negotiations with Italy for an armistice. 17 Aug., Messina taken. 3 Sept., Italy surrenders unconditionally. 4 Sept., the allies disembark on the Italian mainland. 8 Sept., allied armistice with Italy made public. 10 Sept., Germany occupies N Italy and Rome. 12-13 Sept., Free French troops disembark in Corsica.

**1943** 13 Jan., General Leclerc joins Free French forces from Chad with British Eighth Army. 14-27 Jan., Casablanca Conference: allies demand 'unconditional surrender' by Germany, Italy and Japan. 23 Jan., British take Tripoli. 10 Feb., Ferhat Abbas: *Manifesto of the Algerian People*. 21 Feb., allied armies in N Africa placed under General Eisenhower. 16-29 March, battle of the Mareth Line, Tunisia. 24 March, interview between General de Gaulle and General Giraud at Casablanca. 12 May, Germans surrender in Tunisia. 30 May, General de Gaulle arrives in Algiers. 31 May, further interview between de Gaulle and Giraud. 3 June, Generals de Gaulle and Giraud, co-Chairmen of newly formed French Committee of National Liberation, (*Comité Français de la Libération Nationale*)(*CFLN*).

## THE EAST & AUSTRALASIA

**1942** 2 Jan, Japanese take Manila.
19 Jan., Japanese invade Burma.
15 Feb., Japan receives surrender of
Singapore, together with the rest of
Malaya. March, US General Douglas
Macarthur makes Australia the
allied base in the Pacific. 8 March,
Japan takes Java. 10 March, Japan
takes Rangoon. 11 March, Sir
Stafford Cripps sent to India with
'Cripps offer': reiterates dominion
status for India after the war:
provision for constituent assembly.
Apr., Japanese bomb Vizagapatam,
India. Japanese fleet controls Bay
of Bengal: British fleet retires to
EA bases: Japanese in full control
of Malaya and Dutch East Indies.
12 Apr., USAAF bombs Tokyo. 1
May, Japanese take Mandalay:
Burma road cut. 6 May, US
surrenders in the Philippines. 7-11
May, battle of the Coral Sea: air
battle between Japanese and US
fleets. 4-6 June, battle of Midway:
Japanese fleet crippled: Japanese
momentum checked. 7 Aug., US
troops land in Guadalcanal. 7 Aug.,
All-India Congress Committee
rejects 'Cripps offer': Viceroy
imprisons INC committee: short
rising with violence follows. Nov.,
naval battle of Guadalcanal:
Japanese defeated. 26 Nov.,
Churchill, Stalin and Roosevelt meet
in Teheran. Malayan Peoples' anti-
Japanese Army (MPAJA) founded:
about 3,000 jungle fighters. D.S.
Senanayake, Leader of the Ceylon
State Council.
**1942–5** Burma under Japanese rule.
**1942–6** W African troops serving
in Burma.
**1943** Feb., Japanese evacuate
Guadalcanal. 2 March, Japanese
defeated in Battle of the Bismarck
Sea. 1 Aug., Japanese declare
Burma an independent sovereign
state: Ba Maw, Prime Minister. 25
Aug., South-East Asia Command
(SEAC) set up at Peradeniya, Ceylon,
under Lord Mountbatten. 14 Oct.,
Japan declares the Philippines
independent. Nov., Conference of
Greater East Asia held in Tokyo:
includes representatives from China,
Manchukuo, Siam, Philippines,
Burma and 'Free India'. 20 Nov.,
US troops disembark at Tarawa.
1-24 Dec., Teheran Conference:
Churchill, Roosevelt and Stalin plan
defeat of Germany. 16 Dec., US
troops disembark in New Britain.
22 Dec., Syria and Lebanon given
independence by France. Famine
in Bengal.

## THE AMERICAS

**1942** 1 Jan., Washington Pact signed
by twenty-six United Nations not to
make separate peace with Germany.
28 Jan., all American republics
except Argentina sever diplomatic
relations with the Axis. 6 Feb.,
Combined Chiefs of Staff appointed
by Britain and US. May, Mexico
declares war on the Axis. 3 June,
Japan invades Aleutian Is. 5 June,
US declares war on Bulgaria. 11
June, US extends lease-lend to USSR.
Brazil declares war on the Axis.
**1942–6** Juan Antonio Ríos,
President of Chile.

**1943** 18 May–1 June, Hot Springs
Conference: United Nations Relief
and Rehabilitation Administration
(UNRRA) founded. 4 June,
military *coup d'état* in Argentina:
Colonel Juan D. Perón, Minister of
Labour: General Arturo Rawson,
President: fascist type government
instituted. 10 June, the Komintern
dissolved. 11-24 Aug., Quebec
Conference to plan further allied
strategy in the Far East. Oct.,
foreign ministers of Britain, Russia
and US prepare agreement for
making alliance into permanent body
of United Nations. Constitutional
reform in British Guiana. Volcano
Paricutin erupts, reaching 1500 feet
in eight weeks. Enlightened labour
code introduced in Brazil.

## RELIGION & CULTURE

**1942** 16 Apr., Malta awarded the
George Cross for heroism under air
attack. First electronic computer made
in US. The nuclear reactor invented.
University of Ceylon chartered.
OXFAM founded by Professor Gilbert
Murray.
**1942–4** William Temple, Abp of
Canterbury.

**1943** 20 Apr., Jews massacred in
Warsaw. 22 May, the Third
International (Communist) dissolved.
8 Sept., many churches in Russia re-
opened: Holy Synod permitted to
meet: Ecclesiastical Academy of
Moscow revived: Metropolitan Sergius
elected 'Patriarch of Moscow and All
Russia'. Worker-priest movement
founded in France. Nuffield
Foundation instituted. Streptomycin
discovered. The aqualung invented.

| WESTERN & NORTHERN EUROPE | CENTRAL & SOUTHERN EUROPE | AFRICA |
|---|---|---|

**1943** 12 Oct., Portugal grants Britain military facilities in the Azores. 13 Nov., Italy recognized by the allies as a co-belligerent: declares war on Germany. 4 Dec., Communist government formed by Marshal Tito in Yugoslavia. 20 Dec., the Falange Movement dissolved in Spain.

**1943** 17 Sept., French Provisional Consultative Assembly constituted in Algiers. 22-26 Nov., Cairo Conference of Britain, China and USA.

**1944** Feb.–March, Don basin liberated. 1 Feb., Laval announces that Frenchmen from 16 to 65, and women from 18 to 45, can be conscripted for work in Germany. 8 Feb., monetary agreement between France and Britain. 10 March, Ireland declines to break off diplomatic relations with the Axis. Apr.–May, Crimea liberated. 21 Apr., General Giraud dismissed from command of *FFL*. 29 Apr., meeting between Laval and Hitler. 3 June, the allies enter Rome. 6 June, allies disembark in Normandy. 12 June, the Germans start using flying bombs. 22 June, Stalin orders general offensive: Warsaw shortly reached: eastern Prussia attacked: Rumania and Bulgaria taken and compelled to make war on Germany: Hungary taken. 27 June, Cherbourg liberated. 9 July, Caen liberated. 15 Aug., allied armies under de Lattre de Tassigny and Patch disembark in S France. 20 Aug., Marshal Pétain arrested by the Germans. 24 Aug., first French troops under General Leclerc enter Paris. 25 Aug., von Choltitz surrenders to General Leclerc. 26 Aug., General de Gaulle enters Paris. 4 Sept., Lyons liberated. 5 Sept., Brussels liberated. 6 Sept., provisional government set up in Paris (*Gouvernement Provisoire de la Republique Française*)(*GPRF*) (1944–7): de Gaulle, Provisional President (–1945). 12 Sept., Le Havre liberated. 19-28 Sept., battle of Arnhem: allied progress halted. 20 Sept., Prince Charles, Regent of Belgium. 9 Oct., Moscow Conference between Churchill and Stalin. 23 Nov., Strasbourg liberated. 10 Dec., de Gaulle and Bidault sign agreement in Moscow. 17-28 Dec., German offensive in Luxembourg. Germans launch 387 U-boats.

**1944** 4 Jan.–18 May, battle of Monte Cassino. 12 Jan., Count Ciano and Marshal de Bono executed. 19 March, Germany occupies Hungary. May, allied offensive in Italy. 11 May, French under General Juin take Garigliano. 21 May, allies breach Hitler Line in Italy. 4 June, Rome taken. 20 July, abortive attempt on Hitler's life. 2 Aug., diplomatic relations between Germany and Turkey broken off. 22 Aug., Florence liberated. 18 Sept., Sofia taken. 29 Sept., Switzerland forbids export of munitions to Germany. 13 Oct., Athens liberated. 15 Oct., Hungary requests an armistice. 21 Oct., Belgrade liberated. 10 Nov., National Assembly meets in Belgrade. 18 Nov., Tirana liberated. 29 Nov., Hungary again asks for an armistice. 25 Dec., Churchill visits Athens.

**1944** 11 Jan., Moroccan Nationalists demand independence: Ahmad Balafrej arrested: riots ensue. 30 Jan.–8 Feb., Brazzaville conference on French policy in Africa promises decolonization. 20 Feb., *Force Publique* mutinies at Luluabourg. March, *AML* (*Amis du Manifeste et de la Liberté*) founded by Ferhat Abbas rapidly gains ½m. members in Algeria. 7 March, France allots to Algerian Muslims fifteen places in the National Assembly, and seven in the Council of the Republic. 16 March, Nationalist mob attacks meeting of 5,000 garment workers in Johannesburg. 21 Apr., ordinance issued in Algiers on organization. 8 Oct., Nahas Pasha dismissed by King Farouk: Ahmad Maher Pasha, Prime Minister. Dec., Tanganyika Government publishes *An Outline of Post-War Development Proposals*. Nyasaland African Congress (NAC) formed.

**1945** 1 Jan., German offensive in Lorraine. 2-12 Jan., Yalta Conference. 12 Jan., second Russian offensive opened: eastern Prussia seized. 16 Jan., economic agreement between France and USA. March, Russia denounces Russo-Turkish pact of 1921. 4 March, the allies reach the Rhine.

**1945** 20 Jan., Hungary granted an armistice. 13 Feb., Russians take Budapest. 7 March, the allies take Cologne. 30 March, Russians take Danzig. 13 Apr., Russians take Vienna. 16 Apr., Russian assault on Berlin begun. 23 Apr., allies reach Berlin. 28 Apr., Mussolini and his mistress lynched. 30 Apr., Hitler d.: Admiral Dönitz takes control.

**1945** 1 Jan., Wafd boycott Egyptian general election: premier, Ahmad Pasha. 20 Feb., de Gaulle declines to meet Roosevelt in Algiers. 24 Feb., Ahmad Pasha assassinated after Egyptian declaration of war on Germany. March, Arab League inaugurated in Cairo. Apr., Central African Council set up in Salisbury for Rhodesias and Nyasaland.

## THE EAST & AUSTRALASIA  THE AMERICAS  RELIGION & CULTURE

**1943** Japanese shipping losses ten times their annual new building.
**1943—7** Viscount (later Earl) Wavell, Viceroy of India.

**1944** 31 Jan., the allies disembark in the Marshall Is.  14 March, Turkey stops delivery of chrome to Germany.  30 March, economic agreement between Japan and Russia.  2 May, British financial aid given to China.  27 May, allies begin to take New Guinea.  21-24 June, conference at Chungking on the Pacific.  12 July, US occupies Guam.  29 Sept., US seizes Leyte, Philippine Is., from Japan: 22-25 Oct., Japanese fleet heavily defeated.  2 Nov., Iran refuses oil concessions to USSR.  Dec., Lord Soulbury's mission in Ceylon to determine future constitutional development.  US seizes Saipan, Mariana Is., from Japan: 1300 miles from Tokyo, thus enabling US to bomb Japan.  Communist Party (CP) of Ceylon founded.

**1944** Feb., more than 100 German agents captured in Chile.  28 Feb., US places oil embargo on Spain.  1 July, British and US ambassadors recalled from Argentina.  1-22 July, Bretton Woods Conference on monetary and financial affairs.  7-8 July, meeting between de Gaulle and Roosevelt. 21 Aug.—7 Oct., Dumbarton Oaks Conference.  31 Oct., general strike in Buenos Aires.  7 Nov., F.D.Roosevelt re-elected US President for a fourth term.  President Martínez unseated in El Salvador by students and military: military government ensues.  W Indian Chambers of Commerce propose economic federation.  Constitutional reform in Jamaica, virtually with responsible government: Labour Party under Bustamante gains majority.  Family Allowance Act passed in Canada.  Conscription introduced in Canada for overseas service.  Argentina declares war on Japan.
**1944—8** Ramon Grau San Martin again President of Cuba.

**1944** Protestant monastery founded at Taizé, France, by Pastor Roger Schutz.  UK Education Act introduced by R.A. Butler.  The kidney machine invented.

**1945** 10 Jan., Turkish constitution revised.  14 Jan., Turkey opens the Straits to the allies.  23 Jan., allies re-open the Burma Road.  Feb., Turkey declares war on Germany and Japan: Turkey joins UN as an ally.  18 Feb.—14 March, US takes Iwojima Is., c. 900 miles from Tokyo: desperately defended by 23,000 Japanese, fighting to the last man.

**1945** 6-18 Jan., Hot Springs Conference.  21 Feb.—4 March, Pan-American Conference in Mexico.  March, Argentina declares war on Germany.  12 Apr., President Roosevelt d.; succ., his Vice-President, Harry S. Truman (Dem.)(—1953).  25 Apr.—26 June, UN Conference negotiates UN Charter at San Francisco: forty-eight nations attend.

**1945** 26 Oct., Croatian bishops protest against ill-treatment by Tito.  World Zionist Congress held: demands admission of 1m. Jews into Palestine.  Shintoism ceases to be the state religion in Japan.  Pius XII College founded at Roma: later University of Basutoland, Bechuanaland and Swaziland.  The nuclear bomb invented.  Computers invented.

## WESTERN & NORTHERN EUROPE

## CENTRAL & SOUTHERN EUROPE

## AFRICA

**1945** 31 March, 1st French Army under de Lattre de Tassigny crosses the Rhine. 30 Apr., women vote for the first time in France. 8 May, Germans sign unconditional surrender to allies near Reims. 21 May, Labour Party leaves coalition in Britain: Conservatives remain in office under Churchill (−27 July). 5 July, general election in Britain: counting of poll delayed by postal votes from the forces. 23 July−14 Aug., trial of Marshal Pétain: death sentence commuted to imprisonment for life. 27 July, Labour Party in office in Britain: C.R.Attlee, Prime Minister (−1951). 15 Oct., Laval executed. 21 Oct., elections and constitutional referendum in France. 14 Nov., de Gaulle again appointed head of French government. 13 Dec., Franco-British agreement on the Middle East. 27 Dec., foreign ministers of Britain, US and USSR agree in Moscow to provisional democratic government in Korea.

**1945** 1 May, Tito occupies Trieste. 2 May, Berlin garrison surrenders to the allies. 22 June, Germany partitioned into occupation zones between Britain, France, US and USSR. 17 July−2 Aug., Potsdam Conference: Japan warned to make peace or suffer 'prompt and utter destruction'. Nov.−1946, Nuremberg trial of principal Nazi leaders. Portuguese constitution revised: National Assembly increased from ninety to 120 members.

**1945** 22 Aug., Madagascar to send five representatives to French Parliament. 16 Sept., Spain evacuates Tangier. 23 Sept., Egypt demands revision of Anglo-Egyptian treaty, end of military occupation, and control of Sudan. 4 Nov., six African representatives sent for *AOF* to French Constituent Assembly. Rising against French begins in Algeria. First African appointed to Zanzibar Legislative Council. First African members appointed to Tanganyika Legislative Council.

# THE EAST & AUSTRALASIA

**1945** 24 Feb., US recovers Manila.
March, General Aung San, at request
of Lord Mountbatten, organizes
mutiny in Burmese army and
uprisings of civilians against Japanese.
March *ff.*, frequent air attacks on
Japan: 40% of more than sixty
cities destroyed. 25 March, France
grants autonomy to Indo-China.
6-7 Apr., Japanese fleet destroyed
in battle of Okinawa. 19 May,
negotiations between France, Syria
and Lebanon break down. June,
official conversations begin on
Indian independence: general
election follows. 1-2 June, Britain
occupies Lebanon and Syria. 6 Aug.,
first atomic bomb destroys
Hiroshima. 2 Aug., all Burma
liberated by British troops. 8 Aug.,
Russia declares war on Japan:
immediate advance into Manchuria:
many prisoners taken. 9 Aug.,
atomic bomb destroys Nagasaki. 13
Aug., 1500 allied aircraft raid Tokyo.
15 Aug., Emperor of Japan
broadcasts to his people, stating
intention to end the war. 16 Aug.,
numerous riots in India begin. 2
Sept., formal surrender of Japan to
US General MacArthur, Supreme
Commander for the Allied Powers
(SCAP),(in charge until Apr. 1951):
Americans use opportunity to
restore Japan economically as a
bulwark against Communism.
Korea placed under US and USSR
administration. 9 Sept., USSR
intervenes in Azerbaijan. 15 Sept.,
Ho Chi Minh forms government in
Vietnam. Oct., civilian
government restored in Burma.
Soulbury Commission Report on
Ceylon published: cabinet with
bicameral legislature proposed.
SCAP frees political prisoners in
Japan: Japanese CP inaugurated.
Nov., Malay Nationalist Party (MNP)
founded. Dec., Malay Democratic
Union (MDU), chiefly Chinese,
founded. 5 Dec., Singapore
Conference on Indo-China and
Indonesia. British Military
Administration set up in Malaya
following Japanese defeat: some
7,000 MPAJA fighters hand over
weapons and receive gratuities.
Bank of New Zealand nationalized.
**1945–6** Further Welfare State
legislation in New Zealand.
**1945–7** Trial of Japanese war
criminals ends with sentence of
death on seven persons, and eighteen
to periods of imprisonment: little
impression made on population.
H.R.H. the Duke of Gloucester,
Governor-General of Australia.

# THE AMERICAS

**1945** 26 June, UN Charter signed.
24 Aug., lend-lease ended. Sept.,
H.S.Truman announces Fair Deal
programme. Oct., military *coup
d'état* by young officers in Venezuela:
attempt at democratic government to
1948 under Rómulo Betancourt and
Rómulo Gallegos. 9 Oct., Perón
overthrown by military *coup*: Perón
imprisoned: 17 Oct., released: 18
Oct., restored (–1946). 29 Oct.,
Brazilian army forces Vargas to
resign. New constitution in
Guatemala. Peru declares war on the
Axis.
**1945–50** Juan José Arévala,
President of Guatemala.

# RELIGION & CULTURE

**1945–61** Geoffrey Francis Fisher, Abp
of Canterbury.
**1945–7** Conakry, Guinea, greatly
expanded.

1945—1947

WESTERN &
NORTHERN EUROPE
CENTRAL &
SOUTHERN EUROPE
AFRICA

**1946** 20 Jan., de Gaulle resigns. 29 Jan., Félix Gouin becomes French Prime Minister. 26 Feb., French frontier with Spain closed. 1 March, Bank of England nationalized. 25 Apr.—12 July, Preparatory Peace Conference in Paris. 30 Apr., Stalin complains that the West is planning a new war. 2 June, elections in France. 11 June, Gouin ministry falls. 23 June, Georges Bidault, Prime Minister of France. 7 July, Russia demands common defence of the Straits with Turkey. 29 July—15 Oct., Paris Peace Conference: twenty-one nations meet to draft peace treaties with Axis: no agreement reached on Germany and Austria. 1 Aug., negotiations between France and Vietnam at Fontainebleau. 2 Aug., Ferhat Abbas, in French National Constituent Assembly, proposes an Algerian republic federated with France. 12 Aug., Stalin demands Russian share in control of the Dardanelles. 6 Nov., National Health Act comes into force in Britain. 16 Dec., Léon Blum, Prime Minister of France. Colonial Economic and Development Committee set up in Britain.

**1946** 2 Jan., King Zog of Albania deposed. 3 Jan., Saar mines sequestered by France. 12 Jan., Albania proclaimed a republic. 1 Feb., Hungary made a republic. 31 March, elections in Greece favour the Royalists. 18 Apr., Tsaldaris, Prime Minister of Greece. 9 May, Victor Emmanuel III of Italy abdicates: succ. Umberto II. 26 May, Communists returned in increased strength at Czechoslvak general election. 2 June, referendum in Italy hostile to the monarchy: 3 June, Umberto II abdicates. 18 June, republic proclaimed in Italy; 28 June, Enrico de Nicola, first President. 1 Sept., plebiscite in Greece confirms the monarchy: civil war follows. 8 Sept., Bulgaria votes to become a republic. 19 Sept., Churchill recommends European union in speech at Zurich. 30 Sept., Nuremberg tribunal pronounces sentences on principal Nazi war criminals. Dec., Spain formally banned from UN. 2 Dec., Britain and US agree on an economic merger of their zones in Germany. 18 Dec., UN Security Council Commission of Inquiry sent to Greece.

**1946** Feb., general strike in Cairo. 29 March, new constitution in Gold Coast with African majority in legislature. Apr., Britain proposes Greater Somalia under British trusteeship. Somali Youth League grows rapidly. 7 May, French citizenship extended to all colonial subjects. 8 May, nationalist riots in Algeria. 16 May, British troops in Egypt begin to withdraw from Cairo and Alexandria to the Canal Zone. Sept., Jomo Kenyatta returns to Kenya after fifteen years abroad. Williamson Diamond Mine, Mwadui, Tanganyika, found to be the largest in the world. Nov., unsuccessful British mission under Lord Stansgate to Cairo to revise Anglo-Egyptian treaty. Ibn Saud visits Cairo. 9 Dec., Iranian troops enter Azerbaijan: Tabriz occupied.

**1947** 1 Jan., coal mines nationalized in Britain. 12 Jan., Vincent Auriol elected President of France (—1954): Fourth Republic inaugurated (—1958). 22 Jan., Paul Ramadier, premier of France. 10 Feb., Treaty of Paris between France, Bulgaria, Finland, Hungary, Italy and Rumania. 4 March, Franco-British treaty of alliance signed at Dunkirk. 5 March, USSR refuses international control of atomic research. 10 March—24 Apr., Moscow Conference of foreign ministers on Germany and Austria: a failure.

**1947** 1 Feb., Alcide de Gasperi forms coalition in Italy. 1 Apr., George II of Greece d.: succ Paul I. 6 July, Spanish law provides for restoration of the monarchy on Franco's death. 10 July, Czechoslovakia declines Marshall Aid. 22-27 Aug., Tripartite Conference on the Ruhr. 5 Oct., elections ratify the union of the Saar to France. 25-31 Dec., battle of Konitza against Greek Communists. 27 Dec., CP proscribed in Greece. 30 Dec., Michael 1 of Rumania abdicates: republic proclaimed.

**1947** 1 Jan., new constitution effective in Nigeria: self-governing subject to certain restrictions. 21 Jan., Smuts declines to put SWA under UN trusteeship. 26 Jan., Egypt severs diplomatic relations with Britain. 30 Jan., Ground Nut Scheme started at Kongwa, Tanganyika. 30 March, serious strike in Madagascar. 5 Aug., riots in Tunisia. Abdelkrim given asylum in Egypt: Maghreb Office opened in Cairo to co-ordinate nationalistic movements. SA Bureau of Race Relations set up.

## THE EAST & AUSTRALASIA      THE AMERICAS      RELIGION & CULTURE

**1945–9** Joseph Chifley, Federal Prime Minister of Australia. **1945–51** 170,000 displaced persons from Europe settled in Australia. **1946** Jan., Japanese Emperor formally renounces any claim to semi-divine status. 21-22 Feb., violent risings in Bombay and other towns in India: Indian Navy mutinies. 8 March, French troops disembark at Tonkin. 18 March, French troops enter Hanoi. 22 March, Britain declares Transjordan independent as Jordan. 1 Apr., Federated and Unfederated States in Malaya, Penang and Malacca, made the Malayan Union. 25 May, Amir Abdallah proclaimed King of Jordan. 30 June, 'Black Saturday': British arrest Palestine Jewish leaders. 4 July, Philippine Is become independent: US gives grant of $600m. for reconstruction: US given military bases for ninety-nine years. Sept., coalition cabinet formed in Burma. 24 Sept., Arabs and Jews decline to participate in London Conference on Palestine. Oct., Muslim League members join Indian Executive Council. Oct., new Japanese Constitution promulgated: Emperor made a constitutional monarch: war abjured; 'all forms of feudalism' abolished; House of Peers made 'House of Councillors' subject to sexennial election. 15 Nov., agreement between Holland and Indonesia. Dec., Burmese delegation invited to London to discuss future of Burma. 9 Dec., Indian Constituent Assembly meets: boycotted by Muslim League. 20 Dec., general rebellion in Tonkin. Malayan Indian Congress (MIC) founded. Anglo-American Committee of Inquiry on Palestine. **1946–56** Japanese population c. 90m., rising by 1m. annually.

**1947** 27 Jan., agreement signed in London by British and Burmese: constituent assembly to be elected to determine future. 20 Feb., British government announces that India will become independent in June 1948: Lord Wavell recalled: succ. as Viceroy, Lord Mountbatten. 3 March, martial law proclaimed in Palestine. 25 March, Holland recognizes independence of Indonesia. 19 May, Vietminh attack on Saigon. 3 June, Lord Mountbatten announces that British government accepts partition

**1946** 31 Jan., Gen. Enrico Dutra, President of Brazil (–1950). 1 Feb., Trygve Lie elected Secretary-General of UN. 16 Feb., USSR spy ring discovered in Canada. 24 Feb., Col. Juan Domingo Perón becomes President of Argentina: Evita (María Eva Duarte) Perón, his wife, virtual Minister of Labour. 5 March, Churchill's Fulton speech denounces Russian aggression: calls on West to resist. 12 Apr., Viscount Alexander of Tunis, Governor-General of Canada (–1952). Sept., new constitution in Brazil. 1 Dec., Valdes becomes President of Mexico. 5 Dec., New York made UN headquarters. 14 Dec., UN rejects SA proposal to incorporate SWA in the Union. 30 Dec., UN Atomic Energy Commission approves Bernard Baruch's proposal for world control of atomic weapons. Barbados obtains partly responsible government. Mexican Corn Commission created to develop better seed: increased crops by 60% in next twelve years. Banks and telephones nationalized in Argentina. Argentine Institute for Promotion of Exchange established. First Five Year Plan for economic self-sufficiency launched in Argentina. President's Temporary Commission on Employee Loyalty created in US. Canadian Citizenship Act passed: henceforward British citizens born outside Canada subjected to naturalization laws. **1946–50** Dumarsais Estimé, President of Haiti. **1946–52** Gabriel González Videla, President of Chile, with Popular Front government. Miguel Alemán, President of Mexico. Mexican–US border closed on account of foot-and-mouth disease. **1946–58** Conservatives again in power in Colombia. **1947** 7 Jan., General George Marshall, US Secretary of State. 12 March, H.S.Truman enunciates 'Truman Doctrine' to Congress: aid to be given to Greece and Turkey against Communist infiltration: $300m. and $100m. respectively appropriated. 7 Apr., CP forbidden in New York State. 7 May, Brazil proscribes the CP. 5 June, General George Marshall outlines Marshall Plan for European recovery in speech at Harvard (Marshall Aid).

**1946** 11 Oct., Abp Stephinac imprisoned for opposing Communism in Yugoslavia. International Christian Conference held at Cambridge to promote closer relations between Protestants and Orthodox. Arts Council instituted in UK. Zionist Congress held in Basle.

**1947** 14 Sept., Poland ends concordat with the Vatican. Return to militant Bolshevism in Russia; atheistic propaganda stepped up: dialectical materialism preached as the only rational doctrine. Dead Sea Scrolls discovered. University College of the Gold Coast established. First supersonic aircraft flight. Edinburgh Festival instituted.

## WESTERN & NORTHERN EUROPE

## CENTRAL & SOUTHERN EUROPE

## AFRICA

**1947** 14 Apr., de Gaulle creates his own party, *Rassemblement du Peuple Français* (*RPF*). 20 Apr., Christian X of Denmark d.: succ. Frederick IX. 1 May, heavy industries nationalized in Britain. 6 June–1 July, strikes in France. 2 July, USSR refuses Marshall Aid. 6 Aug., Sir Stafford Cripps announces austerity programme in Britain. 20 Aug., Britain suspends free convertibility of the dollar. 22 Sept., Paris Conference of sixteen nations accepts Marshall Aid. 29 Oct., Benelux Customs Union instituted. 10 Nov.–10 Dec., strikes and riots in France. 12 Nov., communist demonstrations at Marseilles. 23 Nov., Robert Schuman replaces Ramadier as premier of France. Dec., Ceylon Independence Act passed in London, making Ceylon a self-governing Dominion in the British Commonwealth. Overseas Food Corporation set up. Colonial Development Corporation established.

**1947** East African High Commission established. *Société de colonisation Belge du Katanga* founded to promote immigration of Belgian agriculturalists.

**1948** 1 Jan., railways nationalized in Britain. 3 Jan., French convention with the Saar. 24 Jan., the *franc* devalued: free gold market in France. 10 Feb., French frontier with Spain reopened. 17 March, treaty of Brussels. 1 Apr., electricity nationalized in Britain. 26 July, André Marie succ. Schuman as premier of France. 26 Aug., Britain declines to join a European Assembly. 4 Sept., Queen Wilhelmina of the Netherlands abdicates: succ. Queen Juliana. 7 Sept., Schuman forms a new cabinet in France: collapses immediately. 11 Sept., Queuille premier of France. 18 Sept., riots in Grenoble following a visit by de Gaulle. 4-29 Oct., strikes and bomb outrages in France.

**1948** 10 Feb., Greek rebels bomb Salonica. 25 Feb., Communists seize power in Czechoslovakia. 10 March, Jan Masaryk commits suicide. 31 March, Russian blockade of Berlin begun. 1 Apr., USSR interferes with road and rail traffic entering West Berlin. 16 Apr., Organization for European Economic Cooperation (OEEC) established. 10 May, Luigi Einaudi elected President of Italy. 20 June, Greek offensive begins against the rebels. 4 July, Yugoslavia expelled from the Kominform. 24 July, USSR stops all surface traffic between Berlin and West Germany: allies reply with air lift (–Sept. 1949). 20 Aug., Greek rebels defeated at Grammos. 10 Nov., Britain and US return Ruhr mines and steelworks to German control: France protests. 28 Dec., agreement between Britain, France and US on Ruhr industries.

**1948** Jan., Four Power Commission visits Somalia: riots in Mogadishu. 26 Jan.–11 Feb., boycott of European goods on Gold Coast. 28 Feb., serious riots in Gold Coast. Apr., elections for Algerian Assembly: results believed rigged. 26 May, Smuts defeated in SA general election: Nationalist Afrikaner Party wins on *apartheid* platform: 3 June, D.F.Malan, Prime Minister. 23 Sept., Ethiopia resumes control of Reserved Areas in Somalia: Somalis appeal to UN for a united Somalia. Nov., Léopold Senghor founds *Bloc Démocratique Sénégalais.*
**1948–9** Egypt, with other Arab countries, at war with Israel.

## THE EAST & AUSTRALASIA | THE AMERICAS | RELIGION & CULTURE

of India and Pakistan: independence brought forward to 14 Aug. 1947: accepted by INC, Muslim League and the Sikhs. 1 July, general mobilisation against Communists in China. 20 July, following breakdown of talks, Dutch occupy Batavia. 15 Aug., India and Pakistan both proclaimed independent: Pandit Jawarharlal Nehru, Prime Minister of India: Liaqat Ali Khan, Prime Minister of Pakistan: mob violence between Hindus and Muslims. 15 Aug.–1948 June, Earl Mountbatten of Burma, Governor-General of India. 10 Sept., Ho Chi-Minh refuses French peace proposals. 9 Oct., French offensive against Tonkin. 26 Oct., Kashmir annexed to India. Nov., India and Pakistan at war in Kashmir. 30 Nov., violent demonstrations in Palestine against partition. 2 Dec., battles between Arabs and Jews in Palestine. 10 Dec., Burma independent. General election in Ceylon: United National Party (UNP) gains overwhelming majority. First Six Year Plan (1947–53) published in Ceylon. Pan-Malayan Federation of Labour founded under Communist auspices. Malayan population 4.9m. US aid to Japan over $400m. New Zealand ratifies Statute of Westminster (1931).
**1947–53** Sir William McKell, Governor-General of Australia.
**1948** Jan.–May, violence in Palestine. 17 Jan., armistice between Holland and Indonesia. 30 Jan., Mahatma Gandhi murdered. Feb., Russian sponsored meeting of Asian and Australian Communists in Calcutta. 4 Feb., Ceylon becomes formally independent: Ceylon Parliament opened by Duke of Gloucester. 17 Feb., Imam Yahya of Yemen assassinated. 14 March, Imam Ahmad installed in Yemen: rigid personal dictatorship ensues. 15 March, treaty between Britain and Jordan. 21 March, Communist offensive against Nanking. 22 Apr., Jews seize Haifa. 1 May, N Korea proclaimed a People's Republic. 14 May, Arab and Egyptian troops enter Palestine. 14-15 May, State of Israel proclaimed. 15 May, British Mandate in Palestine terminated. 17 May, Jordanian troops take the Old City of Jerusalem. 20 May, first Vietnamese government installed. 18 June, following numerous murders, State of Emergency proclaimed in Malaya. Terrorism follows. MCP, MPAJA and Old Comrade's Associations banned.

**1947** 23 June, Taft-Hartley, or Labour-Management Relations Act passed by Congress. 26 July, new US Department of Defence created. 2 Sept., Inter-American Defence Pact signed at Río de Janeiro. 29 Nov., UN approves the partition of Palestine. Dec.. Rómulo Gallegos President of Venezuela. 30 Dec., Kashmir question referred to UN Security Council. Delegate conference on federation of Leeward and Windward Is. Montego Bay Conference, with a view to the Federation of the W Indies. Oil strike at Leduc, Alberta.

**1948** 30 March–30 Apr., Pan-American Conference at Bogotá. 3 Apr., US Economic Co-operation Act gives legislative form to Marshall Plan. 15 July, UN Security Council orders a cease-fire in Palestine. 20 July, Communist leaders in US arrested. 24 Aug., USSR closes its consulates in New York and San Francisco. Nov., *coup d'état* by young officers in Venezuela. 2 Nov., H.S.Truman re-elected President of US. 15 Nov.–1957 21 June, L.S. St Laurent, Canadian Prime Minister. Dec., military *coup d'état* in Venezuela: three-man junta (–1952). Communists outlawed in Chile. Railways, hitherto British owned, nationalized in Argentina.
**1948–51** $12,000m. spent or lent by US in backing Marshall Plan.
**1948–52** Carlos Prío Socarrás, President of Cuba.

**1948** 4 Aug., law against the Catholic Church in Rumania. 22 Aug., World Council of Churches (WCC) instituted in Amsterdam by representatives of 147 churches from forty-four countries. 2 Dec., Uniate Church proscribed in Rumania. 27 Dec., Cardinal Mindszenty, Primate of Hungary, arrested. World Jewish Congress held at Montreux. World Health Organization established: first Assembly held at Geneva. T.D. Lysenko denounces anti-Michurin geneticists in USSR: purge of scientists follows. Wilfrid Thesiger crosses the Empty Quarter. Transistors invented. Long playing records first made.

| WESTERN & NORTHERN EUROPE | CENTRAL & SOUTHERN EUROPE | AFRICA |
| --- | --- | --- |

**1949** 1 Feb., clothes rationing ends in Britain. 14 Apr., Council of Europe inaugurated. 18 Apr., Eire leaves the British Commonwealth. 27 Apr., King George VI assumes the title of Head of the Commonwealth. 1 May, gas nationalized in Britain. 5 May, Statute of Council of Europe signed by ten nations in London. 18 Sept., Britain devalues sterling. 19 Sept., the *franc* devalued. 5 Oct., Queuille government falls. 28 Oct., Georges Bidault, Prime Minister of France.

**1949** 16 Feb., customs union in western occupied Germany. 24 Feb., armistice between Egypt and Israel signed in Rhodes: Egypt retains Gaza strip and parts of S Palestine. 31 March, rebel offensive in Macedonia and Thrace. 6 May, provisional government set up in W Germany. 12 May, end of Russian blockade of Berlin. 8 Aug., Council of Europe inaugurated in Strasbourg. 9 Aug., Greece joins Council of Europe. 14 Aug., Greek rebels defeated in Vitsi Mts. 28 Aug., Greek forces occupy Grammos Mts. 15 Sept., Konrad Adenauer becomes Chancellor of W Germany. 7 Oct., German Democratic Republic proclaimed. 16 Oct., hostilities suspended in Greece.

**1949** Jan., violent racial riots in Durban. Jan.–Aug., Coussey Committee on constitutional reforms in Gold Coast. June, Convention People's Party, (CPP), founded in Ghana by Kwame Nkrumah. 25 June, Mixed Tribunal ended in Egypt. 29 June, SA Citizenship Act suspends automatic grant of citizenship to Commonwealth Immigrants: bans marriages of mixed race. Dec., Socialist Party founded in Egypt. 2 Dec., Mathew Commission, under Sir Charles Mathew, appointed to recommend new constitution for Tanganyika. Disappointing harvest in Ground Nut Scheme.

**1948** 21 June, Mr Rajagopalachari, Governor-General of India (−24 Jan. 1950). 15 Aug., Korea proclaimed a republic in Seoul: Syngman Rhee, President. Communist rising in Burma. 25 Aug., Vietminh defeated. 9 Sept., Korean People's Democratic Republic proclaimed in N Korea: claims authority throughout country. 13-18 Sept., Indian troops occupy Hyderabad. 17 Sept., Israeli terrorists murder UN mediator, Count Bernadotte. 26 Sept., Chinese Communists take Nan, capital of Shantung. 17 Oct., Israeli offensive in the Negev. 31 Oct., Chinese Communists take Mukden. 29 Dec., Holland occupies Jakarta: Indonesian Government arrested. Ceylon Defence Agreement with UK: provides bases fro RN and RAF. Federation of Malaya Agreement: affects all states of the abandoned Malayan Union, except Singapore, which remains a Crown Colony. Rocket range built at Woomera, S Australia.
**1948–54** Lord Soulbury, Governor-General of Ceylon.
**1949** 15 Jan., Chinese Communists penetrate Tientsin. 21 Jan., Chiang Kai-shek loses all power in mainland China: Communists gradually extend control. 22 Jan., Chinese Communists take Peking. Feb., Malayan Chinese Association (MCA) formed. 16 Feb., Chaim Weizmann elected President of Israel. 8 March, Vietnam independent. 13 March, armistice between India and Pakistan in Kashmir. 23 March, armistice between Israel and Lebanon. 25 March, Chinese Communists occupy Moncay. 30 March–1 Apr., military *coup* in Syria: Colonel Zaim takes power. 3 Apr., armistice between Israel and Jordan. 11 May, Siam renamed Thailand. 29 June, US withdraws last troops from Korea. The Dutch evacuate Jakarta. 19 July, Laos independent. 9 Aug., Turkey joins Council of Europe. 14 Aug., further military *coup* in Syria: Colonel Zaim executed. 21 Sept., Chinese People's Republic proclaimed. 23 Oct., Phat Diem occupied. 8 Nov., Cambodia independent. 23 Nov., US mission sent to Saigon. 8 Dec., Chiang Kai-shek establishes Nationalist government in Formosa. 14 Dec., Jerusalem made capital of Israel. 19 Dec., further military *coup* in Syria. 30 Dec., France hands over power in Vietnam.

**1949** 7 Jan., Dean Acheson becomes Secretary of State in USA. 31 March, Newfoundland joined to Canada as a province. 4 Apr., North Atlantic Treaty signed in Washington by Belgium, Britain, Canada, Denmark, France, Holland, Iceland, Italy, Norway and US: NATO comes into being: 350m. people represented. 11 May, Israel admitted to UN. 21 Sept., UN makes Italian Somalia a trusteeship for ten years under Italy. 20 Oct., Yugoslavia admitted to UN in spite of USSR opposition. 21 Nov., UN votes for the independence of Libya. 9 Dec., UN votes for the internationalization of Jerusalem. Civil cases in Canada no longer appealable before Judicial Committee of the Privy Council. Earthquake in Ecuador. US economic mission to Haiti.

**1949** 3-8 Feb., Cardinal Mindszenty tried in Budapest and sentenced to life imprisonment. 25 Feb.–8 March, trial of Protestant pastors in Bulgaria. 16 June, Czechoslovak police seize the Archbishop's residence in Prague. 26 June, the Church 'nationalized' in Slovakia. 13 July, Pope Pius XII excommunicates Communists and Communist sympathisers. 30 Oct., *modus vivendi* agreed between Church and State in Czechoslovakia. 4 Dec., fresh conflict between Church and State in Czechoslovakia. Faculty of Theology created in University of Ankara. Cortisone and neomycin discovered. University College of N Staffordshire (later Keele University) founded. University of Malaya established. Istanbul University founded.

**1950** 23 Feb., general election in Britain: Labour majority eight. 1 March, K.Fuchs, atomic spy, sentenced to imprisonment. 7 March, Iceland joins Council of Europe. 11 May, British, French and US foreign ministers discuss future of Germany in London. 24 June, Bidault government falls in France. 29 June, Conference of Paris opened. 4-11 July, Henri Queuille attempts to form ministry in France. 11 July, René Pleven, premier of France. 22 July, Léopold III returns to Belgium after six years' exile: violent agitation follows. Aug., British government gives instructions to wind up Ground Nut Scheme: £30m. lost. 1 Aug., Léopold III of Belgium abdicates: succ. Baudouin I. 29 Oct., Gustav V of Sweden d.: succ. Gustav VI Adolphus.

**1950** 4 Jan., agitation amongst agricultural workers in the Po valley. 21 March, Chancellor Adenauer proposes economic union between France and Germany. 21 May, diplomatic relations between Greece and Yugoslavia restored. 15 June, W Germany joins Council of Europe. 1 July, European Payments Union instituted. 6 July, frontier treaty between East Germany and Poland.

**1950** Jan. or Feb., Mohammed Ben Bella becomes leader of clandestine *Organisation Secrète* (*OS*) in Algeria. 12 Jan., state of emergency in Gold Coast following strikes. 29 Jan., race riots in the Rand. 30 Jan., riots in the Ivory Coast. 1 Apr., Britain returns Somalia to Italy. 1 May, *anti-apartheid* demonstration in Johannesburg: eighteen killed, thirty wounded. 11 Sept., Field-Marshal Smuts d. 13 Dec., SA declines to place SWA under UN trusteeship.

**1951** 15 Feb., steel nationalized in Britain. 13 March, Henri Queuille again Prime Minister of France. 26 May, Britain applies to the Hague Court on oil conflicts in Iran.

**1951** 18 Apr., European Coal and Steel Treaty signed by Belgium, France, Holland, Italy, Luxembourg and W Germany. 2 May, W Germany joins Council of Europe.

**1951** 19 Jan., six members for SWA take seats for the first time in SA Parliament. Feb. Yundum Egg Scheme collapses in Gambia. SA protests against appointment of

## THE EAST & AUSTRALASIA    THE AMERICAS    RELIGION & CULTURE

**1949** Indian and Pakistani (Citizenship) Act, Ceylon disenfranchises majority of plantation workers in Ceylon. Malayan Races Liberation Movement and Min Yuen (Masses Movement) inaugurated. Economic Stabilization Programme instituted in Japan. Government of New Zealand finances Maori land development from public funds. Over 50,000 Yemeni Jews flown to Israel.
**1949—** R.G. Menzies, Australian Federal Prime Minister (second term).
**1950** 6 Jan., Communist China recognized by Britain. 9 Jan., Conference of Commonwealth Foreign Ministers opens in Colombo. 26 Jan., India made a republic: Dr Rajendra Prasad, first President. 31 Jan., battle of Hué. 14 Feb., thirty year treaty of alliance between China and USSR. 1 March, Chiang Kai-shek proclaimed President of Nationalist China in Taiwan. 17 March, rising in Vietnam against American aid. 27 March, Vietminh offensive in Cochinchina. 24 Apr., Jordan annexes the West Bank area of Palestine. 14 May, Turkish Republican Party, in power since 1922, defeated at elections by Democrats: Celal Bayar, President of Turkey: Adnam Menderes, Prime Minister. 26 June, North Korean army with full Russian support, crosses 38th parallel into S Korea. 15 Sept., US troops disembark in Korea. 18 Sept., Vietminh take Dong-Khe. 26 Sept., UN forces take Seoul: President Syngman Rhee re-establishes government in capital. 4 Oct., French and Vietnamese troops evacuate Cao-bang; and, 18 Oct., Lang-son. 21 Oct., China invades Tibet. 5 Nov., China intervenes in Korea. 24 Nov., ineffective UN offensive in N Korea repelled by Chinese 'volunteers'. 3 Dec., UN forces in Korea retreat. 6 Dec., Marshal de Lattre de Tassigny appointed High Commissioner for Indo-China. 24 Dec., Chinese Army crosses the 38th parallel in Korea. Agricultural population of China 81%. Population of Singapore over 1m., of whom 80% Chinese. Japanese population 90m. Communist Party Dissolution Act disallowed by High Court of Australia.
**1951** 3 Jan., UN troops evacuate Seoul. 13-17 Jan., Vietminh checked N of Hanoi in UN counter-offensive. 13 Feb., Colombo Conference of British Commonwealth countries on SE Asia opens.

**1950** 31 Jan., US Atomic Energy Commission ordered by President Truman to construct hydrogen bomb. 16 March, Dean G. Acheson makes proposals to USSR to end cold war. 6 June, Trygve Lie re-appointed UN Secretary-General: announces twenty year peace plan. 27 June, President Truman announces US air and naval forces sent to aid S Korea: Australia, Britain, Netherlands and New Zealand follow suit and then other countries. 7 July, UN Security Council requests US to establish unified command in Korea: General Douglas MacArthur given supreme command. 12 Sept., General Marshall made US Defence Secretary. 30 Oct., rising in Puerto Rico. 4 Dec., C.R.Attlee visits Washington. 13 Dec., Marshall Aid to Britain ended. 19 Dec., General Eisenhower accepts command of NATO forces. US Defence Production Act: Economic Stabilization Agency established. Communists become dominant in Guatemala. President of Haiti unseated by army: succ. Col. Paul Magloire (—1956). Population of Brazil 51.9m.
**1950—4** Senator Joseph R. McCarthy campaigns against alleged Communists. Col. Jacopo Arbenz, President of Guatemala: attempts made at agrarian reform and control of foreign companies. Getulio Vargas, President of Brazil.
**1950—6** Oscar Osorio, President of El Salvador.
**1950—8** Colonel Marcos Pérez Jiménez, dictator of Venezuela.

**1951** 30 Jan., UN condemns Chinese aggression in Korea. 21-24 March, Bermuda Conference between Britain and US. 1 Sept., ANZUS (Australia, New Zealand and US) Pact signed in San Francisco.

**1950** 21 Jan., many clergy arrested in Czechoslovakia. 17 Aug., Pope Pius XII, *Humani generis*: existentialism and other theories condemned. 5 July, Papal Nuncio expelled from Rumania. 1 Nov., Pope Pius XII proclaims the bodily Assumption of the Blessed Virgin Mary a dogma of the Church. Ethiopia appoints Abuna (Patriarch) independently of Cairo for the first time. Holy Year observed by the Roman Catholic Church. National Council of Churches of Christ instituted in USA. University College of Addis Ababa founded.

**1951** 10 March, Abp Beran of Prague banished from his diocese by the government. 2 June, Pius XII: encyclical *Evangelii Praecones*, on missions. International Astronautical Federation instituted in London.

**1951** 23 June, USSR proposes armistice in Korea. 23 July, Marshal Pétain d. 11 Aug., Pleven again premier of France. 25 Oct., general election in Britain: Churchill, Prime Minister (−1955).

**1951** President Carmona of Portugal d.: succ. Marshal Craveiro Lopes (−1958).

Kwame Nkrumah as Chief Minister in the Gold Coast. 27 Oct., Egypt denounces 1936 treaty with Britain and 1896 agreement on the Sudan: King Farouk proclaimed King of the Sudan. Nov., Britain agrees to federation of the Rhodesias and Nyasaland. 1 Nov., riots in Casablanca. 17 Nov.–12 Dec., unrest among Meru tribe in N Tanganyika. Nov.–1952 Guerrilla war against British forces in Canal Zone. 1 Dec., Kingdom of Libya becomes independent under King Idris I al-Sanusi. CPP triumphant in Gold Coast election.

**1952** 7 Jan., Pleven government falls in France. 20 Jan., Edgar Faure, Prime Minister of France. 31 Jan., new austerity programme announced in Britain. 6 Feb., George VI of England d.: succ. Elizabeth II. 28 Feb., Faure's ministry falls. 11 March–23 Dec., Antoine Pinay, Prime Minister of France. 27-31 May, European Defence Community treaty signed in Paris. 28 May, violent Communist demonstrations in Paris. 23 Dec., Pinay government resigns.

**1952** 18 Feb., Greece joins NATO. 20-25 Feb., NATO Council meets in Lisbon: European Defence Community (ECD) plan approved: Morocco and Tunisia join. 16 June, recruitment of new army announced in E Germany. 22 July, new constitution in Poland. 10 Aug., first meeting of the European Coal and Steel Community. 24 Sept., constitution revised in Rumania.

**1952** 4 Jan., riots in the Canal Zone. 17 Jan., risings in Bizerta and Ferryville. 18 Jan., Habib Bourguiba and other nationalist leaders arrested in Tunisia. 19 Jan., British occupy Ismailia. 22-24 Jan., risings in Qayrawan, Sousse and Tebourba. 26 Jan., large scale incendiarism in Cairo: 277 fires: army intervenes to restore order. 20 March, constitutional crisis in SA following the High Court's judgement that segregation is unlawful. 28 March–15 Apr., tercentenary of arrival of van Riebeeck celebrated in SA: thousands of Bantu protest: numerous riots follow. 23 July, Committee of Free Officers under Nasser (Gamal Abd al-Nasr) seizes power in Egypt: General Neguib (Muhammad Naquib), Commander-in-Chief. 26 July, King Farouk forced to abdicate: infant Fuad II proclaimed King. 11 Sept., Eritrea federated with Ethiopia. 20 Oct., 'Mau Mau' rising in Kenya (−1955). 18 Nov., the Sultan of Morocco demands restoration of sovereignty. 28 Nov., meetings of more than ten 'natives' forbidden in SA. 8 Dec., riots in Casablanca.

| THE EAST & AUSTRALASIA | THE AMERICAS | RELIGION & CULTURE |
|---|---|---|

**1951** 7 March, Premier Razmara of Iran murdered. 14 March, S Korea re-occupies Seoul. 15 March, oil nationalized in Iran. 11 Apr., General MacArthur relieved of command in Korea. 12-25 Apr., strikes and riots in Abadan. 27 Apr., Mussadeq, Prime Minister of Persia. 23 May, Tibet surrenders to China. 24 May, Mussadeq sends ultimatum to the Anglo-Iranian Oil Co. to leave Abadan within six days. 27 May—14 June, massive UN counter-attack in Korea. 20 June, Iran seizes Anglo-Iranian oil installations. 1 July, Colombo Plan comes into effect. 8 July, Korean armistice talks begin at Kaesong. 20 July, King Abdallah of Jordan assassinated in Jerusalem. 9 Sept., Chinese troops enter Lhasa. 1 Oct., British personnel evacuated from Iran. 6 Oct., Sir Henry Gurney, British High Commissioner, assassinated near Kuala Lumpur: succ. Sir Gerald Templer (−1954). 10 Oct., Korean armistice talks resumed at Pan Mun Jom. 14 Nov., French and Vietnamese troops take Hoa Binh. 28 Nov., Col Shishakly seizes power in Syria. 6 Dec., Communist risings in Iran. Independence of Malaya Party (IMP) founded by Dato Oun. 120,000 Jews migrate to Israel from Iraq.

**1952** 13 Jan., British Consulates closed in Iran. 4 Feb., Hoa Binh evacuated. 18 Feb., Turkey joins NATO. 28 Apr., end of US occupation of Japan. May, D.S. Senanayake, Ceylon premier, killed by a fall from his horse: succ. his son, Dudley Senanayake. May, elections in Ceylon: UNP gains 54 seats: opposition parties 26. 21 July, Vietminh massacre at St Jacques. 31 July, Mussadeq reduces the powers of the Shah. 15 Sept., agreement between China and USSR on Port Arthur. 22 Oct., Iran breaks off diplomatic relations with Britain. 30 Oct.—18 Nov., Operation 'Lorraine' in Tonkin. 1 Nov., US explodes hydrogen bomb at Eniwetok Atoll. 21 Nov., Vietminh offensive begins in Laos. High grade uranium deposits found in S Australia.

**1951** 8 Sept., Peace of San Francisco signed between Allies and Japan: China and Formosa not invited: Czechoslovakia, Poland and USSR decline to sign. Security Pact also signed between Japan and US. 20 Sept., NATO Council meets in Ottawa: Greece and Turkey invited to join. 3 Oct., Vargas, President of Brazil. 10 Oct., US Mutual Security Act passed. 11 Nov., Perón successful in Argentine elections. 16 Dec., office of president in Uruguay replaced by a nine man council. Twenty-Second Amendment to the US Constitution forbids any President to serve more than two terms. Elections in Bolivia: success of *Movimento Nacional Revolucionista* (MNR) annulled by military and conservatives.

**1952** 28 Feb., Vincent Massey, first Canadian born Governor-General of Canada (−1959). 10 March, General Fulgencio Batista seizes power as President of Cuba (−1959). 9 Apr., revolution in Bolivia: Victor Paz Estenssoro takes power. 14 Apr., UN Security Council declines to intervene in Tunisia. 14 June, the first atomic submarine laid down. 27 June, US McCarran Act revises immigration laws. 6 July, Adolfo Ruiz Cortines, President of Mexico (−1958). 26 July, Evita Perón d. 4 Nov., General Dwight D. Eisenhower (Rep.) elected President of US: Congress: 221 Republicans, 211 Democrats; Senate: 48 Republicans, 47 Democrats. 3 Dec., Marcos Pérez Jiménez seizes power in Venezuela. Agrarian Law in Guatemala to assist small farmers.

**1951** Electricity first produced from atomic power, in USA. The 'Festival of Britain', inspired by Herbert Morrison, held in London. Yaoundé Cathedral begun.

**1952** Jericho excavated by Dame Kathleen Kenyon. Archaeological finds begin to be tested by radio-carbon 14. The 'pill' (phosphorated hesperidin) first made.

1953–1954

WESTERN &
NORTHERN EUROPE

CENTRAL &
SOUTHERN EUROPE

AFRICA

**1953** 9 Jan.–21 May, René Mayer, premier of France. 12 Feb., USSR severs diplomatic relations with Israel. 5 March, Stalin announced to be dead. 14 March, Khrushchev succ. Stalin as Secretary-General of the Communist Party. 16-31 March, Marshal Tito visits Britain. 17 March, steel denationalized in Britain. 27 March, partial amnesty granted to prisoners in Russia. 17 Apr., road transport denationalized in Britain. 27 Apr.–18 May, French merchant marine officers on strike. 15 June, USSR restores diplomatic relations with Israel and Yugoslavia. 26 June–1954, Joseph Laniel, premier of France. July, Beria expelled from the Communist Party. 5 Aug., Russia announces she can make H bombs. 23 Dec., René Coty elected President of France (–1959). Beria executed with six of his henchmen.

**1954** 20 June–1955 5 Feb., Mendès-France premier of France. 19-22 Aug., Brussels Conference on European Defence Community. 30 Aug., French Assembly rejects proposal for a European Defence Community. 28 Sept.–3 Oct., Nine Power Conference in London. 5 Oct., agreement of London between Italy and Yugoslavia on Trieste. 11 Oct., beginning of the Western European Union in Brussels. 23 Oct., Franco-German agreement of Paris on the Saar. Germany and Italy join NATO. Occupation of Germany ended. 29 Nov.–2 Dec., Moscow Conference of Communist satellites on European security. 16 Dec., USSR threatens to break off diplomatic relations with France; and, 20 Dec., with Britain.

**1953** 13 Jan., new constitution in Yugoslavia. 2 Feb., Czech government re-organized on Russian model. 28 Feb., treaty of friendship between Greece, Turkey and Yugoslavia. 19 March, W Germany ratifies the Bonn Agreement and the Treaty of Paris. 28 May, USSR ends Control Commission in E Germany. 1 June, political commissars suppressed in Yugoslavia. 17 June, anti-Communist riots in E Germany. 18 Oct., violent riots in Poland in support of Cardinal Wyszynski. 4-6 Nov., violent riots in Trieste. 5 Dec., Italy and Yugoslavia withdraw troops from near Trieste. 30 Dec., frontier agreement between Bulgaria and Greece.

**1954** 21 Jan.–18 Feb., Four-Power Conference at Berlin. 26 Feb., W German constitution revised to permit re-armament. 8 May–21 July, conference on Asian affairs at Geneva. 3 July, food rationing ended in Britain. 21 July, agreement in Geneva on Indo-China. 9 Aug., treaty of Bled between Greece, Turkey and Yugoslavia. 16 Aug., EOKA suspends campaign of violence in Cyprus. 9 Nov., Col. Grivas (*alias* Dhigenis) arrives in Cyprus from Rhodes: organizes EOKA, movement to unite Cyprus with Greece, in support of Archbishop Makarios.

**1953** 23 Jan., Rally of the Liberation made the sole political party in Egypt. 10 Feb., Neguib voted dictatorial powers in Egypt. 12 Feb., Anglo-Egyptian agreement on the Sudan. 28 March, Libya joins Arab League. 8 Apr., Jomo Kenyatta and five others convicted of 'managing' Mau Mau. 15 Apr., Nationalists in SA elections maintain majority in record 87.8% poll. 18 June, republic proclaimed in Egypt: Neguib, President: Nasser, Vice-President. 1 Aug., Federation of the Rhodesias and Nyasaland inaugurated. 15 Aug., Pasha of Marrakesh rebels against the Sultan of Morocco. 16 Aug., risings in principal Moroccan towns. 20 Aug., France deposes Sultan of Morocco: puppet, Muhammad b. Arafa, installed. 24 Aug., Kenya government calls on Mau Mau to surrender. 24 Dec., emergency proclaimed against Mau Mau in Tanganyika. Julius Nyerere elected President of Tanganyika African Association. Dr. Albert Margai becomes Chief Minister of Sierra Leone.

**1954** 1 Jan., SA Bantu Education Act comes into force. 9 Jan., first all-Sudanese government formed. 3 Feb., first Parliament of the Federation of Central Africa (FCA) opened. 1 March, Sudanese Parliament opened: violent anti-Egyptian demonstrations in Khartoum. 21 March, Joseph Kasavubu elected President of *ABAKO*. Apr., Gold Coast constitution revision. Nigeria re-organized as a Federation. 18 Apr., Nasser seizes power in Egypt. 31 May, state of emergency declared in Buganda. 7 July, Tanganyika African National Union (TANU) formed, replacing TAA. 27 July, Anglo-Egyptian agreement on the Suez Canal. 31 July, Mendès-France visits Tunisia: internal autonomy granted. 9 Sept., Libya grants US air bases. 19 Oct., Anglo-Egyptian agreement on evacuation of Canal Zone. 29 Oct., Muslim Brotherhood proscribed in Egypt. 1 Nov., nationalist rising begins in Algeria, with bitter civil war (–1962). 17 Nov., Nasser made Head of State in Egypt. 30 Nov., Malan retires: J.G.Strijdom elected leader of SA Nationalist Party. 7 Dec., leaders of the Muslim Brotherhood executed in Egypt. 1944 Anglo-Ethiopian agreement revised. Ethiopian Navy established.

## THE EAST & AUSTRALASIA

**1953** 19 Jan., Vietminh offensive begins in Annam. 26 March, Franco-Vietnamese offensive begins S of the Red River. 17 July, French and Vietnamese troops raid Lang-son. 27 July, armistice in Korea. 11 Aug., French and Vietnamese evacuate Na-Sam. 16 Aug., the Shah of Iran flees to Baghdad. 13 Oct., Sir John Kotelawala replaces Dudley Senanayake as Ceylonese premier. 14 Oct., Qibyah incident between Israel and Jordan. 15-19 Oct., National Congress held in Vietnam. 22 Oct., agreement between France and Laos. 29 Nov., Ho Chi-Minh sets out armistice conditions. 30 Nov., King Ibn Saud d.: succ. Saud. 5 Dec., diplomatic relations between Britain and Iran restored. Alliance Party formed in Malaya. Chinese population 602 m.

**1954** 3 Feb.–7 May, battle of Dien Bien Phu: French defeated. March, US explodes hydrogen bomb near Bikini: Japanese fishing-boat accidentally receives fall-out: strong anti-American feeling in Japan. 8 March, defence agreement between Japan and US. Apr., the Queen and the Duke of Edinburgh visit Ceylon. 2 Apr., mutual defence pact between Pakistan and Turkey. 28 Apr.–2 May, Colombo Conference of Asiatic powers. 7 May, French lose Dien Bien Phu to Vietnamese Communist rebels. 19 May, mutual assistance pact between Pakistan and US. 27 July, armistice signed at Tonkin. 10 Aug., union between Holland and Indonesia ended. 31 Aug., international agreement on Iranian oil. 8 Sept., SE Asia Defence Treaty and Pacific Charter signed by Australia, Britain, France, New Zealand, Pakistan, Philippines, Thailand and US: SEATO set up. 20 Sept., new constitution in China. 8 Oct., Hanoi occupied by Communist force. 9 Oct., French evacuate Hanoi. 21 Oct., French possessions in India ceded to Republic of India. 2 Dec., security pact between China and US. 29 Dec., Cambodia becomes independent.
**1954–62** Sir Oliver Goonetilleke, Governor-General of Ceylon.

## THE AMERICAS

**1953** Jan., new constitution in Venezuela: president given unlimited powers. 7 Apr., Dag Hammarskjöld elected UN Secretary-General. 15 Apr., risings against Perón in Argentina. 25 May, first atomic bomb exploded in US. 1 June, new constitution in Jamaica. 13 June, Rojas Pinilla, President of Colombia: venal and incompetent administration (–1957). 26 July, abortive revolt in Cuba led by Fidel Castro. 15 Sept., UN refuses to admit Communist China. 8-9 Oct., British troops sent to British Guiana following local uprisings. 4-8 Dec., Bermuda Conference between Britain, France and US. 8 Dec., President Eisenhower proposes international control for atomic energy. Fidel Castro makes abortive attempt to overthrow government of Fulgencio Batista in Cuba. US programme of aid to Bolivia initiated.
**1953–8** José Figueres, President of Costa Rica.

**1954** 8 March, President Chaves of Paraguay deposed by military *coup*. 13 May, US St Lawrence Seaway Act passed: provides for canal connecting St Lawrence R. with Great Lakes. 17 May, US Supreme Court declares racial segregation in schools contrary to the Constitution. 18 June–2 July, Conservative rebellion in Guatemala: President Arbenz flees: military dictatorship to 1966. July, Carlos Castillo Armas, President of Guatemala. 24 Aug., President Vargas of Brazil dismissed: commits suicide: succ. Café Filho. 2 Dec., Senator McCarthy's activities condemned by US Senate. US Communist Control Act outlaws Communist Party. American troops first sent to Vietnam. Seventh Fleet and US Marines sent to Laos.

## RELIGION & CULTURE

**1953** 13 Jan., anti-Jewish campaign in Russia. 13 Feb., Catholic Church in Poland put under state control. 29 May, Mt Everest climbed for the first time by Edmund Hillary and Norkey Tensing. 28 Sept., Cardinal Wyszynski, Primate of Poland, arrested. J.Weiner proves the 'Piltdown Man' a hoax. Spanish concordat with the Vatican. The Samaritans founded by the Rev. Chad Varah. Myxomatosis plague kills millions of rabbits.

**1954** 7-11 July, Evangelical Church Congress at Leipzig. 25 Nov., Perón opens anti-clerical campaign in Argentina. Billy Graham, evangelist, holds meetings in Berlin, London and New York. Temple of Mithras excavated in City of London.

## WESTERN & NORTHERN EUROPE

## CENTRAL & SOUTHERN EUROPE

## AFRICA

**1955** 8 Feb., N.A.Bulganin, Prime Minister of USSR. 23 Feb.–1956 24 Jan., Edgar Faure, premier of France. 4 Apr., Britain joins Baghdad pact. 6 Apr., Churchill resigns; 7 Apr.–1957 Anthony Eden, Prime Minister. 9 Apr., USSR denounces 1942 treaty with Britain and 1944 treaty with France. 15 May, allied peace treaty with Austria. 26 May, Conservatives win British general election. 6 Nov., Declaration of La Celle St Cloud: France to terminate Moroccan protectorate.

**1956** 23 Jan., Bulganin proposes twenty-year friendship pact to US. 28 Jan.–1961 21 May, Guy Mollet, premier of France. 25 Feb., 'De-Stalinization' begins in Russia: 'cult of personality' disowned. 2 Aug., Britain rejects request of Federation of Central Africa for independence. 2 Aug., Tripartite Declaration by Britain, France and US against nationalization of Suez Canal. 16-23 Aug., Suez Canal Conference in London. 27 Oct., Franco-German agreement on the Saar. 5 Nov., USSR threatens rocket attacks if Britain and France do not cease fire at Suez.

**1955** 29 Apr., Giovanni Gronchi, President of Italy. 6 May, W European Union inaugurated. 9 May, W Germany joins NATO. 14 May, E European Defence Treaty signed at Warsaw. 18-23 July, Summit Conference of Britain, France, US and USSR at Geneva to discuss disarmament and reunification of Germany. 5 Sept., bombs thrown at the house where Mustafa Kemal was born in Salonica. Spain admitted to UN.

**1956** 1 Jan., NATO Air Forces become operational in S Europe. 8 March, W Germany reintroduces conscription. 22 Aug., surrender terms for EOKA announced by Cyprus government. 23 Oct.–22 Nov., anti-Communist rising in Hungary brutally suppressed by USSR.

**1955** 18 Jan., Kenya government offers surrender terms to Mau Mau. 21 Jan., prolonged crisis over Entrenched Clauses of SA Act begins. Feb.–1956 Jan., Jacques Soustelle, Governor-General of Algeria. 2 March, mutual defensive alliance between Egypt and Syria. 24 March, new constitution in Tanganyika. 27 Apr., commercial agreement between Egypt and USSR. June, Jacques Soustelle proposes integration of Algeria with France. 4 July, Britain offers to return Simonstown to SA while retaining the right to use it. 30 Oct., puppet Sultan of Morocco abdicates. 18 Nov., Sultan Muhammad V restored in Morocco. Dec., Professor Bilsen produces plan for independence of Congo after thirty years. 10 Dec., United Tanganyika Party (UTP) inaugurated.

**1956** Jan., oil first struck at Oloibiri, Nigeria. Jan.–Feb., Queen Elizabeth II visits Nigeria. 1 Jan., the Sudan proclaimed an independent republic. 1 Feb., SA requests USSR to withdraw consulates. 27 Feb., SA Act abrogates Entrenched Clauses protecting Cape Coloured voters. 2 March, Morocco becomes independent. 9 March, British Togoland votes to be absorbed into Gold Coast. 20 March, France makes Tunisia independent: Habib Bourguiba, first President. 7 Apr., Spanish Morocco made independent and re-united with Morocco. 21 Apr., Egypt, Saudi Arabia and Yemen sign military alliance. 3 June Nasser elected President of Egypt. 18 June, Britain evacuates Canal Zone. 5 July, Sultan of Morocco recognized as ruler over Tangier. 19-20 July, Britain and USA inform Egypt they cannot finance Aswan High Dam. 12 Aug., Nasser nationalizes Suez Canal. 23 Oct., Ben Bella and other Algerian Arab leaders arrested. 29 Oct., Israel invades Sinai Desert. 31 Oct., Anglo French bombardment of Egypt. 31 Oct., Lord Malvern (Sir G. Huggins) resigns after twenty-three continuous years as Prime Minister of S Rhodesia: succ. Sir Roy Welensky. 5 Nov., British troops land in Egypt. 7 Nov., Anglo-French cease-fire in Egypt. 15 Nov., UN emergency force arrives in Egypt. 5 Dec., British and French begin withdrawal from Egypt. 19 Dec., preliminary hearing of 150

| THE EAST & AUSTRALASIA | THE AMERICAS | RELIGION & CULTURE |
|---|---|---|

**1955** 24 Feb., Baghdad defence pact between Iraq and Turkey. 17-24 Apr., Bandoeng Conference attended by twenty-four African and Asian states. July, Federal general election in Malaya: Alliance Party gains 51 out of 52 possible seats. 26 Sept., Republic of S Vietnam proclaimed. 3 Nov., Iran joins Baghdad pact. Dec., amnesty offered to Communists to cease fighting in Malaya. Ceylon admitted to UN.
**1955—6** D.Marshall, Chief Minister of Singapore.

**1955** Jan., abortive invasion of Costa Rica from Nicaragua. 7 March, Julius Nyerere addresses UN Trusteeship Council. 17 Apr., Vietnam complains to UN of alleged breach of Geneva treaty by Vietminh. 16 Sept., military and naval revolts in Argentina. 19 Sept., Perón resigns and flees: General Lonardi, provisional president. 2 Oct., France withdraws from UN General Assembly following hostile attitude on Algeria. 9 Nov., SA withdraws from UN General Assembly in protest against Cruz report on *apartheid*.
**1955—8** General Pedro Eugenio Aramburu, President of Argentina: constitution of 1853 restored, with other Conservative measures.
**1955—6** Negroes in Alabama boycott public buses in Montgomery, Alabama, on grounds of illegality of segregation.

**1955** July, Commonwealth Law Conference held in London. Sept., Universal Copyright Convention becomes effective. 6 Sept., 73 churches, 8 chapels, 2 convents, 3,584 warehouses and 1,954 shops belonging to Greeks, Armenians and Jews burnt in Istanbul. Poliomyelitis vaccine first made. Duke of Edinburgh's Award scheme inaugurated.

**1956** 29 Feb., Pakistan proclaimed a republic: remains in British Commonwealth. 2 March, General Glubb dismissed from command of the Arab Legion. 31 March, conference of Aden Protectorate rulers to discuss federation opens. Apr., general election in Ceylon: *MEP* (*Mahajana Eksath Peramuna*) (People's United Front) gains 48 out of 56 seats: S.W.R.D. Bandaranaike, premier. 1 Nov., Jordan forbids use of RAF bases against Egypt. 2 Nov., Gaza taken by the British. 18 Dec., Japan admitted to UN. Ceylon abrogates Defence Agreement with UK: RN leave Trincomalee; RAF leave Katunayake. Strong agitation in Ceylon: Sinhalese made the only official language.
**1956—9** Lim Yew Hock, Chief Minister of Singapore.

**1956** March, new Congress elected in Guatemala, followed by bombings and discontent. 4 March, Col. José Maria Lemus, President of El Salvador. 1 Sept., Ponce Enriquez, President of Ecuador. 29 Sept., Gen. Somoza, President of Nicaragua, assassinated: succ. his son, Luis Somoza. Nov., US Supreme Court holds segregation of negroes on buses to be a violation of the Fourteenth Amendment. 6 Nov., Eisenhower re-elected President of USA. Dec.— 1957 Sept., seven different governments in Haiti. 2 Dec., Fidel Castro, with eighty-two men, again attempts a rising in Cuba: guerrilla operations follow. 20 Dec., Nyerere again addresses UN Trusteeship Council. Following court order, University of Alabama admits negro student: mob violence ensues.
**1956—60** Juscelino Kubitschek, President of Brazil.

**1956** 26 Sept., electricity from nuclear power produced for the first time at Marcoule, France. 28 Oct., Cardinal Wyszynski released. 30 Oct., Cardinal Mindszenty released. Sixth Buddhist Council held in Rangoon. Buddha Jayanti year held in Ceylon, to commemorate 2,500th anniversary of Buddha attaining Nirvana. Craveiro Lopes Dam at Biopio completed. Israeli law recognizes the Druzes as a separate religious communit

1956—1958
WESTERN &
NORTHERN EUROPE

CENTRAL &
SOUTHERN EUROPE

AFRICA

**1957** 7-11 Jan., Chou En-lai, Chinese Prime Minister, visits Moscow. 10 Jan.—1963, Harold MacMillan, Prime Minister. 7 Feb., Britain states she will not join proposed European Economic Community. 13 June—30 Sept., Maurice Bourgès-Manoury, premier of France. 26 June—5 July, Commonwealth Prime Ministers' Conference. 4 July, Molotov, Malenkov and Kaganovich expelled from power in USSR. 8 July, following troubles with IRA, Eire interns sixty men. 21 Sept., Haakon VII of Norway d.: succ. Olaf V. 29 Oct., Russians make gesture of peace towards Turkey. 5 Nov.—1958 15 Apr., Félix Gaillard, premier of France.

**1957** 14 March, EOKA offers to suspend hostilities if Abp Makarios is released. 25 March, European Economic Community (EEC) and Euratom treaties signed in Rome: Common Market comes into being. 28 March, Abp Makarios released, subject to not returning to Cyprus. 15 July, General Franco announces monarchy will be restored in Spain on his death or retirement.

Africans, Asians and Europeans accused of treason begun in Johannesburg. **1957** 6 Jan., treaty of friendship between Libya and Tunisia. 9 Jan.—15 Sept., Johannesburg treason trial progresses. 31 Jan., Nasser nationalizes foreign banks, insurance companies and other businesses. 6 Feb., convention signed between France and Morocco. 6 March, Gold Coast becomes independent as Ghana 2 Apr., Britain transfers Simonstown base to SA, while retaining use. 4 Apr., AEF territories obtain financial autonomy and extended powers. 9 Apr., Suez Canal fully re-opened. 5 July, internal self-government instituted in Mauritius. 25 July, Bey of Tunis deposed: Tunisia proclaimed a republic: Habib Bourguiba, first constitutional President. 8 Aug., E and W Regions of Nigeria become self-governing; Alhaji Abubakar Tafewa, Federal Prime Minister. 14 Aug., Sultan of Morocco takes title of King. 17 Dec., charges against sixty-one accused withdrawn in Johannesburg trial.

**1958** 31 Jan., French Assembly votes a *loi-cadre* for Algeria. 22 Feb., Britain and US agree on the establishment of missile bases in Britain. 15 March, USSR issues four-point peace plan. 27 March, N.Khruschev, Prime Minister of USSR. 15 May, General de Gaulle declares his views on Algeria. 16-28 May, Pflimlin, premier of France. 19 May, press conference given by General de Gaulle. 1 June, General de Gaulle, Prime Minister of France. 24 July, life peerages (other than for Law Lords) first created in Britain. 28 July, Baghdad Pact members meet in London without Iraq. 11 Aug., British agreement with Muscat and Oman on military and economic aid. 23 and 31 Aug., racial disturbances in Nottingham, and Notting Hill, London. 28 Sept., referendum on the French constitution: Fifth Republic

**1958** 1 Jan., W German forces join NATO. 3 Feb., Benelux Economic Union formed. 24 Feb.—27 Apr., UN Conference on the Law of the Sea held in Geneva. 24 May, Committee of Public Safety formed in Corsica. 1-14 Sept., UN Conference at Geneva on Peaceful Uses of Atomic Energy. 9 Nov., Treaty of Montreux renewed for twenty years. 28 Dec., European Monetary Agreement replaces European Payments Union. **1958—73** Rear-Admiral Amérigo Deus Rodrigues Tomás, President of Portugal.

**1958** 14 Jan., Ifni and Spanish Sahara made Spanish metropolitcan provinces. 29 Jan., economic and technical agreement between Egypt and USSR. 4 March, first locally produced oil leaves Algeria. 5 March, United Arab Republic (UAR) proclaimed with Egypt and Syria as provinces: 8 March, joined by Yemen. Apr., Conference for Maghreb Unity held in Tangier. 27 Apr., Togo becomes independent: Sylvanus Olympio, President. 13 May, Committee of Public Safety formed in Algiers. June, UN Good Offices Committee visits SWA. 17 June, agreement between France and Tunisia. 19 June, end of blockade of French troops in Tunisia. July, Nyerere prosecuted for criminal libel. Aug., General de Gaulle announces independence for all French colonies at Brazzaville.

**1957** 30 Jan., Imam of Yemen declines to recognize Aden Protectorate boundaries. 6 March, Israel hands over Gaza strip to UN troops. 11 July, the Agha Khan d.: succ. Karim. 27 Aug., Japan makes first atomic test. 31 Aug., Federation of Malaya becomes independent: Tunku Abdul Rahman, Paramount Ruler: Tengku Abdul Rahman, Chief Minister. 4 Sept., economic union between Egypt and Syria. 15 Sept., conference between Syria and Turkey at Damascus: Russians threaten Turkey with war. Malayan population 6.3m.

**1958** 12 Jan., treaties of friendship, commerce and cultural co-operation between China and Yemen. 27-30 Jan., Baghdad Pact Council meets at Ankara. 2 May, state of emergency proclaimed in Aden. 9 May, riots in Tripoli, Lebanon. 22-26 May, strikes and communal rioting in Ceylon. 27 May, state of emergency and curfew proclaimed in Ceylon. 14 July, King Faysal of Iraq and other members of the royal family assassinated: republic proclaimed. 15 July, US troops called in to support Lebanese government. 17 July, British troops called in to protect independence in Jordan. 31 July– 3 Aug., Khrushchev visits Peking. 1 Aug., State of Singapore created.

**1957** 5 Jan., Eisenhower enunciates 'Eisenhower Doctrine' in Congress: Russian efforts to dominate Middle East denounced: USSR assured that they need not fear US aggression. 8 Jan., UN agreement with Egypt on clearing of Suez Canal. 30 Jan., UN General Assembly votes against *apartheid* in SA. 10 June, Canadian general elections: overwhelming Conservative victory, gaining 210 seats out of 275. 21 June, J.G. Diefenbaker, Canadian Prime Minister. July, Castillo Armas assassinated: makeshift governments in Guatemala. 1 Aug., Federation of the West Indies established. 15 Aug., Dr Cheddi Jagan, Chief Minister in British Guiana. 9 Sept., Eisenhower signs Civil Rights Act: Commission on Civil Rights and Civil Rights Division of Department of Justice set up. Sept., François Duvalier elected President of Haiti. Sept., following admission of nine negro students to Central High School at Little Rock, Arkansas, Governor Orval E. Faubus sends National Guard to exclude them: disturbance ensues: 23 Sept., President Eisenhower sends Federal troops to enforce court order to withdraw National Guard. 26 Sept., Dag Hammarskjöld re-elected UN Secretary-General. 10 Oct., J.F. Dulles states that, in the case of a Russian attack on Turkey, US would defend Turkey. North American Air Defence Command set up by Canada and US.

**1958** 1 Jan., *coup d'état* by young officers in Venezuela: Jiménez exiled: Rómulo Betancourt, President. Feb., General Miguel Ydígoras Fuentes elected President of Guatemala. 5 Apr., Fidel Castro makes 'total war' against President Batista. May, Vice-President Richard Nixon of US visits Peru: angry student demonstrations. 6 July, Alaska becomes the forty-ninth US State. Aug., Lleras Camargo elected President of Colombia with Liberal administration. 4 Aug., first US nuclear submarine passes under N Pole. Sept., Governor Faubus attempts to close all Little Rock schools. 31 Dec., Fulgencio Batista's government overthrown by Fidel Castro in Cuba.
**1958–** Adolfo López Mateos, President of Mexico.
**1958–62** Arturo Frondizi, President of Argentina.

**1957** 4 Apr., SA Native Laws Amendment Act forbids Africans to worship in European churches. 27 Apr., Pius XII: encyclical *Fidei Domum*, on nationalism. 29 July, International Atomic Energy Agency instituted. 4 Oct., USSR launches Sputnik I, unmanned spacecraft. First Conference of European Rabbis held. International Geophysical Year.

**1958** 5 July–9 Aug., Lambeth Conference of Anglican Church. United Church of Christ formed in USA by Congregationalists and Evangelicals. United Presbyterian Church formed in USA. Conversations on church unity held between Anglicans and Methodists. Hovercraft invented. US launches Vanguard and Explorer satellites.
**1958–63** John XXIII (Roncalli), Pope.

1958–1960

WESTERN &
NORTHERN EUROPE

CENTRAL &
SOUTHERN EUROPE

AFRICA

constitution agreed other than in Guinea. 5 Nov., General de Gaulle announces five year plan for Algeria. 21 Dec., General de Gaulle elected President of France and the French Community.

**1959** 8 Jan., General de Gaulle installed as President (–1969): Michel Debré, premier of France. 19 Feb., London agreement between Britain, Greece and Turkey on independence for Cyprus. 24 March, air services agreement between Britain and USSR: 28 March, cultural and technical agreement. 16 May, Conference of Paris on US aircraft incident: *détente* follows. 5-10 June, NATO Atlantic Congress in London. 17 June, Eamonn de Valéra elected President of Ireland. 16 Sept., General de Gaulle offers Algeria secession, integration or self-government in association with France. 8 Oct., Conservatives obtain increased majority in British general election. Dec., meeting of the 'Big Four' powers in Paris.

**1959** 13 Jan., trade agreement between Spain and US. 1 March, Abp Makarios returns to Cyprus. 30 March, agreement between Italy and US on tactical nuclear weapons. 6 May, military agreement between Greece and US. 20 Nov., EFTA (European Free Trade Association) convention agreed. 4 Dec., state of emergency ended in Cyprus.

**1958** 24 Aug., J.G.Strijdom d.: H.F. Verwoerd, Prime Minister of SA. 16 Sept., Provisional Algerian Government established in Cairo: Ferhat Abbas, Prime Minister. 25 Sept., all *AOF* territories except Guinea vote for independence within French community. 29 Sept., French Guinea given immediate independence Seku Touré, President. Oct., Madagascar (Malgache) independent as a Republic. 12 Oct., remaining indictments in SA treason trial withdrawn. 17 Nov., military *coup* in the Sudan led by General Ibrahim Abboud. 23 Nov., the (former French Soudan independent as a republic. 23 Nov., Seku Touré and Kwame Nkrumah announce paper union of Guinea and Ghana. 1 Dec., Central African Republic (former Oubangui-Chari) proclaimed a republic. 4 Dec Ivory Coast declared independent as a republic. Severe famine in Eritrea and Tigre following drought and locusts. Parmehutu Party founded in Rwanda. Uprona Party founded in Burundi.

**1958–61** Sir R.Turnbull, Governor of Tanganyika.

**1959** 13 Jan., General de Gaulle announces amnesty for Algerian insurgents. 17 Jan., abortive Federation of Mali (Senegal, Soudan Upper Volta and Dahomey) announced. 23 Jan., H.F.Verwoerd explains SA Bantustan policy in Parliament. 20 Feb.–3 March, disturbances in Nyasaland. 26 Feb.– 20 May, disturbances in S Rhodesia. 15 March, Northern Region of Nigeria becomes self-governing. 24 March, Bantu Self-Government Bill introduced in SA Parliament. Apr., Jomo Kenyatta released. 7-12 Apr., conference of Congolese political parties at Luluabourg: Patrice Lumumba demands independence in Jan. 1961. May, Umtala made capital of Transkei. 16-19 July, Presidents Nkrumah, Sekou Touré and Tubman meet at Saniguelli, Liberia, to plan union of free African states. 11-12 Dec., meeting of French Community at St Louis, Senegal: Senegal and Soudan demand independence: Community collapses

**1960** 14 Jan., USSR reduces armed forces by 1.2m. to 2.4m. 16-18 Jan., unsuccessful conference on Cyprus in London. 18 Jan., Brussels Conference on the Congo agrees to independence in June.

**1960** 19 Jan., trade agreement between Britain and Hungary. 6 Feb., Spain grants US oil companies concessions in Spanish Sahara. 11 Feb., wheat agreement between Poland and US.

**1960** 1 Jan., Cameroun independent 9 Jan., construction of Aswan High Dam begun. 3 Feb., H.MacMillan's 'wind of change' speech in Cape Town condemns *apartheid*. 13 Feb., first French atomic bomb exploded in the Sahara.

**1959** 11 Feb., Federation of Arab Emirates of the South inaugurated at al-Ittihad, near Aden. 28 Feb., trade agreement between China and USSR reported. 11 March, ten-year commercial treaty between Britain and Persia. 13 March, state of emergency ended in Ceylon. 17 March, Tibet rises abortively against Chinese: Dalai Lama flees to India. 28 Apr., 700 Iraqi Kurds seek political asylum in Turkey: number eventually reaches 1200. 1 May, US aircraft from base in Turkey brought down in USSR: crisis ensues. Sept., President Eisenhower pays official visit to Ankara. 25 Sept., S.W.R.D.Bandaranaike, premier of Ceylon, shot; 26 Sept., d. 9 Oct., Baghdad Pact renamed CENTO (Central Treaty Organization): seat established at Ankara.
**1959–** Lee Kuan-Yew, Prime Minister of Singapore.

**1960** Jan., Japan agrees ten-year Security Pact with US. 16 March, Syngman Rhee re-elected President of S Korea. 19 March, general election in Ceylon: UNP gain 50 seats; SLFP 46 seats; other parties

**1959** 1 Jan., Castro's guerrillas take Havana: Batista flees: Manuel Urrutia temporary President: Castro, Prime Minister: reforms begin, followed by cold war with US. 16 Feb., Fidel Castro becomes Prime Minister of Cuba. 5 March, US joins Baghdad Pact. 25 Apr., Queen Elizabeth II opens the St Lawrence Seaway. 26 Apr., abortive Cuban attempt to provoke rising in Panama. 24 May, John Foster Dulles d. June, Dominican rebels, with Cuban aid, make abortive attempt on Dominica. Aug., Haiti repels invasion by Fidel Castro. 21 Aug., Hawaii declared the fiftieth State of US. 15 Sept., Georges Vanier, Governor-General of Canada. 10 Nov., UN General Assembly condemns *apartheid* and any other form of racial discrimination. Virgina Supreme Court states closure of schools a violation of the State Constitution.
**1959–60** Fidel Castro carries out revolutionary programme in Cuba: US protests at expropriation of US property. US creates Inter-American Development Bank to aid Latin America.
**1960** 11 Jan., US protests at expropriation of US property in Cuba. March, National Agrarian Institute created in Venezuela to take over great estates. 10 Apr., US Civil Rights Bill for negroes.

**1959** 25 Jan., Pope John XXIII summons Second Vatican Council, with especial aim of promoting church unity. 2 June, USSR rocket begins orbit round sun. 3 July, Pope John XXIII orders the French worker-priest movement to cease operation. USSR sends out spacecraft carrying monkeys and dogs; Oct., obtains photographs of hidden side of the moon. First atomic passenger vessel and submarine launched. *Zinjanthropus* skull discovered at Olduvai by Mrs. L.S.B. Leakey. The *Manchester Guardian* renamed the *Guardian.* Anti-Jewish incidents in Germany.

**1960** 7 Aug.–4 Dec., friction between Church and State in Cuba. Nov.–Dec., Abp of Canterbury visits Jerusalem, the Ecumenical Patriarch in Istanbul and the Pope in Rome. Cardinal Stephinac d. Lasers discovered.

## WESTERN & NORTHERN EUROPE

## CENTRAL & SOUTHERN EUROPE

## AFRICA

**1960** 24 Jan., riots in France. 3 Feb., Michel Debré voted full powers; 5 Feb., French cabinet re-organized. March, Khrushchev visits France. Apr., General de Gaulle visits Britain and US. 8 May, L.I.Brzeshnov becomes President of USSR. 25 Aug., USSR Communist party condemns Chinese Communism. 1 Nov., Britain announces US granted facilities for Polaris submarines at Holy Loch.

**1960** 11-12 March, EFTA conference in Vienna. 15 March–29 Apr., 7-27 June, Ten-Power Disarmament Conference at Geneva. 8 Apr., treaty between W Germany and Holland. 14 Apr., E Germany announces completion of collectivization of agriculture. 3 May, EFTA treaty comes into operation. 1 July, Cyprus agrees to grant Britain military bases. 16 Aug., Cyprus proclaimed an independent republic: admitted to British Commonwealth and UN: Abp Makarios, first President. 30 Aug., E Germany begins partial blockade of W Berlin.

**1960** 21 March, demonstration following Pan-African Congress at Sharpeville: 67 Africans killed, 180 wounded. 30 March–31 Aug., State of Emergency in SA. 9 Apr., attempt to murder Dr Verwoerd. 27 Apr., Sierra Leone independent. 13-27 May, riots, strikes, lock-outs and terrorism in Algeria. 17 May, Kariba Dam opened. 6 June, Portugal sends 600 troops to Angola. 15 June, Madagascar independent as Malagasy Republic. 20 June, Mali independent 26 June, British Somaliland independent. 30 June, Congo (L) declared independent: general chaos ensues. 1 July, Ghana declared a republic. Katanga secedes from Congo (L) under Moise Tshombé. 1 July, Somali Republic, including former British and Italian territory, proclaimed. Aug., Senegal becomes independent of Mali: Dahomey and Niger independent. 8 Aug., S Kasai secedes from Congo (L) under Albert Kalondji. 11 Aug., Chad independent 24-28 Aug., foreign mercenaries expelled from Congo (L). 1 Sept., following constitutional changes, Nyerere forms government in Tanganyika: responsible government achieved. 13-20 Sept., UN intervention in Katanga results in cease-fire. 14 Sept., Col. Joseph Mobutu seizes power in Congo (L). 1 Oct., Federation of Nigeria independent. 5 Oct., SA referendum favours a republic. 27 Nov., Mauritania becomes independent. 9-13 Dec., General de Gaulle visits Algeria: riots in Algiers, Oran and elsewhere. 12 Dec., Mafeking made capital of Tswana Bantustan. 13 Dec unsuccessful attempt of group of army officers to seize power in Ethiopia. 24 Dec., Ghana, Guinea, Mali Union announced.

**1961** 1 Jan., the farthing ceases to be legal tender in Britain. 30 Apr., Mayor of Evian assassinated during preparations for conference there between France and *FLN*. 19 May, agreement between Britain and USSR on peaceful use of atomic energy. 20 May–13 June, talks between France and *FLN* at Evian. 31 May, Generals Challe and Zeller sentenced to life imprisonment. 31 May–2 June, President Kennedy visits Paris. 13 June–1962 19 March, Evian talks continued. Aug.–1962 March, numerous bomb incidents in France and Algeria. 8 Sept., attempt on life of General de Gaulle. 17 Oct., Algerians riot in Paris. 30 Oct., the corpse of Stalin removed from the Lenin mausoleum.

**1961** 27 Jan.–19 July, inconclusive talks on Austro-Italian frontiers. 30 Jan., European conference on space opened at Strasbourg. 3 Feb., trade agreements between Albania and China. 2 March–14 Apr., UN Conference on Diplomatic Intercourse and Immunities. 21 March–9 Sept., Three-Power Conference of Britain, USA and USSR on Discontinuance of Nuclear Weapon Tests. 17-18 Aug., Berlin Wall round E Berlin erected. 24 Oct., new constitution renames the island the State of Malta. 6 Nov., Portugal institutes a Common Market with its Overseas Territories.

**1961** 3-7 Jan., Casablanca Conference of African powers: African Charter announced. 6 Jan., UN Secretary-General visits SA for talks on *apartheid*. 6-8 Jan., in Algeria, and 8 Jan. in France, referendum on self-determination of Algeria: majority in favour. 17 Jan., inconclusive general election in Zanzibar. 28 Jan., Rwanda becomes a republic. 4 Feb., civil war starts in Angola. 14 Feb., the *rand*, decimal currency, introduced in SA. 26 Feb. Muhammad V of Morocco d.: succ. Hasan II. 8 Apr., Kwame Nkrumah makes 'Dawn Speech' in Accra. 21-26 Apr., military revolt in Algeria. 27 Apr., Sierra Leone becomes independent within the British Commonwealth.

## THE EAST & AUSTRALASIA

25 seats: Dudley Senananyanke again premier. 21 March, Chiang Kai-shek re-elected President of Nationalist China. 27 Apr., Syngman Rhee resigns from Presidency of S Korea. 23 May, Israel announces capture of Adolf Eichmann, former chief of the Gestapo. 27 May, military *coup d'état* in Turkey: General Jemal Gürsel takes control: President Bayar and Prime Minister Menderes imprisoned, and all members of their government: new government claims to restore democracy: military junta takes power as Committee of National Union: policy of friendship with USSR and alliance with US. 9 June, typhoon strikes Hong Kong. 12 June, new constitution in Turkey abolishes parts of 1924 constitution. 20 July, general election in Ceylon: UNP 30 seats; SLFP 75 seats: 21 July, Mrs. Sirimavo Bandaranaike premier: first woman to be a Prime Minister. 10-24 Sept., Baghdad meeting of oil producing countries sets up OPEC (Organization of Petroleum Exporting Countries). 14 Oct., trial of Adnan Menderes and his followers begun in Turkey. 25 Oct., Patriarch Athenagoras gives evidence in trial of Menderes and others. 13 Nov., General Gürsel purges Committee of National Union: fourteen members of the military junta dismissed out of thirty-eight: committee reduced to twenty-four. Dec., Turkey obtains loan of $130m. from US for construction of steel works. Population of mainland China estimated *c.* 680m. Federal Republic of Germany loans Turkey 400m. Deutsche marks for engineering development.

**1961** 1 Jan., Sinhalese made the official language in Ceylon. 9 Apr., Ngo Dinh Diem elected President of S Vietnam. 25 June, Iraq claims Kuwait as an 'integral part' of the country. 2 July–19 Sept., British troops occupy Kuwait frontier with Iraq. 9 July, new constitution adopted in Turkey by referendum: national assembly with 450 deputies: senate with 150 elected senators with 15 appointed by the president. 17 Sept., Adnan Menderes and two others hanged. 28 Sept., *coup d'état* in Syria: secedes from UAR. 15 Oct., general elections in Turkey: General Gürsel, President: Ismet Inönü, Prime Minister. 17-19 Dec., India takes Goa from Portugal.

## THE AMERICAS

**1960** 21 Apr., Brasilia, new capital of Brazil, inaugurated. 21 May–23 June, earthquakes, volcanic eruptions and tidal waves in Chile. 27 May, US ends aid to Cuba. July–Aug., Cuba expropriates US firms. 1 July, four year economic plan launched in Venezuela. 19 Aug., US prohibits countries receiving US aid from buying sugar from Cuba. Sept., Act of Bogotá: US grants $5m. aid to Latin America. 2 Sept., Cuba recognizes Communist China; 1952 military aid treaty with US denounced. 19 Oct., US places embargo on shipments to Cuba. 4 Nov., John Fitzgerald Kennedy elected President of US by majority of 118,000 out of 68m. votes. Illiteracy in Honduras 70%. Population of Mexico 34.3m. National Association for Advancement of Coloured People boycotts retail stores which practise segregation at lunch counters. **1960–1** Negroes appointed for the first time to posts in US public administration. US actively seeking overthrow of Fidel Castro, dictator of Cuba.

**1961** 3 Jan., US breaks off diplomatic relations with Cuba: followed by twelve American countries. Feb., USSR Deputy Prime Minister Mikoyan visits Cuba: large scale economic and military aid agreed. 17 Feb., agreement between UN and Congo (L) on intervention in Katanga. 1 March, US Peace Corps instituted by President Kennedy. General elections in British Honduras: George Price, first Prime Minister. 7 Apr., abortive UN motion on SWA. 17 Apr., some 1500 Cuban refugees, armed and drilled in US, attempt invasion of Cuba at Bay of Pigs: fail: 1200 taken prisoner: US pays $53m. in compensation. 30 May, Rafael Leonidas Trujillo, dictator of Dominican Republic, assassinated.

## RELIGION & CULTURE

**1960** Intense archaeological work put in hand in Nubia before submersion of the area by the Aswan High Dam. Churchill College, Cambridge, founded.

**1961** 12 Apr., Major Yuri Gagarin, Russian citizen, first man to travel in space round the Earth. 14 July, Pope John XXIII: encyclical *Mater et Magistra,* on Catholic social teaching. 10 Sept., Pope John XXIII appeals for world peace on radio and television. 24 Sept.–1 Oct., Pan-Orthodox Conference held in Rhodes. 19 Nov., WCC meets in Delhi: joined by Russian Orthodox: attended by Roman Catholic observers. International Missionary Council integrated in WCC. Dec., Pope John XXIII: encyclical *Aeterna Dei* on Christian unity. Synagogues closed in Moscow. University of Sussex founded. **1961–74** Arthur Michael Ramsey, Abp of Canterbury.

1961–1963

WESTERN &
NORTHERN EUROPE

CENTRAL &
SOUTHERN EUROPE

AFRICA

**1961** 31 May, SA becomes a Republic outside the British Commonwealth: C.R.Swart, first President: many African countries decline recognition on account of *apartheid.* 30 June, Johannesburg treason trial ends with acquittal of accused. 19-22 July, riots between French and Tunisians at Bizerta. 21 Aug., all restrictions on Jomo Kenyatta lifted in Kenya. 1 Oct., French withdraw troops from Bizerta town. 18 Sept., Dag Hammarskjöld killed in aircraft crash following visit to Congo (L). 8-9 Dec., Tanganyika independent within the British Commonwealth: Sir Richard Turnbull, Governor-General: Julius Nyerere, Prime Minister.

**1962** 14 Jan., common agricultural policy of EEC approved. 18 Jan., Ireland requests membership of EEC. 8 Feb., riots in Paris organized by *OAS.* 19 March, cease-fire in Algeria agreed at Evian. 8 Apr., cease-fire in Algeria approved in French referendum by 17.5m. to 1.7m.: General de Gaulle given full powers to deal with Algeria. 1 May, Norway requests membership of EEC. 1 July, British Commonwealth Immigrants Act comes into force. 22 Aug., attempt on General de Gaulle's life in Paris. 4-9 Sept., General de Gaulle visits Federal Germany. 19 Sept., Commonwealth Prime Ministers' Conference approves British application to join EEC. 6 Oct., Pompidou cabinet falls: requested by General de Gaulle to continue in office. 28 Oct., French referendum on universal suffrage for presidential elections. 18-25 Nov., French general election: Gaullists confirmed in power. 13 Dec., Pompidou again French premier.

**1962** 9 Feb., Spain requests membership of EEC. 3 March, State of Malta formally comes into being: Dr Borg Olivier, Prime Minister. 4 June, Portugal applies to join EEC. 11 July, Spanish cabinet re-organized after five years of office. 1 Nov., Greece joins EEC as an associate member.

**1962** 9 March, new constitution in Congo (L). 19 March, French cease-fire in Algeria. 5 May, proposed Transkei constitution signed by 129 chiefs. 31 May, terrorism ceases in Algeria. 1 July, Rwanda and Burundi become independent. 3 July, Algeria becomes independent. Aug., Northern Sotho Bantustan created. 2 Aug., Katanga approves U Thant's plan for end of Katanga secession. Attempt on President Nkrumah's life fails. 20 Sept., ZAPU banned in S Rhodesia. 27 Sept., Prevention Detention Act in Tanganyika. 2 Oct., Nkrumah declines life presidency, but agrees to one-party state. 9 Oct., Uganda becomes independent. 21 Oct., Egyptian five-year treaty with Yemen 40,000 troops sent to support Republicans. 9 Dec., Tanganyika proclaimed a republic: Julius Nyerere, first President. 22 Dec., Comoro Is. granted internal self-government. 28 Dec., UN troops take Elizabethville: Katanga secession ended. FRELIMO, Mozambique nationalist organization, set up in Dar es Salaam by Eduardo Mondlane.

**1963** 14 Jan., General de Gaulle objects to British admission to EEC. 29 Jan., British admission to EEC abandoned. 14 Feb., Harold Wilson elected leader of British Parliamentary Labour Party. 1 March–5 Apr., miners' strike in France. 2 July, Franco-German treaty of co-operation ratified.

**1963** 17 Feb., disarmament talks resumed in Geneva. 20 Feb., USSR proposes non-aggression pact between NATO and Warsaw Pact countries in Geneva. 7 March, trade agreement between W Germany and Poland. 7 Apr., new constitution in Yugoslavia. 9 Apr., President Makarios announces that union with Greece is no longer an object of policy.

**1963** 13 Jan., President Sylvanus Olympio of Togo found murdered outside US Embassy, Lomé. 14 Jan., one party government proposed in Tanganyika. 17 Jan., Nicholas Grunitzky, President of Togo. 3 Apr., S Rhodesia demands independence: 9 Apr., refused by Britain. 19 Apr., Nkrumah publishes scheme for African unity.

## THE EAST & AUSTRALASIA  THE AMERICAS  RELIGION & CULTURE

**1961** 20 Sept., U Thant elected
Acting Secretary-General of UN.
Negro 'Freedom Riders' campaign
in US for desegregation on inter-
state buses: 22 Sept., Inter-State
Commerce Commission requires end
of such discrimination. Population
of Latin America c. 208m. 13 Dec.,
Brazilian government takes powers
to prevent left wing coup.
**1961–4** Goulart, President of
Brazil.

**1962** Jan., abortive threat of a
military *coup d'état* in Ceylon. 5
Feb., Turkey requests membership
of EEC. 22 Feb., supporters of
Menderes attempt *coup d'état* in
Turkey: suppressed the next day. 1
March, new constitution in Pakistan.
11 May, Dr Sarvepalli Radhakrishnan
elected President of India. 31 May,
Adolf Eichmann hanged at Ramleh.
8 June, Ayub Khan sworn President
of Pakistan. 27 Sept., Yemen
military *coup* gains highland area
only: Egypt intervenes in immediate
support. 20 Oct., China attacks
India. 21 Nov., cease-fire between
China and India. W.Gopallawa,
Governor-General of Ceylon.

**1962** 9 Jan., trade pact between Cuba
and USSR. 27 Feb., West Indies
Federation formed. March, elections
in Argentina: overwhelming vote in
favour of Perón's supporters:
elections annulled by military: 29
March, Arturo Frondizi elected
President, but imprisoned. 10 June,
Socialist Haya de la Torre elected
President of Peru: election annulled
by army. 28 June, UN General
Assembly demands independence
and universal franchise in S Rhodesia.
6 Aug., Jamaica becomes
independent. 10 Aug., U Thant's
plan for federal constitution in
Congo (L) published. 31 Aug.,
Trinidad and Tobago become
independent. 2 Sept., USSR agrees
to provide arms for Cuba. 25 Sept.,
Fidel Castro announces intention of
USSR to establish a fishing base in
Cuba. Oct., US Navy blockades Cuba
to prevent further building of USSR
missile sites: USSR removes nuclear
missiles from Cuba. US continues
boycott of Cuba. 22 Oct., President
Kennedy announces discovery of
USSR rocket bases in Cuba, with
range from Canada to Peru:
dismantling of bases demanded. 26
Oct., Kennedy rejects Khrushchev's
offer to dismantle Cuban rocket
bases if US will demolish bases in
Turkey. 30 Nov., U Thant elected
UN Secretary-General. Fernando
Belaúnde, President of Peru.

**1962** 1 Apr., Pope John XXIII orders
retention of Latin as the language of
the Roman Catholic Church. 30 July,
Abp of Canterbury visits Patriarch of
Moscow. 13 Aug., Anglican Abp of
West Africa and Bp of Accra expelled
from Ghana. 11 Oct., Second Vatican
Council, attended by more than 2,000
bishops, opened in Rome: attended
by Orthodox and other observers.
Exclusive Brethren expel 8,000
English members for refusing to
abandon contact with non-members.
1100 Mormon missionaries campaign
in England. US Supreme Court rules
reading of prayers in US state schools
unconstitutional.

**1963** 18 Jan., Aden Colony joins
Federation of S Arabia. 8 Feb.,
Col. Aref takes power in Iraq
following military *coup*. 2 March,
border agreement between China and
Pakistan. 8 March, *coup* in Syria
establishes National Council of
Revolution. 30 March, fighting in
Plain of Jars, Laos.

**1963** 14 Jan., President Kennedy
announces Cuban rocket crisis at an
end. 3 Apr., negro agitation
campaign against segregation begins
at Birmingham, Alabama. 9 May,
state of emergency proclaimed in
British Guiana. 11 May, negro
leaders' houses bombed by
segregationists in Birmingham,
Alabama.

**1963** 9 Feb., Abp of Lvov released by
USSR after eighteen years'
imprisonment. 11 Apr., Pope John
XXIII: encyclical *Pacem in terris*.
16 June, Valentina Tereshkova,
Russian, first woman to enter space.
4 Oct., Abp Beran of Prague released
after twelve years' imprisonment.

## WESTERN & NORTHERN EUROPE

## CENTRAL & SOUTHERN EUROPE

## AFRICA

**1963** 5 July, China and USSR begin ideological discussions in Moscow. 31 July, British Peerage Act enables renunciation of titles within six months or on succession: hereditary women peers and all Scottish peers admitted to the House of Lords. 5 Aug., test ban treaty signed in Moscow between Britain, USA and USSR: followed by some 100 other states, excluding China and France. 8 Aug., Great Train Robbery in Britain: £2½m. stolen.    19 Oct.–1964 Sir Alec Douglas-Home, Prime Minister, following retirement of Harold MacMillan. 20 Dec., French constitution reformed.

**1964** 27 Jan., France recognizes Communist China. 15 July, Anastas Mikoyan becomes President of USSR. 4-11 Sept., Ian Smith visits London for talks on Rhodesia. 14 Oct., Kosygin becomes Prime Minister of USSR. 15 Oct.–1970, James Harold Wilson, Prime Minister, with initial Labour majority of four. 16 Dec., vaunted 'statement of intent' signed in London by government, employers and trade unions.

**1963** 16-19 May, General de Gaulle visits Greece.

**1964** 11 Feb., fighting between Greeks and Turks in Limassol, Cyprus. 6 March, Paul I of Greece d.: succ. Constantine II.    9 March, heavy fighting at Ktima, Cyprus. 11 March, SA withdraws from International Labour Organization. 4 Apr., Cyprus abrogates treaty of 1959 with Britain and Turkey. 3-4 July, General de Gaulle visits W Germany. 13 Aug., General Grivas takes command of Greek Cypriot forces. 21 Sept., Malta becomes independent within the British Commonwealth. 6 Dec., President Segui of Italy resigns: succ. Giuseppe Saragat.

**1963** 3 May, SA government takes discretionary powers against subversion: May–Nov., 543 persons detained under ninety-day clause. 22-26 May, conference of thirty African Heads of State in Addis Ababa: charter of Organization of African Unity (OAU) approved. 5 June, Kenyatta, Nyerere and Obote meet in Nairobi to discuss East African federation. 2 July, Sultan Abdallah of Zanzibar d.: succ. Jamshid. 10 Aug., Nigeria made a federal republic. 2 Oct., Dr Nnamdi Azikiwe elected President of Nigeria. 4 Oct., Kabaka Mutesa II of Buganda elected President of Uganda. 10 Dec. Zanzibar becomes independent. 12 Dec., Kenya independent. 31 Dec., Federation of Central Africa dissolved.

**1964** 8 Jan., Dr J.B.Danquah and other members of Ghanaian opposition detained without trial. 11-19 Jan., many thousand Tutsi massacred in Rwanda. 12 Jan., revolution in Zanzibar: 'Field-Marshal John Okello seizes power: Shaikh Obedi Karume acclaimed President. 20 Jan., troops mutiny in Dar es Salaam. 21 Jan., Nyerere requests British troops to restore order. 24 Jan., troops mutiny in Kenya: British troops requested. 25 Jan., British troops disembark in Dar es Salaam. 3 Feb., following referendum Ghana becomes a one-party state. 13 Apr., Ian Smith becomes Prime Minister of S Rhodesia. 22 Apr., treaty of union between Tanganyika and Zanzibar. 12 June, Nelson Mandela and seven other SA nationalists sentenced to life imprisonment. 2-3 Aug., fifty persons killed in disturbances caused in Malawi by prophetess Alice Lenshina. 5 Aug., rebels in Congo (L) take Stanleyville. 7 Sept., rebels declare People's Republic of Congo at Stanleyville. 25 Sept., armed subversion begun by FRELIMO in Mozambique. 24 Oct., N Rhodesia becomes independent as Zambia: Dr Kaunda, first President. 25 Oct., Field-Marshal Abboud assumes sole power in Sudan. Wilson warns Rhodesia against any unilateral declaration of independence. 29 Oct., Tanganyika and Zanzibar renamed Tanzania. 30 Oct., civilian caretaker government in the Sudan. 12 Dec., Kenya becomes a republic: Jomo Kenyatta, first President. 22 Dec., General Christopher Soglo takes power in Dahomey. Arab 'Summit Conference' in Cairo: sets up Palestine Liberation Organization.

## THE EAST & AUSTRALASIA

**1963** 17 May, Iraq, Syria and UAR agree to form federation. 21 May, abortive rising of army cadets in Turkey. 10 June, civil war in Iraq between Arabs and Kurds. 1 Nov., army seizes control in S Vietnam. 18 Nov., military *coup* in Iraq. 10 Dec., bomb outrage at Aden airport: emergency declared. Australian population 11m.: 2m. in Sydney, and nearly 2m. in Melbourne: includes 2m. immigrants since the war.

**1964** 21 Feb., attempt to murder Prime Minister Inönü of Turkey fails. 1 March, threat of alleged right-wing *coup d'état* in Ceylon: state of emergency proclaimed: Parliament prorogued until July. 28 March, King Saud of Saudi Arabia grants full powers to Crown Prince Faisal. 27 May, Lal Bahadur Shastri becomes Prime Minister of India. Aug., new coalition government of SLFP and LSSP in Ceylon: Mrs S.Bandaranaike again premier. 2 Aug., N Vietnam torpedo boats attack US warships off Tonkin. 5 Aug., US bombs N Vietnam. 10 Oct., Emperor opens first Olympic Games to be held in Japan. 1 Nov., Vietcong attack air base at Hoa Binh: US aircraft destroyed. 2 Nov., King Saud of Saudi Arabia deposed: succ. Faisal. First Legislative Council elected in Papua and New Guinea.

## THE AMERICAS

**1963** 19 June, President Kennedy warns Congress of necessity for action on civil rights. 18 July, UN Special Committee on *apartheid* recommends embargo on oil and arms for SA. 31 July, UN Security Council demands independence for Portuguese colonies. Elections in Argentina: supporters of Perón banned: Dr Arturo Illia, President. 5 Aug., Nuclear Test Ban Treaty signed by Britain, US and USSR: most other states, except France and China, follow. 7 Aug., UN Security Council bans sale of arms to SA. 28 Aug., negro civil rights demonstration in Washington. 4 Sept., further riots in Birmingham, Alabama. 22 Nov., President Kennedy assassinated: succ. Lyndon B. Johnson (−1969).

**1964** 9 Jan., riots against US in Panama. 4 March, UN appoints peace-keeping force for Cyprus. 16-19 March, General de Gaulle visits Mexico. 2 Apr., Marshal Castello Branco proclaims himself President of Brazil: President Goulart flees into exile: civilian cabinet appointed to combat inflation with austerity. 2 July, US Civil Rights Act passed. 19 July, negro rioting in Harlem, New York. 23 July, negro riots in Brooklyn, New York. 26 July, negro rioting in Rochester, USA. 4 Sept., Eduardo Frei, President of Chile. 14 Oct., Dr Martin Luther King awarded Nobel Peace Prize. 3 Nov., L.B. Johnson elected President of US in landslide victory. Victor Paz Estenssoro overthrown in Bolivia: General René Barrientos, President: military reformist government ensues. 4 Dec., Alex Quaison-Sackey, Ghanaian delegate, elected President of UN General Assembly.

## RELIGION & CULTURE

**1963** 25 Oct., Vatican Council agrees to a fixed date for Easter provided that other Christian bodies concur. Vatican Council approves the use of vernacular in the liturgy, except for the Canon of the Mass. Further Anglican and Methodist conversations on unity.
**1963–** Paul VI (Montini), Pope.
**1963–75** John Carmel, Cardinal Heenan, Abp of Westminster.

**1964** 4-7 Jan., Pope Paul VI visits the Holy Places: holds meeting with Ecumenical Patriarch of Constantinople. 31 July, US spacecraft sends back 4,000 photographs from the Moon. 11 Aug., Alice Lenshina, leader of N Rhodesian Lumpa Church, surrenders after causing some 500 deaths. 15 Sept., Vatican agreement with Hungary signed. 19 Oct., twenty-two Uganda martyrs canonized in Rome. 2-5 Dec., Pope Paul VI visits Bombay. 6 Dec., Roman Catholic Hierarchy of England and Wales authorizes joint prayers with other Christians.

| WESTERN & NORTHERN EUROPE | CENTRAL & SOUTHERN EUROPE | AFRICA |
|---|---|---|

**1965** 14 Jan., Prime Ministers of Ireland and N Ireland meet for first time in more than forty years. 24 Jan., Sir Winston Churchill d. 28 Jan.–6 Feb., financial agreement between Belgium and Congo (L). 24 Feb., atomic electricity station inaugurated at Chinon. 4 March, Afro-Asian student demonstrations in Moscow. 17 March, British Prices and Incomes Board established. 26 May, military service in France reduced to eight months. 10 June, 750th anniversary of Magna Carta celebrated. 17-25 June, Commonwealth Prime Ministers' Conference in London: Vietnam peace delegation appointed. 22 June, 700th anniversary of British Parliament celebrated. 30 June, EEC agricultural policy discussions broken down by France. 22 July, Edward Heath elected leader of the Conservative Party. 4-11 Oct., Ian Smith in London for talks on Rhodesia. 25 Oct., France begins boycott of EEC meetings. 9 Nov., death penalty for murder abolished in Britain. 5-19 Dec., General de Gaulle re-elected for seven years. 9 Dec., N.A.Podgorny becomes President of USSR.

**1966** 9 Jan., cabinet changes in France. 18-24 Jan., Sir Hugh Beadle, Chief Justice of Rhodesia, visits London for talks. 30 Jan., France ceases boycott of EEC. 31 Jan., Britain imposes complete trade ban on Rhodesia. 1 Feb., women given legal equality with their husbands in France. 1 March, France announces withdrawal from NATO of troops stationed in Federal Germany. 30 March, France announces that after one year she will not accept US troops on her soil. 31 March, Labour Party increases majority in British general election. 20-30 June, General de Gaulle visits USSR; 30 June, treaty of co-operation signed. 24 July, EEC agrees on common agricultural policy. 31 July, British Colonial Office abolished: responsibilities taken over by Commonwealth Office. 1 Aug., first Parliamentary Commissioner (Ombudsman), Sir Edward Compton, nominated in Britain. 21 Oct., Aberfan mine tip disaster in Wales.

**1965** 24 Feb., 5,000 students riot in Madrid demanding free student unions. 8 Apr., twenty-year treaty between Poland and USSR. 24 Apr., General Humberto Delgado, Portuguese opposition leader, found murdered in Spain. 23 July, Cyprus electoral law deprives Turkish Cypriots of communal voting rights. 25 July, Admiral Tomás re-elected President of Portugal for seven years. 30 Aug., UN World Population Conference in Belgrade. 8 Sept., Rhodesian diplomatist accredited to Lisbon in spite of British protests.

**1966** 17 Jan., US loses hydrogen bomb in air collision over Spain. 21 Jan., Spain forbids NATO powers, other than Britain, to fly over. 27 Jan.–25 Aug., disarmament conference at Geneva. 4 March, Spain reduces censorship of the press. 16 June, Chou En-lai, Prime Minister of China, visits Rumania; 24 June, Albania. 4-8 July, Warsaw Pact Conference in Bucharest. 1 Nov., Albanian Communist Party calls on true Communists to break with USSR: alliance with China affirmed. 14 Dec., referendum on new constitution in Spain.

**1965** 9 Jan., new government formed in Burundi by Pierre Ngendadumwe; 15 Jan., assassinated. 6 Feb., death of Dr J.B.Danquah, former leader of the opposition in Ghana, made public. 9 Feb., Sudan African National Union (SANU) appeals to end fighting in S Sudan. 10-12 Feb., *Organisation Commune Africaine et Malgache (OCAM)* created. 28 Feb., Gambia becomes independent. 1 March, Seretse Khama, Prime Minister of Bechuanaland, wins general election. 9 March, OAU *ad hoc* Commission on the Congo. 7 May, Rhodesian Front Party, under Ian Smith, wins general election. 19 June, Col. Houari Boumédienne seizes power in Algeria. 5 July, single party government formally adopted in Tanzania. 29 July, Franco-Algerian oil agreement. 4 Sept., Dr Albert Schweitzer d. at Lambarène. 3 Oct., Grégoire Mayibanda elected President of Rwanda. 25-30 Oct., Harold Wilson, British Prime Minister, visits Rhodesia. 26 Oct.–6 Nov., East and Central African countries set up East African Economic Community. 11 Nov., Ian Smith unilaterally proclaims Rhodesia independent. 25 Nov., General Mobutu deposes J.Kasabuvu, becoming President of Congo (L). 22 Dec., General Christophe Soglo seizes power in Dahomey.

**1966** 1 Jan., Col. Jean Bedel Bokassa seizes power in CAR. 4 Jan., Col. Sangoulé Lamizana seizes power in Upper Volta. 15 Jan., Ibo military *coup d'état* in Nigeria. 17 Jan., General Aguiyi Ironsi takes power in Nigeria. 20 Jan., murder of Sir Abubakar Tafawa Balewa, and other leading Nigerian personalities, becomes known. 22 Feb., Milton Obote seizes power in Uganda. 24 Feb., Kwame Nkrumah overthrown in Ghana by army and police: General J.A.Ankrah heads military government. 15 Apr., Uganda becomes a republic: Dr Milton Obote, President. 17 Apr., abortive military *coup* in Ghana. 10-24 May, constitutional crisis in Uganda: 24 May, Obote seizes royal palace: Kabaka escapes. 30 June, Léopoldville renamed Kinshasa. 6 July, Malawi becomes a republic: Dr Hastings Banda, first President. 8 July, Prince Charles Ndizewe (later Ntare V) seizes power in Burundi. 29 July, military counter-*coup* in Nigeria: Lieut.-Col. Yakubu Gowon takes over.

## THE EAST & AUSTRALASIA

**1965** 21 Jan., Prime Minister of Persia assassinated. 26 Jan., riots follow declaration of Hindi as official language in India. 7 Feb., US begins bombing of N Vietnam following N Vietnamese raids on US bases. 13 Feb., Mr Urgüplü, Prime Minister of Turkey. 17-24 Feb., President Nyerere visits Peking. 3 March, Abd al-Qawi Makkawi appointed Chief Minister in Aden. 6 March, Afro-Asian student demonstrations in Peking. 22 March, General election in Ceylon: 18-year-olds first given franchise: new UNP government under Dudley Senanayake. 23 March, US and S Vietnam use tear gas against N Vietnam. 9 Apr. 1 July, hostilities between India and Pakistan. 22 June, treaty between Japan and S Korea. 26 July, Maldive Is. independent: Britain retains control of Gan. 5 Aug.–22 Sept., renewed hostilities between India and Pakistan. 9 Aug., Singapore becomes independent from Malaya. 25 Sept., following violent disorders, Aden constitution suspended. 2 Oct., campaign of violence in Aden begins. 10 Oct., Demirel, Prime Minister of Turkey.

**1966** 4-10 Jan., Pakistan President and Indian Prime Minister meet for talks on Kashmir at Tashkent. 7-17 Jan., USSR delegation attempts to bring about peace in Vietnam. 11 Jan., Lal Bahadur Shastri, Prime Minister of India, d. suddenly in Tashkent. 19 Jan., Mrs. Indira Gandhi, Prime Minister of India. 14 Feb., Australia introduces decimal currency. 23 Feb., military *coup* in Syria. 1 March, rising in Assam. 28 March, Cevdet Sunay, President of Turkey. 13 May, President Aref of Iraq killed in air crash: 16 Apr., succ. his brother, General Rahman Aref. 1 June, Bangkok agreement between Indonesia and Malaya. 18 Aug., the 'cultural revolution' begins in China. 13 Dec., US bombs Hanoi: protests at civilian casualties.

## THE AMERICAS

**1965** 20 Jan., President L.B.Johnson inaugurated: calls on US to build the Great Society. 1-5 Feb., Dr Martin Luther King, negro leader, arrested with 300 others in Dallas, Texas. 7 March, negro civil rights march from Selma to Montgomery, Alabama. 10 March, Dr Martin Luther King again arrested. 24 March, US spacecraft lands on the Moon. 24 March, second negro civil rights march on Montgomery, Alabama. 25 Apr., military *junta* deposes civilian government in Dominican Republic: US send 22,000 Marines to prevent establishment of a Communist government. 11-17 Aug., serious negro riots in Los Angeles. 16 Oct., demonstrations in USA against war in Vietnam. 13 Nov., UN Security Council condemns Rhodesian unilateral declaration of independence (UDI). 17 Nov., following breach of diplomatic relations by eight African states, UN Security Council orders Britain to put down Rhodesian rebellion. 20 Nov., UN Security Council orders oil embargo on Rhodesia. Civil war in Dominican Republic: US sends in Marines to halt strife.

**1966** 7-8 Feb., President Johnson meets S Vietnam leaders in Honolulu. 6 March, Dr Julio Mendez elected President of Guatemala. 1 May, Dr Carlos Lleras Restrepo elected President of Columbia. 26 May, British Guiana becomes independent as Guyana. 1 June, Dr Joaquin Balaguer elected President of Dominica. 28 June, Dr Arturo Illia removed from Presidency of Argentina: succ. General Juan Carlos Onganía. 12-21 July, race riots in Chicago, Cleveland and Brooklyn, USA. 27 Sept., race riots in San Francisco. 27 Oct., UN General Assembly votes to terminate SA Mandate over SWA. 30 Nov., Barbados becomes independent. 2 Dec., U Thant re-elected UN Secretary-General. 16 Dec., UN General Assembly recommends sanctions against Rhodesia.

## RELIGION & CULTURE

**1965** 21 Feb., Malcolm X, Black Muslim leader, assassinated in New York. 4 Oct., Pope Paul VI addresses UN General Assembly. 24 Oct., worker-priest movement in France allowed to restart. 8 Dec., Second Vatican Council ends. Universities of Warwick and Kent instituted. University College, Cambridge, founded. Edward White, US citizen, first man to walk in space. The Pope and the Ecumenical Patriarch of Constantinople mutually withdraw the excommunication of their respective bodies. Israel Museum opened.

**1966** 1 Jan., Pope Paul VI appeals for peace in Vietnam. 18 March, Pope Paul VI relaxes conditions for mixed marriages. 22-23 March, Abp of Canterbury pays official visit to the Vatican. 14 June, the Vatican abolishes the *Index Expurgatorius*.

| WESTERN & NORTHERN EUROPE | CENTRAL & SOUTHERN EUROPE | AFRICA |
|---|---|---|

**1966** 10 Nov., Harold Wilson announces Britain will again seek admission to EEC. 1-9 Dec., Premier Kosygin of USSR visits France. 2-4 Dec., Ian Smith and J.Harold Wilson meet on HMS *Tiger*. 4 Dec., 'working document' approved by British cabinet.

**1967** 15 Jan., Harold Wilson and George Brown tour EEC capitals. 27 Jan., treaty between Britain, US and USSR bans nuclear weapons in outer space. 6-13 Feb., A.N. Kosygin, Prime Minister of USSR, visits Britain. 5-12 March, general election in France: Gaullist majority of one. 29 March, first French nuclear powered submarine launched. 11 May, Britain, Denmark and Ireland formally apply to join EEC. 27 July, Sexual Offences Act tolerates homosexuality in Britain. 9 Oct., census in France, showing 50m. inhabitants. 10 Oct., British Road Safety Act introduces breath tests. 18 Dec., France vetoes British admission to EEC.

**1968** 16 Jan., UK announces withdrawal of forces from Persian Gulf and Far East. 23 Jan., coalition government formed in Denmark. 7 Feb., strikes in Flemish-speaking schools and universities in Belgium. 27 Feb., emergency legislation in Britain to stem Asian immigration into Britain: more than 1m. recent coloured immigrants already in Britain. 22 March, formation of French revolutionary student movement of '22 mars'. 27 Apr., Abortion Act comes into force in UK. 2 May, student riots begin at Nanterre; and, 3 May, in Latin quarter, Paris. 13 May, peace talks on Vietnam in Paris (−1973). 14 May−26 June, serious strikes throughout France.

**1967** 24-30 Jan., President Podgorny of USSR visits Rome. 21 Feb., disarmament conference re-opened in Geneva. 21 Apr., Constantine Kollias, Prime Minister of Greece, following military *coup*. 28 May, summit meeting of EEC in Rome. 6-12 Sept., General de Gaulle visit Poland. 10 Sept., overwhelming vote in Gibraltar referendum to remain British. 10 Oct., elections to the *Cortes* held in Spain. 15 Nov.−8 Dec., crisis between Greeks and Turks in Cyprus. 14 Dec., King Constantine of Greece goes into exile in Rome following military take-over.

**1968** 5 Jan., A.Dubcek elected First Secretary of Czech CP. 30 Jan., student riots in Warsaw. 8-9 Feb., further student riots in Warsaw. 25 Feb., President Makarios re-elected in Cyprus. 11-15 March, student riots in Poland. 5 May, Spain closes frontier at Gibraltar in protest against continued British presence. 14-18 May, General de Gaulle visits Rumania. 20 Aug., USSR troops occupy Czechoslovakia. 11 Sept., USSR troops leave Prague. 26 Sept., Professor Marcelle Caetano succ. Dr Salazar as Prime Minister of Portugal. 9-13 Oct., Ian Smith and Harold Wilson meet on HMS *Fearless* off Gibraltar: discussions abortive.

**1966** 25 Aug., riots in Djibouti during General de Gaulle's visit. 6 Sept., Dr Verwoerd, SA Prime Minister, assassinated. 13 Sept., B.J. Vorster, Prime Minister of SA. 30 Sept., Bechuanaland becomes independent as Republic of Botswana first President, Sir Seretse Khama. 4 Oct., Basutoland becomes independent as Kingdom of Lesotho: Moshoeshoe II takes title of King. 29 Nov., Capt. Michel Micombero seizes power in Burundi: republic proclaimed.

**1967** 1 Jan., Congo (K) government seizes *Union Minière* assets. 12 Jan., Lieut.-Col. Etienne Eyadéma seizes power in Togo. 5 Feb., Nyerere makes 'Arusha declaration', stating Tanzanian political aims. 19 March, referendum in Djibouti: territory votes to remain in the French Community. 24 March, Lieut.-Col. Juxon-Smith leads military *coup* in Sierra Leone. 28 May, Nigerian government re-organizes federation into twelve states. 30 May, Lieut.-Col. Odumegwu Ojukwu proclaims former eastern Region of Nigeria independent as Biafra: civil war ensues. 6 June, East African Community established by Kenya, Tanzania and Uganda. 13 June, French Somaliland renamed the 'French Coast of the Afars and Issas'. 30 June−1 July, Tshombé kidnapped in an aircraft and taken to Algiers. 5 July−5 Nov., military rising in E and N Congo (K). 28 Oct., Kenya and Somalia agree to cease border fighting. 12 Dec., Britain and UAR resume diplomatic relations. 17 Dec., military *coup d'état* in Dahomey led by Commandant Maurice Kouandète.

**1968** 1 Jan., Malawi sends diplomatic mission to SA. 19 Jan., Capt. Kérékou becomes President of Military Revolutionary Committee in Dahomey. 20-24 Feb., OAU Conference of Ministers at Addis Ababa condemns Britain for not taking Rhodesia by force: France condemned for refusing to decolonize Djibouti: *apartheid* denounced vigorously. 24-27 Feb., Sir Alec Douglas-Home and Lord Goodman visit Salisbury for secret talks. March-April., guerrillas attack Rhodesia from Zambia. 12 March, Mauritius independent. 2 Apr., Charter of Union of C African States, Congo (K), Chad and CAR, signed at Bangui: creates common market. 10 Apr., J.J.Fouché, President of SA.

**1967** 10 Feb., violent riots in Aden: curfew imposed. 6 March, Svetlana, daughter of J.Stalin, requests political asylum at US Embassy in Delhi. 2-7 Apr., abortive UN mission to Aden. 2 May, servicemen's families withdrawn from Aden. 6-27 May, rioting in Kowloon, Hongkong. 9 May, Dr Zakir Husain, President of India. 10 May, Sir Humphrey Trevelyan becomes High Commissioner in Aden. 22 May, Egypt closes Gulf of Aqaba to Israel. 5-10 June, the 'Six-Day War' between neighbouring Arab States and Israel. 17 June, China explodes her first hydrogen bomb. 20 June, Federal Army units mutiny in Aden. 5 Sept., Sir H.Trevelyan offers to talk with Aden nationalists. 25 Sept., nationalist parties in Aden propose cease-fire. 5 Nov., President Sallal of Yemen deposed: three-man presidential committee formed. 26 Nov., People's Republic of S Yemen proclaimed in Aden.

**1967** 2 Feb., General Somoza, Jr., elected President of Nicaragua. 14 Feb., Latin American nations sign treaty in Mexico City banning nuclear weapons. 15 March, Marshal Costa Silva, President of Brazil. 19 May, UN General Assembly resolves to set up council to administer SWA. 11 June, negro riots in Florida. 20 June, negro riots at Atlanta, Georgia. 9 July, negro riots in Kansas City. 14-24 July, serious race riots in many US cities. 24-26 July, General de Gaulle visits Quebec, Canada. 29 Sept., President Johnson makes peace proposals for Vietnam. 9 Oct., Che Guevara (*alias* Lynch) reported killed by Bolivian troops while carrying on guerrilla campaign in the Andes. 17 Nov., UN General Assembly recommends sanctions against Portugal until she frees her overseas territories.

**1967** 20 March, Paul VI: encyclical *Populorum Progressio.* 12 May, Papal Pro-Nuncio protests against Guinea's compulsory Africanization of the clergy. 27 May-1 June, seventy-three priests and fifty-five nuns expelled from Guinea. 27 Sept.–29 Oct., synod held in Rome. 2 Dec., first human heart transplanted at Groote Schuur. Hospital, Cape Town. 11 Dec., first public flight of Franco-British aircraft *Concorde* 001 from Toulouse.

**1968** 10 Jan., J.G.Gorton, Prime Minister of Australia. 21 Jan., raid from N Korea on Seoul. 23 Jan., N Korea seizes USN ship *Pueblo.* 28 March, anti-American riots in Tokyo. 17-21 Apr., Prime Minister Kosygin of USSR visits Pakistan and India. 17 July, General Hasan al-Bakr seizes power in Iraq. 31 Aug., some 12,000 killed by earthquakes in Iran. 13 Oct., Chinese CP expels President Liu Shao-chi.

**1968** 4 Apr., Rev. Martin Luther King, US civil rights leader, assassinated. 10 Apr., Civil Rights Bill passed in US. 21 Apr., Pierre Trudeau (Lib.) succ. as Prime Minister of Canada. 29 May, UN Security Council imposes mandatory sanctions on Rhodesia. 5 June, Senator Robert Kennedy shot in Los Angeles. 1 July, nuclear non-proliferation treaty signed at UN by UK, US, USSR and fifty-eight other states. 22 July, state of siege proclaimed in Bolivia. 23 Aug., UN Security Council condemns USSR intervention in Czechoslovakia. 25 Aug., first French H bomb exploded in the Pacific. Oct., President Belaúnde deposed by military *coup* in Peru: General Velasco Alvorado, dictator: radical agrarian reforms instituted.

**1968** 2 Feb., Pope Paul sends message to General Gowon on Biafra. 26 Feb.–9 March, Commonwealth Education Conference in Lagos. 24 Apr., International Olympic Committee excludes SA from the Olympic Games in Mexico. 29 July, Pope Paul VI: encyclical *Humanae Vitae,* on contraception. 2 Sept., oil pipe-line 1,058 miles long opened from Dar es Salåam to Ndola. 26 Sept., censorship of plays ended in UK.
**1968–74** Cecil Day Lewis, Poet Laureate.

1968–1969

WESTERN &
NORTHERN EUROPE

CENTRAL &
SOUTHERN EUROPE

AFRICA

**1968** 23-30 May, general elections in France: Gaullists win 349 out of 482 seats. 29 May, General de Gaulle quits Paris without warning. 30 May, large Communist procession from the Bastille to St Lazare in Paris. 31 May, French Assembly dissolved. 9 July, Couve de Murville, premier of France. 5 Sept., UK Trades Union Congress rejects statutory incomes policy. 5 and 6 Oct., riots in Londonderry by civil rights demonstrators: beginning of period of violence in N Ireland. 13 Nov., currency crisis in France. 16 Nov., civil rights demonstration in Londonderry. 21 Nov., House of Lords approves White Paper on its reform: no result ensues. 22 Nov., Northern Irish government announces reform programme. 30 Nov., Protestant demonstration led by Rev. Ian Paisley halts civil rights march in Armagh.

**1969** 1 Jan., France places an embargo on arms and aircraft for Israel. 7-15 Jan., Commonwealth Conference in London: Uganda announces intention to expel 40,000 Asians. 19 Apr., riots in Londonderry; 20 Apr., army in N Ireland ordered to guard key installations; 21 Apr., riots in Belfast. 28 Apr., French referendum on reform of the Senate rejected by majority of 52.87%: General de Gaulle resigns immediately: Alain Poher, President *ad int.* 28 Apr., Capt. O'Neill resigns premiership of N Ireland: succ. Major Chichester-Clark. 12 May, UK Representation of the People Act reduces voting age to eighteen. 15 June, Georges Pompidou elected President of France with 58% of votes (−1974): Jacques Chaban-Delmas, Prime Minister. 18 June, UK government abandons Trades Union Reform Bill. July, cyclone kills twenty-six people in Brittany. 10 Aug., the *franc* devalued. 12 Aug., serious riots in N Ireland between Catholics and Protestants: army called in to control security. 5 Nov., anti-*apartheid* demonstration at Springboks Rugby match against Oxford University in London. 1 Dec., following UK application for membership, EEC agree to open negotiations in June 1970. 16 and 18 Dec., UK Parliament abolishes death penalty for murder. 26-31 Dec., three gunboats leave Cherbourg secretly, for Haifa.

**1969** 1 Jan., federal government inaugurated in Czechoslovakia, with regional Czech and Slovak governments. 16 Jan., in Prague, a student, Jan Palach, burns himself to death in protest against control of the press. 24 Jan., martial law proclaimed in Spain (−25 March) following riots and student unrest. Riot at London School of Economics. 23 Feb.−2 March, President Nixon tours Europe. 5 March, Dr Gustav Heinemann elected President of Germany. 28 March, anti-USSR demonstrations in Prague. 30 May, new constitution in Gibraltar. 23 July, Prince Juan Carlos sworn in as future King of Spain. 27 Sept., reformist ministers dismissed in Czechoslovakia. 3 Oct., limited restoration of civil liberties in Greece. 21 Oct., Willy Brandt made Chancellor of W Germany. 24 Oct., the *mark* revalued.

**1968** 18 Apr., Col. Juxon-Smith, President, overthrown by military in Sierra Leone: Sir Banja Tejan-Sie, Chief Justice, Governor-General *ad int.* 19 Apr., Mulungushi Reforms announced in Zambia. 21 May, abortive conference at Kampala on a cease-fire in Biafra. 23 July, Israeli aircraft high-jacked by Palestinian commandos and taken to Algiers. 2 Aug., Lieut. Augustin Poignet takes power in Congo (B) *ad int.* 6 Sept., Swaziland becomes independent: constitutional monarchy under King Sobhuza II. 13-16 Sept., OAU Summit Conference in Algiers: majority condemn secession of Biafra. 1 Oct., SA publishes constitution for Ovamboland, SWA. 12 Oct., (Spanish) Equatorial Guinea independent: Francisco Macia Nguema, first President. 18 Oct., Rhodesia rejects *Fearless* proposals. 19 Nov., military *coup* in Mali. 22 Nov., Lieut. Moussa Traoré, President of Mali. Capt. Alfred Raôul, President *ad int* of Congo (B).

**1969** 3 Feb., Dr Eduardo Mondlane, FRELIMO leader, assassinated in Dar es-Salaam: succ. Dr Uria Simango. 2 Apr., General Ankrah, President of National Council of Liberation, Ghana, deposed for alleged corruption: succ. General Akwasi Afrifa. 21 May, new Rhodesian constitution published. 25 May, Col. Jaafar al-Nimeiri leads successful military *coup* in Khartoum. 29 June, Moise Tshombé d. at Algiers. 30 June, Spain returns Ifni to Morocco. 5 July, Tom Mboya, Kenyan political leader, assassinated. 23 Aug., Ghanaian Constituent Assembly promulgates new constitution. 1 Sept., King Idris I of Libya overthrown in military *coup* led by Col. Moamer Qadafi. 7 Sept., following general election, Dr Kofi Busia forms government in Ghana. 25 Sept., agreement between EA Economic Community and EEC signed at Arusha. 8 Oct., Vendaland Bantustan, Transvaal, inaugurated. 15 Oct., President Ali Shirmarke of Somalia assassinated. 30 Oct., Libya asks Britain to withdraw military bases. 10 Dec., military *coup* in Dahomey.

| THE EAST & AUSTRALASIA | THE AMERICAS | RELIGION & CULTURE |

**1968** 5 Nov., Richard Nixon elected President of US.

**1969** 26 Feb.—13 March, conference on constitutional reform in Pakistan. 2 March, clash between Chinese and USSR troops on R. Ussuri. 11 March, Mrs. Golda Meir, Prime Minister of Israel (−1974). 31 March, General Yahya Khan, President of Pakistan. 3 May, Dr Zakir Husain, President of India, d.: succ. Varaha Giri. 15 May, state of emergency in Malaysia. 2 June, Australian aircraft carrier cuts US destroyer in half during manoeuvres in the China Sea. 20 July, N Vietnam rejects US peace proposal. 3 Sept., Ho Chi-Minh, President of N Vietnam, d.: succ. Ton Dac Thang. 8 Nov., UAR destroyers bombard Israeli-occupied Sinai. 17 Nov., Japanese students demonstrate against US bases in Japan.

**1969** 10 March, James Earl Ray sentenced to ninety-nine years' imprisonment for murder of Rev., Martin Luther King. 12 March—11 Apr., troubles in Anguilla, WI. 4 Apr., talks on peace in the Middle East at UN between France, UK, US and USSR. 21 July, Neil Armstrong, US astronaut, is first man to set foot on the moon. Sept., US ambassador to Brazil kidnapped: set free after release of fifteen guerrilla prisoners. 26 Sept., President Salinas of Bolivia overthrown by General Ovando. 15 Oct., widespread demonstrations in US against Vietnam war. 24 Nov., Lieut. William Calley charged with murder of Vietnamese civilians at My Lai (16 March 1968). Population of Latin America *c.* 272m. **1969—74** Richard Nixon (Rep.), President of US.

**1969** 15 Feb., fertilization in a test tube of a human *ovum* reported in Cambridge, England. 9 May, Vatican publishes revision of *Roman Calendar,* arousing considerable controversy. 8 July, Convocations of Canterbury and York reject scheme for unity with Methodists. 31 July—2 Aug., Pope Paul VI visits Uganda. 22 Sept., World Islamic Conference begins at Rabat, Morocco. 11-28 Oct., Synod held in Rome.

## WESTERN & NORTHERN EUROPE

## CENTRAL & SOUTHERN EUROPE

## AFRICA

**1970** 19 Jan., H.Wilson pays tribute in Parliament to 'magnanimity in victory' of General Gowon. 9 Feb., forty-one killed by an avalanche in Val d'Isère, France. 13 Feb., Cambridge students riot in an hotel against a Greek tourist meeting. 28-29 May, demonstrations in Paris. 10-15 June, newspaper strike in Britain. 15 June, general strike in France. A.Gerismar, leader of the *'Gauche Prolétarienne'*, arrested. 18 June, Conservatives win British general election: Edward Heath, Prime Minister (–1974). 30 June, Britain, Denmark, Ireland and Norway apply for membership of EEC. 19 Oct., major British oil find in the N Sea. 9 Nov., General de Gaulle d.

**1971** 13 Jan., cabinet re-shuffle in France: Ministry of the Environment established. 20 Jan.–8 March, Post Office strike in UK. 5 Feb., first soldier killed in riots in Belfast. 11 Feb., treaty banning firing of atomic weapons from sea-bed signed in London, Moscow and Washington, and by forty other nations. 15 Feb., decimal currency introduced in UK after over 150 years' discussion. 23 Feb., Rolls-Royce aircraft and marine divisions nationalized. 20 March, Brian Faulkner, Prime Minister of N Ireland. 21 May, Heath and Pompidou announce identity of view on UK entry into EEC. 6 Aug., UK Industrial Relations Act passed: sets up National Industrial Relations Court: bitterly opposed by Trades Unions. 20 Aug., UK auctions oil and gas concessions in N Sea. 6 Sept., British Trades Union Congress rejects terms for UK entry into EEC.

**1970** 20 Jan., Chinese and US ambassadors hold talks in Warsaw. 21 Feb., Palestinian guerrillas blow up a Swiss aircraft in Germany. 19 March, first meeting of Heads of E and W Germany at Erfurt. 3-8 June, SA Prime Minister visits Portugal. 7 July, treaty of friendship between Rumania and USSR. 4 Dec., state of emergency in Spain following strikes and demonstrations by Basque separatists. 7 Dec., treaty between Poland and W Germany recognizing the Oder-Neisse line frontier. 13 Dec., rioting in Poland against high prices.

**1971** 7 Feb., female adult suffrage introduced in Switzerland. 12 June, government formed in Malta by Dom Mintoff. 23 June, UK entry to EEC agreed in Luxembourg. 30 June, Yugoslav constitution revised. 19 Aug., NATO headquarters transferred from Malta to Naples. 3 Sept., Four-Power agreement on Berlin. 23 Jan., Radio Johannesberg gives details of USSR naval forces in virtual control of Red Sea and Indian Ocean.

**1970** 1 Jan., Trade Licensing Act becomes effective in Uganda: foreign traders restricted to specific commodities. 12 Jan., General Effiong requests armistice in Biafra. 15 Jan., Biafran war ends. Feb., estimated that 12,000 rebels had deserted FRELIMO. 1 Feb.–mid-Apr frequent clashes between UAR and Israel on the Suez Canal. 12 Feb., Israel bombs Cairo: seventy killed. 2 March, Rhodesia unilaterally proclaimed a republic: eleven out of thirteen countries withdraw their consulates leaving only Portugal and SA. 14 Apr., Clifford Dupont nominated President of Rhodesia. 1 May, 'Common Man's Charter' announced in Uganda. 11 June, Zulu Territorial Authority set up in SA. 24 June, Gambia becomes a republic. 21 July, Aswan High Dam begins operation. 31 Aug., former Chief Justice Sir Edward Akufo-Addo elected President of Ghana. 15 Sept., SA Prime Minister states that Bantustans may request independence at any time. 28 Sept., President Nasser d.: succ. Anwar Sadat. 26-28 Oct., construction of Tanzania-Zambia railway begun, with funds loaned by China. 4 Nov., Ivory Coast agrees to a 'dialogue' with SA. UAR, Libya and Sudan agree to federate. 19-21 Nov., co-operative agreement signed between Madagascar and SA. 2 Dec., increase in autonomy granted in Angola and Mozambique. 16 Dec., state of emergency in Eritrea: insurgents alleged to be from 2,000 to 10,000.

**1971** 25 Jan., General Idi Amin leads military *coup* in Uganda. 4 Feb., UAR extends cease-fire with Israel to 7 March: offers to open Suez Canal in return for Israeli withdrawal from Sinai: refused by Israel. 17 Feb., Congo (K) refuses 'dialogue' with SA. 18 Feb., Algerian government nationalizes French petroleum installations. 5 March, SA announces self-rule for Tswanaland. 18 March, UAR rejects Israeli border proposals. 22 March, Ghanaian Foreign Minister indicates readiness to visit SA. 23-29 March, CAR, Ghana, Ivory Coast, and Madagascar accept SA policy of 'dialogue'. 17 Apr., Federation of Arab Republics, including UAR, Libya and Syria announced. 23 July, Vice-President William Tolbert sworn President of Liberia. 27 Oct., official name of Congo (K) changed to Republic of Zaïre. 3 Nov., Transkei Territorial Government authority

## THE EAST & AUSTRALASIA

## THE AMERICAS

## RELIGION & CULTURE

**1970** 20 Jan., unsuccessful *coup d'état* in Iraq. 30 Jan., fighting between Israel and Syria. 6 Feb., Egypt sinks Israeli naval vessel at Eilat: Israel sinks Egyptian minesweepers. 10-21 Feb., Jordan attempts to increase control of Palestinian guerrillas. 11 March, civil war with Kurds ended in Iraq. 30 Apr., US and Vietnam attack Communists in Cambodia. 12 May, Israel attacks guerrillas in Lebanon. 4 June, Tonga becomes an independent kingdom within the Commonwealth. 7 June–27 Sept., fighting in Jordan between Palestinian guerrillas and army. 28 June, US withdrawal from Cambodia begins. 7 Aug., US plan for ninety-day cease-fire accepted by UAR, Israel and Jordan. 6 Sept., four aircraft high-jacked by Palestinian guerrillas. 9 Oct., Cambodia declared the Khmer Republic. 10 Oct., Fiji becomes independent within the British Commonwealth. Qabus b.Said usurps his father, Said b.Taimur, as Sultan of Oman and Muscat.

**1970** 23 Feb., Guyana (formerly British Guiana) becomes a republic within the British Commonwealth. 23 Feb.–4 March, President Pompidou visits US. 3 March, UN Security Council condemns Rhodesia's 'purported assumption of republican status'. 6-8 March, US diplomat kidnapped in Guatemala. 11-15 March, Japanese Consul-General held by guerrillas in Brazil. 31 March–6 Apr., West German ambassador to Guatemala kidnapped and murdered by guerrillas. 4 May, serious student riot at Kent State University sets off strikes at other US campuses. 29 May, former President Aramburu of Argentina kidnapped, and then killed. 22 June, President Ibarra of Ecuador becomes dictator. 5 July, Luis Echeverría elected President of Mexico. 11 July, W German ambassador kidnapped in Brazil; 16 June, released following freeing of forty political prisoners. 31 July, Tupamaro guerrillas in Uruguay kidnap and kill US police adviser. 5 Sept., Dr Salvador Allende elected President of Chile: first Marxist candidate to attain Presidency by free democratic election. 5 Oct.–3 Dec., J.Cross, British Trade Commissioner kidnapped by Quebec separatists in Montreal. 6 Oct., General Torres, President of Bolivia. 11 Oct., P. Laporte, Quebec Minister of Labour, kidnapped and then murdered by Quebec extremists. 7 Dec., Swiss ambassador kidnapped in Brazil.

**1970** 11 Jan., Pope Paul states genocide is feared in Biafra following end of hostilities. 27 Apr., J.-P.Sartre becomes editor of *La cause du peuple*. May, conference of 183 Catholic bishops in Brasilia: 159 vote for declaration urging social and penal reforms in Brazil. 14 May, World Exhibition held at Osaka, Japan. 10 July, Bp James Walsh released after twelve years' imprisonment in China as an alleged US spy. 3 Sept., WCC announces donation of $200,000 (about £80,000) to oppressed racial groups, including nineteen African revolutionary movements. 20 Sept., USSR space spacecraft lands on the Moon.

**1971** 14-22 Jan., Commonwealth Conference in Singapore. 8 Feb.–24 March, S Vietnam troops invade Laos. 10 March, general election in India gives Mrs Gandhi a landslide majority. William MacMahon becomes Prime Minister of Australia. 12 March, Dr Nihat Erim, Prime Minister of Turkey. 26 March, Shaikh Mujibur Rahman declares East Pakistan independent as Bangladesh. Grave cholera epidemic among refugees follows. 5-23 Apr., abortive *coup* by People's Liberation Front in Ceylon. 10 Apr., US table tennis team visits China: beginning of relaxation in relations between China and US. 3 July, first general election in Indonesia for sixteen years. 13-19 July, fighting between Jordanian army and Palestinian guerrillas: some 1,500 guerrillas captured. 18 July, six Persian Gulf Trucial States agree to federate.

**1971** 5 Jan., Dr Jarring, UN mediator, holds talks at UN with Egypt, Israel and Jordan. 8 Jan.–9 Sept., British Ambassador to Uruguay kidnapped by Tupamaro guerrillas. 21 Apr., President François Duvalier of Haiti d.: succ. his son, Jean, aged nineteen. 25 Apr., 200,000 people march peacefully on Washington to demand end to Vietnam war. 15 Aug., US suspends conversion of dollars into gold: ninety-day price freeze imposed. 22 Aug., President Juan Torres of Bolivia deposed in military *coup* led by Col. Hugo Banzer. 6 Sept., more than 100 Tupamaro guerrillas escape from prison in Montevideo. 25 Oct., UN General Assembly admits China: Taiwan expelled. 12 Nov., President Nixon announces end of US offensives in Vietnam. 1 Dec., state of emergency following riots in Chile. 18 Dec., US devalues the dollar. 31 Dec., Dr Kurt Waldheim succ. as Secretary-General of UN.

**1971** 20 Feb., Spanish bishops demand separation of Church and State. 28 Sept., Cardinal Mindszenty reaches Rome after fifteen years in the US Embassy, Budapest. 30 Sept.–6 Nov., Synod held in Rome.

## WESTERN & NORTHERN EUROPE

## CENTRAL & SOUTHERN EUROPE

## AFRICA

**1971** 24 Sept., UK expels 105 USSR diplomats and officials for espionage. 4 Oct., British Labour Party Conference votes against entry to EEC. 5 Oct., Emperor Hirohito of Japan visits London. 13 Oct., British Conservative Party Conference votes for entry into EEC. 28 Oct., House of Commons, by 356 votes against 244, and House of Lords by 451 votes agains 58, agree to UK entry into EEC.

**1972** 9 Jan.–27 Feb., coal miners strike in UK. 22 Jan., Denmark, Eire, Norway and UK accepted for entry into EEC. 30 Jan., 'Bloody Sunday' in N Ireland: thirteen civilians killed in Londonderry during demonstrations. 2 Feb., IRA blow up British Embassy in Dublin. 22 Feb., IRA kill seven people including a Catholic chaplain at Aldershot. 19-20 March, President Pompidou visits UK for talks on EEC. 30 March, direct rule imposed in N Ireland: Stormont Parliament suspended: William Whitelaw, Secretary of State. 10 Apr., Biological Weapons Convention signed by UK, US, USSR and then by ninety other nations. 14 May, UDA (Ulster Defence Association) set up first Protestant 'no-go' area in Belfast. 22-29 May, President Nixon visits Moscow: first US President to do so. 29 May, IRA order cease-fire in N Ireland: Provisional IRA continues strife. 22 June, minimum lending rate replaces bank rate in UK. 26 June, Provisional IRA announce cease-fire in N Ireland. 5 July, Pierre Messmer, Prime Minister of France. 9 July, Provisional IRA ends cease-fire. 1 Sept., Iceland unilaterally extends its fishing limits from twelve to fifty miles: beginning of the 'Cod War'. 18 Sept., first Ugandan Asian exiles reach UK: major resettlement ensues. 24 Sept., referendum in Norway gains majority against entry into EEC. 2 Oct., British Labour Party Conference rejects opposition to entry into EEC. 7 Dec., referendum in Eire deletes provision in constitution giving special position to RC Church.

**1973** 1 Jan., Denmark, Eire and UK join EEC. 27 Jan., agreement to cease-fire in Vietnam signed in Paris. 14 Feb.–23 March, gas workers strike in UK. 8 March, IRA explode car bombs in London. N Irish referendum overwhelmingly favours continuing union with UK. 11 March, Eire, Italy and UK float their currencies.

**1972** 24 Feb., twenty-year treaty of friendship between Hungary and Rumania. 21 March, George Papadopoulos becomes Regent of Greece. 26 March, Malta and UK make agreement on defence. 29 March, Berlin Wall opened after six years. 27 Apr., ex-President Kwame Nkrumah of Ghana d. in Bucharest. 7 May, coalition formed in Italy under Giulio Andreotti. 5 Sept., two members of Israeli Olympic team killed, and nine taken as hostages, by Palestinian guerrillas at Munich. 15 Sept., trade agreement between Spain and USSR.

**1973** 6 Jan., 'Revolutionary Workers' explode bombs in Lisbon to protest against wars in Portuguese colonies. 15 Jan., Mrs. Golda Meir, Prime Minister of Israel, received in audience at the Vatican. 2 Feb., W German government introduces exchange control. 1 June, monarchy abolished in Greece. 9 June, Admiral Luis Carrero Blanco made Prime

extends to 1½m. Xhosa living outside the territory. 15-24 Nov., abortive talks between Britain and Rhodesia.

**1972** 9 Jan.–11 March, Peace Commission in Rhodesia. 13 Jan., Dr Busia deposed by military *coup* in Ghana: Col. Acheampong takes power. 4 Feb., President Kaunda of Zambia bans United Progressive Party: leader, Simon Kapwepwe and 120 members arrested. 25 Feb., one party state announced in Zambia. 1 March, new constitution in Morocco. 6-9 March, UN Secretary-General visits SA and SWA for discussions on SWA. 27 March, regional government agreed for S Sudan. 7 Apr., Vice-President Abedi Karume of Zanzibar murdered in reprisal for enforced marriages. 14 Apr., the Very Rev. Gonville ffrench-Beytagh, Dean of Johannesburg, acquitted by SA appeal court. 29 Apr., ex-King Ntare V of Burundi killed in attempted *coup*: 50,000 persons said to be killed. 2 June, anti-*apartheid* demonstrations by students outside Anglican Cathedral in Cape Town. 6 June, 427 miners killed by explosion at Wankie Colliery, Rhodesia. 18 July, President Sadat requests USSR to remove some 20,000 'advisory' personnel. 4 Aug., President Amin requests UK to take in all Ugandan Asians within ninety days. 16 Aug., abortive attempt by Moroccan Air Force to destroy aircraft carrying King Hasan. 18 Sept., General Amin gives 8,000 Asians forty-eight hours to leave Uganda. 8 Oct., General Ramantsoa takes over power in Madagascar. 26 Oct., Major Kérékou becomes President of Dahomey.

**1973** 9 Jan., following terrorist attacks, Rhodesia closes border with Zambia. 11 Feb., UN mission visits Rhodesia. 20 Jan., Amilcar Cabral, nationalist leader in Portuguese Guinea, murdered. 5 July, General Juvenal Habyalimana takes power in Rwanda. Terrorists kidnap 273 persons, of whom 191 African children, in attack on Jesuit mission in Rhodesia.

# THE EAST & AUSTRALASIA    THE AMERICAS    RELIGION & CULTURE

**1971** 9 Aug., treaty of friendship and co-operation between India and USSR. 12 Oct., Iran celebrates 2,500 years of monarchy. 17 Oct., Thanom Kittiachorn takes over in bloodless *coup* in Thailand. 1 Dec., Union of Arab Emirates (of the Persian Gulf) proclaimed. 3 Dec., Pakistan attacks India. 14 Dec., E Pakistan asks India for cease-fire: 16 Dec., surrender: 17 Dec., cease-fire in W Pakistan.

**1972** 12 Jan., Shaikh Mujibur Rahman becomes Prime Minister of Bangladesh. 30 Jan., Pakistan withdraws from British Commonwealth in protest against recognition of Bangladesh. 21-28 Feb., President Nixon visits China. 18 Apr., Bangladesh formally admitted to British Commonwealth. 1 March, Timothy Davey, aged 14, sentenced for drug smuggling in Turkey. 13 March, China and UK resume diplomatic relations after twenty-two years. 14 March, Marshal Nol, President of Cambodia. 17 March, defence pact between Bangladesh and India. 17 Apr., Ferit Melen, Prime Minister of Turkey. 21 Apr., Zulfikar Ali Bhutto inaugurated as President of Pakistan with new constitution. 22 May, Ceylon changes name to Sri Lanka. 1 June, oilfields nationalized in N Iraq. 5 July, Kakuei Tanaka, Prime Minister of Japan. 2 July, agreement between India and Pakistan on mutual problems. 23 Sept., martial law proclaimed in Philippines. 27 Sept.–13 Oct., border fighting between N and S Yemen. 29 Oct.–2 Nov., Sir Alec Douglas-Home, Foreign Secretary, visits China. 23 Dec., President Pak Cheng-hi of S Korea re-elected.

**1972** 1 Jan., US agrees to supply jet fighting aircraft to Israel. 29 June, US Supreme Court rules the death penalty contrary to the constitution. 10-13 Aug., conference of non-aligned countries at Georgetown, Guyana. 25 Aug., China vetoes entry of Bangladesh to UN. 1 Sept., trade agreement between Japan and US at Honolulu. 7 Nov., President Nixon re-elected in USA (–1974). 17 Nov., ex-President Perón returns to Argentina. 23 Dec., disastrous earthquake at Managua, Nicaragua.

**1972** 29 March–30 Dec., Tutankhamun Exhibition in London: visited by about 1.6m. people. 6 July, Titian's *Death of Actaeon* bought for the nation in UK for £1,763,000. 16 July, Dimitrios elected Patriarch of Constantinople. 5 Oct., Congregationalists and English Presbyterians unite as the United Reformed Church in England and Wales. 30 Nov., European missionaries expelled from Uganda.

**1973** 12 Feb., last US troops leave Vietnam. 13 Feb., Japanese yen floated. 7 March, Shaikh Mujibur Rahman wins first general election in Bangladesh. 13 March, Fahri Koruturk elected President of Turkey. 17 July, General Sardar Muhammad Daud Khan deposes King of Afghanistan. 12 Aug., Mr Bhutto becomes Prime Minister of Pakistan.

**1973** 8 Jan., US suspends hostilities in Vietnam. Watergate trial opened in Washington. 13 Feb., US dollar devalued. 27 Feb.–6 May, Red Indian siege of Wounded Knee, S Dakota. 10 March, Sir Richard Sharples, Governor of Bermuda, murdered. 30 Apr., President Nixon admits responsibility for Watergate bugging.

**1973** 5 March, Pope Paul limits Conclave of Cardinals to 120. 27 May, USSR joins Universal Copyright Convention. 29 Sept., exhibition of archaeological finds from China at the Royal Academy, London (–1974).

## WESTERN & NORTHERN EUROPE

## CENTRAL & SOUTHERN EUROPE

## AFRICA

**1973** 2 Apr., UK publishes N Ireland Emergency Provisions Bill. 30 May, Erskine Childers elected President of Eire. 28 June, Unionists gain majority in N Irish election. 15 Sept., King Gustav VI Adolf of Sweden d.: succ. Carl XVI Gustav. 12 Nov., miners begin over-time ban in UK. 13 Oct., state of emergency proclaimed in UK because of fuel crisis. 12 Dec., ASLEF train drivers' strike begins in UK.

Minister of Spain: General Franco remains Head of State. 19 Aug., Greece proclaimed a republic: George Papadopoulos, President. 25 Nov., President George Papadopoulos of Greece overthrown by General Phaidon Gizikis. 20 Dec., Admiral Carrero Blanco, Prime Minister of Spain, murdered: succ. Carlos Arias Navarro, 29 Dec.

**1973** 30 Aug., Kenya bans hunting elephants and sale of ivory. 1 Sept., Libya announces 51% take-over of US oil concessions. 12 Sept., terrorists seize ninety-three Africans in Rhodesia.

**1974** 1 Jan., three day working week introduced in Britain. 9-10 Jan., emergency sitting of UK Parliament. 28 Feb., UK general election: minority Parliament, with Labour as largest party, elected. 4 March, J. H. Wilson again Prime Minister (–1976). 17 Feb., J. H. Wilson announces 'great new social contract' between Labour Party and TUC. 27 Feb., new constitution agreed in Sweden. 5 March, new cabinet announced in UK. 11 March, state of emergency in UK ended. 20 March, gunman attacks Princess Anne and Captain Mark Phillips in the Mall. 2 Apr., President Pompidou d. 19 May, Valéry Giscard d'Estaing elected President of France. 29 May, N. Ireland placed under direct rule from Westminster. 27 June, President Nixon begins visit to USSR. 1 July, Walter Scheel elected President of Germany. 10 Oct., UK general election: Labour obtain majority of three. 16 Nov., Erskine Childers, President of Ireland, d. 25 Nov., IRA proscribed in Britain. 29 Nov., Cearbhall O'Dalaigh made President of Ireland.

**1974** 21 Apr. Senator Edward Kennedy addresses students at Moscow University. 25 Apr., military coup in Portugal: Dr Caetano over-thrown: General António de Spinola, President. 12 May, Italy votes in plebiscite to retain divorce law. 23 June, Dr Rudolf Kirschläger elected President of Austria. 9 July, President Spinola dismisses Portuguese Cabinet. 13 July, Col. Vasco Gonçalves takes office as President of Portugal. 15 July, President Makarios of Cyprus overthrown: Nicos Sampson appointed President. 19 July, General Franco temporarily hands over power to Prince Juan Carlos. 20 July, Türks invade Cyprus, 23 July, Glafcos Clerides sworn Acting President in Cyprus: 24 July, Constantine Karamanlis sworn Prime Minister of Greece. 14 -16 Aug., renewed hostilities in Cyprus. 2 Sept., General Franco resumes power. 30 Sept., General Spinola resigns: General Francisco Costa Gomes appointed President of Portugal. 7 Dec., President Makarios returns to office in Cyprus. 8 Dec., 62% of electors in Greece vote aginst restoration of the monarchy.

**1974** 18 Jan., Disengagement agreement on the Suez Canal between Egypt and Israel. 8 Feb., military coup in Upper Volta. 27 Feb., Ethiopian army gains control of Asmara: government resigns. 15 Apr., Hamani Diori, President of Niger, deposed. 17 Apr., army takes power in Niger: Col. Seyni Kountie, Head of State. 24 Apr., general election in SA: Nationalists increase majority. 28 Apr., USA and Egypt resume diplomatic relations. 12 June, President Nixon visits Cairo. 29 June, army takes control of all Ethiopia. 10 Sept., Guinea-Bissau becomes independent. 12 Sept., Emperor Haile Selassie deposed by army: kept in solitary imprison-ment. 20 Sept., FRELIMO government takes office in Mozambique . 25 Sept., new cabinet in Egypt: Dr Abdal-Aziz Hejazi, Prime Minister. 26 Oct., summit meeting of Arab Heads of State at Rabat. 24 Nov., sixty prominent persons executed with-out trial in Ethiopia. 11 Dec., Ian Smith releases all political detainees.

| THE EAST & AUSTRALASIA | THE AMERICAS | RELIGION & CULTURE |
|---|---|---|

**1973** 6 Oct., Day of Atonement (Yom Kippur) war between Arabs and Israel begins: Sinai and Golan Heights invaded. 7 Oct., Arab states announce 5% cut in oil production: oil crisis caused in Europe and USA. 22 Oct., cease-fire between Israel and UAR.

**1973** 27 May, Argentina grants amnesty to political prisoners. 4 June, President Nixon declines to release tape recordings concerning Watergate. 10 July, Bahama Is. become independent. 1 Aug., Barbados, Guyana, Jamaica and Trinidad form an economic community. 3 Sept., Dr Henry Kissinger made Secretary of State. 11 Sept., military *coup* in Chile: President Allende commits suicide: General Augusto Pinochet takes power with military government. 23 Sept., General Perón elected President of Argentina. 10 Oct., Vice-President Spiro Agnew of USA resigns, following plea of guilty to tax evasion charge: succ. Gerald Ford, 6 Dec. 21 Oct., impeachment of President Nixon first demanded.

**1974** 27 Jan., Queen Elizabeth II begins visit to Australasia. 22-25 Feb., Islamic Summit Conference at Lahore: Pakistan recognizes Bangladesh: determination to liberate Jerusalem affirmed. 2 March, military rule ended in Burma: U Ne Win, President. 15 May, Israeli army attacks school at Maalot, Lebanon. 16 May, Israeli bomb seven Palestinian refugee camps in Lebanon. 18 May, general election in Australia: Labour win: Gough Whitlam, Prime Minister. 24 Aug., Fakhruddin Ali sworn as President of India. 31 Aug., Norman Kirk, Prime Minister of New Zealand, d. 6 Sept., Wallace Rowling appointed Prime Minister of New Zealand. 24 Dec., John Stonehouse, Labour MP, re-appears in Australia. 25 Dec., Darwin, Australia, wrecked by a cyclone.

**1974** 4 Feb., Grenada, W.I., becomes independent within the Commonwealth. 15 March, General Ernesto Geisel sworn as President of Brazil. 21 Apr., elections in Colombia: Alfonso López Michelson, President. 19 June, NATO Foreign Ministers in Ottawa issue twenty-fifth anniversary declaration of Atlantic principles. 26 June, General Ugarte becomes Head of State in Chile. 1 July, Senora Perón sworn President of Argentina. 8 July, general election in Canada won by Liberals. 24 July, US Supreme Court orders President Nixon to surrender sixty-four tapes to Washington district court. 5 Aug., President Nixon admits he withheld information *re* Watergate scandal. 8 Aug., President Nixon resigns. 9 Aug., Gerald Ford sworn as President of USA. 20 Aug., Nelson Rockefeller nominated Vice-President of USA. 8 Sept., President Ford grants pardon to Richard Nixon for all offences he may have committed in office. 6 Nov., Democrats make massive gains in US general election. 20 Nov., John Stonehouse, Labour MP, reported missing in Florida.

**1974** 2 Feb., anti-Confucius campaign announced in China. 13 Feb., Alexander Solzhenitsyn, novelist, deported from Russia. 19 Apr., *Mona Lisa* exhibited on loan in Tokyo. 11 June, Abp of Birmingham suspends RC priest for praising an IRA hunger striker as 'a great man'. July, UK Parliament approves Bill to remove disqualification of RCs from becoming Lord Chancellor. Nov., Vatican relaxes ban on Freemasons, provided they are not anti-clerical. 15 Nov., Abp Michael Ramsey retires: succ. Abp Donald Coggan. 4 Dec., Church of England (Worship and Doctrine) Measure passed: power given to change Anglican liturgy. 24 Dec., Paul VI inaugurates Holy Year (−1975). Controversy *re* publication of R.H.S. Crossman's diaries.

## WESTERN & NORTHERN EUROPE

**1975** 19 Jan., Arab gunmen injure 20 persons at Orly airport, near Paris. 20 Jan., UK announces abandonment of projected Channel Tunnel. 20 Jan., France agrees to supply Egypt with Mirage aircraft. Anglo-Iranian trade agreement signed. 31 Jan., National Enterprise Board set up in UK. 17 Feb., UK-USSR agreement on economic, scientific and industrial co-operation. 10 March, EEC leaders confer in Dublin. 18 March, UK cabinet agrees to remain in EEC. 29 May, President Ford attends NATO meeting in Brussels. 30 July – 1 Aug., summit conference on European security at Helsinki: declaration on peaceful co-operation signed by 31 nations. 3 Oct.–7 Nov., Dr Tiede Herrema, Dutch businessman, held captive by IRA terrorists. 22 Oct., economic agreement between Saudi Arabia and UK. 24 Oct., women in Iceland paralyse country with almost 100% one day strike. 28 Oct., terrorist bomb attack in Belfast and other capitals. 3 Nov., first oil from N. Sea landed in Britain. 7 Nov., UK borrows £975m from IMF. 15-17 Nov., leaders of France, Germany, Italy, Japan, UK and USA hold economic conference at Rambouillet. 5 Dec., detention without trial ended in N Ireland.

**1976** 1 Jan., British National Oil Corporation comes into being. 12 Jan., French cabinet reshuffled. 19 Jan., House of Commons approves devolution policy for Scotland and Wales by 295 votes to 37, opposition abstaining 24-27 Jan., talks in London on Icelandic fisheries. 3 Feb., George Thomas replaces Selwyn Lloyd as Speaker. 18 Feb., Iceland breaks off diplomatic relations with Britain following numerous incidents in

## CENTRAL & SOUTHERN EUROPE

**1975** 5 Feb., manifesto signed by 500 senior civil servants demands democratization in Spain. 11 March, ex-President Spinola flees from Portugal. 12 March, Armed Forces Movement in Portugal sets up Supreme Revolutionary Council. Apr., Social Democratic Party established in Spain. 25 Apr., general election in Portugal: Socialists 37.9%; People's Party 26.6%; Communists 12.5%. 27 Apr., state of emergency declared in Spanish Basque provinces. 7 June, new constitution announced in Greece. 20 June, Konstantinos Tsatsos sworn in as President of Greece. 25 July, triumvirate takes control in Portugal, dismissing cabinet. 4 Sept., Egypt and Israel agree at Geneva on Israeli withdrawal in Sinai. 28 Oct., terrorist bomb attacks in Lisbon and Valencia. 30 Oct., Prince Juan Carlos assumes office as Head of State in Spain during mortal illness of General Franco. 20 Nov., General Franco d. 22 Nov., Juan Carlos I proclaimed King of Spain.

**1976** 6 Jan., Co-operation agreement between Czecho-Slovakia and Turkey. 7 Jan.– 11 Feb., Aldo Moro forms government in Italy after five attempts. 21 Jan., new constitution in Albania affirms 'Marxism-Leninism and proletarian internationalism.' 2-16 Feb., sixteen nation conference on pollution of Mediterranean in Barcelona concluded by a treaty. 26 Feb., agreement on new constitution reached in Portugal.

## AFRICA

**1975** 1 Jan., J. Callaghan, British Foreign Secretary, begins visit to Zambia and SA. 15 Jan., Portugal signs agreements with three liberation movements giving independence to Angola. 11 Feb., President Ratsimandrava of Madagascar assassinated. 28 Feb., Lomé Convention between EEC and 46 developing nations on trade, aid and co-operation. 21 March, Military Council in Ethiopia abolishes the Crown. 13 Apr., President Tombalbaye of Chad assassinated. 16 Apr., new cabinet in Egypt under Mamduh Muhammad Salim. 11 June, Dennis Hills, British lecturer, sentenced to death in Uganda for describing President Amin as a 'village tyrant'. 15 June, Lieut. Col. Didier Ratsiraka becomes President of Madagascar. 25 June, Mozambique becomes independent: Samora Machel, first President. 5 July, Cape Verde Is. become independent: Aristides Pereira, first President. 6 July, Comoro Is. become independent, Mayotte remaining subject to France by its free choice: Sheikh Muhammad Abdallah, first President. 10 July, Hills released and deported from Uganda. 12 July São Tomé and Principé become independent: Pinto da Costa, first President. 29 July –2 Aug., OAU Summit Meeting in Kampala. 29 July, General Gowon deposed in Nigeria: Brigadier Murtala Muhammad becomes Head of State. 25 Aug., SA Prime Minister Vorster and President Kaunda of Zambia preside at opening of constitutional talks between Rhodesia and ANC on Victoria Falls railway bridge. 1 Sept., constitutional conference on future of Namibia (SWA) opened at Windhoek. Oct., construction begun of military and political academy at Monduli, near Arusha, Tanzania, with Chinese aid. 10 Oct., new Supreme Military Council set up in Ghana. 10 Nov., Angola becomes independent: divided between three warring factions. 14 Nov., Mauritania, Morocco and Spanish Sahara reach agreement on future of Spanish Sahara. 1 Dec., Ian Smith and Joshua Nkomo sign declaration of intent to negotiate a constitutional settlement in Rhodesia.

**1976** 2 Jan., Ali Soilih elected Head of State in Comoro Is. 5 Jan., mutual defence treaty between Libya and Togo announced 14 Jan., John J. Wrathall sworn President of Rhodesia. 23 Jan., SA troops reported withdrawing from Angola. 28 Jan., state emergency declared in Zambia. 30 Jan., Eritrean Liberation Front claimed to be in control of greater part of country. 3 Feb., state boundaries in Nigeria redrawn: state increased from 12 to 19. 9 Feb., Universi of Zambia closed because of student unre

## THE EAST & AUSTRALASIA

**1975** 18 Jan., Chou En-lai re-elected
Prime Minister of China. 26 Jan.,
Sheikh Mujibur Rahman becomes
President of Bangladesh. 10 Feb.,
National Awami Party (opposition)
banned in Pakistan. 2 March, Shah of
Iran announces formation of National
Political Resurrection Movement to
incorporate all political movements.
6 March, 8 Palestinians hold 10
Israeli hostages in Tel Aviv hotel: 18
people killed. 25 March, King Faisal
of Saudi Arabia assassinated: assassin,
Prince Faisal Musaid, subsequently
beheaded publicly: succ. Khalid b.
Abd al-Aziz. 7-12 May, Queen
Elizabeth II visits Honolulu, Hong
Kong and Japan. 20 May, Fiame
Mata'afa, Prime Minister of W Samoa
d.: succ. Tupua Tamasese Leolofi IV.
4 June, five year plan announced in
Saudi Arabia. 12 June, Mrs Indira
Ghandhi found guilty of corrupt
electoral practices. 26 June, size of
emergency declared in India: Mrs
Gandhi arrests political opponents.
15 Aug., Sheikh Mujibur Rahman of
Bangladesh assassinated with his
family: Khondakar Moshtaque Ahmad
sworn as President. 21 Aug., Portuguese
admit loss of control to liberation
groups in Timor. 1 Sept., Bougainville
Is. declares itself independent as
Republic of N. Solomons. 16 Sept.,
Papua-New Guinea becomes
independent within the British
Commonwealth. 1 Oct., name of
Ellice Is. changed to Tuvalu. 28 Oct.,
terrorist bomb attacks in Beirut and
Jerusalem. 10-11 Nov., all street names
referring to UN changed in Israel.
11 Nov., Gough Whitlam dismissed by
Governor-General of Australia:
Malcolm Fraser made caretaker Prime
Minister pending general election.
25 Nov., Surinam becomes indepen-
dent. 29 Nov., NZ National Party
defeats Labour Party in general
election: Robert Muldoon, Prime
Minister. 1-5 Dec., President Ford
visits China. 3 Dec., King of Laos
abdicates: People's Democratic
Republic set up. 13 Dec., Australian
Liberal-National Country Party
defeats Labour Party led by Gough
Whitlam.

**1976** 2 Jan., Solomon Is. become
internally self-governing. 8 Jan., Chou
En-lai, Prime Minister of China, d.
14 Jan., Tun Haji Abdul Razak, Prime
Minister of Malaysia, d.: 15 Jan., succ.
Datuk Hussein, his brother-in-law.
7 Feb., Hua Kuo-feng, Acting Prime
Minister of China. 14 Feb., cease-fire
in Lebanon. March, Muslim officers in
Lebanese army attempt to seize power.
Apr., numerous violent demonstrations
in Chinese cities. 2 Apr., further cease-

## THE AMERICAS

**1975** 5 Feb., USA cuts off aid to
Turkey for delaying agreement on
Cyprus. 27 Apr.–2 May, Queen
Elizabeth II visits Jamaica. 29 Apr.–
6 May, Commonwealth Prime
Ministers' Conference held at
Kingston, Jamaica. 29 Aug., President
Juan Velasco Alvarado deposed in
Peru: succ. General Francisco
Morales Bermudez. 2 Oct., Emperor
Hirohito of Japan begins state visit
to USA. 28 Oct., terrorist bomb
attacks in New York, Washington and
Chicago. 10 Nov., UN General
Assembly denounces Zionism as 'a
form of racism and racial discrimin-
ation.' 19 Dec., US Senate votes end
to military aid to anti-communists in
Angola.

**1976** 3 Jan., UN International
Convenant on Economic, Social and
Cultural Rights comes into force. 10 Jan.,
Chile announces establishment of
consultative Council of State. 11 Jan.,
three-man junta takes power in Chile.
23-25 Jan., P. Trudeau visits Mexico:
26-29 Jan., Cuba: 29 Jan.–2 Feb.,
Venezuela. 24 Jan., treaty between
Spain and US allowing US bases in
Spain. Feb., scandal in US concerning
alleged bribery by Lockheed Aircraft

## RELIGION & CULTURE

**1975** Feb., Elijah Muhammad, leader
of 70,000 'Black Muslims' in USA, d.
Apr., Common Catechism issued by
Roman Catholic and Protestant
theologians. 30 May, Christian
Institute of SA declared by the
government an 'affected organization.'
June, Anglican General Synod in
Canada votes in favour of ordaining
women. 16 June, Rt. Rev. Richard
Wood, Bp of Damaraland, expelled
from SA. July, several women ordained
by American Episcopalians as priests:
Bishops' Conference in Chicago declares
ordinations invalid. 3 July, Anglican
Synod in London accepts that women
may become priests, but defers action
indefinitely. 15, Abp of Canterbury
issues 'Call to the Nation' to return to
religion. 22 Oct., two USSR space
probes land on the planet *Venus*.
27 Nov., Pope Paul VI expresses
'passionate condemnation' of execution
of Basque separatists. Amnesty
International estimates a total of some
10,000 political and religious prisoners
in USSR.

**1976** 21 Jan., *Concorde* service from
London to Bahrein, and from London
to Rio de Janeiro inaugurated. 1-6 Feb.,
Islam-Christian dialogue held in Libya
under patronage of Libyan government
and the Vatican: Vatican re-affirms
demand for an internationally guaranteed
status for Jerusalem. 17 Feb., Dom
George Basil Hume, OSB, appointed
Archbishop of Westminster. 18 Feb.,
Abuna Tewoflos of Ethiopia deposed and
arrested for peculation together with

## WESTERN & NORTHERN EUROPE

fishing grounds. 10-12 March, seven S Moluccan terrorists tried in Holland. 16 March, H. J. Wilson announces resignation as Prime Minister. 23-25 March, seven more S Moluccan terrorists tried. 25 March, UK Prevention of Terrorism (Temporary Provisions) Bill strengthens existing legislation against IRA. 5 Apr., (L). J. Callaghan appointed UK Prime Minister following defeat of M. Foot and D. Healey in ballot for leadership of UK Labour Party. 7 Apr., UK government loses over-all majority. 6 May, widespread Conservative gains at UK local elections. 10-11 May, Franco-African conference in Paris. 1 June, interim agreement between Iceland and UK on Icelandic fisheries. 21 July, British ambassador in Dublin assassinated by IRA. 28 July, UK breaks off diplomatic relations with Uganda. 6 Aug., following prolonged drought, Drought Bill enacted in UK: dryest period recorded since records began in 1727. 27 Aug., cabinet re-organized in France: Raymond Barre, Prime Minister. 16 Sept., Emergency Powers Bill passed by Irish Parliament. 19 Sept., general election in Sweden: Social Democratic Party defeated after forty years in office: coalition of centre-right parties takes office: Thorbjörn Fälldin, Prime Minister. 28 Sept., sterling crisis in UK: £1 drops to $1.63. 30 Sept., UK Labour Party conference demands national-isation of clearing banks, insurance companies and one merchant bank. 23 Oct., President of Ireland resigns. 7 Nov., UK government announces intention to borrow almost $2,000 million from the IMF. 9 Nov., Dr Patrick Hillery elected President of Ireland unopposed.

## CENTRAL & SOUTHERN EUROPE

2 Apr., new constitution in Portugal. 25 Apr., general election in Portugal: Socialist and Popular Democratic Parties gain majority. 20-21 July, elections in Italy: Christian Democrats retain office. 24 June, Mr Vorster and Dr Kissinger hold talks on Rhodesia in Bavaria. 26 June, Polish workers riot against government proposals to increase food prices. 27 June, General António dos Santos Ramalho Eanes elected President of Portugal. 1 July, Carlos Arias Navarro, Prime Minister of Spain, resigns. 5 July, Suárez González sworn Prime Minister of Spain. 8 July, new Spanish cabinet announced. 16 July, Dr Mário Soares appointed Prime Minister of Portugal. 4-6 Sept., Mr Vorster and Dr Kissinger hold further talks on Rhodesia in Zurich.

## AFRICA

13 Feb., General Murtala Ramat Muhammad, Nigerian Head of State, assassinated: succ. Lieut. Gen. Olusegun Obasanjo. 27-28 Feb., Polisario (Saharan Arab Democratic) Republic (former Spanish Sahara) proclaimed: recognized by seventeen African countries, but not by fourteen others. March, Tanzanian government dismisses 9,496 civil servants, being 20% of their number. 5 March, Muhammad Lamine Ould Ahmad appointed Prime Minister of Polisario. 8-18 March, 21,000 Egyptians expelled from Libya. 14 March, Egypt announces intention to abrogate 1975 Treaty of Friendship and Co-operation with USSR. 20 March, border between Benin and Togo re-opened. 31 March, Colonel Maphera Dlamini appointed Prime Minister of Swaziland. 2 May, riots at Tadjourah. June-Aug., SA constitutional conference on future of SWA (Namibia). 16-24 June, mob violence in SA against compulsory Afrikaans in Bantu schools: 176 persons killed. 27 June, *Air France* airbus with largely Jewish passengers hijacked near Athens by Palestinian terrorists landed at Entebbe. 27 June, National Charter adopted in Algeria. 28 June, President Siyad Barrah proclaims Somalia a one-party state. 30 June, 47 passengers from hijacked aircraft released in Entebbe. 2 July, attempted coup in Sudan, said to be organized by Libya. 3-4 July, Israeli commando of 200 seizes Entebbe airport briefly, releasing remaining hijacked passengers. 4 July, Mrs Dora Bloch murdered in Kampala hospital. 14 July, Chinese hand over Tanzam Railway a year ahead of schedule. 15 July, defence agreement announced between Saudi Arabia and Sudan. 5-7 Sept., five African Presidents and Rhodesian African nationalist leaders meet in Dar es Salaam. 16 Sept., President Sadat of Egypt re-elected for five years. 24 Sept., Ian Smith broadcasts 'package deal' to include majority rule in Rhodesia within two years. 17-20 Oct., President Jean Bedel Bokassa of CAR converted to Islam: changes name to Salah al-Din Ahmad Bokassa. 26 Oct., Transkei declared independent by SA: not recognized by any other state: Chief Kaiser Daliwenga Matanzima, Prime Minister. 28 Oct. 14 Dec., Geneva Conference on future of Rhodesia attended by African Nationalists and Rhodesian Front Party under British chairmanship. 1 Nov., President Michel Micombero overthrown in Burundi: succ Lieut. Col. Jean-Baptiste Bagaza. 9 Nov., new cabinet in Egypt, with General Mamdouh Salem as Prime Minister. 4 Dec., CAR proclaimed the Central African Empire: President Bokassa proclaimed Emperor Bokassa I: Ange Patassé, Prime Minister.

## THE EAST & AUSTRALASIA

fire in Lebanon. 5-6 Apr., violent riots in Peking. 8 Apr., Iran breaks off diplomatic relations with Cuba. 9-12 Apr., Vorster visits Israel. 6 May, United Arab Amirates agree to set up combined armed forces. 28-29 June, Seychelles becomes an independent republic: James Mancham, first President. 17 July, East Timor incorporated into Indonesia. 9 Sept., Palestine admitted as a member of the Arab League. 9 Sept., Mao Tse-tung, Chairman of Communist China, d. 7 Oct., Hua Kuo-feng elected Chairman of Chinese Communist Party in succ. to Chairman Mao. 24 December, Takeo Fukuda becomes Prime Minister of Japan.

## THE AMERICAS

Coporation. 1 Feb., General Jorge Fernandes Maldonado Prime Minister of Peru. 15 Feb., new constitution in Cuba. 24 March, President Isabel Martinez de Perón overthrown in Argentine: 29 March, General Jorge Rafael Videla sworn President. 28 May, US-USSR Treaty limiting underground nuclear explosions signed. 12 June, President Juan María Bordaberry of Uruguay deposed by armed forces: Dr Alberto Demichelli appointed President *ad int.* 19 June, state of emergency declared in Jamaica following riots. 2 July, US Supreme Court rules death penalty to be lawful. 4 July, José López Portillo elected President of Mexico. 16 July, capital punishment abolished in Canada, except for desertion and mutiny in time of war. 1 Sept., Dr Aparicio Mendez sworn President of Uruguay. 2 Nov., Jimmy Carter elected President of USA: Democrats retain majority in House of Representatives.

## RELIGION & CULTURE

other bishops. 12 May, fee-paying private schools abolished in Algeria. 24 May, *Concorde* services from London and from Paris to Washington inaugurated. 20 July, US Spacecraft lands on planet *Mars*. 28 July, new Spanish concordat with the Vatican: right of Spanish head of state to appoint bishops discontinued. 10-18 Aug., World Council of Churches meets in Geneva sixth allocation of grants 'to combat racism.' 29 Aug., Abu Melaku Wolde-Mikhail invested as Abuna Tekla Haimanot of Ethiopia: rejected as unlawful by Coptic Patriarch and Synod of Alexandria.

# INDEX

Dates before Christ are all shown with the letters BC. Dates after Christ are not marked AD unless a sequence of dates spans BC and AD, e.g. 14 BC—AD 27.

All entries are in strict alphabetical order, but where the Arabic definite article al- precedes a name, it has been ignored. All saints are listed under that title.

Wherever they are in use, surnames determine the order in which persons are listed. Where they are not in use, the first (and following) names, or the name by which a person is most generally known, determine the order.

Abu Bakr al-Khwarizmi, c. 993 or 1002
Abu Bakr Muhammad b. Ali Muhyi al-Din b. Arabi. 1165-1240
Abu Bakr Muhammad b. Yahya b. Bajjah, 1238
Abu Bakr Muhammad b. Zakariya al-Razi (Rhazes), 865-925
Abu Bakr al-Quzman, 1160
Abu Bakr b. Umar, 977-1070
Abu al-Dhahab, 1771-3
Abu al-Faiz Khan, 1740
Abu al-Faraj b. al-Ibri (Barhebraeus), 1226-84
Abu al-Faraj al-Isfahani, 897-967
Abu Faris, 1393-1433
Abu Hamid al-Ghazzali, 1058-1111, *ante* 1150
Abu Hamid Muhammad al-Mazini, 1080/1-1169/70
Abu Hammu Musa I, 1307-18
Abu Hammu Musa II, 1358-89
Abu Hanifah al-Numan b. Thabit, c. 696-767
Abu al-Hasan Ali al-Ashari, 935/6
Abu al-Hasan Ali al-Masudi, 956
Abu al-Hasan Ali b. al-Nafis, c. 1288-9
Abu Mahalli, 1610-13
Abu al-Husayn Muhammad b. Ahmad al-Jubayr, 1145-1217
Abu Imran Musa b. Maymun, 1135-1204
Abu Inan, 1357
Abu Jafar Muhammad b. Jarir al-Tabari, 838-923
Abu al-Mahasin b. Taghri-Birdi, 1411-69
Abu Mansur al-Yasa, 790-823
Abu Mansur Nizar al-Aziz, caliph, 975-96
Abu Marwan Abd al-Malik b. Ali al-Ala, 1091/4-1162
Abu Melaku Wolde—Mikhail, 1976
Abu Midyan al-Ghawth, 1198
Abu al-Misk Kafur, 946-68
Abu Muhammad Abd al-Haqq b. Sabin, c. 1217-69
Abu Muhammad Abd al-Haqq, Marinid, 1196-1217
Abu Muslim, 747-54
Abu Nuwas, poet, c. 810
Abu al-Qasim al-Azafi, 1256-75
Abu al-Qasim of Darfur, 1739-52
Abu al-Qasim Khalaf b. Abbas al-Zahrawi, c. 1013
Abu al-Qasim Unujur, 946-66
Abu al-Rabi, 1308-10
Abu al-Rayhan Muhammad b. Ahmad al-Biruni, 973-1038
Abu Rukna, 1006
Abu Said, Ilkhan of Persia, 1316-65
Abu Said, Timurid, 1452-69
Abu Said Uthman, 1310-31
Abu Simbel, c. 594-588 BC
Abu Sulayman al-Darani, 849/50
Abu Sufian, 625
Abu Tamin Maadd al-Muizz, 952-75
Abu Tamman, philologist, c. 796-843
Abu Thabit, 1307-8
Abu Ubaid Abdallah b. Abd al-Aziz al-Bakri, 1094
Abu Ubaydah Muslim, c. 900-50
Abu Umar Uthman, 1435-87
Abu Uthman Amr b. Bakr al-Jahiz, 868/9
Abu al-Wafa Muhammad al-Buzjani al-Hasib, 940-97/8
Abu al-Walid Ahmad b. Zaydun, 1003-71
Abu Yahya b. al-Batriq, 796-806
Abu Yaqub b. Abd al-Mumin, 1163-84
Abu Yaqub, Marinid, 1302-7
Abu Yazid, 921-7
Abu Yusuf, c. 798
Abu Yusuf b. Abu Yaqub, 1184-99
Abu Yusuf Aruj b. Yaqub (Barbarossa), 1514

Abu Yusuf Yaqub b. Ishaq al-Kindi, c. 850
Abu al-Walid Muhammad b. Ahmad b. Rushd (Averroes), 1126-98
Abu Zakaria Yahya I, Hafsid, 1228-49
Abu Zayan, 1303-7
Abu Zayd, 916
Abulfatah Agung of Bantam, 1651-83
Abulistin, 1277
Abusir, pyramid, c. *post* 2480 BC
Abydos, 202 BC, 989; tablet, c. 1309-1291 BC
Abyssinia, c. 550, 1891; *see* Axum *and* Ethiopia
Acacius of Constantinople, 484
*Académie Française*, 1635
*Académie de France*, 1668, 1893
*Académie de Musique*, 1671
*Académie des Sciences*, 1699
academies, 830, 1065-7
*Academy*, 387 BC
Academy, Roman, 1468
Academy of Fine Arts, Spanish, 1752
Academy of History, Spanish, 1738
Academy of Medicine, Spanish, 1734
Academy of Moral and Political Sciences, 1856
Academy of Painting, 1101-25
Academy of Sciences in Paris, 1658; Russia, 1725; Spain, 1714
Academy of Theology, 1615
Acadia, 1578, 1611, 1632, 1654, 1667, 1671, 1713, 1750, 1755
Acarnania, 426 BC
*Accademia dei Lincei*, 1609
*Accío Catalana*, 1923
Accra, c. 1300, 1576, 1652, c. 1680, 1809, 1961; Bp of, 1962
acetylene, 1863
Achaemenean dynasty, c. 700-675 BC
Achaemenes, c. 700-675 BC
Achaemenes, satrap, 460 BC
Achaean invasion of Crete c. 1400 BC
Achaean League, 146 BC
Acheans, 228 BC, 208 BC, 197 BC
Achaia, 336 BC, 198 BC, 109
Achaios, 223-220 BC
Acheampong, Colonel, 1972
Acheh, c. 8 or 9-23, 1025, 1599, 1607-36, 1619, 1782, 1784; relations with Britain, 1762, 1764, 1772; Johore, 1540, 1582, 1613, 1623, 1629; Malacca, 1568, 1615, 1616, 1628, 1629; Portuguese, 1523, 1547, 1587
Acheh, Sultanate, c. 1515-30, 1564, 1668, 1819
Acheson, Dean G., 1949
Achila, 710, 714
Achilles, Roman general, 292-3
Achin, 1570
Achyutaraya of Vijayanagar, 1529-42
Acilius Aureolus, 261-8
Acre, 877, 1100, 1104, 1180, 1189, 1229, 1250-4, 1277, 1291, 1318, 1705, 1772, 1799
Acro-Corinth, 243 BC
Acropolis, c. 1400 BC, 7th-6th c. BC, 561-556/5 BC, c. *post* 450 BC, 435 BC
Act of Amnesty, Ireland, 1798
Act of Explanation, 1663
Act of Mediation, 1803
Act of Oblivion, 1604
Act of Settlement, 1701
Act of Supremacy, 1534, 1559, 1560
Act of Uniformity, 1549, 1552, 1559, 1560, 1662
Act of Union, 1706
*Action Française*, 1898, 1926
Actium, 31 BC
Acton, John, Lord, 1834-1902
Adad-Nirari II, 911-891 BC
Adad-Nirari III, 810-783 BC
Adal, c. 1416, 1445, 1473-4, 1488-1518, 1516, 1520, 1527

Adalbert, 950
Adalbert, Abp of Bremen, 1062-5
Adalia, 1361, 1391
Adam, Hon. John, 1823
Adam, Robert, 1728-92
Adam of Bremen, c. 1078
Adam of St Victor, 1130-80
Adamawa, c. 1300
Adams, John, US president, 1795-1801
Adams, John Quincy, US president, 1825-9
Adams, Samuel, 1722-1803
Adams, Will, 1600
Addams, Jane, 1889
Addington, Henry, 1801
Addis Ababa, 1890, 1917, 1933, 1936, 1937, 1941, 1950, 1963, 1968; treaty, 1896
Addison, Joseph, 1672-1719
Adelaide, Australia, 1840, 1861-2, 1870, 189*
Adelaide, Princess of Kiev, 1089
Adelaide, regent, 995-9
Adelard of Bath, 1126
Adeodatus, pope, 672-6
Aden, c. 1 BC, 356, 1488, 1513, 1547, 1837, 1877, 1934; Colony, 1963, 1965, 1967; Protectorate, 1956-1958
Adenauer, Konrad, 1949-50
Ader, Clément, 1897
Adham Khan, 1562
Adherbal, 116 BC*f*
Adiabene, 197
Adicran, c. 570 BC
al-Adid, caliph, 1160-71
Adige, 1915; Pass, 1805
al-Adil (I) Ayyubid, 1193-1215
al-Adil II, 1238-40
al-Adil al-Mustain, caliph, 1412
Aal-Adil I Saif al-Din, 1199-1218
Adil Shah of Persia, 1747-8
Adil-Shahi dynasty, 1489
Adina, mosque, 1368
Adlan of the Funj, 1606-11
Adolf, son of Rudolf of Austria, 1282
Adolf Frederick II of Sweden, 1751-71
Adolf of Nassau, emperor, 1292-8
Adoptionist heresy, c. 645, *ante* 782, 785, 79*
Adowa, 1896, 1935
Adramythion, 1205
Adrenalin, 1901
Adrian, patriarch, 1700
Adrian I, pope, 772-95
Adrian II, pope, 867-72
Adrian III, pope, 884-5
Adrian IV, pope, 1154-9
Adrian V, pope, 1276
Adrian VI, pope, 1520-3
Adriatic, c. 550 BC, 325 BC, 1240
Adrianople, 324, 378, 914, 1205, 1360-1, 13*
1423, 1453, 1828, 1878, 1913, 1920; peac*
1712, 1713; treaties, 1545, 1829
Adud al-Dawlah, 949-83
Adulis (Massawa), 247 BC, c. 524, 530
Adumu, 688 BC
Advances to Settlers Act in NZ, 1894
'Adventurers' Act', 1642
Advisory Council, Cairo, 1829
Aedh, King of Scots, 877-8
*aediles*, 449 BC, 366 BC
Aedui, 58 BC
Aegaean, c. 500 BC, 165, 258, 617-9, 906; seafarers, c. 800 BC, 477 BC
Aegina, 462 BC, 446 BC, 389 BC, 210 BC
Aelia Capitolina, 131
Aelius Gallus, c. 25-24 BC
*Aeterna Dei*, 1961
*Aeterni Patris*, 1621, 1879
Aelle, 560-88
Aemilianus, M. Aemilius, 253

Aeolis, 497 BC
Aequi, c. 460 BC, 389 BC
Aeschines, orator, 389-314 BC
Aeschylus, tragedian, 525-456 BC
Aetius, 428-54
Aetolia, Aetolians, 198 BC, 189 BC
Aetolian League, 212 BC
Aezanas, King of Axum, c. 320-55
Afdal b. al-Badr, 1094-1121
Affairs of the Faith, congregation, 1592
affirmation, in place of oath, 1883
Afghan Chiefs, 1525, 1529
Afghan Wars, 1838, 1841, 1878, 1919
Afghanistan, 547 BC, 331-330 BC, 312 BC,
    962, 1200-9, 1256, 1380-93, 1383, 1530, 1535,
    1677-98, 1764, 1783, 1818, 1838, 1842, 1845,
    1863, 1868, 1887, 1915, 1937; treaty with
    Britain, 1809, 1919; relations with Britain,
    1878, 1879, 1880, 1881; Germany, 1926;
    India, 1893, 1895; Isfahan, 1722-1729;
    Persia, 1720-1724, 1729, 1730, 1738-39,
    1829, 1855, 1869, 1920; Russia, 1869, 1873,
    1878, 1882, 1921, 1926; Turkey, 1726, 1923
Afonso I of Portugal, 1139-85
Afonso II of Portugal, 1211-23
Afonso III of Portugal, 1245-79
Afonso IV of Portugal, 1325-57
Afonso V of Portugal, 1438-81
Afonso VI of Portugal, 1656-68
Africa, 149-146 BC, 121-6, c. 1500, 1884-5;
    Central, c. 800, c. 1600, 1846; East, c. 106, c.
    740, c. 766, 1105, 1119, 1171, 1488-90 or 91,
    1528, 1540, 1562-91, c. 1600, 1636, 1652,
    1660, 1670, c. 1763-80, c. 1839, 1886, 1890,
    1935, 1939, 1941, 1942; Interior, c. post 500;
    exploration of, 1798; North, 739-40, 902-8,
    1086, 12th c., 143, 1279-1370, 1524-95, 1780,
    1941; North-West, 952-75; South, (see South
    Africa); South-West, (see South-West
    Africa); West, 1352-3, post 1562, 1578-85, c.
    1600, 1664-6, 1780-2, 1793-4, 1869-74, 1882;
    relations with France, 1832, 1843, 1845,
    1859, 1912
Africa, Association for Promoting the
    Discovery of the Internal Parts, 1788
African Charter, 1961
African Committee in Jamaica, 1914
African National Council, 1912, 1926
African Union, 1919
African troops, treatment of, 1067, 1939-45; in
    Burma, 1942-6
Africanization of clergy, 1967
Africanus, 355
Afridis, 1674
Afrifa, Akwasi, general, 1969
Afrikaans (language), 1925
Afrikaner Bond, 1903; Party, 1948
Afrikaners, 1921
Afro-Asian demonstrations, 1965
*Afrique Equatoriale Française*, 1908, 1916,
    1957
*Afrique Occidentale Française*, 1890-4, 1895,
    1917, 1920, 1945, 1958
Afroun, Algeria, 1840
Afshars, 1727; dynasty, 1736-95
Afyon Karahissar, 1300
Afzal Khan, 1659
Aga Muhammad Khan of Persia, 1794-7
Agadir (Cadiz), 1100 BC, 1505
Agadir (Morocco), 1911
Agadja of Abomey, c. 1723
Agala, Visigoth, 549
Agapetus II, pope, 946-55
Agate, James, 1877-1947
Agatharcides of Cnidus, 2nd c. BC, c. 130 BC
Agathias, historian, 522-88
Agatho, pope, 678-81

Agathocles, King of Taxila, c. 190-180 BC
Agathocleş of Syracuse, c. 320 BC*f*
Agathon, tragedian, c. 448-400 BC
Agenais, 1279
Agesilaus 397-376 BC
Aggrey, Dr, 1927
Agha Khan, 760
Agha Khan II, 1840-1906
Agha Khan III, 1887-1957
Aghlabid dynasty, 800-11, 831, 837, 843, 878,
    902, 909
Agilulf, 591, 593
Agincourt, 1415
Agis, King of Sparta, 406 BC, 331 BC
Agisymba, c. 86 BC
Agnes, Empress, Regent, 1056-1106
Agnew, Spiro, 1973
Agora, c. 594/3 BC
Agra, 1489, 1526, 1538, 1555, 1565, 1605,
    1632, 1648, 1658, 1854
Agrarian Code in Russia, 1922
Agrarian Law in Guatemala, 1952
Agricola, 77-93
Agricultural Adjustment Act in US, 1933
Agricultural Exhibition, German, 1904
agricultural experimental stations, 1887; policy
    of the EEC, 1962, 1965; prices, 1920-1
Agricultural Holdings Act, 1875
agricultural implements, ploughs, c. *ante* 3000
    BC, *ante* 1000 BC, c. 750 BC, c. 1 BC;
    reapers, AD 1st c., 1840; seed drills, c. *ante*
    3000 BC
Agricultural Loan Banks, c. 550-527 BC
agriculture, early development in Britain, c. 750
    BC, 1 BC: China, *ante* 2000 BC; Germany,
    AD *post* 100; Italy, *post* c. 177 BC, c. 40 BC;
    Mexico, 13th c.
agriculture, financial aid, 1839; improvements,
    1279-1325, 1845-1906; monopoly in Russia,
    1929; slash and burn, 6th c.
Agrigentum, 485 BC, 446 BC, 406 BC, 313 BC,
    307 BC, 262 BC, 213 BC
Agrippa, 31 BC*f*
Agrippina, 29-58
Aguadello, 1509
Aguascalientes, Mexico, 1914
Aguilar, Spaniard, 1511-19
Agung, Sultan, of Mataram, 1613-45
Ahab, 869-850 BC
Ahaz, 735-733 BC
Ahaziah, c. 850-849 BC
Ahenobarbus, L. Domitius, 5 BC
Ahiram, 13th c. BC
Ahmad Baba, 1627
Ahmad, Bahri Mamluk Sultan, 1342
Ahmad, Ikhshidid ruler, 968-9
Ahmad, Ilkhan of Persia, 1281-4
Ahmad, Imam of Yemen, 1948
Ahmad I, Ottoman Sultan, 1603-17
Ahmad III, Ottoman Sultan, 1703-30
Ahmad b. Arif, c. 1141
Ahmad al-Badawi, 1276
Ahmad Bakr b. Musa of Fur, c. 1682-1722
Ahmad Balafrej, 1926-44
Ahmad of Bareilly, 1831
Ahmad b. Buwayh, 945
Ahmad b. Fadhlan b. Hammad, 921
Ahmad Gailani, 1648-55
Ahmad Gran, 1525-43
Ahmad b. Hanbal, 855
Ahmad b. al-Hasan, 1541-73
Ahmad al-Inglisi, c. 1700
Ahmad al-Jazzar, 1780-1804
Ahmad Keuprulu, 1661-76
Ahmad Khan, Shah of Afghanistan, 1747-
    73
Ahmad Maher Pasha, 1944-5

Ahmad Nizam Shah, 1490-1508
Ahmad al-Nuwayri, 1332
Ahmad al-Qalqashandi, 1418
Ahmad Riayet Shah of Johore, 1761-70
Ahmad al-Rifai, 1175
Ahmad Shah, Bahmani Sultan, 1422-35
Ahmad Shah of Delhi, 1754
Ahmad Shah of Gujarat, 1411-41
Ahmad Taj al-Din of Kedah, 1798-1843
Ahmad al-Tijani, 1737/8-1815
Ahmad b. Tulun, 868-84
Ahmad Zogu (Zog) of Albania, 1924-46
Ahmadabad, 1411-41, 1573, 1657
Ahmadiyyah dervish order, 1276
Ahmadiyyah movement, c. 1838-1908
Ahmadnagar, 1490, 1508, 1600, 1601, 1616,
    1630, 1631, 1637, 1683; relations with
    Bijapur, 1543, 1558, 1564, 1570, 1574, 1595
Ahmadu Sefu, 1864-84
Ahmadu Shehu, 1875
Ahom Kingdom, 1229, 1253
al-Ahsa, 899
Ahsan Shah, 1334-5
Ai Ti, Han Emperor, 6-1 BC
Aidan, 603
Aidhab, 1182
Aigos-Potamos, 405 BC
Ailat, 1182
Ain Jalut, 1260
Ain Shams, 640
Ainsworth, William Harrison, 1805-82
Ainu, 8th c.
air, density found, 1638; weighed, 1643
air-pump, 1652, 1764
aircraft, early powered flights, 1897, 1903,
    1909, 1919, 1920, 1927; fighter, 1915;
    commercial, 1936; supersonic, 1947
aircraft involved in terrorism, 1968, 1970
*Air France*, 1976
Aire, France, 1198
Airlangga, 1010, 1019, 1028-37, 1042
air-raids, 1941, 1942
Airship R101, 1930
airships, dirigible, 1952, 1898
Aisne, battle, 1914
Aitken, William (Lord Beaverbrook),
    1879-1964
Aix-en-Provence (Aquae Sextiae), 102 BC
Aix-la-Chapelle, 796-804, 1205, 1257-73, 1794;
    Assembly, 797, 828, 978; Congress, 1818;
    treaties, 1668, 1748, 1749
Ajanta cave paintings, 5th to 6th c.
Ajatashatru, 494 BC
Ajit Singh, Sikh, 1707-8
Ajmer, 1192, 1558, 1561, 1679
Ajnadain, battle, 634
Ajuran Somali, c. 1624
Akan, c. 1200
Akbar, son of Aurangzeb, 1681-1704
Akbar, Mughul emperor, 1542-1605
Akbar II, Mughul, 1806-37
Akerman, treaty, 1826
Akhenaten, Pharaoh, c. 1367-c. 1350 BC
Akhmim, c. 870
Akka see Acre
Akkad, c. 2371-2230 BC, 648 BC, 616 BC, 539
    BC
Akkar, 1019
Akroinion, 739
Akufo-Addo, Sir Edward, 1970
Akwamu, c. 1680
Ala al-Din, *ante* 1316
Ala al-Din II, Bahmani, 1435-75
Ala al-Din Ali, Bahri Mamluk Sultan, 1376-81
Ala al-Din Hasan Shah al-Wali al-Bahmani,
    1347-58
Ala al-Din Husain of Ghur, 1151

Au Lac, 316 BC, 258-207 BC
Auber, Daniel F.E., 1782-1871
Auberoche, 1345
Aubert, Neret and Gayot, Messrs, 1706, 1718
Aubert, Thomas, of Dieppe, 1508
Aubigné, Françoise d', 1635-1719
*Aucassin and Nicolette*, c. 1200-50
Auckland NZ, 1854, 1886, 1917
Auckland, Earl of 1836-42
Audaghost, c. 9th c., 921, c. 990, c. 1000, 1055
Auden, Wystan Hugh, 1907-73
Audubon, John James, 1780-1851
*Audiencia* (Crown Court), 1511
Aughrim, 1691
Augsburg, 1518, 1552, 1805; Confession, 1530;
  League, 1686, 1688-97; treaty, 1534
Augurs, 300 BC
Augustinian nuns, 1639
Augustinians, Portuguese, 1131-2, 1572, c.
  1596, c. 1598-1612
Augustowo, battle, 1914
Augustus (Octavianus), 30 BC-AD 14
Augustus II of Poland, 1697-1733
Augustus III of Poland, 1733
Augustus I of Saxony, 1694-1733
'Auld Lawis', 1286-1386
Aulne, Baron de l', 1727-81
Aumale, Duc d', 1843-7
Aung San, general, 1945
Aungier, Gerald, 1669-77
l'Aunis, 1371-3
Aurangabad, 1682
Aurangzeb, 1636-1707
Auray, 1364
Aurelian, 271-5
Aurelius Antoninus (Marcus Aurelius), 121-180
Aureolus, 261-8
Aurès, 144-52, 539
*Auriga* of Delphi, c. 478 BC
Auriol, Vincent, President of France, 1947-54
*Aurora*, 1917
Ausonius, poet, 309-92
auspices, 318-20
Aussa, sultanate, 1577, 1590
austerity in Britain, 1947
Austerlitz, 1805
Austin, Alfred, 1835-1913
Austin, Stephen, F., 1821
Australia, 1606, 1629, 1770, 1783, 1791,
  1799-1878, 1802-3, 1817, 1831, 1835,
  1839-44, 1855, 1870, 1874, 1876, 1880, 1885,
  1888, 1889, 1901, 1903, 1908, 1914, 1919,
  1926, 1930, 1950, 1954, 1966; S, 1836, 1840,
  1850, 1858, 1876, 1952, 1974; W, 1837, 1870,
  1893; relations with NZ, 1951; USA, 1951;
  Commonwealth of, 1891, 1900, 1901, 1911;
  Navy, 1907-8, 1909, 1969
Australian Federal Convention, 1897, 1898;
  Council, 1897; Parliament, 1901
Australian Communists, 1948
Australian Federation Conference, 1893
Australians in 1st World War, 1916, 1918
Austrasia, 575, 622, 643, 743
Austria, 16 BC, c. 490, 1156, 1246, 1247, 1262,
  1352, 1358, 1466, 1490, 1521, 1551, 1618,
  1821, 1829, 1846-57, 1860, 1864, 1865, 1870,
  1876, 1878, 1881, 1885, 1892, 1908, 1918-21,
  1931, 1934, 1935, 1946, 1947, 1955;
  Protestants in, 1626-8; relations with
  Albania, 1897, 1916; Bavaria, 1745, 1805;
  Britain, 1716, 1741, 1755, 1800, 1808, 1887,
  1903; France, 1493, 1516, 1736, 1738, 1744,
  1756, 1792-1813, 1859, 1866, 1869, 1917;
  Germany, 1872, 1873, 1879, 1882, 1892,
  1910, 1914, 1917, 1918, 1931 1936; Hungary,
  1459, 1477, 1481, 1541, 1551, 1606, 1677-82,
  1867, 1936; Italy, 1866, 1869, 1882, 1887,

1879, 1915-18, 1930-6; Poland, 1733-4, 1846;
  Prussia, 1726, 1741-6, 1756-63, 1778, 1790,
  1791, 1833, 1853, 1866; Rumania, 1883,
  1918; Russia, 1736, 1738, 1746, 1757,
  1809-13, 1833, 1854, 1855, 1872, 1873, 1877,
  1897, 1903, 1914-18; Serbia, 1881, 1885,
  1905-7, 1910, 1914, 1915; Switzerland, 1474,
  1813; Tunis, 1725; Turkey, 1533, 1593-1601,
  1606, 1625, 1663, 1682, 1683-98, 1714, 1716,
  1718, 1726, 1771, 1775, 1787, 1788, 1903,
  1910; United Provinces, 1715; USA, 1921
Austro-German peace offer, 1916
Austro-Hungary, 1904, 1914, 1918
Austro-Italian frontier, 1961
Austro-Russian affairs, 1903; agreement, 1780,
  1796; convention, 1804, 1850
Austro-Turkish agreement, 1909; treaty, 1791
Asturiani, 363
Authorized Version of the Bible, 1611
autocratic government, 405 BC, 1653
autogyro, 1923
automobile (motor car), 1844-1929
Automobile Association, 1905
autonomy in France, 1108-24; Spain, 1914
autopsies performed, c. 1145
Autun Cathedral, 1132
Auvergne, 125-121 BC, 260, 863-5, 1422
Ava, 1364-1555, 1371, 1385-1425, 1388, 1393,
  1401, 1406, 1414, 1441, 1446, 1486, 1507,
  1524, 1527, 1538, 1554, 1555, 1581, 1605,
  1634, 1658, 1750, 1753, 1763-83, 1767,
  1782, 1823, 1824, 1830
avalanches, 1970
Avaricum (Bourges), 52 BC
Avars, 6th c. BC, 6th c., 550, 562, 567,
  591-602, 596, 616, 619, 626, 788-96, 796; rela-
  tions with Byzantium, 569-71, 579-82, 619
Avaugour, Baron d', 1661-3
Avebury, c. 1900 BC
d'Aveiro, João Afonso, c. 1485-6
Averroes of Córdoba, 1126-98
Aversa, 1029, 1042, 1528
Avicenna, 980-1037
Avidius Cassius, 175
Avignon, 734, 1348, 1365, 1367, 1370, 1379,
  1398, 1402, 1545, 1688; Seat of Papacy,
  1309-78
Avila, 1091, 1465; Junta of, 1520
Avitus, 455-6
Aviz, House of, 1385
Avogadro, Amadeo, 1776-1856
Avon, Earl of, 1897-1976
Awallini dynasty of Haggaro, c. 1780
Awel-Marduk, 563-560 BC
Axim, fort, 1642
Axios valley, *post* 279 BC
Axis, Rome-Berlin, 1936, 1940, 1942, 1943,
  1945, 1946
Axum, 1st c. BC, c. 20 BC-AD 15, c. 3rd-4th c.,
  c. 320-55, c. 330, c. 340-78, c. 350, c. 420,
  519, 523, 525, 531, 570 or 571, 575, 615, 629,
  1615, 1690, 1905-10
Ay, Pharaoh, c. 1339-c. 1335 BC
Ayacucno, Peru, 1824
Ayia Laura, 963
Ayum Wuruk of Majapahit, 1389
Aylesford, battle, c. 455
Aylmer, Lord, 1831-5
Ayr, 1307
Ayub Khan, of Pakistan, 1932
Ayuthia, city, 1563, 1568, 1760, 1766, 1767;
  kingdom, 1350, 1356
Ayyubid dynasty in Egypt, 1169-1252
Azam, son of Aurangzeb, 1707
Azaña, Manuel, 1936
Azariah (Uzziah), 783 BC
Azerbaijan, 1136-1225 c. 1225, 1385-6, 1421,

1429, 1434, 1918, 1945, 1946
al-Azhar mosque, 970, c. 975
al-Azhar students, 1777
Azikiwe, Nnamdi, 1904-63
al-Aziz, 1125, 1193-8
al-Aziz Jamal al-Din Yusuf, 1438
Azores, Is., 1431, 1445, 1582, 1591, 1829-31,
  1832, 1943,
Azov, 1637, 1641, 1642, 1695, 1696, 1699,
  1700, 1711, 1736; Sea of, c. 830
Azraqi movement, 698 or 9
Aztecs, c. 500, 1168, 13th c., 1375

Ba Maw, Dr, of Burma, 1937-43
Baabullah of Ternate, 1570-84
Baal (Baal Melqart), c. 842 BC
Baalbek, 975, 1400
Baasha, c. 900 BCf
Bab, The, 1850
Bab al-Mandab, 25-24 BC
Babba Campestris, c. 20 BC
Baba Nanak, Sikh, 1468-1539
Babba Zaki of Kano, 1768-76
Babington, Anthony, 1586
Babington, Thomas, 1800-59
Babur (Zahir al-Din Muhammad), 1504-30
Babur Mirza, Timurid, 1452-7
Babylon (and Babylonians), c. 1225 BCf, 8th
  and 7th c. BC, 710-705 BC, 689 BC, 648 BC,
  610 BC, 539 BC, 521 BC, 482 BC, c. 460 BC,
  388 BC, 331 BC, 312 BC, 141 BC, 127 BC,
  115 f, 641; Fortress of, 640; relations with
  Assyria, 626-615 BCf; Judah, c. 597 BCf,
  539 BC
Babylonian Captivity, 587-538 BC; Chronicles,
  626 BC
Babylonian dynasties, 1st, c. 1894-1595 BC,
  IVth, c. 1162-1046 BC; Vth, c. 1046-1015
  BC; IXth, 746-734 BC, Xth, 732-627 BC;
  XIth, 626-539 BC
Bacchiads, 747-657 BC
Bach, Carl Philipp Emanuel, 1714-88
Bach, Johann Christian, 1735-82
Bach, Johan Sebastian, 1685-1750
Bachkirs, 1709
Bacon, Sir Francis, 1561-1628
Bacon, Nathaniel, 1676
Bacon, Roger, c. 1214-92
Bactria, 547 BC, 5th c. BC, 331-330 BCf, 261
  BCf, 227-189 BC, 210-205 BCf, c. 175 BC,
  167 BC, c. 140-130 BC, c. 25-50
Bactrian Greek dynasty, c. 228-167 BC
Badajoz, 1086, c. 1258, 1811, 1812, 1936;
  Treaty, 1801
Badakhshan, 1530, 1646, 1647, 1873
Badami, *post* 550-c. 850
Baden, 1622, 1804, 1805, 1818, 1849, 1870;
  treaty, 1714, 1717
Baden-Powell, Robert, Lord, 1857-1941
Badhan of Yemen, 628
Badi Dign el Qom of Sennar, 1611-16
Badoglio, Marshal, 1943
Badr, battle, 624
Badr al Jamali, 1073-7; mosque and
  mausoleum, 1085
Baecula, 208 BC
Baeda Mariam of Ethiopia, 1468-78
Baetica, 27 BC, 54, 580-5
Baéz, Buenaventura, 1844-82
Baffin Is., 1576-8
Bagamoyo, 1857-9
Bagaudae (Burgundians), 269, 285-6, 367,
  409-19, 435-7
Bagaza, Jean-Baptiste, 1976
Bagehot, Walter, 1826-77
Baghavand, 1735

baronetcy, 1611
barons in England, 1126, 1131, 1214, 1244, 1258, 1262, 1263, 1308, 1311, 1312, 1315, 1318, 1321
Barotseland, 1847, 1878
Barra, Francisco de la, of Mexico, 1910
Barrackpur, 1824, 1857
Barre, J. A. L. de la, 1682-5
Barre, Raymond, 1976
Barres, Auguste Maurice, 1862-1923
Barreto, Francisco, 1569
Barrie, Sir James Matthew, 1860-1937
Barrientos, René, general, 1964
Barrier Treaty, 1785
Barros, Justo Rufino, 1871-85
Barry, Mme du, 1769-74
Barry, Sir Charles, 1795-1860
Bart, Jean, 1694
Barth, Heinrich, 1850-1
Barth, Karl, 1886-1965
Barthou, Jean Luis, 1934
Bartók, Béla, 1881-1945
Barton, Edmund, 1901-3
Baruch, Bernard, 1946
Bärwald, treaty, 1631
al-Basasiri, 1958-60
Bashir al-Shihabi, Amir of Lebanon, 1763-1850
Basil I, emperor, 867-86
Basil II, 976-1025
Basilica Aemilia, c. 50 BC
Basilica Porcia, 184 BC
Basilicata, 1857
Basilides, gnostic, c. 130
Basilikon Doron, 1599
Basiliscos, 474-6
Basle, 1432, 1433, 1459, 1501, 1897; cathedral 1010; treaty 1795
Basques, 1718, 1765, 1833, 1841, 1970, 1975
Basra, 634, 656, 770, c. 970, 1770, 1775-6, 1914, 1915
Bass, George, 1798
Bass Strait, 1798
Bassein, Bombay, 1762, 1775, 1852
Bassein, Burma, 1402, 1530-4, 1756, 1852
Bassi, Matteo di, 1526
Bastarnes, 392
Bastarnes, 2nd c. BC
Bastille prison, 1789, 1968
Basuto, Basutos, Basutoland, c. 1830, 1843, 1848, 1851, 1858, 1865, 1871, 1945; independent, 1966; see also Lesotho
Batalha Abbey, Portugal, 1385; Dominican convent, 1388
Batalpin, 1858
Batavia, 1629
Batavia, 1617, 1619, 1634, 1642, 1645, 1646, c. 1670-82, 1707, 1740-3, 1747, 1786; statutes of, 1642
relations with Dutch, 1674, 1795, 1947; Macassar, 1653, 1660
Batavian Republic, 1798, 1803-6
Batavians, 69
Bateson, William, 1861-1926
Bath, 973
Bath, Earl of, 1746
Bathory, Gabriel, of Transylvania, 1613-29
Bathory, Sigismund, 1595
Bathory, Stephen, 1571-86
baths, 25-12 BC; public, c. 940
Bathurst, Australia, 1841
Bathurst, Gambia, c. 1618
Batinite sect, c. 874
Batinite Qarmatian sect, c. 890
Batista, Fulgencio, 1933-59
battering-ram used, c. 2000 BC
Batlle y Ordóñez, José, 1886-1915
Batn-al-Hagar, 525-404 BC

Batoka plateau, c. 650
Bato of Dalmatia, 9
al-Batrun, 1289
Battambang, c. 1800
Batticaloa, fort, 1656
Battle of Britain, 1940
'Battle of the Diamond', 1795
'Battle of the Eclipse', 585 BC
Battle of the Elephant, 570 or 71
Battle of the Masts, 655
Battle of the Standard, 1138
Batu, Khan of Kipchak, 1227-55
Batu Sawar, 1587, 1613, c. 1617, 1673
Batu Serai, 1227
Batum, 1878, 1915, 1920
Bauchi, 1902; plateau, c. 900
Baudouin I of Belgium, 1950
Baugé, 1421
Bautzen, treaty, 1350
Bavaria, 500, 595, c. 600, 728, 741-52, 787, 900, 1047, 1139, 1142, 1156, 1492, 1532, 1732, 1778, 1805, 1807, 1813, 1818, 1850, 1870; Catholic, 1569; Republic, 1918; relations with Austria, 1745, 1805; France, 1622, 1646, 1647, 1733, 1741-8; Spain, 1741; Sweden, 1646, 1647
Bavaria, Duke of, 1741-9; Prince of, 1698-9
Bax, Sir Arnold Edward, 1883-1953
Baxter, Richard, 1615-91
Bay of Islands, 1814, 1837
Bayar, Celal, of Turkey, 1950-60
Bayard, Chevalier, 1524
Bayazid I, Ottoman, 1389-1403
Bayazid II, Ottoman, 1481-1512
Bayazid al-Bistani, c. 875
Bayazid, son of Sulayman, 1559-61
Baybars (al-Malik al-Zahir), 1260-77
Baybars II, Bahri Mamluk Sultan, 1308-9
Bayeux, 1082-7, 1088
Bayinnaung of Burma, 1538-81
Bayle, Pierre, 1647-1706
Bayley, Hon. W. Butterworth, 1828
Bayliss, W., 1902
Bayonne, 1140, 1292, 1369, 1375, 1522
Bayreuth, 1779
Baza, 1324
Beachy Head, 1690
Beaconsfield (Benjamin Disraeli), Earl of, 1804-81
Beadle, Sir Hugh, 1966
beads, ante 2000 BC; trade in, ante 1st c., c. 650, c. 11th c., 1292
Beagle, 1831
'beaker' folk, c. 1900 BC
Beardsley, Aubrey, 1872-98
Béarn, 1620
Beaton, cardinal, 1546
Beatty, David, earl, 1871-1936
Beaudelaire, Charles Pierre, 1821-67
Beaufort family, 1425
Beaufort, Henry, 1413
Beaufort, Lebanon, 1289
Beauharnais, Eugène, 1805
Beauharnois, Charles, Marquis de, 1726-49
Beauharnois Fort, 1728
Beaulieu, edict, 1576
Beaumarchais, P. A. Caron de, 1732-99
Beaumont, Francis, 1584-1616
Beauvais, 1099, 1108-9, 1180, 1471
Beauvoir, Simone de, 1908-
beaver wool, post 1580
Beaverbrook, Lord, 1879-1964
Bec, 1078-93
Beccaria, Cesare, 1735-93
Beccaria, Giovanni Battista, 1716-81
Becher, Johann Joachim, 1635-82
Bechuanaland, 1802, 1885, 1945, 1966; see also

Botswana
Becket, St Thomas see St Thomas Becket
Becquerel, Henri, 1896
Bedde, c. 1300
Bede, The Venerable, c. 673-735
Bedmore, Mysore, 1783
Beduin, c. 605, 627, 630-1
Beecroft, J., 1840-53
Beerbohm, Sir Max, 1872-1952
beer-making, c. 2500 BC
beet sugar, 1747
Beethoven, Ludvig van, 1770-1827
Beeton, Isabella, 1836-65
Begemder, 1570, 1788, 1852, 1853
'Beggars' Summons', 1559
beggary, ordinance against, 1724
Bègne, Lambert le, 1187
Behaim, Martin, 1459-1506
Behn, Afra, 1640-89
Behring, Vitus, 1725
Behring Straits, 1725
Beirut (Berytus), 200-55, 551, 975, 1110, 1182, 1285, 1291, 1835, 1840, 1874, 1918, 1919
Beith, Maj.-Gen. John Hay (Ian Hay), 1876-1952
Beja, 404-369 BC, ante 300 BC, c. 250-350, c. 320-55, c. 450, 453, c. 690, 831, 834, 854
Beke, 1840
Bela I of Hungary, 1060-3
Bela II of Hungary, 1131-41
Bela III of Hungary, 1173-96
Bela IV of Hungary, 1241
Belaunde, Fernando, 1962-8
Belecazar, Sebastián de, 1536-7
Belem, convent of, 1499, 1520
Belezina, 905
Belfast, 1975
Belgae, c. 200 BC, 57 BCf, c. 1 BC
Belgaum, 1473
Belgian Congo see Congo, Belgian
Belgic tribesmen, post 200
Belgium, 481-511, 1600, 1683, 1789, 1790, 1830, 1831, 1839, 1866, 1880, 1891, 1898, 1904, 1908, 1913, 1914, 1918, 1921, 1936, 1951, 1968; relations with Congo (L), 1965; France, 1708, 1792, 1794, 1914, 1920; Germany, 1892, 1914, 1916, 1940, 1942; Holland, 1831; Persia, 1898
Belgrade, 1440, 1456, 1521, 1688, 1914, 1915, 1944, 1965; University, 1864; relations with Russia, 1789, 1811; Turks, 1690, 1716-18, 1739
Belisarius, 494-565
Bell, Alexander Graham, 1847-1922
Bell, Gertrude, 1868-1926
Bell, John, 1859
Bellay, Joachim du, c. 1524-60
Belle Isle, 1524
Belle-Ile, 1761
Belli, Giuseppe Gioacchino, 1791-1863
Bellini, Giovanni, 1422-1516
Bello, Francesco, c. 1450-1505
Belloc, Hilaire, 1870-1953
Belluno, 1420
Belmont, Lebanon, 1157
Belshazzar (Bel-shar-usur), 554-539 BC
Bemba, c. 1869-70
Bembo, Cardinal Pietro, 1470-1547
Bemoin, 1486
Benares, treaty, 1773; Sanscrit College, 1794
Benavente, Jacinto, 1866-1954
Benavides, Oscar, marshal, 1933-9
Benburh, Tyrone, 1646
Bencoolen, 1824
Bendelhara, Office of, ante 1445
Bender, 1771
Benedict, Order of St, c. 480-547, 547, 630,

Bindusara, 297 BC, 273 BC
Binnya Dala of Hanthawaddy, 1747-57
Binnya F. Law of Hanthawaddy, 1331
Binnya Kyan of Hanthawaddy, 1450-3
Binnya Ran I of Hanthawaddy, 1426-46
Binnya Ran II of Hanthawaddy, 1492-1526
Binnya U, 1353-85
Binnya Waru of Hanthawaddy, 1446-50
Binnyadhamaraza of Hanthawaddy, 1423-6
Bintang, c. 1513, 1526, 1677-85
Binyon, Laurence, 1869-1943
Biological Weapons Convention, 1972
Biopio, 1956
Birch, James, 1875-6
bireme, c. 700 BC, c. 500 BC
Birger Jarl, 1249-66
Birger of Sweden, 1290-1318
Birgham-on-Tweed, treaty, 1290
Birkenhead, 1st Earl, 1872-1932
Birmingham, Alabama, 1963
Birmingham, England, 1898
biro pen, 1938
Biron, regent in Russia, 1740
Birrell, Augustine, 1850-1933
al-Biruni, 976-1012, 1031-40
Biscay, Bay of, 1631
bishoprics, 540, 1540
bishops, granted rights, 633; English, 1553,
    1559, 1688, 1689; Napoleonic, 1808
Biskra, 683
Bismarck, Otto E. L., Prince von, 1815-98
Bismarck Sea, battle, 1943
Bissagos Is., 1462
Bissau, 1696, c. 1700, 1825
Bithynia, 216 BC, 183 BC, 74 BC, 112 or 113,
    258; under Ottomans, 1231-88, 1288-1326
Bitlis, 1916
Bito dynasty in Uganda, c. 1500
Bittideva, c. 1110-41
Bittiga, c. 1110-41
Biu, amirate, c. 1535-80
Bizerta, 1770, 1785, 1942, 1952, 1961
Bizet, Georges, 1838-75
Björkö, treaty, 1905
Blachernae, 491-518
'Black Acts', 1584
Black Death, 1346, 1348-1400, 1353
'Black Dragon Society', Japan, 1901
'Black Friday', Germany, 1927
Black Hills, Dakota, 1742
Black Hole of Calcutta, 1756
Black Lions, 1936
'Black Madonna', 1382
'Black Muslims', 1975
Black Prince, 1355-76
Black Reichswehr, 1923
'Black Saturday', 1946
Black Sea, c. 650 BC, c. 514-512 BC, c. 150,
    512, 1392, 1739, 1774, 1814, 1856, 1871,
    1914, 1919
Black Shirt troops, 1937
Black Stone of Mecca, 930, 951
Black Troops in (French) Africa, 1918
'Black-and-Tans', 1919-21
Blackmore, Richard Doddridge, 1825-1900
Blackstone, Sir William, 1723-80
Blackwood, Algernon, 1869-1951
Blake, Robert, Admiral, 1599-1627
Blake, William, 1757-1827
Blanche of Castile, 1226
Blanche of Lancaster, 1359
Blanco, Antonio Guzmán, 1870-88
Blanco, Castello, 1825-90
Blantyre, 1876
Blasphemy of Sirmium, 357
Blavatsky, Mme Helena Petrovna, 1875
Blaxland, Gregory, 1813
Bled, treaty, 1954

Bledisloe Commission, 1938
Blemmyes, 284
Bléneau, battle, 1642
Blenheim, 1704; Palace, 1705
Blériot, Louis, 1872-1936
Blessed Virgin Mary, 1858, 1950
Blida, 1830
Bligh, Capt William, 1806-8
Bliss, Sir Arthur, 1891-1975
'Blitz' by air, 1940
Bloc Démocratique Sénégalais, 1948
Bloch, Dora, 1976
blockade, strategic, 1915, 1918, 1960, 1962
Bloemfontein, 1854, 1900
Blois, 1234, 1576, 1588; house of, 1365;
    ordinance, 1579; treaty, 1504
Blois, Charles de, 1341-64
blood, circulation of, 1628
'Blood Bath of Bubat', 1350
'Blood Bath of Stockhold', 1520
Bloody Assize, 1685
'Bloody Sunday' in London, 1887; Ulster,
    1972
'Bloody Week' in Paris, 1871
Blore Heath, battle, 1459
Blow, Dr John, 1649-1708
blowlamp, 1880
Blucher, Gerhard von, 1742-1819
Blucher locomotive, 1814
Blue Mountains, 1813
Blum Léon, 1872-1950
Blum-Violette reforms, 1936
Blunt, Lady Anne, 1879
Blunt, Wilfrid Scawen, 1840-1922
Boadicea (Boudicca), 61
Board of Agriculture, 1793, 1818
Board of Education in England and Wales,
    1899
Board of Trade in England, 1780; NZ, 1915;
    Spain, 1503
Board of Trade and Plantations, 1696
boats, c. ante 3000 BC, c. 2500 BC, c. 600
    BC
Bobadilla, Francisco, 1500
'bobbies', 1829
Bobbio, monastery, c. 612
Boccaccio, Giovanni, 1313-75
Boccherini Luigi, 1743-1805
Bocchus (I), 108-105 BC
Bocchus II, 38-33 BC
Bocskay, Stephen, 1604-6
Bodapaya of Burma, 1782-1819
Bodiam, 1385
Bodleian Library, 1613-18
Bodley, Sir Thomas, 1545-1613
Boeotia, 447 BC, 404-403 BC, 395 BC, 376 BC,
    339 BC, 293 BC
Boer commandos, 1715
Boer republic, 1881
Boer Wars, 1842-3, 1881, 1899-1902
Boers, 1833, 1839, 1881, 1899, 1900, 1901
Boethius, c. 523-5
Boethius (Boece), Hector, 1465-1536
Bogador, C, 1433-4
Bogdan, 1504
Bogland Act, 1771
Bogolepov, Russian minister, 1901
Bogomils, 1084
Bogoris (Boris) of Bulgaria, 852-89
Bogotá, 1538, 1549, 1794, 1819, 1861, 1948;
    Act of, 1960
Bogud, 42 and 38 BC
Bohemia, 195-192 BC, 6f, post 100, 805-6,
    1035, 1041, 1047, 1055, 1627, 1631, 1741,
    1783; Kingdom, 1212, 1276, 1307, 1318;
    disturbances, 1423, 1434, 1547, 1618, 1680;
    reformers, c. 1390, 1403, 1415, 1419-36,
    1444, 1609;

relations with Moravia, 1197, 1222;
    Poland, 830, 967, 1003-4, 1039, 1108;
    Prussia, 1744, 1757
Bohémond, Prince of Antioch, 1098, 1104-8
Bohémond III of Antioch, 1164
Bohr, Niels, 1885-1962
Boiardo, Matteo Maria, c. 1440-94
Boii, 283 BC, 236 BC, 195-192 BC
Boileau, Nicholas, 1636-1711
Bois, W. E. Burghardt du, 1868-1963
Boisay, Jacques René de, 1685
Bokassa, Jean Bedel, 1966, 1976
Boleslaus I of Bohemia, 929
Boleslaw the Curly, 1146
Boleslaw the Modest of Cracrow, 1243-79
Boleslaw I of Poland, 992-1025
Boleslaw II of Poland, 1058-79
Boleslaw III of Poland, 1102-38
Boleyn, Anne, 1533-6
Bolingbroke, Viscount, 1704-17
Bolivar, Simón, 1783-1830
Bolivia, post c. 1438, 1538, 1545, 1776, 1780,
    1825, 1835, 1864, 1922, 1937, 1951, 1952,
    1953, 1968;
    relations with Brazil, 1903; Chile, 1874,
    1879, 1883, 1904; Paraguay, 1935, 1938;
    Peru, 1839, 1873, 1879; Uruguay, 1932-5
Bolland, J., 1596-1665
Bologna, c. ante 1000 BC, c. 550 BC, c. 350
    BC, 1088, 14th c., 1431, 1530, 1547, 1549,
    1838; treaty, 1515
Bolsheviks, 1903, 1917, 1918, 1920
Bolshevism in USSR, 1947
Boma, Congo, 1877
bombs, atomic, 1945, 1952, 1953, 1960; flying,
    1944; hydrogen, 1950, 1953, 1954, 1966,
    1967, 1968; nuclear, 1945
Bombay, 1661, 1662, 1720, 1798, 1802, 1837,
    1853, 1862, 1872, 1885, 1946, 1964;
    Presidency, 1708, 1773, 1819; University,
    1857
Bombay Burma Trading Corp. case, 1886
Bombay Times, 1838
Bomilcar, c. 308 BC
Bon, cape, 468
Bonar Law, Andrew see Law
'Bond of 1844', 1844
Bondone, Giotto de, 1334
Bône, 1034, 1153, 1830, 1914
Bongaya, treaty, 1668
Boniface, count of Africa, 427
Boniface VI, antipope, 896
Boniface VII, antipope, 974-85
Boniface II, pope, 530-2
Boniface III, pope, 607
Boniface IV, pope, 608-15
Boniface V, pope, 619-25
Boniface VIII, pope, 1294-1303
Boniface IX, pope, 1389-1404
Boniface of Montferrat, 1204-7
Bonifacio, José, 1822
Bonilla, Policarpo, of Honduras, 1894-9
Bonington, Richard Parkes, 1802-28
Bonn Agreement, 1953
Bonnets, Sweden, 1772
Bonneuil, 616
Bononia, 189 BC, 43 BC
Bonosus, 280
book binding, 8th or 9th c.; publishing, c. 50
    BC, 1st c.
Book of Canons, Scottish, 1635
Book of Mormon, 1830
books, import duty, 1480; printed, 835, 1474;
    under permit, 1558
booksellers, 891
Boone, Daniel, 1734-1820
Booth, Willim, 1865
Borabodur temples, c. 850-900

Caledon, Earl of, 1807
Caledonia, Caledonians, 193, late 2nd c., 209, 843
calendar, 74-5, 1026, 1699; Babylonian, 747 BC, c. 388-367 BC; Egyptian, 237 BC; Greek, 433 BC; Gregorian, 1074-5, 1582, 1700, 1752, 1923; Julian, 46 BC, 30 BC, 1700; Muslim, 622; Persian, 1074-5; Roman, 191 BC, 153 BC, c. 125 BC, 697
Calgary, Canada, 1918
Cali, Columbia, 1537
Calicut, 1443, 1444, 1488, 1498, 1502, 1513, 1570
California, 1769, 1830, 1845, 1846, 1848, 1850, 1859; Lower, 1853
Caligula, 37-41
Caliphate, 1087, 1180-1225, 1924; Abbasid, 755, 778, 798, 813-6, 817, 819-22, 836, 868-84, 871, 910-24, 945, 1056; of Córdoba, 929-1031; dominated by Turks, 1055; in Egypt, 1324; Umayyad, 660-749, 695
Caliphs, orthodox, 632-61
Calixtus III, antipope, 1168-78
Calixtus II, pope, 1119-24
Calixtus IV, pope, 1455-8
Callaecia, 2 BC
Callaghan, (L.) James, Prime Minister, 1912–
Callao, Peru, 1864
Calles, Plutarco Elías, 1924-35
Calley, William, Lieut., 1969
Callières, Louis Hector de, 1699-1705
Callimachus, poet and grammarian, c. 305-250 BCf.
Callinicum, 531
Callisthenes, 360-327 BC
Calonne, C. A. de, 1787-1802
Calvin (Cauvin), John, 1509-64
Calvinism, 1541, 1549, 1559-73, 1570; attacked by Arminians, 1604-19
Calvinist riots, 1566; union with Lutherans, 1608; war with Catholics, 1583-4
Calvinists in France, 1559
Camacho, Manuel Avila, 1940-6
Cámara de las Indias, 1600
Camargo, Marie-Anne de, 1710-70
Camargo, Lleras, 1958
Camarines Is., 1573
camb pottery, c. 2500 BC
Cambay, 1297
Cambo, c. 1568, 1569
Cambodia, 635, post 681, c. post 706, 802-1432, c. 950, 1001-11, 1051, 1065, 1131, 1149, 1177, 1220, 1282, 1284, 1863, 1867, 1884, 1949, 1954, 1970; relations with Sri Vijaya, 1012; war with Champa, 1190, 1203-20
Cambrai, 1677, 1917; league, 1508, 1509; peace, 1529
Cambridge, England, 1209, 1231, 1381, 1497, 1969, 1970; university, 1281-4, 1510-14
Cambridge, Mass., 1639
Cambridge Platform, 1646
Cambuskenneth, 1326
Cambyses I, c. 600-559 BC
Cambyses II, 538-522 BC
Camden, Texas, 1780
Camden, William, 1551-1623
camels in use, in Arabia, c. 15th-13th c. BC, c. 854 BC; Egypt, 7th c. BC, c. 525 BC: Sahara, 11th c. BC, 1st c.; S Sahara, c. 7th c.; in army corps, 296, 496-523; for transport, c. 115, 747-514 BC-AD c. 300, c. 300-400
camera, box, 1888; cinema, 1895; photographic, 1826
Camerinum, 295 BC
Cameron, Sir Donald, 1925-31
Cameroon, 1916, 1924
Cameroons, R., c. 1588

Cameroun, c. 470 BC, 1434, 1845, 1868, 1882, 1916, 1917, 1927, 1933-46, 1940; independent, 1960
Camisard rebellion, 1702-4
Camlan, battle, c. 537
Cammaerts, Emile, 1878-1955
Camoens, Luis de, c. 1524-80
Campanello, Tommaso, 1568-1639
Campania, c. 750 BC, c. 650 BC, 350-270 BCf, 217 BC, 83 BC
Campbell, Thomas, 1777-1844
Campbell-Bannerman, Sir Henry, 1836-1908
Campbells, 1645
Camperdown, 1797
camphor, 916
Campion, Edmund, 1580-1
Campion, Thomas, 1567-1620
Campo-Formio, treaty, 1797
Campos Salles, Manoel de, 1898-1902
Campus Martius, 220 BC
Camulodunum (Colchester), 40, 43
Camus, Albert, 1913-61
Canaan invaded, c. 1100 BC
*Canada*, HMS, 1742
Canada and Canadians, 1578, 1713, 1760, 1768, 1774, 1776, 1780, 1820-4, 1832, 1837, 1847-50, 1853, 1859, 1864-8, 1917, 1920-1, 1925-35, 1940, 1949, 1957, 1967; constitution, 1789, 1791; Expeditionary Force, 1914, 1917; kingdom, 1867, 1870; laws, 1773; Legislative Assembly, 1792, 1814, 1818, 1819; Navy, 1910; Supreme Court, 1876; Canada, British, 1823; Catholic, 1773; French, 1756, 1793, 1796, 1868; Lower, 1792, 1812, 1814, 1823, 1833, 1835, 1838, 1840; Upper, 1792, 1794, 1811, 1823, 1828, 1832, 1834, 1837, 1840; relations with American rebels, 1776; Britain, 1828, 1869, 1871, 1899, 1937; Germany, 1939; USA, 1818, 1842, 1846, 1866, 1871-80, 1879, 1881-5, 1922, 1923, 1935, 1938, 1940, 1941, 1957; USSR, 1946
Canadian Broadcasting Corporation, 1936
Canadian Citizenship Act, 1946
Canadian Lead, Ballarat, 1853
Canadian Northern Railway, 1917
Canadian Pacific Railway, 1885
Canadian Radio Commission, 1932
canal locks, 50 BC, 983, 1396
Canal du Midi, 1661-81
Canale, Antonio, (Canaletto), 1697-1768
Canalejas y Mendez, José, 1911
Canaletto *see* Canale
Canals, in Britain, 1759, 1790, 1824-9; China, c. post 589, 983, 1411, 1415; Erie, 1817-25; Huron, 1855; Kiel, 1895; du Midi, 1661-81; Mughul, 1818; Nahrawan, 659; Nile-Red Sea, 280 BC, 641-2, 747-514; Oder-Spree, 1661-8; Panama, 1880, 1892; Rideau, 1826; Suez, 1854, 1859, 1869; Trajan's, 658-64
Canary Is., 1402, 1418, 1424, 1435, 1476-1524, 1477, 1480
cancer, 548
Cancha Rayada, 1818
Candia, 1669
Cange, Charles du, 1610–88
Cannae, battle, 216 BC
Cannes, 1815
Canning, Charles John Viscount, 1856-62
Canning, George, 1770-1827
Canning, Sir Stratford *see* Stratford de Redcliffe, Lord
cannons, 1346; foundry for, 1613
Cano, Alonso, 1601-67
canon law, 1550; in Russia, 1650-3
canonization of saints, 1170
Canons of St Victor, 1113
Canopus, Decree of, 237 BC

Canossa, 1077
Canova, Antonio, 1757-1822
Cánovas del Castillo, Antonio, 1875-97
Canso, Nova Scotia, 1745
Cantanduanes Is., 1573
*Cantar de mío Cid*, c. 1150
Canterbury, 602, 632, 634, 805, 851, 1109, 1130, 1170, 1174, 1220, 1277, 1283, 1378-1411, 1423, 1520; treaties, 1189, 1416
Canterbury, Convocation of, 1852
Canterbury, NZ, 1850
Canterbury and York, convocation, 1969
*Cantilène de Ste Eulalie*, c. 890
Canton, 196 BC, 226, 629, 879, c. 1119, 1517, 1918-22, 1924, 1936, 1940
Cantonese Chinese, 1854
Cantons, Swiss, 1316
Canute, King of England, 1014-35
Canute II (Hardicanute), 1040-2
Canute VI of Denmark, 1182-1202
Cao-bang, 1950
Cap Rouge, R., 1541
Cape *see* Cape Colony
Cape Castle, fort, 1642; Coast, 1652; Coast Castle, c. 1662 or 3, 1667, 1752; Patriots, 1779
Cape Colony, 1652, 1662, 1670-96, 1672, 1677, 1682-3, c. 1685, 1688, 1715, c. 1730, 1746, 1753, 1803-6, 1806, 1814, 1820, 1822, 1827, 1833, 1834, 1844, 1846, 1848, 1850, 1853, 1855, 1860, 1865, 1871, 1872, 1894, 1904, 1934,; British occupation, 1795-1803; Indians arrive, 1667
Cape Horn, 1811
Cape Mount, c. 1602
Cape St Vincent, 1833
Cape Town, 1663, 1801, 1805, 1825, 1908-9, 1921, 1927, 1960, 1972; castle, 1666-7
Cape Verde Is., 1460, 1466 independent republic, 1975
Capek, Karel, 1890-1938
Capêlo, Brito, 1877
Capet dynasty, 987-1328
Capet, Hugh, 987-996
Capitol, Rome, c. 460 BC, 390 BC
Capitol, Washington, 1792-1830
capitulations in China, 1921; Egypt, 1937; Persia, 1928
Capodistrias, Augustine, 1831-2; John, of Greece, 1827-31
Caporetto, 1915, 1917
Cappadocia, c. 650 BC, c. 600 BC, 550 BC, 104 BC, 95 BC, 17, 161, 607, 878, 1389
Capri, 26
Caprivi, Georg Leo, count, 1890-4
Capsa, 107 BC
Captain of the Fortress of Malacca, 1571
Captain-General of Brazil, 1549
Capua, c. 650 BC, c. post 450 BC, 343 BC, 334 BC, 314 BC, 211 BC, c. 100 BC, 1058
Capuchin Friars, 1630
car rallies, 1930
Carabobo, 1821
Caracas, 1750, 1810, 1812, 1813, 1935
Caracas Co., 1728
Caracalla, 211-17; baths of, c. 206
Carafa, Cardinal, 1542
Caratacus, 43
Carausius, M. Aurelius, 286-290
caravan routes, 128 BC, c. 7th or 8th c.
caravel, 1440
carburettor, 1893
Carcassonne, 1320-2
Carchemish, 877 BC, 605 BC
Cardenas, Lázaro, 1934
Cardiff, 1106
Cardwell, Edward, 1813-86
Carelia, 1721

Crispi, Francesco, 1819-1901
Crispus, 326
Cristofori, Bartolommeo, 1665-1731
Critias, orator, 403 BC
Critolaus, 146 BC
Croatia, 1076, 1699, 1941; bps, 1945
Croats, *post* 600
Croce, Benedetto, 1866-1962
Croesus, 560-546 BC
Croissenbrun, 1260
Crome, John, 1769-1821
Cromer, Lord, 1883-1907
Crompton, Samuel, 1779
Cromwell, Oliver, 1599-1658
Cromwell, Richard, 1658-9
Cromwell, Thomas, 1533-40
Crookes, W., 1900
Cross, J., Trade Commissioner, 1970
cross-bow, 4th c. BC
Crossman, R. H. S., 1976
Crosthwaite, Sir Charles, 1887-90
Crovan, Godfrey, 1075-1265
Crowder, Enoch, general, 1921-3
Crown Colonies, British, 1624, 1691, 1763-9,
    1802, 1808, 1821, 1856, 1860, 1885, 1923,
    1925, 1948
Crown Land Ordinance in Kenya, 1902
Crown Point, 1731
Crowther, Samuel Ajayi, bp, 1809-91
crucifixion forbidden, 315
Crucifixion of Jesus Christ, 30 or 33, 1032
Cruikshank, George, 1792-1878
Crusaders, 1115, 1124, 1142, 1144, 1156,
    1161-9, 1182, 1192, 1193-1229, 1204,
    1219-21, 1229, 1244, 1263-71, 1291
Crusades, first, 1095-9; second, 1147-9; third,
    1189-93; fourth, 1202-4; fifth, 1217-21;
    sixth, 1227-9; seventh, 1248-54; eighth, 1270;
    against Ottoman Turks, 1454-5, 1463, 1500;
    Waldenses, 1488
Cruz report, 1955
Cruzat y Góngora, Fausto, 1690-1701
Crystal Palace, London, 1851
Ctesibius, c. 265 BC
Ctesiphon, 160-143 BC, *post* 56-c. 37 BC, 36,
    116, 164, 198, 260, 264, 283, 614, 627, 637,
    1915
Cuauhtemoc of Mexico, 1520-1
Cuba, 1492-3, 1494, 1504, 1504, 1515, 1854,
    1868-78, 1886, 1895, 1898, 1917, 1921, 1976;
    rebellions, 1906, 1933, 1953;
    relations with Communist China, 1960; Iran,
    1976; USA, 1898, 1901, 1959-61; USSR,
    1961, 1962
Cuddalore, naval battle, 1782
Cuenca, 1177
Cuilean, King of Scots, 967-71
Cuitlahuac of Mexico, 1520
Culloden, 1746
Cult of Attis, *ante* 50; Baal (Saturn), 217 BC;
    Bacchus, 186 BC; Cybele, 205 BC; Isis, 19;
    Isis and Sarapis, c. 100 BC; 'personality',
    1956; Reason, 1793; Tanith (Caelestis), 217
    BC; Tooth Relic of Buddha, 12th-16th c.;
    Venus, 217 BC; Zeus, 167 BC
'cultural revolution' in China, 1966
Cumae, c. 1052 BC, 428 BC, 180 BC
Cuman Khan Kotyan, 1238
Cumberland, 1000, 1092, 1157; Duke of,
    1745-7
Cumbria, 945
Cunard Line, 1839-40
cuneiform script, 74-5
Cunobelin (Cymbeline), 40
Curcuas, John, 933, 944
Curie, Marie, 1867-1934
Curie, Pierre, 1859-1906
currency, 1523-1027 BC, c. 500 BC, c. 115

BC-c. AD 300, 212, c. 250, 271, 292, 498,
    1230, 1302, 1329-32, 1835, 1857, 1961; in
    Australia, 1966; England, 1551, 1560, 1561,
    1696, (decimal) 1971; France, 1640; India,
    1715-17 *see also* coinage and minting
Curtius, Q., 41-54
Curtin, John, 1941-5
Curzola, 1297
Curzon of Kedleston, Marquess, 1859-1925
Cusa, Cardinal Nicholas de, 1401-64
customs dues, 17, 1160; irregularities, 1926;
    tariffs, 1782; unions, 1852, 1854, 1931, 1949
Custozza, battle, 1866
Cuthbert of Wessex, 752
Cuthred of Mercia, 798-805
Cuthred of Wessex, 740-56
Cuyo, 1814-17
Cuyp, Albert, 1605-91
Cuzco, c. 1000, c. 1200, 1527, 1533
Cyaxares I, c. 721-675 BC
Cyaxares II, 653-585 BC
Cyclades, 394 BC, 727
cyclones, 1969
Cylon, c. 550 BC
Cymbeline, 40
Cyme, 474 BC
Cynaxa, 401 BC
Cynegils of Wessex, 611-43
Cynewulf, poet, 750
Cynewulf of Wessex, 757-86
Cynocephalo, 364
Cynric, c. 622-60
Cypriots, Greek, 1964, 1967; Turkish, 1965,
    1967
Cyprus, 710 BCf, c. 570-526 BC, 546 BC, 498
    BC, 454 BCf, 36 BC, 115, 649, 747, 805, 965,
    1155 or 6, 1184, 1195, 1248, 1270, 1343,
    1383, 1424-6, 1426, 1954-9, 1964; taken by
    Crusaders, 1189, 1191; under Egypt, 1427;
    Republic, 1960;
    relations with Britain 1878, 1914, 1925, 1960,
    1964; Greece, 1954, 1963, 1967; Turks, c.
    1185, 1570, 1964, 1967, 1974, 1975; Venice,
    1473, 1489
Cypselos, c. 657 BC
Cyrenaica, 274 BC, 97 BCf, 767, 1911, 1916,
    1925, 1941
Cyrene, c. 630 BC, c. 588 BC, c. 570-526 BC,
    314 BC, 74 BC, 36 BC, 115
Cyril of Salonica, 860-9
*Cyropaedia*, 4th c. BC
Cyrus I, 640-600 BC
Cyrus II (The Great), 559-529 BC
Cyrus, satrap of Lydia, 406-401 BC
Cyrus (al-Muqauqis), 631
Cythera, 424 BC
Cyzicus, c. 675 BC, 410 BC
Czartoryski, Adam, 1770-1861
Czech faculties in Prague, 1881; government in
    exile, 1939; rebellion, 1848; refugees in
    Russia, 1918, 1919
Czechoslovakia, 1918, 1920, 1921, 1924, 1925,
    1935, 1942, 1946-51, 1969, 1976,
    constitution, 1953;
    relations with Germany, 1939; USSR, 1934,
    1935, 1942, 1968, 1969
Czechs, 1355, 1421, 1433
Czernowitz, 1914, 1916
Czerny, Karl, 1791-1857
Czestochowa, 1382, end of 14th c.


Dabarwa, fortress, 1578
Dabhol, 1351
Dacia, Dacians, c. 62, 86, 101-2, 165, 271, 376,
    470
Dafydd ap Llywelyn, 1240-6
Daghestan, 1741-2

Dagobert I, 623-39
Dagobert II, 675-9
Dagobert III, 711-15
Dagon (Rangoon), 1755
Daguerre, Louis J. M., 1839
daguerrotype process, 1839
Dahomey, 1625, c. 1650, c. 1680, 1724, 1729,
    1747, c. 1776, 1781, 1841, 1849, 1960,
    1964-9, 1976; under French, 1892, 1894
Dai Abu Abdallah, 893, 902-8
Dai Viet, 1128-50
Daiakku (Deioces), c. 740 BC
*Dáil Eireann*, 1919, 1922
Dailino, treaty, 1619
*Daily Courant*, 1702
*Daily Express*, 1900
*Daily Mail*, 1896
*Daily Mirror*, 1904
*Daily Telegraph*, 1908
Daimler, Gottlieb, 1834-1900
Daing Chelak of Bugis, 1728-45
Daing Kemboja of Bugis, 1745-77
Daing Merewah of the Bugis, 1722-8
Daing Parani, c. 1721
Dairen, 1898
Dairy Board, NZ, 1923
Dakar, 1863, 1938, 1940
Dakin of the Funj, 1596-86
Dakotas, 1742
Dalada Maligava, Kandy, 1815
Daladier, Edouard, 1933-40
Dalai Lama, Tibet, c. 1447, 1645, 1653, 1715,
    1908, 1910, 1911, 1959
Dalaigh, Cearbhall O'., President of Ireland,
    1974
Dale, Sir Thomas, 1611-16
Dalhousie, Earl of, 1820-56
Dallas, Texas, 1965
Dalmatia, 129 BC, 6, 9, 379, 481, 535, 554,
    804, 877, 1241, 1358, 1409, 1437; Lower, 155
    BC
Dalny (Dairen), 1898
Dalriada kingdom, 470, 842
Dalry, 1306
Dalton, John, 1766-1844
Damão, 1530
Damaraland, 1850
Damascus, c. *post* 900 BC, 858-824 BC, c. *ante*
    815 BC, 604 BC, 105, 614, 635, 695, 705,
    711, 969, 975, 1095-1104, 1154, 1174, 1184,
    1193, 1211-82, 1279, c. 1288-9, 1300, 1755,
    1771, 1908, 1918, 1957; ruled by Crusaders,
    1126, 1139, 1147-9; French, 1920, 1925;
    Mongols, 1400, 1401; Ottoman Turks, 1516,
    1517-1697
Damasus II, pope, 1047-8
Dambadeniya, 1232-1326
Dambara, 1670
Dambwa, c. 620
Damdam, c. 1220
Damien, 578-604
Damett, Thomas, 1437
Damietta, 853, 1218, 1219-21, 1249, 1250,
    1309-40
Dampier, William, 1652-1715
dams, c. 2000 BC, 5th c., 1902, 1959, 1960
Dan Juma of Gumel, c. 1749-54
Danakil, 9th-11th c.
Danby, Earl of, 1673-9
*dane-geld*, 991
Danelaw, 886, 917
Danes, 500, 810, 835, 851, 870, 878, 1069-70,
    1331, 1627, 1690; invading Britain, 793, 865,
    874, 893, 910, 911-18, 913-15, 927, 980, 988,
    991, 993, 997-9, 1002, 1003-14, 1007-9, 1009,
    1018, 1044; fleet, 875; seamen, c. 1471-80 *see
    also* Denmark
Danewerk, 1331

relations with Brandenburg, 1682, 1700; EEC, 1967, 1970, 1972, 1973; France, 1742, 1807, 1902; Germany, 1848, 1864, 1940; Hanse towns, 1362, 1370, 1534; Holy Roman Empire, 1629, 1701; Iceland, 1874, 1903, 1918; Schleswig, 1767, 1863, 1864; Sweden, 1332, 1389, 1397, 1497, 1561-8, 1564, 1570, 1611, 1613, 1643, 1644, 1645, 1657, 1658, 1674, 1676, 1679, 1700, 1712, 1719, 1720, 1756, 1814, 1850; United Provinces, 1625, 1666, 1674, 1701
Denonville, Marquis de, 1685
dental drill, 1790
Dentatus, M. Curius, 290-284 BC
dentures, c. 1845
Denyu, Jean, of Honfleur, 1506
Deogaon, treaty, 1803
Deogiri (Daulatabad), 1318, 1499
Deorai, Pass of, 1659
Department of Defence, US, 1947
*Départements* of France, 1790
depression, economic, 1895, 1896; industrial, 1837, 1847-8
Depretis, Agostino, 1876-87
Deptford, London, 1890
Derbend, 1722, 1735
Derby, 1745
Derby, Earl of, 1851-68
Derby, Lord, 1344, 1345
Déroulède, Paul, 1846-1914
Dertosa, 215 BC
Dervish convents, 1184; monasteries, *post* 1184; suppression, 1926
Dervishes in the Sudan, 1885, 1894
Descartes, René, 1596-1650
Deschanel, Paul, 1920
Desmarest, Nicholas, 1725-1815
Desmond, Earl of, 1468; lands, 1586; revolts, 1569-73, 1579-83
Despenser, Hugh, 1315-26
Despotate of Epirus, 1204; Mistra, 1348, 1417; Morea, 1460
Dessalines, 1804-6
Dessau, 1525, 1626
'De-Stalinization' in USSR, 1956
Destour Party in Tunisia, 1920
Detroit, 1704, 1813
Dettingen, 1743
Deusdedit, pope, 615-18
Deutero-Malays, c. 300 BC
Deva (Chester), 71, 84
Devagri, *ante* 1316
devaluation of currency, dollar, 1933; franc, 1936-8, 1948, 1969; pound sterling, 1949, 1966
Devanampiya, 250-210 BC
Devapala, 9th c.
Devaraya I of Vijayanagar, c. 1406-22
Devaraya II of Vijayanagar, 1422-46
Devlin, Patrick, Lord, 1905-
Devon, 981-2, 988, 1549; Earl of, 1455
Devonshire, (4th) Duke of, 1756; (8th) Duke of, 1916-21
Dexippus, 267
Dey of Algiers, 1827, 1830
Dhammazedi of Hanthawaddy, 1472-92
Dhanga, c. 950-99
Dhar, 1305
Dharanindravarman II, c. 1155
Dharmapala, end of 8th c., c. 810
Dharmapala of Kotte, 1557-80
Dharmat, 1658
Dharmatunga (Vishnu), c. 775-82
Dharmavamca, c. 991-1007
Dhillika (Delhi), 736
Dhlo-Dhlo, Rhodesia, c. 1700
Dhu al-Nun al-Misri, 860

Dhu-Nuwas, *ante* 523-5
Dia Aliamen, c. 7th c.
Dia Kossoi of Kukia, c. 1009-10
*diadochi*, 323 BC
Diaghilev, Serge, 1872-1929
Diagne, Blaise, 1918
*Dialogus de scaccario*, 1178-9
Diamang Co., 1920
Diamond Jubilee of Queen Victoria, 1897
diamonds, *ante* 1700, 1727, 1869, 1931
*Diana*, Russian vessel, 1854
Diana (Artemis), 356 BC
Diarmait, High King of Ireland, 544-65
Dias, Bartholemeu, 1488
Dias, Ferreira, 1892
Díaz, Porfirio, 1830-1915
Díaz de Bivar, Rodrigo (El Cid), 1081
Dicey, Albert Venn, 1835-1922
Dickens, Charles, 1811-70
Dictatus Papae, 1075
Diderot, Dénis, 1713-84
Didier, Lombard king, 756-74
Didius Iulianus, 193
Diefenbaker, John George, 1895-1957
Dien Bien Phu, battle, 1954
Dien Nham, poetess, c. 1100
Dieppe, 1589, 1942
Dieppois, 1364
diet in China, c. 400-100 BC
dieticians, 994
Diet of Augsburg, 1500, 1530, 1548, 1555; Basle, 1433; Caslar, 1421; Constance, 1507; Copenhagen, 1660; Cremona, 1225; Forchheim, 1077; Frankfurt, 1257-73, 1344, 1427, 1558; Lublin, 1569; Mayence, 1184, 1235; Nuremburg, 1211, 1274, 1422, 1438, 1523; Oberlahnstein, 1400; Oldensee, 1527; Piotrkow, 1493; Prague, 1444; Pressburg, 1687; Roncaglia, 1158; Ratisbon, 1541, 1608, 1623, 1803; Skoplje, 1349; Spier, 1148; Spires, 1526, 1529; Västeras, 1527; Verona, 1184; Worms, 1495, 1521; Würzburg, 1165
Dig, India, 1804
Digambara sect, 2nd c.
Diggers' Republic, 1870
Dijon, 1513, 1630, 1788, 1814
Dilke, Sir Charles Wentworth, 1789-1865
Dillingen University, 1563
Dimas, cape, 1137
Dimitri, brother of Tsar Feodor, usurper, 1591-1606; second usurper, 1608
Dimitri of Kiev, 1075
Dimitri II of Moscow, 1359-80
Dimitrios, Patriarch, 1972
dimple-based pottery, c. 825 ± 150
*Din Ilahi*, 1582
Dinant, 1466, 1675
*dinar* (coin), 774
Dingaan, 1828-40
Dingiswayo, c. 1820
Dinis Dias, 1448
Dinshaway incident, 1906
Dio Cassius, c. 150-235
Dio Chrysostom, 30-117
Diocletian, 284-305, 313
Diodotos, c. 250 BC
Diodotos II, 230-227 BC
Diogenes, Cynic, 413-323 BC
Diogenes, Laertius, 2nd or 3rd c.
Diogenes, navigator, c. 41-54
Diogo I of Kongo, 1556
Dion of Syracuse, 357-354 BC
Dionysius, bp, 247-84
Dionysius of Halicarnassus, c. 40-30 BC
Dionysius of Fourna, 1670-c. 1745-6
Dionysius the Little, 1
Dionysius of Syracuse, 406-367 BC

Dionysius the Younger, 357-345 BC
Diori, Hamani, President of Niger, 1974
Dioscorides, 809-73, 951
Dioscorus, pope, 530
Dioscorus of Alexandria, 444-51
Diospolis, c. 1991-? c. 1786 BC
Dipa Negara of Jogyakarta, 1825-30
diptheria, anti-, serum, 1894
Diplomatic Intercourse and Immunities, 1961
diptychs, 1089
Directory in Paris, 1795, 1797, 1799
*dirham* (coin), 637, 695
Diriyah, 1818
Dis, 249 BC, 207 BC
disarmament, British Plan, 1933; Conferences, 1926, 1932, 1933, 1934, 1966, 1967; naval, 1921-2, 1927; talks, 1963
Disney, Walt, 1901-66
Disraeli, Benjamin, 1804-81
dissolution of monasteries, 1536, 1539, 1540, 1554
Diu, 1509, 1535, 1538
divine right of kings, 1599
diving bell, 1690
divorce, 331, 1533, 1816, 1857
Diwan Mulraj, 1848
Djibouti, 1869, 1966-8
Djidjelli, 1514
Djoser, Pharaoh, c. 2700 BC
Djougachvili, Joseph V. (Stalin), 1879-1953
Dnieper, R., 6th c., 7th c., 13th c., 1500, 1681, 1772; Valley, 2nd c. BC
Doab, 1258-9
Do-Bama Asi-ayon Confederation, 1935
Dobroie, 1708
Dorbruja, 660, 679
Dobson, Austin, 1840-1921
Docket Is., 1604
dock workers, 1877
Dodawa, 1826
Dodgson, C. L. (Lewis Carroll), 1832-98
Döffingen, 1388
Doge, Office of, 742
Doges, Palace of, 1578
Dogger Bank incident, 1904; battle, 1915
Dohnányi, Ernö von, 1887-1960
Dol, 1076
Dolabella, 24
Dolabella, P. Cornelius, 283 BC
Dolgorouki, Princes, 1726-30
dolichocephalic people, c. 1500-1100 BC
dollar, American, 1933, 1947, 1971
Dolfuss, Engelbert, 1892-1934
Döllinger, J. J. I., 1799-1890
Dom João (Dharmapala), 1557-80
Domazlice, 1431
Dome of the Rock, 687-91
*Domesday Book*, 1086
Domfront, 1048
Dominica, 1761, 1814, 1821, 1844, 1861-5, 1864-82, 1905-30, 1916-24, 1930-61, 1937, 1939, 1959, 1965; Republic, 1809
Dominican Order, 1216, 1217, 1250, 1278, 1360, 1587, 1588; in Mozambique, 1577
Dominican Republic, 1492
Dominions, British, 1926, 1947
Dominions Office, 1925
Domitian, 81-96
Domitius Alexander, 305
Don, basin, 1942, 1944; R., 4th c. BC, c. 370, c. 650, 1237-8, 1395
Don John of Austria, 1576-8
Don John of Austria, 1669-79
Don Pacifico, 1850
Donald I, King of Scots, 860-3
Donald II, King of Scots, 889-900
Donald Bane of Scotland, 1093-7

George III of Georgia, 1154-84
George VI of Georgia, 1401
George XII of Georgia, 1799
George I of Greece, 1913; as Prince of Greece, 1899
George II of Greece, 1922-47
George Louis of Hanover, 1698-1727
George of Podiebrad, 1448-71
Georgia, 330, 1054, 1063, 1219-23, c. 1225, 1238, 1386, 1400, 1403, 1722-3, 1799, 1800, 1803
Georgia, USA, c. 1650, 1663, 1732; State, 1733, 1734, 1774, 1779
Georgian Bay, 1610
Georgetown, Guyana, 1972
Gepids, c. 300, 567
Gerald of Kildare, 1477-1531
Gérard, François, 1770-1837
Gerard of Cremona, 1187
Gerard the Great, 1331
Gerbert, bp, 991-1003
Gerizim, Mt, c. early 4th c. BC
Germaine, Anne Louise, 1766-1817
German, Sir Edward, 1862-1936
German Army Act, 1911
German Centre (Catholic) Party, 1870
German Democratic Republic (East), 1949-53, 1960, 1970
German East Africa, 1885, 1886, 1891, 1894, 1896, 1897, 1905-7, 1906 12, c. 1909, 1915, 1916, 1917 see Tanganyika
German Evangelical Church, 1933
German Federal Republic (West), 1949-56 1970, 1973;
  relations with France, 1961, 1966; Holland, 1960, NATO, 1955, 1958; Poland, 1963, 1970; Turkey, 1960
German (language), 1932
German National Assembly, 1849
German Navy Acts, 1898, 1900, 1906, 1908
German Navy League, 1898
German South West Africa, 1907, 1914
German tribal laws, 802
Germanicus (Drusus), 9-23
German-Portuguese treaty, 1886
German-Russian agreement, 1911
Germans, c. 200 BC, c. 65-60 BCf, 8-7 BC, 9, post 100, post 150, 165
Germantown, Pa, 1683, 1739, 1777
Germanus, patriarch, 730
Germany, 4-5, c. 455, 741-52, 814, 843, 870, 953-5, 1063, 1077, 1109, 1189, 1191, 1222, 1242, 1332, 1338, 1411, 1423, 1431, 1451-2, 1650, 1690, 1732, 1803, 1846, 1863, 1871-6, 1881, 1883, 1890, 1902-5, 1918-21, 1926, 1927, 1931-5, 1938-49, 1954, 1970; S, 1449, 1524, 1531, 1741, 1852, 1867; W, 1114; Constitution, 1816; Diet, 1816, 1851, 1866; Parliament, 1850; partitioned, 1945; reunification plans, 1955; emigration, 1709; merchants, 1343; overseas possessions, 1919; struggle between Protestants and Catholics, 1557; Air Force, 1940; Army, 1522, 1695, 1887, 1893, 1913, 1916, 1941; Federation, 1848, 1849, 1863, 1866, 1870; National Association, 1859; Navy, 1853, 1897, 1914-18, 1937; Workers' Association, 1863; relations with Afghanistan, 1926; Africa, 1884, 1885, 1885-1911, 1892; Argentina, 1945; Austria, 1872, 1873, 1879, 1882, 1887, 1892, 1910, 1914, 1917, 1918, 1931, 1936, 1938; Britain, 1875, 1895, 1899, 1900, 1914-18, 1933, 1937, 1939; Canada, 1939; China, 1921, 1941; Czechoslovakia, 1939; Denmark, 1848, 1864, 1940; Egypt, 1945; France, 1674, 1688, 1693, 1870-3, 1914-18, 1921, 1923, 1939, 1940, 1944, 1950; Greece, 1916, 1941; Holland, 1940; Italy,

1882, 1887, 1888, 1914, 1916, 1939, 1940; Japan, 1895, 1914, 1919, 1936, 1940; Norway, 1940; Persia, 1924; Poland, 967-72, 1005, 1007, 1018, 1028, 1886, 1917, 1921, 1925, 1934, 1935, 1939; Portugal, 1916; Prussia, 1866, 1873; Rumania, 1893, 1914, 1917, 1918, 1940; Russia, 1872-5, 1887, 1894, 1905, 1907, 1914, 1917, 1918, 1921; Serbia, 1893, 1915; Spain, 1892, 1893, 1936; Sweden, 1710; Togoland, 1884; Turkey, 1888, 1895, 1903, 1910, 1914, 1941, 1944, 1945; US, 1899, 1917, 1921, 1939, 1941; USSR, 1939, 1941
Gerona, 785, 793, 1212
Gershwin, George, 1898-1937
Gerson, Jean C. de, 1363-1428
Gerstungen, peace, 1074
Gertrude of Hungary, 1213
Gesner, Konrad, 1565
Gesta Regum Francorum, post 727
Gestapo, German, 1942, 1960
Gesualdo, Carlo, 1560-1613
Geta, 211, 212
Getae, 291 BC
Gethsemane, 1919
Gettysburg, battle, 1863
Gex, 1601
Ghadr conspiracy, 1915
Ghali, Butros, of Egypt, 1910
Ghana, 2nd c., c. 790, ante 800, c. 990, 1062, 1077, 1087, c. 1200, 1203, 1240, 1325; (modern), 1949, 1957, 1958, 1962, 1964, 1966, 1971, 1972, 1975; Constituent assembly, 1969; Republic, 1960 see also Gold Coast
Ghangchun, 1905
Ghassan, c. 544
Ghassanids, 312 BC, c. 87-62 BC, 24 BC, 9 BC, 70-106, 529, 630-1
Ghaylan al-Dimashqi, 724-43
Ghazan, 1295
al-Ghazi, c. 1001, 1119
Ghazi I of Iraq, 1933-9
Ghazi Malik of Delhi, 1320
Ghazna, 977, 988/9, 991, 1019, 1148-1215, 1160, 1173, 1214, 1739, 1818, 1839
Ghaznavid dynasty, 976-1186; empire, 962
Ghaznavids, 1186
Ghent, 1338, 1382, 1534, 1539-40, 1576, 1678, 1792, 1794; treaty, 1814
Chibellines, Tuscan, 1260, 1275, 1301
Ghiberti, Lorenzo, 1378-1455
Ghilzai rebellion, 1801-2
Ghirlandaio, Domenico, 1449-94
Ghiyas al-Din, Bahmani Sultan, 1397
Ghiyas al-Din, Ulugh Khan, 1266-86
Ghiyas al-Din of Ghur, 1173-1203
Ghiyas al-Din of Malwa, 1469-1501
Ghiyas al-Din Tughluq Shah, 1320-5
Ghiyath al-Din of Herat, 1370-81
Ghorid dynasty, 1148-1215
Ghulam Qadir, 1787
Ghur, 1173
Ghuzz, 1153, 1160, 1185, 1204
Ghuzz Turks, c. 1000
Giannone, Pietro, 1676-1748
Gibeah, c. post 1020 BC
Gibbon, Edward, 1737-94
Gibbons, Grinling, 1648-1721
Gibbons, Orlando, 1583-1625
Gibbons vs. Ogden, 1824
Gibbs, James, 1674-1754
Gibraltar (Jabal al-Tariq), 711, 1310, 1333, 1340, 1462, 1502, 1601, 1704, 1713, 1721, 1725, 1727, 1739, 1779, 1780, 1785, 1943, 1967, 1969;
  relations with Spain, 1968
Gide, André P. G., 1869-1951

Gideon, c. 1150-c. 1100 BC
Gien, 1642
Giffard (airshops), 1852
Gijón, 1937
Gil, Portes, of Mexico, 1928
Gilbert, Sir Humphrey, 1539-83
Gilbert, William, 1544-1603
Gilbert, Sir W. S., 1836-1911
Gilbert of Ockham, 1329
Gilbert de la Porrée, 1148
Gilbertine Order, 1131
Gildas, ante 504-70
Gildon, c. 386-98
Gilead, c. 629-628 BC
Gill, Eric Rowland, 1882-1940
Gioberti, Vincenzo, 1801-52
Giolitti, Giovanni, 1892-1909
Giordani, Pietro, 1774-1848
Giotto di Bondone, c. 1267-1337
Gipps, Sir George, 1838-46
Giralda tower, Seville, 1184
Giraldo, Giovanni Battista, 1504-73
Giraldus Cambrensis, 1147-1220
Giraud, General, 1943-4
Giraudoux, Jean, 1882-1944
Giri, Varaha, president of India, 1969
Giric, king of Scots, 878-89
Girivraja, c. 642 or 600 BC
Girl Guide movement, 1909
Girondins, 1792, 1793
Girton College, Cambridge, 1869
Giscard d'Estaing, Valéry, 1974-
Giselle, d. of Charles the Simple, 911
Gissing, George, 1857-1830
Gisors, 1198; Affair of, 1109-13; Peace of, 1115, 1119; Treaty of, 1113
Giurgevo, 1595
Giusti, Giuseppe, 1809-50
Giza, pyramid, post 2580 BC
Gizah, 860
Gizikis, Phaidon, 1973
Gladstone, William Ewart, 1809-98
Glamorgan, 1093; treaty, 1645
Glanville, Ranulf de, 1180
Glarus, 1352
Glaser, Eduard, 1882-94
Glasgow, 573, c. 1115, 1571; University, 1451
Glasgow Missionary Society, 1796
glass industry, post 250; taxed, 1767
glass, perspex, 1930
glass manufacture in China, 5th c. BC; with lead, post c. 1500 BC; in Mesopotamia, ante 2000 BC
glass-blowing, 2nd-1st c. BC, post 50 BC, 1292
Glatz, 1742
Glauber, J. R., 1604-88
glazes, feldspar, ante 1000 BC
glazing of bricks and tiles, c. ante 1000 BC
Glen Grey Act in SA, 1894
Glencoe, 1692
Glendower (Owain Glyndwr), 1400-9
Glidden, Carlos, 1873
gliders, man-carrying, 1852
Glinka, Mikhail Ivanovitch, 1804-57
Gloucester, 878; Abbey, 1089, 1331, 1337, 1377, 1450; Duke of, 1397; Parliament, 1407; Statute of, 1278
Gloucester, Duke of, 1945-8
Gloucester, Humphrey, Duke of, 1422-47
Gloucester Hall, Oxford, 1289
Glubb, General, 1956
Gluck, Christoph Willibald, 1714-87
Glycerius, 473
Glyndwr, Owain, 1400-9
Gmünden, 1514
Gnam-ri Srong Btsan, c. 630
Gniesno, archbishopric, 1000
Gnyan-tsan, c. 461

Go Oc Eo, 1st–6th c.
Goa, 1351, 1440, 1472; under Portugal, 1510, 1517, 1542, 1557, 1560, 1570, 1572, 1579, 1600, 1603, 1607, 1614, 1615, 1639, 1649, 1683, 1686, 1752, 1759, 1820, 1835; part of India, 1961
Gobad, 1884
Gobelins, 1601, 1667
Gobi desert, 6th–7th c., 1211
Gobineau, Arthur, 1816–62
Gobir, c. 1715, 1781, 1803; kings of, c. 630
Goblet, René, 1886–7
Goddala, 1042
Godebeot, Richard, 1167
Godeheu, M., 1754
Goderich, Viscount, 1827–8
Gödesberg, 1938
*Godey's Lady's Book*, 1830
Godfrey of Bouillon, 1096–9
Go-Diago, 1331
Godless League, 1937
Gödöllö, 1849
Godomar, 524
Godoy, Manuel de, 1792–1806
Godunov, Boris, 1588–1605
Godwin, Earl of Wessex, 1051–3
Goering, Hermann, 1893–1946
Goethe, Johann Wolfgang von, 1749–1832
Gogh, Vincent Willem van, 1853–90
Gogol, Nicolai, 1809–52
Gojemasu of Kano, 1095–1130
Gojjam, 1840, 1853, 1882
Gok Turks (Tu-chueh), 546
Gokcha, 1825
Gokhale, G. K., 1912–15
Gokomere culture, 530 ± 120–840 ± 100
Golab Singh, 1846
Golan Heights, 1973
Golconda, 1518, 1543, 1564, 1589, 1590, 1635–6, 1647, 1656, 1676, 1685, 1687
gold, c. *post* 600 BC, 5th c. BC, c. 450 BC, 4th c. BC, 1st–6th c., c. 200, c. 300–400, c. 734–50, 742, *ante* 800, c. 11th c., c. 1120, 14th–15th c., 1360, 15th c., 16th c., 1699, 18th c., 1841, 1851, 1894, 1922; booms, *post* 1515, 1693, 1848–9, 1856, 1863, 1893, 1896; diggers, 1854; free market, 1948; mines, 854, 16th c.; trade, 1440, *post* 1531–1650; standard, 1816, 1900, 1914, 1925, 1931, 1933
Gold Coast, c. 1400, 1595, 1657, 1737–41, 1821, 1835, 1850, 1872, 1879, 1897, 1946–50, 1954–7; British, 1828–43, 1843, 1850, 1852, 1901 *see also* Ghana
Gold Rush, 1859
'Golden Act' in Scotland, 1592
Golden Bull, 1356
Golden Fleece, Order, 1429
Golden Hill, battle, 1770
*Golden Hind*, 1577–80
Golden Horde, 1227
Golden Jubilee of Queen Victoria, 1887
Golden Temple, Amritsar, 1577
Goldie, Sir George, 1879
Goldoni, Carlo, 1707–93
Goldsmith, Oliver, 1728–74
Goldwater, Barry, 1909–
Golitsyn, Prince, premier, 1916
Golitsyne, Prince Vassili, 1682–6
Göllheim, battle, 1298
Goltz, von der, 1882
Gomba, c. 1770
Gomes, General Costa, President of Portugal, 1974
Gomes, Manuel Teixeira, 1923–5
Gómez, José Miguel, of Cuba, 1909–13
Gómez, Juan Vicente, 1857–1935
Gommiani, Francesco, 1687–1762
Gompers, Samuel, 1881

Gonçalves, Col. Vasco, President of Portugal, 1974
Concourt, Edmond de, 1822–96
Goncourt, Jules de, 1822–70
Gondar, c. 1633, 1667–82, 1704, 1838, c. 1847, 1887, 1941
Condeband, 501
Gondi, Jean François Paul de, 1614–78
Gondokoro, 1863, 1867, 1871
Gondophernes, c. 20–48, c. 48
Gonfaloniere, Florence, 1421–9, 1429–33, 1434–64, 1464–91, 1502–12, 1512–13, 1513–16, 1516–19, 1519–23
Gonja, Ghana, c. 1200
Conzaga, Louis, 1328
Gonzaga dynasty of Mantua, 1328
González, Fernán, 970
González, Manuel, of Mexico, 1880–4
González, Súarez, 1976
Good Hope, Cape of, 1488, 1497
'Good Neighbour' policy of US, 1933
Goodman, Lord, 1968
Goonetilleke, Sir Oliver, 1954–62
Gopala, 8th c., c. 750, end of 8th c.
Gopallawa, W., 1962
Gordian I, 235–8
Gordian II, 238
Gordian III, 238–44
Gordon, Adam Lindsay, 1833–70
Gordon, Charles George, general, 1874–85
Gordon Memorial College, 1902
Gordon riots, 1780
Gore, Charles, bp, 1853–1932
Gorée, 1621, 1692, 1783, 1880
Goremykin, Russian Prime Minister, 1906
Gorgias of Sicily, *post* 450–392 BC
Gorizia, 1500
Gorki, Maxim, 1868–1936
Gorm of Denmark, 900–35
Gorton, J. G., 1968
Gosford, Earl of, 1835–8
*Gospel* of St John, c. 95
*Gospel* of St Luke, c. 80
*Gospel* of St Mark, c. 65
*Gospel* of St Matthew, c. 85
Gospels translated, c. 362
Gosse, Sir Edmund William, 1849–1928
Gotarzes, 40–46
Götenburg, 1619
Gotha, 1526
'Gothic' arch, 861
Gothic kingdom, 9
Gothland, 1564
Goths, c. 150, c. 200, 213–14, 256, 269–70, 332, 386, 392, 451, 470–90; in Balkans, c. 220, 258, 263, 377; Italy, 535, 537–8, 552, 555
Gottfried, c. 700
Göttingen, 1762; University, 1737
Gough, Hugh, Viscount, 1841, 1849
Gouin, Félix, 1946
Goulart, president of Brazil, 1961–4
Gounaris, prime minister of Greece, 1915
Gounod, Charles François, 1818–93
Gouveia, Fr, 1563
*Gouvernement Provisoire de la République Française*, 1944
'Government' chiefs in Rwanda, 1911
Government of India Act, 1858, 1921, 1935
Government of Ireland Act, 1920
Governor of the South, 1571
Governor-General of Australia, 1850
Govind Singh, Sikh, 1675–1708
Govinda III, 783–814
Govindachandra, c. 1100–60
Gowa, Prince of, 1605
Gower, John, poet, c. 1325–1408
Gowon, Yakubu, general, President of Nigeria, 1934

Gowrie, Lord, 1936–44
Gowrie Conspiracy, 1600
Goya y Lucientes, F. José de, 1746–1828
Gozzi, Carlo, Count, 1720–1806
Gozzi, Gasparo, Count, 1713–86
'Graces' toleration, 1627
*Graf Zeppelin*, 1929
Grafton, Duke of, 1767–70
Graham, Billy, 1918–
Grahame, Kenneth, 1859–1932
Grahi, 1230–70
Grahovo, battle, 1858
Grailly, Jean de, 1364
Grama of Lan Na, c. 1315
Grammar Schools Act, 1840
Grammos, 1948, 1949
Gran Chaco, 1938
Gran Colombia, Republic, 1819
Granada, 1012–90, 1090, 1144, 1246, 1319, 1481, 1490, 1491, 1523, 1531, 1568; Christian kingdom, 1238; Nasrid dynasty, 1232–1492; treaty, 1500
Granada, W. I., 1974
Granadine Confederation, 1858–61, 1861
Granados, Enrique, 1868–1916
Grand Alliance, 1689, 1690, 1696
Grand Army, 1805
Grand Jury, 1166
'Grand Ministry' in France, 1881
Grand Pensionary of Holland, 1620
Grand Pré, 1755
Grand Remonstrance, 1641
Grand Trunk Railway, 1919
Grand Trunk Road in India, 1839
Grande-Chartreuse, 1084
Grandidier, Alfred, 1836–1921
Grand-Masterships in Spain, 1487–94
Grandson, 1476
Grange (Patrons of Husbandry), 1866
Granica, battle, 334 BC
Grant, James Augustus, 1827–92
Grant, Ulysses S., US president, 1869–77
Granville, Earl, 1815–91
Granville Town, 1787
Granville-Barker, Harley, 1877–1946
graphite pencil, 1565
Gratian, emperor, 367–83
Gratianus, John, 1045
Grattan, Henry, 1775
Gratz, agreement, 1616
Graupner, Christoph, 1683–1760
Gravel Pits Lead, Ballarat, 1853
Gravelines, 1520, 1558, 1658
gravity, law of, 1682
Gray, Capt. Robert, 1792
Gray, Thomas, 1716–91
Graz, 1449–62
Great Ardra, 1698, 1724
'Great Army' of Danes, 865, 869
Great Australian Bight, 1840
Great Barrier Reef, 1770
'Great Black War', 1826
Great Britain *see* Britain and British
Great Charter, 1682
Great Comneni, dynasty, 1204
Great Council, 1258
*Great Eastern*, 1866
'Great Emigration', 1843
Great Exhibition, 1851
Great Famine in Ireland, 1845–8
Great Fire of London, 1666
Great Khan, 1229–59
Great Lakes, 1610–13, 1817, 1954
Great Latin War, 340 BC
Great Mosque of Shiraz, 875
Great Plague in London, 1665
Great St Bernard, 1035–89

Haakon IV of Norway, 1217-63
Haakon V of Norway, 1299-1319
Haakon VII of Norway, 1905-57
Haarlem, 1573
Habashat, Yemeni Arab tribe, c. 550
Habakkuk, prophet, c. 650-627 BC
Habe Kings of Katsina, c. 1100
*Habeas Corpus* in England, 1433, 1679, 1696, 1715, 1722; Ireland, 1866, 1881; Quebec, 1784
Habib b. Abi Ubaida, c. 734-50
Habiballah, brigand, 1929
Habiballah Khan of Afghanistan, 1901-19
Habyalimane, Juvenal, general, 1973
Hadden Rig, 1542
Hadeland, 994
Hadendowa, 1831-2
Hadhramaut, 1st c. BC, c. 300; Kingdom, c. 450 BC-c. AD 100
al-Hadi, caliph, 785-6
*Hadiqat al-Akhbar*, 1858
*hadith*, 810-70
Hadley, James, 1731
Hadrian, 117-38
Hadrian's wall, 122-7, 193, late 2nd c., 205, 208, 367
haemophilia, 1904
Hafioum-Kara-Hissar, 1922
al-Hafiz, 1130-49
Hafiz, Persian poet, c. 1320-9
Hafsid dynasty of Tunis, 1228-1574, 1270, 1520, 1540
Haggai, prophet, 520 BC
Haggard, Sir Henry Rider, 1856-1925
Hagia Triada, c. 1900 BC, c. 1400 BC
Hague, 1759-60, 1795; agreement, 1698; alliance, 1710; Conferences, 1899, 1907, 1922, 1929, 1930; Congress, 1684; Convention on Territorial Waters, 1883; Court, 1922, 1951; treaties, 1625, 1659, 1668, 1678, 1701, 1794; Royal library, 1734-8
Haguenau, 1814; treaty, 1330
Haidar Ali of Mysore, 1763-82
Haifa, 1100, 1250-4, 1948, 1969
Haig, Douglas, Earl, 1861-1928
Haile Selassie I of Ethiopia, 1930-75 *see also* Ras Tafari
Hainan, 1939
Hainault, 1345, 1424, 1428
Haiphong, 1867
Hairun, Sultan of Ternate, 1564-70
Haiti, WI, 1492, 1510, 1801, 1804, 1806, 1814, 1816, 1820, 1822, 1825, 1839, 1843, 1908-15, 1915, 1937, 1949, 1956, 1959; N, 1808-20; S, 1808-18, 1818; Spanish, 1821
*hajib* (court chamberlain), 976
Hajipur, 1574
Haj Amin al-Husaini, 1897-1974
al-Hajj Omar, 1854-64
al-Hajjaj, 692-712
al-Hajjaj b. Yusuf, 689
al-Hajjaj b. Yusuf b. Matar, 786-833
Hajji Khalfah, 1658
al-Hakam I, amir, 796-822
al-Hakam II, caliph, 961-76
al-Hakim, caliph, 1005-21
al-Hakim, Mosque of, 990-1012
Hakluyt, Richard, c. 1552-1616
Hakodate, Japan, 1854, 1855, 1857
Halberstadt, 1622
Haldane, Richard B., Lord, 1912
Haldimand, Lt-Gen. F., 1778-91
Hale, Sir Matthew, 1609-76
Halévy, Elie, 1870-1937
Halévy, Joseph, 1869-70
Haliartos, 395 BC
Halibut Fisheries Treaty, 1923

Halicarnassus, c. 484-429 BC, 333 BC
Halidon Hill, 1333
Halifax, George Savile, Marquess of, 1679
Halifax, Charles Montagu, Earl, 1714
Halifax, 2nd Viscount, 1839-1934
Halifax, Nova Scotia, 1749
Halingyi, 1st c. (or *ante*) BC
Hall, Swabia, 1230
al-Hallaj, 922
Hallam, Henry, 1777-1859
Halle, 1806; University, 1694
Halley, Edmund, 1693
Hallstatt culture, c. 900-700 BC
Hals, Frans, 1580-1666
Halys, R., 585 BC, 546 BC
Ham, fortress, 1846
Hama, 1130, 1400
Hamadan, 1387, 1630, 1724, 1732, 1916
Hamadhan, 1037
Hamah, 1260, 1273-1332, c. 1296
Hamath, 858-824 BC
Hamburg, c. 811, 831, 888, 1813, 1849; Bank of, 1619; treaty, 1638
Hamdanids, 944, 947-67, 961
Hamdan Qarmat, c. 890
Hamdillahi, 1863
Hamel, 1918
Hamilcar, 311 BC
Hamilcar, son of Hanno, c. 480 BC
Hamilcar Barca, 247-230 BC
Hamilton, Alexander, 1757-1804
Hamilton Harty, Sir H., *see* Harty
Hamilton, William, 1788-1856
Hammadids, 1007-52
al-Hammah, 1482
Hammarskjöld, Dag, 1905-61
Hammer-Purgstall, Josef von, 1774-1856
Hammond, John, 1872-1949
Hammudid dynasty, 1025
Hammurabi, c. 1792-1750 BC, ?c. 1690 BC
Hampden, John, 1636-43
Hampton Court, 1647; conference, 1604; treaty, 1562
Hamud, Sayyid, Sultan of Zanzibar, 1895
Hamzah al-Isfahani, c. 961
*Hamziya*, Swahili poem, 1652
Han dynasty, 206 BC-AD 220; Later, 24-220, 947-50; states, c. 200 BC, 160-140 BC, 133-119 BC, 108 BC, 58 BC, 1 BC, 73, 78
Han Fei Tzu, c. 233 BC
Han Kan, artist, c. 600-50
Han Yu, essayist, 768-825
Hanau, battle, 1813
Handel, George Frederick, 1685-1759
Handl, Jakob, 1550-91
Hangchow, 1126, 1276
Hangoud, naval battle, 1714
Hanifite school of jurisprudence, 767
Hankow, 555-87, 1852, 1926, 1938
Hannak, 1520
Hannibal, 247-183 BC
Hanno, c. 470 BC
Hanoi, c. 150, 1258, 1287, 1371, 1697, 1700, 1867, 1873, 1946, 1951, 1954, 1966
Hanover, 1692, 1715, 1719, 1755, 1757, 1803, 1806, 1837, 1849, 1851, 1853, 1855, 1866
Hanoverian dynasty, 1714
Hans II of Denmark and Norway, 1481-1513
Hanse confederation (Hanseatic League), 1367, 1370, 1392, 1432, 1438-41, 1441, 1451-7, 1474, 1487, 1494, 1498, 1534, 1535, 1859
Hanseatic market, 1252; merchants, 1347; towns, 1362
Hanthawaddy, 1287-1539; under Burma, 1539-50; under Burmese Toungoo dynasty, 1551-1740
*Hanukkah*, feast, 164 BC

Hao, Chou capital, c. 770 BC
Hapsburgs, 1324, 1330, 1335, 1364, 1415, 1438-1806, 1491, 1516, 1551, 1617, 1687, 1919
Haqq al-Din of Ifat, c. 1325-86
Har Dayal, 1915
Hara castle, 1637, 1638
Haradatta, Raja of Baran, 1018
*hara-kiri*, 1185
Harald II of Denmark, 814-27
Harald Hardrada, c. *post* 1035, 1047-66
Harald Harfager, c. 866-72
*haram* of Mecca, 630
Harappan Culture, c. 3000-c. 1500 BC, c. 1700 BC
Harar, 1520, 1559, 1567, 1569, 1577, 1647, 1875, 1880, 1886, 1887, 1894
Harbin, 1898
Harcourt, Sir Henry Vernon, 1894
Harcourt, Robert, 1609-27
Hardar Ali, 1781
Hardicanute, 1040-2
Hardie, Keir, 1856-1915
Harding, Warren G., US president, 1865-1923
Hardinge, Sir Henry, 1844-8
Hardinge, Lord, 1910-12
Hardy, Thomas, 1840-1928
hardwood, c. 969-936 BC
Haremhab, Pharaoh, c. 1335-? c. 1308 BC
Harfleur, 1120, 1415
Hargobind, Sikh, 1606-45
Hargreaves, James, 1765
Harihara I of Vijayanagar, 1336-1354/5
Harihara II, 1377-1404
*harim*, 1595-1603
Harim, 1158, 1164, 1260
Harington, Sir John, 1597
Haripunjaya (Lamphun), 8th c., 1001-11
al-Harith II b. Jabalah, 529-69
al-Harith (Aretas III), c. 87-62 BC
Harith b. Suraj, 734
Harithath IV (Aretas IV), 9 BC-AD 40
Harivarman I, 802-9
Harivarman IV, 1074-81
Harlech, 1284
Harlem, New York, 1964
Harley, Robert, 1704-11
Harmsworth, Alfred, Viscount, 1865-1922
Harold, Earl of East Anglia, 1053
Harold, Earl of Orkney, 1196
Harold, Earl of Wessex, 1045-65; as King of England, 1066
Harold Bluetooth of Denmark, 936-86
Harold I of England, 1035-40
Harold II of England, 1066
Harold Fair Hair, 863-933
Harpalus, 324 BC
Harper's Ferry, 1859
Harran, 616 BC, 607, 1104
Harris, Townsend, US consul, 1856
Harrison, Benjamin, US president, 1889-93
Harrison, William Henry, US president, 1841
Harsha, c. 606-47
Harsha of Kashmir, 1089-1111
Harshavarman I, 912-c. 922
Harshavarman III, 1066
Harsiyotef, 404-369 BC
Hartford, 1639
Harty, Sir Herbert Hamilton, 1879-1941
Harun of Egypt, 896-904
Harun b. al-Mahdi, 782
Harun al-Rashid, caliph, 786-c. 830
Harvard College, 1636; as University, 1869, 1947
harvest failure in Britain, 1313, 1830, 1879; Russia, 1920 and 1921
Harvey, William, 1578-1651

al-Hasa, c. 887
al-Hasan, Bahri Mamluk Sultan, 1347-1361
Hasan Agha, 1536
al-Hasan b. Ahmad al-Hamdani, 945
al-Hasan b. Ahmad of Malindi, c. 1598
al-Hasan b. Ali b. Abi al-Husayn al-Kalbi, 948-65
al-Hasan b. Ali, Zairite, 1135
Hasan al-Bakr, general, 1968
Hasan al-Banna, 1929
al-Hasan b. Caliph Ali, 661, c. 669, 785
al-Hasan of Mombasa, 1614-15
Hasan II of Morocco, 1961-72
Hasan b. al-Numan al-Ghassani, 693-700
al-Hasan b. al-Sabbah, 1090-1124
al-Hasan b. Sulaiman II, c. 1191-1215
al-Hasan b. Talut, c. 1277-94
Hasan b. Thabit, poet, 563
Hasan Pasha, 1544-52
Hasdrubal, 228-207 BC
hashshashun, see Assassins
Hashepsowe, Pharaoh, c. 1490-c. 1468 BC
Hastenbeck, battle, 1757
Hastings, battle, 1066
Hastings, Lady Flora, 1839
Hastings, Warren, 1772-1818
Hatch Act, US, 1887, 1939
Hatfield Chase, battle, 632
Hatim al-Tai, c. 605
Hatra, 241
Hatshepsut, Queen, c. 1500 BC
Hatt-i-humaioun, 1856
Hattusilis II, 1275-1250 BC
Hauran, 542-570
Hausa, c. 1200
Hausa dynasty of Daura, c. 900-1911
Hausaland, c. 1067
Haussman, Georges Eugène, baron, 1809-91
Haut-Sénégal-Niger, 1904
Havana, 1762, 1829, 1898, 1959; Company, 1740; Conference, 1940; Province, 1897
Havelock, General Sir Henry, 1857
Hawaii, 1778, 1893, 1898, 1959
Hawker, Robert Stephen, 1803-75
Hawkins, Sir Anthony Hope, 1863-1933
Hawkins, Sir John, 1562-7
Hawkins, William, 1530
Hawkins, Capt. William, 1608
Hawksmoor, Nicholas, 1661-1763
Hawley-Smoot tariff, 1932
Hawthorne, Nathaniel, 1804-68
Hay, Ian, see Beith
Haya de la Torre, 1962
Haydn, Franz Josef, 1732-1809
Hayes, Rutherford B., US president, 1877-81
Hayles, abbey, 1246, 1270
Hay-Pounceforte treaty, 1901
Hayter, bp, 1755
Hazlitt, William, 1778-1830
al-Hazm, fort, early 18th c.
Head, Sir Edmund W., 1854-61
Healey, Denis, 1976
heart transplants, 1967
hearth tax, 1793
Heath, Edward, 1916-
Heath Robinson, 1872-1944
'Heavenly Khan', 629-30
Heber, Reginald, bp, 1783-1826
Hébertists, 1794
Hebrew alphabet, c. 1010 BC; language, 4th c. BC; scriptures, c. 250 BC
Hebrews in Egypt, c. 1500-c. 1250 BC
Hebrides, 820, 1098-1103, 1263
Hecataeus, 510 BC
Hecatomnos, 356 BC
Hedley, William, 1813
Hedvig of Poland, 1384-6

Heemskerck, 1642
Heenan, John Carmel, Cardinal, 1963-75
Hegel, Georg Wilhelm Friedrich, 1770-1831
Hehe, 1897-8
Heian period in Japan, 794-1185
Heian-kyo (Miyako, Kyoto), 794
Heidelberg, 1688; University, 1386
Heights of Abraham, 1759
Heilbronn, League of, 1633, 1635
Heimwehr, Fascist, 1931
Heine, Heinrich, 1799-1856
Heinemann, Dr Gustav, 1969
Heinsius, Anthony, 1679-1720
Hejazi, Dr Abd al-Aziz, 1974
Helen of Adiabene, c. 43
Helena, empress, 327
Helena, empress, 913-59
Heligoland, 1890
Heliocles, c. 140-130 BC
helium, 1897
Hellenes, c. 480 BC
Hellenization of the Jews, 175 BC
heller, 1230
Hellespont, c. 514-512 BC, 498 BCff, 411 BC, 387 BC, 337 BCf
helmets, iron, 1390-1410
Héloise, 1101-64
Helsingborg, 1362
Helsingfors, 1713 see also Helsinki
Helsinki (formerly Helsingfors), 1550, 1918, 1975
Helvetian Confessions, 1536, 1566
Helvetic Republic, 1798; relations with France, 1798
Helvetii, c. 65-60 BCf
Helvétius, Claude Adrian, 1715-71
Helvidius Priscus, 75
Hemachandra, 1089-1173
Hemu, usurper of Delhi, 1556
Hendon Police College, 1934
Hengist, c. 450-88
Henle, Peter, 1509
Henoticon, 482, 484
Henri de Hainault, 1208
Henrietta Maria of France, 1625
Henrique, son of Afonso I of Kongo, 1521
Henrique of Portugal (Cardinal Henry), 1578-80
Henry, Colonel, 1898
Henry, Prince of Asturias, 1386
Henry, Prince of Wales, 1612
Henry, Count of Burgundy, 1095
Henry I, emperor, 919-36
Henry II, emperor, 1002-24
Henry III, emperor, 1037-56
Henry IV, emperor, 1056-1106
Henry V, emperor, 1099-1125
Henry VI, emperor, 1186-97
Henry, Prince, Duke of Normandy, 1170-83
Henry VII, King of Romans, 1220-35
Henry of Bavaria, 1278
Henry the Bearded of Silesia, 1231-8
Henry of Blois, ? 1101-71
Henry of Carinthia, 1307-10
Henry III of Castile and León, 1390-1406
Henry IV of Castile, 1454-74
Henry II of Cyprus, 1286
Henry I of England, 1091-1135
Henry II of England, 1151-89
Henry III of England, 1216-72
Henry IV of England, 1399-1413
Henry V of England, 1411-22
Henry VI of England, 1422-71
Henry VII of England, 1485-1509
Henry VIII of England, 1509-47
Henry of Flanders, 1205-16
Henry I of France, 1031-60

Henry II of France, 1551-9
Henry III of France, 1573-89
Henry IV of France and Navarre, 1580-1610
Henry of Guise, 1585-8
Henry Jasimirgott, 1142
Henry of Lancaster, 1346-92
Henry the Lion, 1139-95
Henry VII of Luxembourg, 1308-13
Henry the Navigator, 1394-1460
Henry the Pious of Poland, 1238-41
Henry the Proud of Saxony, 1126-39
Henry the Quarrelsome, 984
Henry of Trastamare, 1365-79
Henty, George Alfred, 1832-1902
Hepburn Act in US, 1906
Heraclea, 280 BC, 806
Heracleonas, 641
Heraclian dynasty, 610-711
Heraclitus, philosopher, c. 540-475 BC
Heraclius, 610-41
Heraclius, patriarch, 1185
Herat, 540, 652, 874, 1148-1215, 1245-1389, 1265, 1351, 1381, 1407, 1452-7, 1457, 1530, 1597, 1727, 1750, 1816, 1818, 1837, 1838, 1856, 1863, 1871
Herbert, George, 1593-1633
Herbert of Cherbury, Edward, Lord, 1583-1648
Herbert de Vermandcis, 927-35
herbs, medicinal, 951
Herculano de Cavalho, A., 1810-77
Herculanum, 79; excavated, 1706
Herder, Johann Gottfried von, 1744-1803
Heredia, José Maria de, 1842-1905
Hereford, 1217
Herefordshire, 1055
Herero, rising of, 1904-8
heresy, legislation against, 1220-38
heretical gatherings, 331; worship, 383
heretics, burning of, 1751
Hereward the Wake, 1070
Hermaeum, cape, 255
Herman of Luxembourg, 1081-8
Hermas, c. 140
Hermenigild, 580-5
hermits, 1637
Hermits of St Augustine, Order, 1256
Hernici, c. 360 BC, 311 BC
Hero of Alexandria, 1st c.
Herod, King of Judaea, 40-4 BC
Herod Antipas, 6
Herod Archelaus, 4 BC, 6
Herodes Atticus, 160
Herodotus, historian, c. 484-429 BC
Herophilos, physician, 285 BC
Héroult, scientist, 1886
Herrenhausen, treaty, 1725, 1727
Herrama, Dr Tiede, 1975
Herrera, José Joaquín, 1844-51
Herrick, Robert, 1591-1674
Herriot, Edouard, 1924-32
Herschel, Sir William, 1738-1822
Herschel, Sir John Frederick William, 1792-1871
Herter, Christian Archibald, 1895-
Hertling, Count von, 1917
Hertz, Heinrich, 1857-94
Hertzog, James B. M., 1924-39
Heruli, 267
Herzogovina, 1465-6, 1875, 1878, 1908
Herzl, Theodor, 1860-1904
Heseltine, Philip (Warlock, Peter), 1894-1930
Hesiod, poet, c. 750 BC
Hess, Rudolph, 1894-1941
Hesse, 719, 1526, 1532, 1866
Hesse-Cassel, 1806, 1850
Hesse-Darmstadt, 1828

Jaoli, Raja, 1655
Japan, 660 BC, 6th c. BC, 1st c., mid 6th c.,
645, early 8th c., 12th c., 1267, 1274, 1281,
1387, 1393, 15th c., 1534-82, 1542, c. 1578,
1582-90, 1638, 1855, 1862, 1870, 1890, 1899,
1904-5, 1911, 1918, 1925, 1930-6,
1940-5, 1951, 1956, 1957; constitution, 1881,
1889; administration, 1192; Cabinet and
Privy Council, 1885; Emperor, 1945, 1946,
1964; internal affairs, 1900, 1927, 1946;
military affairs, 1900, 1936; navy, 1914,
1941, 1944, 1945; world trade, 1868-97,
1914; Christianity in, 1560, 1587, 1597, 1612,
1614, 1616, 1873; Heiau period, 794-1185;
Minamoto period, 1185; myths, 8th c.
relations with Argentina, 1944; Britain, 1854,
1858, 1863, 1921, 1922; Burma, 1942-5;
Ceylon, 1941; China, 1598, 1638, 1869, 1894,
1895, 1914, 1922, 1928-32, 1936-40;
England, 1613, 1623, 1673, 1846, 1858;
France, 1858, 1863, 1895, 1921; Germany,
1895, 1914, 1919, 1936, 1940; Italy, 1940;
Java, 1942; Korea, 1592-8, 1597, 1598, 1876,
1885, 1894, 1904-5, 1907-10; Korea S, 1065;
Malaya, post 1918; Netherlands, 1616, 1638,
1863; Portuguese traders, 1639; Russia and
USSR, 1852, 1858, 1875, 1895, 1901, 1904-5,
1905, 1918, 1925, 1938-41, 1944, 1945; Siam,
1940; Turkey, 1945; USA, 1853-8, 1863,
1922, 1924, 1941-7, 1952, 1954, 1960, 1969,
1972
Japara, 1511, 1574; Queen of, 1550
*Jardin de Plantes*, Paris, 1790
Jarnac, 1569
Jaroslav, Grand Duke of Kiev, 1018-54
Jarring, Dr, of UN, 1971
Jarrow, monastery, 794
Jars, Plain of, Laos, 1963
Jask, Persia, 1620
Jason, 372-370 BC
Jaswant Rao Holkar of Indore, 1800-11
Jaswant Singh of Marwar, 1678
Jat peasants, 1669, 1681, 1688
*Jatakas*, 300 BC
Jats, 1027
Jatt (or Zott), rebellion, 834
al-Jauf, 554 BC
Jaunpur, 1394, 1398, 1399, 1494, 1538
Jaurès, Jean, 1859-1914
Java, c. 78, 5th c., c. 420, 640, c. 671-92, c.
732-c. 822, 750-832, 774, c. 780-800, 802,
1811, 1874, 1908, 1927, 1937; coffee, 1696,
1720; sugar, 1870-80; Dutch, 1595, 1755,
1816; English, 1811; new kingdom, 1222,
1275, 1293, 1309-27, 1322, 1331-51, 1350;
fleet, 1573, 1574; literature, c. 991-1007;
princes, 1813; wars of succession, 1704-8,
1717-23, 1749-55, 1755
Java E, kingdom, c. 929, c. 990, 992, 1006,
1010, 1019, 1042, c. 1178, 1331-51;
relations with China, 614; Japan, 1942
Java N, c. 1680
Java Man, 1937
Javakas, 1247, 1263
Jawhar al-Siqilli, general, 969
Jaworow, 1675
Jaxartes provinces, 713-5
Jaxartes, R., 329 BC
Jay, John, 1794
Jaya Harivarman I, 1149
Jaya Indravarman II, 1081-1113
Jaya Indravarman IV, 1166-7
Jaya Indravarman V, 1190
Jaya Paramesvaravarman, 1226-c. 1252
Jayabhaya of Kadiri, 1135-60
Jayadeva, *post* 1100
Jayadevi, *post* 681
Jayakatwang, 1293
Jayanagara, c. 1295-1328

Jayapala, Shahiya ruler, 1000
Jayavarman I of Cambodia, 635-*post* 681
Jayavarman II of Cambodia, 802-50
Jayavarman III of Cambodia, 850-77
Jayavarman IV of Cambodia, c. 928-41
Jayavarman V of Cambodia, 968-1001
Jayavarman VI of Cambodia, 1080-1112
Jayavarman VII of Cambodia, 1181-c. 1218
Jayavarman of Funan, 478-514
Jayaviravarman, c. 1003-6
Jaysh of Egypt, 895-6
al-Jazair Bani Mazranna, c. 950
Jazar, Amir of Lebanon, 1775-1804
jazz in USA, 1916
Jeanne I of Naples, 1343-82
Jeanne II of Naples, 1414-35
Jeanne de Navarre, 1284
Jeanneret, Charles Edward, 1887-1965
Jeans, Sir James, 1877-1946
Jebel Druze see Jabal al-Duruz
Jebel Nefusa, 1209
Jebusites, c. *post* 1000 BC
Jedburgh Abbey, 1118
Jeddah, 1924
Jefferies, Richard, 1848-87
Jefferson, Thomas, 1743-1826
Jeffreys, Chief Justice, 1685
Jehoahaz, King of Israel, c. 815-801 BC
Jehoahaz, King of Judah, c. 609 BC
Jehoash, 801-786 BC
Jehoiakim, c. 609-598 BC
Jehoiachin, c. 597 BC
Jehoram, King of Israel, c. 849-842 BC
Jehoram, King of Judah, c. 849-842 BC
Jehosaphat, 873-849 BC
Jehovah's Witnesses in USA, 1874
Jehu, c. 842-815 BC
Jelal al-Din, Khwarazmshah, 1220-31
Jem, brother of Bayazid II, 1481
Jemappes, 1792
Jemdet-Nasr culture, c. 2800-2500 BC
Jen Tsung (Chia Ching), emperor, 1796-1821
Jéna, 1806; University, 1558
Jenisseisk, Siberia, 1618
Jenkinson, Anthony, 1559-63
Jenne, 14th-15th, 1471-7, c. 1650
Jenner, Edward, 1749-1823
Jerba, 1153
Jeremiah, prophet, c. 642-587 BC
Jericho, 747, 1918, 1952
Jerma oasis, 19 BC
Jeroboam I, c. 922-901 BC
Jeroboam II, c. 786-746 BC
Jerome, Jerome Klapka, 1859-1927
Jerome of Prague, 1416
Jerusalem, c. *post* 1000 BC, c. 800-783 BC, c.
*ante* 701 BC, c. 688 BC, c. 604 BC, c. 597
BC, 169 BC, 4 BC, 40, c. 43, 66, 131, 327,
614, 638, 1100, 1158, 1672, 1827, 1917, 1919,
1928, 1949, 1951, 1960; besieged, c. 589-568
BC, 63 BC; retaken, 445-433 BC, 37 BC;
Citadel, 1532; Crown of, 1277; Holy Places,
327; Old City, 1948; under Crusaders, 1099,
1229; Fatimids, 1098; Saladin, 1187; Turks,
1070, 1244; Wilhelm II, 1897; Arab
determination to liberate, 1974
Jesu, Thomas de, 1613
Jesuit Colleges, 1548, 1550, 1556, 1559;
missionaries, 1534-82; c. 1560, 1561, 1574,
1583, 1588, 1590-2, 1595, 1605, 1623-69,
1624, 1625, 1628; schools, 1565; University,
1559, 1759
Jesuits (Society of Jesus), 1534, 1542, 1588,
1601, 1615, 1640; females, 1609, 1630; in
Canada, 1800, 1824, 1888; attacked, 1656,
1741, 1750-3, 1762, 1879, 1880; banned,
1551, 1594; expelled, 1759, 1760, 1767, 1847,
1872; restored, 1814, 1836, 1904; suppressed,
1773, 1856, 1932

Jesus Christ, 4 BC-AD 30 or 33
'jet' engine, 1937
Jevons, William Stanley, 1835-82
jewellery, 3rd to 1st c. BC
Jewish Agency, 1920
Jewish Disabilities Act, 1858; Law, 167 BC, c.
47; National Fund, 1901; scriptures, 167 BC
Jews, c. 595/4 BC, 587-538 BC, *post* 437 BC,
410 BC, 198 BC, 150-129 BC, 47 BC, 1st c.,
41, *ante* 523, 629, 681, 10th c., 1182, 1656,
1851, 1882; in Algeria, 1870; England, 1290,
1422; Holland, 1796; Morocco, c. 1200,
1864; Poland, 1334; Russia, 1742, 1881-2,
1882;
relations with Arabs, 1946, 1947, 1973;
rebellions, 66, 115, 116, 131; massacres,
1506, 1881-2, 1943; persecution of, 19, 38,
49, 70, 132-4, 612, 616, 627, 635-6, 996-1021,
1008-14, 1106-43, 1302, 1306, 1349, 1391,
1403, 1414, 1492, 1495, 1790-2; riots against,
1921, 1929 see also Anti-Semitism in
Germany and Alexandria, home of Jewry
Jezebel, 869-842 BC
Jezreel, c. 842 BC
Jibril b. Bakhtishu, c. 830
jib—sails, 1st c. BC
Jiddah, 699, 1431-2
Jie, c. mid 17th c.
*Jihad*, c. 1725, 1804, 1831, 1866
Jijakarta, 1937
Jijhoti (Bundelkand), 9th c.
Jiménez, Juan Ramon, 1881-1958
Jiménez, Marcos Pérez, 1950-8
Jimma, 1882
Jimmu Tenno, 660 BC
Jingereber Mosque, 1327
Jingi, fortress, 1649
Jivanjee, A. M., 1909
Jiyuto Party in Japan, 1881
Joachim, Joseph, 1831-1907
Joan of Arc, 1411-31; beatified, 1909;
canonized, 1920
Joanna, d. of Ferdinand II, 1496, 1504
João, Dom, of Portugal, 1808-21
Joash (or Jehoash), c. 837-800 BC
Job, Abp of Novgorod, 1589
Jobst of Moravia, 1394-1411
Jochi, Khan of Kipchak, 1207-27
Jodhpur, 1678, 1707, 1817-18
Jodo-Shinshu sect, 12th c., 1133-1212
Joffre, Joseph, Marshal, 1852-1931
Jogues, Fr Isaac, 1646
Jogyakarta, 1755, 1792-1810, 1825-30
Johannesburg, 1900, 1941, 1944, 1950, 1956,
1957, 1961, 1971
Johannsen, Wilhelm, 1857-1927
John, Duke of Albany, 1514-24
John, Augustus Edwin, 1879-1961
John, Archduke, of Austria, 1848-9
John, Duke of Bedford, 1422-35
John, Duke of Brittany, 1341
John, Lord Cobham, 1417
John, antipope, 844
John XVI, antipope, 997-8
John XXIII, antipope, 1410-15
John II, pope, 533-5
John III, pope, 560 or 61-74
John IV, pope, 640-2
John V, pope, 685-6
John VI, pope, 701-5
John VII, pope, 705-7
John VIII, pope, 872-82
John IX, pope, 898-900
John X, pope, 914-28
John XI, pope, 931-5
John XII, pope, 955-63
John XIII, pope, 965-72
John XIV, pope, 984-5
John XV, pope, 985-96
John XVII, pope, 1003

Laporte, P., 1970
Larache, 1270, 1471, 1911
Largs, 1263
Larissa, 370 BC, 1083
Larne, 1315
Larousse, Pierre, 1817-75
Larsa, dynasty of, c. 2025-1763 BC
Larut, c. 1840, 1862, 1872
Larut R., 1885
Las Navas de Tolosa, 1212
Las Salmas, battle, 1538
Lascarid dynasty, 1204-61
lasers, 1960
Laski, Harold Joseph, 1893-1950
Lassalle, Ferdinand, 1825-64
Lasso, Ordando di, c. 1532-94
Lassus, Roland de, c. 1532-94
Lasta, 1190-1225, 1533
Lateran Synod, 649; Treaty, 1929
lathe, c. 300 BC; screw, AD c. 1800
*latifundia, post* c. 177 BC
Latimer, Hugh, bp, 1485-1555
Latin America, 1959-60, 1960, 1967
Latin citizens' rights, 73-4; language, 180 BC,
   c. 150 BC, c. 25, *post* 200, c. 700, 1696, c.
   1700, *ante* 1800, 1962; missionaries, 866,
   869; League, c. 509 BC, c. 360 BC; States,
   1098; 'villages', c. 1000 BC
Latin quarter, Paris, 1968
Latini, Brunetto, poet, 1230-94
Latlns, 496 BCf, 356 BCf, 340 BCf, 1417
Latins in Constantinople, 1182, 1192; army,
   1259; emperors, 1204-61
Latium, c. 650 BC, 280 BC
Lattre de Tassigny, de, Marshal, 1944-50
Latvia, 1918, 1929, 1940
Laud, William, Abp, 1628-45
laudanum extracted, c. 2500 BC
Lauenburg, 1864, 1865
Lauffeld, battle, 1747
Laurier, Sir Wilfrid, 1896-1911
Laurion, 485
Lausanne, 590, 1235, 1448, 1927, 1932
Lausanne, treaty, 1912, 1923, 1924
Lautaro, 1553
Lautulae, 315 BC
Lauzun, Marshal, 1690
Laval, François de, bp, 1674
Laval, Gustav de, 1877
Laval, Pierre, 1883-1945
Laval-Montmorency, F. X. de, 1659
Lavapura (Lopburi), 7th c.
Lavater, Johann Kaspar, 1741-1801
Lavery, Sir John, 1857-1941
Lavigerie, Cardinal, 1890
Lavoisier, Antoine Laurent, 1743-94
Law, Andrew Bonar, 1858-1923
Law, John, 1716-21
Law, William, 1686-1761
law code of Scotland, 1286-1386
Law Commission, Indian, 1833
Law of Guarantees in Italy, 1871
law of nations, 5th c. BC
law schools, 1045, 1234
Law of the Sea Conference, 1958
lawn mower, 1830
Lawn Tennis Championships, 1877
Lawrence, antipope, 498-505
Lawrence, David Herbert, 1885-1930
Lawrence, Sir John, 1864-9
Lawrence, Sir Thomas, 1769-1830
Lawrence, Thomas Edward, 1888-1935
*Laws of Reform* in Mexico, 1859
Lawson, William, 1813
Layard, Sir Henry, 1817-94
Laybach, congress, 1821
Lazarist School, Damascus, 1795
Lazarists, 1624, 1755

Lazarus of Serbia, 1372, 1387
Lazica, 546, 589
Le dynasty, 980-1005, 1427-1772
Le Brun, Charles, 1619-90
Le Cateau, 1914
'Le Corbusier', architect, 1887-1965
Le Fanu, Joseph Sheridan, 1814-73
*Le Frigorifique*, 1856-7
Le Goulet, peace, 1200
Le Havre, 1562, 1563, 1944
Le Jeune, Fr Paul, 1632
Le Mans, 1425
Le Nain, Antoine, 1588-1648
Le Nain, Louis, 1593-1648
Le Nain, Matthieu, 1607-77
Le Nôtre, André, 1613-1700
*Le Petit Trianon*, 1762-8
Le Play, Frederic, 1806-82
Le Thanh Tong, 1459-97
Le Valais, 1814
Le Van, architect, 1661
Le Veneur, cardinal, 1533
Le Verrier, Urbain J. J., 1846
Le Zoute, Belgium, 1926
Leacock, Stephen, 1869-1944
lead known, c. 3000 BC; used in bronze and
   glass, c. 1500 BC
lead trust in US, 1887
League of Delos, 477 BC, 468 BC
League of Dresden, 1551
League of Marbach, 1405
League of Nations, 1919, 1920, 1925, 1926,
   1931-9; Assembly, 1920; S America, 1826
League of the Three Emperors, 1881, 1884,
   1887
League of Three Kings, 1849
League of Verona, 1164, 1167
Leakey, Louis S. B., 1903-73
Leakey, Mrs. L. S. B. 1959
leap year, 237 BC
Lear, Edward, 1812-88
Lease-Lend Act in US, 1941, 1942, 1945
Lebanon, 1099, 1544, 1590-1635, c. 1737, 1780,
   1831-40, 1839, 1841, 1860, 1861, 1925, 1941,
   1943, 1945, 1958;
   relations with Israel, 1949, 1970, 1974, 1976;
   USA, 1958; Republic, 1926
Lebanon cedar-wood, c. *post* 2620 BC, c. 1482
   BC
Lebna Dengel of Ethiopia, 1508-40
Lebrun, Albert, 1932-40
Lech, R., 1632
Lechfeld, 966
Lecky, W. E. H., 1838-1903
Leclerc, General, 1943-4
Leclerc, George Louis, 1707-88
Ledi Savadaw, Buddhist, c. 1910
Leduc, Alberta, 1947
Lee, Robert E., general, 1807-70
Lee Kuan-Yew, 1959—
Leek, treaty, 1318
Leeward Is., 1871, 1883, 1932, 1936, 1947
legal codes, c. 526 BC, c. 517 BC; reforms, c.
   622 BC
Legations in Italy, 1860
Legazpi, Miguel Lopez de, 1565-71
*Leges Henrici*, 1113-18
Legge, James, 1755
Leghorn, 1421
Legion of Honour in France, 1802
Legislative Assembly of France, 1791, 1804,
   1815, 1849
Legislative Commission in Russia, 1767-8
Legislative Council Act in Britain, 1853
Legislative Councils in Kenya, 1907;
   Mozambique, 1907; NZ, 1940; Paris, 1795; S
   Rhodesia, 1898
Legnano, 1176

Leguía, Augusto, of Peru, 1908-30
Léhar, Franz, 1870-1948
Leibniz, Gottfried Wilhelm, 1646-1716
Leicester, 1414; Earl of, 1785
Leif, son of Eric the Red, 999
Leigh, Capt. Charles, 1602-6
Leighton, Frederick, Lord, 1880-90
Leik Munhtaw of Hanthawaddy, 1453
Leinster, 1170, 1176
Leipzig, 1631, 1806, 1954; battle, 1813;
   university, 1409
Leiria, 1254
Leith, 1544; treaty, 1560
Leigh, Sir George, 1800
Leix, 1556
Leland, John, c. 1506-52
Lelvar culture, c. 1000-900 BC
Lely, Sir Peter, 1618-80
Lemnos, 394 BC, 917, 1479, 1657
Lemtuna, c. 9th c., c. 1035, 1042
Lemus, José Maria, 1956
Lena, Siberia, 1912
Lenclos, Ninon de, 1620-1705
Lend-Lease *see* Lease-Lend
Lenin, Nikolai, 1870-1924
Lenin mausoleum, 1961
Leningrad, 1941, 1942; Academy, 1727
Lennox, Earl of, 1570-1
Lens, France, 1648
Lenshina, Alice, 1964
Leo I, emperor, 457-74
Leo II, emperor 474
Leo III, emperor, 717-26
Leo IV, emperor, 775-80
Leo V, emperor, 813-20
Leo VI, emperor, 886-912
Leo II, pope, 681-3
Leo III, pope, 795-816
Leo IV, pope, 847-55
Leo V, pope 903
Leo VI, pope 928-9
Leo VII, pope 936-9
Leo VIII, pope, 963-5
Leo IX, pope, 1048-54
Leo X, pope, 1512-20
Leo XI, pope, 1605
Leo XII, pope, 1823-9
Leo XIII, pope, 1878-1903
'Leo Africanus', 1518 (or 20)
Leo I of Lesser Armenia, 1129-37
Leo of Salonika, c. 829-56
Leo of Tripoli, pirate, 904, 917
Leofric, Earl of Mercia, 1056
León, 569, 10th c., 914, 981, 988, 1029, 1037,
   1065, 1170-80, 1188, 1230, c. 1250, 1303
Leoncavallo, Ruggiero, 1858-1919
Leonidas, 480 BC
Leonine dynasty, 457-581
Leontini, 213 BC
Leontinoi, 345 BC
Leontius, emperor, 695-8
Leontopolis, c. 181 BC
*Leopard*, HMS, 1807
Leopardi, Giacomo, 1798-1837
Leopold I, Duke of Austria, 1292-1315
Leopold III, Duke of Austria, 1379-86
Leopold III, Margrave of Austria, 1139
Leopold I, emperor, 1657-1705
Leopold II, emperor, 1790-2
Léopold I of Belgium, 1831-53
Léopold II of Belgium, 1865-1909
Léopold III of Belgium, 1934-50
Leopold of Hohenzollern, 1870
Léopoldville, 1966
Leosthenes, 323-322 BC
Leovigild, 568-86
Lepanto, naval battle, 1571
Lepidus, 78 BC, 44 BC

Maine R., 481-511
Maine, Sir Henry, 1822-88
Maine USA, 1814, 1820
*Maine*, USN, 1898
Maintenon, Marquise de, 1635-1719
Mainz University, 1477
Maipú, Chile, 1818
Maisara, 739-40
Maison Carrée, 16 BC
Maisonneuve, Sieur de, 1642
Maistre, Joseph de, 1754-1821
Maitland, Sir Frederick, 1850-1906
Maitland, Sir Thomas, 1805-11
Maitrakas, c. 490
maize, 9th c. BC, c. 1500, c. 1629
Majapahit, 1293-1309, c. 1295, 1309, 1331-64,
    1364, 1365, 1520
Majid, Sultan of Zanzibar, 1856-70
Maji-Maji uprising, 1905
Majorca, 1229
Major-Generals in England, 1655, 1656
Majorian, 457-61
Majuba Hill, battle, 1881
Makalle, Ethiopia, 1935
Makam Tauhid, c. *ante* 1641
Makarios, Abp, 1954-76
Makhzumi dynasty, c. 897/8-1285
Makhzumi Sultanate, 1277, 1285
Makololo, c. 1823
Makran, 1594, 1870-1
Makua, c. 1580-90
Malabar, 10th c., 1663, 1921
Malacca, 1350, c. 1390, c. 1400, 1414,
    1488-1511, 1548, 1557, 1613, 1824, 1826,
    1830-2, 1946; Straits of, 1513;
    visited by, Arakanese, 1549; British, 1795;
    Bugis, 1756, 1784; Chinese, 1403, 1409;
    Javanese, 1550, 1574; Portuguese, 1509,
    1511, 1530, 1536-40; Siamese, 1445-56;
    relations with Acheh, 1568, 1615, 1616, 1628,
    1629; Dutch, 1606, 1637, 1640, 1641, 1662,
    1818; Johore, 1515-24, 1517, 1523, 1551,
    1587, 1606, 1607-36, 1610, 1616, 1637
Malachi, prophet, c. 450 BC
Malachy, 845, 848
Málaga, 1025, 1487, 1810, 1937
Malagasy, c. 945
Malagasy Republic, 1960 *see also* Madagascar
    *and* Malgache
Malakoff, battle, 1855
Malalas, John, c. 575
Malamir of Bulgaria, 831-852
Malan, D. F., 1948-54
malaria, 396 BC, 212 BC, 1857-1932; bacillus,
    1897
Malavas (Malloi), 325 BC
Malawi, c. 1845, 1964; republic, 1966;
    relations with SA, 1968
Malawi, L., c. 1768
Malay Collieries Ltd, 1913
Malay Democratic Union, 1945
Malay Kingdom of Malacca, c. 1400-1511
Malay Nationalist Party, 1945
Malay peninsula, 774, 1075, 1284, 1401, 1414,
    1456
Malay States, end of 1st c. BC, 1787, 1946
Malaya, 1st c. BC, 1680, 1825-6, 1874, c. 1890,
    1895, 1948, 1955, 1965, Federation, 1957;
    immigrants from China, c. 1830-40, 1850;
    immigrants from India, c. 1870; industries,
    rubber, 1877, 1896, 1910; tin, 1850, c.
    1880-1900, 1904, 1912, university, 1949;
    relations with Britain, 1945; Indonesia, 1966;
    Japan, 1941, 1942; Siam, 1897
Malayan Chinese Ass., 1949; Communist
    Party, 1927, 1948; Indian Congress, 1946;
    Labour Code, 1912; Peoples' Anti-Japanese
    Army, 1942, 1945, 1948; Races Liberation

Movement, 1949; Schools, 1816; Union,
    1946
Malays, peninsular, 1247, 1788, 1824, 1850
Malaysia, 6th c. BC, c. 300 BC, 671-81, 1275,
    1292, c. 1300, 1969; fleet, 154
Malayu, 644-5, 683-6, 1292, 1295, 1377
Malcolm, Sir John, 1800-19
Malcolm X, Black Muslim, 1965
Malcolm I, of Scotland, 942-54
Malcolm II, of Scotland, 1005-34
Malcolm III, of Scotland, 1058-93
Malcolm IV, of Scotland, 1153-65
Malchus II, of Ghassan, 40-70
Maldive Is., 955-1014, 1007, 1505, 1965
Maldon, 991
Maldonado, Jorge Fernandes, 1976
Malenkov, Russian politician, 1957
Malesherbes, C. G. de L. de, 1744-94
Malestroit, treaty, 1343
Malfante, 1447
Malgache, 1958, *see also* Madagascar *and*
    Malagasy
Malherbe, François de, 1555-1628
Mali, 1240, c. 1270, c. 1285-1300, 1307-32, c.
    1322-6, c. 1341-60, 1473
Mali, Federation of, 1959, 1968; independent,
    1960
al-Malik al-Afdal, 1193
Malik Ahmad of Junnar, 1490
Malik, b. Anas, c. 715-95
al-Malik al-Ashraf of Damascus, 1520
al-Malik al-Ashraf Qalil, 1290-3
Malik Ayaz, 1507
Malik Dinar, 1185
Malik Kabur, 1302-16
al-Malik al-Adil Muhammad b. Sulaiman, c.
    1412-21
al-Malik al-Mansur Qalaun, 1279-90
Malik al-Salik of Perlak, 1297
al-Malik al-Zahir Baybars, 1260-77
Malikite rite, 849
Malikite school of jurisprudence, c. 715-95
Malikshah, 1072-92
Malindi, c. 1415, 1417-19, 1421-2, 1498, 1509,
    1541-2, 1588, *post* 1612, c. 1699
Malines, 1920-6
Mallarmé, Stéphane, 1842-98
Mallikarjuna of Vijayanagar, 1447-65
Malloi (Malavas), 325 BC
Mallorca, 1339
Mallu b. Yusuf of Bijapur, 1534-5
Malmö, 1848
Malolos, Philippine Is, 1899
Malory, Sir T., 1485
Malpighi, Marcello, 1628-94
Malplaquet, 1709
Malta, 869, 902, 916, 1090, 1530, 1564, 1565,
    1798, 1835; independent, 1964; State of,
    1961, 1962;
    relations with Britain, 1800, 1803, 1878,
    1942, 1971, 1972
Malte-Brun, Conrad, 1775-1826
Malthus, Thomas Robert, 1766-1834
*Malus Intercursus*, 1506
Malvern, Sir G. Huggins, Lord, 1956
Malwa, 1018-60, *ante* 1236, 1310, 1344-50,
    1398, 1531-2, 1658, 1737, 1738; Kingdom,
    1401
Mamduh Muhammad Salim, Prime Minister of
    Egypt, 1975
Mamertines, 289 BC
Mamluk Sultans of Egypt, 1260-1517
Mamluks in Egypt, 1773, 1804, 1811
al-Mamun, Caliph, 813-33
Man, Is. of, 1000, 1075, 1098-1103, 1290, 1293,
    1313
Man Singh, 1592
Managua, Nicaragua, 1931, 1972

Manasseh, c. 687/6-642 BC
Manavamma, 684
Mancham, James, 1976
Manchester, c. 72-4, 1759, 1819, 1830, 1867,
    1899; university, 1880
*Manchester Guardian*, 1821, 1959
Manchu dynasty, 1644-1912, 1912, 1918
Manchukuo, Republic, 1932, 1938, 1939, 1943
Manchuria, 237, 1217, 1602, 1618, 1690, 1896,
    1902, 1904-5, 1907, 1910, 1918-22, 1931,
    1945; N, 1858; S, 1914
Manchurian Chinese, mid-6th c.
Manchus, 1602, 1618, 1621, 1637, 1638, 1645,
    1673, 1681, 1683, 1690, 1696
Mancini, Pascal-Stanislaus, 1817-88
Manco Capac, Inca, 12th or 13th c.
*Mancomunitat* of Catalonia, 1914, 1925
Manda, 1678
Mandalay, 1857-61, 1859-85, 1872, 1875, 1891,
    1942
Mandela, Nelson, 1964
Mandingo Empire of Jenne, c. 1043; language,
    1836
Mandingos, 2nd c., 4th c.-750, 1325
Mandu, 1305, 1405-35
Manes; gnostic, 242,76
Manet, Edouard, 1832-83
Manetho, historian, c. 323-245 BC
Manfred of Sicily, 1254-82
Mangalore, 1791; treaty, 1784
Mangbetu dynasty, 1815
Mangray of Lan Na, 1296-1315
Manhattan Is, 1624, 1626
Mani, 273 or 4
Maniakes, George, *post* 1040-43
Manichaeans and Manichaeism, 242-76, c. 297,
    c. 305, 382, 780, 843
Manila, 1571, 1574, 1584, 1590, 1600, 1603,
    1609, 1645, 1762, 1823, 1863, 1869, 1898,
    1899, 1942, 1945
Manilius, 1st c.
Manin, Daniele, 1804-57
manioc (cassava), c. 1629
Manipur, 1733, 1758, 1770, 1824; Rajah of,
    1558
Manitoba, 1870; Lake, 1740
Mannheim, 1795; Union, 1727
Manning, Henry E., cardinal, 1808-92
Mannlicher rifle, 1878
Mannu dynasty, c. 1040
Mannu dynasty of Futa Toro, c. 1250-1300
manors in China, 317-409
Manpower and Citizens Assn., 1936
Mansa Ule of Mali, c. 1255-70
Mansard, Jules Hardouin-, 1646-1708
Mansbridge, Albert, 1876-1952
Mansfield, 1622
al-Mansur, caliph, 754-57
al-Mansur, son of Abd al-Jamil, c. 1512
al-Mansur, (Abu Abbas Ismail), 946-52
al-Mansur, Almohad, 1184-99
al-Mansur, Fakhr al-Din Uthman, 1413
al-Mansur al-Muhammad, 1198-9
al-Mansur b. Bulukin, 984-96
Mansur Shah, Sultan of Malacca, c. 1456-77
al-Mansura, 1250
al-Mansuria, 947, 1302
Mantanzima, Chief Kaiser, 1976
Mantegna, Andrea, 1431-1506
Mantes, edict, 1591
Mantinea, battles, 418 BC, 362 BC
Mantua, c. 550 BC, 603, 1328, 1630, 1797;
    Congress of, 1439; Duke of, 1627, 1681
Manu, 'Laws' or Code, between 200 BC and
    AD 200, c. 100 BC
Manuel I, Comnenos, 1143-80
Manuel II, Palaeologos, 1391-1423

Manuel of Epirus, 1230
Manuel I of Portugal, 1485-1521
Manuel II of Portugal, 1908-10
Manufacturers' Encouragement Act, Australia, 1902
Manumission of slaves, 2 BC, 19, 321, 1776
Manyakheta, 815-77
Manzikart, battle, 1071
Manzoni, Alessandro, 1785-1873
Mao Tse-Tung, 1921-7, 1976
Maoris, c. 925, c. 1350, 1769, 1809, 1815, 1819, 1820, 1821-30, 1835, 1837, 1840, 1844-5, 1845, 1852, 1854, 1858, 1860-4, 1863, 1865, 1872, 1881, 1896, 1921, 1949
Mao-Yi, painter, c. 1100-70
map making, 6th c. BC, 7 BC
Maphera Dlamini, 1976
Mapungubwe, c. ante 1100, c. 1500
Mapungubwe culture, 1058±65, 1388±60, 1428±60
al-Maqdisi, geographer, 985-6
Maqs, 955
Mar, Earls of, 1571-2, 1715-16
Mar Petrus, bp, c. 840
Mar Shimun, 339
Marabout cults, 12th c.
Maracaibo, L, 1918
Maraghah, 120-74, 1259, 1265
Maranhão, N, 1560
Maranhão Co., Brazil, 1678-84
Marat, Jean Paul, 1793
Maratha peoples, 1655, 1668-9, 1683, 1714-20, 1737, 1740-1, 1742, 1758, 1760, 1761, 1771, 1773, 1779-82, 1790, 1795, 1798, 1802, 1815, 1817
Marathon, 490 BC
Marbodus, 9
Marburg, 1527, 1829
*Marbury vs. Madison*, 1803
Marca Hispanica, 865
Marcabru, troubadour, c. 1130-48
Marcel, Etienne, 1356-8
Marcellus, M. Claudius, 222 BC, 212 BC
Marcellus II, pope, 1555
March, Earl of, 1328
Marchand, Jean Baptiste, 1897-8
Marchew, Ethiopia, 1936
Marcian, emperor, 450-7
Marcian of Heraclea, c. 400
Marcianopolis, 376
Marcion, gnostic, c. 120
Marcionite heresy, c. 144
Marco Polo, 1254-1324
Marcomanni, 6, 89, 167, 172, 177-80, 295
Marconi, Gugliemo, 1874-1937
Marcos, Abuna of Ethiopia, 1692
Marcoule, France, 1956
Marcus Aurelius, 121-80
Mardawij b. Ziyar, 928-1042
Mardonius, 492 BC
Marduk-kabit-aheshu, c. 1162-1152 BC
Mardyke, 1657
Marengo, 1800
Mareshah, battle of, c. 913-873 BC
Mareth Line, battle, 1943
Marey, Jules Etienne, 1893
Margai, Dr Albert, 1953
Margai, Sir Milton, 1895-1964
Margaret, sister of Henry II, of France, 1559
Margaret, d. of Henry VII, 1502
Margaret, Maid of Norway, 1286-90
Margaret, Queen of Scotland, 1068-9
Margaret of Anjou, 1444; as Queen of England, 1445-71
Margaret of Burgundy, 1477
Margaret the Great, 1387-1412
Margaret of Hainault, 1253

Marggraf, Andreas, 1747
Margus R., 285
Mari dynasty, c. 1850-1761 BC
*María*, 1785
Maria of Braganza, 1746
María Cristina de las Mercedes, 1885-1902
María Christina, of Spain, 1833-85
Maria of Hungary, 1382-5
Maria I, of Portugal, 1777-1807
Maria II, of Portugal, 1826-53
Maria Sophia of Portugal, 1687
Maria Teresa of France, 1683
Maria Theresa dollars, 1780, 1862
Maria Theresa of Hapsburg, 1740-80
Mariana, regent of Spain, 1665-89
Mariano, battle, 1554
Marib dam, c. 650 BC, c. 610-115 BC, c. 450, 542, 543
Marie, André, 1948
Marie-Antoinette, 1770-93
Marie-Françoise of Savoy, 1666-83
Marie-Louise of Austria, 1810
Marienburg, 1309, 1457; treaty, 1656
Mariette, Auguste, 1821-81
Marignano, 1515
Marillac, Louise de, 1634
Marinid dynasty of Fez, 1196-1464, 1274 or 5, 1276
Marinus I, pope, 882-4
Marinus II, pope, 942-6
Marischal, Earl, 1719, 1750-61
Maristan (hospital) at Cairo, 1284
Maritime Alps, 14 BC
Maritz, Gert, 1836
Maritza, R, 1371
Marius C., 108-86 BC
Marj Dabiq, battle, 1516
Marj Rahit, 634
Marj-al-Suffar, 635, 1303
mark (currency), 1096, 1969
Mark Anthony, 49-43 BC
Market Bosworth, 1485
Marlborough, Duke of, 1703-22; Duchess of, 1710
Marlborough, Statute, 1267
Marlowe, Christopher, 1564-93
Marmora, sea, 512
Marmoutiers, abbey, 372
Marne R., c. 200 BC, 481-511; battle, 1914
Maronites, 1841, 1860; students, 1584
Marot, Clemont, 1495-1544
al-Marqab, 1062, 1285
Marquette Range, Mich., 1845
Marquises Is., Polynesia, 1842
Marrakesh, 1070, 1146-7, 1150-90, 1266, 1269, 1525, 1591-1654, 1610-13, 1907
marriage, mixed, 1897, 1949, 1966
marriage age, 1929
marriage laws in Rome, 19 BC, 9 BC
marriages, register of, 1538
Married Women's Property Act, 1870
Marryat, Frederick, 1792-1848
*Mars*, planet, 1976
Marsden, Rev. Samuel, 1814
Marseilles, c. 600 BC, 838, 1309-40, 1524, 1533, 1536, 1720, 1815, 1832, 1904, 1934, 1947
Marshall, Alfred, 1842-1924
Marshall, D., 1955-6
Marshall, George, general, 1947-50
Marshall, John, 1755-1838
Marshall Is., 1944
Marshall Plan (Aid), 1947, 1948, 1949
Marshals of France, 1804
Marsi, 325 BC, 311 BC
Marsilio of Padua, c. 1275-1342
Marston Moor, battle, 1644

Martoban, 1296, 1519, 1538, 1541, 1593, 1615-17, 1852
Martel, Charles, 714-41
Martí, José, 1895-8
Martial, poet, c. 40-c. 104
Martin I, pope, 649-55
Martin IV, pope, 1281-5
Martin V, pope, 1417-31
Martin I, of Aragon, 1395-1410
Martín-García Is., 1838
Martínez, Maximiliano H., 1930-44
Martinique, WI, 1674, 1794, 1839, 1902
Martius Turbo, 116
Martorell, 1114
Marvel, Andrew, 1621-78
Marw, 1037
Marwan I b. al. Hakim, caliph, 684-5
Marwar, 1681
Marx, Karl, 1818-83
Marx, Wilhelm, 1923-7
Marxism, 1970
Marxist Party in Russia, 1883
Mary, Queen of Scots, 1542-87
Mary, Duchess of Suffolk, 1514
Mary, Princess of Teck, 1867-1953
Mary, d, of Duke of York, 1677 (later Mary II)
Mary of Burgundy, 1482
Mary I of England, 1550-8
Mary II of England, 1688-94
Mary of Lorraine, 1554-9
Maryland, 1634, 1649
*Masafent* in Ethiopia, 1769-1855
Masai, c. post 1675, c. post 1775, c. 1890
Masaryk, Jan, 1948
Masaryk, Thomas, 1850-1937
Mascara, Algeria, 1701-91, 1835
Mashivo, Abe, 1853
Mashona, 1892
Mashonaland, 530±120-840±100, 1867
Masinissa, 104-150 BC
Maslamah, c. 717
Masonic Lodges in England, 1717; France, 1721, 1773; Germany, 1733
Masovia, 1300-5
Maspéro, Gaston C. C., 1846-1916
Mass, 1378-84, 1560, 1569, 1649, 1963
Massachusetts, 1629, 1631, 1646, 1679, 1684, 1691, 1765, 1772, 1820; Bay Co., 1629
Massacre Is., 1736
Massada, 42 BC, 73
Massagetes, c. 520 BC
Massawa, 247 BC, 634, 854, 1520-6, 1541, 1557, 1846, 1941
Massé, Ennemond, 1611
Massenet, Jules E. F., 1842-1912
Massey, Vincent, 1927-59
Massey, William Ferguson, 1856-1925
Massina, 1810-14, 1850
Masters, John, 1914—
Masters and Servants Act, 1846
Masties, Berber Chief, 476
al-Masudi, c. 915, c. 940
Masulipatam, 1611, 1759
Matabele, 1831, 1836, 1888, 1893
Mataka, Yao chief, 1898
Matamba, 1590
Matapan, battle, 1717, 1941
Matara, Ceylon, 1796
Mataram, 1588, 1602, 1613-45, 1619, 1622, 1634, 1646, 1677, 1704-8, 1740-3, 1743, 1755 *and see* Surakarta
Mataram, King of, c. 929-47
match trust in US, 1889
matches, safety, 1852
Mateos, Adolfo López, 1958—
*Mater et magistra*, 1961
Maternus, c. 86 BC
mathematics in Babylonia, 18th c. or 17th c.

Muhammad **Khudabanda** of Persia, 1578-87
Muhammad V, of Morocco, 1955-61
Muhammad Lamine Ould Ahmad, 1976
Muhammad b. **Muhammad** b. Tarkhan Abu
    Nasr al-**Farabi**, 950
Muhammad b. **Musa** al-Khwarizmi, 780-c. 850
Muhammad b. **Muslim** al-Dinawari, 889
Muhammad al-**Nafs** al-Zakiyah, 762
Muhammad b. **Nasir**, 1212
Muhammad b. **Nusayr**, 874
Muhammad **Pasha**, 1607
Muhammad b. al-**Qasim**, 710
Muhammad **Quli** of Golconda, 1580-1611
Muhammad **Reza**, Shah of Iran, 1941, 1975
Muhammad **Said** of Egypt, 1854-63
Muhammad b. **Saud**, 1765
Muhammad **Shah** Bahmani, 1472-3
Muhammad **Shah** of the Deccan, 1719-48
Muhammad **Shah** of Delhi, 1434
Muhammad **Shah** of Persia, 1834-48
Muhammad al-**Shaikh** al-Portugali, 1470-1524
Muhammad **Soqolly**, 1566-79
Muhammad **Sultan**, 1676 or 7
Muhammad **Tewfiq**, 1879-92
Muhammad b. **Tumert**, c. 1078-c. 1130
Muhammad b. **Tughj**, 935-46
Muhammad b. **Tughluq**, 1325-51
Muhammad b. **Uthman** al-Mazrui, 1739-46
Muhammad b. **Yusuf** al- Kindi, 897-961
Muhammad b. **Yusuf** b. Nasr, 1232-73
Muhammad **Zahir** Shah, 1933
Muhammad **Bello** of Sokoto, 1817-37
Muhammadu **Korau** of Katsina, c.
    1492/3-1541/2
Mühlberg, battle, 1547
Muhldorf, battle, 1322
al-Muhtadi, caliph, 869-70
al-Muizz b. Badis, 1048, 1053
al-Muizz, Fatimid caliph, 969-75
Muizz al-Dawlah, 945
Muizz al-Din Qaiqabad, 1286-90
Mujahid b. Muhammad, 1373-8
Mujapahit, 1389, 1401-6
Mujibur Rahman, President of Bangla Desh,
    1975
Mu-jung tribes, 281, 289
Mukali, 1217
Mukden, 1905, 1928, 1931, 1948
Mukran, 643, 710
al-Muktafi, 1138
al-Muktafi, caliph, 902-8
Mukurra, c. 540, c. 550
Mularaja, c. 942-97
Mulavarman, c. 400
Muldoon, Robert, 1975
Müller, Hermann, 1928
Müller, Paul, 1939
Multan, 713, 1001-24, 1004-6, 1027, 1175-6,
    1241-2, 1328, 1398, 1649, 1751, 1818-19,
    1848
Muluccha, R., 107 BC
Mulungushi Reforms, 1968
Mumtaz Mahal, 1612-31
Münchengrätz, Conference, 1833
Munda, 46-45 BC
al-Mundhir, amir of Córdoba, 886-8
al-Mundhir I, 418-62
al-Mundhir III, 505-54
al-Mundhir of Ghassan, 580
Mundosir, treaty, 1818
Mundy, Peter, 1630-3
Mungo Park, 1771-1806
Munich, 1559, 1609, 1632, 1742, 1782, 1805,
    1871, 1918, 1919, 1923; Agreement, 1938
Munich, Abp of, 1871
Municipal Corporations Act, 1835, 1882;
    Reform Act, Irish 1840
Munnings, Sir Alfred, 1878-1959

Munster, 1586
Münster, 1225, 1534, 1535, 1566, 1644
al-Muntasir, caliph, 861-2
Münzer, Thomas, 1524-5
Muong Nai, Kingdom, 1223
al-Muqtadi, caliph, 1075-94
al-Muqtadir, caliph, 908-32
al-Muqtafi, caliph, 1136-60
al-Murabitun, *see* Almoravid dynasty
Murad I, Ottoman Sultan, 1359-89
Murad II, Ottoman Sultan, 1421-51
Murad III, Ottoman Sultan, 1574-95
Murad IV, Ottoman Sultan, 1623-40
Murad V, Ottoman Sultan, 1876
Murad Bakhsh, 1646-61
Murano, 1292
Murasaki Shikibu, 11th c.
Murashu family, 460-400 BC
Murat, Joachim, 1808-15
Muratori, Lodovico Antonio, 1672-1750
Murchakhar, 1729
Murcia, 1126, 1150, 1358
Murdoch, Duke of Albany, 1420-4
Murena, 25 BC
Muret, 1213
Murillo, Bartholomé Estaban, 1617-82
Murillo, Bravo, in Spain, 1851
Muristan hospital, 801
Muromachi, 1339-1573
Murray, George Gilbert, 1866-1957
Murray, James, 1764-6
Murray, John, 1778-1843
Mursa, battle, 351
Murtala Muhammad, President of Nigeria,
    1975-6
Murshid Quli Khan of Bengal, 1713-27
Murshid Quli Khan of Deccan, 1656
Murshidabad, 1757
Mursilis II, 1334-1306 BC
Murszteg, 1903
al-Murtada, caliph, 908
Murtada al-Zabidi, 1732-91
Musa, Ottoman, 1410-13
Musa Mzuri, 1823
Musa b. Nusayr, c. 705-15
Musa Pasha of Egypt, 1631
Musa b. Sulaiman of Darfur, c. 1670-82
Musa II of Mali, 1374-8
Musabaat Arabs, 1747-8
Muscat, 1551, 1587, 1650, 1784, 1841, 1958
Muscovy, Grand Dukes, 1328-1480
Muscovy Company, 1555, 1567
muskets, c. 1578, 1819
Muslim b. al-Hajjaj, 875
Muslim b. Said al-Kilabi, 724
Muslim Brotherhood, 1929, 1932, 1954; fleets,
    717-18, 805; imposter, c. 1080; inscription in
    EA, 1105; League, 1934, 1940, 1946, 1947;
    persecutions, 1106-43, 1490, 1790-2;
    Muslims, 625, 628, 641, 643, 649/50, 674,
    1825, 1889;
    relations with Byzantium, 629, 635, 640,
    717-8; Algerian, 1944; Andalusian, *post*
    1248; Meccan, 615; in China, 1855-73,
    1864-5; Chinese Turkestan, 1845; Ethiopia,
    1668, 1862; India, 1175-1340, 1339, 1916,
    1920, 1924, 1929, 1930, 1941; Mombasa,
    1631; Spain, 1302, 1340, 1499, 1502, 1525,
    1567, 1568
Mussadeq, premier of Persia, 1951
Musset, Alfred, de, 1810-57
Mussolini, Benito, 1883-1945
al-Mustadi, caliph, 1170-80
Mustafa I, Ottoman Sultan, 1617-23
Mustafa II, Ottoman Sultan, 1695-1703
Mustafa III, Ottoman Sultan, 1757-74
Mustafa IV, Ottoman Sultan, 1807-8
Mustafa Kamil, 1874-1908

Mustafa Kemal Ataturk, 1919-55
Mustafa Keuprulu, 1691
Mustafa Pasha Fahmi, 1895-1908
al-Musta'in, caliph, 862-6
al-Mustakfi, caliph, 944-6
al-Mustanjid, caliph, 1160-70
al-Mustansir, caliph, 1226-42
al-Mustansiriyah, 1234
al-Mustarshid, caliph, 1118-35
al-Mustasim, Abbasid, 1242-58
al-Mustazhir, caliph, 1094-1118
al-Mutadid, caliph, 892-902
Mutah, 629
al-Mutamid, caliph, 870-902
al-Mutamid, King of Seville, 1068-91
al-Mutanabbi, poet, 915-65
al-Mutasim, caliph, 833-42
al-Mutawakkil I, caliph, 809-61
al-Mutawakkil II, caliph, 1261
Mutawallis c. 1306-1282 BC
Mutazilite dogma, c. 725, 827, 833, 935/6;
    persecutions, 849; sect, 868/9, 915/6
al-Mutazz, caliph, 866-9
Mutesa II, of Buganda, 1963
al-Muti, caliph, 946-74
Mutina, 43 BC
mutinies, naval, 1797, 1905, 1917, 1918, 1921,
    1946
Mutiny Act, 1689
mutiny in Brazil, 1935; Burmese army, 1945;
    CFS, 1895; French army, 1917; India, 1824,
    1857
Mutota, Rozvi King, c. 1440
al-Muttaqi, caliph, 940-4
Muttu Swamu of Kandy, 1803
Mutual Security Act, US, 1951
Muwaffaq al-Din Abu al-Abbas Ahmad b. Abi
    Usaybiah, 1203-70
al-Muzaffar Ahmad, 1421
Muzaffar al-Din of Persia, 1896-1906
Muzaffar Jajji, Sultan, 1346-7
Muzaffar Shah, 1391-1407
Muzaffar Shah, Sultan, 1445-c. 1456
Muzaffar Shah of Johore, 1564-9
Muzaffarid dynasty of Persia, 1313-93
Muzaffarids, Somalia, c. 1500, c. 1624
Mwadui, Tanganyika, 1946
Mwanga, Kabaka of Buganda, 1889-97
Mwene Mutapa (Monomotapa), c. 1440
My Lai, Vietnam, 1969
Mycales, Cape, 479 BC
Mycenaean civilization, c. 1400-1100 BC
Myingondaing, Prince of Burma, 1866
Myingun, Prince of Burma, 1866
Myinsaing, 1301
Mylae, 260 BC
Mylapore, 68
Myonnesus, 191-190 BC
Myriocephalon, 1176
Myron, sculptor, c. 470-430 BC
Mysia, 216 BC, 538
Mysore, 297 BC, 1st half 12th c., c. 1110-41,
    1190, 1764, 1781, 1792, 1799, 1811, 1831,
    1881
mystery religions, 7th-6th c. BC
Mysilene, 428 BCf, 1462
Mytton, 1319
myxomatosis, 1953
Mzizima (Dar es Salaam), 12th c.


Nabataean Arabia, 105; nomads, *post* 600 BC,
    c. 500 BC, 31-30 BC; script, 40-70, c. *ante*
    300
Nablus, 1918
'Nabonassar' (Nabu-nasir) calendar, c. 388-367
    BC
Naboniduus (Nabu-na-id), 556-539 BC

Nabu-apal-usur (Nabopolassar), 627-612 BC
Nabu-nasir, 747 BC
Nachtigal, Gustave, 1869-74
Nadad, c. 901-900 BC
al-Nadim, 988
Nadir Khan of Afghanistan, 1929-33
Nadir Quli, Shah of Persia, 1727-47
Nadoungmya of Pagan, 1210-34
Naevius, Cn., poet, c. 270-200 BC
Naga, c. 20 BC
Nagabhata II, 816
*Nagarakertama*, 1365
Nagardjuna, 70
Nagarkot (Kangra), 1337
Nagasaki, 1597, 1638, 1640, 1805, 1853, 1854, 1855, 1945
Nagpur, 1816, 1817, 1853
Nahas Pasha, 1927-44
Nahrawan Canal, 659
Nail of Funj, 1534-51
Nairobi, 1908, 1921, 1927, 1938, 1963
Najaf, 1920
Najd, 1792, 1879
Najera, 1367
Najib al-Daula, 1761-70
Najran, c. 500, 523, 635-6
Nakatomina-Kamatari (Fujiwara Kamatari), 645
Namaqaland, 1682-3
Namibia, 1975
Namiembali of Mangbetu, 1815
Namier, Sir Lewis Bernstein, 1886-1960
Namur, 1421, 1695, 1794
Nan, Shantung, 1948
Nana Fadnavis, Maratha, 1795-1800
Nan-Chao, kingdom, 1253, 1441; state, 8th c., c. 800
Nancy, 1475
Nanda dynasty, c. 4th c. BC, 322 BC
Nandabayin, 1581-99
Nander, 1708
Nandi, 1309-27
Nandi Field Force, 1905
Nandivardhana, *post* 401 BC
Naning, 1831-2
Nanking, 1126, 1645, 1659, 1690, 1841, 1853, 1864, 1911, 1927, 1931, 1937, 1939, 1940, 1948
Nansen, Fridtjof, 1861-1930
Nantes, 579; edict, 1622, 1626, 1669, 1685
Nanterre, France, 1968
Nanto-Bordelaise Co., 1839
Nao Nihal Singh of Lahore, 1840
Naod of Ethiopia, 1494-8
Napata-Meroe, c. 920 BC, c. 751-730 BC, c. 633 BCf., c. 595 BC, 328-308 BC, 23 BC
Napier, Sir Charles, 1842-3
Napier, Sir George, 1838
Napier, John, 1550-1617
Napier, Sir Robert, 1868
Naples (Neapolis). 428 BC. 327 BC. 536, 543, 552, 837, 856, 1291, 1298-1300, 1318, 1319, 1347-50, 1381, 1486, 1546, 1600, 1714, 1849, 1860, 1871; constitution, 1848; rebellions, 1647, 1820; University, c. 1000-50, 1224; under Aragon, 1282, 1501, subject to Austria, 1707, 1713, 1821; relations with France, 1495, 1501, 1798, 1799, 1801, 1805, 1806; under Spanish rule, 1442, 1504, 1527, 1556, 1734, 1735
Naples, Duke of, 1029
Napoleon Buonaparte, 1769-1821, 1840
Napoleon III, of France, 1836-73
Nara, early, 8th c.
Narapati of Ava, 1443-69
Narapatisitha of Pagan, 1173-1210

Narasa Nakaya of Vijayanager, 1490-1503
Narasimha of Vijayanager, 1490-1
Naratheinka of Pagan, 1170-3
Narathihapati of Pagan, 1254-87
Narathu of Pagan, 1167-70
Narathu of Pinya, 1359-64
Narawara of Burma, 1672-3
Narbonese Gaul, 125-121 BC
Narbonne, 109 BC, 720, 732, 737, 759, 1272
Nares, James, 1715-83
Nariño, Antonio, 1794
Narnaul, Patiala, 1672
Narnia, 299 BC
Narses of Byzantium, 551
Narses of Persia, 275-302
Narva, 1700, 1703, 1890
Nárvaez, Pánfilo de, 1528
Nárváez, Ramón María, 1800-68
Na-Sam, 1953
Naseby, battle, 1645
Nash, John, 1752-1835
Nash, Paul, 1889-1946
*Nashville*, US Navy, 1903
al-Nasir, Almahad, 1199-1222
al-Nasir, caliph, 1180-1225
al-Nasir, Bahri Mamluk Sultan, 1293-1340
Nasir al-Din, Sultan, 1246-66
Nasir al-Din of Malwa, 1500-12
Nasir al-Din of Persia, 1848-96
Nasir al-Din al-Tusi, 1201-74
Nasir Khan, 1758
al-Nasir Muhammad, Burji Mamluk, 1495-8
al-Nasir Nasir al-Din Faraj, 1398-1412
Nasir-i-Khusraw, 1046-9
al-Nasiriyah, school, 1304
*Naskhi* script, c. *ante* 300, c. 1200
Nasr, 913-43
Nasr b. Sayyar, 738-40
Nasrid dynasty of Granada, 1232-1492
Nasrullah Khan of Afghanistan, 1919
Nasser (Gamal Abd al-Nasr), 1918-70
Nastasan, 328-308 BC
Natakamani, c. 20 BC-AD 15
Natal, 1823, 1837, 1842, 1843, 1844, 1846, 1856, 1870, 1871, 1893, 1897
Natchez Indians, 1731
National Academy at New York, 1863
National Agrarian Institute, Venezuela, 1960
*National Apostasy*, 1833
National Assembly of Algeria, 1944, 1948; France, 1789-92; Greece, 1843; Persia, 1906, 1908; Portugal, 1935, 1945
National Assn., for the Advancement of Coloured Peoples, 1908, 1960
National Australian Federation, 1891
National Awami Party, 1975
National Banking Act in US, 1863, 1864
National Central Library, 1916
National Coalition Party in SA, 1933
National Confederation of Labour in Spain, 1888
National Congress in Vietnam, 1953
National Consultative Com. in France, 1941
National Council of Churches of Christ, 1950
National Council of Revolution (in Syria), 1963
National Debt in England, 1693, 1719, 1786
National Emergency Com., of WI, 1940
National Enterprise Board, 1975
National Federation of Employers, 1873
National Gallery, Dublin, 1915; London, 1832-8, 1915
National Government in UK, 1931, 1935
National Guard, Paris, 1830; US, 1957
National Health Act, UK, 1946; Ins., Bill in UK, 1911; Service in NZ, 1938
National Industrial Recovery Act, 1933

National Institute of Economic and Social Research, 1938
National Land League in Ireland, 1878
National League in Poland, 1895
National Liberal Party in Germany, 1866
National Mortgage Corp. of NZ, 1933
National Muhammadan Assn., 1877
National Party of Indonesia, 1929
National Patriotic Society, 1821
National Political Resurrection Movement, 1975
National Portrait Gallery, London, 1857
National Resources Mobilization Act, 1940
National Savings Movement, 1916
National Schools in Burma, 1921
National Socialist Party (NAZI), 1919, 1932
National Socialist Party in Poland, 1878
National Status Act in SA, 1934
'National Tribute' to Parnell, 1882
National Trust, UK, 1895
National Union Party, Portugal, 1930
National University of Ireland, 1908
Nationalist Party SA, 1923, 1953, 1954
Nationalization of finance, 1957, 1976; industry, 1912, 1916, 1918, 1946-51; oil industry, 1938, 1951, 1971, 1972; railways, 1919, 1933, 1937, 1948
Native Affairs, Dept, 1891
Native Authority Ordinance, 1926
Native Courts in Uganda, 1909
Native Laws Amendment Act SA, 1957
Native Representation Act, SA, 1936
NATO, 1949, 1950, 1951, 1952, 1954, 1958, 1963, 1966, 1971; Air Forces, 1956; Atlantic Congress, 1959
Natural History Museum, London, 1881; Paris, 1635
Natural Products Marketing Act, 1935
Naucratis, c. 663 BC
Naulochus, 36 BC
Naungdawgi of Burma, 1760-3
Naupactus, 429 BC, 217 BC
Nauplia, 7th c. BC
Naval Conference, London, 1936; Convention of London, 1936; Defence Act, 1889; Disarmament Conf., 1934
Navarino, battle, 1827
Navarre, 813, 859, 905, 937, 1045, 1355, 1379, 1529, 1834; Company of, 1382-1402; dynasty in France, 1589-1793; relations with Aragon, 1140, 1206, 1212, 1485; France, 1234-1512, 1365, 1521, 1607; part of Spain, 1512, 1515
Navarro, Carlos Arias, 1973, 1976
navies, early, c. 597 BC, 485 BC
Navigation Act, 1651, 1654, 1660, 1665, 1670, 1849
navigation schools, 1415, 1701
Navy Board in England, 1546
Nawab Dost Ali, 1740-1
Nawrahtaminye of Sagaing, 1350
Naxos, *post* c. 750 BC, 7th-6th c. BC, c. 500 BCf
Nayapala, 1038
Nazareth, 976, 1182, 1263
Nazis and Nazism, 1919, 1932, 1933, 1935, 1937, 1938, 1941, 1945, 1946
al-Nazzam, 845
Ndebele, 1892
Ndhlambi, 1819
Ndizewe, Prince Charles, 1966
Ndola, 1968
Ndongo, 1563, 1590, 1618
Neale, John Mason, 1818-66
Neapolis (Naples), 428 BC, 327 BC
Near East, 1854, 1887, 1921
Nearchus, 325 BC

Nebraska, 1854, 1867
Nebuchadrezzar I, 1124–1103 BC
Nebuchadrezzar II, 614–562 BC
Nebuchadrezzar III, 522 BC
Nebuchadrezzar IV, 521 BC
Necho II, Pharaoh, c. 610–595 BC
Nechtan, c. 710
Nechtansmere, 685
Necker, Jacques, 1732–1804
Nectan MacDerili, 596–617
Nectanebo I, Pharaoh, c. 404–360 BC
Nectanebo II, Pharaoh, 360–341 BC
Needham, John, 1713–81
Neerwinden, 1693
Nefusa, 757–923
Negapatam, Madras, 1781
'Negative Confession', 1581
Negeb, c. 783 BC
Negev, 1948
Negombo, Ceylon, 1640
Negrais, Burma, 1756, 1759
Negri Sembilan, 1896
negroes in N. America, 1760, 1861–5, 1866,
    1955–6, 1957, 1960–7; S. America, c. 1800;
    Haiti, 1844; Morocco, 1688–9; W. Indies,
    1764, 1789, 1791
Negropontus, 1470
Nehemiah, 443–428 BC
Nehru, Jawarharlal, 1939
Nehru Report, 1928
Nelson, Horatio, Lord, 1798–1805
Nemours, Duc de, 1831
Nennius, c. 800
Neo-Babylonian dynasty, 626 BC
Neo-Confucianism, 1032–85
Neo-Hittite Kingdoms, 745–720 BC
Neolithic civilization in Scotland, c. 2500 BC;
    tools in Italy, 3rd millenium BC
neomycin, 1949
Neonya Mariam of Ethiopia, 1372–82
Neo-Platonist school, 175–250, 1021 58
Nepal, c. 629–50, 647, 703, 878, 1768, 1790–1,
    1814
Nepherites I, of Mendes, 399 BC
Nepos, C., historian, 1st c. BC
Nepotianus, 350
Neptune, planet, 1846
Nequib (Muhammad Naquib), 1952–3
Nerchinsk, treaty, 1689, 1727
Nergal-shar-usur, 560 BC
Neri, St Philip, 1515–95
Nero, 29–68
*Neronia* festival, 60
Nerva, 96–8
Nervii, 57 BC
Nesbit, battle, 1355
Nesbit Moor, battle, 1402
Nestorian missionaries, 635; monk, 1287
Nestorianism, 428–31, 489, 843, 1138
Nestorius, 428–51
Netherlands, 1482, 1506, 1529, c. 1540, 1543,
    1548, 1565, 1572, 1585, 1642, 1697, 1713,
    1812, 1950; English merchants, 1359; with
    Japan, 1616, 1638, 1863; Spain, 1555, 1563,
    1567, 1572, 1576, 1579, 1667–8, *see also*
    Dutch, Holland and United Provinces
Netherlands, Austrian, 1746, 1789, 1792;
    Spanish, 1576–8, 1578, 1670, 1700, 1701,
    1715
Netherlands, East Indies, 1618–23
Netherlands, India, 1609–17
Neuburg, 1614, 1624; treaty, 1379
Neuchâtel, 1907, 1713, 1814, 1856
Neuhäusel, 1685
Neuilly, treaty, 1919
Neuilly-sur-Marne, 1202–4
Neuss, 1474

Neustadt, 1770
Neustria, c. 680–6, 686–714, 716–9
Neutrality Act, US, 1937, 1939
neutrons, 1934
Neuve Chapelle, 1915
Neva, R., 1240, 1703
Nevada, 1846, 1848, 1864
Neville family, 1453
Neville's Cross, 1346
Nevinson, Christopher R. W., 1889–1946
Nevis Is., 1628, 1629, 1882
Nevsky, Alexander, 1236–63
New Amsterdam, 1605–6, 1624, 1664
New Britain, Bismarck Arch., 1943
New Brunswick, 1818, 1837, 1864, 1866, 1867
New Caledonia, 1853
New College, Oxford, 1367, 1380
New Deal policies in US, 1933
New Deal, Canada, 1935
New Delhi, 1916
New Economic Policy in Russia, 1921
New England (-ers), c. 1001, 1497, 1600–43,
    1605–6, 1629–40, c. 1640, 1643–98, 1675–6,
    1690, 1704, 1708, 1722–4, 1735, 1755, 1760–3,
    1812, 1814; treaty with New France, 1705
New English Co., 1698–1702, 1708
New France, 1578, 1605–6, 1607, 1610–13,
    1634, 1636–9, 1637, 1647, 1654, 1663, 1690–3,
    1700–60, 1711, 1721, 1734, 1753–4, 1755,
    1756, 1762; Company of, 1627, 1700, 1704;
    Superior Council of, 1665, 1700; treaty with
    New England, 1705
New Granada, 1717, 1819, 1830–58
New Guinea, 1542, 1606, 1883, 1944, 1964;
    German, 1914
New Hampshire, 1679
New Holland, 1770
New Jersey, 1776
New Jerusalem, monastery, 1657
New Lanark, 1800
New Mexico, 1846, 1848
New Model Army, 1645
New Orleans, 1718, 1794–5, 1815
New Plymouth, 1620, 1841
New Rajagriha (Rajgir), c. 522–494 BC
New South Wales, 1762–1827, 1770, 1779,
    1808, 1821, 1838–43, 1850, 1857, 1859, 1870,
    1888; Legislative Assembly, 1854; Legislative
    Council, 1824, 1828; Parliament, 1891
New Spain, 1519, 1522, 1535
*New Statesman and Nation*, 1913
New Testament, 862, 1849, 1881
New World, 1493, 1494
New York, 1605–6, 1624, 1643, 1664, 1672–4,
    1690, 1765, 1770, 1776, 1788–90, 1830, 1872,
    1882, 1946, 1948, 1954, 1965; militia, 1709;
    State, 1709–10, 1947
*New York Herald*, 1835, 1870
'*New Youth*' journal in China, 1915
New Zealand, c. 925, c. 1150±, c. 1350, 1643,
    1646, 1769, *post* 1800, 1814, 1833–40, 1854,
    1860–4, 1868, 1869, 1872, 1879, 1885, 1889,
    1893–6, 1901, 1914–18, 1918, 1935–9,
    1947–51, 1954; Constitution, 1846, 1852;
    Dominion, 1907; land policy, 1912; meat
    trade, 1882, 1922; parliament, 1890, 1898,
    1914, 1940; politics, 1910; famine, 1926;
    relationship with Samoa, 1919, 1925; S
    Island, 1642
New Zealand Association, 1837; Company,
    1840, 1841, 1845; Legion, 1933
*New Zealander's First Book*, 1815
Newark, 1216, 1646
Newbolt, Sir Henry, 1862–1938
Newbury, 1643
Newcastle, 1640; treaty, 1334
Newcastle, Duke of, 1754–62

'Newcastle Programme', 1891
Newcomen, Thomas, 1705
Newfoundland, c. 1001, c. 1471–80, 1472, c.
    1494, 1497, 1500, 1501, 1506, 1508, 1524,
    1578, 1583, 1713, 1759, 1762, 1797, 1855,
    1864, 1866, 1933, 1940, 1949; fish, 1510;
    fishing grounds, 1501, c. 1504, 1514, *post*
    1714, *post* 1715
Newman, John Henry, Cardinal, 1801–90
Newmarket, 1647
Newspaper Stamp Act, 1712
newspapers, 1690, 1702, 1703, 1704, 1739,
    1855, 1885
Newton, Sir Isaac, 1642–1727
Nezib, 1839
Ngami, L., c. 1823
Ngarsishia of Pinya, 1343–50
Ngazargarmu, c. 1470, 1472–1504
Ngazaunggyan fortress, 1278, 1283
Ngendadumwe, Pierre, 1965
Ngo Dinh Diem, 1961
Ngolo, 1556, 1580, 1585
Ngola dynasty of Ndongo, c. 1500, 1579
Ngong Hills, c. *post* 1775
Ngoni, c. early 15th c., 1835, c. 1845, 1898
Nguema, Francisco Macia, 1968
Ni Taijo (Litan), 1392
Ni-Tsan, 1301–74
Niagara, 1727; Falls, 1895
Niall of Ireland, 380
Nicaea, 198 BC, 325, 1035, 1077, 1095, 1096,
    1208
Nicaean empire, 1204–61, 1246
Nicaragua, 1838, 1855, 1863–93, 1912–33, 1916,
    1927–33, 1933, 1955, 1972
Nice, 813, 1543, 1691, 1705, 1860, 1940; truce,
    1538
Nicene Creed, 381
Nicephorus I, 802–11
Nicephorus Botaniates, 1078–81
Nicephorus Gregoras, 1295–1359
Nicephorus Ouranos, 996
Nicephorus Phocas, 960–9
Nichiren, preacher, 1222–82
Nichiren sect, 12th c.
Nicholas V, anti-pope, 1328–30
Nicholas, Cardinal of Cues, 1451–2
Nicholas, patriarch, 907
Nicholas I, pope, 858–67
Nicholas II, pope, 1059–61
Nicholas III, pope, 1277–80
Nicholas IV, pope, 1288–92
Nicholas V, pope, 1447–55
Nicholas of Denmark, 1604–34
Nicholas I, of Montenegro, 1910
Nicolas I, of Russia, 1825–55
Nicolas II, of Russia, 1894–1918
nickel mining, 1883
Nicobar Is., 1025
Nicola, Enrico de, 1946
Nicolaiev, c. 1100 BC
Nicomedes II, 95 BC
Nicomedia, c. 290, 1204
Nicopolis, 66 BC, 1396
Nicuesa, Diego de, 1509
Nidwald, 1291
*Niebelunglied*, c. 1160
Niebuhr, Barthold, 1776–1831
Niebuhr, Carsten, 1761
Niemen, R., 1812
Niemirow, treaty, 1737
Nien Fei, 1855–68
Nienschantz, 1703
Nieppe, 1918
Niesse, Silesia, 1769
Nieszawa, Statute of, 1454
Nietsche, Friedrich Wilhelm, 1844–1900

Oaxaca, Mexico, 1806
Obadiah, prophet, c. 500 BC
Obasanjo, Olusegun, 1976
Oberammergau, 1634
Obiri Yeboa, Asantehene, c. 1600-97
Obock, 1862, 1869
Obote, Milton, 1963-6
Obregon, Álvaro, of Mexico, 1914-28
O'Brien, Smith, 1848
observatories, *ante* 830 or 831, 1074-5, 1201-74, 1259, 1271, 1576
*Observer, The*, 1908-42
O'Casey, Sean, 1884-1964
Ockeghem, Jean de, composer, c. 1430-95
O'Connell, Daniel, 1775-1847
Octavia, 40-32 BC
Octavianus, son of Alberic, 955-63
Octavius, C., (Octavian), 45 BC-AD 27
Octennial Act in Ireland, 1768
October Diploma of Austria, 1860
October Revolution in Russia, 1917
oculists, 873
Oda Nobunaga, 1534-82
Odaenathus, 260-4
Odeon, 445 BC; of Herodes Atticus, 160
Oder, R, 992-1025, 1648
Oder-Neisse line, 1970
Oder-Spree canal, 1661-8
Odessa, 1905, 1918, 1941
Odilo, bp, 994
Odo, bp of Bayeux, 1082-7, 1088
Odo, Abp of Canterbury, 942-58
Odo, Count of Paris, 888-98
O'Donnell, 1601
O'Donnell, Leopold, 1809-67
Odovacar, 476-93
Odryses, 429 BC, 351 BC
Oea, 69
Oeland, naval battle, 1676
*Oeuvre des Noirs*, 1839
Offa the Great of Mercia, 757-96
Offaly, 1556
Offaly, Thomas, Lord, 1534-5
Offa's Dyke, c. 784
Offenbach, Jacques, 1819-80
Ogata Korin, c. 1657-1716
Ogdensburg, 1940
Oghuz Turks, 1072
Ogiso dynasty of Benin, c. 900
Oglethorpe, James, general, 1732
Ogodai, 1227-41
Ogul Gaimysh, 1248-51
Oguola, Oba of Benin, c. 1280
O'Higgins, Bernardo, of Chile, 1817
Ohio R, 1748, 1749, 1787, 1791; State, 1795, 1803
Ohlenshläger, Adam Gottlob, 1779-1850
Ohm, Georg Simon, 1787-1854
Ohm's law, 1827
oil, crude, 1829
oil concessions, 1901, 1925, 1944, 1965; embargo, 1944, 1965; industry in Africa, 1956, 1958, 1971; N. America, 1872, 1947; S. America, 1911, 1918; Britain, 1970; Far East, 1883, 1886, 1896; Near East, 1907, 1951, 1954; N Sea, 1975; USSR, 1873; pipelines, 1935, 1968
Oil Creek, Penn., 1859
oil for scent-making, c. 2500 BC
Oirat, 1207
Oise R., 481-511
Ojeda, Alonso, de, 1509
Ojukwu, Odumegwu, Lt. Col., 1967
Oka R, 13th c.
Okello, John, 1964
Oken, Lorenz, 1779-1851

Okhotsk, sea, 1639
*Okhrana* (secret police), 1880
Okinawa, 1846, 1945
Oklahoma, 1539
Okuma Shigenobu, 1881
Olaf V, of Denmark, 1376-87
Olaf of Norway, 994
Olaf V, of Norway, 1957
Olaf Trygvasson, 995-1000
Olbia, c. 646 BC
Old Age Pensions, 1908
Old Catholic Congress, 1871
Old Comrade's Associations, 1948
'Old Man of the Mountains', 1192
Old Pretender, 1701-16
Old Testament, c. 10th c. BC, 404, 678, 809-73
Oldenburg, 1667, 1853
Olduvai, 1959
Oleg, prince, 907, 912
Oleg, son of Sviatoslav I, 972
Oléron, treaty, 1287
Olga, Queen, Regent of Greece, 1920
Olga of Russia, 945-69
Olgierd of Lithuania, 1345-77
Olid, Cristóbal de, 1523
Olier, Canon, 1642
oligarchy, 411 BC
Olinda, 1630-54
Oliphant, Margaret, 1828-97
Oliva, peace, 1660
Olivares, Count-Duke of, 1621-65
olive cultivation, 8th-6th c. BC, 81 BC, 81-96, 1561
olive oil, c. 969-936 BC
Oljeitu Ilkhan of Persa, 1304-16
Olivier, Dr Borg, 1962
Ollivier, Emile, 1870
Olmedo, 1445
Olmütz, convention, 1850; peace, 1479
Oloibiri, Nigeria, 1956
Olugh-beg, 1447-9
Olybrius, 472
*Olympeion*, c. 132-131 BC, 129
Olympia, 468-457 BC; Era, c. 776 BC
Olympic Games, c. 776 BC, 392 BC, 388 BC, 364 BC, 393, 394
Olympic Games (modern), 1896, 1908, 1964, 1968
Olympius, exarch, 650-2
Olympus, 365 BC, 357 BC
Olynthus, 386 BC
O'Malley, Lady, 1891-1974
Oman, 689, 1784, 1805, 1840, 1848, 1958
Oman, Sir Charles William C., 1860-1948
Omani Arabs, 1650, c. 1651, 1652, 1660, 1661, 1670, 1679, 1688, 1698, 1699, c. 1700, 1723, 1727, 1744, 1745, 1822
Omar of Kanem, 1394-8
Ombudsman in UK, 1966
Omdurman, 1884, 1898
omnibuses, 1829
O'More, Rory, 1641
Omri, c. 876-869 BC
Omsk, 1717, 1918, 1919
Omurtag, Khan of Bulgars, 814-831
On, city, c. *post* 2480 BC
One Big Union (OBU), 1918
O'Neil, Conn, 1542
O'Neill, Hugh, 1603
O'Neill, John, 1870
O'Neill, Shane, 1559-67
O'Neill, Terence, Captain, 1969
Onganía, Juan Carlos, 1966
Onondagas, 1655
Ontario, L., 1726
Opera, Paris, 1821
Ophellas, 309 BC

ophthalmoscope, 1850
ophthalmy, 777-857, c. 850, 1188-9, 1256, c. 1296
Opie, John, 1761-1807
Opis, 539 BC
Opium, 1800, 1839
Opoku Ware, Asantehene, 1731-42
Oporto, 1661, 1757, 1809, 1820, 1832, 1868, 1871, 1891, 1927
Oppenheim, Edward Phillips, 1866-1946
*Opritchina*, 1564
Oran, 1509, 1708, 1732, 1830, 1940, 1960
Orange, Prince of, 1795
Orange Free State, 1836, 1854, 1857, 1865, 1900; River, 1848
Orange lodges in Ireland, 1795
Orange Order in Ireland, 1837, 1845
Oranmiyan, c. 1176
Oratorians, 1575, 1613
Oratory of Divine Love, 1516
Orchomenum, 365 BC
Orchomenus, 86 BC
Orczy, Baroness, 1865-1947
Ord, Sir Harry, 1867-73
Order of Christ, Portugal, 1312
Order of Merit, 1902
Order of Preachers *see* Dominicans
Orde's Commercial Resolutions, 1784-5
*Ordinem vestrum*, 1245
*ordonnances*, 1830
Ordoño II, León, 910-24
Ordos, 385-431, 407-31
Örebro, 1812
Oregon, 1818, 1841-6, 1859
Orekhevo-Zonieva, Moscow, 1885
Orel, USSR, 1941, 1943
Orenburg, 4th c. BC, 1391, 1735, 1773
Oresme, Nicole, c. 1323-82
*Orestes*, 408 BC
Orford, Earl of, 1714
organ, hydraulic, c. 265 BC
organ-builders, 1683-1753
*Organisation Armée Secrète*, 1962
*Organisation Commune Africaine et Malgache*, 1965
*Organisation Secrète*, 1950
Organization of African Unity, 1963, 1965, 1968; Summit Conference, 1968, 1975
Organization for European Economic Cooperation, 1948
Organization of Petroleum Exporting Countries, 1960
*Orgbureau* in Russia, 1918
Orhogbua of Benin, c. 1550-78
Oriental and African Studies, School, 1916
Oriental Co., 1719
oriental trade, c. 215
Origen, 185-254
Orinoco, R, 1595, 1816
Orissa (Kalinga) 297 BC, 1592, 1727, 1751, 1918
Orkhan, 1352
Orkhon Basin, 6th-7th c.
Orkney Is., c. 600, 785-850, 1098-1103, 1266
Orlando, Vittorio, 1917
Orléanists, 1411, 1412, 1413, *see also* Armagnacs
Orléans, 838, 1422, 1428-9, 1561; besieged by Catholics, 1563
Orléans, Dukes of, 1344, 1485-8, 1715, 1793, 1830, 1852; family, 1885
Orléansville, 1843
Orly, 1975
Ormond Peace, 1646
Orodes II, *post* 56-c. 37 BC
Orontes, R, 300 BC, 1142
Oropos, 366 BC

Orpen, Sir William, 1878–1931
orphanages in China, 1247
Orsini family, 1486
Orsini, Felice, 1858
Orsini, John, 1328
Orsini, Napoleon, 1334
Orsza, 1514
Ortega y Gasset, 1883–1955
Orvieto Cathedral, c. 1129–1330
Osaka, 1582–90, 1616, 1854, 1970; merchants, 1846–67
Osbald of Northumbria, 796
Osberht of Northumbria, 848–66
Osborne, Sir Thomas, 1631–1712
Osborne, Dorothy, 1627–95
Oscan language, 180 BC
Oscans, c. *post* 450 BC, 428 BC, 278–275 BCf
Oscar I, of Sweden, 1859
Oscar II, of Sweden, 1872–1907
Osei Tutu, Asantehene, 1697–1712 or 17
*Osiander*, 1612
Osiander, André, 1498–1552
Osiris-Apis cult, 3rd c. BC
Oslo, 1811 formerly Christiania, 1925
Osnabrück, 1644
Osney Abbey, 1222
Osorio, Oscar, 1950–6
Osorkon I, Pharaoh, c. 924–c. 888 BC
Osorkon II, Pharaoh, c. 881–c. 852 BC
Osred I, of Northumbria, 705–16
Osred II, of Northumbria, 788–90
Osrhoene, 164, 197
Osric of Deira, 632–3
Osric of Northumbria, 718–29
Osroes, 106–29
Ost, Pierre van, 1379–98
Ostend, 1601, 1604, 1722, 1794, 1876–8; Manifesto, 1854
Ostia, 69 BC, 846, 849
Ostrogoths, c. 200, 257, c. 370, 376, *ante* 461, 470, 471–3, 477–83, c. 500; at war with Byzantium, 535–54; in Italy, 406, 487, 554
Ostrolenka, battle, 1831
Osu, 1650
Osuna, Duke of, 1618–20
Oswald of Northumbria, 632–42
Oswego, 1726, 1727, 1756, 1758
Oswine of Deira, 642–51
Oswulf of Northumbria, 758
Oswy of Bernicia, 642–70
Oswy of Deira, 655–70
Oswy of Mercia, 656–9
Otago, NZ, 1848, 1863
Otchakov, 1738, 1783
Otfried of Wissemburg, 862
Otho, 69
Otho de la Roche, 1205
Oti Akenten, Asantehene, c. 1630–60
Otranto, 1480, 1481, 1509
Otrar, 1405
Ottawa, 1535, 1642, 1646, 1857, 1932, 1951; Agreement, 1937; valley, 1807
Otterburn, 1388
Otto, Duke of Bavaria, 1070–1
Otto, King of Bavaria, 1886–1913
Otto, Prince of Bavaria, 1832–67; as King of Greece, 1832–62
Otto I, emperor, 934–73
Otto II, emperor, 973–83
Otto III, emperor, 983–1002
Otto IV, emperor, 1197–1218
Otto of Wittelsbach, 1208, 1308
Ottokar I, of Bohemia, 1197–1230
Ottokar II, of Bohemia, 1247–78
Ottoman Bank, 1896
Ottoman dynasty in Asia Minor, 1288–1366 *and see* Turkey *and* Turks

Oubangui-Chari, 1958
Ouchy, treaty, 1912
Oudenarde, 1582; battle, 1708
Oudh, c. 320–35, 1774, 1797, 1800, 1856; Tenancy Act, 1868
Oudja oasis, 1844
Oudney, explorer, 1821–5
*Oulojenie*, legal code, 1648–9
Oura mines, 1771
Ourgla, Algeria, 1852
Ouseley, Sir F. A. G., 1825–89
outriggers used, 3rd c. BC
Ou-yang Hsiu, 1007–72
Ovamboland, SWA, 1968
Ovando, General, 1969
Overseas Food Corporation, 1947
Overseas of the Poor, 1601
over-time ban, 1973
Overweg, explorer, 1851
Ovid, 43 BC, 8
Oviedo, 791–842, 1388, 1937
Oviedo, André de, bp, 1557
Ovimbundu, c. 1840, *ante* 1854
Owain the Great, 1137–70
Owain ap Thomas, 1370–8
Owen, Robert, 1771–1858
Owen's College, Manchester, 1880
Oxenstierna, Sweden, 1632–44
Oxenstjerna, Jöns Bengtston, 1465
OXFAM, 1942
Oxford, 1016, 1136, 1177, 1201, 1209, 1474, 1480, 1488, 1490, 1555, 1556, 1642; Assembly of, 1018; Earl of, 1711–15; Parliament of, 1681; Provisions of, 1258, 1261; University, c. 1130, c. 1224–53, 1230, 1447; University Rugby team, 1969
Oxford and Asquith, Earl of, 1852–1928
Oxford Group, 1939
Oxford Movement, 1833
Oxinden, Sir George, 1664
Oxus R., c. 126 BC, c. 425
oxygen, 1774
Oyo, 1729–60, 1781, 1792, 1811, 1830, 1888
Ozolna, Oba, c. 1484–1504


*Pacem in terris*, 1963
Pachacuti, Inca, 1438–71
Pachua, Mexico, 1552
Pacific Charter, 1954; coast of USA, 1790–5, 1803; Ocean, 1513, 1520, 1921, 1942, 1944, 1968; Railway Bill, 1862
pacifism, 1940
Pacorus, 77, 105
'Pact' in SA, 1923, 1924
*Pactum Hludovicianum*, 817
Paderborn, assembly, 777; cathedral, 1143
Paderewski, Ignacy Jan, 1860–1941
Padetha Raza, poet and playwright, 1714–33
Padua, 602, 1222, 1368, 1404–5, 1423, 1918
Paduka Tuan of Malacca, 1510–11
Paeligni, 325 BC, 311 BC
Paetus, consul, 198 BC
Páez, José Antonio, 1823–63
Paez, Pedro, 1618
Pagan, King of Burma, 1846–53
Pagan city, Burma, c. 849, 1044–77, 1225, 1299, 1542; dynasty, 1044–1287; Kingdom, 1271, 1283, 1287, 1312
pagan sacrifices, 341, 356, 361; worship, 392
Paganini, Niccolò, 1782–1840
Paganini, Alessandro de, 1485
Pahang, 16th c., 1607–36, 1858–63, 1889, 1896
Pahlevi dynasty, 1925
Paine, Thomas, 1737–1809

Painlevé, Paul, 1917
paint, duty on, 1766
'painted-grey ware', c. 1100–c. 500 BC
Pais, Fr, 1603–74
Pais, Sidónio, 1917–18
Paisley, Rev. Ian, 1968
Paisiello, Giovanni, 1741–1816
Pak Cheng-hi of S. Korea, 1972
Pakenham, Edward, 1815
Pakistan, 1933, 1940, 1947, 1954, 1956, 1962, 1968; constitution, 1969; relations with Britain, 1966, 1972; Communist China, 1963, 1947, 1949, 1965, 1971, 1972; Turkey, 1954; US, 1954
Pakistan, E, becomes Bangladesh, 1971; W, relations with India, 1971
Pakubuwana I, of Mataram, 1705–19
Pakubuwana II, of Mataram, 1725–49
Pakubuwana III, of Mataram, 1749–88
Pakubuwana IV, of Surakarta, 1788–1820
Pala dynasty, 8th c., 1199
Palace Guard in Spain, 1512
Palach, Jan, Czech student, 1969
Palaeologi dynasty, 1261–1453
Palafitte, c. *post* 2000 BC
Palais Marie in Petrograd, 1917
Palatinate (of the Rhine), 1302, 1545, 1689, 1709, 1732, 1778
Palencia, c. 1212
Palembang, c. 150, 670–3, 683–6, 685–9, 1025
Palermo, 830–1, 1052, 1071, 1072, 1169–85, 1258, 1820, 1860, 1943; Royal Chapel, 1140
Palestine, c. 1250–c. 1200 BC, c. 1200–c. 1000 BC, c. 386–383 BC, 201–200 BC, 47 BC, 40, 634, 976, 1175, 1834, 1917, 1918, 1937, 1947, 1948; Anglo-American Committee of Inquiry, 1946; Archaeological Museum, 1929; home for Jews, 1945, 1946; British White Paper, 1938, 1939; British Mandate, 1923, 1948; Liberation Organization, 1964, 1975, 1976
relations with Arab countries, 1948, *see also* Israel
Palestine Foundation Fund, 1921
Palestinians, 1968, 1970, 1971
Palestrina, Pierluigi de, 1525–94
Palestro, 1859
Paley, William, 1743–1805
Palgrave, William Gifford, 1861
Pali dynasty, 8th c.; language, late 12th c.
Palladio, Andrea, 1508–80
Pallava dynasty, *post* 550–c. 850, c. 600–25, 684
*pallium*, 1435
Palluan et Frontenac, Comte de, 1672–99
Palma, 1276
Palma, Arturo Alessandri, 1920–38
Palma, Estrada, of Cuba, 1902–6
Palma, Majorca, 1380
Palmerston, Lord, 1846–65
palm-oil, 1841
Palmyra, 1100 BC, 42–41 BC, 9 BC, 17, 130, 262, 273, 1805
Pamiers, bp of, 1302
Pamir Mts, 749–50, 1217
Pamplona, 533, 778, 924, 1521, 1814
Pamphylia, 468 BC, 102 BC, 76 BC, 43
Pan Mun Jom, 1951
Pan Pan, early, 3rd c.
Pan Tchao, 84
Pan-African Congress, 1960
Panama, 1513, 1530, 1535, 1572, 1637, 1699, 1850, 1903, 1959; canal, 1880, 1892, 1901, 1903, 1904, 1914; City, 1903; Isthmus, 1846; relations with USA, 1939, 1964
Pan-American Conferences, 1889, 1938, 1945, 1948
Panangkaran, c. 760–80
Pan-Anglican Synod, 1867

Panchor, 1699-1718
Pando, José Hannel, 1899-1904
Pandurpur, 1815
Pandya Dynasty, *post* 550-c. 850; Kingdom, 1263, 1288-93, 1334
Pandyans, 9th c., 907-49, 985-1014
Pangal, 1420
Pangalos, Theodore, 1926
Pangasinan, 1574
Pan-German League, 1891
Pangkor, 1874
Pan-Hellenic congress, 371 BC; League, 307 BC
Panion, 200 BC
Panipat, battles, 1526, 1556, 1761
Panium, battle, 198 BC
Panjdeh Oasis, 1885
Panjim, 1759
Pankhurst, Emmeline, 1903
Pan-Malayan Federation of Labour, 1947
Pannonia, 16 BCf, 6f, 167, 193, 258, 314, 378, 830, 870-85
Panormes (Palermo), 397 BC, 254 BCf
Pan-Orthodox Conference, 1961
Pan-Russian Congress of Soviets, 1917; government, 1918
Pan-Slav Congress, 1848, 1892
Pantaenus, c. *ante* 155
Pantainos, *post* 106
Pantaleon, c. 190-180 BC
Pantheon, Greece, 1801-3
Panthéon, Paris, 1764-90, 1791
*Panther*, gunboat, 1911
Pantocrator, church, c. 1124
Panungulan, c. 780-800
Papadopoulos, George, 1972
Papal Authority, 1139-85, 1535; Bulls, 1231, 1279, 1301, 1302, 1306, 1312, 1314, 1317, 1343, 1484, 1508, 1520, 1564, 1570, 1571, 1621, 1622, 1642, 1665, 1705, 1713, 1839; decrees, 1075; elections, 1059; embassies, 1520,; encyclicals, 1832, 1879, 1891, 1906, 1907, 1924, 1926, 1931, 1937, 1951, 1957, 1961, 1963, 1967, 1968; legates, 1182, 1221, 1411, 1518; missions, 786; palace at Avignon, 1316-91; supremacy, 1369
Papal Nuncio, 1521, 1542, 1645, 1873, 1880, 1950; Pro-Nuncio, 1967 *see also* Vatican
Papal States, 785, 1240, 1265, 1353-7, 1357, 1358-67, 1378, 1403, 1809, 1848, 1849, 1860
paper, duty on, 1766
paper, made and used, 2nd c. BC; in China, c. 100 BC, c. 100; Italy, c. 1268-76; Morocco, c. 1100; Samarqand, c. 750; Spain, c. 1150
paper mills, 794, c. 900
paper money, 1st c. BC, 3rd c., 1294, 1730, 1764, 1883
Paphlagonia, 396-395 BC, 1130
Papin, Denis, 1707
Papinian, 212
Papinius Statius, P., c. 61-96
Papirius Cursor, 293 BC
Pappus, mathematician, c. 285
Papua, 1964
Papua Act, 1903
Papua New Guinea. 1975
papyrus, Greco-Arabic, 709
papyrus reed, c. 2500 BC
parachutes, 1480, 1797, 1912
Paradise of Wisdom, 850
paraffin, 1850
Paraguay, 1537, 1588, 1753, 1811, 1813, 1814-40, 1865-70, 1870-1954, 1928; relations with Argentina, 1864-70; Bolivia, 1935, 1938; Brazil, 1864-70, 1870; Uruguay, 1864-70
Parakrama Bahu I, of Ceylon, 1153-86
Parakrama Bahu VI, of Kotte, 1412-67

Parakrama Bahu VIII, of Kotte, 1484-1508
Paramardi (Parmal), 1203
Parameswara, c. 1390, c. 1400, 1405, 1411, 1414
'paramountcy' of native interests, 1929
Parana, Argentina, 1852, 1853
Parantaka I, 907-49
parchment, 2nd c. BC
Pardon and Oblivion, Act, 1652
Paré, Ambroise, 1509-90
Parénda, Ahmadnagar, 1630
*Parens Scientiarum*, 1231
Parians, c. 680 BC
Parícutin, volcano, 1943
Paris, 360, 486, 885, 978, 1277, 1370, 1413, 1418, 1539-41, 1571, 1590, 1648, 1652, 1717, 1775, 1814, 1815, 1819, 1832, 1842, 1843, 1848, 1870, 1871, 1879, 1895, 1907, 1914, 1917, 1918, 1921, 1940, 1944; taken by Normans, 845, 856-61, 886-7; Conferences, 1919, 1946, 1947, 1950, 1959; treaties, 1229, 1259, 1303, 1320, 1623, 1657, 1762, 1763, 1805, 1808, 1812, 1814, 1815, 1817, 1856, 1898, 1947, 1953; Communist demonstrations, 1952, 1960; Opera, 1861-74; riots, 1720, 1787, 1789, 1795, 1820, 1830, 1839, 1848, 1849, 1867, 1927, 1962, 1967; Parliament of, c. 1250, 1551, 1666, 1714, 1762, 1771, 1774, 1787; University, 1136, 1229, 1253f., 1257, 1311-12, 1325, 1332, 1381, 1394, 1405, 1517, 1528
Paris, Matthew, *post* 1259
parish, poor, 1536
Parisot de la Vallette, Jean, 1494-1568
Park, Mungo, 1771-1806
Parkau, 1683
Parker, Admiral, 1841
Parkes, Sir Henry, 1815-90
Parliament, English, 1265, 1310, 1375, 1377, 1380, 1386, 1414, 1517, 1584, 1603, 1610-11, 1657, 1658, 1664, 1679, 1693, 1832, 1833, 1858, 1965; 'Addled', 1614; 'Barebones', 1653; 'Cavalier', 1661-79; 'Convention', 1660, 1689; 'Good', 1376; 'Long', 1640, 1659; 'Merciless', 1388; 'Model', 1295; 'Protectorate', 1654-6; 'Rump', 1648, 1653; 'Short', 1640; relations with Charles I, 1626, 1628, 1629; relations with Monarchy, 1689
Parliament, Triennial, 1693, 1694; exclusion of Crown Offices, 1695
Parliament Act in Britain, 1910, 1911
Parliament of Dublin, 1320; Gloucester, 1467; Union, 1707, 1719, 1965, 1969; Lincoln, 1316; Paris, 1368, 1594; at Scone, 1320; in Scotland, 1173, 1326, 1399, 1466; of York, 1318, 1322
Parliamentary Commission in Ceylon, 1927; Commissioner, 1966; forces (Roundheads), 1642-7, 1652; Labour Party, 1963; Reform Act, 1867;
Parma, 183 BC, 1248, 1325-7, 1515, 1734, 1735, 1752, 1761, 1802, 1831, 1859, 1860; Duchy of, 1633, 1636, 1731
Parma, Duke of, 1731
Parmal (Paramardi), 1203
Parmehutu Party, Rwanda, 1958
Parmoutier, Jean, 1530
Parnell, Charles Stewart, 1846-91
Paros, 489 BC
Parr, Katherine, 1543-8
Parratt, Sir Walter, 1841-1924
Parry, Sir C. H. H. 1848-1914
Parsons, Robert, 1580
Parthamasiris, 113
Parthamaspates, 116
Parthenon, c. 447-432 BC, 1687
Parthenopean Republic, 1799
Parthia and Parthians, 547 BC, c. 250 BC,

211-191 BCf, 141 BC, *post* 56-c. 37 BC, 2, 6-9, 18, c. 48, 75, 112, 133; relations with Rome, 92 BC, 68 BC, 36 BC, 23 BC, 1 BCf, 37, 51, 62f, 163, 197
Parthian dynasty, c. 250 BC, c. 200 BC
*Parti Communiste Algérien*, c. 1920
*Parti du Peuple Algérien*, 1937, 1939
*Partido Nacional Revolucionario*, 1929
Pasai, 1523; Princes of, 1414
Pasargadae, 559-530 BC
Pascal, *ante* 1150
Pascal, antipope, 687-92
Pascal, Blaise, 1623-62
*Pascendi Gregis*, 1907
Paschal III, antipope, 1164-8
Paschal I, pope, 817-24
Paschal II, pope, 1099-1118
Pasha of Marrakesh, 1953
Pashas of Egypt, 1517-1798
Pashas of Timbuktu, Moroccan, 1591-1654, 1618
Pasiteles, sculptor, c. 90-50 BC
Passarowitz, treaty, 1718
Passau, 942; treaty, 1552
Passchendaele, battle, 1917
passenger vessel, atomic, 1959
*Passion Play*, Oberammergau, 1634
passive, resistance, 1907
Pasteur, Louis, 1822-95
Pasteur Institute, Brazzaville, 1908
pasteurisation, 1864
*Pastor aeternus*, 1870
Pastoral Protection Society, 1855
*Pastoralis cura*, 1314
'Pastry Cook' war, 1838
Pasuruan, 1616
Pataliputra, 494 BC, 250 BC
Patan, 1178
Patani, 1629
Patapan of Sanjaya, 832
*Pataria*, 1056
Patassé, Ange, 1976
Patch, General, 1944
Pate, sultanate, 1204, c. 1291-1399, 1569, 1678, 1679, 1686, 1688, 1727, 1728, 1729, 1807, 1848
Pater, Walter Horatio, 1839-94
*Pater Patriae*, 2 BC
Paterson, Willian, 1694
Pathans, 1812, 1814-15, 1897
Patiala, Sikh state, 1767
Patih Yunus of Demak, 1511
Patino, 1726-36
Patmore, Coventry, 1823-96
Patna, 1574, 1630-3
Patriarch of Jerusalem, 800
'Patriarch' of the Jews, 70
patriarchate of Moscow, 1700
Patriarchs of E Church, 1443, 1511, 1561
Patriot Party in Ireland, 1772
Patriotic Union in Spain, 1926
Patriots in Ireland, 1689, 1690
Patristic studies, 1618
Patrons of Husbandry, 1866
Patton, George Smith, general, 1885-1945
Pau, 1788
Paul II, pope, 1464-71
Paul III, pope, 1534-49
Paul IV, pope, 1555-9
Paul V, pope, 1605-21
Paul VI, pope, 1897-; earlier ref., see 711
Paul, St Vincent de, 1576-1660
Paul, bp of Samosata, 264-73
Paul of Aegina, c. 650
Paul the Deacon, 720-99
Paul I, of Greece, 1947-64
Paul I, of Russia, 1796-1801
Paul-Boncour, French premier, 1932

Pausanias, geographer, 2nd c., 160
Pausanias, 472 BC
Pausanias, 404-403 BC
Pavia, battle, 1525; besieged, 773; cathedral, 1488; treaties, 754, 756, 1617; university, 1361
Pavía, Capt-Gen., of Castile, 1874
paw paw, c. 1629
Paxos, 230 BC
Pazzi, 1476, 1478; Pazzi Chapel, 1430-46
P-document of Hexateuch, post 520 BC
Peace, Perpetual, 1435, 1515
Peace Conference, 1919, 1946
Peace Corps, US, 1961
Peaceful Uses of Atomic Energy, 1958
Peacock Throne, 1628, 1739
Peada of Mercia, c. 655-6
Pearce, Franklin, US president, 1853-7
Pearce Commission, 1972
Pearl Harbour, Hawaii, 1887, 1941
Peary, Robert E., 1909
peasant popular movements, post 150
peasant risings in S. America, 1810; Bohemia, 1783; China, 18, 874, 878, 1855-68; Egypt, c. 161; England, 1381; France, 1358; Germany, 1524; India, 1669; Lebanon, 1858; Oura, 1771; Russia, 1902; Switzerland, 1513
Peasant's Revolt, 1381
Pedir, 1523
Pedrell, Felipe, 1841-1922
Pedro I, of Brazil, 1821-31
Pedro II, of Brazil, 1831-89
Peel, Sir Robert, 1788-1850
'peelers', 1829
Peerage Act, UK, 1963
peerages, life, in Britain, 1958
Pegau, battle, 1080
Pegu, 825, 1287, 1356, 1371, 1385-1425, 1388, 1401, 1406, 1409, 1486, 1496, 1503, 1511, 1534-6, 1538, 1551, 1593, 1599, 1633, 1634, 1740, 1757, 1852, 1853, 1854, 1930
Péguy, Charles, 1873-1914
Peikthanomyo (Vishnu City), 1st c. BC
Peipous, Lake, 1242
Peirce, C. S. 1839-1914
Peixoto, Florians, of Brazil, 1891
Pekah, c. 737-732 BC
Pekahiah, c. 738-737 BC
Peking, 129 BC, 1125, 1368, 1403-24, 1411, 1414, 1419, 1420, 1424-44, 1550, 1638, 1644, 1651-94, 1653, 1690, 1722, 1727, 1729, 1853-5, 1860, 1900, 1902, 1908, 1918-22, 1919, 1921, 1937, 1940, 1949, 1958, 1965, 1976; treaty, 1901, 1925; university, 1902
'Peking Man,' 1920
Pekrovsk tomb, c. 1300-1200 BC
Pelagianism, c. 360-420, 431; heretical, 416, 529; orthodox, 415
Pelagius, c. 360-420
Pelagius I, pope, 556-60 or 61
Pelagius II, pope, 578 or 9-90
Pelayo of Asturia, 718
Pelham, Hon. Henry, 1743-54
Pellegrini, Carlo, 1839-89
Pelloux, Luigi, 1898
Peloponnese, 455-454 BC, 446 BCf, 303 BC, 215-214 BC, 397, 783, 1715
Peloponnesian League, c. 550-500 BC, 431-421 BC, 405 BC, 396 BC, 371 BC
Pelsart, Capt. François, 1629
Pelusium, 605 BC, 373 BC, 31-30 BC, 640, 859
Pemay, Pharaoh, c. 788-c. 782 BC
Pemba, c. 730, post 1612, 1644, 1747, 1872, 1890
Pembroke, Earls of, 1170-1307
Penal Code in Britain, 1823
Penang, 1786, 1788, 1791, 1797, 1800, 1805, 1816, 1818/9, 1821, 1832, 1946; Presidency,

1826; Residency, 1830
pencil, graphite, 1565
Penda of Mercia, c. 626-55; King of Wessex, 645-8
Pendeles, monastery, 1578
Pendleton Civil Service Act, 1883
penicillin, 1928, 1940
Penn, William, 1682
Penna, Affonso, of Brazil, 1906-9
Pennsylvania, 1709, 1776; state, 1778; University, 1740, 1755
Pennsylvania Rock Oil Co., 1854
Penrith, 927
pensions, state, in China, 8th c.; old age in Britain, 1908; NZ, 1898, 1938
Pentapolis, 642-3
Pentateuch, end of 2nd c. BC; translated, c. 362; authority denied, 1862
Penthièvre, 1365
Pentlands rising, 1666
'People's Budget', 1909, 1910
People's Charter, 1838, 1839
People's Council in Dutch EI, 1918, 1922; Indonesia, 1931
People's Liberation Front, (Ceylon), 1971
People's Party of Indonesia, 1931
People's Republic of Congo, 1964
People's Republic of S. Yemen, 1967
People's United Front in Ceylon, 1956
Peoria, Ill., USA, 1854
Pépin I, c. 680-6
Pépin II, 686-714
Pépin, son of Charlemagne, 809-14
Pépin of Aquitaine, 838
Pépin Ie Bref, 741-68
pepper, 17th c., 1619, 1840
Pepys, Samuel, 1633-1703
Pera, 1580, 1581, 1774, 1831
Peradeniya, Ceylon, 1943
Perak, ante 1st c., 1540, 1607-36, 1728, 1740 or 2, 1742, 1816, 1820, 1822, 1826, 1874, 1884, 1896; Sultan of, 1817
Perceval, Spencer, 1809-12
Percy family, 1402, 1403, 1406, 1453
Perdicaris incident, 1904
Perdiccas, 368-321 BC
Pereira, Aristides, 1975
Pereira, Fr Julian, 1576-7
Perennis, 185
Perfectus of Córdoba, 850
Pergamum, 208 BC, 201-200 BCf, c. 160 BC, 133 BCf, 85 BC; Great Altar, c. 197-159 BC
Pergolesi, Giovanni Battista, 1710-36
Periander, 627-585 BC
Pericles, 448-429 BC
Périer, Casimir Pierre, 1777-1832
Périgueux, cathedral, 984-1047, treaty, 1311
Perim Is., 1798, 1858
Periplus of the Erythraean Sea, c. 106
Perkins, W. H., 1856
Perlak, 1292
Perlis, Malaya, 1547, 1771, 1842, 1910, 1930
'Permanent Settlement' of Bengal, 1793
Pernambuco, 1521, 1530, 1630, 1935
Perón, Evita, 1946-52
Perón, Juan D., colonel, 1895-1974
Péronne, Agreement, 1192
Pérouse, 593
Pérouse, Comte de la, 1788
'Perpetual Arrangement', 1474; Edict, 1577; Peace, 1495
Perpignan, 1324, 1542, 1642
Perry, US Commodore, 1853-4
Persepolis, 520-460 BC, 649/50
Perseus, 179 BC
Pershing, John Joseph, 1860-
Persia, 550 BC, 520 BC, c. 350 or 400 BC, 345 BC, 237-8, 241, 481-3, 503-13, 531, c. 550,

570 or 71, 575, 7th c., 611, 626, 867-908, 1001-24, 1210, 1231, 1256, 1260, 1380-93, 1383, 1387, 1407, 1505, 1529, 1618-19, 1637, 1650, 1736, 1743-4, 1802, 1837, 1838, 1856, 1862, 1864, 1870, 1901, 1907, 1924, 1929, 1935; constitution, 1906, 1927;
relations with Afghanistan, 1720-4, 1729, 1730, 1737-8, 1739, 1829, 1869, 1920; Athens, 454 BC, 449-448 BC, 355 BCf; Belgium, 1898; Britain, 1598, 1800, 1808, 1814, 1834-8, 1855, 1932; Byzantium, 524-31, 532, 539-62, 572, 603, 624, 628, 630; Carthage, c. 484-483 BC; Dutch, 1623, 1645; Egypt, 525 BCf, 486 BC, 454 BC, 399 BC, c. 386-383 BCf, 378 BC, 343 BC, 618 or 9; England, 1561-3, 1616-17; France, 1664, 1708, 1806-9; Germany, 1924; Greece, 5th c. BC, 498 BC, 480 BC; Rome, 232, 244, 296, 297, 359-76, 384, 420-1, 503-5, 546; see also Iran; Russia, 1664, 1708, 1715, 1723, 1724, 1734, 1796, 1813, 1825-8, 1920, 1927; Sparta, 372-359 BC, 366 BCf; Turcomans, 1857-61; Turkey, 1534, 1555, 1587, 1590, 1597, 1602, 1603, 1612, 1616-18, 1630, 1635, 1639, 1724-7, 1727, 1730-2, 1736, 1743-5, 1745, 1821-3, 1926; USA, 1911, 1922-5, see also Iran
Persian Gulf, c. post 516 BC, 325 BC, 115-16, 1856, 1968; language as lingua franca, 1279-1368
Perso-Baluch Boundary Commission, 1896
Perso-Russian agreement, 1921
Perso-Turkish boundary, 1843, 1847
perspex glass, 1930
Perth, Scotland, 1298, 1313, 1559, 1644; treaty, 1266
Perth, W. Australia, 1829
Pertinax, P. Helvius, c. 186, 192
Peru, c. 3000 BC, c. 1200 BC, 9th c. BC, 300 BC, ante 1 BC, c. 300-800, 12th c., post c. 1438, 1528, post 1531-1650, 1637, 1776, 1820-4, 1835, 1841, 1945, 1968; constitution, 1920; disastrous rain, 1878, 1884, 1891, 1918, 1925, 1932, 1939; navy, 1818; S, 1780; Upper, 1776;
relations with Bolivia, 1839, 1873, 1879; Chile, 1820, 1836, 1875, 1879, 1880, 1881, 1883; Spain, 1862-6, 1864; USA, 1958
Perugia, 1345-1430
Perugini, P. Vanuchi, 1446-1524
Peruvian culture, 4th c. BC, c. 300 AD
Peruvian-Bolivian Confederation, 1835
Peruz, 675
Pescadores Is., 1895
Pescennius Niger, 193
Peshawar, 85, c. post 110, 1001, 1674, 1767, 1791, 1834, 1837, 1855, 1857
peshwa, office of, 1720
Peshwa Baji Rao II, 1802-19
Pest, Hungary, 1240, 1684, 1873
Pestalozzi, Johann Friedrich, 1746-1827
Petah Tikvah, 1878
Pétain, Philippe, Marshal, 1916-51
Petchenègues, 1049-53, 1089-91, 1121-2
Peter, Coptic Patriarch, 477
Peter, Metropolitan of Moscow, 1925
Peter II, of Aragon, 1196-1213
Peter III of Aragon, 1262-85
Peter IV of Aragon, 1336-87
Peter I of Castile, 1350-69
Peter I of Brazil, 1822
Peter of Alexandria, c. 300-11
Peter of Bulgaria, 927-68
Peter I of Cyprus, 1361-9
Peter II of Cyprus, 1369
Peter the Hermit, 1096
Peter of Hungary, 1045
Peter Kara Georgevitch of Serbia, 1903-21; as

*porphyria*, 1788, 1811
porphyry, c. 40
Porphyry, c. 232-304
Porsenna, c. 509 BC
Port Arthur, 1894, 1895, 1898, 1904-5, 1905, 1952
Port Jackson, NZ, 1788
Port Natal, 1689
Port Philip, Australia, 1857
Port Royal (Annapolis), 1604, 1609, 1613, 1627, 1633, 1637, 1653, 1655, 1704, 1707, 1708, 1710
Port Swettenham, *ante* 3rd c.
port wine, 1703, 1756
Porte, 1771, 1811-18, 1824, 1848
Porteous riots, 1736
Portes-aux-Fer, Algeria, 1839
Portillo, José López, 1976
Portland, Duke of, 1783-1807
Portland Bill, 1652
Porto, da Silva, traveller, 1847
Porto, Silva, artist, 1850-93
Porto Bello, 1637
Porto Novo, 1781, 1861
Portobello, 1739
Portsmouth, England, 1338
Portsmouth (New Hampshire), treaty, 1905
Portugal, c. 2500 BC, 27 BC; County of, 1095, 1097; Kingdom, 1212, 1254, 1279-1325, 1340, 1415, 1433-8, 1437, 1480, 1484-1508, 1507, 1513, 1713, 1752, 1763, 1769, 1782, 1806, 1815, 1834, 1836, 1869, 1878, 1879-81, 1898, (Bankrupt), 1902; capital, 1064; constitution, 1838, 1840, 1976; fleet, 1279-1325, 1500-1600, 1501, 1508, 1511, 1547, 1568, 1578, 1582, 1587, 1601; internal strife, 1820, 1832, 1847, 1868; Republic, 1910, 1912, 1914, 1919-21, 1933, 1935, 1961, 1962, 1967, 1974; liberal movement, 1829-31, 1832, 1833; Armed Forces Movement, 1975; slave trade, 1513-15, 1526, c. 1550, 1612, 1641; interests in Africa, 1471, 1512, c. 1535, 1543, 1557, 1558, 1563, 1580, 1585, 1590-3, 1609, 1610, 1618, 1633-5, 1644, 1723, 1832, 1845, 1891, 1892, 1908, 1913-18, 1917, 1973; expeditions in the Atlantic, 1424, 1445, 1466, 1471, 1485, 1493, c. 1500, c. 1521, 1831; in Ceylon, 1636, 1656; Far East, 1504, 1505, 1526, 1542, 1568, 1578, c. 1579, 1615-17, 1639, 1641, 1832; India, 1510, 1570, 1600, 1686, 1832; trading stations, 1519, 1530, 1531, 1544;
relations with Angola, 17th c., 1612, 1641, 1648, 1665, 1960, 1970; Brazil, 1641, 1788, 1807, 1808, 1815, 1825; Britain, 1797, 1801, 1808, 1890, 1899, 1943; Castile, 1128, 1143, 1267, 1380, 1411; Dutch, 1623-38, 1640, 1642, 1644, 1648; England, 1294, 1373, 1386, 1620, 1653, 1662, 1704; France, 1641, 1712, 1724-38, 1797, 1801, 1807, 1811, 1817, 1831, 1857; Germany, 1916; Kongo, 1489-91, 1508, 1526, 1571; Mombasa, 1498, 1505, 1528, 1554, 1569, 1588, 1614, 1632, 1651, 1728, 1729, 1769-70; Mozambique, 1498, 1508, 1560, 1970; Ottomans, 1717; Pate, 1679, 1727-9; Rhodesia, 1965, 1970; SA, 1928, 1970; Spain, 1383, 1529, 1536, 1568, 1580, 1582, 1619, 1636, 1640, 1641, 1663, 1668, 1680, 1715, 1752, 1762, 1797, 1801, 1942; United Provinces, 1641; Vatican, 1753
Poseidonius of Apamaea, c. 135 BC
Posen, 1703, 1793, 1806, 1815
Poson, 863
*Post mortem* examination, 14th c.
Post Office, British, 1971; Savings Bank, 1861
postage stamps, 1840
postal services, 695, c. 912, 1482, 1873; parcels, 1880; penny, 1680, 1840

Posthumus, 285-60
Posthumus, Vladislav, 1440-57
potatoes, 1586
potatoes, sweet, c. 1629
Potchefstroom, 1844
*Potemkin*, Russian Vessel, 1905
Potemkin, G. A., 1774-88
Potgeiter, 1836
Potidaea, 432 BC
Potosí, Mt, 1545; town, 1547
Potsdam, 1745-7, 1806, 1910; Conference, 1945; edict, 1685
potter's wheel, c. 700 BC, c. 600 BC
pottery from Ukraine, c. 2000 BC; reaches China, c. 1700 BC; red-glazed, c. 50; Stamped Ware, 1st-6th cc.; Roman, 2nd-3rd cc.; Egyptian, 2nd-3rd cc.
Pougatchev, pretender, 1773-4
Pouget, Bertrand du, 1325-7
Poussin, Nicholas, 1594-1665
Poutrincourt, Sieur de, 1607
power of the courts, 1179
Powicke, Sir Maurice, 1879-1963
Powis, 1039, 1208, 1257
Poynings, Sir Edward, 1494
*Prabodha-chandrodaya*, 1065
Prabu Amangkural I of Mataram, 1645-77
Prado, convention, 1728
Prado, Manuel, of Peru, 1939-45
Praeneste, c. 360 BC
*praetor peregrinus*, 240 BC
Praetorian Guard, 41, 193
*praetors*, c. 500 BC, 366 BC
*Pragmatic Sanction*, 1438
Pragmatic Sanction, 554, 1261, 1461, 1713, 1722, 1731, 1732, 1738, 1745, 1830
Prague, 975, 1348, 1415, 1418, 1421, 1423, 1427, 1433, 1618, 1631, 1648, 1741, 1744, 1747, 1848, 1893, 1918, 1938, 1949, 1968, 1969; Abp of, 1410; Cathedral, 1344; Congress, 1813; treaties, 1562, 1635, 1866; University, 1402, 1881
Praguerie, 1440
Prairie Farm Assistance Act, 1939
Prambanan temples, c. 1050
Pramodavardhani, Queen, c. 838-51
Prasad, Dr Rajendra, 1950
Prate, Giovanni, 1815-84
Pratihara dynasty, 725f, 910-40, 1019
Pratiharas, 712
Praxiteles, sculptor, c. 370-330 BC
Prayaga (Allahabad), c. 320-35, 643
*Prayer Book* in Scotland, 1637
prayers in US schools, 1962
predestination, doctrine of, 1604-19
preference, imperial, 1902, 1913
Premis, Nubia, c. 203
Premonstratentian Order, 1120
Preobrajenski Regiment, 1741, 1820
Prés, Joaquin des, c. 1450-1521
Presbyterian Church, in England, 1643; of England, 1876, 1972; of Ireland, 1642; United, 1900
Presbyterianism, 1541, 1925; in Scotland, 1581, 1592, 1599, 1690, 1900, 1929
Prescott, Gen. Robert, 1797-1807
Prescott, William, 1796-1859
Preservation of Ancient Monuments, Society for the, 1877
Presidency of the EIC, 1613
press, Arabic, 1514, 1702
press, freedom of, 1735, 1740, 1781, 1789, 1828, 1868, 1966
Press Act, 1662
Pressburg, treaty, 1491, 1805
'Prester John', 1165
Preston, 1648, 1715
Prestonpans, 1745

Pretoria, 1856, 1877; treaty, 1881
Pretorius, Marthinius, 1840-57
Prevention of Crime Bill, 1882
Preventive Detention Act, 1962
Prevesa, 1538
Prevost, Sir George, 1812-16
Prévost d'Exiles, Antoine, 1697-1763
Priapatius, 191-176 BC
Price, George, 1961
Prices and Incomes Board, UK, 1965
Prices and Trade Board, Wartime, 1939
Pride's Purge, 1648
Priestley, Joseph, 1733-1804
priests, marriage of, 1092, 1123
Prim, Juan, 1814-70
*Primeiro de Janeiro*, 1868
Primitive Methodists, 1932
Primo de Rivera, Miguel, 1923-30
Primrose League, 1882
Prince Edward Is., 1799, 1851, 1864
Prince Imperial, 1856-79
Prince of Wales Fort, 1731
Princeton university, 1748
Principé, 1908, 1975 *and see* São Tomé
*Principia Mathematica*, 1687
printers on strike, in France, 1539-41, 1571
printing, from wood blocks, c. 770; in Scotland, 1507
printing press, 1476, 1537, 1639, 1808; machine, 1814; moveable, 1453-5; rotary, 1851
printing-shop, 1450, 1474
Priscillian heresy, c. 370, 380
Priscus, 598-9
Prisons Act, W Indian, 1838
Prithviraja, 1191-2
privateers, 1564, 1570, 1574, 1817
Privilege of Albano, 1112
'Privilege of the Union', 1287, 1348
*Privilegia Judaeorum*, 1357
privileges, commercial, 992, 1111, 1169, 1234, 1343, 1488, 1749; ecclesiastical, 1603-5; of Nobility in France, 1789; of Nobility in Russia, 1765
Privy Chancery in Russia, 1699
Privy Council, 1784-1801, 1890, 1931, 1949
Probus, 271-82
Probus, Henry, of Cracow, 1289-90
Proclus, 438-85
*proconsul*, 327 BC
Procopius, usurper, 365-6
Procopius, historian, c. 500-*post* 562
Procopius the Great, 1426-34
proctors, clerical, 1372
Prodicus of Ceos, grammarian, 5th c. BC
productivity, industrial, 1938
Progressive League, Barbados, 1935
Progressive Party, German, 1861
Progressive Party, S Rhodesia, 1926
Prohibition Act, Canada, 1878
Prohibition, US, 1869, 1920, 1933
Prokofiev, Sergei, 1891-1953
Proletariat Party, Polish, 1885
Prome, 1st c. BC, c. 94, 1287, 1401, 1412, 1538, 1542, 1551, 1608, 1824, 1852, 1887
Promenade Concerts, 1895
Promontory Point, Utah, 1869
propaganda, antireligious, 1925
*Propaganda* College in Rome, 1627
*Propagation of the Faith, Sacred Congregation*, 1613, 1622, 1817
Propagation of the Faith, Society, 1822
Propanca, 1365
propeller, screw, 1838
Propertius, c. 50-c. 16 BC
Propylaea, 437-432 BC
Prosperine, 249 BC, 207 BC
Protagoras, 480-410 BC

Santo Domingo, 1511, 1527, 1791, 1801, 1814, 1822, 1843, 1844, 1861, 1865, 1904; City, 1936
Santo Domingo Co., 1757
Santo Stefano, Hieronomo de, /496
Santos, 1591
Sanusi, 1915
al-Sanusi, Shaykh of Algeria, 1837
Sanusiyah confraternity, 1837, 1843
São Mameda, 1128
São Paulo, 1710, 1932
São Tomé, 1475, 1485, 1908, 1909; independent with Principé Is , 1975
São Vicente (Santos), 1532
Saône valley, 481-511
Sappho, poetess, c. 650-560 BC
Saracens, c. 400
Saragat, Guiseppe, 1964
Saragossa, 380, 533, 750, 788, 1039-1141, 1091, 1108, 1111, 1118, 1119-1520, 1162-96, 1707, 1710, 1809; treaty, 1529
Sarai, 1395
Sarakole Empire, 920-1050
Saratoga, USA, 1746, 1777
Sarazin, Jacques, 1592-1660
Sarbakuse, 1771
Sarbat Khalsa, 1761-90
Sarda Act in India, 1929
Sardar Muhammad Daud Khan, 1973
Sardica, 809
Sardinia, 259 BC, 238 BC, 227 BC, 215 BC, 177-176 BC, 19, 809-10, 902, 1016, 1133, 1174-5, 1267, 1295, 1306, 1323, 1324, 1708, 1713, 1714, 1717, 1720, 1735, 1743, 1747, 1793, 1798, 1850, 1855, 1857
Sardis, c. 650 BC, 546 BC, 498 BCff, 261 BC, 215-213 BC, 1097
*Sarekat Dagang Islam* movement, 1911, 1917, 1921
Sarfaraz of Bengal, 1738-40
Sargent, John Singer, 1856-1925
Sargon I of Akkadia, c. 2371-2316 BC
Sargon II, of Assyria, 721-705 BC
Sarmatia, Sarmatians, 2nd half of 3rd c. BC, c. 50, 165
Sarmatian culture, 4th c. BC, 3rd to 1st c. BC
Sarmiento, D. F., of Argentina, 1868-74
Sarno, 1460
Saronica, Gulf, 389 BC
Sarpi, Fra Paolo, 1552-1623
Sarrail, General, 1924
Sarraut, Albert, 1933-6
Sarsa Dengel of Ethiopia, 1563-97
Sarto, Andrea del, 1488-1530
Sartre, Jean-Paul, 1970
Saskatchewan, Canada, 1882, 1885; River, 1750
Sassanid Dynasty, 226-641, 611-33, 637, 675; embassy to China, 638
Satavahana (Andhra), dynasty, 1st c. BC-AD 2nd c.; Kingdom, c. 126, c. 130, c. 225
satellites, 1958
*sati* (suttee), 510, 1830
Satiru, Nigeria, 1906
Satisfaction, Act of, 1653
Satnami Hindu sect, 1672
Satrap, satrapy, 546 BC, c *ante* 530, 412 BC, 387-386 BC
Satshuma clan, 1846-67
Saucourt-en-Vimeu, 881
Saud, King of Saudi Arabia, 1953-64
Saudi Arabia (formerly Hijaz), 1756, 1926, 1927, 1934, 1956, 1975, 1976
Saugor Is., 1803
Saul, c. 1020-c. 1000 BC
Sauley, Louis Félicien de, 1807-80
Saumur, 1611

Saurashtra rulers, 1143-72
Savannah, 1778, 1864
savings banks, 1778
Savona, 1809
Savonarola, Girolamo de, 1486-98
Savoy, 1536, 1559, 1562, 1600, 1623, 1655, 1690, 1696, 1703, 1713, 1714, 1771, 1821, 1834, 1860, 1940; relations with France, 1623, 1630, 1696, 1701, 1704, 1736, 1792; war with Spain, 1614, 1617
Savoy, Duke of, 1602, 1615, 1696, 1713
Saw E of Hantawaddy, 1331
Saw Hnuit, 1297-1301
Saw O ot Hanthawaddy, 1310-24
Saw Zein of Hanthawaddy, 1324-31
Sawba of Hsenwei, 1408, 1412
Sawlu of Pagan, 1077-84
saw-mills, 1734
Sawyn of Burma, 1315-23
Saxe-Coburg-Gotha, 1819-61, 1831
Saxe-Weimar, 1638
Saxo Grammaticus, 1140-1206
Saxons, c. 258, 880, 1074; in Britain, 290, late 3rd c., 367, 408, 441-2, 491; in France, 355, 628-39, 719-38, 741-52, 772-6, 777-85, 793-805, 805
Saxony, 782-5, 1073, 1085, 1121, 1138, 1532, 1539, 1635, 1719, 1733, 1741, 1746, 1755, 1806, 1849, 1850; Elector of, 1631; Electorate, 1652; relations with Prussia, 1744, 1745, 1756, 1762, 1866; Sweden, 1636, 1702, 1706, 1715
Saya San, 1930
Sayf al-Dawlah Abu al-Hasan Ali, 944-67
Sayyids of Delhi, 1414-50
Sbeitla, 647
Scaevola, M., 148 BC
Scaevola, Q. M., c. 95 BC
Scaliger, Joseph Justus, 1540-1609
Scaliger, Jules César, 1458-1558
scaling ladders, wheeled, c. 2500 BC
Scandinavia, 1579, 1712, 1930
scandium, 1879
Scania, 1676
Scapa Flow, 1919, 1939
Scapula, 47-52
Scarlatti, Alessandro, 1659-1725
Scarlatti, Domenico, 1685-1757
scent making, c. 2500 BC
Scetis, 330, late 4th c., 817, 1069
Schadow, Johann Gottfried, 1764-1850
Scheel, Walter, 1974
Scheyern, treaty, 1532
Schiller, Johann C. F. von, 1759-1805
Schism, Great, 1378, 1391, 1395, 1408
Schism Act, 1713
Schlegel, August Wilhelm von, 1767-1845
Schlegel, Karl Wilhelm Friedrich von, 1772-1829
Schleicher, Kurt von, 1932
Schliermacher, Friedrich D. E., 1768-1834
Schliemann, Heinrich, 1870
Schleswig, 934, 1435, 1844, 1846, 1848, 1850, 1863, 1864, 1865
Schleswig-Holstein, 1767
Schmalkalden, League of, 1530, 1531, 1534, 1539, 1546, 1547
Schnaebelš, frontier official, 1880
Schnoudi of Atripe, 333-451
Schomberg, Marshal, 1689
Schönberg, Arnold, 1874-1951
Schönbrunn, palace, 1619, 1696, treaty, 1805
Schonen, 1332, 1360
Schongauer, Martin, c. 1445-c. 1499
School of Medicine in Cairo, 1827
school of oriental studies, 1250

School of war in Paris, 1777
School of Engineering, 1816
Schopenhauer, Arthur, 1788-1860
Schubert, Franz Peter, 1797-1828
Schuman, Robert, premier, 1947-8
Schumann, Robert, 1810-56
Schuschnigg, Kurt, 1934-5
Schütz, Heinrich, 1585-1672
Schutz, Roger, pastor, 1944
Schweidnitz, 1761, 1762
Schweitzer, Albert, 1875-1965
Schwyz, 1291
Sciath Nechtain, 848
Scilli, 180
Scipio Aemilianus, 147-133 BC
Scipio Africanus, 218-190 BC
Scipio, L. Barbatus, 298-295 BC
Scone, Abbey, 1113, 1651; Council of, 1357; Stone of, 1296
Scopas, sculptor, c. 385-340 BC
scorched earth policy, 1901
Scordisci, 114 BCf
Scot, Michael, c. 1236
Scotland and Scots, c. 2500 BC, c. 800 BC, 82-3, c. 142-3, 193, 343, 927, 937, 1092, 1173 1204, 1251, 1263, 1266, 1289, 1312, 1313, 1318, 1322, 1495, 1650, 1654, 1699, 1822, 1941; Colonists, 1627, 1628; Crown of, 1292; education, 1696; Highlands, 1725, 1943; Peerage, 1963; Western Isles, 1098-1103, 1719; in Ulster, 1690; relations with England, 1209, 1278, 1296-1302, 1310-14, 1323, 1327, 1369, 1371, 1383, 1389, 1423-9, 1438, 1448, 1464, 1488-1513, 1495-7, 1513, 1542, 1544-5, 1639-41, 1645-8, 1679; union with England, 1607, 1654, 1689, 1706, 1707; France, 1295, 1354, 1389, 1423-9, 1560, 1583; Papacy, 1320, 1323, 1329, 1546, 1560; Parliamentary army, 1643; Spain, 1719
Scots College in Rome, 1600; Sydney, 1831
Scott, Dred, 1857
Scott, Sir George Gilbert, 1811-78
Scott, Sir Giles Gilbert, 1880-1960
Scott, Capt R. F., 1912
Scott, Sir Walter, 1771-1832
Scott, Winfield, general, 1832
Scottish Bible, 1579
Scottish Clans, 1745, 1746; independence, 1189; judicial system, 1808, 1815, 1824; kingdoms, c. 500; landowners, 1496; Parliament, 1543, 1560, 1584, 1612, 1639, 1640, 1689, 1707; Parliamentary Reform Bill, 1832; peers, 1707
Scottish Martyrs, 1793
Scottish Grand Committee, 1894
Scottish Home Rule Association, 1886
Scott-Moncrieff Commission, 1899
scourging in Rome, 195 BC
screw propeller, 1838
screwdriver, c. 1780
screw-jack, c. 1480
Scriabin, Alexander N., 1871-1915
scripts, Roman and Arabic, 1907, 1926, 1928
scrolls, 1st c.
Scrope, Richard, Abp, 1405
Scullin, James, 1929-31
Sculpture and Painting, Academy of, 1648
scutage tax, 1159, 1214
Scythia, Scythians, c. mid 8th c. BC, c. 678 BC, 653-585 BC, c. 638 BC, c. 514-512 BC, 4th c. BC, 2nd half of 3rd c. BC, c. 140-130 BC, c. 126 BC, 538
Scythian culture, c. 1200-700 BC, c. 700-550 BC, c. 550-450 BC, c. 350-250BC
Scutari, 782
seal hunting, 1803; protection, 1826
Sealand, c. 1750-1600 BC, 627 BC

Shaw, T. E. (Lawrence of Arabia), 1888–1935
Shawnee Indians, 1811
Shayban, Tulunid ruler, 904–5
Shayista Khan of Bengal, 1660–94
al-Shaykh Zahir al-Al Umar c. 1737–72
Shearers' Union in Australia, 1889
Sheba, c. *ante* 961 BC *see also* Saba
Shechem, c. 1200
sheep-breeding, 1745, 1793–7
sheep-shearing by machine, c. 1879
sheep-shearers, 1890
Shela, 1813
Shelburne, Earl of, 1782–4
Shell Co., 1907
Shelley, Percy Bysshe, 1792–1822
Shen Tsung, 1068–85
Shen Tsung, emperor, 1573–1619
Sheng Tsu (Kang-Hsi), emperor, 1663–1722
Shenshi, 384–417, 756–62
Shensi, N, 1934
Shensi province, 58 BC
Sheppey, Isle of, 835
Sher Khan, 1527–45
Sher Singh of Lahore, 1840
Sherborne, 705, 893, 1078, c. 1430
Sherbrooke, Sir John, 1816–18
Sheridan, Richard Brinsley, 1751–1816
Sheriff Hutton, Yorkshire, 1484
Sheriffdoms in Scotland, 1296
Sheriffmuir, 1715
Sherley, Sir Anthony and Sir Robert, 1598
Sherman, William T., general, 1820–91
Shesh-bazzar, 539 BC
Shetland Is., c. 600, 785–850, 1266
Shi'as, 765, 1544
Shibtu, c. 1780
Shih Ching-tang, 936
Shih Hu, 333–49
Shih Huang-Ti (Cheng), c. 247 BC, c. 221 BC
Shih Lo, 314–33
Shih Tung, Ming emperor, 1521–66
Shihab al-Din Ghuri, 1401–5
al-Shii, 911
Shi'ism in Bijapur, 1502, 1557–79; Egypt, 1171; Persia, 1736
Shi'ite dynasty, 788–974; sects, 680, 744
Shi'ite Hamdanid dynasty, 929–91
Shilluk, 1826
Shiloh, *post* 1050 BC; battle, 1862
Shimabara, Japan, 1637
Shimoda, Japan, 1854, 1855, 1856, 1857
Shimonoseki, battle, 1185; Strait, Japan, 1863; treaty, 1895
Shin Bohmai, Shan Queen, 1426, 1427–40
Shin Saw Bu, Lady of Hanthwaddy, 1453–72
Shingon sect, 774–835
Shintoism, 1945
Ship Money, 1634, 1635, 1636, 1639
shipbuilding, c. 2500 BC, c. 2000 BC, c. 1500 BC, c. 1000 BC, 800 BC, c. 700 BC, 1st c. BC, 1415, 1705, 1812, 1885
Shipka Pass, 1878
Shipton, Eric, 1907—
Shir Ali Khan of Afghanistan, 1863–79
Shiraz, 934, 935–6, 977–82, 1148, c. 1225, 1387, 1724, 1725, 1750, 1781
Shire, 1861–4
Shirkuh, Saljuq, 1164
Shirmarke, Ali, of Somalia, 1969
Shishakly, Colonel, 1951
Shishunaga, 413 BC, c. 4th c. BC
Shoa, c. 897/8–1285, 1277, 1531, 1841, 1853, 1865
shogunate, 1192, 1562, 1867
Shoguns of Japan, 1399–1573
Sholapur, 1685
Sholes, Christopher L., 1873

Shona culture, c. *ante* 1100; settlers, c. 11th c.
Shore, Sir John, 1793–8
Shoshenk I, Pharaoh, c. 945–924 BC
Shoshenk III, Pharaoh, c. 827–c. 788 BC
Shoshenk IV, Pharaoh, c. 782–745 BC
Shostakovich, Dimitri, 1906–
Shotoku, Prince, 604–21
Showa (Prince Hirohito), 1926
Shrewsbury, 1403; Parliament, 1398; treaty, 1267
Shrewsbury, Duke of, 1714
Shu Han dynasty, 221–63; population 140
Shuja, son of Shahjahan, 1657–8
Shuja al-Daula of Bengal, 1727–38
Shuja al-Mulk of Afghanistan, 1805–42
Shun-chih, Manchu emperor, 1644–62
Shunga dynasty, c. 185 BC
Shute, Nevil, 1899–1960
Shwebo, 1752
Shwedagon pagoda, c. 563–483 BC
Shwenankyawtshin of Ava, 1502–27
Shwetanngtet of Sagaing, 1336–40
Siak, Sumatra, 1540
Siam, Siamese, c. 1300, 1350, 1401, 1456, 1511, 1581, 1688, 1773, c. 1800, 1816, 1822, 1825 or 6, 1855, 1896, 1897, 1917; army, 1445; fleet, 1862; relations with Burma, 1548, 1559,-1563, 1568, 1585, 1593, 1760, 1766, 1767, 1770, 1775, 1776, 1785, 1787, 1791, 1943; France, 1941; Japan, 1940; Kedah, 18th c., 1821, 1831; Toungoo, 1599, 1605 *see also* Thailand
Siam-reap, c. 1800
Sian-Fu, 635
Siang-yang, 1267–72
Siao Ho, c. 193 BC
Sibawahi, philologist, c. 758–91
Sibelius, Jean J. C., 1865–1957
Siberia, c. 500–300 or 200 BC, 1581, 1584, 1699, 1809, 1822, 1928; prisoners sent to, 1709, 1741, 1863
Sibylline oracle, 216 BC
Sicard, Claud, 1677–1726
'Sicilian Vespers', 1282
Sicily, 8th–6th c. BC, *post* 550 BC, c. 499 BC, c. 480 BC, 424 BCf, 380 BC, 313 BCf, 278–275 BC, 135 BCf, 535, 554, 668 or 9, 827, 917, 1009, 1236–7, 1249, 1253, 1258, 1302, 1672, 1783, 1809, 1848, 1849, 1860, 1943; Muslims, 912–16; under Anjou, 1266, 1282; Arabs, 652, 909; Aragon, 1291, 1296, 1372; Holy Roman Emp., 1191, 1194, 1221, 1229; Normans, 1118–23, 1127, 1147; Savoy, 1713, 1714; attacked by Spain, 1646, 1718, 1735 relations with Rome, 261 BC, 241 BC, 227 BC
Sicilies, Two, 1793, 1796, 1805, 1806
Sickert, Walter Richard, 1860–1942
sickles in Switzerland, c. 1000 BC
Siculus, Diodorus, c. 59 BC
Sicyon, 251 BC
Sidama, 1887–94
*Siddhanta*, 771
Siddons, Sarah, 1755–1831
Sidgwick, Henry, 1838–1900
Sidi Barrani, 1940
Sidi Bel Abbes, 1843
Sidi Brahim, Algeria, 1845
Sidmouth, Viscount, 1801
Sidney, Algernon, 1683
Sidney, Sir Henry, 1556–71
Sidney, Sir Philip, 1554–86
Sidon, 604 BC, *post* 50 BC, c. 595–570 BCf, 1110, 1227–8, 1250–4, 1291, 1772, 1918
Sidonius Apollinaris, 430–80
Sidqi, General in Iraq, 1936–7
Sie, Sung empress, 1274–6

siege towers, c. 800 BC
Siemens, Ernest Werner von, 1816–92
Siemens, Sir William, 1823–83
Siena, 1245, 1423, 1472, 1625
Sienkiewicz, Henry, 1847–1916
Sierra Leone, c. 1400, 1448, c. 1602, 1663, 1672, 1792, 1808, 1821, 1842, 1850, 1882, 1924, 1927, 1931, 1953, 1967, 1968; independent, 1960, 1961
Sietah, nomad republic, 1775
*Siete Partidas*, 1348
Sievershausen, battle, 1553
Sieyès, Emmanuel Joseph, 1799
Siffin, battle, 657
Sigea, c. 607 BC, 510 BC
Sigeberht of Wessex, 756–7
Sigebert, 573–5
Siger of Brabant, 1270–7
Sigismond, 516–23
Sigismund, son of Charles IV, 1387–1437
Sigismund of Austria, 1469
Sigismund, John, of Brandenburg, 1608–19
Sigismund Malatesta, 1462–3
Sigismund I of Poland, 1506–48
Sigismund II of Poland, 1548–72
Sigismund III of Poland, 1587–1632
Sigismund of Transylvania, 1540–71
signalling forts, 81
*Signoria* of Milan, 1277
Sijilmasa, c. 705, 742, 771–976, 790–823, 933, 935, 976, 985, c. 1045, 1055, 1274
Sijistan, 867–908
Sikandar of Bijapur, 1673–86
Sikandar Ghazi, Sultan, 1489–1517
Sikandar of Kashmir, 1393–1416
Sikandar Shah, 1368
Sikh wars, 1845, 1848
Sikhs, 1606–45, 1675–1708, 1710, 1761–90, 1762, 1764, 1773, 1829, 1831, 1834, 1847, 1849, 1947
Sikkim, 1888
Sikorski, General, 1943
Silanus, 109 BC
Silberman, Gottfried, 1683–1753
'silent trade', c. *post* 500
Silesia, 820, 1300–5, 1428, 1443, 1460, 1627, 1633, 1763, 1921, 1922; under Prussia, 1740–8
Silistria, 972
silk, artificial, 1887; cultivation, 1147; trade, 1645
silk-weaving, c. 2000 BC
Sillery, Quebec, 1639
Silva, Costa, marshal, 1967
Silva, José da, 1705–39
Silva, Simão da, 1512
Silva y Figueroa, Garcia de, 1618–19
Silvanus, 355
silver, 630 BC, *post* 550 BC, 485 BC, 4th c. BC, 15th c., 16th c., *post* 1531–1650, 1545, 1619–21, 1696, 18th c., 1859, 1873
Silver Jubilee of George V, 1935
Silvester III, antipope, 1045–6
Simancas, 932
Simango, Dr Uria, 1969
Simbirsk, 1670
Simcoe, Col. J. G., 1792–6
Simeon, Grand Prince of Moscow, 1341–53
Simeon of Bulgaria, 893–927
Simeon II of Bulgaria, 1941
Simeon the Proud of Russia, 1353
Simnel, Lambert, 1487
Simon, Sir John, 1873–1954
Simon, Jules, 1877
Simon, R., 1678
Simon Commission on Burma, 1931; India, 1927; Report on India, 1930